Essentials of Accounting

Fourth Edition

Select Material From:

Financial Accounting

Fifth Edition

Kimmel Weygandt Kieso

and

Managerial Accounting

Fourth Edition

Weygandt Kimmel Kieso

To order books or for customer service, please call 1(800)-CALL-WILEY (225-5945).

Printed in the United States of America.

ISBN 978-0-470-50829-9

10 9 8 7 6 5 4 3

about the authors

Paul D. Kimmel, PhD, CPA, received his bachelor's degree from the University of Minnesota and his doctorate in accounting from the University of Wisconsin. He is an Associate Professor at the University of Wisconsin—Milwaukee, and has public accounting experience with Deloitte & Touche (Minneapolis). He was the recipient of the UWM School of Business Advisory Council Teaching Award, the Reggie Taite Excellence in Teaching Award, and a three-time winner of the Outstanding Teaching Assistant Award at the University of Wisconsin. He is also a recipient of the Elijah Watts Sells Award for Honorary Distinction for his results on the CPA exam. He is a member of the American Accounting Association and the Institute of Management Accountants and has published articles in *Accounting Review, Accounting Horizons, Advances in Management Accounting, Managerial Finance, Issues in Accounting Education, Journal of Accounting Education*, as well as other journals. His research interests include accounting for financial instruments and innovation in accounting education. He has published papers and given numerous talks on incorporating critical thinking into accounting education, and helped prepare a catalog of critical thinking resources for the Federated Schools of Accountancy.

Jerry J. Weygandt, PhD, CPA, is Arthur Andersen Alumni Emeritus Professor of Accounting at the University of Wisconsin—Madison. He holds a Ph.D. in accounting from the University of Illinois. Articles by Professor Weygandt have appeared in the *Accounting Review, Journal of Accounting Research, Accounting Horizons, Journal of Accountancy*, and other academic and professional journals. These articles have examined such financial reporting issues as accounting for price-level adjustments, pensions, convertible securities, stock option contracts, and interim reports. Professor Weygandt is author of other accounting and financial reporting books and is a member of the American Accounting Association, the American Institute of Certified Public Accountants, and the Wisconsin Society of Certified Public Accountants. He has served on numerous committees of the American Accounting Association and as a member of the editorial board of the *Accounting Review*; he also has served as President and Secretary-Treasurer of the American Accounting Association. In addition, he has been actively involved with the American Institute of Certified Public Accountants and has been a member of the Accounting Standards Executive Committee (AcSEC) of that organization. He has served on the FASB task force that examined the reporting issues related to accounting for income taxes and served as a trustee of the Financial Accounting Foundation. Professor Weygandt has received the Chancellor's Award for Excellence in Teaching and the Beta Gamma Sigma Dean's Teaching Award. He is on the board of directors of M & I Bank of Southern Wisconsin. He is the recipient of the Wisconsin Institute of CPA's Outstanding Educator's Award and the Lifetime Achievement Award. In 2001 he received the American Accounting Association's Outstanding Accounting Educator Award.

Donald E. Kieso, PhD, CPA, received his bachelor's degree from Aurora University and his doctorate in accounting from the University of Illinois. He has served as chairman of the Department of Accountancy and is currently the KPMG Emeritus Professor of Accountancy at Northern Illinois University. He has public accounting experience with Price Waterhouse & Co. (San Francisco and Chicago) and Arthur Andersen & Co. (Chicago) and research experience with the Research Division of the American Institute of Certified Public Accountants (New York). He has done postdoctorate work as a Visiting Scholar at the University of California at Berkeley and is a recipient of NIU's Teaching Excellence Award and four Golden Apple Teaching Awards. Professor Kieso is the author of other accounting and business books and is a member of the American Accounting Association, the American Institute of Certified Public Accountants, and the Illinois CPA Society. He has served as a member of the Board of Directors of the Illinois CPA Society, the AACSB's Accounting Accreditation Committees, the State of Illinois Comptroller's Commission, as Secretary-Treasurer of the Federation of Schools of Accountancy, and as Secretary-Treasurer of the American Accounting Association. Professor Kieso is currently serving on the Board of Trustees and Executive Committee of Aurora University, as a member of the Board of Directors of Kishwaukee Community Hospital, and as Treasurer and Director of Valley West Community Hospital. From 1989 to 1993 he served as a charter member of the national Accounting Education Change Commission. He is the recipient of the Outstanding Accounting Educator Award from the Illinois CPA Society, the FSA's Joseph A. Silvoso Award of Merit, the NIU Foundation's Humanitarian Award for Service to Higher Education, a Distinguished Service Award from the Illinois CPA Society, and in 2003 an honorary doctorate from Aurora University.

Acknowledgments

Financial Accounting has benefited greatly from the input of focus group participants, manuscript reviewers, those who have sent comments by letter or e-mail, ancillary authors, and proofers. We greatly appreciate the constructive suggestions and innovative ideas of reviewers and the creativity and accuracy of the ancillary authors and checkers.

PRIOR EDITIONS

Thanks to the following reviewers and focus group participants of prior editions of Financial Accounting:

Dawn Addington, *Central New Mexico Community College;* Solochidi Ahiarah, *Buffalo State College;* Sheila Ammons, *Austin Community College;* Thomas G. Amyot, *College of Santa Rose;* Cheryl Bartlett, *Central New Mexico Community College;* Victoria Beard, *University of North Dakota;* Angela H. Bell, *Jacksonville State University;* John A. Booker, *Tennessee Technological University;* Robert L. Braun, *Southeastern Louisiana University;* Daniel Brickner, *Eastern Michigan University;* Sarah Ruth Brown, *University of North Alabama;* and James Byrne, *Oregon State University.*

Judy Cadle, *Tarleton State University*; David Carr, *Austin Community College*; Jack Cathey, *University of North Carolina–Charlotte*; Andy Chen, *Northeast Illinois University;* Jim Christianson, *Austin Community College*; Laura Claus, *Louisiana State University*; Leslie A. Cohen, *University of Arizona*; Teresa L. Conover, *University of North Texas*; Janet Courts, *San Bernadino Valley College;* Helen Davis, *Johnson and Wales University*; Cheryl Dickerson, *Western Washington University*; George M. Dow, *Valencia Community College–West*; Kathy J. Dow, *Salem State College*; and Lola Dudley, *Eastern Illinois University.*

Mary Emery, *St. Olaf College*; Martin L. Epstein, *Central New Mexico Community College;* Larry R. Falcetto, *Emporia State University*; Scott Fargason, *Louisiana State University*; Janet Farler, *Pima Community College;* Sheila D. Foster, *The Citadel*; Jessica J. Frazier, *Eastern Kentucky University;* Norman H. Godwin, *Auburn University*; David Gotlob, *Indiana University-Purdue University–Fort Wayne*; Emmett Griner, *Georgia State University;* Leon J. Hanouille, *Syracuse University*; Kenneth M. Hiltebeitel, *Villanova University*; Harry Hooper, *Santa Fe Community College;* Judith A. Hora, *University of San Diego*; and Carol Olson Houston, *San Diego State University.*

Norma Jacobs, *Austin Community College;* Marianne L. James, *California State University–Los Angeles*; Stanley Jenne, *University of Montana;* Christopher Jones, *George Washington University;* Jane Kaplan, *Drexel University*; John E. Karayan, *California State University–Pomona;* Susan Kattelus, *Eastern Michigan University*; Dawn Kelly, *Texas Tech University;* Cindi Khanlarian, *University of North Carolina–Greensboro;* Robert Kiddoo, *California State University–Northridge;* Robert J. Kirsch, *Southern Connecticut State University;* Frank Korman, *Mountain View College*; and Jerry G. Kreuze, *Western Michigan University.*

John Lacey, *California State University–Long Beach*; Doug Laufer, *Metropolitan State College of Denver*; Keith Leeseberg, *Manatee Community College*; Glenda Levendowski, *Arizona State University;* Seth Levine, *DeVry University*; James Lukawitz, *University of Memphis*; Noel McKeon, *Florida Community College*; P. Merle Maddocks, *University of Alabama Huntsville*; Janice Mardon, *Green River Community College*; John Marts, *University of North Carolina–Wilmington*; Alan Mayer-Sommer, *Georgetown University*; Barbara Merino, *University of North Texas;* Jeanne Miller, *Cypress College;* Robert Miller, *California State University–Fullerton;* Elizabeth Minbiole, *Northwood University; and* Marguerite Muise, *Santa Ana College;* James Neurath, *Central Michigan University;* and Gale E. Newell, *Western Michigan University.*

Suzanne Ogilby, *Sacramento State University;* Sarah N. Palmer, *University of North Carolina–Charlotte;* Patricia Parker, *Columbus State Community College;* Charles Pier, *Appalachian State University;* Meg Pollard, *American River College;* Franklin J. Plewa, *Idaho State University;* John Purisky, *Salem State College;* Donald J. Raux, *Siena College;* Judith Resnick, *Borough of Manhattan Community College;* Mary Ann Reynolds, *Western Washington University;* Carla Rich, *Pensacola Junior College;* Ray Rigoli, *Ramapo College of New Jersey;* Jeff Ritter, *St. Norbert College;* Brandi Roberts, *Southeastern Louisiana University;* Patricia A. Robinson, *Johnson and Wales University;* Nancy Rochman, *University of Arizona;* and Marc A. Rubin, *Miami University.*

Alfredo Salas, *El Paso Community College;* Christine Schalow, *California State University–San Bernadino*; Michael Schoderbek, *Rutgers University*; Richard Schroeder, *University of North Carolina–Charlotte*; Jerry Searfoss, *University of Utah;* Cindy Seipel, *New Mexico State University*; Anne E. Selk,*University of Wisconsin–Green Bay;* William

Seltz, *University of Massachusetts*; Suzanne Sevalstad, *University of Nevada*; Mary Alice Seville, *Oregon State University*; Donald Smillie, *Southwest Missouri State University;* Aileen Smith, *Stephen F. Austin State University*; Talitha Smith, *Auburn University;* William E. Smith, *Xavier University*; Will Snyder, *San Diego State University;* Teresa A. Speck, *St. Mary's University of Minnesota*; Charles Stanley, *Baylor University*; Ron Stone, *California State University–Northridge*; Gary Stout, *California State University–Northridge*; and Ellen L. Sweatt, *Georgia Perimeter College.*

Pamadda Tantral, *Fairleigh Dickinson University*; Andrea B. Weickgenannt, *Northern Kentucky University*; David P. Weiner, *University of San Francisco;* Frederick Weis, *Claremont McKenna College*; T. Sterling Wetzel, *Oklahoma State University*; Allan Young, *DeVry University*; Michael F. van Breda, *Texas Christian University*; Linda G. Wade, *Tarleton State University*; Stuart K. Webster, *University of Wyoming*; V. Joyce Yearley, *New Mexico State University.*

FIFTH EDITION

Thanks to the following reviewers, focus group participants, and others who provided suggestions for the Fifth Edition:

Gilda Agacer, *Monmouth University*
C. Richard Aldridge, *Western Kentucky University*
Joseph Antenucci, *Youngstown State University*
Brian Baick, *Montgomery College*
Timothy Baker, *California State University—Fresno*
Benjamin Bean, *Utah Valley State College*
Charles Bokemeier, *Michigan State University*
Charles Bunn, *Wake Technical Community College*
Thane Butt, *Champlain College*
Sandra Byrd, *Missouri State University*
Julia Camp, *University of Massachusetts—Boston*
Jack Cathey, *University of North Carolina—Charlotte*
Patrick Christensen, *Butte College*
Leslie Cohen, *University of Arizona*
Samantha Cox, *Wake Technical Community College*
Dori Danko, *Grand Valley State University*
Lisa Gillespie, *Loyola University—Chicago*
Sam Isley, *Wake Technical Community College*
Doulas Larson, *Salem State College*
Sara Melendy, *Gonzaga University*
Sherry Mirbod, *Montgomery College*
Andrew Morgret, *University of Memphis*
Michelle Moshier, *SUNY Albany*
Jim Neurath, *Central Michigan University*
Garth Novack, *Utah State University*
John A. Rude, *Bloomsburg University*
Bill N. Schwartz, *Stevens Institute of Technology*
Pam Smith, *Northern Illinois University*
Chris Solomon, *Trident Technical College*
Gracelyn Stuart, *Palm Beach Community College*
William Talbot, *Montgomery College*
Diane Tanner, *University of North Florida*
Steve Teeter, *Utah Valley State College*
Joan Van Hise, *Fairfield University*

ANCILLARY AUTHORS, CONTRIBUTORS, AND PROOFERS

We sincerely thank the following individuals for their hard work in preparing the content that accompanies this textbook:

LuAnn Bean, *Florida Institute of Technology*
Richard Campbell, *University of Rio Grande*
James M. Emig, *Villanova University*
Larry R. Falcetto, *Emporia Sate University*
Anthony Falgiani, *Western Illinois University*
Janet Farler, *Pima Community College*
Cecelia M. Fewox, *College of Charleston*
Coby Harmon, *University of California, Santa Barbara*
Harry Howe, *State University of New York—Geneseo*
Rick Lillie, *California State University—San Bernardino*
Laura McNally
Yvonne Phang, *Borough of Manhattan Community College*
Rex Schildhouse, *San Diego Community College*
Ellen L. Sweatt, *Georgia Perimeter College*
Dick D. Wasson, *Southwestern College*
Bernie Weinrich, *Lindenwood University*

We also greatly appreciate the expert assistance provided by the following individuals in checking the accuracy of the content that accompanies this textbook:

Terry Elliott, *Morehead State University*
Jill Misuraca, *Central Connecticut State University*
John Plouffe, *California State University—Los Angeles*
Ed Schell, *University of Hawaii at Manoa*
Alice Sineath, *Forsyth Technical Community College*
Teresa Speck, *Saint Mary's University of Minnesota*
Lynn Stallworth, *Appalachian State University*
Sheila Viel, *University of Wisconsin—Milwaukee*

We appreciate the exemplary support and professional commitment given us by Wiley's editorial and marketing personnel: Chris DeJohn, associate publisher; Julia Flohr, senior marketing manager; Carly DeCandia, assistant marketing manager; Allie Morris, senior media editor; Brian Kamins, associate editor; Ed Brislin, project editor; Alana Filopovich, marketing assistant; Ann Torbert and Terry Ann Kremer, development editors; Karyn Morrison, permissions editor; and Jen Battista, media assistant. Thanks also to the talented people who turned the material into the physical textbook:

Ann Berlin, vice-president of higher education production and manufacturing; Harry Nolan, creative director; Pam Kennedy, director of production and manufacturing; Dorothy Sinclair, production services manager; Trish McFadden, senior production editor; Madelyn Lesure, senior designer; Sandra Rigby, senior illustration editor; Elle Wagner, senior photo editor; Suzanne Ingrao of Ingrao Associates, project editor; Jane Shifflet, product manager at Aptara; and Amanda Grant, project manager at Elm Street Publishing Services.

Finally, our thanks for the support provided by the management of John Wiley & Sons, Inc.—especially Joe Heider, Vice President of Product and e-Business Development; Bonnie Lieberman, Senior Vice President of the College Division; and Will Pesce, President and Chief Executive Officer.

We thank Tootsie Roll Industries and Hershey Foods Corporation for permitting us the use of their 2007 Annual Reports for our specimen financial statements and accompanying notes.

We appreciate and encourage suggestions and comments from users. Please feel free to email any one of us at *AccountingAuthors@yahoo.com*.

Paul D. Kimmel
Milwaukee, Wisconsin

Jerry J. Weygandt
Madison, Wisconsin

Donald E. Kieso
DeKalb, Illinois

TOOLS FOR STUDENT SUCCESS

Financial Accounting, 5th Edition, provides many proven pedagogical tools to help students learn accounting concepts and apply them to decision making in the business world. The **Student Owner's Manual** at the book's companion site describes all the learning tools of the book in detail. Here are a few key features.

Learning How to Use the Text

- Students who take the new online **Learning Styles Quiz** will identify their learning style. Pages xxiii and xxiv list learning strategies and tips for the seven learning styles, and page xxv shows resources in WileyPLUS and the textbook that relate to those learning styles.

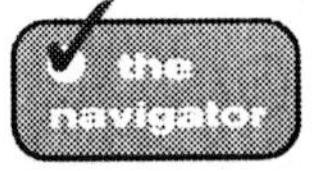

- **The Navigator** guides students through each chapter by pulling all the learning tools together into a learning system. Throughout the chapter, **The Navigator** prompts students to use the learning aids and to set priorities as they study.
- Marginal notes in blue in Chapter 1 explain how to use the text's learning tools to help achieve success in the course.

Understanding the Context

- **Study Objectives**, listed at the beginning of each chapter, reappear in the margins and again in the **Summary of Study Objectives**.
- A **Feature Story** helps students understand how the chapter topic relates to the real world of accounting and business and illustrates the necessity of sound accounting as the basis of informed decisions.
- A **Chapter Preview** links the Feature Story to the major topics of the chapter and provides a road map to the chapter.

preview of chapter 2

If you are thinking of purchasing Best Buy stock, or any stock, how can you decide what the stock is worth? If you manage J. Crew's credit department, how should you determine whether to extend credit to a new customer? If you are a financial executive of IBM, how do you decide whether your company is generating adequate cash to expand operations without borrowing? Your decision in each of these situations will be influenced by a variety of considerations. One of them should be your careful analysis of a company's financial statements. The reason: Financial statements offer relevant and reliable information, which will help you in your decision making.

In this chapter we take a closer look at the balance sheet and introduce some useful ways for evaluating the information provided by the financial statements. We also examine the financial reporting concepts underlying the financial statements.

A Further Look At Financial Statements

The Classified Balance Sheet	Using the Financial Statements	Financial Reporting Concepts
• Current assets • Long-term investments • Property, plant, and equipment • Intangible assets • Current liabilities • Long-term liabilities • Stockholders' equity	• Ratio analysis • Using the income statement • Using the statement of stockholders' equity • Using a classified balance sheet • Using the statement of cash flows	• The standard-setting environment • Characteristics of useful information • Assumptions and principles • Constraints

TOOLS FOR STUDENT SUCCESS

Learning the Material

- Emphasis on accounting experiences of **real companies and business situations throughout.**
- Three types of **Insight** boxes highlight ethics, investor, and international perspectives. These stories provide glimpses into how real companies make decisions using accounting information. In addition, **Accounting Across the Organization** boxes provide glimpses of how individuals in non-accounting functions use accounting information in their decision making.
- The **Insight** boxes and the **Accounting Across the Organization** boxes end with a question, which tests students' understanding of the real-world application in the box. Guideline answers for these questions appear at the end of the **Broadening Your Perspective** section at the end of the chapter.
- **Color illustrations**, including **infographics**, create "visual anchors" that help students visualize and apply accounting concepts.
- **Do It! exercises** appear at key breaks in the chapter narrative. These mini demonstration problems invite students to test their understanding of the just-completed section before they proceed to the next one.

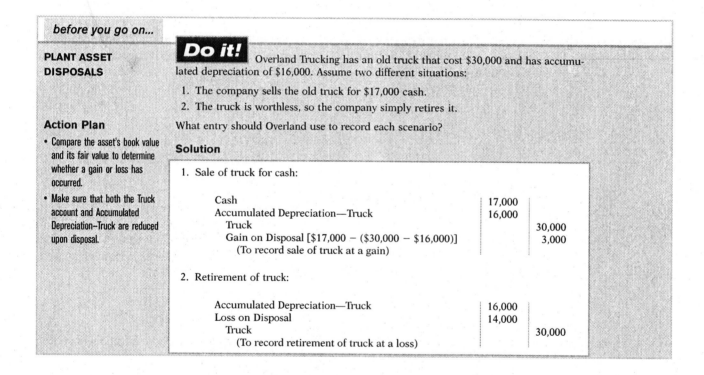

before you go on...

PLANT ASSET DISPOSALS

Do it! Overland Trucking has an old truck that cost $30,000 and has accumulated depreciation of $16,000. Assume two different situations:

1. The company sells the old truck for $17,000 cash.
2. The truck is worthless, so the company simply retires it.

What entry should Overland use to record each scenario?

Action Plan

- Compare the asset's book value and its fair value to determine whether a gain or loss has occurred.
- Make sure that both the Truck account and Accumulated Depreciation–Truck are reduced upon disposal.

Solution

1. Sale of truck for cash:

Cash	17,000	
Accumulated Depreciation—Truck	16,000	
Truck		30,000
Gain on Disposal [$17,000 − ($30,000 − $16,000)]		3,000
(To record sale of truck at a gain)		

2. Retirement of truck:

Accumulated Depreciation—Truck	16,000	
Loss on Disposal	14,000	
Truck		30,000
(To record retirement of truck at a loss)		

- **Accounting equation analyses** in the margin next to key journal entries reinforce understanding of the impact of an accounting transaction on the financial statements. They also report the **cash effect** of each transaction to reinforce understanding of the difference between cash effects and accrual accounting.
- **Helpful Hints, Alternative Terminology,** and blue-highlighted **key terms and concepts** help focus students on key concepts as they study the material.
- In the margins, **International Notes** and **Ethics Notes** provide a convenient way to expose students to international and ethics issues. The Fifth Edition greatly expands the number of these notes.

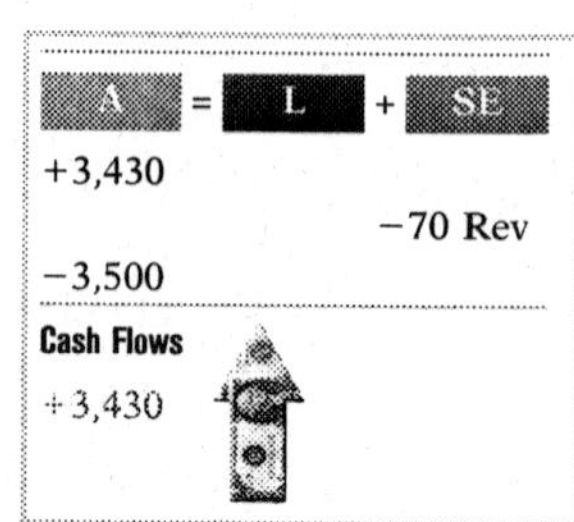

A = L + SE
+3,430
−70 Rev
−3,500
Cash Flows
+3,430

- New in this edition, text sections titled **"Keeping an Eye on Cash"** highlight differences between accrual accounting and cash accounting while increasing the student's understanding of the statement of cash flows. This feature aids the student's ability to evaluate accrual accounting and to use cash-basis numbers as tools of analysis when appropriate.

KEEPING AN EYE ON CASH

Free cash flow is closely monitored by analysts and investors for many reasons and in a variety of ways. One measure that is gaining increased attention is "price to free cash flow." This is a variant of the price to earnings (P-E) ratio, which has been a staple of analysts for a long time. The difference is that rather than divide the company's stock price by its earnings per share (an accrual-accounting–based number), the price to free cash flow ratio divides the company's stock price by its free cash flow per share. A high measure suggests that the stock price is high relative to the company's ability to generate cash. A low measure indicates that the company's stock might be a bargain.

The average price to free cash flow ratio for companies in the Standard and Poor's 500-stock index was recently 22. At the same time, the following companies reported measures way below the average. While you should not use this measure as the sole factor in choosing a stock, it can serve as a useful screen by which to identify companies that merit further investigation.

- **Decision tools** useful for analyzing and solving business problems are presented and then summarized in **Decision Toolkits**. Just before the chapter summary, a **Using the Decision Toolkit** exercise asks students to use the decision tools presented in the chapter and takes them through the problem-solving steps.

Putting It Together

At the end of each chapter are several features useful for review and reference.

- A **Summary of Study Objectives** reviews the main points of the chapter.
- The **Decision Toolkit—A Summary** presents in one place the decision tools used throughout the chapter.
- A **Glossary** of key terms gives definitions with page references to the text.
- A **Comprehensive Do It problem**, with an **Action Plan**, gives students another opportunity to study a detailed solution to a representative problem before they do homework assignments.

Comprehensive Do it!

DuPage Company purchased a factory machine at a cost of $18,000 on January 1, 2010. DuPage expected the machine to have a salvage value of $2,000 at the end of its 4-year useful life.

Instructions

Prepare a depreciation schedule using the straight-line method.

Action Plan

- Under the straight-line method, apply the depreciation rate to depreciable cost.

Solution to Comprehensive Do it!

DUPAGE COMPANY
Depreciation Schedule—Straight-Line Method

	Computation					End of Year	
Year	Depreciable Cost (a)	×	Depreciation Rate (b)	=	Annual Depreciation Expense	Accumulated Depreciation	Book Value (c)
2010	$16,000		25%		$4,000	$ 4,000	$14,000
2011	16,000		25		4,000	8,000	10,000

Developing Skills Through Practice

Each chapter is supported by a full complement of homework material. **Self-Study Questions, Questions, Brief Exercises, Do It! Review exercises, Exercises**, and three sets of **Problems** (one of which is at the book's website) are all keyed to the Study Objectives. In addition:

- Questions marked with the **Tootsie Roll** send students to find information in Tootsie Roll's 2007 annual report printed in the book.
- Certain Questions, Exercises, and Problems make use of the decision tools presented in the chapter. These are marked with the icon . Also, certain Questions, Exercises, and Problems show applications of accounting issues for business functions across the organization. These are marked with the icon .
- A **Comprehensive Problem** (in Chapters 5-11) combines material of the current chapter with previous chapters so that students understand how "it all fits together." Each of these problems requires the recording of transaction and adjusting entries, and culminates in the preparation of financial statements.

Comprehensive Problem

CP9 Pinkerton Corporation's trial balance at December 31, 2010, is presented on page xxx. All 2010 transactions have been recorded except for the items described after the trial balance.

- A **Continuing Cookie Chronicle** problem in every chapter traces the growth of an entrepreneurial venture. Each week students apply their newly acquired accounting skills to solve the financial reporting issues faced by this small business.
- Certain Exercises and Problems can be solved using the Excel supplement that is available to accompany the text and are identified by these icons.
- Other Exercises and Problems can be solved with the **General Ledger Software** available with the text and are marked with this icon. GLS

Expanding and Applying Knowledge

Broadening Your Perspective at the end of each chapter offers a wealth of resources for those instructors who want to broaden the learning experience by bringing in more real-world decision making, analysis, and critical thinking activities.

broadening your perspective

Financial Reporting and Analysis

FINANCIAL REPORTING PROBLEM: ***Tootsie Roll Industries, Inc.***

BYP4-1 The financial statements of Tootsie Roll are presented in Appendix A at the end of this book.

Instructions

(a) Using the consolidated income statement and balance sheet, identify items that may result in adjusting entries for prepayments.

- A **Financial Reporting Problem** directs students to study various aspects of the 2007 financial statements of Tootsie Roll Industries, Inc., which are printed in Chapter 1 (in simplified form) and in Appendix A (in full)

- A **Comparative Analysis Problem** offers the opportunity to compare and contrast the financial reporting of Tootsie Roll Industries, Inc., with a competitor Hershey Foods Corporation.
- **Research Cases** direct students to the *Wall Street Journal* and other business periodicals and references for further study and analysis of key topics. All Research Cases in this edition are *new*.

- **Interpreting Financial Statements** problems offer mini-cases that ask students to read parts of financial statements of actual companies and use the decision tools of the chapter to interpret them. Some of these cases, indicated by a globe icon, focus on specific situations faced by actual international companies.

- **Financial Analysis on the Web** problems guide students to websites from which they can mine and analyze information related to the chapter topic.
- **Decision Making Across the Organization** cases help promote group collaboration and build decision-making and business communication skills by requiring teams of students to consider business problems from various functional perspectives.

- **Communication Activities** provide practice in written communication, a skill much in demand among employers.

- **Ethics Cases** ask students to analyze situations, identify the ethical issues involved, and decide on an appropriate course of action.
- A new **"All About You" Activity** offers students an opportunity to link the accounting concepts learned in the chapter to some aspect of personal finance such as applying for a student loan, protecting themselves from identity theft, and the use of credit cards. These topics provide great opportunities for classroom discussion.

"ALL ABOUT YOU" ACTIVITY

BYP2-10 Every company needs to plan in order to move forward. Its top management must consider where it wants the company to be in three to five years. Like a company, you need to think about where you want to be three to five years from now, and you need to start taking steps now in order to get there.

Instructions

Provide responses to each of the following items.

(a) Where would you like to be working in three to five years? Describe your plan for

what are learning styles?

Have you ever repeated something to yourself over and over to help remember it? Or does your best friend ask you to draw a map to someplace where the two of you are planning to meet, rather than just *tell* her the directions? If so, then you already have an intuitive sense that people learn in different ways.

Researchers in learning theory have developed various categories of learning styles. Some people, for example, learn best by reading or writing. Others learn best by using various senses–seeing, hearing, feeling, tasting, or even smelling.

When you understand how you learn best, you can make use of learning strategies that will optimize the time you spend studying. To find out what your particular learning style is, go to the book's companion site at **www.wiley.com/college/kimmel** and take the learning styles quiz you find there. The quiz will help you determine which is your primary learning style:

Visual learner	**Auditory learner**	**Haptic learner**	**Olfactory learner**
Print learner	**Interactive learner**	**Kinesthetic learner**	

Then, consult the information below and on the following pages for study tips for each learning style. This information will help you better understand your learning style and how to apply it to the study of accounting.

Study Tips for Visual Learners

If you are a **Visual Learner** you prefer to work with images and diagrams. It is important that you *see* information.

Visual Learning:

- Draw charts/diagrams during lecture.
- Examine textbook figures and graphs.
- Look at images and videos on WileyPLUS and other websites.
- Pay close attention to charts, drawings, and handouts your instructors use.
- Underline; use different colors
- Use symbols, flow charts, graphs, different arrangements on the page, white spaces.

Visual Reinforcement:

- Make flashcards by drawing tables/charts on one side and definition or description on the other side
- Use art-based worksheets. Cover labels on images in text and then rewrite the labels.
- Use colored pencils/markers and colored paper to organize information into types.
- Convert your lecture notes into "page pictures." To do this:
  - Use the visual learning strategies outlined above.
  - Reconstruct images in different ways.
  - Redraw pages from memory.
  - Replace words with symbols and initials.
  - Draw diagrams where appropriate.
  - Practice turning your visuals back into words.

If visual learning is your weakness: If you are **not** a Visual Learner but want to improve your visual learning, try re-keying tables/charts from the textbook.

Study Tips for Print Learners

If you are a **Print Learner**, reading will be important but writing will be much more important.

Print Learning:

- Write text lecture notes during lecture.
- Read relevant topics in textbook, especially textbook tables.
- Look at text descriptions in animations and websites.
- Use lists and headings.
- Use dictionaries, glossaries, and definitions.
- Read handouts, textbooks, and supplementary library readings.
- Use lecture notes.

Print Reinforcement:

- Rewrite your notes from class and copy classroom handouts in your own handwriting.
- Make your own flashcards.
- Write out essays summarizing lecture notes or textbook topics.
- Develop mnemonics.
- Identify word relationships.
- Create tables with information extracted from textbook or lecture notes.
- Use text-based worksheets or crossword puzzles.
- Write out words again and again.
- Reread notes silently.
- Rewrite ideas and principles into other words.
- Turn charts, diagrams, and other illustrations into statements.
- Practice writing exam answers.
- Practice with multiple-choice questions.
- Write paragraphs, especially beginnings and endings.
- Write your lists in outline form.
- Arrange your words into hierarchies and points.

If print learning is your weakness: If you are **not** a Print Learner but want to improve your print learning, try covering labels of figures from the textbook and writing in the labels.

Study Tips for Auditory Learners

If you are an **Auditory Learner**, then you prefer listening as a way to learn information. Hearing will be very important, and sound helps you focus.

Auditory Learning:

- Make audio recordings during lecture.
- Do not skip class. Hearing the lecture is essential to understanding.
- Play audio files provided by instructor and textbook.
- Listen to narration of animations.
- Attend lecture and tutorials.
- Discuss topics with students and instructors.
- Explain new ideas to other people.

- Leave spaces in your lecture notes for later recall.
- Describe overheads, pictures, and visuals to somebody who was not in class.

Auditory Reinforcement:

- Record yourself reading the notes and listen to the recording.
- Write out transcripts of the audio files.
- Summarize information that you have read, speaking out loud.
- Use a recorder to create self-tests.
- Compose "songs" about information.
- Play music during studying to help focus.
- Expand your notes by talking with others and with information from your textbook
- Read summarized notes out loud.
- Explain your notes to another auditory learner.
- Talk with the instructor.
- Spend time in quiet places recalling the ideas.
- Say your answers out loud.

If auditory learning is your weakness: If you are **not** an Auditory Learner but want to improve your auditory learning, try writing out the scripts from pre-recorded lectures.

✓Study Tips for Interactive Learners

If you are an **Interactive Learner**, you will want to share your information. A study group will be important.

Interactive Learning:

- Ask a lot of questions during lecture or laboratory meetings.
- Contact other students, via email or discussion forums, and ask them to explain what they learned.

Interactive Reinforcement:

- "Teach" the content to a group of other students.
- Talking to an empty room may seem odd, but it will be effective for you.
- Discuss information with others, making sure that you both ask and answer questions.
- Work in small group discussions, making a verbal and written summary of what others say.

If interactive learning is your weakness: If you are **not** an Interactive Learner but want to improve your interactive learning, try asking your study partner questions and then repeating them to the instructor.

✓Study Tips for Haptic Learners

If you are a **Haptic Learner**, you prefer to work with your hands. It is important to physically manipulate material.

Haptic Learning:

- Take blank paper to lecture to draw charts/tables/diagrams.
- Using the textbook, run your fingers along the figures and graphs to get a "feel" for shapes and relationships.

Haptic Reinforcement:

- Trace words and pictures on flash cards.
- Perform electronic exercises that involve drag-and-drop activities.
- Alternate between speaking and writing information.
- Observe someone performing a task that you would like to learn.
- Make sure you have freedom of movement while studying.

If haptic learning is your weakness: If you are **not** a Haptic Learner but want to improve your haptic learning, try spending more time in class working with formulas, financial statements, and tables while speaking or writing down information.

✓Study Tips for Kinesthetic Learners

If you are a **Kinesthetic Learner** it will be important that you involve your body during studying.

Kinesthetic Learning:

- Ask permission to get up and move during lecture.
- Participate in role playing activities, in the classroom.
- Use all your senses
- Go to labs, take field trips
- Listen to real-life examples
- Pay attention to applications
- Use hands-on approaches
- Use trial-and-error methods

Kinesthetic Reinforcement:

- Make flash cards, place them on the floor and move your body around them.
- Move while you are "teaching" the material to others.
- Put examples in your summaries.
- Use case studies and applications to help with principles and abstract concepts.
- Talk about your notes with another Kinesthetic person.
- Use pictures and photographs that illustrate an idea.
- Write practice answers.
- Role-play the exam situation.

If kinesthetic learning is your weakness: If you are **not** a Kinesthetic Learner but want to improve your kinesthetic learning, try using flash cards to reconstruct balance sheets, income statements, cash flow statements, etc.

✓Study Tips for Olfactory Learners

If you are an **Olfactory Learner**, then you will prefer to use the senses of smell and test to reinforce learning. This is a rare learning modality.

Olfactory Learning:

- During lecture, use different scented markers to identify different types of information.

Olfactory Reinforcement:

- Rewrite notes with scented markers.
- If possible, go back to the computer lab to do your studying.
- Burn aromatic candles while studying.
- Try to associate the material that you're studying with a pleasant taste or smell.

If olfactory learning is your weakness: If you are **not** an **Olfactory Learner**, but want to improve your olfactory learning, try burning an aromatic candle or incense while you study or eating cookies during study sessions.

WileyPLUS and Textbook Resources for Various Learning Styles

RESOURCES	Visual	Print	Auditory	Interactive	Haptic	Kinesthetic	Olfactory*
Content of textbook		✓					
The Navigator/Feature Story/Preview	✓	✓					
Study Objectives		✓					
Infographics/Illustrations	✓	✓					
Accounting Equation Analyses	✓	✓	✓	✓	✓	✓	
Decision Toolkits/Decision Toolkit Summaries	✓	✓		✓			
Do It! Exercises/Comprehensive Do It! Problem/Action Plan	✓	✓		✓	✓	✓	
Summary of Study Objectives		✓					
Glossary/Self-study questions		✓		✓	✓	✓	
Questions/Exercises/Problems	✓	✓		✓			
Alternate versions of exercises & problems (B exercises; Problem sets B & C)	✓	✓		✓			
Financial Reporting/ Comparative Analysis Problems	✓	✓		✓	✓	✓	
Writing activities–Exercises and Problems marked with a pencil icon	✓	✓		✓	✓	✓	
Exploring the Web activity	✓	✓	✓	✓	✓	✓	
Communication Activity		✓		✓	✓	✓	
AAY Activity		✓		✓	✓	✓	
Practice quizzes		✓		✓	✓	✓	
Flash cards	✓	✓	✓	✓	✓	✓	
Audio Reviews/Video Clips/Clicker Content			✓	✓	✓	✓	
Flash Tutorial Reviews (Comprehensive Do It!/ Accounting Cycle/Annual Report)	✓	✓	✓	✓	✓	✓	
Crossword Puzzles	✓	✓		✓	✓	✓	
Excel Templates/Excel Working Papers	✓	✓		✓	✓	✓	
Checklist of Key Figures	✓	✓					
Peachtree/Quickbooks/GLS	✓	✓		✓	✓	✓	
Self-study/Self-test web quizzes	✓	✓		✓	✓	✓	

**To improve your learning using your olfactory modality, look at the resources recommended for your other most preferred learning styles. Then, pair olfactory study techniques with other resources, to enhance your learning. For example, you can burn aromatic candles while working on Flash tutorial reviews or Excel templates in WileyPLUS, or you can use scented markers to create flashcards.*

brief contents

1 Introduction to Financial Statements **2**

2 A Further Look at Financial Statements **46**

3 The Accounting Information System **100**

4 Fraud, Internal Control, and Cash **160**

5 Managerial Accounting **220**

6 Cost Volume Profit **270**

7 Budgetary Planning **308**

8 Budgetary Control and Responsibility Accounting **352**

9 Incremental Analysis **406**

10 Planning for Capital Investments **442**

11 Pricing **480**

appendixes

A Specimen Financial Statements: Tootsie Roll Industries, Inc. **A-1**

B Specimen Financial Statements: Hershey Foods Corporation **B-1**

C Time Value of Money **C-1**

D Standards of Ethical Conduct for Management Accountants **D-1**

indices

Company Index **I-1**

Subject Index **I-3**

chapter 1

Introduction to Financial Statements

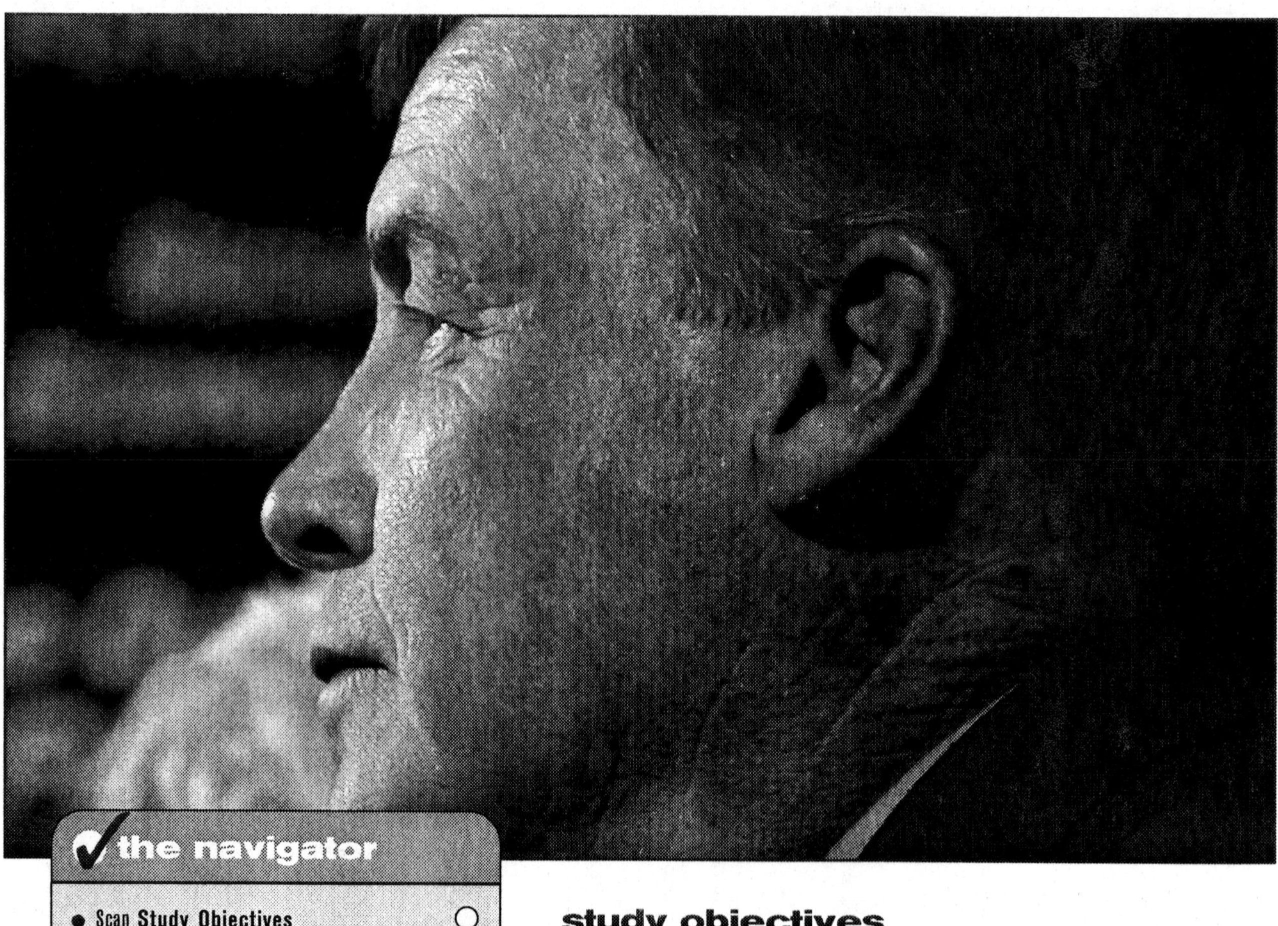

the navigator

- Scan Study Objectives ○
- Read Feature Story ○
- Scan Preview ○
- Read Text and Answer **Do it!** p. 5 ○ p. 11 ○ p. 18 ○ p. 23 ○
- Work Using the Decision Toolkit ○
- Review Summary of Study Objectives ○
- Work Comprehensive **Do it!** p. 26 ○
- Answer Self-Study Questions ○
- Complete Assignments ○

The Navigator is a learning system designed to prompt you to use the learning aids in the chapter and to set priorities as you study.

study objectives

After studying this chapter, you should be able to:

1. Describe the primary forms of business organization.
2. Identify the users and uses of accounting information.
3. Explain the three principal types of business activity.
4. Describe the content and purpose of each of the financial statements.
5. Explain the meaning of assets, liabilities, and stockholders' equity, and state the basic accounting equation.
6. Describe the components that supplement the financial statements in an annual report.

the navigator

feature story

Knowing the Numbers

Many students who take this course do not plan to be accountants. If you are in that group, you might be thinking, "If I'm not going to be an accountant, why do I need to know accounting?" In response, consider this quote from Harold Geneen, the former chairman of IT&T: "To be good at your business, you have to know the numbers—cold." Success in any business comes back to the numbers. You will rely on them to make decisions, and managers will use them to evaluate your performance. That is true whether your job involves marketing, production, management, or information systems.

In business, accounting and financial statements are the means for communicating the numbers. If you don't know how to read financial statements, you can't really know your business.

Many companies spend significant resources teaching their employees basic accounting so that they can read financial statements and understand how their actions affect the company's financial results. One such company is Springfield ReManufacturing Corporation (SRC). When Jack Stack and 11 other managers purchased SRC for 10 cents a share, it was a failing division of International Harvester. Jack's 119 employees were counting on him for their livelihood. He decided that for the company to survive, every employee needed to think like a businessperson and to act like an owner. To accomplish this, all employees at SRC took basic accounting courses and participated in weekly reviews of the company's financial statements. SRC survived, and eventually thrived. To this day, every employee (now numbering more than 1,000) undergoes this same training.

Many other companies have adopted this approach, which is called "open-book management." Even in companies that do not practice open-book management, employers generally assume that managers in all areas of the company are "financially literate."

Taking this course will go a long way to making you financially literate. In this book you will learn how to read and prepare financial statements, and how to use basic tools to evaluate financial results. In this first chapter we will introduce you to the financial statements of a real company whose products you are probably familiar with—Tootsie Roll. Tootsie Roll's presentation of its financial results is complete, yet also relatively easy to understand.

Tootsie Roll started off humbly in 1896 in a small New York City candy shop owned by an Austrian immigrant, Leo Hirshfield. The candy's name came from his five-year-old daughter's nickname—"Tootsie." Today the Chicago-based company produces more than 49 million Tootsie Rolls and 16 million Tootsie Pops *each day*. In fact, Tootsie Pops are at the center of one of science's most challenging questions: How many licks does it take to get to the Tootsie Roll center of a Tootsie Pop? The answer varies: Licking machines created at Purdue University and the University of Michigan report an average of 364 and 411 licks, respectively. In studies using human lickers, the answer ranges from 144 to 252. We recommend that you take a few minutes today away from your studies to determine your own results.

Source: Tootsie Roll information adapted from *www.tootsie.com*.

On the World Wide Web
Springfield ReManufacturing Corporation: *www.srcreman.com*
Tootsie Roll Industries: *www.tootsie.com*

preview of chapter 1

How do you start a business? How do you determine whether your business is making or losing money? How should you finance expansion–should you borrow, should you issue stock, should you use your own funds? How do you convince lenders to lend you money or investors to buy your stock? Success in business requires making countless decisions, and decisions require financial information.

The purpose of this chapter is to show you what role accounting plays in providing financial information. The content and organization of the chapter are as follows.

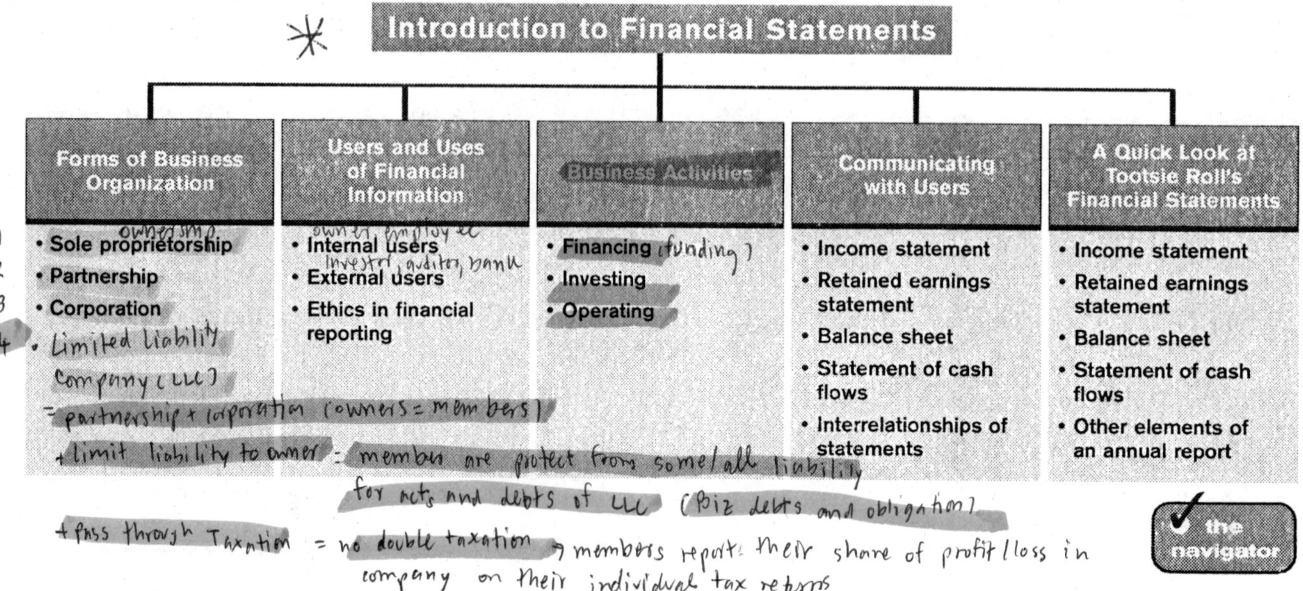

Forms of Business Organization

study objective 1

Describe the primary forms of business organization.

Essential terms are printed in blue. They are defined again in the **glossary** at the end of the chapter.

Suppose you graduate with a marketing degree and open your own marketing agency. One of your initial decisions is what organizational form your business will have. You have three choices—sole proprietorship, partnership, or corporation.

You will probably choose the sole proprietorship form for your marketing agency. A business owned by one person is a **sole proprietorship**. It is **simple to set up** and **gives you control** over the business. Small owner-operated businesses such as barber shops, law offices, and auto repair shops are often sole proprietorships, as are farms and small retail stores.

Another possibility is for you to join forces with other individuals to form a partnership. A business owned by two or more persons associated as partners is a **partnership**. Partnerships often are formed because one individual does not have **enough economic resources** to initiate or expand the business. Sometimes **partners bring unique skills or resources** to the partnership. You and your partners should formalize your duties and contributions in a written partnership agreement. Retail and service-type businesses, including professional practices (lawyers, doctors, architects, and certified public accountants), often organize as partnerships.

Alternative Terminology notes present synonymous terms that you may come across in practice.

Alternative Terminology
Stockholders are sometimes called *shareholders*.

As a third alternative, you might organize as a corporation. A business organized as a separate legal entity owned by stockholders is a **corporation**. As an investor in a corporation you receive shares of stock to indicate your ownership claim. Buying stock in a corporation is often more attractive than investing in a partnership because shares of stock are **easy to sell** (transfer ownership). Selling a proprietorship or partnership interest is much more involved. Also, individuals can become **stockholders** by investing relatively small amounts of money. Therefore, it is **easier for corporations to raise funds**. Successful corporations often have thousands of stockholders, and their stock is traded on organized stock exchanges like the New York Stock Exchange. Many businesses start as sole proprietorships or partnerships and eventually incorporate. For example, in 1896 Leo Hirshfield started Tootsie Roll as a sole proprietorship, and by 1919 the company had incorporated.

Other factors to consider in deciding which organizational form to choose are **taxes and legal liability**. If you choose a sole proprietorship or partnership, you generally receive more favorable tax treatment than a corporation. However, proprietors and partners are personally liable for all debts of the business; corporate stockholders are not. In other words, corporate stockholders generally pay higher taxes but have no personal liability. We will discuss these issues in more depth in a later chapter. Illustration 1-1 highlights the three types of organizations and the advantages of each.

Illustrations like this one convey information in pictorial form to help you visualize and apply the ideas as you study.

Illustration 1-1 Forms of business organization

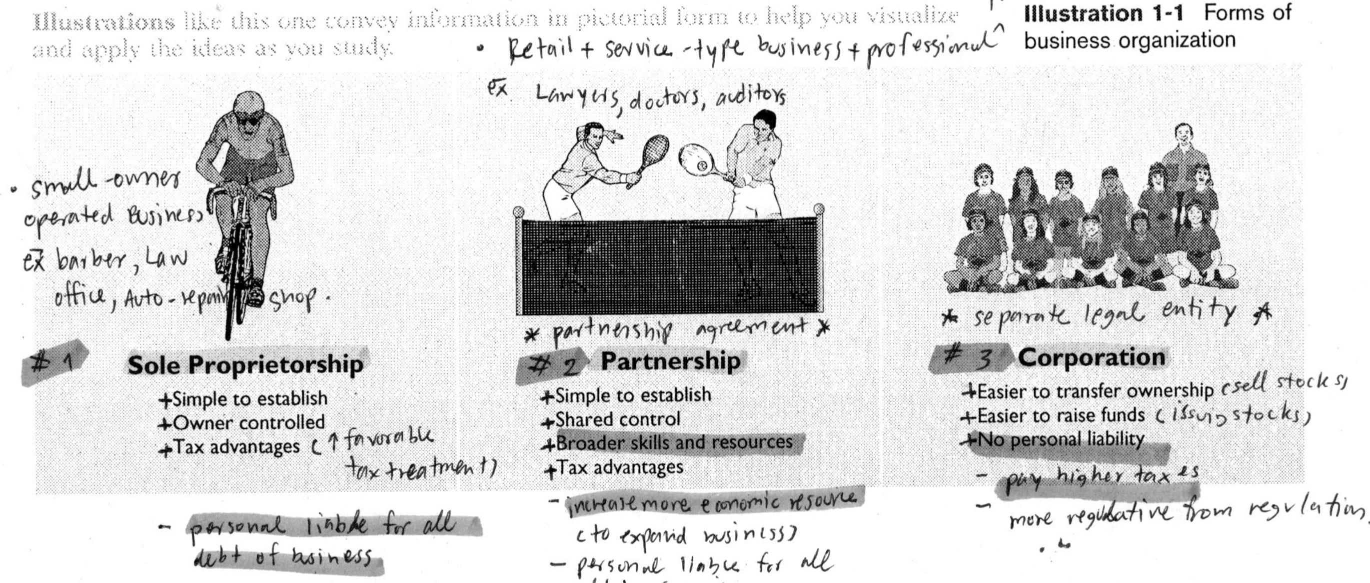

The combined number of proprietorships and partnerships in the United States is more than five times the number of corporations. However, the revenue produced by corporations is eight times greater. Most of the largest enterprises in the United States—for example, Coca-Cola, ExxonMobil, General Motors, Citigroup, and Microsoft—are corporations. Because the majority of U.S. business is transacted by corporations, the emphasis in this book is on the corporate form of organization.

Before You Go On... Do it! exercises prompt you to stop and review the key points you have just studied.

before you go on...

Do it! Identify each of the following organizational characteristics with the organizational form or forms with which it is associated.

BUSINESS ORGANIZATION FORMS

1. Easier to raise funds
2. Simple to establish
3. No personal legal liability
4. Tax advantages
5. Easier to transfer ownership

Action Plan

- Know which organizational form best matches the business type, size, and preferences of the owner(s).

Action Plans give you tips about how to approach the problem.

Solution

1. Easier to raise funds: Corporation.
2. Simple to establish: Sole proprietorship and partnership.
3. No personal legal liability: Corporation.
4. Tax advantages: Sole proprietorship and partnership.
5. Easier to transfer ownership: Corporation.

Users and Uses of Financial Information

study objective 2

Identify the users and uses of accounting information.

The purpose of financial information is to provide inputs for decision making. Accounting is the information system that identifies, records, and communicates the economic events of an organization to interested users. **Users** of accounting information can be divided broadly into two groups: internal users and external users.

INTERNAL USERS

Internal users of accounting information are managers who plan, organize, and run a business. These include **marketing managers, production supervisors, finance directors, and company officers**. In running a business, managers must answer many important questions, as shown in Illustration 1-2.

Illustration 1-2
Questions that internal users ask

Questions Asked by Internal Users

Finance
Is cash sufficient to pay dividends to Microsoft stockholders?

Marketing
What price for an Apple iPod will maximize the company's net income?

Human Resources
Can we afford to give General Motors employees pay raises this year?

Management
Which PepsiCo product line is the most profitable? Should any product lines be eliminated?

To answer these and other questions, you need detailed information on a timely basis. For internal users, accounting provides internal reports, such as financial comparisons of operating alternatives, projections of income from new sales campaigns, and forecasts of cash needs for the next year. In addition, companies present summarized financial information in the form of financial statements.

Accounting Across the Organization

Accounting can serve as a useful recruiting tool even for the human resources department. Rhino Foods, located in Burlington, Vermont, is a manufacturer of specialty ice cream. Its corporate website includes the following:

> "Wouldn't it be great to work where you were part of a team? Where your input and hard work made a difference? Where you weren't kept in the dark about what management was thinking? . . . Well–it's not a dream! It's the way we do business . . . Rhino Foods believes in family, honesty and open communication–we really care about and appreciate our employees–and it shows. Operating results are posted and monthly group meetings inform all employees about what's happening in the Company. Employees also share in the Company's profits, in addition to having an excellent comprehensive *benefits* package."

Source: www.rhinofoods.com/workforus/workforus.html.

What are the benefits to the company and to the employees of making the financial statements available to all employees? Answers to questions appear on the last page of the chapter (p. 44).

Accounting Across the Organization stories show applications of accounting information in various business functions.

EXTERNAL USERS

There are several types of **external users** of accounting information. **Investors** (owners) use accounting information to make decisions to buy, hold, or sell stock. **Creditors** such as suppliers and bankers use accounting information to evaluate the risks of selling on credit or lending money. Some questions that investors and creditors may ask about a company are shown in Illustration 1-3.

Illustration 1-3
Questions that external users ask

Questions Asked by External Users

Investors
Is General Electric earning satisfactory income?

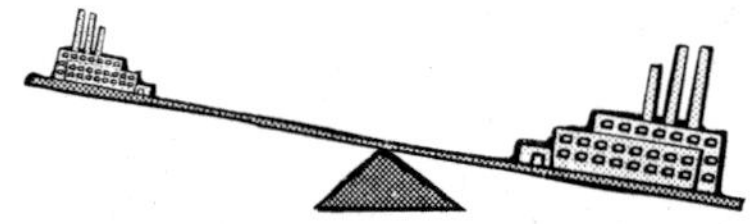

Investors
How does Disney compare in size and profitability with Time Warner?

Creditors
Will United Airlines be able to pay its debts as they come due?

The information needs and questions of other external users vary considerably. **Taxing authorities**, such as the Internal Revenue Service, want to know whether the company complies with the tax laws. **Customers** are interested in whether a company like General Motors will continue to honor product warranties and otherwise support its product lines. **Labor unions** such as the Major League Baseball Players Association want to know whether the owners have the ability to pay increased wages and benefits. **Regulatory agencies**, such as the Securities and Exchange Commission or the Federal Trade Commission, want to know whether the company is operating within prescribed rules. For example, Enron, Dynegy, Duke Energy, and other big energy-trading companies reported record profits at the same time as California was paying extremely high prices for energy and suffering from blackouts. This disparity caused regulators to investigate the energy traders to make sure that the profits were earned by legitimate and fair practices.

Accounting Across the Organization

One question that accounting students frequently ask is, "How will the study of accounting help me?" It should help you a great deal, because a working knowledge of accounting is desirable for virtually every field of endeavor. Some examples of how accounting is used in business careers include:

General management: Imagine running Ford Motors, Massachusetts General Hospital, California State University–Fullerton, a McDonald's franchise, a Trek bike shop. All general managers need to understand accounting data in order to make wise business decisions.

Marketing: A marketing specialist at a company like Procter & Gamble develops strategies to help the sales force be successful. But making a sale is meaningless unless it is a profitable sale. Marketing people must be sensitive to costs and benefits, which accounting helps them quantify and understand.

Finance: Do you want to be a banker for Citicorp, an investment analyst for Goldman Sachs, a stock broker for Merrill Lynch? These fields rely heavily on accounting. In all of them you will regularly examine and analyze financial statements. In fact, it is difficult to get a good job in a finance function without two or three courses in accounting.

Real estate: Are you interested in being a real estate broker for Prudential Real Estate? Because a third party–the bank–is almost always involved in financing a real estate transaction, brokers must understand the numbers involved: Can the buyer afford to make the payments to the bank? Does the cash flow from an industrial property justify the purchase price? What are the tax benefits of the purchase?

How might accounting help you?

ETHICS IN FINANCIAL REPORTING

People won't gamble in a casino if they think it is "rigged." Similarly, people won't "play" the stock market if they think stock prices are rigged. In recent years the financial press has been full of articles about financial scandals at Enron, WorldCom, HealthSouth, and AIG. As more scandals came to light, a mistrust of financial reporting in general seemed to be developing. One article in the *Wall Street Journal* noted that "repeated disclosures about questionable accounting practices have bruised investors' faith in the reliability of earnings reports, which in turn has sent stock prices tumbling."[1] Imagine trying to carry on a business or invest money if you could not depend on the financial statements to be honestly prepared. Information would have no credibility. There is no doubt that a sound, well-functioning economy depends on accurate and dependable financial reporting.

[1]"U.S. Share Prices Slump," *Wall Street Journal* (February 21, 2002).

United States regulators and lawmakers were very concerned that the economy would suffer if investors lost confidence in corporate accounting because of unethical financial reporting. In 2002 Congress passed the **Sarbanes-Oxley Act (SOX)** to reduce unethical corporate behavior and decrease the likelihood of future corporate scandals. As a result of SOX, top management must now certify the accuracy of financial information. In addition, penalties for fraudulent financial activity are much more severe. Also, SOX increased the independence of the outside auditors who review the accuracy of corporate financial statements, and increased the oversight role of boards of directors.

Ethics Note Circus-founder P.T. Barnum is alleged to have said, "Trust everyone, but cut the deck." What Sarbanes-Oxley does is to provide measures that (like cutting the deck of playing cards) help ensure that fraud will not occur.

Effective financial reporting depends on sound ethical behavior. To sensitize you to ethical situations and to give you practice at solving ethical dilemmas, we address ethics in a number of ways in this book: (1) A number of the *Feature Stories* and other parts of the text discuss the central importance of ethical behavior to financial reporting. (2) *Business Insight boxes* with an ethics perspective highlight ethics situations and issues in actual business settings. (3) At the end of the chapter, an *Ethics Case* simulates a business situation and asks you to put yourself in the position of a decision maker in that case.

When analyzing these various ethics cases and your own ethical experiences, you should apply the three steps outlined in Illustration 1-4.

Illustration 1-4 Steps in analyzing ethics cases

Solving an Ethical Dilemma

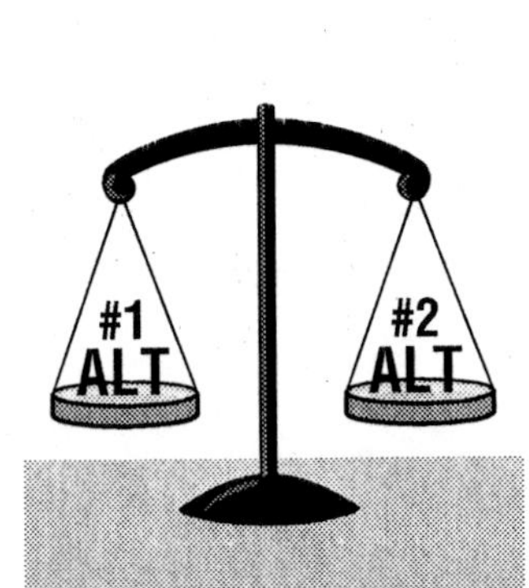

1. Recognize an ethical situation and the ethical issues involved.

Use your personal ethics to identify ethical situations and issues. Some businesses and professional organizations provide written codes of ethics for guidance in some business situations.

2. Identify and analyze the principal elements in the situation.

Identify the *stakeholders*—persons or groups who may be harmed or benefited. Ask the question: What are the responsibilities and obligations of the parties involved?

3. Identify the alternatives, and weigh the impact of each alternative on various stakeholders.

Select the most ethical alternative, considering all the consequences. Sometimes there will be one right answer. Other situations involve more than one right solution; these situations require you to evaluate each alternative and select the best one.

International Insight

Accounting plays an important role for a wide range of business organizations worldwide. Just as the integrity of the numbers matters for business, it matters at least as much for not-for-profit organizations. Proper control and reporting help ensure that money is used the way donors intended. Donors are less inclined to give to an organization if they think the organization is subject to waste or theft. The accounting challenges of some large international not-for-profits rival those of the world's largest businesses. For example, billions of dollars were donated for relief of the tsunami victims of India and Sri Lanka. To assist in that effort, one international accounting firm volunteered to help create a system that would investigate allegations of fraud or waste. Another accounting system proposed by the United Nations would enable donors to track donations via the Web. In addition, the United Nations created rules to protect employees who report possible fraudulent activity.

What benefits does a sound accounting system provide to a not-for-profit organization?

Business Insights provide examples of business situations from various perspectives—ethics, investor, and international.

Business Activities

study objective 3

Explain the three principal types of business activity.

All businesses are involved in three types of activity—financing, investing, and operating. For example, Leo Hirshfield the founder of Tootsie Roll, obtained cash through financing to start and grow his business. Some of this **financing** came from personal savings, and some likely came from outside sources like banks. Hirshfield then **invested** the cash in equipment to run the business, such as mixing equipment and delivery vehicles. Once this equipment was in place, he could begin the **operating** activities of making and selling candy.

The **accounting information system** keeps track of the results of each of the various business activities—financing, investing, and operating. Let's look in more detail at each type of business activity.

FINANCING ACTIVITIES

Financing

It takes money to make money. The two primary sources of outside funds for corporations are borrowing money and issuing (selling) shares of stock in exchange for cash.

Tootsie Roll Industries may borrow money in a variety of ways. For example, it can take out a loan at a bank or borrow directly from investors by issuing debt securities called bonds. Persons or entities to whom Tootsie Roll owes money are its **creditors**. Amounts owed to creditors—in the form of debt and other obligations—are called **liabilities**. Specific names are given to different types of liabilities, depending on their source. Tootsie Roll may have a **note payable** to a bank for the money borrowed to purchase delivery trucks. Debt securities sold to investors that must be repaid at a particular date some years in the future are **bonds payable**.

A corporation may also obtain funds by selling shares of stock to investors. **Common stock** is the term used to describe the total amount paid in by stockholders for the shares they purchase.

The claims of creditors differ from those of stockholders. If you loan money to a company, you are one of its creditors. In lending money, you specify a payment schedule (e.g., payment at the end of three months). As a creditor, you have a legal right to be paid at the agreed time. In the event of nonpayment, you may legally force the company to sell property to pay its debts. In the case of financial difficulty, creditor claims must be paid before stockholders' claims.

Stockholders, on the other hand, have no claim to corporate cash until the claims of creditors are satisfied. If you buy a company's stock instead of loaning it money, you have no legal right to expect any payments until all of its creditors are paid. However, many corporations make payments to stockholders on a regular basis as long as there is sufficient cash to cover required payments to creditors. These payments to stockholders are called **dividends**.

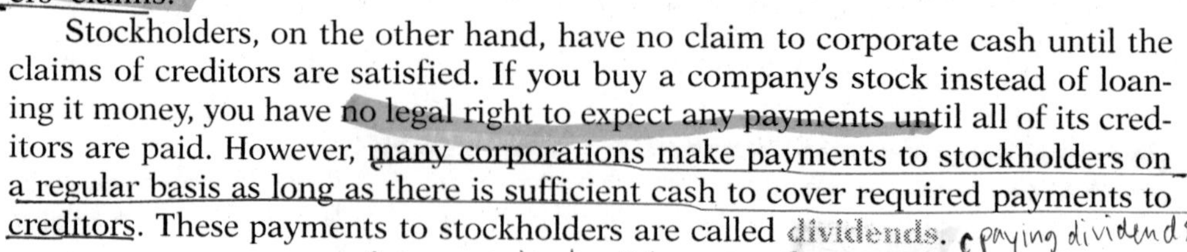

INVESTING ACTIVITIES

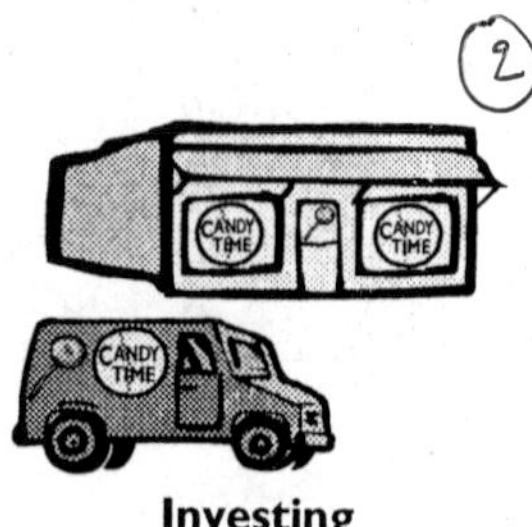

Investing

Once the company has raised cash through financing activities, it will then use that cash in investing activities. Investing activities involve the purchase of the resources a company needs in order to operate. A growing company purchases many resources, such as computers, delivery trucks, furniture, and buildings. Resources owned by a business are called **assets**. Different types of assets are given different names. Tootsie Roll's mixing equipment is a type of asset referred to as **property, plant, and equipment**.

Alternative Terminology
Property, plant, and equipment is sometimes called *fixed assets*.

Cash is one of the more important assets owned by Tootsie Roll or any other business. If a company has excess cash that it does not need for a while, it might choose to invest in securities (stocks or bonds) of other corporations. **Investments** are another example of an investing activity.

OPERATING ACTIVITIES

Operating

Once a business has the assets it needs to get started, it can begin its operations. Tootsie Roll is in the business of selling all things that taste, look, or smell like candy. It sells Tootsie Rolls, Tootsie Pops, Blow Pops, Caramel Apple Pops, Mason Dots, Mason Crows, Sugar Daddy, and Sugar Babies. We call amounts earned on the sale of these products *revenues*. **Revenue** is the increase in assets resulting from the sale of a product or service in the normal course of business. For example, Tootsie Roll records revenue when it sells a candy product.

Revenues arise from different sources and are identified by various names depending on the nature of the business. For instance, Tootsie Roll's primary source of revenue is the sale of candy products. However, it also generates interest revenue on debt securities held as investments. Sources of revenue common to many businesses are **sales revenue**, **service revenue**, and **interest revenue**.

The company purchases its longer-lived assets through investing activities as described earlier. Other assets with shorter lives, however, result from operating activities. For example, supplies are assets used in day-to-day operations. Goods available for future sales to customers are assets called **inventory**. Also, if Tootsie Roll sells goods to a customer and does not receive cash immediately, then the company has a right to expect payment from that customer in the near future. This right to receive money in the future is called an **account receivable**.

Before Tootsie Roll can sell a single Tootsie Roll, Tootsie Pop, or Blow Pop, it must purchase sugar, corn syrup, and other ingredients, mix these ingredients, process the mix, and wrap and ship the finished product. It also incurs costs like salaries, rents, and utilities. All of these costs, referred to as *expenses*, are necessary to produce and sell the product. In accounting language, **expenses** are the cost of assets consumed or services used in the process of generating revenues.

Expenses take many forms and are identified by various names depending on the type of asset consumed or service used. For example, Tootsie Roll keeps track of these types of expenses: **cost of goods sold** (such as the cost of ingredients); **selling expenses** (such as the cost of salespersons' salaries); **marketing expenses** (such as the cost of advertising); **administrative expenses** (such as the salaries of administrative staff, and telephone and heat costs incurred at the corporate office); **interest expense** (amounts of interest paid on various debts); and **income taxes** (corporate taxes paid to government).

Tootsie Roll may also have liabilities arising from these expenses. For example, it may purchase goods on credit from suppliers; the obligations to pay for these goods are called **accounts payable**. Additionally, Tootsie Roll may have **interest payable** on the outstanding amounts owed to the bank. It may also have **wages payable** to its employees and **sales taxes payable**, **property taxes payable**, and **income taxes payable** to the government.

Tootsie Roll compares the revenues of a period with the expenses of that period to determine whether it earned a profit. When revenues exceed expenses, **net income** results. When expenses exceed revenues, a **net loss** results.

before you go on...

BUSINESS ACTIVITIES

Do it! Classify each item as an asset, liability, common stock, revenue, or expense.

1. Cost of renting property
2. Truck purchased
3. Notes payable
4. Issuance of ownership shares
5. Amount earned from providing service
6. Amounts owed to suppliers

Action Plan

- Classify each item based on its economic characteristics. Proper classification of items is critical if accounting is to provide useful information.

Solution

1. Cost of renting property: Expense.
2. Truck purchased: Asset.
3. Notes payable: Liabilities.
4. Issuance of ownership shares: Common stock.
5. Amount earned from providing service: Revenue.
6. Amounts owed to suppliers: Liabilities.

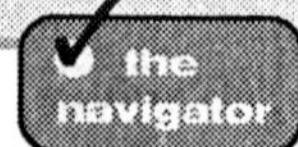

Communicating with Users

study objective 4

Describe the content and purpose of each of the financial statements.

Assets, liabilities, expenses, and revenues are of interest to users of accounting information. This information is arranged in the format of four different **financial statements**, which form the backbone of financial accounting:

- To present a picture at a point in time of what your business owns (its assets) and what it owes (its liabilities), you prepare a **balance sheet.**
- To show how successfully your business performed during a period of time, you report its revenues and expenses in an **income statement.**
- To indicate how much of previous income was distributed to you and the other owners of your business in the form of dividends, and how much was retained in the business to allow for future growth, you present a **retained earnings statement.**
- To show where your business obtained cash during a period of time and how that cash was used, you present a **statement of cash flows.**

International Note The primary types of financial statements required by international accounting standards (IFRS) and U.S. accounting standards (GAAP) are the same. Neither IFRS nor GAAP is very specific regarding format requirements for the primary financial statements. However, in practice, some format differences do exist in presentations commonly employed by IFRS companies compared to GAAP companies.

To introduce you to these statements, we have prepared the financial statements for a marketing agency, Sierra Corporation.

INCOME STATEMENT

The income statement reports the success or failure of the company's operations for a period of time. To indicate that its income statement reports the results of operations for a **period of time**, Sierra dates the income statement "For the Month Ended October 31, 2010." The income statement lists the company's revenues followed by its expenses. Finally, Sierra determines the net income (or net loss) by deducting expenses from revenues. Sierra Corporation's income statement is shown in Illustration 1-5.

Illustration 1-5 Sierra Corporation's income statement

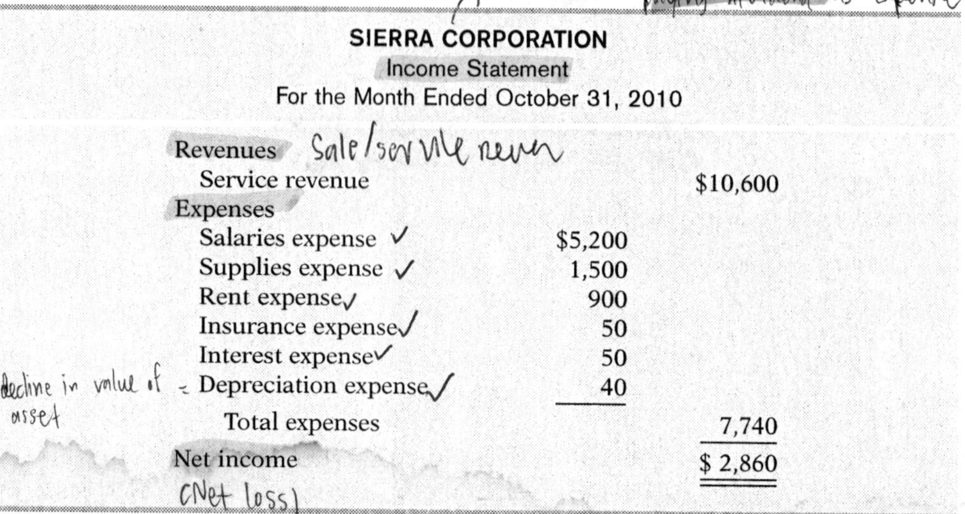

SIERRA CORPORATION
Income Statement
For the Month Ended October 31, 2010

Revenues		
Service revenue		$10,600
Expenses		
Salaries expense	$5,200	
Supplies expense	1,500	
Rent expense	900	
Insurance expense	50	
Interest expense	50	
Depreciation expense	40	
Total expenses		7,740
Net income		$ 2,860

Helpful Hint The heading identifies the company, the type of statement, and the time period covered. Sometimes another line indicates the unit of measure–e.g., "in thousands" or "in millions."

Why are financial statement users interested in net income? Investors are interested in Sierra's past net income because it provides useful information for predicting future net income. Investors buy and sell stock based on their beliefs about Sierra's future performance. If you believe that Sierra will be successful in the future and that this will result in a higher stock price, you should buy its stock. Creditors also use the income statement to predict future earnings. When a bank loans money to a company, it believes that it will be repaid in the future. If it didn't think it would be repaid, it wouldn't loan the money. Therefore, prior to making the loan the bank loan officer uses the income statement as a source of information to predict whether the company will be profitable enough to repay its loan.

Amounts received from issuing stock are not revenues, and amounts paid out as dividends are not expenses. As a result, they are not reported on the income statement. For example, Sierra Corporation does not treat as revenue the $10,000 of cash received from issuing new stock, nor does it regard as a business expense the $500 of dividends paid.

Ethics Note When companies find errors in previously released income statements, they restate those numbers. Perhaps because of the increased scrutiny caused by Sarbanes-Oxley, in a recent year companies filed a record 1,195 restatements.

Decision Toolkits summarize the financial decision-making process.

DECISION CHECKPOINTS	INFO NEEDED FOR DECISION	TOOL TO USE FOR DECISION	HOW TO EVALUATE RESULTS
Are the company's operations profitable?	Income statement	The income statement reports on the success or failure of the company's operations by reporting its revenues and expenses.	If the company's revenue exceeds its expenses, it will report net income; otherwise it will report a net loss.

RETAINED EARNINGS STATEMENT

If Sierra is profitable, at the end of each period it must decide what portion of profits to pay to shareholders in dividends. In theory it could pay all of its current-period profits, but few companies do this. Why? Because they want to retain part of the profits to allow for further expansion. High-growth companies, such as Google and Cisco Systems, often pay no dividends. Retained earnings is the net income retained in the corporation.

The retained earnings statement shows the amounts and causes of changes in retained earnings during the period. The time period is the same as that covered by the income statement. The beginning retained earnings amount appears on the first line of the statement. Then the company adds net income and deducts dividends to determine the retained earnings at the end of the period. If a company has a net loss, it deducts (rather than adds) that amount in the retained earnings statement. Illustration 1-6 presents Sierra Corporation's retained earnings statement.

Illustration 1-6 Sierra Corporation's retained earnings statement

SIERRA CORPORATION
Retained Earnings Statement
For the Month Ended October 31, 2010

Retained earnings, October 1	$ 0
Add: Net income	2,860
	2,860
Less: Dividends	500
Retained earnings, October 31	$2,360

Helpful Hint The heading of this statement identifies the company, the type of statement, and the time period covered by the statement.

By monitoring the retained earnings statement, financial statement users can evaluate dividend payment practices. Some investors seek companies, such as Dow Chemical, that have a history of paying high dividends. Other investors seek companies, such as Amazon.com, that reinvest earnings to increase the company's growth instead of paying dividends. Lenders monitor their corporate customers' dividend payments because any money paid in dividends reduces a company's ability to repay its debts.

DECISION TOOLKIT

DECISION CHECKPOINTS	INFO NEEDED FOR DECISION	TOOL TO USE FOR DECISION	HOW TO EVALUATE RESULTS
What is the company's policy toward dividends and growth?	Retained earnings statement	How much of this year's income did the company pay out in dividends to shareholders?	A company striving for rapid growth will pay a low (or no) dividend.

BALANCE SHEET

study objective 5

Explain the meaning of assets, liabilities, and stockholders' equity, and state the basic accounting equation.

The **balance sheet** reports assets and claims to assets at a specific **point** in time. Claims to assets are subdivided into two categories: claims of creditors and claims of owners. As noted earlier, claims of creditors are called **liabilities**. Claims of owners are called **stockholders' equity**.

Illustration 1-7 shows the relationship among the categories on the balance sheet in equation form. This equation is referred to as the **basic accounting equation**.

Illustration 1-7 Basic accounting equation

Assets = Liabilities + Stockholders' Equity

This relationship is where the name "balance sheet" comes from. Assets must balance with the claims to assets.

As you can see from looking at Sierra's balance sheet in Illustration 1-8, the balance sheet presents the company's financial position as of a specific date—in this case, October 31, 2010. It lists assets first, followed by liabilities and stockholders' equity. Stockholders' equity is comprised of two parts: (1) common stock

Illustration 1-8 Sierra Corporation's balance sheet

Helpful Hint The heading of a balance sheet must identify the company, the statement, and the date.

SIERRA CORPORATION
Balance Sheet
October 31, 2010

Assets		
Cash		$15,200
Accounts receivable		200
Advertising supplies		1,000
Prepaid insurance		550
Office equipment, net		4,960
Total assets		$21,910
Liabilities and Stockholders' Equity		
Liabilities		
Notes payable	$ 5,000	
Accounts payable	2,500	
Salaries payable	1,200	
Unearned revenue	800	
Interest payable	50	
Total liabilities		$ 9,550
Stockholders' equity		
Common stock	10,000	
Retained earnings	2,360	
Total stockholders' equity		12,360
Total liabilities and stockholders' equity		$21,910

and (2) retained earnings. As noted earlier, common stock results when the company sells new shares of stock; retained earnings is the net income retained in the corporation. Sierra has common stock of $10,000 and retained earnings of $2,360, for total stockholders' equity of $12,360.

Creditors analyze a company's balance sheet to determine the likelihood that they will be repaid. They carefully evaluate the nature of the company's assets and liabilities. For example, does Sierra have assets that could be easily sold to repay its debts? Sierra's managers use the balance sheet to determine whether cash on hand is sufficient for immediate cash needs. They also look at the relationship between debt and stockholders' equity to determine whether the company has a satisfactory proportion of debt and common stock financing.

DECISION TOOLKIT

DECISION CHECKPOINTS	INFO NEEDED FOR DECISION	TOOL TO USE FOR DECISION	HOW TO EVALUATE RESULTS
Does the company rely primarily on debt or stockholders' equity to finance its assets?	Balance sheet	The balance sheet reports the company's resources and claims to those resources. There are two types of claims: liabilities and stockholders' equity.	Compare the amount of debt versus the amount of stockholders' equity to determine whether the company relies more on creditors or owners for its financing.

Ethics Insight

What topic has performers such as Tom Waits, Clint Black, Sheryl Crow, and Madonna so concerned that they are pushing for new laws regarding its use? Accounting. Recording-company accounting to be more precise. Musicians receive royalty payments based on the accounting done by their recording companies. Many performers say that the recording companies–either intentionally or unintentionally–have very poor accounting systems, which, the performers say, has resulted in many inaccurate royalty payments. They would like to see laws created that would hit the recording companies with stiff fines for accounting errors.

What is one way that some of these disputes might be resolved?

STATEMENT OF CASH FLOWS

The primary purpose of a **statement of cash flows** is to provide financial information about the cash receipts and cash payments of a business for a specific period of time. To help investors, creditors, and others in their analysis of a company's cash position, the statement of cash flows reports the cash effects of a company's **operating**, **investing**, and **financing** activities. In addition, the statement shows the net increase or decrease in cash during the period, and the amount of cash at the end of the period.

Users are interested in the statement of cash flows because they want to know what is happening to a company's most important resource. The statement of cash flows provides answers to these simple but important questions:

- Where did cash come from during the period?
- How was cash used during the period?
- What was the change in the cash balance during the period?

The statement of cash flows for Sierra, in Illustration 1-9, shows that cash increased $15,200 during the month. This increase resulted because operating activities (services to clients) increased cash $5,700, and financing activities increased cash $14,500. Investing activities used $5,000 of cash for the purchase of equipment.

Illustration 1-9 Sierra Corporation's statement of cash flows

SIERRA CORPORATION
Statement of Cash Flows
For the Month Ended October 31, 2010

Cash flows from operating activities		
Cash receipts from operating activities	$11,200	
Cash payments for operating activities	(5,500)	
Net cash provided by operating activities		$ 5,700
Cash flows from investing activities		
Purchased office equipment	(5,000)	
Net cash used by investing activities		(5,000)
Cash flows from financing activities		
Issuance of common stock	10,000	
Issued note payable	5,000	
Payment of dividend	(500)	
Net cash provided by financing activities		14,500
Net increase in cash		15,200
Cash at beginning of period		0
Cash at end of period		$15,200

Helpful Hint The heading of this statement identifies the company, the type of statement, and the time period covered by the statement. Negative numbers are shown in parentheses.

DECISION TOOLKIT

DECISION CHECKPOINTS	INFO NEEDED FOR DECISION	TOOL TO USE FOR DECISION	HOW TO EVALUATE RESULTS
Does the company generate sufficient cash from operations to fund its investing activities?	Statement of cash flows	The statement of cash flows shows the amount of cash provided or used by operating activities, investing activities, and financing activities.	Compare the amount of cash provided by operating activities with the amount of cash used by investing activities. Any deficiency in cash from operating activities must be made up with cash from financing activities.

INTERRELATIONSHIPS OF STATEMENTS

Because the results on some financial statements become inputs to other statements, the statements are interrelated. Illustration 1-10 shows the interrelationships for Sierra's financial statements, which we describe below.

1. The retained earnings statement depends on the results of the income statement. Sierra reported net income of $2,860 for the period. It adds the net income amount to the beginning amount of retained earnings in order to determine ending retained earnings.
2. The balance sheet and retained earnings statement also are interrelated: Sierra reports the ending amount of $2,360 on the retained earnings statement as the retained earnings amount on the balance sheet.
3. Finally, the statement of cash flows relates to information on the balance sheet. The statement of cash flows shows how the cash account changed during the period. It shows the amount of cash at the beginning of the period, the sources and uses of cash during the period, and the $15,200 of cash at the end of the period. The ending amount of cash shown on the statement of cash flows must agree with the amount of cash on the balance sheet.

Study these interrelationships carefully. To prepare financial statements you must understand the sequence in which these amounts are determined, and how each statement impacts the next.

Illustration 1-10 Sierra Corporation's financial statements

Helpful Hint Note that final sums are double-underlined, and negative amounts (in the statement of cash flows) are presented in parentheses.

Helpful Hint The arrows in this illustration show interrelationships of the four financial statements.

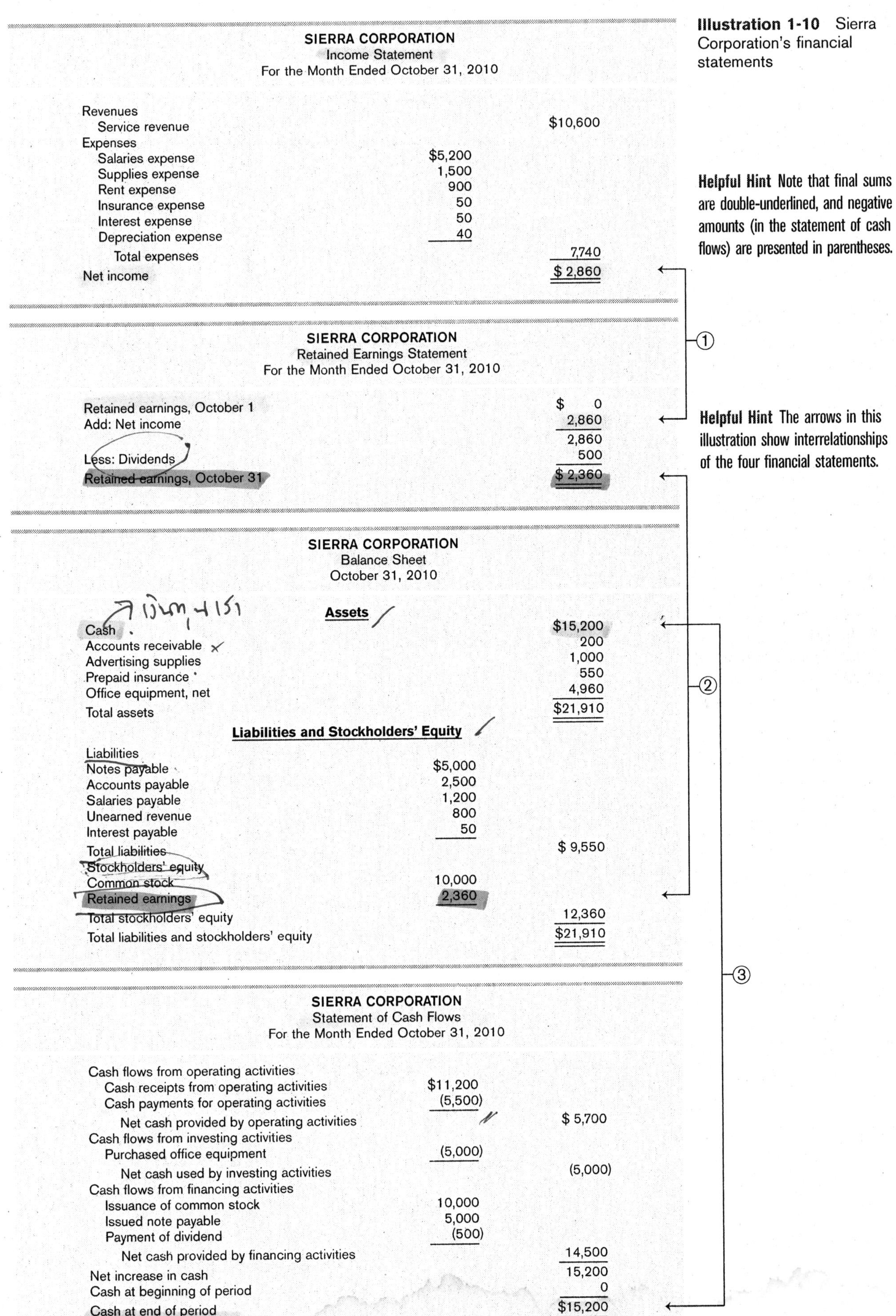

SIERRA CORPORATION
Income Statement
For the Month Ended October 31, 2010

Revenues		
Service revenue		$10,600
Expenses		
Salaries expense	$5,200	
Supplies expense	1,500	
Rent expense	900	
Insurance expense	50	
Interest expense	50	
Depreciation expense	40	
Total expenses		7,740
Net income		$ 2,860

SIERRA CORPORATION
Retained Earnings Statement
For the Month Ended October 31, 2010

Retained earnings, October 1	$ 0
Add: Net income	2,860
	2,860
Less: Dividends	500
Retained earnings, October 31	$ 2,360

SIERRA CORPORATION
Balance Sheet
October 31, 2010

Assets		
Cash		$15,200
Accounts receivable		200
Advertising supplies		1,000
Prepaid insurance		550
Office equipment, net		4,960
Total assets		$21,910
Liabilities and Stockholders' Equity		
Liabilities		
Notes payable	$5,000	
Accounts payable	2,500	
Salaries payable	1,200	
Unearned revenue	800	
Interest payable	50	
Total liabilities		$ 9,550
Stockholders' equity		
Common stock	10,000	
Retained earnings	2,360	
Total stockholders' equity		12,360
Total liabilities and stockholders' equity		$21,910

SIERRA CORPORATION
Statement of Cash Flows
For the Month Ended October 31, 2010

Cash flows from operating activities		
Cash receipts from operating activities	$11,200	
Cash payments for operating activities	(5,500)	
Net cash provided by operating activities		$ 5,700
Cash flows from investing activities		
Purchased office equipment	(5,000)	
Net cash used by investing activities		(5,000)
Cash flows from financing activities		
Issuance of common stock	10,000	
Issued note payable	5,000	
Payment of dividend	(500)	
Net cash provided by financing activities		14,500
Net increase in cash		15,200
Cash at beginning of period		0
Cash at end of period		$15,200

before you go on...

FINANCIAL STATEMENTS

Do it!

CSU Corporation began operations on January 1, 2010. The following information is available for CSU Corporation on December 31, 2010: Service revenue $17,000

Accounts receivable	1,800	Common stock	10,000	Supplies	4,000
Accounts payable	2,000	Retained earnings	?	Supplies expense	200
Building rental expense	9,000	Equipment	16,000	Cash	1,400
Notes payable	5,000	Insurance expense	1,000	Dividends	600

Prepare an income statement, a retained earnings statement, and a balance sheet using this information.

Action Plan

- Report the revenues and expenses for a period of time in an income statement.
- Show the amounts and causes (net income and dividends) of changes in retained earnings during the period in the retained earnings statement.
- Present the assets and claims to those assets at a specific point in time in the balance sheet.

Solution

CSU CORPORATION
Income Statement
For the Year Ended December 31, 2010

Revenues		
Service revenue		$17,000
Expenses		
Rent expense	$9,000	
Insurance expense	1,000	
Supplies expense	200	
Total expenses		10,200
Net income		$ 6,800

CSU CORPORATION
Retained Earnings Statement
For the Year Ended December 31, 2010

Retained earnings, January 1	$ 0
Add: Net income	6,800
	6,800
Less: Dividends	600
Retained earnings, December 31	$6,200

CSU CORPORATION
Balance Sheet
December 31, 2010

Assets		
Cash		$ 1,400
Accounts receivable		1,800
Supplies		4,000
Equipment		16,000
Total assets		$23,200
Liabilities and Stockholders' Equity		
Liabilities		
Notes payable	$ 5,000	
Accounts payable	2,000	
Total liabilities		$ 7,000
Stockholders' equity		
Common stock	10,000	
Retained earnings	6,200	
Total stockholders' equity		16,200
Total liabilities and stockholders' equity		$23,200

A Quick Look at Tootsie Roll's Financial Statements

The same relationships that you observed among the financial statements of Sierra Corporation are evident in the 2007 financial statements of Tootsie Roll Industries, Inc., which are presented in Illustrations 1-11 through 1-14. We have simplified the financial statements to assist your learning. Tootsie Roll's **actual financial statements** are presented in **Appendix A** at the end of the book.

Before we dive in, we need to explain two points:

1. Note that numbers are reported in thousands on Tootsie Roll's financial statements—that is, the last three 000s are omitted. Thus, Tootsie Roll's net income in 2007 is $51,625,000, not $51,625.
2. Tootsie Roll, like most companies, presents its financial statements for more than one year. Financial statements that report information for more than one period are called **comparative statements**. Comparative statements allow users to compare the financial results of the business from one accounting period with those of previous periods.

WILEY PLUS
Tootsie Roll Annual Report Walkthrough

Helpful Hint The percentage change in any amount from one year to the next is calculated as follows:

$$\frac{\text{Change during period}}{\text{Previous value}}$$

Thus, the percentage change in income is:

$$\frac{\text{Change in income}}{\text{Previous year's income}}$$

INCOME STATEMENT

Tootsie Roll's income statement is presented in Illustration 1-11. It reports total revenues in 2007 of $497,717,000. It then subtracts three types of expenses—cost of goods sold; selling, marketing, and administrative expenses; and income tax expense—to arrive at net income of $51,625,000. This is a 21.7% decrease from income for the previous year.

Illustration 1-11 Tootsie Roll's income statement

TOOTSIE ROLL INDUSTRIES, INC.
Income Statements
For the Years Ended December 31, 2007, and December 31, 2006
(in thousands)

	2007	2006
Revenues		
Sales revenue	$492,742	$495,990
Other revenues	4,975	5,150
Total revenues	497,717	501,140
Expenses		
Cost of goods sold	327,695	311,267
Selling, marketing, and administrative expenses, and other	92,855	95,158
Income tax expense	25,542	28,796
Total expenses	446,092	435,221
Net income	$ 51,625	$ 65,919

RETAINED EARNINGS STATEMENT

Illustration 1-12 (next page) presents Tootsie Roll's retained earnings statement. (Many companies present changes in retained earnings in a broader report called the Statement of Stockholders' Equity.) Find the line "Retained earnings, December 31, 2006." This number, $169,233,000, agrees with the retained earnings balance from the December 31, 2006, balance sheet.

As you proceed down the retained earnings statement, the next figure is net income of $51,625,000. Tootsie Roll distributed dividends of $64,106,000. The ending balance of retained earnings is $156,752,000 on December 31, 2007. Find

Illustration 1-12 Tootsie Roll's retained earnings statement

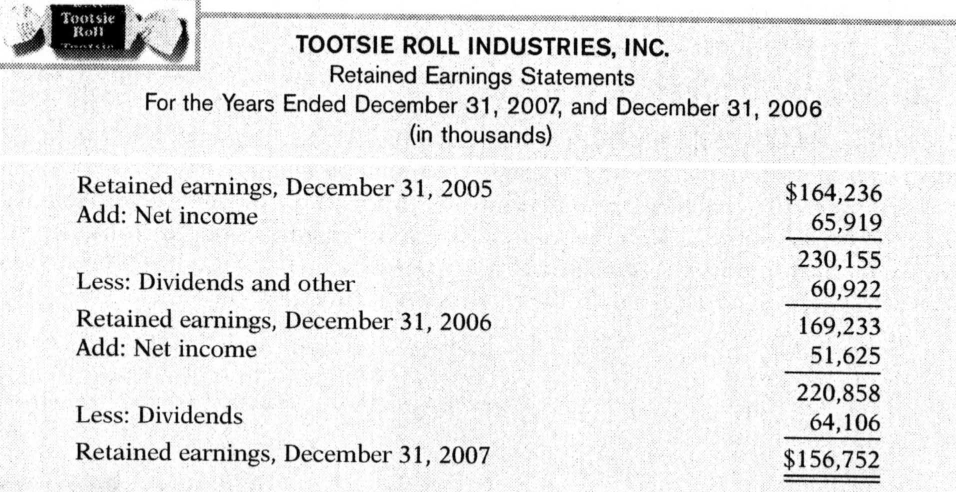

TOOTSIE ROLL INDUSTRIES, INC.
Retained Earnings Statements
For the Years Ended December 31, 2007, and December 31, 2006
(in thousands)

Retained earnings, December 31, 2005	$164,236
Add: Net income	65,919
	230,155
Less: Dividends and other	60,922
Retained earnings, December 31, 2006	169,233
Add: Net income	51,625
	220,858
Less: Dividends	64,106
Retained earnings, December 31, 2007	$156,752

this amount of retained earnings near the bottom of Tootsie Roll's balance sheet for December 31, 2007 (Illustration 1-13).

BALANCE SHEET

As shown in its balance sheet in Illustration 1-13, Tootsie Roll's assets include the kinds previously mentioned in our discussion of Sierra Corporation. These

Illustration 1-13 Tootsie Roll's balance sheet

TOOTSIE ROLL INDUSTRIES, INC.
Balance Sheets
December 31, 2007, and December 31, 2006
(in thousands)

Assets	**2007**	**2006**
Cash	$ 57,606	$ 55,729
Investments	41,307	23,531
Accounts receivable	35,284	39,007
Inventories	57,402	63,957
Prepaid expenses	6,551	6,489
Property, plant, and equipment, net	201,401	202,898
Other assets	413,174	400,028
Total assets	$812,725	$791,639
Liabilities and Stockholders' Equity		
Liabilities		
Accounts payable	$ 11,572	$ 13,102
Dividends payable	4,344	4,300
Accrued liabilities	42,056	43,802
Income taxes payable	0	1,007
Bonds payable	7,500	7,500
Employee benefits payable	53,027	50,383
Other liabilities	55,996	40,864
Total liabilities	174,495	160,958
Stockholders' equity		
Common stock	481,478	461,448
Retained earnings	156,752	169,233
Total stockholders' equity	638,230	630,681
Total liabilities and stockholders' equity	$812,725	$791,639

are cash, inventories, and property, plant, and equipment, plus other types of assets that we will discuss in later chapters, such as prepaid expenses. Tootsie Roll's total assets increased from $791,639,000 on December 31, 2006, to $812,725,000 on December 31, 2007. Its liabilities include accounts payable as well as items not yet discussed, such as employee benefits payable.

You can see that Tootsie Roll relies far more on equity financing than on debt—it has more than three times as much stockholders' equity as it has liabilities. As you learn more about financial statements we will discuss how to interpret the relationships and changes in financial statement items.

STATEMENT OF CASH FLOWS

Tootsie Roll's balance sheet shows that cash was $55,729,000 at December 31, 2006, and $57,606,000 at December 31, 2007. Thus, Tootsie Roll's cash increased $1,877,000 during 2007. The reasons for this increase can be determined by examining the statement of cash flows in Illustration 1-14. Tootsie Roll generated $90,064,000 from its operating activities during 2007. Its investing activities included capital expenditures (purchases of property, plant, and equipment) as well as purchases and sales of investment securities. The net effect of its investment activities is an outflow of cash of $43,345,000. Its financing activities involve the repurchase of its own common stock and the payment of cash dividends. In all, the net effect of the cash generated from its operating and financing activities, less the cash used in its investing activities, was a increase in cash of $1,877,000.

Illustration 1-14 Tootsie Roll's statement of cash flows

TOOTSIE ROLL INDUSTRIES, INC.
Statements of Cash Flows
For the Years Ended December 31, 2007, and December 31, 2006
(in thousands)

	2007	2006
Cash flows from operating activities		
Cash receipts from operating activities	$500,315	$455,647
Cash payments for operating activities	(410,251)	(399,991)
Net cash provided by operating activities	90,064	55,656
Cash flows from investing activities		
Capital expenditures and acquisitions	(14,767)	(39,207)
Purchase of investment securities	(59,132)	(35,663)
Sales of investment securities and other	30,554	85,896
Net cash provided (used) in investing activities	(43,345)	11,026
Cash flows from financing activities		
Repayment of bank loan	—	(32,001)
Repurchase of common stock	(27,300)	(30,694)
Dividends paid in cash	(17,542)	(17,264)
Net cash (used) by financing activities	(44,842)	(79,959)
Net increase (decrease) in cash	1,877	(13,277)
Cash at beginning of year	55,729	69,006
Cash at end of year	$57,606	$55,729

study objective 6

Describe the components that supplement the financial statements in an annual report.

OTHER ELEMENTS OF AN ANNUAL REPORT

U.S. companies that are publicly traded must provide shareholders with an **annual report**. The annual report always includes the financial statements introduced in this chapter. The annual report also includes other important information such as a management discussion and analysis section, notes to the financial statements, and an independent auditor's report. No analysis of a company's financial situation and prospects is complete without a review of these items.

Management Discussion and Analysis

The **management discussion and analysis (MD&A)** section covers various financial aspects of a company, including **its ability to pay near-term obligations, its ability to fund operations and expansion, and its results of operations**. Management must highlight favorable or unfavorable trends and identify significant events and uncertainties that affect these three factors. This discussion obviously involves a number of subjective estimates and opinions. A brief excerpt from the MD&A section of Tootsie Roll's annual report is presented in Illustration 1-15.

Illustration 1-15 Tootsie Roll's management discussion and analysis

TOOTSIE ROLL INDUSTRIES, INC.
Management's Discussion and Analysis of
Financial Condition and Results of Operations

The Company has a relatively straight-forward financial structure and has historically maintained a conservative financial position. Except for an immaterial amount of operating leases, the Company has no special financing arrangements or "off-balance sheet" special purpose entities. Cash flows from operations plus maturities of short term investments are expected to be adequate to meet the Company's overall financing needs, including capital expenditures, in 2008.

Managerial statement provide boarder info than financial statement.

Notes to the Financial Statements

Explanatory notes and supporting schedules accompany every set of financial statements and are an integral part of the statements. The **notes to the financial statements** clarify the financial statements, and provide additional detail. Information in the notes does not have to be quantifiable (numeric). Examples of notes are descriptions of the significant accounting policies and methods used in preparing the statements, explanations of uncertainties and contingencies, and various statistics and details too voluminous to be included in the statements. The notes are essential to understanding a company's operating performance and financial position.

Illustration 1-16 is an excerpt from the notes to Tootsie Roll's financial statements. It describes the methods that Tootsie Roll uses to account for revenues.

Illustration 1-16 Notes to Tootsie Roll's financial statements

TOOTSIE ROLL INDUSTRIES, INC.
Notes to Financial Statements

Revenue recognition
Revenue, net of applicable provisions for discounts, returns, allowances, and certain advertising and promotional costs, is recognized when products are delivered to customers based on a customer purchase order, and collectibility is reasonably assured.

Auditor's Report

An **auditor's report** is prepared by an independent outside auditor. It states the auditor's opinion as to the fairness of the presentation of the financial position and results of operations and their conformance with generally accepted accounting standards.

An **auditor** is an accounting professional who conducts an independent examination of a company's financial statements. Only accountants who meet certain criteria and thereby attain the designation Certified Public Accountant (CPA) may perform audits. If the auditor is satisfied that the financial statements provide a fair representation of the company's financial position and results of operations in accordance with generally accepted accounting principles, then the auditor expresses an **unqualified opinion.** If the auditor expresses anything other than an unqualified opinion, then readers should only use the financial statements with caution. That is, without an unqualified opinion, we cannot have complete confidence that the financial statements give an accurate picture of the company's financial health.

Illustration 1-17 is an excerpt from the auditor's report from Tootsie Roll's 2007 annual report. Tootsie Roll received an unqualified opinion from its auditor, PricewaterhouseCoopers.

TOOTSIE ROLL INDUSTRIES, INC.
Excerpt from Auditor's Report

To the Board of Directors and Shareholders of Tootsie Roll Industries, Inc.

In our opinion, the accompanying consolidated balance sheets and the related consolidated statements of earnings, comprehensive earnings, retained earnings, and cash flows present fairly, in all material respects, the financial position of Tootsie Roll Industries, Inc. and its subsidiaries at December 31, 2007 and 2006, and the results of their operations and their cash flows for each of the three years in the period ended December 31, 2007, in conformity with accounting principles generally accepted in the United States of America.

Illustration 1-17 Excerpt from auditor's report on Tootsie Roll's financial statements

before you go on...

Do it!

COMPONENTS OF ANNUAL REPORTS

State whether each of the following items is most closely associated with the management discussion and analysis (MD&A), the notes to the financial statements, or the auditor's report.

1. Descriptions of significant accounting policies
2. Unqualified opinion
3. Explanations of uncertainties and contingencies
4. Description of ability to fund operations and expansion
5. Description of results of operations
6. Certified Public Accountant (CPA)

Action Plan

- Realize that financial statements provide information about a company's performance and financial position.
- Be familar with the other elements of the annual report in order to gain a fuller understanding of a company.

Solution

1. Descriptions of significant accounting policies: Notes.
2. Unqualified opinion: Auditor's report.
3. Explanations of uncertainties and contingencies: Notes.
4. Description of ability to fund operations and expansion: MD&A.
5. Description of results of operations: MD&A.
6. Certified Public Accountant (CPA): Auditor's report.

USING THE DECISION TOOLKIT

Using the Decision Toolkit exercises ask you to use information from financial statements to make financial decisions.

Hershey Foods Corporation, located in Hershey, Pennsylvania, is the leading North American manufacturer of chocolate—for example, Hershey's Kisses, Reese's Peanut Butter Cups, Kit Kat, and Take 5 bars. Imagine that you are considering the purchase of shares of Hershey's common stock.

Instructions

Answer these questions related to your decision whether to invest.

(a) What financial statements should you request from the company?
(b) What should these financial statements tell you?
(c) Should you request audited financial statements? Explain.
(d) Appendix B at the end of this book contains financial statements for Hershey Foods. What comparisons can you make between Tootsie Roll and Hershey in terms of their respective results from operations and financial position?

Solution

(a) Before you invest, you should investigate the income statement, retained earnings statement, statement of cash flows, and balance sheet.
(b) You would probably be most interested in the income statement because it tells about past performance and thus gives an indication of future performance. The retained earnings statement provides a record of the company's dividend history. The statement of cash flows reveals where the company is getting and spending its cash. This is especially important for a company that wants to grow. Finally, the balance sheet reveals the relationship between assets and liabilities.
(c) You would want audited financial statements. These statements indicate that a CPA (certified public accountant) has examined and expressed an opinion that the statements present fairly the financial position and results of operations of the company. Investors and creditors should not make decisions without studying audited financial statements.
(d) Many interesting comparisons can be made between the two companies. Tootsie Roll is smaller, with total assets of $812,725,000 versus $4,247,113,000 for Hershey, and it has lower revenue—$497,717,000 versus $4,946,716,000 for Hershey. In addition, Tootsie Roll's cash provided by operating activities of $90,064,000 is less than Hershey's $778,836,000.

While useful, these basic measures are not enough to determine whether one company is a better investment than the other. In later chapters you will learn of tools that will allow you to compare the relative profitability and financial health of these and other companies.

Summary of Study Objectives

1 Describe the primary forms of business organization. A sole proprietorship is a business owned by one person. A partnership is a business owned by two or more people associated as partners. A corporation is a separate legal entity for which evidence of ownership is provided by shares of stock.

2 Identify the users and uses of accounting information. Internal users are managers who need accounting information to plan, organize, and run business operations. The primary external users are investors and creditors. Investors (stockholders) use accounting information to help them decide whether to buy, hold, or sell shares of a company's stock. Creditors (suppliers and bankers) use accounting information to assess the risk of granting credit or loaning money to a business. Other groups who have an indirect interest in a business are taxing authorities, customers, labor unions, and regulatory agencies.

3 Explain the three principal types of business activity. Financing activities involve collecting the necessary funds to support the business. Investing activities involve acquiring the resources necessary to run the business. Operating activities involve putting the resources of the business into action to generate a profit.

4 Describe the content and purpose of each of the financial statements. An income statement presents the revenues and expenses of a company for a specific period of time. A retained earnings statement summarizes the changes in retained earnings that have occurred for a specific period of time. A balance sheet reports the assets, liabilities, and stockholders' equity of a business at a specific date. A statement of cash flows summarizes information concerning the cash inflows (receipts) and outflows (payments) for a specific period of time.

5 Explain the meaning of assets, liabilities, and stockholders' equity, and state the basic accounting equation. Assets are resources owned by a business. Liabilities are the debts and obligations of the business. Liabilities represent claims of creditors on the assets of the business. Stockholders' equity represents the claims of owners on the assets of the business. Stockholders' equity is subdivided into two parts: common stock and retained earnings. The basic accounting equation is: Assets = Liabilities + Stockholders' Equity.

6 Describe the components that supplement the financial statements in an annual report. The management discussion and analysis provides management's interpretation of the company's results and financial position as well as a discussion of plans for the future. Notes to the financial statements provide additional explanation or detail to make the financial statements more informative. The auditor's report expresses an opinion as to whether the financial statements present fairly the company's results of operations and financial position.

DECISION TOOLKIT *A SUMMARY*

DECISION CHECKPOINTS	INFO NEEDED FOR DECISION	TOOL TO USE FOR DECISION	HOW TO EVALUATE RESULTS
Are the company's operations profitable?	Income statement	The income statement reports on the success or failure of the company's operations by reporting its revenues and expenses.	If the company's revenue exceeds its expenses, it will report net income; otherwise it will report a net loss.
What is the company's policy toward dividends and growth?	Retained earnings statement	How much of this year's income did the company pay out in dividends to shareholders?	A company striving for rapid growth will pay a low (or no) dividend.
Does the company rely primarily on debt or stockholders' equity to finance its assets?	Balance sheet	The balance sheet reports the company's resources and claims to those resources. There are two types of claims: liabilities and stockholders' equity.	Compare the amount of debt versus the amount of stockholders' equity to determine whether the company relies more on creditors or owners for its financing.
Does the company generate sufficient cash from operations to fund its investing activities?	Statement of cash flows	The statement of cash flows shows the amount of cash provided or used by operating activities, investing activities, and financing activities.	Compare the amount of cash provided by operating activities with the amount of cash used by investing activities. Any deficiency in cash from operating activities must be made up with cash from financing activities.

Glossary

Accounting *(p. 6)* The information system that identifies, records, and communicates the economic events of an organization to interested users.

Annual report *(p. 21)* A report prepared by corporate management that presents financial information including financial statements, notes, a management discussion and analysis section, and an independent auditor's report.

Assets *(p. 10)* Resources owned by a business.

Auditor's report *(p. 22)* A report prepared by an independent outside auditor stating the auditor's opinion as to the fairness of the presentation of the financial position and results of operations and their conformance with generally accepted accounting standards.

Balance sheet *(p. 14)* A financial statement that reports the assets and claims to those assets at a specific point in time.

Basic accounting equation *(p. 14)* Assets = Liabilities + Stockholders' Equity.

Certified Public Accountant (CPA) *(p. 23)* An individual who has met certain criteria and is thus allowed to perform audits of corporations.

Common stock *(p. 10)* Term used to describe the total amount paid in by stockholders for the shares they purchase.

Comparative statements *(p. 19)* A presentation of the financial statements of a company for more than one year.

Corporation *(p. 4)* A business organized as a separate legal entity having ownership divided into transferable shares of stock.

Dividends *(p. 10)* Payments of cash from a corporation to its stockholders.

Expenses *(p. 11)* The cost of assets consumed or services used in the process of generating revenues.

Income statement *(p. 12)* A financial statement that presents the revenues and expenses and resulting net income or net loss of a company for a specific period of time.

Liabilities *(p. 10)* The debts and obligations of a business. Liabilities represent the amounts owed to creditors.

Management discussion and analysis (MD&A) *(p. 22)* A section of the annual report that presents management's views on the company's ability to pay near-term obligations, its ability to fund operations and expansion, and its results of operations.

Net income *(p. 11)* The amount by which revenues exceed expenses.

Net loss *(p. 11)* The amount by which expenses exceed revenues.

Notes to the financial statements *(p. 22)* Notes that clarify information presented in the financial statements, as well as expand upon it where additional detail is needed.

Partnership *(p. 4)* A business owned by two or more persons associated as partners.

Retained earnings *(p. 13)* The amount of net income retained in the corporation.

Retained earnings statement *(p. 13)* A financial statement that summarizes the amounts and causes of changes in retained earnings for a specific period of time.

Revenue *(p. 11)* The increase in assets that result from the sale of a product or service in the normal course of business.

Sarbanes-Oxley Act *(p. 9)* Regulations passed by Congress in 2002 to try to reduce unethical corporate behavior.

Sole proprietorship *(p. 4)* A business owned by one person.

Statement of cash flows *(p. 15)* A financial statement that provides financial information about the cash receipts and cash payments of a business for a specific period of time.

Stockholders' equity *(p. 14)* The owners' claim on total assets.

Comprehensive Do it!

The Comprehensive Do It! is a final review before you begin homework.

Jeff Andringa, a former college hockey player, quit his job and started Ice Camp, a hockey camp for kids ages 8 to 18. Eventually he would like to open hockey camps nationwide. Jeff has asked you to help him prepare financial statements at the end of his first year of operations. He relates the following facts about his business activities.

In order to get the business off the ground, he decided to incorporate. He sold shares of common stock to a few close friends, as well as buying some of the shares himself. He initially raised $25,000 through the sale of these shares. In addition, the company took out a $10,000 loan at a local bank.

Ice Camp purchased, for $12,000 cash, a bus for transporting kids. The company also bought hockey goals and other miscellaneous equipment with $1,500 cash. The company earned camp tuition during the year of $100,000 but had collected only $80,000 of this amount. Thus, at the end of the year its customers still owed $20,000. The company rents time at a local rink for $50 per hour. Total rink rental costs during the year were $8,000, insurance was $10,000, salary expense was $20,000, and administrative expenses totaled $9,000, all of which were paid in cash. The company incurred $800 in interest expense on the bank loan, which it still owed at the end of the year.

The company paid dividends during the year of $5,000 cash. The balance in the corporate bank account at December 31, 2010, was $49,500.

Instructions

Using the format of the Sierra Corporation statements in this chapter, prepare an income statement, retained earnings statement, balance sheet, and statement of cash flows. (*Hint:* Prepare the statements in the order stated to take advantage of the flow of information from one statement to the next, as shown in Illustration 1-10 on page 17.)

Action Plan

- On the income statement: Show revenues and expenses for a period of time.
- On the retained earnings statement: Show the changes in retained earnings for a period of time.
- On the balance sheet: Report assets, liabilities, and stockholders' equity at a specific date.
- On the statement of cash flows: Report sources and uses of cash from operating, investing, and financing activities for a period of time.

Solution to Comprehensive Do it!

ICE CAMP
Income Statement
For the Year Ended December 31, 2010

Revenues		
Camp tuition revenue		$100,000
Expenses		
Salaries expense	$20,000	
Insurance expense	10,000	
Administrative expense	9,000	
Rink rental expense	8,000	
Interest expense	800	
Total expenses		47,800
Net income		$ 52,200

ICE CAMP
Retained Earnings Statement
For the Year Ended December 31, 2010

Retained earnings, January 1, 2010	$ 0
Add: Net income	52,200
	52,200
Less: Dividends	5,000
Retained earnings, December 31, 2010	$47,200

ICE CAMP
Balance Sheet
December 31, 2010

Assets

Cash	$49,500
Accounts receivable	20,000
Bus	12,000
Equipment	1,500
Total assets	$83,000

Liabilities and Stockholders' Equity

Liabilities		
Bank loan payable	$10,000	
Interest payable	800	
Total liabilities		$10,800
Stockholders' equity		
Common stock	25,000	
Retained earnings	47,200	
Total stockholders' equity		72,200
Total liabilities and stockholders' equity		$83,000

Solution continues on next page.

ICE CAMP
Statement of Cash Flows
For the Year Ended December 31, 2010

Cash flows from operating activities		
Cash receipts from operating activities	$80,000	
Cash payments for operating activities	(47,000)	
Net cash provided by operating activities		$33,000
Cash flows from investing activities		
Purchase of bus	(12,000)	
Purchase of equipment	(1,500)	
Net cash used by investing activities		(13,500)
Cash flows from financing activities		
Issuance of bank loan payable	10,000	
Issuance of common stock	25,000	
Dividends paid	(5,000)	
Net cash provided by financing activities		30,000
Net increase in cash		49,500
Cash at beginning of period		0
Cash at end of period		$49,500

This would be a good time to look at the **Student Owner's Manual** at the beginning of the book. Knowing the purpose of the different types of homework will help you understand what each contributes to your accounting skills and competencies.

The tool icon indicates that an activity employs one of the decision tools presented in the chapter. The indicates that an activity relates to a business function beyond accounting. The pencil icon indicates that an activity requires written communication.

Self-Study Questions

Answers are at the end of the chapter.

(SO 1) 1. Which is not one of the three forms of business organization?
(a) Sole proprietorship. (c) Partnership.
(b) Creditorship. (d) Corporation.

(SO 1) 2. Which is an advantage of corporations relative to partnerships and sole proprietorships?
(a) Lower taxes.
(b) Harder to transfer ownership.
(c) Reduced legal liability for investors.
(d) Most common form of organization.

(SO 2) 3. Which statement about users of accounting information is *incorrect*?
(a) Management is considered an internal user.
(b) Taxing authorities are considered external users.
(c) Present creditors are considered external users.
(d) Regulatory authorities are considered internal users.

(SO 2) 4. Which of the following did *not* result from the Sarbanes-Oxley Act?
(a) Top management must now certify the accuracy of financial information.
(b) Penalties for fraudulent activity increased.
(c) Independence of auditors increased.
(d) Tax rates on corporations increased.

5. Which is not one of the three primary business activities? (SO 3)
(a) Financing. (c) Advertising.
(b) Operating. (d) Investing.

6. Which of the following is an example of a financing activity? (SO 3)
(a) Issuing shares of common stock.
(b) Selling goods on account.
(c) Buying delivery equipment.
(d) Buying inventory.

7. Net income will result during a time period when: (SO 4)
(a) assets exceed liabilities.
(b) assets exceed revenues.
(c) expenses exceed revenues.
(d) revenues exceed expenses.

(SO 4) 8. The financial statements for Harold Corporation contained the following information.

Accounts receivable	$ 5,000
Sales revenue	75,000
Cash	15,000
Salaries expense	20,000
Rent expense	10,000

What was Harold's net income?
(a) $60,000.
(b) $15,000.
(c) $65,000.
(d) $45,000.

(SO 4, 5) 9. What section of a cash flow statement indicates the cash spent on new equipment during the past accounting period?
(a) The investing section.
(b) The operating section.
(c) The financing section.
(d) The cash flow statement does not give this information.

(SO 4, 5) 10. Which statement presents information as of a specific point in time?
(a) Income statement.
(b) Balance sheet.
(c) Statement of cash flows.
(d) Retained earnings statement.

(SO 5) 11. Which financial statement reports assets, liabilities, and stockholders' equity?
(a) Income statement.
(b) Retained earnings statement.
(c) Balance sheet.
(d) Statement of cash flows.

12. Stockholders' equity represents: (SO 5)
(a) claims of creditors.
(b) claims of employees.
(c) the difference between revenues and expenses.
(d) claims of owners.

13. As of December 31, 2007, Stoneland Corporation has assets of $3,500 and stockholders' equity of $2,000. What are the liabilities for Stoneland Corporation as of December 31, 2007? (SO 5)
(a) $1,500.
(b) $1,000.
(c) $2,500.
(d) $2,000.

14. The element of a corporation's annual report that describes the corporation's accounting methods is the: (SO 6)
(a) notes to the financial statements.
(b) management discussion and analysis.
(c) auditor's report.
(d) income statement.

15. The element of the annual report that presents an opinion regarding the fairness of the presentation of the financial position and results of operations is/are the: (SO 6)
(a) income statement.
(b) auditor's opinion.
(c) balance sheet.
(d) comparative statements.

Go to the book's companion website, **www.wiley.com/college/kimmel**, to access additional Self-Study Questions.

Questions

1. What are the three basic forms of business organizations?

2. What are the advantages to a business of being formed as a corporation? What are the disadvantages?

3. What are the advantages to a business of being formed as a partnership or sole proprietorship? What are the disadvantages?

4. "Accounting is ingrained in our society and is vital to our economic system." Do you agree? Explain.

5. Who are the internal users of accounting data? How does accounting provide relevant data to the internal users?

6. Who are the external users of accounting data? Give examples.

7. What are the three main types of business activity? Give examples of each activity.

8. Listed here are some items found in the financial statements of Ellyn Toth, Inc. Indicate in which financial statement(s) each item would appear.
(a) Service revenue.
(b) Equipment.
(c) Advertising expense.
(d) Accounts receivable.
(e) Common stock.
(f) Wages payable.

9. Why would a bank want to monitor the dividend payment practices of the corporations it lends money to?

10. "A company's net income appears directly on the income statement and the retained earnings statement, and it is included indirectly in the company's balance sheet." Do you agree? Explain.

11. What is the primary purpose of the statement of cash flows?

12. What are the three main categories of the statement of cash flows? Why do you think these categories were chosen?

13. What is retained earnings? What items increase the balance in retained earnings? What items decrease the balance in retained earnings?

14. What is the basic accounting equation?

15. (a) Define the terms *assets, liabilities,* and *stockholders' equity.*
(b) What items affect stockholders' equity?

16. Which of these items are liabilities of White Glove Cleaning Service?
(a) Cash.
(b) Accounts payable.
(c) Dividends.
(d) Accounts receivable.

(e) Supplies.
(f) Equipment.
(g) Salaries payable.
(h) Service revenue.
(i) Rent expense.

17. How are each of the following financial statements interrelated? (a) Retained earnings statement and income statement. (b) Retained earnings statement and balance sheet. (c) Balance sheet and statement of cash flows.

18. What is the purpose of the management discussion and analysis section (MD&A)?

19. Why is it important for financial statements to receive an unqualified auditor's opinion?

20. What types of information are presented in the notes to the financial statements?

21. The accounting equation is: Assets = Liabilities + Stockholders' Equity. Appendix A, at the end of this book, reproduces Tootsie Roll's financial statements. Replacing words in the equation with dollar amounts, what is Tootsie Roll's accounting equation at December 31, 2007?

Brief Exercises

Describe forms of business organization. (SO 1)

BE1-1 Match each of the following forms of business organization with a set of characteristics: sole proprietorship (SP), partnership (P), corporation (C).

(a) _____ Shared control, tax advantages, increased skills and resources.
(b) _____ Simple to set up and maintains control with founder.
(c) _____ Easier to transfer ownership and raise funds, no personal liability.

Identify users of accounting information. (SO 2)

BE1-2 Match each of the following types of evaluation with one of the listed users of accounting information.

1. Trying to determine whether the company complied with tax laws.
2. Trying to determine whether the company can pay its obligations.
3. Trying to determine whether a marketing proposal will be cost effective.
4. Trying to determine whether the company's net income will result in a stock price increase.
5. Trying to determine whether the company should employ debt or equity financing.

(a) _____ Investors in common stock.
(b) _____ Marketing managers.
(c) _____ Creditors.
(d) _____ Chief Financial Officer.
(e) _____ Internal Revenue Service.

Classify items by activity. (SO 3, 4)

BE1-3 Indicate in which part of the statement of cash flows each item would appear: operating activities (O), investing activities (I), or financing activities (F).

(a) _____ Cash received from customers.
(b) _____ Cash paid to stockholders (dividends).
(c) _____ Cash received from issuing new common stock.
(d) _____ Cash paid to suppliers.
(e) _____ Cash paid to purchase a new office building.

Determine effect of transactions on stockholders' equity. (SO 4)

BE1-4 Presented below are a number of transactions. Determine whether each transaction affects common stock (C), dividends (D), revenue (R), expense (E), or does not affect stockholders' equity (NSE). Provide titles for the revenues and expenses.

(a) Costs incurred for advertising.
(b) Assets received for services performed.
(c) Costs incurred for insurance.
(d) Amounts paid to employees.
(e) Cash distributed to stockholders.
(f) Assets received in exchange for allowing the use of the company's building.
(g) Costs incurred for utilities used.
(h) Cash purchase of equipment.
(i) Issued common stock for cash.

Prepare a balance sheet. (SO 4, 5)

BE1-5 In alphabetical order below are balance sheet items for Mantle Company at December 31, 2010. Prepare a balance sheet following the format of Illustration 1-8.

Accounts payable	$75,000
Accounts receivable	81,000
Cash	22,000
Common stock	28,000

BE1-6 Eskimo Pie Corporation markets a broad range of frozen treats, including its famous Eskimo Pie ice cream bars. The following items were taken from a recent income statement and balance sheet. In each case identify whether the item would appear on the balance sheet (BS) or income statement (IS).

Determine where items appear on financial statements.
(SO 4, 5)

(a) _____ Income tax expense.
(b) _____ Inventories.
(c) _____ Accounts payable.
(d) _____ Retained earnings.
(e) _____ Property, plant, and equipment.
(f) _____ Net sales.
(g) _____ Cost of goods sold.
(h) _____ Common stock.
(i) _____ Receivables.
(j) _____ Interest expense.

BE1-7 Indicate which statement you would examine to find each of the following items: income statement (I), balance sheet (B), retained earnings statement (R), or statement of cash flows (C).

Determine proper financial statement.
(SO 4)

(a) Revenue during the period.
(b) Supplies on hand at the end of the year.
(c) Cash received from issuing new bonds during the period.
(d) Total debts outstanding at the end of the period.

BE1-8 Use the basic accounting equation to answer these questions.

Use basic accounting equation.
(SO 5)

(a) The liabilities of Cummings Company are $90,000 and the stockholders' equity is $230,000. What is the amount of Cummings Company's total assets?
(b) The total assets of Haldeman Company are $170,000 and its stockholders' equity is $90,000. What is the amount of its total liabilities?
(c) The total assets of Dain Co. are $800,000 and its liabilities are equal to one-fourth of its total assets. What is the amount of Dain Co.'s stockholders' equity?

BE1-9 At the beginning of the year, Fuqua Company had total assets of $800,000 and total liabilities of $500,000.

Use basic accounting equation.
(SO 5)

(a) If total assets increased $150,000 during the year and total liabilities decreased $80,000, what is the amount of stockholders' equity at the end of the year?
(b) During the year, total liabilities increased $100,000 and stockholders' equity decreased $70,000. What is the amount of total assets at the end of the year?
(c) If total assets decreased $90,000 and stockholders' equity increased $110,000 during the year, what is the amount of total liabilities at the end of the year?

BE1-10 Indicate whether each of these items is an asset (A), a liability (L), or part of stockholders' equity (SE).

Identify assets, liabilities, and stockholders' equity.
(SO 5)

(a) Accounts receivable.
(b) Salaries payable.
(c) Equipment.
(d) Office supplies.
(e) Common stock.
(f) Notes payable.

BE1-11 Which is *not* a required part of an annual report of a publicly traded company?

Determine required parts of annual report.
(SO 6)

(a) Statement of cash flows.
(b) Notes to the financial statements.
(c) Management discussion and analysis.
(d) All of these are required.

Do it! Review

WILEY PLUS

Do it! 1-1 Identify each of the following organizational characteristics with the organizational form or forms with which it is associated.

Identify benefits of business organization forms.
(SO 1)

1. Easier to transfer ownership
2. Easier to raise funds
3. More owner control
4. Tax advantages
5. No personal legal liability

Do it! 1-2 Classify each item as an asset, liability, common stock, revenue, or expense.

Classify business activities.
(SO 3)

1. Issuance of ownership shares
2. Land purchased
3. Amounts owed to suppliers
4. Bonds payable
5. Amount earned from selling a product
6. Cost of advertising

Prepare financial statements.
(SO 4)

Do it! 1-3 Cougar Corporation began operations on January 1, 2010. The following information is available for Cougar Corporation on December 31, 2010.

Accounts payable	$ 5,000	Notes payable	$ 7,000
Accounts receivable	3,000	Rent expense	10,000
Advertising expense	2,000	Retained earnings	?
Cash	3,100	Service revenue	25,000
Common stock	15,000	Supplies	1,900
Dividends	2,500	Supplies expense	1,700
Equipment	27,800		

Prepare an income statement, a retained earnings statement, and a balance sheet for Cougar Corporation.

Identify components of annual reports.
(SO 6)

Do it! 1-4 Indicate whether each of the following items is most closely associated with the management discussion and analysis (MD&A), the notes to the financial statements, or the auditor's report.

1. Description of ability to pay near-term obligations
2. Unqualified opinion
3. Details concerning liabilities, too voluminous to be included in the statements
4. Description of favorable and unfavorable trends
5. Certified Public Accountant (CPA)
6. Descriptions of significant accounting policies

Exercises

Match items with descriptions.
(SO 1, 2, 4, 6)

E1-1 Here is a list of words or phrases discussed in this chapter:

1. Corporation	4. Partnership	7. Accounts payable
2. Creditor	5. Stockholder	8. Auditor's opinion
3. Accounts receivable	6. Common stock	

Instructions

Match each word or phrase with the best description of it.

_____ (a) An expression about whether financial statements are presented in conformance with generally accepted accounting principles.
_____ (b) A business enterprise that raises money by issuing shares of stock.
_____ (c) The portion of stockholders' equity that results from receiving cash from investors.
_____ (d) Obligations to suppliers of goods.
_____ (e) Amounts due from customers.
_____ (f) A party to whom a business owes money.
_____ (g) A party that invests in common stock.
_____ (h) A business that is owned jointly by two or more individuals but does not issue stock.

Identify business activities.
(SO 3)

E1-2 All businesses are involved in three types of activities—financing, investing, and operating. Listed below are the names and descriptions of companies in several different industries.

Abitibi Consolidated Inc.—manufacturer and marketer of newsprint
Cal State–Northridge Stdt Union—university student union
Oracle Corporation—computer software developer and retailer
Sportsco Investments—owner of the Vancouver Canucks hockey club
Grant Thornton LLP—professional accounting and business advisory firm
Southwest Airlines—discount airline

Instructions

(a) For each of the above companies, provide examples of (1) a financing activity, (2) an investing activity, and (3) an operating activity that the company likely engages in.
(b) Which of the activities that you identified in (a) are common to most businesses? Which activities are not?

E1-3 The Long Run Golf & Country Club details the following accounts in its financial statements.

Classify accounts.
(SO 3, 4)

	(a)	(b)
Accounts payable and accrued liabilities	_____	_____
Accounts receivable	_____	_____
Property, plant, and equipment	_____	_____
Food and beverage operations revenue	_____	_____
Golf course operations revenue	_____	_____
Inventory	_____	_____
Long-term debt	_____	_____
Office and general expense	_____	_____
Professional fees expense	_____	_____
Wages and benefits expense	_____	_____

Instructions

(a) Classify each of the above accounts as an asset (A), liability (L), stockholders' equity (SE), revenue (R), or expense (E) item.

(b) Classify each of the above accounts as a financing activity (F), investing activity (I), or operating activity (O). If you believe a particular account doesn't fit in any of these activities, explain why.

E1-4 This information relates to Denson Co. for the year 2010.

Prepare income statement and retained earnings statement.
(SO 4)

Retained earnings, January 1, 2010	$64,000
Advertising expense	1,800
Dividends paid during 2010	6,000
Rent expense	10,400
Service revenue	53,000
Utilities expense	2,400
Salaries expense	30,000

Instructions

After analyzing the data, prepare an income statement and a retained earnings statement for the year ending December 31, 2010.

E1-5 The following information was taken from the 2006 financial statements of pharmaceutical giant Merck and Co. All dollar amounts are in millions.

Prepare income statement and retained earnings statement.
(SO 4)

Retained earnings, January 1, 2006	$37,980.0
Materials and production expense	6,001.1
Marketing and administrative expense	8,165.4
Dividends	3,318.7
Sales revenue	22,636.0
Research and development expense	4,782.9
Tax expense	1,787.6
Other revenue	2,677.1

Instructions

(a) After analyzing the data, prepare an income statement and a retained earnings statement for the year ending December 31, 2006.

(b) Suppose that Merck decided to reduce its research and development expense by 50%. What would be the short-term implications? What would be the long-term implications? How do you think the stock market would react?

E1-6 Presented here is information for Willingham Inc. for 2010.

Prepare a retained earnings statement.
(SO 4)

Retained earnings, January 1	$130,000
Revenue from legal services	400,000
Total expenses	170,000
Dividends	82,000

Instructions

Prepare the 2010 retained earnings statement for Willingham Inc.

E1-7 Consider each of the following independent situations.

Interpret financial facts.
(SO 4)

(a) The retained earnings statement of Hollis Corporation shows dividends of $68,000, while net income for the year was $75,000.

(b) The statement of cash flows for Zhiang Corporation shows that cash provided by operating activities was $10,000, cash used in investing activities was $110,000, and cash provided by financing activities was $130,000.

Instructions

For each company provide a brief discussion interpreting these financial facts. For example, you might discuss the company's financial health or its apparent growth philosophy.

Identify financial statement components and prepare income statement.
(SO 4)

E1-8 The following items and amounts were taken from Wayside Inc.'s 2010 income statement and balance sheet.

______	Cash and short-term investments	$ 84,700	______	Receivables	88,419
______	Retained earnings	123,192	______	Sales revenue	584,951
______	Cost of goods sold	438,458	______	Income taxes payable	6,499
______	Selling, general, and administrative expenses	115,131	______	Accounts payable	49,384
______	Prepaid expenses	7,818	______	Franchising revenues	4,786
______	Inventories	$ 64,618	______	Interest expense	1,994

Instructions

(a) In each, case, identify on the blank line whether the item is an asset (A), liability (L), stockholder's equity (SE), revenue (R), or expense (E) item.
(b) Prepare an income statement for Wayside Inc. for the year ended December 31, 2010.

Calculate missing amounts.
(SO 4, 5)

E1-9 Here are incomplete financial statements for Garrett, Inc.

GARRETT, INC.
Balance Sheet

Assets		Liabilities and Stockholders' Equity	
Cash	$ 5,000	Liabilities	
Inventory	10,000	Accounts payable	$ 5,000
Building	45,000	Stockholders' equity	
Total assets	$60,000	Common stock	(a)
		Retained earnings	(b)
		Total liabilities and stockholders' equity	$60,000

Income Statement

Revenues	$85,000
Cost of goods sold	(c)
Administrative expenses	10,000
Net income	$ (d)

Retained Earnings Statement

Beginning retained earnings	$10,000
Add: Net income	(e)
Less: Dividends	5,000
Ending retained earnings	$25,000

Instructions

Calculate the missing amounts.

Compute net income and prepare a balance sheet.
(SO 4, 5)

E1-10 Forest Park is a private camping ground near the Lathom Peak Recreation Area. It has compiled the following financial information as of December 31, 2010.

Revenues during 2010: camping fees	$132,000	Dividends	$ 9,000
Revenues during 2010: general store	25,000	Notes payable	50,000
Accounts payable	11,000	Expenses during 2010	129,000
Cash	8,500	Supplies	2,500
Equipment	114,000	Common stock	40,000
		Retained earnings (1/1/2010)	5,000

Instructions

(a) Determine Forest Park's net income for 2010.

(b) Prepare a retained earnings statement and a balance sheet for Forest Park as of December 31, 2010.

(c) Upon seeing this income statement, Steve Shatner, the campground manager immediately concluded, "The general store is more trouble than it is worth—let's get rid of it." The marketing director isn't so sure this is a good idea. What do you think?

Identify financial statement components and prepare an income statement.
(SO 4, 5)

E1-11 Kellogg Company is the world's leading producer of ready-to-eat cereal and a leading producer of grain-based convenience foods such as frozen waffles and cereal bars. The following items were taken from its 2006 income statement and balance sheet. All dollars are in millions.

____	Retained earnings	$3,630.4	____	Long-term debt	$ 3,053.0
____	Cost of goods sold	6,081.5	____	Inventories	823.9
____	Selling and administrative expenses	3,059.4	____	Net sales	10,906.7
____	Cash	410.6	____	Accounts payable	910.4
____	Notes payable	1,268.0	____	Common stock	104.6
____	Interest expense	307.4	____	Income tax expense	466.5
			____	Other revenue	13.2

Instructions

Perform each of the following.

(a) In each case identify whether the item is an asset (A), liability (L), stockholders' equity (SE), revenue (R), or expense (E).

(b) Prepare an income statement for Kellogg Company for the year ended December 31, 2006.

Prepare a statement of cash flows.
(SO 5)

E1-12 This information is for Damon Corporation for the year ended December 31, 2010.

Cash received from lenders	$20,000
Cash received from customers	60,000
Cash paid for new equipment	35,000
Cash dividends paid	8,000
Cash paid to suppliers	18,000
Cash balance 1/1/10	12,000

Instructions

(a) Prepare the 2010 statement of cash flows for Damon Corporation.

(b) Suppose you are one of Damon's creditors. Referring to the statement of cash flows, evaluate Damon's ability to repay its creditors.

Prepare a statement of cash flows.
(SO 5)

E1-13 The following data are derived from the 2006 financial statements of Southwest Airlines. All dollars are in millions. Southwest has a December 31 year-end.

Cash balance, January 1, 2006	$2,280
Cash paid for repayment of debt	607
Cash received from issuance of common stock	260
Cash received from issuance of long-term debt	300
Cash received from customers	9,081
Cash paid for property and equipment	1,399
Cash paid for dividends	14
Cash paid for repurchase of common stock	800
Cash paid for goods and services	7,583

Instructions

(a) After analyzing the data, prepare a statement of cash flows for Southwest Airlines for the year ended December 31, 2006.

(b) Discuss whether the company's cash from operations was sufficient to finance its investing activities. If it was not, how did the company finance its investing activities?

Correct an incorrectly prepared balance sheet.
(SO 5)

E1-14 Mike Paul is the bookkeeper for Benelli Company. Mike has been trying to get the balance sheet of Benelli Company to balance. It finally balanced, but now he's not sure it is correct.

BENELLI COMPANY
Balance Sheet
December 31, 2010

Assets		Liabilities and Stockholders' Equity	
Cash	$20,500	Accounts payable	$16,000
Supplies	9,500	Accounts receivable	(12,000)
Equipment	40,000	Common stock	40,000
Dividends	8,000	Retained earnings	34,000
Total assets	$78,000	Total liabilities and stockholders' equity	$78,000

Instructions

Prepare a correct balance sheet.

Classify items as assets, liabilities, and stockholders' equity and prepare accounting equation.
(SO 5)

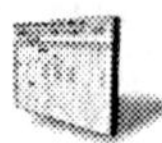

E1-15 The following items were taken from the balance sheet of Nike, Inc.

1. Cash	$ 828.0	7. Inventories	$1,633.6
2. Accounts receivable	2,120.2	8. Income taxes payable	118.2
3. Common stock	890.6	9. Property, plant, and equipment	1,586.9
4. Notes payable	146.0	10. Retained earnings	3,891.1
5. Other assets	1,722.9	11. Accounts payable	763.8
6. Other liabilities	2,081.9		

Instructions

Perform each of the following.

(a) Classify each of these items as an asset, liability, or stockholders' equity and determine the total dollar amount for each classification. (All dollars are in millions.)
(b) Determine Nike's accounting equation by calculating the value of total assets, total liabilities, and total stockholders' equity.
(c) To what extent does Nike rely on debt versus equity financing?

Use financial statement relationships to determine missing amounts.
(SO 5)

E1-16 The summaries of data from the balance sheet, income statement, and retained earnings statement for two corporations, Elder Corporation and Holden Enterprises, are presented below for 2010.

	Elder Corporation	Holden Enterprises
Beginning of year		
Total assets	$110,000	$130,000
Total liabilities	70,000	(d)
Total stockholders' equity	(a)	70,000
End of year		
Total assets	(b)	180,000
Total liabilities	120,000	55,000
Total stockholders' equity	50,000	(e)
Changes during year in retained earnings		
Dividends	(c)	5,000
Total revenues	215,000	(f)
Total expenses	165,000	80,000

Instructions

Determine the missing amounts. Assume all changes in stockholders' equity are due to changes in retained earnings.

Classify various items in an annual report.
(SO 6)

E1-17 The annual report provides financial information in a variety of formats including the following.

Management discussion and analysis (MD&A)
Financial statements
Notes to the financial statements
Auditor's opinion

Instructions

For each of the following, state in what area of the annual report the item would be presented. If the item would probably not be found in an annual report, state "Not disclosed."

(a) The total cumulative amount received from stockholders in exchange for common stock.
(b) An independent assessment concerning whether the financial statements present a fair depiction of the company's results and financial position.
(c) The interest rate that the company is being charged on all outstanding debts.
(d) Total revenue from operating activities.
(e) Management's assessment of the company's results.
(f) The names and positions of all employees hired in the last year.

Exercises: Set B

Visit the book's companion website, at **www.wiley.com/college/kimmel**, and choose the Student Companion site, to access Exercise Set B.

Problems: Set A

Determine forms of business organization.

(SO 1)

P1-1A Presented below are five independent situations.

(a) Three physics professors at MIT have formed a business to improve the speed of information transfer over the Internet for stock exchange transactions. Each has contributed an equal amount of cash and knowledge to the venture. Although their approach looks promising, they are concerned about the legal liabilities that their business might confront.
(b) Daniel Remington, a college student looking for summer employment, opened a bait shop in a small shed at a local marina.
(c) Terry Hill and Bill Mayo each owned separate shoe manufacturing businesses. They have decided to combine their businesses. They expect that within the coming year they will need significant funds to expand their operations.
(d) Alexis, Danny, and Robert recently graduated with marketing degrees. They have been friends since childhood. They have decided to start a consulting business focused on marketing sporting goods over the Internet.
(e) Stan McGlone wants to rent CD players and CDs in airports across the country. His idea is that customers will be able to rent equipment and CDs at one airport, listen to the CDs on their flights, and return the equipment and CDs at their destination airport. Of course, this will require a substantial investment in equipment and CDs, as well as employees and locations in each airport. Stan has no savings or personal assets. He wants to maintain control over the business.

Instructions

In each case explain what form of organization the business is likely to take—sole proprietorship, partnership, or corporation. Give reasons for your choice.

Identify users and uses of financial statements.

(SO 2, 4, 5)

P1-2A Financial decisions often place heavier emphasis on one type of financial statement over the others. Consider each of the following hypothetical situations independently.

(a) The North Face, Inc. is considering extending credit to a new customer. The terms of the credit would require the customer to pay within 30 days of receipt of goods.
(b) An investor is considering purchasing common stock of Amazon.com. The investor plans to hold the investment for at least 5 years.
(c) Chase Manhattan is considering extending a loan to a small company. The company would be required to make interest payments at the end of each year for 5 years, and to repay the loan at the end of the fifth year.
(d) The president of Campbell Soup is trying to determine whether the company is generating enough cash to increase the amount of dividends paid to investors in this and future years, and still have enough cash to buy equipment as it is needed.

Instructions

In each situation, state whether the decision maker would be most likely to place primary emphasis on information provided by the income statement, balance sheet, or statement of cash flows. In each case provide a brief justification for your choice. Choose only one financial statement in each case.

Prepare an income statement, retained earnings statement, and balance sheet; discuss results.
(SO 4, 5)

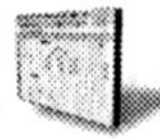

P1-3A On June 1 Eckersley Service Co. was started with an initial investment in the company of $26,200 cash. Here are the assets and liabilities of the company at June 30, and the revenues and expenses for the month of June, its first month of operations:

Cash	$ 4,600	Notes payable	$12,000
Accounts receivable	4,000	Accounts payable	500
Revenue	7,000	Supplies expense	1,000
Supplies	2,400	Gas and oil expense	600
Advertising expense	400	Utilities expense	300
Equipment	29,000	Wage expense	1,400

Marginal check figures (in blue) provide a key number to let you know you are on the right track.
(a) Net income $3,300
Ret. earnings $1,300
Tot. assets $40,000

In June, the company issued no additional stock, but paid dividends of $2,000.

Instructions

(a) Prepare an income statement and a retained earnings statement for the month of June and a balance sheet at June 30, 2010.
(b) Briefly discuss whether the company's first month of operations was a success.
(c) Discuss the company's decision to distribute a dividend.

Determine items included in a statement of cash flows, prepare the statement, and comment.
(SO 4, 5)

P1-4A Presented below is selected financial information for Maris Corporation for December 31, 2010.

Inventory	$ 25,000	Cash paid to purchase equipment	$ 10,000
Cash paid to suppliers	108,000	Equipment	40,000
Building	200,000	Revenues	100,000
Common stock	50,000	Cash received from customers	132,000
Cash dividends paid	9,000	Cash received from issuing common stock	22,000

Instructions

(a) Net increase $27,000

(a) Determine which items should be included in a statement of cash flows and then prepare the statement for Maris Corporation.
(b) Comment on the adequacy of net cash provided by operating activities to fund the company's investing activities and dividend payments.

Comment on proper accounting treatment and prepare a corrected balance sheet.
(SO 4, 5)

P1-5A Penington Corporation was formed on January 1, 2010. At December 31, 2010, Trent Radinsky, the president and sole stockholder, decided to prepare a balance sheet, which appeared as follows.

PENINGTON CORPORATION
Balance Sheet
December 31, 2010

Assets		Liabilities and Stockholders' Equity	
Cash	$20,000	Accounts payable	$30,000
Accounts receivable	50,000	Notes payable	15,000
Inventory	33,000	Boat loan	18,000
Boat	24,000	Stockholders' equity	64,000

Trent willingly admits that he is not an accountant by training. He is concerned that his balance sheet might not be correct. He has provided you with the following additional information.

1. The boat actually belongs to Radinsky, not to Penington Corporation. However, because he thinks he might take customers out on the boat occasionally, he decided to list it as an asset of the company. To be consistent he also listed as a liability of the corporation his personal loan that he took out at the bank to buy the boat.
2. The inventory was originally purchased for $21,000, but due to a surge in demand Trent now thinks he could sell it for $33,000. He thought it would be best to record it at $33,000.
3. Included in the accounts receivable balance is $12,000 that Trent loaned to his brother 5 years ago. Trent included this in the receivables of Penington Corporation so he wouldn't forget that his brother owes him money.

Instructions

Tot. assets $79,000

(a) Comment on the proper accounting treatment of the three items above.
(b) Provide a corrected balance sheet for Penington Corporation. (*Hint:* To get the balance sheet to balance, adjust stockholders' equity.)

Problems: Set B

Determine forms of business organization.

(SO 1)

P1-1B Presented below are five independent situations.

(a) Sally Quayle, a college student looking for summer employment, opened a vegetable stand along a busy local highway. Each morning she buys produce from local farmers, then sells it in the afternoon as people return home from work.

(b) Jack Nabb and Kevin Klein each owned separate swing-set manufacturing businesses. They have decided to combine their businesses and try to expand their reach beyond their local market. They expect that within the coming year they will need significant funds to expand their operations.

(c) Three chemistry professors at FIU have formed a business to employ bacteria to clean up toxic waste sites. Each has contributed an equal amount of cash and knowledge to the venture. The use of bacteria in this situation is experimental, and legal obligations could result.

(d) Lois Shore has run a successful, but small cooperative health food store for over 20 years. The increased sales of her store have made her believe that the time is right to open a national chain of health food stores across the country. Of course, this will require a substantial investment in stores, inventory, and employees in each store. Lois has no savings or personal assets. She wants to maintain control over the business.

(e) Megan Piper and Brett Tanner recently graduated with masters degrees in economics. They have decided to start a consulting business focused on teaching the basics of international economics to small business owners interested in international trade.

Instructions

In each case explain what form of organization the business is likely to take—sole proprietorship, partnership, or corporation. Give reasons for your choice.

Identify users and uses of financial statements.

(SO 2, 4, 5)

P1-2B Financial decisions often place heavier emphasis on one type of financial statement over the others. Consider each of the following hypothetical situations independently.

(a) An investor is considering purchasing common stock of the Bally Total Fitness company. The investor plans to hold the investment for at least 3 years.

(b) Boeing is considering extending credit to a new customer. The terms of the credit would require the customer to pay within 60 days of receipt of goods.

(c) The president of Northwest Airlines is trying to determine whether the company is generating enough cash to increase the amount of dividends paid to investors in this and future years, and still have enough cash to buy new flight equipment as it is needed.

(d) Bank of America is considering extending a loan to a small company. The company would be required to make interest payments at the end of each year for 5 years, and to repay the loan at the end of the fifth year.

Instructions

In each of the situations above, state whether the decision maker would be most likely to place primary emphasis on information provided by the income statement, balance sheet, or statement of cash flows. In each case provide a brief justification for your choice. Choose only one financial statement in each case.

Prepare an income statement, retained earnings statement, and balance sheet; discuss results.

(SO 4, 5)

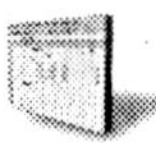

(a) Net income $3,500
Ret. earnings $1,800
Tot. assets $77,200

P1-3B Labette Delivery was started on May 1 with an investment of $45,000 cash. To "jump start" its sales, the company spent significant money on advertising. Following are the assets and liabilities of the company on May 31, 2010, and the revenues and expenses for the month of May, its first month of operations.

Accounts receivable	$ 6,200	Notes payable	$28,000
Service revenue	9,800	Wage expense	2,200
Advertising expense	800	Equipment	57,300
Accounts payable	2,400	Repair expense	500
Cash	13,700	Fuel expense	2,400
		Insurance expense	400

No additional common stock was issued in May, but a dividend of $1,700 in cash was paid.

Instructions

(a) Prepare an income statement and a retained earnings statement for the month of May and a balance sheet at May 31, 2010.

(b) Briefly discuss whether the company's first month of operations was a success.
(c) Discuss the company's decision to distribute a dividend.

Determine items included in a statement of cash flows, prepare the statement, and comment.
(SO 4, 5)

P1-4B Presented below are selected financial statement items for Eaton Corporation for December 31, 2010.

Inventory	$ 55,000	Cash paid to purchase equipment	$ 34,000
Cash paid to suppliers	154,000	Equipment	40,000
Building	400,000	Revenues	200,000
Common stock	20,000	Cash received from customers	178,000
Cash dividends paid	9,000	Cash received from issuing bonds payable	35,000

Instructions

(a) Net increase $16,000

(a) Determine which items should be included in a statement of cash flows, and then prepare the statement for Eaton Corporation.
(b) Comment on the adequacy of net cash provided by operating activities to fund the company's investing activities and dividend payments.

Comment on proper accounting treatment and prepare a corrected income statement.
(SO 4, 5)

P1-5B Houston Corporation was formed during 2009 by Glenda Lee. Glenda is the president and sole stockholder. At December 31, 2010, Glenda prepared an income statement for Houston Corporation. Glenda is not an accountant, but she thinks she did a reasonable job preparing the income statement by looking at the financial statements of other companies. She has asked you for advice. Glenda's income statement appears as follows.

HOUSTON CORPORATION
Income Statement
For the Year Ended December 31, 2010

Accounts receivable	$17,000
Revenue	50,000
Rent expense	12,000
Insurance expense	7,000
Vacation expense	2,000
Net income	58,000

Glenda has also provided you with these facts.

1. Included in the revenue account is $3,000 of revenue that the company earned and received payment for in 2009. She forgot to include it in the 2009 income statement, so she put it in this year's statement.
2. Glenda operates her business out of the basement of her parents' home. They do not charge her anything, but she thinks that if she paid rent it would cost her about $12,000 per year. She, therefore, included $12,000 of rent expense in the income statement.
3. To reward herself for a year of hard work, Glenda went to Greece. She did not use company funds to pay for the trip, but she reported it as an expense on the income statement since it was her job that made her need the vacation.

Instructions

(a) Net income $40,000

(a) Comment on the proper accounting treatment of the three items above.
(b) Prepare a corrected income statement for Houston Corporation.

Problems: Set C

Visit the book's companion website at **www.wiley.com/college/kimmel** and choose the Student Companion site to access Problem Set C.

Continuing Cookie Chronicle

CCC1 Natalie Koebel spent much of her childhood learning the art of cookie-making from her grandmother. They spent many happy hours mastering every type of cookie imaginable and later devised new recipes that were both healthy and delicious. Now at the start of her second year in college, Natalie is investigating possibilities for starting her own business as part of the entrepreneurship program in which she is enrolled.

A long-time friend insists that Natalie has to include cookies in her business plan. After a series of brainstorming sessions, Natalie settles on the idea of operating a cookie-making school. She will start on a part-time basis and offer her services in people's homes. Now that she has started thinking about it, the possibilities seem endless. During the fall, she will concentrate on holiday cookies. She will offer group sessions (which will probably be more entertainment than education) and individual lessons. Natalie also decides to include children in her target market. The first difficult decision is coming up with the perfect name for her business. She settles on "Cookie Creations," and then moves on to more important issues.

This serial problem starts in Chapter 1 and continues in every chapter. You can also find this problem at the book's companion website. **www.wiley.com/college/kimmel.**

Instructions

(a) What form of business organization—proprietorship, partnership, or corporation—do you recommend that Natalie use for her business? Discuss the benefits and weaknesses of each form that Natalie might consider.

(b) Will Natalie need accounting information? If yes, what information will she need and why? How often will she need this information?

(c) Identify specific asset, liability, revenue, and expense accounts that Cookie Creations will likely use to record its business transactions.

(d) Should Natalie open a separate bank account for the business? Why or why not?

(e) Natalie expects she will have to use her car to drive to people's homes and to pick up supplies, but she also needs to use her car for personal reasons. She recalls from her first-year accounting course something about keeping business and personal assets separate. She wonders what she should do for accounting purposes. What do you recommend?

broadening your perspective

Financial Reporting and Analysis

FINANCIAL REPORTING PROBLEM: *Tootsie Roll Industries Inc.*

BYP1-1 Simplified 2007 financial statements of Tootsie Roll Industries, Inc. are given in Illustrations 1-11 through 1-14.

Instructions

Refer to Tootsie Roll's financial statements to answer the following questions.

(a) What were Tootsie Roll's total assets at December 31, 2007? At December 31, 2006?

(b) How much cash did Tootsie Roll have on December 31, 2007?

(c) What amount of accounts payable did Tootsie Roll report on December 31, 2007? On December 31, 2006?

(d) What were Tootsie Roll's sales revenue in 2007? In 2006?

(e) What is the amount of the change in Tootsie Roll's net income from 2006 to 2007?

COMPARATIVE ANALYSIS PROBLEM: *Tootsie Roll vs. Hershey Foods*

BYP1-2 Financial statements of Hershey Foods Corporation are presented in Appendix B, and Tootsie Roll's simplified financial statements are presented in Illustrations 1-11 through 1-14.

Instructions

(a) Based on the information in these financial statements, determine the following for each company.

(1) Total assets at December 31, 2007.
(2) Net property, plant, and equipment at December 31, 2007.
(3) Sales revenue for 2007.
(4) Net income for 2007.

(b) What conclusions concerning the two companies can you draw from these data?

RESEARCH CASE

BYP1-3 The September 24, 2007, issue of *BusinessWeek* includes an article by Lindsey Gerdes titled "The Best Places to Launch a Career." It provides interesting information regarding the job opportunities for accounting students.

Instructions

Read the article and answer the following questions.

(a) What position did each of the "Big Four" (the four largest international accounting firms) receive in the survey?
(b) To what did the article attribute the accounting firms' success?
(c) What did Deloitte and Touche name as its most desirable trait for a new employee?
(d) What was the starting salary for a new employee at Deloitte and Touche?
(e) At the time the article was written in 2007, how much had the number of students graduating with accounting degrees increased relative to 2002?

INTERPRETING FINANCIAL STATEMENTS

BYP1-4 Xerox was not having a particularly pleasant year. The company's stock price had already fallen in the previous year from $60 per share to $30. Just when it seemed things couldn't get worse, Xerox's stock fell to $4 per share. The data below were taken from the statement of cash flows of Xerox. All dollars are in millions.

Cash used in operating activities		$ (663)
Cash used in investing activities		(644)
Financing activities		
Dividends paid	$ (587)	
Net cash received from issuing debt	3,498	
Cash provided by financing activities		2,911

Instructions

Analyze the information above, and then answer the following questions.

(a) If you were a creditor of Xerox, what reaction might you have to the above information?
(b) If you were an investor in Xerox, what reaction might you have to the above information?
(c) If you were evaluating the company as either a creditor or a stockholder, what other information would you be interested in seeing?
(d) Xerox decided to pay a cash dividend. This dividend was approximately equal to the amount paid in the previous year. Discuss the issues that were probably considered in making this decision.

FINANCIAL ANALYSIS ON THE WEB

BYP1-5 ***Purpose:*** Identify summary information about companies. This information includes basic descriptions of the company's location, activities, industry, financial health, and financial performance.

Address: **http://biz.yahoo.com/i**, or go to **www.wiley.com/college/kimmel**

Steps

1. Type in a company name, or use the index to find company name.
2. Choose **Quote**, then choose **Profile**, then choose **Income Statement**. Perform instructions (a) and (b) below.
3. Choose **Industry** to identify others in this industry. Perform instructions (c)–(e) below.

Instructions

Answer the following questions.

(a) What was the company's net income? Over what period was this measured?
(b) What was the company's total sales? Over what period was this measured?
(c) What is the company's industry?
(d) What are the names of four companies in this industry?
(e) Choose one of the competitors. What is this competitor's name? What were its sales? What was its net income?

Critical Thinking

DECISION MAKING ACROSS THE ORGANIZATION

BYP1-6 Kim Walters recently accepted a job in the production department at Tootsie Roll. Before she starts work, she decides to review the company's annual report to better understand its operations.

Instructions

Use the annual report provided in Appendix A to answer the following questions.

(a) What CPA firm performed the audit of Tootsie Roll's financial statements?
(b) What was the amount of Tootsie Roll's earnings per share in 2007?
(c) What are the company's net sales in foreign countries in 2007?
(d) What did management suggest as the cause of the decrease in the sales in 2007?
(e) What were net sales in 2003?
(f) How many shares of Class B common stock have been authorized?
(g) How much cash was spent on capital expenditures in 2007?
(h) Over what life does the company depreciate its buildings?
(i) What was the value of raw material and supplies inventory in 2006?

COMMUNICATION ACTIVITY

BYP1-7 Diane Wynne is the bookkeeper for Bates Company, Inc. Diane has been trying to get the company's balance sheet to balance. She finally got it to balance, but she still isn't sure that it is correct.

BATES COMPANY, INC.
Balance Sheet
For the Month Ended December 31, 2010

Assets		**Liabilities and Stockholders' Equity**	
Equipment	$20,500	Common stock	$12,000
Cash	10,500	Accounts receivable	(6,000)
Supplies	2,000	Dividends	(2,000)
Accounts payable	(5,000)	Notes payable	14,000
		Retained earnings	10,000
Total assets	$28,000	Total liabilities and stockholders' equity	$28,000

Instructions

Explain to Diane Wynne in a memo (a) the purpose of a balance sheet, and (b) why this balance sheet is incorrect and what she should do to correct it.

ETHICS CASE

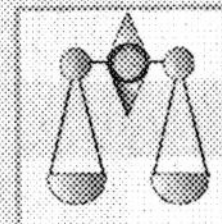

BYP1-8 Rules governing the investment practices of individual certified public accountants prohibit them from investing in the stock of a company that their firm audits. The Securities and Exchange Commission became concerned that some accountants were violating this rule. In response to an SEC investigation, PricewaterhouseCoopers fired 10 people and spent $25 million educating employees about the investment rules and installing an investment tracking system.

Instructions

Answer the following questions.

(a) Why do you think rules exist that restrict auditors from investing in companies that are audited by their firms?
(b) Some accountants argue that they should be allowed to invest in a company's stock as long as they themselves aren't involved in working on the company's audit or consulting. What do you think of this idea?
(c) Today a very high percentage of publicly traded companies are audited by only four very large public accounting firms. These firms also do a high percentage of the consulting work that is done for publicly traded companies. How does this fact complicate the decision regarding whether CPAs should be allowed to invest in companies audited by their firm?

(d) Suppose you were a CPA and you had invested in IBM when IBM was not one of your firm's clients. Two years later, after IBM's stock price had fallen considerably, your firm won the IBM audit contract. You will not in any way be involved in working with the IBM audit, which will be done by one of your firm's other offices in a different state. You know that your firm's rules, as well as U.S. law, require that you sell your shares immediately. If you do sell immediately, you will sustain a large loss. Do you think this is fair? What would you do?
(e) Why do you think PricewaterhouseCoopers took such extreme steps in response to the SEC investigation?

"ALL ABOUT YOU" ACTIVITY

BYP1-9 Some people are tempted to make their finances look worse to get financial aid. Companies sometimes also manage their financial numbers in order to accomplish certain goals. Earnings management is the planned timing of revenues, expenses, gains, and losses to smooth out bumps in net income. In managing earnings, companies' actions vary from being within the range of ethical activity, to being both unethical and illegal attempts to mislead investors and creditors.

Instructions
Provide responses for each of the following questions.
(a) Discuss whether you think each of the following actions (adapted from *www.finaid.org/fafsa/maximize.phtml*) to increase the chances of receiving financial aid is ethical.
  (i) Spend down the student's assets and income first, before spending parents' assets and income.
  (ii) Accelerate necessary expenses to reduce available cash. For example, if you need a new car, buy it before applying for financial aid.
  (iii) State that a truly financially dependent child is independent.
  (iv) Have a parent take an unpaid leave of absence for long enough to get below the "threshold" level of income.
(b) What are some reasons why a *company* might want to overstate its earnings?
(c) What are some reasons why a *company* might want to understate its earnings?
(d) Under what circumstances might an otherwise ethical person decide to illegally overstate or understate earnings?

Answers to Insight and Accounting Across the Organization Questions

p. 7
Q: What are the benefits to the company and to the employees of making the financial statements available to all employees?
A: If employees can read and use financial reports, a company will benefit in the following ways. The *marketing department* will make better decisions about products to offer and prices to charge. The *finance department* will make better decisions about debt and equity financing and how much to distribute in dividends. The *production department* will make better decisions about when to buy new equipment and how much inventory to produce. The *human resources department* will be better able to determine whether employees can be given raises. Finally, *all employees* will be better informed about the basis on which they are evaluated, which will increase employee morale.

p. 8
Q: How might accounting help you?
A: You will need to understand financial reports in any enterprise with which you are associated. Whether you become a manager, a doctor, a lawyer, a social worker, a teacher, an engineer, an architect, or an entrepreneur, a working knowledge of accounting is relevant.

p. 9
Q: What benefits does a sound accounting system provide to a not-for-profit organization?
A: Accounting provides at least two benefits to not-for-profit organizations. First, it helps to ensure that money is used in the way that donors intended. Second, it assures donors that their money is not going to waste, and thus increases the likelihood of future donations.

p. 15
Q: What is one way that some of these disputes might be resolved?
A: Frequently, when contractual payments depend on accounting-based financial results, interested parties employ outside auditors to evaluate whether the financial information has been prepared fairly and accurately. The musicians would like auditors to have easy access to inventory and manufacturing information of the recording companies.

Answers to Self-Study Questions

1. b 2. c 3. d 4. d 5. c 6. a 7. d 8. d 9. a 10. b 11. c 12. d 13. a 14. a 5. b

Remember to go back to the navigator box on the chapter-opening page and check off your completed work.

chapter 2

A Further Look at Financial Statements

the navigator

- Scan Study Objectives ○
- Read Feature Story ○
- Scan Preview ○
- Read Text and answer **Do it!** p. 52 ○ p. 53 ○ p. 63 ○ p. 70 ○
- Work Using the Decision Toolkit ○
- Review Summary of Study Objectives ○
- Work Comprehensive **Do it!** p. 75 ○
- Answer Self-Study Questions ○
- Complete Assignments ○

study objectives

After studying this chapter, you should be able to:

1 Identify the sections of a classified balance sheet.

2 Identify and compute ratios for analyzing a company's profitability.

3 Explain the relationship between a retained earnings statement and a statement of stockholders' equity.

4 Identify and compute ratios for analyzing a company's liquidity and solvency using a balance sheet.

5 Use the statement of cash flows to evaluate solvency.

6 Explain the meaning of generally accepted accounting principles.

7 Discuss financial reporting concepts.

Just Fooling Around?

Few people could have predicted how dramatically the Internet would change the investment world. One of the most interesting results is how it has changed the way ordinary people invest their savings. More and more people are striking out on their own, making their own investment decisions.

Two early pioneers in providing investment information to the masses were Tom and David Gardner, brothers who created an online investor bulletin board called The Motley Fool. The name comes from Shakespeare's *As You Like It.* The fool in Shakespeare's plays was the only one who could speak unpleasant truths to kings and queens without being killed. Tom and David view themselves as 21st-century "fools," revealing the "truths" of Wall Street to the small investor, who they feel has been taken advantage of by Wall Street insiders. Their online bulletin board enables investors to exchange information and insights about companies.

Critics of these bulletin boards contend that they are high-tech rumor mills. They suggest that the fervor created by bulletin board chatter causes investors to bid up stock prices to unreasonable levels. Because bulletin board participants typically use aliases, there is little to stop people from putting misinformation on the board to influence a stock's price. For example, the stock of PairGain Technologies jumped 32 percent in a single day as a result of a bogus takeover rumor on an investment bulletin board. Some observers are concerned that small investors–ironically, the very people the Gardner brothers are trying to help–will be hurt the most by misinformation and intentional scams.

To show how these bulletin boards work, suppose that in a recent year you had $10,000 to invest. You were considering Best Buy Company, the largest seller of electronics equipment in the United States. You scanned the Internet investment bulletin boards and found messages posted by two different investors. Here are excerpts from actual postings during the same recent year.

> *From: "TMPVenus":* "Where are the prospects for positive movement for this company? Poor margins, poor management, astronomical P/E!"

> *From "broachman":* "I believe that this is a LONG TERM winner, and presently at a good price."

One says sell, and one says buy. Whom should you believe? If you had taken "broachman's" advice and purchased the stock, the $10,000 you invested would have been worth over $300,000 five years later. Best Buy was one of America's best-performing stocks during that period of time.

Deciding what information to rely on is becoming increasingly complex. For example, shortly before its share price completely collapsed, nearly every professional analyst who followed Enron was recommending its stock as a "buy."

Rather than getting swept away by rumors, investors must sort out the good information from the bad. One thing is certain–as information services such as The Motley Fool increase in number, gathering information will become even easier. Evaluating it will be the harder task.

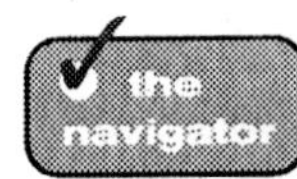

On the World Wide Web
The Motley Fool: www.fool.com.
Best Buy Company: www.bestbuy.com

preview of chapter 2

If you are thinking of purchasing Best Buy stock, or any stock, how can you decide what the stock is worth? If you manage J. Crew's credit department, how should you determine whether to extend credit to a new customer? If you are a financial executive of IBM, how do you decide whether your company is generating adequate cash to expand operations without borrowing? Your decision in each of these situations will be influenced by a variety of considerations. One of them should be your careful analysis of a company's financial statements. The reason: Financial statements offer relevant and reliable information, which will help you in your decision making.

In this chapter we take a closer look at the balance sheet and introduce some useful ways for evaluating the information provided by the financial statements. We also examine the financial reporting concepts underlying the financial statements.

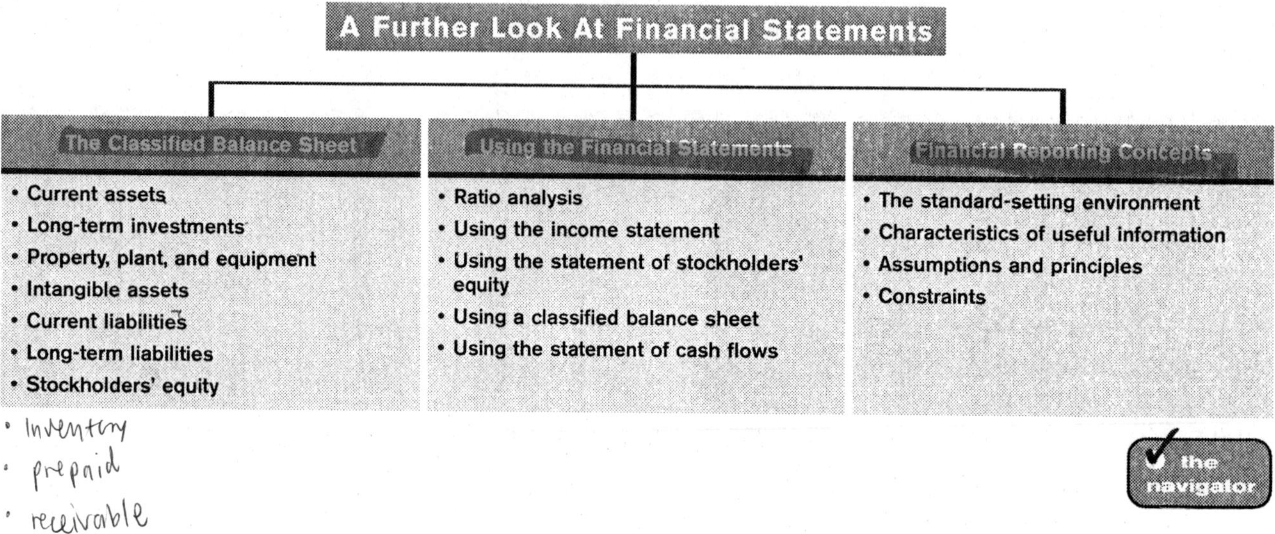

the navigator

In Chapter 1 we introduced the four financial statements. In this section we review the financial statements and present tools that are useful for evaluating them. We begin by introducing the classified balance sheet.

A Further Look At Financial Statements
The Classified Balance Sheet
• Current assets
• Long-term investments
• Property, plant, and equipment
• Intangible assets
• Current liabilities
• Long-term liabilities
• Stockholders' equity
Using the Financial Statements
• Ratio analysis
• Using the income statement
• Using the statement of stockholders' equity
• Using a classified balance sheet
• Using the statement of cash flows
Financial Reporting Concepts
• The standard-setting environment
• Characteristics of useful information
• Assumptions and principles
• Constraints

The Classified Balance Sheet

study objective 1

Identify the sections of a classified balance sheet.

In Chapter 1 you learned that a balance sheet presents a snapshot of a company's financial position at a point in time. The balance sheet in Chapter 1 listed individual asset, liability and stockholders' equity items in no particular order. To improve users' understanding of a company's financial position, companies often use a classified balance sheet. A **classified balance sheet** groups together similar assets and similar liabilities, using a number of standard classifications and sections. This is useful because items within a group have similar economic characteristics. A classified balance sheet generally contains the standard classifications listed in Illustration 2-1.

Illustration 2-1 Standard balance sheet classifications

Assets	Liabilities and Stockholders' Equity
Current assets	Current liabilities
Long-term investments	Long-term liabilities
Property, plant, and equipment	Stockholders' equity
Intangible assets	

These groupings help readers determine such things as (1) whether the company has enough assets to pay its debts as they come due, and (2) the claims of short- and long-term creditors on the company's total assets. Many of these groupings can be seen in the balance sheet of Franklin Corporation shown in Illustration 2-2. In the sections that follow, we explain each of these groupings.

CURRENT ASSETS

Current assets are assets that a company expects to convert to cash or use up within one year or its operating cycle, whichever is longer. In Illustration 2-2, Franklin Corporation had current assets of $22,100. For most businesses the cut-off for classification as current assets is one year from the balance sheet date. For example, accounts receivable are current assets because the company will

Illustration 2-2 Classified balance sheet

FRANKLIN CORPORATION
Balance Sheet
October 31, 2010

Assets			
Current assets			
Cash		$ 6,600	
Short-term investments		2,000	
Accounts receivable		7,000	
Notes receivable		1,000	
Inventories		3,000	
Supplies		2,100	
Prepaid insurance		400	
Total current assets			$22,100
Long-term investments			
Investment in stock of Walters Corp.		5,200	
Investment in real estate		2,000	7,200
Property, plant, and equipment			
Land		10,000	
Office equipment	$24,000		
Less: Accumulated depreciation	5,000	19,000	29,000
Intangible assets			
Patents			3,100
Total assets			$61,400
Liabilities and Stockholders' Equity			
Current liabilities			
Notes payable		$11,000	
Accounts payable		2,100	
Salaries payable		1,600	
Unearned revenue		900	
Interest payable		450	
Total current liabilities			$16,050
Long-term liabilities			
Mortgage payable		10,000	
Notes payable		1,300	
Total long-term liabilities			11,300
Total liabilities			27,350
Stockholders' equity			
Common stock		14,000	
Retained earnings		20,050	
Total stockholders' equity			34,050
Total liabilities and stockholders' equity			$61,400

Helpful Hint Recall that the accounting equation is Assets = Liabilities + Stockholders' Equity.

collect them and convert them to cash within one year. Supplies is a current asset because the company expects to use them up in operations within one year.

Some companies use a period longer than one year to classify assets and liabilities as current because they have an operating cycle longer than one year. The operating cycle of a company is the average time that it takes to go from cash to cash in producing revenue—to purchase inventory, sell it on account, and then collect cash from customers. For most businesses this cycle takes less than a year, so they use a one-year cutoff. But, for some businesses, such as vineyards or airplane manufacturers, this period may be longer than a year. **Except where noted, we will assume that companies use one year to determine whether an asset or liability is current or long-term.**

Common types of current assets are (1) cash, (2) short-term investments (such as short-term U.S. government securities), (3) receivables (notes receivable, accounts receivable, and interest receivable), (4) inventories, and (5) prepaid expenses (insurance and supplies). **Companies list current assets in the order in which they expect to convert them into cash.** *Follow this rule when doing your homework.*

Illustration 2-3 presents the current assets of Southwest Airlines Co.

Illustration 2-3 Current assets section

SOUTHWEST AIRLINES CO.
Balance Sheet (partial)
(in millions)

Current assets	
Cash and cash equivalents	$1,390
Short-term investments	369
Accounts receivable	241
Inventories	181
Prepaid expenses and other current assets	420
Total current assets	$2,601

As explained later in the chapter, a company's current assets are important in assessing its short-term debt-paying ability.

LONG-TERM INVESTMENTS

Alternative Terminology Long-term investments are often referred to simply as *investments*.

Long-term investments are generally: (1) investments in stocks and bonds of other corporations that are held for more than one year, and (2) long-term assets such as land or buildings that a company is not currently using in its operating activities. In Illustration 2-2 Franklin Corporation reported total long-term investments of $7,200 on its balance sheet.

Yahoo! Inc. reported long-term investments on its balance sheet as shown in Illustration 2-4.

Illustration 2-4 Long-term investments section

YAHOO!

YAHOO! INC.
Balance Sheet (partial)
(in thousands)

Long-term investments	
Long-term investments in marketable securities	$90,266

PROPERTY, PLANT, AND EQUIPMENT

Property, plant, and equipment are assets with relatively long useful lives that a company is currently using in operating the business. This category includes land, buildings, machinery and equipment, delivery equipment, and furniture. In Illustration 2-2 Franklin Corporation reported property, plant, and equipment of $29,000.

Alternative Terminology Property, plant, and equipment is sometimes called *fixed assets* or *plant assets*.

Depreciation is the practice of allocating the cost of assets to a number of years. Companies do this by systematically assigning a portion of an asset's cost as an expense each year (rather than expensing the full purchase price in the year of purchase). The assets that the company depreciates are reported on the balance sheet at cost less accumulated depreciation. The **accumulated depreciation** account shows the total amount of depreciation that the company has expensed thus far in the asset's life. In Illustration 2-2 Franklin Corporation reported accumulated depreciation of $5,000.

Illustration 2-5 presents the property, plant, and equipment of Cooper Tire & Rubber Company.

International Note In 2007 China adopted international financial reporting standards. This was done in an effort to reduce fraud and increase investor confidence in financial reports. Under these standards, many items, such as property, plant, and equipment, may be reported at current market values, rather than historical cost.

Illustration 2-5 Property, plant, and equipment section

COOPER TIRE & RUBBER COMPANY
Balance Sheet (partial)
(in thousands)

Property, plant, and equipment		
Land and land improvements	$ 41,553	
Buildings	298,706	
Machinery and equipment	1,636,091	
Molds, cores, and rings	268,158	$2,244,508
Less: Accumulated depreciation		1,252,692
		$ 991,816

INTANGIBLE ASSETS

Many companies have assets that do not have physical substance yet often are very valuable. We call these assets **intangible assets**. One common intangible is goodwill. Others include patents, copyrights, and trademarks or trade names that give the company **exclusive right** of use for a specified period of time. Franklin Corporation reported intangible assets of $3,100.

Illustration 2-6 shows the intangible assets of media giant Time Warner, Inc.

Helpful Hint Sometimes intangible assets are reported under a broader heading called *"Other assets."*

Illustration 2-6 Intangible assets section

TIME WARNER, INC.
Balance Sheet (partial)
(in millions)

Intangible assets	
Goodwill	$40,953
Film library	2,690
Customer lists	2,540
Cable television franchises	38,048
Sports franchises	262
Brands, trademarks, and other intangible assets	8,313
	$92,806

before you go on...

ASSETS SECTION OF BALANCE SHEET

Do it! Baxter Hoffman recently received the following information related to Hoffman Corporation's December 31, 2010, balance sheet.

Prepaid expenses	$ 2,300	Inventory	$3,400
Cash	800	Accumulated depreciation	2,700
Property, plant, and equipment	10,700	Accounts receivable	1,100

Prepare the assets section of Hoffman Corporation's balance sheet.

Action Plan

- Present current assets first. Current assets are cash and other resources that the company expects to convert to cash or use up within one year.
- Present current assets in the order in which the company expects to convert them into cash.
- Subtract accumulated depreciation from property, plant, and equipment to determine net property, plant, and equipment.

Solution

HOFFMAN CORPORATION
Balance Sheet (partial)
December 31, 2010

Assets		
Current assets		
Cash	$ 800	
Accounts receivable	1,100	
Inventory	3,400	
Prepaid expenses	2,300	
Total current assets		$ 7,600
Property, plant, and equipment	10,700	
Less: Accumulated depreciation	2,700	8,000
Total assets		$15,600

CURRENT LIABILITIES

In the liabilities and stockholders' equity section of the balance sheet, the first grouping is current liabilities. **Current liabilities** are obligations that the company is to pay within the coming year or operating cycle, whichever is longer. Common examples are accounts payable, wages payable, bank loans payable, interest payable, and taxes payable. Also included as current liabilities are current maturities of long-term obligations—payments to be made within the next year on long-term obligations. In Illustration 2-2 Franklin Corporation reported five different types of current liabilities, for a total of $16,050.

Within the current liabilities section, companies usually list notes payable first, followed by accounts payable. Other items then follow in the order of their magnitude. In your homework, you should present notes payable first, followed by accounts payable, and then other liabilities in order of magnitude.

Illustration 2-7 shows the current liabilities section adapted from the balance sheet of Marcus Corporation.

Illustration 2-7 Current liabilities section

MARCUS CORPORATION
Balance Sheet (partial)
(in thousands)

Current liabilities	
Notes payable	$ 239
Accounts payable	24,242
Current maturities of long-term debt	57,250
Other current liabilities	27,477
Taxes payable	11,215
Accrued compensation payable	6,720
Total current liabilities	$127,143

LONG-TERM LIABILITIES

Long-term liabilities are obligations that a company expects to pay **after** one year. Liabilities in this category include bonds payable, mortgages payable, long-term notes payable, lease liabilities, and pension liabilities. Many companies report long-term debt maturing after one year as a single amount in the balance sheet and show the details of the debt in notes that accompany the financial statements. Others list the various types of long-term liabilities. In Illustration 2-2 Franklin Corporation reported long-term liabilities of $11,300. In your homework, list long-term liabilities in the order of their magnitude.

Illustration 2-8 shows the long-term liabilities that Procter & Gamble Company reported in its balance sheet.

Illustration 2-8 Long-term liabilities section

THE PROCTER & GAMBLE COMPANY
Balance Sheet (partial)
(in millions)

Long-term liabilities	
Long-term debt	$23,375
Deferred income taxes	12,015
Other noncurrent liabilities	5,147
Total long-term liabilities	$40,537

STOCKHOLDERS' EQUITY

Stockholders' equity consists of two parts: common stock and retained earnings. Companies record as **common stock** the investments of assets into the business by the stockholders. They record as **retained earnings** the income retained for use in the business. These two parts, combined, make up **stockholders' equity** on the balance sheet. In Illustration 2-2 Franklin reported common stock of $14,000 and retained earnings of $20,050.

Alternative Terminology Common stock is sometimes called *capital stock*.

before you go on...

Do it!

BALANCE SHEET CLASSIFICATIONS

The following financial statement items were taken from the financial statements of Callahan Corp.

_____	Salaries payable	_____	Investment in real estate
_____	Service revenue	_____	Delivery truck
_____	Dividends payable	_____	Accumulated depreciation
_____	Goodwill	_____	Depreciation expense
_____	Short-term investments	_____	Retained earnings
_____	Mortgage note payable due in 3 years	_____	Unearned revenue

Match each of the items to its proper balance sheet classification, shown below. If the item would not appear on a balance sheet, use "NA."

Current assets (CA)	Current liabilities (CL)
Long-term investments (LTI)	Long-term liabilities (LTL)
Property, plant, and equipment (PPE)	Stockholders' equity (SE)
Intangible assets (IA)	

Action Plan

- Analyze whether each financial statement item is an asset, liability, or stockholders' equity item.
- Determine if asset and liability items are current or long-term.

Solution

CL	Salaries payable	LTI	Investment in real estate
NA	Service revenue	PPE	Delivery truck
CL	Dividends payable	PPE	Accumulated depreciation
IA	Goodwill	NA	Depreciation expense
CA	Short-term investments	SE	Retained earnings
LTL	Mortgage note payable due in 3 years	CL	Unearned revenue

Using the Financial Statements

In Chapter 1 we introduced the four financial statements. We discussed how these statements provide information about a company's performance and financial position. In this chapter we extend this discussion by showing you specific tools that you can use to analyze financial statements in order to make a more meaningful evaluation of a company.

RATIO ANALYSIS

Ratio analysis expresses the relationship among selected items of financial statement data. A **ratio** expresses the mathematical relationship between one quantity and another. The relationship is expressed in terms of either a percentage, a rate, or a simple proportion.

To illustrate, Best Buy has current assets of $9,081 million and current liabilities of $6,301 million. We can determine a relationship between these accounts by dividing current assets by current liabilities, to get 1.44. The alternative means of expression are:

Percentage: Current assets are 144% of current liabilities.

Rate: Current assets are 1.44 times as great as current liabilities.

Proportion: The relationship of current assets to current liabilities is 1.44:1.

For analysis of the primary financial statements, we classify ratios as follows.

Illustration 2-9 Financial ratio classifications

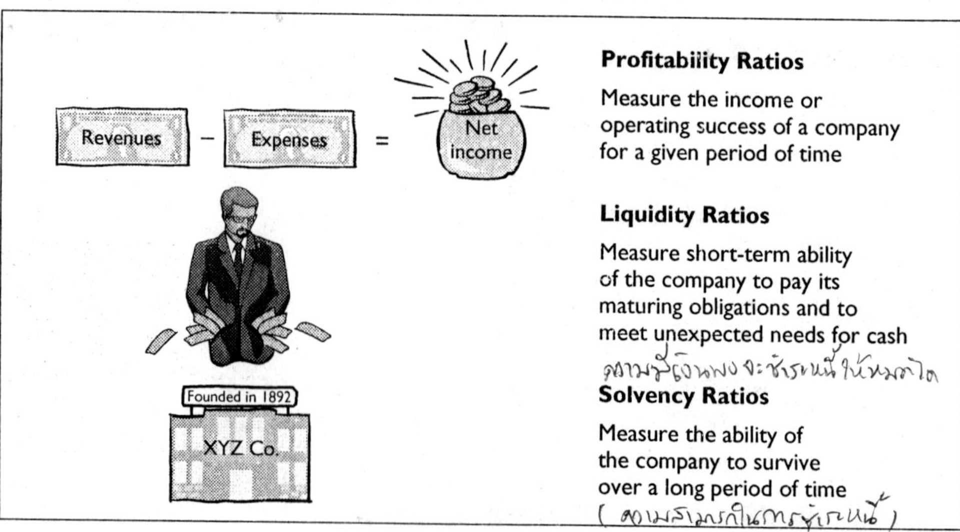

Revenues
–
Expenses
=
Net income
Profitability Ratios
Measure the income or operating success of a company for a given period of time
Liquidity Ratios
Measure short-term ability of the company to pay its maturing obligations and to meet unexpected needs for cash
Founded in 1892
XYZ Co.
Solvency Ratios
Measure the ability of the company to survive over a long period of time

Ratios can provide clues to underlying conditions that may not be apparent from examination of the individual items on the financial statements. However, a single ratio by itself is not very meaningful. Accordingly, in this and the following chapters we will use various comparisons to shed light on company performance:

1. **Intracompany comparisons** covering two years for the same company.
2. **Industry-average comparisons** based on average ratios for particular industries.
3. **Intercompany comparisons** based on comparisons with a competitor in the same industry.

USING THE INCOME STATEMENT

Best Buy Company generates profits for its stockholders by selling electronics. The income statement reports how successful it is at generating a profit from its sales. The income statement reports the amount earned during the period (revenues) and the costs incurred during the period (expenses). Illustration 2-10 shows a simplified income statement for Best Buy.

study objective 2

Identify and compute ratios for analyzing a company's profitability.

Illustration 2-10 Best Buy's income statement

BEST BUY CO., INC.
Income Statements
For the Years Ended March 3, 2007, and February 25, 2006 (in millions)

	2007	2006
Revenues		
Net sales and other revenue	$35,934	$30,848
Expenses		
Cost of goods sold	27,165	23,122
Selling, general, and administrative expenses	6,640	6,005
Income tax expense	752	581
Total expenses	34,557	29,708
Net income	$ 1,377	$ 1,140

From this income statement we can see that Best Buy's sales and net income both increased during the period. Net income increased from $1,140 million to $1,377 million. Best Buy's primary competitor is Circuit City. Circuit City reported a net loss of $10.2 million for the year ended February 28, 2007.

To evaluate the profitability of Best Buy, we will use ratio analysis. Profitability ratios measure the operating success of a company for a given period of time.

EARNINGS PER SHARE. Earnings per share (EPS) measures the net income earned on each share of common stock. We compute EPS by dividing **net income** by the **average number of common shares outstanding during the year**. Stockholders usually think in terms of the number of shares they own or plan to buy or sell, so stating net income earned as a per share amount provides a useful perspective for determining the investment return. Advanced accounting courses present more refined techniques for calculating earnings per share.

For now, a basic approach for calculating earnings per share is to divide earnings available to common stockholders by average common shares outstanding during the year. What is "earnings available to common stockholders"? It is an earnings amount calculated as net income less dividends paid on another type of stock, called preferred stock (Net income − Preferred stock dividends).

By comparing earnings per share of **a single company over time**, one can evaluate its relative earnings performance from the perspective of a stockholder—that is, on a per share basis. It is very important to note that comparisons of earnings per share across companies are **not meaningful** because of the wide variations in the numbers of shares of outstanding stock among companies.

Illustration 2-11 shows the earnings per share calculation for Best Buy in 2007 and 2006, based on the information presented below. (Note that to simplify our calculations, we assumed that any change in the number of shares for Best Buy occurred in the middle of the year.)

(in millions)	2007	2006
Net income	$1,377	$1,140
Preferred stock dividends	–0–	–0–
Shares outstanding at beginning of year	485	493
Shares outstanding at end of year	481	485

Illustration 2-11 Best Buy earnings per share

$$\text{Earnings per Share} = \frac{\text{Net Income} - \text{Preferred Stock Dividends}}{\text{Average Common Shares Outstanding}}$$

($ and shares in millions)	2007	2006
Earnings per share	$\frac{\$1,377 - \$0}{(481 + 485)/2} = \$2.85$	$\frac{\$1,140 - \$0}{(485 + 493)/2} = \$2.33$

DECISION TOOLKIT

DECISION CHECKPOINTS	INFO NEEDED FOR DECISION	TOOL TO USE FOR DECISION	HOW TO EVALUATE RESULTS
How does the company's earnings performance compare with that of previous years?	Net income available to common stockholders and average common shares outstanding	$\text{Earnings per share} = \frac{\text{Net income} - \text{Preferred stock dividends}}{\text{Average common shares outstanding}}$	A higher measure suggests improved performance, although the number is subject to manipulation. Values should not be compared across companies.

USING THE STATEMENT OF STOCKHOLDERS' EQUITY

study objective 3

Explain the relationship between a retained earnings statement and a statement of stockholders' equity.

As discussed in Chapter 1, the retained earnings statement describes the changes in retained earnings during the year. This statement adds net income and then subtracts dividends from the beginning retained earnings to arrive at ending retained earnings.

Stockholders' equity is comprised of two parts: retained earnings and common stock. Therefore, the stockholders' equity of most companies is affected by factors other than just changes in retained earnings. For example, the company may issue or retire shares of common stock. Most companies, therefore, use what is called a statement of stockholders' equity, rather than a retained earnings statement, so that they can report **all changes** in stockholders' equity accounts. Illustration 2-12 is a simplified statement of stockholders' equity for Best Buy.

Illustration 2-12 Best Buy's statement of stockholders' equity

BEST BUY CO., INC.
Statement of Stockholders' Equity
(in millions)

	Common Stock	Retained Earnings
Balances at February 28, 2004	$ 868	$2,554
Issuance of common stock	117	
Net income		984
Dividends		(137)
Other adjustments		63
Balances at February 26, 2005	985	3,464
Repurchase of common stock	(293)	
Net income		1,140
Dividends		(151)
Other adjustments		112
Balances at February 25, 2006	692	4,565
Repurchase of common stock	(214)	
Net income		1,377
Dividends		(174)
Other adjustments		(45)
Balances at March 3, 2007	$ 478	$5,723

We can observe from this financial statement that Best Buy's common stock increased during the first year as the result of issuance of common stock. It declined in the second and third years as the result of repurchasing shares of stock. Another observation from this financial statement is that Best Buy paid an increasing amount of dividends each year. This is a recent practice for Best Buy. Prior to 2003, it did not pay dividends, even though it was profitable and could do so. You might wonder why Best Buy paid no dividends during prior years when it was profitable. In fact, in a prior year, two Best Buy stockholders discussed this question about the company's dividend policy on an investor bulletin board. Here are excerpts:

> *From "Katwoman":* "Best Buy has a nice price increase. Earnings are on the way up. But why no dividends?"
>
> *From "AngryCandy":* "I guess they feel they can make better use of the money by investing back in the business. They still view Best Buy as a rapidly growing company and would prefer to invest in expanding the infrastructure (building new stores, advertising, etc.) than in paying out dividends . . . . If Best Buy gets to the stage of 'stable, big company' with little room for expansion, then I'm sure you'll see them elect to pay out a dividend."

AngryCandy's response is an excellent explanation of the thought process that management goes through in deciding whether to pay a dividend. Management must evaluate what its cash needs are. If it has uses for cash that will increase the value of the company (for example, building a new, centralized warehouse), then it should retain cash in the company. However, if it has more cash than it has valuable opportunities, it should distribute its excess cash as a dividend.

USING A CLASSIFIED BALANCE SHEET

You can learn a lot about a company's financial health by also evaluating the relationship between its various assets and liabilities. Illustration 2-13 provides a simplified balance sheet for Best Buy.

Illustration 2-13 Best Buy's balance sheet

BEST BUY CO., INC.
Balance Sheets
(in millions)

Assets	**March 3, 2007**	**February 25, 2006**
Current assets		
Cash and cash equivalents	$ 1,205	$ 748
Receivables	548	449
Merchandise inventories	4,028	3,338
Other current assets	3,300	3,450
Total current assets	9,081	7,985
Property and equipment	4,904	4,836
Less: Accumulated depreciation	1,966	2,124
Net property and equipment	2,938	2,712
Other assets	1,551	1,167
Total assets	$13,570	$11,864
Liabilities and Stockholders' Equity		
Current liabilities		
Accounts payable	$ 3,934	$ 3,234
Accrued liabilities	1,486	1,347
Accrued income taxes	489	703
Other current liabilities	60	418
Accrued compensation payable	332	354
Total current liabilities	6,301	6,056
Long-term liabilities		
Long-term debt	590	178
Other long-term liabilities	478	373
Total long-term liabilities	1,068	551
Total liabilities	7,369	6,607
Stockholders' equity		
Common stock	478	692
Retained earnings	5,723	4,565
Total stockholders' equity	6,201	5,257
Total liabilities and stockholders' equity	$13,570	$11,864

study objective 

Identify and compute ratios for analyzing a company's liquidity and solvency using a balance sheet.

Liquidity

Suppose you are a banker at CitiGroup considering lending money to Best Buy, or you are a sales manager at Hewlett-Packard interested in selling computers to Best Buy on credit. You would be concerned about Best Buy's liquidity—its ability to pay obligations expected to become due within the next year or operating cycle. You would look closely at the relationship of its current assets to current liabilities.

WORKING CAPITAL. One measure of liquidity is working capital, which is the difference between the amounts of current assets and current liabilities:

Illustration 2-14 Working capital

Working Capital = Current Assets − Current Liabilities

When current assets exceed current liabilities, working capital is positive. When this occurs, there is greater likelihood that the company will pay its liabilities. When working capital is negative, a company might not be able to pay short-term creditors, and the company might ultimately be forced into bankruptcy. Best Buy had working capital in 2007 of $2,780 million ($9,081 million − $6,301 million).

CURRENT RATIO. Liquidity ratios measure the short-term ability of the company to pay its maturing obligations and to meet unexpected needs for cash. One liquidity ratio is the current ratio, computed as current assets divided by current liabilities.

The current ratio is a more dependable indicator of liquidity than working capital. Two companies with the same amount of working capital may have significantly different current ratios. Illustration 2-15 shows the 2007 and 2006 current ratios for Best Buy and for Circuit City, along with the 2007 industry average.

Illustration 2-15 Current ratio

$$\text{Current Ratio} = \frac{\text{Current Assets}}{\text{Current Liabilities}}$$

	2007	2006
Best Buy ($ in millions)	$\frac{\$9,081}{\$6,301} = 1.44:1$	$\frac{\$7,985}{\$6,056} = 1.32:1$
Circuit City	1.68:1	1.75:1
Industry average	1.21:1	

What does the ratio actually mean? Best Buy's 2007 current ratio of 1.44:1 means that for every dollar of current liabilities, Best Buy has $1.44 of current assets. Best Buy's current ratio increased in 2007. When compared to the industry average of 1.21:1, Best Buy's liquidity seems adequate, although it is less than that of Circuit City.

One potential weakness of the current ratio is that it does not take into account the **composition** of the current assets. For example, a satisfactory current ratio does not disclose whether a portion of the current assets is tied up in slow-moving inventory. The composition of the current assets matters because a dollar of cash is more readily available to pay the bills than is a dollar of inventory. For example, suppose a company's cash balance declined while its merchandise inventory increased substantially. If inventory increased because the company is having difficulty selling its products, then the current ratio might not fully reflect the reduction in the company's liquidity.

Ethics Note A company that has more current assets than current liabilities can increase the ratio of current assets to current liabilities by using cash to pay off some current liabilities. This gives the appearance of being more liquid. Do you think this move is ethical?

Accounting Across the Organization

There actually is a point where a company can be too liquid–that is, it can have too much working capital. While it is important to be liquid enough to be able to pay short-term bills as they come due, a company does not want to tie up its cash in extra inventory or receivables that are not earning the company money.

By one estimate from the REL Consultancy Group, the thousand largest U.S. companies have on their books cumulative excess working capital of $764 billion. Based on this figure, companies could have reduced debt by 36% or increased net income by 9%. Given that managers throughout a company are interested in improving profitability, it is clear that they should have an eye toward managing working capital. They need to aim for a "Goldilocks solution"–not too much, not too little, but just right.

Source: K. Richardson, "Companies Fall Behind in Cash Management," *Wall Street Journal*, June 19, 2007.

What can various company managers do to ensure that working capital is managed efficiently to maximize net income?

Solvency

Now suppose that instead of being a short-term creditor, you are interested in either buying Best Buy's stock or extending the company a long-term loan. Long-term creditors and stockholders are interested in a company's solvency—its ability to pay interest as it comes due and to repay the balance of a debt due at its maturity. Solvency ratios measure the ability of the company to survive over a long period of time.

DEBT TO TOTAL ASSETS RATIO. The debt to total assets ratio is one source of information about long-term debt-paying ability. It measures the percentage of total financing provided by creditors rather than stockholders. Debt financing is more risky than equity financing because debt must be repaid at specific points in time, whether the company is performing well or not. Thus, the higher the percentage of debt financing, the riskier the company.

Helpful Hint Some users evaluate solvency using a ratio of liabilities divided by stockholders' equity. The higher this "debt to equity" ratio, the lower is a company's solvency.

We compute the debt to total assets ratio as total debt (both current and long-term liabilities) divided by total assets. The higher the percentage of total liabilities (debt) to total assets, the greater the risk that the company may be unable to pay its debts as they come due. Illustration 2-16 shows the debt to total assets ratios for Best Buy and Circuit City, along with the 2007 industry average.

Illustration 2-16 Debt to total assets ratio

$$\text{Debt to Total Assets Ratio} = \frac{\text{Total Liabilities}}{\text{Total Assets}}$$

	2007	2006
Best Buy ($ in millions)	$\frac{\$7,369}{\$13,570} = 54\%$	$\frac{\$6,607}{\$11,864} = 56\%$
Circuit City	55%	52%
Industry average	21%	

The 2007 ratio of 54% means that every dollar of assets was financed by 54 cents of debt. Best Buy's ratio exceeds the industry average of 21%, and is approximately the same as Circuit City's ratio of 55%. The higher the ratio, the lower the equity "buffer" available to creditors if the company becomes insolvent. Thus, from the creditors' point of view, a high ratio of debt to total assets is undesirable. Best Buy's solvency appears roughly the same as that of Circuit City but significantly lower than the average company in the industry.

The adequacy of this ratio is often judged in the light of the company's earnings. Generally, companies with relatively stable earnings, such as public utilities, can support higher debt to total assets ratios than can cyclical companies with widely fluctuating earnings, such as many high-tech companies. In later chapters you will learn additional ways to evaluate solvency.

Investor Insight

Debt financing differs greatly across industries and companies. Here are some debt to total assets ratios for selected companies:

	Debt to Total Assets Ratio
American Pharmaceutical Partners	19%
Callaway Golf Company	20%
Microsoft	21%
Sears Holdings Corporation	73%
Eastman Kodak Company	78%
General Motors Corporation	94%

? Discuss the difference in the debt to total assets ratio of Microsoft and General Motors.

DECISION TOOLKIT

DECISION CHECKPOINTS	INFO NEEDED FOR DECISION	TOOL TO USE FOR DECISION	HOW TO EVALUATE RESULTS
Can the company meet its near-term obligations?	Current assets and current liabilities	Current ratio = Current assets	Higher ratio suggests favorable liquidity.
Can the company meet its long-term obligations?	Total debt and total assets	Debt to total = Total liabilities	Lower value suggests favorable solvency.

USING THE STATEMENT OF CASH FLOWS

study objective 5

Use the statement of cash flows to evaluate solvency.

Investors, creditors, and others want to know what is happening to a company's most liquid resource—its cash. In fact, people often say that "cash is king" because if a company cannot generate cash, it will not survive. Neither the income statement nor the balance sheet is prepared using a "cash basis" of accounting. Consequently, they do not answer many important questions about a company's cash. Instead, the **statement of cash flows** provides financial information about the sources and uses of a company's cash.

To aid in the analysis of cash, the statement of cash flows reports the cash effects of (1) a company's **operating activities**, (2) its **investing activities**, and (3) its **financing activities**. Sources of cash matter. For example, you would feel much better about a company's health if you knew that most of its cash was generated by operating its business rather than by borrowing cash from lenders. Illustration 2-17 (page 62) shows a simplified statement of cash flows for Best Buy.

Illustration 2-17 Best Buy's statement of cash flows

BEST BUY CO., INC.
Statement of Cash Flows
(in millions)

	For fiscal year ending	
	March 3, 2007	**February 25, 2006**
Cash flows provided by operating activities		
Cash receipts from operating activities	$35,864	$30,805
Cash payments for operating activities	34,102	29,065
Net cash provided (used) by operations	1,762	1,740
Cash flows provided by investing activities		
(Increase) decrease in property and plant	(733)	(648)
Other cash inflow (outflow)	(59)	(79)
Net cash provided (used) by investing	(792)	(727)
Cash flows provided by financing activities		
Issue of equity securities	248	337
Increase (decrease) in borrowing	12	(33)
Dividends	(174)	(151)
Repurchase of common stock	(599)	(772)
Net cash provided (used) by financing	(513)	(619)
Net increase (decrease) in cash and equivalents	457	394
Cash and equivalents at start of year	748	354
Cash and equivalents at year-end	$ 1,205	$ 748

If you were a creditor of Best Buy, you would want to know where it would get cash to pay you. If you have a long-term interest in Best Buy as a stockholder, you would want information regarding the company's ability to generate cash over the long run to meet its cash needs for growth.

Companies generally get cash from two sources: operating activities and financing activities. In the early years of a company's life it typically does not generate enough cash from operating activities to meet its investing needs, so it issues stock or borrows money. Established companies, however, often meet most cash needs with cash from operations. Best Buy's cash provided by operating activities was sufficient to meet its needs for acquisitions of property, plant, and equipment. For example, in 2007 cash provided by operating activities was $1,762 million, whereas cash spent on property, plant, and equipment was $733 million.

KEEPING AN EYE ON CASH

In the statement of cash flows, cash provided by operating activities is intended to indicate the cash-generating capability of the company. Analysts have noted, however, that **cash provided by operating activities fails to take into account that a company must invest in new property, plant, and equipment** (capital expenditures) just to maintain its current level of operations. Companies also must at least **maintain dividends at current levels** to satisfy investors. A measurement to provide additional insight regarding a company's cash-generating ability is free cash flow. **Free cash flow** describes the cash remaining from operating activities after adjusting for capital expenditures and dividends paid.

Consider the following example: Suppose that MPC produced and sold 10,000 personal computers this year. It reported $100,000 cash provided by operating activities. In order to maintain production at 10,000 computers, MPC invested $15,000 in equipment. It chose to pay $5,000 in dividends. Its free cash flow was $80,000 ($100,000 − $15,000 − $5,000). The company could use this $80,000 to purchase new assets to expand the business, to pay off debts, or to increase its dividend distribution. In practice, analysts often calculate free cash flow with the formula shown below. (Alternative definitions also exist.)

Free Cash Flow = Cash Provided by Operations − Capital Expenditures − Cash Dividends

We can calculate Best Buy's free cash flow as follows (dollars in millions).

Cash provided by operating activities	$1,762
Less: Expenditures on property, plant, and equipment	733
Dividends paid	174
Free cash flow	$ 855

Best Buy generated free cash flow of $855 million which is available for the acquisition of new assets, the retirement of stock or debt, or the payment of additional dividends. Long-term creditors consider a high free cash flow amount an indication of solvency. Circuit City's free cash flow for 2007 is $10.5 million. This lack of free cash flow calls into question Circuit City's ability to repay its long-term obligations as they come due.

DECISION TOOLKIT

DECISION CHECKPOINTS	INFO NEEDED FOR DECISION	TOOL TO USE FOR DECISION	HOW TO EVALUATE RESULTS
How much cash did the company generate to expand operations, pay off debts, or distribute dividends?	Cash provided by operating activities, cash spent on fixed assets, and cash dividends	Free cash flow = Cash provided by operations − Capital expenditures − Cash dividends	Significant free cash flow indicates greater potential to finance new investment and pay additional dividends.

before you go on...

Do it! The following information is available for Ozone Inc.

RATIO ANALYSIS

	2010	2009
Current assets	$ 88,000	$ 60,800
Total assets	400,000	341,000
Current liabilities	40,000	38,000
Total liabilities	120,000	150,000
Net income	100,000	50,000
Cash provided by operating activities	110,000	70,000
Preferred stock dividends	10,000	10,000
Common stock dividends	5,000	2,500
Expenditures on property, plant, and equipment	45,000	20,000
Shares outstanding at beginning of year	60,000	40,000
Shares outstanding at end of year	120,000	60,000

(a) Compute earnings per share for 2010 and 2009 for Ozone, and comment on the change. Ozone's primary competitor, Frost Corporation, had earnings per share of $2 in 2010. Comment on the difference in the ratios of the two companies.

(b) Compute the current ratio and debt to total assets ratio for each year, and comment on the changes.

(c) Compute free cash flow for each year, and comment on the changes.

Action Plan

- Use the formula for earnings per share (EPS): (Net income − Preferred stock dividends) ÷ (Average common shares outstanding).
- Use the formula for the current ratio: Current assets ÷ Current liabilities.
- Use the formula for the debt to total assets ratio: Total liabilities ÷ Total assets.
- Use the formula for free cash flow: Cash provided by operating activities − Capital expenditures − Cash dividends.

Solution

(a) Earnings per share

2010	2009
$\frac{(\$100{,}000 - \$10{,}000)}{(120{,}000 + 60{,}000)/2} = \$1.00$	$\frac{(\$50{,}000 - \$10{,}000)}{(60{,}000 + 40{,}000)/2} = \$0.80$

Ozone's profitability, as measured by the amount of income available to each share of common stock, increased by 25% [($1.00 − $0.80) ÷ $0.80] during 2010. Earnings per share should not be compared across companies because the number of shares issued by companies varies widely. Thus, we cannot conclude that Frost Corporation is more profitable than Ozone based on its higher EPS.

(b)	2010	2009
Current ratio	$\frac{\$88{,}000}{\$40{,}000} = 2.20{:}1$	$\frac{\$60{,}800}{\$38{,}000} = 1.60{:}1$
Debt to total assets ratio	$\frac{\$120{,}000}{\$400{,}000} = 30\%$	$\frac{\$150{,}000}{\$341{,}000} = 44\%$

The company's liquidity, as measured by the current ratio, improved from 1:60:1 to 2.20:1. Its solvency also improved, as measured by the debt to total assets ratio, which declined from 44% to 30%.

(c) Free cash flow

2010: $110,000 − $45,000 − ($10,000 + $5,000) = $50,000
2009: $70,000 − $20,000 − ($10,000 + $2,500) = $37,500

The amount of cash generated by the company above its needs for dividends and capital expenditures increased from $37,500 to $50,000.

Financial Reporting Concepts

In Chapter 1 you learned about the four financial statements, and in this chapter we introduced you to some basic ways to interpret those statements. In this last section we will discuss concepts that underly these financial statements. It would be unwise to make business decisions based on financial statements without understanding the implications of these concepts.

THE STANDARD-SETTING ENVIRONMENT

study objective 

Explain the meaning of generally accepted accounting principles.

How does Best Buy decide on the type of financial information to disclose? What format should it use? How should it measure assets, liabilities, revenues, and expenses? The answers are found in a set of rules and practices having substantial authoritative support, referred to as **generally accepted accounting principles (GAAP)**. Various standard-setting bodies, in consultation with the accounting profession and the business community, determine these guidelines:

The **Securities and Exchange Commission (SEC)** is the agency of the U.S. government that oversees U.S. financial markets and accounting standard-setting bodies.

The Public Company Accounting Oversight Board (PCAOB) determines auditing standards and reviews auditing firms.

The Financial Accounting Standards Board (FASB) is the primary accounting standard-setting body in the United States.

The International Accounting Standards Board (IASB) issues standards (IFRS) that have been adopted by many countries outside of the United States.

The FASB and IASB have worked closely to try to minimize the differences in their standards. Recently the SEC announced that foreign companies that wish to have their shares traded on U.S. stock exchanges will no longer have to prepare reports that conform with U.S. accounting standards, as long as their reports conform with international accounting standards. Also, the SEC proposed that it will allow some U.S companies to adopt IFRS as early as 2009. The SEC also laid out a roadmap by which all U.S. companies will be required to switch to IFRS by 2016. The adoption of IFRS by U.S. companies would make it easier for investors to compare U.S. and foreign companies, as well as for U.S. companies to raise capital in international markets.

International Note Over 100 countries use international standards (called IFRS). For example, all companies in the European Union follow international standards. The differences between U.S. and international standards are not generally significant. In this book, we highlight any major differences using International Notes like this one.

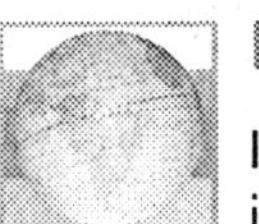

International Insight

If you think that accounting standards don't matter, consider recent events in South Korea. For many years, international investors complained that the financial reports of South Korean companies were inadequate and inaccurate. Accounting practices there often resulted in huge differences between stated revenues and actual revenues. Because investors did not have faith in the accuracy of the numbers, they were unwilling to pay as much for the shares of these companies relative to shares of comparable companies in different countries. This difference in share price was often referred to as the "Korean discount."

In response, Korean regulators decided that, beginning in 2011, companies will have to comply with international accounting standards. This change was motivated by a desire to "make the country's businesses more transparent" in order to build investor confidence and spur economic growth. Many other Asian countries, including China, India, Japan, and Hong Kong, have also decided either to adopt international standards or to create standards that are based on the international standards.

Source: Evan Ramstad, "End to 'Korea Discount'?" *Wall Street Journal*, March 16, 2007.

What is meant by the phrase "make the country's businesses more transparent"? Why would increasing transparency spur economic growth?

CHARACTERISTICS OF USEFUL INFORMATION

In establishing guidelines for reporting financial information, the FASB believes that the overriding consideration should be the generation of financial information **useful** for making business decisions. To be useful, information should possess these characteristics: relevance, reliability, comparability, and consistency.

Relevance

Accounting information is considered relevant if it would make a difference in a business decision. For example, the information in Best Buy's financial statements is considered relevant because it provides a basis for forecasting Best Buy's future earnings. Accounting information is also relevant to business decisions because it confirms or corrects prior expectations. Financial statements provide

study objective 

Discuss financial reporting concepts.

relevant information that helps **predict** future events and **provide feedback** about prior expectations for the financial health of the company.

For accounting information to be relevant it must be **timely**. That is, it must be available to decision makers before it loses its capacity to influence decisions. The SEC requires that public companies provide their annual reports to investors within 60 days of their year-end.

Reliability

Reliability of information means that the information can be depended on. To be reliable, accounting information must be **verifiable**—we must be able to prove that it is free of error. Also, the information must be a **faithful representation** of what it purports to be—it must be factual. If Best Buy's income statement reports sales of $20 billion when it actually had sales of $10 billion, then the statement is not a faithful representation of Best Buy's financial performance. Finally, accounting information must be **neutral**—it cannot be selected, prepared, or presented to favor one set of interested users over another. As noted in Chapter 1, to ensure reliability, certified public accountants audit financial statements.

Comparability

In accounting, comparability results when different companies use the same accounting principles. U.S. accounting standards are relatively comparable because they are based on certain basic principles and assumptions. However, these principles and assumptions allow for some variation in methods. For example, there are a variety of ways to report inventory. Often these different methods result in different amounts of net income. To make comparison across companies easier, each company **must disclose** the accounting methods used.

Accounting Across the Organization

Another issue related to comparability is the accounting time period. An accounting period that is one-year long is called a **fiscal year**. But a fiscal year need not match the calendar year. For example, a company could end its fiscal year on April 30, rather than December 31.

Why do companies choose the particular year-ends that they do? For example, why doesn't every company use December 31 as the accounting year-end? Many companies choose to end their accounting year when inventory or operations are at a low. This is advantageous because compiling accounting information requires much time and effort by managers, so they would rather do it when they aren't as busy operating the business. Also, inventory is easier and less costly to count when its volume is low.

Some companies whose year-ends differ from December 31 are Delta Air Lines, June 30; Walt Disney Productions, September 30; and Dunkin' Donuts, Inc., October 31. In the notes to its financial statements, Best Buy states that its accounting year-end is the Saturday nearest the end of February.

What problems might Best Buy's year-end create for analysts?

Consistency

To compare Best Buy's net income over several years, you would need to know that it used the same accounting principles from year to year. Consistency means that a company uses the same accounting principles and methods from year to year. Thus, if a company selects one inventory accounting method in the first year of operations, it is expected to continue to use that same method in succeeding years.

A company *may* change to a new method of accounting if management can justify that the new method produces more useful financial information. In the year in which the change occurs, the change must be disclosed in the notes to the financial statements so that users of the statements are aware of the lack of consistency.

Illustration 2-18 summarizes the characteristics that make accounting information useful.

Illustration 2-18
Characteristics of useful information

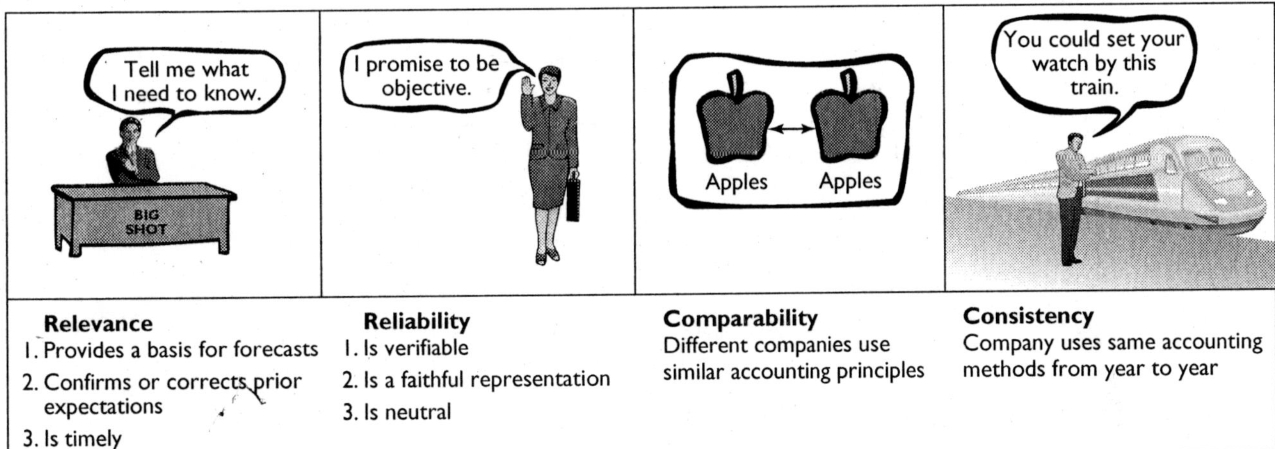

Tell me what I need to know.
BIG SHOT
I promise to be objective.
Apples
Apples
You could set your watch by this train.
Relevance
1. Provides a basis for forecasts
2. Confirms or corrects prior expectations
3. Is timely
Reliability
1. Is verifiable
2. Is a faithful representation
3. Is neutral
Comparability
Different companies use similar accounting principles
Consistency
Company uses same accounting methods from year to year

ASSUMPTIONS AND PRINCIPLES IN FINANCIAL REPORTING

To develop accounting standards, the FASB relies on some key assumptions and principles.

Monetary Unit Assumption

The **monetary unit assumption** requires that only those things that can be expressed in money are included in the accounting records. Because the exchange of money is fundamental to business transactions, it makes sense that we measure a business in terms of money.

However, the monetary unit assumption also means that certain important information needed by investors, creditors, and managers is not reported in the financial statements. For example, customer satisfaction is important to every business, but it is not easily quantified in dollar terms; thus it is not reported in the financial statements.

Economic Entity Assumption

The **economic entity assumption** states that every economic entity can be separately identified and accounted for. For example, suppose you are a stockholder of Best Buy. The amount of cash you have in your personal bank account and the balance owed on your personal car loan are not reported in Best Buy's balance sheet. In order to accurately assess Best Buy's performance and financial position, it is important that we not blur it with your personal transactions, or the transactions of any other person (especially its managers) or other company.

Ethics Note The importance of the economic entity assumption is illustrated by scandals involving Adelphia. In this case, senior company employees entered into transactions that blurred the line between the employees' financial interests and those of the company. For example, Adelphia guaranteed over $2 billion of loans to the founding family.

Time Period Assumption

Next, notice that the income statement, retained earnings statement, and statement of cash flows all cover periods of one year, and the balance sheet is prepared at the end of each year. The **time period assumption** states that the life of a business can be divided into artificial time periods and that useful reports covering those periods can be prepared for the business. All companies report financial results at least annually. Many also report every three months (quarterly) to stockholders, and many prepare monthly statements for internal purposes.

Going Concern Assumption

The **going concern assumption** states that the business will remain in operation for the foreseeable future. Of course many businesses do fail, but in general, it is reasonable to assume that the business will continue operating. If going concern is not assumed, then the company should state property and equipment at their liquidation value (selling price less cost of disposal), rather than at their cost. Only when liquidation of the business appears likely is the going concern assumption inappropriate.

Illustration 2-19 shows these four accounting assumptions graphically.

Illustration 2-19
Accounting assumptions

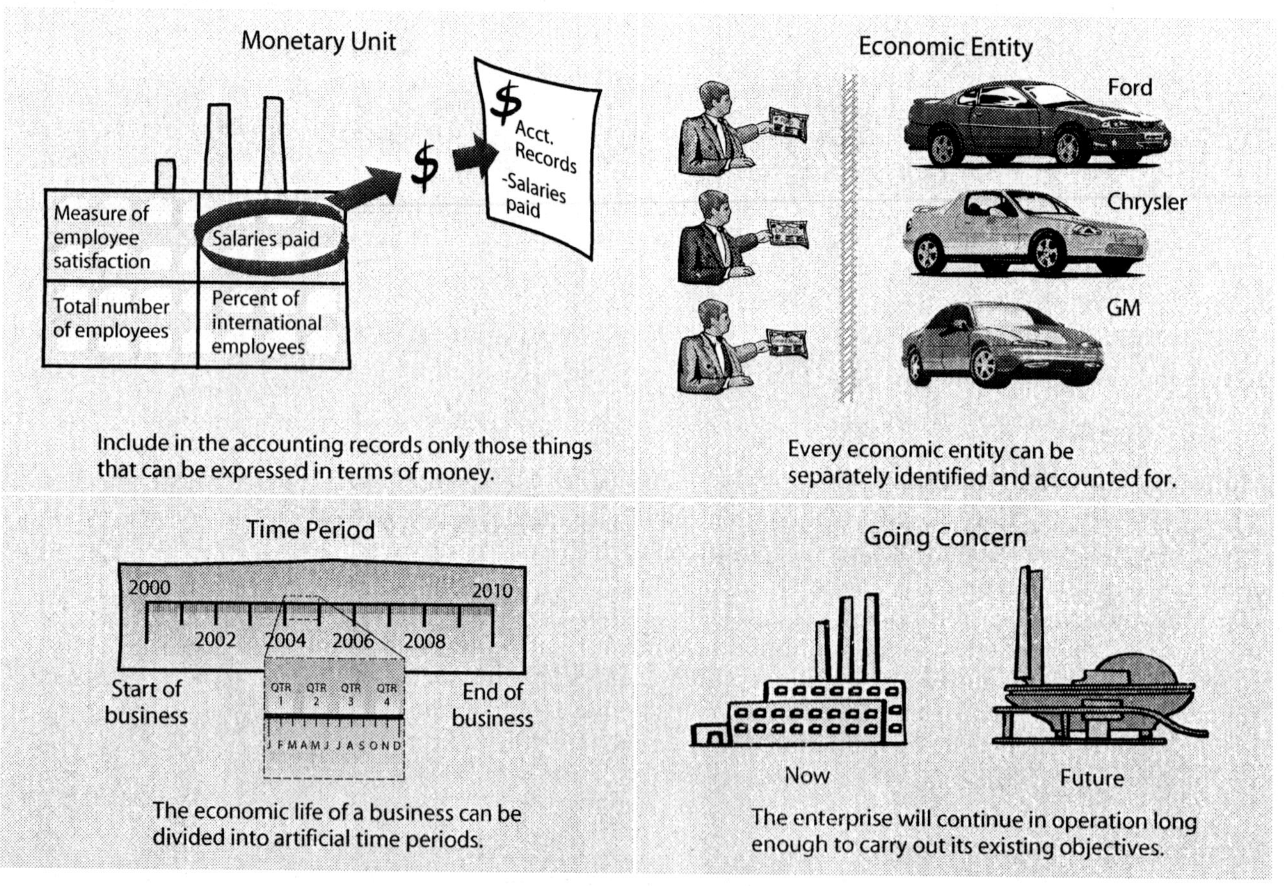

Cost Principle

The **cost principle** dictates that assets be recorded at their cost. This is true not only at the time the asset is purchased, but also over the time the asset is held. For example, if Best Buy were to purchase some land for $30,000, the company would initially report it on the balance sheet at $30,000. But what would Best Buy do if, by the end of the next year, the land had increased in value to $40,000? Under the cost principle the company would continue to report the land at $30,000.

Proponents of the cost principle state that cost is the best measure because it can be easily verified from transactions between two parties, whereas market value is often subjective. However, the cost principle is often criticized as being irrelevant. Critics contend that market value would be more useful to financial decision makers. The FASB now requires that certain investment securities be recorded at their market value. In choosing between cost and market value, the FASB weighed the reliability of cost figures against the relevance of market value.

In addition, to encourage broader use of market values in the financial statements, a new accounting standard gives companies the option to use market value to account for a wide range of items. This change makes U.S. standards more similar to international standards, which already gave foreign companies this option.

International Note The results of a recent survey by Deloitte & Touche LLP (USA) show that approximately 20% of CFOs and senior finance professionals (representing about 300 U.S. companies) would consider adopting International Financial Reporting Standards, if given a choice by the U.S. Securities and Exchange Commission.

Full Disclosure Principle

The **full disclosure principle** requires that companies disclose all circumstances and events that would make a difference to financial statement users. Some important financial information is not easily reported on the face of the statements. For example, Best Buy has debt outstanding. Investors and creditors would like to know the terms of the debt; that is, when does it mature, what is its interest rate, and is it renewable? Also, Best Buy might be sued by one of its customers. Investors and creditors might not know about this lawsuit. If an important item cannot reasonably be reported directly in one of the four types of financial statements, then it should be discussed in notes that accompany the statements. Some investors who lost money in Enron, WorldCom, and Global Crossing complained that the lack of full disclosure regarding some of the companies' transactions caused the financial statements to be misleading.

Illustration 2-20 depicts these two accounting principles.

Illustration 2-20
Accounting principles

Cost

Record assets at cost.

Full Disclosure

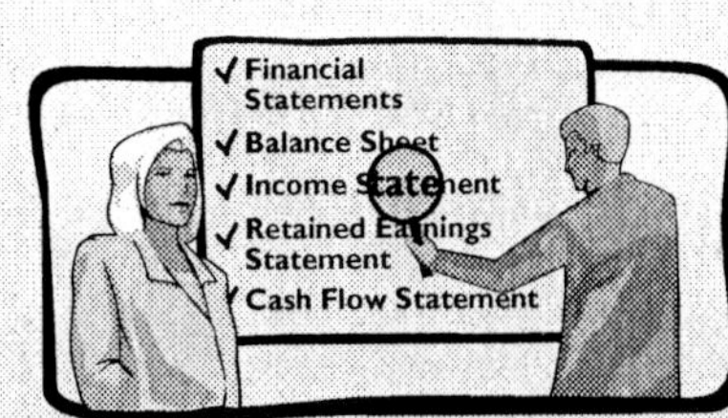

√ Financial Statements
√ Balance Sheet
√ Income Statement
√ Retained Earnings Statement
√ Cash Flow Statement

Disclose circumstances and events that make a difference to financial statement users.

CONSTRAINTS IN ACCOUNTING

Efforts to provide useful financial information can be costly to a company. Therefore, the profession has agreed upon **constraints** to ensure that companies apply accounting rules in a reasonable fashion, from the perspectives of both the company and the user. The constraints are materiality and conservatism.

Materiality

Materiality relates to a financial statement item's impact on a company's overall financial condition and operations. An item is **material** when its **size** makes it likely to influence the decision of an investor or creditor. It is **immaterial** if it is too small to impact a decision maker. In short, if the item does not make a difference, the company does not have to follow GAAP in reporting it. To determine the materiality of an amount—that is, to determine its financial significance—the company compares the item with such items as total assets, sales revenue, and net income.

To illustrate, assume that Best Buy made a $100 error in recording revenue. Best Buy's total revenue is almost $36 billion; thus a $100 error is not material.

Conservatism

Conservatism in accounting means that when preparing financial statements, a company should choose the accounting method that will be least likely to overstate assets or income. It does not mean, however, that a company should intentionally understate assets or income.

A common application of the conservatism constraint is in valuing inventories. Companies normally record inventories at their cost. Conservatism, however, requires that companies write down inventories to market value if market value is below cost. Conservatism also requires that when the market value of inventory exceeds cost, the company should not increase the value of the inventory on the books, but instead keep it at cost. This practice results in lower net income on the income statement and a lower amount reported for inventory on the balance sheet.

Illustration 2-21 graphically depicts the two constraints.

Illustration 2-21
Accounting constraints

Materiality

Companies do not have to follow GAAP for small amounts.

Conservatism

When in doubt, choose the solution that will be least likely to overstate assets and income.

before you go on...

FINANCIAL ACCOUNTING CONCEPTS AND PRINCIPLES

Do it! The following are characteristics, assumptions, principles, or constraints that guide the FASB when it creates accounting standards.

Relevance	Time period assumption
Reliability	Going concern assumption
Comparability	Cost principle
Consistency	Full disclosure principle
Monetary unit assumption	Materiality
Economic entity assumption	Conservatism

Match each item above with a description below.

1. ________ Ability to easily evaluate one company's results relative to another's.
2. ________ Belief that a company will continue to operate for the foreseeable future.
3. ________ The judgment concerning whether an item is large enough to matter to decision makers.
4. ________ The reporting of all information that would make a difference to financial statement users.

5. _______ The practice of preparing financial statements at regular intervals.
6. _______ The quality of information that indicates the information makes a difference in a decision.
7. _______ A belief that items should be reported on the balance sheet at the price that was paid to acquire the item.
8. _______ A company's use of the same accounting principles and methods from year to year.
9. _______ The use of accounting methods that do not overstate assets or income.
10. _______ Tracing accounting events to particular companies.
11. _______ The desire to minimize errors and bias in financial statements.
12. _______ Reporting only those things that can be measured in dollars.

Action Plan

- Understand the need for conceptual guidelines in accounting.
- List the characteristics of useful financial information.
- Review the assumptions, principles, and constraints that comprise the guidelines in accounting.

Solution

1. Comparability
2. Going concern assumption
3. Materiality
4. Full disclosure principle
5. Time period assumption
6. Relevance
7. Cost principle
8. Consistency
9. Conservatism
10. Economic entity assumption
11. Reliability
12. Monetary unit assumption

USING THE DECISION TOOLKIT

In this chapter we evaluated a home electronics giant, Best Buy. Tweeter Home Entertainment sold consumer electronics products from 154 stores on the East Coast under various names. It specialized in products with high-end features. Tweeter filed for bankruptcy in June 2007 and was acquired by another company in July 2007. Financial data for Tweeter, prior to its bankruptcy, are provided below.

	September 30	
(amounts in millions)	**2006**	**2005**
Current assets	$146.4	$158.2
Total assets	258.6	284.0
Current liabilities	107.1	119.0
Total liabilities	190.4	201.1
Total common stockholders' equity	68.2	82.9
Net income (loss)	(16.5)	(74.4)
Cash provided (used) by operating activities	15.6	(26.7)
Capital expenditures (net)	17.4	22.2
Dividends paid	0	0
Average shares of common stock (millions)	25.2	24.6

Instructions

Using the data provided, answer the following questions and discuss how these results might have provided an indication of Tweeter's financial troubles.

1. Calculate the current ratio for Tweeter for 2006 and 2005 and discuss its liquidity position.
2. Calculate the debt to total assets ratio and free cash flow for Tweeter for 2006 and 2005 and discuss its solvency.

3. Calculate the earnings per share for Tweeter for 2006 and 2005, and discuss its change in profitability.
4. Best Buy's accounting year-end was February 28, 2007; Tweeter's was September 30, 2006. How does this difference affect your ability to compare their profitability?

Solution

1. Current ratio:

   2006: $146.4 ÷ $107.1 = 1.37:1 *2005:* $158.2 ÷ $119.0 = 1.33:1

   Tweeter's liquidity improved slightly from 2005 to 2006, but in both years it would most likely have been considered inadequate. In 2006 Tweeter had only $1.37 in current assets for every dollar of current liabilities. Sometimes larger companies, such as Best Buy and Circuit City, can function with lower current ratios because they have alternative sources of working capital. But a company of Tweeter's size would normally want a higher ratio.

2. Debt to total assets:

   2006: $190.4 ÷ $258.6 = 73.6% *2005:* $201.1 ÷ $284.0 = 70.8%

   Tweeter's solvency, as measured by its debt to total assets ratio, declined from 2005 to 2006. Its ratio of 73.6% meant that every dollar of assets was financed by 73.6 cents of debt. For a retailer, this is extremely high reliance on debt. This low solvency suggests Tweeter's ability to meet its debt payments was questionable.

   Free cash flow:

   2006: $15.6 − $17.4 − $0 = −$1.8 million
   2005: −$26.7 − $22.2 − $0 = −$48.9 million

   Tweeter's free cash flow was negative in both years. The company did not generate enough cash from operations even to cover its capital expenditures, and it was not paying a dividend. While this is not unusual for new companies in their early years, it is also not sustainable for very long. Part of the reason that its debt to assets ratio, discussed above, was so high was that it had to borrow money to make up for its deficient free cash flow.

3. Loss per share:

   2006: −$16.5 ÷ 25.2 = −$0.65 per share
   2005: −$74.4 ÷ 24.6 = −$3.02 per share

   Tweeter's loss per share declined substantially. However, this was little consolation for its shareholders, who experienced losses in previous years as well. The company's lack of profitability, combined with its poor liquidity and solvency, increased the likelihood that it would eventually file for bankruptcy.

4. Tweeter's income statement covers 7 months not covered by Best Buy's. Suppose that the economy changed dramatically during this 7-month period, either improving or declining. This change in the economy would be reflected in Tweeter's income statement but would not be reflected in Best Buy's income statement until the following March, thus reducing the usefulness of a comparison of the income statements of the two companies.

Summary of Study Objectives

1 Identify the sections of a classified balance sheet. In a classified balance sheet, companies classify assets as current assets; long-term investments; property, plant, and equipment; and intangibles. They classify liabilities as either current or long-term. A stockholders' equity section shows common stock and retained earnings.

2 Identify and compute ratios for analyzing a company's profitability. Profitability ratios, such as earnings per share (EPS), measure aspects of the operating success of a company for a given period of time.

3 Explain the relationship between a retained earnings statement and a statement of stockholders' equity. The retained earnings statement presents the factors that changed the retained earnings balance during the period. A statement of stockholders' equity presents the factors that changed stockholders' equity during the period, including those that changed retained earnings. Thus, a statement of stockholders' equity is more inclusive.

4 Identify and compute ratios for analyzing a company's liquidity and solvency using a balance sheet. Liquidity ratios, such as the current ratio, measure the short-term ability of a company to pay its maturing obligations and to meet unexpected needs for cash. Solvency ratios, such as the debt to total assets ratio, measure the ability of an enterprise to survive over a long period.

5 Use the statement of cash flows to evaluate solvency. Free cash flow indicates a company's ability to generate cash from operations that is sufficient to pay debts, acquire assets, and distribute dividends.

6 Explain the meaning of generally accepted accounting principles. Generally accepted accounting principles are a set of rules and practices recognized as a general guide for financial reporting purposes. The basic objective of financial reporting is to provide information that is useful for decision making.

7 Discuss financial reporting concepts. To be judged useful, information should have relevance, reliability, comparability, and consistency.

The *monetary unit assumption* requires that companies include in the accounting records only transaction data that can be expressed in terms of money. The *economic entity assumption* states that economic events can be identified with a particular unit of accountability. The *time period assumption* states that the economic life of a business can be divided into artificial time periods and that meaningful accounting reports can be prepared for each period. The *going concern assumption* states that the enterprise will continue in operation long enough to carry out its existing objectives and commitments.

The *cost principle* states that companies should record assets at their cost. The *full disclosure principle* dictates that companies disclose circumstances and events that matter to financial statement users.

The major constraints are materiality and conservatism.

DECISION TOOLKIT A SUMMARY

DECISION CHECKPOINTS	INFO NEEDED FOR DECISION	TOOL TO USE FOR DECISION	HOW TO EVALUATE RESULTS
How does the company's earnings performance compare with that of previous years?	Net income available to common stockholders and average common shares outstanding	Earnings per share = $\frac{\text{Net income} - \text{Preferred stock dividends}}{\text{Average common shares outstanding}}$	A higher measure suggests improved performance, although the number is subject to manipulation. Values should not be compared across companies.
Can the company meet its near-term obligations?	Current assets and current liabilities	Current ratio = $\frac{\text{Current assets}}{\text{Current liabilities}}$	Higher ratio suggests favorable liquidity.
Can the company meet its long-term obligations?	Total debt and total assets	Debt to total assets ratio = $\frac{\text{Total liabilities}}{\text{Total assets}}$	Lower value suggests favorable solvency.
How much cash did the company generate to expand operations, pay off debts, or distribute dividends?	Cash provided by operating activities, cash spent on fixed assets, and cash dividends	Free cash flow = Cash provided by operations − Capital expenditures − Cash dividends	Significant free cash flow indicates greater potential to finance new investment and pay additional dividends.

Glossary

Classified balance sheet *(p. 48)* A balance sheet that contains a number of standard classifications and sections.

Comparability *(p. 66)* Ability to compare the accounting information of different companies because they use the same accounting principles.

Conservatism *(p. 70)* The approach of choosing an accounting method, when alternatives exist, that will least likely overstate assets and net income.

Consistency *(p. 66)* Use of the same accounting principles and methods from year to year within a company.

Cost principle *(p. 68)* An accounting principle that states that companies should record assets at their cost.

Current assets *(p. 49)* Cash and other resources that companies reasonably expect to convert to cash or use up within one year or the operating cycle, whichever is longer.

Current liabilities *(p. 52)* Obligations that a company reasonably expects to pay within the next year or operating cycle, whichever is longer.

Current ratio *(p. 59)* A measure used to evaluate a company's liquidity and short-term debt-paying ability; computed as current assets divided by current liabilities.

Debt to total assets ratio *(p. 60)* Measures the percentage of total financing provided by creditors; computed as total debt divided by total assets.

Earnings per share (EPS) *(p. 55)* A measure of the net income earned on each share of common stock; computed as net income minus preferred stock dividends divided by the average number of common shares outstanding during the year.

Economic entity assumption *(p. 67)* An assumption that every economic entity can be separately identified and accounted for.

Financial Accounting Standards Board (FASB) *(p. 65)* The primary accounting standard-setting body in the United States.

Free cash flow *(p. 62)* Cash remaining from operating activities after adjusting for capital expenditures and dividends paid.

Full disclosure principle *(p. 69)* Accounting principle that dictates that companies disclose circumstances and events that make a difference to financial statement users.

Generally accepted accounting principles (GAAP) *(p. 64)* A set of rules and practices, having substantial authoritative support, that the accounting profession recognizes as a general guide for financial reporting purposes.

Going concern assumption *(p. 68)* The assumption that the company will continue in operation for the foreseeable future.

Intangible assets *(p. 51)* Assets that do not have physical substance.

International Accounting Standards Board (IASB) *(p. 65)* An accounting standard-setting body that issues standards adopted by many countries outside of the United States.

Liquidity *(p. 58)* The ability of a company to pay obligations that are expected to become due within the next year or operating cycle.

Liquidity ratios *(p. 59)* Measures of the short-term ability of the company to pay its maturing obligations and to meet unexpected needs for cash.

Long-term investments *(p. 50)* Generally, (1) investments in stocks and bonds of other corporations that companies hold for more than one year, and (2) long-term assets, such as land and buildings, not currently being used in the company's operations.

Long-term liabilities (Long-term debt) *(p. 53)* Obligations that a company expects to pay after one year.

Materiality *(p. 69)* The constraint of determining whether an item is large enough to likely influence the decision of an investor or creditor.

Monetary unit assumption *(p. 67)* An assumption that requires that only those things that can be expressed in money are included in the accounting records.

Operating cycle *(p. 50)* The average time required to go from cash to cash in producing revenues.

Profitability ratios *(p. 55)* Measures of the operating success of a company for a given period of time.

Property, plant, and equipment *(p. 51)* Assets with relatively long useful lives that companies use in operating the business and are not intended for resale.

Public Company Accounting Oversight Board (PCAOB) *(p. 65)* The group charged with determining auditing standards and reviewing the performance of auditing firms.

Ratio *(p. 54)* An expression of the mathematical relationship between one quantity and another; may be expressed as a percentage, a rate, or a proportion.

Ratio analysis *(p. 54)* A technique for evaluating financial statements that expresses the relationship among selected items of financial statement data.

Relevance *(p. 65)* The quality of information that indicates the information makes a difference in a decision.

Reliability *(p. 66)* The quality of information that gives assurance that it is free of error, is factual, and is neutral.

Securities and Exchange Commission (SEC) *(p. 64)* The agency of the U.S. government that oversees U.S. financial markets and accounting standard-setting bodies.

Solvency *(p. 60)* The ability of a company to pay interest as it comes due and to repay the balance of debt at its maturity.

Solvency ratios *(p. 60)* Measures of the ability of the company to survive over a long period of time.

Statement of stockholders' equity *(p. 56)* A financial statement that presents the factors that caused stockholders' equity to change during the period, including those that caused retained earnings to change.

Time period assumption *(p. 68)* An assumption that the life of a business can be divided into artificial time periods and that useful reports covering those periods can be prepared for the business.

Working capital *(p. 59)* The difference between the amounts of current assets and current liabilities.

Comprehensive Do it!

Listed here are items taken from the income statement and balance sheet of Circuit City Stores, Inc. for the year ended February 28, 2007. Certain items have been combined for simplification. Amounts are given in millions.

Long-term debt, excluding current installments	$ 50.5
Cash and cash equivalents	141.1
Selling, general, and administrative expenses	2,933.6
Common stock	454.9
Accounts payable	922.2
Prepaid expenses and other current assets	723.3
Property and equipment, net	921.0
Cost of goods sold	9,501.4
Current portion of long-term debt	7.2
Interest expense	1.5
Other long-term liabilities	451.5
Retained earnings	1,336.3
Merchandise inventory	1,636.5
Net sales and operating revenues	12,456.9
Accounts receivable, net	382.6
Income tax expense	30.5
Other assets	202.7
Accrued expenses and other current liabilities	784.6

Instructions

Prepare an income statement and a classified balance sheet using the items listed. Do not use any item more than once.

Action Plan

- In preparing the income statement, list revenues, then expenses.
- In preparing a classified balance sheet, list current assets in order of liquidity.

Solution to Comprehensive Do it!

CIRCUIT CITY STORES, INC.
Income Statement
For the Year Ended February 28, 2007
(in millions)

Net sales and operating revenues		$12,456.9
Cost of goods sold	$9,501.4	
Selling, general, and administrative expenses	2,933.6	
Interest expense	1.5	
Income tax expense	30.5	
Total expenses		12,467.0
Net loss		$ (10.1)

CIRCUIT CITY STORES, INC.
Balance Sheet
February 28, 2007
(in millions)

Assets		
Current assets		
Cash and cash equivalents	$ 141.1	
Accounts receivable, net	382.6	
Merchandise inventory	1,636.5	
Prepaid expenses and other current assets	723.3	
Total current assets		$2,883.5
Property and equipment, net		921.0
Other assets		202.7
Total assets		$4,007.2
Liabilities and Stockholders' Equity		
Current liabilities		
Accounts payable	$ 922.2	
Accrued expenses and other current liabilities	784.6	
Current portion of long-term debt	7.2	
Total current liabilities		$1,714.0
Long-term liabilities		
Other long-term liabilities	451.5	
Long-term debt, excluding current installments	50.5	502.0
Total liabilities		2,216.0
Stockholders' equity		
Common stock	454.9	
Retained earnings	1,336.3	
Total stockholders' equity		1,791.2
Total liabilities and stockholders' equity		$4,007.2

Self-Study Questions

Answers are at the end of the chapter.

(SO 1) 1. In a classified balance sheet, assets are usually classified as:
(a) current assets; long-term assets; property, plant, and equipment; and intangible assets.
(b) current assets; long-term investments; property, plant, and equipment; and common stock.
(c) current assets; long-term investments; tangible assets; and intangible assets.
(d) current assets; long-term investments; property, plant, and equipment; and intangible assets.

2. Current assets are listed: (SO 1)
(a) by order of expected conversion to cash.
(b) by importance.
(c) by longevity.
(d) alphabetically.

3. The correct order of presentation in a classified balance sheet for the following current assets is: (SO 1)
(a) accounts receivable, cash, prepaid insurance, inventories.
(b) cash, inventories, accounts receivable, prepaid insurance.

(c) cash, accounts receivable, inventories, prepaid insurance.
(d) inventories, cash, accounts receivable, prepaid insurance.

(SO 1) 4. A company has purchased a tract of land. It expects to build a production plant on the land in approximately 5 years. During the 5 years before construction, the land will be idle. The land should be reported as:
(a) property, plant, and equipment.
(b) land expense.
(c) a long-term investment.
(d) an intangible asset.

(SO 2) 5. Which is an indicator of profitability?
(a) Current ratio.
(b) Earnings per share.
(c) Debt to total assets ratio.
(d) Free cash flow.

(SO 2) 6. For 2010 Stoneland Corporation reported net income $26,000; net sales $400,000; and average shares outstanding 6,000. There were preferred stock dividends of $2,000. What was the 2010 earnings per share?
(a) $4.00
(b) $0.06
(c) $16.67
(d) $66.67

(SO 3) 7. The balance in retained earnings is *not* affected by:
(a) net income.
(b) net loss.
(c) issuance of common stock.
(d) dividends.

(SO 4) 8. Which of these measures is an evaluation of a company's ability to pay current liabilities?
(a) Earnings per share.
(b) Current ratio.
(c) Both (a) and (b).
(d) None of the above.

(SO 2, 4) 9. The following ratios are available for Leer Inc. and Stable Inc.

	Current Ratio	Debt to Assets Ratio	Earnings per Share
Leer Inc.	2:1	75%	$3.50
Stable Inc.	1.5:1	40%	$2.75

Compared to Stable Inc., Leer Inc. has:
(a) higher liquidity, higher solvency, and higher profitability.
(b) lower liquidity, higher solvency, and higher profitability.
(c) higher liquidity, lower solvency, and higher profitability.
(d) higher liquidity and lower solvency, but profitability cannot be compared based on information provided.

10. Companies can use free cash flow to: (SO 5)
(a) pay additional dividends.
(b) acquire property, plant, and equipment.
(c) pay off debts.
(d) All of the above.

11. Generally accepted accounting principles are: (SO 6)
(a) a set of standards and rules that are recognized as a general guide for financial reporting.
(b) usually established by the Internal Revenue Service.
(c) the guidelines used to resolve ethical dilemmas.
(d) fundamental truths that can be derived from the laws of nature.

12. What organization issues U.S. accounting standards? (SO 6)
(a) Financial Accounting Standards Board.
(b) International Accounting Standards Committee.
(c) International Auditing Standards Committee.
(d) None of the above.

13. What is the primary criterion by which accounting information can be judged? (SO 7)
(a) Consistency.
(b) Predictive value.
(c) Usefulness for decision making.
(d) Comparability.

14. Verifiability is an ingredient of: (SO 7)

	Reliability	Relevance
(a)	Yes	Yes
(b)	No	No
(c)	Yes	No
(d)	No	Yes

15. What accounting constraint refers to the tendency of accountants to resolve uncertainty in a way least likely to overstate assets and net income? (SO 7)
(a) Comparability.
(b) Materiality.
(c) Conservatism.
(d) Consistency.

Go to the book's companion website, **www.wiley.com/college/kimmel**, to access additional Self-Study Questions.

Questions

1. What is meant by the term *operating cycle?*
2. Define current assets. What basis is used for ordering individual items within the current assets section?
3. Distinguish between long-term investments and property, plant, and equipment.
4. How do current liabilities differ from long-term liabilities?

5. Identify the two parts of stockholders' equity in a corporation and indicate the purpose of each.

6. (a) Glenda Rosen believes that the analysis of financial statements is directed at two characteristics of a company: liquidity and profitability. Is Glenda correct? Explain.
   (b) Are short-term creditors, long-term creditors, and stockholders primarily interested in the same characteristics of a company? Explain.

7. Name ratios useful in assessing (a) liquidity, (b) solvency, and (c) profitability.

8. Jack Pine, the founder of Waterboots Inc., needs to raise $500,000 to expand his company's operations. He has been told that raising the money through debt will increase the riskiness of his company much more than issuing stock. He doesn't understand why this is true. Explain it to him.

9. What do these classes of ratios measure?
   (a) Liquidity ratios.
   (b) Profitability ratios.
   (c) Solvency ratios.

10. Holding all other factors constant, indicate whether each of the following signals generally good or bad news about a company.
   (a) Increase in earnings per share.
   (b) Increase in the current ratio.
   (c) Increase in the debt to total assets ratio.
   (d) Decrease in free cash flow.

11. Which ratio or ratios from this chapter do you think should be of greatest interest to:
   (a) a pension fund considering investing in a corporation's 20-year bonds?
   (b) a bank contemplating a short-term loan?
   (c) an investor in common stock?

12. (a) What are generally accepted accounting principles (GAAP)?
   (b) What body provides authoritative support for GAAP?

13. (a) What is the basic objective of financial reporting?
   (b) Identify the characteristics of useful accounting information.

14. Jan Leonard, the president of King Company, is pleased. King substantially increased its net income in 2010 while keeping its unit inventory relatively the same. Joe Morton, chief accountant, cautions Jan, however. Morton says that since King changed its method of inventory valuation, there is a consistency problem and it is difficult to determine whether King is better off. Is Morton correct? Why or why not?

15. What is the distinction between comparability and consistency?

16. Describe the two constraints inherent in the presentation of accounting information.

17. Your roommate believes that international accounting standards are uniform throughout the world. Is your roommate correct? Explain.

18. What purpose does the going concern assumption serve?

19. Laurie Belk is president of Better Books. She has no accounting background. Belk cannot understand why market value is not used as the basis for accounting measurement and reporting. Explain what basis is used and why.

20. What is the economic entity assumption? Give an example of its violation.

21. What was Tootsie Roll's largest current asset, largest current liability, and largest item under "Other assets" at December 31, 2007?

Brief Exercises

Classify accounts on balance sheet. (SO 1)

BE2-1 The following are the major balance sheet classifications:

Current assets (CA)	Current liabilities (CL)
Long-term investments (LTI)	Long-term liabilities (LTL)
Property, plant, and equipment (PPE)	Common stock (CS)
Intangible assets (IA)	Retained earnings (RE)

Match each of the following accounts to its proper balance sheet classification.

CL Accounts payable	CL Income tax payable
CA Accounts receivable	LTI Investment in long-term bonds
PPE Accumulated depreciation	PPE Land
PPE Building	CA Merchandise inventory
CA Cash	IA Patent
IA Goodwill	CA Supplies

Prepare the current assets section of a balance sheet. (SO 1)

BE2-2 A list of financial statement items for Rondelli Company includes the following: accounts receivable $14,000; prepaid insurance $3,300; cash $10,400; supplies $3,800, and short-term investments $8,200. Prepare the current assets section of the balance sheet listing the items in the proper sequence.

BE2-3 The following information (in millions of dollars) is available for Limited Brands for 2007: Sales revenue \$10,671; net income \$676; preferred stock dividend \$0; average shares outstanding 402 million. Compute the earnings per share for Limited Brands for 2007.

Compute earnings per share. (SO 2)

BE2-4 For each of the following events affecting the stockholders' equity of Haulmarke, indicate whether the event would: increase retained earnings (IRE), decrease retained earnings (DRE), increase common stock (ICS), or decrease common stock (DCS).

Identify items affecting stockholders' equity. (SO 3)

_____ (a) Issued new shares of common stock.
_____ (b) Paid a cash dividend.
_____ (c) Reported net income of \$75,000.
_____ (d) Reported a net loss of \$20,000.

BE2-5 These selected condensed data are taken from a recent balance sheet of Bob Evans Farms (in millions of dollars).

Calculate liquidity ratios. (SO 4)

Cash	\$ 29.3
Accounts receivable	20.5
Inventories	28.7
Other current assets	24.0
Total current assets	\$ 102.5
Total current liabilities	\$ 201.2

Compute working capital and the current ratio.

BE2-6 Danny's Books & Music Inc. reported the following selected information at March 31.

Calculate liquidity and solvency ratios. (SO 4, 5)

	2010
Total current assets	\$262,787
Total assets	439,832
Total current liabilities	293,625
Total liabilities	376,002
Cash provided by operating activities	55,472

Calculate (a) the current ratio, (b) the debt to total assets ratio, and (c) free cash flow for March 31, 2010. The company paid dividends of \$15,000 and spent \$24,787 on capital expenditures.

BE2-7 Indicate whether each statement is *true* or *false*.

Recognize generally accepted accounting principles. (SO 6)

(a) GAAP is a set of rules and practices established by accounting standard-setting bodies to serve as a general guide for financial reporting purposes.
(b) Substantial authoritative support for GAAP usually comes from two standards-setting bodies: the FASB and the IRS.

BE2-8 The accompanying chart shows the qualitative characteristics of accounting information. Fill in the blanks.

Identify characteristics of useful information. (SO 7)

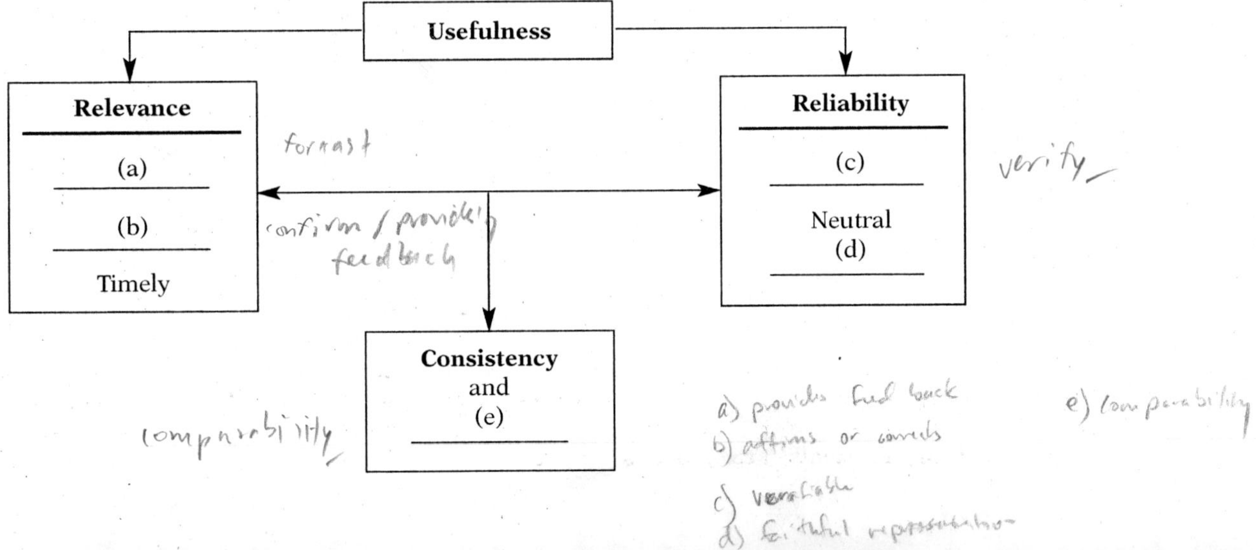

Identify characteristics of useful information. (SO 7)

BE2-9 Given the *characteristics* of useful accounting information, complete each of the following statements.

(a) For information to be ____, it should have predictive or feedback value, and it must be presented on a timely basis.

(b) ____ is the quality of information that gives assurance that it is free of error and bias; it can be depended on.

(c) ____ means using the same accounting principles and methods from year to year within a company.

Identify characteristics of useful information. (SO 7)

BE2-10 Here are some qualitative characteristics of accounting information:

1. Predictive value
2. Neutral
3. Verifiable
4. Timely

Match each qualitative characteristic to one of the following statements.

____ (a) Accounting information should help users make predictions about the outcome of past, present, and future events.

____ (b) Accounting information cannot be selected, prepared, or presented to favor one set of interested users over another.

____ (c) Accounting information must be proved to be free of error.

____ (d) Accounting information must be available to decision makers before it loses its capacity to influence their decisions.

Define full disclosure principle (SO 7)

BE2-11 The full disclosure principle dictates that:

(a) financial statements should disclose all assets at their cost.

(b) financial statements should disclose only those events that can be measured in dollars.

(c) financial statements should disclose all events and circumstances that would matter to users of financial statements.

(d) financial statements should not be relied on unless an auditor has expressed an unqualified opinion on them.

Identify constraints that have been violated. (SO 7)

BE2-12 Gantner Company uses these accounting practices:

(a) Inventory is reported at cost when market value is lower.

(b) Small tools are recorded as plant assets and depreciated.

(c) The income statement shows paper clips expense of $10.

Indicate the accounting constraint, if any, that each practice has violated.

Do it! Review

WILEY PLUS

Prepare assets section of balance sheet. (SO 1)

Do it! 2-1 Theremin Corporation has collected the following information related to its December 31, 2010, balance sheet.

Accounts receivable	$22,000	Equipment	$180,000
Accumulated depreciation	45,000	Inventory	58,000
Cash	13,000	Supplies	9,000

Prepare the assets section of Theremin Corporation's balance sheet.

Classify financial statement items by balance sheet classification. (SO 1)

Do it! 2-2 The following financial statement items were taken from the financial statements of de Vries Corp.

____ Trademarks	____ Inventories
____ Current maturities of long-term debt	____ Accumulated depreciation
____ Interest revenue	____ Land improvements
____ Taxes payable	____ Common stock
____ Long-term marketable debt securities	____ Advertising expense
____ Unearned consulting fees	____ Mortgage note payable due in 3 years

Match each of the financial statement items to its proper balance sheet classification. (See E2-1, on page 81, for a list of the balance sheet classifications.) If the item would not appear on a balance sheet, use "NA."

Compute ratios and analyze.
(SO 4, 5)

Do it! 2-3 The following information is available for Allotrope Corporation.

	2010	2009
Current assets	$ 54,000	$ 36,000
Total assets	240,000	205,000
Current liabilities	24,000	33,000
Total liabilities	72,000	100,000
Net income	80,000	40,000
Cash provided by operating activities	90,000	56,000
Preferred stock dividends	6,000	6,000
Common stock dividends	3,000	1,500
Expenditures on property, plant, and equipment	27,000	12,000
Shares outstanding at beginning of year	40,000	30,000
Shares outstanding at end of year	75,000	40,000

(a) Compute earnings per share for 2010 and 2009 for Allotrope, and comment on the change. Allotrope's primary competitor, Triatomic Corporation, had earnings per share of $1 per share in 2010. Comment on the difference in the ratios of the two companies.
(b) Compute the current ratio and debt to total assets ratio for each year, and comment on the changes.
(c) Compute free cash flow for each year, and comment on the changes.

Identify financial accounting concepts and principles.
(SO 7)

Do it! 2-4 The following are characteristics, assumptions, principles, or constraints that guide the FASB when it creates accounting standards.

Relevance	Time period assumption
Reliability	Going concern assumption
Comparability	Cost principle
Consistency	Full disclosure principle
Monetary unit assumption	Materiality
Economic entity assumption	Conservatism

Match each item above with a description below.

1. __________ Items not easily quantified in dollar terms are not reported in the financial statements.
2. __________ Accounting information must be verifiable, neutral, and a faithful representation of what it purports to measure.
3. __________ Personal transactions are not mixed with the company's transactions.
4. __________ Choosing the accounting method least likely to overstate assets or income.
5. __________ A company's use of the same accounting principles from year to year.
6. __________ Assets are recorded and reported at original purchase price.
7. __________ Accounting information should be timely, should help users predict future events, and should provide feedback about prior expectations.
8. __________ The life of a business can be divided into artificial segments of time.
9. __________ The reporting of all information that would make a difference to financial statement users.
10. __________ The judgment concerning whether an item's size makes it likely to influence a decision maker.
11. __________ Assumes a business will remain in operation for the foreseeable future.
12. __________ Different companies use the same accounting principles.

Exercises

Classify accounts on balance sheet.
(SO 1)

E2-1 The following are the major balance sheet classifications.

Current assets (CA)	Current liabilities (CL)
Long-term investments (LTI)	Long-term liabilities (LTL)
Property, plant, and equipment (PPE)	Common stock (CS)
Intangible assets (IA)	Retained earnings (RE)

Instructions
Classify each of the following financial statement items taken from Remington Corporation's balance sheet.

____ Accounts payable and accrued liabilities	____ Income taxes payable
____ Accounts receivable	____ Inventories
____ Accumulated depreciation	____ Investments
____ Buildings	____ Land
____ Cash and short-term investments	____ Long-term debt
____ Dividends payable	____ Materials and supplies
____ Goodwill	____ Office equipment and furniture
	____ Prepaid expenses

Classify financial statement items by balance sheet classification.
(SO 1)

E2-2 The major balance sheet classifications are listed in E2-1, on page 81.

Instructions
Classify each of the following financial statement items based upon the major balance sheet classifications listed in E2-1.

____ Prepaid expenses	____ Land held for future use
____ Machinery and equipment	____ Patents
____ Trademarks	____ Bonds payable
____ Dividends payable	____ Common stock
____ Taxes payable	____ Accumulated depreciation
____ Retained earnings	____ Unearned revenue
____ Accounts receivable	____ Inventory

Classify items as current or noncurrent, and prepare assets section of balance sheet.
(SO 1)

E2-3 The following items were taken from the December 31, 2006, assets section of the Boeing Company balance sheet. (All dollars are in millions.)

Inventories	$ 8,105	Other current assets	$ 2,837
Notes receivable—due after December 31, 2007	12,605	Property, plant, and equipment	19,310
Notes receivable—due before December 31, 2007	370	Cash and cash equivalents	6,118
		Accounts receivable	5,285
Accumulated depreciation	11,635	Other noncurrent assets	3,786
Intangible assets	4,745	Short-term investments	268

Instructions
Prepare the assets section of a classified balance sheet, listing the current assets in order of their liquidity.

Prepare assets section of a classified balance sheet.
(SO 1)

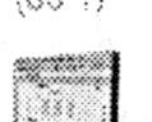

E2-4 The following information (in thousands of dollars) is available for H.J. Heinz Company—famous for ketchup and other fine food products—for the year ended May 2, 2007.

Prepaid expenses	$ 132,561	Inventories	$1,197,957
Land	51,950	Buildings and equipment	4,002,913
Other current assets	38,736	Cash and cash equivalents	652,896
Intangible assets	4,139,872	Accounts receivable	996,852
Other noncurrent assets	875,999	Accumulated depreciation	2,056,710

Instructions
Prepare the assets section of a classified balance sheet, listing the items in proper sequence and including a statement heading.

Prepare a classified balance sheet.
(SO 1)

E2-5 These items are taken from the financial statements of Cleland Co. at December 31, 2010.

Building	$105,800
Accounts receivable	12,600
Prepaid insurance	4,680
Cash	11,840
Equipment	82,400
Land	61,200
Insurance expense	780
Depreciation expense	5,300
Interest expense	2,600
Common stock	62,000

Retained earnings (January 1, 2010)	$40,000
Accumulated depreciation—building	45,600
Accounts payable	9,500
Note payable	93,600
Accumulated depreciation—equipment	18,720
Interest payable	3,600
Bowling revenues	14,180

Instructions

Prepare a classified balance sheet. Assume that $13,600 of the note payable will be paid in 2011.

Prepare a classified balance sheet.
(SO 1)

E2-6 The following items were taken from the 2006 financial statements of Texas Instruments, Inc. (All dollars are in millions.)

Common stock	$2,624	Cash and cash equivalents	$1,183
Prepaid expenses	181	Accumulated depreciation	3,801
Property, plant, and equipment	7,751	Accounts payable	560
Other current assets	745	Other noncurrent assets	1,839
Other current liabilities	1,475	Noncurrent liabilities	492
Long-term investments	287	Retained earnings	8,736
Short-term investments	2,534	Accounts receivable	1,774
Note payable in 2007	43	Inventories	1,437

Instructions

Prepare a classified balance sheet in good form as of December 31, 2006.

Compute and interpret profitability ratio.
(SO 2)

E2-7 The following information is available for Callaway Golf Company for the years 2006 and 2005. (Dollars are in thousands, except share information.)

	2006	2005
Net sales	$1,017,907	$998,093
Net income (loss)	23,290	13,284
Total assets	845,947	764,498
Share information		
Shares outstanding at year-end	67,954,213	70,495,136
Preferred dividends	-0-	-0-

There were 69,111,349 shares outstanding at the end of 2004.

Instructions

(a) What was the company's earnings per share for each year?
(b) Based on your findings above, how did the company's profitability change from 2005 to 2006?
(c) Suppose the company had paid dividends on preferred stock and on common stock during the year. How would this affect your calculation in part (a)?

Prepare financial statements.
(SO 1, 3, 4)

E2-8 These financial statement items are for Barone Corporation at year-end, July 31, 2010.

Salaries payable	$ 2,080
Salaries expense	51,700
Utilities expense	22,600
Equipment	18,500
Accounts payable	4,100
Commission revenue	66,100
Rent revenue	8,500
Long-term note payable	1,800
Common stock	16,000
Cash	29,200
Accounts receivable	9,780
Accumulated depreciation	6,000
Dividends	4,000
Depreciation expense	4,000
Retained earnings (beginning of the year)	35,200

Instructions

(a) Prepare an income statement and a retained earnings statement for the year. Barone Corporation did not issue any new stock during the year.
(b) Prepare a classified balance sheet at July 31.
(c) Compute the current ratio and debt to total assets ratio.
(d) Suppose that you are the president of Allied Equipment. Your sales manager has approached you with a proposal to sell $20,000 of equipment to Barone. He would like to provide a loan to Barone in the form of a 10%, 5-year note payable. Evaluate how this loan would change Barone's current ratio and debt to total assets ratio, and discuss whether you would make the sale.

Compute liquidity ratios and compare results.
(SO 4)

E2-9 Nordstrom, Inc. operates department stores in numerous states. Selected financial statement data (in millions of dollars) for the year ended February 3, 2007, follow.

	End of Year	Beginning of Year
Cash and cash equivalents	$ 403	$ 463
Receivables (net)	684	640
Merchandise inventory	997	956
Other current assets	658	815
Total current assets	$2,742	$2,874
Total current liabilities	$1,433	$1,623

Instructions

(a) Compute working capital and the current ratio at the beginning of the year and at the end of the current year.
(b) Did Nordstrom's liquidity improve or worsen during the year?
(c) Using the data in the chapter, compare Nordstrom's liquidity with Best Buy's.

Compute liquidity measures and discuss findings.
(SO 4)

E2-10 The chief financial officer (CFO) of Greenstem Corporation requested that the accounting department prepare a preliminary balance sheet on December 30, 2010, so that the CFO could get an idea of how the company stood. He knows that certain debt agreements with its creditors require the company to maintain a current ratio of at least 2:1. The preliminary balance sheet is as follows.

GREENSTEM CORP.
Balance Sheet
December 30, 2010

Current assets			Current liabilities		
Cash	$30,000		Accounts payable	$ 25,000	
Accounts receivable	30,000		Salaries payable	15,000	$ 40,000
Prepaid insurance	10,000	$ 70,000	Long-term liabilities		
Property, plant, and equipment (net)		190,000	Notes payable		80,000
			Total liabilities		120,000
Total assets		$260,000	Stockholders' equity		
			Common stock	100,000	
			Retained earnings	40,000	140,000
			Total liabilities and stockholders' equity		$260,000

Instructions

(a) Calculate the current ratio and working capital based on the preliminary balance sheet.
(b) Based on the results in (a), the CFO requested that $25,000 of cash be used to pay off the balance of the accounts payable account on December 31, 2010. Calculate the new current ratio and working capital after the company takes these actions.
(c) Discuss the pros and cons of the current ratio and working capital as measures of liquidity.
(d) Was it unethical for the CFO to take these steps?

E2-11 The following data were taken from the 2007 and 2006 financial statements of American Eagle Outfitters. (All dollars are in thousands.)

Compute and interpret solvency ratios.

(SO 4, 5)

	2007	2006
Current assets	$1,198,254	$1,076,781
Total assets	1,987,484	1,605,649
Current liabilities	460,464	351,487
Total liabilities	570,172	450,097
Total stockholders' equity	1,417,312	1,155,552
Cash provided by operating activities	749,268	480,419
Capital expenditures	225,939	81,545
Dividends paid	61,521	42,058

Instructions

Perform each of the following.

(a) Calculate the debt to total assets ratio for each year.

(b) Calculate the free cash flow for each year.

(c) Discuss American Eagle's solvency in 2007 versus 2006.

(d) Discuss American Eagle's ability to finance its investment activities with cash provided by operating activities, and how any deficiency would be met.

E2-12 Presented below are the assumptions and principles discussed in this chapter.

Identify accounting assumptions and principles.

(SO 7)

1. Full disclosure principle.
2. Going concern assumption.
3. Monetary unit assumption.
4. Time period assumption.
5. Cost principle.
6. Economic entity assumption.

Instructions

Identify by number the accounting assumption or principle that is described below. Do not use a number more than once.

_____ (a) Is the rationale for why plant assets are not reported at liquidation value. (*Note:* Do not use the cost principle.)

_____ (b) Indicates that personal and business record-keeping should be separately maintained.

_____ (c) Assumes that the dollar is the "measuring stick" used to report on financial performance.

_____ (d) Separates financial information into time periods for reporting purposes.

_____ (e) Indicates that companies should not record in the accounts market value changes subsequent to purchase.

_____ (f) Dictates that companies should disclose all circumstances and events that make a difference to financial statement users.

E2-13 Ghosh Co. had three major business transactions during 2010.

Identify the assumption or principle that has been violated.

(SO 7)

(a) Reported at its market value of $260,000 merchandise inventory with a cost of $208,000.

(b) The president of Ghosh Co., Dipak Ghosh, purchased a truck for personal use and charged it to his expense account.

(c) Ghosh Co. wanted to make its 2010 income look better, so it added 2 more weeks to the year (a 54-week year). Previous years were 52 weeks.

Instructions

In each situation, identify the assumption or principle that has been violated, if any, and discuss what the company should have done.

Exercises: Set B

Visit the book's companion website, at **www.wiley.com/college/kimmel**, and choose the Student Companion site, to access Exercise Set B.

Problems: Set A

Prepare a classified balance sheet.
(SO 1)

P2-1A The following items are taken from the 2006 balance sheet of Yahoo! Inc. (All dollars are in thousands.)

Intangible assets	$3,374,379
Common stock	5,292,545
Property and equipment, net	1,101,379
Accounts payable	109,130
Other assets	459,988
Long-term investments	2,827,720
Accounts receivable	930,964
Prepaid expenses and other current assets	217,779
Short-term investments	1,031,528
Retained earnings	3,868,065
Cash and cash equivalents	1,569,871
Long-term debt	749,915
Accrued expenses and other current liabilities	1,046,882
Unearned revenue—current	317,982
Other long-term liabilities	129,089

Tot. current assets $3,750,142
Tot. assets $11,513,608

Instructions

Prepare a classified balance sheet for Yahoo! Inc. as of December 31, 2006.

Prepare financial statements.
(SO 1, 3)

P2-2A These items are taken from the financial statements of Finn Corporation for 2010.

Retained earnings (beginning of year)	$31,000
Utilities expense	2,000
Equipment	66,000
Accounts payable	18,300
Cash	12,900
Salaries payable	3,000
Common stock	13,000
Dividends	12,000
Service revenue	72,000
Prepaid insurance	3,500
Repair expense	1,800
Depreciation expense	3,300
Accounts receivable	14,200
Insurance expense	2,200
Salaries expense	37,000
Accumulated depreciation	17,600

Net income $25,700
Tot. assets $79,000

Instructions

Prepare an income statement, a retained earnings statement, and a classified balance sheet as of December 31, 2010.

Prepare financial statements.
(SO 1, 3)

P2-3A You are provided with the following information for Kiley Enterprises, effective as of its April 30, 2010, year-end.

Accounts payable	$ 834
Accounts receivable	810
Building, net of accumulated depreciation	1,537
Cash	1,270
Common stock	900
Cost of goods sold	990
Current portion of long-term debt	450
Depreciation expense	335
Dividends	325
Equipment, net of accumulated depreciation	1,220
Income tax expense	165

Income taxes payable	$ 135
Interest expense	400
Inventories	967
Land	2,100
Long-term debt	3,500
Prepaid expenses	12
Retained earnings, beginning	1,600
Revenues	4,600
Selling expenses	210
Short-term investments	1,200
Wages expense	700
Wages payable	222

Instructions

(a) Prepare an income statement and a retained earnings statement for Kiley Enterprises for the year ended April 30, 2010.

(b) Prepare a classified balance sheet for Kiley Enterprises as of April 30, 2010.

Net income	$1,800
Tot. current assets	$4,259
Tot. assets	$9,116

Compute ratios; comment on relative profitability, liquidity, and solvency.

(SO 2, 4, 5)

P2-4A Comparative financial statement data for Bedene Corporation and Groneman Corporation, two competitors, appear below. All balance sheet data are as of December 31, 2010.

	Bedene Corporation	Groneman Corporation
	2010	2010
Net sales	$1,900,000	$620,000
Cost of goods sold	1,175,000	340,000
Operating expenses	303,000	98,000
Interest expense	9,000	3,800
Income tax expense	85,000	36,000
Current assets	407,200	190,336
Plant assets (net)	532,000	139,728
Current liabilities	66,325	40,348
Long-term liabilities	108,500	29,620
Cash from operating activities	138,000	36,000
Capital expenditures	90,000	20,000
Dividends paid	36,000	15,000
Average number of shares outstanding	100,000	50,000

Instructions

(a) Comment on the relative profitability of the companies by computing the net income and earnings per share for each company for 2010.

(b) Comment on the relative liquidity of the companies by computing working capital and the current ratios for each company for 2010.

(c) Comment on the relative solvency of the companies by computing the debt to total assets ratio and the free cash flow for each company for 2010.

Compute and interpret liquidity, solvency, and profitability ratios.

(SO 2, 4, 5)

P2-5A Here and on page 88 are financial statements of Edmiston Company.

EDMISTON COMPANY
Income Statement
For the Year Ended December 31, 2010

Net sales	$2,218,500
Cost of goods sold	1,012,400
Selling and administrative expenses	906,000
Interest expense	98,000
Income tax expense	69,000
Net income	$ 133,100

EDMISTON COMPANY
Balance Sheet
December 31, 2010

Assets	
Current assets	
Cash	$ 60,100
Short-term investments	74,000
Accounts receivable (net)	169,800
Inventory	125,000
Total current assets	428,900
Plant assets (net)	625,300
Total assets	$1,054,200
Liabilities and Stockholders' Equity	
Current liabilities	
Accounts payable	$ 180,000
Income taxes payable	35,500
Total current liabilities	215,500
Bonds payable	200,000
Total liabilities	415,500
Stockholders' equity	
Common stock	350,000
Retained earnings	288,700
Total stockholders' equity	638,700
Total liabilities and stockholders' equity	$1,054,200

Additional information: The cash provided by operating activities for 2010 was $190,800. The cash used for capital expenditures was $92,000. The cash used for dividends was $31,000. The average number of shares outstanding during the year was 50,000.

Instructions

(a) Compute the following values and ratios for 2010. (We provide the results from 2009 for comparative purposes.)
   (i) Working capital. (2009: $160,500)
   (ii) Current ratio. (2009: 1.65:1)
   (iii) Free cash flow. (2009: $48,700)
   (iv) Debt to total assets ratio. (2009: 31%)
   (v) Earnings per share. (2009: $3.15)

(b) Using your calculations from part (a), discuss changes from 2009 in liquidity, solvency, and profitability.

Compute and interpret liquidity, solvency, and profitability ratios.
(SO 2, 4, 5)

P2-6A Condensed balance sheet and income statement data for Lark Corporation are presented here.

LARK CORPORATION
Balance Sheets
December 31

Assets	**2010**	**2009**
Cash	$ 25,000	$ 20,000
Receivables (net)	70,000	62,000
Other current assets	80,000	73,000
Long-term investments	75,000	60,000
Plant and equipment (net)	510,000	470,000
Total assets	$760,000	$685,000
Liabilities and Stockholders' Equity		
Current liabilities	$ 75,000	$ 70,000
Long-term debt	80,000	90,000
Common stock	330,000	300,000
Retained earnings	275,000	225,000
Total liabilities and stockholders' equity	$760,000	$685,000

LARK CORPORATION
Income Statements
For the Years Ended December 31

	2010	2009
Sales	$750,000	$670,000
Cost of goods sold	440,000	400,000
Operating expenses (including income taxes)	240,000	220,000
Net income	$ 70,000	$ 50,000

Additional information:

Cash from operating activities	$87,000	$60,000
Cash used for capital expenditures	$45,000	$38,000
Dividends paid	$20,000	$15,000
Average number of shares outstanding	33,000	30,000

Instructions

Compute these values and ratios for 2009 and 2010.

(a) Earnings per share.
(b) Working capital.
(c) Current ratio.
(d) Debt to total assets ratio.
(e) Free cash flow.
(f) Based on the ratios calculated, discuss briefly the improvement or lack thereof in financial position and operating results from 2009 to 2010 of Lark Corporation.

Compute ratios and compare liquidity, solvency, and profitability for two companies.

(SO 2, 4, 5)

P2-7A Selected financial data of two competitors, Target and Wal-Mart, are presented here. (All dollars are in millions.)

	Target (2/3/07)	Wal-Mart (1/31/07)
	Income Statement Data for Year	
Net sales	$59,490	$344,992
Cost of goods sold	39,399	264,152
Selling and administrative expenses	14,315	64,001
Interest expense	572	1,529
Other income (loss)	(707)	3,658
Income taxes	1,710	6,365
Net income	$ 2,787	$ 12,603

	Target	Wal-Mart
	Balance Sheet Data (End of Year)	
Current assets	$14,706	$ 46,588
Noncurrent assets	22,643	104,605
Total assets	$37,349	$151,193
Current liabilities	$11,117	$ 51,754
Long-term debt	10,599	37,866
Total stockholders' equity	15,633	61,573
Total liabilities and stockholders' equity	$37,349	$151,193
Cash from operating activities	$4,862	$20,209
Cash paid for capital expenditures	3,928	15,666
Dividends declared and paid on common stock	380	2,802
Average shares outstanding (millions)	869	4,168

Instructions

For each company, compute these values and ratios.

(a) Working capital.
(b) Current ratio.

(c) Debt to total assets ratio.
(d) Free cash flow.
(e) Earnings per share.
(f) Compare the liquidity, solvency, and profitability of the two companies.

Comment on the objectives and qualitative characteristics of financial reporting.
(SO 6, 7)

P2-8A A friend of yours, Cindy Estes, recently completed an undergraduate degree in science and has just started working with a biotechnology company. Cindy tells you that the owners of the business are trying to secure new sources of financing which are needed in order for the company to proceed with development of a new health care product. Cindy said that her boss told her that the company must put together a report to present to potential investors.

Cindy thought that the company should include in this package the detailed scientific findings related to the Phase I clinical trials for this product. She said, "I know that the biotech industry sometimes has only a 10% success rate with new products, but if we report all the scientific findings, everyone will see what a sure success this is going to be! The president was talking about the importance of following some set of accounting principles. Why do we need to look at some accounting rules? What they need to realize is that we have scientific results that are quite encouraging, some of the most talented employees around, and the start of some really great customer relationships. We haven't made any sales yet, but we will. We just need the funds to get through all the clinical testing and get government approval for our product. Then these investors will be quite happy that they bought in to our company early!"

Instructions

(a) What is financial reporting? Explain to Cindy what is meant by generally accepted accounting principles.
(b) Comment on how Cindy's suggestions for what should be reported to prospective investors conforms to the qualitative characteristics of accounting information. Do you think that the things that Cindy wants to include in the information for investors will conform to financial reporting guidelines?

Problems: Set B

Prepare a classified balance sheet.
(SO 1)

P2-1B The following items are from the 2006 balance sheet of Kellogg Company. (All dollars are in millions.)

Common stock	$ 396.9
Other assets	5,471.4
Notes payable—current	1,268.0
Other current assets	247.7
Current maturities of long-term debt	723.3
Cash and cash equivalents	410.6
Other long-term liabilities	1,571.8
Retained earnings	1,672.1
Accounts payable	910.4
Other current liabilities	1,118.5
Accounts receivable, net	944.8
Property, net	2,815.6
Inventories	823.9
Long-term debt	3,053.0

Tot. current assets $2,427.0
Tot. assets $10,714.0

Instructions

Prepare a classified balance sheet for Kellogg Company as of December 31, 2006.

Prepare financial statements.
(SO 1, 3)

P2-2B These items are taken from the financial statements of Pinson, Inc.

Prepaid insurance	$ 1,800
Equipment	31,000
Salaries expense	36,000
Utilities expense	2,100
Accumulated depreciation	8,600
Accounts payable	10,200
Cash	5,300

Accounts receivable	$ 5,500
Salaries payable	2,000
Common stock	5,900
Depreciation expense	4,300
Retained earnings (beginning)	14,000
Dividends	3,600
Service revenue	53,000
Repair expense	2,900
Insurance expense	1,200

Instructions

Prepare an income statement, a retained earnings statement, and a classified balance sheet as of December 31, 2010.

Net income $6,500
Tot. assets $35,000

Prepare financial statements.
(SO 1, 3)

P2-3B You are provided with the following information for Milner Corporation, effective as of its April 30, 2010, year-end.

Accounts payable	$ 2,400
Accounts receivable	9,150
Accumulated depreciation	6,600
Depreciation expense	2,200
Cash	21,955
Common stock	20,000
Dividends	2,800
Equipment	25,050
Sales revenue	21,450
Income tax expense	1,100
Income taxes payable	300
Interest expense	350
Interest payable	175
Long-term notes payable	5,700
Prepaid rent	380
Rent expense	760
Retained earnings, beginning	13,960
Salaries expense	6,840

Instructions

(a) Prepare an income statement and a retained earnings statement for Milner Corporation for the year ended April 30, 2010.

(b) Prepare a classified balance sheet for Milner as of April 30, 2010.

(c) Explain how each financial statement interrelates with the others.

Net income $10,200
Tot. current assets $31,485
Tot. assets $49,935

Compute ratios; comment on relative profitability, liquidity, and solvency.
(SO 2, 4, 5)

P2-4B Comparative statement data for Smyth Company and James Company, two competitors, are presented below. All balance sheet data are as of December 31, 2010.

	Smyth Company	James Company
	2010	2010
Net sales	$450,000	$898,000
Cost of goods sold	260,000	620,000
Operating expenses	134,000	55,000
Interest expense	6,000	10,000
Income tax expense	10,000	65,000
Current assets	180,000	700,000
Plant assets (net)	600,000	800,000
Current liabilities	75,000	300,000
Long-term liabilities	190,000	200,000
Cash from operating activities	36,000	180,000
Capital expenditures	20,000	50,000
Dividends paid	4,000	15,000
Average number of shares outstanding	200,000	400,000

Instructions

(a) Comment on the relative profitability of the companies by computing the net income and earnings per share for each company for 2010.

(b) Comment on the relative liquidity of the companies by computing working capital and the current ratios for each company for 2010.

(c) Comment on the relative solvency of the companies by computing the debt to total assets ratio and the free cash flow for each company for 2010.

Compute and interpret liquidity, solvency, and profitability ratios.

(SO 2, 4, 5)

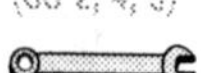

P2-5B The financial statements of Windsor Company are presented here.

WINDSOR COMPANY
Income Statement
For the Year Ended December 31, 2010

Net sales	$700,000
Cost of goods sold	400,000
Selling and administrative expenses	150,000
Interest expense	7,800
Income tax expense	43,000
Net income	$ 99,200

WINDSOR COMPANY
Balance Sheet
December 31, 2010

Assets	
Current assets	
Cash	$ 23,100
Short-term investments	34,800
Accounts receivable (net)	106,200
Inventory	155,000
Total current assets	319,100
Plant assets (net)	465,300
Total assets	$784,400
Liabilities and Stockholders' Equity	
Current liabilities	
Accounts payable	$120,200
Income taxes payable	29,000
Total current liabilities	149,200
Bonds payable	130,000
Total liabilities	279,200
Stockholders' equity	
Common stock	170,000
Retained earnings	335,200
Total stockholders' equity	505,200
Total liabilities and stockholders' equity	$784,400

Cash from operating activities	$ 71,300
Capital expenditures	$ 42,000
Dividends paid	$ 10,000
Average number of shares outstanding	65,000

Instructions

(a) Compute the following values and ratios for 2010. (We provide the results from 2009 for comparative purposes.)

(i) Current ratio. (2009: 2.4:1)

(ii) Working capital. (2009: $178,000)

(iii) Debt to total assets ratio. (2009: 31%)
(iv) Free cash flow. (2009: $13,000)
(v) Earnings per share. (2009: $1.35)

(b) Using your calculations from part (a), discuss changes from 2009 in liquidity, solvency, and profitability.

Compute and interpret liquidity, solvency, and profitability ratios.

(SO 2, 4, 5)

P2-6B Condensed balance sheet and income statement data for Pratt Corporation are presented below.

PRATT CORPORATION
Balance Sheets
December 31

Assets	**2010**	**2009**
Cash	$ 40,000	$ 24,000
Receivables (net)	90,000	55,000
Other current assets	74,000	73,000
Long-term investments	78,000	70,000
Plant and equipment (net)	525,000	427,000
Total assets	$807,000	$649,000

Liabilities and Stockholders' Equity	**2010**	**2009**
Current liabilities	$ 93,000	$ 75,000
Long-term debt	90,000	70,000
Common stock	370,000	340,000
Retained earnings	254,000	164,000
Total liabilities and stockholders' equity	$807,000	$649,000

PRATT CORPORATION
Income Statements
For the Years Ended December 31

	2010	**2009**
Sales	$760,000	$800,000
Cost of goods sold	420,000	400,000
Operating expenses (including income taxes)	200,000	237,000
Net income	$140,000	$163,000
Cash from operating activities	$165,000	$178,000
Cash used for capital expenditures	85,000	45,000
Dividends paid	50,000	43,000
Average number of shares outstanding	370,000	320,000

Instructions

Compute the following values and ratios for 2009 and 2010.

(a) Earnings per share.
(b) Working capital.
(c) Current ratio.
(d) Debt to total assets ratio.
(e) Free cash flow.
(f) Based on the ratios calculated, discuss briefly the improvement or lack thereof in the financial position and operating results of Pratt from 2009 to 2010.

Compute ratios and compare liquidity, solvency, and profitability for two companies.

(SO 2, 4, 5)

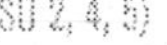

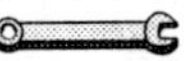

P2-7B Selected financial data of two competitors, Blockbuster Inc. and Movie Gallery, Inc., in 2006 are presented on page 94. (All dollars are in millions.)

	Blockbuster Inc.	Movie Gallery, Inc.
	Income Statement Data for Year	
Net sales	$ 5,524	$2,542
Cost of goods sold	2,476	1,012
Selling and administrative expenses	2,755	1,431
Interest expense	102	120
Other expense	212	3
Income tax expense (refund)	(76)	2
Net income (loss)	$ 55	$ (26)

	Blockbuster Inc.	Movie Gallery, Inc.
	Balance Sheet Data (End of Year)	
Current assets	$ 1,566	$ 239
Property, plant, and equipment (net)	580	243
Intangible assets	835	297
Other assets	156	374
Total assets	$ 3,137	$1,153
Current liabilities	$ 1,395	$ 268
Long-term debt	851	1,122
Total stockholders' equity	891	(237)
Total liabilities and stockholders' equity	$ 3,137	$1,153
Cash from operating activities	$329	$(10)
Cash used for capital expenditures	79	20
Dividends paid	11	-0-
Average shares outstanding	189.0	31.8

Instructions

For each company, compute these values and ratios.

(a) Working capital.

(b) Current ratio. (Round to two decimal places.)

(c) Debt to total assets ratio.

(d) Free cash flow.

(e) Earnings per share.

(f) Compare the liquidity, profitability, and solvency of the two companies.

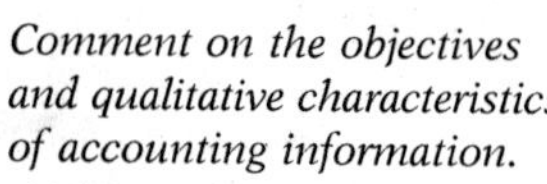

Comment on the objectives and qualitative characteristics of accounting information.
(SO 6, 7)

P2-8B Net Nanny Software International Inc., headquartered in Vancouver, specializes in Internet safety and computer security products for both the home and commercial markets. In a recent balance sheet, it reported a deficit (negative retained earnings) of US $5,678,288. It has reported only net losses since its inception. In spite of these losses, Net Nanny's common shares have traded anywhere from a high of $3.70 to a low of $0.32 on the Canadian Venture Exchange.

Net Nanny's financial statements have historically been prepared in Canadian dollars. Recently, the company adopted the U.S. dollar as its reporting currency.

Instructions

(a) What is the objective of financial reporting? How does this objective meet or not meet Net Nanny's investor's needs?

(b) Why would investors want to buy Net Nanny's shares if the company has consistently reported losses over the last few years? Include in your answer an assessment of the relevance of the information reported on Net Nanny's financial statements.

(c) Comment on how the change in reporting information from Canadian dollars to U.S. dollars likely affected the readers of Net Nanny's financial statements. Include in your answer an assessment of the comparability of the information.

Problems: Set C

Visit the book's companion website at **www.wiley.com/college/kimmel** and choose the Student Companion site to access Problem Set C.

Continuing Cookie Chronicle

(*Note:* This is a continuation of the Cookie Chronicle from Chapter 1.)

CCC2 After investigating the different forms of business organization, Natalie Koebel decides to operate her business as a corporation, Cookie Creations Inc., and she begins the process of getting her business running.

Go to the book's companion website, **www.wiley.com/college/kimmel,** to find the completion of this problem.

broadening your perspective

FINANCIAL REPORTING PROBLEM: *Tootsie Roll Industries, Inc.*

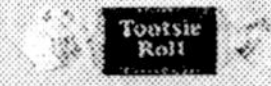

BYP2-1 The financial statements of Tootsie Roll Industries, Inc., appear in Appendix A at the end of this book.

Instructions

Answer the following questions using the Consolidated Balance Sheet and the Notes to Consolidated Financial Statements section.

(a) What were Tootsie Roll's total current assets at December 31, 2007, and December 31, 2006?

(b) Are the assets included in current assets listed in the proper order? Explain.

(c) How are Tootsie Roll's assets classified?

(d) What were Tootsie Roll's current liabilities at December 31, 2007, and December 31, 2006?

COMPARATIVE ANALYSIS PROBLEM: *Tootsie Roll vs. Hershey Foods*

BYP2-2 The financial statements of Hershey Foods appear in Appendix B, following the financial statements for Tootsie Roll in Appendix A. Assume Hershey's average number of shares outstanding was 228,652,000, and Tootsie Roll's was 54,980,000.

Instructions

(a) For each company calculate the following values for 2007.

(1) Working capital.
(2) Current ratio.
(3) Debt to total assets ratio
(4) Free cash flow.
(5) Earnings per share.

(*Hint:* When calculating free cash flow, **do not** consider business acquisitions to be part of capital expenditures.)

(b) Based on your findings above, discuss the relative liquidity, solvency, and profitability of the two companies.

RESEARCH CASE

BYP 2-3 The January 2008 edition of *Strategic Finance* includes an article by Curtis C. Verschoor titled "ERC Says Ethics Risk Landscape Still Treacherous."

Instructions

Read the article and answer the following questions.

(a) In 2007 what percentage of employees in the survey said that they had personally observed violations of company ethics standards, policy, or the law? How did this percentage compare with 2005 and 2003?

(b) What were the three most frequent types of observed misconduct, and what percentage of employees observed each type of behavior?
(c) What percentage of employees who witnessed misconduct did not report it through company channels? What were the two most common reasons given for not reporting?
(d) What are the key elements of an effective ethics and compliance program?

INTERPRETING FINANCIAL STATEMENTS

BYP2-4 The following information was reported by Gap, Inc. in its 2006 annual report.

	2006	2005	2004	2003	2002
Total assets (millions)	$8,544	$8,821	$10,048	$10,713	$10,283
Working capital	$2,757	$3,297	$4,062	$4,156	$2,972
Current ratio	2.21:1	2.70:1	2.81:1	2.63:1	2.08:1
Debt to total assets ratio	.39:1	.38:1	.51:1	.57:1	.66:1
Earnings per share	$0.94	$1.26	$1.29	$1.15	$0.55

(a) Determine the overall percentage decrease in Gap's total assets from 2002 to 2006. What was the average decrease per year?
(b) Comment on the change in Gap's liquidity. Does working capital or the current ratio appear to provide a better indication of Gap's liquidity? What might explain the change in Gap's liquidity during this period?
(c) Comment on the change in Gap's solvency during this period.
(d) Comment on the change in Gap's profitability during this period. How might this affect your prediction about Gap's future profitability?

FINANCIAL ANALYSIS ON THE WEB

BYP2-5 ***Purpose:*** Identify summary liquidity, solvency, and profitability information about companies, and compare this information across companies in the same industry.

Address: **http://biz.yahoo.com/i**, or go to **www.wiley.com/college/kimmel**

Steps

1. Type in a company name, or use the index to find a company name. Choose **Profile**. Choose **Key Statistics**. Perform instruction (a) below.
2. Go back to **Profile**. Click on the company's particular industry behind the heading "Industry." Perform instructions (b), (c), and (d).

Instructions

Answer the following questions.
(a) What is the company's name? What was the company's current ratio and debt to equity ratio (a variation of the debt to total assets ratio)?
(b) What is the company's industry?
(c) What is the name of a competitor? What is the competitor's current ratio and its debt to equity ratio?
(d) Based on these measures: Which company is more liquid? Which company is more solvent?

BYP2-6 The opening story described the dramatic effect that investment bulletin boards are having on the investment world. This exercise will allow you to evaluate a bulletin board discussing a company of your choice.

Address: **http://biz.yahoo.com/i**, or go to **www.wiley.com/college/kimmel**

Steps

1. Type in a company name, or use the index to find a company name.
2. Choose **Msgs** or **Message Board**. (for messages).
3. Read the ten most recent messages.

Instructions

Answer the following questions.
(a) State the nature of each of these messages (e.g., offering advice, criticizing company, predicting future results, ridiculing other people who have posted messages).
(b) For those messages that expressed an opinion about the company, was evidence provided to support the opinion?
(c) What effect do you think it would have on bulletin board discussions if the participants provided their actual names? Do you think this would be a good policy?

Critical Thinking

DECISION MAKING ACROSS THE ORGANIZATION

BYP2-7 As a financial analyst in the planning department for Steigner Industries, Inc., you have been requested to develop some key ratios from the comparative financial statements. This information is to be used to convince creditors that Steigner Industries, Inc. is liquid, solvent, and profitable, and that it deserves their continued support. Lenders are particularly concerned about the company's ability to continue as a going concern.

Here are the data requested and the computations developed from the financial statements:

	2010	2009
Current ratio	3.1	2.1
Working capital	Up 22%	Down 7%
Free cash flow	Up 25%	Up 18%
Debt to total assets ratio	0.60	0.70
Net income	Up 32%	Down 8%
Earnings per share	$2.40	$1.15

Instructions

Steigner Industries, Inc. asks you to prepare brief comments stating how each of these items supports the argument that its financial health is improving. The company wishes to use these comments to support presentation of data to its creditors. With the class divided into groups, prepare the comments as requested, giving the implications and the limitations of each item separately, and then the collective inference that may be drawn from them about Steigner's financial well-being.

COMMUNICATION ACTIVITY

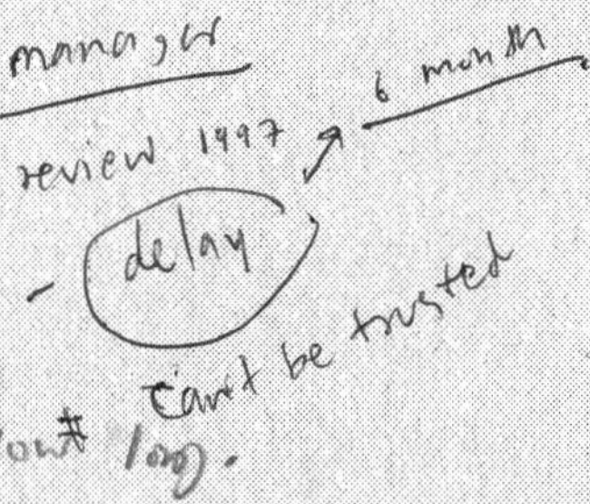

BYP2-8 T. J. Rains is the chief executive officer of Tomorrow's Products. T. J. is an expert engineer but a novice in accounting.

Instructions

Write a letter to T. J. Rains that explains (a) the three main types of ratios; (b) examples of each, how they are calculated, and what they measure; and (c) the bases for comparison in analyzing Tomorrow's Products' financial statements.

ETHICS CASE

BYP2-9 A May 20, 2002, *Business Week* story by Stanley Holmes and Mike France entitled "Boeing's Secret" discusses issues surrounding the timing of the disclosure of information at the giant airplane manufacturer. To summarize, on December 11, 1996, Boeing closed a giant deal to acquire another manufacturer, McDonnell Douglas. Boeing paid for the acquisition by issuing shares of its own stock to the stockholders of McDonnell Douglas. In order for the deal not to be revoked, the value of Boeing's stock could not decline below a certain level for a number of months after the deal.

The article suggests that during the first half of 1997 Boeing suffered significant cost overruns because of severe inefficiencies in its production methods. Had these problems been disclosed in the quarterly financial statements during the first and second quarter of 1997, the company's stock most likely would have plummeted, and the deal would have been revoked. Company managers spent considerable time debating when the bad news should be disclosed. One public relations manager suggested that the company's problems be revealed on the date of either Princess Diana's or Mother Teresa's funeral, in the hope that it would be lost among those big stories that day. Instead, the company waited until October 22 of that year to announce a $2.6 billion write-off due to cost overruns. Within one week the company's stock price had fallen 20%, but by this time the McDonnell Douglas deal could not be reversed.

Instructions

Answer the following questions. Although it is not required in order to answer the questions, you may want to read the *Business Week* article.

(a) Who are the stakeholders in this situation?

(b) What are the ethical issues?

(c) What assumptions or principles of accounting are relevant to this case?
(d) Do you think it is ethical to try to "time" the release of a story so as to diminish its effect?
(e) What would you have done if you were the chief executive officer of Boeing?
(f) Boeing's top management maintains that it did not have an obligation to reveal its problems during the first half of 1997, and that it wouldn't do anything differently today. What implications does this have for investors and analysts who follow Boeing's stock?

"ALL ABOUT YOU" ACTIVITY

BYP2-10 Every company needs to plan in order to move forward. Its top management must consider where it wants the company to be in three to five years. Like a company, you need to think about where you want to be three to five years from now, and you need to start taking steps now in order to get there.

Instructions

Provide responses to each of the following items.

(a) Where would you like to be working in three to five years? Describe your plan for getting there by identifying between five and 10 specific steps that you need to take in order to get there.
(b) In order to get the job you want, you will need a résumé. Your résumé is the equivalent of a company's annual report. It needs to provide relevant and reliable information about your past accomplishments so that employers can decide whether to "invest" in you. Do a search on the Internet to find a good résumé format. What are the basic elements of a résumé?
(c) A company's annual report provides information about a company's accomplishments. In order for investors to use the annual report, the information must be reliable; that is, users must have faith that the information is accurate and believable. How can you provide assurance that the information on your résumé is reliable?
(d) Prepare a résumé assuming that you have accomplished the five to 10 specific steps you identified in part (a).Also, provide evidence that would give assurance that the information is reliable.

? *Answers to Insight and Accounting Across the Organization Questions*

p. 60

Q: What can various company managers do to ensure that working capital is managed efficiently to maximize net income?

A: Marketing and sales managers must understand that by extending generous repayment terms they are expanding the company's receivables balance and slowing the company's cash flow. Production managers must strive to minimize the amount of excess inventory on hand. Managers must coordinate efforts to speed up the collection of receivables, while also ensuring that the company pays its payables on time, but never too early.

p. 61

Q: Discuss the difference in the debt to total assets ratio of Microsoft and General Motors.

A: Microsoft has a very low debt to total assets ratio. The company is in a rapidly changing industry and thus should try to minimize the risk associated with increased debt. Also, because Microsoft generates significant amounts of cash and has minimal needs for large investments in plant assets, it does not need to borrow a lot of cash. General Motors needs to make huge investments in plant assets, and it has a very large credit operation. Thus it has large borrowing needs.

p. 65

Q: What is meant by the phrase "make the country's businesses more transparent"? Why would increasing transparency spur economic growth?

A: Transparency refers to the extent to which outsiders have knowledge regarding a company's financial performance and financial position. If a company lacks transparency, its financial reports do not adequately inform investors of critical information that is needed to make investment decisions. If corporate transparency is increased, investors will be more willing to supply the financial capital that businesses need in order to grow, which would spur the country's economic growth.

p. 66

Q: What problems might Best Buy's year-end create for analysts?

A: First, if Best Buy's competitors use a different year-end, then when you compare their financial results, you are not comparing performance over the same period of time or financial position at the same point in time. Also, by not picking a particular date, the number of weeks in Best Buy's fiscal year will change. For example, fiscal years 2005 and 2006 had 52 weeks, but fiscal year 2007 had 53 weeks.

Answers to Self-Study Questions

1. d 2. a 3. c 4. c 5. b 6. a 7. c 8. b 9. d 10. d 11. a 12. a 13. c 14. c 15. c

✓ Remember to go back to the navigator box on the chapter-opening page and check off your completed work.

chapter 3

The Accounting Information System

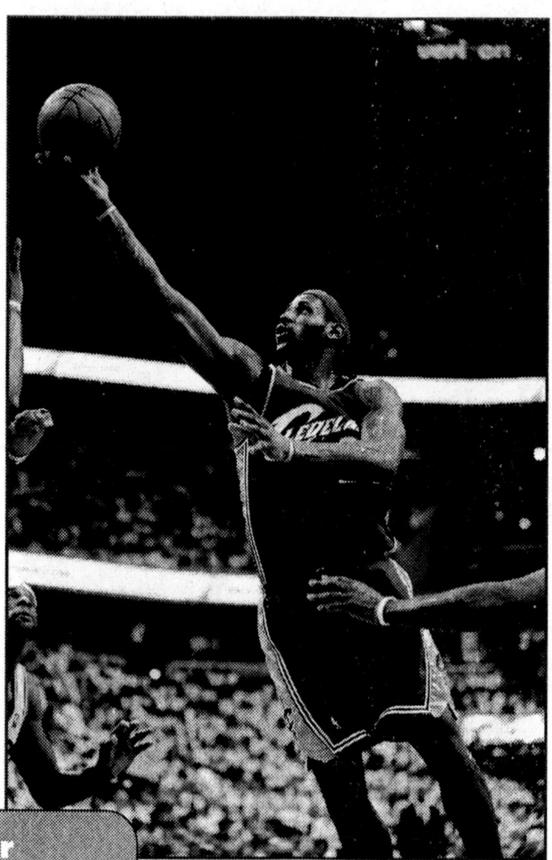

the navigator

- Scan Study Objectives ○
- Read Feature Story ○
- Scan Preview ○
- Read Text and answer **Do it!** p. 110 ○ p. 115 ○ p. 118 ○ p. 128 ○
- Work Using the Decision Toolkit ○
- Review Summary of Study Objectives ○
- Work Comprehensive **Do it!** p. 133 ○
- Answer Self-Study Questions ○
- Complete Assignments ○

study objectives

After studying this chapter, you should be able to:

1 Analyze the effect of business transactions on the basic accounting equation.
2 Explain what an account is and how it helps in the recording process.
3 Define debits and credits and explain how they are used to record business transactions.
4 Identify the basic steps in the recording process.
5 Explain what a journal is and how it helps in the recording process.
6 Explain what a ledger is and how it helps in the recording process.
7 Explain what posting is and how it helps in the recording process.
8 Explain the purposes of a trial balance.
9 Classify cash activities as operating, investing, or financing.

Accidents Happen

How organized are you financially? Take a short quiz. Answer *yes* or *no* to each question:

- Does your wallet contain so many cash machine receipts that you've been declared a walking fire hazard?
- Is your wallet such a mess that it is often faster to fish for money in the crack of your car seat than to dig around in your wallet?
- Was Lebron James playing high school basketball the last time you balanced your bank account?
- Have you ever been tempted to burn down your house so you don't have to try to find all of the receipts and records that you need to fill out your tax returns?

If you think it is hard to keep track of the many transactions that make up *your* life, imagine what it is like for a major corporation like Fidelity Investments. Fidelity is one of the largest mutual fund management firms in the world. If you had your life savings invested at Fidelity Investments, you might be just slightly displeased if, when you called to find out your balance, the representative said, "You know, I kind of remember someone with a name like yours sending us some money–now what did we do with that?"

To ensure the accuracy of your balance and the security of your funds, Fidelity Investments, like all other companies large and small, relies on a sophisticated accounting information system. That's not to say that Fidelity or any other company is error-free. In fact, if you've ever really messed up your checkbook register, you may take some comfort from one accountant's mistake at Fidelity Investments. The accountant failed to include a minus sign while doing a calculation, making what was actually a $1.3 billion loss look like a $1.3 billion gain–yes, *billion!* Fortunately, like most accounting errors, it was detected before any real harm was done.

No one expects that kind of mistake at a company like Fidelity, which has sophisticated computer systems and top investment managers. In explaining the mistake to shareholders, a spokesperson wrote, "Some people have asked how, in this age of technology, such a mistake could be made. While many of our processes are computerized, accounting systems are complex and dictate that some steps must be handled manually by our managers and accountants, and people can make mistakes."

On the World Wide Web
Fidelity Investments: www.fidelity.com

preview of chapter 3

As indicated in the Feature Story, a reliable information system is a necessity for any company. The purpose of this chapter is to explain and illustrate the features of an accounting information system. The organization and content of the chapter are as follows.

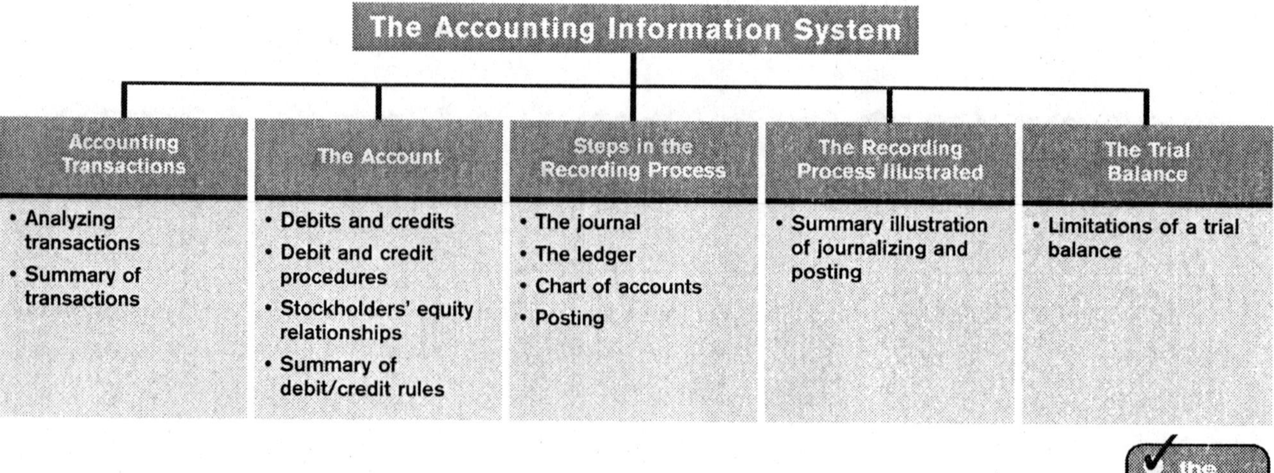

the navigator

The Accounting Information System

The system of collecting and processing transaction data and communicating financial information to decision makers is known as the **accounting information system.** Factors that shape these systems include: the nature of the company's business, the types of transactions, the size of the company, the volume of data, and the information demands of management and others.

Most businesses use computerized accounting systems—sometimes referred to as electronic data processing (EDP) systems. These systems handle all the steps involved in the recording process, from initial data entry to preparation of the financial statements. In order to remain competitive, companies continually improve their accounting systems to provide accurate and timely data for decision making. For example, in a recent annual report, Tootsie Roll states, "We also invested in additional processing and data storage hardware during the year. We view information technology as a key strategic tool, and are committed to deploying leading edge technology in this area." In addition, many companies have upgraded their accounting information systems in response to the requirements of Sarbanes-Oxley.

In this chapter we focus on a manual accounting system because the accounting concepts and principles do not change whether a system is computerized or manual, and manual systems are easier to illustrate. However, many of the homework problems in this and subsequent chapters can also be done using the computerized general ledger package that supplements this text.

Accounting Transactions

To use an accounting information system, you need to know which economic events to recognize (record). Not all events are recorded and reported in the financial statements. For example, suppose General Motors hired a new employee or purchased a new computer. Are these events entered in its accounting records? The first event would not be recorded, but the second event would. We call economic events that require recording in the financial statements **accounting transactions.**

An accounting transaction occurs when assets, liabilities, or stockholders' equity items change as a result of some economic event. The purchase of a computer by General Motors, the payment of rent by Microsoft, and the sale of advertising space by Sierra Corporation are examples of events that change a company's assets, liabilities, or stockholders' equity. Illustration 3-1 summarizes the decision process companies use to decide whether or not to record economic events.

Illustration 3-1
Transaction identification process

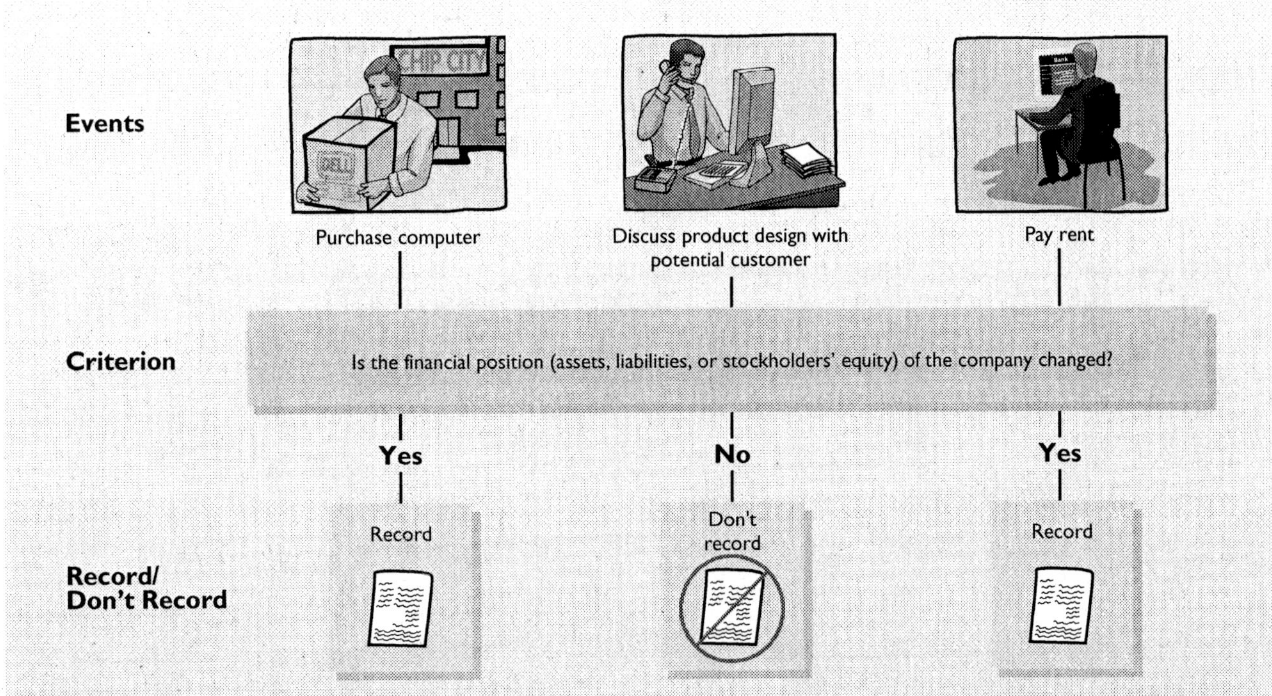

ANALYZING TRANSACTIONS

In Chapter 1 you learned the basic accounting equation:

study objective 1
Analyze the effect of business transactions on the basic accounting equation.

Assets = Liabilities + Stockholders' Equity

In this chapter you will learn how to analyze transactions in terms of their effect on assets, liabilities, and stockholders' equity. **Transaction analysis** is the process of identifying the specific effects of economic events on the accounting equation.

The accounting equation must always balance. Each transaction has a dual (double-sided) effect on the equation. For example, if an individual asset is increased, there must be a corresponding:

Decrease in another asset, *or*
Increase in a specific liability, *or*
Increase in stockholders' equity.

Two or more items could be affected when an asset is increased. For example, if a company purchases a computer for $10,000 by paying $6,000 in cash and signing a note for $4,000, one asset (computer) increases $10,000, another asset (cash) decreases $6,000, and a liability (notes payable) increases $4,000.

The result is that the accounting equation remains in balance—assets increased by a net $4,000 and liabilities increased by $4,000, as shown below.

Assets	=	Liabilities	+	Stockholders' Equity
+$10,000		+$4,000		
− 6,000				
$ 4,000	=	$4,000		

Chapter 1 presented the financial statements for Sierra Corporation for its first month. You should review those financial statements (on page 17) at this time. To illustrate how economic events affect the accounting equation, we will examine events affecting Sierra Corporation during its first month.

In order to analyze the transactions for Sierra Corporation, we will expand the basic accounting equation. This will allow us to better illustrate the impact of transactions on stockholders' equity. Recall from the balance sheets in Chapters 1 and 2 that stockholders' equity is comprised of two parts: common stock and retained earnings. Common stock is affected when the company issues new shares of stock in exchange for cash. Retained earnings is affected when the company earns revenue, incurs expenses, or pays dividends. Illustration 3-2 shows the expanded equation.

Illustration 3-2 Expanded accounting equation

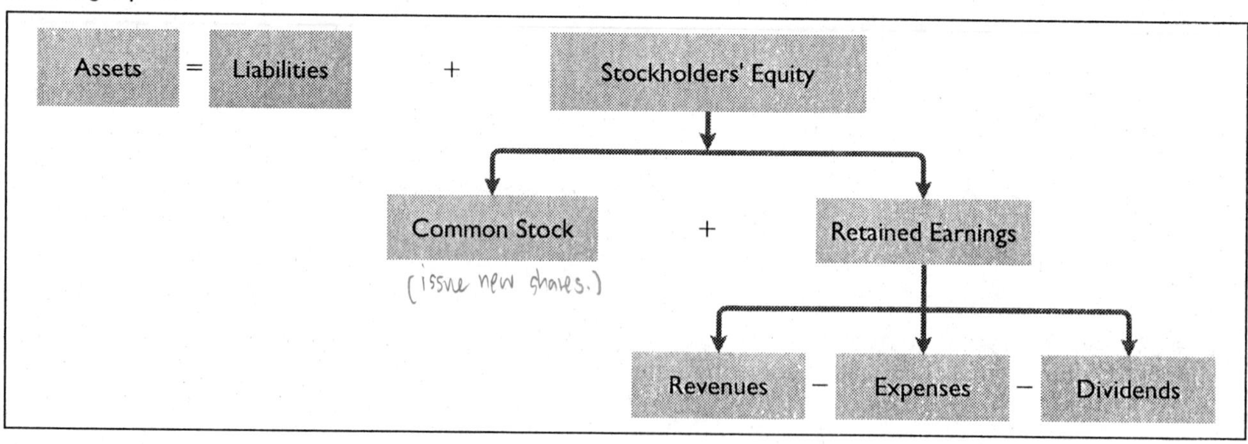

If you are tempted to skip ahead after you've read a few of the following transaction analyses, don't do it. Each has something unique to teach, something you'll need later. (We assure you that we've kept them to the minimum needed!)

EVENT (1). INVESTMENT OF CASH BY STOCKHOLDERS. On October 1 cash of $10,000 is invested in the business by investors in exchange for $10,000 of common stock. This event is an accounting transaction because it results in an increase in both assets and stockholders' equity. There is an increase of $10,000 in the asset Cash and an increase of $10,000 in Common Stock on the books of Sierra Corporation. The effect of this transaction on the accounting equation is:

	Assets	=	Liabilities	+	Stockholders' Equity	
	Cash	=			Common Stock	
(1)	+$10,000	=			+$10,000	Issued stock

The equation is in balance after the issuance of common stock. Keeping track of the source of each change in stockholders' equity is essential for later accounting activities. In particular, items recorded in the revenue and expense columns are used for the calculation of net income.

EVENT (2). NOTE ISSUED IN EXCHANGE FOR CASH. On October 1 Sierra borrowed $5,000 from Castle Bank by signing a 3-month, 12%, $5,000 note payable. This transaction results in an equal increase in assets and liabilities: Cash (an asset) increases $5,000, and Notes Payable (a liability) increases $5,000. The specific effect of this transaction and the cumulative effect of the first two transactions are:

	Assets	=	Liabilities	+	Stockholders' Equity
	Cash	=	Notes Payable	+	Common Stock
	$10,000				$10,000
(2)	+5,000		+$5,000		
	$15,000	=	$5,000	+	$10,000
			$15,000		

Total assets are now $15,000, and stockholders' equity plus the new liability also total $15,000.

EVENT (3). PURCHASE OF OFFICE EQUIPMENT FOR CASH. On October 2 Sierra purchased office equipment by paying $5,000 cash to Superior Equipment Sales Co. This event is a transaction because an equal increase and decrease in Sierra's assets occur: Office Equipment (an asset) increases $5,000, and Cash (an asset) decreases $5,000.

	Assets			=	Liabilities	+	Stockholders' Equity
	Cash	+	Office Equipment	=	N/P	+	Common Stock
	$15,000				$5,000		$10,000
(3)	−5,000		+$5,000				
	$10,000	+	$5,000	=	$5,000	+	$10,000
	$15,000				$15,000		

The total assets are now $15,000, and stockholders' equity plus the liability also total $15,000.

EVENT (4). RECEIPT OF CASH IN ADVANCE FROM CUSTOMER. On October 2 Sierra received a $1,200 cash advance from R. Knox, a client. This event is a transaction because Sierra received cash (an asset) for advertising services that are expected to be completed by Sierra in the future. Although Sierra received cash, **it does not record revenue until it has performed the work**. In some industries, such as the magazine and airline industries, customers are expected to prepay. These companies have a liability to the customer until they deliver the magazines or provide the flight. When the company eventually provides the product or service, it records the revenue.

Since Sierra received cash prior to performance of the service, Sierra has a liability for the work due. Cash increases by $1,200, and a liability, Unearned Service Revenue, increases by an equal amount.

	Assets		=	Liabilities		+	Stockholders' Equity
	Cash	+ Office Equip.	=	N/P	+ Unearned Service Revenue	+	Common Stock
	$10,000	$5,000		$5,000			$10,000
(4)	+1,200				+$1,200		
	$11,200	+ $5,000	=	$5,000	+ $1,200	+	$10,000

EVENT (5). SERVICES PROVIDED FOR CASH. On October 3 Sierra received $10,000 in cash from Copa Company for advertising services performed. This event is a transaction because Sierra received an asset (cash) in exchange for services.

Advertising service is the principal revenue-producing activity of Sierra. **Revenue increases stockholders' equity.** This transaction, then, increases both assets and stockholders' equity. Cash is increased $10,000, and revenues (specifically, Service Revenue) is increased $10,000. The new balances in the equation are:

	Assets		=	Liabilities		+	Stockholders' Equity				
								Retained Earnings			
	Cash	+ Office Equip.	=	N/P	+ Unearned Serv. Rev.	+	Common Stock	+ Rev.	− Exp.	− Div.	
	$11,200	$5,000		$5,000	$1,200		$10,000				
(5)	+10,000							+$10,000			Service Revenue
	$21,200	+ $5,000	=	$5,000	+ $1,200	+	$10,000	+ $10,000			
	$26,200						$26,200				

Often companies provide services "on account." That is, they provide service for which they are paid at a later date. Revenue, however, is earned when services are performed. Therefore, revenues would increase when services are performed, even though cash has not been received. Instead of receiving cash, the company receives a different type of asset, an **account receivable**. Accounts receivable represent the right to receive payment at a later date. Suppose that Sierra had provided these services on account rather than for cash. This event would be reported using the accounting equation as:

Assets	=	Liabilities	+	Stockholders' Equity	
Accounts Receivable	=			Revenues	
+$10,000				+$10,000	Service Revenue

Later, when Sierra collects the $10,000 from the customer, Accounts Receivable declines by $10,000, and Cash increases by $10,000.

Assets		=	Liabilities	+	Stockholders' Equity
Cash	Accounts Receivable				
+$10,000	−$10,000				

Note that in this case, revenues is not affected by the collection of cash. Instead we record an exchange of one asset (Accounts Receivable) for a different asset (Cash).

EVENT (6). PAYMENT OF RENT. On October 3 Sierra Corporation paid its office rent for the month of October in cash, $900. This rent payment is a transaction because it results in a decrease in an asset, cash.

Rent is an expense incurred by Sierra Corporation in its effort to generate revenues. **Expenses decrease stockholders' equity.** Sierra records the rent payment by decreasing cash and increasing expenses to maintain the balance of the accounting equation. To record this transaction, Sierra decreases Cash $900, and increases expense (specifically, Rent Expense) $900. The effect of this payment on the accounting equation is:

	Assets			=	Liabilities			+	Stockholders' Equity							
											Retained Earnings					
	Cash	+	Office Equip.	=	N/P	+	Unearned Serv. Rev.	+	Common Stock	+	Rev.	−	Exp.	−	Div.	
	$21,200		$5,000		$5,000		$1,200		$10,000		$10,000					
(6)	−900												−$900			Rent Expense
	$20,300	+	$5,000	=	$5,000	+	$1,200	+	$10,000	+	$10,000	−	$900			
	$25,300				$25,300											

EVENT (7). PURCHASE OF INSURANCE POLICY FOR CASH. On October 4 Sierra paid $600 for a one-year insurance policy that will expire next year on September 30. In this transaction the asset Cash is decreased $600. Payments of expenses that will benefit more than one accounting period are identified as assets called prepaid expenses or prepayments. Therefore the asset Prepaid Insurance is increased $600. The balance in total assets did not change; one asset account decreased by the same amount that another increased.

	Assets					=	Liabilities			+	Stockholders' Equity						
													Retained Earnings				
	Cash	+	Prepaid Insurance	+	Office Equip.	=	N/P	+	Unearned Serv. Rev.	+	Common Stock	+	Rev.	−	Exp.	−	Div.
	$20,300				$5,000		$5,000		$1,200		$10,000		$10,000		$900		
(7)	−600		+$600														
	$19,700	+	$600	+	$5,000	=	$5,000	+	$1,200	+	$10,000	+	$10,000	−	$900		
	$25,300						$25,300										

EVENT (8). PURCHASE OF SUPPLIES ON ACCOUNT. On October 5 Sierra purchased a three-month supply of advertising materials on account from Aero Supply for $2,500. In this case, "on account" means that the company receives goods or services that it will pay for at a later date. Supplies, an asset, increases $2,500 by this transaction. Accounts Payable, a liability, increases $2,500, to indicate the amount due to Aero Supply. The effect on the equation is:

	Assets							=	Liabilities					+	Stockholders' Equity						
																	Retained Earnings				
	Cash	+	Supplies	+	Prepd. Insur.	+	Office Equip.	=	N/P	+	Accounts Payable	+	Unearned Serv. Rev.	+	Common Stock	+	Rev.	−	Exp.	−	Div.
	$19,700				$600		$5,000		$5,000				$1,200		$10,000		$10,000		$900		
(8)			+$2,500								+$2,500										
	$19,700	+	$2,500	+	$600	+	$5,000	=	$5,000	+	$2,500	+	$1,200	+	$10,000	+	$10,000	−	$900		
	$27,800								$27,800												

EVENT (9). HIRING OF NEW EMPLOYEES. On October 9 Sierra hired four new employees to begin work on October 15. Each employee will receive a weekly salary of $500 for a five-day work week, payable every two weeks. Employees will receive their first paychecks on October 26. On the date Sierra hires the employees, there is no effect on the accounting equation because the assets, liabilities, and stockholders' equity of the company have not changed. **An accounting transaction has not occurred.** At this point there is only an agreement that the employees will begin work on October 15. [See Event (11) for the first payment.]

EVENT (10). PAYMENT OF DIVIDEND. On October 20 Sierra paid a $500 dividend. **Dividends** are a reduction of stockholders' equity but not an expense. Dividends are not included in the calculation of net income. Instead, a dividend is a distribution of the company's assets to its stockholders. This dividend transaction affects assets (Cash) and stockholders' equity (Dividends) by $500.

	Assets				=	Liabilities			+	Stockholders' Equity			
											Retained Earnings		
	Cash	+ Supp.	+ Prepd. Insur.	+ Office Equip.	=	N/P	+ A/P	+ Unearned Serv. Rev.	+	Common Stock	+ Rev.	− Exp.	− Div.
	$19,700	$2,500	$600	$5,000		$5,000	$2,500	$1,200		$10,000	$10,000	$900	
(10)	−500												− $500
	$19,200	+ $2,500	+ $600	+ $5,000	=	$5,000	+ $2,500	+ $1,200	+	$10,000	+ $10,000	− $900	− $500
	$27,300									$27,300			

EVENT (11). PAYMENT OF CASH FOR EMPLOYEE SALARIES. Employees have worked two weeks, earning $4,000 in salaries, which were paid on October 26. Salaries are an expense which reduce stockholders' equity. This event is a transaction because assets and stockholders' equity are affected. Thus, Cash is decreased $4,000 and expenses (specifically, Salaries Expense) is increased $4,000.

Investor Insight

While most companies record transactions very carefully, the reality is that mistakes still happen. For example, bank regulators fined Bank One Corporation (now Chase) $1.8 million because they felt that the unreliability of the bank's accounting system caused it to violate regulatory requirements.

Also, in recent years Fannie Mae, the government-chartered mortgage association, announced a series of large accounting errors. These announcements caused alarm among investors, regulators, and politicians because they fear that the errors may suggest larger, undetected problems. This is important because the home-mortgage market depends on Fannie Mae to buy hundreds of billions of dollars of mortgages each year from banks, thus enabling the banks to issue new mortgages.

Finally, before a major overhaul of its accounting system, the financial records of Waste Management Company were in such disarray that of the company's 57,000 employees, 10,000 were receiving pay slips that were in error.

The Sarbanes-Oxley Act of 2002 was created to minimize the occurrence of errors like these by increasing every employee's responsibility for accurate financial reporting.

? In order for these companies to prepare and issue financial statements, their accounting equations (debits and credits) must have been in balance at year-end. How could these errors or misstatements have occurred?

	Assets				=	Liabilities			+	Stockholders' Equity				
											Retained Earnings			
	Cash	+ Supp.	+ Prepd. Insur.	+ Office Equip.	=	N/P	+ A/P	+ Unearned Serv. Rev.	+	Common Stock	+ Rev.	− Exp.	− Div.	
	$19,200	$2,500	$600	$5,000		$5,000	$2,500	$1,200		$10,000	$10,000	$ 900	$500	
(11)	−4,000											− 4,000		Salaries
	$15,200 +	$2,500 +	$600 +	$5,000	=	$5,000 +	$2,500 +	$1,200	+	$10,000	+ $10,000	− $4,900	− $500	Expenses
	$23,300									$23,300				

SUMMARY OF TRANSACTIONS

Illustration 3-3 summarizes the transactions of Sierra Corporation to show their cumulative effect on the basic accounting equation. It includes the transaction number in the first column on the left. The right-most column shows the specific effect of any transaction that affects stockholders' equity. Remember that Event (9) did not result in a transaction, so no entry is included for that event. The illustration demonstrates three important points:

1. Each transaction is analyzed in terms of its effect on assets, liabilities, and stockholders' equity.
2. The two sides of the equation must always be equal.
3. The cause of each change in stockholders' equity must be indicated.

Illustration 3-3 Summary of transactions

	Assets				=	Liabilities			+	Stockholders' Equity				
											Retained Earnings			
	Cash	+ Supp.	+ Prepd. Insur.	+ Office Equip.	=	N/P	+ A/P	+ Unearned Serv. Rev.	+	Common Stock	+ Rev.	− Exp.	− Div.	
(1)	+$10,000				=					+$10,000				Issued stock
(2)	+5,000					+$5,000								
(3)	−5,000			+$5,000										
(4)	+1,200							+$1,200						
(5)	+10,000										+$10,000			Service Revenue
(6)	−900											−$ 900		Rent Expense
(7)	−600		+$600											
(8)		+$2,500					+ $2,500							
(10)	−500												−$500	Dividends
(11)	−4,000											−4,000		Salaries Expense
	$15,200 +	$2,500 +	$600 +	$5,000	=	$5,000 +	$2,500 +	$1,200	+	$10,000	+ $10,000	− $4,900	− $500	
	$23,300									$23,300				

DECISION TOOLKIT

DECISION CHECKPOINTS	INFO NEEDED FOR DECISION	TOOL TO USE FOR DECISION	HOW TO EVALUATE RESULTS
Has an accounting transaction occurred?	Details of the event	Accounting equation	If the event affected assets, liabilities, or stockholders' equity, then record as a transaction.

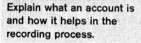

before you go on...

TRANSACTION ANALYSIS

Do it! A tabular analysis of the transactions made by Roberta Mendez & Co., a certified public accounting firm, for the month of August is shown below. Each increase and decrease in stockholders' equity is explained.

	Assets			=	Liabilities	+	Stockholders' Equity					
									Retained Earnings			
	Cash	+	Office Equipment	=	Accounts Payable	+	Common Stock	+	Revenue	−	Expenses	
1.	+$25,000						+$25,000					Issued Stock
2.			+$7,000	=	+$7,000							
3.	+8,000								+$8,000			Service Revenue
4.	−850										−$850	Rent Expense
	$32,150	+	$7,000	=	$7,000	+	$25,000	+	$8,000	−	$850	
	$39,150						$39,150					

Action Plan

- Analyze the tabular analysis to determine the nature and effect of each transaction.
- Keep the accounting equation in balance.
- Remember that a change in an asset will require a change in another asset, a liability, or in stockholders' equity.

Describe each transaction that occurred for the month.

Solution

1. The company issued shares of stock to stockholders for $25,000 cash.
2. The company purchased $7,000 of office equipment on account.
3. The company received $8,000 of cash in exchange for services performed.
4. The company paid $850 for this month's rent.

The Account

study objective 2

Explain what an account is and how it helps in the recording process.

Rather than using a tabular summary like the one in Illustration 3-3 for Sierra Corporation, an accounting information system uses accounts. An **account** is an individual accounting record of increases and decreases in a specific asset, liability, stockholders' equity, revenue, or expense item. For example, Sierra Corporation has separate accounts for Cash, Accounts Receivable, Accounts Payable, Service Revenue, Salaries Expense, and so on. (Note that whenever we are referring to a specific account, we capitalize the name.)

In its simplest form, an account consists of three parts: (1) the title of the account, (2) a left or debit side, and (3) a right or credit side. Because the alignment of these parts of an account resembles the letter T, it is referred to as a **T account**. The basic form of an account is shown in Illustration 3-4.

Illustration 3-4 Basic form of account

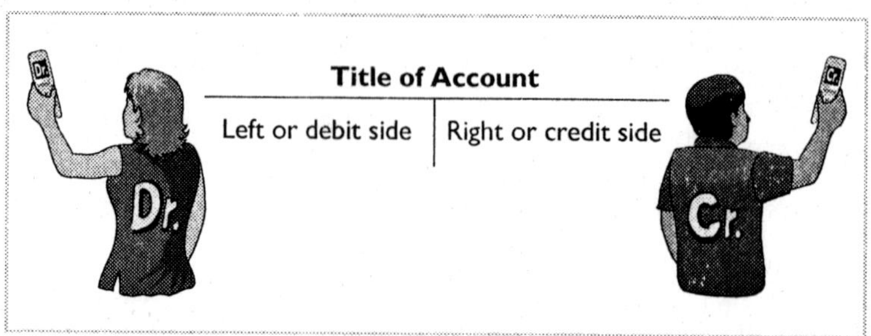

We use this form of account often throughout this book to explain basic accounting relationships.

DEBITS AND CREDITS

study objective 3

Define debits and credits and explain how they are used to record business transactions.

The term **debit** indicates the left side of an account, and **credit** indicates the right side. They are commonly abbreviated as **Dr.** for debit and **Cr.** for credit. They **do not** mean increase or decrease, as is commonly thought. We use the terms *debit* and *credit* repeatedly in the recording process to describe **where** entries are made in accounts. For example, the act of entering an amount on the left side of an account is called **debiting** the account. Making an entry on the right side is **crediting** the account.

When comparing the totals of the two sides, an account shows a **debit balance** if the total of the debit amounts exceeds the credits. An account shows a **credit balance** if the credit amounts exceed the debits. Note the position of the debit side and credit side in Illustration 3-4.

The procedure of recording debits and credits in an account is shown in Illustration 3-5 for the transactions affecting the Cash account of Sierra Corporation. The data are taken from the Cash column of the tabular summary in Illustration 3-3.

Illustration 3-5 Tabular summary and account form for Sierra Corporation's Cash account

Tabular Summary

Cash
$10,000
5,000
−5,000
1,200
10,000
−900
−600
−500
−4,000
$15,200

Account Form

	Cash		
(Debits)	10,000	(Credits)	5,000
	5,000		900
	1,200		600
	10,000		500
			4,000
Balance (Debit)	15,200		

Every positive item in the tabular summary represents a receipt of cash; every negative amount represents a payment of cash. **Notice that in the account form we record the increases in cash as debits, and the decreases in cash as credits.** For example, the $10,000 receipt of cash (in red) is debited to Cash, and the −$5,000 payment of cash (in blue) is credited to Cash.

Having increases on one side and decreases on the other reduces recording errors and helps in determining the totals of each side of the account as well as the account balance. The balance is determined by netting the two sides (subtracting one amount from the other). The account balance, a debit of $15,200, indicates that Sierra had $15,200 more increases than decreases in cash. That is, since it started with a balance of zero, it has $15,200 in its Cash account.

DEBIT AND CREDIT PROCEDURES

International Note Rules for accounting for specific events sometimes differ across countries. For example, European companies rely less on historical cost and more on fair value than U.S. companies. Despite the differences, the double-entry accounting system is the basis of accounting systems worldwide.

Each transaction must affect two or more accounts to keep the basic accounting equation in balance. In other words, **for each transaction, debits must equal credits**. The equality of debits and credits provides the basis for the double-entry accounting system.

Under the **double-entry system**, the two-sided effect of each transaction is recorded in appropriate accounts. This system provides a logical method for recording transactions. The double-entry system also helps to ensure the accuracy of the recorded amounts and helps to detect errors such as those at Fidelity Investments as discussed in the Feature Story. If every transaction is recorded with equal debits and credits, then the sum of all the debits to the accounts must equal the sum of all the credits. The double-entry system for determining the equality of the accounting equation is much more efficient than the plus/minus procedure used earlier.

Dr./Cr. Procedures for Assets and Liabilities

In Illustration 3-5 for Sierra Corporation, increases in Cash—an asset—were entered on the left side, and decreases in Cash were entered on the right side. We know that both sides of the basic equation (Assets = Liabilities + Stockholders' Equity) must be equal. It therefore follows that increases and decreases in liabilities will have to be recorded *opposite from* increases and decreases in assets. Thus, increases in liabilities must be entered on the right or credit side, and decreases in liabilities must be entered on the left or debit side. The effects that debits and credits have on assets and liabilities are summarized in Illustration 3-6.

Illustration 3-6 Debit and credit effects–assets and liabilities

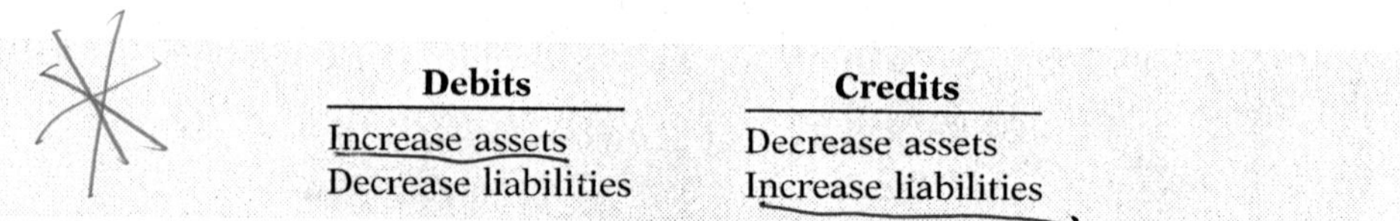

Debits	Credits
Increase assets	Decrease assets
Decrease liabilities	Increase liabilities

Asset accounts normally show debit balances. That is, debits to a specific asset account should exceed credits to that account. Likewise, **liability accounts normally show credit balances**. That is, credits to a liability account should exceed debits to that account. The **normal balances** may be diagrammed as in Illustration 3-7.

Illustration 3-7 Normal balances–assets and liabilities

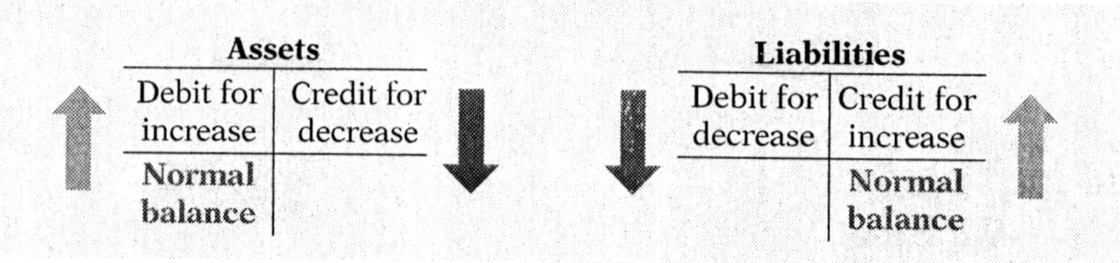

Helpful Hint The normal balance is the side where increases in the account are recorded.

Knowing which is the normal balance in an account may help when you are trying to identify errors. For example, a credit balance in an asset account such as Land or a debit balance in a liability account such as Wages Payable usually indicates errors in recording. Occasionally, however, an abnormal balance may be correct. The Cash account, for example, will have a credit balance when a company has overdrawn its bank balance (written a check that "bounced"). In automated accounting systems, the computer is programmed to flag violations of the normal balance and to print out error or exception reports. In manual systems, careful visual inspection of the accounts is required to detect normal balance problems.

Dr./Cr. Procedures for Stockholders' Equity

In Chapter 1 we indicated that stockholders' equity is comprised of two parts: common stock and retained earnings. In the transaction events earlier in this chapter, you saw that revenues, expenses, and the payment of dividends affect retained earnings. Therefore, the subdivisions of stockholders' equity are: common stock, retained earnings, dividends, revenues, and expenses.

COMMON STOCK. Common stock is issued to investors in exchange for the stockholders' investment. The Common Stock account is increased by credits and decreased by debits. For example, when cash is invested in the business, Cash is debited and Common Stock is credited. The effects of debits and credits on the Common Stock account are shown in Illustration 3-8.

Debits	Credits
Decrease Common Stock	Increase Common Stock

Illustration 3-8 Debit and credit effects–Common Stock

The normal balance in the Common Stock account may be diagrammed as in Illustration 3-9.

Common Stock	
Debit for decrease	Credit for increase
	Normal balance

Illustration 3-9 Normal balance–Common Stock

RETAINED EARNINGS. Retained earnings is net income that is retained in the business. It represents the portion of stockholders' equity that has been accumulated through the profitable operation of the company. Retained Earnings is increased by credits (for example, by net income) and decreased by debits (for example, by a net loss), as shown in Illustration 3-10.

Debits	Credits
Decrease Retained Earnings	Increase Retained Earnings

Illustration 3-10 Debit and credit effects–Retained Earnings

The normal balance for Retained Earnings may be diagrammed as in Illustration 3-11.

Retained Earnings	
Debit for decrease	Credit for increase
	Normal balance

Illustration 3-11 Normal balance–Retained Earnings

DIVIDENDS. A dividend is a distribution by a corporation to its stockholders. The most common form of distribution is a cash dividend. Dividends result in a reduction of the stockholders' claims on retained earnings. Because dividends reduce stockholders' equity, increases in the Dividends account are recorded with debits. As shown in Illustration 3-12, the Dividends account normally has a debit balance.

Dividends	
Debit for increase	Credit for decrease
Normal balance	

Illustration 3-12 Normal balance–Dividends

REVENUES AND EXPENSES. When a company earns revenues, stockholders' equity is increased. Revenue accounts are increased by credits and decreased by debits.

Expenses decrease stockholders' equity. Thus, expense accounts are increased by debits and decreased by credits. The effects of debits and credits on revenues and expenses are shown in Illustration 3-13.

Illustration 3-13 Debit and credit effects–revenues and expenses

Debits	Credits
Decrease revenue	Increase revenue
Increase expenses	Decrease expenses

Credits to revenue accounts should exceed debits; debits to expense accounts should exceed credits. Thus, **revenue accounts normally show credit balances, and expense accounts normally show debit balances**. The normal balances may be diagrammed as in Illustration 3-14.

Illustration 3-14 Normal balances–revenues and expenses

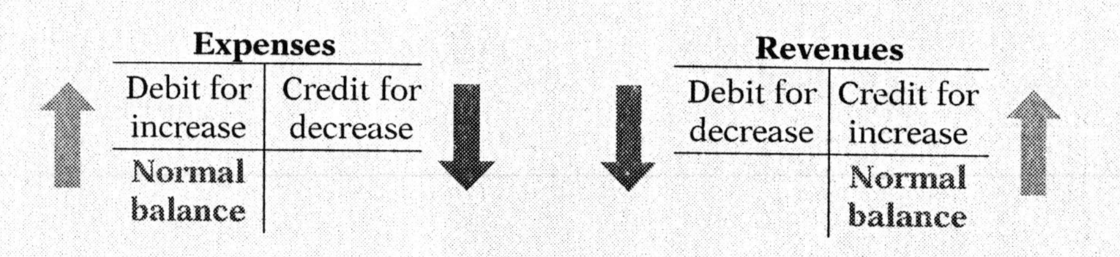

Investor Insight

The Chicago Cubs baseball team has these major revenue and expense accounts:

Revenues	Expenses
Admissions (ticket sales)	Players' salaries
Concessions	Administrative salaries
Television and radio	Travel
Advertising	Ballpark maintenance

 Do you think that the Chicago Bears football team would be likely to have the same major revenue and expense accounts as the Cubs?

STOCKHOLDERS' EQUITY RELATIONSHIPS

Companies report the subdivisions of stockholders' equity in various places in the financial statements:

- Common stock and retained earnings: in the stockholders' equity section of the balance sheet.
- Dividends: on the retained earnings statement.
- Revenues and expenses: on the income statement.

Dividends, revenues, and expenses are eventually transferred to retained earnings at the end of the period. As a result, a change in any one of these three items affects stockholders' equity. Illustration 3-15 shows the relationships of the accounts affecting stockholders' equity.

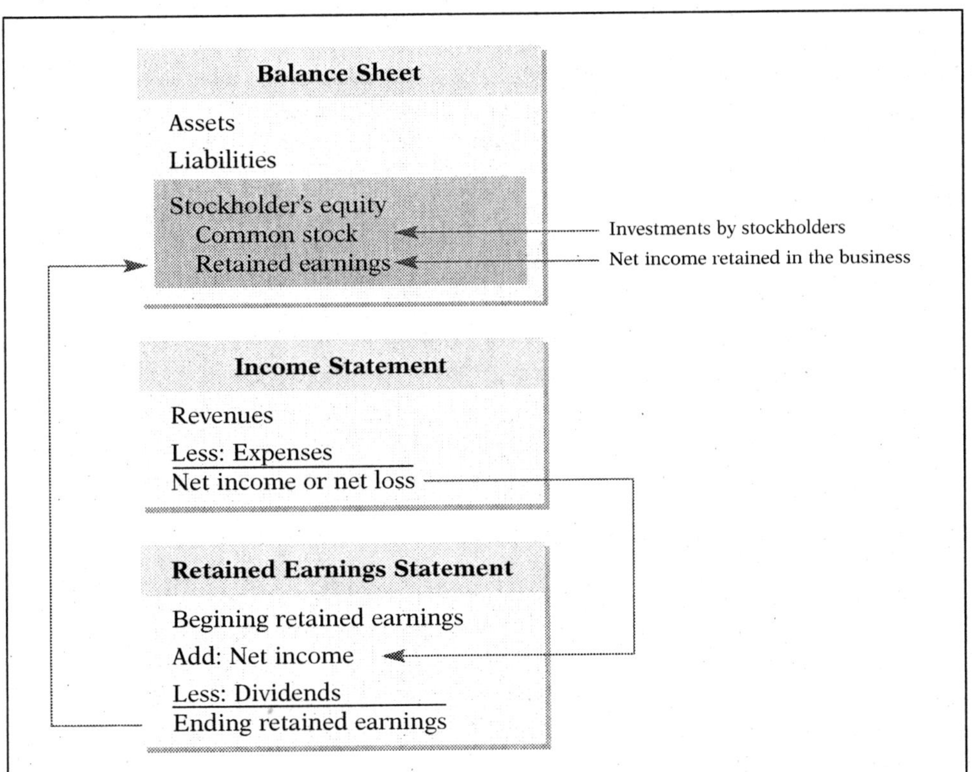

Illustration 3-15 Stockholders' equity relationships

SUMMARY OF DEBIT/CREDIT RULES

Illustration 3-16 summarizes the debit/credit rules and effects on each type of account. **Study this diagram carefully.** It will help you understand the fundamentals of the double-entry system. No matter what the transaction, total debits must equal total credits in order to keep the accounting equation in balance.

Illustration 3-16 Summary of debit/credit rules

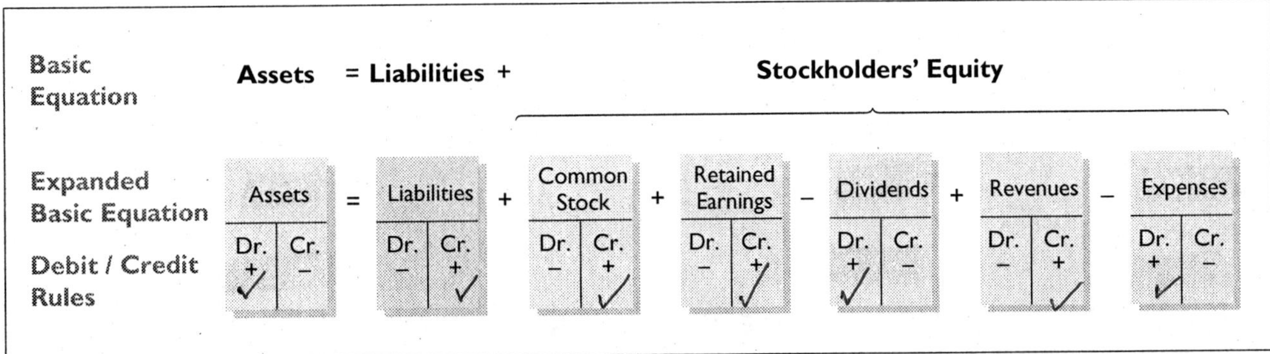

before you go on...

Do it! Kate Browne, president of Hair It Is Inc., has just rented space in a shopping mall for the purpose of opening and operating a beauty salon. Long before opening day and before purchasing equipment, hiring assistants, and remodeling the space, Kate was strongly advised to set up a double-entry set of accounting records in which to record all of her business transactions.

Identify the balance sheet accounts that Hair It Is Inc. will likely need to record the transactions necessary to establish and open for business. Also, indicate whether the normal balance of each account is a debit or a credit.

DEBITS AND CREDITS FOR BALANCE SHEET ACCOUNTS

Action Plan

- First identify asset accounts for each different type of asset invested in the business.

Action Plan (cont.)

- Then identify liability accounts for debts incurred by the business.
- Remember that Hair It Is Inc. will need only one stockholders' equity account for common stock when it begins the business. The other stockholders' equity accounts will be needed only after the business is operating.

Solution

Hair It Is Inc. would likely need the following accounts in which to record the transactions necessary to establish and ready the beauty salon for opening day: Cash (debit balance); Equipment (debit balance); Supplies (debit balance); Accounts Payable (credit balance); Notes Payable (credit balance), if the business borrows money; and Common Stock (credit balance).

study objective  4

Identify the basic steps in the recording process.

Steps in the Recording Process

Although it is possible to enter transaction information directly into the accounts, few businesses do so. Practically every business uses these basic steps in the recording process:

1. Analyze each transaction in terms of its effect on the accounts.
2. Enter the transaction information in a journal.
3. Transfer the journal information to the appropriate accounts in the ledger (book of accounts).

The actual sequence of events begins with the transaction. Evidence of the transaction comes in the form of a **source document**, such as a sales slip, a check, a bill, or a cash register tape. This evidence is analyzed to determine the effect of the transaction on specific accounts. The transaction is then entered in the **journal**. Finally, the journal entry is transferred to the designated accounts in the **ledger**. The sequence of events in the recording process is shown in Illustration 3-17.

Ethics Note Business documents provide evidence that transactions actually occurred. International Outsourcing Services, LLC, was accused of submitting fraudulent documents (store coupons) to companies such as Kraft Foods and PepsiCo for reimbursement of as much as $250 million. Ensuring that all recorded transactions are backed up by proper business documents reduces the likelihood of fraudulent activity.

Illustration 3-17 The recording process

The Recording Process

Analyze each transaction

Enter transaction in a journal

Transfer journal information to ledger accounts

study objective  5

Explain what a journal is and how it helps in the recording process.

THE JOURNAL

Transactions are initially recorded in chronological order in **journals** before they are transferred to the accounts. For each transaction the journal shows the debit and credit effects on specific accounts. (In a computerized system, journals are kept as files, and accounts are recorded in computer databases.)

Companies may use various kinds of journals, but every company has at least the most basic form of journal, a general journal. **The journal makes three significant contributions to the recording process:**

1. It discloses in one place the **complete effect of a transaction**.
2. It provides a **chronological record** of transactions.
3. It **helps to prevent or locate errors** because the debit and credit amounts for each entry can be readily compared.

Entering transaction data in the journal is known as journalizing. To illustrate the technique of journalizing, let's look at the first three transactions of Sierra Corporation in equation form.

On October 1, Sierra issued common stock in exchange for $10,000 cash:

Assets	=	**Liabilities** +	**Stockholders' Equity**	
Cash	=		Common Stock	
+$10,000			+$10,000	Issued stock

On October 1, Sierra borrowed $5,000 by signing a note:

Assets	=	**Liabilities** +	**Stockholders' Equity**
Cash	=	Notes Payable	
+$5,000		+$5,000	

On October 2, Sierra purchased office equipment for $5,000:

Assets		=	**Liabilities**	+	**Stockholders' Equity**
Cash	Office Equipment				
−$5,000	+$5,000				

Sierra makes separate journal entries for each transaction. A complete entry consists of: (1) the date of the transaction, (2) the accounts and amounts to be debited and credited, and (3) a brief explanation of the transaction. These transactions are journalized in Illustration 3-18 (on page 118).

Note the following features of the journal entries.

1. The date of the transaction is entered in the Date column.
2. The account to be debited is entered first at the left. The account to be credited is then entered on the next line, indented under the line above. The indentation differentiates debits from credits and decreases the possibility of switching the debit and credit amounts.
3. The amounts for the debits are recorded in the Debit (left) column, and the amounts for the credits are recorded in the Credit (right) column.
4. A brief explanation of the transaction is given.

Illustration 3-18
Recording transactions in journal form

GENERAL JOURNAL

Date		Account Titles and Explanation	Debit	Credit
2010				
Oct.	1	Cash	10,000	
		Common Stock		10,000
		(Issued stock for cash)		
	1	Cash	5,000	
		Notes Payable		5,000
		(Issued 3-month, 12% note payable for cash)		
	2	Office Equipment	5,000	
		Cash		5,000
		(Purchased office equipment for cash)		

It is important to use correct and specific account titles in journalizing. Erroneous account titles lead to incorrect financial statements. Some flexibility exists initially in selecting account titles. The main criterion is that each title must appropriately describe the content of the account. For example, a company could use any of these account titles for recording the cost of delivery trucks: Delivery Equipment, Delivery Trucks, or Trucks. Once the company chooses the specific title to use, however, it should record under that account title all subsequent transactions involving the account.

Accounting Across the Organization

Bryan Lee is head of finance at Microsoft's Home and Entertainment Division. In recent years the division lost over $4 billion, mostly due to losses on the original Xbox videogame player. With the Xbox 360 videogame player, Mr. Lee hoped the division would become profitable. He set strict goals for sales, revenue, and profit. "A manager seeking to spend more on a feature such as a disk drive has to find allies in the group to cut spending elsewhere, or identify new revenue to offset the increase," he explains.

For example, Microsoft originally designed the new Xbox to have 256 megabytes of memory. But the design department said that amount of memory wouldn't support the best special effects. The purchasing department said that adding more memory would cost $30–which was 10% of the estimated selling price of $300. But the marketing department "determined that adding the memory would let Microsoft reduce marketing costs and attract more game developers, boosting royalty revenue. It would also extend the life of the console, generating more sales." Microsoft doubled the memory to 512 megabytes.

Source: Robert A. Guth, "New Xbox Aim for Microsoft: Profitability," *Wall Street Journal*, May 24, 2005, p. C1.

? In what ways is this Microsoft division using accounting to assist in its effort to become more profitable?

before you go on...

JOURNAL ENTRIES

Do it! The following events occurred during the first month of business of Hair It Is Inc., Kate Browne's beauty salon:

1. Issued common stock to shareholders in exchange for $20,000 cash.
2. Purchased $4,800 of equipment on account (to be paid in 30 days).
3. Interviewed three people for the position of beautician.

In what form (type of record) should the company record these three activities? Prepare the entries to record the transactions.

Solution

Each transaction that is recorded is entered in the general journal. The three activities are recorded as follows.

1. Cash	20,000	
Common Stock		20,000
(Issued stock for cash)		
2. Equipment	4,800	
Accounts Payable		4,800
(Purchased equipment on account)		
3. No entry because no transaction occurred.		

Action Plan

- Record the transactions in a journal, which is a chronological record of the transactions.
- Make sure to provide a complete and accurate representation of the transactions' effects on the assets, liabilities, and stockholders' equity of the business.

THE LEDGER

Explain what a ledger is and how it helps in the recording process.

The entire group of accounts maintained by a company is referred to collectively as the **ledger**. The ledger keeps in one place all the information about changes in specific account balances.

Companies may use various kinds of ledgers, but every company has a general ledger. A **general ledger** contains all the assets, liabilities, stockholders' equity, revenue, and expense accounts, as shown in Illustration 3-19. Whenever we use the term *ledger* in this textbook without additional specification, it will mean the general ledger.

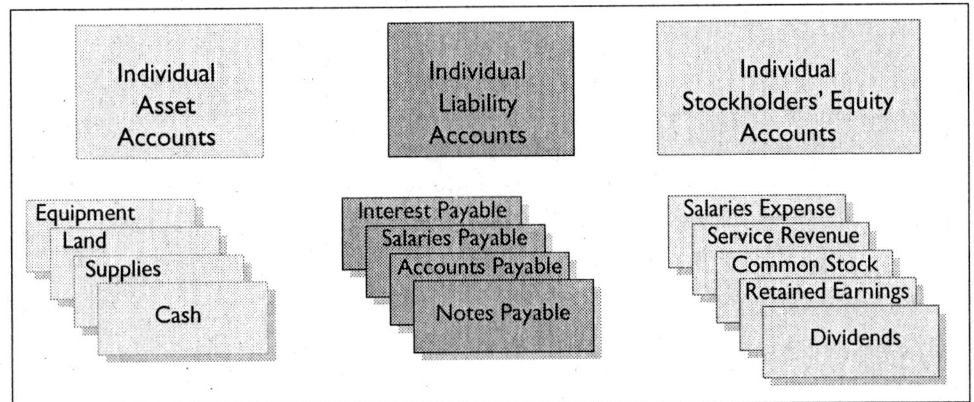

Illustration 3-19 The general ledger

CHART OF ACCOUNTS

The number and type of accounts used differ for each company, depending on the size, complexity, and type of business. For example, the number of accounts depends on the amount of detail desired by management. The management of one company may want one single account for all types of utility expense.

Another may keep separate expense accounts for each type of utility expenditure, such as gas, electricity, and water. A small corporation like Sierra Corporation will not have many accounts compared with a corporate giant like Ford Motor Company. Sierra may be able to manage and report its activities in 20 to 30 accounts, whereas Ford requires thousands of accounts to keep track of its worldwide activities.

Most companies list the accounts in a chart of accounts. They may create new accounts as needed during the life of the business. Illustration 3-20 shows the chart of accounts for Sierra Corporation in the order that they are typically listed (assets, liabilities, stockholders' equity, revenues, and expenses). **Accounts shown in red are used in this chapter**; accounts shown in black are explained in later chapters.

Illustration 3-20 Chart of accounts for Sierra Corporation

SIERRA CORPORATION—CHART OF ACCOUNTS

Assets	Liabilities	Stockholders' Equity	Revenues	Expenses
Cash	Notes Payable	Common Stock	Service Revenue	Salaries Expense
Accounts Receivable	Accounts Payable	Retained Earnings		Supplies Expense
Advertising Supplies	Interest Payable	Dividends		Rent Expense
Prepaid Insurance	Unearned Service Revenue	Income Summary		Insurance Expense
Office Equipment	Salaries Payable			Interest Expense
Accumulated Depreciation—Office Equipment				Depreciation Expense

POSTING

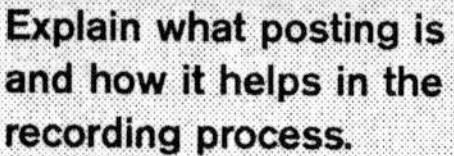

Explain what posting is and how it helps in the recording process.

The procedure of transferring journal entry amounts to ledger accounts is called posting. **This phase of the recording process accumulates the effects of journalized transactions in the individual accounts.** Posting involves these steps:

1. In the ledger, enter in the appropriate columns of the debited account(s) the date and debit amount shown in the journal.
2. In the ledger, enter in the appropriate columns of the credited account(s) the date and credit amount shown in the journal.

The Recording Process Illustrated

Illustrations 3-21 through 3-31 on the following pages show the basic steps in the recording process using the October transactions of Sierra Corporation. Sierra's accounting period is a month. A basic analysis and a debit–credit analysis precede the journalizing and posting of each transaction. Study these transaction analyses carefully. **The purpose of transaction analysis is first to identify the type of account involved and then to determine whether a debit or a credit to the account is required.** You should always perform this type of analysis before preparing a journal entry. Doing so will help you understand the journal entries discussed in this chapter as well as more complex journal entries to be described in later chapters.

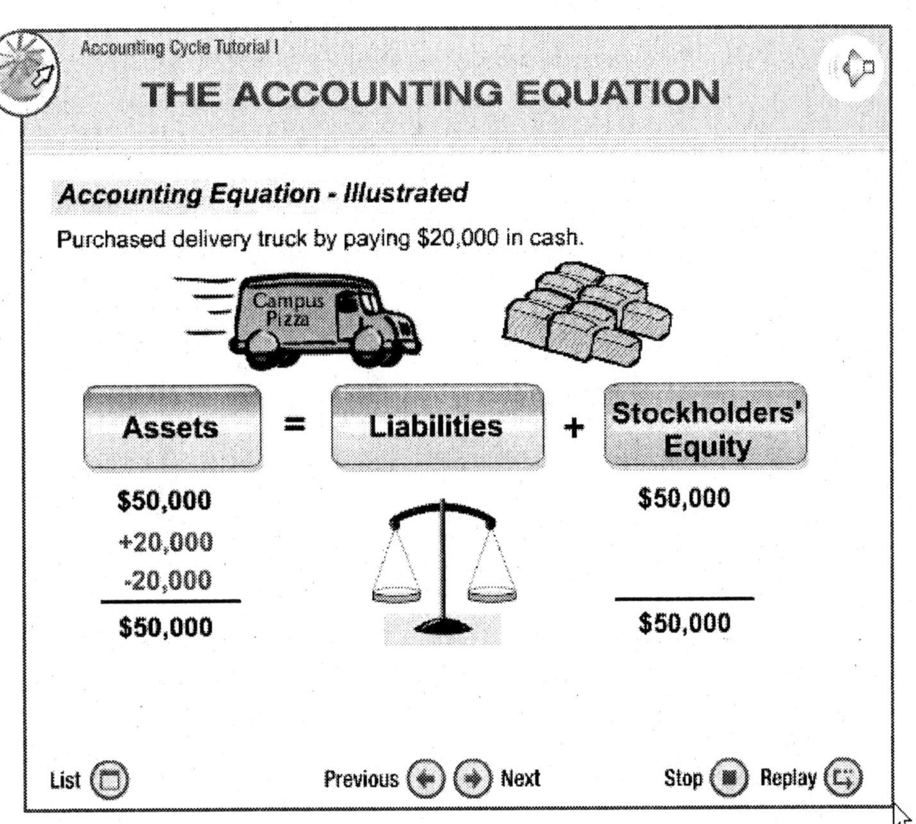

Accounting Cycle Tutorial

The diagrams in Illustrations 3-21 to 3-31 review the accounting cycle. If you would like additional practice, an Accounting Cycle Tutorial is available on WileyPLUS. The illustration to the left is an example of a screen from the tutorial.

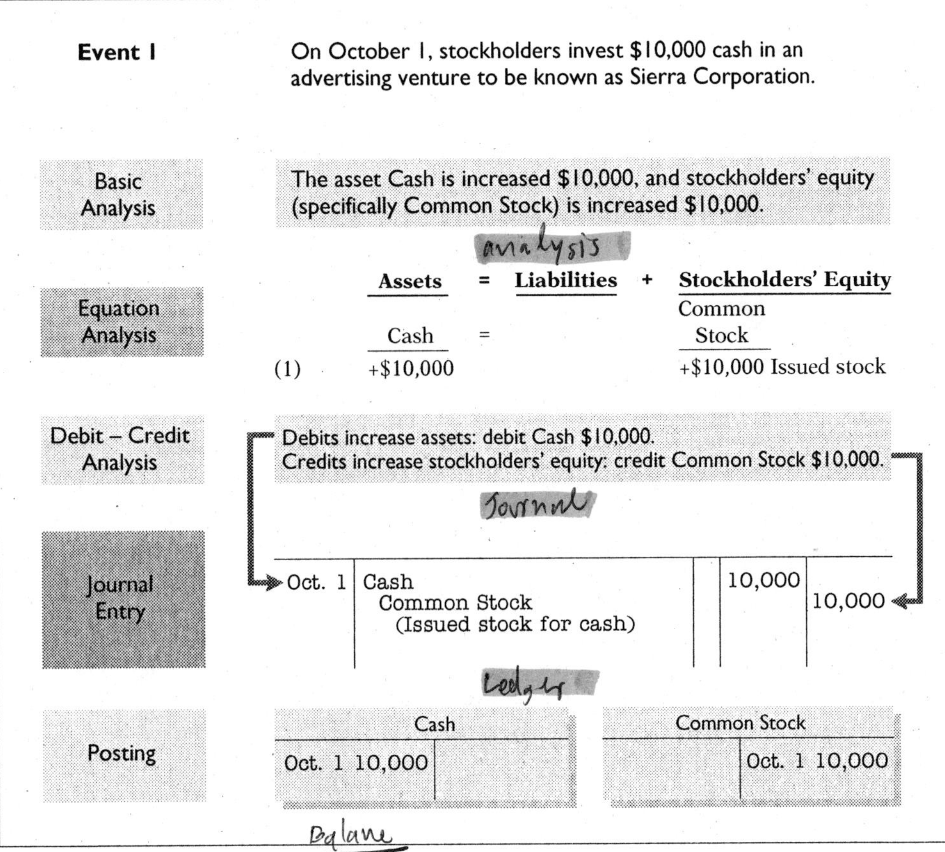

Event 1
On October 1, stockholders invest $10,000 cash in an advertising venture to be known as Sierra Corporation.
Basic Analysis
The asset Cash is increased $10,000, and stockholders' equity (specifically Common Stock) is increased $10,000.
Equation Analysis
Assets = Liabilities + Stockholders' Equity
Cash = Common Stock
(1) +$10,000 +$10,000 Issued stock
Debit – Credit Analysis
Debits increase assets: debit Cash $10,000.
Credits increase stockholders' equity: credit Common Stock $10,000.
Journal Entry
Oct. 1 Cash 10,000
Common Stock 10,000
(Issued stock for cash)
Posting
Cash
Oct. 1 10,000
Common Stock
Oct. 1 10,000

Illustration 3-21
Investment of cash by stockholders

Illustration 3-22 Issue of note payable

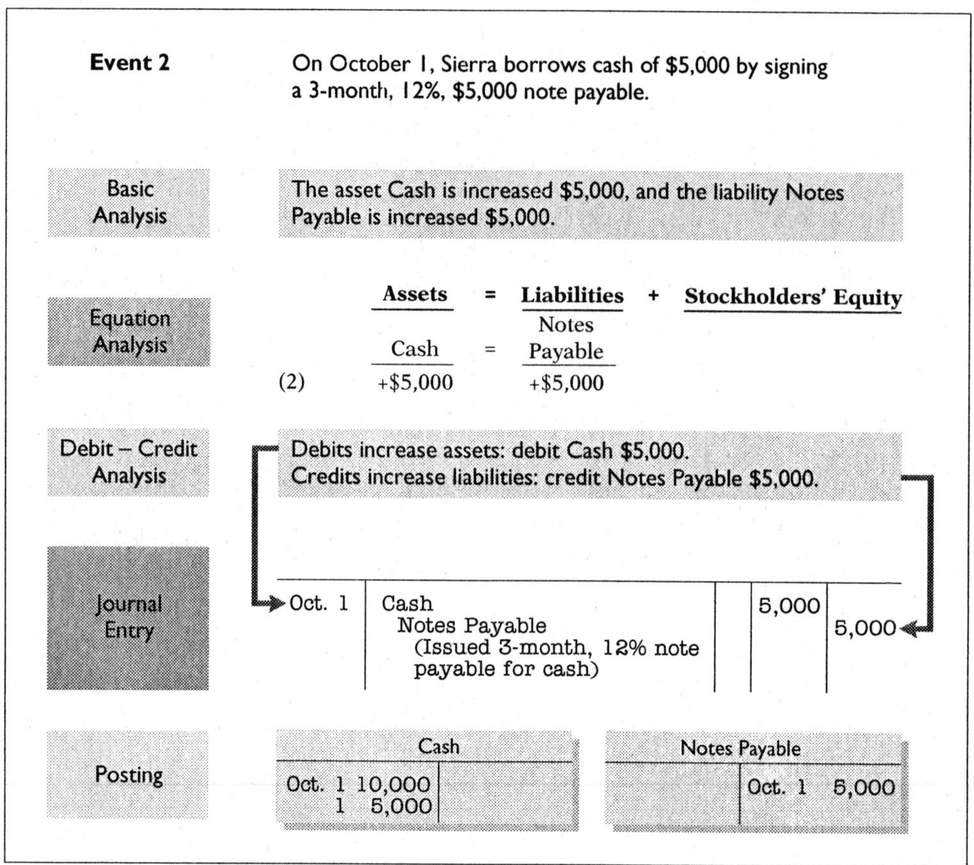

Event 2
On October 1, Sierra borrows cash of $5,000 by signing a 3-month, 12%, $5,000 note payable.
Basic Analysis
The asset Cash is increased $5,000, and the liability Notes Payable is increased $5,000.
Equation Analysis
Assets = Liabilities + Stockholders' Equity
Cash = Notes Payable
(2) +$5,000 +$5,000
Debit – Credit Analysis
Debits increase assets: debit Cash $5,000.
Credits increase liabilities: credit Notes Payable $5,000.
Journal Entry
Oct. 1 Cash 5,000
Notes Payable 5,000
(Issued 3-month, 12% note payable for cash)
Posting
Cash
Oct. 1 10,000
1 5,000
Notes Payable
Oct. 1 5,000

Illustration 3-23 Purchase of office equipment

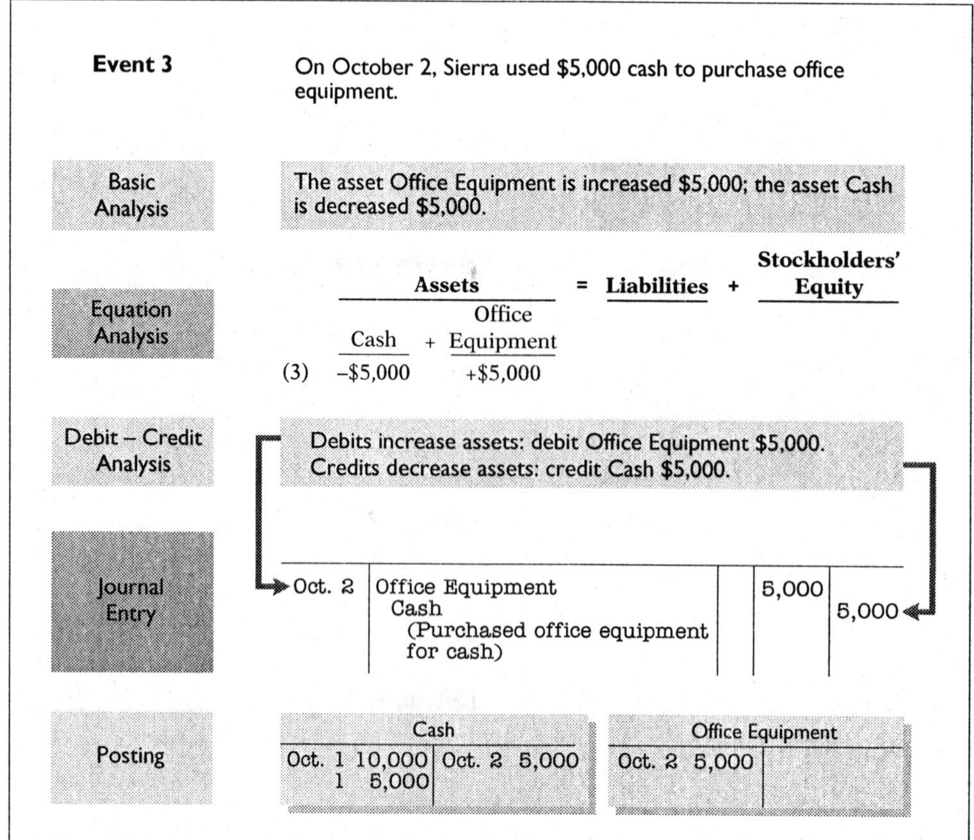

Event 3
On October 2, Sierra used $5,000 cash to purchase office equipment.
Basic Analysis
The asset Office Equipment is increased $5,000; the asset Cash is decreased $5,000.
Equation Analysis
Assets = Liabilities + Stockholders' Equity
Cash + Office Equipment
(3) –$5,000 +$5,000
Debit – Credit Analysis
Debits increase assets: debit Office Equipment $5,000.
Credits decrease assets: credit Cash $5,000.
Journal Entry
Oct. 2 Office Equipment 5,000
Cash 5,000
(Purchased office equipment for cash)
Posting
Cash
Oct. 1 10,000 Oct. 2 5,000
1 5,000
Office Equipment
Oct. 2 5,000

Illustration 3-24
Receipt of cash in advance from customer

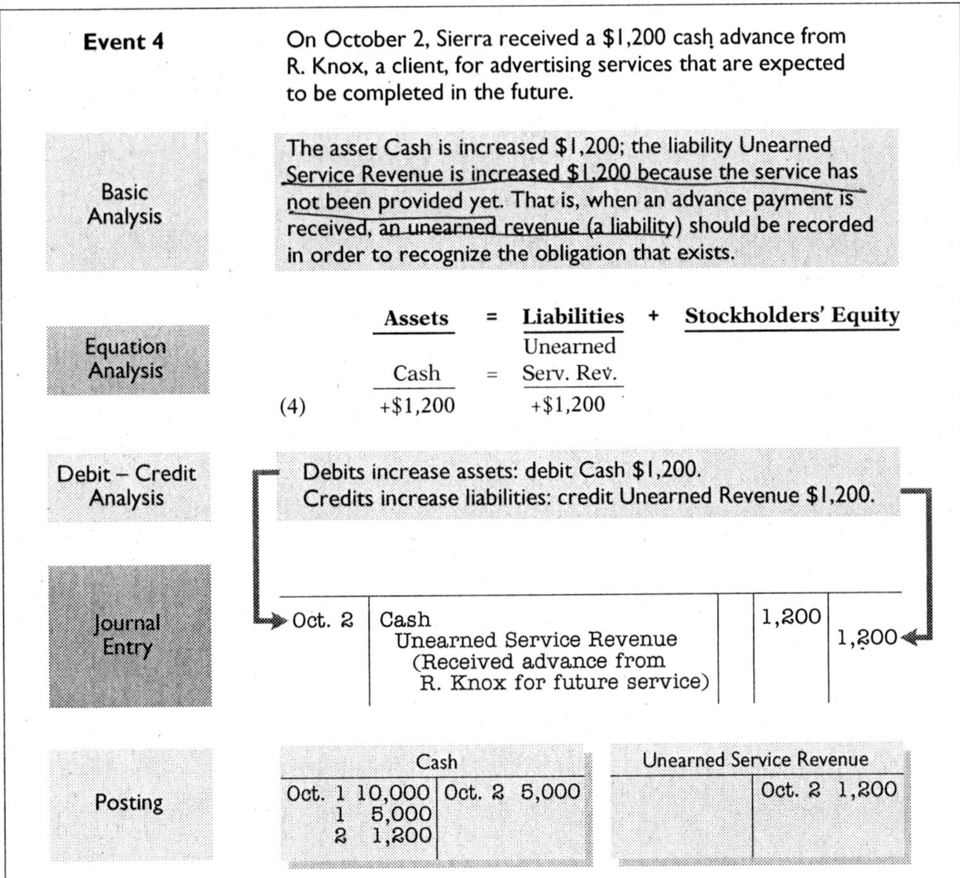

Event 4
On October 2, Sierra received a $1,200 cash advance from R. Knox, a client, for advertising services that are expected to be completed in the future.
Basic Analysis
The asset Cash is increased $1,200; the liability Unearned Service Revenue is increased $1,200 because the service has not been provided yet. That is, when an advance payment is received, an unearned revenue (a liability) should be recorded in order to recognize the obligation that exists.
Equation Analysis
Assets = Liabilities + Stockholders' Equity
Cash = Unearned Serv. Rev.
(4) +$1,200 +$1,200
Debit – Credit Analysis
Debits increase assets: debit Cash $1,200.
Credits increase liabilities: credit Unearned Revenue $1,200.
Journal Entry
Oct. 2 Cash 1,200
Unearned Service Revenue 1,200
(Received advance from R. Knox for future service)
Posting
Cash
Oct. 1 10,000 Oct. 2 5,000
1 5,000
2 1,200
Unearned Service Revenue
Oct. 2 1,200

Helpful Hint Many liabilities have the word "payable" in their title. But note that Unearned Service Revenue is considered a liability even though the word *payable* is not used.

Illustration 3-25
Services provided for cash

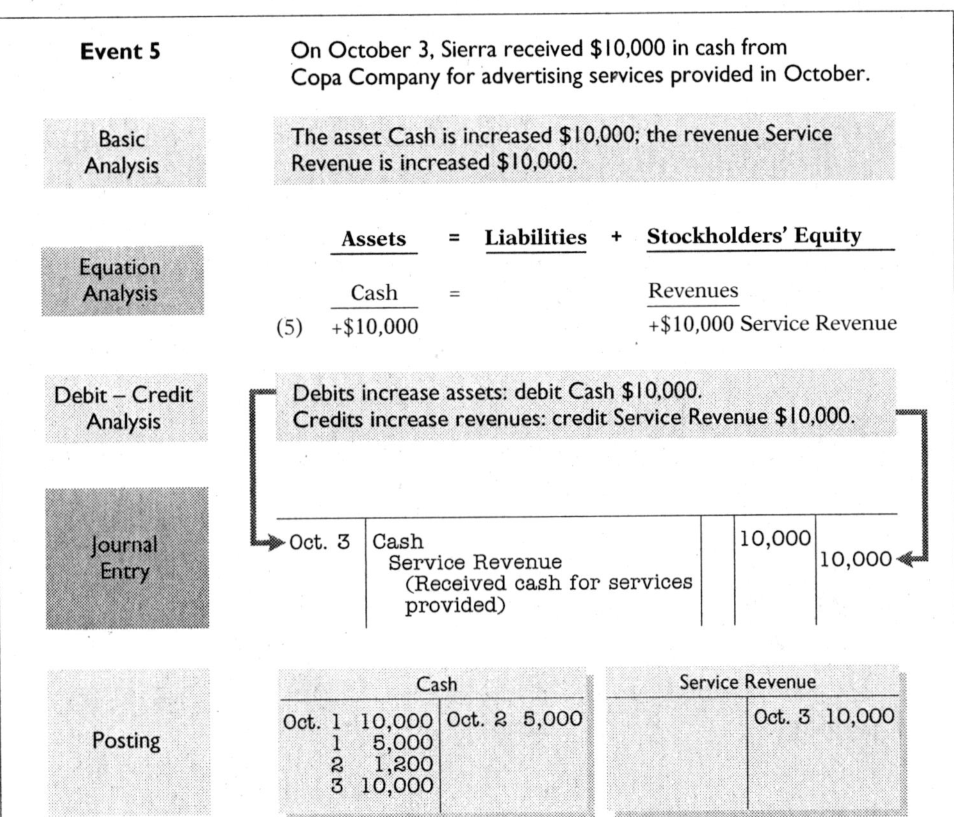

Event 5
On October 3, Sierra received $10,000 in cash from Copa Company for advertising services provided in October.
Basic Analysis
The asset Cash is increased $10,000; the revenue Service Revenue is increased $10,000.
Equation Analysis
Assets = Liabilities + Stockholders' Equity
Cash = Revenues
(5) +$10,000 +$10,000 Service Revenue
Debit – Credit Analysis
Debits increase assets: debit Cash $10,000.
Credits increase revenues: credit Service Revenue $10,000.
Journal Entry
Oct. 3 Cash 10,000
Service Revenue 10,000
(Received cash for services provided)
Posting
Cash
Oct. 1 10,000 Oct. 2 5,000
1 5,000
2 1,200
3 10,000
Service Revenue
Oct. 3 10,000

Illustration 3-26
Payment of rent with cash

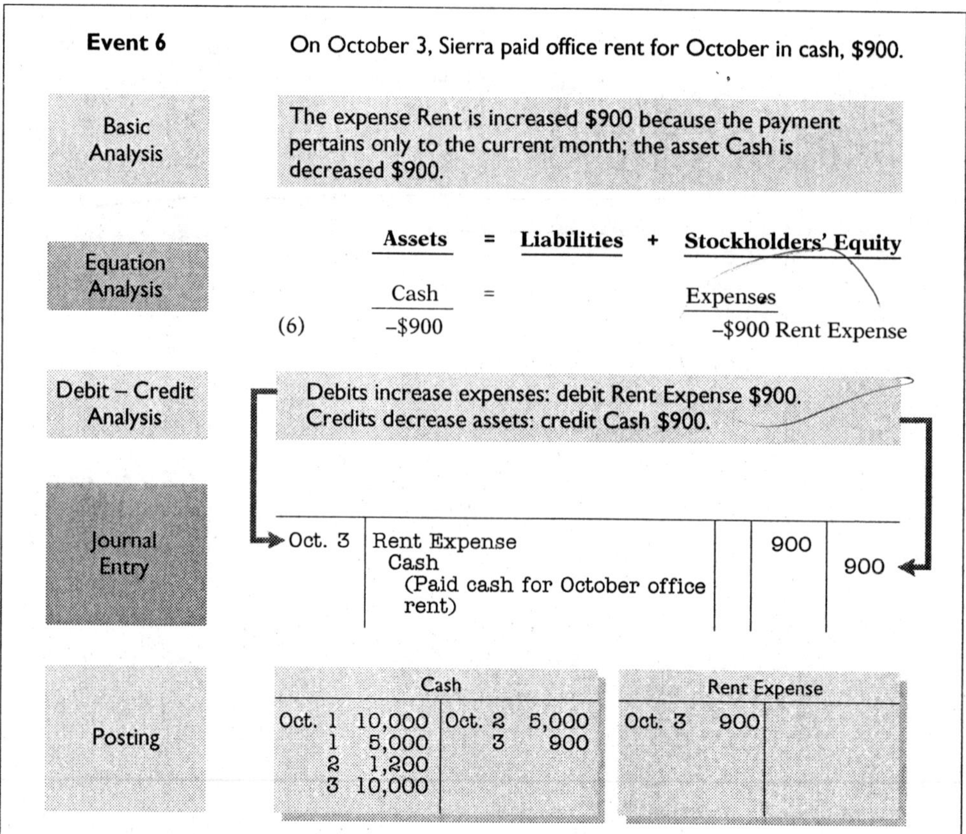

Event 6 On October 3, Sierra paid office rent for October in cash, $900.

Basic Analysis The expense Rent is increased $900 because the payment pertains only to the current month; the asset Cash is decreased $900.

Equation Analysis

	Assets	=	Liabilities	+	Stockholders' Equity
	Cash	=			Expenses
(6)	−$900				−$900 Rent Expense

Debit – Credit Analysis Debits increase expenses: debit Rent Expense $900. Credits decrease assets: credit Cash $900.

Journal Entry

Date	Account		Debit	Credit
Oct. 3	Rent Expense		900	
	Cash			900
	(Paid cash for October office rent)			

Posting

Cash			
Oct. 1	10,000	Oct. 2	5,000
1	5,000	3	900
2	1,200		
3	10,000		

Rent Expense			
Oct. 3	900		

Illustration 3-27
Purchase of insurance policy with cash

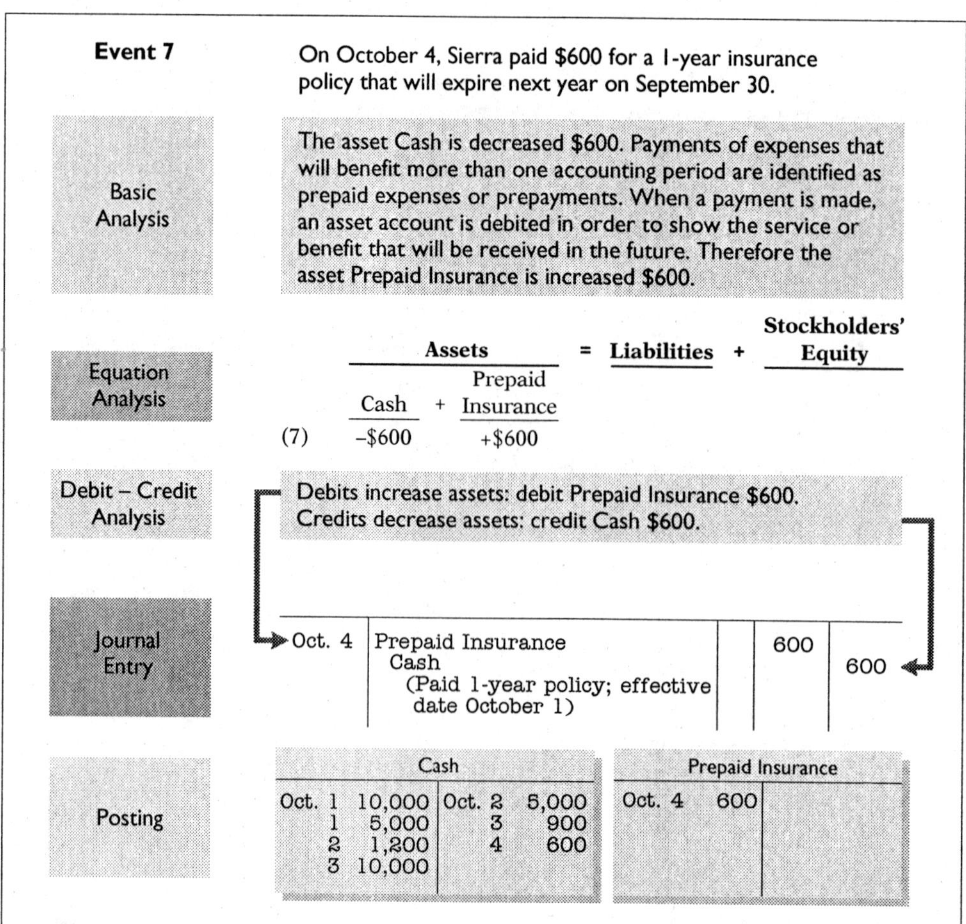

Event 7 On October 4, Sierra paid $600 for a 1-year insurance policy that will expire next year on September 30.

Basic Analysis The asset Cash is decreased $600. Payments of expenses that will benefit more than one accounting period are identified as prepaid expenses or prepayments. When a payment is made, an asset account is debited in order to show the service or benefit that will be received in the future. Therefore the asset Prepaid Insurance is increased $600.

Equation Analysis

	Assets			=	Liabilities	+	Stockholders' Equity
	Cash	+	Prepaid Insurance				
(7)	−$600		+$600				

Debit – Credit Analysis Debits increase assets: debit Prepaid Insurance $600. Credits decrease assets: credit Cash $600.

Journal Entry

Date	Account		Debit	Credit
Oct. 4	Prepaid Insurance		600	
	Cash			600
	(Paid 1-year policy; effective date October 1)			

Posting

Cash			
Oct. 1	10,000	Oct. 2	5,000
1	5,000	3	900
2	1,200	4	600
3	10,000		

Prepaid Insurance			
Oct. 4	600		

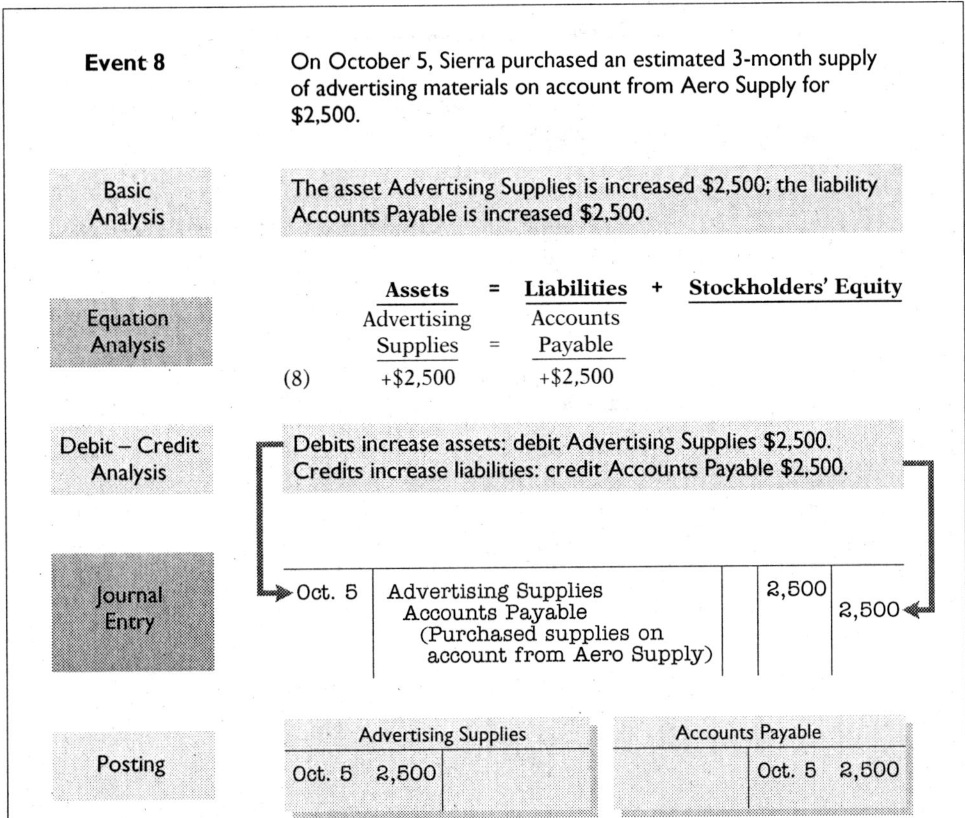

Event 8
On October 5, Sierra purchased an estimated 3-month supply of advertising materials on account from Aero Supply for $2,500.
Basic Analysis
The asset Advertising Supplies is increased $2,500; the liability Accounts Payable is increased $2,500.
Equation Analysis
Assets = Liabilities + Stockholders' Equity
Advertising Supplies = Accounts Payable
(8) +$2,500 +$2,500
Debit – Credit Analysis
Debits increase assets: debit Advertising Supplies $2,500.
Credits increase liabilities: credit Accounts Payable $2,500.
Journal Entry
Oct. 5 Advertising Supplies 2,500
Accounts Payable 2,500
(Purchased supplies on account from Aero Supply)
Posting
Advertising Supplies
Oct. 5 2,500
Accounts Payable
Oct. 5 2,500

Illustration 3-28 Purchase of supplies on account

Illustration 3-29 Hiring of new employees

Event 9

On October 9, Sierra hired four employees to begin work on October 15. Each employee is to receive a weekly salary of $500 for a 5-day work week, payable every 2 weeks — first payment made on October 26.

Basic Analysis

An accounting transaction has not occurred. There is only an agreement that the employees will begin work on October 15. Thus, a debit–credit analysis is not needed because there is no accounting entry. (See transaction of October 26 for first entry.)

Illustration 3-30
Payment of dividend

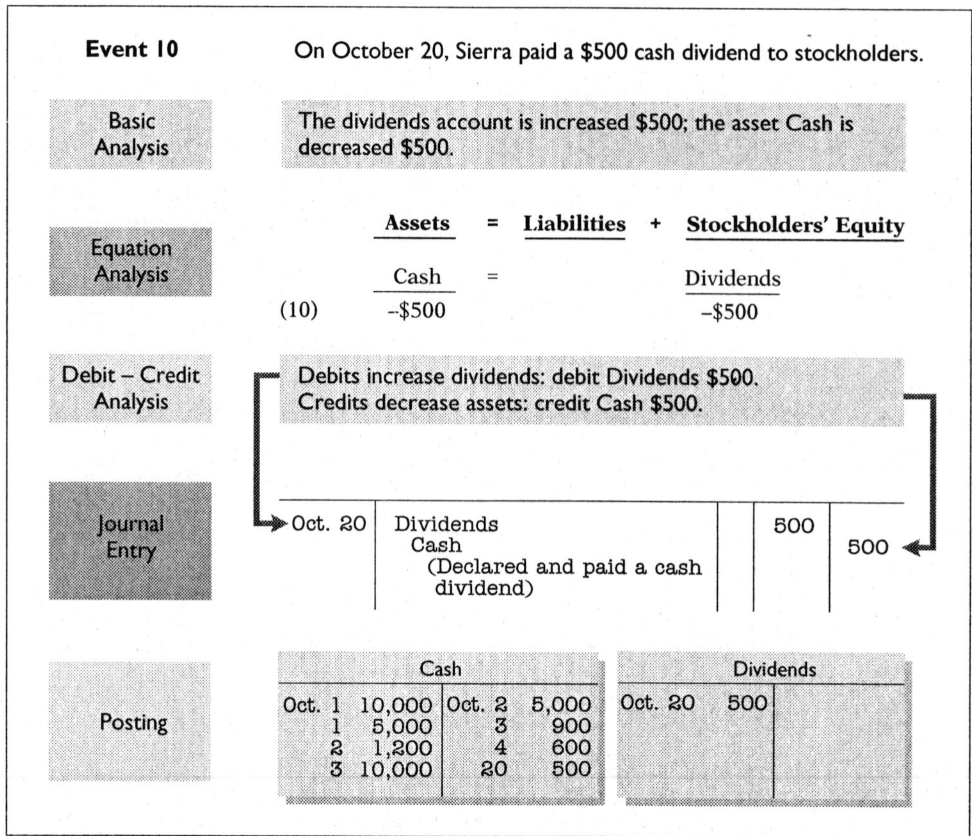

Event 10 On October 20, Sierra paid a $500 cash dividend to stockholders.

Basic Analysis: The dividends account is increased $500; the asset Cash is decreased $500.

Equation Analysis:

	Assets	=	Liabilities	+	Stockholders' Equity
	Cash	=			Dividends
(10)	–$500				–$500

Debit – Credit Analysis: Debits increase dividends: debit Dividends $500. Credits decrease assets: credit Cash $500.

Journal Entry:

Date	Account	Debit	Credit
Oct. 20	Dividends	500	
	Cash		500
	(Declared and paid a cash dividend)		

Posting:

Cash

Oct. 1	10,000	Oct. 2	5,000
1	5,000	3	900
2	1,200	4	600
3	10,000	20	500

Dividends

Oct. 20	500	

Illustration 3-31 Payment of cash for employee salaries

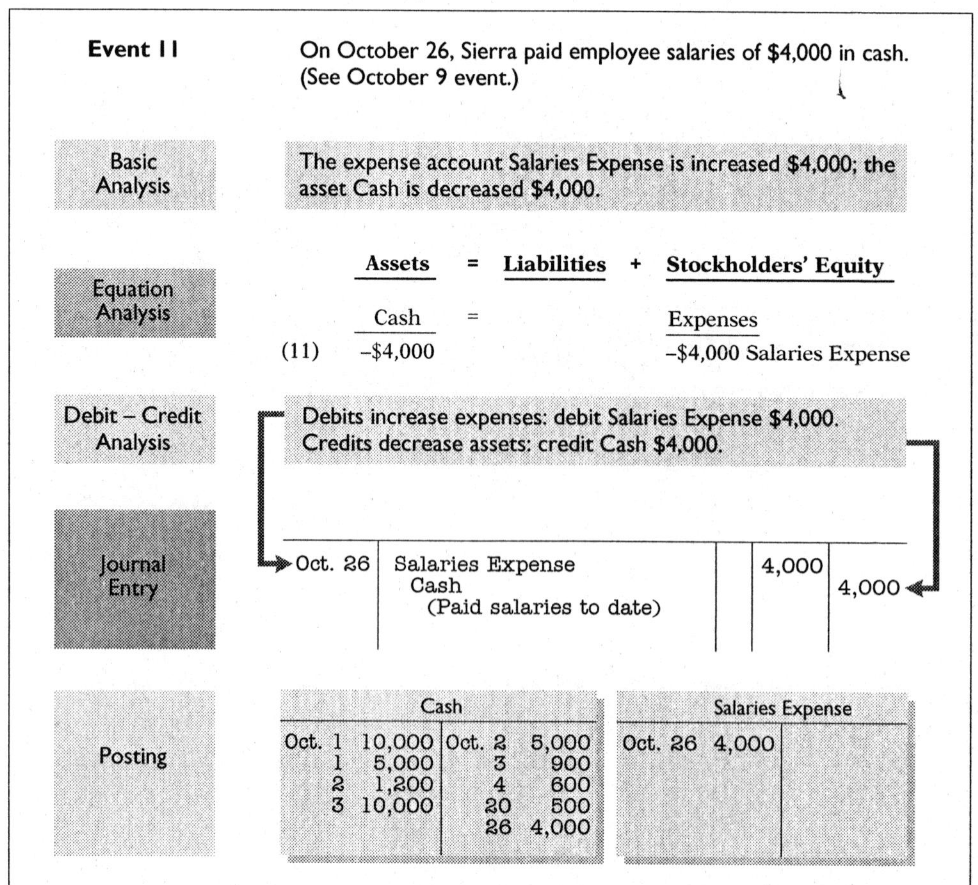

Event 11 On October 26, Sierra paid employee salaries of $4,000 in cash. (See October 9 event.)

Basic Analysis: The expense account Salaries Expense is increased $4,000; the asset Cash is decreased $4,000.

Equation Analysis:

	Assets	=	Liabilities	+	Stockholders' Equity
	Cash	=			Expenses
(11)	–$4,000				–$4,000 Salaries Expense

Debit – Credit Analysis: Debits increase expenses: debit Salaries Expense $4,000. Credits decrease assets: credit Cash $4,000.

Journal Entry:

Date	Account	Debit	Credit
Oct. 26	Salaries Expense	4,000	
	Cash		4,000
	(Paid salaries to date)		

Posting:

Cash

Oct. 1	10,000	Oct. 2	5,000
1	5,000	3	900
2	1,200	4	600
3	10,000	20	500
		26	4,000

Salaries Expense

Oct. 26	4,000	

SUMMARY ILLUSTRATION OF JOURNALIZING AND POSTING

The journal for Sierra Corporation for the month of October is summarized in Illustration 3-32. The ledger is shown in Illustration 3-33 (on page 128) with all balances highlighted in red.

Illustration 3-32 General journal for Sierra Corporation

GENERAL JOURNAL

Date		Account Titles and Explanation	Debit	Credit
2010				
Oct.	1	Cash	10,000	
		Common Stock		10,000
		(Issued stock for cash)		
	1	Cash	5,000	
		Notes Payable		5,000
		(Issued 3-month, 12% note payable for cash)		
	2	Office Equipment	5,000	
		Cash		5,000
		(Purchased office equipment for cash)		
	2	Cash	1,200	
		Unearned Service Revenue		1,200
		(Received advance from R. Knox for future service)		
	3	Cash	10,000	
		Service Revenue		10,000
		(Received cash for services provided)		
	3	Rent Expense	900	
		Cash		900
		(Paid cash for October office rent)		
	4	Prepaid Insurance	600	
		Cash		600
		(Paid 1-year policy; effective date October 1)		
	5	Advertising Supplies	2,500	
		Accounts Payable		2,500
		(Purchased supplies on account from Aero Supply)		
	20	Dividends	500	
		Cash		500
		(Paid a cash dividend)		
	26	Salaries Expense	4,000	
		Cash		4,000
		(Paid salaries to date)		

Illustration 3-33 General ledger for Sierra Corporation

GENERAL LEDGER

Cash

Oct. 1	10,000	Oct. 2	5,000
1	5,000	3	900
2	1,200	4	600
3	10,000	20	500
		26	4,000
Bal.	**15,200**		

Unearned Service Revenue

		Oct. 2	1,200
		Bal.	**1,200**

Advertising Supplies

Oct. 5	2,500		
Bal.	**2,500**		

Common Stock

		Oct. 1	10,000
		Bal.	**10,000**

Prepaid Insurance

Oct. 4	600		
Bal.	**600**		

Dividends

Oct. 20	500		
Bal.	**500**		

Office Equipment

Oct. 2	5,000		
Bal.	**5,000**		

Service Revenue

		Oct. 3	10,000
		Bal.	**10,000**

Notes Payable

		Oct. 1	5,000
		Bal.	**5,000**

Salaries Expense

Oct. 26	4,000		
Bal.	**4,000**		

Accounts Payable

		Oct. 5	2,500
		Bal.	**2,500**

Rent Expense

Oct. 3	900		
Bal.	**900**		

before you go on...

POSTING

Do it! Selected transactions from the journal of Faital Inc. during its first month of operations are presented below. Post these transactions to T accounts.

Date		Account Titles	Debit	Credit
July	1	Cash	30,000	
		Common Stock		30,000
	9	Accounts Receivable	6,000	
		Service Revenue		6,000
	24	Cash	4,000	
		Accounts Receivable		4,000

Action Plan

- Journalize transactions to keep track of financial activities (receipts, payments, receivables, payables, etc.).
- To make entries useful, classify and summarize them by posting the entries to specific ledger accounts.

Solution

Cash

July 1	30,000		
24	4,000		

Accounts Receivable

July 9	6,000	July 24	4,000

Common Stock

		July 1	30,000

Service Revenue

		July 9	6,000

✓ the navigator

The Trial Balance

study objective 8

Explain the purposes of a trial balance.

A **trial balance** lists accounts and their balances at a given time. A company usually prepares a trial balance at the end of an accounting period. The accounts are listed in the order in which they appear in the ledger. Debit balances are listed in the left column and credit balances in the right column. The totals of the two columns must be equal.

The trial balance proves the mathematical equality of debits and credits after posting. Under the double-entry system this equality occurs when the sum of the debit account balances equals the sum of the credit account balances. **A trial balance may also uncover errors in journalizing and posting.** For example, a trial balance may well have detected the error at Fidelity Investments discussed in the Feature Story. **In addition, a trial balance is useful in the preparation of financial statements.**

These are the procedures for preparing a trial balance:

1. List the account titles and their balances.
2. Total the debit column and total the credit column.
3. Verify the equality of the two columns.

Illustration 3-34 presents the trial balance prepared from the ledger of Sierra Corporation. Note that the total debits, $28,700, equal the total credits, $28,700.

Illustration 3-34 Sierra Corporation trial balance

SIERRA CORPORATION
Trial Balance
October 31, 2010

	Debit	Credit
Cash	$15,200	
Advertising Supplies	2,500	
Prepaid Insurance	600	
Office Equipment	5,000	
Notes Payable		$ 5,000
Accounts Payable		2,500
Unearned Service Revenue		1,200
Common Stock		10,000
Dividends	500	
Service Revenue		10,000
Salaries Expense	4,000	
Rent Expense	900	
	$28,700	$28,700

Helpful Hint Note that the order of presentation in the trial balance is:
Assets
Liabilities
Stockholders' equity
Revenues
Expenses

LIMITATIONS OF A TRIAL BALANCE

A trial balance does not prove that all transactions have been recorded or that the ledger is correct. Numerous errors may exist even though the trial balance column totals agree. For example, the trial balance may balance even when any of the following occurs: (1) a transaction is not journalized, (2) a correct journal entry is not posted, (3) a journal entry is posted twice, (4) incorrect accounts are used in journalizing or posting, or (5) offsetting errors are made in recording the amount of a transaction. In other words, as long as equal debits and credits are posted, even to the wrong account or in the wrong amount, the total debits will equal the total credits. Nevertheless, despite these limitations, the trial balance is a useful screen for finding errors and is frequently used in practice.

Ethics Note An *error* is the result of an unintentional mistake; it is neither ethical nor unethical. An *irregularity* is an intentional misstatement, which *is* viewed as unethical.

DECISION TOOLKIT

DECISION CHECKPOINTS	INFO NEEDED FOR DECISION	TOOL TO USE FOR DECISION	HOW TO EVALUATE RESULTS
How do you determine that debits equal credits?	All account balances	Trial balance	List the account titles and their balances; total the debit and credit columns; verify equality.

KEEPING AN EYE ON CASH

The Cash account shown below reflects all of the inflows and outflows of cash that occurred during October. We have also provided a description of each transaction that affected the cash account.

Cash

Oct.	1	10,000	Oct.	2	5,000
	1	5,000		3	900
	2	1,200		4	600
	3	10,000		20	500
				26	4,000
Bal.		15,200			

1. Oct. 1 Issued stock for $10,000 cash.
2. Oct. 1 Issued note payable for $5,000 cash.
3. Oct. 2 Purchased office equipment for $5,000 cash.
4. Oct. 2 Received $1,200 cash in advance from customer.
5. Oct. 3 Received $10,000 cash for services provided.
6. Oct. 3 Paid $900 cash for October rent.
7. Oct. 4 Paid $600 cash for one-year insurance policy.
8. Oct. 20 Paid $500 cash dividend to stockholders.
9. Oct. 26 Paid $4,000 cash salaries.

The cash account and the related cash transactions indicate why cash changed during October. However, to make this information useful for analysis, it is summarized in a statement of cash flows. The statement of cash flows classifies each transaction as an operating activity, an investing activity, or a financing activity. A user of this statement can then determine the amount of cash provided by operations, the amount of cash used for investing purposes, and the amount of cash provided by financing activities.

study objective 

Classify cash activities as operating, investing, or financing.

Operating activities are the types of activities the company performs to generate profits. Sierra Corporation is a marketing agency, so its operating activities involve providing marketing services. Activities 4, 5, 6, 7, and 9 relate to cash received or spent to directly support its marketing services.

Investing activities include the purchase or sale of long-lived assets used in operating the business, or the purchase or sale of investment securities (stocks and bonds of companies other than Sierra). Activity 3, the purchase of office equipment, is an investment activity.

The primary types of *financing activities* are borrowing money, issuing shares of stock, and paying dividends. The financing activities of Sierra Corporation are activities 1, 2, and 8.

USING THE DECISION TOOLKIT

The Kansas Farmers' Vertically Integrated Cooperative, Inc. (K-VIC), was formed by over 200 northeast Kansas farmers in the late 1980s. Its purpose is to use raw materials, primarily grain and meat products grown by K-VIC's members, to process this material into end-user food products, and to distribute the products nationally. Profits not needed for expansion or investment are returned to the members annually, on a pro-rata basis, according to the market value of the grain and meat products received from each farmer.

Assume that the following trial balance was prepared for K-VIC.

KANSAS FARMERS' VERTICALLY INTEGRATED COOPERATIVE, INC.
Trial Balance
December 31, 2010
(in thousands)

	Debit	Credit
Accounts Receivable	$ 712,000	
Accounts Payable		$ 37,000
Advertising and Promotion Payable		141,000
Buildings	365,000	
Cash	32,000	
Cost of Goods Sold	2,384,000	
Current Maturity of Long-Term Debt		12,000
Inventories	1,291,000	
Land	110,000	
Long-Term Debt		873,000
Machinery and Equipment	63,000	
Notes Payable to Members		495,000
Retained Earnings		822,000
Sales Revenue		3,741,000
Salaries and Wages Payable		62,000
Selling and Administrative Expense	651,000	
Trucking Expense	500,000	
	$6,108,000	$6,183,000

Because the trial balance is not in balance, you have checked with various people responsible for entering accounting data and have discovered the following.

1. The purchase of 35 new trucks, costing $7 million and paid for with cash, was not recorded.
2. A data entry clerk accidentally deleted the account name for an account with a credit balance of $472 million, so the amount was added to the Long-Term Debt account in the trial balance.
3. December cash sales revenue of $75 million was credited to the Sales Revenue account, but the other half of the entry was not made.
4. $50 million of selling expenses were mistakenly charged to Trucking Expense.

Instructions

Answer these questions.

(a) Which mistake(s) have caused the trial balance to be out of balance?

(b) Should all of the items be corrected? Explain.

(c) What is the name of the account the data entry clerk deleted?

(d) Make the necessary corrections and prepare a correct trial balance with accounts listed in proper order.

(e) On your trial balance, write BAL beside the accounts that go on the balance sheet and INC beside those that go on the income statement.

Solution

(a) Only mistake #3 has caused the trial balance to be out of balance.

(b) All of the items should be corrected. The misclassification error (mistake #4) on the selling expense would not affect bottom-line net income, but it does affect the amounts reported in the two expense accounts.

(c) There is no Common Stock account, so that must be the account that was deleted by the data entry clerk.

(d) and (e):

KANSAS FARMERS' VERTICALLY INTEGRATED COOPERATIVE, INC.
Trial Balance
December 31, 2010
(in thousands)

	Debit	Credit	
Cash ($32,000 − $7,000 + $75,000)	$ 100,000		BAL
Accounts Receivable	712,000		BAL
Inventories	1,291,000		BAL
Land	110,000		BAL
Machinery and Equipment	70,000		BAL
Buildings	365,000		BAL
Notes Payable to Members		$ 495,000	BAL
Accounts Payable		37,000	BAL
Advertising and Promotion Payable		141,000	BAL
Salaries and Wages Payable		62,000	BAL
Current Maturity of Long-Term Debt		12,000	BAL
Long-Term Debt ($873,000 − $472,000)		401,000	BAL
Common Stock		472,000	BAL
Retained Earnings		822,000	BAL
Sales Revenue		3,741,000	INC
Cost of Goods Sold	2,384,000		INC
Selling and Administrative Expense	701,000		INC
Trucking Expense	450,000		INC
	$6,183,000	$6,183,000	

Summary of Study Objectives

1 Analyze the effect of business transactions on the basic accounting equation. Each business transaction must have a dual effect on the accounting equation. For example, if an individual asset is increased, there must be a corresponding (a) decrease in another asset, or (b) increase in a specific liability, or (c) increase in stockholders' equity.

2 Explain what an account is and how it helps in the recording process. An account is an individual accounting record of increases and decreases in specific asset, liability, and stockholders' equity items.

3 Define debits and credits and explain how they are used to record business transactions. The terms *debit* and *credit* are synonymous with *left* and *right*. Assets, dividends, and expenses are increased by debits and decreased by credits. Liabilities, common stock, retained earnings, and revenues are increased by credits and decreased by debits.

4 Identify the basic steps in the recording process. The basic steps in the recording process are: (a) analyze each transaction in terms of its effect on the accounts, (b) enter the transaction information in a journal, and (c) transfer the journal information to the appropriate accounts in the ledger.

5 Explain what a journal is and how it helps in the recording process. The initial accounting record of a transaction is entered in a journal before the data are entered in the accounts. A journal (a) discloses in one place the complete effect of a transaction, (b) provides a chronological record of transactions, and (c) prevents or locates errors because the debit and credit amounts for each entry can be readily compared.

6 Explain what a ledger is and how it helps in the recording process. The entire group of accounts maintained by a company is referred to collectively as a ledger. The ledger keeps in one place all the information about changes in specific account balances.

7 Explain what posting is and how it helps in the recording process. Posting is the procedure of transferring journal entries to the ledger accounts. This phase of the recording process accumulates the effects of journalized transactions in the individual accounts.

8 Explain the purposes of a trial balance. A trial balance is a list of accounts and their balances at a given time. The primary purpose of the trial balance is to prove the mathematical equality of debits and credits after posting. A trial balance also uncovers errors in journalizing and posting and is useful in preparing financial statements.

9 Classify cash activities as operating, investing, or financing. Operating activities are the types of activities the company uses to generate profits. Investing activities relate to the purchase or sale of long-lived assets used in operating the business, or to the purchase or sale of investment securities (stock and bonds of other companies). Financing activities are borrowing money, issuing shares of stock, and paying dividends.

DECISION TOOLKIT A SUMMARY

DECISION CHECKPOINTS	INFO NEEDED FOR DECISION	TOOL TO USE FOR DECISION	HOW TO EVALUATE RESULTS
Has an accounting transaction occurred?	Details of the event	Accounting equation	If the event affected assets, liabilities, or stockholders' equity, then record as a transaction.
How do you determine that debits equal credits?	All account balances	Trial balance	List the account titles and their balances; total the debit and credit colums; verify equality.

Glossary

Account *(p. 110)* An individual accounting record of increases and decreases in specific asset, liability, stockholders' equity, revenue or expense items.

Accounting information system *(p. 102)* The system of collecting and processing transaction data and communicating financial information to interested parties.

Accounting transactions *(p. 102)* Events that require recording in the financial statements because they affect assets, liabilities, or stockholders' equity.

Chart of accounts *(p. 120)* A list of a company's accounts.

Credit *(p. 111)* The right side of an account.

Debit *(p. 111)* The left side of an account.

Double-entry system *(p. 111)* A system that records the dual effect of each transaction in appropriate accounts.

General journal *(p. 117)* The most basic form of journal.

General ledger *(p. 119)* A ledger that contains all asset, liability, stockholders' equity, revenue, and expense accounts.

Journal *(p. 116)* An accounting record in which transactions are initially recorded in chronological order.

Journalizing *(p. 117)* The procedure of entering transaction data in the journal.

Ledger *(p. 119)* The group of accounts maintained by a company.

Posting *(p. 120)* The procedure of transferring journal entry amounts to the ledger accounts.

T account *(p. 110)* The basic form of an account.

Trial balance *(p. 129)* A list of accounts and their balances at a given time.

Comprehensive Do it!

Bob Sample and other student investors opened Campus Carpet Cleaning, Inc. on September 1, 2010. During the first month of operations the following transactions occurred.

Sept.	1	Stockholders invested $20,000 cash in the business.
	2	Paid $1,000 cash for store rent for the month of September.
	3	Purchased industrial carpet-cleaning equipment for $25,000, paying $10,000 in cash and signing a $15,000 6-month, 12% note payable.
	4	Paid $1,200 for 1-year accident insurance policy.
	10	Received bill from the *Daily News* for advertising the opening of the cleaning service, $200.
	15	Performed services on account for $6,200.
	20	Paid a $700 cash dividend to stockholders.
	30	Received $5,000 from customers billed on September 15.

The chart of accounts for the company is the same as for Sierra Corporation except for the following additional accounts: Cleaning Equipment and Advertising Expense.

Instructions

(a) Journalize the September transactions.
(b) Open ledger accounts and post the September transactions.
(c) Prepare a trial balance at September 30, 2010.

Action Plan

- Proceed through the accounting cycle in the following sequence:

1. Make separate journal entries for each transaction.
2. Note that all debits precede all credit entries.
3. In journalizing, make sure debits equal credits.
4. In journalizing, use specific account titles taken from the chart of accounts.
5. Provide an appropriate explanation of each journal entry.
6. Arrange ledger in statement order, beginning with the balance sheet accounts.
7. Post in chronological order.
8. Prepare a trial balance, which lists accounts in the order in which they appear in the ledger.
9. List debit balances in the left column and credit balances in the right column.

Solution to Comprehensive **Do it!**

(a) **GENERAL JOURNAL**

Date	Account Titles and Explanation	Debit	Credit
2010			
Sept. 1	Cash	20,000	
	Common Stock		20,000
	(Issued stock for cash)		
2	Rent Expense	1,000	
	Cash		1,000
	(Paid September rent)		
3	Cleaning Equipment	25,000	
	Cash		10,000
	Notes Payable		15,000
	(Purchased cleaning equipment for cash and 6-month, 12% note payable)		
4	Prepaid Insurance	1,200	
	Cash		1,200
	(Paid 1-year insurance policy)		
10	Advertising Expense	200	
	Accounts Payable		200
	(Received bill from *Daily News* for advertising)		
15	Accounts Receivable	6,200	
	Service Revenue		6,200
	(Services performed on account)		
20	Dividends	700	
	Cash		700
	(Declared and paid a cash dividend)		
30	Cash	5,000	
	Accounts Receivable		5,000
	(Collection of accounts receivable)		

(b) **GENERAL LEDGER**

Cash

Debit		Credit	
Sept. 1	20,000	Sept. 2	1,000
30	5,000	3	10,000
		4	1,200
		20	700
Bal.	12,100		

Common Stock

Debit		Credit	
		Sept. 1	20,000
		Bal.	20,000

Accounts Receivable

Debit		Credit	
Sept. 15	6,200	Sept. 30	5,000
Bal.	1,200		

Dividends

Debit		Credit	
Sept. 20	700		
Bal.	700		

Prepaid Insurance			
Sept. 4	1,200		
Bal.	1,200		

Service Revenue			
		Sept. 15	6,200
		Bal.	6,200

Cleaning Equipment			
Sept. 3	25,000		
Bal.	25,000		

Advertising Expense			
Sept. 10	200		
Bal.	200		

Notes Payable			
		Sept. 3	15,000
		Bal.	15,000

Rent Expense			
Sept. 2	1,000		
Bal.	1,000		

Accounts Payable			
		Sept. 10	200
		Bal.	200

(c)

CAMPUS CARPET CLEANING, INC.
Trial Balance
September 30, 2010

	Debit	Credit
Cash	$12,100	
Accounts Receivable	1,200	
Prepaid Insurance	1,200	
Cleaning Equipment	25,000	
Notes Payable		$15,000
Accounts Payable		200
Common Stock		20,000
Dividends	700	
Service Revenue		6,200
Advertising Expense	200	
Rent Expense	1,000	
	$41,400	$41,400

Self-Study Questions

Answers are at the end of this chapter.

(SO 1) 1. The effects on the basic accounting equation of performing services for cash are to:
(a) increase assets and decrease stockholders' equity.
(b) increase assets and increase stockholders' equity.
(c) increase assets and increase liabilities.
(d) increase liabilities and increase stockholders' equity.

2. Genesis Company buys a $900 machine on credit. (SO 1) This transaction will affect the:
(a) income statement only.
(b) balance sheet only.
(c) income statement and retained earnings statement only.
(d) income statement, retained earnings statement, and balance sheet.

(SO 1) 3. Which of the following events is *not* recorded in the accounting records?
(a) Equipment is purchased on account.
(b) An employee is terminated.
(c) A cash investment is made into the business.
(d) Company pays dividend to stockholders.

(SO 1) 4. During 2010, Gibson Company assets decreased $50,000 and its liabilities decreased $90,000. Its stockholders' equity therefore:
(a) increased $40,000.
(b) decreased $140,000.
(c) decreased $40,000.
(d) increased $140,000.

(SO 2) 5. Which statement about an account is *true?*
(a) In its simplest form, an account consists of two parts.
(b) An account is an individual accounting record of increases and decreases in specific asset, liability, and stockholders' equity items.
(c) There are separate accounts for specific assets and liabilities but only one account for stockholders' equity items.
(d) The left side of an account is the credit or decrease side.

(SO 3) 6. Debits:
(a) increase both assets and liabilities.
(b) decrease both assets and liabilities.
(c) increase assets and decrease liabilities.
(d) decrease assets and increase liabilities.

(SO 3) 7. A revenue account:
(a) is increased by debits.
(b) is decreased by credits.
(c) has a normal balance of a debit.
(d) is increased by credits.

(SO 3) 8. Which accounts normally have debit balances?
(a) Assets, expenses, and revenues.
(b) Assets, expenses, and retained earnings.
(c) Assets, liabilities, and dividends.
(d) Assets, dividends, and expenses.

(SO 3) 9. Paying an account payable with cash affects the components of the accounting equation in the following way.
(a) Decreases stockholders' equity and decreases liabilities.
(b) Increases assets and decreases liabilities.
(c) Decreases assets and increases stockholders' equity.
(d) Decreases assets and decreases liabilities.

10. Which is *not* part of the recording process? (SO 4)
(a) Analyzing transactions.
(b) Preparing a trial balance.
(c) Entering transactions in a journal.
(d) Posting transactions.

11. Which of these statements about a journal is *false?* (SO 5)
(a) It contains only revenue and expense accounts.
(b) It provides a chronological record of transactions.
(c) It helps to locate errors because the debit and credit amounts for each entry can be readily compared.
(d) It discloses in one place the complete effect of a transaction.

12. A ledger: (SO 6)
(a) contains only asset and liability accounts.
(b) should show accounts in alphabetical order.
(c) is a collection of the entire group of accounts maintained by a company.
(d) provides a chronological record of transactions.

13. Posting: (SO 7)
(a) normally occurs before journalizing.
(b) transfers ledger transaction data to the journal.
(c) is an optional step in the recording process.
(d) transfers journal entries to ledger accounts.

14. A trial balance: (SO 8)
(a) is a list of accounts with their balances at a given time.
(b) proves that proper account titles were used.
(c) will not balance if a correct journal entry is posted twice.
(d) proves that all transactions have been recorded.

15. A trial balance will *not* balance if: (SO 8)
(a) a correct journal entry is posted twice.
(b) the purchase of supplies on account is debited to Supplies and credited to Cash.
(c) a $100 cash dividend is debited to Dividends for $1,000 and credited to Cash for $100.
(d) a $450 payment on account is debited to Accounts Payable for $45 and credited to Cash for $45.

Go to the book's companion website, **www.wiley.com/college/kimmel**, to access additional Self-Study Questions.

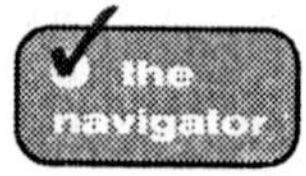

Questions

1. Describe the accounting information system and the steps in the recording process.

2. Can a business enter into a transaction that affects only the left side of the basic accounting equation? If so, give an example.

3. Are the following events recorded in the accounting records? Explain your answer in each case.
(a) A major stockholder of the company dies.
(b) Supplies are purchased on account.
(c) An employee is fired.
(d) The company pays a cash dividend to its stockholders.

4. Indicate how each business transaction affects the basic accounting equation.
(a) Paid cash for janitorial services.
(b) Purchased equipment for cash.

(c) Issued common stock to investors in exchange for cash.
(d) Paid an account payable in full.

5. Why is an account referred to as a T account?

6. The terms *debit* and *credit* mean "increase" and "decrease," respectively. Do you agree? Explain.

7. Steve Rondelli, a fellow student, contends that the double-entry system means each transaction must be recorded twice. Is Steve correct? Explain.

8. Marie Likert, a beginning accounting student, believes debit balances are favorable and credit balances are unfavorable. Is Marie correct? Discuss.

9. State the rules of debit and credit as applied to (a) asset accounts, (b) liability accounts, and (c) the common stock account.

10. What is the normal balance for each of these accounts?
(a) Accounts Receivable.
(b) Cash.
(c) Dividends.
(d) Accounts Payable.
(e) Service Revenue.
(f) Salaries Expense.
(g) Common Stock.

11. Indicate whether each account is an asset, a liability, or a stockholders' equity account, and whether it would have a normal debit or credit balance.
(a) Accounts Receivable.
(b) Accounts Payable.
(c) Equipment.
(d) Dividends.
(e) Supplies.

12. For the following transactions, indicate the account debited and the account credited.
(a) Supplies are purchased on account.
(b) Cash is received on signing a note payable.
(c) Employees are paid salaries in cash.

13. For each account listed here, indicate whether it generally will have debit entries only, credit entries only, or both debit and credit entries.
(a) Cash.
(b) Accounts Receivable.
(c) Dividends.
(d) Accounts Payable.
(e) Salaries Expense.
(f) Service Revenue.

14. Tootsie Roll What are the normal balances for the following accounts of Tootsie Roll Industries? (a) Accounts Receivable. (b) Income Taxes Payable. (c) Sales. (d) Selling, Marketing, and Administrative Expenses.

15. What are the basic steps in the recording process?

16. (a) When entering a transaction in the journal, should the debit or credit be written first?
(b) Which should be indented, the debit or the credit?

17. (a) Can accounting transaction debits and credits be recorded directly in the ledger accounts?
(b) What are the advantages of first recording transactions in the journal and then posting to the ledger?

18. Journalize these accounting transactions.
(a) Stockholders invested $12,000 in the business in exchange for common stock.
(b) Insurance of $800 is paid for the year.
(c) Supplies of $1,500 are purchased on account.
(d) Cash of $7,500 is received for services rendered.

19. (a) What is a ledger?
(b) Why is a chart of accounts important?

20. What is a trial balance and what are its purposes?

21. Pete Riser is confused about how accounting information flows through the accounting system. He believes information flows in this order:
(a) Debits and credits are posted to the ledger.
(b) Accounting transaction occurs.
(c) Information is entered in the journal.
(d) Financial statements are prepared.
(e) Trial balance is prepared.
Indicate to Pete the proper flow of the information.

22. Two students are discussing the use of a trial balance. They wonder whether the following errors, each considered separately, would prevent the trial balance from balancing. What would you tell them?
(a) The bookkeeper debited Cash for $600 and credited Wages Expense for $600 for payment of wages.
(b) Cash collected on account was debited to Cash for $800, and Service Revenue was credited for $80.

Brief Exercises

BE3-1 Presented below are three economic events. On a sheet of paper, list the letters (a), (b), and (c) with columns for assets, liabilities, and stockholders' equity. In each column, indicate whether the event increased (+), decreased (−), or had no effect (NE) on assets, liabilities, and stockholders' equity.
(a) Purchased supplies on account.
(b) Received cash for providing a service.
(c) Expenses paid in cash.

Determine effect of transactions on basic accounting equation.
(SO 1)

Determine effect of transactions on basic accounting equation. (SO 1)

BE3-2 During 2010, Bleeker Corp. entered into the following transactions.
1. Borrowed $60,000 by issuing bonds.
2. Paid $9,000 cash dividend to stockholders.
3. Received $17,000 cash from a previously billed customer for services provided.
4. Purchased supplies on account for $3,100.

Using the following tabular analysis, show the effect of each transaction on the accounting equation. Put explanations for changes to Stockholders' Equity in the right-hand margin. For Retained Earnings, use separate columns for Revenues, Expenses, and Dividends if necessary. Use Illustration 3-3 (page 109) as a model.

Assets				=	**Liabilities**			+	**Stockholders' Equity**		
Cash	+	Accounts Receivable	+ Supplies	=	Accounts Payable	+	Bonds Payable	+	Common Stock	+	Retained Earnings

Determine effect of transactions on basic accounting equation. (SO 1)

BE3-3 During 2010, Estes company entered into the following transactions.
1. Purchased property, plant, and equipment for $286,176 cash.
2. Issued common stock to investors for $137,590 cash.
3. Purchased inventory of $77,662 on account.

Using the following tabular analysis, show the effect of each transaction on the accounting equation. Put explanations for changes to Stockholders' Equity in the right-hand margin. For Retained Earnings, use separate columns for Revenues, Expenses, and Dividends if necessary. Use Illustration 3-3 (page 109) as a model.

Assets					=	**Liabilities**	+	**Stockholders' Equity**		
Cash	+	Inventory	+	Property, Plant, and Equipment	=	Accounts Payable	+	Common Stock	+	Retained Earnings

Indicate debit and credit effects. (SO 3)

BE3-4 For each of the following accounts indicate the effect of a debit or a credit on the account and the normal balance.

(a) Accounts Payable. (d) Accounts Receivable.
(b) Advertising Expense. (e) Retained Earnings.
(c) Service Revenue. (f) Dividends.

Identify accounts to be debited and credited. (SO 3)

BE3-5 Transactions for Marquis Company for the month of June are presented next. Identify the accounts to be debited and credited for each transaction.

June 1 Issues common stock to investors in exchange for $5,000 cash.
2 Buys equipment on account for $1,100.
3 Pays $500 to landlord for June rent.
12 Bills Jeff Gore $700 for welding work done.

Journalize transactions. (SO 5)

BE3-6 Use the data in BE3-5 and journalize the transactions. (You may omit explanations.)

Identify steps in the recording process. (SO 4)

BE3-7 Terry Rolen, a fellow student, is unclear about the basic steps in the recording process. Identify and briefly explain the steps in the order in which they occur.

Indicate basic debit–credit analysis. (SO 4)

BE3-8 Ankiel Corporation has the following transactions during August of the current year. Indicate (a) the basic analysis and (b) the debit–credit analysis illustrated on pages 121–126.

Aug. 1 Issues shares of common stock to investors in exchange for $10,000.
4 Pays insurance in advance for 3 months, $1,500.
16 Receives $900 from clients for services rendered.
27 Pays the secretary $500 salary.

Journalize transactions. (SO 5)

BE3-9 Use the data in BE3-8 and journalize the transactions. (You may omit explanations.)

Post journal entries to T accounts. (SO 7)

BE3-10 Selected transactions for Martinez Company are presented on page 139 in journal form (without explanations). Post the transactions to T accounts.

Date	Account Title	Debit	Credit
May 5	Accounts Receivable	3,800	
	Service Revenue		3,800
12	Cash	1,900	
	Accounts Receivable		1,900
15	Cash	2,000	
	Service Revenue		2,000

Prepare a trial balance. (SO 8)

BE3-11 From the ledger balances below, prepare a trial balance for Trowman Company at June 30, 2010. All account balances are normal.

Accounts Payable	$ 3,000	Service Revenue	$8,600
Cash	5,400	Accounts Receivable	3,000
Common Stock	18,000	Salaries Expense	4,000
Dividends	1,200	Rent Expense	1,000
Equipment	15,000		

Prepare a corrected trial balance. (SO 8)

BE3-12 An inexperienced bookkeeper prepared the following trial balance that does not balance. Prepare a correct trial balance, assuming all account balances are normal.

PETTENGILL COMPANY
Trial Balance
December 31, 2010

	Debit	Credit
Cash	$20,800	
Prepaid Insurance		$ 3,500
Accounts Payable		2,500
Unearned Revenue	1,800	
Common Stock		10,000
Retained Earnings		6,400
Dividends		5,000
Service Revenue		25,600
Salaries Expense	14,600	
Rent Expense		2,400
	$37,200	$55,400

Do it! Review

Prepare tabular analysis. (SO 1)

Do it! 3-1 Transactions made by Orlando Carbrera Co. for the month of March are shown below. Prepare a tabular analysis which shows the effects of these transactions on the expanded accounting equation, similar to that shown in Illustration 3-3 (page 109).

1. The company provided $20,000 of services for customers on account.
2. The company received $20,000 in cash from customers who had been billed for services [in transaction (1)].
3. The company received a bill for $2,000 of advertising, but will not pay it until a later date.
4. Orlando Carbrera Co. paid a cash dividend of $5,000.

Identify normal balances. (SO 2, 3)

Do it! 3-2 Josh Borke has just rented space in a strip mall. In this space, he will open a photography studio, to be called "Picture This!" A friend has advised Josh to set up a double-entry set of accounting records in which to record all of his business transactions.

Identify the balance sheet accounts that Josh will likely need to record the transactions needed to open his business (a corporation). Indicate whether the normal balance of each account is a debit or credit.

Record business activities.
(SO 4, 5)

Do it! 3-3 Josh Borke engaged in the following activities in establishing his photography studio, Picture This!:

1. Opened a bank account in the name of Picture This! and deposited $8,000 of his own money into this account in exchange for common stock.
2. Purchased photography supplies at a total cost of $1,100. The business paid $400 in cash, and the balance is on account.
3. Obtained estimates on the cost of photography equipment from three different manufacturers.

In what form (type of record) should Josh record these three activities? Prepare the entries to record the transactions.

Post transactions.
(SO 6, 7)

Do it! 3-4 Josh Borke recorded the following transactions during the month of April.

Apr. 3	Cash	3,400	
	Photography Revenue		3,400
Apr. 16	Rent Expense	600	
	Cash		600
Apr. 20	Salaries Expense	300	
	Cash		300

Post these entries to the Cash account of the general ledger to determine the ending balance in cash. The beginning balance in cash on April 1 was $1,600.

Exercises

Analyze the effect of transactions.
(SO 1)

E3-1 Selected transactions for Ruiz Advertising Company, Inc., are listed here.

1. Issued common stock to investors in exchange for cash received from investors.
2. Paid monthly rent.
3. Received cash from customers when service was provided.
4. Billed customers for services performed.
5. Paid dividend to stockholders.
6. Incurred advertising expense on account.
7. Received cash from customers billed in (4).
8. Purchased additional equipment for cash.
9. Purchased equipment on account.

Instructions

Describe the effect of each transaction on assets, liabilities, and stockholders' equity. For example, the first answer is: (1) Increase in assets and increase in stockholders' equity.

Analyze the effect of transactions on assets, liabilities, and stockholders' equity.
(SO 1)

E3-2 McBride Company entered into these transactions during May 2010.

1. Purchased computers for office use for $30,000 from Dell on account.
2. Paid $4,000 cash for May rent on storage space.
3. Received $12,000 cash from customers for contracts billed in April.
4. Provided computer services to Brieske Construction Company for $5,000 cash.
5. Paid Southern States Power Co. $11,000 cash for energy usage in May.
6. Stockholders invested an additional $40,000 in the business in exchange for common stock of the company.
7. Paid Dell for the computers purchased in (1).
8. Incurred advertising expense for May of $1,000 on account.

Instructions

Using the following tabular analysis, show the effect of each transaction on the accounting equation. Put explanations for changes to Stockholders' Equity in the right-hand margin. Use Illustration 3-3 (page 109) as a model.

Assets					=	Liabilities	+	Stockholders' Equity						
										Retained Earnings				
Cash	+	Accounts Receivable	+	Office Equipment	=	Accounts Payable	+	Common Stock	+	Revenues	−	Expenses	−	Dividends

E3-3 During 2010, its first year of operations as a delivery service, Lopez Corp. entered into the following transactions.

Determine effect of transactions on basic accounting equation. (SO 1)

1. Issued shares of common stock to investors in exchange for $100,000 in cash.
2. Borrowed $45,000 by issuing bonds.
3. Purchased delivery trucks for $60,000 cash.
4. Received $16,000 from customers for services provided.
5. Purchased supplies for $4,200 on account.
6. Paid rent of $5,600.
7. Performed services on account for $10,000.
8. Paid salaries of $28,000.
9. Paid a dividend of $11,000 to shareholders.

Instructions

Using the following tabular analysis, show the effect of each transaction on the accounting equation. Put explanations for changes to Stockholders' Equity in the right-hand margin. Use Illustration 3-3 (page 109) as a model. ("P/P/E" refers to Property, Plant, and Equipment.)

Assets								=	**Liabilities**			+	**Stockholders' Equity**						
															Retained Earnings				
Cash	+	Accounts Receivable	+	Supplies	+	P/P/E		=	Accounts Payable	+	Bonds Payable	+	Common Stock	+	Revenues	–	Expenses	–	Dividends

E3-4 A tabular analysis of the transactions made during August 2010 by Witten Company during its first month of operations is shown below. Each increase and decrease in stockholders' equity is explained.

Analyze transactions and compute net income. (SO 1)

	Assets							=	**Liabilities**	+	**Stockholders' Equity**							
													Retained Earnings					
	Cash	+	A/R	+	Supp.	+	Office Equip.	=	Accounts Payable	+	Common Stock	+	Rev.	–	Exp.	–	Div.	
1.	+$20,000										+$20,000							Com. Stock
2.	−1,000						+$5,000		+$4,000									
3.	−750				+$750													
4.	+4,400		+$5,400										+$9,800					Serv. Rev.
5.	−1,500								−1,500									
6.	−2,000																−$2,000	Div.
7.	−800														−$ 800			Rent Exp.
8.	+450		−450															
9.	−3,000														−3,000			Sal. Exp.
10.									+500						−500			Util. Exp.

Instructions

(a) Describe each transaction.
(b) Determine how much stockholders' equity increased for the month.
(c) Compute the net income for the month.

E3-5 The tabular analysis of transactions for Witten Company is presented in E3-4.

Prepare an income statement, retained earnings statement, and balance sheet. (SO 1)

Instructions

Prepare an income statement and a retained earnings statement for August and a classified balance sheet at August 31, 2010.

E3-6 Selected transactions for Loving Home, an interior decorator corporation, in its first month of business, are as follows.

Identify debits, credits, and normal balances and journalize transactions. (SO 3, 5)

1. Issued stock to investors for $15,000 in cash.
2. Purchased used car for $8,000 cash for use in business.
3. Purchased supplies on account for $300.
4. Billed customers $3,600 for services performed.
5. Paid $200 cash for advertising start of the business.

6. Received $1,100 cash from customers billed in transaction (4).
7. Paid creditor $300 cash on account.
8. Paid dividends of $400 cash to stockholders.

Instructions

(a) For each transaction indicate (a) the basic type of account debited and credited (asset, liability, stockholders' equity); (b) the specific account debited and credited (Cash, Rent Expense, Service Revenue, etc.); (c) whether the specific account is increased or decreased; and (d) the normal balance of the specific account. Use the following format, in which transaction 1 is given as an example.

	Account Debited				Account Credited			
Transaction	**(a) Basic Type**	**(b) Specific Account**	**(c) Effect**	**(d) Normal Balance**	**(a) Basic Type**	**(b) Specific Account**	**(c) Effect**	**(d) Normal Balance**
1	Asset	Cash	Increase	Debit	Stockholders' equity	Common Stock	Increase	Credit

(b) Journalize the transactions. Do not provide explanations.

Analyze transactions and determine their effect on accounts.
(SO 3)

E3-7 This information relates to Pickert Real Estate Agency.

Oct. 1 Stockholders invest $30,000 in exchange for common stock of the corporation.
2 Hires an administrative assistant at an annual salary of $42,000.
3 Buys office furniture for $4,600, on account.
6 Sells a house and lot for M.E. Petty; commissions due from Petty, $10,800 (not paid by Petty at this time).
10 Receives cash of $140 as commission for acting as rental agent renting an apartment.
27 Pays $700 on account for the office furniture purchased on October 3.
30 Pays the administrative assistant $3,500 in salary for October.

Instructions

Prepare the debit–credit analysis for each transaction as illustrated on pages 121–126.

Journalize transactions.
(SO 5)

E3-8 Transaction data for Pickert Real Estate Agency are presented in E3-7.

Instructions

Journalize the transactions. Do not provide explanations.

Post journal entries and prepare a trial balance.
(SO 7, 8)

E3-9 Transaction data and journal entries for Pickert Real Estate Agency are presented in E3-7 and E3-8.

Instructions

(a) Post the transactions to T accounts.
(b) Prepare a trial balance at October 31, 2010.

Analyze transactions, prepare journal entries, and post transactions to T accounts.
(SO 1, 5, 7)

E3-10 Selected transactions for A. B. Coors Corporation during its first month in business are presented below.

Sept. 1 Issued common stock in exchange for $20,000 cash received from investors.
5 Purchased equipment for $10,000, paying $2,000 in cash and the balance on account.
25 Paid $5,000 cash on balance owed for equipment.
30 Paid $500 cash dividend.

A. B. Coors's chart of accounts shows: Cash, Equipment, Accounts Payable, Common Stock, and Dividends.

Instructions

(a) Prepare a tabular analysis of the September transactions. The column headings should be: Cash + Equipment = Accounts Payable + Stockholders' Equity. For transactions affecting stockholders' equity, provide explanations in the right margin, as shown on page 109.
(b) Journalize the transactions. Do not provide explanations.
(c) Post the transactions to T accounts.

Journalize transactions from T accounts and prepare a trial balance.
(SO 5, 8)

E3-11 The T accounts on page 143 summarize the ledger of Sutton's Gardening Company, Inc. at the end of the first month of operations.

Cash

Apr.	1	15,000	Apr.	15	900
	12	700		25	3,500
	29	800			
	30	600			

Unearned Revenue

			Apr.	30	600

Accounts Receivable

Apr.	7	3,400	Apr.	29	800

Common Stock

			Apr.	1	15,000

Supplies

Apr.	4	5,200			

Service Revenue

			Apr.	7	3,400
				12	700

Accounts Payable

Apr.	25	3,500	Apr.	4	5,200

Salaries Expense

Apr.	15	900			

Instructions

(a) Prepare in the order they occurred the journal entries (including explanations) that resulted in the amounts posted to the accounts.

(b) Prepare a trial balance at April 30, 2010. (*Hint:* Compute ending balances of T accounts first.)

Post journal entries and prepare a trial balance.

(SO 7, 8)

E3-12 Selected transactions from the journal of Gipson Inc. during its first month of operations are presented here.

Date		Account Titles	Debit	Credit
Aug.	1	Cash	5,000	
		Common Stock		5,000
	10	Cash	1,700	
		Service Revenue		1,700
	12	Office Equipment	6,200	
		Cash		1,200
		Notes Payable		5,000
	25	Accounts Receivable	3,100	
		Service Revenue		3,100
	31	Cash	600	
		Accounts Receivable		600

Instructions

(a) Post the transactions to T accounts.

(b) Prepare a trial balance at August 31, 2010.

Journalize transactions from T accounts and prepare a trial balance.

(SO 5, 8)

E3-13 Here is the ledger for Brumbaugh Co.

Cash

Oct.	1	7,000	Oct.	4	400
	10	750		12	1,500
	10	8,000		15	250
	20	800		30	300
	25	2,000		31	500

Common Stock

			Oct.	1	7,000
				25	2,000

Accounts Receivable

Oct.	6	800	Oct.	20	800
	20	920			

Dividends

Oct.	30	300			

Supplies

Oct.	4	400	Oct.	31	180

Service Revenue

			Oct.	6	800
				10	750
				20	920

Furniture

Oct.	3	3,000			

Store Wages Expense

Oct.	31	500			

Notes Payable

			Oct.	10	8,000

Supplies Expense

Oct.	31	180			

Accounts Payable

Oct.	12	1,500	Oct.	3	3,000

Rent Expense

Oct.	15	250			

Instructions

(a) Reproduce the journal entries for only the transactions that ***occurred on October 1, 10, and 20***, and provide explanations for each.

(b) Prepare a trial balance at October 31, 2010. (*Hint:* Compute ending balances of T accounts first.)

Analyze errors and their effects on trial balance.
(SO 8)

E3-14 The bookkeeper for Biggio Corporation made these errors in journalizing and posting.

1. A credit posting of $400 to Accounts Receivable was omitted.
2. A debit posting of $750 for Prepaid Insurance was debited to Insurance Expense.
3. A collection on account of $100 was journalized and posted as a debit to Cash $100 and a credit to Accounts Payable $100.
4. A credit posting of $300 to Property Taxes Payable was made twice.
5. A cash purchase of supplies for $250 was journalized and posted as a debit to Supplies $25 and a credit to Cash $25.
6. A debit of $395 to Advertising Expense was posted as $359.

Instructions

For each error, indicate (a) whether the trial balance will balance; if the trial balance will not balance, indicate (b) the amount of the difference, and (c) the trial balance column that will have the larger total. Consider each error separately. Use the following form, in which error 1 is given as an example.

Error	(a) In Balance	(b) Difference	(c) Larger Column
1	No	$400	Debit

Prepare a trial balance and financial statements.
(SO 8)

E3-15 The accounts in the ledger of Thornton Delivery Service contain the following balances on July 31, 2010.

Accounts Receivable	$13,400	Prepaid Insurance	$ 1,800
Accounts Payable	8,400	Repair Expense	1,200
Cash	?	Service Revenue	15,500
Delivery Equipment	59,360	Dividends	700
Gas and Oil Expense	758	Common Stock	40,000
Insurance Expense	600	Salaries Expense	7,428
Notes Payable, due 2013	28,450	Salaries Payable	900
		Retained Earnings (July 1, 2010)	5,200

Instructions

(a) Prepare a trial balance with the accounts arranged as illustrated in the chapter, and fill in the missing amount for Cash.

(b) Prepare an income statement, a retained earnings statement, and a classified balance sheet for the month of July 2010.

Identify normal account balance and corresponding financial statement.
(SO 3)

E3-16 The following accounts, in alphabetical order, were selected from the 2007 financial statements of Krispy Kreme Doughnuts, Inc.

Accounts payable	Interest income
Accounts receivable	Inventories
Common stock	Prepaid expenses
Depreciation expense	Property and equipment
Interest expense	Revenues

Instructions

For each account, indicate (a) whether the normal balance is a debit or a credit, and (b) the financial statement—balance sheet or income statement—where the account should be presented.

Classify transactions as cash-flow activities.
(SO 9)

E3-17 Review the transactions listed in E3-1 for Ruiz Advertising Company, and classify each transaction as either an operating activity, investing activity, or financing activity, or if no cash is exchanged, as a non-cash event.

Classify transactions as cash-flow activities.
(SO 9)

E3-18 Review the transactions listed in E3-3 for Lopez Corp. and classify each transaction as either an operating activity, investing activity, or financing activity, or if no cash is exchanged, as a non-cash event.

Exercises: Set B

Visit the book's companion website, at **www.wiley.com/college/kimmel,** and choose the Student Companion site, to access Exercise Set B.

Problems: Set A

P3-1A On April 1 Flint Hills Travel Agency Inc. was established. These transactions were completed during the month.

Analyze transactions and compute net income.

(SO 1)

1. Stockholders invested $25,000 cash in the company in exchange for common stock.
2. Paid $900 cash for April office rent.
3. Purchased office equipment for $2,800 cash.
4. Purchased $200 of advertising in the *Chicago Tribune*, on account.
5. Paid $500 cash for office supplies.
6. Earned $10,000 for services provided: Cash of $1,000 is received from customers, and the balance of $9,000 is billed to customers on account.
7. Paid $400 cash dividends.
8. Paid *Chicago Tribune* amount due in transaction (4).
9. Paid employees' salaries $1,200.
10. Received $9,000 in cash from customers billed previously in transaction (6).

Instructions

(a) Prepare a tabular analysis of the transactions using these column headings: Cash, Accounts Receivable, Supplies, Office Equipment, Accounts Payable, Common Stock, and Retained Earnings (with separate columns for Revenues, Expenses, and Dividends). Include margin explanations for any changes in Retained Earnings.

(a) Cash $23,000
Ret. earnings $ 7,300

(b) From an analysis of the Retained Earnings columns, compute the net income or net loss for April.

P3-2A Diana Kuhlmann started her own consulting firm, Kuhlmann Consulting Inc., on May 1, 2010. The following transactions occurred during the month of May.

Analyze transactions and prepare financial statements.

(SO 1)

May	1	Stockholders invested $15,000 cash in the business in exchange for common stock.
	2	Paid $700 for office rent for the month.
	3	Purchased $500 of supplies on account.
	5	Paid $150 to advertise in the *County News*.
	9	Received $1,000 cash for services provided.
	12	Paid $200 cash dividend.
	15	Performed $4,200 of services on account.
	17	Paid $2,500 for employee salaries.
	20	Paid for the supplies purchased on account on May 3.
	23	Received a cash payment of $1,500 for services provided on account on May 15.
	26	Borrowed $5,000 from the bank on a note payable.
	29	Purchased office equipment for $2,000 paying $200 in cash and the balance on account.
	30	Paid $150 for utilities.

Instructions

(a) Show the effects of the previous transactions on the accounting equation using the following format. Assume the note payable is to be repaid within the year.

(a) Cash $18,100
Ret. earnings $ 1,500

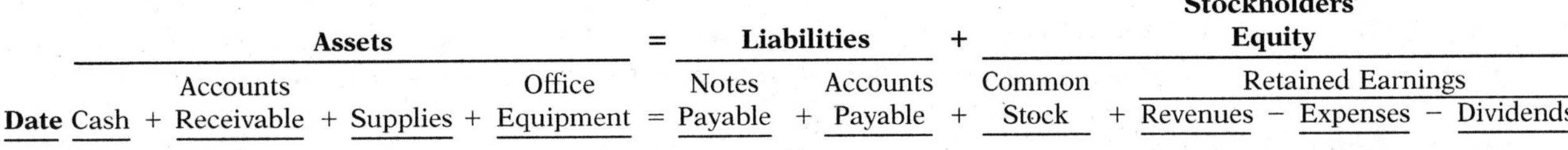

	Assets				=	Liabilities		+	Stockholders' Equity			
										Retained Earnings		
Date	Cash	+ Accounts Receivable	+ Supplies	+ Office Equipment	=	Notes Payable	+ Accounts Payable	+	Common Stock	+ Revenues	− Expenses	− Dividends

(b) Net income $1,700

Include margin explanations for any changes in Retained Earnings.
(b) Prepare an income statement for the month of May.
(c) Prepare a classified balance sheet at May 31, 2010.

Analyze transactions and prepare an income statement, retained earnings statement, and balance sheet.
(SO 1)

P3-3A Dick Reber created a corporation providing legal services, Dick Reber Inc., on July 1, 2010. On July 31 the balance sheet showed: Cash $4,000; Accounts Receivable $2,500; Supplies $500; Office Equipment $5,000; Accounts Payable $4,200; Common Stock $6,200; and Retained Earnings $1,600. During August the following transactions occurred.

1. Collected $1,500 of accounts receivable due from customers.
2. Paid $2,700 cash for accounts payable due.
3. Earned revenue of $5,400, of which $3,000 is collected in cash and the balance is due in September.
4. Purchased additional office equipment for $4,000, paying $400 in cash and the balance on account.
5. Paid salaries $1,400, rent for August $900, and advertising expenses $350.
6. Paid a cash dividend of $700.
7. Received $5,000 from Standard Federal Bank; the money was borrowed on a 4-month note payable.
8. Incurred utility expenses for the month on account $450.

(a) Cash $7,050
Ret. earnings $3,200

(b) Net income $2,300

Instructions

(a) Prepare a tabular analysis of the August transactions beginning with July 31 balances. The column heading should be: Cash + Accounts Receivable + Supplies + Office Equipment = Notes Payable + Accounts Payable + Common Stock + Retained Earnings. (Use separate Revenue, Expense, and Dividend columns). Include margin explanations for any changes in Retained Earnings.
(b) Prepare an income statement for August, a retained earnings statement for August, and a classified balance sheet at August 31.

Journalize a series of transactions.
(SO 3, 5)
GLS

P3-4A Four Oaks Miniature Golf and Driving Range Inc. was opened on March 1 by Tiger Woodley. These selected events and transactions occurred during March.

Mar.	1	Stockholders invested $50,000 cash in the business in exchange for common stock of the corporation.
	3	Purchased Arnie's Golf Land for $38,000 cash. The price consists of land $23,000, building $9,000, and equipment $6,000. (Record this in a single entry.)
	5	Advertised the opening of the driving range and miniature golf course, paying advertising expenses of $1,600 cash.
	6	Paid cash $2,400 for a 1-year insurance policy.
	10	Purchased golf clubs and other equipment for $4,700 from Golden Bear Company, payable in 30 days.
	18	Received golf fees of $1,200 in cash from customers for golf fees earned.
	19	Sold 100 coupon books for $25 each in cash. Each book contains ten coupons that enable the holder to play one round of miniature golf or to hit one bucket of golf balls. (*Hint:* The revenue is not earned until the customers use the coupons.)
	25	Paid a $500 cash dividend.
	30	Paid salaries of $700.
	30	Paid Golden Bear Company in full for equipment purchased on March 10.
	31	Received $800 in cash from customers for golf fees earned.

The company uses these accounts: Cash, Prepaid Insurance, Land, Buildings, Equipment, Accounts Payable, Unearned Golf Revenue, Common Stock, Retained Earnings, Dividends, Golf Revenue, Advertising Expense, and Salaries Expense.

Instructions

Journalize the March transactions, including explanations.

P3-5A Sunflower Architects incorporated as licensed architects on April 1, 2010. During the first month of the operation of the business, these events and transactions occurred:

Journalize transactions, post, and prepare a trial balance.
(SO 3, 5, 6, 7, 8)

Apr.	1	Stockholders invested $15,000 cash in exchange for common stock of the corporation.
	1	Hired a secretary-receptionist at a salary of $375 per week, payable monthly.
	2	Paid office rent for the month $900.
	3	Purchased architectural supplies on account from Spring Green Company $1,000.
	10	Completed blueprints on a carport and billed client $1,500 for services.
	11	Received $500 cash advance from J. Madison to design a new home.
	20	Received $2,300 cash for services completed and delivered to M. Svetlana.
	30	Paid secretary-receptionist for the month $1,500.
	30	Paid $300 to Spring Green Company for accounts payable due.

The company uses these accounts: Cash, Accounts Receivable, Supplies, Accounts Payable, Unearned Revenue, Common Stock, Service Revenue, Salaries Expense, and Rent Expense.

Instructions

(a) Journalize the transactions, including explanations.
(b) Post to the ledger T accounts.
(c) Prepare a trial balance on April 30, 2010.

(c) Cash $15,100
Tot. trial balance $20,000

P3-6A This is the trial balance of Slocombe Company on September 30.

Journalize transactions, post, and prepare a trial balance.
(SO 3, 5, 6, 7, 8)

SLOCOMBE COMPANY
Trial Balance
September 30, 2010

	Debit	Credit
Cash	$ 8,300	
Accounts Receivable	2,600	
Supplies	2,100	
Equipment	8,000	
Accounts Payable		$ 5,100
Unearned Revenue		900
Common Stock		15,000
	$21,000	$21,000

The October transactions were as follows.

Oct.	5	Received $1,300 in cash from customers for accounts receivable due.
	10	Billed customers for services performed $5,100.
	15	Paid employee salaries $1,400.
	17	Performed $600 of services for customers who paid in advance in August.
	20	Paid $1,500 to creditors for accounts payable due.
	29	Paid a $300 cash dividend.
	31	Paid utilities $500.

Instructions

(a) Prepare a general ledger using T accounts. Enter the opening balances in the ledger accounts as of October 1. Provision should be made for these additional accounts: Dividends, Service Revenue, Salaries Expense, and Utilities Expense.
(b) Journalize the transactions, including explanations.
(c) Post to the ledger accounts.
(d) Prepare a trial balance on October 31, 2010.

(d) Cash $ 5,900
Tot. trial balance $24,800

Prepare a correct trial balance.
(SO 8)

P3-7A This trial balance of Titus Co. does not balance.

TITUS CO.
Trial Balance
June 30, 2010

	Debit	Credit
Cash		$ 3,090
Accounts Receivable	$ 3,460	
Supplies	800	
Equipment	3,000	
Accounts Payable		3,666
Unearned Revenue	1,200	
Common Stock		9,000
Dividends	800	
Service Revenue		3,480
Salaries Expense	3,600	
Office Expense	910	
	$13,770	$19,236

Each of the listed accounts has a normal balance per the general ledger. An examination of the ledger and journal reveals the following errors:

1. Cash received from a customer on account was debited for $590, and Accounts Receivable was credited for the same amount. The actual collection was for $950.
2. The purchase of a printer on account for $340 was recorded as a debit to Supplies for $340 and a credit to Accounts Payable for $340.
3. Services were performed on account for a client for $800. Accounts Receivable was debited for $80 and Service Revenue was credited for $800.
4. A debit posting to Salaries Expense of $500 was omitted.
5. A payment on account for $206 was credited to Cash for $206 and credited to Accounts Payable for $260.
6. Payment of a $600 cash dividend to Titus's stockholders was debited to Salaries Expense for $600 and credited to Cash for $600.

Instructions

Tot. trial balance $16,830

Prepare the correct trial balance. (*Hint:* All accounts have normal balances.)

Journalize transactions, post, and prepare a trial balance.
(SO 3, 5, 6, 7, 8)

P3-8A The Star-Lite Theater Inc. was recently formed. It began operations in March 2010. The Star-Lite is unique in that it will show only triple features of sequential theme movies. On March 1, the ledger of The Star-Lite showed: Cash $16,000; Land $38,000; Buildings (concession stand, projection room, ticket booth, and screen) $22,000; Equipment $16,000; Accounts Payable $12,000; and Common Stock $80,000. During the month of March the following events and transactions occurred.

Mar.	2	Rented the three Star Wars movies (*Star Wars®, The Empire Strikes Back*, and *The Return of the Jedi*) to be shown for the first three weeks of March. The film rental was $10,000; $2,000 was paid in cash and $8,000 will be paid on March 10.
	3	Ordered the first three *Star Trek* movies to be shown the last 10 days of March. It will cost $400 per night.
	9	Received $9,200 cash from admissions.
	10	Paid balance due on *Star Wars* movies rental and $2,600 on March 1 accounts payable.
	11	Hired J. Carne to operate the concession stand. Carne agrees to pay The Star-Lite Theater 15% of gross receipts, payable monthly.
	12	Paid advertising expenses $900.
	20	Received $7,100 cash from customers for admissions.
	20	Received the *Star Trek* movies and paid rental fee of $4,000.
	31	Paid salaries of $3,800.

31 Received statement from J. Carne showing gross receipts from concessions of $10,000 and the balance due to The Star-Lite of $1,500 for March. Carne paid half the balance due and will remit the remainder on April 5.

31 Received $20,000 cash from customers for admissions.

In addition to the accounts identified above, the chart of accounts includes: Accounts Receivable, Admission Revenue, Concession Revenue, Advertising Expense, Film Rental Expense, and Salaries Expense.

Instructions

(a) Using T accounts, enter the beginning balances to the ledger.
(b) Journalize the March transactions, including explanations.
(c) Post the March journal entries to the ledger.
(d) Prepare a trial balance on March 31, 2010.

(d) Cash $31,750
Tot. trial balance $127,200

P3-9A The bookkeeper for Sandy McClain's dance studio made the following errors in journalizing and posting.

Analyze errors and their effects on the trial balance.
(SO 8)

1. A credit to Supplies of $600 was omitted.
2. A debit posting of $300 to Accounts Payable was inadvertently debited to Accounts Receivable.
3. A purchase of supplies on account of $450 was debited to Supplies for $540 and credited to Accounts Payable for $540.
4. A credit posting of $350 to Wages Payable was posted twice.
5. A debit posting to Wages Payable for $250 and a credit posting to Cash for $250 were made twice.
6. A debit posting for $1,200 of Dividends was inadvertently posted to Travel Expense instead.
7. A credit to Service Revenue for $450 was inadvertently posted as a debit to Service Revenue.
8. A credit to Accounts Receivable of $250 was credited to Accounts Payable.

Instructions

For each error, indicate (a) whether the trial balance will balance; (b) the amount of the difference if the trial balance will not balance; and (c) the trial balance column that will have the larger total. Consider each error separately. Use the following form, in which error 1 is given as an example.

Error	(a) In Balance	(b) Difference	(c) Larger Column
1.	No	$600	Debit

Problems: Set B

P3-1B Hermesch Window Washing Inc. was started on May 1. Here is a summary of the May transactions.

Analyze transactions and compute net income.
(SO 1)

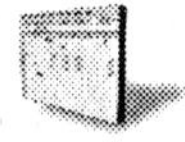

1. Stockholders invested $20,000 cash in the company in exchange for common stock.
2. Purchased equipment for $7,000 cash.
3. Paid $700 cash for May office rent.
4. Paid $400 cash for supplies.
5. Purchased $750 of advertising in the *Beacon News* on account.
6. Received $5,800 in cash from customers for service.
7. Paid a $500 cash dividend.
8. Paid part-time employee salaries $1,700.
9. Paid utility bills $140.
10. Provided service on account to customers $1,000.
11. Collected cash of $240 for services billed in transaction (10).

Instructions

(a) Prepare a tabular analysis of the transactions using these column headings: Cash, Accounts Receivable, Supplies, Equipment, Accounts Payable, Common Stock, and Retained Earnings (with separate columns for Revenues, Expenses, and Dividends). Revenue is called Service Revenue. Include margin explanations for any changes in Retained Earnings.

(b) Net income $3,510

(b) From an analysis of the Retained Earnings columns, compute the net income or net loss for May.

Analyze transactions and prepare financial statements.
(SO 1)

GLS

P3-2B Richard Mordica started his own delivery service, Speedy Service Inc., on June 1, 2010. The following transactions occurred during the month of June.

June	1	Stockholders invested $15,000 cash in the business in exchange for common stock.
	2	Purchased a used van for deliveries for $15,000. Richard paid $2,000 cash and signed a note payable for the remaining balance.
	3	Paid $500 for office rent for the month.
	5	Performed $2,400 of services on account.
	9	Paid $300 in cash dividends.
	12	Purchased supplies for $150 on account.
	15	Received a cash payment of $750 for services provided on June 5.
	17	Purchased gasoline for $200 on account.
	20	Received a cash payment of $1,500 for services provided.
	23	Made a cash payment of $800 on the note payable.
	26	Paid $250 for utilities.
	29	Paid for the supplies purchased on account on June 12.
	30	Paid $750 for employee salaries.

(a) Cash $12,500

Instructions

(a) Show the effects of the previous transactions on the accounting equation using the following format. Assume the note payable is to be repaid within the year.

	Assets				=	Liabilities		+	Stockholders' Equity			
										Retained Earnings		
Date	Cash	+ Accounts Receivable	+ Supplies	+ Delivery Van	=	Notes Payable	+ Accounts Payable	+	Common Stock	+ Revenues	− Expenses	− Dividends

Include margin explanations for any changes in Retained Earnings.

(b) Net income $2,200

(b) Prepare an income statement for the month of June.

(c) Prepare a classified balance sheet at June 30, 2010.

Analyze transactions and prepare an income statement, retained earnings statement, and balance sheet.
(SO 1)

GLS

P3-3B Nancy Grey opened Grey Company, a veterinary business in Neosho, Wisconsin, on August 1, 2010. On August 31 the balance sheet showed: Cash $9,000; Accounts Receivable $1,700; Supplies $600; Office Equipment $5,000; Accounts Payable $3,600; Common Stock $12,000; and Retained Earnings $700. During September the following transactions occurred.

1. Paid $3,400 cash for accounts payable due.
2. Received $1,600 from customers in payment of accounts receivable.
3. Purchased additional office equipment for $5,100, paying $1,000 in cash and the balance on account.
4. Earned revenue of $9,500, of which $2,300 is paid in cash and the balance is due in October.
5. Declared and paid a $600 cash dividend.
6. Paid salaries $900, rent for September $800, and advertising expense $250.
7. Incurred utility expenses for the month on account $170.
8. Received $5,000 from Hilldale Bank on a 6-month note payable.

Instructions

(a) Cash $10,950
Ret. earnings $ 7,480

(a) Prepare a tabular analysis of the September transactions beginning with August 31 balances. The column headings should be: Cash + Accounts Receivable + Supplies + Office Equipment = Notes Payable + Accounts Payable + Common Stock + Retained Earnings. Include margin explanations for any changes in Retained Earnings.

(b) Prepare an income statement for September, a retained earnings statement for September, and a classified balance sheet at September 30, 2010.

P3-4B RV Haven was started on April 1 by Tom Larkin. These selected events and transactions occurred during April.

Journalize a series of transactions.

(SO 3, 5)

Apr.	1	Stockholders invested $70,000 cash in the business in exchange for common stock.
	4	Purchased land costing $50,000 for cash.
	8	Purchased advertising in local newspaper for $1,200 on account.
	11	Paid salaries to employees $2,700.
	12	Hired park manager at a salary of $3,000 per month, effective May 1.
	13	Paid $6,000 for a 1-year insurance policy.
	17	Paid $600 cash dividends.
	20	Received $5,000 in cash from customers for admission fees.
	25	Sold 100 coupon books for $75 each. Each book contains ten coupons that entitle the holder to one admission to the park. (*Hint*: The revenue is not earned until the coupons are used.)
	30	Received $7,900 in cash from customers for admission fees.
	30	Paid $500 of the balance owed for the advertising purchased on account on April 8.

The company uses the following accounts: Cash, Prepaid Insurance, Land, Accounts Payable, Unearned Admissions, Common Stock, Dividends, Admission Revenue, Advertising Expense, and Salaries Expense.

Instructions

Journalize the April transactions, including explanations.

P3-5B Sammy Baden incorporated Baden Consulting, an accounting practice, on May 1, 2010. During the first month of operations, these events and transactions occurred.

Journalize transactions, post, and prepare a trial balance.

(SO 3, 5, 6, 7, 8)

May	1	Stockholders invested $50,000 cash in exchange for common stock of the corporation.
	2	Hired a secretary-receptionist at a salary of $2,000 per month.
	3	Purchased $800 of supplies on account from Fleming Supply Company.
	7	Paid office rent of $1,100 for the month.
	11	Completed a tax assignment and billed client $1,000 for services provided.
	12	Received $4,200 advance on a management consulting engagement.
	17	Received cash of $3,600 for services completed for Goodman Co.
	31	Paid secretary-receptionist $2,000 salary for the month.
	31	Paid 50% of balance due Fleming Supply Company.

The company uses the following chart of accounts: Cash, Accounts Receivable, Supplies, Accounts Payable, Unearned Revenue, Common Stock, Service Revenue, Salaries Expense, and Rent Expense.

Instructions

(a) Journalize the transactions, including explanations.
(b) Post to the ledger T accounts.
(c) Prepare a trial balance on May 31, 2010.

(c) Cash $54,300
Tot. trial balance $59,200

P3-6B The trial balance of Capaldo Dry Cleaners on June 30 is given here.

Journalize transactions, post, and prepare a trial balance.

(SO 3, 5, 6, 7, 8)

CAPALDO DRY CLEANERS
Trial Balance
June 30, 2010

	Debit	Credit
Cash	$12,532	
Accounts Receivable	10,536	
Supplies	3,512	
Equipment	25,950	
Accounts Payable		$15,800
Unearned Revenue		1,730
Common Stock		35,000
	$52,530	$52,530

The July transactions were as follows.

July	8	Received $5,189 in cash on June 30 accounts receivable.
	9	Paid employee salaries $2,100.
	11	Received $6,100 in cash for services provided.
	14	Paid creditors $10,750 of accounts payable.
	17	Purchased supplies on account $720.
	22	Billed customers for services provided $4,700.
	30	Paid employee salaries $3,114, utilities $1,767, and repairs $492.
	31	Paid $400 cash dividend.

Instructions

(a) Prepare a general ledger using T accounts. Enter the opening balances in the ledger accounts as of July 1. Provision should be made for the following additional accounts: Dividends, Dry Cleaning Revenue, Repair Expense, Salaries Expense, and Utilities Expense.

(b) Journalize the transactions, including explanations.

(c) Post to the ledger accounts.

(d) Prepare a trial balance on July 31, 2010.

(d) Cash $ 5,198
Tot. trial balance $53,300

Prepare a correct trial balance.

(SO 8)

P3-7B This trial balance of Schumaker Company does not balance.

SCHUMAKER COMPANY
Trial Balance
May 31, 2010

	Debit	Credit
Cash	$ 6,340	
Accounts Receivable		$ 2,750
Prepaid Insurance	700	
Equipment	8,000	
Accounts Payable		4,100
Property Taxes Payable	750	
Common Stock		5,700
Retained Earnings		6,000
Service Revenue	7,690	
Salaries Expense	4,200	
Advertising Expense		1,100
Property Tax Expense	900	
	$28,580	$19,650

Your review of the ledger reveals that each account has a normal balance. You also discover the following errors.

1. The totals of the debit sides of Prepaid Insurance, Accounts Payable, and Property Tax Expense were each understated $100.
2. Transposition errors were made in Accounts Receivable and Service Revenue. Based on postings made, the correct balances were $2,570 and $7,960, respectively.
3. A debit posting to Salaries Expense of $400 was omitted.
4. An $800 cash dividend was debited to Common Stock for $800 and credited to Cash for $800.
5. A $350 purchase of supplies on account was debited to Equipment for $350 and credited to Cash for $350.
6. A cash payment of $450 for advertising was debited to Advertising Expense for $45 and credited to Cash for $45.
7. A collection from a customer for $240 was debited to Cash for $240 and credited to Accounts Payable for $240.

Instructions

Prepare the correct trial balance, assuming all accounts have normal balances. (*Note:* The chart of accounts also includes the following: Dividends and Supplies.)

Cash $ 6,285
Tot. trial balance $25,320

P3-8B Granada Theater Inc. was recently formed. All facilities were completed on March 31. On April 1, the ledger showed: Cash $6,300; Land $10,000; Buildings (concession stand, projection room, ticket booth, and screen) $8,000; Equipment $6,000; Accounts Payable $2,300; Mortgage Payable $8,000; and Common Stock $20,000. During April, the following events and transactions occurred.

Journalize transactions, post, and prepare a trial balance.
(SO 3, 5, 6, 7, 8)

Apr.	2	Paid film rental fee of $800 on first movie.
	3	Ordered two additional films at $900 each.
	9	Received $4,900 cash from admissions.
	10	Paid $2,000 of mortgage payable and $1,200 of accounts payable.
	11	Hired M. Gavin to operate the concession stand. Gavin agrees to pay Granada Theater 17% of gross receipts, payable monthly.
	12	Paid advertising expenses $460.
	20	Received one of the films ordered on April 3 and was billed $900. The film will be shown in April.
	25	Received $3,000 cash from customers for admissions.
	29	Paid salaries $1,900.
	30	Received statement from M. Gavin showing gross receipts of $2,000 and the balance due to Granada Theater of $340 for April. Gavin paid half of the balance due and will remit the remainder on May 5.
	30	Prepaid $1,000 rental fee on special film to be run in May.

In addition to the accounts identified above, the chart of accounts shows: Accounts Receivable, Prepaid Rentals, Admission Revenue, Concession Revenue, Advertising Expense, Film Rental Expense, Salaries Expense.

Instructions

(a) Enter the beginning balances in the ledger T accounts as of April 1.
(b) Journalize the April transactions, including explanations.
(c) Post the April journal entries to the ledger T accounts.
(d) Prepare a trial balance on April 30, 2010.

(d) Cash $ 7,010
Tot. trial balance $36,240

P3-9B A first year co-op student working for UR Here.com recorded the transactions for the month. He wasn't exactly sure how to journalize and post, but he did the best he could. He had a few questions, however, about the following transactions.

Analyze errors and their effects on the trial balance.
(SO 8)

1. Cash received from a customer on account was recorded as a debit to Cash of $360 and a credit to Accounts Receivable of $630, instead of $360.
2. A service provided for cash was posted as a debit to Cash of $2,000 and a credit to Service Revenue of $2,000.
3. A debit of $880 for services provided on account was neither recorded nor posted. The credit was recorded correctly.
4. The debit to record $1,000 of cash dividends was posted to the Salary Expense account.
5. The purchase, on account, of a computer that cost $2,500 was recorded as a debit to Supplies and a credit to Accounts Payable.
6. A cash payment of $495 for salaries was recorded as a debit to Dividends and a credit to Cash.
7. Payment of month's rent was debited to Rent Expense and credited to Cash, $850.
8. Issue of $7,000 of common shares was credited to the Common Stock account, but no debit was recorded.

Instructions

(a) Indicate which of the above transactions are correct, and which are incorrect.
(b) For each error identified in (a), indicate (1) whether the trial balance will balance; (2) the amount of the difference if the trial balance will not balance; and (3) the trial balance column that will have the larger total. Consider each error separately. Use the following form, in which transaction 1 is given as an example.

Error	(1) In Balance	(2) Difference	(3) Larger Column
1.	No	$270	Credit

Problems: Set C

Visit the book's companion website at **www.wiley.com/college/kimmel** and choose the Student Companion site to access Problem Set C.

Continuing Cookie Chronicle

(*Note:* This is a continuation of the Cookie Chronicle from Chapters 1 and 2.)

CCC3 In November 2009 after having incorporated Cookie Creations Inc., Natalie begins operations. She has decided to not pursue the offer to supply cookies to Biscuits. Instead she will focus on offering cooking classes.

Go to the book's companion website, **www.wiley.com/college/kimmel,** to find the completion of this problem.

broadening your perspective

Financial Reporting and Analysis

FINANCIAL REPORTING PROBLEM: *Tootsie Roll Industries*

BYP3-1 The financial statements of Tootsie Roll in Appendix A at the back of this book contain the following selected accounts, all in thousands of dollars.

Common Stock	$ 24,586
Accounts Payable	11,572
Accounts Receivable	32,371
Selling, Marketing, and Administrative Expenses	97,821
Prepaid Expenses	6,551
Property, Plant, and Equipment	201,401
Net Sales	492,742

Instructions

(a) What is the increase and decrease side for each account? What is the normal balance for each account?

(b) Identify the probable other account in the transaction and the effect on that account when:
   (1) Accounts Receivable is decreased.
   (2) Accounts Payable is decreased.
   (3) Prepaid Expenses is increased.

(c) Identify the other account(s) that ordinarily would be involved when:
   (1) Interest Expense is increased.
   (2) Property, Plant, and Equipment is increased.

COMPARATIVE ANALYSIS PROBLEM: *Tootsie Roll vs. Hershey Foods*

BYP3-2 The financial statements of Hershey Foods appear in Appendix B, following the financial statements for Tootsie Roll in Appendix A.

Instructions

(a) Based on the information contained in these financial statements, determine the normal balance for:

Tootsie Roll Industries	Hershey Foods
(1) Accounts Receivable	(1) Inventories
(2) Property, Plant, and Equipment	(2) Provision for Income Taxes
(3) Accounts Payable	(3) Accrued Liabilities
(4) Retained Earnings	(4) Common Stock
(5) Net Sales	(5) Interest Expense

(b) Identify the other account ordinarily involved when:
  (1) Accounts Receivable is increased.
  (2) Notes Payable is decreased.
  (3) Machinery is increased.
  (4) Interest Income is increased.

RESEARCH CASE

BYP3-3 Sid Cato provides critiques of corporate annual reports. He maintains a website at **www.sidcato.com** that provides many useful resources for those who are interested in preparing or using annual reports.

Instructions

Go to the website and answer the following questions.

(a) Read the section, "What makes a good annual report?" and choose which three factors you think are most important. Explain why you think each item is important.
(b) For the most recent year, which companies were listed in the section "Producers of the best annuals for (*most recent year*)"?
(c) What potential benefits might a company gain by receiving a high rating from Sid Cato's organization?

INTERPRETING FINANCIAL STATEMENTS

BYP3-4 Chieftain International, Inc., is an oil and natural gas exploration and production company. A recent balance sheet reported $208 million in assets with only $4.6 million in liabilities, all of which were short-term accounts payable.

During the year, Chieftain expanded its holdings of oil and gas rights, drilled 37 new wells, and invested in expensive 3-D seismic technology. The company generated $19 million cash from operating activities and paid no dividends. It had a cash balance of $102 million at the end of the year.

Instructions

(a) Name at least two advantages to Chieftain from having no long-term debt. Can you think of disadvantages?
(b) What are some of the advantages to Chieftain from having this large a cash balance? What is a disadvantage?
(c) Why do you suppose Chieftain has the $4.6 million balance in accounts payable, since it appears that it could have made all its purchases for cash?

BYP3-5 Doman Industries Ltd., whose products are sold in 30 countries worldwide, is an integrated Canadian forest products company.

Doman sells the majority of its lumber products in the United States, and a significant amount of its pulp products in Asia. Doman also has loans from other countries. For example, the Company borrowed US$160 million at an annual interest rate of 12%. Doman must repay this loan, and interest, in U.S. dollars.

One of the challenges global companies face is to make themselves attractive to investors from other countries. This is difficult to do when different accounting rules in different countries blur the real impact of earnings. For example, in a recent year Doman reported a loss of $2.3 million, using Canadian accounting rules. Had it reported under U.S. accounting rules, its loss would have been $12.1 million.

Many companies that want to be more easily compared with U.S. and other global competitors have switched to U.S. accounting principles. Canadian National Railway, Corel, Cott, Inco, and Thomson Corporation are but a few examples of large Canadian companies whose financial statements are now presented in U.S. dollars, adhere to U.S. GAAP, or are reconciled to U.S. GAAP.

Instructions

(a) Identify advantages and disadvantages that companies should consider when switching to U.S. reporting standards.
(b) Suppose you compare Doman Industries to a U.S.-based competitor. Do you believe the use of country-specific accounting policies would hinder your ability to compare the companies? If so, explain how.

(c) Suppose you compare Doman Industries to a Canadian-based competitor. If the companies apply generally acceptable Canadian accounting policies differently, how could this affect your ability to compare their financial results?

(d) Do you see any significant distinction between comparing statements prepared using generally accepted accounting principles of different countries and comparing statements prepared using generally accepted accounting principles of the same country (e.g. U.S.) but that apply the principles differently?

FINANCIAL ANALYSIS ON THE WEB

BYP3-6 ***Purpose:*** This activity provides information about career opportunities for CPAs.

Address: **www.icpas.org/students.htm**, or go to **www.wiley.com/college/kimmel**

Steps

1. Go to the address shown above.
2. Click on **High School**, then **CPA101** for parts a, b, and c.
3. Click **College** to answer part d.

Instructions

Answer the following questions.

(a) What does CPA stand for? Where do CPAs work?

(b) What is meant by "public accounting"?

(c) What skills does a CPA need?

(d) What is the salary range for a CPA at a large firm during the first three years? What is the salary range for chief financial officers and treasurers at large corporations?

Critical Thinking

DECISION MAKING ACROSS THE ORGANIZATION

BYP3-7 Donna Dye operates Double D Riding Academy, Inc. The academy's primary sources of revenue are riding fees and lesson fees, which are provided on a cash basis. Donna also boards horses for owners, who are billed monthly for boarding fees. In a few cases, boarders pay in advance of expected use. For its revenue transactions, the academy maintains these accounts: Cash, Accounts Receivable, Unearned Revenue, Riding Revenue, Lesson Revenue, and Boarding Revenue.

The academy owns 10 horses, a stable, a riding corral, riding equipment, and office equipment. These assets are accounted for in the following accounts: Horses, Building, Riding Corral, Riding Equipment, and Office Equipment.

The academy employs stable helpers and an office employee, who receive weekly salaries. At the end of each month, the mail usually brings bills for advertising, utilities, and veterinary service. Other expenses include feed for the horses and insurance. For its expenses, the academy maintains the following accounts: Hay and Feed Supplies, Prepaid Insurance, Accounts Payable, Salaries Expense, Advertising Expense, Utilities Expense, Veterinary Expense, Hay and Feed Expense, and Insurance Expense.

Donna Dye's sole source of personal income is dividends from the academy. Thus, the corporation declares and pays periodic dividends. To account for stockholders' equity in the business and dividends, two accounts are maintained: Common Stock and Dividends.

During the first month of operations an inexperienced bookkeeper was employed. Donna Dye asks you to review the following eight entries of the 50 entries made during the month. In each case, the explanation for the entry is correct.

May	1	Cash	15,000	
		Unearned Revenue		15,000
		(Issued common stock in exchange for $15,000 cash)		
	5	Cash	250	
		Lesson Revenue		250
		(Received $250 cash for lesson fees)		

May	7	Cash	500	
		Boarding Revenue		500
		(Received $500 for boarding of horses beginning June 1)		
	9	Hay and Feed Expense	1,500	
		Cash		1,500
		(Purchased estimated 5 months' supply of feed and hay for $1,500 on account)		
	14	Riding Equipment	80	
		Cash		800
		(Purchased desk and other office equipment for $800 cash)		
	15	Salaries Expense	400	
		Cash		400
		(Issued check to Donna Dye for personal use)		
	20	Cash	145	
		Riding Revenue		154
		(Received $154 cash for riding fees)		
	31	Veterinary Expense	75	
		Accounts Receivable		75
		(Received bill of $75 from veterinarian for services provided)		

Instructions

With the class divided into groups, answer the following.

(a) For each journal entry that is correct, so state. For each journal entry that is incorrect, prepare the entry that should have been made by the bookkeeper.

(b) Which of the incorrect entries would prevent the trial balance from balancing?

(c) What was the correct net income for May, assuming the bookkeeper originally reported net income of $4,500 after posting all 50 entries?

(d) What was the correct cash balance at May 31, assuming the bookkeeper reported a balance of $12,475 after posting all 50 entries?

COMMUNICATION ACTIVITY

BYP3-8 Clean Sweep Company offers home cleaning service. Two recurring transactions for the company are billing customers for services provided and paying employee salaries. For example, on March 15 bills totaling $6,000 were sent to customers, and $2,000 was paid in salaries to employees.

Instructions

Write a memorandum to your instructor that explains and illustrates the steps in the recording process for each of the March 15 transactions. Use the format illustrated in the text under the heading "The Recording Process Illustrated" (pp. 120–126).

ETHICS CASES

BYP3-9 Monica Geller is the assistant chief accountant at BIT Company, a manufacturer of computer chips and cellular phones. The company presently has total sales of $20 million. It is the end of the first quarter and Monica is hurriedly trying to prepare a general ledger trial balance so that quarterly financial statements can be prepared and released to management and the regulatory agencies. The total credits on the trial balance exceed the debits by $1,000.

In order to meet the 4 P.M. deadline, Monica decides to force the debits and credits into balance by adding the amount of the difference to the Equipment account. She chose Equipment because it is one of the larger account balances; percentage-wise it will be the least misstated. Monica plugs the difference! She believes that the difference is quite small and will not affect anyone's decisions. She wishes that she had another few days to find the error but realizes that the financial statements are already late.

Instructions

(a) Who are the stakeholders in this situation?
(b) What ethical issues are involved?
(c) What are Monica's alternatives?

BYP3-10 The July 28, 2007, issue of the *Wall Street Journal* includes an article by Kathryn Kranhold titled "GE's Accounting Draws Fresh Focus on News of Improper Sales Bookings."

Instructions

Read the article and answer the following questions.

(a) What improper activity did the employees at GE engage in?
(b) Why might the employees have engaged in this activity?
(c) What were the implications for the employees who engaged in this activity?
(d) What does it mean to "restate" financial results? Why didn't GE restate its results to correct for the improperly reported locomotive sales?

"ALL ABOUT YOU" ACTIVITY

BYP3-11 In their annual reports to stockholders, companies must report or disclose information about all liabilities, including potential liabilities related to environmental clean-up. There are many situations in which you will be asked to provide personal financial information about your assets, liabilities, revenue, and expenses. Sometimes you will face difficult decisions regarding what to disclose and how to disclose it.

Instructions

Suppose that you are putting together a loan application to purchase a home. Based on your income and assets, you qualify for the mortgage loan, but just barely. How would you address each of the following situations in reporting your financial position for the loan application? Provide responses for each of the following questions.

(a) You signed a guarantee for a bank loan that a friend took out for $20,000. If your friend doesn't pay, you will have to pay. Your friend has made all of the payments so far, and it appears he will be able to pay in the future.
(b) You were involved in an auto accident in which you were at fault. There is the possibility that you may have to pay as much as $50,000 as part of a settlement. The issue will not be resolved before the bank processes your mortgage request.
(c) The company at which you work isn't doing very well, and it has recently laid off employees. You are still employed, but it is quite possible that you will lose your job in the next few months.

Answers to Insight and Accounting Across the Organization Questions

p. 108

Q: In order for these companies to prepare and issue financial statements, their accounting equations (debit and credits) must have been in balance at year-end. How could these errors or misstatements have occurred?

A: A company's accounting equation (its books) can be in balance yet its financial statements have errors or misstatements because of the following: entire transactions were not recorded; transactions were recorded at wrong amounts; transactions were recorded in the wrong accounts; transactions were recorded in the wrong accounting period. Audits of financial statements uncover some, but obviously not all, errors or misstatements.

p. 114

Q: Do you think that the Chicago Bears football team would be likely to have the same major revenue and expense accounts as the Cubs?

A: Because their businesses are similar—professional sports—many of the revenue and expense accounts for the baseball and football teams might be similar.

p. 118

Q: In what ways is this Microsoft division using accounting to assist in its effort to become more profitable?

A: The division has used accounting to set very strict sales, revenue, and profit goals. In addition, the managers in this division use accounting to keep a tight reign on product costs. Also, accounting serves as the basis of communication so that the marketing managers and product designers can work with production managers, engineers, and accountants to create an exciting product within specified cost constraints.

Answers to Self-Study Questions

1. b 2. b 3. b 4. a 5. b 6. c 7. d 8. d 9. d 10. b 11. a 12. c 13. d 14. a 15. c

Remember to go back to the navigator box on the chapter-opening page and check off your completed work.

chapter 4

Fraud, Internal Control, and Cash

the navigator

- Scan Study Objectives ○
- Read Feature Story ○
- Scan Preview ○
- Read Text and Answer **Do it!** p. 172 ○ p. 176 ○ p. 185 ○ p. 190 ○
- Work Using the Decision Toolkit ○
- Review Summary of Study Objectives ○
- Work Comprehensive **Do it!** p. 196 ○
- Answer Self-Study Questions ○
- Complete Assignments ○

study objectives

After studying this chapter, you should be able to:

1. Define fraud and internal control.
2. Identify the principles of internal control activities.
3. Explain the applications of internal control principles to cash receipts.
4. Explain the applications of internal control principles to cash disbursements.
5. Prepare a bank reconciliation.
6. Explain the reporting of cash.
7. Discuss the basic principles of cash management.
8. Identify the primary elements of a cash budget.

Minding the Money in Moose Jaw

If you're ever looking for a cappuccino in Moose Jaw, Saskatchewan, stop by Stephanie's Gourmet Coffee and More, located on Main Street. Staff there serve, on average, 650 cups of coffee a day, including both regular and specialty coffees, not to mention soups, Italian sandwiches, and a wide assortment of gourmet cheesecakes.

"We've got high school students who come here, and students from the community college," says owner/manager Stephanie Mintenko, who has run the place since opening it in 1995. "We have customers who are retired, and others who are working people and have only 30 minutes for lunch. We have to be pretty quick."

That means that the cashiers have to be efficient. Like most businesses where purchases are low-cost and high-volume, cash control has to be simple.

"We have an electronic cash register, but it's not the fancy new kind where you just punch in the item," explains Ms. Mintenko. "You have to punch in the prices." The machine does keep track of sales in several categories, however. Cashiers punch a button to indicate whether each item is a beverage, a meal, or a charge for the cafe's Internet connections. An internal tape in the machine keeps a record of all transactions; the customer receives a receipt only upon request.

There is only one cash register. "Up to three of us might operate it on any given shift, including myself," says Ms. Mintenko.

She and her staff do two "cashouts" each day–one with the shift change at 5:00 p.m. and one when the shop closes at 10:00 p.m. At each cashout, they count the cash in the register drawer. That amount, minus the cash change carried forward (the float), should match the shift total on the register tape. If there's a discrepancy, they do another count. Then, if necessary, "we go through the whole tape to find the mistake," she explains. "It usually turns out to be someone who punched in $18 instead of $1.80, or something like that."

Ms. Mintenko sends all the cash tapes and float totals to a bookkeeper, who double-checks everything and provides regular reports. "We try to keep the accounting simple, so we can concentrate on making great coffee and food."

preview of chapter 4

As the story about recording cash sales at Stephanie's Gourmet Coffee and More indicates, control of cash is important to ensure that fraud does not occur. Companies also need controls to safeguard other types of assets. For example, Stephanie's undoubtedly has controls to prevent the theft of food and supplies, and controls to prevent the theft of tableware and dishes from its kitchen.

In this chapter, we explain the essential features of an internal control system and how it prevents fraud. We also describe how those controls apply to a specific asset–cash. The applications include some controls with which you may be already familiar, such as the use of a bank.

The content and organization of Chapter 4 are as follows.

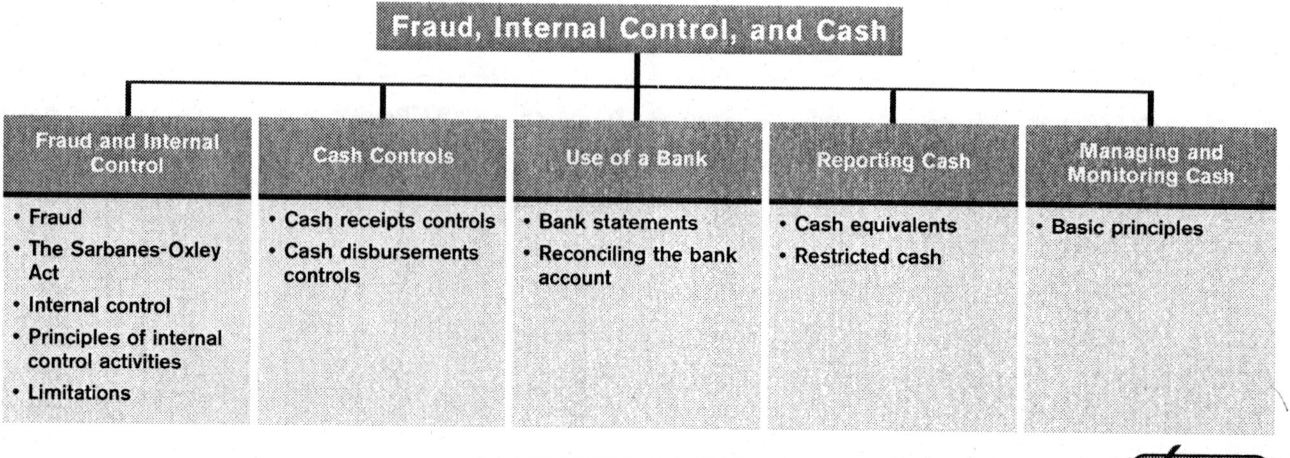

Fraud and Internal Control

study objective 1

Define fraud and internal control.

The Feature Story describes many of the internal control procedures used by Stephanie's Gourmet Coffee and More. These procedures are necessary to discourage employees from fraudulent activities.

FRAUD

A **fraud** is a dishonest act by an employee that results in personal benefit to the employee at a cost to the employer. Examples of fraud reported in the financial press include:

- A bookkeeper in a small company diverted $750,000 of bill payments to a personal bank account over a three-year period.
- A shipping clerk with 28 years of service shipped $125,000 of merchandise to himself.
- A computer operator embezzled $21 million from Wells Fargo Bank over a two-year period.
- A church treasurer "borrowed" $150,000 of church funds to finance a friend's business dealings.

Why does fraud occur? The three main factors that contribute to fraudulent activity are depicted by the **fraud triangle** in Illustration 4-1 (next page).

The most important element of the fraud triangle is **opportunity**. For an employee to commit fraud, the workplace environment must provide opportunities that an employee can exploit. Opportunities occur when the workplace lacks sufficient controls to deter and detect fraud. For example, inadequate

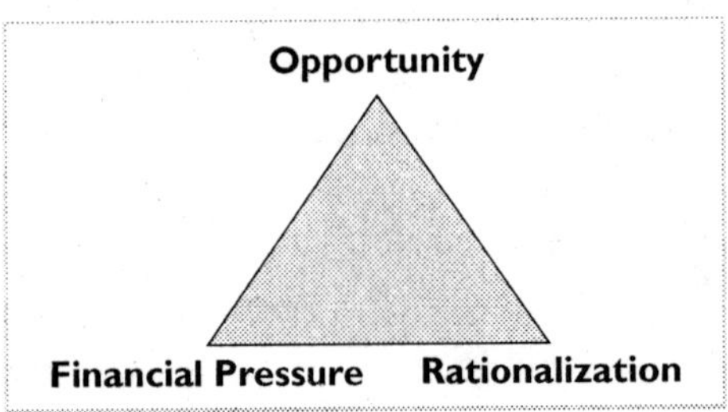

Illustration 4-1 Fraud triangle

monitoring of employee actions can create opportunities for theft and can embolden employees because they believe they will not be caught.

A second factor that contributes to fraud is **financial pressure**. Employees sometimes commit fraud because of personal financial problems caused by too much debt. Or they might commit fraud because they want to lead a lifestyle that they cannot afford on their current salary.

The third factor that contributes to fraud is **rationalization**. In order to justify their fraud, employees rationalize their dishonest actions. For example, employees sometimes justify fraud because they believe they are underpaid while the employer is making lots of money. These employees feel justified in stealing because they believe they deserve to be paid more.

THE SARBANES-OXLEY ACT

What can be done to prevent or to detect fraud? After numerous corporate scandals came to light in the early 2000s, Congress addressed this issue by passing the **Sarbanes-Oxley Act of 2002 (SOX)**. Under SOX, all publicly traded U.S. corporations are required to maintain an adequate system of internal control. Corporate executives and boards of directors must ensure that these controls are reliable and effective. In addition, independent outside auditors must attest to the adequacy of the internal control system. Companies that fail to comply are subject to fines, and company officers can be imprisoned. SOX also created the Public Company Accounting Oversight Board (PCAOB), to establish auditing standards and regulate auditor activity.

One poll found that 60% of investors believe that SOX helps safeguard their stock investments. Many say they would be unlikely to invest in a company that fails to follow SOX requirements. Although some corporate executives have criticized the time and expense involved in following the SOX requirements, SOX appears to be working well. For example, the chief accounting officer of Eli Lily noted that SOX triggered a comprehensive review of how the company documents controls. This review uncovered redundancies and pointed out controls that needed to be added. In short, it added up to time and money well spent. And the finance chief at General Electric noted, "We have seen value in SOX. It helps build investors' trust and gives them more confidence."[1]

INTERNAL CONTROL

Internal control consists of all the related methods and measures adopted within an organization to safeguard its assets, enhance the reliability of its accounting records, increase efficiency of operations, and ensure compliance with

[1] "Corporate Regulation Must Be Working—There's a Backlash," *Wall Street Journal*, June 16, 2004, p. C1; and Judith Burns, "Is Sarbanes-Oxley Working?" *Wall Street Journal*, June 21, 2004, pp. R8–R9.

laws and regulations. Internal control systems have five primary components as listed below.[2]

- **A control environment.** It is the responsibility of top management to make it clear that the organization values integrity and that unethical activity will not be tolerated. This component is often referred to as the "tone at the top."
- **Risk assessment.** Companies must identify and analyze the various factors that create risk for the business and must determine how to manage these risks.
- **Control activities.** To reduce the occurrence of fraud, management must design policies and procedures to address the specific risks faced by the company.
- **Information and communication.** The internal control system must capture and communicate all pertinent information both down and up the organization, as well as communicate information to appropriate external parties.
- **Monitoring.** Internal control systems must be monitored periodically for their adequacy. Significant deficiencies need to be reported to top management and/or the board of directors.

PRINCIPLES OF INTERNAL CONTROL ACTIVITIES

study objective 2

Identify the principles of internal control activities.

Each of the five components of an internal control system is important. Here, we will focus on one component, the control activities. The reason? These activities are the backbone of the company's efforts to address the risks it faces, such as fraud. The specific control activities used by a company will vary, depending on management's assessment of the risks faced. This assessment is heavily influenced by the size and nature of the company.

The six principles of control activities are as follows.

- Establishment of responsibility
- Segregation of duties
- Documentation procedures
- Physical controls
- Independent internal verification
- Human resource controls

We explain these principles in the following sections. You should recognize that they apply to most companies and are relevant to both manual and computerized accounting systems.

In the explanations that follow, we have added "Anatomy of a Fraud" stories that describe some recent real-world frauds. At the end of each story, we discuss the missing control activity that, had it been in place, is likely to have prevented or uncovered the fraud.[3]

Establishment of Responsibility

An essential principle of internal control is to assign responsibility to specific employees. **Control is most effective when only one person is responsible for a given task.**

---

[2]The Committee of Sponsoring Organizations of the Treadway Commission, "Internal Control—Integrated Framework," *www.coso.org/publications/executive_summary_integrated_framework.htm* (accessed March 2008).

[3]The "Anatomy of a Fraud" stories on pages 165–171 are adapted from *Fraud Casebook: Lessons from the Bad Side of Business*, edited by Joseph T. Wells (Hoboken, NJ: John Wiley & Sons, Inc., 2007). Used by permission. The names of some of the people and organizations in the stories are fictitious, but the facts in the stories are true.

To illustrate, assume that the cash on hand at the end of the day in a Safeway supermarket is $10 short of the cash rung up on the cash register. If only one person has operated the register, the shift manager can quickly determine responsibility for the shortage. If two or more individuals have worked the register, it may be impossible to determine who is responsible for the error. In the Feature Story, the principle of establishing responsibility does not appear to be strictly applied by Stephanie's, since three people operate the cash register on any given shift.

Establishing responsibility often requires limiting access only to authorized personnel, and then identifying those personnel. For example, the automated systems used by many companies have mechanisms such as identifying passcodes that keep track of who made a journal entry, who rang up a sale, or who entered an inventory storeroom at a particular time. Use of identifying passcodes enables the company to establish responsibility by identifying the particular employee who carried out the activity.

It's your shift now. I'm turning in my cash drawer and heading home.

Transfer of cash drawers

ANATOMY OF A FRAUD

Maureen Frugali was a training supervisor for claims processing at Colossal Healthcare. As a standard part of the claims processing training program, Maureen created fictitious claims for use by trainees. These fictitious claims were then sent to Accounts Payable. After the training claims had been processed, she was to notify the accounts payable department of all fictitious claims, so that they would not be paid. However, she did not inform Accounts Payable about every fictitious claim. She created some fictitious claims for entities that she controlled (that is, she would receive the payment), and she let Accounts Payable pay her.

Total take: $11 million

THE MISSING CONTROL

Establishment of responsibility. The healthcare company did not adequately restrict the responsibility for authoring and approving claims transactions. The training supervisor should not have been authorized to create claims in the company's "live" system.

Source: Adapted from Wells, *Fraud Casebook* (2007), pp. 61–70.

Segregation of Duties

Segregation of duties is indispensable in an internal control system. There are two common applications of this principle:

1. Different individuals should be responsible for related activities.
2. The responsibility for record-keeping for an asset should be separate from the physical custody of that asset.

The rationale for segregation of duties is this: **The work of one employee should, without a duplication of effort, provide a reliable basis for evaluating the work of another employee.** For example, the personnel that design and program computerized systems should not be assigned duties related to day-to-day use of the system. Otherwise, they could design the system to benefit them personally and conceal the fraud through day-to-day use.

SEGREGATION OF RELATED ACTIVITIES. Making one individual responsible for related activities increases the potential for errors and irregularities.

For example, companies should assign related *purchasing activities* to different individuals. Related purchasing activities include ordering merchandise, order approval, receiving goods, authorizing payment, and paying for goods or services. Various frauds are possible when one person handles related purchasing activities. For example:

- If a purchasing agent can order goods without supervisory approval, the likelihood of the agent receiving kickbacks from suppliers increases.
- If an employee who orders goods also handles receipt of the goods (and invoice) as well as payment authorization, he or she might authorize payment for a fictitious invoice.

These abuses are less likely to occur when companies divide the purchasing tasks.

Similarly, companies should assign related *sales activities* to different individuals. Related selling activities include making a sale, shipping (or delivering) the goods to the customer, billing the customer, and receiving payment. Various frauds are possible when one person handles related sales transactions. For example:

- If a salesperson can make a sale without obtaining supervisory approval, he or she might make sales at unauthorized prices to increase sales commissions.
- A shipping clerk who also has access to accounting records could ship goods to himself.
- A billing clerk who handles billing and cash receipts could understate the amount billed for sales made to friends and relatives.

These abuses are less likely to occur when companies divide the sales tasks: the salespeople make the sale; the shipping department ships the goods on the basis of the sales order; and the billing department prepares the sales invoice after comparing the sales order with the report of goods shipped.

ANATOMY OF A FRAUD

Lawrence Fairbanks, the assistant vice-chancellor of communications at Aesop University was allowed to make purchases for his department of under $2,500 without external approval. Unfortunately, he also sometimes bought items for himself, such as expensive antiques and other collectibles. How did he do it? He replaced the vendor invoices he received with fake vendor invoices that he created. The fake invoices had descriptions that were more consistent with the communications department's operations. He submitted these fake invoices to the accounting department as the basis for their journal entries and to Accounts Payable as the basis for payment.

Total take: $475,000

THE MISSING CONTROL

Segregation of duties. The university had not properly segregated related purchasing activities. Lawrence was ordering items, receiving the items, and receiving the invoice. By receiving the invoice, he had control over the documents that were used to account for the purchase and thus was able to substitute a fake invoice.

Source: Adapted from Wells, *Fraud Casebook* (2007), pp. 3–15.

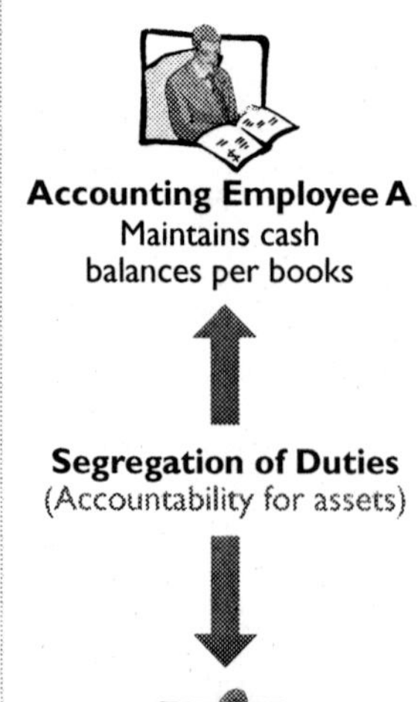

SEGREGATION OF RECORD-KEEPING FROM PHYSICAL CUSTODY. The accountant should have neither physical custody of the asset nor access to it. Likewise, the custodian of the asset should not maintain or have access to the accounting records. **The custodian of the asset is not likely to convert the asset to personal use when one employee maintains the record of the asset, and a different employee has physical custody of the asset.** The separation of accounting responsibility from the custody of assets is especially important for cash and inventories because these assets are very vulnerable to fraud.

ANATOMY OF A FRAUD

Angela Bauer was an accounts payable clerk for Aggasiz Construction Company. She prepared and issued checks to vendors and reconciled bank statements. She perpetrated a fraud in this way: She wrote checks for costs that the company had not actually incurred (e.g., fake taxes). A supervisor then approved and signed the checks. Before issuing the check, though, Angela would "white-out" the payee line on the check and change it to personal accounts that she controlled. She was able to conceal the theft because she also reconciled the bank account. That is, nobody else ever saw that the checks had been altered.

Total take: $570,000

THE MISSING CONTROL

Segregation of duties. Aggasiz Construction Company did not properly segregate recordkeeping from physical custody. Angela had physical custody of the checks, which essentially was control of the cash. She also had recording-keeping responsibility because she prepared the bank reconciliation.

Source: Adapted from Wells, *Fraud Casebook* (2007), pp. 100–107.

Documentation Procedures

Documents provide evidence that transactions and events have occurred. At Stephanie's Gourmet Coffee and More, the cash register tape is the restaurant's documentation for the sale and the amount of cash received. Similarly, a shipping document indicates that the goods have been shipped, and a sales invoice indicates that the company has billed the customer for the goods. By requiring signatures (or initials) on the documents, the company can identify the individual(s) responsible for the transaction or event. Companies should document transactions when the transaction occurs.

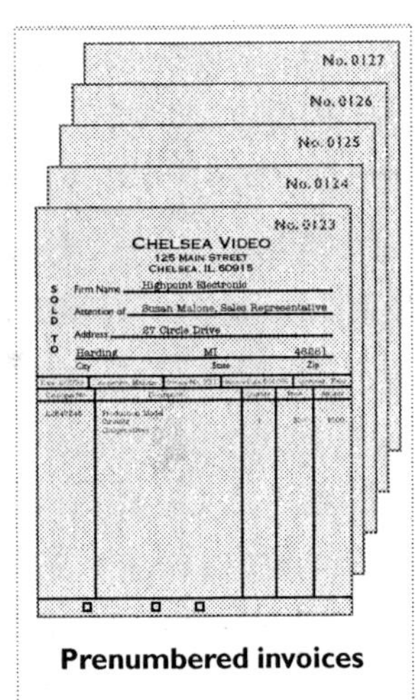

Prenumbered invoices

Companies should establish procedures for documents. First, whenever possible, companies should use **prenumbered documents, and all documents should be accounted for**. Prenumbering helps to prevent a transaction from being recorded more than once, or conversely, from not being recorded at all. Second, the control system should require that employees **promptly forward source documents for accounting entries to the accounting department. This control measure helps to ensure timely recording of the transaction** and contributes directly to the accuracy and reliability of the accounting records.

ANATOMY OF A FRAUD

To support their reimbursement requests for travel costs incurred, employees at Mod Fashions Corporation's design center were required to submit receipts. The receipts could include the detailed bill provided for a meal, or the credit card receipt provided when the credit card payment is made, or a copy of the employee's monthly credit card bill that listed the item. A number of the designers who frequently traveled together came up with a fraud scheme: They submitted claims for the same expenses. For example, if they had a meal together that cost $200, one person submitted the detailed meal bill, another submitted the credit card receipt, and a third submitted a monthly credit card bill showing the meal as a line item. Thus, all three received a $200 reimbursement.

Total take: $75,000

THE MISSING CONTROL

Documentation procedures. Mod Fashions should require the original, detailed receipt. It should not accept photocopies, and it should not accept credit card statements. In addition, documentation procedures could be further improved by requiring the use of a corporate credit card (rather than personal credit card) for all business expenses.

Source: Adapted from Wells, *Fraud Casebook* (2007), pp. 79–90.

Physical Controls

Use of physical controls is essential. *Physical controls* relate to the safeguarding of assets and enhance the accuracy and reliability of the accounting records. Illustration 4-2 shows examples of these controls.

Illustration 4-2 Physical controls

Physical Controls

Safes, vaults, and safety deposit boxes for cash and business papers

Locked warehouses and storage cabinets for inventories and records

Computer facilities with pass key access or fingerprint or eyeball scans

Alarms to prevent break-ins

Television monitors and garment sensors to deter theft

Time clocks for recording time worked

ANATOMY OF A FRAUD

At Centerstone Health, a large insurance company, the mailroom each day received insurance applications from prospective customers. Mailroom employees scanned the applications into electronic documents before the applications were processed. Once the applications are scanned they can be accessed online by authorized employees.

Insurance agents at Centerstone Health earn commissions based upon successful applications. The sales agent's name is listed on the application. However, roughly 15% of the applications are from customers who did not work with a sales agent. Two friends–Alex, an employee in record keeping, and Parviz, a sales agent–thought up a way to perpetrate a fraud. Alex identified scanned applications that did not list a sales agent. After business hours, he entered the mailroom and found the hardcopy applications that did not show a sales agent. He wrote in Parviz's name as the sales agent and then rescanned the application for processing. Parviz received the commission, which the friends then split.

Total take: $240,000

> **THE MISSING CONTROL**
>
> *Physical controls.* Centerstone Health lacked two basic physical controls that could have prevented this fraud. First, the mailroom should have been locked during nonbusiness hours, and access during business hours should have been tightly controlled. Second, the scanned applications supposedly could be accessed only by authorized employees using their password. However, the password for each employee was the same as the employee's user ID. Since employee user ID numbers were available to all other employees, all employees knew all other employees' passwords. Thus, Alex could enter the system using another employee's password and access the scanned applications.
>
> *Source:* Adapted from Wells, *Fraud Casebook* (2007), pp. 316–326.

Independent Internal Verification

Most internal control systems provide for **independent internal verification.** This principle involves the review of data prepared by employees. To obtain maximum benefit from independent internal verification:

1. Companies should verify records periodically or on a surprise basis.
2. An employee who is independent of the personnel responsible for the information should make the verification.
3. Discrepancies and exceptions should be reported to a management level that can take appropriate corrective action.

Independent internal verification is especially useful in comparing recorded transactions with existing assets. The reconciliation of the cash register tape with the cash in the register at Stephanie's Gourmet Coffee and More is an example of this internal control principle. Another common example is the reconciliation of a company's cash balance per books with the cash balance per bank and the verification of the perpetual inventory records through a count of physical inventory. Illustration 4-3 shows the relationship between this principle and the segregation of duties principle.

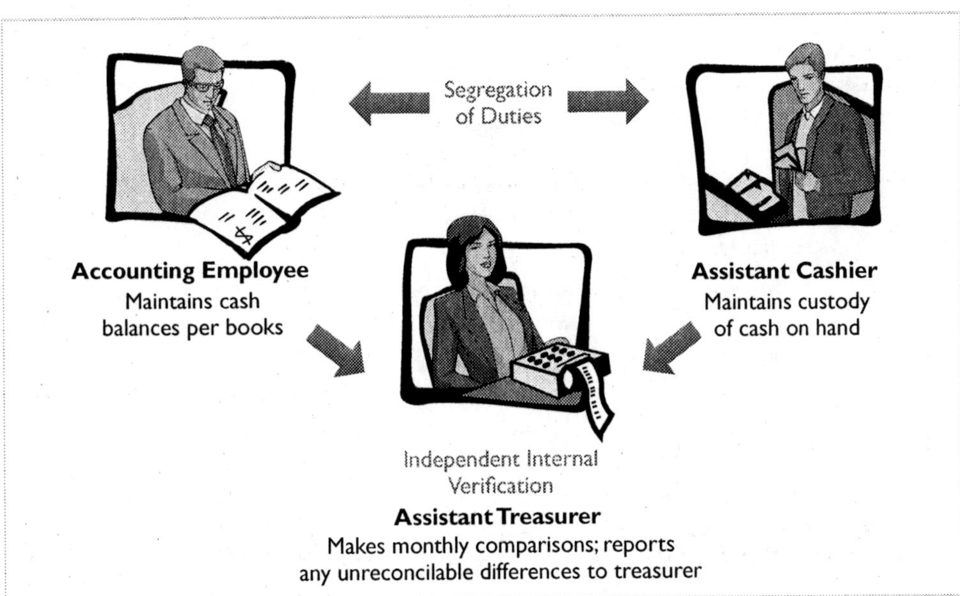

Illustration 4-3 Comparison of segregation of duties principle with independent internal verification principle

Large companies often assign independent internal verification to internal auditors. **Internal auditors** are company employees who continuously evaluate the effectiveness of the company's internal control systems. They review the activities of departments and individuals to determine whether prescribed internal controls are being followed. They also recommend improvements when needed. In fact, most fraud is discovered by the company through internal mechanisms such as existing internal controls and internal audits. For example, the fraud at WorldCom, involving billions of dollars, was uncovered by an internal auditor.

ANATOMY OF A FRAUD

Bobbi Jean Donnelly, the office manager for Mod Fashions Corporation's design center, was responsible for preparing the design center budget and reviewing expense reports submitted by design center employees. Her desire to upgrade her wardrobe got the better of her, and she enacted a fraud that involved filing expense-reimbursement requests for her own personal clothing purchases. She was able to conceal the fraud because she was responsible for reviewing all expense reports, including her own. In addition, she sometimes was given ultimate responsibility for signing off on the expense reports when her boss was "too busy." Also, because she controlled the budget, when she submitted her expenses, she coded them to budget items that she knew were running under budget, so that they would not catch anyone's attention.

Total take: $275,000

THE MISSING CONTROL

Independent internal verification. Bobbi Jean's boss should have verified her expense reports. When asked what he thought her expenses for a year were, the boss said about $10,000. At $115,000 per year, her actual expenses were more than ten times what would have been expected. However, because he was "too busy" to verify her expense reports or to review the budget, he never noticed.

Source: Adapted from Wells, *Fraud Casebook* (2007), pp. 79–90.

Human Resource Controls

Human resource control activities include the following.

If I take a vacation they will know that I've been stealing.

1. **Bond employees who handle cash.** **Bonding** involves obtaining insurance protection against theft by employees. It contributes to the safeguarding of cash in two ways: First, the insurance company carefully screens all individuals before adding them to the policy and may reject risky applicants. Second, bonded employees know that the insurance company will vigorously prosecute all offenders.
2. **Rotate employees' duties and require employees to take vacations.** These measures deter employees from attempting thefts since they will not be able to permanently conceal their improper actions. Many banks, for example, have discovered employee thefts when the employee was on vacation or assigned to a new position.
3. **Conduct thorough background checks.** Many believe that the most important and inexpensive measure any business can take to reduce employee theft and fraud is for the human resources department to conduct thorough background checks. Two tips: (1) Check to see whether job applicants actually

graduated from the schools they list. (2) Never use the telephone numbers for previous employers given on the reference sheet; always look them up yourself.

ANATOMY OF A FRAUD

Ellen Lowry was the desk manager and Josephine Rodriquez was the head of housekeeping at the Excelsior Inn, a luxury hotel. The two best friends were so dedicated to their jobs that they never took vacations, and they frequently filled in for other employees. In fact, Ms. Rodriquez, whose job as head of housekeeping did not include cleaning rooms, often cleaned rooms herself, "just to help the staff keep up." These two "dedicated" employees, working as a team, found a way to earn a little more cash. Ellen, the desk manager, provided significant discounts to guests who paid with cash. She kept the cash and did not register the guest in the hotel's computerized system. Instead, she took the room out of circulation "due to routine maintenance." Because the room did not show up as being used, it did not receive a normal housekeeping assignment. Instead, Josephine, the head of housekeeping, cleaned the rooms during the guests' stay.

Total take: $95,000

THE MISSING CONTROL

Human resource controls. Ellen, the desk manager, had been fired by a previous employer after being accused of fraud. If the Excelsior Inn had conducted a thorough background check, it would not have hired her. The hotel fraud was detected when Ellen missed work for a few days due to illness. A system of mandatory vacations and rotating days off would have increased the chances of detecting the fraud before it became so large.

Source: Adapted from Wells, *Fraud Casebook* (2007), pp. 145–155.

Accounting Across the Organization

Under SOX, a company needs to keep track of employees' degrees and certifications to ensure that employees continue to meet the specified requirements of a job. Also, to ensure proper employee supervision and proper separation of duties, companies must develop and monitor an organizational chart. When one corporation went through this exercise it found that out of 17,000 employees, there were 400 people who did not report to anyone, and they had 35 people who reported to each other. In addition, if an employee complains of an unfair firing and mentions financial issues at the company, HR must refer the case to the company audit committee and possibly to its legal counsel.

Why would unsupervised employees or employees who report to each other represent potential internal control threats?

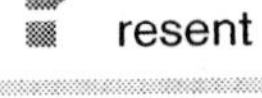

LIMITATIONS OF INTERNAL CONTROL

Companies generally design their systems of internal control to provide **reasonable assurance** of proper safeguarding of assets and reliability of the accounting records. The concept of reasonable assurance rests on the premise that the costs of establishing control procedures should not exceed their expected benefit.

Helpful Hint Controls may vary with the risk level of the activity. For example, management may consider cash to be high risk and maintaining inventories in the stockroom as lower risk. Thus management would have stricter controls for cash.

To illustrate, consider shoplifting losses in retail stores. Stores could eliminate such losses by having a security guard stop and search customers as they leave the store. But store managers have concluded that the negative effects of such a procedure cannot be justified. Instead, stores have attempted to control shoplifting losses by less costly procedures: They post signs saying, "We reserve the right to inspect all packages" and "All shoplifters will be prosecuted." They use hidden TV cameras and store detectives to monitor customer activity, and they install sensor equipment at exits.

The **human element** is an important factor in every system of internal control. A good system can become ineffective as a result of employee fatigue, carelessness, or indifference. For example, a receiving clerk may not bother to count goods received and may just "fudge" the counts. Occasionally, two or more individuals may work together to get around prescribed controls. Such **collusion** can significantly reduce the effectiveness of a system, eliminating the protection offered by segregation of duties. No system of internal control is perfect.

The size of the business also may impose limitations on internal control. A small company, for example, may find it difficult to segregate duties or to provide for independent internal verification.

Ethics Insight

A study by the Association of Certified Fraud Examiners indicates that businesses with fewer than 100 employees are most at risk for employee theft. Nearly 46% of frauds occurred at companies with fewer than 100 employees. The average loss at small companies was $98,000, which was only slightly less than the average fraud at companies with more than 10,000 employees. A $100,000 loss can threaten the very existence of a small company.

Source: 2004 Report to the Nation on Occupational Fraud and Abuse, Association of Certified Fraud Examiners, *http://www.cfenet.com/pdfs/2004RttN.pdf*, p. 6.

? Why are small companies more susceptible to employee theft?

DECISION TOOLKIT

DECISION CHECKPOINTS	INFO NEEDED FOR DECISION	TOOL TO USE FOR DECISION	HOW TO EVALUATE RESULTS
Are the company's financial statements supported by adequate internal controls?	Auditor's report, management discussion and analysis, articles in financial press	The principles of internal control activities are (1) establishment of responsibility, (2) segregation of duties, (3) documentation procedures, (4) physical controls, (5) independent internal verification, and (6) human resource controls.	If any indication is given that these or other controls are lacking, use the financial statements with caution.

before you go on...

CONTROL ACTIVITIES

Do it! Identify which control activity is violated in each of the following situations, and explain how the situation creates an opportunity for a fraud.

1. The person with primary responsibility for reconciling the bank account is also the company's accountant and makes all bank deposits.

2. Wellstone Company's treasurer received an award for distinguished service because he had not taken a vacation in 30 years.
3. In order to save money on order slips, and to reduce time spent keeping track of order slips, a local bar/restaurant does not buy prenumbered order slips.

Solution

1. Violates the control activity of segregation of duties. Record-keeping should be separate from physical custody. As a consequence, the employee could embezzle cash and make journal entries to hide the theft.
2. Violates the control activity of human resource controls. Key employees, such as a treasurer, should be required to take vacations. The treasurer, who manages the company's cash, might embezzle cash and use his position to conceal the theft.
3. Violates the control activity of documentation procedures. If pre-numbered documents are not used, then it is virtually impossible to account for the documents. As a consequence, an employee could write up a dinner sale, receive the cash from the customer, and then throw away the order slip and keep the cash.

Action Plan

- Familiarize yourself with each of the control activities listed on page 164.
- Understand the nature of the frauds that each control activity is intended to address.

Cash Controls

Cash is the one asset that is readily convertible into any other type of asset. It also is easily concealed and transported, and is highly desired. Because of these characteristics, **cash is the asset most susceptible to fraudulent activities**. In addition, because of the large volume of cash transactions, numerous errors may occur in executing and recording them. To safeguard cash and to ensure the accuracy of the accounting records for cash, effective internal control over cash is critical.

CASH RECEIPTS CONTROLS

study objective 3

Explain the applications of internal control principles to cash receipts.

Illustration 4-4 (page 174) shows how the internal control principles explained earlier apply to cash receipts transactions. As you might expect, companies vary considerably in how they apply these principles. To illustrate internal control over cash receipts, we will examine control activities for a retail store with both over-the-counter and mail receipts.

Over-the-Counter Receipts

In retail businesses, control of over-the-counter receipts centers on cash registers that are visible to customers. A cash sale is rung-up on a cash register with the amount clearly visible to the customer. This activity prevents the cashier from ringing up a lower amount and pocketing the difference. The customer receives an itemized cash register receipt slip and is expected to count the change received. The cash register's tape is locked in the register until a supervisor removes it. This tape accumulates the daily transactions and totals.

At the end of the clerk's shift, the clerk counts the cash and sends the cash and the count to the cashier. The cashier counts the cash, prepares a deposit slip, and deposits the cash at the bank. The cashier also sends a duplicate of the deposit slip to the accounting department to indicate cash received. The supervisor removes the cash register tape and sends it to the accounting department as the basis for a journal entry to record the cash received. The tape is compared to the deposit slip for any discrepancies. Illustration 4-5 (page 175) summarizes this process.

Cash Receipts Controls

Establishment of Responsibility
Only designated personnel are authorized to handle cash receipts (cashiers)

Physical Controls
Store cash in safes and bank vaults; limit access to storage areas; use cash registers

Segregation of Duties
Different individuals receive cash, record cash receipts, and hold the cash

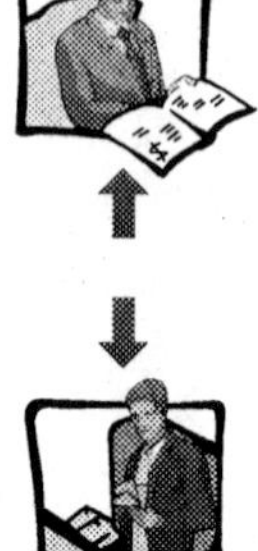

Independent Internal Verification
Supervisors count cash receipts daily; treasurer compares total receipts to bank deposits daily

Documentation Procedures
Use remittance advice (mail receipts), cash register tapes, and deposit slips

Human Resource Controls
Bond personnel who handle cash; require employees to take vacations; conduct background checks

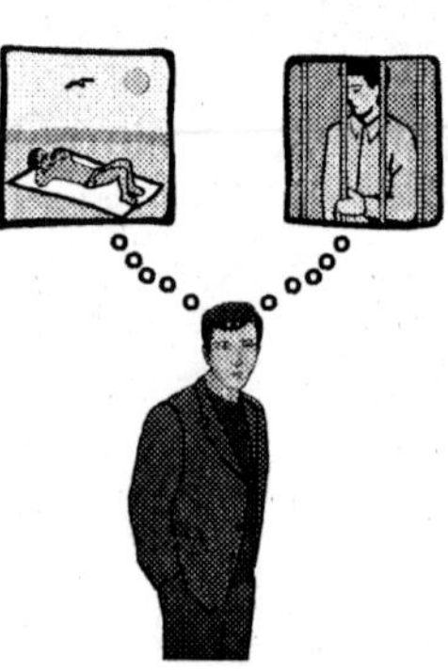

Illustration 4-4
Application of internal control principles to cash receipts

This system for handling cash receipts uses an important internal control principle—segregation of record-keeping from physical custody. The supervisor has access to the cash register tape, but **not** to the cash. The clerk and the cashier have access to the cash, but **not** to the register tape. In addition, the cash register tape provides documentation and enables independent internal verification with the deposit slip. Use of these three principles of internal control (segregation of record-keeping from physical custody, documentation, and independent internal verification) provides an effective system of internal control. Any attempt at fraudulent activity should be detected unless there is collusion among the employees.

In some instances, the amount deposited at the bank will not agree with the cash recorded in the accounting records based on the cash register tape. These differences often result because the clerk hands incorrect change back to the retail customer. In this case, the difference between the actual cash and the amount reported on the cash register tape is reported in a Cash Over and Short account. For example, suppose that the cash register tape indicated sales of $6,956.20 but

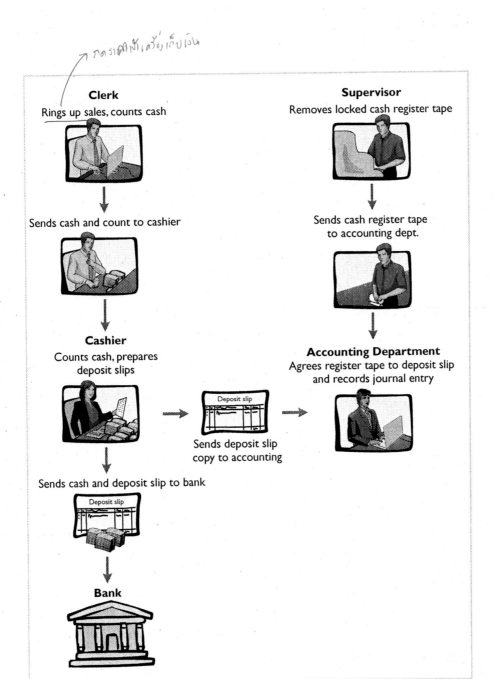

Clerk
Rings up sales, counts cash

Sends cash and count to cashier

Cashier
Counts cash, prepares deposit slips

Deposit slip

Sends deposit slip copy to accounting

Sends cash and deposit slip to bank

Deposit slip

Bank

Supervisor
Removes locked cash register tape

Sends cash register tape to accounting dept.

Accounting Department
Agrees register tape to deposit slip and records journal entry

Illustration 4-5 Control of over-the-counter receipts

Helpful Hint Flowcharts such as this one enhance the understanding of the flow of documents, the processing steps, and the internal control procedures.

the amount of cash was only $6,946.10. A cash shortfall of $10.10 exists. To account for this cash shortfall and related cash, the company makes the following entry.

Cash	6,946.10	
Cash Over and Short	10.10	
Sales Revenue		6,956.20
(To record cash shortfall)		

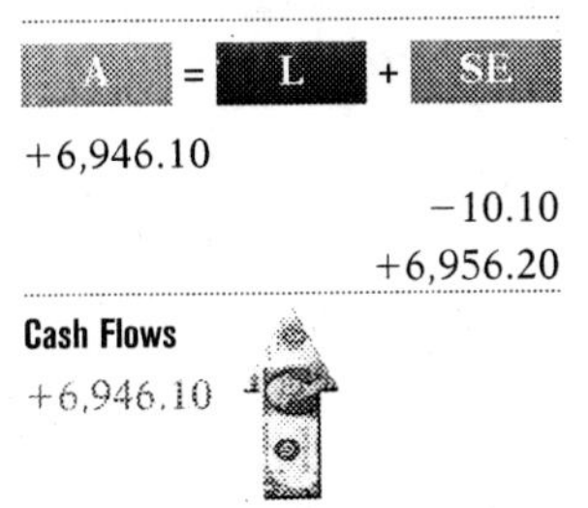

Cash Over and Short is an income statement item. It is reported as miscellaneous expense when there is a cash shortfall, and as miscellaneous revenue when there is an overage. Clearly, the amount should be small. Any material amounts in this account should be investigated.

Mail Receipts

All mail receipts should be opened in the presence of at least two mail clerks. These receipts are generally in the form of checks. A mail clerk should endorse each check "For Deposit Only." This restrictive endorsement reduces the likelihood that someone could divert the check to personal use. Banks will not give an individual cash when presented with a check that has this type of endorsement.

The mail-receipt clerks prepare, in triplicate, a list of the checks received each day. This list shows the name of the check issuer, the purpose of the payment, and the amount of the check. Each mail clerk signs the list to establish responsibility for the data. The original copy of the list, along with the checks, is then sent to the cashier's department. A copy of the list is sent to the accounting department for recording in the accounting records. The clerks also keep a copy.

This process provides excellent internal control for the company. By employing two clerks, the chance of fraud is reduced; each clerk knows he or she is being observed by the other clerk(s). To engage in fraud, they would have to collude. The customers who submit payments also provide control, because they will contact the company with a complaint if they are not properly credited for payment. Because the cashier has access to cash but not the records, and the accounting department has access to records but not cash, neither can engage in undetected fraud.

before you go on...

Do it!

CONTROL OVER CASH RECEIPTS

L. R. Cortez is concerned about the control over cash receipts in his fast-food restaurant, Big Cheese. The restaurant has two cash registers. At no time do more than two employees take customer orders and ring up sales. Work shifts for employees range from 4 to 8 hours. Cortez asks your help in installing a good system of internal control over cash receipts.

Action Plan

- Differentiate among the internal control principles of (1) establishment of responsibility, (2) physical controls, and (3) independent internal verification.
- Design an effective system of internal control over cash receipts.

Solution

Cortez should assign a cash register to each employee at the start of each work shift, with register totals set at zero. Each employee should be instructed to use only the assigned register and to ring up all sales. Each customer should be given a receipt. At the end of the shift, the employee should do a cash count. A separate employee should compare the cash count with the register tape, to be sure they agree. In addition, Cortez should install an automated system that would enable the company to compare orders rung up on the register to orders processed by the kitchen.

CASH DISBURSEMENTS CONTROLS

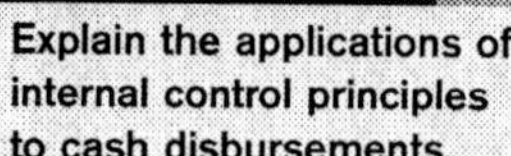

Explain the applications of internal control principles to cash disbursements.

Companies disburse cash for a variety of reasons, such as to pay expenses and liabilities or to purchase assets. **Generally, internal control over cash disbursements is more effective when companies pay by check, rather than by cash.** One exception is **for incidental amounts that are paid out of petty cash.**[4]

Companies generally issue checks only after following specified control procedures. Illustration 4-6 shows how principles of internal control apply to cash disbursements.

[4]We explain the operation of a petty cash fund in the appendix to this chapter on pages 193–195.

Cash Disbursements Controls

Establishment of Responsibility

Only designated personnel are authorized to sign checks (treasurer) and approve vendors

Physical Controls

Store blank checks in safes, with limited access; print check amounts by machine in indelible ink

Segregation of Duties

Different individuals approve and make payments; check signers do not record disbursements

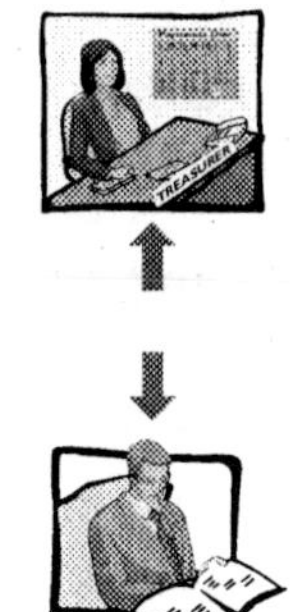

Independent Internal Verification

Compare checks to invoices; reconcile bank statement monthly

Documentation Procedures

Use prenumbered checks and account for them in sequence; each check must have an approved invoice; require employees to use corporate credit cards for reimbursable expenses; stamp invoices "paid."

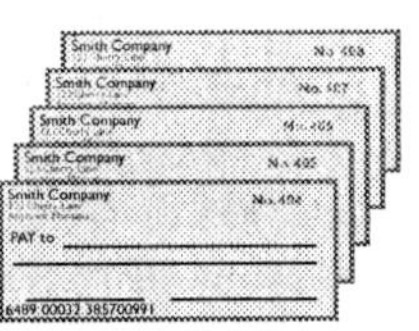

Human Resource Controls

Bond personnel who handle cash; require employees to take vacations; conduct background checks

Illustration 4-6
Application of internal control principles to cash disbursements

Voucher System Controls

Most medium and large companies use vouchers as part of their internal control over cash disbursements. A **voucher system** is a network of approvals by authorized individuals, acting independently, to ensure that all disbursements by check are proper.

The system begins with the authorization to incur a cost or expense. It ends with the issuance of a check for the liability incurred. A **voucher** is an authorization form prepared for each expenditure in a voucher system. Companies require vouchers for all types of cash disbursements except those from petty cash.

The starting point in preparing a voucher is to fill in the appropriate information about the liability on the face of the voucher. The vendor's invoice provides most of the needed information. Then, an employee in accounts payable records the voucher (in a journal called a **voucher register**) and files it according to the date on which it is to be paid. The company issues and sends a check on that date, and stamps the voucher "paid." The paid voucher is sent to the accounting department for recording (in a journal called the **check register**). A voucher system involves two journal entries, one to issue the voucher and a second to pay the voucher.

The use of a voucher system improves internal control over cash disbursements. First, the authorization process inherent in a voucher system establishes responsibility. Each individual has responsibility to review the underlying documentation to ensure that it is correct. In addition, the voucher system keeps track of the documents that back up each transaction. By keeping these documents in one place, a supervisor can independently verify the authenticity of each transaction. Consider, for example, the case of Aesop University presented on page 166. Aesop did not use a voucher system for transactions under $2,500. As a consequence, there was no independent verification of the documents, which enabled the employee to submit fake invoices to hide his unauthorized purchases.

Petty Cash Fund

Ethics Note Internal control over a petty cash fund is strengthened by: (1) having a supervisor make surprise counts of the fund to confirm whether the paid vouchers and fund cash equal the imprest amount, and (2) canceling or mutilating the paid vouchers so they cannot be resubmitted for reimbursement.

As you learned earlier in the chapter, better internal control over cash disbursements is possible when companies make payments by check. However, using checks to pay such small amounts as those for postage due, employee working lunches, and taxi fares is both impractical and a nuisance. A common way of handling such payments, while maintaining satisfactory control, is to use a petty cash fund. A **petty cash fund** is a cash fund used to pay relatively small amounts. We explain the operation of a petty cash fund in the appendix at the end of this chapter.

Ethics Insight

A recent study by the Association of Certified Fraud Examiners found that two-thirds of all employee thefts involved a fraudulent disbursement by an employee. The most common form (28.3% of cases) was fraudulent billing schemes. In these, the employee causes the company to issue a payment to the employee by submitting a bill for nonexistent goods or services, purchases of personal goods by the employee, or inflated invoices. The following graph shows various types of fraudulent disbursements and the median loss from each.

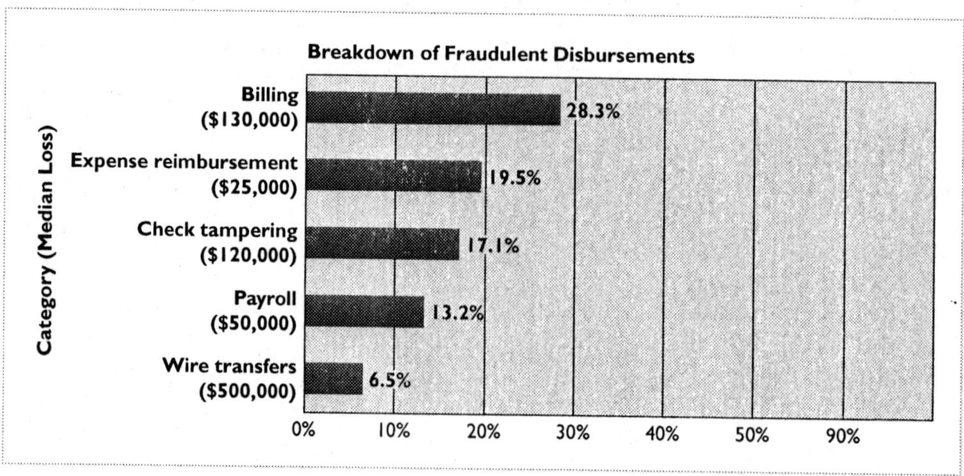

Source: 2006 Report to the Nation on Occupational Fraud and Abuse, Association of Certified Fraud Examiners, *www.acfe.com/documents/2006_rttn.pdf*, p. 14.

How can companies reduce the likelihood of fraudulent disbursements?

Control Features: Use of a Bank

The use of a bank contributes significantly to good internal control over cash. A company can safeguard its cash by using a bank as a depository and clearinghouse for checks received and checks written. The use of a bank minimizes the amount of currency that must be kept on hand. It also facilitates control of cash because a double record is maintained of all bank transactions—one by the business and the other by the bank. The asset account Cash maintained by the company is the "flip-side" of the bank's liability account for that company. A **bank reconciliation** is the process of comparing the bank's balance with the company's balance, and explaining the differences to make them agree.

Many companies have more than one bank account. For efficiency of operations and better control, national retailers like Wal-Mart and Target often have regional bank accounts. Similarly, a company such as ExxonMobil with more than 100,000 employees may have a payroll bank account as well as one or more general bank accounts. In addition, a company may maintain several bank accounts in order to have more than one source for short-term loans.

BANK STATEMENTS

Each month, the company receives from the bank a **bank statement** showing its bank transactions and balances.[5] For example, the statement for Laird Company in Illustration 4-7 (on page 180) shows the following: (1) checks paid and other debits that reduce the balance in the depositor's account, (2) deposits and other credits that increase the balance in the depositor's account, and (3) the account balance after each day's transactions.

Remember that bank statements are prepared from the *bank's* perspective. For example, every deposit the bank receives is an increase in the bank's liabilities (an account payable to the depositor). Therefore, in Illustration 4-7, National Bank and Trust *credits* to Laird Company every deposit it received from Laird. The reverse occurs when the bank "pays" a check issued by Laird Company on its checking account balance: Payment reduces the bank's liability and is therefore *debited* to Laird's account with the bank.

Helpful Hint Essentially, the bank statement is a copy of the bank's records sent to the customer for periodic review.

The bank statement lists in numerical sequence all paid checks along with the date the check was paid and its amount. Upon paying a check, the bank stamps the check "paid"; a paid check is sometimes referred to as a **canceled check**. In addition, the bank includes with the bank statement memoranda explaining other debits and credits it made to the depositor's account.

A check that is not paid by a bank because of insufficient funds in a bank account is called an **NSF check** (not sufficient funds). The bank uses a debit memorandum when a previously deposited customer's check "bounces" because of insufficient funds. In such a case, the customer's bank marks the check NSF (not sufficient funds) and returns it to the depositor's bank. The bank then debits (decreases) the depositor's account, as shown by the symbol NSF in Illustration 4-7, and sends the NSF check and debit memorandum to the depositor as notification of the charge. The NSF check creates an account receivable for the depositor and reduces cash in the bank account.

[5] Our presentation assumes that a company makes all adjustments at the end of the month. In practice, a company may also make journal entries during the month as it receives information from the bank regarding its account.

Illustration 4-7 Bank statement

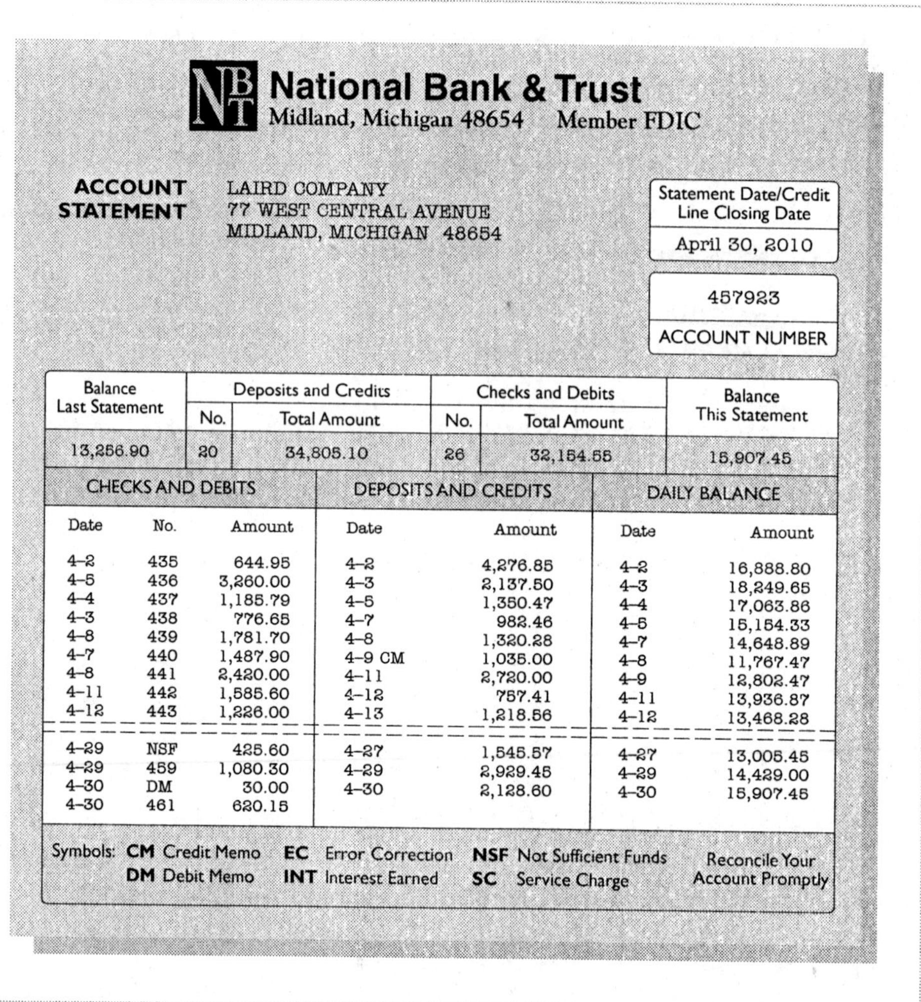

National Bank & Trust
Midland, Michigan 48654 Member FDIC

ACCOUNT STATEMENT

LAIRD COMPANY
77 WEST CENTRAL AVENUE
MIDLAND, MICHIGAN 48654

Statement Date/Credit Line Closing Date: April 30, 2010

457923
ACCOUNT NUMBER

Balance Last Statement	Deposits and Credits		Checks and Debits		Balance This Statement
	No.	Total Amount	No.	Total Amount	
13,256.90	20	34,805.10	26	32,154.55	15,907.45

CHECKS AND DEBITS			DEPOSITS AND CREDITS		DAILY BALANCE	
Date	No.	Amount	Date	Amount	Date	Amount
4-2	435	644.95	4-2	4,276.85	4-2	16,888.80
4-5	436	3,260.00	4-3	2,137.50	4-3	18,249.65
4-4	437	1,185.79	4-5	1,350.47	4-4	17,063.86
4-3	438	776.65	4-7	982.46	4-5	15,154.33
4-8	439	1,781.70	4-8	1,320.28	4-7	14,648.89
4-7	440	1,487.90	4-9 CM	1,035.00	4-8	11,767.47
4-8	441	2,420.00	4-11	2,720.00	4-9	12,802.47
4-11	442	1,585.60	4-12	757.41	4-11	13,936.87
4-12	443	1,226.00	4-13	1,218.56	4-12	13,468.28
4-29	NSF	425.60	4-27	1,545.57	4-27	13,005.45
4-29	459	1,080.30	4-29	2,929.45	4-29	14,429.00
4-30	DM	30.00	4-30	2,128.60	4-30	15,907.45
4-30	461	620.15				

Symbols: **CM** Credit Memo **EC** Error Correction **NSF** Not Sufficient Funds
DM Debit Memo **INT** Interest Earned **SC** Service Charge

Reconcile Your Account Promptly

RECONCILING THE BANK ACCOUNT

study objective 5

Prepare a bank reconciliation.

Because the bank and the company maintain independent records of the company's checking account, you might assume that the respective balances will always agree. In fact, the two balances are seldom the same at any given time. Therefore it is necessary to make the balance per books agree with the balance per bank—a process called **reconciling the bank account**. The lack of agreement between the balances has two causes:

1. **Time lags** that prevent one of the parties from recording the transaction in the same period.
2. **Errors** by either party in recording transactions.

Time lags occur frequently. For example, several days may elapse between the time a company pays by check and the date the bank pays the check. Similarly, when a company uses the bank's night depository to make its deposits, there will be a difference of one day between the time the company records the receipts and the time the bank does so. A time lag also occurs whenever the bank mails a debit or credit memorandum to the company.

The incidence of errors depends on the effectiveness of the internal controls maintained by the company and the bank. Bank errors are infrequent. However, either party could accidentally record a $450 check as $45 or $540. In addition, the bank might mistakenly charge a check drawn by C. D. Berg to the account of C. D. Burg.

Reconciliation Procedure

In reconciling the bank account, it is customary to reconcile the balance per books and balance per bank to their adjusted (correct or true) cash balances. **To obtain maximum benefit from a bank reconciliation, an employee who has no other responsibilities related to cash should prepare the reconciliation.** When companies do not follow the internal control principle of independent internal verification in preparing the reconciliation, cash embezzlements may escape unnoticed. For example, in the Anatomy of a Fraud box at the top of page 167, a bank reconciliation by someone other than Angela Bauer might have exposed her embezzlement.

Illustration 4-8 shows the reconciliation process. The starting point in preparing the reconciliation is to enter the balance per bank statement and balance per books on a schedule. The following steps should reveal all the reconciling items that cause the difference between the two balances.

Helpful Hint Deposits in transit and outstanding checks are reconciling items because of time lags.

Illustration 4-8 Bank reconciliation adjustments

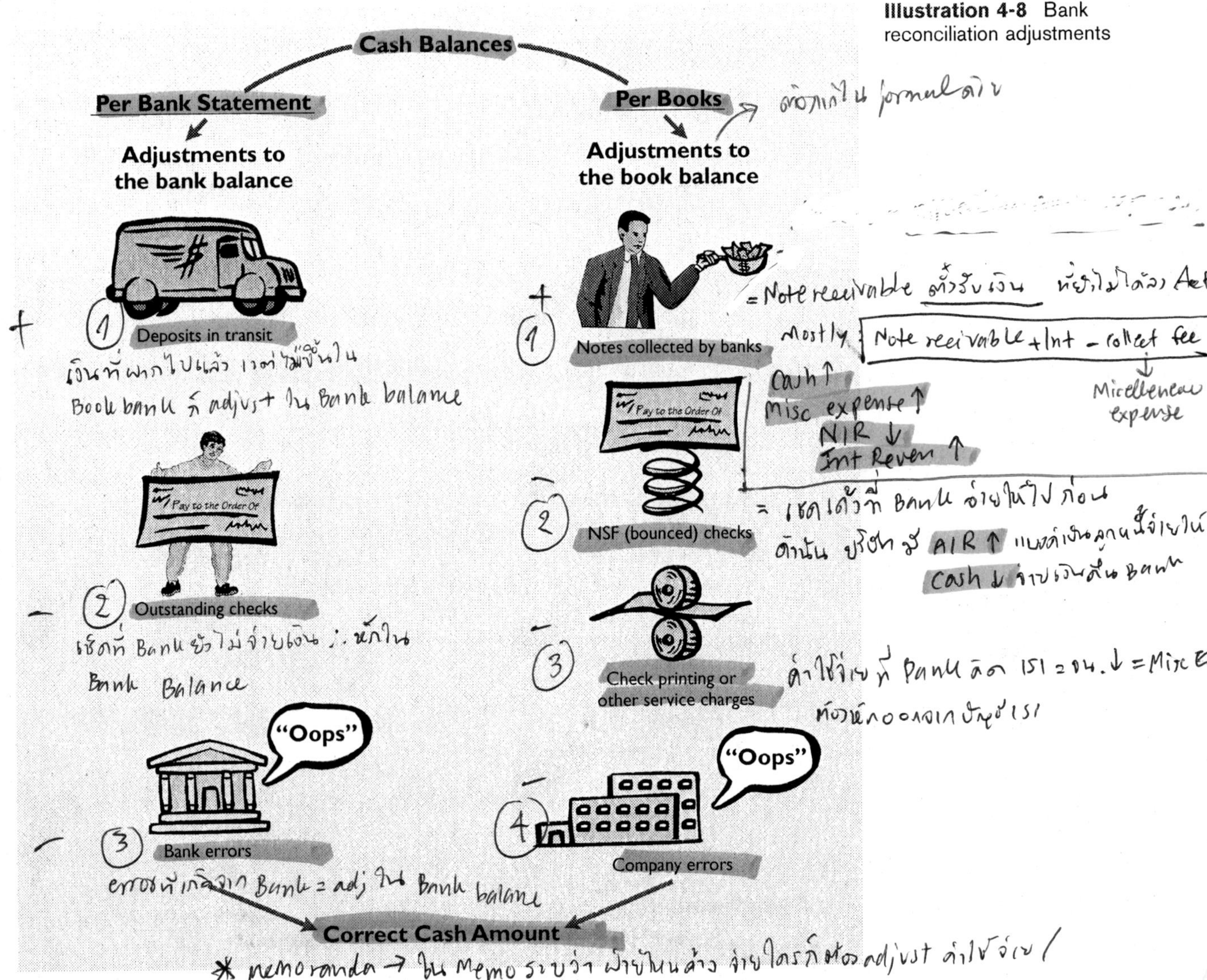

Step 1. Deposits in transit. Compare the individual deposits on the bank statement with the deposits in transit from the preceding bank reconciliation and with the deposits per company records or copies of duplicate deposit slips. Deposits recorded by the depositor that have not been

recorded by the bank represent **deposits in transit**. Add these deposits to the balance per bank.

Step 2. Outstanding checks. Compare the paid checks shown on the bank statement or the paid checks returned with the bank statement with (a) checks outstanding from the preceding bank reconciliation, and (b) checks issued by the company as recorded in the cash payments journal. Issued checks recorded by the company that have not been paid by the bank represent **outstanding checks**. Deduct outstanding checks from the balance per the bank.

Step 3. Errors. Note any errors discovered in the previous steps and list them in the appropriate section of the reconciliation schedule. For example, if the company mistakenly recorded as $159 a paid check correctly written for $195, the company would deduct the error of $36 from the balance per books. All errors made by the depositor are reconciling items in determining the adjusted cash balance per books. In contrast, all errors made by the bank are reconciling items in determining the adjusted cash balance per the bank.

Step 4. Bank memoranda. Trace bank memoranda to the depositor's records. The company lists in the appropriate section of the reconciliation schedule any unrecorded memoranda. For example, the company would deduct from the balance per books a $5 debit memorandum for bank service charges. Similarly, it would add to the balance per books a $32 credit memorandum for interest earned.

Bank Reconciliation Illustrated

Helpful Hint Note in the bank statement that the bank has paid checks No. 459 and 461, but check No. 460 is not listed. Thus, this check is outstanding. If a complete bank statement were provided, checks No. 453 and 457 also would not be listed. Laird obtains the amounts for these three checks from its cash payments records.

Illustration 4-7 presented the bank statement for Laird Company. It shows a balance per bank of $15,907.45 on April 30, 2010. On this date the balance of cash per books is $11,589.45. From the foregoing steps, Laird determines the following reconciling items.

Step 1. Deposits in transit: April 30 deposit (received by bank on May 1).	$2,201.40
Step 2. Outstanding checks: No. 453, $3,000.00; No. 457, $1,401.30; No. 460, $1,502.70.	5,904.00
Step 3. Errors: Check No. 443 was correctly written by Laird for $1,226.00 and was correctly paid by the bank. However, Laird recorded the check as $1,262.00.	36.00
Step 4. Bank memoranda:	
(a) Debit—NSF check from J. R. Baron for $425.60	425.60
(b) Debit—Printing company checks charge, $30	30.00
(c) Credit—Collection of note receivable for $1,000 plus interest earned $50, less bank collection fee $15	1,035.00

Illustration 4-9 (next page) shows Laird's bank reconciliation.

Entries from Bank Reconciliation

Helpful Hint These entries are adjusting entries. In prior chapters, we considered Cash an account that did not require adjustment because we had not yet explained a bank reconciliation.

The depositor (that is, the company) next must record each reconciling item used to determine the **adjusted cash balance per books**. If the company does not journalize and post these items, the Cash account will not show the correct balance. The adjusting entries for the Laird Company bank reconciliation on April 30 are as follows.

COLLECTION OF NOTE RECEIVABLE. This entry involves four accounts. Assuming that the interest of $50 has not been recorded and the collection fee is charged

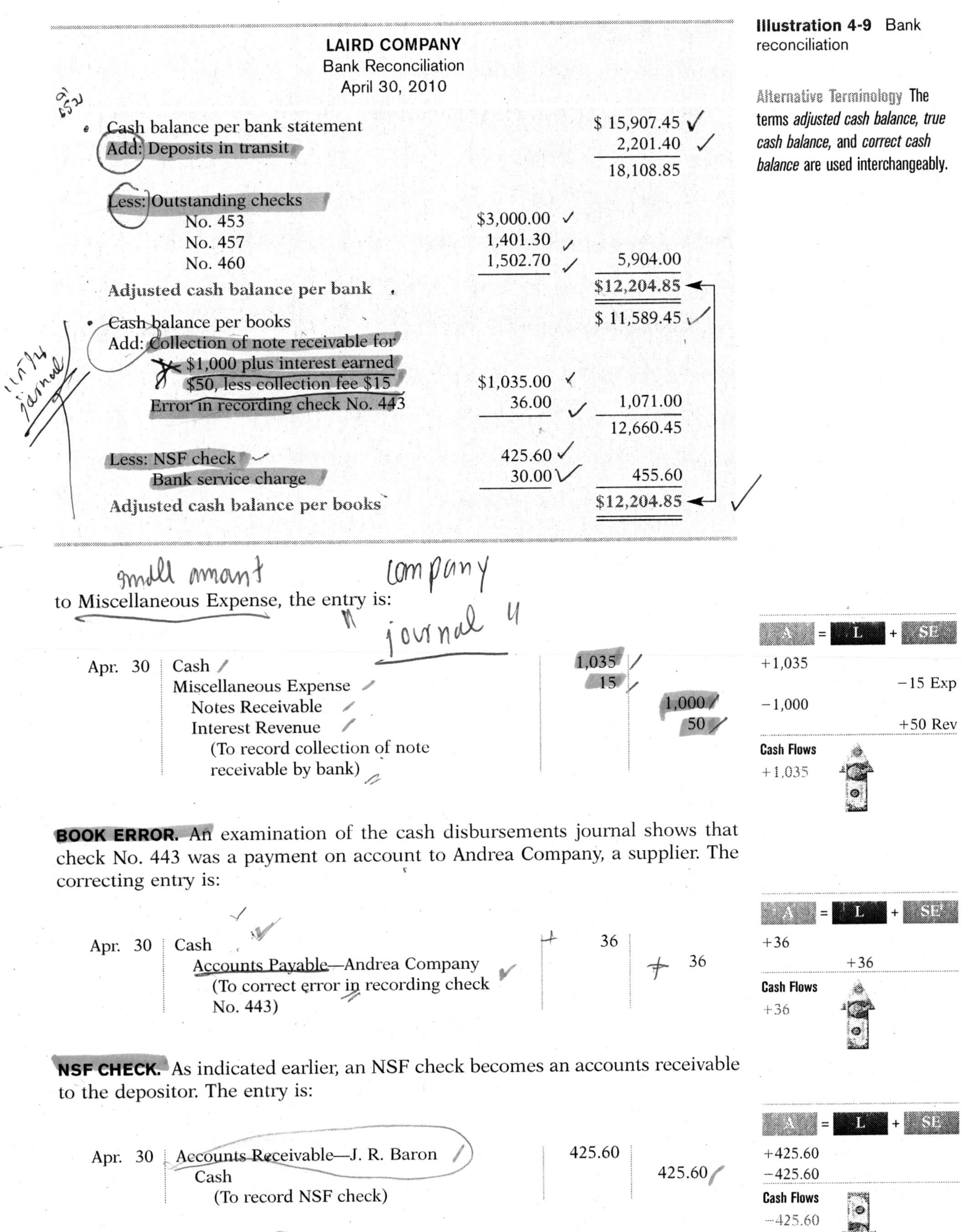

Illustration 4-9 Bank reconciliation

LAIRD COMPANY
Bank Reconciliation
April 30, 2010

Cash balance per bank statement		$ 15,907.45
Add: Deposits in transit		2,201.40
		18,108.85
Less: Outstanding checks		
No. 453	$3,000.00	
No. 457	1,401.30	
No. 460	1,502.70	5,904.00
Adjusted cash balance per bank		**$12,204.85**
Cash balance per books		$ 11,589.45
Add: Collection of note receivable for $1,000 plus interest earned $50, less collection fee $15	$1,035.00	
Error in recording check No. 443	36.00	1,071.00
		12,660.45
Less: NSF check	425.60	
Bank service charge	30.00	455.60
Adjusted cash balance per books		**$12,204.85**

Alternative Terminology The terms *adjusted cash balance, true cash balance,* and *correct cash balance* are used interchangeably.

to Miscellaneous Expense, the entry is:

Apr. 30	Cash	1,035	
	Miscellaneous Expense	15	
	Notes Receivable		1,000
	Interest Revenue		50
	(To record collection of note receivable by bank)		

A = L + SE: +1,035; −15 Exp; −1,000; +50 Rev

Cash Flows +1,035

BOOK ERROR. An examination of the cash disbursements journal shows that check No. 443 was a payment on account to Andrea Company, a supplier. The correcting entry is:

Apr. 30	Cash	36	
	Accounts Payable—Andrea Company		36
	(To correct error in recording check No. 443)		

A = L + SE: +36; +36

Cash Flows +36

NSF CHECK. As indicated earlier, an NSF check becomes an accounts receivable to the depositor. The entry is:

Apr. 30	Accounts Receivable—J. R. Baron	425.60	
	Cash		425.60
	(To record NSF check)		

A = L + SE: +425.60; −425.60

Cash Flows −425.60

BANK SERVICE CHARGES. Companies typically debit to Miscellaneous Expense the check printing charges (DM) and other bank service charges (SC) because

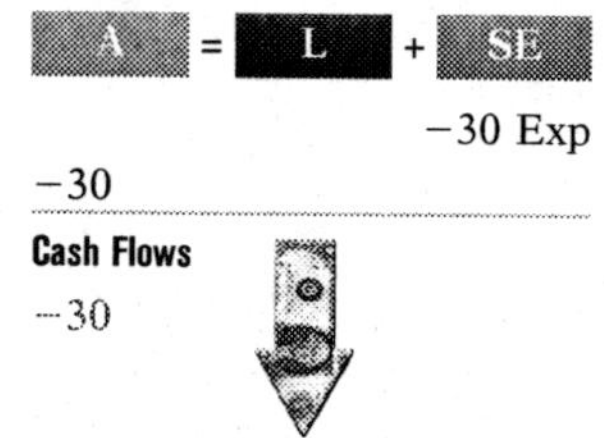

they are usually small in amount. Laird's entry is:

Apr. 30	Miscellaneous Expense	30	
	Cash		30
	(To record charge for printing company checks)		

The foregoing entries could also be combined into one compound entry.

After Laird posts the entries, the Cash account will appear as in Illustration 4-10. The adjusted cash balance in the ledger should agree with the adjusted cash balance per books in the bank reconciliation in Illustration 4-9.

Illustration 4-10
Adjusted balance in cash account

Cash				
Apr. 30	Bal.	11,589.45	Apr. 30	425.60
30		1,035.00	30	30.00
30		36.00		
Apr. 30	Bal.	12,204.85		

What entries does the bank make? If the company discovers any bank errors in preparing the reconciliation, it should notify the bank so the bank can make the necessary corrections on its records. The bank does not make any entries for deposits in transit or outstanding checks. Only when these items reach the bank will the bank record these items.

Electronic Funds Transfer (EFT) System

It is not surprising that companies and banks have developed approaches to transfer funds among parties without the use of paper (deposit tickets, checks, etc.). Such procedures, called **electronic funds transfers (EFTs)**, are disbursement systems that use wire, telephone, or computers to transfer cash balances from one location to another. Use of EFT is quite common. For example, many employees receive no formal payroll checks from their employers. Instead, employers send electronic payroll data to the appropriate banks. Also, individuals now frequently make regular payments such as those for house, car, and utilities by EFT.

EFT transfers normally result in better internal control since no cash or checks are handled by company employees. This does not mean that opportunities for fraud are eliminated. In fact, the same basic principles related to internal control apply to EFT transfers. For example, without proper segregation of duties and authorizations, an employee might be able to redirect electronic payments into a personal bank account and conceal the theft with fraudulent accounting entries.

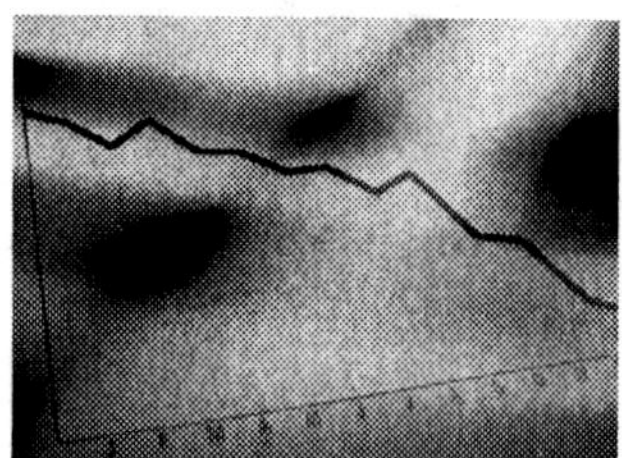

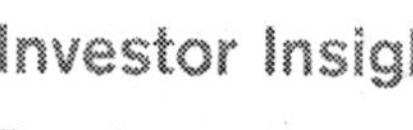

Investor Insight

Poor internal controls can cost a company money even if no theft occurs. For example, Eastman Kodak Co., SunTrust Banks Inc., and Toys "R" Us Inc. all recently reported material weaknesses in internal controls. When a company announces that it has deficiencies in its internal controls, its stock price often falls.

Under the Sarbanes-Oxley Act companies must evaluate their internal controls systems and report on any deficiencies. Some analysts estimate that as many as 10% of all publicly traded companies will report weaknesses in their internal controls. The estimate for smaller companies is even higher.

Source: William M. Bulkeley and Robert Tomsho, "Kodak to Get Auditors Adverse View," *Wall Street Journal Online* (January 27, 2005).

Why would a company's stock price fall if it reports deficiencies in its internal controls?

before you go on...

Do it! Sally Kist owns Linen Kist Fabrics. Sally asks you to explain how she should treat the following reconciling items when reconciling the company's bank account: (1) a debit memorandum for an NSF check, (2) a credit memorandum for a note collected by the bank, (3) outstanding checks, and (4) a deposit in transit.

BANK RECONCILIATION

Action Plan

- Understand the purpose of a bank reconciliation.
- Identify time lags and explain how they cause reconciling items.

Solution

Sally should treat the reconciling items as follows.

(1) NSF check: Deduct from balance per books.
(2) Collection of note: Add to balance per books.
(3) Outstanding checks: Deduct from balance per bank.
(4) Deposit in transit: Add to balance per bank.

Reporting Cash

study objective 

Explain the reporting of cash.

Cash consists of coins, currency (paper money), check, money orders, and money on hand or on deposit in a bank or similar depository. Companies report cash in two different statements: the balance sheet and the statement of cash flows. The balance sheet reports the amount of cash available at a given point in time. The statement of cash flows shows the sources and uses of cash during a period of time. The cash flow statement was introduced in Chapters 1 and 2 and will be discussed in much detail in a later chapter. In this section we discuss some important points regarding the presentation of cash in the balance sheet.

When presented in a balance sheet, cash on hand, cash in banks, and petty cash are often combined and reported simply as **Cash**. Because it is the most liquid asset owned by the company, cash is listed first in the current assets section of the balance sheet.

CASH EQUIVALENTS

Many companies use the designation "Cash and cash equivalents" in reporting cash. (See Illustration 4-11 for an example.) **Cash equivalents** are short-term, highly liquid investments that are both:

1. Readily convertible to known amounts of cash, and
2. So near their maturity that their market value is relatively insensitive to changes in interest rates.

Illustration 4-11 Balance sheet presentation of cash

Delta

DELTA AIR LINES, INC.
Balance Sheet (partial)
December 31, 2007
(in millions)

Assets	
Current assets	
Cash and cash equivalents	$2,648
Short-term investments	138
Restricted cash	520
Accounts receivable, net	1,066
Parts inventories	262
Prepaid expenses and other	606
Total current assets	$5,240

Ethics Note Recently some companies were forced to restate their financial statements because they had too broadly interpreted which types of investments could be treated as cash equivalents. By reporting these items as cash equivalents, the companies made themselves look more liquid.

Examples of cash equivalents are Treasury bills, commercial paper (short-term corporate notes), and money market funds. All typically are purchased with cash that is in excess of immediate needs.

Occasionally a company will have a net negative balance in its bank account. In this case, the company should report the negative balance among current liabilities. For example, farm equipment manufacturer Ag-Chem recently reported "Checks outstanding in excess of cash balances" of $2,145,000 among its current liabilities.

RESTRICTED CASH

A company may have restricted cash, cash that is not available for general use but rather is restricted for a special purpose. For example, landfill companies are often required to maintain a fund of restricted cash to ensure they will have adequate resources to cover closing and clean-up costs at the end of a landfill site's useful life. McKesson Corp. recently reported restricted cash of $962 million to be paid out as the result of investor lawsuits.

Cash restricted in use should be reported separately on the balance sheet as restricted cash. If the company expects to use the restricted cash within the next year, it reports the amount as a current asset. When this is not the case, it reports the restricted funds as a noncurrent asset.

Illustration 4-11 shows restricted cash reported in the financial statements of Delta Air Lines. The company is required to maintain restricted cash as collateral to support insurance obligations related to workers' compensation claims. Delta does not have access to these funds for general use, and so it must report them separately, rather than as part of cash and cash equivalents.

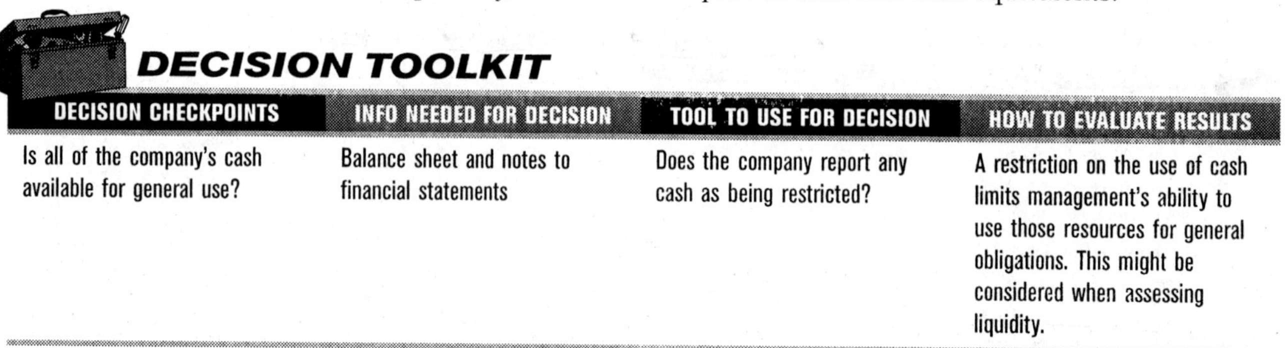

DECISION TOOLKIT

DECISION CHECKPOINTS	INFO NEEDED FOR DECISION	TOOL TO USE FOR DECISION	HOW TO EVALUATE RESULTS
Is all of the company's cash available for general use?	Balance sheet and notes to financial statements	Does the company report any cash as being restricted?	A restriction on the use of cash limits management's ability to use those resources for general obligations. This might be considered when assessing liquidity.

Managing and Monitoring Cash

Many companies struggle, not because they fail to generate sales, but because they can't manage their cash. A real-life example of this is a clothing manufacturing company owned by Sharon McCollick. McCollick gave up a stable, high-paying marketing job with Intel Corporation to start her own company. Soon she had more orders from stores such as JC Penney and Dayton Hudson (now Target) than she could fill. Yet she found herself on the brink of financial disaster, owing three mortgage payments on her house and $2,000 to the IRS. Her company could generate sales, but it was not collecting cash fast enough to support its operations. The bottom line is that a business must have cash.[6]

A merchandising company's operating cycle is generally shorter than that of a manufacturing company. Illustration 4-12 shows the cash to cash operating cycle of a merchandising operation.

---

[6]Adapted from T. Petzinger, Jr., "The Front Lines—Sharon McCollick Got Mad and Tore Down a Bank's Barriers," *Wall Street Journal* (May 19, 1995), p. B1.

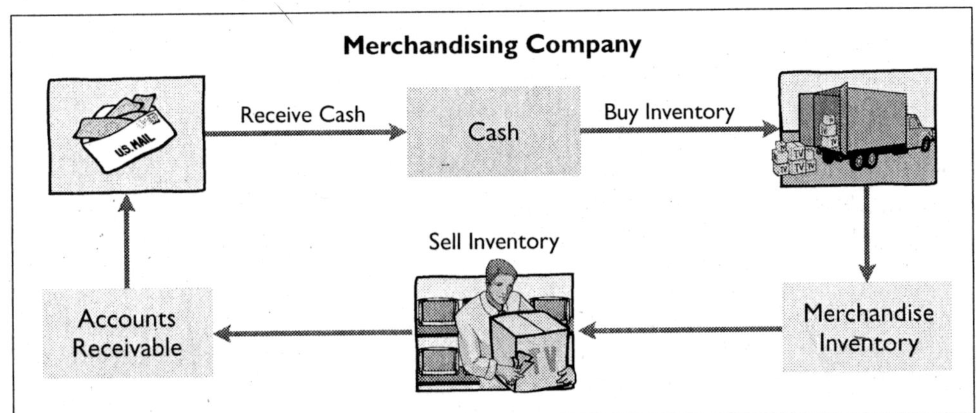

Illustration 4-12
Operating cycle of a merchandising company

To understand cash management, consider the operating cycle of Sharon McCollick's clothing manufacturing company. First, it purchases cloth. Let's assume that it purchases the cloth on credit provided by the supplier, so the company owes its supplier money. Next, employees convert the cloth to clothing. Now the company also owes its employees money. Next, it sells the clothing to retailers, on credit. McCollick's company will have no money to repay suppliers or employees until it receives payments from customers. In a manufacturing operation there may be a significant lag between the original purchase of raw materials and the ultimate receipt of cash from customers.

Managing the often-precarious balance created by the ebb and flow of cash during the operating cycle is one of a company's greatest challenges. The objective is to ensure that a company has sufficient cash to meet payments as they come due, yet minimize the amount of non-revenue-generating cash on hand.

BASIC PRINCIPLES OF CASH MANAGEMENT

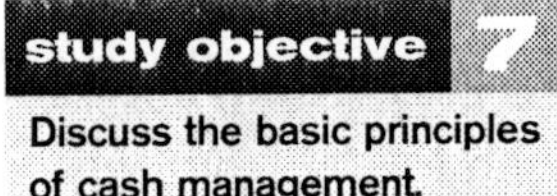

study objective 7
Discuss the basic principles of cash management.

Management of cash is the responsibility of the company treasurer. Any company can improve its chances of having adequate cash by following five basic principles of cash management.

1. **Increase the speed of receivables collection.** Money owed Sharon McCollick by her customers is money that she can't use. The more quickly customers pay her, the more quickly she can use those funds. Thus, rather than have an average collection period of 30 days, she may want an average collection period of 15 days. However, she must carefully weigh any attempt to force her customers to pay earlier against the possibility that she may anger or alienate customers. Perhaps her competitors are willing to provide a 30-day grace period. As noted in another chapter, one common way to encourage customers to pay more quickly is to offer cash discounts for early payment under such terms as 2/10, n/30.
2. **Keep inventory levels low.** Maintaining a large inventory of cloth and finished clothing is costly. It ties up large amounts of cash, as well as warehouse space. Increasingly, companies are using techniques to reduce the inventory on hand, thus conserving their cash. Of course, if Sharon McCollick has inadequate inventory, she will lose sales. The proper level of inventory is an important decision.
3. **Delay payment of liabilities.** By keeping track of when her bills are due, Sharon McCollick's company can avoid paying bills too early. Let's say her supplier allows 30 days for payment. If she pays in 10 days, she has lost the use of that cash for 20 days. Therefore, she should use the full payment period. But she should not "stretch" payment past the point that could damage her credit rating (and future borrowing ability). Sharon McCollick's

company also should conserve cash by taking cash discounts offered by suppliers, when possible.

4. **Plan the timing of major expenditures.** To maintain operations or to grow, all companies must make major expenditures, which normally require some form of outside financing. In order to increase the likelihood of obtaining outside financing, McCollick should carefully consider the timing of major expenditures in light of her company's operating cycle. If at all possible, she should make any major expenditure when the company normally has excess cash—usually during the off-season.
5. **Invest idle cash.** Cash on hand earns nothing. An important part of the treasurer's job is to ensure that the company invests any excess cash, even if it is only overnight. Many businesses, such as Sharon McCollick's clothing company, are seasonal. During her slow season, when she has excess cash, she should invest it.

   To avoid a cash crisis, however, it is very important that investments of idle cash be highly liquid and risk-free. A *liquid investment* is one with a market in which someone is always willing to buy or sell the investment. A *risk-free investment* means there is no concern that the party will default on its promise to pay its principal and interest. For example, using excess cash to purchase stock in a small company because you heard that it was probably going to increase in value in the near term is totally inappropriate. First, the stock of small companies is often illiquid. Second, if the stock suddenly decreases in value, you might be forced to sell the stock at a loss in order to pay your bills as they come due. The most common form of liquid investments is interest-paying U.S. government securities.

International Note International sales complicate cash management. For example, if Nike must repay a Japanese supplier 30 days from today in Japanese yen, Nike will be concerned about how the exchange rate of U.S. dollars for yen might change during those 30 days. Often corporate treasurers make investments known as *hedges* to lock in an exchange rate to reduce the company's exposure to exchange-rate fluctuation.

Illustration 4-13 summarizes these five principles of cash management.

Illustration 4-13 Five principles of sound cash management

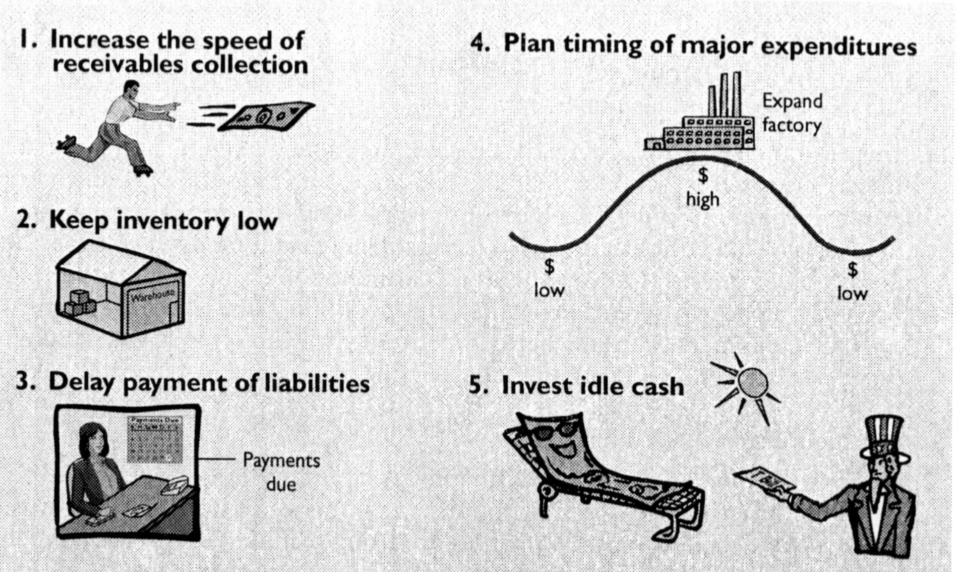

KEEPING AN EYE ON CASH

Because cash is so vital to a company, **planning the company's cash needs** is a key business activity. It enables the company to plan ahead to cover possible cash shortfalls and to make investments of idle funds. The **cash budget** shows anticipated cash flows, usually over a one- to two-year period. In this section we introduce the basics of cash budgeting. More advanced discussion of cash budgets and budgets in general is provided in managerial accounting texts.

study objective 8

Identify the primary elements of a cash budget.

As shown below, the cash budget contains three sections—cash receipts, cash disbursements, and financing—and the beginning and ending cash balances.

ANY COMPANY
Cash Budget

Beginning cash balance	$X,XXX
Add: Cash receipts (itemized)	X,XXX
Total available cash	X,XXX
Less: Cash disbursements (itemized)	X,XXX
Excess (deficiency) of available cash over cash disbursements	X,XXX
Financing needed	X,XXX
Ending cash balance	$X,XXX

The **Cash receipts** section includes expected receipts from the company's principal source(s) of cash, such as cash sales and collections from customers on credit sales. This section also shows anticipated receipts of interest and dividends, and proceeds from planned sales of investments, plant assets, and the company's capital stock.

The **Cash disbursements** section shows expected payments for inventory, labor, overhead, and selling and administrative expenses. This section also includes projected payments for income taxes, dividends, investments, and plant assets.

The **Financing** section shows expected borrowings and the repayment of the borrowed funds plus interest. The financing entry is needed when there is a cash deficiency or when the cash balance is less than management's minimum required balance.

Companies must prepare the data in the cash budget in sequence because the ending cash balance of one period becomes the beginning cash balance for the next period. They obtain data for preparing the cash budget from other budgets and from information provided by management. In practice, companies often prepare cash budgets for the next 12 months on a monthly basis.

To minimize detail, we will assume that Hayes Company prepares an annual cash budget by quarters. Preparing a cash budget requires making some assumptions. For example, Hayes makes assumptions regarding collection of accounts receivable, sales of securities, payments for materials and salaries, and purchases of property, plant, and equipment. The accuracy of the cash budget is very dependent on the accuracy of these assumptions.

On the next page, we present the cash budget for Hayes Company. The budget indicates that the company will need $3,000 of financing in the second quarter to maintain a minimum cash balance of $15,000. Since there is an excess of available cash over disbursements of $22,500 at the end of the third quarter, Hayes will repay the borrowing, plus $100 interest, in that quarter.

A cash budget contributes to more effective cash management. For example, it can show when a company will need additional financing, well before the actual need arises. Conversely, it can indicate when the company will have excess cash available for investments or other purposes.

HAYES COMPANY
Cash Budget
For the Year Ending December 31, 2010

	Quarter			
	1	2	3	4
Beginning cash balance	$ 38,000	$ 25,500	$ 15,000	$ 19,400
Add: Cash receipts				
Collections from customers	168,000	198,000	228,000	258,000
Sale of securities	2,000	0	0	0
Total receipts	170,000	198,000	228,000	258,000
Total available cash	208,000	223,500	243,000	277,400
Less: Cash disbursements				
Inventory	23,200	27,200	31,200	35,200
Salaries	62,000	72,000	82,000	92,000
Selling and administrative expenses (excluding depreciation)	94,300	99,300	104,300	109,300
Purchase of truck	0	10,000	0	0
Income tax expense	3,000	3,000	3,000	3,000
Total disbursements	182,500	211,500	220,500	239,500
Excess (deficiency) of available cash over disbursements	25,500	12,000	22,500	37,900
Financing				
Borrowings	0	3,000	0	0
Repayments—plus $100 interest	0	0	3,100	0
Ending cash balance	$ 25,500	$ 15,000	$ 19,400	$ 37,900

DECISION TOOLKIT

DECISION CHECKPOINTS	INFO NEEDED FOR DECISION	TOOL TO USE FOR DECISION	HOW TO EVALUATE RESULTS
Will the company be able to meet its projected cash needs?	Cash budget (typically available only to management)	The cash budget shows projected sources and uses of cash. If cash uses exceed internal cash sources, then the company must look for outside sources.	Two issues: (1) Are management's projections reasonable? (2) If outside sources are needed, are they available?

before you go on...

CASH BUDGET

Do it! Martian Company's management wants to maintain a minimum monthly cash balance of $15,000. At the beginning of March the cash balance is $16,500; expected cash receipts for March are $210,000; and cash disbursements are expected to be $220,000. How much cash, if any, must Martian borrow to maintain the desired minimum monthly balance?

Solution

Beginning cash balance	$ 16,500
Add: Cash receipts for March	210,000
Total available cash	226,500
Less: Cash disbursements for March	220,000
Excess of available cash over cash disbursements	6,500
Financing	8,500
Ending cash balance	$ 15,000

To maintain the desired minimum cash balance of $15,000, Martian Company must borrow $8,500 of cash.

Action Plan

- Add the beginning cash balance to receipts to determine total available cash.
- Subtract disbursements to determine excess or deficiency.
- Compare excess or deficiency with desired minimum cash to determine borrowing needs.

Presented below is hypothetical financial information for Mattel Corporation. Included in this information is financial statement data from the year ended December 31, 2009, which should be used to evaluate Mattel's cash position.

Selected Financial Information
Year Ended December 31, 2009
(in millions)

Net cash provided by operations	$325
Capital expenditures	162
Dividends paid	80
Total expenses	680
Depreciation expense	40
Cash balance	206

Also provided are projected data which are management's best estimate of its sources and uses of cash during 2010. This information should be used to prepare a cash budget for 2010.

Projected Sources and Uses of Cash
(in millions)

Beginning cash balance	$206
Cash receipts from sales of product	355
Cash receipts from sale of short-term investments	20
Cash payments for inventory	357
Cash payments for selling and administrative expense	201
Cash payments for property, plant, and equipment	45
Cash payments for taxes	17

Mattel Corporation's management believes it should maintain a balance of $200 million cash.

Instructions

(a) Using the hypothetical projected sources and uses of cash information presented above, prepare a cash budget for 2010 for Mattel Corporation.

(b) Comment on the company's cash adequacy, and discuss steps that might be taken to improve its cash position.

Solution

(a)

MATTEL CORPORATION
Cash Budget
For the Year 2010
(in millions)

Beginning cash balance		$206
Add: Cash receipts		
From sales of product	$355	
From sale of short-term investments	20	375
Total available cash		581
Less: Cash disbursements		
Payments for inventory	357	
Payments for selling and administrative costs	201	
Payments for property, plant, and equipment	45	
Payments for taxes	17	
Total disbursements		620
Excess (deficiency) of available cash over disbursements		(39)
Financing needed		239
Ending cash balance		$200

(b) Using these hypothetical data, Mattel's cash position appears adequate. For 2010 Mattel is projecting a cash shortfall. This is not necessarily of concern, but it should be investigated. Given that its primary line of business is toys, and that most toys are sold during December, we would expect Mattel's cash position to vary significantly during the course of the year. After the holiday season it probably has a lot of excess cash. Earlier in the year, when it is making and selling its product but has not yet been paid, it may need to borrow to meet any temporary cash shortfalls.

If Mattel's management is concerned with its cash position, it could take the following steps: (1) Offer its customers cash discounts for early payment, such as 2/10, n/30. (2) Implement inventory management techniques to reduce the need for large inventories of such things as the plastics used to make its toys. (3) Carefully time payments to suppliers by keeping track of when payments are due, so as not to pay too early. (4) If it has plans for major expenditures, time those expenditures to coincide with its seasonal period of excess cash.

Summary of Study Objectives

1 Define fraud and internal control. A fraud is a dishonest act by an employee that results in personal benefit to the employee at a cost to the employer. The fraud triangle refers to the three factors that contribute to fraudulent activity by employees: opportunity, financial pressure, and rationalization. Internal control consists of all the related methods and measures adopted within an organization to safeguard its assets, enhance the reliability of its accounting records, increase efficiency of operations, and ensure compliance with laws and regulations.

2 Identify the principles of internal control activities. The principles of internal control are: establishment of responsibility; segregation of duties; documentation procedures; physical controls; independent internal verification; and human resource controls.

3 Explain the applications of internal control principles to cash receipts. Internal controls over cash receipts include: (a) designating only personnel such as cashiers to handle cash; (b) assigning the duties of receiving cash, recording cash, and having custody of cash to different individuals; (c) obtaining remittance advices for mail receipts, cash register tapes for over-the-counter receipts, and deposit slips for bank deposits; (d) using company safes and bank vaults to store cash with access limited to authorized personnel, and using cash registers in executing over-the-counter receipts; (e) making independent daily counts of register receipts and daily comparisons of total receipts with total deposits; and (f) bonding personnel who handle cash and requiring them to take vacations.

4 **Explain the applications of internal control to cash disbursements.** Internal controls over cash disbursements include: (a) having only specified individuals such as the treasurer authorized to sign checks; (b) assigning the duties of approving items for payment, paying the items, and recording the payment to different individuals; (c) using prenumbered checks and accounting for all checks, with each check supported by an approved invoice; after payment, stamping each approved invoice "paid"; (d) storing blank checks in a safe or vault with access restricted to authorized personnel, and using a machine with indelible ink to imprint amounts on checks; (e) comparing each check with the approved invoice before issuing the check, and making monthly reconciliations of bank and book balances; and (f) bonding personnel who handle cash, requiring employees to take vacations, and conducting background checks.

5 **Prepare a bank reconciliation.** In reconciling the bank account, it is customary to reconcile the balance per books and the balance per bank to their adjusted balance. The steps reconciling the cash account are to determine deposits in transit, outstanding checks, errors by the depositor or the bank, and unrecorded bank memoranda.

6 **Explain the reporting of cash.** Cash is listed first in the current assets section of the balance sheet. Companies often report cash together with cash equivalents. Cash restricted for a special purpose is reported separately as a current asset or as a noncurrent asset, depending on when the company expects to use the cash.

7 **Discuss the basic principles of cash management.** The basic principles of cash management include: (a) increase the speed of receivables collection, (b) keep inventory levels low, (c) delay payment of liabilities, (d) plan timing of major expenditures, and (e) invest idle cash.

8 **Identify the primary elements of a cash budget.** The three main elements of a cash budget are the cash receipts section, cash disbursements section, and financing section.

the navigator

DECISION TOOLKIT A SUMMARY

DECISION CHECKPOINTS	INFO NEEDED FOR DECISION	TOOL TO USE FOR DECISION	HOW TO EVALUATE RESULTS
Are the company's financial statements supported by adequate internal controls?	Auditor's report, management discussion and analysis, articles in financial press	The principles of internal control activities are (1) establishment of responsibility, (2) segregation of duties, (3) documentation procedures, (4) physical controls, (5) independent internal verification, and (6) human resource controls.	If any indication is given that these or other controls are lacking, use the financial statements with caution.
Is all of the company's cash available for general use?	Balance sheet and notes to financial statements	Does the company report any cash as being restricted?	A restriction on the use of cash limits management's ability to use those resources for general obligations. This might be considered when assessing liquidity.
Will the company be able to meet its projected cash needs?	Cash budget (typically available only to management)	The cash budget shows projected sources and uses of cash. If cash uses exceed internal cash sources, then the company must look for outside sources.	Two issues: (1) Are management's projections reasonable? (2) If outside sources are needed, are they available?

appendix

Operation of the Petty Cash Fund

study objective 9

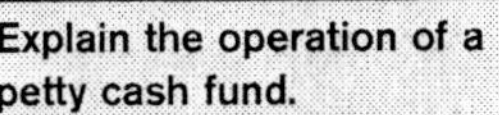
Explain the operation of a petty cash fund.

The operation of a petty cash fund involves (1) establishing the fund, (2) making payments from the fund, and (3) replenishing the fund.

ESTABLISHING THE PETTY CASH FUND

Two essential steps in establishing a petty cash fund are: (1) appointing a petty cash custodian who will be responsible for the fund, and (2) determining the size of the fund. Ordinarily, a company expects the amount in the fund to cover anticipated disbursements for a three- to four-week period.

When the company establishes the petty cash fund, it issues a check payable to the petty cash custodian for the stipulated amount. If Laird Company decides to establish a $100 fund on March 1, the entry in general journal form is:

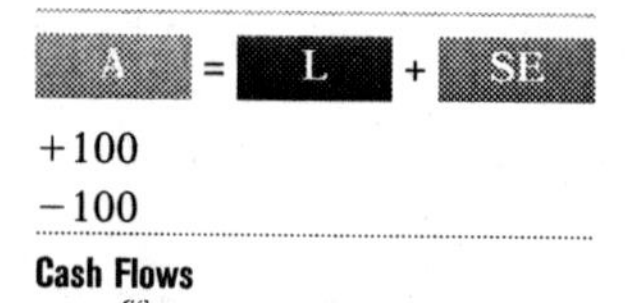

Mar.	1	Petty Cash	100	
		Cash		100
		(To establish a petty cash fund)		

Ethics Note Petty cash funds are authorized and legitimate. In contrast, "slush" funds are unauthorized and hidden (under the table).

The fund custodian cashes the check and places the proceeds in a locked petty cash box or drawer. Most petty cash funds are established on a fixed-amount basis. Moreover, the company will make no additional entries to the Petty Cash account unless the stipulated amount of the fund is changed. For example, if Laird Company decides on July 1 to increase the size of the fund to $250, it would debit Petty Cash $150 and credit Cash $150.

MAKING PAYMENTS FROM PETTY CASH

The custodian of the petty cash fund has the authority to make payments from the fund that conform to prescribed management policies. Usually management limits the size of expenditures that come from petty cash and does not permit use of the fund for certain types of transactions (such as making short-term loans to employees).

Helpful Hint From the standpoint of internal control, the receipt satisfies two principles: (1) establishing responsibility (signature of custodian), and (2) documentation procedures.

Each payment from the fund must be documented on a prenumbered petty cash receipt (or petty cash voucher). The signatures of both the custodian and the individual receiving payment are required on the receipt. If other supporting documents such as a freight bill or invoice are available, they should be attached to the petty cash receipt.

The custodian keeps the receipts in the petty cash box until the fund is replenished. As a result, the sum of the petty cash receipts and money in the fund should equal the established total at all times. This means that management can make surprise counts at any time by an independent person, such as an internal auditor, to determine the correctness of the fund.

The company does not make an accounting entry to record a payment at the time it is taken from petty cash. It is considered both inexpedient and unnecessary to do so. Instead, the company recognizes the accounting effects of each payment when the fund is replenished.

REPLENISHING THE PETTY CASH FUND

Helpful Hint Replenishing involves three internal control procedures: segregation of duties, documentation procedures, and independent internal verification.

When the money in the petty cash fund reaches a minimum level, the company replenishes the fund. The petty cash custodian initiates a request for reimbursement. This individual prepares a schedule (or summary) of the payments that have been made and sends the schedule, supported by petty cash receipts and other documentation, to the treasurer's office. The receipts and supporting documents are examined in the treasurer's office to verify that they were proper payments from the fund. The treasurer then approves the request, and a check is prepared to restore the fund to its established amount. At the same time, all supporting documentation is stamped "paid" so that it cannot be submitted again for payment.

To illustrate, assume that on March 15 the petty cash custodian requests a check for $87. The fund contains $13 cash and petty cash receipts for postage

$44, supplies $38, and miscellaneous expenses $5. The entry, in general journal form, to record the check is:

Mar. 15	Postage Expense	44	
	Supplies	38	
	Miscellaneous Expense	5	
	Cash		87
	(To replenish petty cash fund)		

A	=	L	+	SE
				−44 Exp
+38				
				−5 Exp
−87				

Cash Flows
−87

Note that the reimbursement entry does not affect the Petty Cash account. Replenishment changes the composition of the fund by replacing the petty cash receipts with cash, but it does not change the balance in the fund.

Occasionally, in replenishing a petty cash fund the company may need to recognize a cash shortage or overage. To illustrate, assume in the preceding example that the custodian had only $12 in cash in the fund plus the receipts as listed. The request for reimbursement would therefore be for $88, and the following entry would be made.

Mar. 15	Postage Expense	44	
	Supplies	38	
	Miscellaneous Expense	5	
	Cash Over and Short	1	
	Cash		88
	(To replenish petty cash fund)		

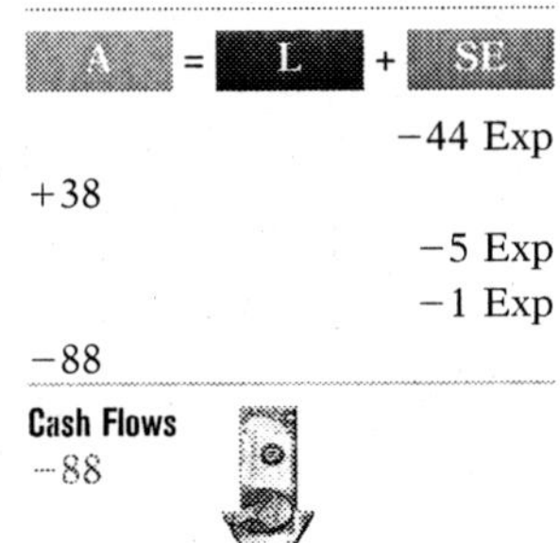

Conversely, if the custodian had $14 in cash, the reimbursement request would be for $86, and Cash Over and Short would be credited for $1. A debit balance in Cash Over and Short is reported in the income statement as miscellaneous expense; a credit balance is reported as miscellaneous revenue. The company closes Cash Over and Short to Income Summary at the end of the year.

Companies should replenish a petty cash fund **at the end of the accounting period, regardless of the cash in the fund.** Replenishment at this time is necessary in order to recognize the effects of the petty cash payments on the financial statements.

Internal control over a petty cash fund is strengthened by (1) having a supervisor make surprise counts of the fund to ascertain whether the paid vouchers and fund cash equal the designated amount, and (2) canceling or mutilating the paid vouchers so they cannot be resubmitted for reimbursement.

Summary of Study Objective for Appendix

9 Explain the operation of a petty cash fund. In operating a petty cash fund, a company establishes the fund by appointing a custodian and determining the size of the fund. The custodian makes payments from the fund for documented expenditures. The company replenishes the fund as needed, and at the end of each accounting period. Accounting entries to record payments are made each time the fund is replenished.

Glossary

Bank reconciliation *(p. 179)* The process of comparing the bank's account balance with the company's balance, and explaining the differences to make them agree.

Bank statement *(p. 179)* A statement received monthly from the bank that shows the depositor's bank transactions and balances.

Bonding *(p. 170)* Obtaining insurance protection against theft by employees.

Cash *(p. 185)* Resources that consist of coins, currency, checks, money orders, and money on hand or on deposit in a bank or similar depository.

Cash budget *(p. 188)* A projection of anticipated cash flows, usually over a one- to two-year period.

Cash equivalents *(p. 185)* Short-term, highly liquid investments that can be converted to a specific amount of cash.

Deposits in transit *(p. 182)* Deposits recorded by the depositor that have not been recorded by the bank.

Electronic funds transfer (EFT) *(p. 184)* A disbursement system that uses wire, telephone, or computer to transfer cash from one location to another.

Fraud *(p. 162)* A dishonest act by an employee that results in personal benefit to the employee at a cost to the employer.

Fraud triangle *(p. 162)* The three factors that contribute to fraudulent activity by employees: opportunity, financial pressure, and rationalization.

Internal auditors *(p. 170)* Company employees who continuously evaluate the effectiveness of the company's internal control systems.

Internal control *(p. 163)* All the related methods and measures adopted within an organization to safeguard its assets and enhance the reliability of its accounting records, increase efficiency of operation, and ensure compliance with laws and regulations.

NSF check *(p. 179)* A check that is not paid by a bank because of insufficient funds in a bank account.

Outstanding checks *(p. 182)* Checks issued and recorded by a company that have not been paid by the bank.

Petty cash fund *(p. 178)* A cash fund used to pay relatively small amounts.

Restricted cash *(p. 186)* Cash that is not available for general use, but instead is restricted for a particular purpose.

Sarbanes-Oxley Act of 2002 (SOX) *(p. 163)* Law that requires companies to maintain adequate systems of internal control.

Treasurer *(p. 187)* Employee responsible for the management of a company's cash.

Voucher *(p. 177)* An authorization form prepared for each expenditure in a voucher system.

Voucher system *(p. 177)* A network of approvals by authorized individuals acting independently to ensure that all disbursements by check are proper.

Comprehensive Do it!

Trillo Company's bank statement for May 2010 shows these data.

Balance May 1	$12,650	Balance May 31	$14,280
Debit memorandum:		Credit memorandum:	
NSF check	175	Collection of note receivable	505

The cash balance per books at May 31 is $13,319. Your review of the data reveals the following.

1. The NSF check was from Hup Co., a customer.
2. The note collected by the bank was a $500, 3-month, 12% note. The bank charged a $10 collection fee. No interest has been previously accrued.
3. Outstanding checks at May 31 total $2,410.
4. Deposits in transit at May 31 total $1,752.
5. A Trillo Company check for $352 dated May 10 cleared the bank on May 25. This check, which was a payment on account, was journalized for $325.

Instructions

(a) Prepare a bank reconciliation at May 31.
(b) Journalize the entries required by the reconciliation.

Action Plan

- Follow the four steps used in reconciling items (p. 181–182).
- Work carefully to minimize mathematical errors in the reconciliation.
- Prepare entries based on reconciling items per books.
- Make sure the cash ledger balance after posting the reconciling entries agrees with the adjusted cash balance per books.

Solution to Comprehensive Do it!

(a)

Cash balance per bank statement		$14,280
Add: Deposits in transit		1,752
		16,032
Less: Outstanding checks		2,410
Adjusted cash balance per bank		$13,622
Cash balance per books		$13,319
Add: Collection of note receivable $500, plus $15 interest less collection fee $10		505
		13,824
Less: NSF check	$175	
Error in recording check	27	202
Adjusted cash balance per books		$13,622

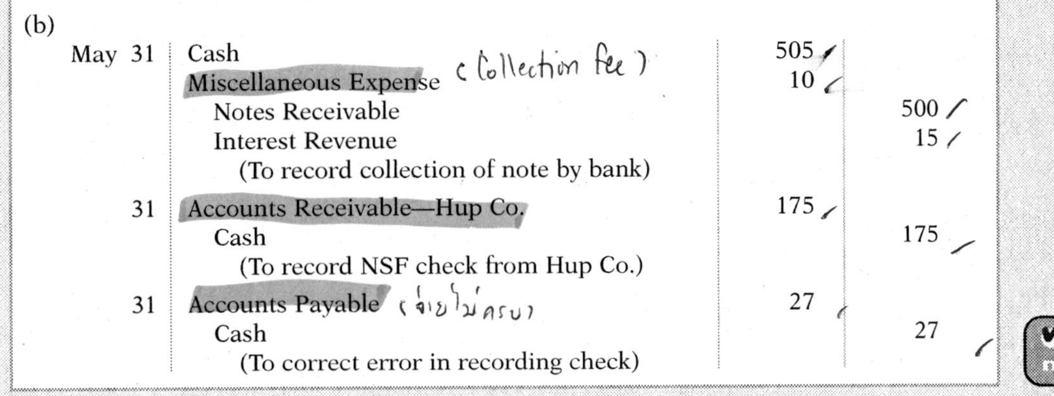

(b)

Date	Account	Debit	Credit
May 31	Cash	505	
	Miscellaneous Expense	10	
	Notes Receivable		500
	Interest Revenue		15
	(To record collection of note by bank)		
31	Accounts Receivable—Hup Co.	175	
	Cash		175
	(To record NSF check from Hup Co.)		
31	Accounts Payable	27	
	Cash		27
	(To correct error in recording check)		

Note: All Questions, Exercises, and Problems marked with an asterisk relate to material in the appendix to the chapter.

Self-Study Questions

WILEY PLUS

Answers are at the end of the chapter.

(SO 1) 1. Which of the following is *not* an element of the fraud triangle?
   (a) Rationalization.
   (b) Financial pressure.
   (c) Segregation of duties.
   (d) Opportunity.

(SO 1) 2. Internal control is used in a business to enhance the accuracy and reliability of its accounting records and to:
   (a) safeguard its assets.
   (b) create fraud.
   (c) analyze financial statements.
   (d) determine employee bonuses.

(SO 2) 3. The principles of internal control do *not* include:
   (a) establishment of responsibility.
   (b) documentation procedures.
   (c) financial performance measures.
   (d) independent internal verification.

(SO 2) 4. Physical controls do *not* include:
   (a) safes and vaults to store cash.
   (b) independent bank reconciliations.
   (c) locked warehouses for inventories.
   (d) bank safety deposit boxes for important papers.

(SO 1) 5. Which of the following was *not* a result of the Sarbanes-Oxley Act?
   (a) Companies must file financial statements with the Internal Revenue Service.
   (b) All publicly traded companies must maintain adequate internal controls.
   (c) The Public Company Accounting Oversight Board was created to establish auditing standards and regulate auditor activity.
   (d) Corporate executives and board of directors must ensure that controls are reliable and effective, and they can be fined or imprisoned for failure to do so.

6. Permitting only designated personnel such as cashiers to handle cash receipts is an application of the principle of: (SO 3)
   (a) documentation procedures.
   (b) establishment of responsibility.
   (c) independent internal verification.
   (d) other controls.

7. The use of prenumbered checks in disbursing cash is an application of the principle of: (SO 4)
   (a) establishment of responsibility.
   (b) segregation of duties.
   (c) physical controls.
   (d) documentation procedures.

8. The control features of a bank account do *not* include: (SO 4)
   (a) having bank auditors verify the correctness of the bank balance per books.
   (b) minimizing the amount of cash that must be kept on hand.
   (c) providing a double record of all bank transactions.
   (d) safeguarding cash by using a bank as a depository.

9. Which of the following control activities is *not* relevant to when a company uses a computerized (rather than manual) accounting system? (SO 2)
   (a) Establishment of responsibility.
   (b) Segregation of duties.
   (c) Independent internal verification.
   (d) All of these control activities are relevant to a computerized system.

10. In a bank reconciliation, deposits in transit are: (SO 5)
   (a) deducted from the book balance.
   (b) added to the book balance.
   (c) added to the bank balance.
   (d) deducted from the bank balance.

(SO 6) 11. Which of the following items in a cash drawer at November 30 is *not* cash?
(a) Money orders.
(b) Coins and currency.
(c) A customer check dated December 1.
(d) A customer check dated November 28.

(SO 6) 12. Which statement correctly describes the reporting of cash?
(a) Cash cannot be combined with cash equivalents.
(b) Restricted cash funds may be combined with Cash.
(c) Cash is listed first in the current assets section.
(d) Restricted cash funds cannot be reported as a current asset.

(SO 7) 13. Which of the following would *not* be an example of good cash management?
(a) Provide discounts to customers to encourage early payment.
(b) Invest temporary excess cash in stock of a small company.
(c) Carefully monitor payments so that payments are not made early.
(d) Employ just-in-time inventory methods to keep inventory low.

14. Which of the following is *not* one of the sections of a cash budget? (SO 8)
(a) Cash receipts section.
(b) Cash disbursements section.
(c) Financing section.
(d) Cash from operations section.

*15. A check is written to replenish a $100 petty cash fund when the fund contains receipts of $94 and $2 in cash. In recording the check: (SO 9)
(a) Cash Over and Short should be debited for $4.
(b) Petty Cash should be debited for $94.
(c) Cash should be credited for $94.
(d) Petty Cash should be credited for $4.

Go to the book's companion website, **www.wiley.com/college/kimmel**, to access additional Self-Study Questions.

Questions

1. A local bank reported that it lost $150,000 as the result of an employee fraud. Randal Smith is not clear on what is meant by an "employee fraud." Explain the meaning of fraud to Randal and give an example of frauds that might occur at a bank.
2. Fraud experts often say that there are three primary factors that contribute to employee fraud. Identify the three factors and explain what is meant by each.
3. Identify and describe the five components of a good internal control system.
4. "Internal control is concerned only with enhancing the accuracy of the accounting records." Do you agree? Explain.
5. Discuss how the Sarbanes-Oxley Act has increased the importance of internal control to all employees in a company.
6. What principles of internal control apply to most business enterprises?
7. In the corner grocery store, all sales clerks make change out of one cash register drawer. Is this a violation of internal control? Why?
8. Gloria Modine is reviewing the principle of segregation of duties. What are the two common applications of this principle?
9. How do documentation procedures contribute to good internal control?
10. What internal control objectives are met by physical controls?
11. (a) Explain the control principle of independent internal verification.
(b) What practices are important in applying this principle?
12. As the company accountant, explain the following ideas to the management of Keane Company.
(a) The concept of reasonable assurance in internal control.
(b) The importance of the human factor in internal control.
13. Discuss the human resources department's involvement in internal controls.
14. Commerford Inc. owns the following assets at the balance sheet date.

Cash in bank—savings account	$ 8,000
Cash on hand	1,100
Cash refund due from the IRS	1,000
Checking account balance	12,000
Postdated checks	500

What amount should be reported as Cash in the balance sheet?
15. What principle(s) of internal control is (are) involved in making daily cash counts of over-the-counter receipts?
16. Assume that Kohl's Department Stores installed new electronic cash registers in its stores. How do cash registers improve internal control over cash receipts?
17. At Unruh Wholesale Company two mail clerks open all mail receipts. How does this strengthen internal control?
18. "To have maximum effective internal control over cash disbursements, all payments should be made by check." Is this true? Explain.
19. Rondelli Company's internal controls over cash disbursements provide for the treasurer to sign checks imprinted by a checkwriter after comparing the check

with the approved invoice. Identify the internal control principles that are present in these controls.

20. How do these principles apply to cash disbursements:
    (a) Physical controls?
    (b) Documentation controls?

21. What is the essential feature of an electronic funds transfer (EFT) procedure?

22. "The use of a bank contributes significantly to good internal control over cash." Is this true? Why?

23. Stanley Delong is confused about the lack of agreement between the cash balance per books and the balance per bank. Explain the causes for the lack of agreement to Stanley, and give an example of each cause.

24. Describe the basic principles of cash management.

25. Julie Ellis asks your help concerning an NSF check. Explain to Julie (a) what an NSF check is, (b) how it is treated in a bank reconciliation, and (c) whether it will require an adjusting entry on the company's books.

26.
    (a) "Cash equivalents are the same as cash." Do you agree? Explain.
    (b) How should restricted cash funds be reported on the balance sheet?

27. What was Tootsie Roll's balance in cash and cash equivalents at December 31, 2007? Did it report any restricted cash? How did Tootsie Roll define cash equivalents?

*28. (a) Identify the three activities that pertain to a petty cash fund, and indicate an internal control principle that is applicable to each activity.
    (b) When are journal entries required in the operation of a petty cash fund?

Brief Exercises

BE4-1 Match each situation with the fraud triangle factor (opportunity, financial pressure, or rationalization) that best describes it.

Identify fraud-triangle concepts. (SO 1)

(a) An employee's monthly credit card payments are nearly 75% of their monthly earnings.
(b) An employee earns minimum wage at a firm that has reported record earnings for each of the last five years.
(c) An employee has an expensive gambling habit.
(d) An employee has check writing and signing responsibilities for a small company, and is also responsible for reconciling the bank account.

BE4-2 Deb Baden is the new owner of Birk Co. She has heard about internal control but is not clear about its importance for her business. Explain to Deb the four purposes of internal control, and give her one application of each purpose for Birk Co.

Explain the importance of internal control. (SO 1)

BE4-3 The internal control procedures in Payton Company make the following provisions. Identify the principles of internal control that are being followed in each case.

Identify internal control principles. (SO 2)

(a) Employees who have physical custody of assets do not have access to the accounting records.
(b) Each month the assets on hand are compared to the accounting records by an internal auditor.
(c) A prenumbered shipping document is prepared for each shipment of goods to customers.

BE4-4 Beaty Company has the following internal control procedures over cash receipts. Identify the internal control principle that is applicable to each procedure.

Identify the internal control principles applicable to cash receipts. (SO 3)

(a) All over-the-counter receipts are registered on cash registers.
(b) All cashiers are bonded.
(c) Daily cash counts are made by cashier department supervisors.
(d) The duties of receiving cash, recording cash, and having custody of cash are assigned to different individuals.
(e) Only cashiers may operate cash registers.

BE4-5 While examining cash receipts information, the accounting department determined the following information: opening cash balance $150, cash on hand $1,125.74, and cash sales per register tape $990.83. Prepare the required journal entry based upon the cash count sheet.

Make journal entry using cash count sheet. (SO 3)

BE4-6 Newell Company has the following internal control procedures over cash disbursements. Identify the internal control principle that is applicable to each procedure.

Identify the internal control principles applicable to cash disbursements. (SO 4)

(a) Company checks are prenumbered.
(b) The bank statement is reconciled monthly by an internal auditor.

(c) Blank checks are stored in a safe in the treasurer's office.
(d) Only the treasurer or assistant treasurer may sign checks.
(e) Check signers are not allowed to record cash disbursement transactions.

Identify the control features of a bank account. (SO 4)

BE4-7 Brent Bosch is uncertain about the control features of a bank account. Explain the control benefits of (a) a check and (b) a bank statement.

Indicate location of reconciling items in a bank reconciliation. (SO 5)

BE4-8 The following reconciling items are applicable to the bank reconciliation for Gammill Co. Indicate how each item should be shown on a bank reconciliation.
(a) Outstanding checks.
(b) Bank debit memorandum for service charge.
(c) Bank credit memorandum for collecting a note for the depositor.
(d) Deposit in transit.

Identify reconciling items that require adjusting entries. (SO 5)

BE4-9 Using the data in BE4-8, indicate (a) the items that will result in an adjustment to the depositor's records and (b) why the other items do not require adjustment.

Prepare partial bank reconciliation. (SO 5)

BE4-10 At July 31 Eidman Company has this bank information: cash balance per bank $7,300; outstanding checks $762; deposits in transit $1,350; and a bank service charge $40. Determine the adjusted cash balance per bank at July 31.

Analyze outstanding checks. (SO 5)

BE4-11 In the month of November, Hickox Company Inc. wrote checks in the amount of $9,750. In December, checks in the amount of $11,880 were written. In November, $8,800 of these checks were presented to the bank for payment, and $10,889 in December. What is the amount of outstanding checks at the end of November? At the end of December?

Explain the statement presentation of cash balances. (SO 6)

BE4-12 Luzinski Company has these cash balances: cash in bank $12,742; payroll bank account $6,000; and plant expansion fund cash $25,000. Explain how each balance should be reported on the balance sheet.

Prepare a cash budget. (SO 8)

BE4-13 The following information is available for Eusey Company for the month of January: expected cash receipts $62,000; expected cash disbursements $67,000; cash balance on January 1, $12,000. Management wishes to maintain a minimum cash balance of $8,000. Prepare a basic cash budget for the month of January.

Prepare entry to replenish a petty cash fund. (SO 9)

***BE4-14** On March 20 Pineda's petty cash fund of $100 is replenished when the fund contains $19 in cash and receipts for postage $40, supplies $26, and travel expense $15. Prepare the journal entry to record the replenishment of the petty cash fund.

Do it! Review

WILEY PLUS

Identify violations of control activities. (SO 2)

Do it! 4-1 Identify which control activity is violated in each of the following situations, and explain how the situation creates an opportunity for fraud or inappropriate accounting practices.

1. Once a month the sales department sends sales invoices to the accounting department to be recorded.
2. Jay Margan orders merchandise for Rice Lake Company; he also receives merchandise and authorizes payment for merchandise.
3. Several clerks at Dick's Groceries use the same cash register drawer.

Design system of internal control over cash receipts. (SO 3)

Do it! 4-2 Javier Vasquez is concerned with control over mail receipts at Javy's Sporting Goods. All mail receipts are opened by Nick Swisher. Nick sends the checks to the accounting department, where they are stamped "For Deposit Only." The accounting department records and deposits the mail receipts weekly. Javier asks your help in installing a good system of internal control over mail receipts.

Explain treatment of items in bank reconciliation. (SO 5)

Do it! 4-3 Linus Hugt owns Linus Blankets. Linus asks you to explain how he should treat the following reconciling items when reconciling the company's bank account.

1. Outstanding checks
2. A deposit in transit
3. The bank charged to our account a check written by another company
4. A debit memorandum for a bank service charge

Do it! 4-4 Rally Corporation's management wants to maintain a minimum monthly cash balance of $9,000. At the beginning of September the cash balance is $12,300; expected cash receipts for September are $97,200; cash disbursements are expected to be $115,000. How much cash, if any, must Rally borrow to maintain the desired minimum monthly balance? Determine your answer by using the basic form of the cash budget.

Prepare a cash budget.
(SO 8)

Exercises

WILEY PLUS

E4-1 Bank employees use a system known as the "maker-checker" system. An employee will record an entry in the appropriate journal, and then a supervisor will verify and approve the entry. These days, as all of a bank's accounts are computerized, the employee first enters a batch of entries into the computer, and then the entries are posted automatically to the general ledger account after the supervisor approves them on the system.

Access to the computer system is password-protected and task-specific, which means that the computer system will not allow the employee to approve a transaction or the supervisor to record a transaction.

Identify the principles of internal control.
(SO 2)

Instructions
Identify the principles of internal control inherent in the "maker-checker" procedure used by banks.

E4-2 Gambino's Pizza operates strictly on a carryout basis. Customers pick up their orders at a counter where a clerk exchanges the pizza for cash. While at the counter, the customer can see other employees making the pizzas and the large ovens in which the pizzas are baked.

Identify the principles of internal control.
(SO 2)

Instructions
Identify the six principles of internal control and give an example of each principle that you might observe when picking up your pizza. (*Note:* It may not be possible to observe all the principles.)

E4-3 The following control procedures are used in Falk Company for over-the-counter cash receipts.

List internal control weaknesses over cash receipts and suggest improvements.
(SO 2, 3)

1. Cashiers are experienced; thus, they are not bonded.
2. All over-the-counter receipts are registered by three clerks who share a cash register with a single cash drawer.
3. To minimize the risk of robbery, cash in excess of $100 is stored in an unlocked attaché case in the stock room until it is deposited in the bank.
4. At the end of each day the total receipts are counted by the cashier on duty and reconciled to the cash register total.
5. The company accountant makes the bank deposit and then records the day's receipts.

Instructions
(a) For each procedure, explain the weakness in internal control and identify the control principle that is violated.
(b) For each weakness, suggest a change in the procedure that will result in good internal control.

E4-4 The following control procedures are used in Karina's Boutique Shoppe for cash disbursements.

List internal control weaknesses for cash disbursements and suggest improvements.
(SO 2, 4)

1. Each week Karina leaves 100 company checks in an unmarked envelope on a shelf behind the cash register.
2. The store manager personally approves all payments before signing and issuing checks.
3. The company checks are unnumbered.
4. After payment, bills are "filed" in a paid invoice folder.
5. The company accountant prepares the bank reconciliation and reports any discrepancies to the owner.

Instructions
(a) For each procedure, explain the weakness in internal control and identify the internal control principle that is violated.
(b) For each weakness, suggest a change in the procedure that will result in good internal control.

Identify internal control weaknesses for cash disbursements and suggest improvements.
(SO 2, 4)

E4-5 At Ratliff Company checks are not prenumbered because both the purchasing agent and the treasurer are authorized to issue checks. Each signer has access to unissued checks kept in an unlocked file cabinet. The purchasing agent pays all bills pertaining to goods purchased for resale. Prior to payment, the purchasing agent determines that the goods have been received and verifies the mathematical accuracy of the vendor's invoice. After payment, the invoice is filed by vendor and the purchasing agent records the payment in the cash disbursements journal. The treasurer pays all other bills following approval by authorized employees. After payment, the treasurer stamps all bills "paid," files them by payment date, and records the checks in the cash disbursements journal. Ratliff Company maintains one checking account that is reconciled by the treasurer.

Instructions

(a) List the weaknesses in internal control over cash disbursements.
(b) Identify improvements for correcting these weaknesses.

Prepare bank reconciliation and adjusting entries.
(SO 5)

E4-6 Juan Ortiz is unable to reconcile the bank balance at January 31. Juan's reconciliation is shown here.

Cash balance per bank	$3,660.20
Add: NSF check	470.00
Less: Bank service charge	25.00
Adjusted balance per bank	$4,105.20
Cash balance per books	$3,975.20
Less: Deposits in transit	590.00
Add: Outstanding checks	770.00
Adjusted balance per books	$4,155.20

Instructions

(a) What is the proper adjusted cash balance per bank?
(b) What is the proper adjusted cash balance per books?
(c) Prepare the adjusting journal entries necessary to determine the adjusted cash balance per books.

Determine outstanding checks.
(SO 5)

E4-7 At April 30 the bank reconciliation of Guardado Company shows three outstanding checks: No. 254 $650, No. 255 $700, and No. 257 $410. The May bank statement and the May cash payments journal are given here.

Bank Statement Checks Paid

Date	Check No.	Amount
5-4	254	$650
5-2	257	410
5-17	258	159
5-12	259	275
5-20	261	500
5-29	263	480
5-30	262	750

Cash Payments Journal Checks Issued

Date	Check No.	Amount
5-2	258	$159
5-5	259	275
5-10	260	925
5-15	261	500
5-22	262	750
5-24	263	480
5-29	264	360

Instructions

Using step 2 in the reconciliation procedure (see page 182), list the outstanding checks at May 31.

Prepare bank reconciliation and adjusting entries.
(SO 5)

E4-8 The following information pertains to Gilmore Company.

1. Cash balance per bank, July 31, $7,328.
2. July bank service charge not recorded by the depositor $40.
3. Cash balance per books, July 31, $7,280.
4. Deposits in transit, July 31, $2,700.
5. Note for $2,000 collected for Gilmore in July by the bank, plus interest $36 less fee $20. The collection has not been recorded by Gilmore, and no interest has been accrued.
6. Outstanding checks, July 31, $772.

Instructions

(a) Prepare a bank reconciliation at July 31, 2010.
(b) Journalize the adjusting entries at July 31 on the books of Gilmore Company.

E4-9 This information relates to the Cash account in the ledger of Hadaway Company.

Prepare bank reconciliation and adjusting entries. (SO 5)

Balance September 1—$16,400; Cash deposited—$64,000
Balance September 30—$17,600; Checks written—$62,800

The September bank statement shows a balance of $16,422 at September 30 and the following memoranda.

Credits		Debits	
Collection of $1,800 note plus interest $30	$1,830	NSF check: J. Hower	$560
Interest earned on checking account	45	Safety deposit box rent	50

At September 30 deposits in transit were $4,826 and outstanding checks totaled $2,383.

Instructions
(a) Prepare the bank reconciliation at September 30, 2010.
(b) Prepare the adjusting entries at September 30, assuming (1) the NSF check was from a customer on account, and (2) no interest had been accrued on the note.

E4-10 The cash records of Haig Company show the following.

Compute deposits in transit and outstanding checks for two bank reconciliations. (SO 5)

For July:

1. The June 30 bank reconciliation indicated that deposits in transit total $750. During July the general ledger account Cash shows deposits of $16,900, but the bank statement indicates that only $15,600 in deposits were received during the month.
2. The June 30 bank reconciliation also reported outstanding checks of $940. During the month of July, Haig Company books show that $17,500 of checks were issued, yet the bank statement showed that $16,400 of checks cleared the bank in July.

For September:

3. In September deposits per bank statement totaled $25,900, deposits per books were $26,400, and deposits in transit at September 30 were $2,200.
4. In September cash disbursements per books were $23,700, checks clearing the bank were $24,000, and outstanding checks at September 30 were $2,100.

There were no bank debit or credit memoranda, and no errors were made by either the bank or Haig Company.

Instructions
Answer the following questions.
(a) In situation 1, what were the deposits in transit at July 31?
(b) In situation 2, what were the outstanding checks at July 31?
(c) In situation 3, what were the deposits in transit at August 31?
(d) In situation 4, what were the outstanding checks at August 31?

E4-11 Kane Inc.'s bank statement from Western Bank at August 31, 2010, gives the following information.

Prepare bank reconciliation and adjusting entries. (SO 5)

Balance, August 1	$16,400	Bank debit memorandum:	
August deposits	73,000	Safety deposit box fee	$ 25
Checks cleared in August	68,678	Service charge	50
Bank credit memorandum:		Balance, August 31	20,692
Interest earned	45		

A summary of the Cash account in the ledger for August shows the following: balance, August 1, $16,900; receipts $77,000; disbursements $73,570; and balance, August 31, $20,330. Analysis reveals that the only reconciling items on the July 31 bank reconciliation were a deposit in transit for $5,000 and outstanding checks of $4,500. In addition, you determine that there was an error involving a company check drawn in August: A check for $400 to a creditor on account that cleared the bank in August was journalized and posted for $40.

Instructions
(a) Determine deposits in transit.
(b) Determine outstanding checks. (*Hint*: You need to correct disbursements for the check error.)
(c) Prepare a bank reconciliation at August 31.
(d) Journalize the adjusting entry(ies) to be made by Kane Inc. at August 31.

E4-12 A new accountant at Nicholsen Inc. is trying to identify which of the amounts shown on page 204 should be reported as the current asset "Cash and cash equivalents" in the year-end balance sheet, as of April 30, 2010.

Identify reporting of cash. (SO 6)

1. $60 of currency and coin in a locked box used for incidental cash transactions.
2. A $10,000 U.S. Treasury bill, due May 31, 2010.
3. $300 of April-dated checks that Nicholson has received from customers but not yet deposited.
4. An $85 check received from a customer in payment of its April account, but post-dated to May 1.
5. $2,500 in the company's checking account.
6. $4,500 in its savings account.
7. $75 of prepaid postage in its postage meter.
8. A $25 IOU from the company receptionist.

Instructions

(a) What balance should Nicholsen report as its "Cash and cash equivalents" balance at April 30, 2010?

(b) In what account(s) and in what financial statement(s) should the items not included in "Cash and cash equivalents" be reported?

Review cash management practices.
(SO 7)

E4-13 Adams, Loomis, and Vogt, three law students who have joined together to open a law practice, are struggling to manage their cash flow. They haven't yet built up sufficient clientele and revenues to support their legal practice's ongoing costs. Initial costs, such as advertising, renovations to their premises, and the like, all result in outgoing cash flow at a time when little is coming in. Adams, Loomis, and Vogt haven't had time to establish a billing system since most of their clients' cases haven't yet reached the courts, and the lawyers didn't think it would be right to bill them until "results were achieved."

Unfortunately, Adams, Loomis, and Vogt's suppliers don't feel the same way. Their suppliers expect them to pay their accounts payable within a few days of receiving their bills. So far, there hasn't even been enough money to pay the three lawyers, and they are not sure how long they can keep practicing law without getting some money into their pockets.

Instructions

Can you provide any suggestions for Adams, Loomis, and Vogt to improve their cash management practices?

Prepare a cash budget for two months.
(SO 8)

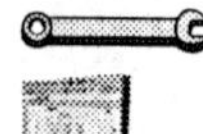

E4-14 Mayfield Company expects to have a cash balance of $46,000 on January 1, 2010. These are the relevant monthly budget data for the first two months of 2010.

1. Collections from customers: January $75,000, February $146,000
2. Payments to suppliers: January $40,000, February $75,000
3. Wages: January $30,000, February $40,000. Wages are paid in the month they are incurred.
4. Administrative expenses: January $21,000, February $31,000. These costs include depreciation of $1,000 per month. All other costs are paid as incurred.
5. Selling expenses: January $15,000, February $20,000. These costs are exclusive of depreciation. They are paid as incurred.
6. Sales of short-term investments in January are expected to realize $12,000 in cash. Mayfield has a line of credit at a local bank that enables it to borrow up to $25,000. The company wants to maintain a minimum monthly cash balance of $20,000.

Instructions

Prepare a cash budget for January and February.

Prepare journal entries for a petty cash fund.
(SO 9)

***E4-15** During October, Eastern Light Company experiences the following transactions in establishing a petty cash fund.

Oct. 1	A petty cash fund is established with a check for $100 issued to the petty cash custodian.			
31	A count of the petty cash fund disclosed the following items:			
	Currency			$7.00
	Coins			0.40
	Expenditure receipts (vouchers):			
	Office supplies		$26.10	
	Telephone, Internet, and fax		16.40	
	Postage		42.00	
	Freight-out		6.80	
31	A check was written to reimburse the fund and increase the fund to $200.			

Instructions

Journalize the entries in October that pertain to the petty cash fund.

*E4-16 Otto Company maintains a petty cash fund for small expenditures. These transactions occurred during the month of August.

Journalize and post petty cash fund transactions. (SO 9)

Aug. 1 Established the petty cash fund by writing a check on Central Bank for $200.

15 Replenished the petty cash fund by writing a check for $175. On this date, the fund consisted of $25 in cash and these petty cash receipts: freight-out $74.40, entertainment expense $41, postage expense $33.70 and miscellaneous expense $27.50.

16 Increased the amount of the petty cash fund to $400 by writing a check for $200.

31 Replenished the petty cash fund by writing a check for $283. On this date, the fund consisted of $117 in cash and these petty cash receipts: postage expense $145, entertainment expense $90.60, and freight-out $46.40.

Instructions

(a) Journalize the petty cash transactions.
(b) Post to the Petty Cash account.
(c) What internal control features exist in a petty cash fund?

Exercises: Set B

Visit the book's companion website, at **www.wiley.com/college/kimmel**, and choose the Student Companion site, to access Exercise Set B.

Problems: Set A

P4-1A Cherokee Theater is in the Federal Mall. A cashier's booth is located near the entrance to the theater. Two cashiers are employed. One works from 1:00 to 5:00 P.M., the other from 5:00 to 9:00 P.M. Each cashier is bonded. The cashiers receive cash from customers and operate a machine that ejects serially numbered tickets. The rolls of tickets are inserted and locked into the machine by the theater manager at the beginning of each cashier's shift.

Identify internal control weaknesses for cash receipts. (SO 2, 3)

After purchasing a ticket, the customer takes the ticket to a doorperson stationed at the entrance of the theater lobby some 60 feet from the cashier's booth. The doorperson tears the ticket in half, admits the customer, and returns the ticket stub to the customer. The other half of the ticket is dropped into a locked box by the doorperson.

At the end of each cashier's shift, the theater manager removes the ticket rolls from the machine and makes a cash count. The cash count sheet is initialed by the cashier. At the end of the day, the manager deposits the receipts in total in a bank night deposit vault located in the mall. In addition, the manager sends copies of the deposit slip and the initialed cash count sheets to the theater company treasurer for verification and to the company's accounting department. Receipts from the first shift are stored in a safe located in the manager's office.

Instructions

(a) Identify the internal control principles and their application to the cash receipts transactions of Cherokee Theater.
(b) If the doorperson and cashier decided to collaborate to misappropriate cash, what actions might they take?

Identify internal control weaknesses in cash receipts and cash disbursements. (SO 2, 3, 4)

P4-2A Scottsdale Middle School wants to raise money for a new sound system for its auditorium. The primary fund-raising event is a dance at which the famous disc jockey Jay Dee will play classic and not-so-classic dance tunes. Steve Cerra, the music and theater instructor, has been given the responsibility for coordinating the fund-raising efforts. This is Steve's first experience with fund-raising. He decides to put the eighth-grade choir in charge of the event; he will be a relatively passive observer.

Steve had 500 unnumbered tickets printed for the dance. He left the tickets in a box on his desk and told the choir students to take as many tickets as they thought they could sell for $5 each. In order to ensure that no extra tickets would be floating around, he told them to dispose of any unsold tickets. When the students received payment for the tickets, they were to bring the cash back to Steve, and he would put it in a locked box in his desk drawer.

Some of the students were responsible for decorating the gymnasium for the dance. Steve gave each of them a key to the money box and told them that if they took money out to purchase materials, they should put a note in the box saying how much they took and what it was used for. After two weeks the money box appeared to be getting full, so Steve asked Emily Polzin to count the money, prepare a deposit slip, and deposit the money in a bank account Steve had opened.

The day of the dance, Steve wrote a check from the account to pay Jay Dee. The DJ said, however, that he accepted only cash and did not give receipts. So Steve took $200 out of the cash box and gave it to Jay. At the dance Steve had Lisa Depriest working at the entrance to the gymnasium, collecting tickets from students and selling tickets to those who had not pre-purchased them. Steve estimated that 400 students attended the dance.

The following day Steve closed out the bank account, which had $250 in it, and gave that amount plus the $180 in the cash box to Principal Skinner. Principal Skinner seemed surprised that, after generating roughly $2,000 in sales, the dance netted only $430 in cash. Steve did not know how to respond.

Instructions

Identify as many internal control weaknesses as you can in this scenario, and suggest how each could be addressed.

Prepare a bank reconciliation and adjusting entries.
(SO 5)

P4-3A On July 31, 2010, Fenton Company had a cash balance per books of $6,140. The statement from Jackson State Bank on that date showed a balance of $7,695.80. A comparison of the bank statement with the cash account revealed the following facts.

1. The bank service charge for July was $25.
2. The bank collected a note receivable of $1,500 for Fenton Company on July 15, plus $30 of interest. The bank made a $10 charge for the collection. Fenton has not accrued any interest on the note.
3. The July 31 receipts of $1,193.30 were not included in the bank deposits for July. These receipts were deposited by the company in a night deposit vault on July 31.
4. Company check No. 2480 issued to H. Coby, a creditor, for $384 that cleared the bank in July was incorrectly entered in the cash payments journal on July 10 for $348.
5. Checks outstanding on July 31 totaled $1,980.10.
6. On July 31 the bank statement showed an NSF charge of $690 for a check received by the company from P. Figura, a customer, on account.

Instructions

(a) Cash bal. $6,909.00

(a) Prepare the bank reconciliation as of July 31.
(b) Prepare the necessary adjusting entries at July 31.

Prepare a bank reconciliation and adjusting entries from detailed data.
(SO 5)

P4-4A The bank portion of the bank reconciliation for Hunsaker Company at October 31, 2010, is shown here and on the next page.

HUNSAKER COMPANY
Bank Reconciliation
October 31, 2010

Cash balance per bank	$12,367.90
Add: Deposits in transit	1,530.20
	13,898.10

Less: Outstanding checks

Check Number	Check Amount	
2451	$ 1,260.40	
2470	720.10	
2471	844.50	
2472	426.80	
2474	1,050.00	4,301.80
Adjusted cash balance per bank		$ 9,596.30

The adjusted cash balance per bank agreed with the cash balance per books at October 31. The November bank statement showed the following checks and deposits.

Bank Statement

Checks			Deposits	
Date	**Number**	**Amount**	**Date**	**Amount**
11-1	2470	$ 720.10	11-1	$ 1,530.20
11-2	2471	844.50	11-4	1,211.60
11-5	2474	1,050.00	11-8	990.10
11-4	2475	1,640.70	11-13	2,575.00
11-8	2476	2,830.00	11-18	1,472.70
11-10	2477	600.00	11-21	2,945.00
11-15	2479	1,750.00	11-25	2,567.30
11-18	2480	1,330.00	11-28	1,650.00
11-27	2481	695.40	11-30	1,186.00
11-30	2483	575.50	Total	$16,127.90
11-29	2486	900.00		
	Total	$12,936.20		

The cash records per books for November showed the following.

Cash Payments Journal

Date	Number	Amount	Date	Number	Amount
11-1	2475	$1,640.70	11-20	2483	$ 575.50
11-2	2476	2,830.00	11-22	2484	829.50
11-2	2477	600.00	11-23	2485	974.80
11-4	2478	538.20	11-24	2486	900.00
11-8	2479	1,705.00	11-29	2487	398.00
11-10	2480	1,330.00	11-30	2488	800.00
11-15	2481	695.40	Total		$14,429.10
11-18	2482	612.00			

Cash Receipts Journal

Date	Amount
11-3	$ 1,211.60
11-7	990.10
11-12	2,575.00
11-17	1,472.70
11-20	2,954.00
11-24	2,567.30
11-27	1,650.00
11-29	1,186.00
11-30	1,218.00
Total	$15,824.70

The bank statement contained two bank memoranda:

1. A credit of $2,242 for the collection of a $2,100 note for Hunsaker Company plus interest of $157 and less a collection fee of $15. Hunsaker Company has not accrued any interest on the note.
2. A debit for the printing of additional company checks $85.

At November 30 the cash balance per books was $10,991.90 and the cash balance per bank statement was $17,716.60. The bank did not make any errors, but **Hunsaker Company made two errors.**

(a) Cash bal. $13,094.90

Instructions

(a) Using the four steps in the reconciliation procedure described on pages 181–182, prepare a bank reconciliation at November 30, 2010.

(b) Prepare the adjusting entries based on the reconciliation. (*Note:* The correction of any errors pertaining to recording checks should be made to Accounts Payable. The correction of any errors relating to recording cash receipts should be made to Accounts Receivable.)

Prepare a bank reconciliation and adjusting entries.
(SO 5)

P4-5A Shellankamp Company of Canton, Iowa, spreads herbicides and applies liquid fertilizer for local farmers. On May 31, 2010, the company's cash account per its general ledger showed a balance of $6,738.90.

The bank statement from Canton State Bank on that date showed the following balance.

CANTON STATE BANK

Checks and Debits	Deposits and Credits	Daily Balance
XXX	XXX	5-31 7,112.00

A comparison of the details on the bank statement with the details in the cash account revealed the following facts.

1. The statement included a debit memo of $40 for the printing of additional company checks.
2. Cash sales of $833.15 on May 12 were deposited in the bank. The cash receipts journal entry and the deposit slip were incorrectly made for $839.15. The bank credited Shellankamp Company for the correct amount.
3. Outstanding checks at May 31 totaled $276.25, and deposits in transit were $1,880.15.
4. On May 18, the company issued check No. 1181 for $685 to R. Delzer, on account. The check, which cleared the bank in May, was incorrectly journalized and posted by Shellankamp Company for $658.
5. A $2,700 note receivable was collected by the bank for Shellankamp Company on May 31 plus $110 interest. The bank charged a collection fee of $20. No interest has been accrued on the note.
6. Included with the cancelled checks was a check issued by Shellman Company to P. Jonet for $360 that was incorrectly charged to Shellankamp Company by the bank.
7. On May 31, the bank statement showed an NSF charge of $380 for a check issued by Natalie Fong, a customer, to Shellankamp Company on account.

(a) Cash bal. $9,076.90

Instructions

(a) Prepare the bank reconciliation at May 31, 2010.

(b) Prepare the necessary adjusting entries for Shellankamp Company at May 31, 2010.

Prepare a cash budget.
(SO 8)

P4-6A You are provided with the following information taken from Weinberger Inc.'s March 31, 2010, balance sheet.

Cash	$ 8,000
Accounts receivable	20,000
Inventory	36,000
Property, plant, and equipment, net of depreciation	120,000
Accounts payable	22,400
Common stock	150,000
Retained earnings	11,600

Additional information concerning Weinberger Inc. is as follows.

1. Gross profit is 25% of sales.
2. Actual and budgeted sales data:

March (actual)	$50,000
April (budgeted)	70,000

3. Sales are both cash and credit. Cash collections expected in April are:

March	$20,000	(40% of $50,000)
April	42,000	(60% of $70,000)
	$62,000	

4. Half of a month's purchases are paid for in the month of purchase and half in the following month. Cash disbursements expected in April are:

Purchases March	$22,400
Purchases April	28,100
	$50,500

5. Cash operating costs are anticipated to be $11,700 for the month of April.
6. Equipment costing $2,500 will be purchased for cash in April.
7. The company wishes to maintain a minimum cash balance of $8,000. An open line of credit is available at the bank. All borrowing is done at the beginning of the month, and all repayments are made at the end of the month. The interest rate is 12% per year, and interest expense is accrued at the end of the month and paid in the following month.

Instructions
Prepare a cash budget for the month of April. Determine how much cash Weinberger Inc. must borrow, or can repay, in April.

Apr. borrowings $2,700

P4-7A Fogelberg Corporation prepares monthly cash budgets. Here are relevant data from operating budgets for 2010.

Prepare a cash budget.
(SO 8)

	January	February
Sales	$360,000	$400,000
Purchases	120,000	130,000
Salaries	84,000	95,000
Administrative expenses	72,000	75,000
Selling expenses	79,000	88,000

All sales and purchases are on account. Budgeted collections and disbursement data are given below. All other expenses are paid in the month incurred except for administrative expenses, which include $1,000 of depreciation per month.

Other data.

1. Collections from customers: January $332,000; February $378,000.
2. Payments for purchases: January $110,000; February $125,000.
3. Other receipts: January: collection of December 31, 2009, notes receivable $15,000; February: proceeds from sale of securities $6,000
4. Other disbursements: February $12,000 cash dividend

The company's cash balance on January 1, 2010, is expected to be $52,000. The company wants to maintain a minimum cash balance of $50,000.

Instructions
Prepare a cash budget for January and February.

Jan. 31 cash bal. $55,000

P4-8A Frederickson Company is a very profitable small business. It has not, however, given much consideration to internal control. For example, in an attempt to keep clerical and office expenses to a minimum, the company has combined the jobs of cashier and bookkeeper. As a result, Kenny Dillon handles all cash receipts, keeps the accounting records, and prepares the monthly bank reconciliations.

Prepare a comprehensive bank reconciliation with theft and internal control deficiencies.
(SO 2, 3, 4, 5)

The balance per the bank statement on October 31, 2010, was $18,380. Outstanding checks were: No. 62 for $126.75, No. 183 for $180, No. 284 for $253.25, No. 862 for $190.71, No. 863 for $226.80, and No. 864 for $165.28. Included with the statement was a credit memorandum of $200 indicating the collection of a note receivable for Frederickson Company by the bank on October 25. This memorandum has not been recorded by Frederickson.

The company's ledger showed one cash account with a balance of $21,892.72. The balance included undeposited cash on hand. Because of the lack of internal controls, Kenny took for personal use all of the undeposited receipts in excess of $3,795.51. He then prepared the following bank reconciliation in an effort to conceal his theft of cash.

Cash balance per books, October 31		$21,892.72
Add: Outstanding checks		
No. 862	$190.71	
No. 863	226.80	
No. 864	165.28	482.79
		22,375.51
Less: Undeposited receipts		3,795.51
Unadjusted balance per bank, October 31		18,580.00
Less: Bank credit memorandum		200.00
Cash balance per bank statement, October 31		$18,380.00

Instructions

(a) Cash bal. $21,032.72

(a) Prepare a correct bank reconciliation. (*Hint:* Deduct the amount of the theft from the adjusted balance per books.)

(b) Indicate the three ways that Kenny attempted to conceal the theft and the dollar amount involved in each method.

(c) What principles of internal control were violated in this case?

Problems: Set B

Identify internal control principles for cash disbursements.

(SO 2, 4)

P4-1B Celtic Company recently changed its system of internal control over cash disbursements. The system includes the following features.

1. Instead of being unnumbered and manually prepared, all checks must now be prenumbered and written by using the new checkwriter purchased by the company.
2. Before a check can be issued, each invoice must have the approval of Jane Bell, the purchasing agent, and Dick McRae, the receiving department supervisor.
3. Checks must be signed by either Frank Person, the treasurer, or Sara Goss, the assistant treasurer. Before signing a check, the signer is expected to compare the amounts of the check with the amounts on the invoice.
4. After signing a check, the signer stamps the invoice "paid" and inserts within the stamp, the date, check number, and amount of the check. The "paid" invoice is then sent to the accounting department for recording.
5. Blank checks are stored in a safe in the treasurer's office. The combination to the safe is known by only the treasurer and assistant treasurer.
6. Each month the bank statement is reconciled with the bank balance per books by the assistant chief accountant.
7. All employees who handle or account for cash are bonded.

Instructions

Identify the internal control principles and their application to cash disbursements of Celtic Company.

Identify internal control weaknesses in cash receipts.

(SO 2, 3)

P4-2B The board of trustees of a local church is concerned about the internal accounting controls pertaining to the offering collections made at weekly services. They ask you to serve on a three-person audit team with the internal auditor of the university and a CPA who has just joined the church. At a meeting of the audit team and the board of trustees you learn the following.

1. The church's board of trustees has delegated responsibility for the financial management and audit of the financial records to the finance committee. This group pre-

pares the annual budget and approves major disbursements but is not involved in collections or recordkeeping. No audit has been made in recent years because the same trusted employee has kept church records and served as financial secretary for 15 years. The church does not carry any fidelity insurance.

2. The collection at the weekly service is taken by a team of ushers who volunteer to serve for 1 month. The ushers take the collection plates to a basement office at the rear of the church. They hand their plates to the head usher and return to the church service. After all plates have been turned in, the head usher counts the cash received. The head usher then places the cash in the church safe along with a notation of the amount counted. The head usher volunteers to serve for 3 months.
3. The next morning the financial secretary opens the safe and recounts the collection. The secretary withholds \$150–\$200 in cash, depending on the cash expenditures expected for the week, and deposits the remainder of the collections in the bank. To facilitate the deposit, church members who contribute by check are asked to make their checks payable to "Cash."
4. Each month the financial secretary reconciles the bank statement and submits a copy of the reconciliation to the board of trustees. The reconciliations have rarely contained any bank errors and have never shown any errors per books.

Instructions

(a) Indicate the weaknesses in internal accounting control in the handling of collections.
(b) List the improvements in internal control procedures that you plan to make at the next meeting of the audit team for (1) the ushers, (2) the head usher, (3) the financial secretary, and (4) the finance committee.
(c) What church policies should be changed to improve internal control?

Prepare a bank reconciliation and adjusting entries.

(SO 5)

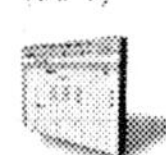

P4-3B On May 31, 2010, Lombard Company had a cash balance per books of \$5,681.50. The bank statement from Community Bank on that date showed a balance of \$7,964.60. A comparison of the statement with the cash account revealed the following facts.

1. The statement included a debit memo of \$70 for the printing of additional company checks.
2. Cash sales of \$786.15 on May 12 were deposited in the bank. The cash receipts journal entry and the deposit slip were incorrectly made for \$796.15. The bank credited Lombard Company for the correct amount.
3. Outstanding checks at May 31 totaled \$1,106.25, and deposits in transit were \$836.15.
4. On May 18 the company issued check No. 1181 for \$685 to N. Habben, on account. The check, which cleared the bank in May, was incorrectly journalized and posted by Lombard Company for \$658.
5. A \$2,500 note receivable was collected by the bank for Lombard Company on May 31 plus \$80 interest. The bank charged a collection fee of \$30. No interest has been accrued on the note.
6. Included with the cancelled checks was a check issued by Lonshek Company to C. Young for \$290 that was incorrectly charged to Lombard Company by the bank.
7. On May 31 the bank statement showed an NSF charge of \$140 for a check issued by K. Uzong, a customer, to Lombard Company on account.

Instructions

(a) Prepare the bank reconciliation as of May 31, 2010.
(b) Prepare the necessary adjusting entries at May 31, 2010.

(a) Cash bal. \$7,984.50

Prepare a bank reconciliation and adjusting entries from detailed data.

(SO 5)

P4-4B The bank portion of the bank reconciliation for Christiansen Company at November 30, 2010, is shown here and on the next page.

CHRISTIANSEN COMPANY
Bank Reconciliation
November 30, 2010

Cash balance per bank	\$14,367.90
Add: Deposits in transit	2,530.20
	16,898.10

Less: Outstanding checks

Check Number	Check Amount	
3451	$ 2,260.40	
3470	1,100.10	
3471	844.50	
3472	1,426.80	
3474	1,050.00	6,681.80
Adjusted cash balance per bank		$10,216.30

The adjusted cash balance per bank agreed with the cash balance per books at November 30. The December bank statement showed the following checks and deposits.

Bank Statement

Checks			Deposits	
Date	**Number**	**Amount**	**Date**	**Amount**
12-1	3451	$ 2,260.40	12-1	$ 2,530.20
12-2	3470	1,100.10	12-4	1,211.60
12-7	3472	1,426.80	12-8	2,365.10
12-4	3475	1,640.70	12-16	2,672.70
12-8	3476	1,300.00	12-21	2,945.00
12-10	3477	2,130.00	12-26	2,567.30
12-15	3479	3,080.00	12-29	2,836.00
12-27	3480	600.00	12-30	1,025.00
12-30	3482	475.50	Total	$18,152.90
12-29	3484	764.00		
12-31	3485	540.80		
	Total	$15,318.30		

The cash records per books for December showed the following.

Cash Payments Journal

Date	Number	Amount	Date	Number	Amount
12-1	3475	$1,640.70	12-20	3482	$ 475.50
12-2	3476	1,300.00	12-22	3483	1,140.00
12-2	3477	2,130.00	12-23	3484	764.00
12-4	3478	538.20	12-24	3485	450.80
12-8	3479	3,080.00	12-30	3486	1,389.50
12-10	3480	600.00	Total		$14,316.10
12-17	3481	807.40			

Cash Receipts Journal

Date	Amount
12-3	$ 1,211.60
12-7	2,365.10
12-15	2,672.70
12-20	2,954.00
12-25	2,567.30
12-28	2,836.00
12-30	1,025.00
12-31	1,190.40
Total	$16,822.10

The bank statement contained two memoranda.

1. A credit of $2,645 for the collection of a $2,500 note for Christiansen Company plus interest of $160 and less a collection fee of $15. Christiansen Company has not accrued any interest on the note.
2. A debit of $819.10 for an NSF check written by J. Waller, a customer. At December 31 the check had not been redeposited in the bank.

At December 31 the cash balance per books was $12,722.30, and the cash balance per bank statement was $19,028.40. The bank did not make any errors, **but Christiansen Company made two errors.**

Instructions

(a) Using the four steps in the reconciliation procedure described on pages 181–182, prepare a bank reconciliation at December 31, 2010.

(a) Cash bal. $14,449.20

(b) Prepare the adjusting entries based on the reconciliation. [*Note:* The correction of any errors pertaining to recording checks should be made to Accounts Payable. The correction of any errors relating to recording cash receipts should be made to Accounts Receivable.]

Prepare a bank reconciliation and adjusting entries.
(SO 5)

P4-5B Greenwood Company of Omaha, Nebraska, provides liquid fertilizer and herbicides to regional farmers. On July 31, 2010, the company's cash account per its general ledger showed a balance of $5,909.70.

The bank statement from Tri-County Bank on that date showed the following balance.

TRI-COUNTY BANK

Checks and Debits	Deposits and Credits	Daily Balance
XXX	XXX	7-31 7,075.80

A comparison of the details on the bank statement with the details in the cash account revealed the following facts.

1. The bank service charge for July was $32.
2. The bank collected a note receivable of $900 for Greenwood Company on July 15, plus $48 of interest. The bank made a $10 charge for the collection. Greenwood has not accrued any interest on the note.
3. The July 31 receipts of $1,339 were not included in the bank deposits for July. These receipts were deposited by the company in a night deposit vault on July 31.
4. Company check No. 2480 issued to N. Teig, a creditor, for $492 that cleared the bank in July was incorrectly entered in the cash payments journal on July 10 for $429.
5. Checks outstanding on July 31 totaled $2,480.10.
6. On July 31, the bank statement showed an NSF charge of $818 for a check received by the company from N. O. Doe, a customer, on account.

Instructions

(a) Prepare the bank reconciliation as of July 31, 2010.

(a) Cash bal. $5,834.70

(b) Prepare the necessary adjusting entries at July 31, 2010.

Prepare a cash budget.
(SO 8)

P4-6B Polk Co. expects to have a cash balance of $26,000 on January 1, 2010. Relevant monthly budget data for the first two months of 2010 are as follows.

Collections from customers: January $70,000; February $160,000
Payments to suppliers: January $45,000; February $75,000
Salaries: January $35,000; February $40,000. Salaries are paid in the month they are incurred.
Selling and administrative expenses: January $27,000; February $35,000. These costs are exclusive of depreciation and are paid as incurred.
Sales of short-term investments in January are expected to realize $7,000 in cash.

Polk has a line of credit at a local bank that enables it to borrow up to $45,000. The company wants to maintain a minimum monthly cash balance of $25,000. Any excess cash above the $25,000 minimum is used to pay off the line of credit.

Instructions

(a) Prepare a cash budget for January and February.

(a) Jan. cash bal. $25,000

(b) Explain how a cash budget contributes to effective management.

Prepare a cash budget.
(SO 8)

P4-7B Ybarra Inc. prepares monthly cash budgets. Shown on page 214 are relevant data from operating budgets for 2010.

	January	February
Sales	$330,000	$400,000
Purchases	110,000	130,000
Salaries	80,000	95,000
Selling and administrative expenses	135,000	150,000

All sales and purchases are on account. Collections and disbursement data are given below. All other items above are paid in the month incurred. Depreciation has been excluded from selling and administrative expenses.

Other data.

1. Collections from customers: January $297,000; February $358,000.
2. Payments for purchases: January $98,000; February $118,000.
3. Other receipts: January: collection of December 31, 2009, interest receivable $2,000; February: proceeds from sale of short-term investments $8,000
4. Other disbursements: February payment of $20,000 for land

The company's cash balance on January 1, 2010, is expected to be $60,000. The company wants to maintain a minimum cash balance of $40,000.

Instructions

Jan. 31 cash bal. $46,000

Prepare a cash budget for January and February.

Prepare a comprehensive bank reconciliation with theft and internal control deficiencies.
(SO 2, 3, 4, 5)

P4-8B McNally Company is a very profitable small business. It has not, however, given much consideration to internal control. For example, in an attempt to keep clerical and office expenses to a minimum, the company has combined the jobs of cashier and bookkeeper. As a result, M. Mordica handles all cash receipts, keeps the accounting records, and prepares the monthly bank reconciliations.

The balance per the bank statement on October 31, 2010, was $13,600. Outstanding checks were: No. 62 for $126.75, No. 183 for $180, No. 284 for $253.25, No. 862 for $190.71, No. 863 for $226.80, and No. 864 for $165.28. Included with the statement was a credit memorandum of $490 indicating the collection of a note receivable for McNally Company by the bank on October 25. This memorandum has not been recorded by McNally Company.

The company's ledger showed one cash account with a balance of $15,847.21. The balance included undeposited cash on hand. Because of the lack of internal controls, Mordica took for personal use all of the undeposited receipts in excess of $2,240. He then prepared the following bank reconciliation in an effort to conceal his theft of cash.

Cash balance per books, October 31		$15,847.21
Add: Outstanding checks		
No. 862	$190.71	
No. 863	226.80	
No. 864	165.28	482.79
		16,330.00
Less: Undeposited receipts		2,240.00
Unadjusted balance per bank, October 31		14,090.00
Less: Bank credit memorandum		490.00
Cash balance per bank statement, October 31		$13,600.00

Instructions

(a) Cash bal. $14,697.21

(a) Prepare a correct bank reconciliation. (*Hint:* Deduct the amount of the theft from the adjusted balance per books.)
(b) Indicate the three ways that Mordica attempted to conceal the theft and the dollar amount pertaining to each method.
(c) What principles of internal control were violated in this case?

Problems: Set C

Visit the book's companion website at **www.wiley.com/college/kimmel** and choose the Student Companion site to access Problem Set C.

Comprehensive Problem

CP4 On December 1, 2010, Moreland Company had the following account balances.

	Debits		Credits
Cash	$18,200	Accumulated Depreciation	$ 3,000
Notes Receivable	2,500	Accounts Payable	6,100
Accounts Receivable	7,500	Common Stock	20,000
Merchandise Inventory	16,000	Retained Earnings	44,700
Prepaid Insurance	1,600		$73,800
Equipment	28,000		
	$73,800		

During December the company completed the following transactions.

Dec. 7 Received $3,200 cash from customers in payment of account (no discount allowed).

12 Purchased merchandise on account from King Co. $12,000, terms 2/10, n/30.

17 Sold merchandise on account $15,000, terms 1/10, n/30. The cost of the merchandise sold was $10,000.

19 Paid salaries $2,500.

22 Paid King Co. in full, less discount.

26 Received collections in full, less discounts, from customers billed on December 17.

Adjustment data:

1. Depreciation $200 per month.
2. Insurance expired $400.
3. Income tax expense was $425. It was unpaid at December 31.

Instructions

(a) Journalize the December transactions. (Assume a perpetual inventory system.)

(b) Enter the December 1 balances in the ledger T accounts and post the December transactions. Use Cost of Goods Sold, Depreciation Expense, Insurance Expense, Salaries Expense, Sales, Sales Discounts, Income Tax Payable, and Income Tax Expense.

(c) The statement from Lyon County Bank on December 31 showed a balance of $22,164. A comparison of the bank statement with the cash account revealed the following facts.

1. The bank collected a note receivable of $2,500 for Moreland Company on December 15.
2. The December 31 receipts of $2,736 were not included in the bank deposits for December. The company deposited these receipts in a night deposit vault on December 31.
3. Checks outstanding on December 31 totaled $1,210.
4. On December 31 the bank statement showed a NSF charge of $800 for a check received by the company from C. Park, a customer, on account.

Prepare a bank reconciliation as of December 31 based on the available information. (*Hint:* The cash balance per books is $21,990. This can be proven by finding the balance in the Cash account from parts (a) and (b).)

(d) Journalize the adjusting entries resulting from the bank reconciliation and adjustment data.

(e) Post the adjusting entries to the ledger T accounts.

(f) Prepare an adjusted trial balance.

(g) Prepare an income statement for December and a classified balance sheet at December 31.

(f) Totals	$89,425
(g) Net income	$ 1,325
Total assets	$72,550

Continuing Cookie Chronicle

(*Note:* This is a continuation of the Cookie Chronicle from Chapters 1 through 3.)

CCC4 Part 1 Natalie is struggling to keep up with the recording of her accounting transactions. She is spending a lot of time marketing and selling mixers and giving her cookie classes. Her friend John is an accounting student who runs his own accounting service. He has asked Natalie if she would like to have him do her accounting. John and Natalie meet and discuss her business.

Part 2 Natalie decides that she cannot afford to hire John to do her accounting. One way that she can ensure that her cash account does not have any errors and is accurate and up-to-date is to prepare a bank reconciliation at the end of each month. Natalie would like you to help her.

Go to the book's companion website, **www.wiley.com/college/kimmel**, to see the completion of this problem.

broadening your perspective

Financial Reporting and Analysis

FINANCIAL REPORTING PROBLEM: *Tootsie Roll Industries Inc.*

BYP4-1 The financial statements of Tootsie Roll are presented in Appendix A of this book, together with an auditor's report—Report of Independent Auditors.

Instructions

Using the financial statements and reports, answer these questions about Tootsie Roll's internal controls and cash.

(a) What comments, if any, are made about cash in the report of the independent auditors?

(b) What data about cash and cash equivalents are shown in the consolidated balance sheet (statement of financial condition)?

(c) What activities are identified in the consolidated statement of cash flows as being responsible for the changes in cash during 2007?

(d) How are cash equivalents defined in the Notes to Consolidated Financial Statements?

(e) Read the section of the report titled "Management's Report on Internal Control Over Financial Reporting." Summarize the statements made in that section of the report.

COMPARATIVE ANALYSIS PROBLEM: *Tootsie Roll vs. Hershey Foods*

BYP4-2 The financial statements of Hershey Foods are presented in Appendix B, following the financial statements for Tootsie Roll in Appendix A.

Instructions

Answer the following questions for each company.

(a) What is the balance in cash and cash equivalents at December 31, 2007?

(b) What percentage of total assets does cash represent for each company over the last two years? Has it changed significantly for either company?

(c) How much cash was provided by operating activities during 2007?

(d) Comment on your findings in parts (a) through (c).

RESEARCH CASE

BYP4-3 The May 13, 2008, issue of the *Wall Street Journal* contains an article by Jeffrey McCracken entitled "Economy Puts Tight Squeeze on RV Makers."

Instructions

Read the article and answer the following questions.

(a) What are the factors that have caused RV sales to decline?

(b) What did Coachmen Industries do to address its cash shortfall? What other steps does the article suggest that the company might take to address its cash shortfall?

(c) What did Fleetwood Enterprises Inc. do to address its cash shortfall? What event does the company have in the near-term that will require significant cash? What other steps is the company considering to address its cash shortfall?

INTERPRETING FINANCIAL STATEMENTS

BYP4-4 The international accounting firm Ernst and Young recently performed a global survey. The results of that survey are summarized in a report titled "Fraud Risk in Emerging Markets." You can find this report at: **http://www.ey.com/Global/assets.nsf/International/FIDS_-_9th_Global_Fraud_Survey_2006/$file/EY_Fraud_Survey_June2006.pdf,** or do an Internet search for "9th Global Fraud Survey—Fraud Risk in Emerging Markets."

Instructions

Read the Executive Summary section, and then skim the remainder of the report to answer the following questions.

(a) What did survey respondents consider to be the top three factors to prevent fraud?
(b) What type of fraud poses the greatest threat in developed markets? What type of fraud poses the greatest threat in emerging markets?
(c) In what three regions are anti-fraud measures most likely to be considered when deciding whether to begin doing business in that region?

FINANCIAL ANALYSIS ON THE WEB

BYP4-5 The Financial Accounting Standards Board (FASB) is a private organization established to improve accounting standards and financial reporting. The FASB conducts extensive research before issuing a "Statement of Financial Accounting Standards," which represents an authoritative expression of generally accepted accounting principles.

Address: **www.fasb.org**, or go to
www.wiley.com/college/kimmel

Steps:

Choose **Facts about FASB**.

Instructions

Answer the following questions.

(a) What is the mission of the FASB?
(b) How are topics added to the FASB technical agenda?
(c) What characteristics make the FASB's procedures an "open" decision-making process?

BYP4-6 The Public Company Accounting Oversight Board (PCAOB) was created as a result of the Sarbanes-Oxley Act. It has oversight and enforcement responsibilities over accounting firms in the U.S.

Address: **http://www.pcaobus.org/**,
or go to **www.wiley.com/college/kimmel**

Instructions

Answer the following questions.

(a) What is the mission of the PCAOB?
(b) Briefly summarize its responsibilities related to inspections.
(c) Briefly summarize its responsibilities related to enforcement.

Critical Thinking

DECISION MAKING ACROSS THE ORGANIZATION

BYP4-7 Alternative Distributor Corp., a distributor of groceries and related products, is headquartered in Medford, Massachusetts.

During a recent audit, Alternative Distributor Corp. was advised that existing internal controls necessary for the company to develop reliable financial statements were inadequate. The audit report stated that the current system of accounting for sales, receivables, and cash receipts constituted a material weakness. Among other items, the report focused on nontimely deposit of cash receipts, exposing Alternative Distributor to potential loss or misappropriation, excessive past due accounts receivable due to lack of collection efforts, disregard of advantages offered by vendors for prompt payment of invoices, absence of appropriate segregation of duties by personnel consistent with appropriate control objectives, inadequate procedures for applying accounting principles, lack of qualified management personnel, lack of supervision by an outside board of directors, and overall poor recordkeeping.

Instructions

(a) Identify the principles of internal control violated by Alternative Distributor Corporation.

(b) Explain why managers of various functional areas in the company should be concerned about internal controls.

COMMUNICATION ACTIVITY

BYP4-8 As a new auditor for the CPA firm of Ticke and Tie, you have been assigned to review the internal controls over mail cash receipts of Proehl Company. Your review reveals that checks are promptly endorsed "For Deposit Only," but no list of the checks is prepared by the person opening the mail. The mail is opened either by the cashier or by the employee who maintains the accounts receivable records. Mail receipts are deposited in the bank weekly by the cashier.

Instructions

Write a letter to S.A. Dykstra, owner of the Proehl Company, explaining the weaknesses in internal control and your recommendations for improving the system.

ETHICS CASES

BYP4-9 As noted in the chapter, banks charge fees of up to $30 for "bounced" checks—that is, checks that exceed the balance in the account. It has been estimated that processing bounced checks costs a bank roughly $1.50 per check. Thus, the profit margin on bounced checks is very high. Recognizing this, some banks have started to process checks from largest to smallest. By doing this, they maximize the number of checks that bounce if a customer overdraws an account. For example, NationsBank (now Bank of America) projected a $14 million increase in fee revenue as a result of processing largest checks first. In response to criticism, banks have responded that their customers prefer to have large checks processed first, because those tend to be the most important. At the other extreme, some banks will cover their customers' bounced checks, effectively extending them an interest-free loan while their account is overdrawn.

Instructions

Answer each of the following questions.

(a) William Preston had a balance of $1,500 in his checking account at First National Bank on a day when the bank received the following five checks for processing against his account.

Check Number	Amount	Check Number	Amount
3150	$ 35	3165	$ 550
3162	400	3166	1,510
		3169	180

Assuming a $30 fee assessed by the bank for each bounced check, how much fee revenue would the bank generate if it processed checks (1) from largest to smallest, (2) from smallest to largest, and (3) in order of check number?

(b) Do you think that processing checks from largest to smallest is an ethical business practice?

(c) In addition to ethical issues, what other issues must a bank consider in deciding whether to process checks from largest to smallest?

(d) If you were managing a bank, what policy would you adopt on bounced checks?

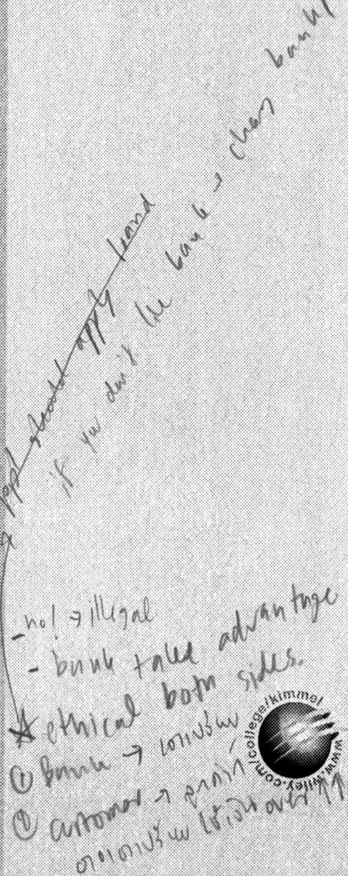

BYP4-10 Fraud Bureau is a free service, established to alert consumers and investors about prior complaints relating to online vendors, including sellers at online auctions,

and to provide consumers, investors, and users with information and news. One of the services it provides is a collection of online educational articles related to fraud.

Address: **www.fraudbureau.com/articles/**, or go to **www.wiley.com/college/kimmel**

Instructions

Go to this site and choose an article of interest to you. Write a short summary of your findings.

"ALL ABOUT YOU" ACTIVITY

BYP4-11 The print and electronic media are full of stories about potential security risks that can arise from your personal computer. It is important to keep in mind, however, that there are also many ways that your identity can be stolen other than from your computer. The federal government provides many resources to help protect you from identity thieves.

Instructions

Go to **http://onguardonline.gov/idtheft.html**, and click on ID Theft Faceoff. Complete the quiz provided there.

Answers to Insight and Accounting Across the Organization Questions

p. 171

Q: Why would unsupervised employees or employees who report to each other represent potential internal control threats?

A. An unsupervised employee may have a fraudulent job (or may even be a fictitious person)—e.g., a person drawing a paycheck without working. Or, if two employees supervise each other, there is no real separation of duties, and they can conspire to defraud the company.

p. 172

Q. Why are small companies more susceptible to employee theft?

A. The high degree of trust often found in small companies makes them more vulnerable. Also, small companies tend to have less sophisticated systems of internal control, and they usually lack internal auditors. In addition, it is very hard to achieve some internal control features, such as segregation of duties, when you have very few employees.

p. 178

Q. How can companies reduce the likelihood of fraudulent disbursements?

A. To reduce the occurrence of fraudulent disbursements a company should follow the procedures discussed in this chapter. These include having only designated personnel sign checks; having different personnel approve payments and make payments; ensuring that check signers do not record disbursements; using prenumbered checks and matching each check to an approved invoice; storing blank checks securely; reconciling the bank statement; and stamping invoices PAID.

p. 184

Q. Why would a company's stock price fall if it reports deficiencies in its internal controls?

A. Internal controls protect against employee theft, but they also provide protection against manipulation of accounting numbers. If a company has poor internal controls, investors will have less confidence that its financial statements are accurate. As a consequence, its stock price will suffer.

Answers to Self-Study Questions

1. c 2. a 3. c 4. b 5. a 6. b 7. d 8. a 9. d 10. c 11. c 12. c 13. b 14. d *15. a

Remember to go back to the navigator box on the chapter-opening page and check off your completed work.

Chapter 5

Managerial Accounting

STUDY OBJECTIVES

After studying this chapter, you should be able to:

1. Explain the distinguishing features of managerial accounting.
2. Identify the three broad functions of management.
3. Define the three classes of manufacturing costs.
4. Distinguish between product and period costs.
5. Explain the difference between a merchandising and a manufacturing income statement.
6. Indicate how cost of goods manufactured is determined.
7. Explain the difference between a merchandising and a manufacturing balance sheet.
8. Identify trends in managerial accounting.

The Navigator

Study Objectives give you a framework for learning the specific concepts covered in the chapter.

The Navigator

Scan **Study Objectives**	☐
Read **Feature Story**	☐
Read **Preview**	☐
Read text and answer **Before You Go On** p. 227 ☐ p. 230 ☐ p. 236 ☐ p. 240	☐
Work **Using the Decision Toolkit**	☐
Review **Summary of Study Objectives**	☐
Work **Demonstration Problem**	☐
Answer **Self-Study Questions**	☐
Complete **Assignments**	☐

The Navigator is a learning system designed to prompt you to use the learning aids in the chapter and to help you set priorities as you study.

Feature Story

The Feature Story helps you picture how the chapter topic relates to the real world of business and accounting. You will find references to the story throughout the chapter.

WHAT A DIFFERENCE A DAY MAKES

In January 1998 Compaq Computer (*www.compaq.com*) had just become the largest seller of personal computers, and it was *Forbes* magazine's "company of the year." Its chief executive, Eckhard Pfeiffer, was riding high. But during the next two years Compaq lost $2 billion. The company was in chaos, and Mr. Pfeiffer was out of a job. What happened?

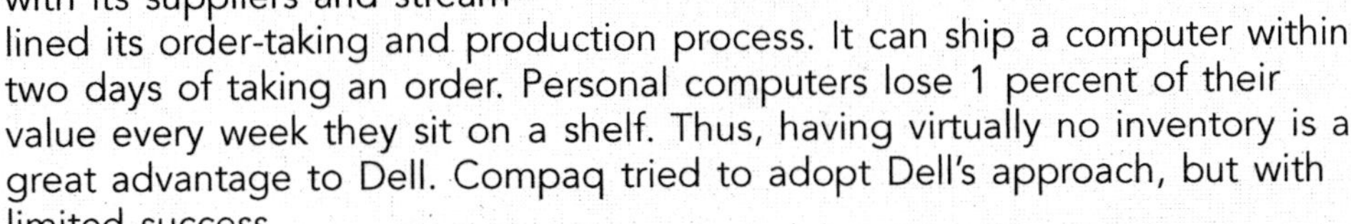

First, Dell happened. Dell Computer (*www.dell.com*) pioneered a new way of making and selling personal computers. Its customers "custom design" their computers over the Internet or phone. Dell reengineered its "supply chain": It coordinated its efforts with its suppliers and streamlined its order-taking and production process. It can ship a computer within two days of taking an order. Personal computers lose 1 percent of their value every week they sit on a shelf. Thus, having virtually no inventory is a great advantage to Dell. Compaq tried to adopt Dell's approach, but with limited success.

The second shock to Compaq came when it acquired a company even larger than itself—Digital Equipment. Mr. Pfeiffer believed that the purchase of Digital, with its huge and respected technical sales force, opened new opportunities for Compaq as a global service company. But combining the two companies proved to be hugely expensive and extremely complicated. Ultimately Compaq decided to merge with Hewlett-Packard (HP) (*www.hp.com*) in order to survive.

After this merger, HP lost significant market share to Dell because its higher cost structure made it hard to compete with Dell on price. Dell created a buzz in the financial press when it decided to enter the computer printing business—a segment that HP had long dominated. Many predicated that Dell would soon take over printers as well. But just when it appeared that Dell could not be beat, HP regained its footing and Dell stumbled. HP reduced its costs by adopting many of Dell's "lean" practices. Thus Dell lost much of its competitive advantage. In addition, computer purchasing habits changed, and Dell wasn't able to adjust fast enough.

The Navigator

Inside Chapter 5

"Inside Chapter" lists boxes in the chapter that should be of special interest to you.

- **Even the Best Have to Get Better** (p. 224)
- **How Many Labor Hours to Build a Car?** (p. 229)
- **Bananas Receive Special Treatment** (p. 239)
- ***All About You:* Outsourcing and Jobs** (p. 241)

Preview of Chapter 5

This chapter focuses on issues illustrated in the Feature Story about Compaq Computer, Hewlett-Packard, and Dell. These include determining and controlling the costs of material, labor, and overhead and the relationship between costs and profits. In a financial accounting course, you learned about the form and content of **financial statements for external users** of financial information, such as stockholders and creditors. These financial statements represent the principal product of financial accounting. Managerial accounting focuses primarily on the preparation of **reports for internal users** of financial information, such as the managers and officers of a company. In today's rapidly changing global environment, managers often make decisions that determine their company's fate—and their own. Managers are evaluated on the results of their decisions. Managerial accounting provides tools for assisting management in making decisions and for evaluating the effectiveness of those decisions.

The content and organization of this chapter are as follows.

The Preview describes the purpose of the chapter and outlines the major topics and subtopics you will find in it.

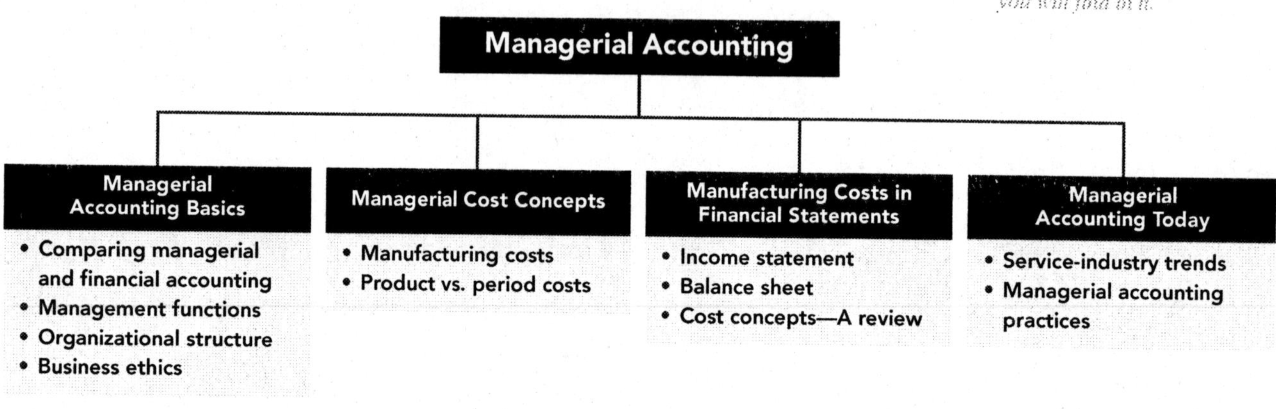

The Navigator

MANAGERIAL ACCOUNTING BASICS

Essential terms and concepts are printed in blue where they first appear and are defined in the end-of-chapter Glossary.

Managerial accounting, also called **management accounting**, is a field of accounting that provides economic and financial information for managers and other internal users. The activities that are part of managerial accounting are as follows.

1. Explaining manufacturing and nonmanufacturing costs and how they are reported in the financial statements.
2. Computing the cost of providing a service or manufacturing a product.
3. Determining the behavior of costs and expenses as activity levels change and analyzing cost–volume–profit relationships within a company.
4. Accumulating and presenting data for management decision making.
5. Determining prices for external and internal transactions.
6. Assisting management in profit planning and formalizing these plans in the form of budgets.
7. Providing a basis for controlling costs and expenses by comparing actual results with planned objectives and standard costs.
8. Accumulating and presenting data for capital expenditure decisions.

Managerial accounting applies to all types of businesses—service, merchandising, and manufacturing. It also applies to all forms of business organizations—

proprietorships, partnerships, and corporations. Not-for-profit entities as well as profit-oriented enterprises need managerial accounting.

In the past, managerial accountants were primarily engaged in cost accounting—collecting and reporting costs to management. Recently that role has changed significantly. First, as the business environment has become more automated, methods to determine the amount and type of cost in a product have changed. Second, managerial accountants are now held responsible for strategic cost management; that is, they assist in evaluating how well the company is employing its resources. As a result, managerial accountants now serve as team members alongside personnel from production, marketing, and engineering when the company makes critical strategic decisions.

Opportunities for managerial accountants to advance within the company are considerable. Financial executives must have a background that includes an understanding of managerial accounting concepts. Whatever your position in the company—marketing, sales, or production, knowledge of managerial accounting greatly improves your opportunities for advancement. As the CEO of Microsoft noted: "If you're supposed to be making money in business and supposed to be satisfying customers and building market share, there are numbers that characterize those things. And if somebody can't sort of speak to me quantitatively about it, then I'm nervous."

Comparing Managerial and Financial Accounting

STUDY OBJECTIVE 1

Explain the distinguishing features of managerial accounting.

There are both similarities and differences between managerial and financial accounting. First, each field of accounting deals with the economic events of a business. Thus, their interests overlap. For example, *determining* the unit cost of manufacturing a product is part of managerial accounting. *Reporting* the total cost of goods manufactured and sold is part of financial accounting. In addition, both managerial and financial accounting require that a company's economic events be quantified and communicated to interested parties.

Illustration 5-1 summarizes the principal differences between financial accounting and managerial accounting. The need for various types of economic data is responsible for many of the differences.

Illustration 5-1
Differences between financial and managerial accounting

Financial Accounting		Managerial Accounting
• External users: stockholders, creditors, and regulators.	**Primary Users of Reports**	• Internal users: officers and managers.
• Financial statements. • Quarterly and annually.	**Types and Frequency of Reports**	• Internal reports. • As frequently as needed.
• General-purpose.	**Purpose of Reports**	• Special-purpose for specific decisions.
• Pertains to business as a whole. • Highly aggregated (condensed). • Limited to double-entry accounting and cost data. • Generally accepted accounting principles.	**Content of Reports**	• Pertains to subunits of the business. • Very detailed. • Extends beyond double-entry accounting to any relevant data. • Standard is relevance to decisions.
• Audit by CPA.	**Verification Process**	• No independent audits.

Management Functions

STUDY OBJECTIVE 2

Identify the three broad functions of management.

Managers' activities and responsibilities can be classified into three broad functions:

1. Planning.
2. Directing.
3. Controlling.

In performing these functions, managers make decisions that have a significant impact on the organization.

Planning requires managers to look ahead and to establish objectives. These objectives are often diverse: maximizing short-term profits and market share, maintaining a commitment to environmental protection, and contributing to social programs. For example, Hewlett-Packard, in an attempt to gain a stronger foothold in the computer industry, has greatly reduced its prices to compete with Dell. A key objective of management is to **add value** to the business under its control. Value is usually measured by the trading price of the company's stock and by the potential selling price of the company.

Directing involves coordinating a company's diverse activities and human resources to produce a smooth-running operation. This function relates to implementing planned objectives and providing necessary incentives to motivate employees. For example, manufacturers such as Campbell Soup Company, General Motors, and Dell must coordinate purchasing, manufacturing, warehousing, and selling. Service corporations such as American Airlines, Federal Express, and AT&T must coordinate scheduling, sales, service, and acquisitions of equipment

MANAGEMENT INSIGHT

Insight boxes illustrate interesting situations in real companies and show how managers make decisions using accounting information. Guideline answers to the critical thinking questions appear on the last page of the chapter.

Even the Best Have to Get Better

Louis Vuitton is a French manufacturer of high-end handbags, wallets, and suitcases. Its reputation for quality and style allows it to charge extremely high prices—for example, $700 for a tote bag. But often in the past, when demand was hot, supply was nonexistent—shelves were empty, and would-be buyers left empty-handed.

Luxury-goods manufacturers used to consider stock-outs to be a good thing, but recently Louis Vuitton changed its attitude. The company adopted "lean" processes used by car manufacturers and electronics companies to speed up production of "hot" products. Work is done by flexible teams, with jobs organized based on how long a task takes. By reducing wasted time and eliminating bottlenecks, what used to take 20 to 30 workers eight days to do now takes 6 to 12 workers one day. Also, production employees who used to specialize on a single task on a single product are now multiskilled. This allows them to quickly switch products to meet demand.

To make sure that the factory is making the right products, within a week of a product launch, Louis Vuitton stores around the world feed sales information to the headquarters in France, and production is adjusted accordingly. Finally, the new production processes have also improved quality. Returns of some products are down by two-thirds, which makes quite a difference to the bottom line when the products are pricey.

Source: Christina Passariello, "Louis Vuitton Tries Modern Methods on Factory Lines," *Wall Street Journal*, October 9, 2006.

What are some of the steps that this company has taken in order to ensure that production meets demand?

and supplies. Directing also involves selecting executives, appointing managers and supervisors, and hiring and training employees.

The third management function, **controlling**, is the process of keeping the company's activities on track. In controlling operations, managers determine whether planned goals are being met. When there are deviations from targeted objectives, managers must decide what changes are needed to get back on track. Recent scandals at companies like Enron, Lucent, and Xerox attest to the fact that companies must have adequate controls to ensure that the company develops and distributes accurate information.

How do managers achieve control? A smart manager in a small operation can make personal observations, ask good questions, and know how to evaluate the answers. But using this approach in a large organization would result in chaos. Unless there is some record of what has happened and what is expected to occur, imagine the president of Dell attempting to determine whether the company is meeting its planned objectives. Thus, large businesses typically use a formal system of evaluation. These systems include such features as budgets, responsibility centers, and performance evaluation reports—all of which are features of managerial accounting.

Decision making is not a separate management function. Rather, it is the outcome of the exercise of good judgment in planning, directing, and controlling.

Organizational Structure

In order to assist in carrying out management functions, most companies prepare **organization charts** to show the interrelationships of activities and the delegation of authority and responsibility within the company. Illustration 5-2 shows a typical organization chart, which outlines the delegation of responsibility.

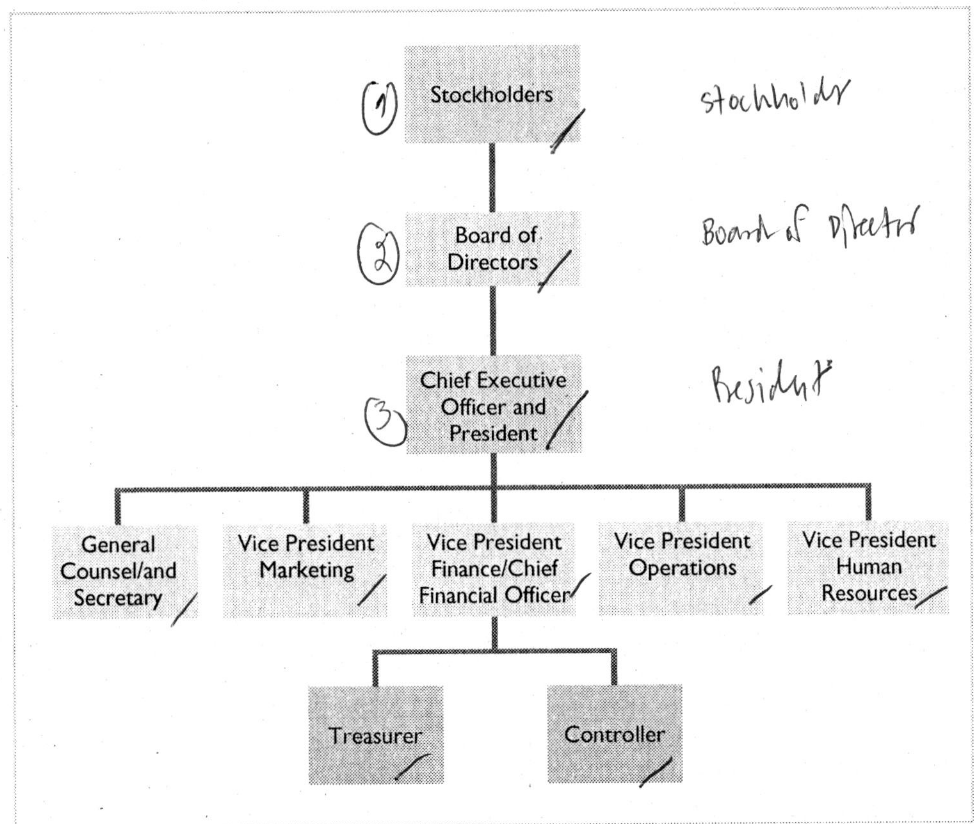

Illustration 5-2 Corporation's organization chart

Stockholders own the corporation, but they manage it indirectly through a **board of directors** they elect. Even not-for-profit organizations have boards of directors. The board formulates the operating policies for the company or organization. The board also selects officers, such as a president and one or more vice presidents, to execute policy and to perform daily management functions.

The **chief executive officer (CEO)** has overall responsibility for managing the business. Obviously, even in a small business, in order to accomplish organizational objectives, the company relies on delegation of responsibilities. As the organization chart on page 225 shows, the CEO delegates responsibilities to other officers. Each member of the organization has a clearly defined role to play.

Responsibilities within the company are frequently classified as either line or staff positions. Employees with **line positions** are directly involved in the company's primary revenue-generating operating activities. Examples of line positions include the vice president of operations, vice president of marketing, plant managers, supervisors, and production personnel. Employees with **staff positions** are involved in activities that support the efforts of the line employees. In a firm like General Electric or ExxonMobil, employees in finance, legal, and human resources have staff positions. While activities of staff employees are vital to the company, these employees are nonetheless there to serve the line employees who engage in the company's primary operations.

The **chief financial officer (CFO)** is responsible for all of the accounting and finance issues the company faces. The CFO is supported by the **controller** and the **treasurer**. The controller's responsibilities include (1) maintaining the accounting records, (2) maintaining an adequate system of internal control, and (3) preparing financial statements, tax returns, and internal reports. The treasurer has custody of the corporation's funds and is responsible for maintaining the company's cash position.

Also serving the CFO is the internal audit staff. The staff's responsibilities include reviewing the reliability and integrity of financial information provided by the controller and treasurer. Staff members also ensure that internal control systems are functioning properly to safeguard corporate assets. In addition, they investigate compliance with policies and regulations, and in many companies they determine whether resources are being used in the most economical and efficient fashion.

The vice president of operations oversees employees with line positions. For example, the company might have multiple plant managers, each of whom would report to the vice president of operations. Each plant would also have department managers, such as fabricating, painting, and shipping, each of whom would report to the plant manager.

Business Ethics

All employees within an organization are expected to act ethically in their business activities. Given the importance of ethical behavior to corporations and their owners (stockholders), an increasing number of organizations provide codes of business ethics for their employees.

Despite these efforts, recent business scandals resulted in massive investment losses and numerous employee layoffs. A recent survey of fraud by international accounting firm KPMG reported a 13% increase in instances of corporate fraud compared to five years earlier. It noted that while employee fraud (such things as expense-account abuse, payroll fraud, and theft of assets) represented 60% of all instances of fraud, financial reporting fraud (the intentional misstatement of financial reports) was the most costly to companies. That should not be surprising given the long list of companies such as Enron, Global Crossing, WorldCom, and others that engaged in massive financial frauds which led to huge financial losses and thousands of lost jobs.

CREATING PROPER INCENTIVES

Companies like Motorola, IBM, and Nike use complex systems to control and evaluate the actions of managers. They dedicate substantial resources to monitor and effectively evaluate the actions of employees. Unfortunately, these systems and controls sometimes unwittingly create incentives for managers to take unethical actions. For example, companies prepare budgets to provide direction. Because the budget is also used as an evaluation tool, some managers try to "game" the budgeting process by underestimating their division's predicted performance so that it will be easier to meet their performance targets. On the other hand, if the budget is set at unattainable levels, managers sometimes take unethical actions to meet the targets in order to receive higher compensation or, in some cases, to keep their jobs.

For example, in recent years, airline manufacturer Boeing was plagued by a series of scandals including charges of over-billing, corporate espionage, and illegal conflicts of interest. Some long-time employees of Boeing blame the decline in ethics on a change in the corporate culture that took place after Boeing merged with McDonnell Douglas. They suggest that evaluation systems implemented after the merger to monitor results and evaluate employee performance made employees believe they needed to succeed no matter what actions were required to do so.

As another example, manufacturing companies need to establish production goals for their processes. Again, if controls are not effective and realistic, problems develop. To illustrate, Schering-Plough, a pharmaceutical manufacturer, found that employees were so concerned with meeting production standards that they failed to monitor the quality of the product, and as a result the dosages were often wrong.

CODE OF ETHICAL STANDARDS

In response to corporate scandals in 2000 and 2001, the U.S. Congress enacted legislation to help prevent lapses in internal control. This legislation, referred to as the Sarbanes-Oxley Act of 2002 (SOX) has important implications for the financial community. One result of SOX was to clarify top management's responsibility for the company's financial statements. CEOs and CFOs must now certify that financial statements give a fair presentation of the company's operating results and its financial condition. In addition, top managers must certify that the company maintains an adequate system of internal controls to safeguard the company's assets and ensure accurate financial reports.

Another result of Sarbanes-Oxley is that companies now pay more attention to the composition of the board of directors. In particular, the audit committee of the board of directors must be comprised entirely of independent members (that is, non-employees) and must contain at least one financial expert.

Finally, to increase the likelihood of compliance with the rules that are part of the new legislation, the law substantially increases the penalties for misconduct.

To provide guidance for managerial accountants, the Institute of Management Accountants (IMA) has developed a code of ethical standards, entitled *IMA Statement of Ethical Professional Practice.* Management accountants should not commit acts in violation of these standards. Nor should they condone such acts by others within their organizations. We include the IMA code of ethical standards in Appendix B at the end of the book. Throughout the book, we will address various ethical issues managers face.

Before You Go On...

Before You Go On... Review It questions at the end of major text sections offer an opportunity to stop and reexamine the key points you have studied.

REVIEW IT

1. Compare financial accounting and managerial accounting and identify the principal differences.
2. Identify and discuss the three broad functions of management.

3. What are staff positions? What are line positions? Give examples.
4. What were some of the regulatory changes enacted under the Sarbanes-Oxley Act?

The Navigator

MANAGERIAL COST CONCEPTS

In order for managers at companies like Dell or Hewlett-Packard to plan, direct, and control operations effectively, they need good information. One very important type of information is related to costs. Managers should ask questions such as the following.

1. What costs are involved in making a product or providing a service?
2. If we decrease production volume, will costs decrease?
3. What impact will automation have on total costs?
4. How can we best control costs?

To answer these questions, managers need reliable and relevant cost information. We now explain and illustrate the various cost categories that companies use.

Manufacturing Costs

STUDY OBJECTIVE 3
Define the three classes of manufacturing costs.

Manufacturing consists of activities and processes that convert raw materials into finished goods. Contrast this type of operation with merchandising, which sells merchandise in the form in which it is purchased. Manufacturing costs are typically classified as shown in Illustration 5-3.

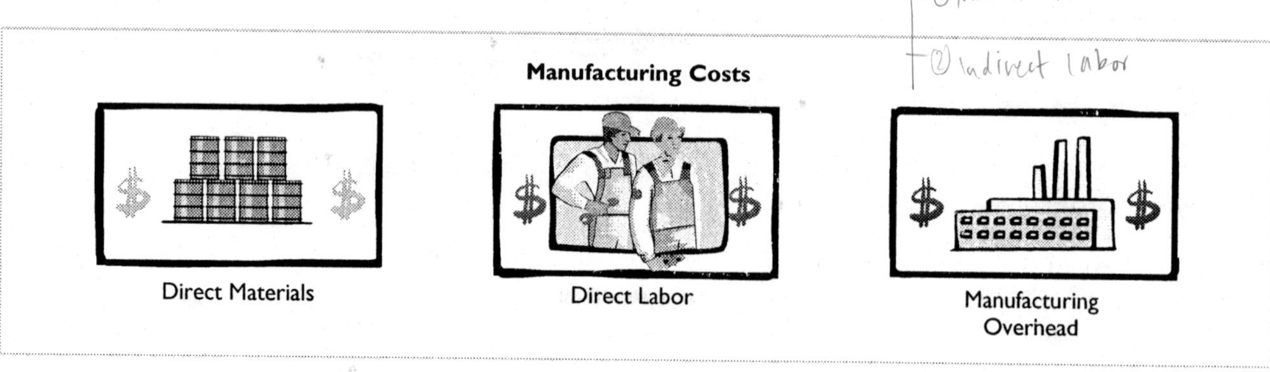

Illustration 5-3
Classifications of manufacturing costs

DIRECT MATERIALS

To obtain the materials that will be converted into the finished product, the manufacturer purchases raw materials. **Raw materials** are the basic materials and parts used in the manufacturing process. For example, auto manufacturers such as General Motors, Ford, and Toyota use steel, plastic, and tires as raw materials in making cars.

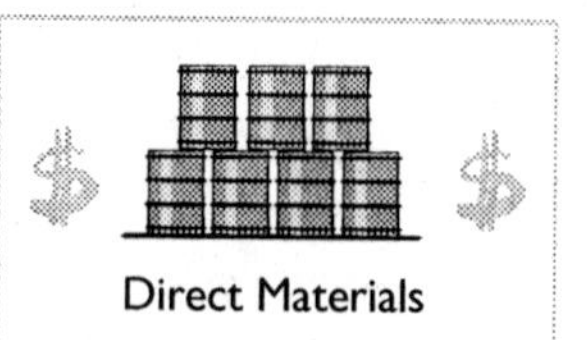

Raw materials that can be physically and directly associated with the finished product during the manufacturing process are **direct materials**. Examples include flour in the baking of bread, syrup in the bottling of soft drinks, and steel in the making of automobiles. Direct materials for Hewlett-Packard and Dell Computer (in the Feature Story) include plastic, glass, hard drives, and processing chips.

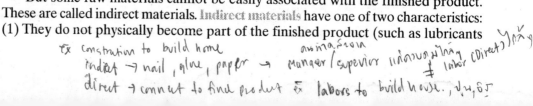

But some raw materials cannot be easily associated with the finished product. These are called indirect materials. **Indirect materials** have one of two characteristics: (1) They do not physically become part of the finished product (such as lubricants

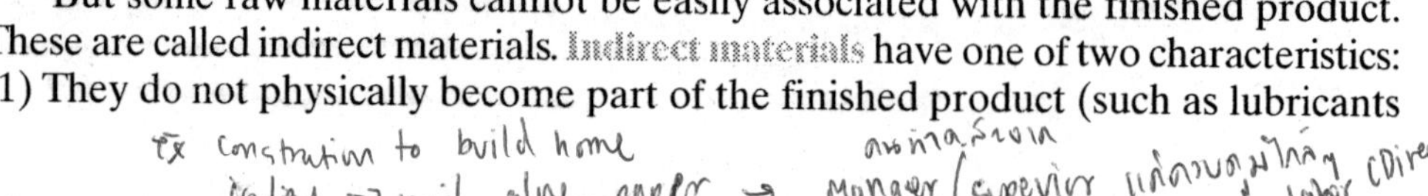

and polishing compounds). Or, (2) they cannot be traced because their physical association with the finished product is too small in terms of cost (such as cotter pins and lock washers). Companies account for indirect materials as part of **manufacturing overhead**.

DIRECT LABOR

The work of factory employees that can be physically and directly associated with converting raw materials into finished goods is **direct labor**. Bottlers at Coca-Cola, bakers at Sara Lee, and typesetters at Aptara Corp. are employees whose activities are usually classified as direct labor. **Indirect labor** refers to the work of employees that has no physical association with the finished product, or for which it is impractical to trace costs to the goods produced. Examples include wages of maintenance people, time-keepers, and supervisors. Like indirect materials, companies classify indirect labor as **manufacturing overhead**.

MANAGEMENT INSIGHT

How Many Labor Hours to Build a Car?

Nissan and Toyota were number 1 and 2 in a recent annual study of labor productivity in the auto industry. But U.S. auto manufacturers showed improvements. Labor represents about 15% of the total cost to make a vehicle. Since Nissan required only 28.46 labor hours per vehicle, it saves about $300 to $450 in labor costs to build a car relative to Ford, the least-efficient manufacturer. General Motors (GM) has shown steady improvement over the years. In 1998 it needed almost 17 more hours of labor than Toyota to build a car; it now needs only 4 more hours than Toyota. Chrysler says that much of its improvement in labor productivity has come from designing cars that are easier to build.

Source: Rick Popely, "Japanese Automakers Lead Big Three in Productivity Review," *Knight Ridder Tribune News Service*, June 1, 2006, p. 1.

Why might Nissan production require significantly fewer labor hours?

MANUFACTURING OVERHEAD

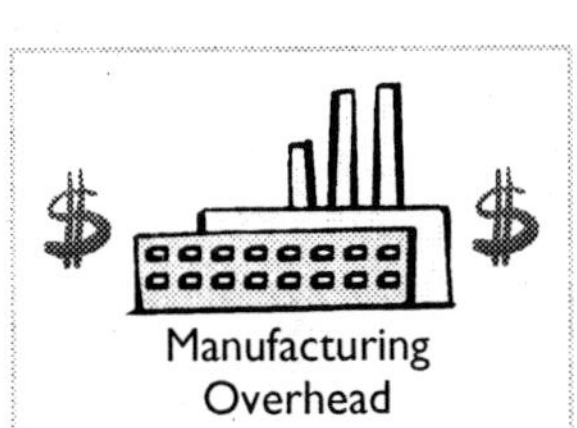

Manufacturing overhead consists of costs that are indirectly associated with the manufacture of the finished product. These costs may also be manufacturing costs that cannot be classified as direct materials or direct labor. Manufacturing overhead includes indirect materials, indirect labor, depreciation on factory buildings and machines, and insurance, taxes, and maintenance on factory facilities.

One study found the following magnitudes of the three different product costs as a percentage of the total product cost: direct materials 54%, direct labor 13%, and manufacturing overhead 33%. Note that the direct labor component is the smallest. This component of product cost is dropping substantially because of automation. In some companies, direct labor has become as little as 5% of the total cost.

Alternative Terminology notes present synonymous terms used in practice.

Allocating materials and labor costs to specific products is fairly straightforward. Good record keeping can tell a company how much plastic it used in making each type of gear, or how many hours of factory labor it took to assemble a part. But allocating overhead costs to specific products presents problems. How much of the purchasing agent's salary is attributable to the hundreds of different products made in the same plant? What about the grease that keeps the machines humming, or the computers that make sure paychecks come out on time? Boiled down to its simplest form, the question becomes: Which products cause the incurrence of which costs? In subsequent chapters we show various methods of allocating overhead to products.

ALTERNATIVE TERMINOLOGY

Some companies use terms such as *factory overhead, indirect manufacturing costs,* and *burden* instead of manufacturing overhead.

Product versus Period Costs

STUDY OBJECTIVE 4

Distinguish between product and period costs.

Each of the manufacturing cost components—direct materials, direct labor, and manufacturing overhead—are product costs. As the term suggests, **product costs** are costs that are a necessary and integral part of producing the finished product. Companies record product costs, when incurred, as inventory. Under the matching principle, these costs do not become expenses until the company sells the finished goods inventory. At that point, the company records the expense as cost of goods sold.

ALTERNATIVE TERMINOLOGY

Product costs are also called *inventoriable* costs.

Period costs are costs that are matched with the revenue of a specific time period rather than included as part of the cost of a salable product. These are nonmanufacturing costs. Period costs include selling and administrative expenses. In order to determine net income, companies deduct these costs from revenues in the period in which they are incurred.

Illustration 5-4 summarizes these relationships and cost terms. Our main concern in this chapter is with product costs.

Illustration 5-4
Product versus period costs

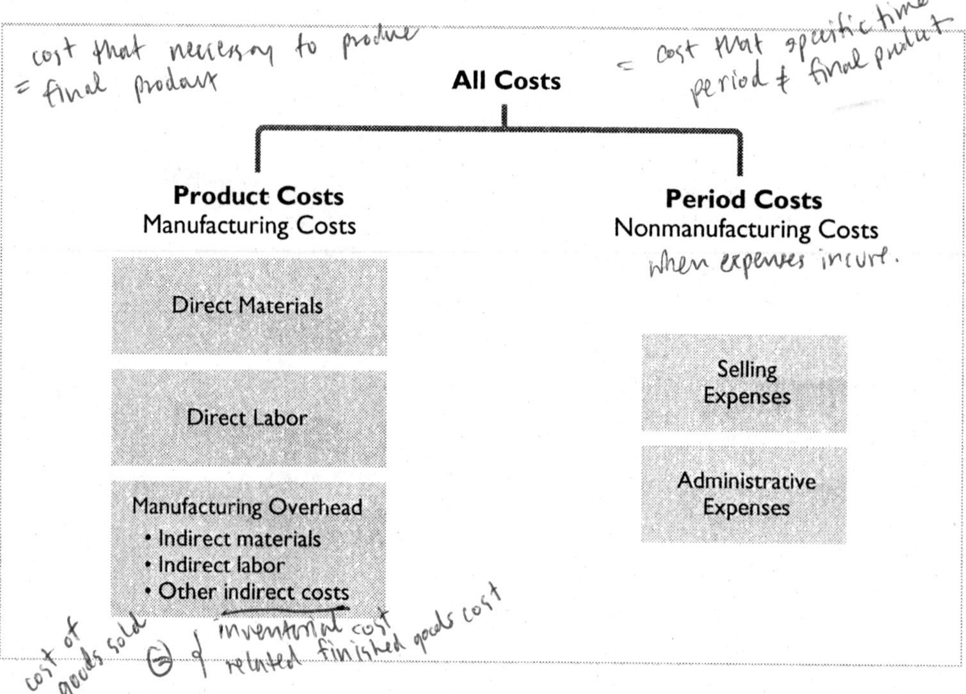

Before You Go On...

REVIEW IT

1. What are the major cost classifications involved in manufacturing a product?
2. What are product and period costs, and what is their relationship to the manufacturing process?

DO IT

Before You Go On... Do It exercises ask you to put to work newly acquired knowledge. The Action Plan outlines the reasoning necessary to complete the exercise. The accompanying Solution (next page) shows how the exercise should be solved.

A bicycle company has these costs: tires, salaries of employees who put tires on the wheels, factory building depreciation, wheel nuts, spokes, salary of factory manager, handlebars, and salaries of factory maintenance employees. Classify each cost as direct materials, direct labor, or overhead.

Action Plan

- Classify as direct materials any raw materials that can be physically and directly associated with the finished product.

- Classify as direct labor the work of factory employees that can be physically and directly associated with the finished product.
- Classify as manufacturing overhead any costs that are indirectly associated with the finished product.

Solution Tires, spokes, and handlebars are direct materials. Salaries of employees who put tires on the wheels are direct labor. All of the other costs are manufacturing overhead.

Related exercise material: BE5-4, BE5-5, BE5-6, BE5-7, E5-2, E5-3, E5-4, E5-5, E5-6, and E5-7.

The Navigator

MANUFACTURING COSTS IN FINANCIAL STATEMENTS

STUDY OBJECTIVE 5

Explain the difference between a merchandising and a manufacturing income statement.

The financial statements of a manufacturer are very similar to those of a merchandiser. For example, you will find many of the same sections and same accounts in the financial statements of Procter & Gamble that you find in the financial statements of Dick's Sporting Goods. The principal differences between their financial statements occur in two places: the cost of goods sold section in the income statement and the current assets section in the balance sheet.

Income Statement

Under a periodic inventory system, the income statements of a merchandiser and a manufacturer differ in the cost of goods sold section. Merchandisers compute cost of goods sold by adding the beginning merchandise inventory to the **cost of goods purchased** and subtracting the ending merchandise inventory. Manufacturers compute cost of goods sold by adding the beginning finished goods inventory to the **cost of goods manufactured** and subtracting the ending finished goods inventory. Illustration 5-5 shows these different methods.

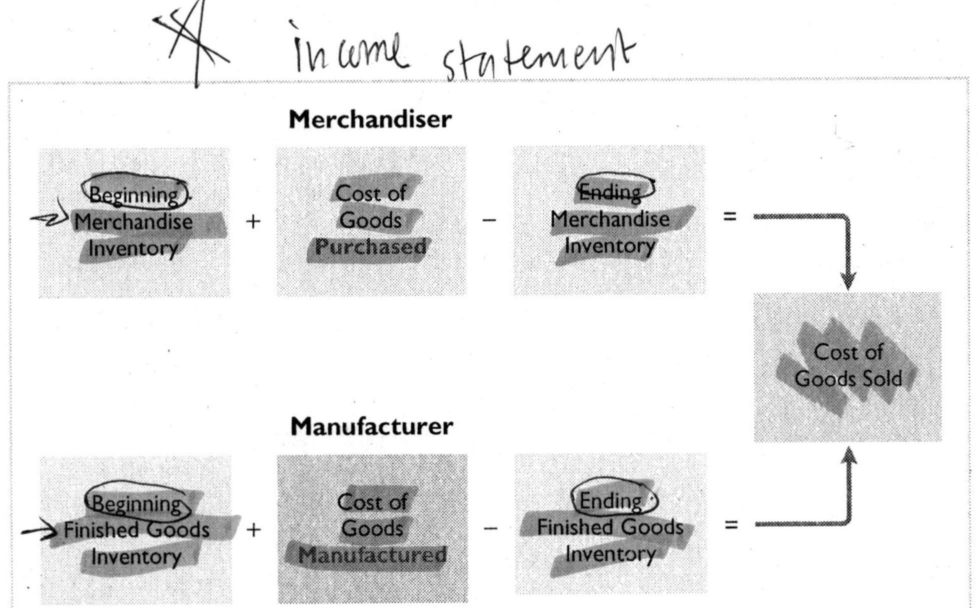

Illustration 5-5
Cost of goods sold components

Helpful Hints clarify concepts being discussed.

HELPFUL HINT

We assume a periodic inventory system in this illustration.

A number of accounts are involved in determining the cost of goods manufa tured. To eliminate excessive detail, income statements typically show only th total cost of goods manufactured. A separate statement, called a Cost of Good Manufactured Schedule, presents the details. (For more information, see the dis cussion on page 233 and Illustration 5-8.)

Illustration 5-6
Cost of goods sold sections of merchandising and manufacturing income statements

Illustration 5-6 shows the different presentations of the cost of goods sold sec tions for merchandising and manufacturing companies. The other sections of an income statement are similar for merchandisers and manufacturers.

MERCHANDISING COMPANY Income Statement (partial) For the Year Ended December 31, 2008		MANUFACTURING COMPANY Income Statement (partial) For the Year Ended December 31, 2008	
Cost of goods sold		Cost of goods sold	
Merchandise inventory, January 1	$ 70,000	**Finished goods inventory, January 1**	$ 90,000
Cost of goods purchased	650,000	**Cost of goods manufactured (see Illustration 5-8)**	370,000
Cost of goods available for sale	720,000	Cost of goods available for sale	460,000
Merchandise inventory, December 31	400,000	**Finished goods inventory, December 31**	80,000
Cost of goods sold	$320,000	Cost of goods sold	$380,000

DETERMINING THE COST OF GOODS MANUFACTURED

STUDY OBJECTIVE 6

Indicate how cost of goods manufactured is determined.

An example may help show how companies determine the cost of goods manufactured. Assume that on January 1 Dell has a number of computers in various stages of production. In total, these partially completed units are called **beginning work in process inventory**. The costs the company assigns to beginning work in process inventory are based on the **manufacturing costs incurred in the prior period.**

Dell first uses the manufacturing costs incurred in the current year to complete the work that was in process on January 1. It then incurs manufacturing costs for production of new orders. The sum of the direct materials costs, direct labor costs, and manufacturing overhead incurred in the current year is the **total manufacturing costs** for the current period.

We now have two cost amounts: (1) the cost of the beginning work in process and (2) the total manufacturing costs for the current period. The sum of these costs is the **total cost of work in process** for the year.

At the end of the year, Dell may have some computers that are only partially completed. The costs of these units become the cost of the **ending work in process inventory**. To find the **cost of goods manufactured**, we subtract this cost from the total cost of work in process. Illustration 5-7 shows the formula for determining the cost of goods manufactured.

Illustration 5-7
Cost of goods manufactured formula

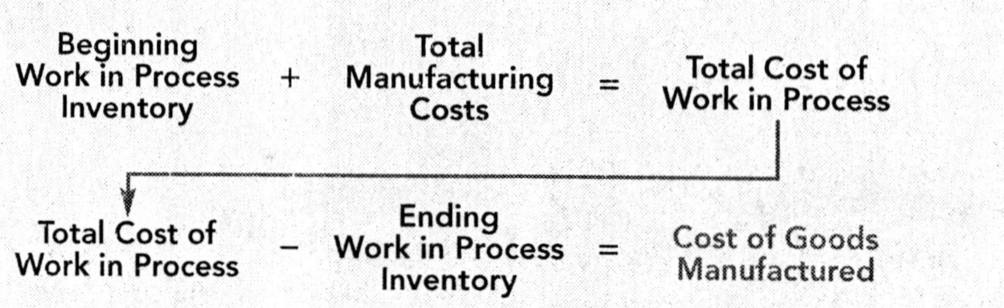

COST OF GOODS MANUFACTURED SCHEDULE

The **cost of goods manufactured schedule** reports cost elements used in calculating cost of goods manufactured. Illustration 5-8 shows the schedule for Olsen Manufacturing Company (using assumed data). The schedule presents detailed data for direct materials and for manufacturing overhead.

Review Illustration 5-7 and then examine the cost of goods manufactured schedule in Illustration 5-8. You should be able to distinguish between "Total manufacturing costs" and "Cost of goods manufactured." The difference is the effect of the change in work in process during the period.

Illustration 5-8
Cost of goods manufactured schedule

OLSEN MANUFACTURING COMPANY Cost of Goods Manufactured Schedule For the Year Ended December 31, 2008			
Work in process, January 1			**$ 18,400**
Direct materials			
Raw materials inventory, January 1	$ 16,700		
Raw materials purchases	152,500		
Total raw materials available for use	169,200		
Less: Raw materials inventory, December 31	22,800		
Direct materials used		$146,400	
Direct labor		175,600	
Manufacturing overhead			
Indirect labor	14,300		
Factory repairs	12,600		
Factory utilities	10,100		
Factory depreciation	9,440		
Factory insurance	8,360		
Total manufacturing overhead		54,800	
Total manufacturing costs			**376,800**
Total cost of work in process			395,200
Less: Work in process, December 31			**25,200**
Cost of goods manufactured			**$370,000**

Often, numbers or categories in the financial statements are highlighted in red type to draw your attention to key information.

Each chapter presents useful information about how decision makers analyze and solve business problems. Decision Toolkits summarize the key features of a decision tool and review why and how to use it.

DECISION TOOLKIT

Decision Checkpoints	Info Needed for Decision	Tool to Use for Decision	How to Evaluate Results
Is the company maintaining control over the costs of production?	Cost of material, labor, and overhead	Cost of goods manufactured schedule	Compare the cost of goods manufactured to revenue expected from product sales.

Balance Sheet

The balance sheet for a merchandising company shows just one category of inventory. In contrast, the balance sheet for a manufacturer may have three inventory accounts, as shown in Illustration 5-9 (page 234).

Illustration 5-9
Inventory accounts for a manufacturer

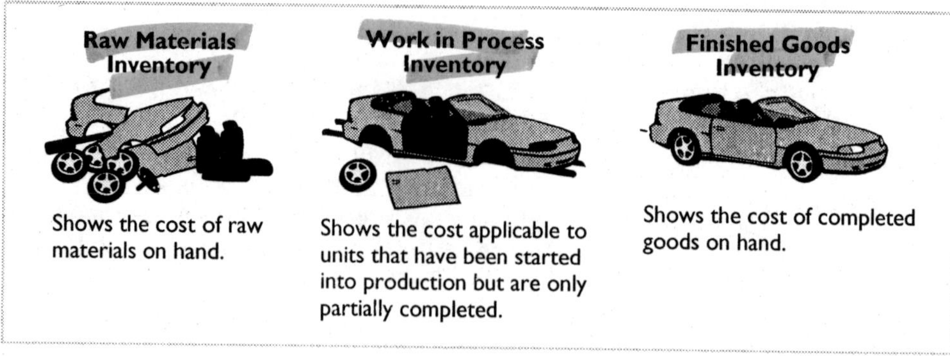

Raw Materials Inventory
Shows the cost of raw materials on hand.
Work in Process Inventory
Shows the cost applicable to units that have been started into production but are only partially completed.
Finished Goods Inventory
Shows the cost of completed goods on hand.

STUDY OBJECTIVE 7

Explain the difference between a merchandising and a manufacturing balance sheet.

Finished Goods Inventory is to a manufacturer what Merchandise Inventory is to a merchandiser. Each of these classifications represents the goods that the company has available for sale.

The current assets sections presented in Illustration 5-10 contrast the presentations of inventories for merchandising and manufacturing companies. Manufacturing companies generally list their inventories in the order of their liquidity—the order in which they are expected to be realized in cash. Thus, finished goods inventory comes first. The remainder of the balance sheet is similar for the two types of companies.

Illustration 5-10
Current assets sections of merchandising and manufacturing balance sheets

MERCHANDISING COMPANY
Balance Sheet
December 31, 2008

Current assets	
Cash	$100,000
Receivables (net)	210,000
Merchandise inventory	**400,000**
Prepaid expenses	22,000
Total current assets	$732,000

MANUFACTURING COMPANY
Balance Sheet
December 31, 2008

Current assets		
Cash		$180,000
Receivables (net)		210,000
Inventories		
Finished goods	**$80,000**	
Work in process	**25,200**	
Raw materials	**22,800**	**128,000**
Prepaid expenses		18,000
Total current assets		$536,000

For expanded coverage, see the appendix at the end of the chapter.

Each step in the accounting cycle for a merchandiser applies to a manufacturer. For example, prior to preparing financial statements, manufacturers make adjusting entries. The adjusting entries are essentially the same as those of a merchandiser. The closing entries are also similar for manufacturers and merchandisers.

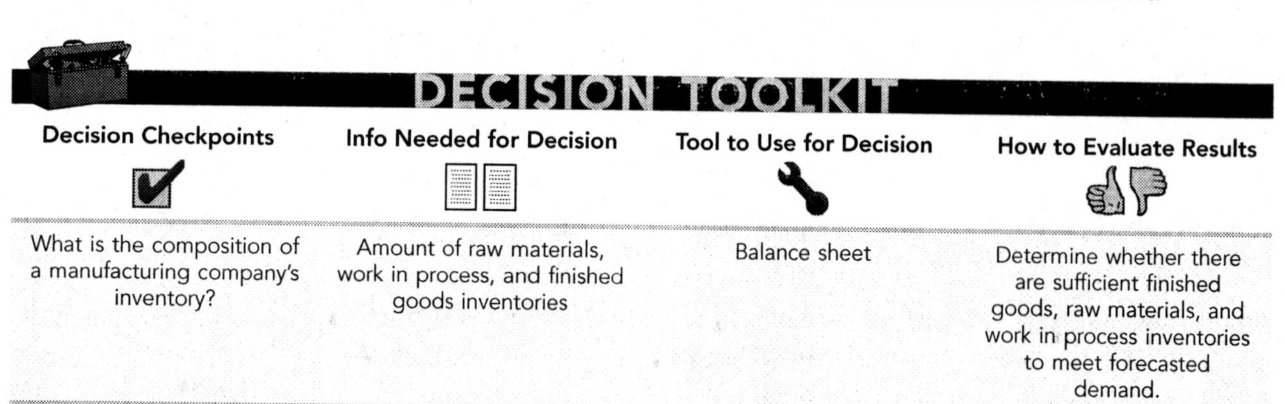

DECISION TOOLKIT

Decision Checkpoints	Info Needed for Decision	Tool to Use for Decision	How to Evaluate Results
What is the composition of a manufacturing company's inventory?	Amount of raw materials, work in process, and finished goods inventories	Balance sheet	Determine whether there are sufficient finished goods, raw materials, and work in process inventories to meet forecasted demand.

Cost Concepts—A Review

You have learned a number of cost concepts in this chapter. Because many of these concepts are new, here we provide an extended example for review.

Assume that Northridge Company manufactures and sells pre-hung metal doors. Recently, it also has decided to start selling pre-hung wood doors. The company will use an old warehouse that it owns to manufacture the new product. Northridge identifies the following costs associated with manufacturing and selling the pre-hung wood doors.

1. The material cost (wood) for each door is $10.
2. Labor costs required to construct a wood door are $8 per door.
3. Depreciation on the factory equipment used to make the wood doors is $25,000 per year.
4. Property taxes on the factory building used to make the wood doors are $6,000 per year.
5. Advertising costs for the pre-hung wood doors total $2,500 per month or $30,000 per year.
6. Sales commissions related to pre-hung wood doors sold are $4 per door.
7. Salaries for employees who maintain the factory facilities are $28,000.
8. The salary of the plant manager in charge of pre-hung wood doors is $70,000.
9. The cost of shipping pre-hung wood doors is $12 per door sold.

Illustration 5-11 shows how Northridge would assign these manufacturing and selling costs to the various categories.

Illustration 5-11
Assignment of costs to cost categories

	Product Costs			
Cost Item	**Direct Materials**	**Direct Labor**	**Manufacturing Overhead**	**Period Costs**
1. Material cost ($10) per door	X			
2. Labor costs ($8) per door		X		
3. Depreciation on factory equipment ($25,000 per year)			X	
4. Property taxes on factory building ($6,000 per year)			X	
5. Advertising costs ($30,000 per year)				X
6. Sales commissions ($4 per door)				X
7. Maintenance salaries (factory facilities) ($28,000 per year)			X	
8. Salary of plant manager ($70,000)			X	
9. Cost of shipping pre-hung doors ($12 per door)				X

Remember that total manufacturing costs are the sum of the **product costs**—direct materials, direct labor, and manufacturing overhead. If Northridge Company produces 10,000 pre-hung wood doors the first year, the total manufacturing costs would be $309,000 as shown in Illustration 5-12.

Illustration 5-12
Computation of total manufacturing costs

Cost Number and Item	Manufacturing Cost
1. Material cost ($10 × 10,000)	$100,000
2. Labor cost ($8 × 10,000)	80,000
3. Depreciation on factory equipment	25,000
4. Property taxes on factory building	6,000
7. Maintenance salaries (factory facilities)	28,000
8. Salary of plant manager	70,000
Total manufacturing costs	**$309,000**

Knowing the total manufacturing costs, Northridge can compute the manufacturing cost per unit. Assuming 10,000 units, the cost to produce one pre-hung wood door is $30.90 ($309,000 ÷ 10,000 units).

In subsequent chapters, we will use extensively the cost concepts discussed in this chapter. Study Illustration 5-11 carefully. If you do not understand any of these classifications, go back and reread the appropriate section in this chapter.

Before You Go On...

REVIEW IT

1. How does the content of an income statement for a merchandiser differ from that for a manufacturer?
2. How do companies report the work in process inventories in the cost of goods manufactured schedule?
3. How does the content of the balance sheet for a merchandiser differ from that for a manufacturer?

MANAGERIAL ACCOUNTING TODAY

STUDY OBJECTIVE 8

Identify trends in managerial accounting.

In recent years, the competitive environment for U.S. business has changed significantly. For example, the airline, financial services, and telecommunications industries have been deregulated. Global competition has intensified. The world economy now has the European Union, NAFTA, and ASEAN. Countries like China and India are becoming economic powerhouses. As indicated earlier, managerial accountants must be forward-looking, acting as advisors and information providers to different members of the organization. Some of the issues they face are discussed below.

Ethics Notes help sensitize you to some of the ethical issues in accounting.

Service-Industry Trends

ETHICS NOTE

Do telecommunications companies have an obligation to provide service to remote or low-user areas for a fee that may be less than the cost of the service?

The Feature Story notes that at the peak of its success as a personal computer manufacturer, Compaq purchased Digital Equipment. Its management believed that the future of computing was in providing computer services, rather than in manufacturing computer hardware. In fact, the U.S. economy in general has shifted toward an emphasis on providing services, rather than goods. Today over 50% of U.S. workers work in service companies, and that percentage is projected to increase in coming years. Much of this chapter focused on manufacturers, but most of the techniques that you will learn in this course apply equally to service companies.

Managers of service companies look to managerial accounting to answer many questions. In some instances the managerial accountant may need to develop new systems for measuring the cost of serving individual customers. In others, companies may need new operating controls to improve the quality and efficiency of specific services. Many of the examples we present in subsequent chapters will be based on service companies.

Managerial Accounting Practices

As discussed earlier, the practice of managerial accounting has changed significantly in recent years to better address the needs of managers. The following sections explain some recent managerial accounting practices.

THE VALUE CHAIN

The value chain refers to all activities associated with providing a product or service. For a manufacturer these include research and development, product design, acquisition of raw materials, production, sales and marketing, delivery, customer relations, and subsequent service. Illustration 5-13 depicts the value chain for a manufacturer. In recent years, companies have made huge strides in analyzing all stages of the value chain in an effort to improve productivity and eliminate waste. Japanese automobile manufacturer Toyota pioneered many of these innovations.

Illustration 5-13
A manufacturer's value chain

In the 1980s many companies purchased giant machines to replace humans in the manufacturing process. These machines were designed to produce large batches of products. In recent years these large-batch manufacturing processes have been recognized as very wasteful. They require vast amounts of inventory storage capacity and considerable movement of materials. Consequently, many companies have reengineered their manufacturing processes. As one example, the manufacturing company Pratt and Whitney has replaced many large machines with smaller, more flexible ones and has begun reorganizing its plants for more efficient flow of goods. Pratt and Whitney was able to reduce the time that its turbine engine blades spend in the grinding section of its factory from 10 days down to 2 hours. It cut the total amount of time spent making a blade from 22 days to 7 days. Analysis of the value chain has made companies far more responsive to customer needs and has improved profitability.

TECHNOLOGICAL CHANGE

Technology has played a large role in the value chain. Computerization and automation have permitted companies to be more effective in streamlining production and thus enhancing the value chain. For example, many companies now employ enterprise resource planning (ERP) software systems to manage their value chain. ERP systems provide a comprehensive, centralized, integrated source of information that companies can use to manage all major business processes, from purchasing to manufacturing to human resources.

In large companies, an ERP system might replace as many as 200 individual software packages. For example, an ERP system can eliminate the need for individual software packages for personnel, inventory management, receivables, and payroll. Because the value chain extends beyond the walls of the company, ERP systems enable a two-way flow of information between a company and its major suppliers, customers, and business partners. Such systems both collect and disperse information throughout the value chain. The largest ERP provider, German corporation SAP AG, has more than 36,000 customers worldwide.

Another example of technological change is **computer-integrated manufacturing (CIM)**. Using CIM, many companies can now manufacture products that are untouched by human hands. An example is the use of robotic equipment in the steel and automobile industries. Workers monitor the manufacturing process by watching instrument panels. Automation significantly reduces direct labor costs in many cases.

Also, the widespread use of computers has greatly reduced the cost of accumulating, storing, and reporting managerial accounting information. Computers now make it possible to do more detailed costing of products, processes, and services than was possible under manual processing.

Technology is also affecting the value chain through business-to-business (B2B) e-commerce on the Internet. The Internet has dramatically changed the way corporations do business with one another. Interorganizational information systems connected over the Internet enable suppliers to share information nearly instantaneously. The Internet has also changed the marketplace, often having the effect of cutting out intermediaries. Industries such as the automobile, airline, hotel, and electronics industries have made commitments to purchase some or all of their supplies and raw materials in the huge B2B electronic marketplaces. For example, Hilton Hotels recently agreed to purchase as much as $1.5 billion of bed sheets, pest control services, and other items from an online supplier, PurchasePro.com.

JUST-IN-TIME INVENTORY METHODS

Many companies have significantly lowered inventory levels and costs using just-in-time (JIT) inventory methods. Under a just-in-time method, goods are manufactured or purchased just in time for use. As noted in the Feature Story, Dell is famous for having developed a system for making computers in response to individual customer requests. Even though each computer is custom-made to meet each customer's particular specifications, it takes Dell less than 48 hours to assemble the computer and put it on a truck. By integrating its information systems with those of its suppliers, Dell reduced its inventories to nearly zero. This is a huge advantage in an industry where products become obsolete nearly overnight.

ETHICS NOTE

Does just-in-time inventory justify "just-in-time" employees obtained through temporary employment services?

QUALITY

JIT inventory systems require an increased emphasis on product quality. If products are produced only as they are needed, it is very costly for the company to have to stop production because of defects or machine breakdowns. Many companies have installed total quality management (TQM) systems to reduce defects in finished products. The goal is to achieve zero defects. These systems require timely data on defective products, rework costs, and the cost of honoring warranty contracts. Often, companies use this information to help redesign the product in a way that makes it less prone to defects. Or they may use the information to reengineer the production process to reduce setup time and decrease the potential for error. TQM systems also provide information on nonfinancial measures such as customer satisfaction, number of service calls, and time to generate reports. Attention to these measures, which employees can control, leads to increased profitability.

MANAGEMENT INSIGHT

Bananas Receive Special Treatment

When it comes to total quality management, few companies can compare with Chiquita Brands International. Grocery store customers are very picky about bananas—bad bananas are consistently the number one grocery store complaint. Because bananas often account for up to 3% of a grocery store's sales, Chiquita goes to great lengths to protect the popular fruit. While bananas are in transit from Central America, "black box" recording devices attached to shipping crates ensure that they are kept in an environment of 90% humidity and an unvarying 55-degree temperature. Upon arrival in the U.S., bananas are ripened in airtight warehouses that use carefully monitored levels of ethylene gas. Regular checks are made of each warehouse using ultrasonic detectors that can detect leaks the size of a pinhole. Says one grocery store executive, "No other item in the store has this type of attention and resources devoted to it."

Source: Devon Spurgeon, "When Grocers in U.S. Go Bananas Over Bad Fruit, They Call Laubenthal," *Wall Street Journal*, August 14, 2000, p. A1.

Why is it important to keep track of costs that are incurred to improve product quality?

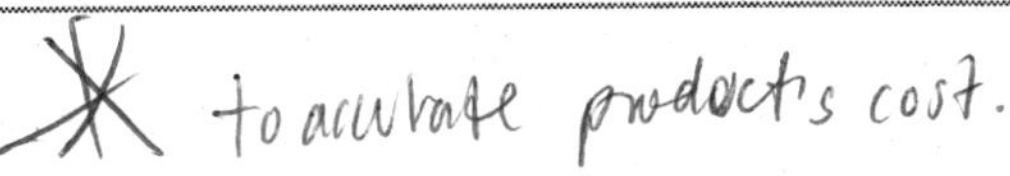

ACTIVITY-BASED COSTING

As discussed earlier, overhead costs have become an increasingly large component of product and service costs. By definition, overhead costs cannot be directly traced to individual products. But to determine each product's cost, overhead must be **allocated** to the various products. In order to obtain more accurate product costs, many companies now allocate overhead using activity-based costing (ABC). Under ABC, companies allocate overhead based on each product's use of activities in making the product. For example, companies can keep track of their cost of setting up machines for each batch of a production process. Then companies can allocate part of the total set-up cost to a particular product based on the number of set-ups that product required.

Activity-based costing is beneficial because it results in more accurate product costing and in more careful scrutiny of all activities in the value chain. For example, if a product's cost is high because it requires a high number of set-ups, management will be motivated to determine how to produce the product using the optimal number of machine set-ups. Both manufacturing and service companies now widely use ABC. Allied Signal and Coca-Cola have both enjoyed improved results from ABC. Fidelity Investments uses ABC to identify which customers cost the most to serve.

THEORY OF CONSTRAINTS

All companies have certain aspects of their business that create "bottlenecks"—constraints that limit the company's potential profitability. An important aspect of managing the value chain is identifying these constraints. The theory of constraints is a specific approach used to identify and manage constraints in order to achieve the company's goals. Automobile manufacturer General Motors has implemented the theory of constraints in all of its North American plants. GM has found that it is most profitable when it focuses on fixing bottlenecks, rather than worrying about whether all aspects of the company are functioning at full capacity. It has greatly improved the company's ability to effectively use overtime labor while meeting customer demand. Chapter 6 discusses an application of the theory of constraints.

BALANCED SCORECARD

As companies implement various business practice innovations, managers sometimes focus too enthusiastically on the latest innovation, to the detriment of other areas of the business. For example, in focusing on improving quality, companies sometimes have lost sight of cost/benefit considerations. Similarly, in focusing on reducing inventory levels through just-in-time, companies sometimes have lost sales due to inventory shortages. The **balanced scorecard** is a performance-measurement approach that uses both financial and nonfinancial measures to evaluate all aspects of a company's operations in an **integrated** fashion. The performance measures are linked in a cause-and-effect fashion to ensure that they all tie to the company's overall objectives.

For example, the company may desire to increase its return on assets, a common financial performance measure (calculated as net income divided by average total assets). It will then identify a series of linked goals. If the company accomplishes each goal, the ultimate result will be an increase in return on assets. For example, in order to increase return on assets, sales must increase. In order to increase sales, customer satisfaction must be increased. In order to increase customer satisfaction, product defects must be reduced. In order to reduce product defects, employee training must be increased. Note the linkage, which starts with employee training and ends with return on assets. Each objective will have associated performance measures.

The use of the balanced scorecard is widespread among well-known and respected companies. For example, Hilton Hotels Corporation uses the balanced scorecard to evaluate the performance of employees at all of its hotel chains. Wal-Mart employs the balanced scorecard, and actually extends its use to evaluation of its suppliers. For example, Wal-Mart recently awarded Welch Company the "Dry Grocery Division Supplier of the Year Award" for its balanced scorecard results.

Before You Go On...

REVIEW IT

1. Describe, in sequence, the main components of a manufacturer's value chain.
2. Why is product quality important for companies that implement a just-in-time inventory system?
3. Explain what is meant by "balanced" in the balanced scorecard approach.

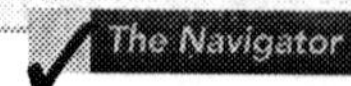

An All About You feature (next page) links some aspect of the chapter topic to your personal life or a financial situation you are likely to face.

Be sure to read **ALL ABOUT YOU: *Outsourcing and Jobs*** on the next page for information on how topics in this chapter apply to you.

all about YOU

Outsourcing and Jobs

As noted in this chapter, because of global competition, companies have become increasingly focused on reducing costs. To reduce costs, and remain competitive, many companies are turning to outsourcing. *Outsourcing* means hiring an outside supplier to provide elements of a product rather than producing them internally.

In many instances, companies outsource jobs to foreign suppliers. This practice has caused considerable concern about the loss of U.S. jobs. Until recently, most of the debate about outsourcing related to manufacturing. Now outsourcing is also taking place in professional services like engineering and accounting. This is occurring because high-speed transmission of large amounts of data over the Internet is now cheap and easy. As a consequence, jobs that once seemed safe from foreign competition are now condidates for outsourcing.

Some Facts

* IBM has expanded beyond information technology into providing advisory services related to outsourcing, which it believes will be a $500 billion market.
* A U.S. professional association of certified public accountants requires that its members notify clients before they share confidential client information with an outside contractor as part of an outsourcing arrangement.
* During a recent two-year period Ford Motor Co. inspected the working conditions at about 160 of the more than 2,000 foreign-owned plants in low-cost countries that supply it with outsourced parts.
* The McKinsey Global Institute predicts that white-collar overseas outsourcing will increase at a rate of 30% to 40% over the next five years. By 2015, the consultancy group Forrester predicts roughly 3.3 million service jobs will have moved offshore, including 1.7 million "back-office" jobs such as payroll processing and accounting, and 473,000 jobs in the information technology industry.
* On the other hand, Hewlett-Packard has begun to "insource" (bring back inhouse) many of the manufacturing operations that it previously outsourced.

About the Numbers

Interestingly, foreign firms doing business in the United States also hire a lot of Americans. In a recent year, U.S. subsidiaries of foreign companies employed approximately 5.3 million Americans. In comparison, in that same year 134,000 Americans lost their jobs due to outsourcing. The following graph shows which countries are the top foreign employers in the United States.

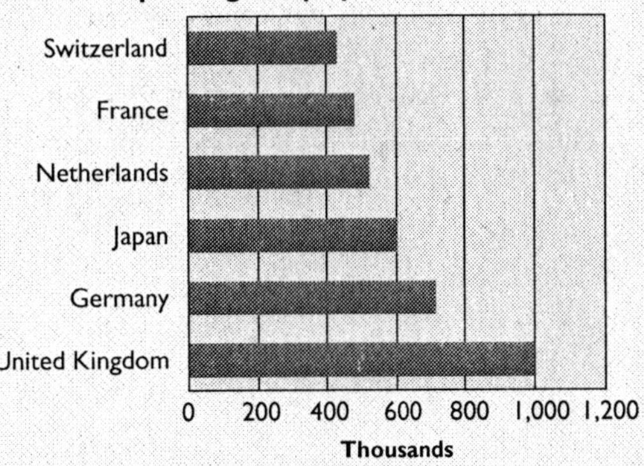

Source for graph: Darren Dahl, "Insourcing 101," *Inc.* Magazine, April 2006, p. 50.

What Do You Think?

Suppose you are the managing partner in a CPA firm with 30 full-time staff. Larger firms in your community have begun to outsource basic tax-return preparation work to India. Should you outsource your basic tax return work to India as well? You estimate that you would have to lay off six staff members if you outsource the work.

YES: The wages paid to Indian accountants are very low relative to U.S. wages. You will not be able to compete unless you outsource.

NO: Tax-return data is highly sensitive. Many customers will be upset to learn that their data is being emailed around the world.

Sources: Jonathan Weil, "Accountants Scrutinize Outsourcing," *Wall Street Journal*, August 11, 2004, p. A2; Jeffrey McCracken, "Ford Probes Work Conditions at Part Makers in China, Mexico," *Wall Street Journal*, April 5, 2006, p. A12; Council on Foreign Affairs, "Backgrounder, Trade: Outsourcing Jobs," February 20, 2004, *www.cfr.org/publication* (accessed June 2006).

The authors' comments on this situation appear on page 269.

Using the Decision Toolkit exercises ask you to use business information and the decision tools presented in the chapter. We encourage you to think through the questions related to the decision before you study the Solution.

Using the Decision Toolkit

Giant Manufacturing Co. Ltd. specializes in manufacturing many different models of bicycles. Assume that the market has responded enthusiastically to a new model, the Jaguar. As a result, the company has established a separate manufacturing facility to produce these bicycles. The company produces 1,000 bicycles per month. Giant's monthly manufacturing cost and other expenses data related to these bicycles are as follows.

1. Rent on manufacturing equipment (lease cost) — $2,000/month
2. Insurance on manufacturing building — $750/month
3. Raw materials (frames, tires, etc.) — $80/bicycle
4. Utility costs for manufacturing facility — $1,000/month
5. Supplies for administrative office — $800/month
6. Wages for assembly line workers in manufacturing facility — $30/bicycle
7. Depreciation on office equipment — $650/month
8. Miscellaneous materials (lubricants, solders, etc.) — $1.20/bicycle
9. Property taxes on manufacturing building — $2,400/year
10. Manufacturing supervisor's salary — $3,000/month
11. Advertising for bicycles — $30,000/year
12. Sales commissions — $10/bicycle
13. Depreciation on manufacturing building — $1,500/month

Instructions

(a) Prepare an answer sheet with the following column headings.

	Product Costs			
Cost Item	**Direct Materials**	**Direct Labor**	**Manufacturing Overhead**	**Period Costs**

Enter each cost item on your answer sheet, placing an "X" mark under the appropriate headings.

(b) Compute total manufacturing costs for the month.

Solution

(a)

	Product Costs			
Cost Item	**Direct Materials**	**Direct Labor**	**Manufacturing Overhead**	**Period Costs**
1. Rent on manufacturing equipment ($2,000/month)			X	
2. Insurance on manufacturing building ($750/month)			X	
3. Raw materials ($80/bicycle)	X			
4. Manufacturing utilities ($1,000/month)			X	
5. Office supplies ($800/month)				X
6. Wages for workers ($30/bicycle)		X		

Cost Item	Product Costs: Direct Materials	Direct Labor	Manufacturing Overhead	Period Costs
7. Depreciation on office equipment ($650/month)				X
8. Miscellaneous materials ($1.20/bicycle)			X	
9. Property taxes on manufacturing building ($2,400/year)			X	
10. Manufacturing supervisor's salary ($3,000/month)			X	
11. Advertising cost ($30,000/year)				X
12. Sales commissions ($10/bicycle)				X
13. Depreciation on manufacturing building ($1,500/month)			X	

(b)

Cost Item	Manufacturing Cost
Rent on manufacturing equipment	$ 2,000
Insurance on manufacturing building	750
Raw materials ($80 × 1,000)	80,000
Manufacturing utilities	1,000
Labor ($30 × 1,000)	30,000
Miscellaneous materials ($1.20 × 1,000)	1,200
Property taxes on manufacturing building ($2,400 ÷ 12)	200
Manufacturing supervisor's salary	3,000
Depreciation on manufacturing building	1,500
Total manufacturing costs	$119,650

The Navigator

The Summary of Study Objectives reiterates the main points related to the Study Objectives. It provides you with an opportunity to review what you have learned.

SUMMARY OF STUDY OBJECTIVES

1 **Explain the distinguishing features of managerial accounting.** The *primary users* of managerial accounting reports are internal users, who are officers, department heads, managers, and supervisors in the company. Managerial accounting issues internal reports as frequently as the need arises. The purpose of these reports is to provide special-purpose information for a particular user for a specific decision. The content of managerial accounting reports pertains to subunits of the business, may be very detailed, and may extend beyond the double-entry accounting system. The reporting standard is relevance to the decision being made. No independent audits are required in managerial accounting.

2 **Identify the three broad functions of management.** The three functions are planning, directing, and controlling. Planning requires management to look ahead and to establish objectives. Directing involves coordinating the diverse activities and human resources of a company to produce a smooth-running operation. Controlling is the process of keeping the activities on track.

3 **Define the three classes of manufacturing costs.** Manufacturing costs are typically classified as either (1) direct materials, (2) direct labor, or (3) manufacturing overhead. Raw materials that can be physically and directly associated with the finished product during the manufacturing process are called direct materials. The work of factory employees that can be physically and directly associated with converting raw materials into finished goods is considered direct labor. Manufacturing overhead consists of costs that are indirectly associated with the manufacture of the finished product.

4 **Distinguish between product and period costs.** Product costs are costs that are a necessary and integral part of producing the finished product. Product costs are also called inventoriable costs. Under the matching principle, these costs do not become expenses until the company sells the finished goods inventory. Period costs are costs that are identified with a specific time period rather than with a salable product. These costs relate to nonmanufacturing costs and therefore are not inventoriable costs.

5 **Explain the difference between a merchandising and a manufacturing income statement.** The difference between a merchandising and a manufacturing income statement is in the cost of goods sold section. A manufacturing cost of goods sold section shows beginning and ending finished goods inventories and the cost of goods manufactured.

6 **Indicate how cost of goods manufactured is determined.** Companies add the cost of the beginning work in process to the total manufacturing costs for the current year to arrive at the total cost of work in process for the year. They then subtract the ending work in process from the total cost of work in process to arrive at the cost of goods manufactured.

7 **Explain the difference between a merchandising and a manufacturing balance sheet.** The difference between a merchandising and a manufacturing balance sheet is in the current assets section. The current assets section of a manufacturing company's balance sheet presents three inventory accounts: finished goods inventory, work in process inventory, and raw materials inventory.

8 **Identify trends in managerial accounting.** Managerial accounting has experienced many changes in recent years. Among these are a shift toward addressing the needs of service companies and improving practices to better meet the needs of managers. Improved practices include a focus on managing the value chain through techniques such as just-in-time inventory and technological applications such as enterprise resource management, computer-integrated manufacturing, and B2B e-commerce. In addition, techniques such as just-in-time inventory, total quality management, activity-based costing, and theory of constraints are improving decision making. Finally, the balanced scorecard is now used by many companies in order to attain a more comprehensive view of the company's operations.

The Navigator

The Decision Toolkit—A Summary reviews the contexts and techniques useful for decision making that were covered in the chapter.

DECISION TOOLKIT—A SUMMARY

Decision Checkpoints	Info Needed for Decision	Tool to Use for Decision	How to Evaluate Results
Is the company maintaining control over the costs of production?	Cost of material, labor, and overhead	Cost of goods manufactured schedule	Compare the cost of goods manufactured to revenue expected from product sales.
What is the composition of a manufacturing company's inventory?	Amount of raw materials, work in process, and finished goods inventories	Balance sheet	Determine whether there are sufficient finished goods, raw materials, and work in process inventories to meet forecasted demand.

APPENDIX Accounting Cycle for a Manufacturing Company

STUDY OBJECTIVE 9

Prepare a worksheet and closing entries for a manufacturing company.

The accounting cycle for a manufacturing company is the same as for a merchandising company when companies use a periodic inventory system. The journalizing and posting of transactions is the same, except for the additional manufacturing inventories and manufacturing cost accounts. Similarly, the preparation of a trial balance and the journalizing and posting of adjusting entries are the same. Some changes, however, occur in using a worksheet and in preparing closing entries.

To illustrate the changes in the worksheet, we will use the cost of goods manufactured schedule for Olsen Manufacturing presented in Illustration 5-8, along with other assumed data. For convenience, we reproduce the cost of goods manufactured schedule in Illustration 5A-1.

Illustration 5A-1
Cost of goods manufactured schedule

OLSEN MANUFACTURING COMPANY Cost of Goods Manufactured Schedule For the Year Ended December 31, 2008			
Work in process, January 1			$ 18,400
Direct materials			
Raw materials inventory, January 1	$ 16,700		
Raw materials purchases	152,500		
Total raw materials available for use	169,200		
Less: Raw materials inventory, December 31	22,800		
Direct materials used		$146,400	
Direct labor		175,600	
Manufacturing overhead			
Indirect labor	14,300		
Factory repairs	12,600		
Factory utilities	10,100		
Factory depreciation	9,440		
Factory insurance	8,360		
Total manufacturing overhead		54,800	
Total manufacturing costs			376,800
Total cost of work in process			395,200
Less: Work in process, December 31			25,200
Cost of goods manufactured			$370,000

Worksheet

When a company uses a worksheet in preparing financial statements, it needs two additional columns for the cost of goods manufactured schedule. As illustrated in the worksheet in Illustration 5A-2 (page 246), we insert debit and credit columns for this schedule before the income statement columns.

In completing the cost of goods manufactured columns, you would enter the beginning inventories of raw materials and work in process as debits. In addition, you would enter all of the manufacturing costs as debits. The reason is that each of these amounts increases cost of goods manufactured. In contrast, you would enter ending inventories for raw materials and work in process as credits in the cost of goods manufactured columns because they have the opposite effect—they decrease cost of goods manufactured. The balancing amount for these columns is the cost of goods manufactured. Note that the amount ($370,000) agrees with the amount reported for cost of goods manufactured in Illustration 5A-1. This amount is also entered in the income statement debit column.

The income statement and balance sheet columns for a manufacturing company are basically the same as for a merchandising company. For example, the treatment of the finished goods inventories is identical with the treatment of merchandise inventory: The beginning inventory appears in the debit column of the income statement, and the ending finished goods inventory appears in the income statement credit column as well as in the balance sheet debit column.

As in the case of a merchandising company, manufacturing companies can prepare financial statements from the statement columns of the worksheet. They also can prepare the cost of goods manufactured schedule directly from the worksheet.

Illustration 5A-2
Partial worksheet

Olsen Manufacturing Company.xls

File Edit View Insert Format Tools Data Window Help

	A	B	C	D	E	F	G	H	I
1									
2		OLSEN MANUFACTURING COMPANY							
3		Worksheet (Partial) For the Year Ended December 31, 2008							
4		Adjusted Trial Balance		Cost of Goods Manufactured		Income Statement		Balance Sheet	
5		Dr.	Cr.	Dr.	Cr.	Dr.	Cr.	Dr.	Cr.
6	Cash	42,500						42,500	
7	Accounts Receivable (Net)	71,900						71,900	
8	Finished Goods Inventory	24,600				24,600	19,500	19,500	
9	Work in Process Inventory	18,400		18,400	25,200			25,200	
10	Raw Material Inventory	16,700		16,700	22,800			22,800	
11	Plant Assets	724.000						724,000	
12	Accumulated Depreciation		278,400						278,400
13	Notes Payable		100,000						100,000
14	Accounts Payable		40,000						40,000
15	Income Taxes Payable		5,000						5,000
16	Common Stock		200,000						200,000
17	Retained Earnings		205,100						205,100
18	Sales		680,000				680,000		
19	Raw Materials Purchases	152,500		152,500					
20	Direct Labor	175,600		175,600					
21	Indirect Labor	14,300		14,300					
22	Factory Repairs	12,600		12,600					
23	Factory Utilities	10,100		10,100					
24	Factory Depreciation	9,440		9,440					
25	Factory Insurance	8,360		8,360					
26	Selling Expenses	114,900				114,900			
27	Administrative Expenses	92,600				92,600			
28	Income Tax Expense	20,000				20,000			
29	Totals	1,508,500	1,508,500	418,000	48,000				
30	Cost of Goods Manufactured				370,000	370,000			
31	Totals			418,000	418,000	622,100	699,500	905,900	828,500
32	Net Income					77,400			77,400
33	Totals					699,500	699,500	905,900	905,900
34									

Closing Entries

The closing entries are different for manufacturing and merchandising companies. Manufacturing companies use a Manufacturing Summary account to close all accounts that appear in the cost of goods manufactured schedule. The balance of the Manufacturing Summary account is the Cost of Goods Manufactured for the period. Manufacturing Summary is then closed to Income Summary.

Companies can prepare the closing entries from the worksheet. As illustrated below, they first prepare the closing entries for the manufacturing accounts. The closing entries for Olsen Manufacturing are as follows.

Date	Account	Debit	Credit
Dec. 31	Work in Process Inventory (Dec. 31)	25,200	
	Raw Materials Inventory (Dec. 31)	22,800	
	Manufacturing Summary		**48,000**
	(To record ending raw materials and work in process inventories)		

(The closing entries continue on the next page.)

Date	Account Titles and Explanation	Debit	Credit
Dec. 31	**Manufacturing Summary**	**418,000**	
	Work in Process Inventory (Jan. 1)		18,400
	Raw Materials Inventory (Jan. 1)		16,700
	Raw Materials Purchases		152,500
	Direct Labor		175,600
	Indirect Labor		14,300
	Factory Repairs		12,600
	Factory Utilities		10,100
	Factory Depreciation		9,440
	Factory Insurance		8,360
	(To close beginning raw materials and work in process inventories and manufacturing cost accounts)		
31	Finished Goods Inventory (Dec. 31)	19,500	
	Sales	680,000	
	Income Summary		699,500
	(To record ending finished goods inventory and close sales account)		
31	Income Summary	622,100	
	Finished Goods Inventory (Jan. 1)		24,600
	Manufacturing Summary		**370,000**
	Selling Expenses		114,900
	Administrative Expenses		92,600
	Income Tax Expense		20,000
	(To close beginning finished goods inventory, manufacturing summary, and expense accounts)		
31	Income Summary	77,400	
	Retained Earnings		77,400
	(To close net income to retained earnings)		

After posting, the summary accounts will show the following.

Illustration 5A-3
Summary accounts for a manufacturing company, after posting

Manufacturing Summary

Date		Debit	Date		Credit
Dec. 31	Close	418,000	Dec. 31	Close	48,000
			31	Close	370,000

Income Summary

Date		Debit	Date		Credit
Dec. 31	Close	622,100	Dec. 31	Close	699,500
31	Close	77,400			

SUMMARY OF STUDY OBJECTIVE FOR APPENDIX

9 **Prepare a worksheet and closing entries for a manufacturing company.** The worksheet for the cost of goods manufactured needs two additional columns. In these columns, manufacturing companies enter the beginning inventories of raw materials and work in process as debits, and the ending inventories as credits. All manufacturing costs are entered as debits. To close all of the accounts that appear in the cost of goods manufactured schedule, manufacturers use a Manufacturing Summary account.

GLOSSARY

Activity-based costing (ABC) A method of allocating overhead based on each product's use of activities in making the product. (p. 239).

Balanced scorecard A performance-measurement approach that uses both financial and nonfinancial measures, tied to company objectives, to evaluate a company's operations in an integrated fashion. (p. 240).

Board of directors The group of officials elected by the stockholders of a corporation to formulate operating policies, select officers, and otherwise manage the company. (p. 226)

Chief executive officer (CEO) Corporate officer who has overall responsibility for managing the business and delegates responsibilities to other corporate officers. (p. 226)

Chief financial officer (CFO) Corporate officer who is responsible for all of the accounting and finance issues of the company. (p. 226)

Controller Financial officer responsible for a company's accounting records, system of internal control, and preparation of financial statements, tax returns, and internal reports. (p. 226)

Cost of goods manufactured Total cost of work in process less the cost of the ending work in process inventory. (p. 232).

Direct labor The work of factory employees that can be physically and directly associated with converting raw materials into finished goods. (p. 229).

Direct materials Raw materials that can be physically and directly associated with manufacturing the finished product. (p. 228).

Enterprise resource planning (ERP) system Software that provides a comprehensive, centralized, integrated source of information used to manage all major business processes. (p. 237).

Indirect labor Work of factory employees that has no physical association with the finished product, or for which it is impractical to trace the costs to the goods produced. (p. 229).

Indirect materials Raw materials that do not physically become part of the finished product or cannot be traced because their physical association with the finished product is too small. (p. 228).

Just-in-time (JIT) inventory Inventory system in which goods are manufactured or purchased just in time for use. (p. 238).

Line positions Jobs that are directly involved in a company's primary revenue-generating operating activities. (p. 226).

Managerial accounting A field of accounting that provides economic and financial information for managers and other internal users. (p. 222).

Manufacturing overhead Manufacturing costs that are indirectly associated with the manufacture of the finished product. (p. 229).

Period costs Costs that are matched with the revenue of a specific time period and charged to expense as incurred. (p. 230).

Product costs Costs that are a necessary and integral part of producing the finished product. (p. 230).

Sarbanes-Oxley Act of 2002 (SOX) Law passed by Congress in 2002 intended to reduce unethical corporate behavior. (p. 227).

Staff positions Jobs that support the efforts of line employees. (p. 226).

Theory of constraints A specific approach used to identify and manage constraints in order to achieve the company's goals. (p. 239).

Total cost of work in process Cost of the beginning work in process plus total manufacturing costs for the current period. (p. 232).

Total manufacturing costs The sum of direct materials, direct labor, and manufacturing overhead incurred in the current period. (p. 232).

Total quality management (TQM) Systems implemented to reduce defects in finished products with the goal of achieving zero defects. (p. 238).

Treasurer Financial officer responsible for custody of a company's funds and for maintaining its cash position. (p. 226).

Value chain All activities associated with providing a product or service. (p. 237).

Demonstration Problem

Demonstration Problems are a final review before you begin homework. An ***Action Plan*** *that appears in the margin gives you tips about how to approach the problem, and the* ***Solution*** *provided demonstrates both the form and content of complete answers.*

Superior Manufacturing Company has the following cost and expense data for the year ending December 31, 2008.

Raw materials, 1/1/08	$ 30,000	Insurance, factory	$ 14,000
Raw materials, 12/31/08	20,000	Property taxes, factory building	6,000
Raw materials purchases	205,000	Sales (net)	1,500,000
Indirect materials	15,000	Delivery expenses	100,000
Work in process, 1/1/08	80,000	Sales commissions	150,000
Work in process, 12/31/08	50,000	Indirect labor	90,000
Finished goods, 1/1/08	110,000	Factory machinery rent	40,000
Finished goods, 12/31/08	120,000	Factory utilities	65,000
Direct labor	350,000	Depreciation, factory building	24,000
Factory manager's salary	35,000	Administrative expenses	300,000

Instructions

(a) Prepare a cost of goods manufactured schedule for Superior Company for 2008.

(b) Prepare an income statement for Superior Company for 2008.

(c) Assume that Superior Company's ledgers show the balances of the following current asset accounts: Cash $17,000, Accounts Receivable (net) $120,000, Prepaid Expenses $13,000, and Short-term Investments $26,000. Prepare the current assets section of the balance sheet for Superior Company as of December 31, 2008.

Solution

(a)

SUPERIOR MANUFACTURING COMPANY
Cost of Goods Manufactured Schedule
For the Year Ended December 31, 2008

Work in process, 1/1			$ 80,000
Direct materials			
Raw materials inventory, 1/1	$ 30,000		
Raw materials purchases	205,000		
Total raw materials available for use	235,000		
Less: Raw materials inventory, 12/31	20,000		
Direct materials used		$215,000	
Direct labor		350,000	
Manufacturing overhead			
Indirect labor	90,000		
Factory utilities	65,000		
Factory machinery rent	40,000		
Factory manager's salary	35,000		
Depreciation on building	24,000		
Indirect materials	15,000		
Factory insurance	14,000		
Property taxes	6,000		
Total manufacturing overhead		289,000	
Total manufacturing costs			854,000
Total cost of work in process			934,000
Less: Work in process, 12/31			50,000
Cost of goods manufactured			$884,000

action plan

- ✔ Start with beginning work in process as the first item in the cost of goods manufactured schedule.
- ✔ Sum direct materials used, direct labor, and total manufacturing overhead to determine total manufacturing costs.
- ✔ Sum beginning work in process and total manufacturing costs to determine total cost of work in process.
- ✔ Cost of goods manufactured is the total cost of work in process less ending work in process.
- ✔ In the cost of goods sold section of the income statement, show beginning and ending finished goods inventory and cost of goods manufactured.
- ✔ In the balance sheet, list manufacturing inventories in the order of their expected realization in cash, with finished goods first.

(b)

SUPERIOR MANUFACTURING COMPANY
Income Statement
For the Year Ended December 31, 2008

Sales (net)		$1,500,000
Cost of goods sold		
Finished goods inventory, January 1	$110,000	
Cost of goods manufactured	884,000	
Cost of goods available for sale	994,000	
Less: Finished goods inventory, December 31	120,000	
Cost of goods sold		874,000
Gross profit		626,000
Operating expenses		
Administrative expenses	300,000	
Sales commissions	150,000	
Delivery expenses	100,000	
Total operating expenses		550,000
Net income		$ 76,000

(c)

SUPERIOR MANUFACTURING COMPANY
Balance Sheet (partial)
December 31, 2008

Current assets		
Cash		$ 17,000
Short-term investments		26,000
Accounts receivable (net)		120,000
Inventories		
Finished goods	$120,000	
Work in process	50,000	
Raw materials	20,000	190,000
Prepaid expenses		13,000
Total current assets		$366,000

*This would be a good time to return to the **Student Owner's Manual** at the beginning of the book (or look at it for the first time if you skipped it before) to read about the various types of homework materials that appear at the ends of chapters. Knowing the purpose of different assignments will help you appreciate what each contributes to your accounting skills and competencies.*

Note: All asterisked Questions, Exercises, and Problems relate to material in the appendix to the chapter.

SELF-STUDY QUESTIONS

Answers are at the end of the chapter.

(SO 1) **1.** Managerial accounting:

a. is governed by generally accepted accounting principles.
b. places emphasis on special-purpose information.
c. pertains to the entity as a whole and is highly aggregated.
d. is limited to cost data.

(SO 2) **2.** The management of an organization performs several broad functions. They are:

a. planning, directing, and selling.
b. planning, directing, and controlling.
c. planning, manufacturing, and controlling.
d. directing, manufacturing, and controlling.

3. Direct materials are a: (SO 3)

	Product Cost	Manufacturing Overhead	Period Cost
a.	Yes	Yes	No
b.	Yes	No	No
c.	Yes	Yes	Yes
d.	No	No	No

(SO 4) **4.** Indirect labor is a:
a. nonmanufacturing cost.
b. raw material cost.
c. product cost.
d. period cost.

(SO 3) **5.** Which of the following costs would a computer manufacturer include in manufacturing overhead?
a. The cost of the disk drives.
b. The wages earned by computer assemblers.
c. The cost of the memory chips.
d. Depreciation on testing equipment.

(SO 3) **6.** Which of the following is *not* an element of manufacturing overhead?
a. Sales manager's salary.
b. Plant manager's salary.
c. Factory repairman's wages.
d. Product inspector's salary.

(SO 5) **7.** For the year, Redder Company has cost of goods manufactured of $600,000, beginning finished goods inventory of $200,000, and ending finished goods inventory of $250,000. The cost of goods sold is:
a. $450,000.
b. $500,000.
c. $550,000.
d. $600,000.

8. A cost of goods manufactured schedule shows beginning and ending inventories for: (SO 6)
a. raw materials and work in process only.
b. work in process only.
c. raw materials only.
d. raw materials, work in process, and finished goods.

9. A manufacturer may report three inventories on its balance sheet: (1) raw materials, (2) work in process, and (3) finished goods. Indicate in what sequence these inventories generally appear on a balance sheet. (SO 7)
a. (1), (2), (3) **c.** (3), (1), (2)
b. (2), (3), (1) **d.** (3), (2), (1)

10. Which of the following managerial accounting techniques attempts to allocate manufacturing overhead in a more meaningful fashion? (SO 8)
a. Just-in-time inventory.
b. Total-quality management.
c. Balanced scorecard.
d. Activity-based costing.

Go to the book's website,
www.wiley.com/college/weygandt,
for Additional Self-Study questions.

QUESTIONS

1. **(a)** "Managerial accounting is a field of accounting that provides economic information for all interested parties." Do you agree? Explain.
(b) Mary Barett believes that managerial accounting serves only manufacturing firms. Is Mary correct? Explain.
2. Distinguish between managerial and financial accounting as to (a) primary users of reports, (b) types and frequency of reports, and (c) purpose of reports.
3. How does the content of reports and the verification of reports differ between managerial and financial accounting?
4. In what ways can the budgeting process create incentives for unethical behavior?
5. Karen Fritz is studying for the next accounting mid-term examination. Summarize for Karen what she should know about management functions.
6. "Decision making is management's most important function." Do you agree? Why or why not?
7. Explain the primary difference between line positions and staff positions, and give examples of each.
8. What new rules were enacted under the Sarbanes-Oxley Act to address unethical accounting practices?
9. Stan Kaiser is studying for his next accounting examination. Explain to Stan what he should know about the differences between the income statements for a manufacturing and for a merchandising company.
10. Terry Lemay is unclear as to the difference between the balance sheets of a merchandising company and a manufacturing company. Explain the difference to Terry.
11. How are manufacturing costs classified?
12. Matt Litkee claims that the distinction between direct and indirect materials is based entirely on physical association with the product. Is Matt correct? Why?
13. Megan Neill is confused about the differences between a product cost and a period cost. Explain the differences to Megan.
14. Identify the differences in the cost of goods sold section of an income statement between a merchandising company and a manufacturing company.
15. The determination of the cost of goods manufactured involves the following factors: (A) beginning work in process inventory, (B) total manufacturing costs, and (C) ending work in process inventory. Identify the meaning of x in the following formulas:
(a) $A + B = x$
(b) $A + B - C = x$
16. Ohmie Manufacturing has beginning raw materials inventory $12,000, ending raw materials inventory $15,000, and raw materials purchases $170,000. What is the cost of direct materials used?
17. Neff Manufacturing Inc. has beginning work in process $26,000, direct materials used $240,000, direct labor $200,000, total manufacturing overhead $180,000, and ending work in process $32,000. What are total manufacturing costs?
18. Using the data in Q17, what are (a) the total cost of work in process and (b) the cost of goods manufactured?

19. In what order should manufacturing inventories be listed in a balance sheet?
20. What is the value chain? Describe, in sequence, the main components of a manufacturer's value chain.
21. What is an enterprise resource planning (ERP) system? What are its primary benefits?
22. Why is product quality important for companies that implement a just-in-time inventory system?
23. Explain what is meant by "balanced" in the balanced scorecard approach.
24. What is activity-based costing, and what are its potential benefits?
*25. How, if at all, does the accounting cycle differ between a manufacturing company and a merchandising company?
*26. What typical account balances are carried into the cost of goods manufactured columns of the manufacturing worksheet?
*27. Prepare the closing entries for (a) ending work in process and raw materials inventories and (b) manufacturing summary. Use XXXs for amounts.

BRIEF EXERCISES

Distinguish between managerial and financial accounting.
(SO 1)

BE5-1 Complete the following comparison table between managerial and financial accounting.

	Financial Accounting	Managerial Accounting
Primary users		
Types of reports		
Frequency of reports		
Purpose of reports		
Content of reports		
Verification		

Identify important regulatory changes.
(SO 2)

BE5-2 The Sarbanes-Oxley Act of 2002 (SOX) has important implications for the financial community. Explain two implications of SOX.

Identify the three management functions.
(SO 2)

BE5-3 Listed below are the three functions of the management of an organization.

1. Planning 2. Directing 3. Controlling

Identify which of the following statements best describes each of the above functions.

(a) _____ requires management to look ahead and to establish objectives. A key objective of management is to add value to the business.
(b) _____ involves coordinating the diverse activities and human resources of a company to produce a smooth-running operation. This function relates to the implementation of planned objectives.
(c) _____ is the process of keeping the activities on track. Management must determine whether goals are being met and what changes are necessary when there are deviations.

Classify manufacturing costs.
(SO 3)

BE5-4 Determine whether each of the following costs should be classified as direct materials (DM), direct labor (DL), or manufacturing overhead (MO).

(a) _____ Frames and tires used in manufacturing bicycles.
(b) _____ Wages paid to production workers.
(c) _____ Insurance on factory equipment and machinery.
(d) _____ Depreciation on factory equipment.

Classify manufacturing costs.
(SO 3)

BE5-5 Indicate whether each of the following costs of an automobile manufacturer would be classified as direct materials, direct labor, or manufacturing overhead.

(a) _____ Windshield.
(b) _____ Engine.
(c) _____ Wages of assembly line worker.
(d) _____ Depreciation of factory machinery.
(e) _____ Factory machinery lubricants.
(f) _____ Tires.
(g) _____ Steering wheel.
(h) _____ Salary of painting supervisor.

Identify product and period costs.
(SO 4)

BE5-6 Identify whether each of the following costs should be classified as product costs or period costs.

(a) _____ Manufacturing overhead.
(b) _____ Selling expenses.
(c) _____ Administrative expenses.
(d) _____ Advertising expenses.
(e) _____ Direct labor.
(f) _____ Direct material.

Classify manufacturing costs. (SO 3)

BE5-7 Presented below are Lang Company's monthly manufacturing cost data related to its personal computer products.

(a)	Utilities for manufacturing equipment	$116,000
(b)	Raw material (CPU, chips, etc.)	$ 85,000
(c)	Depreciation on manufacturing building	$880,000
(d)	Wages for production workers	$191,000

Enter each cost item in the following table, placing an "X" under the appropriate headings.

	Product Costs		
	Direct Materials	**Direct Labor**	**Factory Overhead**
(a)			
(b)			
(c)			
(d)			

Compute total manufacturing costs and total cost of work in process. (SO 6)

BE5-8 Francum Manufacturing Company has the following data: direct labor $229,000, direct materials used $180,000, total manufacturing overhead $208,000, and beginning work in process $25,000. Compute (a) total manufacturing costs and (b) total cost of work in process.

Prepare current assets section. (SO 7)

BE5-9 In alphabetical order below are current asset items for Dieker Company's balance sheet at December 31, 2008. Prepare the current assets section (including a complete heading).

Accounts receivable	$200,000
Cash	62,000
Finished goods	71,000
Prepaid expenses	38,000
Raw materials	73,000
Work in process	87,000

Determine missing amounts in computing total manufacturing costs. (SO 6)

BE5-10 Presented below are incomplete manufacturing cost data. Determine the missing amounts for three different situations.

	Direct Materials Used	Direct Labor Used	Factory Overhead	Total Manufacturing Costs
(1)	$25,000	$61,000	$ 50,000	?
(2)	?	$75,000	$140,000	$296,000
(3)	$55,000	?	$111,000	$310,000

Determine missing amounts in computing cost of goods manufactured. (SO 6)

BE5-11 Use the same data from BE5–10 above and the data below. Determine the missing amounts.

	Total Manufacturing Costs	Work in Process (1/1)	Work in Process (12/31)	Cost of Goods Manufactured
(1)	?	$120,000	$82,000	?
(2)	$296,000	?	$98,000	$321,000
(3)	$310,000	$463,000	?	$715,000

Identify worksheet columns for selected accounts. (SO 9)

***BE5-12** Table Manufacturing Company uses a worksheet in preparing financial statements. The following accounts are included in the adjusted trial balance: Finished Goods Inventory $28,000, Work in Process Inventory $21,600, Raw Materials Purchases $175,000, and Direct Labor $140,000. Indicate the worksheet column(s) to which each account should be extended.

EXERCISES

Identify distinguishing features of managerial accounting.
(SO 1)

E5-1 Chris Martin has prepared the following list of statements about managerial accounting and financial accounting.

1. Financial accounting focuses on providing information to internal users.
2. Analyzing cost-volume-profit relationships is part of managerial accounting.
3. Preparation of budgets is part of financial accounting.
4. Managerial accounting applies only to merchandising and manufacturing companies.
5. Both managerial accounting and financial accounting deal with many of the same economic events.
6. Managerial accounting reports are prepared only quarterly and annually.
7. Financial accounting reports are general-purpose reports.
8. Managerial accounting reports pertain to subunits of the business.
9. Managerial accounting reports must comply with generally accepted accounting principles.
10. Although managerial accountants are expected to behave ethically, there is no code of ethical standards for managerial accountants.

Instructions

Identify each statement as true or false. If false, indicate how to correct the statement.

Classify costs into three classes of manufacturing costs.
(SO 3)

E5-2 Presented below is a list of costs and expenses usually incurred by Burrand Corporation, a manufacturer of furniture, in its factory.

1. Salaries for assembly line inspectors.
2. Insurance on factory machines.
3. Property taxes on the factory building.
4. Factory repairs.
5. Upholstery used in manufacturing furniture.
6. Wages paid to assembly line workers.
7. Factory machinery depreciation.
8. Glue, nails, paint, and other small parts used in production.
9. Factory supervisors' salaries.
10. Wood used in manufacturing furniture.

Instructions

Classify the above items into the following categories: (a) direct materials, (b) direct labor, and (c) manufacturing overhead.

Identify types of cost and explain their accounting.
(SO 3, 4)

E5-3 Coldplay Corporation incurred the following costs while manufacturing its product.

Materials used in product	$100,000	Advertising expense	$45,000
Depreciation on plant	60,000	Property taxes on plant	14,000
Property taxes on store	7,500	Delivery expense	21,000
Labor costs of assembly-line workers	110,000	Sales commissions	35,000
Factory supplies used	13,000	Salaries paid to sales clerks	50,000

Instructions

(a) Identify each of the above costs as direct materials, direct labor, manufacturing overhead, or period costs.
(b) Explain the basic difference in accounting for product costs and period costs.

Determine the total amount of various types of costs.
(SO 3, 4),

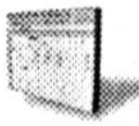

E5-4 Caroline Company reports the following costs and expenses in May.

Factory utilities	$ 11,500	Direct labor	$69,100
Depreciation on factory equipment	12,650	Sales salaries	46,400
Depreciation on delivery trucks	3,800	Property taxes on factory building	2,500
Indirect factory labor	48,900	Repairs to office equipment	1,300
Indirect materials	80,800	Factory repairs	2,000
Direct materials used	137,600	Advertising	18,000
Factory manager's salary	8,000	Office supplies used	2,640

Instructions
From the information, determine the total amount of:

(a) Manufacturing overhead.
(b) Product costs.
(c) Period costs.

Classify various costs into different cost categories.
(SO 3, 4)

E5-5 Sota Company is a manufacturer of personal computers. Various costs and expenses associated with its operations are as follows.

1. Property taxes on the factory building.
2. Production superintendents' salaries.
3. Memory boards and chips used in assembling computers.
4. Depreciation on the factory equipment.
5. Salaries for assembly line quality control inspectors.
6. Sales commissions paid to sell personal computers.
7. Electrical components used in assembling computers.
8. Wages of workers assembling personal computers.
9. Soldering materials used on factory assembly lines.
10. Salaries for the night security guards for the factory building.

The company intends to classify these costs and expenses into the following categories: (a) direct materials, (b) direct labor, (c) manufacturing overhead, and (d) period costs.

Instructions
List the items (1) through (10). For each item, indicate the cost category to which it belongs.

Classify various costs into different cost categories.
(SO 3)

Homework materials related to service companies are indicated by this icon.

E5-6 The administrators of San Diego County's Memorial Hospital are interested in identifying the various costs and expenses that are incurred in producing a patient's X-ray. A list of such costs and expenses in presented below.

1. Salaries for the X-ray machine technicians.
2. Wages for the hospital janitorial personnel.
3. Film costs for the X-ray machines.
4. Property taxes on the hospital building.
5. Salary of the X-ray technicians' supervisor.
6. Electricity costs for the X-ray department.
7. Maintenance and repairs on the X-ray machines.
8. X-ray department supplies.
9. Depreciation on the X-ray department equipment.
10. Depreciation on the hospital building.

The administrators want these costs and expenses classified as: (a) direct materials, (b) direct labor, or (c) service overhead.

Instructions
List the items (1) through (10). For each item, indicate the cost category to which the item belongs.

Classify various costs into different cost categories.
(SO 4)

E5-7 Rapid Delivery Service reports the following costs and expenses in June 2008.

Indirect materials	$ 5,400	Drivers' salaries	$11,000
Depreciation on delivery equipment	11,200	Advertising	1,600
Dispatcher's salary	5,000	Delivery equipment repairs	300
Property taxes on office building	870	Office supplies	650
CEO's salary	12,000	Office utilities	990
Gas and oil for delivery trucks	2,200	Repairs on office equipment	180

Instructions
Determine the total amount of (a) delivery service (product) costs and (b) period costs.

Compute cost of goods manufactured and sold.

(SO 5, 6)

E5-8 Coldplay Corporation incurred the following costs while manufacturing its product.

Materials used in product	$100,000	Advertising expense	$45,000
Depreciation on plant	60,000	Property taxes on plant	14,000
Property taxes on store	7,500	Delivery expense	21,000
Labor costs of assembly-line workers	110,000	Sales commissions	35,000
Factory supplies used	23,000	Salaries paid to sales clerks	50,000

Work-in-process inventory was $12,000 at January 1 and $15,500 at December 31. Finished goods inventory was $60,000 at January 1 and $55,600 at December 31.

Instructions

(a) Compute cost of goods manufactured.

(b) Compute cost of goods sold.

Determine missing amounts in cost of goods manufactured schedule.

(SO 6)

E5-9 An incomplete cost of goods manufactured schedule is presented below.

CEPEDA MANUFACTURING COMPANY
Cost of Goods Manufactured Schedule
For the Year Ended December 31, 2008

Work in process (1/1)			$210,000
Direct materials			
Raw materials inventory (1/1)	$?		
Add: Raw materials purchases	158,000		
Total raw materials available for use	?		
Less: Raw materials inventory (12/31)	12,500		
Direct materials used		$190,000	
Direct labor		?	
Manufacturing overhead			
Indirect labor	$ 18,000		
Factory depreciation	36,000		
Factory utilities	68,000		
Total overhead		122,000	
Total manufacturing costs			?
Total cost of work in process			?
Less: Work in process (12/31)			81,000
Cost of goods manufactured			$510,000

Instructions

Complete the cost of goods manufactured schedule for Cepeda Manufacturing Company.

Determine the missing amount of different cost items.

(SO 6)

E5-10 Manufacturing cost data for Criqui Company are presented below.

	Case A	Case B	Case C
Direct materials used	(a)	$58,400	$130,000
Direct labor	$ 57,000	86,000	(g)
Manufacturing overhead	46,500	81,600	102,000
Total manufacturing costs	185,650	(d)	253,700
Work in process 1/1/08	(b)	16,500	(h)
Total cost of work in process	221,500	(e)	337,000
Work in process 12/31/08	(c)	11,000	70,000
Cost of goods manufactured	185,275	(f)	(i)

Instructions

Indicate the missing amount for each letter (a) through (i).

Determine the missing amount of different cost items, and prepare a condensed cost of goods manufactured schedule.

(SO 6)

E5-11 Incomplete manufacturing cost data for Ikerd Company for 2008 are presented as follows for four different situations.

	Direct Materials Used	Direct Labor Used	Manufacturing Overhead	Total Manufacturing Costs	Work in Process 1/1	Work in Process 12/31	Cost of Goods Manufactured
(1)	$127,000	$140,000	$ 77,000	(a)	$33,000	(b)	$360,000
(2)	(c)	200,000	132,000	$450,000	(d)	$40,000	470,000
(3)	80,000	100,000	(e)	245,000	60,000	80,000	(f)
(4)	70,000	(g)	75,000	288,000	45,000	(h)	270,000

Instructions

(a) Indicate the missing amount for each letter.

(b) Prepare a condensed cost of goods manufactured schedule for situation (1) for the year ended December 31, 2008.

E5-12 Aikman Corporation has the following cost records for June 2008.

Prepare a cost of goods manufactured schedule and a partial income statement.

(SO 5, 6)

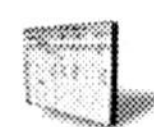

Indirect factory labor	$ 4,500	Factory utilities	$ 400
Direct materials used	20,000	Depreciation, factory equipment	1,400
Work in process, 6/1/08	3,000	Direct labor	30,000
Work in process, 6/30/08	3,800	Maintenance, factory equipment	1,800
Finished goods, 6/1/08	5,000	Indirect materials	2,200
Finished goods, 6/30/08	7,500	Factory manager's salary	3,000

Instructions

(a) Prepare a cost of goods manufactured schedule for June 2008.

(b) Prepare an income statement through gross profit for June 2008 assuming net sales are $87,100.

E5-13 Sara Collier, the bookkeeper for Danner, Cheney, and Howe, a political consulting firm, has recently completed a managerial accounting course at her local college. One of the topics covered in the course was the cost of goods manufactured schedule. Sara wondered if such a schedule could be prepared for her firm. She realized that, as a service-oriented company, it would have no Work-in-Process inventory to consider.

Classify various costs into different categories and prepare cost of services provided schedule.

(SO 4, 5, 6)

Listed below are the costs her firm incurred for the month ended August 31, 2008.

Supplies used on consulting contracts	$ 1,200
Supplies used in the administrative offices	1,500
Depreciation on equipment used for contract work	900
Depreciation used on administrative office equipment	1,050
Salaries of professionals working on contracts	12,600
Salaries of administrative office personnel	7,700
Janitorial services for professional offices	400
Janitorial services for administrative offices	500
Insurance on contract operations	800
Insurance on administrative operations	900
Utilities for contract operations	1,400
Utilities for administrative offices	1,300

Instructions

(a) Prepare a schedule of cost of contract services provided (similar to a cost of goods manufactured schedule) for the month.

(b) For those costs not included in (a), explain how they would be classified and reported in the financial statements.

E5-14 The following information is available for Sassafras Company.

Prepare a cost of goods manufactured schedule and a partial income statement.

(SO 5, 6, 7)

	January 1, 2008	2008	December 31, 2008
Raw materials inventory	$ 21,000		$30,000
Work in process inventory	13,500		17,200
Finished goods inventory	27,000		21,000
Materials purchased		$150,000	
Direct labor		200,000	
Manufacturing overhead		180,000	
Sales		900,000	

Instructions

(a) Compute cost of goods manufactured.

(b) Prepare an income statement through gross profit.

(c) Show the presentation of the ending inventories on the December 31, 2008 balance sheet.

(d) How would the income statement and balance sheet of a merchandising company be different from Sassafras's financial statements?

Indicate in which schedule or financial statement(s) different cost items will appear.

(SO 5, 6, 7)

E5-15 Corbin Manufacturing Company produces blankets. From its accounting records it prepares the following schedule and financial statements on a yearly basis.

(a) Cost of goods manufactured schedule.

(b) Income statement.

(c) Balance sheet.

The following items are found in its ledger and accompanying data.

1. Direct labor
2. Raw materials inventory, 1/1
3. Work in process inventory, 12/31
4. Finished goods inventory, 1/1
5. Indirect labor
6. Depreciation on factory machinery
7. Work in process, 1/1
8. Finished goods inventory, 12/31
9. Factory maintenance salaries
10. Cost of goods manufactured
11. Depreciation on delivery equipment
12. Cost of goods available for sale
13. Direct materials used
14. Heat and electricity for factory
15. Repairs to roof of factory building
16. Cost of raw materials purchases

Instructions

List the items (1)–(16). For each item, indicate by using the appropriate letter or letters, the schedule and/or financial statement(s) in which the item will appear.

Prepare a cost of goods manufactured schedule, and present the ending inventories of the balance sheet.

(SO 6, 7)

E5-16 An analysis of the accounts of Chamberlin Manufacturing reveals the following manufacturing cost data for the month ended June 30, 2008.

Inventories	Beginning	Ending
Raw materials	$9,000	$13,100
Work in process	5,000	7,000
Finished goods	9,000	6,000

Costs incurred: Raw materials purchases $54,000, direct labor $57,000, manufacturing overhead $19,900. The specific overhead costs were: indirect labor $5,500, factory insurance $4,000, machinery depreciation $4,000, machinery repairs $1,800, factory utilities $3,100, miscellaneous factory costs $1,500. Assume that all raw materials used were direct materials.

Instructions

(a) Prepare the cost of goods manufactured schedule for the month ended June 30, 2008.

(b) Show the presentation of the ending inventories on the June 30, 2008, balance sheet.

Determine the amount of cost to appear in various accounts, and indicate in which financial statements these accounts would appear.

(SO 5, 6, 7)

E5-17 Todd Motor Company manufactures automobiles. During September 2008 the company purchased 5,000 head lamps at a cost of $9 per lamp. Todd withdrew 4,650 lamps from the warehouse during the month. Fifty of these lamps were used to replace the head lamps in autos used by traveling sales staff. The remaining 4,600 lamps were put in autos manufactured during the month.

Of the autos put into production during September 2008, 90% were completed and transferred to the company's storage lot. Of the cars completed during the month, 75% were sold by September 30.

Instructions

(a) Determine the cost of head lamps that would appear in each of the following accounts at September 30, 2008: Raw Materials, Work in Process, Finished Goods, Cost of Goods Sold, and Selling Expenses.

(b) Write a short memo to the chief accountant, indicating whether and where each of the accounts in (a) would appear on the income statement or on the balance sheet at September 30, 2008.

E5-18 The following is a list of terms related to managerial accounting practices.

Identify various managerial accounting practices.

(SO 8)

1. Activity-based costing.
2. Just-in-time inventory.
3. Balanced scorecard.
4. Value chain.

Instructions

Match each of the terms with the statement below that best describes the term.

(a) ____ A performance-measurement technique that attempts to consider and evaluate all aspects of performance using financial and nonfinancial measures in an integrated fashion.

(b) ____ The group of activities associated with providing a product or service.

(c) ____ An approach used to reduce the cost associated with handling and holding inventory by reducing the amount of inventory on hand.

(d) ____ A method used to allocate overhead to products based on each product's use of the activities that cause the incurrence of the overhead cost.

***E5-19** Data for Chamberlin Manufacturing are presented in E5-16.

Prepare a partial worksheet for a manufacturing firm.

(SO 9)

Instructions

Beginning with the adjusted trial balance, prepare a partial worksheet for Chamberlin Manufacturing using the format shown in Illustration 5A-2.

EXERCISES: SET B

Visit the book's website at **www.wiley.com/college/weygandt**, and choose the Student Companion site, to access Exercise Set B.

PROBLEMS: SET A

P5-1A Bjerg Company specializes in manufacturing a unique model of bicycle helmet. The model is well accepted by consumers, and the company has enough orders to keep the factory production at 10,000 helmets per month (80% of its full capacity). Bjerg's monthly manufacturing cost and other expense data are as follows.

Classify manufacturing costs into different categories and compute the unit cost.

(SO 3, 4)

Rent on factory equipment	$ 7,000
Insurance on factory building	1,500
Raw materials (plastics, polystyrene, etc.)	75,000
Utility costs for factory	900
Supplies for general office	300
Wages for assembly line workers	43,000
Depreciation on office equipment	800
Miscellaneous materials (glue, thread, etc.)	1,100
Factory manager's salary	5,700
Property taxes on factory building	400
Advertising for helmets	14,000
Sales commissions	7,000
Depreciation on factory building	1,500

Marginal check figures for parts of some problems, in most chapters, provide key numbers to confirm that you are on the right track in your computations.

(a) DM $75,000
DL $43,000
MO $18,100
PC $22,100

Instructions

(a) Prepare an answer sheet with the following column headings.

	Product Costs			
Cost Item	Direct Materials	Direct Labor	Manufacturing Overhead	Period Costs

Enter each cost item on your answer sheet, placing the dollar amount under the appropriate headings. Total the dollar amounts in each of the columns.

(b) Compute the cost to produce one helmet

Classify manufacturing costs into different categories and compute the unit cost.

(SO 3, 4)

P5-2A Copa Company, a manufacturer of stereo systems, started its production in October 2008. For the preceding 3 years Copa had been a retailer of stereo systems. After a thorough survey of stereo system markets, Copa decided to turn its retail store into a stereo equipment factory.

Raw materials cost for a stereo system will total $74 per unit. Workers on the production lines are on average paid $12 per hour. A stereo system usually takes 5 hours to complete. In addition, the rent on the equipment used to assemble stereo systems amounts to $4,900 per month. Indirect materials cost $5 per system. A supervisor was hired to oversee production; her monthly salary is $3,000.

Factory janitorial costs are $1,300 monthly. Advertising costs for the stereo system will be $8,500 per month. The factory building depreciation expense is $7,200 per year. Property taxes on the factory building will be $9,000 per year.

(a) DM $96,200
DL $78,000
MO $17,050
PC $ 8,500

Instructions

(a) Prepare an answer sheet with the following column headings.

	Product Costs			
Cost Item	Direct Materials	Direct Labor	Manufacturing Overhead	Period Costs

Assuming that Copa manufactures, on average, 1,300 stereo systems per month, enter each cost item on your answer sheet, placing the dollar amount per month under the appropriate headings. Total the dollar amounts in each of the columns.

(b) Compute the cost to produce one stereo system.

Indicate the missing amount of different cost items, and prepare a condensed cost of goods manufactured schedule, an income statement, and a partial balance sheet.

(SO 5, 6, 7)

P5-3A Incomplete manufacturing costs, expenses, and selling data for two different cases are as follows.

	Case	
	1	2
Direct Materials Used	$ 7,600	$ (g)
Direct Labor	5,000	8,000
Manufacturing Overhead	8,000	4,000
Total Manufacturing Costs	(a)	18,000
Beginning Work in Process Inventory	1,000	(h)
Ending Work in Process Inventory	(b)	3,000
Sales	24,500	(i)
Sales Discounts	2,500	1,400
Cost of Goods Manufactured	17,000	22,000
Beginning Finished Goods Inventory	(c)	3,300
Goods Available for Sale	18,000	(j)
Cost of Goods Sold	(d)	(k)
Ending Finished Goods Inventory	3,400	2,500
Gross Profit	(e)	7,000
Operating Expenses	2,500	(l)
Net Income	(f)	5,000

Instructions

(a) Indicate the missing amount for each letter.

(b) Ending WIP $4,600

(b) Prepare a condensed cost of goods manufactured schedule for Case 1.

(c) Prepare an income statement and the current assets section of the balance sheet for Case 1. Assume that in Case 1 the other items in the current assets section are as follows: Cash $4,000, Receivables (net) $15,000, Raw Materials $600, and Prepaid Expenses $400.

(c) Current assets $28,000

P5-4A The following data were taken from the records of Stellar Manufacturing Company for the fiscal year ended June 30, 2008.

Prepare a cost of goods manufactured schedule, a partial income statement, and a partial balance sheet.

(SO 5, 6, 7)

Raw Materials Inventory 7/1/07	$ 48,000	Factory Insurance	$ 4,600
Raw Materials Inventory 6/30/08	39,600	Factory Machinery Depreciation	16,000
Finished Goods Inventory 7/1/07	96,000	Factory Utilities	27,600
Finished Goods Inventory 6/30/08	95,900	Office Utilities Expense	8,650
Work in Process Inventory 7/1/07	19,800	Sales	554,000
Work in Process Inventory 6/30/08	18,600	Sales Discounts	4,200
Direct Labor	149,250	Plant Manager's Salary	29,000
Indirect Labor	24,460	Factory Property Taxes	9,600
Accounts Receivable	27,000	Factory Repairs	1,400
		Raw Materials Purchases	96,400
		Cash	32,000

Instructions

(a) Prepare a cost of goods manufactured schedule. (Assume all raw materials used were direct materials.)

(b) Prepare an income statement through gross profit.

(c) Prepare the current assets section of the balance sheet at June 30, 2008.

(a) CGM $367,910

(b) Gross profit $181,790

(c) Current assets $213,100

P5-5A Tombert Company is a manufacturer of computers. Its controller resigned in October 2008. An inexperienced assistant accountant has prepared the following income statement for the month of October 2008.

Prepare a cost of goods manufactured schedule and a correct income statement.

(SO 5, 6)

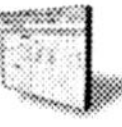

TOMBERT COMPANY
Income Statement
For the Month Ended October 31, 2008

Sales (net)		$780,000
Less: Operating expenses		
Raw materials purchases	$264,000	
Direct labor cost	190,000	
Advertising expense	90,000	
Selling and administrative salaries	75,000	
Rent on factory facilities	60,000	
Depreciation on sales equipment	45,000	
Depreciation on factory equipment	31,000	
Indirect labor cost	28,000	
Utilities expense	12,000	
Insurance expense	8,000	803,000
Net loss		$(23,000)

Prior to October 2008 the company had been profitable every month. The company's president is concerned about the accuracy of the income statement. As his friend, you have been asked to review the income statement and make necessary corrections. After examining other manufacturing cost data, you have acquired additional information as follows.

1. Inventory balances at the beginning and end of October were:

	October 1	October 31
Raw materials	$18,000	$34,000
Work in process	16,000	14,000
Finished goods	30,000	48,000

2. Only 70% of the utilities expense and 60% of the insurance expense apply to factory operations. The remaining amounts should be charged to selling and administrative activities.

(a) CGM $572,200
(b) NI $ 9,000

Instructions

(a) Prepare a schedule of cost of goods manufactured for October 2008.
(b) Prepare a correct income statement for October 2008.

Complete a worksheet; prepare a cost of goods manufactured schedule, an income statement, and a balance sheet; journalize and post the closing entries.

(SO 9)

***P5-6A** Medina Manufacturing Company uses a simple manufacturing accounting system. At the end of its fiscal year on August 31, 2008, the adjusted trial balance contains the following accounts.

Debits		Credits	
Cash	$ 16,700	Accumulated Depreciation	$353,000
Accounts Receivable (net)	62,900	Notes Payable	45,000
Finished Goods Inventory	56,000	Accounts Payable	36,200
Work in Process Inventory	27,800	Income Taxes Payable	9,000
Raw Materials Inventory	37,200	Common Stock	352,000
Plant Assets	890,000	Retained Earnings	205,300
Raw Materials Purchases	236,500	Sales	998,000
Direct Labor	283,900		$1,998,500
Indirect Labor	27,400		
Factory Repairs	17,200		
Factory Depreciation	16,000		
Factory Manager's Salary	40,000		
Factory Insurance	11,000		
Factory Property Taxes	14,900		
Factory Utilities	13,300		
Selling Expenses	96,500		
Administrative Expenses	115,200		
Income Tax Expense	36,000		
	$1,998,500		

Physical inventory accounts on August 31, 2008, show the following inventory amounts: Finished Goods $50,600, Work in Process $23,400, and Raw Materials $44,500.

Instructions

(a) Enter the adjusted trial balance data on a worksheet in financial statement order and complete the worksheet.

(b) CGM $657,300
(c) NI $ 87,600

(b) Prepare a cost of goods manufactured schedule for the year.
(c) Prepare an income statement for the year and a balance sheet at August 31, 2008.
(d) Journalize the closing entries.
(e) Post the closing entries to Manufacturing Summary and to Income Summary.

PROBLEMS: SET B

Classify manufacturing costs into different categories and compute the unit cost.

(SO 3, 4)

P5-1B Hite Company specializes in manufacturing motorcycle helmets. The company has enough orders to keep the factory production at 1,000 motorcycle helmets per month. Hite's monthly manufacturing cost and other expense data are as follows.

Maintenance costs on factory building	$ 600
Factory manager's salary	4,000
Advertising for helmets	8,000
Sales commissions	3,000
Depreciation on factory building	700
Rent on factory equipment	6,000
Insurance on factory building	3,000
Raw materials (plastic, polystyrene, etc.)	20,000
Utility costs for factory	800
Supplies for general office	200
Wages for assembly line workers	44,000
Depreciation on office equipment	500
Miscellaneous materials (glue, thread, etc.)	2,000

Instructions

(a) Prepare an answer sheet with the following column headings.

(a) DM $20,000
DL $44,000
MO $17,100
PC $11,700

	Product Costs			
Cost Item	Direct Materials	Direct Labor	Manufacturing Overhead	Period Costs

Enter each cost item on your answer sheet, placing the dollar amount under the appropriate headings. Total the dollar amounts in each of the columns.

(b) Compute the cost to produce one motorcycle helmet.

Classify manufacturing costs into different categories and compute the unit cost.

(SO 3, 4)

P5-2B Ladoca Company, a manufacturer of tennis rackets, started production in November 2008. For the preceding 5 years Ladoca had been a retailer of sports equipment. After a thorough survey of tennis racket markets, Ladoca decided to turn its retail store into a tennis racket factory.

Raw materials cost for a tennis racket will total $23 per racket. Workers on the production lines are paid on average $13 per hour. A racket usually takes 2 hours to complete. In addition, the rent on the equipment used to produce rackets amounts to $1,300 per month. Indirect materials cost $3 per racket. A supervisor was hired to oversee production; her monthly salary is $3,500.

Factory janitorial costs are $1,400 monthly. Advertising costs for the rackets will be $6,000 per month. The factory building depreciation expense is $8,400 per year. Property taxes on the factory building will be $5,400 per year.

Instructions

(a) Prepare an answer sheet with the following column headings.

(a) DM $46,000
DL $52,000
MO $13,350
PC $ 6,000

	Product Costs			
Cost Item	Direct Materials	Direct Labor	Manufacturing Overhead	Period Costs

Assuming that Ladoca manufactures, on average, 2,000 tennis rackets per month, enter each cost item on your answer sheet, placing the dollar amount per month under the appropriate headings. Total the dollar amounts in each of the columns.

(b) Compute the cost to produce one racket.

Indicate the missing amount of different cost items, and prepare a condensed cost of goods manufactured schedule, an income statement, and a partial balance sheet.

(SO 5, 6, 7)

P5-3B Incomplete manufacturing costs, expenses, and selling data for two different cases are as follows.

	Case 1	Case 2
Direct Materials Used	$ 8,300	$ (g)
Direct Labor	3,000	4,000
Manufacturing Overhead	6,000	5,000
Total Manufacturing Costs	(a)	18,000
Beginning Work in Process Inventory	1,000	(h)
Ending Work in Process Inventory	(b)	2,000
Sales	22,500	(i)
Sales Discounts	1,500	1,200
Cost of Goods Manufactured	15,800	20,000
Beginning Finished Goods Inventory	(c)	4,000
Goods Available for Sale	17,300	(j)
Cost of Goods Sold	(d)	(k)
Ending Finished Goods Inventory	1,200	2,500
Gross Profit	(e)	6,000
Operating Expenses	2,700	(l)
Net Income	(f)	3,200

Instructions

(a) Indicate the missing amount for each letter.

(b) Prepare a condensed cost of goods manufactured schedule for Case 1.

(c) Prepare an income statement and the current assets section of the balance sheet for Case 1. Assume that in Case 1 the other items in the current assets section are as follows: Cash $3,000, Receivables (net) $10,000, Raw Materials $700, and Prepaid Expenses $200.

(c) Current assets $17,600

Prepare a cost of goods manufactured schedule, a partial income statement, and a partial balance sheet.

(SO 5, 6, 7)

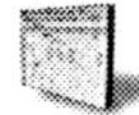

P5-4B The following data were taken from the records of Ruiz Manufacturing Company for the year ended December 31, 2008.

Raw Materials Inventory 1/1/08	$ 47,000	Factory Insurance	$ 7,400
Raw Materials Inventory 12/31/08	44,200	Factory Machinery Depreciation	7,700
		Factory Utilities	12,900
Finished Goods Inventory 1/1/08	85,000	Office Utilities Expense	8,600
		Sales	475,000
Finished Goods Inventory 12/31/08	77,800	Sales Discounts	2,500
		Plant Manager's Salary	30,000
Work in Process Inventory 1/1/08	9,500	Factory Property Taxes	6,100
		Factory Repairs	800
Work in Process Inventory 12/31/08	8,000	Raw Materials Purchases	67,500
		Cash	28,000
Direct Labor	145,100		
Indirect Labor	18,100		
Accounts Receivable	27,000		

Instructions

(a) CGM $299,900

(b) Gross profit $165,400

(c) Current assets $185,000

(a) Prepare a cost of goods manufactured schedule. (Assume all raw materials used were direct materials.)

(b) Prepare an income statement through gross profit.

(c) Prepare the current assets section of the balance sheet at December 31.

Prepare a cost of goods manufactured schedule and a correct income statement.

(SO 5, 6)

P5-5B Agler Company is a manufacturer of toys. Its controller, Joyce Rotzen, resigned in August 2008. An inexperienced assistant accountant has prepared the following income statement for the month of August 2008.

AGLER COMPANY
Income Statement
For the Month Ended August 31, 2008

Sales (net)		$675,000
Less: Operating expenses		
Raw materials purchases	$200,000	
Direct labor cost	160,000	
Advertising expense	75,000	
Selling and administrative salaries	70,000	
Rent on factory facilities	60,000	
Depreciation on sales equipment	50,000	
Depreciation on factory equipment	35,000	
Indirect labor cost	20,000	
Utilities expense	10,000	
Insurance expense	5,000	685,000
Net loss		$(10,000)

Prior to August 2008 the company had been profitable every month. The company's president is concerned about the accuracy of the income statement. As her friend, you have been asked to review the income statement and make necessary corrections. After examining other manufacturing cost data, you have acquired additional information as follows.

1. Inventory balances at the beginning and end of August were:

	August 1	August 31
Raw materials	$19,500	$30,000
Work in process	25,000	21,000
Finished goods	40,000	64,000

2. Only 60% of the utilities expense and 70% of the insurance expense apply to factory operations; the remaining amounts should be charged to selling and administrative activities.

Instructions

(a) Prepare a cost of goods manufactured schedule for August 2008.

(b) Prepare a correct income statement for August 2008.

(a) CGM $478,000
(b) NI $ 20,500

PROBLEMS: SET C

Visit the book's website at **www.wiley.com/college/weygandt**, and choose the Student Companion site, to access Problem Set C.

WATERWAYS CONTINUING PROBLEM

(*Note:* The Waterways Problem begins in Chapter 5 and continues in later chapters. You can also find this problem at the book's Student Companion site.)

The Waterways Problem starts in this chapter and continues in every chapter. You will find the complete problem for each chapter at the book's companion website.

WCP5 Waterways Corporation is a private corporation formed for the purpose of providing the products and the services needed to irrigate farms, parks, commercial projects, and private lawns. It has a centrally located factory in a U.S. city that manufactures the products it markets to retail outlets across the nation. It also maintains a division that provides installation and warranty servicing in six metropolitan areas.

The mission of Waterways is to manufacture quality parts that can be used for effective irrigation projects that also conserve water. By that effort, the company hopes to satisfy its customers, provide rapid and responsible service, and serve the community and the employees who represent them in each community.

The company has been growing rapidly, so management is considering new ideas to help the company continue its growth and maintain the high quality of its products.

Waterways was founded by Will Winkman, who is the company president and chief executive officer (CEO). Working with him from the company's inception was Will's brother, Ben, whose sprinkler designs and ideas about the installation of proper systems have been a major basis of the company's success. Ben is the vice president who oversees all aspects of design and production in the company.

The factory itself is managed by Todd Senter who hires his line managers to supervise the factory employees. The factory makes all of the parts for the irrigation systems. The purchasing department is managed by Hector Hines.

The installation and training division is overseen by vice president Henry Writer, who supervises the managers of the six local installation operations. Each of these local managers hires his or her own local service people. These service employees are trained by the home office under Henry Writer's direction because of the uniqueness of the company's products.

There is a small human resources department under the direction of Sally Fenton, a vice president who handles the employee paperwork, though hiring is actually performed by the separate departments. Sam Totter is the vice president who heads the sales and marketing area; he oversees 10 well-trained salespeople.

The accounting and finance division of the company is headed by Abe Headman, who is the chief financial officer (CFO) and a company vice president; he is a member of the Institute of Management Accountants and holds a certificate in management accounting. He has a small staff of Certified Public Accountants, including a controller and a treasurer, and a staff of accounting input operators who maintain the financial records.

A partial list of Waterway's accounts and their balances for the month of November follows.

Accounts Receivable	$295,000
Advertising Expenses	54,000
Cash	260,000
Depreciation—Factory Equipment	16,800
Depreciation—Office Equipment	2,500
Direct Labor	22,000
Factory Supplies Used	16,850

(*Continued*)

Factory Utilities	10,200
Finished Goods Inventory, November 30	68,300
Finished Goods Inventory, October 31	72,550
Indirect Labor	48,000
Office Supplies Expense	1,400
Other Administrative Expenses	72,000
Prepaid Expenses	41,250
Raw Materials Inventory, November 30	52,700
Raw Materials Inventory, October 31	38,000
Raw Materials Purchases	185,400
Rent—Factory Equipment	47,000
Repairs—Factory Equipment	4,200
Salaries	325,000
Sales	1,350,000
Sales Commissions	40,500
Work in Process Inventory, October 31	52,900
Work in Process Inventory, November 30	42,000

Instructions

(a) Based on the information given, construct an organizational chart of Waterways Corporation

(b) A list of accounts and their values are given above. From this information, prepare a cost of goods manufactured schedule, an income statement, and a partial balance sheet for Waterways Corporation for the month of November.

BROADENING YOUR PERSPECTIVE

DECISION MAKING ACROSS THE ORGANIZATION

BYP5-1 Mismatch Manufacturing Company specializes in producing fashion outfits. On July 31, 2008, a tornado touched down at its factory and general office. The inventories in the warehouse and the factory were completely destroyed as was the general office nearby. Next morning, through a careful search of the disaster site, however, Ross Clarkson, the company's controller, and Catherine Harper, the cost accountant, were able to recover a small part of manufacturing cost data for the current month.

"What a horrible experience," sighed Ross. "And the worst part is that we may not have enough records to use in filing an insurance claim."

"It was terrible," replied Catherine. "However, I managed to recover some of the manufacturing cost data that I was working on yesterday afternoon. The data indicate that our direct labor cost in July totaled $240,000 and that we had purchased $345,000 of raw materials. Also, I recall that the amount of raw materials used for July was $350,000. But I'm not sure this information will help. The rest of our records are blown away."

"Well, not exactly," said Ross. "I was working on the year-to-date income statement when the tornado warning was announced. My recollection is that our sales in July were $1,260,000 and our gross profit ratio has been 40% of sales. Also, I can remember that our cost of goods available for sale was $770,000 for July."

"Maybe we can work something out from this information!" exclaimed Catherine. "My experience tells me that our manufacturing overhead is usually 60% of direct labor."

"Hey, look what I just found," cried Catherine. "It's a copy of this June's balance sheet, and it shows that our inventories as of June 30 are Finished goods $38,000, Work in process $25,000, and Raw materials $19,000."

"Super," yelled Ross. "Let's go work something out."

In order to file an insurance claim, Mismatch Company must determine the amount of its inventories as of July 31, 2008, the date of the tornado touchdown.

Instructions

With the class divided into groups, determine the amount of cost in the Raw Materials, Work in Process, and Finished Goods inventory accounts as of the date of the tornado touchdown.

MANAGERIAL ANALYSIS

BYP5-2 Love All is a fairly large manufacturing company located in the southern United States. The company manufactures tennis rackets, tennis balls, tennis clothing, and tennis shoes, all bearing the company's distinctive logo, a large green question mark on a white flocked tennis ball. The company's sales have been increasing over the past 10 years.

The tennis racket division has recently implemented several advanced manufacturing techniques. Robot arms hold the tennis rackets in place while glue dries, and machine vision systems check for defects. The engineering and design team uses computerized drafting and testing of new products. The following managers work in the tennis racket division.

Andre Agassi, Sales Manager (supervises all sales representatives).
Serena Williams, technical specialist (supervises computer programmers).
Pete Sampras, cost accounting manager (supervises cost accountants).
Andy Roddick, production supervisor (supervises all manufacturing employees).
Venus Williams, engineer (supervises all new-product design teams).

Instructions

(a) What are the primary information needs of each manager?
(b) Which, if any, financial accounting report(s) is each likely to use?
(c) Name one special-purpose management accounting report that could be designed for each manager. Include the name of the report, the information it would contain, and how frequently it should be issued.

REAL-WORLD FOCUS

BYP5-3 Anchor Glass Container Corporation, the third largest manufacturer of glass containers in the U.S., supplies beverage and food producers and consumer products manufacturers nationwide. Parent company Consumers Packaging Inc. *(Toronto Stock Exchange:* CGC) is a leading international designer and manufacturer of glass containers.

The following management discussion appeared in a recent annual report of Anchor Glass.

ANCHOR GLASS CONTAINER CORPORATION
Management Discussion

Cost of Products Sold Cost of products sold as a percentage of net sales was 89.3% in the current year compared to 87.6% in the prior year. The increase in cost of products sold as a percentage of net sales principally reflected the impact of operational problems during the second quarter of the current year at a major furnace at one of the Company's plants, higher downtime, and costs and expenses associated with an increased number of scheduled capital improvement projects, increases in labor, and certain other manufacturing costs (with no corresponding selling price increases in the current year). Reduced fixed costs from the closing of the Streator, Illinois, plant in June of the current year and productivity and efficiency gains partially offset these cost increases.

Instructions

What factors affect the costs of products sold at Anchor Glass Container Corporation?

EXPLORING THE WEB

BYP5-4 The Institute of Management Accountants (IMA) is an organization dedicated to excellence in the practice of management accounting and financial management.

Address: www.imanet.org, or go to **www.wiley.com/college/weygandt**

Instructions

At the IMA's home page, locate the answers to the following questions.

(a) How many members does the IMA have, and what are their job titles?
(b) What are some of the benefits of joining the IMA as a student?
(c) Use the chapter locator function to locate the IMA chapter nearest you, and find the name of the chapter president.

COMMUNICATION ACTIVITY

BYP5-5 Refer to Problem 5–5A and add the following requirement.

Prepare a letter to the president of the company, Sue Tombert, describing the changes you made. Explain clearly why net income is different after the changes. Keep the following points in mind as you compose your letter.

1. This is a letter to the president of a company, who is your friend. The style should be generally formal, but you may relax some requirements. For example, you may call the president by her first name.
2. Executives are very busy. Your letter should tell the president your main results first (for example, the amount of net income).
3. You should include brief explanations so that the president can understand the changes you made in the calculations.

ETHICS CASE

BYP5-6 Wayne Terrago, controller for Robbin Industries, was reviewing production cost reports for the year. One amount in these reports continued to bother him—advertising. During the year, the company had instituted an expensive advertising campaign to sell some of its slower-moving products. It was still too early to tell whether the advertising campaign was successful.

There had been much internal debate as how to report advertising cost. The vice president of finance argued that advertising costs should be reported as a cost of production, just like direct materials and direct labor. He therefore recommended that this cost be identified as manufacturing overhead and reported as part of inventory costs until sold. Others disagreed. Terrago believed that this cost should be reported as an expense of the current period, based on the conservatism principle. Others argued that it should be reported as Prepaid Advertising and reported as a current asset.

The president finally had to decide the issue. He argued that these costs should be reported as inventory. His arguments were practical ones. He noted that the company was experiencing financial difficulty and expensing this amount in the current period might jeopardize a planned bond offering. Also, by reporting the advertising costs as inventory rather than as prepaid advertising, less attention would be directed to it by the financial community.

Instructions

(a) Who are the stakeholders in this situation?
(b) What are the ethical issues involved in this situation?
(c) What would you do if you were Wayne Terrago?

"ALL ABOUT YOU" ACTIVITY

BYP5-7 The primary purpose of managerial accounting is to provide information useful for management decisions. Many of the managerial accounting techniques that you learn in this course will be useful for decisions you make in your everyday life.

Instructions

For each of the following managerial accounting techniques, read the definition provided and then provide an example of a personal situation that would benefit from use of this technique.

(a) Break-even analysis.
(b) Budgeting.
(c) Balanced scorecard.
(d) Capital budgeting.

Answers to Insight and Accounting Across the Organization Questions

Even the Best Have to Get Better, p. 224

Q: What are some of the steps that this company has taken in order to ensure that production meets demand?

A: *The company has organized flexible teams, with jobs arranged by the amount of time a task takes. Employees now are multiskilled, so they can switch between tasks and products. Also, the stores now provide sales data more quickly to the manufacturing facility, so that production levels can be changed more quickly to respond to demand.*

How Many Labor Hours to Build a Car?, p. 229

Q: Why might Nissan production require significantly fewer labor hours?

A: *Nissan's U.S. factories are probably newer than those of Daimler-Chrysler and Ford. Newer factories tend to be more highly automated with less reliance on production-line employees.*

Bananas Receive Special Treatment, p. 239

Q: Why is it important to keep track of costs that are incurred to improve product quality?

A: *Most companies are concerned about product quality, but managers need to consider the cost/benefit tradeoff. If you spend too much on improving product quality, your customers might not be willing to pay the price needed to recover costs. Therefore it is very important that Chiquita closely track all of the costs that it incurs to protect the bananas, to ensure that these costs are factored into the price that it ultimately charges for the bananas.*

Authors' Comments on *All About You*: Outsourcing and Jobs, p. 241

This is a difficult decision. While the direct costs of outsourced tax return preparation may in fact be lower, you must also consider other issues: Will the accuracy of the returns be as high? Will your relationships with your customers suffer due to the loss of direct contact? Will customers resent having their personal information shipped overseas? While you may not want to lay off six employees, you also don't want to put your firm at risk by not remaining competitive.

Perhaps one solution would be to outsource the most basic tasks, and then provide training to the six employees so they can perform higher-skilled services such as tax planning. Many of the techniques that you learn in the remaining chapters of this text will help you evaluate the merits of your various options.

Answers to Self-Study Questions

1. b **2.** b **3.** b **4.** c **5.** d **6.** a **7.** c **8.** a **9.** d **10.** d

Remember to go back to the Navigator box on the chapter-opening page and check off your completed work.

Chapter 6

Cost-Volume-Profit

STUDY OBJECTIVES

After studying this chapter, you should be able to:

1. Distinguish between variable and fixed costs.
2. Explain the significance of the relevant range.
3. Explain the concept of mixed costs.
4. List the five components of cost-volume-profit analysis.
5. Indicate what contribution margin is and how it can be expressed.
6. Identify the three ways to determine the break-even point.
7. Give the formulas for determining sales required to earn target net income.
8. Define margin of safety, and give the formulas for computing it.

The Navigator

- Scan **Study Objectives** ☐
- Read **Feature Story** ☐
- Read **Preview** ☐
- Read text and answer **Before You Go On** p. 279 ☐ p. 285 ☐ p. 288 ☐
- Work **Using the Decision Toolkit** ☐
- Review **Summary of Study Objectives** ☐
- Work **Demonstration Problem** ☐
- Answer **Self-Study Questions** ☐
- Complete **Assignments** ☐

Feature Story

GROWING BY LEAPS AND LEOTARDS

When the last of her three children went off to school, Amy began looking for a job. At this same time, her daughter asked to take dance classes. The nearest dance studio was over 20 miles away, and Amy didn't know how she would balance a new job and drive her daughter to dance class. Suddenly it hit her—why not start her own dance studio?

Amy sketched out a business plan: A local church would rent its basement to her for $6 per hour. The size of the basement limited the number of students she could teach, but the rent was low. Insurance for a small studio was $50 per month. Initially she would teach only classes for young kids since that was all she felt qualified to do. She thought she could charge $2.50 for a one-hour class. There was room for eight students per class. She

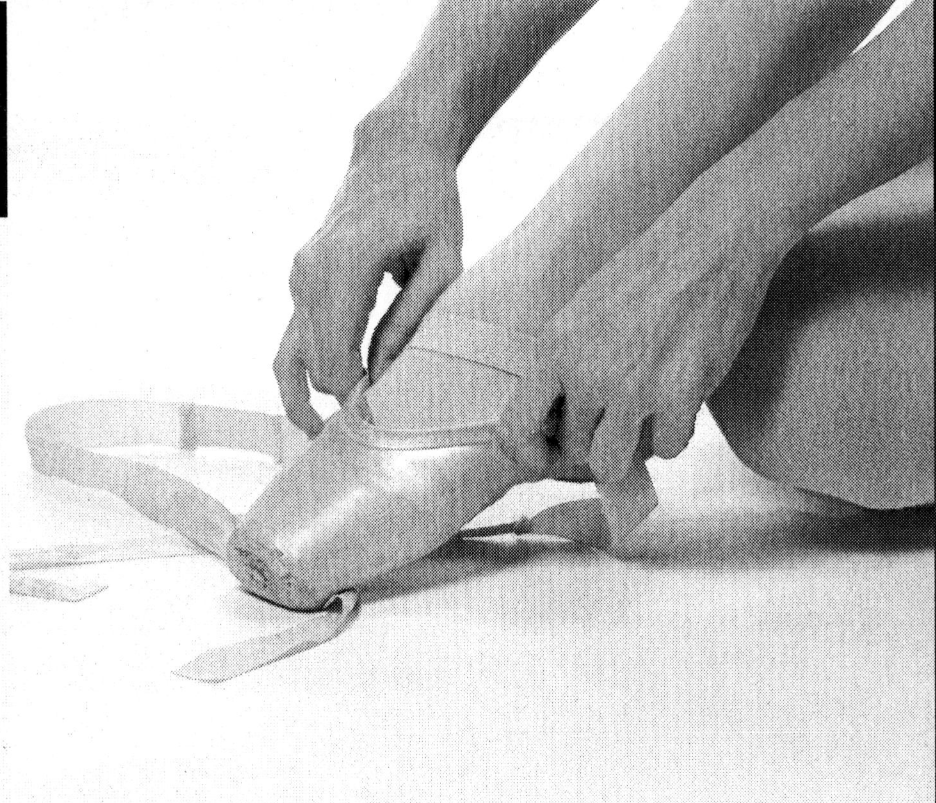

wouldn't get rich—but at least it would be fun, and she didn't have much at risk.

Amy soon realized that the demand for dance classes far exceeded her capacity. She considered renting a bigger space that could serve 15 students per class. But her rent would also increase significantly. Also, rather than paying rent by the hour, she would have to pay $600 per month, even during the summer months when demand for dance classes was low. She also would have to pay utilities—roughly $70 per month.

However, with a bigger space Amy could offer classes for teens and adults. Teens and adults would pay a higher fee—$5 per hour—though the number of students per class would have to be smaller, probably only eight per class. She could hire a part-time instructor at about $18 per hour to teach advanced classes. Insurance costs could increase to $100 per month. In addition, she would need a part-time administrator at $100 per month to keep records. Amy also realized she could increase her income by selling dance supplies such as shoes, towels, and leotards.

Amy laid out a new business plan based on these estimates. If she failed, she stood to lose real money. Convinced she could make a go of it, she made the big plunge.

Her planning paid off: Within 10 years of starting her business in a church basement Amy had over 800 students, seven instructors, two administrators, and a facility with three separate studios.

The Navigator

Inside Chapter 6

- **Woodworker Runs an Efficient Operation for Producing Furniture** (p. 274)
- **Charter Flights Offer a Good Deal** (p. 284)
- **How a Rolling Stones' Tour Makes Money** (p. 288)
- ***All About You:* A Hybrid Dilemma** (p. 289)

Preview of Chapter 6

As the Feature Story indicates, to manage any size business you must understand how costs respond to changes in sales volume and the effect of costs and revenues on profits. A prerequisite to understanding cost-volume-profit (CVP) relationships is knowledge of how costs behave. In this chapter, we first explain the considerations involved in cost behavior analysis. Then we discuss and illustrate CVP analysis.

The content and organization of Chapter 6 are as follows.

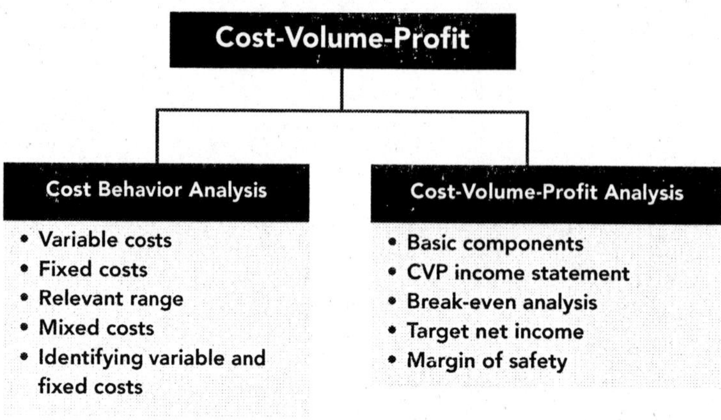

Cost-Volume-Profit
Cost Behavior Analysis
• Variable costs
• Fixed costs
• Relevant range
• Mixed costs
• Identifying variable and fixed costs
Cost-Volume-Profit Analysis
• Basic components
• CVP income statement
• Break-even analysis
• Target net income
• Margin of safety

The Navigator

COST BEHAVIOR ANALYSIS

Cost behavior analysis is the study of how specific costs respond to changes in the level of business activity. As you might expect, some costs change, and others remain the same. For example, for an airline company such as Southwest or United, the longer the flight the higher the fuel costs. On the other hand, Massachusetts General Hospital's costs to staff the emergency room on any given night are relatively constant regardless of the number of patients treated. A knowledge of cost behavior helps management plan operations and decide between alternative courses of action. Cost behavior analysis applies to all types of entities, as the Feature Story about Amy's dance studio indicates.

The starting point in cost behavior analysis is measuring the key business activities. Activity levels may be expressed in terms of sales dollars (in a retail company), miles driven (in a trucking company), room occupancy (in a hotel), or dance classes taught (by a dance studio). Many companies use more than one measurement base. A manufacturer, for example, may use direct labor hours or units of output for manufacturing costs and sales revenue or units sold for selling expenses.

For an activity level to be useful in cost behavior analysis, changes in the level or volume of activity should be correlated with changes in costs. The activity level selected is referred to as the activity (or volume) index. The **activity index** identifies the activity that causes changes in the behavior of costs. With an appropriate activity index, companies can classify the behavior of costs in response to changes in activity levels into three categories: variable, fixed, or mixed.

Variable Costs

STUDY OBJECTIVE 1
Distinguish between variable and fixed costs.

Variable costs are costs that vary **in total** directly and proportionately with changes in the activity level. If the level increases 10%, total variable costs will increase 10%. If the level of activity decreases by 25%, variable costs will decrease 25%. Examples of variable costs include direct materials and direct labor for a manufacturer; cost of goods sold, sales commissions, and freight-out for a merchandiser; and gasoline in airline and trucking companies. A variable cost may also be defined as a cost that **remains the same *per unit* at every level of activity**.

To illustrate the behavior of a variable cost, assume that Damon Company manufactures radios that contain a $10 digital clock. The activity index is the number of radios produced. As Damon manufactures each radio, the total cost of the clocks increases by $10. As part (a) of Illustration 6-1 shows, total cost of the clocks will be $20,000 if Damon produces 2,000 radios, and $100,000 when it produces 10,000 radios. We also can see that a variable cost remains the same per unit as the level of activity changes. As part (b) of Illustration 6-1 shows, the unit cost of $10 for the clocks is the same whether Damon produces 2,000 or 10,000 radios.

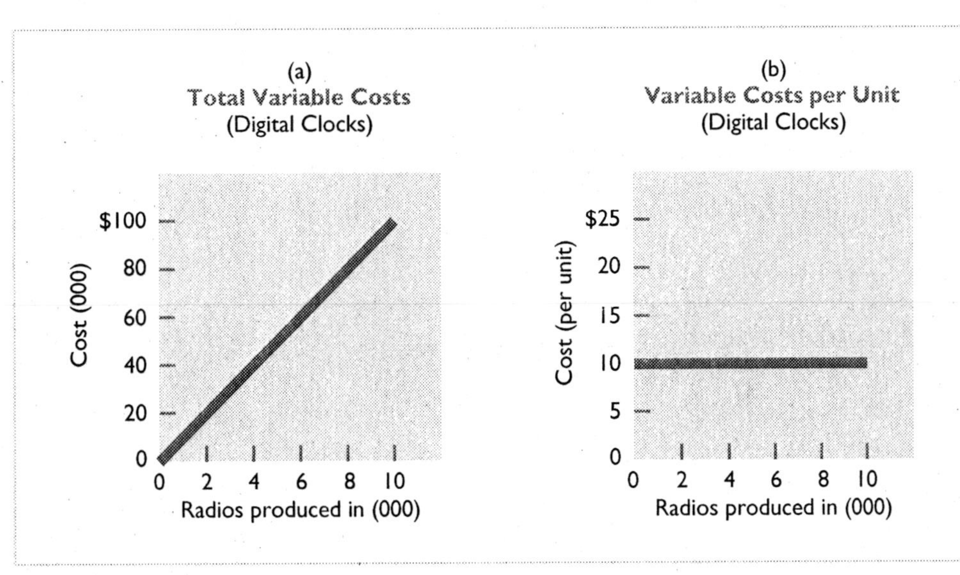

Illustration 6-1
Behavior of total and unit variable costs

HELPFUL HINT
True or false: **Variable cost per unit changes directly and proportionately with changes in activity.**
Answer: **False. Per unit cost remains constant at all levels of activity.**

Companies that rely heavily on labor to manufacture a product, such as Nike or Reebok, or to provide a service, such as Hilton or Marriott, are likely to have many variable costs. In contrast, companies that use a high proportion of machinery and equipment in producing revenue, such as AT&T or Duke Energy Co., may have few variable costs.

Fixed Costs

Fixed costs are costs that **remain the same in total** regardless of changes in the activity level. Examples include property taxes, insurance, rent, supervisory salaries, and depreciation on buildings and equipment. Because total fixed costs remain constant as activity changes, it follows that **fixed costs *per unit* vary inversely with activity: As volume increases, unit cost declines, and vice versa**.

To illustrate the behavior of fixed costs, assume that Damon Company leases its productive facilities at a cost of $10,000 per month. Total fixed costs of the facilities will remain constant at every level of activity, as part (a) of Illustration 6-2 (page 274) shows. But, on a per unit basis, the cost of rent will decline as activity increases, as part (b) of Illustration 6-2 shows. At 2,000 units, the unit cost is $5 ($10,000 ÷ 2,000). When Damon produces 10,000 radios, the unit cost is only $1 ($10,000 ÷ 10,000).

Illustration 6-2
Behavior of total and unit fixed costs

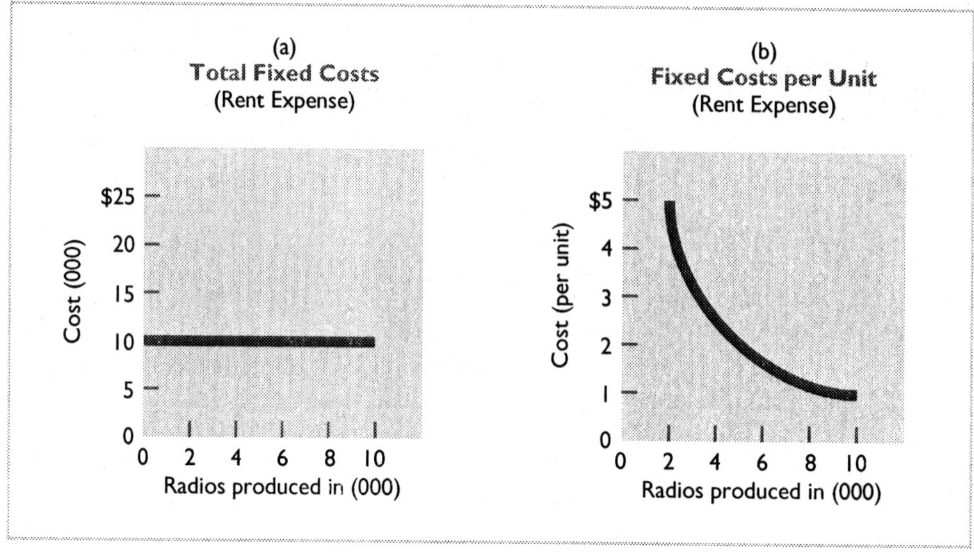

The trend for many manufacturers is to have more fixed costs and fewer variable costs. This trend is the result of increased use of automation and less use of employee labor. As a result, depreciation and lease charges (fixed costs) increase, whereas direct labor costs (variable costs) decrease.

MANAGEMENT INSIGHT

Woodworker Runs an Efficient Operation for Producing Furniture

When Thomas Moser quit teaching communications at Bates College 25 years ago, he turned to what he loved doing—furniture woodworking. Today he has over 120 employees. In a business where profit margins are seldom thicker than wood shavings, cost control is everything. Moser keeps no inventory; he uses customers' 50% deposits on orders to buy the wood. Because computer-driven machines cut most of the standardized parts and joints, "we're free to be inefficient in assembly and finishing work, where the craft is most obviously expressed," says Moser. Direct labor costs are a manageable 30% of revenues. By keeping a tight lid on costs and running an efficient operation, Moser is free to spend most of his time doing what he enjoys most—designing furniture.

Source: Excerpts from "Out of the Woods," *Forbes*, April 5, 1999, p. 74.

Are the costs associated with use of the computer-driven cutting machines fixed or variable?

Relevant Range

STUDY OBJECTIVE 2

Explain the significance of the relevant range.

In Illustration 6-1, part (a) (page 273), a straight line is drawn throughout the entire range of the activity index for total variable costs. In essence, the assumption is that the costs are **linear**. If a relationship is linear (that is, straight-line), then changes in the activity index will result in a direct, proportional change in the variable cost. For example, if the activity level doubles, the cost doubles.

It is now necessary to ask: Is the straight-line relationship realistic? Does the linear assumption produce useful data for CVP analysis?

In most business situations, a straight-line relationship **does not exist** for variable costs throughout the entire range of possible activity. At abnormally low levels of activity, it may be impossible to be cost-efficient. Small-scale operations may not allow the company to obtain quantity discounts for raw materials or to use specialized labor. In contrast, at abnormally high levels of activity, labor costs may increase sharply because of overtime pay. Also at high activity levels, materials costs may jump significantly because of excess spoilage caused by worker fatigue.

As a result, in the real world, the relationship between the behavior of a variable cost and changes in the activity level is often **curvilinear**, as shown in part (a) of Illustration 6-3. In the curved sections of the line, a change in the activity index will not result in a direct, proportional change in the variable cost. That is, a doubling of the activity index will not result in an exact doubling of the variable cost. The variable cost may more than double, or it may be less than double.

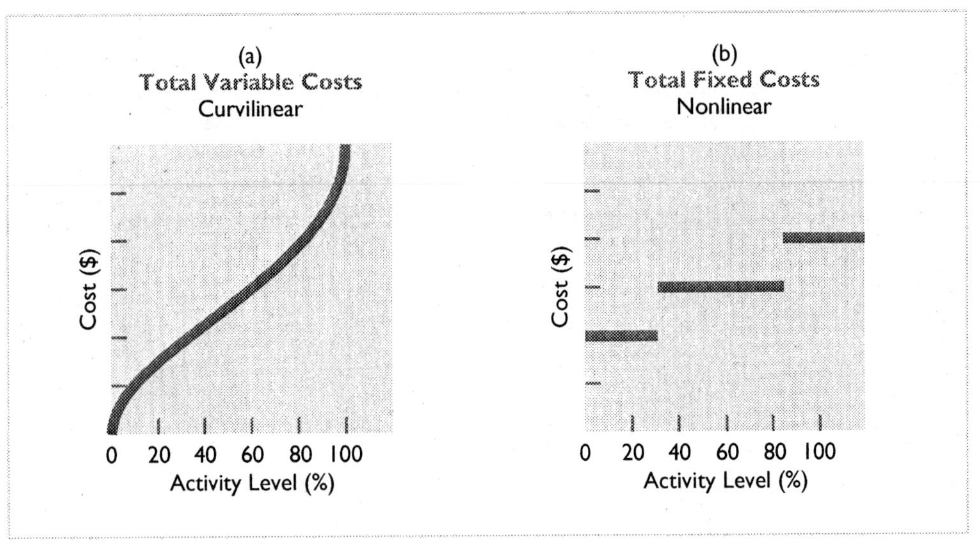

Illustration 6-3
Nonlinear behavior of variable and fixed costs

Total fixed costs also do not have a straight-line relationship over the entire range of activity. Some fixed costs will not change. But it is possible for management to change other fixed costs. For example, in the Feature Story the dance studio's rent was originally variable and then became fixed at a certain amount. It then increased to a new fixed amount when the size of the studio increased beyond a certain point. Illustration 6-3, part (b), shows an example of the behavior of total fixed costs through all potential levels of activity.

For most companies, operating at almost zero or at 100% capacity is the exception rather than the rule. Instead, companies often operate over a somewhat narrower range, such as 40–80% of capacity. The range over which a company expects to operate during a year is called the **relevant range** of the activity index. Within the relevant range, as both diagrams in Illustration 6-4 (page 276) show, a straight-line relationship generally exists for both variable and fixed costs.

HELPFUL HINT
Fixed costs that may be changeable include research, such as new product development, and management training programs.

ALTERNATIVE TERMINOLOGY
The relevant range is also called the *normal* or *practical range.*

Illustration 6-4
Linear behavior within relevant range

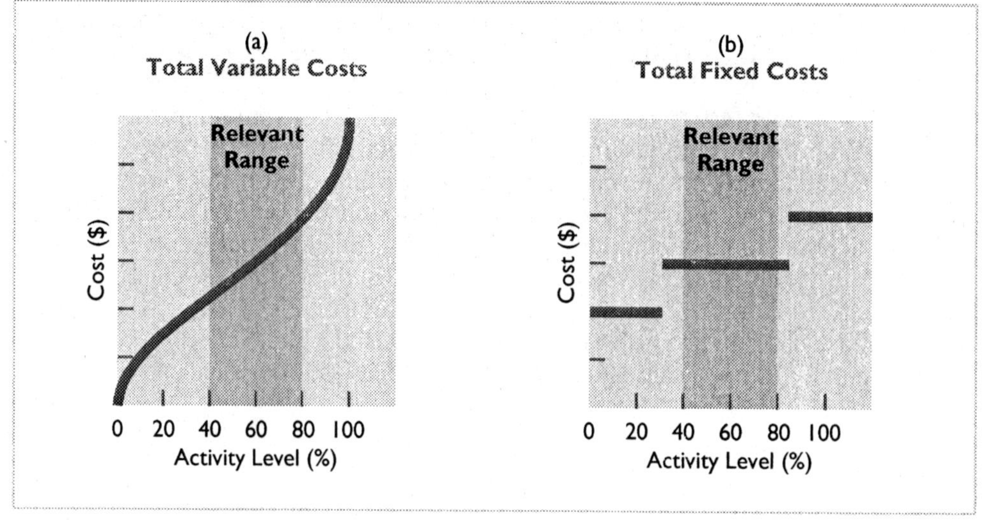

As you can see, although the linear (straight-line) relationship may not be completely realistic, **the linear assumption produces useful data for CVP analysis as long as the level of activity remains within the relevant range.**

Mixed Costs

STUDY OBJECTIVE 3
Explain the concept of mixed costs.

Mixed costs are costs that contain both a variable element and a fixed element. **Mixed costs, therefore, change in total but not proportionately with changes in the activity level.**

The rental of a U-Haul truck is a good example of a mixed cost. Assume that local rental terms for a 17-foot truck, including insurance, are $50 per day plus 50 cents per mile. When determining the cost of a one-day rental, the per day charge is a fixed cost (with respect to miles driven), whereas the mileage charge is a variable cost. The graphic presentation of the rental cost for a one-day rental is as follows.

Illustration 6-5
Behavior of a mixed cost

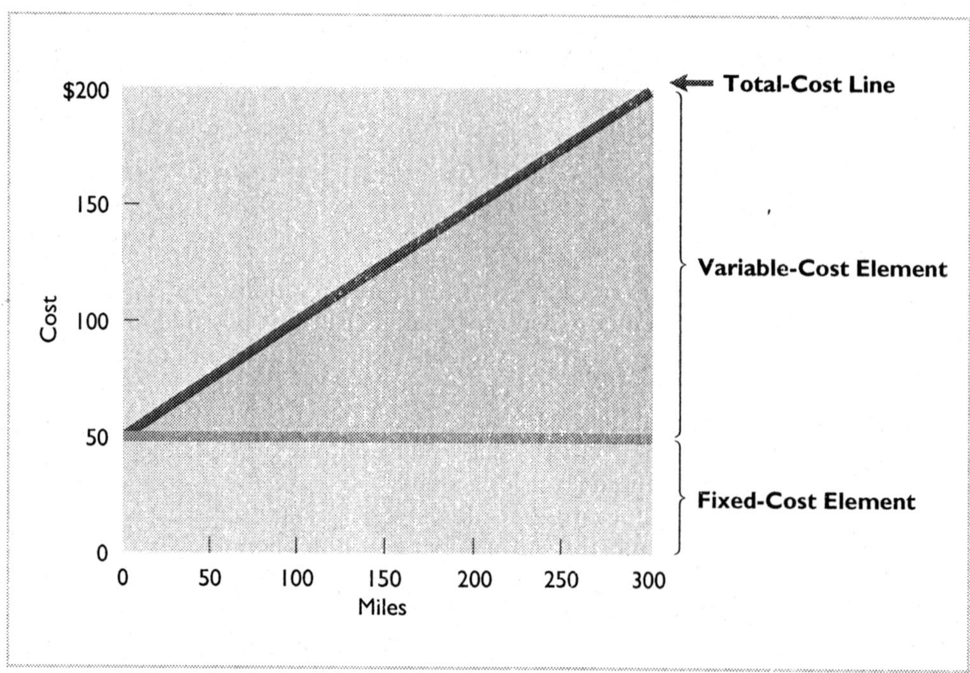

In this case, the fixed-cost element is the cost of having the service available. The variable-cost element is the cost of actually using the service. Another example of a mixed cost is utility costs (electric, telephone, and so on), where there is a flat service fee plus a usage charge.

For purposes of CVP analysis, **mixed costs must be classified into their fixed and variable elements.** How does management make the classification? One possibility is to determine the variable and fixed components each time a mixed cost is incurred. But because of time and cost constraints, this approach is rarely followed. Instead, the usual approach is to collect data on the behavior of the mixed costs at various levels of activity. Analysts then identify the fixed and variable cost components. Companies use various types of analysis. One type of analysis, called the **high-low method**, is discussed below. Other methods, such as the scatter diagram method and least squares regression analysis, are more appropriately explained in cost accounting courses.

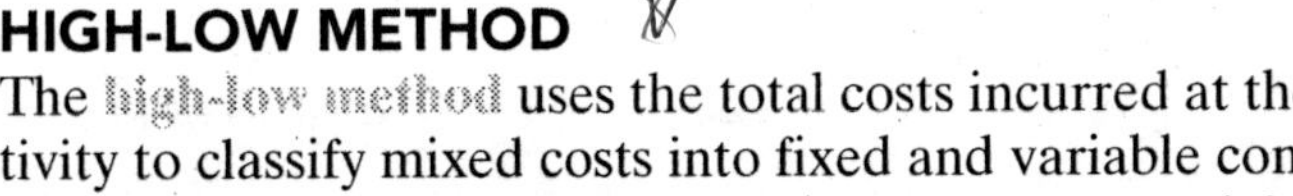

HIGH-LOW METHOD

The **high-low method** uses the total costs incurred at the high and low levels of activity to classify mixed costs into fixed and variable components. The difference in costs between the high and low levels represents variable costs, since only the variable cost element can change as activity levels change.

The steps in computing fixed and variable costs under this method are as follows.

1. Determine variable cost per unit from the following formula.

Change in Total Costs	÷	High minus Low Activity Level	=	Variable Cost per Unit

Illustration 6-6
Formula for variable cost per unit using high-low method

To illustrate, assume that Metro Transit Company has the following maintenance costs and mileage data for its fleet of buses over a 4-month period.

Month	Miles Driven	Total Cost	Month	Miles Driven	Total Cost
January	20,000	$30,000	March	35,000	$49,000
February	40,000	48,000	April	50,000	63,000

Illustration 6-7
Assumed maintenance costs and mileage data

The high and low levels of activity are 50,000 miles in April and 20,000 miles in January. The maintenance costs at these two levels are $63,000 and $30,000, respectively. The difference in maintenance costs is $33,000 ($63,000 − $30,000), and the difference in miles is 30,000 (50,000 − 20,000). Therefore, for Metro Transit, variable cost per unit is $1.10, computed as follows.

$$\$33{,}000 \div 30{,}000 = \$1.10$$

2. Determine the fixed cost by subtracting the total variable cost at either the high or the low activity level from the total cost at that activity level.

For Metro Transit, the computations are shown in Illustration 6-8.

Illustration 6-8
High-low method computation of fixed costs

	A	B	C	D
1		METRO TRANSIT		
2				
3			Activity Level	
4			High	Low
5	Total cost		$63,000	$30,000
6	Less:	Variable costs		
7		50,000 × $1.10	55,000	
8		20,000 × $1.10		22,000
9	Total fixed costs		$8,000	$8,000
10				

Maintenance costs are therefore $8,000 per month plus $1.10 per mile. This is represented by the following formula:

$$\text{Maintenance costs} = \text{Fixed costs} + (\$1.10 \times \text{Miles driven})$$

For example, at 45,000 miles, estimated maintenance costs would be $8,000 fixed and $49,500 variable ($1.10 × 45,000) for a total of $57,500.

The high-low method generally produces a reasonable estimate for analysis. However, it does not produce a precise measurement of the fixed and variable elements in a mixed cost because it ignores other activity levels in the computation.

Importance of Identifying Variable and Fixed Costs

Why is it important to segregate costs into variable and fixed elements? The answer may become apparent if we look at the following four business decisions.

1. If American Airlines is to make a profit when it reduces all domestic fares by 30%, what reduction in costs or increase in passengers will be required? **Answer**: To make a profit when it cuts domestic fares by 30%, American Airlines will have to increase the number of passengers or cut its variable costs for those flights. Its fixed costs will not change.
2. If Ford Motor Company meets workers' demands for higher wages, what increase in sales revenue will be needed to maintain current profit levels? **Answer**: Higher wages at Ford Motor Company will increase the variable costs of manufacturing automobiles. To maintain present profit levels, Ford will have to cut other variable costs or increase the price of its automobiles.
3. If United States Steel Corp.'s program to modernize plant facilities through significant equipment purchases reduces the work force by 50%, what will be the effect on the cost of producing one ton of steel?
   Answer: The modernizing of plant facilities at United States Steel Corp. changes the proportion of fixed and variable costs of producing one ton of steel. Fixed costs increase because of higher depreciation charges, whereas variable costs decrease due to the reduction in the number of steelworkers.
4. What happens if Kellogg Company increases its advertising expenses but cannot increase prices because of competitive pressure?
   Answer: Sales volume must be increased to cover the increase in fixed advertising costs.

Before You Go On...

REVIEW IT

1. What are the effects on (a) a variable cost and (b) a fixed cost due to a change in activity?
2. What is the relevant range, and how do costs behave within this range?
3. What are the steps in applying the high-low method to mixed costs?

DO IT

Helena Company reports the following total costs at two levels of production.

	10,000 units	20,000 units
Direct materials	$20,000	$40,000
Maintenance	8,000	10,000
Depreciation	4,000	4,000

Classify each cost as either variable, fixed, or mixed.

Action Plan

- Recall that a variable cost varies in total directly and proportionately with each change.
- Recall that a fixed cost remains the same in total with each change.
- Recall that a mixed cost changes in total but not proportionately with each change.

Solution Direct materials is a variable cost. Maintenance is a mixed cost. Depreciation is a fixed cost.

Related exercise material: *BE6-1, BE6-2, BE6-3, BE6-4, BE6-5, E6-1, E6-2, E6-3, E6-4, E6-5, and E6-6.*

The Navigator

COST-VOLUME-PROFIT ANALYSIS

STUDY OBJECTIVE 4
List the five components of cost-volume-profit analysis.

Cost-volume-profit (CVP) analysis is the study of the effects of changes in costs and volume on a company's profits. CVP analysis is important in profit planning. It also is a critical factor in such management decisions as setting selling prices, determining product mix, and maximizing use of production facilities.

Basic Components

CVP analysis considers the interrelationships among the components shown in Illustration 6-9.

Illustration 6-9
Components of CVP analysis

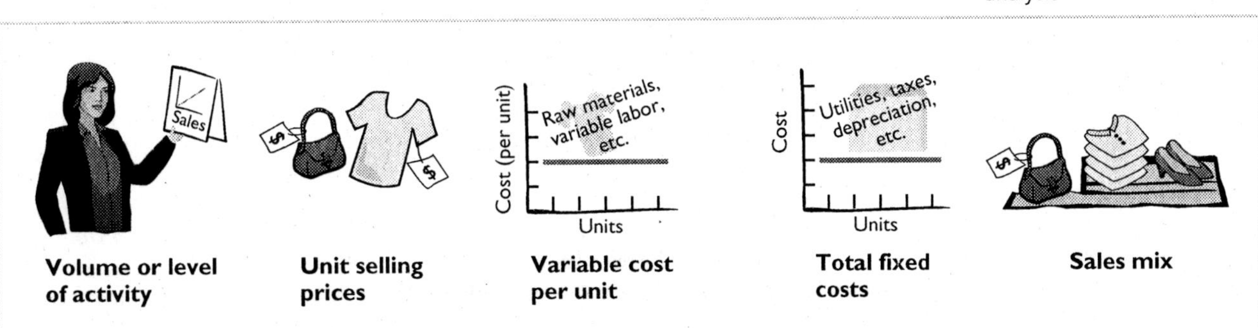

The following assumptions underlie each CVP analysis.

1. The behavior of both costs and revenues is linear throughout the relevant range of the activity index.
2. Costs can be classified accurately as either variable or fixed.
3. Changes in activity are the only factors that affect costs.
4. All units produced are sold.
5. When more than one type of product is sold, the sales mix will remain constant. That is, the percentage that each product represents of total sales will stay the same. Sales mix complicates CVP analysis because different products will have different cost relationships. In this chapter we assume a single product.

When these assumptions are not valid, the CVP analysis may be inaccurate.

CVP Income Statement

STUDY OBJECTIVE 5

Indicate what contribution margin is and how it can be expressed.

Because CVP is so important for decision making, management often wants this information reported in a **CVP income statement** format for internal use. The CVP income statement classifies costs as variable or fixed and computes a contribution margin. **Contribution margin (CM)** is the amount of revenue remaining after deducting variable costs. It is often stated both as a total amount and on a per unit basis.

We will use Vargo Video Company to illustrate a CVP income statement. Vargo Video produces a high-end, progressive-scan DVD player/recorder with up to 160-hour recording capacity and MP3 playback capability. Relevant data for the DVD players sold by this company in June 2008 are as follows.

Illustration 6-10
Assumed selling and cost data for Vargo Video

Unit selling price of DVD player	$500
Unit variable costs	$300
Total monthly fixed costs	$200,000
Units sold	1,600

The CVP income statement for Vargo Video therefore would be reported as follows.

Illustration 6-11
CVP income statement, with net income

VARGO VIDEO COMPANY
CVP Income Statement
For the Month Ended June 30, 2008

	Total	Per Unit
Sales (1,600 DVD players)	$800,000	$500
Variable costs	480,000	300
Contribution margin	**320,000**	**$200**
Fixed costs	200,000	
Net income	**$120,000**	

A traditional income statement and a CVP income statement both report the same net income of $120,000. However a traditional income statement does not classify costs as variable or fixed, and therefore it does not report a contribution margin. In addition, both a total and a per unit amount are often shown on a CVP income statement to facilitate CVP analysis.

In the applications of CVP analysis that follow, we assume that the term "cost" includes all costs and expenses related to production and sale of the product. That is, cost includes manufacturing costs plus selling and administrative expenses.

CONTRIBUTION MARGIN PER UNIT

Vargo Video's CVP income statement shows a contribution margin of $320,000, and a contribution margin per unit of $200 ($500 – $300). The formula for **contribution margin per unit** and the computation for Vargo Video are:

Illustration 6-12
Formula for contribution margin per unit

Unit Selling Price	–	Unit Variable Costs	=	Contribution Margin per Unit
$500	–	$300	=	**$200**

Contribution margin per unit indicates that for every DVD player sold, Vargo has $200 to cover fixed costs and contribute to net income. Because Vargo Video has fixed costs of $200,000, it must sell 1,000 DVD players ($200,000 ÷ $200) before it earns any net income. Vargo's CVP income statement, assuming a zero net income, is as follows.

Illustration 6-13
CVP income statement, with zero net income

VARGO VIDEO COMPANY
CVP Income Statement
For the Month Ended June 30, 2008

	Total	Per Unit
Sales (1,000 DVD players)	$500,000	$500
Variable costs	300,000	300
Contribution margin	**200,000**	**$200**
Fixed costs	200,000	
Net income	$ -0-	

It follows that for every DVD player sold above 1,000 units, net income increases by the amount of the contribution margin per unit, $200. For example, assume that Vargo sold one more DVD player, for a total of 1,001 DVD players sold. In this case Vargo reports net income of $200 as shown in Illustration 6-14.

Illustration 6-14
CVP income statement, with net income

VARGO VIDEO COMPANY
CVP Income Statement
For the Month Ended June 30, 2008

	Total	Per Unit
Sales (1,001 DVD players)	$500,500	$500
Variable costs	300,300	300
Contribution margin	**200,200**	**$200**
Fixed costs	200,000	
Net income	$ 200	

CONTRIBUTION MARGIN RATIO

Some managers prefer to use a contribution margin ratio in CVP analysis. The **contribution margin ratio** is the contribution margin per unit divided by the unit selling price. For Vargo Video, the ratio is as follows.

Illustration 6-15
Formula for contribution margin ratio

Contribution Margin per Unit	÷	Unit Selling Price	=	Contribution Margin Ratio
$200	÷	$500	=	**40%**

The contribution margin ratio of 40% means that $0.40 of each sales dollar ($1 × 40%) is available to apply to fixed costs and to contribute to net income.

This expression of contribution margin is very helpful in determining the effect of changes in sales on net income. For example, if sales increase $100,000, net income will increase $40,000 (40% × $100,000). Thus, by using the contribution margin ratio, managers can quickly determine increases in net income from any change in sales.

We can also see this effect through a CVP income statement. Assume that Vargo Video's current sales are $500,000 and it wants to know the effect of a $100,000 (200-unit) increase in sales. Vargo prepares a comparative CVP income statement analysis as follows.

Illustration 6-16
Comparative CVP income statements

VARGO VIDEO COMPANY
CVP Income Statements
For the Month Ended June 30, 2008

	No Change		With Change	
	Total	**Per Unit**	**Total**	**Per Unit**
Sales	$500,000	$500	$600,000	$500
Variable costs	300,000	300	360,000	300
Contribution margin	200,000	$200	240,000	$200
Fixed costs	200,000		200,000	
Net income	$ -0-		$ 40,000	

Study these CVP income statements carefully. The concepts presented in these statements are used extensively in this and later chapters.

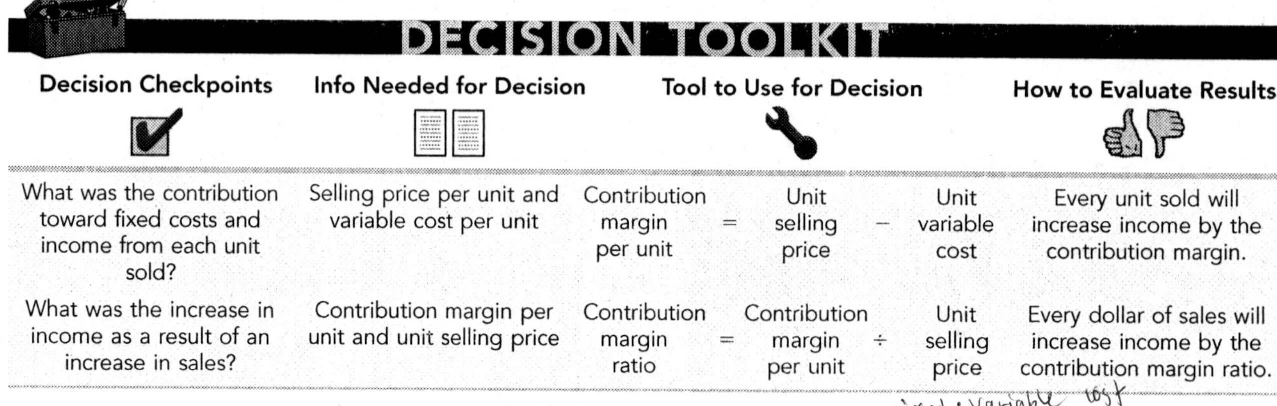
DECISION TOOLKIT

Decision Checkpoints	Info Needed for Decision	Tool to Use for Decision	How to Evaluate Results
What was the contribution toward fixed costs and income from each unit sold?	Selling price per unit and variable cost per unit	Contribution margin per unit = Unit selling price − Unit variable cost	Every unit sold will increase income by the contribution margin.
What was the increase in income as a result of an increase in sales?	Contribution margin per unit and unit selling price	Contribution margin ratio = Contribution margin per unit ÷ Unit selling price	Every dollar of sales will increase income by the contribution margin ratio.

Break-even Analysis

STUDY OBJECTIVE 6
Identify the three ways to determine the break-even point.

A key relationship in CVP analysis is the level of activity at which total revenues equal total costs (both fixed and variable). This level of activity is called the **break-even point**. At this volume of sales, the company will realize no income but will suffer no loss. The process of finding the break-even point is called **break-even analysis**. Knowledge of the break-even point is useful to management when it decides whether to introduce new product lines, change sales prices on established products, or enter new market areas.

The break-even point can be:

1. Computed from a mathematical equation.
2. Computed by using contribution margin.
3. Derived from a cost-volume-profit (CVP) graph.

The break-even point can be expressed either in **sales units** or **sales dollars**.

MATHEMATICAL EQUATION

Illustration 6-17 shows a common equation used for CVP analysis.

Sales	=	Variable Costs	+	Fixed Costs	+	Net Income

Illustration 6-17
Basic CVP equation

Identifying the break-even point is a special case of CVP analysis. Because at the break-even point net income is zero, **break-even occurs where total sales equal variable costs plus fixed costs.**

We can compute the break-even point **in units** directly from the equation by **using unit selling prices** and **unit variable costs.** The computation for Vargo Video is:

Sales	=	Variable Costs	+	Fixed Costs	+	Net Income
\$500Q	=	\$300Q	+	\$200,000	+	\$0

$\$200Q = \$200{,}000$
$Q = 1{,}000 \text{ units}$

where

Q = sales volume in units
\$500 = selling price
\$300 = variable cost per unit
\$200,000 = total fixed costs

Illustration 6-18
Computation of break-even point in units

Thus, Vargo Video must sell 1,000 units to break even.

To find **sales dollars** required to break even, we multiply the units sold at the break-even point times the selling price per unit, as shown below.

1,000 × \$500 = \$500,000 (break-even sales dollars)

CONTRIBUTION MARGIN TECHNIQUE

We know that contribution margin equals total revenues less variable costs. It follows that at the break-even point, **contribution margin must equal total fixed costs.** On the basis of this relationship, we can compute the break-even point using either the contribution margin per unit or the contribution margin ratio.

When a company uses the contribution margin per unit, the formula to compute break-even point in units is fixed costs divided by contribution margin per unit. For Vargo Video the computation is as follows.

Fixed Costs	÷	Contribution Margin per Unit	=	Break-even Point in Units
\$200,000	÷	\$200	=	1,000 units

Illustration 6-19
Formula for break-even point in units using contribution margin

One way to interpret this formula is that Vargo Video generates \$200 of contribution margin with each unit that it sells. This \$200 goes to pay off fixed costs. Therefore, the company must sell 1,000 units to pay off \$200,000 in fixed costs.

When a company uses the contribution margin ratio, the formula to compute break-even point in dollars is fixed costs divided by the contribution margin ratio. We know that the contribution margin ratio for Vargo Video is 40% (\$200 ÷ \$500), which means that every dollar of sales generates 40 cents to pay off fixed costs. Thus, the break-even point in dollars is:

Illustration 6-20
Formula for break-even point in dollars using contribution margin ratio

Fixed Costs	÷	Contribution Margin Ratio	=	Break-even Point in Dollars
$200,000	÷	40%	=	$500,000

ACCOUNTING ACROSS THE ORGANIZATION

Charter Flights Offer a Good Deal

The Internet is wringing inefficiencies out of nearly every industry. While commercial aircraft spend roughly 4,000 hours a year in the air, chartered aircraft spend only 500 hours flying. That means that they are sitting on the ground—not making any money—about 90% of the time. One company, FlightServe, saw a business opportunity in that fact. For about the same cost as a first-class ticket, FlightServe decided to match up executives with charter flights in small "private jets." The executive would get a more comfortable ride and could avoid the hassle of big airports. FlightServe noted that the average charter jet has eight seats. When all eight seats were full, the company would have an 80% profit margin. It would break even at an average of 3.3 full seats per flight.

Source: "Jet Set Go," *The Economist,* March 18, 2000, p. 68.

How did FlightServe determine that it would break even with 3.3 seats full per flight?

GRAPHIC PRESENTATION

An effective way to find the break-even point is to prepare a break-even graph. Because this graph also shows costs, volume, and profits, it is referred to as a **cost-volume-profit (CVP) graph.**

As the CVP graph in Illustration 6-21 (next page) shows, sales volume is recorded along the horizontal axis. This axis should extend to the maximum level of expected sales. Both total revenues (sales) and total costs (fixed plus variable) are recorded on the vertical axis.

The construction of the graph, using the data for Vargo Video, is as follows.

1. Plot the total-sales line, starting at the zero activity level. For every DVD player sold, total revenue increases by $500. For example, at 200 units, sales are $100,000. At the upper level of activity (1,800 units), sales are $900,000. The revenue line is assumed to be linear through the full range of activity.
2. Plot the total fixed cost using a horizontal line. For the DVD players, this line is plotted at $200,000. The fixed cost is the same at every level of activity.
3. Plot the total-cost line. This starts at the fixed-cost line at zero activity. It increases by the variable cost at each level of activity. For each DVD player, variable costs are $300. Thus, at 200 units, total variable cost is $60,000, and the total cost is $260,000. At 1,800 units total variable cost is $540,000, and total cost is $740,000. On the graph, the amount of the variable cost can be derived from the difference between the total cost and fixed cost lines at each level of activity.
4. Determine the break-even point from the intersection of the total-cost line and the total-revenue line. The break-even point in dollars is found by drawing a horizontal line from the break-even point to the vertical axis. The break-even point in units is found by drawing a vertical line from the break-even point to the horizontal axis. For the DVD players, the break-even point is $500,000 of sales, or 1,000 units. At this sales level, Vargo Video will cover costs but make no profit.

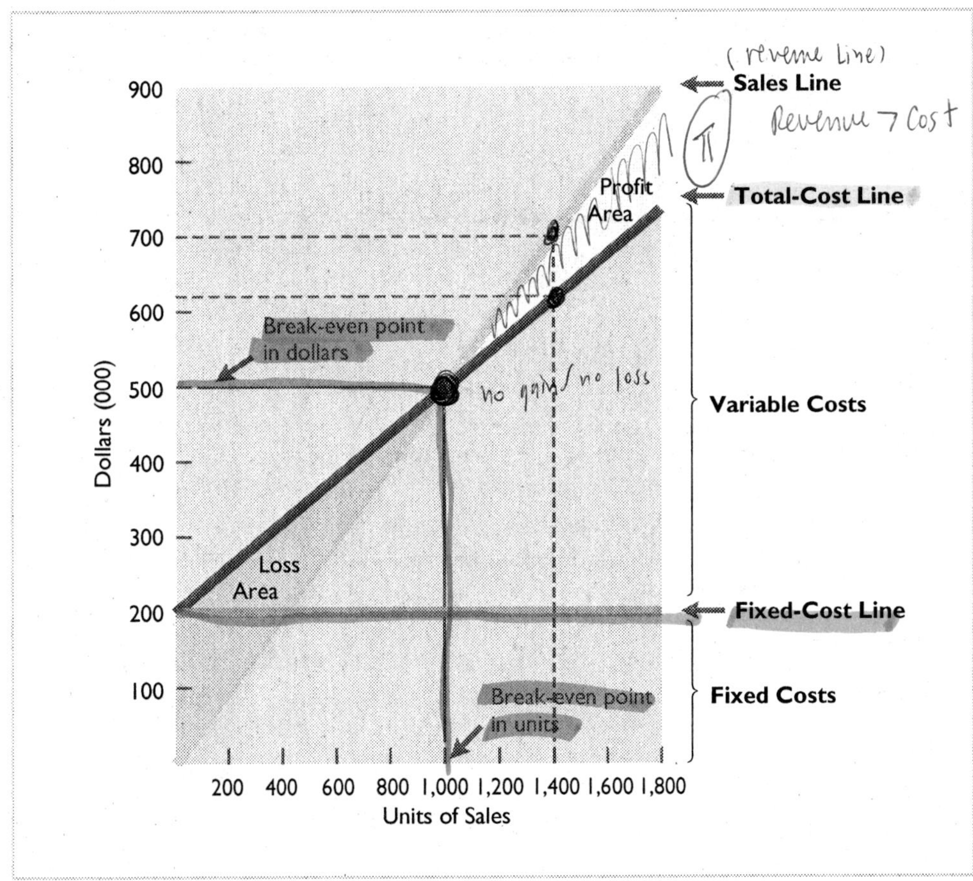

Illustration 6-21
CVP graph

The CVP graph also shows both the net income and net loss areas. Thus, the amount of income or loss at each level of sales can be derived from the total sales and total cost lines.

A CVP graph is useful because the effects of a change in any element in the CVP analysis can be quickly seen. For example, a 10% increase in selling price will change the location of the total revenue line. Likewise, the effects on total costs of wage increases can be quickly observed.

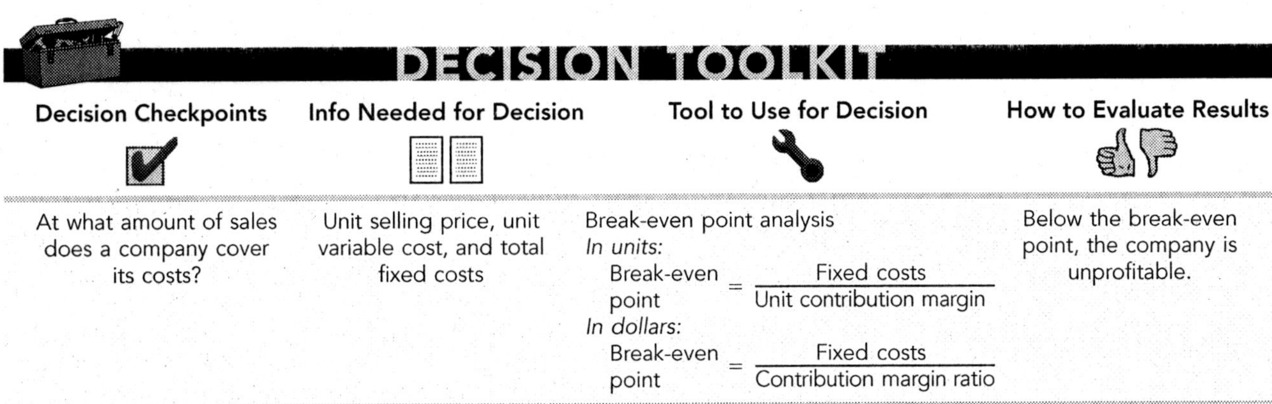

DECISION TOOLKIT

Decision Checkpoints	Info Needed for Decision	Tool to Use for Decision	How to Evaluate Results
At what amount of sales does a company cover its costs?	Unit selling price, unit variable cost, and total fixed costs	Break-even point analysis *In units:* $\text{Break-even point} = \frac{\text{Fixed costs}}{\text{Unit contribution margin}}$ *In dollars:* $\text{Break-even point} = \frac{\text{Fixed costs}}{\text{Contribution margin ratio}}$	Below the break-even point, the company is unprofitable.

Before You Go On...

REVIEW IT

1. What are the assumptions that underlie each CVP application?
2. What is contribution margin, and how can it be expressed?
3. How can the break-even point be determined?

DO IT

Lombardi Company has a unit selling price of $400, variable costs per unit of $240, and fixed costs of $180,000. Compute the break-even point in units using (a) a mathematical equation and (b) contribution margin per unit.

Action Plan

- Apply the formula: Sales = Variable costs + Fixed costs + Net income.
- Apply the formula: Fixed costs ÷ Contribution margin per unit = Break-even point in units.

Solution (a) The equation is $400Q = $240Q + $180,000. The break-even point in units is 1,125 ($180,000 ÷ $160). (b) The contribution margin per unit is $160 ($400 − $240). The formula therefore is $180,000 ÷ $160, and the break-even point in units is 1,125.

Related exercise material: *BE6-6, BE6-7, BE6-8, BE6-9, E6-8, E6-9, E6-10, E6-11, E6-12, and E6-13.*

Target Net Income

STUDY OBJECTIVE 7

Give the formulas for determining sales required to earn target net income.

Rather than simply "breaking even," management usually sets an income objective often called **target net income**. It indicates the sales necessary to achieve a specified level of income. Companies determine the sales necessary to achieve target net income by using one of the three approaches discussed earlier.

MATHEMATICAL EQUATION

We know that at the break-even point no profit or loss results for the company. By adding an amount for target net income to the same basic equation, we obtain the following formula for determining required sales.

Illustration 6-22
Formula for required sales to meet target net income

Required Sales	=	Variable Costs	+	Fixed Costs	+	Target Net Income

Required sales may be expressed in either **sales units** or **sales dollars**. Assuming that target net income is $120,000 for Vargo Video, the computation of required sales in units is as follows.

Illustration 6-23
Computation of required sales

Required Sales	=	Variable Costs	+	Fixed Costs	+	Target Net Income
$500Q	=	$300Q	+	$200,000	+	$120,000

$200Q = $320,000
Q = 1,600

where

Q = sales volume
$500 = selling price
$300 = variable costs per unit
$200,000 = total fixed costs
$120,000 = target net income

The sales dollars required to achieve the target net income is found by multiplying the units sold by the unit selling price [(1,600 × $500) = $800,000].

CONTRIBUTION MARGIN TECHNIQUE

As in the case of break-even sales, we can compute in either units or dollars the sales required to meet a target net income. The formula to compute required sales in units for Vargo Video using the contribution margin per unit is as follows.

Fixed Costs + Target Net Income	÷	Contribution Margin Per Unit	=	Required Sales in Units
($200,000 + $120,000)	÷	$200	=	1,600 units

Illustration 6-24
Formula for required sales in units using contribution margin per unit

This computation tells Vargo that to achieve its desired target net income of $120,000, it must sell 1,600 DVD players.

The formula to compute the required sales in dollars for Vargo Video using the contribution margin ratio is as follows.

Fixed Costs + Target Net Income	÷	Contribution Margin Ratio	=	Required Sales in Dollars
($200,000 + $120,000)	÷	40%	=	$800,000

Illustration 6-25
Formula for required sales in dollars using contribution margin ratio

This computation tells Vargo that to achieve its desired target net income of $120,000, it must generate sales of $800,000.

GRAPHIC PRESENTATION

We also can use the CVP graph in Illustration 6-21 (on page 285) to find the sales required to meet target net income. In the profit area of the graph, the distance between the sales line and the total cost line at any point equals net income. We can find required sales by analyzing the differences between the two lines until the desired net income is found.

For example, suppose Vargo Video sells 1,400 DVD players. Illustration 6-21 shows that a vertical line drawn at 1,400 units intersects the sales line at $700,000 and the total cost line at $620,000. The difference between the two amounts represents the net income (profit) of $80,000.

Margin of Safety

STUDY OBJECTIVE 8
Define margin of safety, and give the formulas for computing it.

The margin of safety is another relationship used in CVP analysis. **Margin of safety** is the difference between actual or expected sales and sales at the break-even point. This relationship measures the "cushion" that management has, allowing it to break even if expected sales fail to materialize. The margin of safety is expressed in dollars or as a ratio.

The formula for stating the **margin of safety in dollars** is actual (or expected) sales minus break-even sales. Assuming that actual (expected) sales for Vargo Video are $750,000, the computation is:

Actual (Expected) Sales	−	Break-even Sales	=	Margin of Safety in Dollars
$750,000	−	$500,000	=	$250,000

Illustration 6-26
Formula for margin of safety in dollars

Vargo's margin of safety is $250,000. Its sales must fall $250,000 before it operates at a loss.

The **margin of safety ratio** is the margin of safety in dollars divided by actual (or expected) sales. The formula and computation for determining the margin of safety ratio are:

Illustration 6-27
Formula for margin of safety ratio

Margin of Safety in Dollars	÷	Actual (Expected) Sales	=	Margin of Safety Ratio
$250,000	÷	$750,000	=	33%

This means that the company's sales could fall by 33% before it would be operating at a loss.

The higher the dollars or the percentage, the greater the margin of safety. Management continuously evaluates the adequacy of the margin of safety in terms of such factors as the vulnerability of the product to competitive pressures and to downturns in the economy.

MANAGEMENT INSIGHT

How a Rolling Stones' Tour Makes Money

Computation of break-even and margin of safety is important for service companies. Consider how the promoter for the Rolling Stones' tour used the break-even point and margin of safety. For example, one outdoor show should bring 70,000 individuals for a gross of $2.45 million. The promoter guarantees $1.2 million to the Rolling Stones. In addition, 20% of gross goes to the stadium in which the performance is staged. Add another $400,000 for other expenses such as ticket takers, parking attendants, advertising, and so on. The promoter also shares in sales of T-shirts and memorabilia for which the promoter will net over $7 million during the tour. From a successful Rolling Stones' tour, the promoter could make $35 million!

What amount of sales dollars are required for the promoter to break even?

Before You Go On...

REVIEW IT

1. What is the equation to compute target net income?
2. What is the formula for computing the margin of safety (a) in dollars and (b) as a ratio?

Be sure to read **ALL ABOUT YOU: *A Hybrid Dilemma*** on the next page for information on how topics in this chapter apply to you.

all about YOU

A Hybrid Dilemma

Have high gas prices got you down? Maybe you should consider a hybrid. These half-gas and half-electric vehicles are generating a lot of interest. They burn less fuel and therefore are easier on the environment. But are they easier on your pocketbook? Is a hybrid car at least a break-even investment, or is it more likely a money-losing proposition?

Some Facts

* Ford plans to sell at least seven different models of hybrid cars, about 250,000 vehicles annually, by the end of the decade.
* Hybrid vehicles typically cost $3,000 to $5,000 more than their conventional counterparts, although for some models the premium is higher.
* Bank of America and Timberland offer $3,000 to employees who purchase hybrids. Google offers $5,000 to employees who purchase cars that get at least 45 miles per gallon.
* The most fuel-efficient hybrids–the Toyota Prius and the Honda Civic–can save about $660 per year in fuel costs relative to a similar conventional car. However some other hybrids provide only slight fuel savings.
* Each gallon of gasoline that is not consumed reduces carbon dioxide emissions by 19 pounds. Many believe carbon dioxide contributes to global warming.
* The federal government initially provided tax credits of up to $3,400 to buyers of hybrids. These credits are to be phased out as automakers reach sales caps determined by the Internal Revenue Service (IRS).

About the Numbers

Sales of hybrid cars started very strong in 2005, but then tapered off. The following graph shows that sales of the Toyota Prius far exceed other brands.

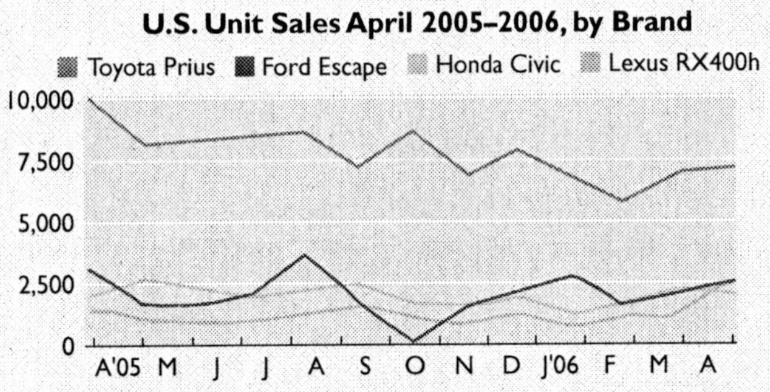

U.S. Unit Sales April 2005–2006, by Brand

Source: J.D. Power and Associates, 2006, "Happening Hybrids," as reported in the *Wall Street Journal*, May 23, 2006.

What Do You Think?

Gas prices are depleting your wallet so fast that you might even have to give up your old car and resort to walking or riding your bike on occasion. Will making the investment in a hybrid slow the outflow from your wallet and spare your feet?

YES: At 44 miles per gallon, I can drive forever without ever having to fill up.

NO: Because of the premium price charged for hybrids, I will never drive enough miles to break even on my investment.

Sources: "The Dollars and Sense of Hybrids," *Consumer Reports*, April, 2006, pp. 18-22.; John D. Stoll and Gina Chon, "Consumer Drive for Hybrid Autos Is Slowing Down," *Wall Street Journal*, April 7, 2006, p. A2. Associated Press, "Bank Workers Get Hybrid Reward," *Wall Street Journal*, June 8, 2006, p. D2.

The authors' comments on this situation appear on page 306.

Using the Decision Toolkit

B.T. Hernandez Company, maker of high-quality flashlights, has experienced steady growth over the last 6 years. However, increased competition has led Mr. Hernandez, the president, to believe that an aggressive campaign is needed next year to maintain the company's present growth. The company's accountant has presented Mr. Hernandez with the following data for the current year, 2007, for use in preparing next year's advertising campaign.

COST SCHEDULES

Variable costs	
Direct labor per flashlight	$ 8.00
Direct materials	4.00
Variable overhead	3.00
Variable cost per flashlight	$15.00
Fixed costs	
Manufacturing	$ 25,000
Selling	40,000
Administrative	70,000
Total fixed costs	$135,000
Selling price per flashlight	$25.00
Expected sales, 2007 (20,000 flashlights)	$500,000

Mr. Hernandez has set the sales target for the year 2008 at a level of $550,000 (22,000 flashlights).

Instructions

(Ignore any income tax considerations.)

(a) What is the projected operating income for 2007?
(b) What is the contribution margin per unit for 2007?
(c) What is the break-even point in units for 2007?
(d) Mr. Hernandez believes that to attain the sales target in the year 2008, the company must incur an additional selling expense of $10,000 for advertising in 2008, with all other costs remaining constant. What will be the break-even point in sales dollars for 2008 if the company spends the additional $10,000?
(e) If the company spends the additional $10,000 for advertising in 2008, what is the sales level in dollars required to equal 2007 operating income?

Solution

(a)

Expected sales	$500,000
Less:	
Variable cost (20,000 flashlights × $15)	300,000
Fixed costs	135,000
Projected operating income	$ 65,000

(b)

Selling price per flashlight	$25
Variable cost per flashlight	15
Contribution margin per unit	$10

(c) Fixed costs ÷ Contribution margin per unit = Break-even point in units
$135,000 ÷ $10 = 13,500 units

(d) Fixed costs ÷ Contribution margin ratio = Break-even point in dollars
$145,000* ÷ 40%** = $362,500

*Fixed costs (from 2007)	$135,000
Additional advertising expense	10,000
Fixed costs (2008)	$145,000

**Contribution margin ratio = Contribution margin per unit ÷ Unit selling price
40% = $10 ÷ $25

(e) Required sales = (Fixed costs + Target net income) ÷ Contribution margin ratio

$525,000 = ($145,000 + $65,000) ÷ 40%

✓ The Navigator

SUMMARY OF STUDY OBJECTIVES

1 **Distinguish between variable and fixed costs.** Variable costs are costs that vary in total directly and proportionately with changes in the activity index. Fixed costs are costs that remain the same in total regardless of changes in the activity index.

2 **Explain the significance of the relevant range.** The relevant range is the range of activity in which a company expects to operate during a year. It is important in CVP analysis because the behavior of costs is assumed to be linear throughout the relevant range.

3 **Explain the concept of mixed costs.** Mixed costs increase in total but not proportionately with changes in the activity level. For purposes of CVP analysis, mixed costs must be classified into their fixed and variable elements. One method that management may use to classify these costs is the high-low method.

4 **List the five components of cost-volume-profit analysis.** The five components of CVP analysis are (a) volume or level of activity, (b) unit selling prices, (c) variable cost per unit, (d) total fixed costs, and (e) sales mix.

5 **Indicate what contribution margin is and how it can be expressed.** Contribution margin is the amount of revenue remaining after deducting variable costs. It is identified in a CVP income statement, which classifies costs as variable or fixed. It can be expressed as a total amount, as a per unit amount, or as a ratio.

6 **Identify the three ways to determine the break-even point.** The break-even point can be (a) computed from a mathematical equation, (b) computed by using a contribution margin technique, and (c) derived from a CVP graph.

7 **Give the formulas for determining sales required to earn target net income.** The general formula for required sales is: Required sales = Variable costs + Fixed costs + Target net income. Two other formulas are: Required sales in units = (Fixed costs + Target net income) ÷ Contribution margin per unit, and Required sales in dollars = (Fixed costs + Target net income) ÷ Contribution margin ratio.

8 **Define margin of safety, and give the formulas for computing it.** Margin of safety is the difference between actual or expected sales and sales at the break-even point. The formulas for margin of safety are: Actual (expected) sales − Break-even sales = Margin of safety in dollars; Margin of safety in dollars ÷ Actual (expected) sales = Margin of safety ratio.

✓ The Navigator

DECISION TOOLKIT—A SUMMARY

Decision Checkpoints	Info Needed for Decision	Tool to Use for Decision	How to Evaluate Results
What was the contribution toward fixed costs and income from each unit sold?	Selling price per unit and variable cost per unit	Contribution margin per unit = Unit selling price − Unit variable cost	Every unit sold will increase income by the contribution margin.
What was the increase in income as a result of an increase in sales?	Contribution margin per unit and unit selling price	Contribution margin ratio = Contribution margin per unit ÷ Unit selling price	Every dollar of sales will increase income by the contribution margin ratio.
At what amount of sales does a company cover its costs?	Unit selling price, unit variable cost, and total fixed costs	Break-even point analysis *In units:* $\text{Break-even point} = \frac{\text{Fixed costs}}{\text{Unit contribution margin}}$ *In dollars:* $\text{Break-even point} = \frac{\text{Fixed costs}}{\text{Contribution margin ratio}}$	Below the break-even point, the company is unprofitable.

GLOSSARY

Activity index The activity that causes changes in the behavior of costs. (p. 272).

Break-even point The level of activity at which total revenues equal total costs. (p. 282).

Contribution margin (CM) The amount of revenue remaining after deducting variable costs. (p. 280).

Contribution margin per unit The amount of revenue remaining per unit after deducting variable costs; calculated as unit selling price minus unit variable cost. (p. 281).

Contribution margin ratio The percentage of each dollar of sales that is available to apply to fixed costs and contribute to net income; calculated as contribution margin per unit divided by unit selling price. (p. 281).

Cost behavior analysis The study of how specific costs respond to changes in the level of business activity. (p. 272).

Cost-volume-profit (CVP) analysis The study of the effects of changes in costs and volume on a company's profits. (p. 279).

Cost-volume-profit (CVP) graph A graph showing the relationship between costs, volume, and profits. (p. 284).

Cost-volume-profit (CVP) income statement A statement for internal use that classifies costs as fixed or variable and reports contribution margin in the body of the statement. (p. 280).

Fixed costs Costs that remain the same in total regardless of changes in the activity level. (p. 273).

High-low method A mathematical method that uses the total costs incurred at the high and low levels of activity to classify mixed costs into fixed and variable components. (p. 277).

Margin of safety The difference between actual or expected sales and sales at the break-even point. (p. 287).

Mixed costs Costs that contain both a variable and a fixed cost element and change in total but not proportionately with changes in the activity level. (p. 276).

Relevant range The range of the activity index over which the company expects to operate during the year. (p. 275).

Target net income The income objective set by management. (p. 286).

Variable costs Costs that vary in total directly and proportionately with changes in the activity level. (p. 273).

Demonstration Problem

Mabo Company makes calculators that sell for $20 each. For the coming year, management expects fixed costs to total $220,000 and variable costs to be $9 per unit.

Instructions

(a) Compute break-even point in units using the mathematical equation.
(b) Compute break-even point in dollars using the contribution margin (CM) ratio.
(c) Compute the margin of safety percentage assuming actual sales are $500,000.
(d) Compute the sales required in dollars to earn net income of $165,000.

Solution

(a) Sales = Variable costs + Fixed costs + Net income
$20Q = $9Q + $220,000 + $0
$11Q = $220,000
Q = 20,000 units

(b) Contribution margin per unit = Unit selling price − Unit variable costs
$11 = $20 − $9
Contribution margin ratio = Contribution margin per unit ÷ Unit selling price
55% = $11 ÷ $20
Break-even point in dollars = Fixed cost ÷ Contribution margin ratio
= $220,000 ÷ 55%
= $400,000

(c) Margin of safety = (Actual sales − Break-even sales) / Actual sales

= ($500,000 − $400,000) / $500,000

= 20%

(d) Required sales = Variable costs + Fixed costs + Net income
$20Q = $9Q + $220,000 + $165,000
$11Q = $385,000
Q = 35,000 units
35,000 units × $20 = $700,000 required sales

action plan

✓ Know the formulas.

✓ Recognize that variable costs change with sales volume; fixed costs do not.

✓ Avoid computational errors.

✓ The Navigator

SELF-STUDY QUESTIONS

WILEY PLUS

Answers are at the end of the chapter.

(SO 1) 1. Variable costs are costs that:
- **a.** vary in total directly and proportionally with changes in the activity level.
- **b.** remain the same per unit at every activity level.
- **c.** Neither of the above.
- **d.** Both (a) and (b) above.

(SO 2) 2. The relevant range is:
- **a.** the range of activity in which variable costs will be curvilinear.
- **b.** the range of activity in which fixed costs will be curvilinear.
- **c.** the range over which the company expects to operate during a year.
- **d.** usually from zero to 100% of operating capacity.

(SO 3) 3. Mixed costs consist of a:
- **a.** variable cost element and a fixed cost element.
- **b.** fixed cost element and a controllable cost element.
- **c.** relevant cost element and a controllable cost element.
- **d.** variable cost element and a relevant cost element.

(SO 3) 4. Kendra Corporation's total utility costs during the past year were $1,200 during its highest month and $600 during its lowest month. These costs corresponded with 10,000 units of production during the high month and 2,000 units during the low month. What are the fixed and variable components of its utility costs using the high-low method?
- **a.** $0.075 variable and $450 fixed.
- **b.** $0.120 variable and $0 fixed.
- **c.** $0.300 variable and $0 fixed.
- **d.** $0.060 variable and $600 fixed.

5. One of the following is *not* involved in CVP analysis. That factor is: (SO 4)
- **a.** sales mix.
- **b.** unit selling prices.
- **c.** fixed costs per unit.
- **d.** volume or level of activity.

6. Contribution margin: (SO 5)
- **a.** is revenue remaining after deducting variable costs.
- **b.** may be expressed as contribution margin per unit.
- **c.** is selling price less cost of goods sold.
- **d.** Both (a) and (b) above.

7. Cournot Company sells 100,000 wrenches for $12 a unit. Fixed costs are $300,000, and net income is $200,000. What should be reported as variable expenses in the CVP income statement? (SO 5)
- **a.** $700,000.
- **b.** $900,000.
- **c.** $500,000.
- **d.** $1,000,000.

8. Gossen Company is planning to sell 200,000 pliers for $4 per unit. The contribution margin ratio is 25%. If Gossen will break even at this level of sales, what are the fixed costs? (SO 6)
- **a.** $100,000.
- **b.** $160,000.
- **c.** $200,000.
- **d.** $300,000.

9. The mathematical equation for computing required sales to obtain target net income is: Required sales = (SO 7)
- **a.** Variable costs + Target net income.
- **b.** Variable costs + Fixed costs + Target net income.

c. Fixed costs + Target net income.
d. No correct answer is given.

(SO 8) **10.** Marshall Company had actual sales of $600,000 when break-even sales were $420,000. What is the margin of safety ratio?
a. 25%. **c.** 33⅓%.
b. 30%. **d.** 45%.

Go to the book's website, **www.wiley.com/college/weygandt**, for Additional Self-Study questions.

QUESTIONS

1. **(a)** What is cost behavior analysis?
(b) Why is cost behavior analysis important to management?

2. **(a)** Jenny Kent asks your help in understanding the term "activity index." Explain the meaning and importance of this term for Jenny.
(b) State the two ways that variable costs may be defined.

3. Contrast the effects of changes in the activity level on total fixed costs and on unit fixed costs.

4. A. J. Hernandez claims that the relevant range concept is important only for variable costs.
(a) Explain the relevant range concept.
(b) Do you agree with A. J.'s claim? Explain.

5. "The relevant range is indispensable in cost behavior analysis." Is this true? Why or why not?

6. Ryan Ricketts is confused. He does not understand why rent on his apartment is a fixed cost and rent on a Hertz rental truck is a mixed cost. Explain the difference to Ryan.

7. How should mixed costs be classified in CVP analysis? What approach is used to effect the appropriate classification?

8. At the high and low levels of activity during the month, direct labor hours are 90,000 and 40,000, respectively. The related costs are $160,000 and $100,000. What are the fixed and variable costs at any level of activity?

9. "Cost-volume-profit (CVP) analysis is based entirely on unit costs." Do you agree? Explain.

10. Jill Nott defines contribution margin as the amount of profit available to cover operating expenses. Is there any truth in this definition? Discuss.

11. Kosko Company's Speedo calculator sells for $40. Variable costs per unit are estimated to be $28. What are the contribution margin per unit and the contribution margin ratio?

12. "Break-even analysis is of limited use to management because a company cannot survive by just breaking even." Do you agree? Explain.

13. Total fixed costs are $25,000 for Haag Inc. It has a contribution margin per unit of $15, and a contribution margin ratio of 25%. Compute the break-even sales in dollars.

14. Nancy Tobias asks your help in constructing a CVP graph. Explain to Nancy (a) how the break-even point is plotted, and (b) how the level of activity and dollar sales at the break-even point are determined.

15. Define the term "margin of safety." If Peine Company expects to sell 1,250 units of its product at $12 per unit, and break-even sales for the product are $12,000, what is the margin of safety ratio?

16. Ortega Company's break-even sales are $600,000. Assuming fixed costs are $180,000, what sales volume is needed to achieve a target net income of $60,000?

17. The traditional income statement for Mallon Company shows sales $900,000, cost of goods sold $500,000, and operating expenses $200,000. Assuming all costs and expenses are 70% variable and 30% fixed, prepare a CVP income statement through contribution margin.

BRIEF EXERCISES

WILEY PLUS

Classify costs as variable, fixed, or mixed.
(SO 1, 3)

BE6-1 Monthly production costs in Pesavento Company for two levels of production are as follows.

Cost	3,000 units	6,000 units
Indirect labor	$10,000	$20,000
Supervisory salaries	5,000	5,000
Maintenance	4,000	7,000

Indicate which costs are variable, fixed, and mixed, and give the reason for each answer.

Diagram the behavior of costs within the relevant range.
(SO 2)

BE6-2 For Loder Company, the relevant range of production is 40–80% of capacity. At 40% of capacity, a variable cost is $4,000 and a fixed cost is $6,000. Diagram the behavior of each cost within the relevant range assuming the behavior is linear.

Diagram the behavior of a mixed cost.
(SO 3)

BE6-3 For Hunt Company, a mixed cost is $20,000 plus $16 per direct labor hour. Diagram the behavior of the cost using increments of 500 hours up to 2,500 hours on the horizontal axis and increments of $20,000 up to $80,000 on the vertical axis.

Determine variable and fixed cost elements using the high-low method.
(SO 3)

BE6-4 Deines Company accumulates the following data concerning a mixed cost, using miles as the activity level.

	Miles Driven	Total Cost		Miles Driven	Total Cost
January	8,000	$14,150	March	8,500	$15,000
February	7,500	13,600	April	8,200	14,490

Compute the variable and fixed cost elements using the high-low method.

Determine variable and fixed cost elements using the high-low method.
(SO 3)

BE6-5 Westerville Corp. has collected the following data concerning its maintenance costs for the past 6 months.

	Units Produced	Total Cost
July	18,000	$32,000
August	32,000	48,000
September	36,000	55,000
October	22,000	38,000
November	40,000	65,000
December	38,000	62,000

Compute the variable and fixed cost elements using the high-low method.

Determine missing amounts for contribution margin.
(SO 5)

BE6-6 Determine the missing amounts.

	Unit Selling Price	Unit Variable Costs	Contribution Margin per Unit	Contribution Margin Ratio
1.	$640	$384	(a)	(b)
2.	$300	(c)	$90	(d)
3.	(e)	(f)	$320	25%

Prepare CVP income statement.
(SO 5)

BE6-7 Bruno Manufacturing Inc. had sales of $2,200,000 for the first quarter of 2008. In making the sales, the company incurred the following costs and expenses.

	Variable	Fixed
Cost of goods sold	$920,000	$440,000
Selling expenses	70,000	45,000
Administrative expenses	86,000	98,000

Prepare a CVP income statement for the quarter ended March 31, 2008.

Compute the break-even point.
(SO 6)

BE6-8 Larissa Company has a unit selling price of $520, variable costs per unit of $286, and fixed costs of $187,200. Compute the break-even point in units using **(a)** the mathematical equation and **(b)** contribution margin per unit.

Compute the break-even point.
(SO 6)

BE6-9 Turgro Corp. had total variable costs of $180,000, total fixed costs of $160,000, and total revenues of $300,000. Compute the required sales in dollars to break even.

Compute sales for target net income.
(SO 7)

BE6-10 For MeriDen Company, variable costs are 60% of sales, and fixed costs are $195,000. Management's net income goal is $75,000. Compute the required sales in dollars needed to achieve management's target net income of $75,000. (Use the contribution margin approach.)

Compute the margin of safety and the margin of safety ratio.
(SO 8)

BE6-11 For Dousmann Company actual sales are $1,200,000 and break-even sales are $840,000. Compute **(a)** the margin of safety in dollars and **(b)** the margin of safety ratio.

Compute the required sales in units for target net income.
(SO 7)

BE6-12 PCB Corporation has fixed costs of $480,000. It has a unit selling price of $6, unit variable cost of $4.50, and a target net income of $1,500,000. Compute the required sales in units to achieve its target net income.

EXERCISES

Define and classify variable, fixed, and mixed costs.
(SO 1, 3)

E6-1 Dye Company manufactures a single product. Annual production costs incurred in the manufacturing process are shown below for two levels of production.

	Costs Incurred			
Production in Units	**5,000**		**10,000**	
Production Costs	**Total Cost**	**Cost/ Unit**	**Total Cost**	**Cost/ Unit**
Direct materials	$8,250	$1.65	$16,500	$1.65
Direct labor	9,500	1.90	19,000	1.90
Utilities	1,500	0.30	2,500	0.25
Rent	4,000	0.80	4,000	0.40
Maintenance	800	0.16	1,100	0.11
Supervisory salaries	1,000	0.20	1,000	0.10

Instructions

(a) Define the terms variable costs, fixed costs, and mixed costs.
(b) Classify each cost above as either variable, fixed, or mixed.

Diagram cost behavior, determine relevant range, and classify costs.
(SO 1, 2)

E6-2 Kozy Enterprises is considering manufacturing a new product. It projects the cost of direct materials and rent for a range of output as shown below.

Output in Units	Rent Expense	Direct Materials
1,000	$ 5,000	$ 4,000
2,000	5,000	6,000
3,000	5,000	7,800
4,000	7,000	8,000
5,000	7,000	10,000
6,000	7,000	12,000
7,000	7,000	14,000
8,000	7,000	16,000
9,000	7,000	18,000
10,000	10,000	23,000
11,000	10,000	28,000
12,000	10,000	36,000

Instructions

(a) Diagram the behavior of each cost for output ranging from 1,000 to 12,000 units.
(b) Determine the relevant range of activity for this product.
(c) Calculate the variable cost per unit within the relevant range.
(d) Indicate the fixed cost within the relevant range.

Determine fixed and variable costs using the high-low method and prepare graph.
(SO 1, 3)

E6-3 The controller of Dugan Industries has collected the following monthly expense data for use in analyzing the cost behavior of maintenance costs.

Month	Total Maintenance Costs	Total Machine Hours
January	$2,400	300
February	3,000	400
March	3,600	600
April	4,500	790
May	3,200	500
June	4,900	800

Instructions

(a) Determine the fixed and variable cost components using the high-low method.
(b) Prepare a graph showing the behavior of maintenance costs, and identify the fixed and variable cost elements. Use 200-hour increments and $1,000 cost increments.

Classify variable, fixed, and mixed costs.
(SO 1, 3)

E6-4 Black Brothers Furniture Corporation incurred the following costs.

1. Wood used in the production of furniture.
2. Fuel used in delivery trucks.

3. Straight-line depreciation on factory building.
4. Screws used in the production of furniture.
5. Sales staff salaries.
6. Sales commissions.
7. Property taxes.
8. Insurance on buildings.
9. Hourly wages of furniture craftsmen.
10. Salaries of factory supervisors.
11. Utilities expense.
12. Telephone bill.

Instructions

Identify the costs above as variable, fixed, or mixed.

Determine fixed and variable costs using the high-low method and prepare graph.

(SO 1, 3)

E6-5 The controller of Gutierrez Industries has collected the following monthly expense data for use in analyzing the cost behavior of maintenance costs.

Month	Total Maintenance Costs	Total Machine Hours
January	$2,800	3,000
February	3,000	4,000
March	3,600	6,000
April	4,500	7,900
May	3,200	5,000
June	5,000	8,000

Instructions

(a) Determine the fixed and variable cost components using the high-low method.

(b) Prepare a graph showing the behavior of maintenance costs, and identify the fixed and variable cost elements. Use 2,000-hour increments and $1,000 cost increments.

Determine fixed, variable, and mixed costs.

(SO 1, 3)

E6-6 Mozena Corporation manufactures a single product. Monthly production costs incurred in the manufacturing process are shown below for the production of 3,000 units. The utilities and maintenance costs are mixed costs. The fixed portions of these costs are $300 and $200, respectively.

Production in Units	3,000
Production Costs	
Direct materials	$ 7,500
Direct labor	15,000
Utilities	1,800
Property taxes	1,000
Indirect labor	4,500
Supervisory salaries	1,800
Maintenance	1,100
Depreciation	2,400

Instructions

(a) Identify the above costs as variable, fixed, or mixed.

(b) Calculate the expected costs when production is 5,000 units.

Explain assumptions underlying CVP analysis.

(SO 4)

E6-7 Jim Thome wants Thome Company to use CVP analysis to study the effects of changes in costs and volume on the company. Thome has heard that certain assumptions must be valid in order for CVP analysis to be useful.

Instructions

Prepare a memo to Jim Thome concerning the assumptions that underlie CVP analysis.

Compute break-even point in units and dollars.

(SO 5, 6)

E6-8 Green with Envy provides environmentally friendly lawn services for homeowners. Its operating costs are as follows.

Depreciation	$1,500 per month
Advertising	$200 per month
Insurance	$2,000 per month
Weed and feed materials	$13 per lawn
Direct labor	$12 per lawn
Fuel	$2 per lawn

Green with Envy charges $60 per treatment for the average single-family lawn.

Instructions

Determine the company's break-even point in **(a)** number of lawns serviced per month and **(b)** dollars.

Compute break-even point.
(SO 5, 6)

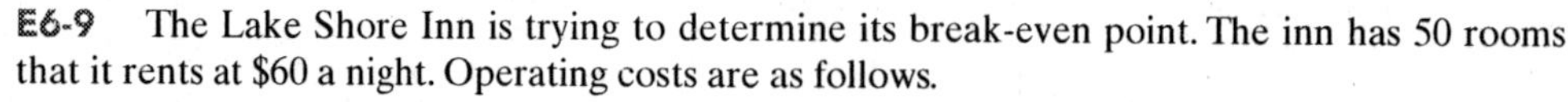

E6-9 The Lake Shore Inn is trying to determine its break-even point. The inn has 50 rooms that it rents at $60 a night. Operating costs are as follows.

Salaries	$7,200 per month
Utilities	$1,500 per month
Depreciation	$1,200 per month
Maintenance	$300 per month
Maid service	$8 per room
Other costs	$28 per room

Instructions

Determine the inn's break-even point in (1) number of rented rooms per month and (2) dollars.

Compute contribution margin and break-even point.
(SO 5, 6)

E6-10 In the month of March, New Day Spa services 570 clients at an average price of $120. During the month, fixed costs were $21,000 and variable costs were 65% of sales.

Instructions

(a) Determine the contribution margin in dollars, per unit, and as a ratio.
(b) Using the contribution margin technique, compute the break-even point in dollars and in units.

Compute break-even point.
(SO 5, 6)

E6-11 Airport Connection provides shuttle service between four hotels near a medical center and an international airport. Airport Connection uses two 10 passenger vans to offer 12 round trips per day. A recent month's activity in the form of a cost-volume-profit income statement is shown below.

Fare revenues (1,440 fares)		$36,000
Variable costs		
Fuel	$5,040	
Tolls and parking	3,100	
Maintenance	500	8,640
Contribution margin		27,360
Fixed costs		
Salaries	13,000	
Depreciation	1,300	
Insurance	1,128	15,428
Net income		$11,932

Instructions

(a) Calculate the break-even point in (1) dollars and (2) number of fares.
(b) Without calculations, determine the contribution margin at the break-even point.

Compute variable cost per unit, contribution margin ratio, and increase in fixed costs.
(SO 5, 6)

E6-12 In 2008, Hadicke Company had a break-even point of $350,000 based on a selling price of $7 per unit and fixed costs of $105,000. In 2009, the selling price and the variable cost per unit did not change, but the break-even point increased to $420,000.

Instructions

(a) Compute the variable cost per unit and the contribution margin ratio for 2008.
(b) Compute the increase in fixed costs for 2009.

Prepare CVP income statements.
(SO 5, 6)

E6-13 NIU Company has the following information available for September 2008.

Unit selling price of video game consoles	$ 400
Unit variable costs	$ 270
Total fixed costs	$52,000
Units sold	620

Instructions

(a) Prepare a CVP income statement that shows both total and per unit amounts.
(b) Compute NIU's break-even point in units.
(c) Prepare a CVP income statement for the break-even point that shows both total and per unit amounts.

E6-14 Lynn Company had $150,000 of net income in 2008 when the selling price per unit was $150, the variable costs per unit were $90, and the fixed costs were $570,000. Management expects per unit data and total fixed costs to remain the same in 2009. The president of Lynn Company is under pressure from stockholders to increase net income by $60,000 in 2009.

Compute various components to derive target net income under different assumptions.

(SO 6, 7)

Instructions

(a) Compute the number of units sold in 2008.
(b) Compute the number of units that would have to be sold in 2009 to reach the stockholders' desired profit level.
(c) Assume that Lynn Company sells the same number of units in 2009 as it did in 2008. What would the selling price have to be in order to reach the stockholders' desired profit level?

E6-15 Moran Company reports the following operating results for the month of August: Sales $350,000 (units 5,000); variable costs $210,000; and fixed costs $90,000. Management is considering the following independent courses of action to increase net income.

Compute net income under different alternatives.

(SO 7)

1. Increase selling price by 10% with no change in total variable costs.
2. Reduce variable costs to 55% of sales.

Instructions

Compute the net income to be earned under each alternative. Which course of action will produce the highest net income?

E6-16 Grissom Company estimates that variable costs will be 60% of sales, and fixed costs will total $800,000. The selling price of the product is $4.

Prepare a CVP graph and compute break-even point and margin of safety.

(SO 6, 8)

Instructions

(a) Prepare a CVP graph, assuming maximum sales of $3,200,000. (*Note*: Use $400,000 increments for sales and costs and 100,000 increments for units.)
(b) Compute the break-even point in (1) units and (2) dollars.
(c) Compute the margin of safety in (1) dollars and (2) as a ratio, assuming actual sales are $2.5 million.

EXERCISES: SET B

Visit the book's website at **www.wiley.com/college/weygandt**, and choose the Student Companion site, to access Exercise Set B.

PROBLEMS: SET A

WILEY PLUS

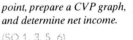

P6-1A Matt Reiss owns the Fredonia Barber Shop. He employs five barbers and pays each a base rate of $1,000 per month. One of the barbers serves as the manager and receives an extra $500 per month. In addition to the base rate, each barber also receives a commission of $5.50 per haircut.

Determine variable and fixed costs, compute break-even point, prepare a CVP graph, and determine net income.

(SO 1, 3, 5, 6)

Other costs are as follows.

Advertising	$200 per month
Rent	$900 per month
Barber supplies	$0.30 per haircut
Utilities	$175 per month plus $0.20 per haircut
Magazines	$25 per month

Matt currently charges $10 per haircut.

barber commission 5.50

Instructions

(a) Determine the variable cost per haircut and the total monthly fixed costs.
(b) Compute the break-even point in units and dollars.
(c) Prepare a CVP graph, assuming a maximum of 1,800 haircuts in a month. Use increments of 300 haircuts on the horizontal axis and $3,000 on the vertical axis.
(d) Determine net income, assuming 1,900 haircuts are given in a month.

VC $6

Prepare a CVP income statement, compute break-even point, contribution margin ratio, margin of safety ratio, and sales for target net income.

(SO 5, 6, 7, 8)

P6-2A Utech Company bottles and distributes Livit, a diet soft drink. The beverage is sold for 50 cents per 16-ounce bottle to retailers, who charge customers 75 cents per bottle. For the year 2008, management estimates the following revenues and costs.

Net sales	$1,800,000	Selling expenses—variable	$70,000
Direct materials	430,000	Selling expenses—fixed	65,000
Direct labor	352,000	Administrative expenses—variable	20,000
Manufacturing overhead—variable	316,000	Administrative expenses—fixed	60,000
Manufacturing overhead—fixed	283,000		

(b) (1) 2,400,000 units
(c) CM ratio # 34%

Instructions

(a) Prepare a CVP income statement for 2008 based on management's estimates.
(b) Compute the break-even point in (1) units and (2) dollars.
(c) Compute the contribution margin ratio and the margin of safety ratio. (Round to full percents.)
(d) Determine the sales dollars required to earn net income of $238,000.

Compute break-even point under alternative courses of action.

(SO 5, 6)

P6-3A Gorham Manufacturing's sales slumped badly in 2008. For the first time in its history, it operated at a loss. The company's income statement showed the following results from selling 600,000 units of product: Net sales $2,400,000; total costs and expenses $2,540,000; and net loss $140,000. Costs and expenses consisted of the amounts shown below.

	Total	Variable	Fixed
Cost of goods sold	$2,100,000	$1,440,000	$660,000
Selling expenses	240,000	72,000	168,000
Administrative expenses	200,000	48,000	152,000
	$2,540,000	$1,560,000	$980,000

Management is considering the following independent alternatives for 2009.

1. Increase unit selling price 20% with no change in costs, expenses, and sales volume.
2. Change the compensation of salespersons from fixed annual salaries totaling $210,000 to total salaries of $60,000 plus a 5% commission on net sales.

Instructions

(a) Compute the break-even point in dollars for 2008.
(b) Alternative 1 # $2,130,435
(b) Compute the break-even point in dollars under each of the alternative courses of action. (Round all ratios to nearest full percent.) Which course of action do you recommend?

Compute break-even point and margin of safety ratio, and prepare a CVP income statement before and after changes in business environment.

(SO 5, 6, 8)

P6-4A Alice Shoemaker is the advertising manager for Value Shoe Store. She is currently working on a major promotional campaign. Her ideas include the installation of a new lighting system and increased display space that will add $34,000 in fixed costs to the $270,000 currently spent. In addition, Alice is proposing that a 5% price decrease ($40 to $38) will produce a 20% increase in sales volume (20,000 to 24,000). Variable costs will remain at $22 per pair of shoes. Management is impressed with Alice's ideas but concerned about the effects that these changes will have on the break-even point and the margin of safety.

Instructions

(a) Compute the current break-even point in units, and compare it to the break-even point in units if Alice's ideas are used.
(b) Current margin of safety ratio # 25%
(b) Compute the margin of safety ratio for current operations and after Alice's changes are introduced. (Round to nearest full percent.)
(c) Prepare a CVP income statement for current operations and after Alice's changes are introduced. Would you make the changes suggested?

Compute contribution margin, fixed costs, break-even point, sales for target net income, and margin of safety ratio.

(SO 5, 6, 7, 8)

P6-5A Poole Corporation has collected the following information after its first year of sales. Net sales were $1,600,000 on 100,000 units; selling expenses $240,000 (40% variable and 60% fixed); direct materials $511,000; direct labor $285,000; administrative expenses $280,000 (20% variable and 80% fixed); manufacturing overhead $360,000 (70% variable and 30% fixed). Top management has asked you to do a CVP analysis so that it can make plans for the coming year. It has projected that unit sales will increase by 10% next year.

Instructions

(a) Compute (1) the contribution margin for the current year and the projected year, and (2) the fixed costs for the current year. (Assume that fixed costs will remain the same in the projected year.)

(b) Compute the break-even point in units and sales dollars for the current year. (b) 119,000 units

(c) The company has a target net income of $310,000. What is the required sales in dollars for the company to meet its target?

(d) If the company meets its target net income number, by what percentage could its sales fall before it is operating at a loss? That is, what is its margin of safety ratio?

PROBLEMS: SET B

Determine variable and fixed costs, compute break-even point, prepare a CVP graph, and determine net income.

(SO 1, 3, 5, 6)

P6-1B The Galena Barber Shop employs four barbers. One barber, who also serves as the manager, is paid a salary of $3,200 per month. The other barbers are paid $1,400 per month. In addition, each barber is paid a commission of $3 per haircut. Other monthly costs are: store rent $700 plus 60 cents per haircut, depreciation on equipment $500, barber supplies 40 cents per haircut, utilities $300, and advertising $100. The price of a haircut is $10.

Instructions

(a) Determine the variable cost per haircut and the total monthly fixed costs. (a) VC $4

(b) Compute the break-even point in units and dollars.

(c) Prepare a CVP graph, assuming a maximum of 1,800 haircuts in a month. Use increments of 300 haircuts on the horizontal axis and $3,000 increments on the vertical axis.

(d) Determine the net income, assuming 1,700 haircuts are given in a month.

Prepare a CVP income statement, compute break-even point, contribution margin ratio, margin of safety ratio, and sales for target net income.

(SO 5, 6, 7, 8)

P6-2B Wilks Company bottles and distributes No-FIZZ, a fruit drink. The beverage is sold for 50 cents per 16-ounce bottle to retailers, who charge customers 70 cents per bottle. For the year 2008, management estimates the following revenues and costs.

Net sales	$2,000,000	Selling expenses—variable	$ 100,000
Direct materials	360,000	Selling expenses—fixed	150,000
Direct labor	590,000	Administrative expenses—variable	40,000
Manufacturing overhead—variable	270,000	Administrative expenses—fixed	78,000
Manufacturing overhead—fixed	220,000		

Instructions

(a) Prepare a CVP income statement for 2008 based on management's estimates.

(b) Compute the break-even point in (1) units and (2) dollars. (b) (1) 2,800,000 units

(c) Compute the contribution margin ratio and the margin of safety ratio. (c) CM ratio # 32%

(d) Determine the sales dollars required to earn net income of $272,000.

Compute break-even point under alternative courses of action.

(SO 5, 6)

P6-3B Milner Manufacturing had a bad year in 2008. For the first time in its history it operated at a loss. The company's income statement showed the following results from selling 60,000 units of product: Net sales $1,500,000; total costs and expenses $1,660,000; and net loss $160,000. Costs and expenses consisted of the following.

	Total	Variable	Fixed
Cost of goods sold	$1,200,000	$780,000	$420,000
Selling expenses	340,000	65,000	275,000
Administrative expenses	120,000	55,000	65,000
	$1,660,000	$900,000	$760,000

Management is considering the following independent alternatives for 2009.

1. Increase unit selling price 20% with no change in costs, expenses, and sales volume.
2. Change the compensation of salespersons from fixed annual salaries totaling $200,000 to total salaries of $30,000 plus a 6% commission on net sales.

Instructions

(b) Alternative 1 # $1,520,000

(a) Compute the break-even point in dollars for 2008.

(b) Compute the break-even point in dollars under each of the alternative courses of action. (Round all ratios to nearest full percent.) Which course of action do you recommend?

Compute break-even point and margin of safety ratio, and prepare a CVP income statement before and after changes in business environment.

(SO 5, 6, 8)

P6-4B Anne Ogilvie is the advertising manager for Thrifty Shoe Store. She is currently working on a major promotional campaign. Her ideas include the installation of a new lighting system and increased display space that will add $51,000 in fixed costs to the $204,000 currently spent. In addition, Anne is proposing that a 6⅔% price decrease (from $30 to $28) will produce an increase in sales volume from 16,000 to 21,000 units. Variable costs will remain at $13 per pair of shoes. Management is impressed with Anne's ideas but concerned about the effects that these changes will have on the break-even point and the margin of safety.

Instructions

(a) Compute the current break-even point in units, and compare it to the break-even point in units if Anne's ideas are used.

(b) Current margin of safety ratio 25%

(b) Compute the margin of safety ratio for current operations and after Anne's changes are introduced. (Round to nearest full percent.)

(c) Prepare a CVP income statement for current operations and after Anne's changes are introduced. Would you make the changes suggested?

Compute contribution margin, fixed costs, break-even point, sales for target net income, and margin of safety ratio.

(SO 5, 6, 7, 8)

P6-5B Washington Corporation has collected the following information after its first year of sales. Net sales were $2,400,000 on 200,000 units; selling expenses $360,000 (30% variable and 70% fixed); direct materials $626,500; direct labor $507,500; administrative expenses $420,000 (40% variable and 60% fixed); manufacturing overhead $540,000 (50% variable and 50% fixed). Top management has asked you to do a CVP analysis so that it can make plans for the coming year. It has projected that unit sales will increase by 20% next year.

Instructions

(a) Compute (1) the contribution margin for the current year and the projected year, and (2) the fixed costs for the current year. (Assume that fixed costs will remain the same in the projected year.)

(b) 215,000 units

(b) Compute the break-even point in units and sales dollars for the current year.

(c) The company has a target net income of $620,000. What is the required sales in dollars for the company to meet its target?

(d) If the company meets its target net income number, by what percentage could its sales fall before it is operating at a loss? That is, what is its margin of safety ratio?

PROBLEMS: SET C

Visit the book's website at **www.wiley.com/college/weygandt**, and choose the Student Companion site, to access Problem Set C.

WATERWAYS CONTINUING PROBLEM

(*Note:* This is a continuation of the Waterways Problem from previous chapters.)

WCP6 The Vice President for Sales and Marketing at Waterways Corporation is planning for production needs to meet sales demand in the coming year. He is also trying to determine how the company's profits might be increased in the coming year. This problem asks you to use cost-volume-profit concepts to help Waterways understand contribution margins of some of its products and to decide whether to mass-produce certain products.

Go to the book's website, **www.wiley.com/college/weygandt,** *to find the remainder of this problem.*

BROADENING YOUR PERSPECTIVE

DECISION MAKING ACROSS THE ORGANIZATION

BYP6-1 Gagliano Company has decided to introduce a new product. The new product can be manufactured by either a capital-intensive method or a labor-intensive method. The manufacturing method will not affect the quality of the product. The estimated manufacturing costs by the two methods are as follows.

	Capital-Intensive	Labor-Intensive
Direct materials	$5 per unit	$5.50 per unit
Direct labor	$6 per unit	$8.00 per unit
Variable overhead	$3 per unit	$4.50 per unit
Fixed manufacturing costs	$2,508,000	$1,538,000

Gagliano's market research department has recommended an introductory unit sales price of $30. The incremental selling expenses are estimated to be $502,000 annually plus $2 for each unit sold, regardless of manufacturing method.

Instructions

With the class divided into groups, answer the following.

(a) Calculate the estimated break-even point in annual unit sales of the new product if Gagliano Company uses the:
  (1) capital-intensive manufacturing method.
  (2) labor-intensive manufacturing method.

(b) Determine the annual unit sales volume at which Gagliano Company would be indifferent between the two manufacturing methods.

(c) Explain the circumstance under which Gagliano should employ each of the two manufacturing methods.

(CMA adapted)

MANAGERIAL ANALYSIS

BYP6-2 The condensed income statement for the Terri and Jerry partnership for 2008 is as follows.

TERRI AND JERRY COMPANY
Income Statement
For the Year Ended December 31, 2008

Sales (200,000 units)		$1,200,000
Cost of goods sold		800,000
Gross profit		400,000
Operating expenses		
Selling	$280,000	
Administrative	160,000	440,000
Net loss		($40,000)

A cost behavior analysis indicates that 75% of the cost of goods sold are variable, 50% of the selling expenses are variable, and 25% of the administrative expenses are variable.

Instructions

(Round to nearest unit, dollar, and percentage, where necessary. Use the CVP income statement format in computing profits.)

(a) Compute the break-even point in total sales dollars and in units for 2008.

(b) Terri has proposed a plan to get the partnership "out of the red" and improve its profitability. She feels that the quality of the product could be substantially improved by spending $0.25 more per unit on better raw materials. The selling price per unit could be increased to only $6.25 because of competitive pressures. Terri estimates that sales volume will increase by 30%. What effect would Terri's plan have on the profits and the break-even point in dollars of the partnership? (Round the contribution margin ratio to two decimal places.)

(c) Jerry was a marketing major in college. He believes that sales volume can be increased only by intensive advertising and promotional campaigns. He therefore proposed the following plan as an alternative to Terri's. (1) Increase variable selling expenses to $0.79 per unit, (2) lower the selling price per unit by $0.30, and (3) increase fixed selling expenses by $35,000. Jerry quoted an old marketing research report that said that sales volume would increase by 60% if these changes were made. What effect would Jerry's plan have on the profits and the break-even point in dollars of the partnership?

(d) Which plan should be accepted? Explain your answer.

REAL-WORLD FOCUS

BYP6-3 The Coca-Cola Company hardly needs an introduction. A line taken from the cover of a recent annual report says it all: If you measured time in servings of Coca-Cola, "a billion Coca-Cola's ago was yesterday morning." On average, every U.S. citizen drinks 363 8-ounce servings of Coca-Cola products each year. Coca-Cola's primary line of business is the making and selling of syrup to bottlers. These bottlers then sell the finished bottles and cans of Coca-Cola to the consumer.

In the annual report of Coca-Cola, the following information was provided.

THE COCA-COLA COMPANY
Management Discussion

Our gross margin declined to 61 percent this year from 62 percent in the prior year, primarily due to costs for materials such as sweeteners and packaging.

The increases [in selling expenses] in the last two years were primarily due to higher marketing expenditures in support of our Company's volume growth.

We measure our sales volume in two ways: (1) gallon shipments of concentrates and syrups and (2) unit cases of finished product (bottles and cans of Coke sold by bottlers).

Instructions

Answer the following questions.

(a) Are sweeteners and packaging a variable cost or a fixed cost? What is the impact on the contribution margin of an increase in the per unit cost of sweeteners or packaging? What are the implications for profitability?

(b) In your opinion, are marketing expenditures a fixed cost, variable cost, or mixed cost to The Coca-Cola Company? Give justification for your answer.

(c) Which of the two measures cited for measuring volume represents the activity index as defined in this chapter? Why might Coca-Cola use two different measures?

EXPLORING THE WEB

BYP6-4 Ganong Bros. Ltd., located in St. Stephen, New Brunswick, is Canada's oldest independent candy company. Its products are distributed worldwide. In 1885, Ganong invented the popular "chicken bone," a cinnamon flavored, pink, hard candy jacket over a chocolate center. The home page of Ganong, listed on the next page, includes information about the company and its products.

Address: www.ganong.com/retail/chicken_bones.html, or go to **www.wiley.com/college/weygandt**

Instructions

Read the description of "chicken bones," and answer the following.

(a) Describe the steps in making "chicken bones."

(b) Identify at least two variable and two fixed costs that are likely to affect the production of "chicken bones."

COMMUNICATION ACTIVITY

BYP6-5 Your roommate asks your help on the following questions about CVP analysis formulas.

(a) How can the mathematical equation for break-even sales show both sales units and sales dollars?

(b) How do the formulas differ for contribution margin per unit and contribution margin ratio?

(c) How can contribution margin be used to determine break-even sales in units and in dollars?

Instructions

Write a memo to your roommate stating the relevant formulas and answering each question.

ETHICS CASE

BYP6-6 Kenny Hampton is an accountant for Bartley Company. Early this year Kenny made a highly favorable projection of sales and profits over the next 3 years for Bartley's hot-selling computer PLEX. As a result of the projections Kenny presented to senior management, they decided to expand production in this area. This decision led to dislocations of some plant personnel who were reassigned to one of the company's newer plants in another state. However, no one was fired, and in fact the company expanded its work force slightly.

Unfortunately Kenny rechecked his computations on the projections a few months later and found that he had made an error that would have reduced his projections substantially. Luckily, sales of PLEX have exceeded projections so far, and management is satisfied with its decision. Kenny, however, is not sure what to do. Should he confess his honest mistake and jeopardize his possible promotion? He suspects that no one will catch the error because sales of PLEX have exceeded his projections, and it appears that profits will materialize close to his projections.

Instructions

(a) Who are the stakeholders in this situation?

(b) Identify the ethical issues involved in this situation.

(c) What are the possible alternative actions for Kenny? What would you do in Kenny's position?

"ALL ABOUT YOU" ACTIVITY

BYP6-7 In the "All About You" feature in this chapter, you learned that cost-volume-profit analysis can be used in making personal financial decisions. The purchase of a new car is one of your biggest personal expenditures. It is important that you carefully analyze your options.

Suppose that you are considering the purchase of a hybrid vehicle. Let's assume the following facts: The hybrid will initially cost an additional $3,000 above the cost of a traditional vehicle. The hybrid will get 40 miles per gallon of gas, and the traditional car will get 30 miles per gallon. Also, assume that the cost of gas is $3 per gallon.

Instructions

Using the facts above, answer the following questions.

(a) What is the variable gasoline cost of going one mile in the hybrid car? What is the variable cost of going one mile in the traditional car?

(b) Using the information in part (a), if "miles" is your unit of measure, what is the "contribution margin" of the hybrid vehicle relative to the traditional vehicle? That is, express the variable cost savings on a per-mile basis.

(c) How many miles would you have to drive in order to break even on your investment in the hybrid car?
(d) What other factors might you want to consider?

Answers to Insight and Accounting Across the Organization Questions

Woodworker Runs an Efficient Operation for Producing Furniture, p. 274

Q: Are the costs associated with use of the computer-driven cutting machines fixed or variable?
A: *The cost of the cutting machine that is recognized through depreciation expense is a fixed cost. The costs of operating (electricity) and maintaining the machine are variable.*

Charter Flights Offer a Good Deal, p. 284

Q: How did FlightServe determine that it would break even with 3.3 seats full per flight?
A: *FlightServe determined its break-even point with the following formula:*
Fixed costs ÷ Contribution margin per seat occupied = Break-even point in seats.

How a Rolling Stones' Tour Makes Money, p. 288

Q: What amount of sales dollars are required for the promoter to break even?
A: *Fixed costs = $1,200,000 + $400,000 = $1,600,000*
Contribution margin ratio = 80%
Break-even sales = $1,600,000 ÷ .80 = $2,000,000

Authors' Comments on *All About You:* A Hybrid Dilemma, p. 289

Just like the break-even analysis that a company would perform on an investment in a new piece of equipment, the break-even analysis of a hybrid car requires a lot of assumptions. After deciding on a car, you need to estimate how many miles you would drive each year and how many years you would own the car. If you trade cars every two or three years, it is unlikely, with the hybrids available today, that you will recoup your initial investment. Your chances of recouping the investment increase the longer you keep the car and the more miles you drive. You need to determine whether you will get a federal tax credit or a rebate from your employer. You also need to estimate what the car would be worth when you sell it. Based on assumed values for the average driver, *Consumer Reports* determined that only the most fuel-efficient hybrids save enough on fuel to cover their additional costs, but individual results will vary depending on the factors mentioned above.

Answers to Self-Study Questions

1. d **2.** c **3.** a **4.** a **5.** c **6.** d **7.** a **8.** c **9.** b **10.** b

Remember to go back to the Navigator box on the chapter-opening page and check off your completed work.

Chapter 7

Budgetary Planning

STUDY OBJECTIVES

After studying this chapter, you should be able to:

1 Indicate the benefits of budgeting.
2 State the essentials of effective budgeting.
3 Identify the budgets that comprise the master budget.
4 Describe the sources for preparing the budgeted income statement.
5 Explain the principal sections of a cash budget.
6 Indicate the applicability of budgeting in nonmanufacturing companies.

The Navigator

- Scan **Study Objectives**
- Read **Feature Story**
- Read **Preview**
- Read text and answer **Before You Go On** p. 315 p. 319 p. 326 p. 329
- Work **Using the Decision Toolkit**
- Review **Summary of Study Objectives**
- Work **Demonstration Problem**
- Answer **Self-Study Questions**
- Complete **Assignments**

Feature Story

THE NEXT AMAZON.COM? NOT QUITE

The bursting of the dot-com bubble resulted in countless stories of dot-com failures. Many of these ventures were half-baked, get-rich-quick schemes, rarely based on sound business practices. Initially they saw money flowing in faster than they knew what to do with—which was precisely the problem. Without proper planning and budgeting, much of the money went to waste. In some cases, failure was actually brought on by rapid, uncontrolled growth.

One such example was online discount bookseller, www.Positively-You.com. One of the website's co-founders, Lyle Bowline, had never run a business. However, his experience as an assistant director of an entrepreneurial center had provided him with knowledge about the do's and don'ts of small business. To minimize costs, he started the company small and simple. He invested $5,000 in computer equipment and ran the business out of his basement. In the early months, even though sales were only about $2,000 a month, the company actually made a profit because it kept its costs low (a feat few other dot-coms could boast of).

Things changed dramatically when the company received national publicity in the financial press. Suddenly the company's sales increased to $50,000 a month—fully 25 times the previous level. The "simple" little business suddenly needed a business plan, a strategic plan, and a budget. It needed to rent office space and to hire employees.

Initially, members of a local book club donated time to help meet the sudden demand. Some put in so much time that eventually the company hired them. Quickly the number of paid employees ballooned. The sudden growth necessitated detailed planning and budgeting. The need for a proper budget was accentuated by the fact that the company's gross profit was only 16 cents on each dollar of goods sold. This meant that after paying for its inventory, the company had only 16 cents of every dollar to cover its remaining operating costs.

Unfortunately, the company never got things under control. Within a few months, sales had plummeted to $12,000 per month. At this level of sales the company could not meet the mountain of monthly expenses that it had accumulated in trying to grow. Ironically, the company's sudden success, and the turmoil it created, appears to have been what eventually caused the company to fail.

The Navigator

Inside Chapter 7

- **Businesses Often Feel Too Busy to Plan for the Future** (p. 312)
- **Which Budget Approach Do You Prefer?** (p. 314)
- **Without a Budget, Can the Games Begin?** (p. 324)
- ***All About You:* Avoiding Personal Financial Disaster** (p. 330)

Preview of Chapter 7

As the Feature Story about Positively-You.com indicates, budgeting is critical to financial well-being. As a student, you budget your study time and your money. Families budget income and expenses. Governmental agencies budget revenues and expenditures. Business enterprises use budgets in planning and controlling their operations.

Our primary focus in this chapter is budgeting—specifically, how budgeting is used as a *planning tool* by management. Through budgeting, it should be possible for management to maintain enough cash to pay creditors, to have sufficient raw materials to meet production requirements, and to have adequate finished goods to meet expected sales.

The content and organization of Chapter 7 are as follows.

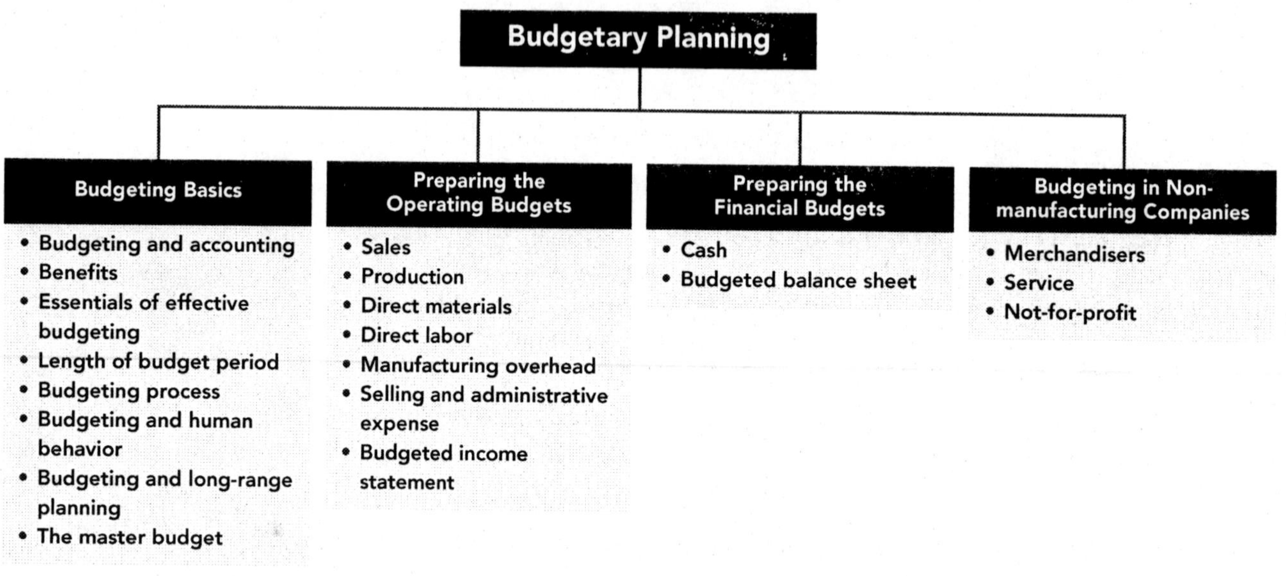

The Navigator

BUDGETING BASICS

One of management's major responsibilities is planning. As explained in Chapter 1, **planning** is the process of establishing enterprise-wide objectives. A successful organization makes both long-term and short-term plans. These plans set forth the objectives of the company and the proposed way of accomplishing them.

A **budget** is a formal written statement of management's plans for a specified future time period, expressed in financial terms. It normally represents the primary method of communicating agreed-upon objectives throughout the organization. Once adopted, a budget becomes an important basis for evaluating performance. It promotes efficiency and serves as a deterrent to waste and inefficiency. We consider the role of budgeting as a **control device** in Chapter 8.

Budgeting and Accounting

Accounting information makes major contributions to the budgeting process. From the accounting records, companies can obtain historical data on revenues, costs, and expenses. These data are helpful in formulating future budget goals.

Normally, accountants have the responsibility for presenting management's budgeting goals in financial terms. In this role, they translate management's plans and communicate the budget to employees throughout the company. They prepare periodic budget reports that provide the basis for measuring performance and comparing actual results with planned objectives. The budget itself, and the administration of the budget, however, are entirely management responsibilities.

The Benefits of Budgeting

The primary benefits of budgeting are:

STUDY OBJECTIVE 1

Indicate the benefits of budgeting.

1. It requires all levels of management to **plan ahead** and to formalize goals on a recurring basis.
2. It provides **definite objectives** for evaluating performance at each level of responsibility.
3. It creates an **early warning system** for potential problems so that management can make changes before things get out of hand.
4. It facilitates the **coordination of activities** within the business. It does this by correlating the goals of each segment with overall company objectives. Thus, the company can integrate production and sales promotion with expected sales.
5. It results in greater **management awareness** of the entity's overall operations and the impact on operations of external factors, such as economic trends.
6. It **motivates personnel** throughout the organization to meet planned objectives.

A budget is an aid to management; it is not a *substitute* for management. A budget cannot operate or enforce itself. Companies can realize the benefits of budgeting only when managers carefully administer budgets.

Essentials of Effective Budgeting

STUDY OBJECTIVE 2

State the essentials of effective budgeting.

Effective budgeting depends on a **sound organizational structure**. In such a structure, authority and responsibility for all phases of operations are clearly defined. Budgets based on **research and analysis** should result in realistic goals that will contribute to the growth and profitability of a company. And, the effectiveness of a budget program is directly related to its **acceptance by all levels of management**.

Once adopted, the budget is an important tool for evaluating performance. Managers should systematically and periodically review variations between actual and expected results to determine their cause(s). However, individuals should not be held responsible for variations that are beyond their control.

Length of the Budget Period

The budget period is not necessarily one year in length. **A budget may be prepared for any period of time.** Various factors influence the length of the budget period. These factors include the type of budget, the nature of the organization, the need for periodic appraisal, and prevailing business conditions. For example, cash may be budgeted monthly, whereas a plant expansion budget may cover a 10-year period.

The budget period should be long enough to provide an attainable goal under normal business conditions. Ideally, the time period should minimize the impact of seasonal or cyclical fluctuations. On the other hand, the budget period should not be so long that reliable estimates are impossible.

The **most common budget period is one year**. The annual budget, in turn, is often supplemented by monthly and quarterly budgets. Many companies use **continuous 12-month budgets**. These budgets drop the month just ended and add a future month. One advantage of continuous budgeting is that it keeps management planning a full year ahead.

The Budgeting Process

The development of the budget for the coming year generally starts several months before the end of the current year. The budgeting process usually begins with the collection of data from each organizational unit of the company. Past performance is often the starting point from which future budget goals are formulated.

The budget is developed within the framework of a **sales forecast**. This forecast shows potential sales for the industry and the company's expected share of such sales. Sales forecasting involves a consideration of various factors: (1) general economic conditions, (2) industry trends, (3) market research studies, (4) anticipated advertising and promotion, (5) previous market share, (6) changes in prices, and (7) technological developments. The input of sales personnel and top management is essential to the sales forecast.

In small companies like Positively-You.com, the budgeting process is often informal. In larger companies, a **budget committee** has responsibility for coordinating the preparation of the budget. The committee ordinarily includes the president, treasurer, chief accountant (controller), and management personnel from each of the major areas of the company, such as sales, production, and research. The budget committee serves as a review board where managers can defend their budget goals and requests. Differences are reviewed, modified if necessary, and reconciled. The budget is then put in its final form by the budget committee, approved, and distributed.

ACCOUNTING ACROSS THE ORGANIZATION

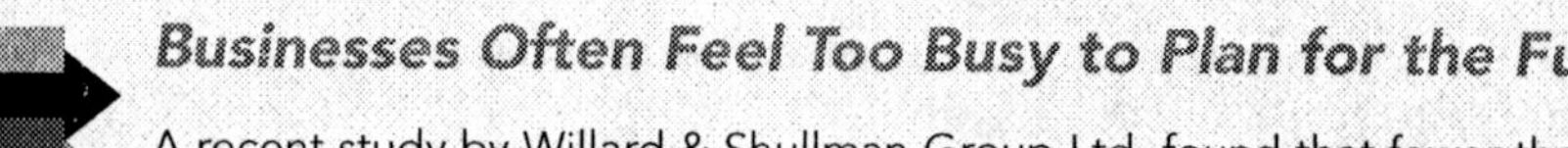

Businesses Often Feel Too Busy to Plan for the Future

A recent study by Willard & Shullman Group Ltd. found that fewer than 14% of businesses with fewer than 500 employees do an annual budget or have a written business plan. In all, nearly 60% of these businesses have no plans on paper at all. For many small businesses the basic assumption is that, "As long as I sell as much as I can, and keep my employees paid, I'm doing OK." A few small business owners even say that they see no need for budgeting and planning. Most small business owners, though, say that they understand that budgeting and planning are critical for survival and growth. But given the long hours that they already work addressing day-to-day challenges, they also say that they are "just too busy to plan for the future."

? Describe a situation in which a business "sells as much as it can" but cannot "keep its employees paid."

Budgeting and Human Behavior

A budget can have a significant impact on human behavior. It may inspire a manager to higher levels of performance. Or, it may discourage additional effort and pull down the morale of a manager. Why do these diverse effects occur? The answer is found in how the budget is developed and administered.

In developing the budget, each level of management should be invited to participate. This "bottom-to-top" approach is referred to as **participative budgeting**.

The advantages of participative budgeting are, first, that lower-level managers have more detailed knowledge of their specific area and thus are able to provide more accurate budgetary estimates. Second, when lower-level managers participate in the budgeting process, they are more likely to perceive the resulting budget as fair. The overall goal is to reach agreement on a budget that the managers consider fair and achievable, but which also meets the corporate goals set by top management. When this goal is met, the budget will provide positive motivation for the managers. In contrast, if the managers view the budget as being unfair and unrealistic, they may feel discouraged and uncommitted to budget goals. The risk of having unrealistic budgets is generally greater when the budget is developed from top management down to lower management than vice versa.

Participative budgeting does, however, have potential disadvantages. First, it is more time-consuming (and thus more costly) than a "top-down" approach, in which the budget is simply dictated to lower-level managers. A second disadvantage is that participative budgeting can foster budgetary "gaming" through budgetary slack. **Budgetary slack** occurs when managers intentionally underestimate budgeted revenues or overestimate budgeted expenses in order to make it easier to achieve budgetary goals. To minimize budgetary slack, higher-level managers must carefully review and thoroughly question the budget projections provided to them by employees whom they supervise. Illustration 7-1 graphically displays the appropriate flow of budget data from bottom to top in an organization.

Illustration 7-1
Flow of budget data from lower levels of management to top levels

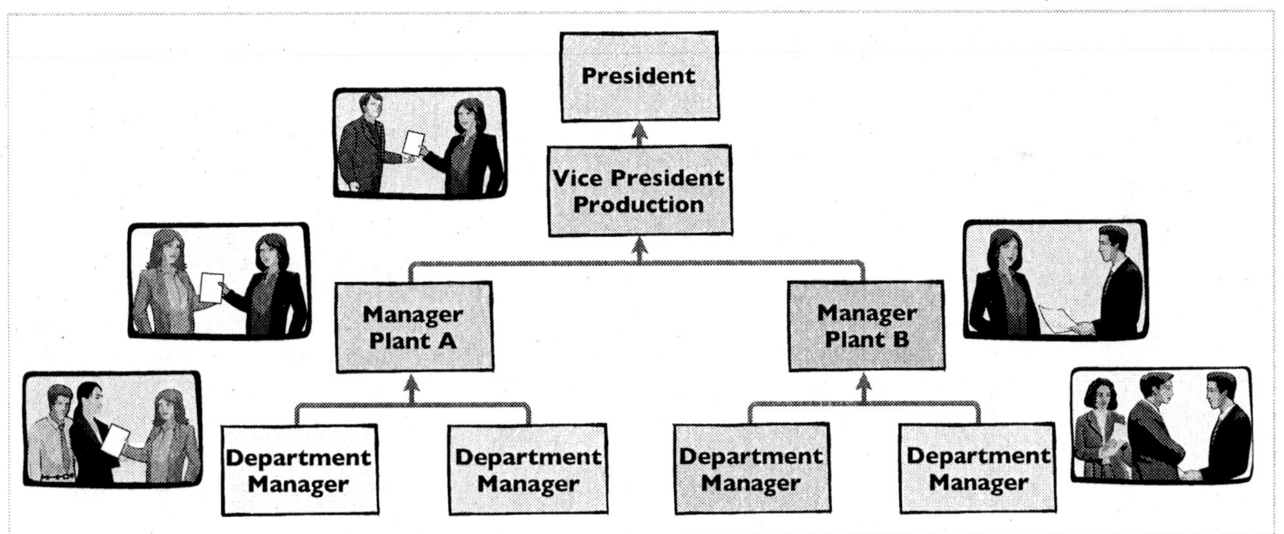

For the budget to be effective, top management must completely support the budget. The budget is an important basis for evaluating performance. It also can be used as a positive aid in achieving projected goals. The effect of an evaluation is positive when top management tempers criticism with advice and assistance. In contrast, a manager is likely to respond negatively if top management uses the budget exclusively to assess blame. A budget should not be used as a pressure device to force improved performance. In sum, a budget can be a manager's friend or a foe.

ETHICS NOTE

Unrealistic budgets can lead to unethical employee behavior such as cutting corners on the job or distorting internal financial reports.

ACCOUNTING ACROSS THE ORGANIZATION

Which Budget Approach Do You Prefer?

Not too long ago, in an effort to revive its plummeting stock, Time Warner's top management determined and publicly announced bold new financial goals for the coming year. Unfortunately, these goals were not reached.

The next year the company got a new CEO who promised, "We will not over promise, and we will deliver." The new budgets were developed with each operating unit setting what it felt were optimistic but attainable goals. In the words of one manager, using this approach created a sense of teamwork: "We're all going forward with our arms locked together."

Source: Carol J. Loomis, "AOL Time Warner's New Math," *Fortune*, February 4, 2002, pp. 98–102.

? What approach did Time Warner use to prepare the old budget? What approach did it use to prepare the new budget?

Budgeting and Long-Range Planning

Budgeting and long-range planning are not the same. One important difference is the **time period involved**. The maximum length of a budget is usually one year, and budgets are often prepared for shorter periods of time, such as a month or a quarter. In contrast, long-range planning usually encompasses a period of at least five years.

HELPFUL HINT

In comparing a budget with a long-range plan: (1) Which has more detail? (2) Which is done for a longer period of time? (3) Which is more concerned with short-term goals? Answers: (1) Budget. (2) Long-range plan. (3) Budget.

A second significant difference is in **emphasis**. Budgeting focuses on achieving specific short-term goals, such as meeting annual profit objectives. **Long-range planning**, on the other hand, identifies long-term goals, selects strategies to achieve those goals, and develops policies and plans to implement the strategies. In long-range planning, management also considers anticipated trends in the economic and political environment and how the company should cope with them.

The final difference between budgeting and long-range planning relates to the **amount of detail presented**. Budgets, as you will see in this chapter, can be very detailed. Long-range plans contain considerably less detail. The data in long-range plans are intended more for a review of progress toward long-term goals than as a basis of control for achieving specific results. The primary objective of long-range planning is to develop the best strategy to maximize the company's performance over an extended future period.

The Master Budget

STUDY OBJECTIVE 3

Identify the budgets that comprise the master budget.

The term "budget" is actually a shorthand term to describe a variety of budget documents. All of these documents are combined into a master budget. The **master budget** is a set of interrelated budgets that constitutes a plan of action for a specified time period.

The master budget contains two classes of budgets. **Operating budgets** are the individual budgets that result in the preparation of the budgeted income statement. These budgets establish goals for the company's sales and production personnel. In contrast, **financial budgets** are the capital expenditure budget, the cash budget, and the budgeted balance sheet. These budgets focus primarily on the cash resources needed to fund expected operations and planned capital expenditures.

Illustration 7-2 pictures the individual budgets included in a master budget, and the sequence in which they are prepared. The company first develops the operating budgets, beginning with the sales budget. Then it prepares the financial budgets. We will explain and illustrate each budget shown in Illustration 7-2 except the capital expenditure budget. That budget is discussed under the topic of capital budgeting in Chapter 10.

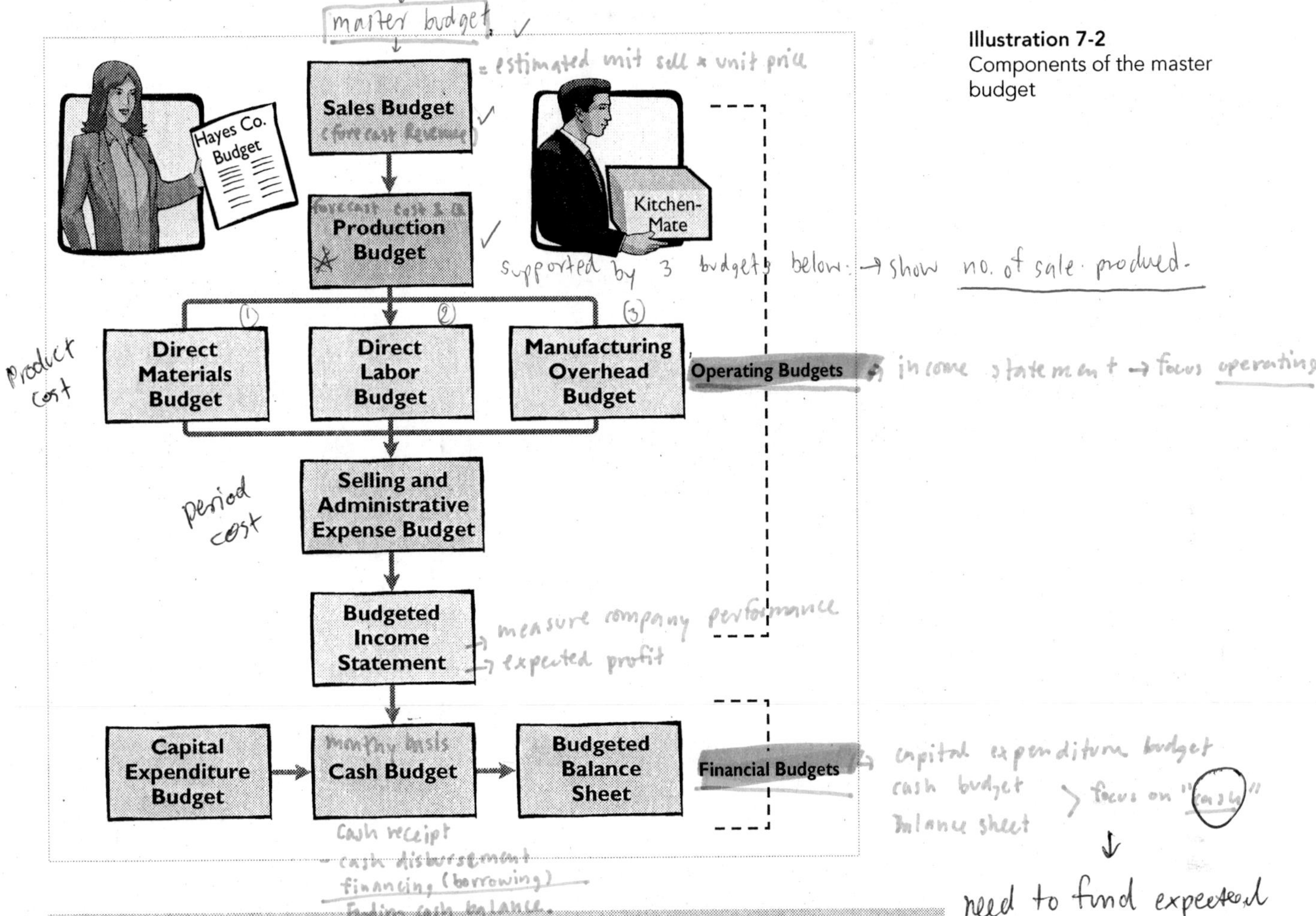

Illustration 7-2
Components of the master budget

Before You Go On...

REVIEW IT

1. What are the benefits of budgeting?
2. What are the factors essential to effective budgeting?
3. How does the budget process work?
4. How does budgeting differ from long-range planning?
5. What is a master budget?

The Navigator

PREPARING THE OPERATING BUDGETS

We use a case study of Hayes Company in preparing the operating budgets. Hayes manufactures and sells a single product, Kitchen-Mate. The budgets are prepared by quarters for the year ending December 31, 2008. Hayes Company begins its annual budgeting process on September 1, 2007, and it completes the budget for 2008 by December 1, 2007.

Sales Budget

HELPFUL HINT

For a retail or manufacturing company, what is the starting point in preparing the master budget, and why? Answer: The sales budget is the starting point for the master budget. It sets the level of activity for other functions such as production and purchasing.

As shown in the master budget in Illustration 7-2, **the sales budget is the first budget prepared.** Each of the other budgets depends on the sales budget. The **sales budget** is derived from the sales forecast. It represents management's best estimate of sales revenue for the budget period. An inaccurate sales budget may adversely affect net income. For example, an overly optimistic sales budget may result in excessive inventories that may have to be sold at reduced prices. In contrast, an unduly conservative budget may result in loss of sales revenue due to inventory shortages.

Forecasting sales is challenging. For example, consider the forecasting challenges faced by major sports arenas, whose revenues depend on the success of the home team. Madison Square Garden's revenues from April to June were $193 million when the Knicks made the NBA playoffs. But revenues were only $133.2 million a couple of years later when the team did not make the playoffs. Or consider the challenges faced by Hollywood movie producers in predicting the complicated revenue stream produced by a new movie. Movie theater ticket sales represent only 20% of total revenue. The bulk of revenue comes from global sales, DVDs, video-on-demand, merchandising products, and videogames, all of which are difficult to forecast.

The sales budget is prepared by multiplying the expected unit sales volume for each product by its anticipated unit selling price. Hayes Company expects sales volume to be 3,000 units in the first quarter, with 500-unit increases in each succeeding quarter. Illustration 7-3 shows the sales budget for the year, by quarters, based on a sales price of $60 per unit.

Illustration 7-3
Sales budget

Hayes Company Sales Budget.xls
File Edit View Insert Format Tools Data Window Help

	A	B	C	D	E	F
1	HAYES COMPANY					
2	Sales Budget					
3	For the Year Ending December 31, 2008					
4		Quarter				
5		1	2	3	4	Year
6	Expected unit sales	3,000	3,500	4,000	4,500	15,000
7	Unit selling price	× $60	× $60	× $60	× $60	× $60
8	Total sales	$180,000	$210,000	$240,000	$270,000	$900,000

Some companies classify the anticipated sales revenue as cash or credit sales and by geographical regions, territories, or salespersons.

Production Budget

The **production budget** shows the units to produce to meet anticipated sales. Production requirements are determined from the following formula.[1]

Illustration 7-4
Production requirements formula

Budgeted Sales Units	+	Desired Ending Finished Goods Units	−	Beginning Finished Goods Units	=	Required Production Units

[1]This formula ignores any work in process inventories, which are assumed to be nonexistent in Hayes Company.

A realistic estimate of ending inventory is essential in scheduling production requirements. Excessive inventories in one quarter may lead to cutbacks in production and employee layoffs in a subsequent quarter. On the other hand, inadequate inventories may result either in added costs for overtime work or in lost sales. Hayes Company believes it can meet future sales requirements by maintaining an ending inventory equal to 20% of the next quarter's budgeted sales volume. For example, the ending finished goods inventory for the first quarter is 700 units (20% × anticipated second-quarter sales of 3,500 units). Illustration 7-5 shows the production budget.

Illustration 7-5
Production budget

Hayes Company Production Budget.xls

File Edit View Insert Format Tools Data Window Help

HAYES COMPANY
Production Budget
For the Year Ending December 31, 2008

	Quarter 1	Quarter 2	Quarter 3	Quarter 4	Year
Expected unit sales (Illustration 9-3)	3,000	3,500	4,000	4,500	
Add: Desired ending finished goods units[a]	700	800	900	1,000[b]	
Total required units	3,700	4,300	4,900	5,500	
Less: Beginning finished goods units	600[c]	700	800	900	
Required production units	**3,100**	**3,600**	**4,100**	**4,600**	**15,400**

[a]20% of next quarter's sales
[b]Expected 2009 first-quarter sales, 5,000 units × 20%
[c]20% of estimated first-quarter 2008 sales units

The production budget, in turn, provides the basis for the budgeted costs for each manufacturing cost element, as explained in the following pages.

Direct Materials Budget

The **direct materials budget** shows both the quantity and cost of direct materials to be purchased. The quantities of direct materials are derived from the following formula.

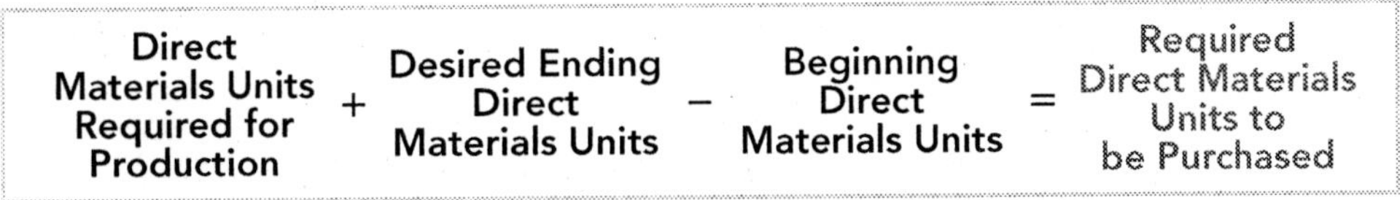

Illustration 7-6
Formula for direct materials quantities

The company then computes the budgeted cost of direct materials to be purchased by multiplying the required units of direct materials by the anticipated cost per unit.

The desired ending inventory is again a key component in the budgeting process. For example, inadequate inventories could result in temporary shutdowns of production. Because of its close proximity to suppliers, Hayes Company maintains an ending inventory of raw materials equal to 10% of the next quarter's production requirements. The manufacture of each Kitchen-Mate requires 2 pounds of raw materials, and the expected cost per pound is $4. Illustration 7-7 (page 318) shows the direct materials budget. Assume that the desired ending direct materials amount is 1,020 pounds for the fourth quarter of 2008.

Illustration 7-7
Direct materials budget

Hayes Company Direct Materials Budget.xls

File Edit View Insert Format Tools Data Window Help

HAYES COMPANY
Direct Materials Budget
For the Year Ending December 31, 2008

	Quarter 1	Quarter 2	Quarter 3	Quarter 4	Year
Units to be produced (Illustration 9-5)	3,100	3,600	4,100	4,600	
Direct materials per unit	× 2	× 2	× 2	× 2	
Total pounds needed for production	6,200	7,200	8,200	9,200	
Add: Desired ending direct materials (pounds)[a]	720	820	920	1,020	
Total materials required	6,920	8,020	9,120	10,220	
Less: Beginning direct materials (pounds)	620[b]	720	820	920	
Direct materials purchases	6,300	7,300	8,300	9,300	
Cost per pound	× $4	× $4	× $4	× $4	
Total cost of direct materials purchases	**$25,200**	**$29,200**	**$33,200**	**$37,200**	**$124,800**

[a]10% of next quarter's production requirements
[b]10% of estimated first-quarter pounds needed for production

Direct Labor Budget

Like the direct materials budget, the **direct labor budget** contains the quantity (hours) and cost of direct labor necessary to meet production requirements. The total direct labor cost is derived from the following formula.

Illustration 7-8
Formula for direct labor cost

Units to be Produced × **Direct Labor Time per Unit** × **Direct Labor Cost per Hour** = **Total Direct Labor Cost**

Direct labor hours are determined from the production budget. At Hayes Company, two hours of direct labor are required to produce each unit of finished goods. The anticipated hourly wage rate is $10. Illustration 7-9 shows these data.

Illustration 7-9
Direct labor budget

Hayes Company Direct Labor Budget.xls

File Edit View Insert Format Tools Data Window Help

HAYES COMPANY
Direct Labor Budget
For the Year Ending December 31, 2008

	Quarter 1	Quarter 2	Quarter 3	Quarter 4	Year
Units to be produced (Illustration 9-5)	3,100	3,600	4,100	4,600	
Direct labor time (hours) per unit	× 2	× 2	× 2	× 2	
Total required direct labor hours	6,200	7,200	8,200	9,200	
Direct labor cost per hour	× $10	× $10	× $10	× $10	
Total direct labor cost	**$62,000**	**$72,000**	**$82,000**	**$92,000**	**$308,000**

HELPFUL HINT

An important assumption in Illustration 7-9 is that the company can add to and subtract from its work force as needed so that the $10 per hour labor cost applies to a wide range of possible production activity.

The direct labor budget is critical in maintaining a labor force that can meet the expected levels of production.

Before You Go On...

REVIEW IT

1. What is the formula to determine required production units?
2. What are the inputs necessary to prepare the direct labor budget?
3. Which budget must be prepared before the direct materials budget?

DO IT

Becker Company estimates that 2008 unit sales will be 12,000 in quarter 1, 16,000 in quarter 2, and 20,000 in quarter 3, at a unit selling price of $30. Management desires to have ending finished goods inventory equal to 15% of the next quarter's expected unit sales. Prepare a production budget by quarter for the first 6 months of 2008.

Action Plan

- Begin with budgeted sales in units.
- Add desired ending finished goods inventory.
- Subtract beginning finished goods inventory.

Solution

BECKER COMPANY
Production Budget
For the Six Months Ending June 30, 2008

	Quarter 1	Quarter 2	Six Months
Expected unit sales	12,000	16,000	
Add: Desired ending finished goods	2,400	3,000	
Total required units	14,400	19,000	
Less: Beginning finished goods inventory	1,800	2,400	
Required production units	12,600	16,600	29,200

Related exercise material: *BE7-3, E7-4, and E7-6.*

The Navigator

Manufacturing Overhead Budget

The **manufacturing overhead budget** shows the expected manufacturing overhead costs for the budget period. As Illustration 7-10 (page 320) shows, **this budget distinguishes between variable and fixed overhead costs.** Hayes Company expects variable costs to fluctuate with production volume on the basis of the following rates per direct labor hour: indirect materials $1.00, indirect labor $1.40, utilities $0.40, and maintenance $0.20. Thus, for the 6,200 direct labor hours to produce 3,100 units, budgeted indirect materials are $6,200 (6,200 × $1), and budgeted indirect labor is $8,680 (6,200 × $1.40). Hayes also recognizes that some maintenance is fixed. The amounts reported for fixed costs are assumed for our example. The accuracy of budgeted overhead cost estimates can be greatly improved by employing activity-based costing.

At Hayes Company, overhead is applied to production on the basis of direct labor hours. Thus, as Illustration 7-10 shows, the budgeted annual rate is $8 per hour ($246,400 ÷ 30,800).

Selling and Administrative Expense Budget

Hayes Company combines its operating expenses into one budget, the **selling and administrative expense budget**. This budget projects anticipated selling and

Illustration 7-10
Manufacturing overhead budget

Hayes Company Manufacturing Overhead Budget.xls

	A	B	C	D	E	F
1	**HAYES COMPANY**					
2	**Manufacturing Overhead Budget**					
3	**For the Year Ending December 31, 2008**					
4		Quarter				
5		1	2	3	4	Year
6	Variable costs					
7	Indirect materials ($1.00/hour)	$ 6,200	$ 7,200	$ 8,200	$ 9,200	$ 30,800
8	Indirect labor ($1.40/hour)	8,680	10,080	11,480	12,880	43,120
9	Utilities ($0.40/hour)	2,480	2,880	3,280	3,680	12,320
10	Maintenance ($0.20/hour)	1,240	1,440	1,640	1,840	6,160
11	Total variable costs	18,600	21,600	24,600	27,600	92,400
12	Fixed costs					
13	Supervisory salaries	20,000	20,000	20,000	20,000	80,000
14	Depreciation	3,800	3,800	3,800	3,800	15,200
15	Property taxes and insurance	9,000	9,000	9,000	9,000	36,000
16	Maintenance	5,700	5,700	5,700	5,700	22,800
17	Total fixed costs	38,500	38,500	38,500	38,500	154,000
18	**Total manufacturing overhead**	**$57,100**	**$60,100**	**$63,100**	**$66,100**	**$246,400**
19	**Direct labor hours (Illustration 9-9)**	**6,200**	**7,200**	**8,200**	**9,200**	**30,800**
20	**Manufacturing overhead rate per direct labor hour ($246,400 ÷ 30,800)**					**$8**
21						

administrative expenses for the budget period. This budget (Illustration 7-11) also classifies expenses as either variable or fixed. In this case, the variable expense rates per unit of sales are sales commissions $3 and freight-out $1. Variable expenses per quarter are based on the unit sales from the sales budget (Illustration 7-3, page 316). For example, Hayes expects sales in the first quarter to be 3,000 units. Thus, Sales Commissions Expense is $9,000 (3,000 × $3), and Freight-out is $3,000 (3,000 × $1). Fixed expenses are based on assumed data. Illustration 7-11 shows the selling and administrative expense budget.

Illustration 7-11
Selling and administrative expense budget

Hayes Company Manufacturing Selling and Administrative Expense Budget.xls

	A	B	C	D	E	F
1	**HAYES COMPANY**					
2	**Selling and Administrative Expense Budget**					
3	**For the Year Ending December 31, 2008**					
4		Quarter				
5		1	2	3	4	Year
6	Budgeted sales in units (Illustration 9-3)	3,000	3,500	4,000	4,500	15,000
7	Variable expenses					
8	Sales commissions ($3 per unit)	$ 9,000	$10,500	$12,000	$ 13,500	$ 45,000
9	Freight-out ($1 per unit)	3,000	3,500	4,000	4,500	15,000
10	Total variable expenses	12,000	14,000	16,000	18,000	60,000
11	Fixed expenses					
12	Advertising	5,000	5,000	5,000	5,000	20,000
13	Sales salaries	15,000	15,000	15,000	15,000	60,000
14	Office salaries	7,500	7,500	7,500	7,500	30,000
15	Depreciation	1,000	1,000	1,000	1,000	4,000
16	Property taxes and insurance	1,500	1,500	1,500	1,500	6,000
17	Total fixed expenses	30,000	30,000	30,000	30,000	120,000
18	**Total selling and administrative expenses**	**$42,000**	**$44,000**	**$46,000**	**$48,000**	**$180,000**
19						

Budgeted Income Statement

STUDY OBJECTIVE 4

Describe the sources for preparing the budgeted income statement.

The **budgeted income statement** is the important end-product of the operating budgets. This budget indicates the expected profitability of operations for the budget period. The budgeted income statement provides the basis for evaluating company performance. Budgeted income statements often act as a call to action. For example, a board member at XM Satellite Radio Holdings felt that budgeted costs were too high relative to budgeted revenues. When management refused to cut its marketing and programming costs, the board member resigned; he felt that without the cuts, the company risked financial crisis.

As you would expect, the budgeted income statement is prepared from the various operating budgets. For example, to find the cost of goods sold, it is first necessary to determine the total unit cost of producing one Kitchen-Mate, as follows.

Illustration 7-12
Computation of total unit cost

	Cost of One Kitchen-Mate			
Cost Element	**Illustration**	**Quantity**	**Unit Cost**	**Total**
Direct materials	7-7	2 pounds	$ 4.00	$ 8.00
Direct labor	7-9	2 hours	$10.00	20.00
Manufacturing overhead	7-10	2 hours	$ 8.00	16.00
Total unit cost				$44.00

Hayes Company then determines cost of goods sold by multiplying the units sold by the unit cost. Its budgeted cost of goods sold is $660,000 (15,000 × $44). All data for the income statement come from the individual operating budgets except the following: (1) interest expense is expected to be $100, and (2) income taxes are estimated to be $12,000. Illustration 7-13 shows the budgeted income statement.

Illustration 7-13
Budgeted income statement

HAYES COMPANY
Budgeted Income Statement
For the Year Ending December 31, 2008

Sales (Illustration 7-3)	$900,000
Cost of goods sold (15,000 × $44)	660,000
Gross profit	240,000
Selling and administrative expenses (Illustration 7-11)	180,000
Income from operations	60,000
Interest expense	100
Income before income taxes	59,900
Income tax expense	12,000
Net income	$ 47,900

DECISION TOOLKIT

Decision Checkpoints	Info Needed for Decision	Tool to Use for Decision	How to Evaluate Results
	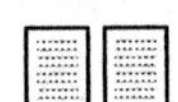		
Has the company met its targets for sales, production expenses, selling and administrative expenses, and net income?	Sales forecasts, inventory levels, projected materials, labor, overhead, and selling and administrative requirements	Master budget—a set of interrelated budgets including sales, production, materials, labor, overhead, and selling and administrative budgets	Results are favorable if revenues exceed budgeted amounts, or if expenses are less than budgeted amounts.

PREPARING THE FINANCIAL BUDGETS

As shown in Illustration 7-2 (page 315), the financial budgets consist of the capital expenditure budget, the cash budget, and the budgeted balance sheet. We will discuss the capital expenditure budget in Chapter 10; the other budgets are explained in the following sections.

Cash Budget

STUDY OBJECTIVE 5

Explain the principal sections of a cash budget.

The **cash budget** shows anticipated cash flows. Because cash is so vital, this budget is often considered to be the most important financial budget.

The cash budget contains three sections (cash receipts, cash disbursements, and financing) and the beginning and ending cash balances, as shown in Illustration 7-14.

Illustration 7-14
Basic form of a cash budget

ANY COMPANY
Cash Budget

Beginning cash balance	$X,XXX
Add: Cash receipts (Itemized)	X,XXX
Total available cash	X,XXX
Less: Cash disbursements (Itemized)	X,XXX
Excess (deficiency) of available cash over cash disbursements	X,XXX
Financing	X,XXX
Ending cash balance	$X,XXX

HELPFUL HINT

Why is the cash budget prepared after the other budgets are prepared? Answer: Because the information generated by the other budgets dictates the expected inflows and outflows of cash.

The **cash receipts section** includes expected receipts from the company's principal source(s) of revenue. These are usually cash sales and collections from customers on credit sales. This section also shows anticipated receipts of interest and dividends, and proceeds from planned sales of investments, plant assets, and the company's capital stock.

The **cash disbursements section** shows expected cash payments. Such payments include direct materials, direct labor, manufacturing overhead, and selling and administrative expenses. This section also includes projected payments for income taxes, dividends, investments, and plant assets.

The **financing section** shows expected borrowings and the repayment of the borrowed funds plus interest. Companies need this section when there is a cash deficiency or when the cash balance is below management's minimum required balance.

Data in the cash budget are prepared in sequence. The ending cash balance of one period becomes the beginning cash balance for the next period. Companies obtain data for preparing the cash budget from other budgets and from information provided by management. In practice, cash budgets are often prepared for the year on a monthly basis.

To minimize detail, we will assume that Hayes Company prepares an annual cash budget by quarters. Its cash budget is based on the following assumptions.

1. The January 1, 2008, cash balance is expected to be $38,000. Hayes wishes to maintain a balance of at least $15,000.
2. Sales (Illustration 7-3, page 316): 60% are collected in the quarter sold and 40% are collected in the following quarter. Accounts receivable of $60,000 at December 31, 2007, are expected to be collected in full in the first quarter of 2008.
3. Short-term investments are expected to be sold for $2,000 cash in the first quarter.

4. Direct materials (Illustration 7-7, page 318): 50% are paid in the quarter purchased and 50% are paid in the following quarter. Accounts payable of $10,600 at December 31, 2007, are expected to be paid in full in the first quarter of 2008.
5. Direct labor (Illustration 7-9, page 318): 100% is paid in the quarter incurred.
6. Manufacturing overhead (Illustration 7-10, page 320) and selling and administrative expenses (Illustration 7-11, page 320): All items except depreciation are paid in the quarter incurred.
7. Management plans to purchase a truck in the second quarter for $10,000 cash.
8. Hayes makes equal quarterly payments of its estimated annual income taxes.
9. Loans are repaid in the earliest quarter in which there is sufficient cash (that is, when the cash on hand exceeds the $15,000 minimum required balance).

In preparing the cash budget, it is useful to prepare schedules for collections from customers (assumption No. 2, previous page) and cash payments for direct materials (assumption No. 4, above). These schedules are shown in Illustrations 7-15 and 7-16.

Illustration 7-15
Collections from customers

HAYES COMPANY
Schedule of Expected Collections from Customers

	Quarter			
	1	2	3	4
Accounts receivable, 12/31/07	$ 60,000			
First quarter ($180,000)	108,000	$ 72,000		
Second quarter ($210,000)		126,000	$ 84,000	
Third quarter ($240,000)			144,000	$ 96,000
Fourth quarter ($270,000)				162,000
Total collections	$168,000	$198,000	$228,000	$258,000

Illustration 7-16
Payments for direct materials

HAYES COMPANY
Schedule of Expected Payments for Direct Materials

	Quarter			
	1	2	3	4
Accounts payable, 12/31/07	$10,600			
First quarter ($25,200)	12,600	$12,600		
Second quarter ($29,200)		14,600	$14,600	
Third quarter ($33,200)			16,600	$16,600
Fourth quarter ($37,200)				18,600
Total payments	$23,200	$27,200	$31,200	$35,200

Illustration 7-17 (page 324) shows the cash budget for Hayes Company. The budget indicates that Hayes will need $3,000 of financing in the second quarter to maintain a minimum cash balance of $15,000. Since there is an excess of available cash over disbursements of $22,500 at the end of the third quarter, the borrowing, plus $100 interest, is repaid in this quarter.

Hayes Company Cash Budget.xls

File Edit View Insert Format Tools Data Window Help

	A	B	C	D	E	F	G	H	I	J
1					HAYES COMPANY					
2					Cash Budget					
3					For the Year Ending December 31, 2008					
4							Quarter			
5		Assumption	1		2		3		4	
6	Beginning cash balance	1	$ 38,000		$ 25,500		$ 15,000		$ 19,400	
7	**Add: Receipts**									
8	Collections from customers	2	168,000		198,000		228,000		258,000	
9	Sale of securities	3	2,000		0		0		0	
10	Total receipts		170,000		198,000		228,000		258,000	
11	Total available cash		208,000		223,500		243,000		277,400	
12	**Less: Disbursements**									
13	Direct materials	4	23,200		27,200		31,200		35,200	
14	Direct labor	5	62,000		72,000		82,000		92,000	
15	Manufacturing overhead	6	53,300	a	56,300		59,300		62,300	
16	Selling and administrative expenses	6	41,000	b	43,000		45,000		47,000	
17	Purchase of truck	7	0		10,000		0		0	
18	Income tax expense	8	3,000		3,000		3,000		3,000	
19	Total disbursements		182,500		211,500		220,500		239,500	
20	Excess (deficiency) of available cash over cash disbursements		25,500		12,000		22,500		37,900	
21	**Financing**									
22	Borrowings		0		**3,000**		0		0	
23	Repayments-plus $100 interest	9	0		0		**3,100**		0	
24	Ending cash balance		$ 25,500		$ 15,000		$ 19,400		$ 37,900	
25										
26	[a]$57,100-$3,800 depreciation									
27	[b]$42,000-$1,000 depreciation									

Illustration 7-17
Cash budget

MANAGEMENT INSIGHT

Without a Budget, Can the Games Begin?

Behind the grandeur of the Olympic Games lies a huge financial challenge—how to keep budgeted costs in line with revenues. For example, the 2006 Winter Olympics in Turin, Italy, narrowly avoided going into bankruptcy before the Games even started. In order for the event to remain solvent, organizers cancelled glitzy celebrations and shifted promotional responsibilities to an Italian state-run agency. Despite these efforts, after the Games were over, the Italian government created a lottery game to cover its financial losses.

As another example, organizers of the 2002 Winter Olympics in Salt Lake City cut budgeted costs by $200 million shortly before the events began. According to the chief operating and financial officer, the organizers went through every line item in the budget, sorting each one into "must have" versus "nice to have." As a result, the Salt Lake City Games produced a surplus of $100 million.

Source: Gabriel Kahn and Roger Thurow, "In Turin, Paying for Games Went Down to the Wire," *Wall Street Journal*, February 10, 2006.

Why does it matter whether the Olympic Games exceed their budget?

A cash budget contributes to more effective cash management. It shows managers when additional financing is necessary well before the actual need arises. And, it indicates when excess cash is available for investments or other purposes.

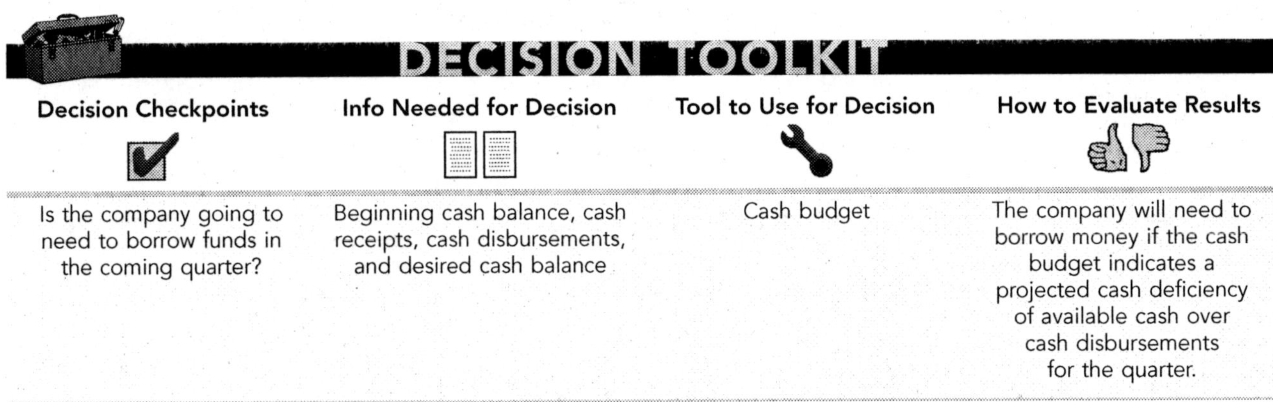

DECISION TOOLKIT

Decision Checkpoints	Info Needed for Decision	Tool to Use for Decision	How to Evaluate Results
Is the company going to need to borrow funds in the coming quarter?	Beginning cash balance, cash receipts, cash disbursements, and desired cash balance	Cash budget	The company will need to borrow money if the cash budget indicates a projected cash deficiency of available cash over cash disbursements for the quarter.

Budgeted Balance Sheet

The budgeted balance sheet is a projection of financial position at the end of the budget period. This budget is developed from the budgeted balance sheet for the preceding year and the budgets for the current year. Pertinent data from the budgeted balance sheet at December 31, 2007, are as follows.

Buildings and equipment	$182,000	Common stock	$225,000
Accumulated depreciation	$ 28,800	Retained earnings	$ 46,480

Illustration 7-18 show Hayes Company's budgeted balance sheet at December 31, 2008.

Illustration 7-18
Budgeted balance sheet

HAYES COMPANY
Budgeted Balance Sheet
December 31, 2008

Assets		
Cash		$ 37,900
Accounts receivable		108,000
Finished goods inventory		44,000
Raw materials inventory		4,080
Buildings and equipment	$192,000	
Less: Accumulated depreciation	48,000	144,000
Total assets		$337,980
Liabilities and Stockholders' Equity		
Accounts payable		$ 18,600
Common stock		225,000
Retained earnings		94,380
Total liabilities and stockholders' equity		$337,980

The computations and sources of the amounts are explained below.

Cash: Ending cash balance $37,900, shown in the cash budget (Illustration 7-17, page 324).

Accounts receivable: 40% of fourth-quarter sales $270,000, shown in the schedule of expected collections from customers (Illustration 7-15, page 323).

Finished goods inventory: Desired ending inventory 1,000 units, shown in the production budget (Illustration 7-5, page 317) times the total unit cost $44 (shown in Illustration 7-12, page 321).

Raw materials inventory: Desired ending inventory 1,020 pounds, times the cost per pound $4, shown in the direct materials budget (Illustration 7-7, page 318).

Buildings and equipment: December 31, 2007, balance $182,000, plus purchase of truck for $10,000 (Illustration 7-17, page 324).

Accumulated depreciation: December 31, 2007, balance $28,800, plus $15,200 depreciation shown in manufacturing overhead budget (Illustration 7-10, page 320) and $4,000 depreciation shown in selling and administrative expense budget (Illustration 7-11, page 320).

Accounts payable: 50% of fourth-quarter purchases $37,200, shown in schedule of expected payments for direct materials (Illustration 7-16, page 323).

Common stock: Unchanged from the beginning of the year.

Retained earnings: December 31, 2007, balance $46,480, plus net income $47,900, shown in budgeted income statement (Illustration 7-13, page 321).

After budget data are entered into the computer, Hayes prepares the various budgets (sales, cash, etc.), as well as the budgeted financial statements. Using spreadsheets, management can also perform "what if" (sensitivity) analyses based on different hypothetical assumptions. For example, suppose that sales managers project that sales will be 10% higher in the coming quarter. What impact does this change have on the rest of the budgeting process and the financing needs of the business? The impact of the various assumptions on the budget is quickly determined by the spreadsheet. Armed with these analyses, managers make more informed decisions about the impact of various projects. They also anticipate future problems and business opportunities. As seen in this chapter, budgeting is an excellent use of electronic spreadsheets.

Before You Go On...

REVIEW IT

1. What are the two classifications of the individual budgets in the master budget?
2. What is the sequence for preparing the budgets that comprise the operating budgets?
3. Identify some of the source documents that would be used in preparing each of the operating budgets.
4. What are the three principal sections of the cash budget?

DO IT

Martian Company management wants to maintain a minimum monthly cash balance of $15,000. At the beginning of March, the cash balance is $16,500, expected cash receipts for March are $210,000, and cash disbursements are expected to be $220,000. How much cash, if any, must be borrowed to maintain the desired minimum monthly balance?

Action Plan

- Write down the basic form of the cash budget, starting with the beginning cash balance, adding cash receipts for the period, deducting cash disbursements, and identifying the needed financing to achieve the desired minimum ending cash balance.
- Insert the data given into the outlined form of the cash budget.

Solution

MARTIAN COMPANY
Cash Budget
For the Month Ending March 31, 2008

Beginning cash balance	$ 16,500
Add: Cash receipts for March	210,000
Total available cash	226,500
Less: Cash disbursements for March	220,000
Excess of available cash over cash disbursements	6,500
Financing	8,500
Ending cash balance	$ 15,000

To maintain the desired minimum cash balance of $15,000, Martian Company must borrow $8,500 of cash.

Related exercise material: *BE7-9, E7-12, E7-13, E7-14, E7-15, and E7-16.*

The Navigator

BUDGETING IN NONMANUFACTURING COMPANIES

STUDY OBJECTIVE 6

Indicate the applicability of budgeting in nonmanufacturing companies.

Budgeting is not limited to manufacturers. Budgets are also used by merchandisers, service enterprises, and not-for-profit organizations.

Merchandisers

As in manufacturing operations, the sales budget for a merchandiser is both the starting point and the key factor in the development of the master budget. The major differences between the master budgets of a merchandiser and a manufacturer are these:

1. A merchandiser **uses a merchandise purchases budget instead of a production budget.**
2. A merchandiser **does not use the manufacturing budgets (direct materials, direct labor, and manufacturing overhead).**

The **merchandise purchases budget** shows the estimated cost of goods to be purchased to meet expected sales. The formula for determining budgeted merchandise purchases is:

Budgeted Cost of Goods Sold	+	Desired Ending Merchandise Inventory	−	Beginning Merchandise Inventory	=	Required Merchandise Purchases

Illustration 7-19
Merchandise purchases formula

To illustrate, assume that the budget committee of Lima Company is preparing the merchandise purchases budget for July 2008. It estimates that budgeted sales will be $300,000 in July and $320,000 in August. Cost of goods sold is expected to be 70% of sales—that is, $210,000 in July (.70 × $300,000) and $224,000 in August (.70 × $320,000). The company's desired ending inventory is 30% of the following month's cost of goods sold. Required merchandise purchases for July are $214,200, computed as follows.

Illustration 7-20
Merchandise purchases budget

LIMA COMPANY
Merchandise Purchases Budget
For the Month Ending July 31, 2008

Budgeted cost of goods sold ($300,000 × 70%)	$ 210,000
Add: Desired ending merchandise inventory ($224,000 × 30%)	67,200
Total	277,200
Less: Beginning merchandise inventory ($210,000 × 30%)	63,000
Required merchandise purchases for July	**$214,200**

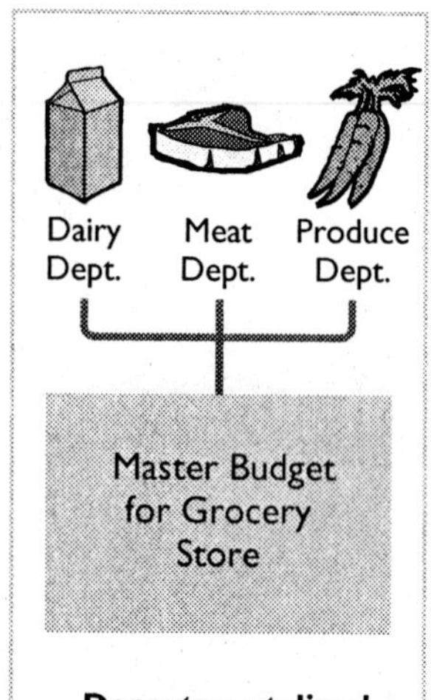

Departmentalized budgets

When a merchandiser is departmentalized, it prepares separate budgets for each department. For example, a grocery store prepares sales budgets and purchases budgets for each of its major departments, such as meats, dairy, and produce. The store then combines these budgets into a master budget for the store. When a retailer has branch stores, it prepares separate master budgets for each store. Then it incorporates these budgets into master budgets for the company as a whole.

Service Enterprises

In a service enterprise, such as a public accounting firm, a law office, or a medical practice, the critical factor in budgeting is **coordinating professional staff needs with anticipated services**. If a firm is overstaffed, several problems may result: Labor costs are disproportionately high. Profits are lower because of the additional salaries. Staff turnover sometimes increases because of lack of challenging work. In contrast, if a service enterprise is understaffed, it may lose revenue because existing and prospective client needs for service cannot be met. Also, professional staff may seek other jobs because of excessive work loads.

Service enterprises can obtain budget data for service revenue from **expected output** or **expected input**. When output is used, it is necessary to determine the expected billings of clients for services provided. In a public accounting firm, for example, output is the sum of its billings in auditing, tax, and consulting services. When input data are used, each professional staff member projects his or her billable time. The firm then applies billing rates to billable time to produce expected service revenue.

Not-for-Profit Organizations

Budgeting is just as important for not-for-profit organizations as for profit-oriented enterprises. The budget process, however, is different. In most cases, not-for-profit entities budget **on the basis of cash flows (expenditures and receipts), rather than on a revenue and expense basis**. Further, the starting point in the process is usually expenditures, not receipts. For the not-for-profit entity, management's task generally is to find the receipts needed to support the planned expenditures. The activity index is also likely to be significantly different. For example, in a not-for-profit entity, such as a university, budgeted faculty positions may be based on full-time equivalent students or credit hours expected to be taught in a department.

For some governmental units, voters approve the budget. In other cases, such as state governments and the federal government, legislative approval is required. After the budget is adopted, it must be followed. Overspending is often illegal. In governmental budgets, authorizations tend to be on a line-by-line basis. That is, the budget for a municipality may have a specified authorization for police and fire protection, garbage collection, street paving, and so on. The line-item authorization of governmental budgets significantly limits the amount of discretion management can exercise. The city manager often cannot use savings from one line item, such as street paving, to cover increased spending in another line item, such as snow removal.

Before You Go On...

REVIEW IT

1. What is the formula for computing required merchandise purchases?
2. How does budgeting in service and not-for-profit organizations differ from budgeting for manufacturers and merchandisers?

Be sure to read **ALL ABOUT YOU: *Avoiding Personal Financial Disaster*** on page 330 for information on how topics in this chapter apply to you.

all about YOU

Avoiding Personal Financial Disaster

You might hear people say that they "need to learn to live within a budget." The funny thing is that most people who say this haven't actually prepared a personal budget, nor do they intend to. Instead, what they are referring to is a vaguely defined, poorly specified, collection of rough ideas of how much they should spend on various aspects of their life. You can't live within or even outside of something that doesn't exist. With that in mind, let's take a look at personal budgets.

Some Facts

* The average American household income is $49,430, before taxes.
* The average family spends $5,375 on food each year. Of this, $3,099 is for food consumed at home, and $2,276 is for food consumed away from home.
* The average family spends $13,283 annually on housing costs. Of this amount, $7,829 is the actual cost of shelter, $2,684 is for utilities, and $1,518 is for furnishings and equipment.
* The average family spends $7,759 per year on transportation. Of this, $3,665 goes to vehicle purchase payments, and $1,235 is spent on fuel. The average family spends only $389 per year on public transportation.

About the Numbers

Obviously people spend their income in different ways. For example, the percentage of your income spent on necessities declines as your income increases. Nonetheless, it is interesting to see how the average family spends its money.

Average U.S. Household Expenditures

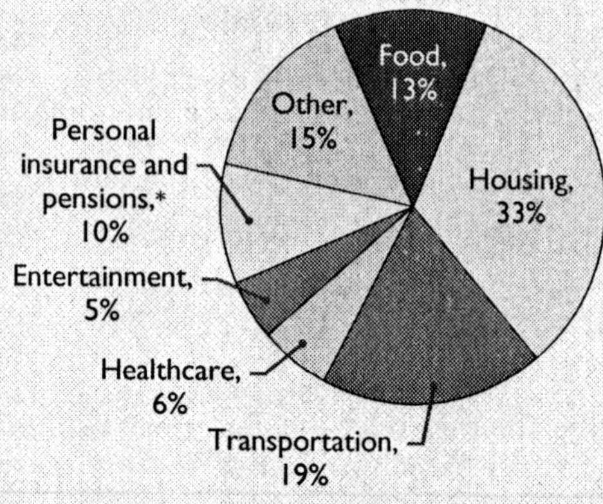

* This includes Social Security tax.

Source: "Consumer Expenditures in 2004," U.S. Department of Labor and U.S. Bureau of Labor Statistics, Report 992, April 2006.

What Do You Think?

Many worksheet templates that are provided for personal budgets for college students treat student loans as an income source. See, for example, the template provided at **http://financialplan.about.com/cs/budgeting/l/blmocolbud.htm**. Based on your knowledge of accounting, is this correct?

YES: Student loans provide a source of cash which can be used to pay costs. As the saying goes, "It all spends the same." Therefore student loans are income.

NO: Student loans must eventually be repaid; therefore they are not income. As the name suggests, they are loans.

The authors' comments on this situation appear on page 351.

Using the Decision Toolkit

The University of Wisconsin and its subunits must prepare budgets. One unique subunit of the University of Wisconsin is Babcock Ice Cream, a functioning producer of dairy products (and famous, at least on campus, for its delicious ice cream).

Assume that Babcock Ice Cream prepares monthly cash budgets. Relevant data from assumed operating budgets for 2008 are:

	January	February
Sales	$460,000	$412,000
Direct materials purchases	185,000	210,000
Direct labor	70,000	85,000
Manufacturing overhead	50,000	65,000
Selling and administrative expenses	85,000	95,000

Babcock sells its ice cream in shops on campus, as well as to local stores. Collections are expected to be 75% in the month of sale, and 25% in the month following sale. Babcock pays 60% of direct materials purchases in cash in the month of purchase, and the balance due in the month following the purchase. All other items above are paid in the month incurred. (Depreciation has been excluded from manufacturing overhead and selling and administrative expenses.)

Other data:

(1) Sales: December 2007, $320,000
(2) Purchases of direct materials: December 2007, $175,000
(3) Other receipts: January—Donation received, $2,000
February—Sale of used equipment, $4,000
(4) Other disbursements: February—Purchased equipment, $10,000
(5) Repaid debt: January, $30,000

The company's cash balance on January 1, 2008, is expected to be $50,000. The company wants to maintain a minimum cash balance of $45,000.

Instructions

(a) Prepare schedules for (1) expected collections from customers and (2) expected payments for direct materials purchases.
(b) Prepare a cash budget for January and February in columnar form.

Solution

(a) (1) **Expected Collections from Customers**

	January	February
December ($320,000)	$ 80,000	$ 0
January ($460,000)	345,000	115,000
February ($412,000)	0	309,000
Totals	$425,000	$424,000

(2) **Expected Payments for Direct Materials**

	January	February
December ($175,000)	$ 70,000	$ 0
January ($185,000)	111,000	74,000
February ($210,000)	0	126,000
Totals	$181,000	$200,000

(b)

BABCOCK ICE CREAM
Cash Budget
For the Two Months Ending February 28, 2008

	January	February
Beginning cash balance	$ 50,000	$ 61,000
Add: Receipts		
Collections from customers	425,000	424,000
Donations received	2,000	0
Sale of used equipment	0	4,000
Total receipts	427,000	428,000
Total available cash	477,000	489,000
Less: Disbursements		
Direct materials	181,000	200,000
Direct labor	70,000	85,000
Manufacturing overhead	50,000	65,000
Selling and administrative expenses	85,000	95,000
Purchase of equipment	0	10,000
Total disbursements	386,000	455,000
Excess (deficiency) of available cash over cash disbursements	91,000	34,000
Financing		
Borrowings	0	11,000
Repayments	30,000	0
Ending cash balance	$ 61,000	$ 45,000

The Navigator

SUMMARY OF STUDY OBJECTIVES

1 **Indicate the benefits of budgeting.** The primary advantages of budgeting are that it (a) requires management to plan ahead, (b) provides definite objectives for evaluating performance, (c) creates an early warning system for potential problems, (d) facilitates coordination of activities, (e) results in greater management awareness, and (f) motivates personnel to meet planned objectives.

2 **State the essentials of effective budgeting.** The essentials of effective budgeting are (a) sound organizational structure, (b) research and analysis, and (c) acceptance by all levels of management.

3 **Identify the budgets that comprise the master budget.** The master budget consists of the following budgets: (a) sales, (b) production, (c) direct materials, (d) direct labor, (e) manufacturing overhead, (f) selling and administrative expense, (g) budgeted income statement, (h) capital expenditure budget, (i) cash budget, and (j) budgeted balance sheet.

4 **Describe the sources for preparing the budgeted income statement.** The budgeted income statement is prepared from (a) the sales budget, (b) the budgets for direct materials, direct labor, and manufacturing overhead, and (c) the selling and administrative expense budget.

5 **Explain the principal sections of a cash budget.** The cash budget has three sections (receipts, disbursements, and financing) and the beginning and ending cash balances.

6 **Indicate the applicability of budgeting in nonmanufacturing companies.** Budgeting may be used by merchandisers for development of a merchandise purchases budget. In service enterprises budgeting is a critical factor in coordinating staff needs with anticipated services. In not-for-profit organizations, the starting point in budgeting is usually expenditures, not receipts.

DECISION TOOLKIT—A SUMMARY

Decision Checkpoints 	Info Needed for Decision 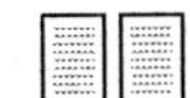	Tool to Use for Decision 	How to Evaluate Results 
Has the company met its targets for sales, production expenses, selling and administrative expenses, and net income?	Sales forecasts, inventory levels, projected materials, labor, overhead, and selling and administrative requirements	Master budget — a set of interrelated budgets including sales, production, materials, labor, overhead, and selling and administrative budgets	Results are favorable if revenues exceed budgeted amounts, or if expenses are less than budgeted amounts.
Is the company going to need to borrow funds in the coming quarter?	Beginning cash balance, cash receipts, cash disbursements, and desired cash balance	Cash budget	The company will need to borrow money if the cash budget indicates a projected cash deficiency of available cash over cash disbursements for the quarter.

GLOSSARY

Budget A formal written statement of management's plans for a specified future time period, expressed in financial terms. (p. 310).

Budget committee A group responsible for coordinating the preparation of the budget. (p. 312).

Budgetary slack The amount by which a manager intentionally underestimates budgeted revenues or overestimates budgeted expenses in order to make it easier to achieve budgetary goals. (p. 313).

Budgeted balance sheet A projection of financial position at the end of the budget period. (p. 325).

Budgeted income statement An estimate of the expected profitability of operations for the budget period. (p. 321).

Cash budget A projection of anticipated cash flows. (p. 322).

Direct labor budget A projection of the quantity and cost of direct labor necessary to meet production requirements. (p. 318).

Direct materials budget An estimate of the quantity and cost of direct materials to be purchased. (p. 317).

Financial budgets Individual budgets that focus primarily on the cash resources needed to fund expected operations and planned capital expenditures. (p. 314).

Long-range planning A formalized process of selecting strategies to achieve long-term goals and developing policies and plans to implement the strategies. (p. 314).

Manufacturing overhead budget An estimate of expected manufacturing overhead costs for the budget period. (p. 319).

Master budget A set of interrelated budgets that constitutes a plan of action for a specific time period. (p. 314).

Merchandise purchases budget The estimated cost of goods to be purchased by a merchandiser to meet expected sales. (p. 327).

Operating budgets Individual budgets that result in a budgeted income statement. (p. 314).

Participative budgeting A budgetary approach that starts with input from lower-level managers and works upward so that managers at all levels participate. (p. 312).

Production budget A projection of the units that must be produced to meet anticipated sales. (p. 316).

Sales budget An estimate of expected sales revenue for the budget period. (p. 316).

Sales forecast The projection of potential sales for the industry and the company's expected share of such sales. (p. 312).

Selling and administrative expense budget A projection of anticipated selling and administrative expenses for the budget period. (p. 319).

Demonstration Problem

Soroco Company is preparing its master budget for 2008. Relevant data pertaining to its sales and production budgets are as follows:

Sales: Sales for the year are expected to total 1,200,000 units. Quarterly sales are 20%, 25%, 30%, and 25% respectively. The sales price is expected to be $50 per unit for the first three quarters and $55 per unit beginning in the fourth quarter. Sales in the first quarter of 2009 are expected to be 10% higher than the budgeted sales volume for the first quarter of 2008.

Production: Management desires to maintain ending finished goods inventories at 25% of the next quarter's budgeted sales volume.

Instructions

Prepare the sales budget and production budget by quarters for 2008.

action plan

- Know the form and content of the sales budget.
- Prepare the sales budget first as the basis for the other budgets.
- Determine the units that must be produced to meet anticipated sales.
- Know how to compute the beginning and ending finished goods units.

Solution

SOROCO COMPANY
Sales Budget
For the Year Ending December 31, 2008

	Quarter				
	1	2	3	4	Year
Expected unit sales	240,000	300,000	360,000	300,000	1,200,000
Unit selling price	× $50	× $50	× $50	× $55	—
Total sales	$12,000,000	$15,000,000	$18,000,000	$16,500,000	$61,500,000

SOROCO COMPANY
Production Budget
For the Year Ending December 31, 2008

	Quarter				
	1	2	3	4	Year
Expected unit sales	240,000	300,000	360,000	300,000	
Add: Desired ending finished goods units	75,000	90,000	75,000	66,000[1]	
Total required units	315,000	390,000	435,000	366,000	
Less: Beginning finished goods units	60,000[2]	75,000	90,000	75,000	
Required production units	255,000	315,000	345,000	291,000	1,206,000

[1]Estimated first-quarter 2009 sales volume 240,000 + (240,000 × 10%) = 264,000; 264,000 × 25%.
[2]25% of estimated first-quarter 2008 sales units (240,000 × 25%).

SELF-STUDY QUESTIONS

Answers are at the end of the chapter.

(SO 1) 1. Which of the following is not a benefit of budgeting?
   a. Management can plan ahead.
   b. An early warning system is provided for potential problems.
   c. It enables disciplinary action to be taken at every level of responsibility.
   d. The coordination of activities is facilitated.

(SO 2) 2. The essentials of effective budgeting do *not* include:
   a. top-down budgeting.
   b. management acceptance.
   c. research and analysis.
   d. sound organizational structure.

3. Compared to budgeting, long-range planning generally has the: (SO 2)
   a. same amount of detail.
   b. longer time period.
   c. same emphasis.
   d. same time period.

4. A sales budget is: (SO 3)
   a. derived from the production budget.
   b. management's best estimate of sales revenue for the year.

c. not the starting point for the master budget.
d. prepared only for credit sales.

(SO 3) 5. The formula for the production budget is budgeted sales in units plus:
a. desired ending merchandise inventory less beginning merchandise inventory.
b. beginning finished goods units less desired ending finished goods units.
c. desired ending direct materials units less beginning direct materials units.
d. desired ending finished goods units less beginning finished goods units.

(SO 3) 6. Direct materials inventories are kept in pounds in Byrd Company, and the total pounds of direct materials needed for production is 9,500. If the beginning inventory is 1,000 pounds and the desired ending inventory is 2,200 pounds, the total pounds to be purchased is:
a. 9,400.
b. 9,500.
c. 9,700.
d. 10,700.

(SO 3) 7. The formula for computing the direct labor budget is to multiply the direct labor cost per hour by the:
a. total required direct labor hours.
b. physical units to be produced.
c. equivalent units to be produced.
d. No correct answer is given.

8. Each of the following budgets is used in preparing the budgeted income statement *except* the: (SO 4)
a. sales budget.
b. selling and administrative budget.
c. capital expenditure budget.
d. direct labor budget.

9. Expected direct materials purchases in Read Company are $70,000 in the first quarter and $90,000 in the second quarter. Forty percent of the purchases are paid in cash as incurred, and the balance is paid in the following quarter. The budgeted cash payments for purchases in the second quarter are: (SO 5)
a. $96,000.
b. $90,000.
c. $78,000.
d. $72,000.

10. The budget for a merchandiser differs from a budget for a manufacturer because: (SO 6)
a. a merchandise purchases budget replaces the production budget.
b. the manufacturing budgets are not applicable.
c. None of the above.
d. Both (a) and (b) above.

Go to the book's website, **www.wiley.com/college/weygandt**, for Additional Self-Study questions.

QUESTIONS

1. **(a)** What is a budget?
(b) How does a budget contribute to good management?
2. Karen Bay and Frank Barone are discussing the benefits of budgeting. They ask you to identify the primary advantages of budgeting. Comply with their request.
3. Tina Haworth asks your help in understanding the essentials of effective budgeting. Identify the essentials for Tina.
4. **(a)** "Accounting plays a relatively unimportant role in budgeting." Do you agree? Explain.
(b) What responsibilities does management have in budgeting?
5. What criteria are helpful in determining the length of the budget period? What is the most common budget period?
6. Megan Pedigo maintains that the only difference between budgeting and long-range planning is time. Do you agree? Why or why not?
7. What is participative budgeting? What are its potential benefits? What are its potential shortcomings?
8. What is budgetary slack? What incentive do managers have to create budgetary slack?
9. Distinguish between a master budget and a sales forecast.
10. What budget is the starting point in preparing the master budget? What may result if this budget is inaccurate?
11. "The production budget shows both unit production data and unit cost data." Is this true? Explain.
12. Cali Company has 15,000 beginning finished goods units. Budgeted sales units are 160,000. If management desires 20,000 ending finished goods units, what are the required units of production?
13. In preparing the direct materials budget for Mast Company, management concludes that required purchases are 64,000 units. If 52,000 direct materials units are required in production and there are 7,000 units of beginning direct materials, what is the desired units of ending direct materials?
14. The production budget of Rooney Company calls for 80,000 units to be produced. If it takes 30 minutes to make one unit and the direct labor rate is $16 per hour, what is the total budgeted direct labor cost?
15. Morales Company's manufacturing overhead budget shows total variable costs of $198,000 and total fixed costs of $162,000. Total production in units is expected to be 160,000. It takes 15 minutes to make one unit, and the direct labor rate is $15 per hour. Express the manufacturing overhead rate as (a) a percentage of direct labor cost, and (b) an amount per direct labor hour.
16. Elbert Company's variable selling and administrative expenses are 10% of net sales. Fixed expenses are $50,000 per quarter. The sales budget shows expected sales of $200,000 and $250,000 in the first and second quarters, respectively. What are the total budgeted selling and administrative expenses for each quarter?

17. For Nolte Company, the budgeted cost for one unit of product is direct materials $10, direct labor $20, and manufacturing overhead 90% of direct labor cost. If 25,000 units are expected to be sold at $69 each, what is the budgeted gross profit?
18. Indicate the supporting schedules used in preparing a budgeted income statement through gross profit for a manufacturer.
19. Identify the three sections of a cash budget. What balances are also shown in this budget?
20. Van Gundy Company has credit sales of $500,000 in January. Past experience suggests that 45% is collected in the month of sale, 50% in the month following the sale, and 5% in the second month following the sale. Compute the cash collections from January sales in January, February, and March.
21. What is the formula for determining required merchandise purchases for a merchandiser?
22. How may expected revenues in a service enterprise be computed?

BRIEF EXERCISES

Prepare a diagram of a master budget. (SO 3)

BE7-1 Noble Manufacturing Company uses the following budgets: Balance Sheet, Capital Expenditure, Cash, Direct Labor, Direct Materials, Income Statement, Manufacturing Overhead, Production, Sales, and Selling and Administrative. Prepare a diagram of the interrelationships of the budgets in the master budget. Indicate whether each budget is an operating or a financial budget.

Prepare a sales budget. (SO 3)

BE7-2 Goody Company estimates that unit sales will be 10,000 in quarter 1; 12,000 in quarter 2; 14,000 in quarter 3; and 18,000 in quarter 4. Using a sales price of $80 per unit, prepare the sales budget by quarters for the year ending December 31, 2008.

Prepare a production budget for 2 quarters. (SO 3)

BE7-3 Sales budget data for Goody Company are given in BE7-2. Management desires to have an ending finished goods inventory equal to 20% of the next quarter's expected unit sales. Prepare a production budget by quarters for the first 6 months of 2008.

Prepare a direct materials budget for 1 month. (SO 3)

BE7-4 Ortiz Company has 1,600 pounds of raw materials in its December 31, 2008, ending inventory. Required production for January and February of 2009 are 4,000 and 5,500 units, respectively. Two pounds of raw materials are needed for each unit, and the estimated cost per pound is $6. Management desires an ending inventory equal to 20% of next month's materials requirements. Prepare the direct materials budget for January.

Prepare a direct labor budget for 2 quarters. (SO 3)

BE7-5 For Everly Company, units to be produced are 5,000 in quarter 1 and 6,000 in quarter 2. It takes 1.5 hours to make a finished unit, and the expected hourly wage rate is $14 per hour. Prepare a direct labor budget by quarters for the 6 months ending June 30, 2008.

Prepare a manufacturing overhead budget. (SO 3)

BE7-6 For Justus Inc. variable manufacturing overhead costs are expected to be $20,000 in the first quarter of 2008 with $4,000 increments in each of the remaining three quarters. Fixed overhead costs are estimated to be $35,000 in each quarter. Prepare the manufacturing overhead budget by quarters and in total for the year.

Prepare a selling and administrative expense budget. (SO 3)

BE7-7 Mize Company classifies its selling and administrative expense budget into variable and fixed components. Variable expenses are expected to be $25,000 in the first quarter, and $5,000 increments are expected in the remaining quarters of 2008. Fixed expenses are expected to be $40,000 in each quarter. Prepare the selling and administrative expense budget by quarters and in total for 2008.

Prepare a budgeted income statement for the year. (SO 4)

BE7-8 Perine Company has completed all of its operating budgets. The sales budget for the year shows 50,000 units and total sales of $2,000,000. The total unit cost of making one unit of sales is $22. Selling and administrative expenses are expected to be $300,000. Income taxes are estimated to be $150,000. Prepare a budgeted income statement for the year ending December 31, 2008.

Prepare data for a cash budget. (SO 5)

BE7-9 Agee Industries expects credit sales for January, February, and March to be $200,000, $260,000, and $310,000, respectively. It is expected that 70% of the sales will be collected in the month of sale, and 30% will be collected in the following month. Compute cash collections from customers for each month.

Determine required merchandise purchases for 1 month. (SO 6)

BE7-10 Palermo Wholesalers is preparing its merchandise purchases budget. Budgeted sales are $400,000 for April and $475,000 for May. Cost of goods sold is expected to be 60% of sales. The company's desired ending inventory is 20% of the following month's cost of goods sold. Compute the required purchases for April.

EXERCISES

WILEY PLUS

E7-1 Black Rose Company has always done some planning for the future, but the company has never prepared a formal budget. Now that the company is growing larger, it is considering preparing a budget.

Explain the concept of budgeting.

(SO 1, 2, 3)

Instructions

Write a memo to Jack Bruno, the president of Black Rose Company, in which you define budgeting, identify the budgets that comprise the master budget, identify the primary benefits of budgeting, and discuss the essentials of effective budgeting.

E7-2 Zeller Electronics Inc. produces and sells two models of pocket calculators, XQ-103 and XQ-104. The calculators sell for $12 and $25, respectively. Because of the intense competition Zeller faces, management budgets sales semiannually. Its projections for the first 2 quarters of 2008 are as follows.

Prepare a sales budget for 2 quarters.

(SO 3)

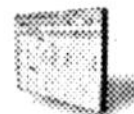

	Unit Sales	
Product	**Quarter 1**	**Quarter 2**
XQ-103	20,000	25,000
XQ-104	12,000	15,000

No changes in selling prices are anticipated.

Instructions

Prepare a sales budget for the 2 quarters ending June 30, 2008. List the products and show for each quarter and for the 6 months, units, selling price, and total sales by product and in total.

E7-3 Roche and Young, CPAs, are preparing their service revenue (sales) budget for the coming year (2008). The practice is divided into three departments: auditing, tax, and consulting. Billable hours for each department, by quarter, are provided below.

Prepare a sales budget for four quarters.

(SO 3, 6)

Department	Quarter 1	Quarter 2	Quarter 3	Quarter 4
Auditing	2,200	1,600	2,000	2,400
Tax	3,000	2,400	2,000	2,500
Consulting	1,500	1,500	1,500	1,500

Average hourly billing rates are: auditing $80, tax $90, and consulting $100.

Instructions

Prepare the service revenue (sales) budget for 2008 by listing the departments and showing for each quarter and the year in total, billable hours, billable rate, and total revenue.

E7-4 Turney Company produces and sells automobile batteries, the heavy-duty HD-240. The 2008 sales budget is as follows.

Prepare quarterly production budgets.

(SO 3)

Quarter	HD-240
1	5,000
2	7,000
3	8,000
4	10,000

The January 1, 2008, inventory of HD-240 is 2,500 units. Management desires an ending inventory each quarter equal to 50% of the next quarter's sales. Sales in the first quarter of 2009 are expected to be 30% higher than sales in the same quarter in 2008.

Instructions

Prepare quarterly production budgets for each quarter and in total for 2008.

E7-5 Moreno Industries has adopted the following production budget for the first 4 months of 2009.

Prepare a direct materials purchases budget.

(SO 3)

Month	Units	Month	Units
January	10,000	March	5,000
February	8,000	April	4,000

Each unit requires 3 pounds of raw materials costing $2 per pound. On December 31, 2008, the ending raw materials inventory was 9,000 pounds. Management wants to have a raw materials inventory at the end of the month equal to 30% of next month's production requirements.

Instructions

Prepare a direct materials purchases budget by month for the first quarter.

Prepare production and direct materials budgets by quarters for 6 months.

(SO 3)

E7-6 On January 1, 2009 the Batista Company budget committee has reached agreement on the following data for the 6 months ending June 30, 2009.

Sales units:	First quarter 5,000; second quarter 6,000; third quarter 7,000
Ending raw materials inventory:	50% of the next quarter's production requirements
Ending finished goods inventory:	30% of the next quarter's expected sales units
Third-quarter production:	7,250 units

The ending raw materials and finished goods inventories at December 31, 2008, follow the same percentage relationships to production and sales that occur in 2009. Three pounds of raw materials are required to make each unit of finished goods. Raw materials purchased are expected to cost $4 per pound.

Instructions

(a) Prepare a production budget by quarters for the 6-month period ended June 30, 2009.
(b) Prepare a direct materials budget by quarters for the 6-month period ended June 30, 2009.

Prepare a direct labor budget.

(SO 3)

E7-7 Neely, Inc., is preparing its direct labor budget for 2008 from the following production budget based on a calendar year.

Quarter	Units	Quarter	Units
1	20,000	3	35,000
2	25,000	4	30,000

Each unit requires 1.6 hours of direct labor.

Instructions

Prepare a direct labor budget for 2008. Wage rates are expected to be $15 for the first 2 quarters and $16 for quarters 3 and 4.

Prepare a manufacturing overhead budget for the year.

(SO 3)

E7-8 Hardin Company is preparing its manufacturing overhead budget for 2008. Relevant data consist of the following.

Units to be produced (by quarters): 10,000, 12,000, 14,000, 16,000.

Direct labor: Time is 1.5 hours per unit.

Variable overhead costs per direct labor hour: Indirect materials $0.70; indirect labor $1.20; and maintenance $0.50.

Fixed overhead costs per quarter: Supervisory salaries $35,000; depreciation $16,000; and maintenance $12,000.

Instructions

Prepare the manufacturing overhead budget for the year, showing quarterly data.

Prepare a selling and administrative expense budget for 2 quarters.

(SO 3)

E7-9 Edington Company combines its operating expenses for budget purposes in a selling and administrative expense budget. For the first 6 months of 2008, the following data are available.

1. Sales: 20,000 units quarter 1; 22,000 units quarter 2.
2. Variable costs per dollar of sales: Sales commissions 5%, delivery expense 2%, and advertising 3%.
3. Fixed costs per quarter: Sales salaries $10,000, office salaries $6,000, depreciation $4,200, insurance $1,500, utilities $800, and repairs expense $600.
4. Unit selling price: $20.

Instructions

Prepare a selling and administrative expense budget by quarters for the first 6 months of 2008.

Prepare a production and a direct materials budget.

(SO 3)

E7-10 Tyson Chandler Company's sales budget projects unit sales of part 198Z of 10,000 units in January, 12,000 units in February, and 13,000 units in March. Each unit of part 198Z requires 2 pounds of materials, which cost $3 per pound. Tyson Chandler Company desires its ending raw materials inventory to equal 40% of the next month's production requirements, and its ending finished goods inventory to equal 25% of the next month's expected unit sales. These goals were met at December 31, 2007.

Instructions

(a) Prepare a production budget for January and February 2008.
(b) Prepare a direct materials budget for January 2008.

Prepare a budgeted income statement for the year.

(SO 3, 4)

E7-11 Fuqua Company has accumulated the following budget data for the year 2008.

1. Sales: 30,000 units, unit selling price $80.
2. Cost of one unit of finished goods: Direct materials 2 pounds at $5 per pound, direct labor 3 hours at $12 per hour, and manufacturing overhead $6 per direct labor hour.
3. Inventories (raw materials only): Beginning, 10,000 pounds; ending, 15,000 pounds.
4. Raw materials cost: $5 per pound.
5. Selling and administrative expenses: $200,000.
6. Income taxes: 30% of income before income taxes.

Instructions

(a) Prepare a schedule showing the computation of cost of goods sold for 2008.
(b) Prepare a budgeted income statement for 2008.

Prepare a cash budget for 2 months.

(SO 5)

E7-12 Garza Company expects to have a cash balance of $46,000 on January 1, 2008. Relevant monthly budget data for the first 2 months of 2008 are as follows.

Collections from customers: January $85,000, February $150,000.

Payments for direct materials: January $50,000, February $70,000.

Direct labor: January $30,000, February $45,000. Wages are paid in the month they are incurred.

Manufacturing overhead: January $21,000, February $25,000. These costs include depreciation of $1,000 per month. All other overhead costs are paid as incurred.

Selling and administrative expenses: January $15,000, February $20,000. These costs are exclusive of depreciation. They are paid as incurred.

Sales of marketable securities in January are expected to realize $10,000 in cash. Garza Company has a line of credit at a local bank that enables it to borrow up to $25,000. The company wants to maintain a minimum monthly cash balance of $20,000.

Instructions

Prepare a cash budget for January and February.

Prepare a cash budget.

(SO 5)

E7-13 Pink Martini Corporation is projecting a cash balance of $31,000 in its December 31, 2007, balance sheet. Pink Martini's schedule of expected collections from customers for the first quarter of 2008 shows total collections of $180,000. The schedule of expected payments for direct materials for the first quarter of 2008 shows total payments of $41,000. Other information gathered for the first quarter of 2008 is: sale of equipment $3,500; direct labor $70,000, manufacturing overhead $35,000, selling and administrative expenses $45,000; and purchase of securities $12,000. Pink Martini wants to maintain a balance of at least $25,000 cash at the end of each quarter.

Instructions

Prepare a cash budget for the first quarter.

Prepare schedules of expected collections and payments.

(SO 5)

E7-14 NIU Company's budgeted sales and direct materials purchases are as follows.

	Budgeted Sales	Budgeted D.M. Purchases
January	$200,000	$30,000
February	220,000	35,000
March	270,000	41,000

NIU's sales are 40% cash and 60% credit. Credit sales are collected 10% in the month of sale, 50% in the month following sale, and 36% in the second month following sale; 4% are uncollectible. NIU's purchases are 50% cash and 50% on account. Purchases on account are paid 40% in the month of purchase, and 60% in the month following purchase.

Instructions

(a) Prepare a schedule of expected collections from customers for March.
(b) Prepare a schedule of expected payments for direct materials for March.

Prepare schedules for cash receipts and cash payments, and determine ending balances for balance sheet.

(SO 5, 6)

E7-15 Environmental Landscaping Inc. is preparing its budget for the first quarter of 2008. The next step in the budgeting process is to prepare a cash receipts schedule and a cash payments schedule. To that end the following information has been collected.

Clients usually pay 60% of their fee in the month that service is provided, 30% the month after, and 10% the second month after receiving service.

Actual service revenue for 2007 and expected service revenues for 2008 are: November 2007, $90,000; December 2007, $80,000; January 2008, $100,000; February 2008, $120,000; March 2008, $130,000.

Purchases on landscaping supplies (direct materials) are paid 40% in the month of purchase and 60% the following month. Actual purchases for 2007 and expected purchases for 2008 are: December 2007, $14,000; January 2008, $12,000; February 2008, $15,000; March 2008, $18,000.

Instructions

(a) Prepare the following schedules for each month in the first quarter of 2008 and for the quarter in total:
  (1) Expected collections from clients.
  (2) Expected payments for landscaping supplies.

(b) Determine the following balances at March 31, 2008:
  (1) Accounts receivable.
  (2) Accounts payable.

Prepare a cash budget for two quarters.

(SO 5, 6)

E7-16 Donnegal Dental Clinic is a medium-sized dental service specializing in family dental care. The clinic is currently preparing the master budget for the first 2 quarters of 2008. All that remains in this process is the cash budget. The following information has been collected from other portions of the master budget and elsewhere.

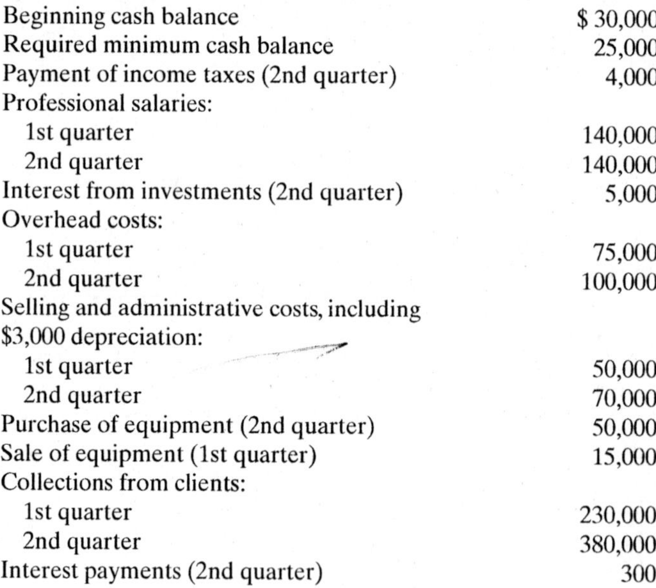

Beginning cash balance	$ 30,000
Required minimum cash balance	25,000
Payment of income taxes (2nd quarter)	4,000
Professional salaries:	
1st quarter	140,000
2nd quarter	140,000
Interest from investments (2nd quarter)	5,000
Overhead costs:	
1st quarter	75,000
2nd quarter	100,000
Selling and administrative costs, including $3,000 depreciation:	
1st quarter	50,000
2nd quarter	70,000
Purchase of equipment (2nd quarter)	50,000
Sale of equipment (1st quarter)	15,000
Collections from clients:	
1st quarter	230,000
2nd quarter	380,000
Interest payments (2nd quarter)	300

Instructions

Prepare a cash budget for each of the first two quarters of 2008.

Prepare a purchases budget and budgeted income statement for a merchandiser.

(SO 6)

SERVICE

E7-17 In May 2008, the budget committee of Dalby Stores assembles the following data in preparation of budgeted merchandise purchases for the month of June.

1. Expected sales: June $500,000, July $600,000.
2. Cost of goods sold is expected to be 70% of sales.
3. Desired ending merchandise inventory is 40% of the following (next) month's cost of goods sold.
4. The beginning inventory at June 1 will be the desired amount.

Instructions

(a) Compute the budgeted merchandise purchases for June.
(b) Prepare the budgeted income statement for June through gross profit.

EXERCISES: SET B

Visit the book's website at **www.wiley.com/college/weygandt**, and choose the Student Companion site, to access Exercise Set B.

PROBLEMS: SET A

Prepare budgeted income statement and supporting budgets.

(SO 3, 4)

P7-1A Danner Farm Supply Company manufactures and sells a pesticide called Snare. The following data are available for preparing budgets for Snare for the first 2 quarters of 2009.

1. Sales: Quarter 1, 28,000 bags; quarter 2, 42,000 bags. Selling price is $60 per bag.
2. Direct materials: Each bag of Snare requires 4 pounds of Gumm at a cost of $4 per pound and 6 pounds of Tarr at $1.50 per pound.
3. Desired inventory levels:

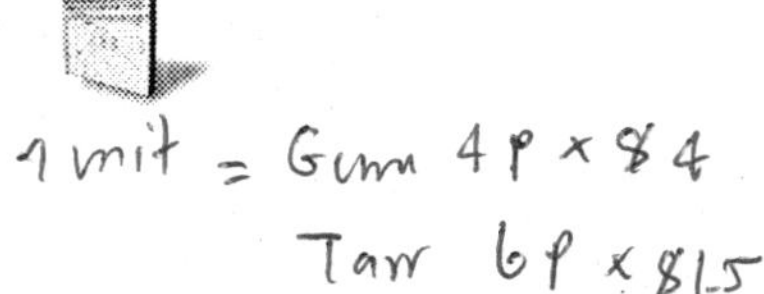

Type of Inventory	January 1	April 1	July 1
Snare (bags)	8,000	12,000	18,000
Gumm (pounds)	9,000	10,000	13,000
Tarr (pounds)	14,000	20,000	25,000

4. Direct labor: Direct labor time is 15 minutes per bag at an hourly rate of $14 per hour.
5. Selling and administrative expenses are expected to be 15% of sales plus $175,000 per quarter.
6. Income taxes are expected to be 30% of income from operations.

Your assistant has prepared two budgets: (1) The manufacturing overhead budget shows expected costs to be 150% of direct labor cost. (2) The direct materials budget for Tarr shows the cost of Tarr purchases to be $297,000 in quarter 1 and $439,500 in quarter 2.

Instructions

Prepare the budgeted income statement for the first 6 months and all required operating budgets by quarters. (*Note:* Use variable and fixed in the selling and administrative expense budget). Do not prepare the manufacturing overhead budget or the direct materials budget for Tarr.

Net Income $600,250
Cost per bag $33.75

Prepare sales, production, direct materials, direct labor, and income statement budgets.

(SO 3, 4)

P7-2A LaRussa Inc. is preparing its annual budgets for the year ending December 31, 2009. Accounting assistants furnish the data shown below.

	Product JB 50	Product JB 60
Sales budget:		
Anticipated volume in units	400,000	200,000
Unit selling price	$20	$25
Production budget:		
Desired ending finished goods units	25,000	15,000
Beginning finished goods units	30,000	10,000
Direct materials budget:		
Direct materials per unit (pounds)	2	3
Desired ending direct materials pounds	30,000	15,000
Beginning direct materials pounds	40,000	10,000
Cost per pound	$3	$4
Direct labor budget:		
Direct labor time per unit	0.4	0.6
Direct labor rate per hour	$12	$12
Budgeted income statement:		
Total unit cost	$12	$21

An accounting assistant has prepared the detailed manufacturing overhead budget and the selling and administrative expense budget. The latter shows selling expenses of $660,000 for product JB 50 and $360,000 for product JB 60, and administrative expenses of $540,000 for product JB 50 and $340,000 for product JB 60. Income taxes are expected to be 30%.

(a) Total sales $13,000,000
(b) Required production units: JB 50, 395,000 JB 60, 205,000
(c) Total cost of direct materials purchases $4,820,000
(d) Total direct labor cost $3,372,000
(e) Net income $1,470,000

Instructions

Prepare the following budgets for the year. Show data for each product. Quarterly budgets should not be prepared.

(a) Sales
(b) Production
(c) Direct materials
(d) Direct labor
(e) Income statement (*Note*: Income taxes are not allocated to the products.)

Prepare sales and production budgets and compute cost per unit under two plans.

(SO 3, 4)

P7-3A Colt Industries had sales in 2008 of $6,400,000 and gross profit of $1,100,000. Management is considering two alternative budget plans to increase its gross profit in 2009.

Plan A would increase the selling price per unit from $8.00 to $8.40. Sales volume would decrease by 5% from its 2008 level. Plan B would decrease the selling price per unit by $0.50. The marketing department expects that the sales volume would increase by 150,000 units.

At the end of 2008, Colt has 40,000 units of inventory on hand. If Plan A is accepted, the 2009 ending inventory should be equal to 5% of the 2009 sales. If Plan B is accepted, the ending inventory should be equal to 50,000 units. Each unit produced will cost $1.80 in direct labor, $1.25 in direct materials, and $1.20 in variable overhead. The fixed overhead for 2009 should be $1,895,000.

Instructions

(c) Unit cost: Plan A $6.75 Plan B $6.22
(d) Gross profit: Plan A $1,254,000 Plan B $1,216,000

(a) Prepare a sales budget for 2009 under each plan.
(b) Prepare a production budget for 2009 under each plan.
(c) Compute the production cost per unit under each plan. Why is the cost per unit different for each of the two plans? (Round to two decimals.)
(d) Which plan should be accepted? (*Hint*: Compute the gross profit under each plan.)

Prepare cash budget for 2 months.

(SO 5)

P7-4A Haas Company prepares monthly cash budgets. Relevant data from operating budgets for 2009 are:

	January	February
Sales	$350,000	$400,000
Direct materials purchases	110,000	130,000
Direct labor	90,000	100,000
Manufacturing overhead	70,000	75,000
Selling and administrative expenses	79,000	86,000

All sales are on account. Collections are expected to be 50% in the month of sale, 30% in the first month following the sale, and 20% in the second month following the sale. Sixty percent (60%) of direct materials purchases are paid in cash in the month of purchase, and the balance due is paid in the month following the purchase. All other items above are paid in the month incurred except for selling and administrative expenses that include $1,000 of depreciation per month.

Other data:

1. Credit sales: November 2008, $260,000; December 2008, $320,000.
2. Purchases of direct materials: December 2008, $100,000.
3. Other receipts: January—Collection of December 31, 2008, notes receivable $15,000; February—Proceeds from sale of securities $6,000.
4. Other disbursements: February—Withdrawal of $5,000 cash for personal use of owner, Dewey Yaeger.

The company's cash balance on January 1, 2009, is expected to be $60,000. The company wants to maintain a minimum cash balance of $50,000.

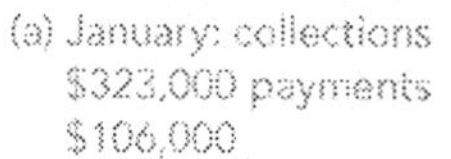

(b) Ending cash balance: January $54,000 February $50,000

Instructions

(a) Prepare schedules for (1) expected collections from customers and (2) expected payments for direct materials purchases.
(b) Prepare a cash budget for January and February in columnar form.

Prepare purchases and income statement budgets for a merchandiser.

(SO 6)

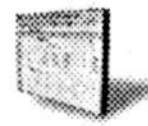

P7-5A The budget committee of Deleon Company collects the following data for its San Miguel Store in preparing budgeted income statements for May and June 2009.

1. Sales for May are expected to be $800,000. Sales in June and July are expected to be 10% higher than the preceding month.
2. Cost of goods sold is expected to be 75% of sales.
3. Company policy is to maintain ending merchandise inventory at 20% of the following month's cost of goods sold.

4. Operating expenses are estimated to be:

Sales salaries	$30,000 per month
Advertising	5% of monthly sales
Delivery expense	3% of monthly sales
Sales commissions	4% of monthly sales
Rent expense	$5,000 per month
Depreciation	$800 per month
Utilities	$600 per month
Insurance	$500 per month

5. Income taxes are estimated to be 30% of income from operations.

Instructions

(a) Prepare the merchandise purchases budget for each month in columnar form.

(b) Prepare budgeted income statements for each month in columnar form. Show in the statements the details of cost of goods sold.

(a) Purchases:
May $612,000
June $673,200
(b) Net income:
May $46,970
June $54,250

P7-6A Glendo Industries' balance sheet at December 31, 2008, is presented below.

Prepare budgeted income statement and balance sheet.

(SO 4, 5)

GLENDO INDUSTRIES
Balance Sheet
December 31, 2008

Assets

Current assets		
Cash		$ 7,500
Accounts receivable		82,500
Finished goods inventory (2,000 units)		30,000
Total current assets		120,000
Property, plant, and equipment		
Equipment	$40,000	
Less: Accumulated depreciation	10,000	30,000
Total assets		$150,000

Liabilities and Stockholders' Equity

Liabilities		
Notes payable		$ 25,000
Accounts payable		45,000
Total liabilities		70,000
Stockholders' equity		
Common stock	$50,000	
Retained earnings	30,000	
Total stockholders' equity		80,000
Total liabilities and stockholders' equity		$150,000

Additional information accumulated for the budgeting process is as follows.

Budgeted data for the year 2009 include the following.

	4th Qtr. of 2009	Year 2009 Total
Sales budget (8,000 units at $35)	$84,000	$280,000
Direct materials used	17,000	69,400
Direct labor	12,500	56,600
Manufacturing overhead applied	10,000	54,000
Selling and administrative expenses	18,000	76,000

To meet sales requirements and to have 3,000 units of finished goods on hand at December 31, 2009, the production budget shows 9,000 required units of output. The total unit cost of production is expected to be $20. Glendo Industries uses the first-in, first-out (FIFO) inventory costing method. Selling and administrative expenses include $4,000 for depreciation on equipment. Interest expense is expected to be $3,500 for the year. Income taxes are expected to be 30% of income before income taxes.

All sales and purchases are on account. It is expected that 60% of quarterly sales are collected in cash within the quarter and the remainder is collected in the following quarter. Direct materials purchased from suppliers are paid 50% in the quarter incurred and the remainder in the following quarter. Purchases in the fourth quarter were the same as the materials used. In 2009, the company expects to purchase additional equipment costing $19,000. It expects to pay $8,000 on notes payable plus all interest due and payable to December 31 (included in interest expense $3,500, above). Accounts payable at December 31, 2009, includes amounts due suppliers (see above) plus other accounts payable of $5,700. In 2009, the company expects to declare and pay a $5,000 cash dividend. Unpaid income taxes at December 31 will be $5,000. The company's cash budget shows an expected cash balance of $7,950 at December 31, 2009.

Instructions

Net income $35,350
Total assets $146,550

Prepare a budgeted income statement for 2009 and a budgeted balance sheet at December 31, 2009. In preparing the income statement, you will need to compute cost of goods manufactured (direct materials + direct labor + manufacturing overhead) and finished goods inventory (December 31, 2009).

PROBLEMS: SET B

Prepare budgeted income statement and supporting budgets.

(SO 3, 4)

P7-1B Krause Farm Supply Company manufactures and sells a fertilizer called Basic II. The following data are available for preparing budgets for Basic II for the first 2 quarters of 2008.

1. Sales: Quarter 1, 40,000 bags; quarter 2, 60,000 bags. Selling price is $60 per bag.
2. Direct materials: Each bag of Basic II requires 6 pounds of Crup at a cost of $4 per pound and 10 pounds of Dert at $1.50 per pound.
3. Desired inventory levels:

Type of Inventory	January 1	April 1	July 1
Basic II (bags)	10,000	15,000	20,000
Crup (pounds)	9,000	12,000	15,000
Dert (pounds)	15,000	20,000	25,000

4. Direct labor: Direct labor time is 15 minutes per bag at an hourly rate of $12 per hour.
5. Selling and administrative expenses are expected to be 10% of sales plus $150,000 per quarter.
6. Income taxes are expected to be 30% of income from operations.

Your assistant has prepared two budgets: (1) The manufacturing overhead budget shows expected costs to be 100% of direct labor cost. (2) The direct materials budget for Dert which shows the cost of Dert purchases to be $682,500 in quarter 1 and $982,500 in quarter 2.

Instructions

Net income $420,000
Cost per bag $45.00

Prepare the budgeted income statement for the first 6 months of 2008 and all required operating budgets by quarters. (*Note*: Use variable and fixed in the selling and administrative expense budget.) Do not prepare the manufacturing overhead budget or the direct materials budget for Dert.

Prepare sales, production, direct materials, direct labor, and income statement budgets.

(SO 3, 4)

P7-2B Mercer Inc. is preparing its annual budgets for the year ending December 31, 2008. Accounting assistants furnish the following data.

	Product LN 35	Product LN 40
Sales budget:		
Anticipated volume in units	300,000	180,000
Unit selling price	$20	$30
Production budget:		
Desired ending finished goods units	30,000	25,000
Beginning finished goods units	20,000	15,000

Table continues on next page

	Product LN 35	Product LN 40
Direct materials budget:		
Direct materials per unit (pounds)	2	3
Desired ending direct materials pounds	50,000	20,000
Beginning direct materials pounds	40,000	10,000
Cost per pound	$2	$3
Direct labor budget:		
Direct labor time per unit	0.5	0.75
Direct labor rate per hour	$12	$12
Budgeted income statement:		
Total unit cost	$11	$20

An accounting assistant has prepared the detailed manufacturing overhead budget and the selling and administrative expense budget. The latter shows selling expenses of $560,000 for product LN 35 and $440,000 for product LN 40, and administrative expenses of $420,000 for product LN 35 and $380,000 for product LN 40. Income taxes are expected to be 30%.

Instructions

Prepare the following budgets for the year. Show data for each product. Quarterly budgets should not be prepared.

(a) Sales
(b) Production
(c) Direct materials
(d) Direct labor
(e) Income statement (*Note*: Income taxes are not allocated to the products.)

(a) Total sales $11,400,000
(b) Required production units: LN 35, 310,000
(c) Total cost of direct materials purchases $3,000,000
(d) Total direct labor cost $3,570,000
(e) Net income $1,890,000

P7-3B Litwin Industries has sales in 2008 of $4,900,000 (700,000 units) and gross profit of $1,187,500. Management is considering two alternative budget plans to increase its gross profit in 2009.

Prepare sales and production budgets and compute cost per unit under two plans.

(SO 3, 4)

Plan A would increase the selling price per unit from $7.00 to $7.60. Sales volume would decrease by 10% from its 2008 level. Plan B would decrease the selling price per unit by 5%. The marketing department expects that the sales volume would increase by 100,000 units.

At the end of 2008, Litwin has 70,000 units on hand. If Plan A is accepted, the 2009 ending inventory should be equal to 90,000 units. If Plan B is accepted, the ending inventory should be equal to 100,000 units. Each unit produced will cost $2.00 in direct materials, $1.50 in direct labor, and $0.50 in variable overhead. The fixed overhead for 2009 should be $975,000.

Instructions

(a) Prepare a sales budget for 2009 under (1) Plan A and (2) Plan B.
(b) Prepare a production budget for 2009 under (1) Plan A and (2) Plan B.
(c) Compute the cost per unit under (1) Plan A and (2) Plan B. Explain why the cost per unit is different for each of the two plans. (Round to two decimals.)
(d) Which plan should be accepted? (*Hint*: Compute the gross profit under each plan.)

(c) Unit cost: Plan A $5.50, Plan B $5.17
(d) Gross profit: Plan A $1,323,000 Plan B $1,184,000

P7-4B Orton Company prepares monthly cash budgets. Relevant data from operating budgets for 2009 are:

Prepare cash budget for 2 months.

(SO 5)

	January	February
Sales	$320,000	$400,000
Direct materials purchases	80,000	110,000
Direct labor	85,000	115,000
Manufacturing overhead	60,000	75,000
Selling and administrative expenses	75,000	80,000

All sales are on account. Collections are expected to be 60% in the month of sale, 30% in the first month following the sale, and 10% in the second month following the sale. Thirty percent (30%) of direct materials purchases are paid in cash in the month of purchase, and the balance due is paid in the month following the purchase. All other items above are paid in the month incurred. Depreciation has been excluded from manufacturing overhead and selling and administrative expenses.

Other data:

1. Credit sales: November 2008, $200,000; December 2008, $280,000.
2. Purchases of direct materials: December 2008, $90,000.

3. Other receipts: January—Collection of December 31, 2008, interest receivable $3,000; February—Proceeds from sale of securities $5,000.
4. Other disbursements: February—payment of $20,000 for land.

The company's cash balance on January 1, 2009, is expected to be $60,000. The company wants to maintain a minimum cash balance of $50,000.

(a) January: collections $296,000
payments $87,000
(b) Ending cash balance:
January $52,000
February $50,000

Instructions

(a) Prepare schedules for (1) expected collections from customers and (2) expected payments for direct materials purchases.

(b) Prepare a cash budget for January and February in columnar form.

Prepare purchases and income statement budgets for a merchandiser.

(SO 6)

P7-5B The budget committee of Urbina Company collects the following data for its Westwood Store in preparing budgeted income statements for July and August 2008.

1. Expected sales: July $400,000, August $450,000, September $500,000.
2. Cost of goods sold is expected to be 64% of sales.
3. Company policy is to maintain ending merchandise inventory at 25% of the following month's cost of goods sold.
4. Operating expenses are estimated to be:

Sales salaries	$40,000 per month
Advertising	4% of monthly sales
Delivery expense	2% of monthly sales
Sales commissions	3% of monthly sales
Rent expense	$3,000 per month
Depreciation	$700 per month
Utilities	$500 per month
Insurance	$300 per month

5. Income taxes are estimated to be 30% of income from operations.

(a) Purchases: July $264,000
August $296,000
(b) Net income: July $44,450
August $53,900

Instructions

(a) Prepare the merchandise purchases budget for each month in columnar form.

(b) Prepare budgeted income statements for each month in columnar form. Show the details of cost of goods sold in the statements.

PROBLEMS: SET C

Visit the book's website at **www.wiley.com/college/weygandt**, and choose the Student Companion site, to access Problem Set C.

WATERWAYS CONTINUING PROBLEM

(This is a continuation of the Waterways Problem from previous chapters.)

WCP7 Waterways Corporation is preparing its budget for the coming year, 2009. The first step is to plan for the first quarter of that coming year. The company has gathered information from its managers in preparation of the budgeting process. This problem asks you to prepare the various budgets that comprise the master budget for 2009.

Go to the book's website,
www.wiley.com/college/weygandt,
to find the remainder of this problem.

BROADENING YOUR PERSPECTIVE

DECISION MAKING ACROSS THE ORGANIZATION

BYP7-1 Lanier Corporation operates on a calendar-year basis. It begins the annual budgeting process in late August when the president establishes targets for the total dollar sales and net income before taxes for the next year.

The sales target is given first to the marketing department. The marketing manager formulates a sales budget by product line in both units and dollars. From this budget, sales quotas by product line in units and dollars are established for each of the corporation's sales districts. The marketing manager also estimates the cost of the marketing activities required to support the target sales volume and prepares a tentative marketing expense budget.

The executive vice president uses the sales and profit targets, the sales budget by product line, and the tentative marketing expense budget to determine the dollar amounts that can be devoted to manufacturing and corporate office expense. The executive vice president prepares the budget for corporate expenses. She then forwards to the production department the product-line sales budget in units and the total dollar amount that can be devoted to manufacturing.

The production manager meets with the factory managers to develop a manufacturing plan that will produce the required units when needed within the cost constraints set by the executive vice president. The budgeting process usually comes to a halt at this point because the production department does not consider the financial resources allocated to be adequate.

When this standstill occurs, the vice president of finance, the executive vice president, the marketing manager, and the production manager meet together to determine the final budgets for each of the areas. This normally results in a modest increase in the total amount available for manufacturing costs and cuts in the marketing expense and corporate office expense budgets. The total sales and net income figures proposed by the president are seldom changed. Although the participants are seldom pleased with the compromise, these budgets are final. Each executive then develops a new detailed budget for the operations in his or her area.

None of the areas has achieved its budget in recent years. Sales often run below the target. When budgeted sales are not achieved, each area is expected to cut costs so that the president's profit target can be met. However, the profit target is seldom met because costs are not cut enough. In fact, costs often run above the original budget in all functional areas (marketing, production, and corporate office).

The president is disturbed that Lanier has not been able to meet the sales and profit targets. He hired a consultant with considerable experience with companies in Lanier's industry. The consultant reviewed the budgets for the past 4 years. He concluded that the product line sales budgets were reasonable and that the cost and expense budgets were adequate for the budgeted sales and production levels.

Instructions

With the class divided into groups, answer the following.

(a) Discuss how the budgeting process employed by Lanier Corporation contributes to the failure to achieve the president's sales and profit targets.

(b) Suggest how Lanier Corporation's budgeting process could be revised to correct the problems.

(c) Should the functional areas be expected to cut their costs when sales volume falls below budget? Explain your answer. (CMA adapted.)

MANAGERIAL ANALYSIS

BYP7-2 Bedner & Flott Inc. manufactures ergonomic devices for computer users. Some of their more popular products include glare screens (for computer monitors), keyboard stands with wrist rests, and carousels that allow easy access to discs. Over the past 5 years, they experienced rapid growth, with sales of all products increasing 20% to 50% each year.

Last year, some of the primary manufacturers of computers began introducing new products with some of the ergonomic designs, such as glare screens and wrist rests, already built in. As a result, sales of Bedner & Flott's accessory devices have declined somewhat. The company believes that the disc carousels will probably continue to show growth, but that the other products will probably continue to decline. When the next year's budget was prepared, increases were built in to research and development so that replacement products could be developed or the company could expand into some other product line. Some product lines being considered are general-purpose ergonomic devices including back supports, foot rests, and sloped writing pads.

The most recent results have shown that sales decreased more than was expected for the glare screens. As a result, the company may have a shortage of funds. Top management has therefore asked that all expenses be reduced 10% to compensate for these reduced sales. Summary budget information is as follows.

Direct materials	$240,000
Direct labor	110,000
Insurance	50,000
Depreciation	90,000
Machine repairs	30,000
Sales salaries	50,000
Office salaries	80,000
Factory salaries (indirect labor)	50,000
Total	$700,000

Instructions

Using the information above, answer the following questions.

(a) What are the implications of reducing each of the costs? For example, if the company reduces direct materials costs, it may have to do so by purchasing lower-quality materials. This may affect sales in the long run.

(b) Based on your analysis in (a), what do you think is the best way to obtain the $70,000 in cost savings requested? Be specific. Are there any costs that cannot or should not be reduced? Why?

REAL-WORLD FOCUS

BYP7-3 Network Computing Devices Inc. was founded in 1988 in Mountain View, California. The company develops software products such as X-terminals, Z-mail, PC X-ware, and related hardware products. Presented below is a discussion by management in its annual report.

NETWORK COMPUTING DEVICES, INC.

Management Discussion

The Company's operating results have varied significantly, particularly on a quarterly basis, as a result of a number of factors, including general economic conditions affecting industry demand for computer products, the timing and market acceptance of new product introductions by the Company and its competitors, the timing of significant orders from large customers, periodic changes in product pricing and discounting due to competitive factors, and the availability of key components, such as video monitors and electronic subassemblies, some of which require substantial order lead times. The Company's operating results may fluctuate in the future as a result of these and other factors, including the Company's success in developing and introducing new products, its product and customer mix, and the level of competition which it experiences. The Company operates with a small backlog. Sales and operating results, therefore, generally depend on the volume and timing of orders received, which are difficult to forecast. The Company has experienced slowness in orders from some customers during the first quarter of each calendar year due to budgeting cycles common in the computer industry. In addition, sales in Europe typically are adversely affected in the third calendar quarter as many European customers reduce their business activities during the month of August.

Due to the Company's rapid growth rate and the effect of new product introductions on quarterly revenues, these seasonal trends have not materially impacted the Company's results of operations to date. However, as the Company's product lines mature and its rate of revenue growth declines, these seasonal factors may become more evident. Additionally, the Company's international sales are denominated in U.S. dollars, and an increase or decrease in the value of the U.S. dollar relative to foreign currencies could make the Company's products less or more competitive in those markets.

Instructions

(a) Identify the factors that affect the budgeting process at Network Computing Devices, Inc.

(b) Explain the additional budgeting concerns created by the international operations of the company.

EXPLORING THE WEB

BYP7-4 Information regarding many approaches to budgeting can be found on the Web. The following activity investigates the merits of "zero-based" budgeting as discussed by Michael LaFaive, Director of the Mackinac Center for Public Policy.

Address: www.mackinac.org/article.aspx?ID=5928, or go to **www.wiley.com/college/weygandt**

Instructions

Read the article at the website and answer the following questions.

(a) How does zero-based budgeting differ from standard budgeting procedures?

(b) What are some potential advantages of zero-based budgeting?

(c) What are some potential disadvantages of zero-based budgeting?

(d) How often do departments in Oklahoma undergo zero-based budgeting?

COMMUNICATION ACTIVITY

BYP7-5 In order to better serve their rural patients, Drs. Dan and Jack Fleming (brothers) began giving safety seminars. Especially popular were their "emergency-preparedness" talks given to farmers. Many people asked whether the "kit" of materials the doctors recommended for common farm emergencies was commercially available.

After checking with several suppliers, the doctors realized that no other company offered the supplies they recommended in their seminars, packaged in the way they described. Their wives, Julie and Amy, agreed to make a test package by ordering supplies from various medical supply companies and assembling them into a "kit" that could be sold at the seminars. When these kits proved a runaway success, the sisters-in-law decided to market them. At the advice of their accountant, they organized this venture as a separate company, called Life Protection Products (LPP), with Julie Fleming as CEO and Amy Fleming as Secretary-Treasurer.

LPP soon started receiving requests for the kits from all over the country, as word spread about their availability. Even without advertising, LPP was able to sell its full inventory every month. However, the company was becoming financially strained. Julie and Amy had about $100,000 in savings, and they invested about half that amount initially. They believed that this venture would allow them to make money. However, at the present time, only about $30,000 of the cash remains, and the company is constantly short of cash.

Julie has come to you for advice. She does not understand why the company is having cash flow problems. She and Amy have not even been withdrawing salaries. However, they have rented a local building and have hired two more full-time workers to help them cope with the increasing demand. They do not think they could handle the demand without this additional help.

Julie is also worried that the cash problems mean that the company may not be able to support itself. She has prepared the cash budget shown on page 350. All seminar customers pay for their products in full at the time of purchase. In addition, several large companies have ordered the kits for use by employees who work in remote sites. They have requested credit terms and have been allowed to pay in the month following the sale. These large purchasers amount to about 25% of the sales at the present time. LPP purchases the materials for the kits about 2 months ahead of time. Julie and Amy are considering slowing the growth of the company by simply purchasing less materials, which will mean selling fewer kits.

The workers are paid weekly. Julie and Amy need about $15,000 cash on hand at the beginning of the month to pay for purchases of raw materials. Right now they have been using cash from their savings, but as noted, only $30,000 is left.

Instructions

Write a response to Julie Fleming. Explain why LPP is short of cash. Will this company be able to support itself? Explain your answer. Make any recommendations you deem appropriate.

LIFE PROTECTION PRODUCTS
Cash Budget
For the Quarter Ending June 30, 2009

	April	May	June
Cash balance, beginning	$15,000	$15,000	$15,000
Cash received			
From prior month sales	5,000	7,500	12,500
From current sales	15,000	22,500	37,500
Total cash on hand	35,000	45,000	65,000
Cash payments			
To employees	3,000	3,000	3,000
For products	25,000	35,000	45,000
Miscellaneous expenses	5,000	6,000	7,000
Postage	1,000	1,000	1,000
Total cash payments	34,000	45,000	56,000
Cash balance	$ 1,000	$ 0	$ 9,000
Borrow from savings	$14,000	$15,000	$ 1,000
Borrow from bank?	$ 0	$ 0	$ 5,000

ETHICS CASE

BYP7-6 You are an accountant in the budgetary, projections, and special projects department of American Conductor, Inc., a large manufacturing company. The president, William Brown, asks you on very short notice to prepare some sales and income projections covering the next 2 years of the company's much heralded new product lines. He wants these projections for a series of speeches he is making while on a 2-week trip to eight East Coast brokerage firms. The president hopes to bolster American's stock sales and price.

You work 23 hours in 2 days to compile the projections, hand deliver them to the president, and are swiftly but graciously thanked as he departs. A week later you find time to go over some of your computations and discover a miscalculation that makes the projections grossly overstated. You quickly inquire about the president's itinerary and learn that he has made half of his speeches and has half yet to make. You are in a quandary as to what to do.

Instructions

(a) What are the consequences of telling the president of your gross miscalculations?
(b) What are the consequences of *not* telling the president of your gross miscalculations?
(c) What are the ethical considerations to you and the president in this situation?

"ALL ABOUT YOU" ACTIVITY

BYP7-7 The "All About You" feature in this chapter emphasizes that in order to get your personal finances under control, you need to prepare a personal budget. Assume that you have compiled the following information regarding your expected cash flows for a typical month.

Rent payment	$ 400	Miscellaneous costs	$110
Interest income	50	Savings	50
Income tax withheld	300	Eating out	150
Electricity bill	22	Telephone and Internet costs	90
Groceries	80	Student loan payments	275
Wages earned	2,000	Entertainment costs	250
Insurance	100	Transportation costs	150

Instructions

Using the information above, prepare a personal budget. In preparing this budget, use the format found at **http://financialplan.about.com/cs/budgeting/l/blbudget.htm**. Just skip any unused line items.

Answers to Insight and Accounting Across the Organization Questions

Business Often Feel Too Busy to Plan for the Future, p. 312

Q: Describe a situation in which a business "sells as much as it can" but cannot "keep its employees paid."

A: *If sales are made to customers on credit and collection is slow, the company may find that it does not have enough cash to pay employees or suppliers. Without these resources, the company will fail to survive.*

Which Budget Approach Do You Prefer?, p. 314

Q: What approach did Time Warner use to prepare the old budget? What approach did it use to prepare the new budget?

A: *Time Warner used a "top-down" approach to prepare the old budget since its goals were determined by top management. It used a participative approach to prepare the new budget since each operating unit set goals.*

Without a Budget, Can the Games Begin?, p. 324

Q: Why does it matter whether the Olympic Games exceed their budget?

A: *If the Olympic Games exceed their budget, taxpayers of the sponsoring community and country will end up footing the bill. Depending on the size of the losses, and the resources of the community, this could produce a substantial burden. As a result, other communities might be reluctant to host the Olympics in the future.*

Authors' Comments on *All About You:* Avoiding Personal Financial Disaster, p. 330

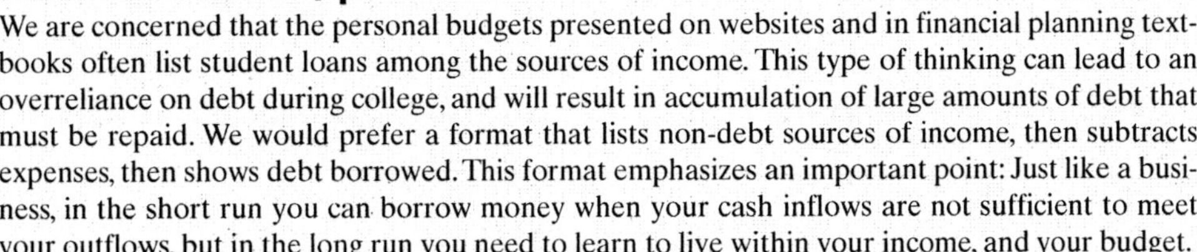

We are concerned that the personal budgets presented on websites and in financial planning textbooks often list student loans among the sources of income. This type of thinking can lead to an overreliance on debt during college, and will result in accumulation of large amounts of debt that must be repaid. We would prefer a format that lists non-debt sources of income, then subtracts expenses, then shows debt borrowed. This format emphasizes an important point: Just like a business, in the short run you can borrow money when your cash inflows are not sufficient to meet your outflows, but in the long run you need to learn to live within your income, and your budget.

Answers to Self-Study Questions

1. c **2.** a **3.** b **4.** b **5.** d **6.** d **7.** a **8.** c **9.** c **10.** d

Remember to go back to the Navigator box on the chapter-opening page and check off your completed work.

Chapter 8

Budgetary Control and Responsibility Accounting

STUDY OBJECTIVES

After studying this chapter, you should be able to:

1 Describe the concept of budgetary control.
2 Evaluate the usefulness of static budget reports.
3 Explain the development of flexible budgets and the usefulness of flexible budget reports.
4 Describe the concept of responsibility accounting.
5 Indicate the features of responsibility reports for cost centers.
6 Identify the content of responsibility reports for profit centers.
7 Explain the basis and formula used in evaluating performance in investment centers.

The Navigator

The Navigator

Scan **Study Objectives**	☐
Read **Feature Story**	☐
Read **Preview**	☐
Read text and answer **Before You Go On** p. 364 ☐ p. 372 ☐ p. 377	☐
Work **Using the Decision Toolkit**	☐
Review **Summary of Study Objectives**	☐
Work **Demonstration Problem**	☐
Answer **Self-Study Questions**	☐
Complete **Assignments**	☐

Feature Story

TRYING TO AVOID AN ELECTRIC SHOCK

Budgets are critical to evaluating an organization's success. They are based on management's expectations of what is most likely to happen in the future. In order to be useful, they must be accurate. But what if management's expectations are wrong? Estimates are never exactly correct, and

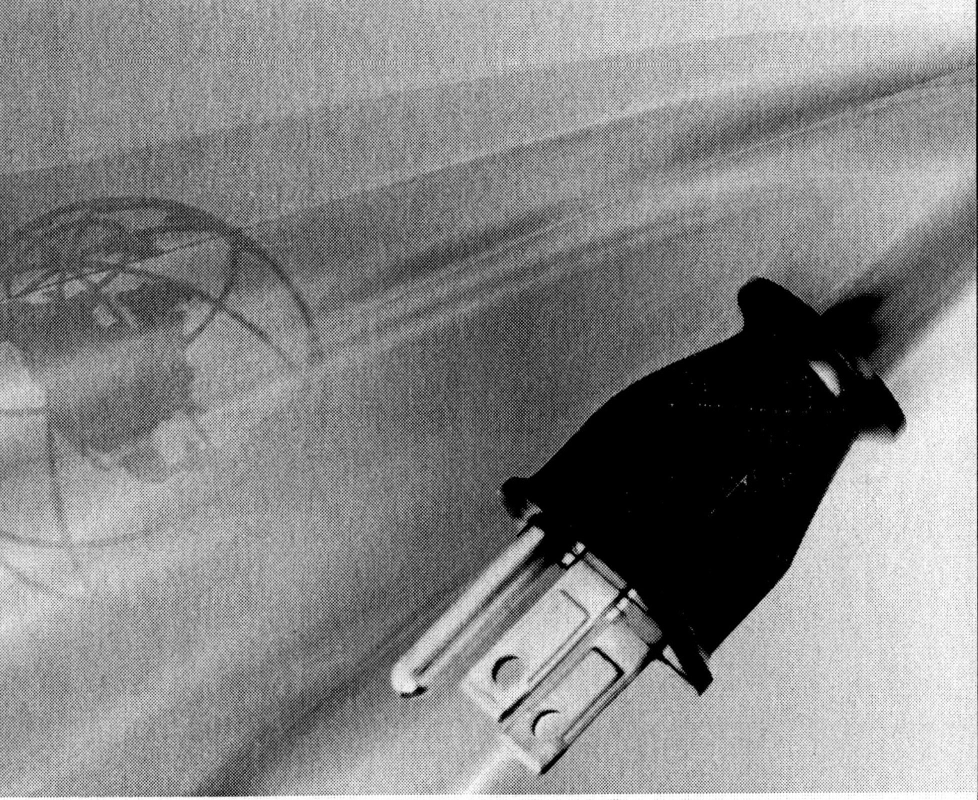

sometimes, especially in volatile industries, estimates can be "off by a mile."

In recent years the electric utility industry has become very volatile. Deregulation, volatile prices for natural gas, coal, and oil, changes in environmental regulations, and economic swings have all contributed to large changes in the profitability of electric utility companies. This means that for planning and budgeting purposes, utilities must plan and budget based on multiple "what if" scenarios that take into account factors beyond management's control. For example, in recent years, Duke Energy Corporation (*www.duke-energy.com*), headquartered in Charlotte, North Carolina, built budgeting and planning models based on three different scenarios of what the future might hold. One scenario assumes that the U.S. economy will slow considerably. A second scenario assumes that the company will experience "pricing pressure" as the market for energy becomes more efficient as a result of more energy being traded in Internet auctions. A third scenario assumes a continuation of the current environment of rapid growth, changing regulation, and large swings in the prices for the fuels the company uses to create energy.

Compounding this budgeting challenge is the fact that changes in many indirect costs can also significantly affect the company. For example, even a tiny change in market interest rates has a huge effect on the company because it has massive amounts of outstanding debt. And finally, as a result of the California energy crisis, there is mounting pressure for government intervention and regulation. This pressure has resulted in setting "rate caps" that limit the amount that utilities and energy companies can charge, thus lowering profits. The bottom line is that for budgeting and planning purposes, utility companies must remain alert and flexible.

✓ The Navigator

Inside Chapter 8

- **Budgets and the Exotic Newcastle Disease** (p. 363)
- **Competition versus Collaboration** (p. 366)
- **Does Hollywood Look at ROI?** (p. 376)
- ***All About You:* Budgeting for Housing Costs** (p. 378)

Preview of Chapter 8

In contrast to Chapter 7, we now consider how budgets are used by management to control operations. In the Feature Story on Duke Energy, we saw that budgeting must take into account factors beyond management's control. This chapter focuses on two aspects of management control: (1) budgetary control and (2) responsibility accounting.

The content and organization of Chapter 8 are as follows.

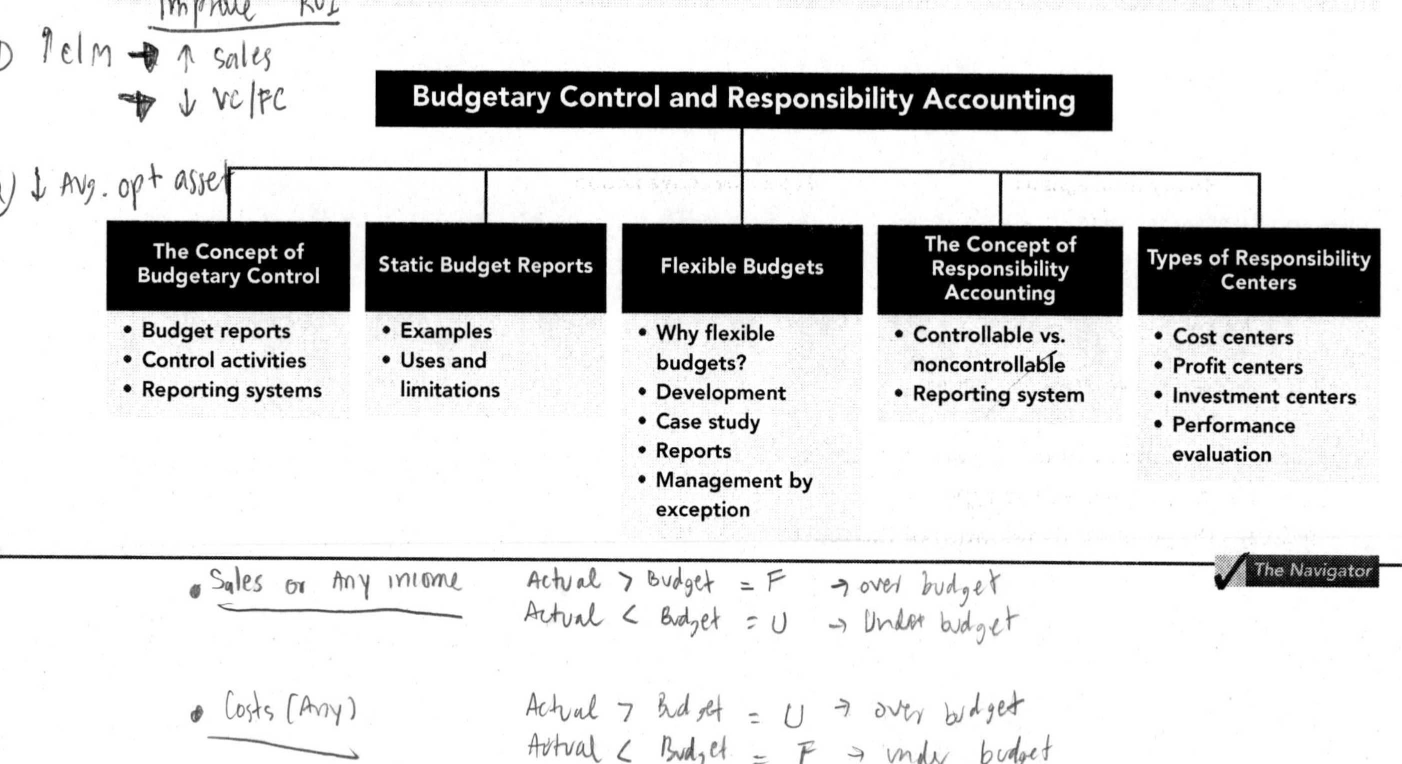

THE CONCEPT OF BUDGETARY CONTROL

STUDY OBJECTIVE 1

Describe the concept of budgetary control.

One of management's major functions is to control company operations. Control consists of the steps taken by management to see that planned objectives are met. We now ask: How do budgets contribute to control of operations?

The use of budgets in controlling operations is known as **budgetary control**. Such control takes place by means of **budget reports** that compare actual results with planned objectives. The use of budget reports is based on the belief that planned objectives lose much of their potential value without some monitoring of progress along the way. Just as your professors give midterm exams to evaluate your progress, so top management requires periodic reports on the progress of department managers toward their planned objectives.

Budget reports provide management with feedback on operations. The feedback for a crucial objective, such as having enough cash on hand to pay bills, may be made daily. For other objectives, such as meeting budgeted annual sales and operating expenses, monthly budget reports may suffice. Budget reports are prepared as frequently as needed. From these reports, management analyzes any differences between actual and planned results and determines their causes. Management then takes corrective action, or it decides to modify future plans.

Budgetary control involves activities shown in Illustration 8-1.

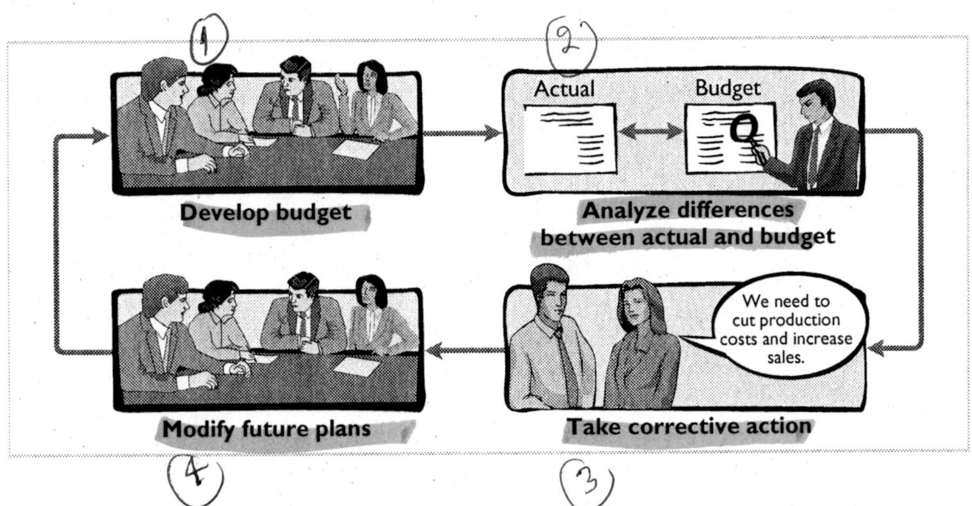

Illustration 8-1
Budgetary control activities

Budgetary control works best when a company has a formalized reporting system. The system does the following:

1. Identifies the name of the budget report, such as the sales budget or the manufacturing overhead budget.
2. States the frequency of the report, such as weekly or monthly.
3. Specifies the purpose of the report.
4. Indicates the primary recipient(s) of the report.

Illustration 8-2 provides a partial budgetary control system for a manufacturing company. Note the frequency of the reports and their emphasis on control. For example, there is a daily report on scrap and a weekly report on labor.

Illustration 8-2
Budgetary control reporting system

Name of Report	Frequency	Purpose	Primary Recipient(s)
Sales	Weekly	Determine whether sales goals are being met	Top management and sales manager
Labor	Weekly	Control direct and indirect labor costs	Vice president of production and production department managers
Scrap	Daily	Determine efficient use of materials	Production manager
Departmental overhead costs	Monthly	Control overhead costs	Department manager
Selling expenses	Monthly	Control selling expenses	Sales manager
Income statement	Monthly and quarterly	Determine whether income objectives are being met	Top management

STATIC BUDGET REPORTS

STUDY OBJECTIVE 2

Evaluate the usefulness of static budget reports.

You learned in Chapter 7 that the master budget formalizes management's planned objectives for the coming year. When used in budgetary control, each budget included in the master budget is considered to be static. A **static budget** is a projection of budget data **at one level of activity.** These budgets do not consider data for different levels of activity. As a result, companies always compare actual results with budget data at the activity level that was used in developing the master budget.

Examples

To illustrate the role of a static budget in budgetary control, we will use selected data prepared for Hayes Company in Chapter 7. Budget and actual sales data for the Kitchen-Mate product in the first and second quarters of 2008 are as follows.

Illustration 8-3
Budget and actual sales data

Sales	First Quarter	Second Quarter	Total
Budgeted	$180,000	$210,000	$390,000
Actual	179,000	199,500	378,500
Difference	$ 1,000	$ 10,500	$ 11,500

The sales budget report for Hayes Company's first quarter is shown below. The right-most column reports the difference between the budgeted and actual amounts.

Illustration 8-4
Sales budget report—first quarter

ALTERNATIVE TERMINOLOGY

The difference between budget and actual is sometimes called a *budget variance*.

HAYES COMPANY
Sales Budget Report
For the Quarter Ended March 31, 2008

Product Line	Budget	Actual	Difference Favorable F Unfavorable U
Kitchen-Mate[a]	$180,000	$179,000	$1,000 U

[a]In practice, each product line would be included in the report.

The report shows that sales are $1,000 under budget—an unfavorable result. This difference is less than 1% of budgeted sales ($1,000 ÷ $180,000 = .0056). Top management's reaction to unfavorable differences is often influenced by the materiality (significance) of the difference. Since the difference of $1,000 is immaterial in this case, we assume that Hayes Company management takes no specific corrective action.

Illustration 8-5 shows the budget report for the second quarter. It contains one new feature: cumulative year-to-date information. This report indicates that sales for the second quarter are $10,500 below budget. This is 5% of budgeted sales ($10,500 ÷ $210,000). Top management may now conclude that the difference between budgeted and actual sales requires investigation.

Illustration 8-5
Sales budget report—second quarter

HAYES COMPANY
Sales Budget Report
For the Quarter Ended June 30, 2008

	Second Quarter			Year-to-Date		
Product Line	Budget	Actual	Difference Favorable F Unfavorable U	Budget	Actual	Difference Favorable F Unfavorable U
Kitchen-Mate	$210,000	$199,500	$10,500 U	$390,000	$378,500	$11,500 U

Management's analysis should start by asking the sales manager the cause(s) of the shortfall. Managers should consider the need for corrective action. For example, management may decide to spur sales by offering sales incentives to customers or by increasing the advertising of Kitchen-Mates. Or, if management concludes that a downturn in the economy is responsible for the lower sales, it may modify planned sales and profit goals for the remainder of the year.

Uses and Limitations

From these examples, you can see that a master sales budget is useful in evaluating the performance of a sales manager. It is now necessary to ask: Is the master budget appropriate for evaluating a manager's performance in controlling costs? Recall that in a static budget, data are not modified or adjusted, regardless of changes in activity. It follows, then, that a static budget is appropriate in evaluating a manager's effectiveness in controlling costs when:

1. The actual level of activity closely approximates the master budget activity level, and/or
2. The behavior of the costs in response to changes in activity is fixed.

A static budget report is, therefore, appropriate for **fixed manufacturing costs** and for **fixed selling and administrative expenses**. But, as you will see shortly, static budget reports may not be a proper basis for evaluating a manager's performance in controlling variable costs.

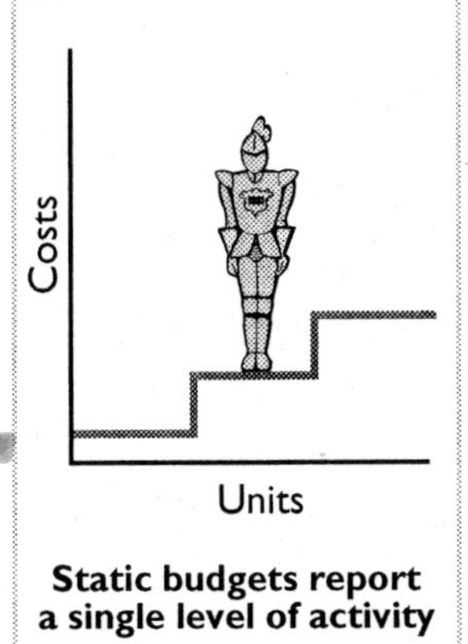

Static budgets report a single level of activity

FLEXIBLE BUDGETS

STUDY OBJECTIVE 3

Explain the development of flexible budgets and the usefulness of flexible budget reports.

In contrast to a static budget, which is based on one level of activity, a **flexible budget** projects budget data for various levels of activity. In essence, **the flexible budget is a series of static budgets at different levels of activity**. The flexible budget recognizes that the budgetary process is more useful if it is adaptable to changed operating conditions.

Flexible budgets can be prepared for each of the types of budgets included in the master budget. For example, Marriott Hotels can budget revenues and net income on the basis of 60%, 80%, and 100% of room occupancy. Similarly, American Van Lines can budget its operating expenses on the basis of various levels of truck miles driven. Likewise, in the Feature Story, Duke Energy can budget revenue and net income on the basis of estimated billions of kwh (kilowatt hours) of residential, commercial, and industrial electricity generated. In the following pages, we will illustrate a flexible budget for manufacturing overhead.

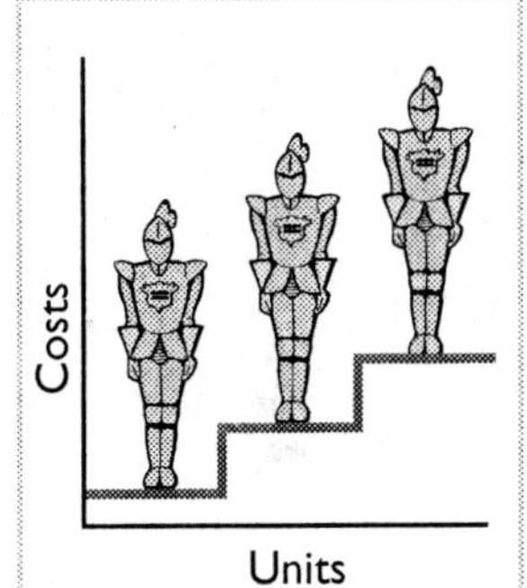

Flexible budgets are static budgets at different activity levels

Why Flexible Budgets?

Assume that you are the manager in charge of manufacturing overhead in the Forging Department of Barton Steel. In preparing the manufacturing overhead budget for 2008, you prepare the following static budget based on a production volume of 10,000 units of steel ingots.

Illustration 8-6
Static overhead budget

BARTON STEEL
Manufacturing Overhead Budget (Static)
Forging Department
For the Year Ended December 31, 2008

Budgeted production in units (steel ingots)	10,000
Budgeted costs	
Indirect materials	$ 250,000
Indirect labor	260,000
Utilities	190,000
Depreciation	280,000
Property taxes	70,000
Supervision	50,000
	$1,100,000

HELPFUL HINT
The master budget described in Chapter 7 is based on a static budget.

Fortunately for the company, the demand for steel ingots has increased, and Barton produces and sells 12,000 units during the year, rather than 10,000. You are elated: Increased sales means increased profitability, which should mean a bonus or a raise for you and the employees in your department. Unfortunately, a comparison of Forging Department actual and budgeted costs has put you on the spot. The budget report is shown below.

Illustration 8-7
Overhead static budget report

Barton Steel.xls

BARTON STEEL
Manufacturing Overhead Static Budget Report
For the Year Ended December 31, 2008

	Budget	Actual	Difference Favorable - F Unfavorable - U	
Production in units	10,000	12,000		
Costs				
Indirect materials	$ 250,000	$ 295,000	**$ 45,000**	U
Indirect labor	260,000	312,000	**52,000**	U
Utilities	190,000	225,000	**35,000**	U
Depreciation	280,000	280,000	**0**	
Property taxes	70,000	70,000	**0**	
Supervision	50,000	50,000	**0**	
	$1,100,000	$1,232,000	**$132,000**	U

HELPFUL HINT
A static budget is not useful for performance evaluation if a company has substantial variable costs.

This comparison uses budget data based on the original activity level (10,000 steel ingots). It indicates that the Forging Department is significantly **over budget** for three of the six overhead costs. And, there is a total unfavorable difference of $132,000, which is 12% over budget ($132,000 ÷ $1,100,000). Your supervisor is very unhappy! Instead of sharing in the company's success, you may find yourself looking for another job. What went wrong?

When you calm down and carefully examine the manufacturing overhead budget, you identify the problem: The budget data are not relevant! At the time the budget was developed, the company anticipated that only 10,000 units of steel ingots would be produced, **not** 12,000. Comparing actual with budgeted variable costs is meaningless. As production increases, the budget allowances for variable costs should increase proportionately. The variable costs in this example are indirect materials, indirect labor, and utilities.

Analyzing the budget data for these costs at 10,000 units, you arrive at the following per unit results.

Illustration 8-8
Variable costs per unit

Item	Total Cost	Per Unit
Indirect materials	$250,000	$25
Indirect labor	260,000	26
Utilities	190,000	19
	$700,000	$70

Illustration 8-9 calculates the budgeted variable costs at 12,000 units.

Illustration 8-9
Budgeted variable costs, 12,000 units

Item	Computation	Total
Indirect materials	$25 × 12,000	$300,000
Indirect labor	26 × 12,000	312,000
Utilities	19 × 12,000	228,000
		$840,000

Because fixed costs do not change in total as activity changes, the budgeted amounts for these costs remain the same. Illustration 8-10 shows the budget report based on the flexible budget for **12,000 units** of production. (Compare this with Illustration 8-7.)

Illustration 8-10
Overhead flexible budget report

Barton Steel.xls
File Edit View Insert Format Tools Data Window Help

BARTON STEEL
Manufacturing Overhead Flexible Budget Report
For the Year Ended December 31, 2008

	Budget	Actual	Difference Favorable - F Unfavorable - U	
Production in units	12,000	12,000		
Variable costs				
Indirect materials	$ 300,000	$ 295,000	$5,000	F
Indirect labor	312,000	312,000	0	
Utilities	228,000	225,000	3,000	F
Total variable costs	840,000	832,000	8,000	F
Fixed costs				
Depreciation	280,000	280,000	0	
Property taxes	70,000	70,000	0	
Supervision	50,000	50,000	0	
Total fixed costs	400,000	400,000	0	
Total costs	$1,240,000	$1,232,000	$8,000	F

This report indicates that the Forging Department's costs are *under budget*—a favorable difference. Instead of worrying about being fired, you may be in line for a bonus or a raise after all! As this analysis shows, the only appropriate comparison is between actual costs at 12,000 units of production and budgeted costs at 12,000 units. Flexible budget reports provide this comparison.

Developing the Flexible Budget

The flexible budget uses the master budget as its basis. To develop the flexible budget, management uses the following steps.

1. Identify the activity index and the relevant range of activity.
2. Identify the variable costs, and determine the budgeted variable cost per unit of activity for each cost.
3. Identify the fixed costs, and determine the budgeted amount for each cost.
4. Prepare the budget for selected increments of activity within the relevant range.

The activity index chosen should significantly influence the costs being budgeted. For manufacturing overhead costs, for example, the activity index is usually the same as the index used in developing the predetermined overhead rate—that is, direct labor hours or machine hours. For selling and administrative expenses, the activity index usually is sales or net sales.

The choice of the increment of activity is largely a matter of judgment. For example, if the relevant range is 8,000 to 12,000 direct labor hours, increments of 1,000 hours may be selected. The flexible budget is then prepared for each increment within the relevant range.

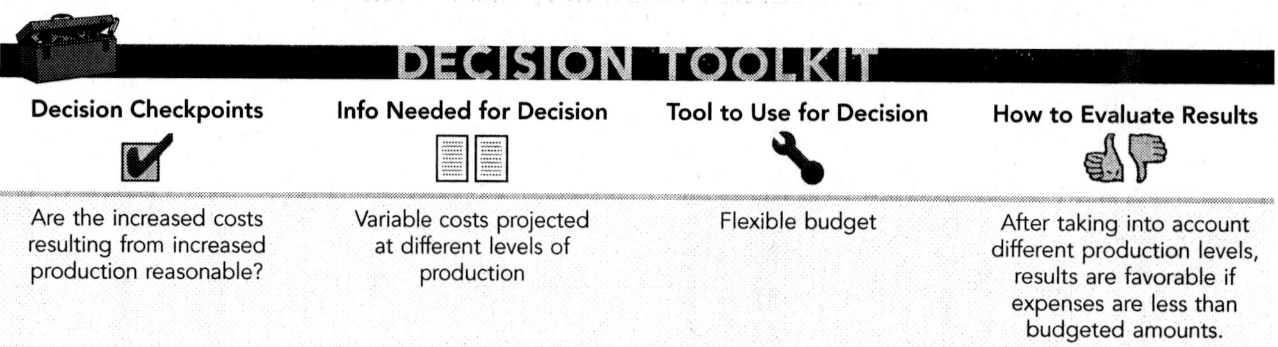

DECISION TOOLKIT

Decision Checkpoints	Info Needed for Decision	Tool to Use for Decision	How to Evaluate Results
Are the increased costs resulting from increased production reasonable?	Variable costs projected at different levels of production	Flexible budget	After taking into account different production levels, results are favorable if expenses are less than budgeted amounts.

Flexible Budget—A Case Study

To illustrate the flexible budget, we use Fox Manufacturing Company. Fox's management uses a **flexible budget for monthly comparisons** of actual and budgeted manufacturing overhead costs of the Finishing Department. The master budget for the year ending December 31, 2008, shows expected annual operating capacity of 120,000 direct labor hours and the following overhead costs.

Illustration 8-11
Master budget data

Variable Costs		Fixed Costs	
Indirect materials	$180,000	Depreciation	$180,000
Indirect labor	240,000	Supervision	120,000
Utilities	60,000	Property taxes	60,000
Total	$480,000	Total	$360,000

The four steps for developing the flexible budget are applied as follows.

STEP 1. **Identify the activity index and the relevant range of activity.** The activity index is direct labor hours. The relevant range is 8,000–12,000 direct labor hours per month.

STEP 2. **Identify the variable costs, and determine the budgeted variable cost per unit of activity for each cost.** There are three variable costs. The variable cost per unit is found by dividing each total budgeted cost by the direct labor hours used in preparing the master budget (120,000 hours). For Fox Manufacturing, the computations are:

Illustration 8-12
Computation of variable costs per direct labor hour

Variable Cost	Computation	Variable Cost per Direct Labor Hour
Indirect materials	$180,000 ÷ 120,000	$1.50
Indirect labor	$240,000 ÷ 120,000	2.00
Utilities	$ 60,000 ÷ 120,000	0.50
Total		$4.00

STEP 3. **Identify the fixed costs, and determine the budgeted amount for each cost.** There are three fixed costs. Since Fox desires **monthly budget data**, it divides each annual budgeted cost by 12 to find the monthly amounts. For Fox Manufacturing, the monthly budgeted fixed costs are: depreciation $15,000, supervision $10,000, and property taxes $5,000.

STEP 4. **Prepare the budget for selected increments of activity within the relevant range.** Management prepares the budget in increments of 1,000 direct labor hours.

Illustration 8-13 shows Fox's flexible budget.

Fox Manufacturing Company.xls

File Edit View Insert Format Tools Data Window Help

FOX MANUFACTURING COMPANY
Monthly Manufacturing Overhead Flexible Budget
Finishing Department
For the Year 2008

	A	B	C	D	E	F
5	Activity level					
6	Direct labor hours	8,000	9,000	10,000	11,000	12,000
7	Variable costs					
8	Indirect materials	$12,000	$13,500	$15,000	$16,500	$18,000
9	Indirect labor	16,000	18,000	20,000	22,000	24,000
10	Utilities	4,000	4,500	5,000	5,500	6,000
11	Total variable costs	32,000	36,000	40,000	44,000	48,000
12	Fixed costs					
13	Depreciation	15,000	15,000	15,000	15,000	15,000
14	Supervision	10,000	10,000	10,000	10,000	10,000
15	Property taxes	5,000	5,000	5,000	5,000	5,000
16	Total fixed costs	30,000	30,000	30,000	30,000	30,000
17	Total costs	$62,000	$66,000	$70,000	$74,000	$78,000
18						

Illustration 8-13
Monthly overhead flexible budget

Fox uses the formula below to determine total budgeted costs at any level of activity.

Fixed Costs + **Variable Costs*** = **Total Budgeted Costs**

*Total variable cost per unit of activity × Activity level.

Illustration 8-14
Formula for total budgeted costs

HELPFUL HINT

Using the data given for Fox, what amount of total costs would be budgeted for 10,600 direct labor hours? Answer: $30,000 fixed + $42,400 variable (i.e, 10,600 × $4) = $72,400 total.

For Fox, fixed costs are $30,000, and total variable cost per direct labor hour is $4. At 9,000 direct labor hours, total budgeted costs are $66,000 [$30,000 + ($4 × 9,000)]. At 8,622 direct labor hours, total budgeted costs are $64,488 [$30,000 + ($4 × 8,622)].

Total budgeted costs can also be shown graphically, as in Illustration 8-15 (page 362). In the graph, the horizontal axis represents the activity index, and costs are indicated on the vertical axis. The graph highlights two activity levels (10,000 and 12,000). As shown, total budgeted costs at these activity levels are $70,000 [$30,000 + ($4 × 10,000)] and $78,000 [$30,000 + ($4 × 12,000)], respectively.

Illustration 8-15
Graphic flexible budget data highlighting 10,000 and 12,000 activity levels

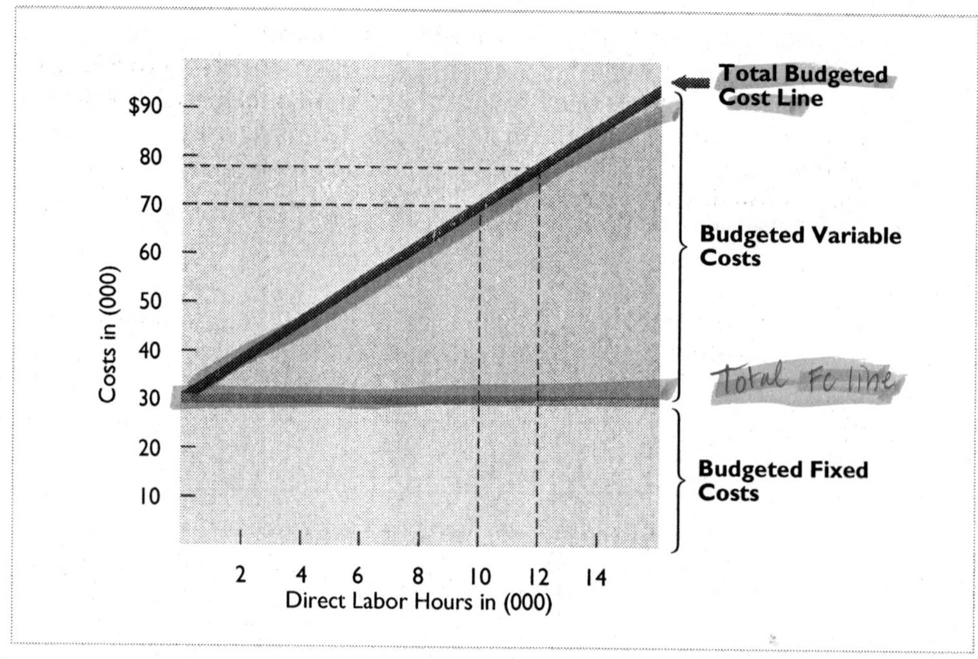

Flexible Budget Reports

Flexible budget reports are another type of internal report. The flexible budget report consists of two sections: (1) production data for a selected activity index, such as direct labor hours, and (2) cost data for variable and fixed costs. The report provides a basis for evaluating a manager's performance in two areas: production control and cost control. Flexible budget reports are widely used in production and service departments.

Illustration 8-16 shows a budget report for the Finishing Department of Fox Company for the month of January. In this month, 9,000 hours are worked. The budget data are therefore based on the flexible budget for 9,000 hours in Illustration 8-13 (page 361). The actual cost data are assumed.

Illustration 8-16
Overhead flexible budget report

Fox Manufacturing Company.xls

File Edit View Insert Format Tools Data Window Help

FOX MANUFACTURING COMPANY
Manufacturing Overhead Flexible Budget Report
Finishing Department
For the Month Ended January 31, 2008

	Budget at	Actual costs at	Difference Favorable - F Unfavorable - U	
Direct labor hours (DLH)	9,000 DLH	9,000 DLH		
Variable costs				
Indirect materials	$13,500	$14,000	$ 500	U
Indirect labor	18,000	17,000	1,000	F
Utilities	4,500	4,600	100	U
Total variable costs	36,000	35,600	400	F
Fixed costs				
Depreciation	15,000	15,000	0	
Supervision	10,000	10,000	0	
Property taxes	5,000	5,000	0	
Total fixed costs	30,000	30,000	0	
Total costs	$66,000	$65,600	$ 400	F

How appropriate is this report in evaluating the Finishing Department manager's performance in controlling overhead costs? The report clearly provides a reliable basis. Both actual and budget costs are based on the activity level worked during January. Since variable costs generally are incurred directly by the department, the difference between the budget allowance for those hours and the actual costs is the responsibility of the department manager.

In subsequent months, Fox Manufacturing will prepare other flexible budget reports. For each month, the budget data are based on the actual activity level attained. In February that level may be 11,000 direct labor hours, in July 10,000, and so on.

Note that this flexible budget is based on a single cost driver. A more accurate budget often can be developed using activity-based costing concepts.

ACCOUNTING ACROSS THE ORGANIZATION

Budgets and the Exotic Newcastle Disease

Exotic Newcastle Disease, one of the most infectious bird diseases in the world, kills so swiftly that many victims die before any symptoms appear. When it broke out in Southern California in 2003, it could have spelled disaster for the San Diego Zoo. "We have one of the most valuable collections of birds in the world, if not *the* most valuable," says Paula Brock, CFO of the Zoological Society of San Diego, which operates the zoo.

Bird exhibits were closed to the public for several months (the disease, which is harmless to humans, can be carried on clothes and shoes). The tires of arriving delivery trucks were sanitized, as were the shoes of anyone visiting the zoo's nonpublic areas. Zookeeper uniforms had to be changed and cleaned daily. And ultimately, the zoo, with $150 million in revenues, spent almost half a million dollars on quarantine measures in 2003.

It worked: no birds got sick. Better yet, the damage to the rest of the zoo's budget was minimized by another protective measure: the monthly budget reforecast. "When we get a hit like this, we still have to find a way to make our bottom line," says Brock. Thanks to a new planning process Brock had introduced a year earlier, the zoo's scientists were able to raise the financial alarm as they redirected resources to ward off the disease. "Because we had timely awareness," she says, "we were able to make adjustments to weather the storm."

Budget reforecasting is nothing new. (The San Diego Zoo's annual static budget was behind the times before Brock took over as CFO in 2001.) But the reaction of the zoo's staff shows the benefits of Brock's immediate efforts to link strategy to the process. It's a move long touted by consultants as a key way to improve people's involvement in budgeting.

"To keep your company on a path, it has to have some kind of map," says Brock. "The budgeting-and-planning process is that map. I cannot imagine an organization feeling in control if it didn't have that sort of discipline."

Source: Tim Reason, "Budgeting in the Real World," *CFO Magazine*, July 12, 2005, *www.cfodirect.com/cfopublic.nsf/vContentPrint/649A82C8FF8AB06B85257037004* (accessed July 2005).

 What is the major benefit of tying a budget to the overall goals of the company?

Management by Exception

Management by exception means that top management's review of a budget report is focused either entirely or primarily on differences between actual results and planned objectives. This approach enables top management to focus on problem areas. For example, many companies now use online reporting systems for employees to file their travel and entertainment expense reports. In addition to cutting reporting time in half, the online system enables managers to quickly analyze variances from travel budgets. This enables companies to cut down on expense account "padding" such as spending too much on meals or falsifying documents for costs that were never actually incurred.

Management by exception does not mean that top management will investigate every difference. For this approach to be effective, there must be guidelines for identifying an exception. The usual criteria are materiality and controllability.

MATERIALITY

Without quantitative guidelines, management would have to investigate every budget difference regardless of the amount. Materiality is usually expressed as a percentage difference from budget. For example, management may set the percentage difference at 5% for important items and 10% for other items. Managers will investigate all differences either over or under budget by the specified percentage. Costs over budget warrant investigation to determine why they were not controlled. Likewise, costs under budget merit investigation to determine whether costs critical to profitability are being curtailed. For example, if maintenance costs are budgeted at $80,000 but only $40,000 is spent, major unexpected breakdowns in productive facilities may occur in the future.

Alternatively, a company may specify a single percentage difference from budget for all items and supplement this guideline with a minimum dollar limit. For example, the exception criteria may be stated at 5% of budget or more than $10,000.

CONTROLLABILITY OF THE ITEM

Exception guidelines are more restrictive for controllable items than for items the manager cannot control. In fact, there may be no guidelines for noncontrollable items. For example, a large unfavorable difference between actual and budgeted property tax expense may not be flagged for investigation because the only possible causes are an unexpected increase in the tax rate or in the assessed value of the property. An investigation into the difference would be useless: the manager cannot control either cause.

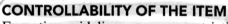

Before You Go On...

REVIEW IT

1. What is the meaning of budgetary control?
2. When is a static budget appropriate for evaluating a manager's effectiveness in controlling costs?
3. What is a flexible budget?
4. How is a flexible budget developed?
5. What are the criteria used in management by exception?

DO IT

Your roommate asks your help in understanding how to compute total budgeted costs at any level of activity. Compute total budgeted costs at 30,000 direct labor hours, assuming that in the flexible budget graph, the fixed cost line and the total budgeted cost line intersect the vertical axis at $36,000 and that the total budget cost line is $186,000 at an activity level of 50,000 direct labor hours.

Action Plan

- Apply the formula: Fixed costs + Variable costs (Total variable costs per unit × Activity level) = Total budgeted costs.

Solution Using the graph, fixed costs are \$36,000, and variable costs are \$3 per direct labor hour [(\$186,000 − \$36,000) ÷ 50,000]. Thus, at 30,000 direct labor hours, total budgeted costs are \$126,000 [\$36,000 + (\$3 × 30,000)].

Related exercise material: *BE8-3, BE8-4, BE8-5, E8-3, E8-4, E8-5, E8-6, and E8-8.*

✓ The Navigator

THE CONCEPT OF RESPONSIBILITY ACCOUNTING

STUDY OBJECTIVE 4

Describe the concept of responsibility accounting.

Like budgeting, responsibility accounting is an important part of management accounting. **Responsibility accounting** involves accumulating and reporting costs (and revenues, where relevant) on the basis of the manager who has the authority to make the day-to-day decisions about the items. Under responsibility accounting, a manager's performance is evaluated on matters directly under that manager's control. Responsibility accounting can be used at every level of management in which the following conditions exist.

1. Costs and revenues can be directly associated with the specific level of management responsibility.
2. The costs and revenues can be controlled by employees at the level of responsibility with which they are associated.
3. Budget data can be developed for evaluating the manager's effectiveness in controlling the costs and revenues.

Illustration 8-17 depicts levels of responsibility for controlling costs.

Illustration 8-17
Responsibility for controllable costs at varying levels of management

HELPFUL HINT

All companies use responsibility accounting. Without some form of responsibility accounting, there would be chaos in discharging management's control function.

Under responsibility accounting, any individual who controls a specified set of activities can be a responsibility center. Thus, responsibility accounting may extend from the lowest level of control to the top strata of management. Once responsibility is established, the company first measures and reports the effectiveness of the individual's performance for the specified activity. It then reports that measure upward throughout the organization.

Responsibility accounting is especially valuable in a decentralized company. **Decentralization** means that the control of operations is delegated to many managers throughout the organization. The term **segment** is sometimes used to identify an area of responsibility in decentralized operations. Under responsibility accounting, companies prepare segment reports periodically, such as monthly, quarterly, and annually, to evaluate managers' performance.

Responsibility accounting is an essential part of any effective system of budgetary control. The reporting of costs and revenues under responsibility accounting differs from budgeting in two respects:

1. A distinction is made between controllable and noncontrollable items.
2. Performance reports either emphasize or include only items controllable by the individual manager.

Responsibility accounting applies to both profit and not-for-profit entities. For-profit entities seek to maximize net income. Not-for-profit entities wish to provide services as efficiently as possible.

MANAGEMENT INSIGHT

Competition versus Collaboration

Many compensation and promotion programs encourage competition among employees for pay raises. To get ahead you have to perform better than your fellow employees. While this may encourage hard work, it does not foster collaboration, and it can lead to distrust and disloyalty. Such results have led some companies to believe that cooperation and collaboration are essential in order to succeed in today's environment. For example, division managers might increase collaboration (and reduce costs) by sharing design and marketing resources or by jointly negotiating with suppliers. In addition, companies can reduce the need to hire and lay off employees by sharing employees across divisions as human resource needs increase and decrease.

As a consequence, many companies now explicitly include measures of collaboration in their performance measures. For example, Procter & Gamble measures collaboration in employees' annual performance reviews. At Cisco Systems the assessment of an employee's teamwork can affect the annual bonus by as much as 20%.

Source: Carol Hymowitz, "Rewarding Competitors Over Collaboration No Longer Makes Sense," *Wall Street Journal*, February 13, 2006.

How might managers of separate divisions be able to reduce division costs through collaboration?

Controllable versus Noncontrollable Revenues and Costs

HELPFUL HINT
Are there more or fewer controllable costs as you move to higher levels of management?
Answer: More.

All costs and revenues are controllable at some level of responsibility within a company. This truth underscores the adage by the CEO of any organization that "the buck stops here." Under responsibility accounting, the critical issue is **whether the cost or revenue is controllable at the level of responsibility with which it is associated**. A cost over which a manager has control is called a **controllable cost**. From this definition, it follows that:

1. All costs are controllable by top management because of the broad range of its authority.
2. Fewer costs are controllable as one moves down to each lower level of managerial responsibility because of the manager's decreasing authority.

In general, **costs incurred directly by a level of responsibility are controllable at that level.** In contrast, costs incurred indirectly and allocated to a responsibility level are **noncontrollable costs** at that level.

HELPFUL HINT
The longer the time span, the more likely that the cost becomes controllable.

Responsibility Reporting System

A **responsibility reporting system** involves the preparation of a report for each level of responsibility in the company's organization chart. To illustrate such a system, we use the partial organization chart and production departments of Francis Chair Company in Illustration 8-18.

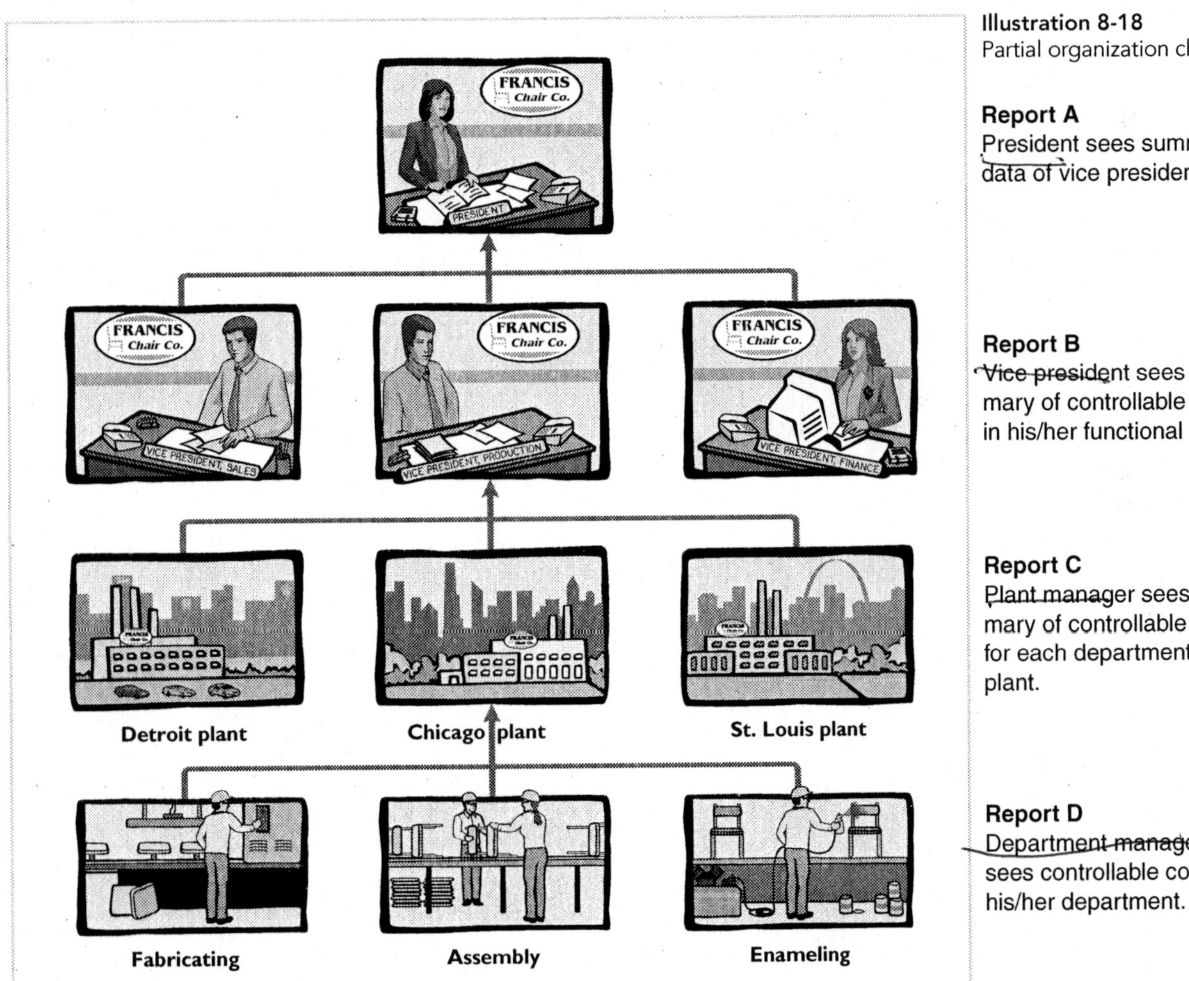

Illustration 8-18
Partial organization chart

Report A
President sees summary data of vice presidents.

Report B
Vice president sees summary of controllable costs in his/her functional area.

Report C
Plant manager sees summary of controllable costs for each department in the plant.

Report D
Department manager sees controllable costs of his/her department.

The responsibility reporting system begins with the lowest level of responsibility for controlling costs and moves upward to each higher level. Illustration 8-19 (page 368) details the connections between levels.

Illustration 8-19
Responsibility reporting system

Report A
President sees summary data of vice presidents.

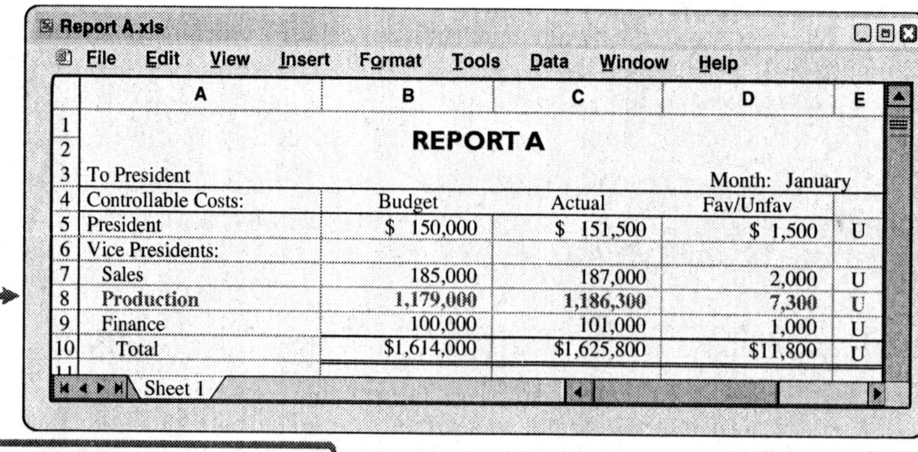

Report A.xls

REPORT A

To President			Month: January	
Controllable Costs:	Budget	Actual	Fav/Unfav	
President	$ 150,000	$ 151,500	$ 1,500	U
Vice Presidents:				
Sales	185,000	187,000	2,000	U
Production	1,179,000	1,186,300	7,300	U
Finance	100,000	101,000	1,000	U
Total	$1,614,000	$1,625,800	$11,800	U

Report B
Vice president sees summary of controllable costs in his/her functional area.

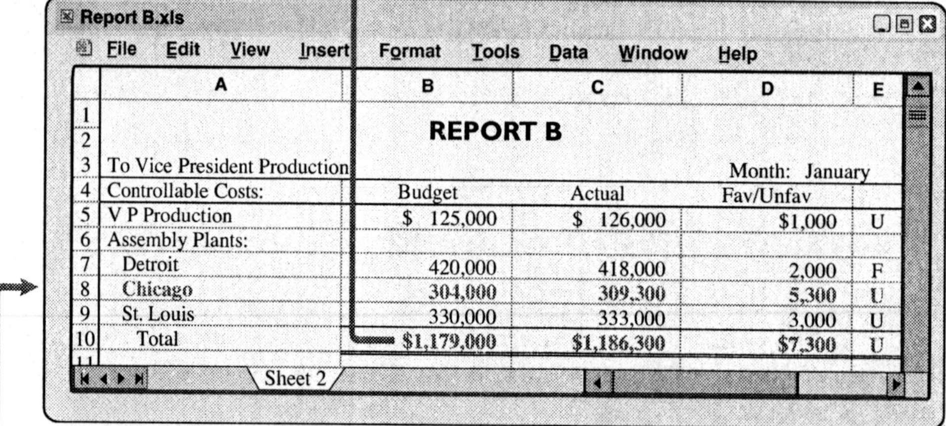

Report B.xls

REPORT B

To Vice President Production			Month: January	
Controllable Costs:	Budget	Actual	Fav/Unfav	
V P Production	$ 125,000	$ 126,000	$1,000	U
Assembly Plants:				
Detroit	420,000	418,000	2,000	F
Chicago	304,000	309,300	5,300	U
St. Louis	330,000	333,000	3,000	U
Total	$1,179,000	$1,186,300	$7,300	U

Report C
Plant manager sees summary of controllable costs for each department in the plant.

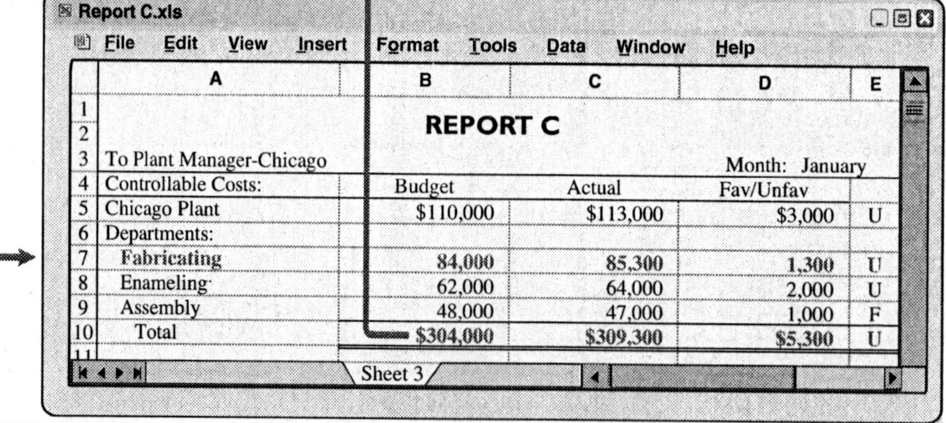

Report C.xls

REPORT C

To Plant Manager-Chicago			Month: January	
Controllable Costs:	Budget	Actual	Fav/Unfav	
Chicago Plant	$110,000	$113,000	$3,000	U
Departments:				
Fabricating	84,000	85,300	1,300	U
Enameling	62,000	64,000	2,000	U
Assembly	48,000	47,000	1,000	F
Total	$304,000	$309,300	$5,300	U

Report D
Department manager sees controllable costs of his/her department.

Report D.xls

REPORT D

To Fabricating Department Manager			Month: January	
Controllable Costs:	Budget	Actual	Fav/Unfav	
Direct Materials	$20,000	$20,500	$ 500	U
Direct Labor	40,000	41,000	1,000	U
Overhead	24,000	23,800	200	F
Total	$84,000	$85,300	$1,300	U

A brief description of the four reports for Francis Chair Company is as follows.

1. **Report D** is typical of reports that go to department managers. Similar reports are prepared for the managers of the Fabricating, Assembly, and Enameling Departments.
2. **Report C** is an example of reports that are sent to plant managers. It shows the costs of the Chicago plant that are controllable at the second level of responsibility. In addition, Report C shows summary data for each department that is controlled by the plant manager. Similar reports are prepared for the Detroit and St. Louis plant managers.
3. **Report B** illustrates the reports at the third level of responsibility. It shows the controllable costs of the vice president of production and summary data on the three assembly plants for which this officer is responsible. Similar reports are prepared for the vice presidents of sales and finance.
4. **Report A** is typical of reports that go to the top level of responsibility—the president. It shows the controllable costs and expenses of this office and summary data on the vice presidents that are accountable to the president.

A responsibility reporting system permits management by exception at each level of responsibility. And, each higher level of responsibility can obtain the detailed report for each lower level of responsibility. For example, the vice president of production in the Francis Chair Company may request the Chicago plant manager's report because this plant is $5,300 over budget.

This type of reporting system also permits comparative evaluations. In Illustration 8-19, the Chicago plant manager can easily rank the department managers' effectiveness in controlling manufacturing costs. Comparative rankings provide further incentive for a manager to control costs.

TYPES OF RESPONSIBILITY CENTERS

There are three basic types of responsibility centers: cost centers, profit centers, and investment centers. These classifications indicate the degree of responsibility the manager has for the performance of the center.

A **cost center** incurs costs (and expenses) but does not directly generate revenues. Managers of cost centers have the authority to incur costs. They are evaluated on their ability to control costs. **Cost centers are usually either production departments or service departments.** Production departments participate directly in making the product. Service departments provide only support services. In a Ford Motor Company automobile plant, the welding, painting, and assembling departments are production departments. Ford's maintenance, cafeteria, and human resources departments are service departments. All of them are cost centers.

A **profit center** incurs costs (and expenses) and also generates revenues. Managers of profit centers are judged on the profitability of their centers. Examples of profit centers include the individual departments of a retail store, such as clothing, furniture, and automotive products, and branch offices of banks.

Like a profit center, an **investment center** incurs costs (and expenses) and generates revenues. In addition, an investment center has control over decisions regarding the assets available for use. Investment center managers are evaluated on both the profitability of the center and the rate of return earned on the funds invested. Investment centers are often associated with subsidiary companies. Utility Duke Energy has operating divisions such as electric utility, energy trading, and natural gas. Investment center managers control or significantly influence investment decisions related to such matters as plant expansion and entry into new market areas. Illustration 8-20 (page 370) depicts the three types of responsibility centers.

HELPFUL HINT

(1) Is the jewelry department of Macy's department store a profit center or a cost center? (2) Is the props department of a movie studio a profit center or a cost center? Answers: (1) Profit center. (2) Cost center.

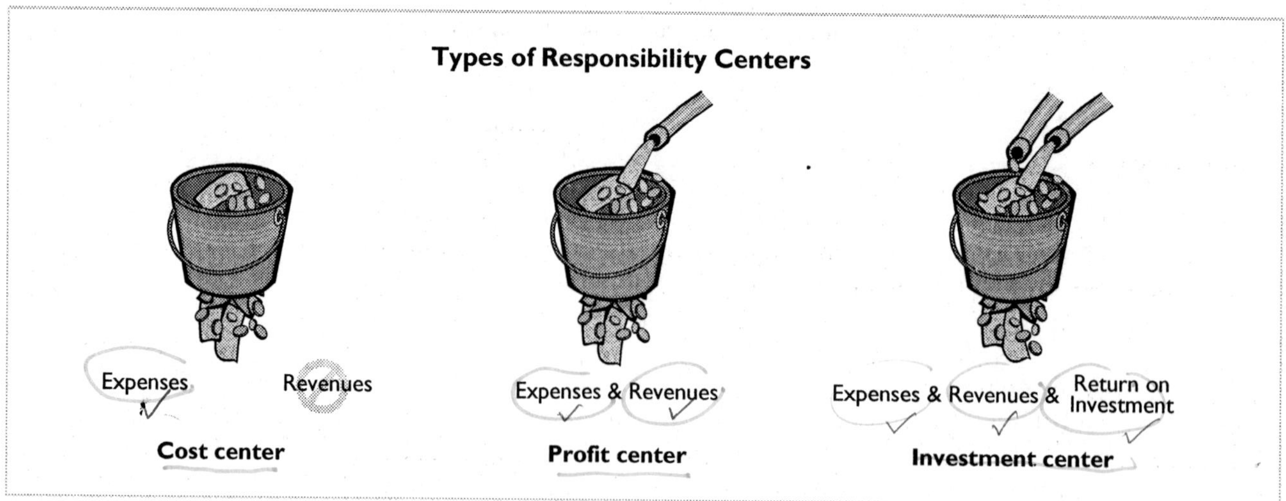

Illustration 8-20
Types of responsibility centers

Responsibility Accounting for Cost Centers

STUDY OBJECTIVE 5

Indicate the features of responsibility reports for cost centers.

The evaluation of a manager's performance for cost centers is based on his or her ability to meet budgeted goals for controllable costs. **Responsibility reports for cost centers compare actual controllable costs with flexible budget data.**

Illustration 8-21 shows a responsibility report. The report is adapted from the flexible budget report for Fox Manufacturing Company in Illustration 8-16 on page 362. It assumes that the Finishing Department manager is able to control all manufacturing overhead costs except depreciation, property taxes, and his own monthly salary of $6,000. The remaining $4,000 ($10,000 – $6,000) of supervision costs are assumed to apply to other supervisory personnel within the Finishing Department, whose salaries are controllable by the manager.

Illustration 8-21
Responsibility report for a cost center

Fox Manufacturing Company.xls

File Edit View Insert Format Tools Data Window Help

FOX MANUFACTURING COMPANY
Finishing Department
Responsibility Report
For the Month Ended January 31, 2008

	A	B	C	D	E
5				Difference	
6	Controllable Cost	Budget	Actual	Favorable - F Unfavorable - U	
7	Indirect materials	$13,500	$14,000	**$ 500**	**U**
8	Indirect labor	18,000	17,000	**$1,000**	**F**
9	Utilities	4,500	4,600	**100**	**U**
10	**Supervision**	**4,000**	**4,000**	**0**	
11		$40,000	$39,600	**$ 400**	**F**
12					

The report in Illustration 8-21 includes **only controllable costs**, and no distinction is made between variable and fixed costs. The responsibility report continues the concept of management by exception. In this case, top management may request an explanation of the $1,000 favorable difference in indirect labor and/or the $500 unfavorable difference in indirect materials.

Responsibility Accounting for Profit Centers

STUDY OBJECTIVE 6

Identify the content of responsibility reports for profit centers.

To evaluate the performance of a profit center manager, upper management needs detailed information about both controllable revenues and controllable costs. The operating revenues earned by a profit center, such as sales, are controllable by the manager. All variable costs (and expenses) incurred by the center are also controllable by the manager because they vary with sales. However, to determine the controllability of fixed costs, it is necessary to distinguish between direct and indirect fixed costs.

DIRECT AND INDIRECT FIXED COSTS

A profit center may have both direct and indirect fixed costs. **Direct fixed costs** relate specifically to one center and are incurred for the sole benefit of that center. Examples of such costs include the salaries established by the profit center manager for supervisory personnel and the cost of a timekeeping department for the center's employees. Since these fixed costs can be traced directly to a center, they are also called **traceable costs. Most direct fixed costs are controllable by the profit center manager.**

In contrast, **indirect fixed costs** pertain to a company's overall operating activities and are incurred for the benefit of more than one profit center. Management allocates indirect fixed costs to profit centers on some type of equitable basis. For example, property taxes on a building occupied by more than one center may be allocated on the basis of square feet of floor space used by each center. Or, the costs of a company's human resources department may be allocated to profit centers on the basis of the number of employees in each center. Because these fixed costs apply to more than one center, they are also called **common costs. Most indirect fixed costs are not controllable by the profit center manager.**

RESPONSIBILITY REPORT

The responsibility report for a profit center shows budgeted and actual **controllable revenues and costs**. The report is prepared using the cost-volume-profit income statement explained in Chapter 6. In the report:

1. Controllable fixed costs are deducted from contribution margin.
2. The excess of contribution margin over controllable fixed costs is identified as **controllable margin**.
3. Noncontrollable fixed costs are not reported.

HELPFUL HINT

Recognize that we are emphasizing *financial* measures of performance. These days companies are also making an effort to stress *nonfinancial* performance measures such as product quality, labor productivity, market growth, materials' yield, manufacturing flexibility, and technological capability.

Illustration 8-22 (page 372) shows the responsibility report for the manager of the Marine Division, a profit center of Mantle Manufacturing Company. For the year, the Marine Division also had $60,000 of indirect fixed costs that were not controllable by the profit center manager.

Controllable margin is considered to be the best measure of the manager's performance **in controlling revenues and costs.** The report in Illustration 8-22 shows that the manager's performance was below budgeted expectations by 10% ($36,000 ÷ $360,000). Top management would likely investigate the causes of this unfavorable result. Note that the report does not show the Marine Division's noncontrollable fixed costs of $60,000. These costs would be included in a report on the profitability of the profit center.

Management also may choose to see **monthly** responsibility reports for profit centers. In addition, responsibility reports may include cumulative year-to-date results.

Illustration 8-22
Responsibility report for profit center

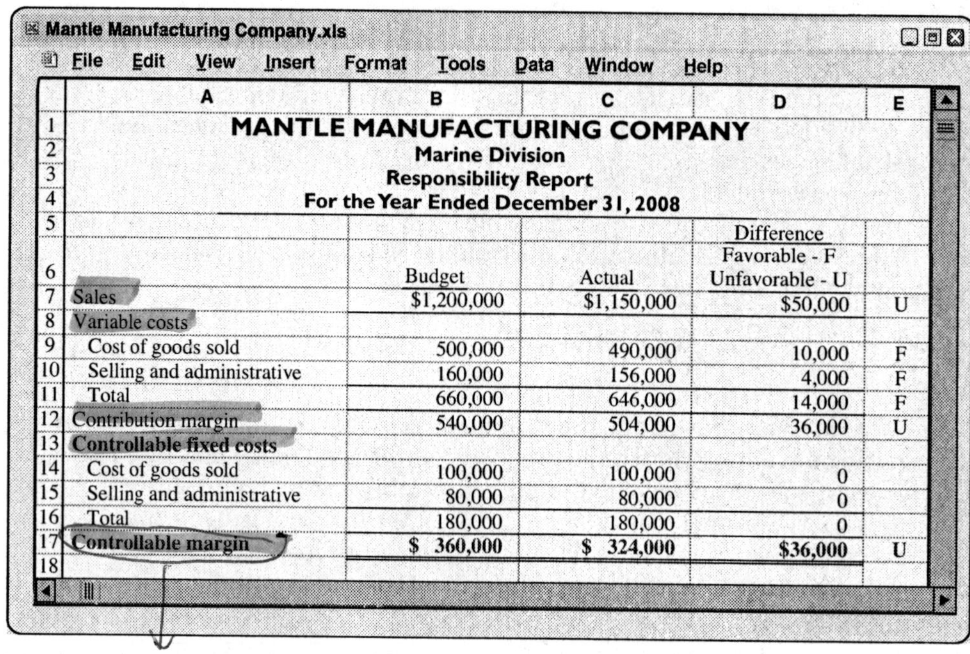

Mantle Manufacturing Company.xls

MANTLE MANUFACTURING COMPANY
Marine Division
Responsibility Report
For the Year Ended December 31, 2008

	Budget	Actual	Difference Favorable - F Unfavorable - U	
Sales	$1,200,000	$1,150,000	$50,000	U
Variable costs				
Cost of goods sold	500,000	490,000	10,000	F
Selling and administrative	160,000	156,000	4,000	F
Total	660,000	646,000	14,000	F
Contribution margin	540,000	504,000	36,000	U
Controllable fixed costs				
Cost of goods sold	100,000	100,000	0	
Selling and administrative	80,000	80,000	0	
Total	180,000	180,000	0	
Controllable margin	**$ 360,000**	**$ 324,000**	**$36,000**	U

DECISION TOOLKIT

Decision Checkpoints	Info Needed for Decision	Tool to Use for Decision	How to Evaluate Results
	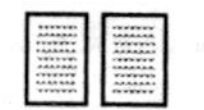		
Have the individual managers been held accountable for the costs and revenues under their control?	Relevant costs and revenues, where the individual manager has authority to make day-to-day decisions about the items	Responsibility reports focused on cost centers, profit centers, and investment centers as appropriate	Compare budget to actual costs and revenues for controllable items.

Before You Go On...

REVIEW IT

1. What conditions are essential for responsibility accounting?
2. What is involved in a responsibility reporting system?
3. What is the primary objective of a responsibility report for a cost center?
4. How does contribution margin differ from controllable margin in a responsibility report for a profit center?

DO IT

Midwest Division operates as a profit center. It reports the following for the year:

	Budgeted	Actual
Sales	$1,500,000	$1,700,000
Variable costs	700,000	800,000
Controllable fixed costs	400,000	400,000
Noncontrollable fixed costs	200,000	200,000

Prepare a responsibility report for the Midwest Division for December 31, 2008.

Action Plan

- Deduct variable costs from sales to show contribution margin.
- Deduct controllable fixed costs from the contribution margin to show controllable margin.
- Do not report noncontrollable fixed costs.

Solution

MIDWEST DIVISION
Responsibility Report
For the Year Ended December 31, 2008

			Difference
	Budget	Actual	Favorable F Unfavorable U
Sales	$1,500,000	$1,700,000	$200,000 F
Variable costs	700,000	800,000	100,000 U
Contribution margin	800,000	900,000	100,000 F
Controllable fixed costs	400,000	400,000	-0-
Controllable margin	$ 400,000	$ 500,000	$100,000 F

Related exercise material: *BE8-7 and E8-13.*

Responsibility Accounting for Investment Centers

STUDY OBJECTIVE 7

Explain the basis and formula used in evaluating performance in investment centers.

As explained earlier, an investment center manager can control or significantly influence the investment funds available for use. Thus, the primary basis for evaluating the performance of a manager of an investment center is **return on investment (ROI)**. The return on investment is considered to be a useful performance measurement because it shows the **effectiveness of the manager in utilizing the assets at his or her disposal.**

RETURN ON INVESTMENT (ROI)

The formula for computing ROI for an investment center, together with assumed illustrative data, is shown in Illustration 8-23.

Controllable Margin	÷	Average Operating Assets	=	Return on Investment (ROI)
$1,000,000	÷	$5,000,000	=	20%

Illustration 8-23
ROI formula

Both factors in the formula are controllable by the investment center manager. Operating assets consist of current assets and plant assets used in operations by the center and controlled by the manager. Nonoperating assets such as idle plant assets and land held for future use are excluded. Average operating assets are usually based on the cost or book value of the assets at the beginning and end of the year.

RESPONSIBILITY REPORT

The scope of the investment center manager's responsibility significantly affects the content of the performance report. Since an investment center is an independent entity for operating purposes, **all fixed costs are controllable by its manager**. For example, the manager is responsible for depreciation on investment center assets. Therefore, more fixed costs are identified as controllable in the performance report for an investment center manager than in a performance report for a profit center manager. The report also shows budgeted and actual ROI below controllable margin.

To illustrate this responsibility report, we will now assume that the Marine Division of Mantle Manufacturing Company is an investment center. It has budgeted and actual average operating assets of $2,000,000. The manager can control $60,000 of fixed costs that were not controllable when the division was a profit center. Illustration 8-24 shows the division's responsibility report.

Illustration 8-24
Responsibility report for investment center

Mantle Manufacturing Company.xls

File Edit View Insert Format Tools Data Window Help

MANTLE MANUFACTURING COMPANY
Marine Division
Responsibility Report
For the Year Ended December 31, 2008

	Budget	Actual	Difference Favorable - F Unfavorable - U	
Sales	$1,200,000	$1,150,000	$ 50,000	U
Variable costs				
Cost of goods sold	500,000	490,000	10,000	F
Selling and administrative	160,000	156,000	4,000	F
Total	660,000	646,000	14,000	F
Contribution margin	540,000	504,000	36,000	U
Controllable fixed costs				
Cost of goods sold	100,000	100,000	0	
Selling and administrative	80,000	80,000	0	
Other fixed costs	**60,000**	**60,000**	**0**	
Total	240,000	240,000	0	
Controllable margin	**$ 300,000**	**$ 264,000**	**$ 36,000**	U
Return on investment	**15.0%**	**13.2%**	**1.8%**	U
	(a)	(b)	(c)	
	(a) $ 300,000 / $2,000,000	(b) $ 264,000 / $2,000,000	(c) $ 36,000 / $2,000,000	

The report shows that the manager's performance based on ROI was below budget expectations by 1.8% (15.0% versus 13.2%). Top management would likely want an explanation of the reasons for this unfavorable result.

JUDGMENTAL FACTORS IN ROI

The return on investment approach includes two judgmental factors:

1. **Valuation of operating assets.** Operating assets may be valued at acquisition cost, book value, appraised value, or market value. The first two bases are readily available from the accounting records.
2. **Margin (income) measure.** This measure may be controllable margin, income from operations, or net income.

Each of the alternative values for operating assets can provide a reliable basis for evaluating a manager's performance as long as it is consistently applied between reporting periods. However, the use of income measures other than controllable margin will not result in a valid basis for evaluating the performance of an investment center manager.

IMPROVING ROI

The manager of an investment center can improve ROI by increasing controllable margin, and/or reducing average operating assets. To illustrate, we will use the following assumed data for the Laser Division of Berra Manufacturing.

Sales	$2,000,000
Variable cost	1,100,000
Contribution margin (45%)	900,000
Controllable fixed costs	300,000
Controllable margin (a)	$ 600,000
Average operating assets (b)	$5,000,000
Return on investment (a) ÷ (b)	**12%**

Illustration 8-25
Assumed data for Laser Division

Increasing Controllable Margin. Controllable margin can be increased by increasing sales or by reducing variable and controllable fixed costs as follows.

1. **Increase sales 10%.** Sales will increase $200,000 ($2,000,000 × .10). Assuming no change in the contribution margin percentage of 45%, contribution margin will increase $90,000 ($200,000 × .45). Controllable margin will increase by the same amount because controllable fixed costs will not change. Thus, controllable margin becomes $690,000 ($600,000 + $90,000). The new ROI is 13.8%, computed as follows.

$$\text{ROI} = \frac{\text{Controllable margin}}{\text{Average operating assets}} = \frac{\$690{,}000}{\$5{,}000{,}000} = \mathbf{13.8\%}$$

Illustration 8-26
ROI computation—increase in sales

An increase in sales benefits both the investment center and the company if it results in new business. It would not benefit the company if the increase was achieved at the expense of other investment centers.

2. **Decrease variable and fixed costs 10%.** Total costs decrease $140,000 [($1,100,000 + $300,000) × .10]. This reduction results in a corresponding increase in controllable margin. Thus, controllable margin becomes $740,000 ($600,000 + $140,000). The new ROI is 14.8%, computed as follows.

$$\text{ROI} = \frac{\text{Controllable margin}}{\text{Average operating assets}} = \frac{\$740{,}000}{\$5{,}000{,}000} = \mathbf{14.8\%}$$

Illustration 8-27
ROI computation—decrease in costs

This course of action is clearly beneficial when waste and inefficiencies are eliminated. But, a reduction in vital costs such as required maintenance and inspections is not likely to be acceptable to top management.

Reducing Average Operating Assets. Assume that average operating assets are reduced 10% or $500,000 ($5,000,000 × .10). Average operating assets become $4,500,000 ($5,000,000 − $500,000). Since controllable margin remains unchanged at $600,000, the new ROI is 13.3%, computed as follows.

$$\text{ROI} = \frac{\text{Controllable margin}}{\text{Average operating assets}} = \frac{\$600{,}000}{\$4{,}500{,}000} = \mathbf{13.3\%}$$

Illustration 8-28
ROI computation—decrease in operating assets

Reductions in operating assets may or may not be prudent. It is beneficial to eliminate overinvestment in inventories and to dispose of excessive plant assets. However, it is unwise to reduce inventories below expected needs or to dispose of essential plant assets.

ACCOUNTING ACROSS THE ORGANIZATION

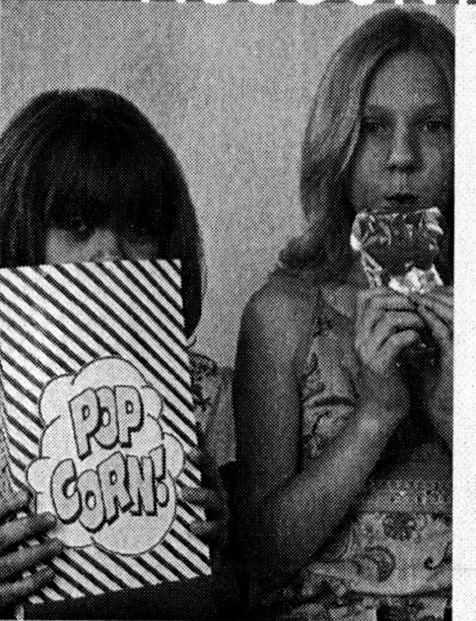

Does Hollywood Look at ROI?

If Hollywood were run like a real business, where things like return on investment mattered, there would be one unchallenged, sacred principle that studio chieftains would never violate: Make lots of G-rated movies.

No matter how you slice the movie business—by star vehicles, by budget levels, by sequels or franchises—by far the best return on investment comes from the not-so-glamorous world of G-rated films. The problem is, these movies represent only 3% of the total films made in a typical year.

Take 2003: According to Motion Picture Association of America statistics, of the 940 movies released that year, only 29 were G-rated. Yet the highest-grossing movie of the year, *Finding Nemo*, was G-rated. . . . On the flip side are the R-rated films, which dominate the total releases and yet yield the worst return on investment. A whopping 646 R-rated films were released in 2003—69% of the total output—but only four of the top-20 grossing movies of the year were R-rated films.

This trend—G-rated movies are good for business but underproduced; R-rated movies are bad for business, and yet overdone—is something that has been driving economists batty for the past several years.

Source: Grainger, David, "The Dysfunctional Family-Film Business," *Fortune*, January 10, 2005, pp. 20–21.

? What might be the reason that movie studios do not produce G-rated movies as much as R-rated ones?

DECISION TOOLKIT

Decision Checkpoints	Info Needed for Decision	Tool to Use for Decision	How to Evaluate Results
Has the investment center performed up to expectations?	Controllable margin (contribution margin minus controllable fixed costs), and average investment center operating assets	Return on investment	Compare actual ROI to expected ROI.

Principles of Performance Evaluation

Performance evaluation is at the center of responsibility accounting. **Performance evaluation** is a management function that compares actual results with budget goals. It involves both behavioral and reporting principles.

BEHAVIORAL PRINCIPLES

The human factor is critical in evaluating performance. Behavioral principles include the following.

1. **Managers of responsibility centers should have direct input into the process of establishing budget goals of their area of responsibility.** Without such input, managers may view the goals as unrealistic or arbitrarily set by top management. Such views adversely affect the managers' motivation to meet the targeted objectives.
2. **The evaluation of performance should be based entirely on matters that are controllable by the manager being evaluated.** Criticism of a manager on matters outside his or her control reduces the effectiveness of the evaluation process. It leads to negative reactions by a manager and to doubts about the fairness of the company's evaluation policies.
3. **Top management should support the evaluation process.** As explained earlier, the evaluation process begins at the lowest level of responsibility and extends upward to the highest level of management. Managers quickly lose faith in the process when top management ignores, overrules, or bypasses established procedures for evaluating a manager's performance.
4. **The evaluation process must allow managers to respond to their evaluations.** Evaluation is not a one-way street. Managers should have the opportunity to defend their performance. Evaluation without feedback is both impersonal and ineffective.
5. **The evaluation should identify both good and poor performance.** Praise for good performance is a powerful motivating factor for a manager. This is especially true when a manager's compensation includes rewards for meeting budget goals.

REPORTING PRINCIPLES

Performance evaluation under responsibility accounting should be based on certain reporting principles. These principles pertain primarily to the internal reports that provide the basis for evaluating performance. Performance reports should:

1. Contain only data that are controllable by the manager of the responsibility center.
2. Provide accurate and reliable budget data to measure performance.
3. Highlight significant differences between actual results and budget goals.
4. Be tailor-made for the intended evaluation.
5. Be prepared at reasonable intervals.

In recent years companies have come under increasing pressure from influential shareholder groups to do a better job of linking executive pay to corporate performance. For example, software maker Siebel Systems unveiled a new incentive plan after lengthy discussions with the California Public Employees' Retirement System. One unique feature of the plan is that managers' targets will be publicly disclosed at the beginning of each year for investors to evaluate.

Before You Go On...

REVIEW IT

1. What is the formula for computing return on investment (ROI)?
2. Identify three actions a manager may take to improve ROI.

The Navigator

Be sure to read **ALL ABOUT YOU: *Budgeting for Housing Costs*** on page 378 for information on how topics in this chapter apply to you.

all about YOU

Budgeting for Housing Costs

In Chapter 7 you learned how to prepare a budget. Budgets are great planning tools, but planning is only one purpose of budgeting. As you learned in this chapter, budgets also are used as the basis of performance evaluation. That is, a company prepares the budget to lay out what it plans on doing, and then it compares its actual results with its plan to see how well it did.

It works the same way for individual budgets. Preparing a personal budget is a great first step. But the real benefit of budgeting comes from comparing your actual results with your personal budget and then making the necessary (and sometimes unpleasant) adjustments. Although unexpected bills can create problems, most financial problems are the result of not controlling routine expenses.

About the Numbers

Housing represents the largest cost for nearly all Americans. The cost of housing as a percentage of income varies considerably across the United States. The following graph shows the percentage of homeowners with mortgages in each state who spend more than 30% of household income on housing costs.

Figure 1. Mortgaged Owners Spending 30% or more of Household Income on Selected Monthly Owner Costs, 2004

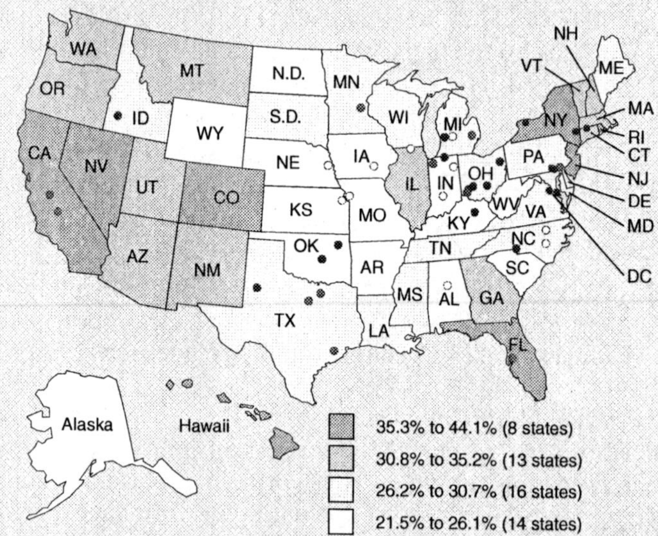

Some Facts

* Most experts encourage people to keep housing costs (mortgage, insurance, and taxes) at approximately 25% to 30% of pre-tax income.
* The U.S. Department of Agriculture estimates that it will cost between $127,080 and $254,400 to raise a child born in 2002 to the age of 18. That amount *does not* include college tuition. Married couples with children file for bankruptcy twice as often as married couples without children.
* Medical bills contribute to one out of five bankruptcies. One out of seven Americans has no health insurance.
* Approximately 40% of American households do not have even $1,000 in cash available for emergencies when unexpected expenses arise.
* Increases in interest rates are causing budget problems for people with adjustable-rate mortgages. As interest rates rose from 2005 to 2006, the number of adjustable-rate mortgages that were at least 90 days past due increased by more than 140%.

What Do You Think?

As noted above, housing is the greatest expense for most people. The percentage of people in the United States who own a home is high compared to many other countries. This is in part the result of U.S. government programs and incentives that encourage home ownership. For example, the interest on a home mortgage is deductible for tax purposes.

Suppose you have just graduated from college and are moving to a new community. Should you immediately buy a new home?

YES: The cost of housing continues to rise. By purchasing a home soon, I can make my housing cost more like a fixed cost, and thus reduce future cost increases. Also I will benefit from the appreciation in my home's value.

NO: I just moved to a new town, so I don't know the market. Also, it is likely that my income will increase in the next few years, so I will be able to afford a better house if I wait a few years. Also, house prices have increased a lot in recent years, but some experts think they may actually decline in some parts of the country. I don't want to get stuck with a house that I can't sell.

Sources: Liz Pullman Weston, "How to Survive 7 Budget Busters," *moneycentral.msn.com/content/Savinganddebt/Learntobudget/P58710.asp*; Amber Kostelac, "Housing Is Affordable in the Hoosier State," *www.incontext.indiana.edu/2005/october/pdfs/housing.pdf*, October 2005 (both accessed August 2006).

The authors' comments on this situation appear on page 405.

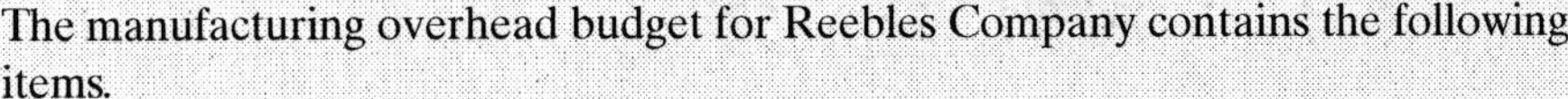

Using the Decision Toolkit

The manufacturing overhead budget for Reebles Company contains the following items.

Variable costs	
Indirect materials	$25,000
Indirect labor	12,000
Maintenance expenses	10,000
Manufacturing supplies	6,000
Total variable	$53,000
Fixed costs	
Supervision	$17,000
Inspection costs	1,000
Insurance expenses	2,000
Depreciation	15,000
Total fixed	$35,000

The budget was based on an estimated 2,000 units being produced. During November, 1,500 units were produced, and the following costs incurred.

Variable costs	
Indirect materials	$25,200
Indirect labor	13,500
Maintenance expenses	8,200
Manufacturing supplies	5,100
Total variable	$52,000
Fixed costs	
Supervision	$19,300
Inspection costs	1,200
Insurance expenses	2,200
Depreciation	14,700
Total fixed	$37,400

Instructions

(a) Determine which items would be controllable by Ed Lopat, the production manager. (Assume "supervision" excludes Lopat's own salary.)

(b) How much should have been spent during the month for the manufacture of the 1,500 units?

(c) Prepare a flexible manufacturing overhead budget report for Mr. Lopat.

(d) Prepare a responsibility report. Include only the costs that would have been controllable by Mr. Lopat. In an attached memo, describe clearly for Mr. Lopat the areas in which his performance needs to be improved.

Solution

(a) Ed Lopat should be able to control all the variable costs and the fixed costs of supervision and inspection. Insurance and depreciation ordinarily are not the responsibility of the department manager.

(b) The total variable cost per unit is $26.50 ($53,000 ÷ 2,000). The total budgeted cost during the month to manufacture 1,500 units is variable costs $39,750 (1,500 × $26.50) plus fixed costs ($35,000), for a total of $74,750 ($39,750 + $35,000).

(c)

REEBLES COMPANY
Production Department
Manufacturing Overhead Budget Report (Flexible)
For the Month Ended November 30, 2008

	Budget at 1,500 units	Actual at 1,500 units	Difference Favorable F Unfavorable U
Variable costs			
Indirect materials	$18,750	$25,200	$ 6,450 U
Indirect labor	9,000	13,500	4,500 U
Maintenance	7,500	8,200	700 U
Manufacturing supplies	4,500	5,100	600 U
Total variable	39,750	52,000	12,250 U
Fixed costs			
Supervision	17,000	19,300	2,300 U
Inspection	1,000	1,200	200 U
Insurance	2,000	2,200	200 U
Depreciation	15,000	14,700	300 F
Total fixed	35,000	37,400	2,400 U
Total costs	$74,750	$89,400	$14,650 U

(d) Because a production department is a cost center, the responsibility report should include only the costs that are controllable by the production manager. In this type of report, no distinction is made between variable and fixed costs. Budget data in the report should be based on the units actually produced.

REEBLES COMPANY
Production Department
Manufacturing Overhead Responsibility Report
For the Month Ended November 30, 2008

Controllable Cost	Budget	Actual	Difference Favorable F Unfavorable U
Indirect materials	$18,750	$25,200	$ 6,450 U
Indirect labor	9,000	13,500	4,500 U
Maintenance	7,500	8,200	700 U
Manufacturing supplies	4,500	5,100	600 U
Supervision	17,000	19,300	2,300 U
Inspection	1,000	1,200	200 U
Total	$57,750	$72,500	$14,750 U

To: Mr. Ed Lopat, Production Manager
From: ________________, Vice-President of Production
Subject: Performance Evaluation for the Month of November

Your performance in controlling costs that are your responsibility was very disappointing in the month of November. As indicated in the accompanying responsibility report, total costs were $14,750 over budget. On a percentage basis, costs were 26% over budget. As you can see, actual costs were over budget for every cost item. In three instances, costs were significantly over budget (indirect materials 34%, indirect labor 50%, and supervision 14%).

Ed, it is imperative that you get costs under control in your department as soon as possible.

I think we need to talk about ways to implement more effective cost control measures. I would like to meet with you in my office at 9 a.m. on Wednesday to discuss possible alternatives.

SUMMARY OF STUDY OBJECTIVES

1 **Describe the concept of budgetary control.** Budgetary control consists of (a) preparing periodic budget reports that compare actual results with planned objectives, (b) analyzing the differences to determine their causes, (c) taking appropriate corrective action, and (d) modifying future plans, if necessary.

2 **Evaluate the usefulness of static budget reports.** Static budget reports are useful in evaluating the progress toward planned sales and profit goals. They are also appropriate in assessing a manager's effectiveness in controlling costs when (a) actual activity closely approximates the master budget activity level, and/or (b) the behavior of the costs in response to changes in activity is fixed.

3 **Explain the development of flexible budgets and the usefulness of flexible budget reports.** To develop the flexible budget it is necessary to: (a) Identify the activity index and the relevant range of activity. (b) Identify the variable costs, and determine the budgeted variable cost per unit of activity for each cost. (c) Identify the fixed costs, and determine the budgeted amount for each cost. (d) Prepare the budget for selected increments of activity within the relevant range. Flexible budget reports permit an evaluation of a manager's performance in controlling production and costs.

4 **Describe the concept of responsibility accounting.** Responsibility accounting involves accumulating and reporting revenues and costs on the basis of the individual manager who has the authority to make the day-to-day decisions about the items. The evaluation of a manager's performance is based on the matters directly under the manager's control. In responsibility accounting, it is necessary to distinguish between controllable and noncontrollable fixed costs and to identify three types of responsibility centers: cost, profit, and investment.

5 **Indicate the features of responsibility reports for cost centers.** Responsibility reports for cost centers compare actual costs with flexible budget data. The reports show only controllable costs, and no distinction is made between variable and fixed costs.

6 **Identify the content of responsibility reports for profit centers.** Responsibility reports show contribution margin, controllable fixed costs, and controllable margin for each profit center.

7 **Explain the basis and formula used in evaluating performance in investment centers.** The primary basis for evaluating performance in investment centers is return on investment (ROI). The formula for computing ROI for investment centers is: Controllable margin ÷ Average operating assets.

DECISION TOOLKIT—A SUMMARY

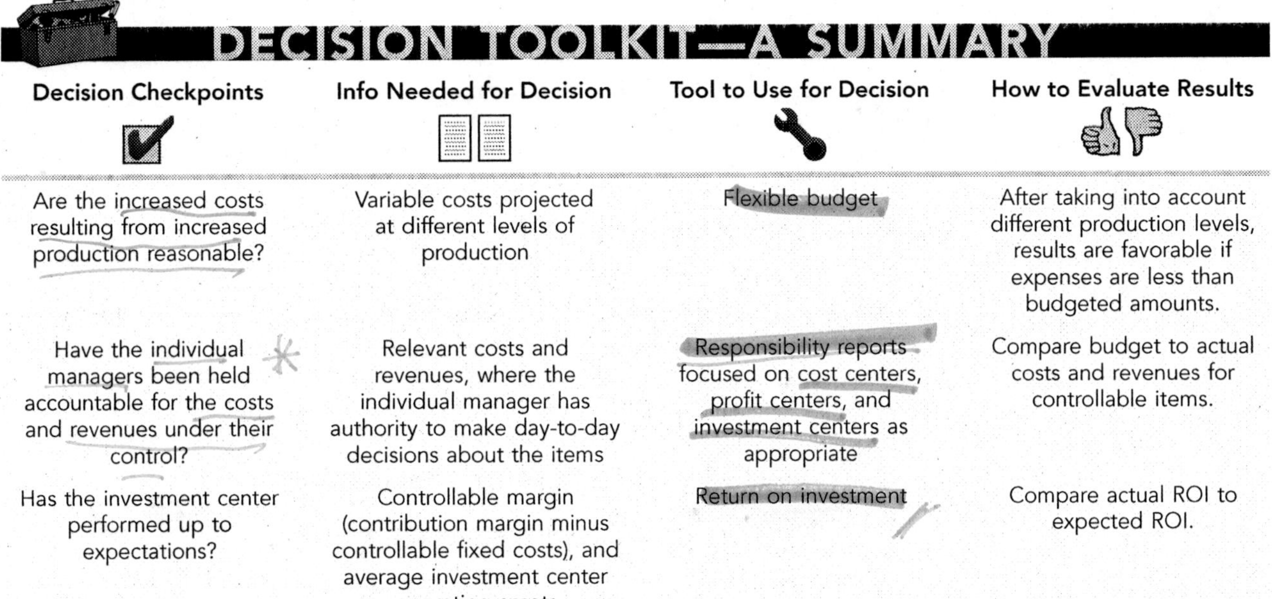

Decision Checkpoints	Info Needed for Decision	Tool to Use for Decision	How to Evaluate Results
Are the increased costs resulting from increased production reasonable?	Variable costs projected at different levels of production	Flexible budget	After taking into account different production levels, results are favorable if expenses are less than budgeted amounts.
Have the individual managers been held accountable for the costs and revenues under their control?	Relevant costs and revenues, where the individual manager has authority to make day-to-day decisions about the items	Responsibility reports focused on cost centers, profit centers, and investment centers as appropriate	Compare budget to actual costs and revenues for controllable items.
Has the investment center performed up to expectations?	Controllable margin (contribution margin minus controllable fixed costs), and average investment center operating assets	Return on investment	Compare actual ROI to expected ROI.

APPENDIX Residual Income—Another Performance Measurement

STUDY OBJECTIVE 8

Explain the difference between ROI and residual income.

Although most companies use ROI in evaluating their investment performance, ROI has a significant disadvantage. To illustrate, let's look at the Electronics Division of Pujols Manufacturing Company. It has an ROI of 20% computed as follows.

Illustration 8A-1
ROI formula

Controllable Margin	÷	Average Operating Assets	=	Return on Investment (ROI)
$1,000,000	÷	$5,000,000	=	20%

The Electronics Division is considering producing a new product, a GPS satellite tracker (hereafter referred to as Tracker), for its boats. To produce Tracker, operating assets will have to increase $2,000,000. Tracker is expected to generate an additional $260,000 of controllable margin. Illustration 8A-2 shows how Tracker will effect ROI.

Illustration 8A-2
ROI comparison

	Without Tracker	Tracker	With Tracker
Controllable margin (a)	$1,000,000	$ 260,000	$1,260,000
Average operating assets (b)	$5,000,000	$2,000,000	$7,000,000
Return on investment [(a) ÷ (b)]	20%	13%	18%

The investment in Tracker reduces ROI from 20% to 18%.

Let's suppose that you are the manager of the Electronics Division and must make the decision to produce or not produce Tracker. If you were evaluated using ROI, you probably would not produce Tracker because your ROI would drop from 20% to 18%. The problem with this ROI analysis is that it ignores an important variable, the minimum rate of return on a company's operating assets. The **minimum rate of return** is the rate at which the Electronics Division can cover its costs and earn a profit. Assuming that the Electronics Division has a minimum rate of return of 10%, it should invest in Tracker because its ROI of 13% is greater than 10%.

Residual Income Compared to ROI

To evaluate performance using the minimum rate of return, companies use the residual income approach. **Residual income** is the income that remains after subtracting from the controllable margin the minimum rate of return on a company's average operating assets. The residual income for Tracker would be computed as follows.

Illustration 8A-3
Residual income formula

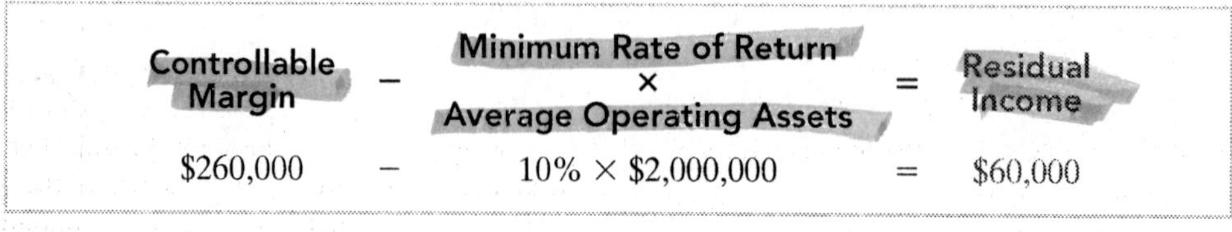

As shown, the residual income related to the Tracker investment is $60,000. Illustration 8A-4 indicates how residual income changes as the additional investment is made.

Illustration 8A-4
Residual income comparison

	Without Tracker	Tracker	With Tracker
Controllable margin (a)	$1,000,000	$260,000	$1,260,000
Average operating assets × 10% (b)	500,000	200,000	700,000
Residual income [(a) − (b)]	$ 500,000	$ 60,000	$ 560,000

This example illustrates how performance evaluation based on ROI can be misleading and can even cause managers to reject projects that would actually increase income for the company. As a result, many companies such as Coca-Cola, Briggs and Stratton, Eli Lilly, and Siemens AG use residual income (or a variant often referred to as economic value added) to evaluate investment alternatives and measure company performance.

Residual Income Weakness

It might appear from the above discussion that the goal of any company should be to maximize the total amount of residual income in each division. This goal, however, ignores the fact that one division might use substantially fewer assets to attain the same level of residual income as another division. For example, we know that to produce Tracker, the Electronics Division of Pujols Manufacturing used $2,000,000 of average operating assets to generate $260,000 of controllable margin. Now let's say a different division produced a product called SeaDog, which used $4,000,000 to generate $460,000 of controllable margin, as shown in Illustration 8A-5.

Illustration 8A-5
Comparison of two products

	Tracker	SeaDog
Controllable margin (a)	$260,000	$460,000
Average operating assets × 10% (b)	200,000	400,000
Residual income [(a) − (b)]	$ 60,000	$ 60,000

If the performance of these two investments were evaluated using residual income, they would be considered equal: Both products have the same total residual income. This ignores, however, the fact that SeaDog required **twice** as many operating assets to achieve the same level of residual income.

SUMMARY OF STUDY OBJECTIVE FOR APPENDIX

8 **Explain the difference between ROI and residual income.** ROI is controllable margin divided by average operating assets. Residual income is the income that remains after subtracting the minimum rate of return on a company's average operating assets. ROI sometimes provides misleading results because profitable investments are often rejected when the investment reduces ROI but increases overall profitability.

GLOSSARY

Budgetary control The use of budgets to control operations. (p. 354).

Controllable cost A cost over which a manager has control. (p. 366).

Controllable margin Contribution margin less controllable fixed costs. (p. 371).

Cost center A responsibility center that incurs costs but does not directly generate revenues. (p. 369).

Decentralization Control of operations is delegated to many managers throughout the organization. (p. 366).

Direct fixed costs Costs that relate specifically to a responsibility center and are incurred for the sole benefit of the center. (p. 371).

Flexible budget A projection of budget data for various levels of activity. (p. 357).

Indirect fixed costs Costs that are incurred for the benefit of more than one profit center. (p. 371).

Investment center A responsibility center that incurs costs, generates revenues, and has control over decisions regarding the assets available for use. (p. 369).

Management by exception The review of budget reports by top management focused entirely or primarily on differences between actual results and planned objectives. (p. 363).

Noncontrollable costs Costs incurred indirectly and allocated to a responsibility center that are not controllable at that level. (p. 367).

Profit center A responsibility center that incurs costs and also generates revenues. (p. 369).

Responsibility accounting A part of management accounting that involves accumulating and reporting revenues and costs on the basis of the manager who has the authority to make the day-to-day decisions about the items. (p. 365).

Responsibility reporting system The preparation of reports for each level of responsibility in the company's organization chart. (p. 367).

Residual income The income that remains after subtracting from the controllable margin the minimum rate of return on a company's average operating assets. (p. 382).

Return on investment (ROI) A measure of management's effectiveness in utilizing assets at its disposal in an investment center. (p. 373).

Segment An area of responsibility in decentralized operations. (p. 366).

Static budget A projection of budget data at one level of activity. (p. 355).

Demonstration Problem

Glenda Company uses a flexible budget for manufacturing overhead based on direct labor hours. For 2008 the master overhead budget for the Packaging Department based on 300,000 direct labor hours was as follows.

Variable Costs		Fixed Costs	
Indirect labor	$360,000	Supervision	$ 60,000
Supplies and lubricants	150,000	Depreciation	24,000
Maintenance	210,000	Property taxes	18,000
Utilities	120,000	Insurance	12,000
	$840,000		$114,000

During July, 24,000 direct labor hours were worked. The company incurred the following variable costs in July: indirect labor $30,200, supplies and lubricants $11,600, maintenance $17,500, and utilities $9,200. Actual fixed overhead costs were the same as monthly budgeted fixed costs.

Instructions

Prepare a flexible budget report for the Packaging Department for July.

Solution to Demonstration Problem

GLENDA COMPANY
Manufacturing Overhead Budget Report (Flexible)
Packaging Department
For the Month Ended July 31, 2008

			Difference
Direct labor hours (DLH)	**Budget 24,000 DLH**	**Actual Costs 24,000 DLH**	**Favorable F Unfavorable U**
Variable costs			
Indirect labor ($1.20)	$28,800	$30,200	$1,400 U
Supplies and lubricants ($0.50)	12,000	11,600	400 F
Maintenance ($0.70)	16,800	17,500	700 U
Utilities ($0.40)	9,600	9,200	400 F
Total variable	67,200	68,500	1,300 U
Fixed costs			
Supervision	$ 5,000	$ 5,000	-0-
Depreciation	2,000	2,000	-0-
Property taxes	1,500	1,500	-0-
Insurance	1,000	1,000	-0-
Total fixed	9,500	9,500	-0-
Total costs	$76,700	$78,000	$1,300 U

action plan

✓ Classify each cost as variable or fixed.

✓ Compute the budgeted cost per direct labor hour for all variable costs.

✓ Use budget data for actual direct labor hours worked.

✓ Determine the difference between budgeted and actual costs.

✓ Identify the difference as favorable or unfavorable.

✓ Determine the difference in total variable costs, total fixed costs, and total costs.

The Navigator

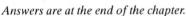

SELF-STUDY QUESTIONS

Answers are at the end of the chapter.

(SO 1) 1. Budgetary control involves all but one of the following:
(a) modifying future plans.
(b) analyzing differences.
(c) using static budgets.
(d) determining differences between actual and planned results.

(SO 2) 2. A static budget is useful in controlling costs when cost behavior is:
(a) mixed. (c) variable.
(b) fixed. (d) linear.

(SO 3) 3. At zero direct labor hours in a flexible budget graph, the total budgeted cost line intersects the vertical axis at $30,000. At 10,000 direct labor hours, a horizontal line drawn from the total budgeted cost line intersects the vertical axis at $90,000. Fixed and variable costs may be expressed as:
(a) $30,000 fixed plus $6 per direct labor hour variable.
(b) $30,000 fixed plus $9 per direct labor hour variable.
(c) $60,000 fixed plus $3 per direct labor hour variable.
(d) $60,000 fixed plus $6 per direct labor hour variable.

(SO 3) 4. At 9,000 direct labor hours, the flexible budget for indirect materials is $27,000. If $28,000 of indirect materials costs are incurred at 9,200 direct labor hours, the flexible budget report should show the following difference for indirect materials:
(a) $1,000 unfavorable.
(b) $1,000 favorable.
(c) $400 favorable.
(d) $400 unfavorable.

5. Under responsibility accounting, the evaluation of a manager's performance is based on matters that the manager: (SO 4)
(a) directly controls.
(b) directly and indirectly controls.
(c) indirectly controls.
(d) has shared responsibility for with another manager.

6. Responsibility centers include: (SO 4)
(a) cost centers.
(b) profit centers.
(c) investment centers.
(d) all of the above.

7. Responsibility reports for cost centers: (SO 5)
(a) distinguish between fixed and variable costs.
(b) use static budget data.
(c) include both controllable and noncontrollable costs.
(d) include only controllable costs.

8. In a responsibility report for a profit center, controllable fixed costs are deducted from contribution margin to show: (SO 6)
(a) profit center margin.
(b) controllable margin.
(c) net income.
(d) income from operations.

(SO 7) **9.** In the formula for return on investment (ROI), the factors for controllable margin and operating assets are, respectively:
(a) controllable margin percentage and total operating assets.
(b) controllable margin dollars and average operating assets.
(c) controllable margin dollars and total assets.
(d) controllable margin percentage and average operating assets.

10. A manager of an investment center can improve ROI by: (SO 7)
(a) increasing average operating assets.
(b) reducing sales.
(c) increasing variable costs.
(d) reducing variable and/or controllable fixed costs.

Go to the book's website,
www.wiley.com/college/weygandt,
for Additional Self-Study questions.

QUESTIONS

1. **(a)** What is budgetary control?
   (b) Greg Gilligan is describing budgetary control. What steps should be included in Greg's description?
2. The following purposes are part of a budgetary reporting system: (a) Determine efficient use of materials. (b) Control overhead costs. (c) Determine whether income objectives are being met. For each purpose, indicate the name of the report, the frequency of the report, and the primary recipient(s) of the report.
3. How may a budget report for the second quarter differ from a budget report for the first quarter?
4. Joe Cey questions the usefulness of a master sales budget in evaluating sales performance. Is there justification for Joe's concern? Explain.
5. Under what circumstances may a static budget be an appropriate basis for evaluating a manager's effectiveness in controlling costs?
6. "A flexible budget is really a series of static budgets." Is this true? Why?
7. The static manufacturing overhead budget based on 40,000 direct labor hours shows budgeted indirect labor costs of $54,000. During March, the department incurs $65,000 of indirect labor while working 45,000 direct labor hours. Is this a favorable or unfavorable performance? Why?
8. A static overhead budget based on 40,000 direct labor hours shows Factory Insurance $6,500 as a fixed cost. At the 50,000 direct labor hours worked in March, factory insurance costs were $6,200. Is this a favorable or unfavorable performance? Why?
9. Kate Coulter is confused about how a flexible budget is prepared. Identify the steps for Kate.
10. Alou Company has prepared a graph of flexible budget data. At zero direct labor hours, the total budgeted cost line intersects the vertical axis at $25,000. At 10,000 direct labor hours, the line drawn from the total budgeted cost line intersects the vertical axis at $85,000. How may the fixed and variable costs be expressed?
11. The flexible budget formula is fixed costs $40,000 plus variable costs of $4 per direct labor hour. What is the total budgeted cost at (a) 9,000 hours and (b) 12,345 hours?
12. What is management by exception? What criteria may be used in identifying exceptions?
13. What is responsibility accounting? Explain the purpose of responsibility accounting.
14. Ann Wilkins is studying for an accounting examination. Describe for Ann what conditions are necessary for responsibility accounting to be used effectively.
15. Distinguish between controllable and noncontrollable costs.
16. How do responsibility reports differ from budget reports?
17. What is the relationship, if any, between a responsibility reporting system and a company's organization chart?
18. Distinguish among the three types of responsibility centers.
19. (a) What costs are included in a performance report for a cost center? (b) In the report, are variable and fixed costs identified?
20. How do direct fixed costs differ from indirect fixed costs? Are both types of fixed costs controllable?
21. Lori Quan is confused about controllable margin reported in an income statement for a profit center. How is this margin computed, and what is its primary purpose?
22. What is the primary basis for evaluating the performance of the manager of an investment center? Indicate the formula for this basis.
23. Explain the ways that ROI can be improved.
24. Indicate two behavioral principles that pertain to (a) the manager being evaluated and (b) top management.

*25. What is a major disadvantage of using ROI to evaluate investment and company performance?

*26. What is residual income, and what is one of its major weaknesses?

BRIEF EXERCISES

WILEY PLUS

BE8-1 For the quarter ended March 31, 2008, Voorhees Company accumulates the following sales data for its product, Garden-Tools: $310,000 budget; $304,000 actual. Prepare a static budget report for the quarter.

Prepare static budget report. (SO 2)

BE8-2 Data for Voorhees Company are given in BE8-1. In the second quarter, budgeted sales were $380,000, and actual sales were $383,000. Prepare a static budget report for the second quarter and for the year to date.

Prepare static budget report for 2 quarters. (SO 2)

BE8-3 In Mussatto Company, direct labor is $20 per hour. The company expects to operate at 10,000 direct labor hours each month. In January 2008, direct labor totaling $203,000 is incurred in working 10,400 hours. Prepare (a) a static budget report and (b) a flexible budget report. Evaluate the usefulness of each report.

Show usefulness of flexible budgets in evaluating performance. (SO 3)

BE8-4 Hannon Company expects to produce 1,200,000 units of Product XX in 2008. Monthly production is expected to range from 80,000 to 120,000 units. Budgeted variable manufacturing costs per unit are: direct materials $4, direct labor $6, and overhead $8. Budgeted fixed manufacturing costs per unit for depreciation are $2 and for supervision are $1. Prepare a flexible manufacturing budget for the relevant range value using 20,000 unit increments.

Prepare a flexible budget for variable costs. (SO 3)

BE8-5 Data for Hannon Company are given in BE8-4. In March 2008, the company incurs the following costs in producing 100,000 units: direct materials $425,000, direct labor $590,000, and variable overhead $805,000. Prepare a flexible budget report for March. Were costs controlled?

Prepare flexible budget report. (SO 3)

BE8-6 In the Assembly Department of Cobb Company, budgeted and actual manufacturing overhead costs for the month of April 2008 were as follows.

Prepare a responsibility report for a cost center. (SO 5)

	Budget	Actual
Indirect materials	$15,000	$14,300
Indirect labor	20,000	20,600
Utilities	10,000	10,750
Supervision	5,000	5,000

All costs are controllable by the department manager. Prepare a responsibility report for April for the cost center.

BE8-7 Eckert Manufacturing Company accumulates the following summary data for the year ending December 31, 2008, for its Water Division which it operates as a profit center: sales—$2,000,000 budget, $2,080,000 actual; variable costs—$1,000,000 budget, $1,050,000 actual; and controllable fixed costs—$300,000 budget, $310,000 actual. Prepare a responsibility report for the Water Division.

Prepare a responsibility report for a profit center. (SO 6)

BE8-8 For the year ending December 31, 2008, Kaspar Company accumulates the following data for the Plastics Division which it operates as an investment center: contribution margin—$700,000 budget, $715,000 actual; controllable fixed costs—$300,000 budget, $309,000 actual. Average operating assets for the year were $2,000,000. Prepare a responsibility report for the Plastics Division beginning with contribution margin.

Prepare a responsibility report for an investment center. (SO 7)

BE8-9 For its three investment centers, Paige Company accumulates the following data:

Compute return on investment using the ROI formula. (SO 7)

	I	II	III
Sales	$2,000,000	$3,000,000	$ 4,000,000
Controllable margin	1,200,000	2,000,000	3,200,000
Average operating assets	5,000,000	8,000,000	10,000,000

Compute the return on investment (ROI) for each center.

BE8-10 Data for the investment centers for Paige Company are given in BE8-9. The centers expect the following changes in the next year: (I) increase sales 15%; (II) decrease costs $200,000; (III) decrease average operating assets $400,000. Compute the expected return on investment (ROI) for each center. Assume center I has a contribution margin percentage of 75%.

Compute return on investment under changed conditions. (SO 7)

Compute ROI and residual income.

(SO 8)

***BE8-11** Wasson, Inc. reports the following financial information.

Average operating assets	$3,000,000
Controllable margin	$ 600,000
Minimum rate of return	9%

Compute the return on investment and the residual income.

Compute ROI and residual income.

(SO 8)

***BE8-12** Presented below is information related to the Santa Clara Division of Cut Wood, Inc.

Contribution margin	$1,200,000
Controllable margin	$ 800,000
Average operating assets	$3,200,000
Minimum rate of return	16%

Compute the Santa Clara's return on investment and residual income.

EXERCISES

WILEY PLUS

Understand the concept of budgetary control.

(SO 1, 2, 3)

E8-1 Jim Thome has prepared the following list of statements about budgetary control.

1. Budget reports compare actual results with planned objectives.
2. All budget reports are prepared on a weekly basis.
3. Management uses budget reports to analyze differences between actual and planned results and determine their causes.
4. As a result of analyzing budget reports, management may either take corrective action or modify future plans.
5. Budgetary control works best when a company has an informal reporting system.
6. The primary recipients of the sales report are the sales manager and the vice-president of production.
7. The primary recipient of the scrap report is the production manager.
8. A static budget is a projection of budget data at one level of activity.
9. Top management's reaction to unfavorable differences is not influenced by the materiality of the difference.
10. A static budget is not appropriate in evaluating a manager's effectiveness in controlling costs unless the actual activity level approximates the static budget activity level or the behavior of the costs is fixed.

Instructions

Identify each statement as true or false. If false, indicate how to correct the statement.

Prepare and evaluate static budget report.

(SO 2)

E8-2 Pargo Company budgeted selling expenses of $30,000 in January, $35,000 in February, and $40,000 in March. Actual selling expenses were $31,000 in January, $34,500 in February, and $47,000 in March.

Instructions

(a) Prepare a selling expense report that compares budgeted and actual amounts by month and for the year to date.
(b) What is the purpose of the report prepared in (a), and who would be the primary recipient?
(c) What would be the likely result of management's analysis of the report?

Prepare flexible manufacturing overhead budget.

(SO 3)

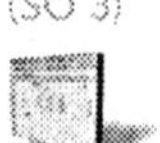

E8-3 Raney Company uses a flexible budget for manufacturing overhead based on direct labor hours. Variable manufacturing overhead costs per direct labor hour are as follows.

Indirect labor	$1.00
Indirect materials	0.50
Utilities	0.40

Fixed overhead costs per month are: Supervision $4,000, Depreciation $1,500, and Property Taxes $800. The company believes it will normally operate in a range of 7,000–10,000 direct labor hours per month.

Instructions
Prepare a monthly manufacturing overhead flexible budget for 2008 for the expected range of activity, using increments of 1,000 direct labor hours.

Prepare flexible budget reports for manufacturing overhead costs, and comment on findings.

(SO 3)

E8-4 Using the information in E8-3, assume that in July 2008, Raney Company incurs the following manufacturing overhead costs.

Variable Costs		Fixed Costs	
Indirect labor	$8,700	Supervision	$4,000
Indirect materials	4,300	Depreciation	1,500
Utilities	3,200	Property taxes	800

Instructions
(a) Prepare a flexible budget performance report, assuming that the company worked 9,000 direct labor hours during the month.
(b) Prepare a flexible budget performance report, assuming that the company worked 8,500 direct labor hours during the month.
(c) Comment on your findings.

Prepare flexible selling expense budget.

(SO 3)

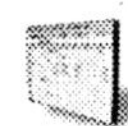

E8-5 Trusler Company uses flexible budgets to control its selling expenses. Monthly sales are expected to range from $170,000 to $200,000. Variable costs and their percentage relationship to sales are: Sales Commissions 5%, Advertising 4%, Traveling 3%, and Delivery 2%. Fixed selling expenses will consist of Sales Salaries $34,000, Depreciation on Delivery Equipment $7,000, and Insurance on Delivery Equipment $1,000.

Instructions
Prepare a monthly flexible budget for each $10,000 increment of sales within the relevant range for the year ending December 31, 2008.

Prepare flexible budget reports for selling expenses.

(SO 3)

E8-6 The actual selling expenses incurred in March 2008 by Trusler Company are as follows.

Variable Expenses		Fixed Expenses	
Sales commissions	$9,200	Sales salaries	$34,000
Advertising	7,000	Depreciation	7,000
Travel	5,100	Insurance	1,000
Delivery	3,500		

Instructions
(a) Prepare a flexible budget performance report for March using the budget data in E8-5, assuming that March sales were $170,000. Expected and actual sales are the same.
(b) Prepare a flexible budget performance report, assuming that March sales were $180,000. Expected sales and actual sales are the same.
(c) Comment on the importance of using flexible budgets in evaluating the performance of the sales manager.

Prepare flexible budget and responsibility report for manufacturing overhead.

(SO 3, 5)

E8-7 Pletcher Company's manufacturing overhead budget for the first quarter of 2008 contained the following data.

Variable Costs		Fixed Costs	
Indirect materials	$12,000	Supervisory salaries	$36,000
Indirect labor	10,000	Depreciation	7,000
Utilities	8,000	Property taxes and insurance	8,000
Maintenance	6,000	Maintenance	5,000

Actual variable costs were: indirect materials $13,800, indirect labor $9,600, utilities $8,700, and maintenance $4,900. Actual fixed costs equaled budgeted costs except for property taxes and insurance, which were $8,200. The actual activity level equaled the budgeted level.

All costs are considered controllable by the production department manager except for depreciation, and property taxes and insurance.

Instructions
(a) Prepare a manufacturing overhead flexible budget report for the first quarter.
(b) Prepare a responsibility report for the first quarter.

Prepare flexible budget report, and answer question.

(SO 2, 3)

E8-8 As sales manager, Terry Dewitt was given the following static budget report for selling expenses in the Clothing Department of Garber Company for the month of October.

GARBER COMPANY
Clothing Department
Budget Report
For the Month Ended October 31, 2008

	Budget	Actual	Difference Favorable F Unfavorable U
Sales in units	8,000	10,000	2,000 F
Variable expenses			
Sales commissions	$ 2,000	$ 2,600	$ 600 U
Advertising expense	800	850	50 U
Travel expense	3,600	4,000	400 U
Free samples given out	1,600	1,300	300 F
Total variable	8,000	8,750	750 U
Fixed expenses			
Rent	1,500	1,500	-0-
Sales salaries	1,200	1,200	-0-
Office salaries	800	800	-0-
Depreciation—autos (sales staff)	500	500	-0-
Total fixed	4,000	4,000	-0-
Total expenses	$12,000	$12,750	$ 750 U

As a result of this budget report, Terry was called into the president's office and congratulated on his fine sales performance. He was reprimanded, however, for allowing his costs to get out of control. Terry knew something was wrong with the performance report that he had been given. However, he was not sure what to do, and comes to you for advice.

Instructions

(a) Prepare a budget report based on flexible budget data to help Terry.

(b) Should Terry have been reprimanded? Explain.

Prepare and discuss a responsibility report.

(SO 3, 5)

E8-9 Pronto Plumbing Company is a newly formed company specializing in plumbing services for home and business. The owner, Paul Pronto, had divided the company into two segments: Home Plumbing Services and Business Plumbing Services. Each segment is run by its own supervisor, while basic selling and administrative services are shared by both segments.

Paul has asked you to help him create a performance reporting system that will allow him to measure each segment's performance in terms of its profitability. To that end, the following information has been collected on the Home Plumbing Services segment for the first quarter of 2008.

	Budgeted	Actual
Service revenue	$25,000	$26,000
Allocated portion of:		
Building depreciation	11,000	11,000
Advertising	5,000	4,200
Billing	3,500	3,000
Property taxes	1,200	1,000
Material and supplies	1,500	1,200
Supervisory salaries	9,000	9,400
Insurance	4,000	3,500
Wages	3,000	3,300
Gas and oil	2,700	3,400
Equipment depreciation	1,600	1,300

Instructions

(a) Prepare a responsibility report for the first quarter of 2008 for the Home Plumbing Services segment.

(b) Write a memo to Paul Pronto discussing the principles that should be used when preparing performance reports.

E8-10 Rensing Company has two production departments, Fabricating and Assembling. At a department managers' meeting, the controller uses flexible budget graphs to explain total budgeted costs. Separate graphs based on direct labor hours are used for each department. The graphs show the following.

State total budgeted cost formulas, and prepare flexible budget graph.

(SO 3)

1. At zero direct labor hours, the total budgeted cost line and the fixed cost line intersect the vertical axis at $40,000 in the Fabricating Department and $30,000 in the Assembling Department.
2. At normal capacity of 50,000 direct labor hours, the line drawn from the total budgeted cost line intersects the vertical axis at $150,000 in the Fabricating Department, and $110,000 in the Assembling Department.

Instructions

(a) State the total budgeted cost formula for each department.

(b) Compute the total budgeted cost for each department, assuming actual direct labor hours worked were 53,000 and 47,000, in the Fabricating and Assembling Departments, respectively.

(c) Prepare the flexible budget graph for the Fabricating Department, assuming the maximum direct labor hours in the relevant range is 100,000. Use increments of 10,000 direct labor hours on the horizontal axis and increments of $50,000 on the vertical axis.

E8-11 Lovell Company's organization chart includes the president; the vice president of production; three assembly plants—Dallas, Atlanta, and Tucson; and two departments within each plant—Machining and Finishing. Budget and actual manufacturing cost data for July 2008 are as follows:

Prepare reports in a responsibility reporting system.

(SO 4)

Finishing Department—Dallas: Direct materials $41,500 actual, $45,000 budget; direct labor $83,000 actual, $82,000 budget; manufacturing overhead $51,000 actual, $49,200 budget.

Machining Department—Dallas: Total manufacturing costs $220,000 actual, $216,000 budget.

Atlanta Plant: Total manufacturing costs $424,000 actual, $421,000 budget.

Tucson Plant: Total manufacturing costs $494,000 actual, $496,500 budget.

The Dallas plant manager's office costs were $95,000 actual and $92,000 budget. The vice president of production's office costs were $132,000 actual and $130,000 budget. Office costs are not allocated to departments and plants.

Instructions

Using the format on page 368, prepare the reports in a responsibility system for:

(a) The Finishing Department—Dallas.

(b) The plant manager—Dallas.

(c) The vice president of production.

E8-12 The Mixing Department manager of Crede Company is able to control all overhead costs except rent, property taxes, and salaries. Budgeted monthly overhead costs for the Mixing Department, in alphabetical order, are:

Prepare a responsibility report for a cost center.

(SO 5)

Indirect labor	$12,000	Property taxes	$ 1,000
Indirect materials	7,500	Rent	1,800
Lubricants	1,700	Salaries	10,000
Maintenance	3,500	Utilities	5,000

Actual costs incurred for January 2008 are indirect labor $12,200; indirect materials $10,200; lubricants $1,650; maintenance $3,500; property taxes $1,100; rent $1,800; salaries $10,000; and utilities $6,500.

Instructions

(a) Prepare a responsibility report for January 2008.

(b) What would be the likely result of management's analysis of the report?

Compute missing amounts in responsibility reports for three profit centers, and prepare a report.

(SO 6)

E8-13 Gonzales Manufacturing Inc. has three divisions which are operated as profit centers. Actual operating data for the divisions listed alphabetically are as follows.

Operating Data	Women's Shoes	Men's Shoes	Children's Shoes
Contribution margin	$240,000	(3)	$180,000
Controllable fixed costs	100,000	(4)	(5)
Controllable margin	(1)	$ 90,000	96,000
Sales	600,000	450,000	(6)
Variable costs	(2)	330,000	250,000

Instructions

(a) Compute the missing amounts. Show computations.

(b) Prepare a responsibility report for the Women's Shoe Division assuming (1) the data are for the month ended June 30, 2008, and (2) all data equal budget except variable costs which are $10,000 over budget.

Prepare a responsibility report for a profit center, and compute ROI.

(SO 6, 7)

E8-14 The Sports Equipment Division of Brandon McCarthy Company is operated as a profit center. Sales for the division were budgeted for 2008 at $900,000. The only variable costs budgeted for the division were cost of goods sold ($440,000) and selling and administrative ($60,000). Fixed costs were budgeted at $100,000 for cost of goods sold, $90,000 for selling and administrative and $70,000 for noncontrollable fixed costs. Actual results for these items were:

Sales	$880,000
Cost of goods sold	
Variable	409,000
Fixed	105,000
Selling and administrative	
Variable	61,000
Fixed	67,000
Noncontrollable fixed	80,000

Instructions

(a) Prepare a responsibility report for the Sports Equipment Division for 2008.

(b) Assume the division is an investment center, and average operating assets were $1,000,000. Compute ROI.

Compute ROI for current year and for possible future changes.

(SO 7)

E8-15 The Green Division of Frizell Company reported the following data for the current year.

Sales	$3,000,000
Variable costs	1,950,000
Controllable fixed costs	600,000
Average operating assets	5,000,000

Top management is unhappy with the investment center's return on investment (ROI). It asks the manager of the Green Division to submit plans to improve ROI in the next year. The manager believes it is feasible to consider the following independent courses of action.

1. Increase sales by $320,000 with no change in the contribution margin percentage.
2. Reduce variable costs by $100,000.
3. Reduce average operating assets by 4%.

Instructions

(a) Compute the return on investment (ROI) for the current year.

(b) Using the ROI formula, compute the ROI under each of the proposed courses of action. (Round to one decimal.)

Prepare a responsibility report for an investment center.

(SO 7)

E8-16 The Medina and Ortiz Dental Clinic provides both preventive and orthodontic dental services. The two owners, Martin Medina and Olga Ortiz, operate the clinic as two separate investment centers: Preventive Services and Orthodontic Services. Each of them is in charge of one of the centers: Martin for Preventive Services and Olga for Orthodontic Services. Each month they prepare an income statement for the two centers to evaluate performance and make decisions about how to improve the operational efficiency and profitability of the clinic.

Recently they have been concerned about the profitability of the Preventive Services operations. For several months it has been reporting a loss. Shown below is the responsibility report for the month of May 2008.

	Actual	Difference from Budget
Service revenue	$ 40,000	$1,000 F
Variable costs:		
Filling materials	5,000	100 U
Novocain	4,000	200 U
Supplies	2,000	250 F
Dental assistant wages	2,500	–0–
Utilities	500	50 U
Total variable costs	14,000	100 U
Fixed costs:		
Allocated portion of receptionist's salary	3,000	200 U
Dentist salary	10,000	500 U
Equipment depreciation	6,000	–0–
Allocated portion of building depreciation	15,000	1,000 U
Total fixed costs	34,000	1,700 U
Operating income (loss)	$ (8,000)	$ 800 U

In addition, the owners know that the investment in operating assets at the beginning of the month was $82,400, and it was $77,600 at the end of the month. They have asked for your assistance in evaluating their current performance reporting system.

Instructions

(a) Prepare a responsibility report for an investment center as illustrated in the chapter.
(b) Write a memo to the owners discussing the deficiencies of their current reporting system.

Prepare missing amounts in responsibility reports for three investment centers.

(SO 7)

E8-17 The Transamerica Transportation Company uses a responsibility reporting system to measure the performance of its three investment centers: Planes, Taxis, and Limos. Segment performance is measured using a system of responsibility reports and return on investment calculations. The allocation of resources within the company and the segment managers' bonuses are based in part on the results shown in these reports.

Recently, the company was the victim of a computer virus that deleted portions of the company's accounting records. This was discovered when the current period's responsibility reports were being prepared. The printout of the actual operating results appeared as follows.

	Planes	Taxis	Limos
Service revenue	$?	$500,000	$?
Variable costs	5,500,000	?	320,000
Contribution margin	?	200,000	480,000
Controllable fixed costs	1,500,000	?	?
Controllable margin	?	80,000	240,000
Average operating assets	25,000,000	?	1,600,000
Return on investment	12%	10%	?

Instructions

Determine the missing pieces of information above.

Compare ROI and residual income.

(SO 8)

***E8-18** Presented below is selected information for three regional divisions of Yono Company.

	Divisions		
	North	**West**	**South**
Contribution margin	$ 300,000	$ 500,000	$ 400,000
Controllable margin	$ 150,000	$ 400,000	$ 225,000
Average operating assets	$1,000,000	$2,000,000	$1,500,000
Minimum rate of return	13%	16%	10%

Instructions

(a) Compute the return on investment for each division.
(b) Compute the residual income for each division.
(c) Assume that each division has an investment opportunity that would provide a rate of return of 19%.
  (1) If ROI is used to measure performance, which division or divisions will probably make the additional investment?
  (2) If residual income is used to measure performance, which division or divisions will probably make the additional investment?

Fill in information related to ROI and residual income.

(SO 8)

***E8-19** Presented below is selected financial information for two divisions of Capital Brewery. You are to supply the missing information for the lettered items.

	Lager	**Lite Lager**
Contribution margin	$500,000	$ 300,000
Controllable margin	200,000	(c)
Average operating assets	(a)	$1,000,000
Minimum rate of return	(b)	13%
Return on investment	25%	(d)
Residual income	$ 90,000	$ 200,000

EXERCISES: SET B

Visit the book's website at **www.wiley.com/college/weygandt**, and choose the Student Companion site, to access Exercise Set B.

PROBLEMS: SET A

Prepare flexible budget and budget report for manufacturing overhead.

(SO 3)

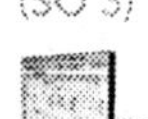

P8-1A Malone Company estimates that 360,000 direct labor hours will be worked during the coming year, 2008, in the Packaging Department. On this basis, the following budgeted manufacturing overhead cost data are computed for the year.

Fixed Overhead Costs		**Variable Overhead Costs**	
Supervision	$ 90,000	Indirect labor	$126,000
Depreciation	60,000	Indirect materials	90,000
Insurance	30,000	Repairs	54,000
Rent	24,000	Utilities	72,000
Property taxes	18,000	Lubricants	18,000
	$222,000		$360,000

It is estimated that direct labor hours worked each month will range from 27,000 to 36,000 hours.

During October, 27,000 direct labor hours were worked and the following overhead costs were incurred.

Fixed overhead costs: Supervision $7,500, Depreciation $5,000, Insurance $2,470, Rent $2,000, and Property taxes $1,500.

Variable overhead costs: Indirect labor $10,360, Indirect materials, $6,400, Repairs $4,000, Utilities $5,700, and Lubricants $1,640.

(a) Total costs: DLH 27,000, $45,500; DLH 36,000, $54,500

Instructions

(a) Prepare a monthly manufacturing overhead flexible budget for each increment of 3,000 direct labor hours over the relevant range for the year ending December 31, 2008.

(b) Total $1,070 U

(b) Prepare a flexible budget report for October.
(c) Comment on management's efficiency in controlling manufacturing overhead costs in October.

Prepare flexible budget, budget report, and graph for manufacturing overhead.

(SO 3)

P8-2A Fultz Company manufactures tablecloths. Sales have grown rapidly over the past 2 years. As a result, the president has installed a budgetary control system for 2008. The following data were used in developing the master manufacturing overhead budget for the Ironing Department, which is based on an activity index of direct labor hours.

Variable Costs	Rate per Direct Labor Hour	Annual Fixed Costs	
Indirect labor	$0.40	Supervision	$42,000
Indirect materials	0.50	Depreciation	18,000
Factory utilities	0.30	Insurance	12,000
Factory repairs	0.20	Rent	24,000

The master overhead budget was prepared on the expectation that 480,000 direct labor hours will be worked during the year. In June, 42,000 direct labor hours were worked. At that level of activity, actual costs were as shown below.

Variable—per direct labor hour: Indirect labor $0.43, Indirect materials $0.49, Factory utilities $0.32, and Factory repairs $0.24.

Fixed: same as budgeted.

Instructions

(a) Prepare a monthly manufacturing overhead flexible budget for the year ending December 31, 2008, assuming production levels range from 35,000 to 50,000 direct labor hours. Use increments of 5,000 direct labor hours.

(a) Total costs: 35,000 DLH, $57,000; 50,000 DLH, $78,000

(b) Prepare a budget report for June comparing actual results with budget data based on the flexible budget.

(b) Budget $66,800 Actual $70,160

(c) Were costs effectively controlled? Explain.
(d) State the formula for computing the total budgeted costs for the Ironing Department.
(e) Prepare the flexible budget graph, showing total budgeted costs at 35,000 and 45,000 direct labor hours. Use increments of 5,000 direct labor hours on the horizontal axis and increments of $10,000 on the vertical axis.

State total budgeted cost formula, and prepare flexible budget reports for 2 time periods.

(SO 2, 3)

P8-3A Zelmer Company uses budgets in controlling costs. The August 2008 budget report for the company's Assembling Department is as follows.

ZELMER COMPANY
Budget Report
Assembling Department
For the Month Ended August 31, 2008

Manufacturing Costs	Budget	Actual	Difference Favorable F Unfavorable U
Variable costs			
Direct materials	$ 48,000	$ 47,000	$1,000 F
Direct labor	54,000	51,300	2,700 F
Indirect materials	24,000	24,200	200 U
Indirect labor	18,000	17,500	500 F
Utilities	15,000	14,900	100 F
Maintenance	9,000	9,200	200 U
Total variable	168,000	164,100	3,900 F
Fixed costs			
Rent	12,000	12,000	–0–
Supervision	17,000	17,000	–0–
Depreciation	7,000	7,000	–0–
Total fixed	36,000	36,000	–0–
Total costs	$204,000	$200,100	$3,900 F

The monthly budget amounts in the report were based on an expected production of 60,000 units per month or 720,000 units per year. The Assembling Department manager is pleased with the report and expects a raise, or at least praise for a job well done. The company president, however, is unhappy with the results for August, because only 58,000 units were produced.

Instructions

(b) Budget $198,400

(c) Budget $215,200
Actual $216,510

(a) State the total monthly budgeted cost formula.
(b) Prepare a budget report for August using flexible budget data. Why does this report provide a better basis for evaluating performance than the report based on static budget data?
(c) In September, 64,000 units were produced. Prepare the budget report using flexible budget data, assuming (1) each variable cost was 10% higher than its actual cost in August, and (2) fixed costs were the same in September as in August.

Prepare responsibility report for a profit center.

(SO 6)

P8-4A Jantzen Manufacturing Inc. operates the Patio Furniture Division as a profit center. Operating data for this division for the year ended December 31, 2008, are as shown below.

	Budget	Difference from Budget
Sales	$2,500,000	$60,000 F
Cost of goods sold		
Variable	1,300,000	41,000 F
Controllable fixed	200,000	6,000 U
Selling and administrative		
Variable	220,000	7,000 U
Controllable fixed	50,000	2,000 U
Noncontrollable fixed costs	70,000	4,000 U

In addition, Jantzen Manufacturing incurs $180,000 of indirect fixed costs that were budgeted at $175,000. Twenty percent (20%) of these costs are allocated to the Patio Furniture Division.

Instructions

(a) Contribution margin $94,000 F
Controllable margin $86,000 F

(a) Prepare a responsibility report for the Patio Furniture Division for the year.
(b) Comment on the manager's performance in controlling revenues and costs.
(c) Identify any costs excluded from the responsibility report and explain why they were excluded.

Prepare responsibility report for an investment center, and compute ROI.

(SO 7)

P8-5A Dinkle Manufacturing Company manufactures a variety of tools and industrial equipment. The company operates through three divisions. Each division is an investment center. Operating data for the Home Division for the year ended December 31, 2008, and relevant budget data are as follows.

	Actual	Comparison with Budget
Sales	$1,500,000	$100,000 favorable
Variable cost of goods sold	700,000	60,000 unfavorable
Variable selling and administrative expenses	125,000	25,000 unfavorable
Controllable fixed cost of goods sold	170,000	On target
Controllable fixed selling and administrative expenses	80,000	On target

Average operating assets for the year for the Home Division were $2,500,000 which was also the budgeted amount.

Instructions

(a) Controllable margin:
Budget $410;
Actual $425

(a) Prepare a responsibility report (in thousands of dollars) for the Home Division.
(b) Evaluate the manager's performance. Which items will likely be investigated by top management?
(c) Compute the expected ROI in 2009 for the Home Division, assuming the following independent changes to actual data.
  (1) Variable cost of goods sold is decreased by 6%.
  (2) Average operating assets are decreased by 10%.
  (3) Sales are increased by $200,000, and this increase is expected to increase contribution margin by $90,000.

P8-6A Nieto Company uses a responsibility reporting system. It has divisions in Denver, Seattle, and San Diego. Each division has three production departments: Cutting, Shaping, and Finishing. The responsibility for each department rests with a manager who reports to the division production manager. Each division manager reports to the vice president of production. There are also vice presidents for marketing and finance. All vice presidents report to the president.

Prepare reports for cost centers under responsibility accounting, and comment on performance of managers.

(SO 4)

In January 2008, controllable actual and budget manufacturing overhead cost data for the departments and divisions were as shown below.

Manufacturing Overhead	Actual	Budget
Individual costs—Cutting Department—Seattle		
Indirect labor	$ 73,000	$ 70,000
Indirect materials	47,700	46,000
Maintenance	20,500	18,000
Utilities	20,100	17,000
Supervision	22,000	20,000
	$183,300	$171,000
Total costs		
Shaping Department—Seattle	$158,000	$148,000
Finishing Department—Seattle	210,000	206,000
Denver division	676,000	673,000
San Diego division	722,000	715,000

Additional overhead costs were incurred as follows: Seattle division production manager—actual costs $52,500, budget $51,000; vice president of production—actual costs $65,000, budget $64,000; president—actual costs $76,400, budget $74,200. These expenses are not allocated.

The vice presidents who report to the president, other than the vice president of production, had the following expenses.

Vice president	Actual	Budget
Marketing	$133,600	$130,000
Finance	109,000	105,000

Instructions

(a) Using the format on page 368, prepare the following responsibility reports.

(1) Manufacturing overhead—Cutting Department manager—Seattle division.

(2) Manufacturing overhead—Seattle division manager.

(3) Manufacturing overhead—vice president of production.

(4) Manufacturing overhead and expenses—president.

(b) Comment on the comparative performances of:

(1) Department managers in the Seattle division.

(2) Division managers.

(3) Vice presidents.

(a) (1) $12,300 U
(2) $27,800 U
(3) $38,800 U
(4) $48,600 U

***P8-7A** Haniwall Industries has manufactured prefabricated houses for over 20 years. The houses are constructed in sections to be assembled on customers' lots. Haniwall expanded into the precut housing market when it acquired Orlando Company, one of its suppliers. In this market, various types of lumber are precut into the appropriate lengths, banded into packages, and shipped to customers' lots for assembly. Haniwall designated the Orlando Division as an investment center.

Compare ROI and residual income.

(SO 8)

Haniwall uses return on investment (ROI) as a performance measure with investment defined as average operating assets. Management bonuses are based in part on ROI. All investments are expected to earn a minimum rate of return of 16%. Orlando's ROI has ranged from 20.1% to 23.5% since it was acquired. Orlando had an investment opportunity in 2008 that had an estimated ROI of 19%. Orlando's management decided against the investment because it believed the investment would decrease the division's overall ROI.

Selected financial information for Orlando are presented on the next page. The division's average operating assets were $12,300,000 for the year 2008.

ORLANDO DIVISION
Selected Financial Information
For the Year Ended December 31, 2008

Sales	$26,000,000
Contribution margin	9,100,000
Controllable margin	2,460,000

Instructions

(a) Calculate the following performance measures for 2008 for the Orlando Division.

(1) Return on investment (ROI).

(2) Residual income.

(b) Would the management of Orlando Division have been more likely to accept the investment opportunity it had in 2008 if residual income were used as a performance measure instead of ROI? Explain your answer.

(CMA, adapted)

PROBLEMS: SET B

Prepare flexible budget and budget report for manufacturing overhead.

(SO 3)

P8-1B Clarke Company estimates that 240,000 direct labor hours will be worked during 2008 in the Assembly Department. On this basis, the following budgeted manufacturing overhead data are computed.

Variable Overhead Costs		Fixed Overhead Costs	
Indirect labor	$ 72,000	Supervision	$ 72,000
Indirect materials	48,000	Depreciation	36,000
Repairs	24,000	Insurance	12,000
Utilities	50,400	Rent	9,000
Lubricants	9,600	Property taxes	6,000
	$204,000		$135,000

It is estimated that direct labor hours worked each month will range from 18,000 to 24,000 hours.

During January, 20,000 direct labor hours were worked and the following overhead costs were incurred.

Variable Overhead Costs		Fixed Overhead Costs	
Indirect labor	$ 6,200	Supervision	$ 6,000
Indirect materials	3,600	Depreciation	3,000
Repairs	1,600	Insurance	1,000
Utilities	3,300	Rent	800
Lubricants	830	Property taxes	500
	$15,530		$11,300

Instructions

(a) Total costs: 18,000 DLH, $26,550; 24,000 DLH, $31,650

(b) Budget, $28,250 Actual, $26,830

(a) Prepare a monthly manufacturing overhead flexible budget for each increment of 2,000 direct labor hours over the relevant range for the year ending December 31, 2008.

(b) Prepare a manufacturing overhead budget report for January.

(c) Comment on management's efficiency in controlling manufacturing overhead costs in January.

Prepare flexible budget, budget report, and graph for manufacturing overhead.

(SO 3)

P8-2B Flaherty Manufacturing Company produces one product, Kebo. Because of wide fluctuations in demand for Kebo, the Assembly Department experiences significant variations in monthly production levels.

The annual master manufacturing overhead budget is based on 300,000 direct labor hours. In July 27,500 labor hours were worked. The master manufacturing overhead budget for the year and the actual overhead costs incurred in July are as follows.

Overhead Costs	Master Budget (annual)	Actual in July
Variable		
Indirect labor	$ 360,000	$32,000
Indirect materials	210,000	17,000
Utilities	90,000	8,100
Maintenance	60,000	5,400
Fixed		
Supervision	150,000	12,500
Depreciation	120,000	10,000
Insurance and taxes	60,000	5,000
Total	$1,050,000	$90,000

Instructions

(a) Prepare a monthly overhead flexible budget for the year ending December 31, 2008, assuming monthly production levels range from 22,500 to 30,000 direct labor hours. Use increments of 2,500 direct labor hours.

(a) Total costs: 22,500 DLH, $81,500; 30,000 DLH, $99,500

(b) Prepare a budget report for the month of July 2008 comparing actual results with budget data based on the flexible budget.

(b) Budget $93,500 Actual $90,000

(c) Were costs effectively controlled? Explain.

(d) State the formula for computing the total monthly budgeted costs in the Assembly Department.

(e) Prepare the flexible budget graph showing total budgeted costs at 25,000 and 27,500 direct labor hours. Use increments of 5,000 on the horizontal axis and increments of $10,000 on the vertical axis.

P8-3B Hardesty Company uses budgets in controlling costs. The May 2008 budget report for the company's Packaging Department is as follows.

State total budgeted cost formula, and prepare flexible budget reports for 2 time periods.

(SO 2, 3)

HARDESTY COMPANY
Budget Report
Packaging Department
For the Month Ended May 31, 2008

Manufacturing Costs	Budget	Actual	Difference Favorable F Unfavorable U
Variable costs			
Direct materials	$ 45,000	$ 47,000	$2,000 U
Direct labor	50,000	53,000	3,000 U
Indirect materials	15,000	15,200	200 U
Indirect labor	12,500	13,000	500 U
Utilities	7,500	7,100	400 F
Maintenance	5,000	5,200	200 U
Total variable	135,000	140,500	5,500 U
Fixed costs			
Rent	8,000	8,000	-0-
Supervision	7,000	7,000	-0-
Depreciation	5,000	5,000	-0-
Total fixed	20,000	20,000	-0-
Total costs	$155,000	$160,500	$5,500 U

The monthly budget amounts in the report were based on an expected production of 50,000 units per month or 600,000 units per year.

The company president was displeased with the department manager's performance. The department manager, who thought he had done a good job, could not understand the unfavorable results. In May, 55,000 units were produced.

Instructions

(b) Budget $168,500

(c) Budget $128,000
Actual $132,400

(a) State the total budgeted cost formula.
(b) Prepare a budget report for May using flexible budget data. Why does this report provide a better basis for evaluating performance than the report based on static budget data?
(c) In June, 40,000 units were produced. Prepare the budget report using flexible budget data, assuming (1) each variable cost was 20% less in June than its actual cost in May, and (2) fixed costs were the same in the month of June as in May.

Prepare responsibility report for a profit center.
(SO 6)

P8-4B Grider Manufacturing Inc. operates the Home Appliance Division as a profit center. Operating data for this division for the year ended December 31, 2008, are shown below.

	Budget	Difference from Budget
Sales	$2,400,000	$90,000 U
Cost of goods sold		
Variable	1,200,000	40,000 U
Controllable fixed	200,000	8,000 F
Selling and administrative		
Variable	240,000	8,000 F
Controllable fixed	60,000	6,000 U
Noncontrollable fixed costs	50,000	2,000 U

In addition, Grider Manufacturing incurs $150,000 of indirect fixed costs that were budgeted at $155,000. Twenty percent (20%) of these costs are allocated to the Home Appliance Division. None of these costs are controllable by the division manager.

Instructions

(a) Contribution margin $122,000 U
Controllable margin $120,000 U

(a) Prepare a responsibility report for the Home Appliance Division (a profit center) for the year.
(b) Comment on the manager's performance in controlling revenues and costs.
(c) Identify any costs excluded from the responsibility report and explain why they were excluded.

Prepare responsibility report for an investment center, and compute ROI.
(SO 7)

P8-5B Jeffery Manufacturing Company manufactures a variety of garden and lawn equipment. The company operates through three divisions. Each division is an investment center. Operating data for the Lawnmower Division for the year ended December 31, 2008, and relevant budget data are as follows.

	Actual	Comparison with Budget
Sales	$2,800,000	$150,000 unfavorable
Variable cost of goods sold	1,400,000	80,000 unfavorable
Variable selling and administrative expenses	300,000	50,000 favorable
Controllable fixed cost of goods sold	270,000	On target
Controllable fixed selling and administrative expenses	130,000	On target

Average operating assets for the year for the Lawnmower Division were $5,000,000 which was also the budgeted amount.

Instructions

(a) Controllable margin:
Budget $880
Actual $700

(a) Prepare a responsibility report (in thousands of dollars) for the Lawnmower Division.
(b) Evaluate the manager's performance. Which items will likely be investigated by top management?
(c) Compute the expected ROI in 2009 for the Lawnmower Division, assuming the following independent changes.
  (1) Variable cost of goods sold is decreased by 15%.
  (2) Average operating assets are decreased by 20%.
  (3) Sales are increased by $500,000 and this increase is expected to increase contribution margin by $200,000.

PROBLEMS: SET C

Visit the book's website at **www.wiley.com/college/weygandt**, and choose the Student Companion site, to access Problem Set C.

WATERWAYS CONTINUING PROBLEM

(*Note:* This is a continuation of the Waterways Problem from previous chapters.)

WCP8 Waterways Corporation is continuing its budget preparations. This problem gives you static budget information as well as actual overhead costs and asks you to calculate amounts related to budgetary control and responsibility accounting.

Go to the book's website, ***www.wiley.com/college/weygandt,*** *to find the completion of this problem.*

BROADENING YOUR PERSPECTIVE

DECISION MAKING ACROSS THE ORGANIZATION

BYP8-1 G-Bar Pastures is a 400-acre farm on the outskirts of the Kentucky Bluegrass, specializing in the boarding of broodmares and their foals. A recent economic downturn in the thoroughbred industry has led to a decline in breeding activities, and it has made the boarding business extremely competitive. To meet the competition, G-Bar Pastures planned in 2008 to entertain clients, advertise more extensively, and absorb expenses formerly paid by clients such as veterinary and blacksmith fees.

The budget report for 2008 is presented below. As shown, the static income statement budget for the year is based on an expected 21,900 boarding days at $25 per mare. The variable expenses per mare per day were budgeted: Feed $5, Veterinary fees $3, Blacksmith fees $0.30, and Supplies $0.55. All other budgeted expenses were either semifixed or fixed.

During the year, management decided not to replace a worker who quit in March, but it did issue a new advertising brochure and did more entertaining of clients.[1]

G-BAR PASTURES
Static Budget Income Statement
Year Ended December 31, 2008

	Actual	Master Budget	Difference
Number of mares	52	60	8*
Number of boarding days	18,980	21,900	2,920*
Sales	$379,600	$547,500	$167,900*

Continued

[1]Data for this case are based on Hans Sprohge and John Talbott, "New Applications for Variance Analysis," *Journal of Accountancy* (AICPA, New York), April 1989, pp. 137–141.

	Actual	Master Budget	Difference
Less: Variable expenses			
Feed	104,390	109,500	5,110
Veterinary fees	58,838	65,700	6,862
Blacksmith fees	6,074	6,570	496
Supplies	10,178	12,045	1,867
Total variable expenses	179,480	193,815	14,335
Contribution margin	200,120	353,685	153,565*
Less: Fixed expenses			
Depreciation	40,000	40,000	-0-
Insurance	11,000	11,000	-0-
Utilities	12,000	14,000	2,000
Repairs and maintenance	10,000	11,000	1,000
Labor	88,000	96,000	8,000
Advertisement	12,000	8,000	4,000*
Entertainment	7,000	5,000	2,000*
Total fixed expenses	180,000	185,000	5,000
Net income	$ 20,120	$168,685	$148,565*

*Unfavorable.

Instructions

With the class divided into groups, answer the following.

(a) Based on the static budget report:

(1) What was the primary cause(s) of the loss in net income?

(2) Did management do a good, average, or poor job of controlling expenses?

(3) Were management's decisions to stay competitive sound?

(b) Prepare a flexible budget report for the year.

(c) Based on the flexible budget report, answer the three questions in part (a) above.

(d) What course of action do you recommend for the management of G-Bar Pastures?

MANAGERIAL ANALYSIS

BYP8-2 Fugate Company manufactures expensive watch cases sold as souvenirs. Three of its sales departments are: Retail Sales, Wholesale Sales, and Outlet Sales. The Retail Sales Department is a profit center. The Wholesale Sales Department is a cost center. Its managers merely take orders from customers who purchase through the company's wholesale catalog. The Outlet Sales Department is an investment center, because each manager is given full responsibility for an outlet store location. The manager can hire and discharge employees, purchase, maintain, and sell equipment, and in general is fairly independent of company control.

Jane Duncan is a manager in the Retail Sales Department. Richard Wayne manages the Wholesale Sales Department. Jose Lopez manages the Golden Gate Club outlet store in San Francisco. The following are the budget responsibility reports for each of the three departments.

	Budget		
	Retail Sales	Wholesale Sales	Outlet Sales
Sales	$ 750,000	$ 400,000	$200,000
Variable costs			
Cost of goods sold	150,000	100,000	25,000
Advertising	100,000	30,000	5,000
Sales salaries	75,000	15,000	3,000
Printing	10,000	20,000	5,000
Travel	20,000	30,000	2,000
Fixed costs			
Rent	50,000	30,000	10,000
Insurance	5,000	2,000	1,000
Depreciation	75,000	100,000	40,000
Investment in assets	$1,000,000	$1,200,000	$800,000

Actual Results			
	Retail Sales	Wholesale Sales	Outlet Sales
Sales	$ 750,000	$ 400,000	$200,000
Variable costs			
Cost of goods sold	195,000	120,000	26,250
Advertising	100,000	30,000	5,000
Sales salaries	75,000	15,000	3,000
Printing	10,000	20,000	5,000
Travel	15,000	20,000	1,500
Fixed costs			
Rent	40,000	50,000	12,000
Insurance	5,000	2,000	1,000
Depreciation	80,000	90,000	60,000
Investment in assets	$1,000,000	$1,200,000	$800,000

Instructions

(a) Determine which of the items should be included in the responsibility report for each of the three managers.

(b) Compare the budgeted measures with the actual results. Decide which results should be called to the attention of each manager.

REAL-WORLD FOCUS

BYP8-3 Computer Associates International, Inc., the world's leading business software company, delivers the end-to-end infrastructure to enable e-business through innovative technology, services, and education. CA has 19,000 employees worldwide and recently had revenue of over $6 billion.

Presented below is information from the company's annual report.

COMPUTER ASSOCIATES INTERNATIONAL

Management Discussion

The Company has experienced a pattern of business whereby revenue for its third and fourth fiscal quarters reflects an increase over first- and second-quarter revenue. The Company attributes this increase to clients' increased spending at the end of their calendar year budgetary periods and the culmination of its annual sales plan. Since the Company's costs do not increase proportionately with the third- and fourth-quarters' increase in revenue, the higher revenue in these quarters results in greater profit margins and income. Fourth-quarter profitability is traditionally affected by significant new hirings, training, and education expenditures for the succeeding year.

Instructions

(a) Why don't the company's costs increase proportionately as the revenues increase in the third and fourth quarters?

(b) What type of budgeting seems appropriate for the Computer Associates situation?

EXPLORING THE WEB

BYP8-4 There are many useful resources regarding budgeting available on websites. The following activity investigates the results of a comprehensive budgeting study performed by a very large international accounting firm.

Address:
www.pwc.com/extweb/pwcpublications.nsf/docid/C2D9FB96F792CFA3852572B10049C87D, or go to **www.wiley.com/college/weygandt**

Steps
Go to the address on the previous page, click on the link to download the full report, and then register to receive the report. (Remove the checkmark to receive future reports.)

Instructions
Scan the report to answer the following questions.

(a) What percentage of respondents report that they are "very satisfied" with their financial planning process?
(b) What are the top six key elements that companies forecast?
(c) What is the percentage of total budget time spent on each of the following budgeting activities?
  (1) Data collection/consolidation
  (2) Analysis
  (3) Strategy/target setting
  (4) Review/approval
  (5) Report preparation
(d) What percentage of firms spend more than four months to complete a budget?
(e) What percentage of surveyed firms update their forecasts on a monthly basis?

COMMUNICATION ACTIVITY

BYP8-5 The manufacturing overhead budget for Edmonds Company contains the following items.

Variable costs		Fixed costs	
Indirect materials	$24,000	Supervision	$18,000
Indirect labor	12,000	Inspection costs	1,000
Maintenance expense	10,000	Insurance expense	2,000
Manufacturing supplies	6,000	Depreciation	15,000
Total variable	$52,000	Total fixed	$36,000

The budget was based on an estimated 2,000 units being produced. During the past month, 1,500 units were produced, and the following costs incurred.

Variable costs		Fixed costs	
Indirect materials	$24,200	Supervision	$19,300
Indirect labor	13,500	Inspection costs	1,200
Maintenance expense	8,200	Insurance expense	2,200
Manufacturing supplies	5,100	Depreciation	14,700
Total variable	$51,000	Total fixed	$37,400

Instructions

(a) Determine which items would be controllable by Mark Farris, the production manager.
(b) How much should have been spent during the month for the manufacture of the 1,500 units?
(c) Prepare a flexible manufacturing overhead budget report for Mr. Farris.
(d) Prepare a responsibility report. Include only the costs that would have been controllable by Mr. Farris. Assume that the supervision cost above includes Mr. Farris's salary of $10,000, both at budget and actual. In an attached memo, describe clearly for Mr. Farris the areas in which his performance needs to be improved.

ETHICS CASE

BYP8-6 National Products Corporation participates in a highly competitive industry. In order to meet this competition and achieve profit goals, the company has chosen the decentralized form of organization. Each manager of a decentralized investment center is measured on the basis of profit contribution, market penetration, and return on investment. Failure to meet the objectives established by corporate management for these measures has not been acceptable and usually has resulted in demotion or dismissal of an investment center manager.

An anonymous survey of managers in the company revealed that the managers feel the pressure to compromise their personal ethical standards to achieve the corporate objectives. For example, at certain plant locations there was pressure to reduce quality control to a level which could not assure that all unsafe products would be rejected. Also, sales personnel were encouraged to use questionable sales tactics to obtain orders, including gifts and other incentives to purchasing agents.

The chief executive officer is disturbed by the survey findings. In his opinion such behavior cannot be condoned by the company. He concludes that the company should do something about this problem.

Instructions

(a) Who are the stakeholders (the affected parties) in this situation?

(b) Identify the ethical implications, conflicts, or dilemmas in the above described situation.

(c) What might the company do to reduce the pressures on managers and decrease the ethical conflicts?

(CMA adapted)

"ALL ABOUT YOU" ACTIVITY

BYP8-7 It is one thing to prepare a personal budget; it is another thing to stick to it. Financial planners have suggested various mechanisms to provide support for enforcing personal budgets. One approach is called "envelope budgeting."

Instructions

Read the article provided at **http://en.wikipedia.org/wiki/Envelope_budgeting**, and answer the following questions.

(a) Summarize the process of envelope budgeting.

(b) Evaluate whether you think you would benefit from envelope budgeting. What do you think are its strengths and weaknesses relative to your situation?

Answers to Insight and Accounting Across the Organization Questions

Budgets and the Exotic Newcastle Disease, p. 363

Q: What is the major benefit of tying a budget to the overall goals of the company?

A: *People working on a budgeting process that is clearly guided and focused by strategic goals spend less time arguing about irrelevant details and more time focusing on the items that matter.*

Competition versus Collaboration, p. 366

Q: How might managers of separate divisions be able to reduce division costs through collaboration?

A: *Division managers might reduce costs by sharing design and marketing resources or by jointly negotiating with suppliers. In addition, they can reduce the need to hire and lay off employees by sharing staff across divisions as human resource needs change.*

Does Hollywood Look at ROI?, p. 376

Q: What might be the reason that movie studios do not produce G-rated movies as much as R-rated ones?

A: *Perhaps Hollywood believes that big-name stars or large budgets, both of which are typical of R-rated movies, sell movies. However, one study recently concluded, "We can't find evidence that stars help movies, and we can't find evidence that bigger budgets increase return on investment." Some film companies are going out of their way to achieve at least a PG rating.*

Authors' Comments on *All About You:* Budgeting for Housing Costs, p. 378

In general, in past years it has been a wise decision to purchase a home rather than to rent. As noted, over time home prices have usually appreciated in most parts of the country. Mortgage interest provides some tax relief, and by purchasing a home you get some control over your housing costs. However, in the current environment the decision is a little more complicated. In some parts of the country, home prices have appreciated so much that some experts suggest that renting is actually a more financially prudent choice, at least in the short term.

If you do purchase a home, do not bite off more than you can chew. In addition to a higher mortgage payment, a more expensive house will result in increased maintenance and utility costs, more spent on insurance premiums, and higher property taxes. Make sure to factor all of these expenses into your budget.

Answers to Self-Study Questions

1. c **2.** b **3.** a **4.** d **5.** a **6.** d **7.** d **8.** b **9.** b **10.** d

Remember to go back to the Navigator box on the chapter-opening page and check off your completed work.

Chapter 9

Incremental Analysis

STUDY OBJECTIVES

After studying this chapter, you should be able to:

1. Identify the steps in management's decision-making process.
2. Describe the concept of incremental analysis
3. Identify the relevant costs in accepting an order at a special price.
4. Identify the relevant costs in a make-or-buy decision.
5. Identify the relevant costs in determining whether to sell or process materials further.
6. Identify the relevant costs to be considered in retaining or replacing equipment.
7. Identify the relevant costs in deciding whether to eliminate an unprofitable segment.

The Navigator

The Navigator

- Scan **Study Objectives**
- Read **Feature Story**
- Read **Preview**
- Read text and answer **Before You Go On** p. 419 p. 420
- Work **Using the Decision Toolkit**
- Review **Summary of Study Objectives**
- Work **Demonstration Problem**
- Answer **Self-Study Questions**
- Complete **Assignments**

Feature Story

MAKE IT OR BUY IT?

When is a manufacturer not a manufacturer? When it outsources. An extension of the classic "make or buy" decision, outsourcing involves hiring other companies to make all or part of a product or to perform services. Who is outsourcing? Nike, General Motors, Sara Lee, and Hewlett-Packard, to name a few. Even a recent trade journal article for small cabinet makers outlined the pros and cons of building cabinet doors and drawers internally, or outsourcing them to other shops.

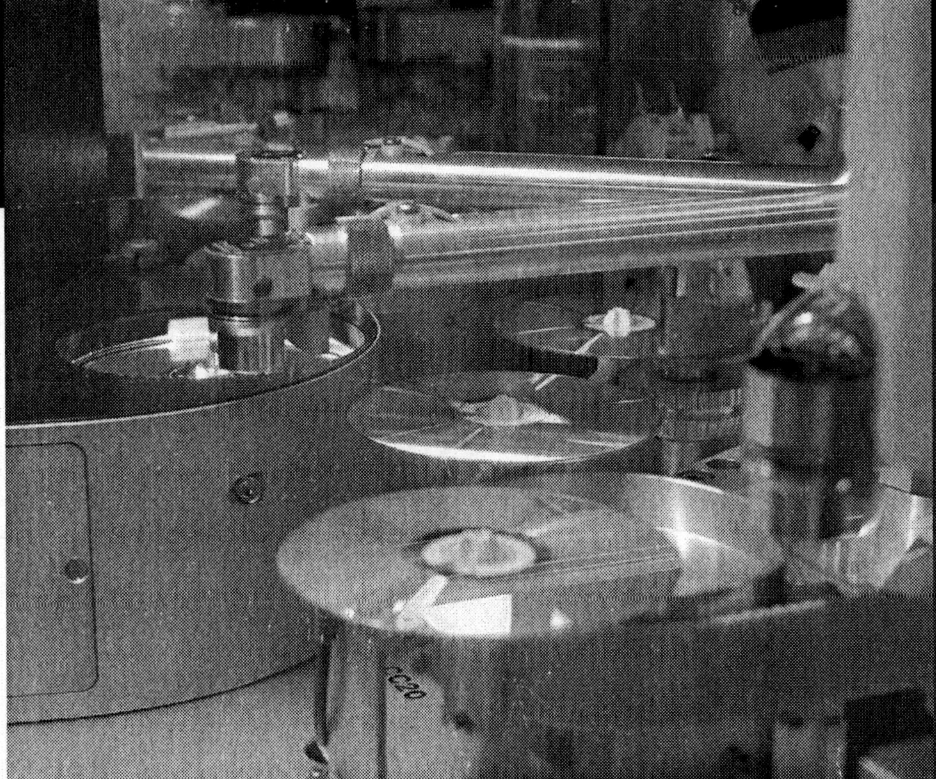

Gibson Greetings, Inc., one of the country's largest sellers of greeting cards, has experienced both the pros and cons of outsourcing. In April one year it announced it would outsource the manufacturing of all of its cards and gift wrap. Gibson's stock price shot up quickly because investors believed the strategy could save the company $10 million a year, primarily by reducing manufacturing costs. But later in the same year Gibson got a taste of the negative side of outsourcing: When one of its suppliers was unable to meet its production schedule, about $20 million of Christmas cards went to stores a month later than scheduled.

Outsourcing is often a point of dispute in labor negotiations. Although many of the jobs lost to outsourcing go overseas, that is not always the case. In fact, a recent trend is to hire out work to vendors located close to the company. This reduces shipping costs and can improve coordination of efforts.

One company that has benefited from local outsourcing is Solectron Corporation in Silicon Valley. It makes things like cell phones, printers, and computers for high-tech companies in the region. To the surprise of many, it has kept thousands of people employed in California, rather than watching those jobs go overseas. What is its secret? It produces high-quality products efficiently. Solectron has to be efficient because it operates on a very thin profit margin—that is, it makes a tiny amount of money on each part—but it makes millions and millions of parts. It has proved the logic of outsourcing as a management decision, both for the companies for whom it makes parts and for its owners and employees.

✓ The Navigator

Inside Chapter 9

- **These Wheels Have Miles Before Installation** (p. 413)
- **Time to Move to a New Neighborhood?** (p. 418)
- **What Is the Real Cost of Packaging Options?** (p. 420)
- ***All About You:* What Is a Degree Worth?** (p. 421)

Preview of Chapter 9

An important purpose of management accounting is to provide managers with relevant information for decision making. Companies of all sorts must make product decisions. Philip Morris decided to cut prices to raise market share. Oral-B Laboratories opted to produce a new, higher priced ($5) toothbrush. General Motors discontinued making the Buick Riviera and announced the closure of its Oldsmobile Division. Quaker Oats decided to sell off a line of beverages, at a price more than one billion dollars less than it paid for that product line only a few years before. Ski manufacturers like Dynastar had to decide whether to use their limited resources to make snowboards instead of downhill skis.

This chapter explains management's decision-making process and a decision-making approach called incremental analysis. The use of incremental analysis is demonstrated in a variety of situations.

The content and organization of this chapter are as follows.

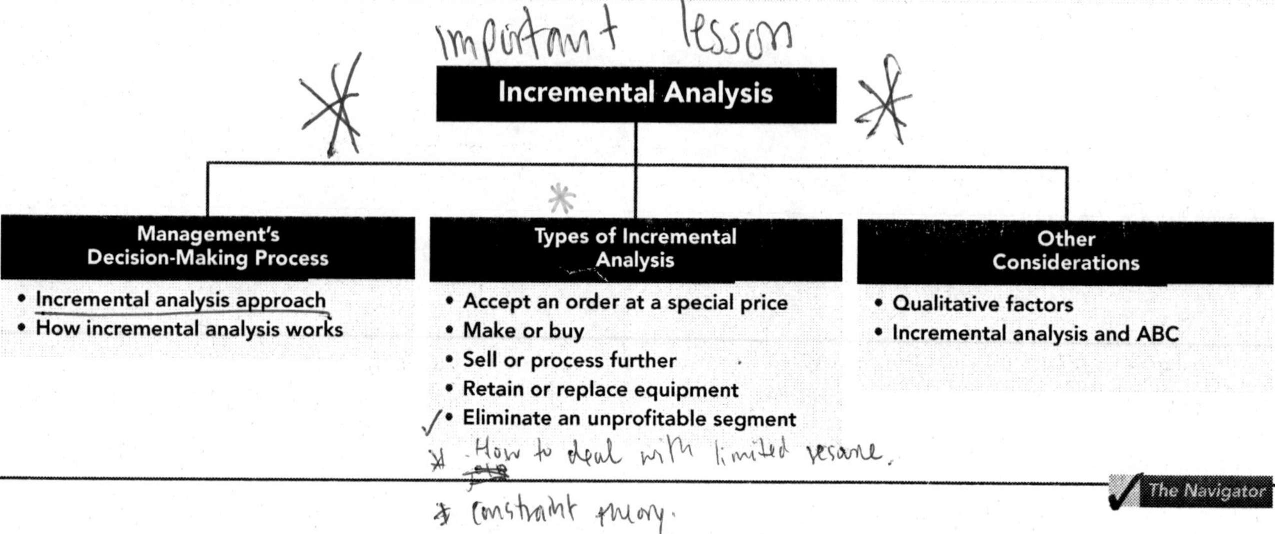

Incremental Analysis
Management's Decision-Making Process
• Incremental analysis approach
• How incremental analysis works
Types of Incremental Analysis
• Accept an order at a special price
• Make or buy
• Sell or process further
• Retain or replace equipment
• Eliminate an unprofitable segment
Other Considerations
• Qualitative factors
• Incremental analysis and ABC
The Navigator

MANAGEMENT'S DECISION-MAKING PROCESS

STUDY OBJECTIVE 1

Identify the steps in management's decision-making process.

Making decisions is an important management function. Management's decision-making process does not always follow a set pattern because decisions vary significantly in their scope, urgency, and importance. It is possible, though, to identify some steps that are frequently involved in the process. These steps are shown in Illustration 9-1 below.

Accounting's contribution to the decision-making process occurs primarily in Steps 2 and 4—evaluating possible courses of action, and reviewing results. In Step 2, for each possible course of action, relevant revenue and cost data are

Illustration 9-1
Management's decision-making process

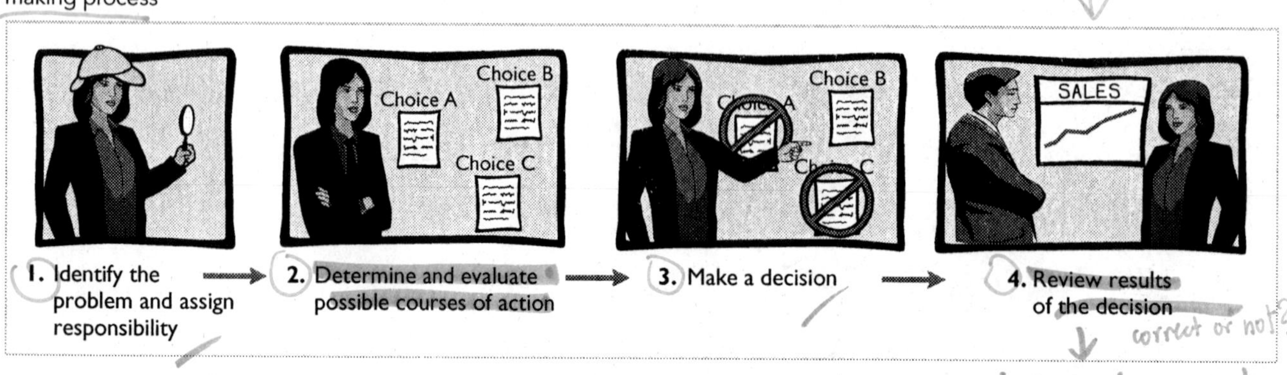

provided. These show the expected overall effect on net income. In Step 4, internal reports are prepared that review the actual impact of the decision.

In making business decisions, management ordinarily considers both financial and nonfinancial information. **Financial** information is related to revenues and costs and their effect on the company's overall profitability. **Nonfinancial** information relates to such factors as the effect of the decision on employee turnover, the environment, or the overall image of the company in the community. Although nonfinancial information can be as important as financial information, we will focus primarily on financial information that is relevant to the decision.

Incremental Analysis Approach

STUDY OBJECTIVE 2

Describe the concept of incremental analysis.

Decisions involve a choice among alternative courses of action. Suppose that you were deciding whether to purchase or lease a car. The financial data relate to the cost of leasing versus the cost of purchasing. For example, leasing would involve periodic lease payments; purchasing would require "up-front" payment of the purchase price. In other words, the financial data relevant to the decision are the data that would vary in the future among the possible alternatives. The process used to identify the financial data that change under alternative courses of action is called **incremental analysis**. In some cases, you will find that when you use incremental analysis, both costs **and** revenues will vary. In other cases, only costs **or** revenues will vary.

Just as your decision to buy or lease a car will affect your future financial situation, similar decisions, on a larger scale, will affect a company's future. Incremental analysis identifies the probable effects of those decisions on future earnings. Such analysis inevitably involves estimates and uncertainty. Gathering data for incremental analyses may involve market analysts, engineers, and accountants. In quantifying the data, the accountant is expected to produce the most reliable information available at the time the decision must be made.

ALTERNATIVE TERMINOLOGY

Incremental analysis is also called *differential analysis* because the analysis focuses on differences.

How Incremental Analysis Works

The basic approach in incremental analysis is illustrated in the following example.

Incremental Analysis.xls

File Edit View Insert Format Tools Data Window Help

	A	B	C	D
1		Alternative A	Alternative B	Net Income Increase (Decrease)
2	Revenues	$125,000	$110,000	$ (15,000)
3	Costs	100,000	80,000	20,000
4	Net income	$ 25,000	$ 30,000	$ 5,000
5				

Illustration 9-2 Basic approach in incremental analysis

This example compares alternative B with alternative A. The net income column shows the differences between the alternatives. In this case, incremental revenue will be $15,000 less under alternative B than under alternative A. But a $20,000 incremental cost saving will be realized.[1] Thus, alternative B will produce $5,000 more net income than alternative A.

In the following pages you will encounter three important cost concepts used in incremental analysis, as defined and discussed in Illustration 9-3 (page 410).

[1]Although income taxes are sometimes important in incremental analysis, they are ignored in the chapter for simplicity's sake.

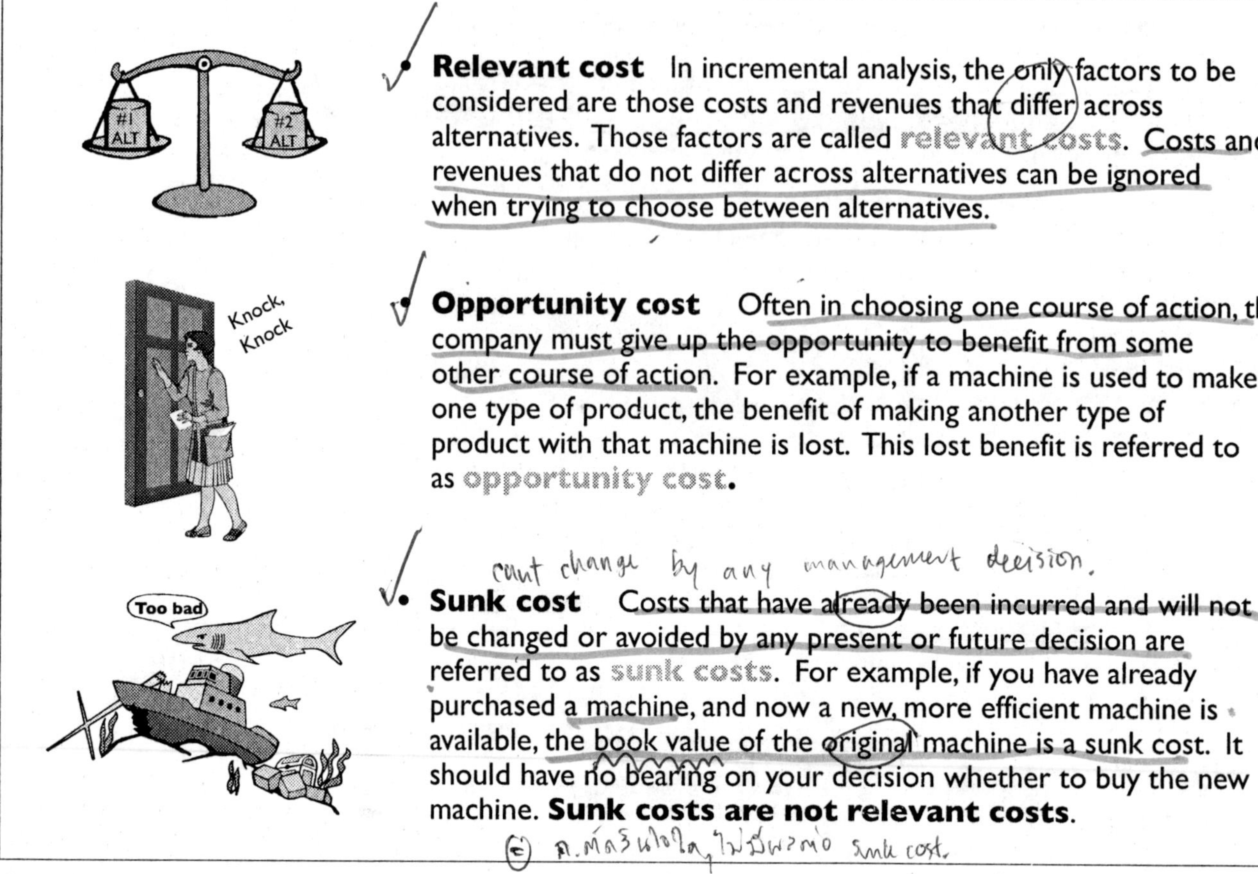

- **Relevant cost** In incremental analysis, the only factors to be considered are those costs and revenues that differ across alternatives. Those factors are called **relevant costs**. Costs and revenues that do not differ across alternatives can be ignored when trying to choose between alternatives.

- **Opportunity cost** Often in choosing one course of action, the company must give up the opportunity to benefit from some other course of action. For example, if a machine is used to make one type of product, the benefit of making another type of product with that machine is lost. This lost benefit is referred to as **opportunity cost.**

- **Sunk cost** Costs that have already been incurred and will not be changed or avoided by any present or future decision are referred to as **sunk costs**. For example, if you have already purchased a machine, and now a new, more efficient machine is available, the book value of the original machine is a sunk cost. It should have no bearing on your decision whether to buy the new machine. **Sunk costs are not relevant costs.**

Illustration 9-3 Key cost concepts in incremental analysis

Incremental analysis sometimes involves changes that at first glance might seem contrary to your intuition. For example, sometimes variable costs **do not change** under the alternative courses of action. Also, sometimes fixed costs **do change**. For example, direct labor, normally a variable cost, is not an incremental cost in deciding between two new factory machines if each asset requires the same amount of direct labor. In contrast, rent expense, normally a fixed cost, is an incremental cost in a decision whether to continue occupancy of a building or to purchase or lease a new building.

TYPES OF INCREMENTAL ANALYSIS

A number of different types of decisions involve incremental analysis. The more common types of decisions are whether to:

1. Accept an order at a special price.
2. Make or buy component parts or finished products.
3. Sell products or process them further.
4. Retain or replace equipment.
5. Eliminate an unprofitable business segment.
6. Allocate limited resources.

We will consider each of these types of decisions in the following pages.

Accept an Order at a Special Price

STUDY OBJECTIVE 3

Identify the relevant costs in accepting an order at a special price.

Sometimes a company may have an opportunity to obtain additional business if it is willing to make a major price concession to a specific customer. To illustrate, assume that Sunbelt Company produces 100,000 automatic blenders per month, which is 80 percent of plant capacity. Variable manufacturing costs are $8 per unit. Fixed manufacturing costs are $400,000, or $4 per unit. The blenders are normally sold directly to retailers at $20 each. Sunbelt has an offer from Mexico Co. (a foreign wholesaler) to purchase an additional 2,000 blenders at $11 per unit. Acceptance of the offer would not affect normal sales of the product, and the additional units can be manufactured without increasing plant capacity. What should management do?

If management makes its decision on the basis of the total cost per unit of $12 ($8 + $4), the order would be rejected, because costs ($12) would exceed revenues ($11) by $1 per unit. However, since the units can be produced within existing plant capacity, the special order **will not increase fixed costs**. Let's identify the relevant data for the decision. First, the variable manufacturing costs will increase $16,000, ($8 × 2,000). Second, the expected revenue will increase $22,000, ($11 × 2,000). Thus, as shown in Illustration 9-4, Sunbelt will increase its net income by $6,000 by accepting this special order.

HELPFUL HINT

This is a good example of different costs for different purposes. In the long run all costs are relevant, but for this decision only costs that change are relevant.

Illustration 9-4
Incremental analysis—accepting an order at a special price

Accepting an order at a special price.xls

File Edit View Insert Format Tools Data Window Help

	A	B	C	D
1		Reject Order	Accept Order	Net Income Increase (Decrease)
2	Revenues	$0	$22,000	$ 22,000
3	Costs	0	16,000	(16,000)
4	Net income	$0	$ 6,000	$ 6,000
5				

Two points should be emphasized: First, we assume that sales of the product in other markets **would not be affected by this special order**. If other sales were affected, then Sunbelt would have to consider the lost sales in making the decision. Second, if Sunbelt is operating **at full capacity**, it is likely that the special order would be rejected. Under such circumstances, the company would have to expand plant capacity. In that case, the special order would have to absorb these additional fixed manufacturing costs, as well as the variable manufacturing costs.

Make or Buy

STUDY OBJECTIVE 4

Identify the relevant costs in a make-or-buy decision.

When a manufacturer assembles component parts in producing a finished product, management must decide whether to make or buy the components. The decision to buy parts or services is often referred to as outsourcing. For example, as discussed in the *Feature Story,* a company such as General Motors Corporation may either make or buy the batteries, tires, and radios used in its cars. Similarly, Hewlett-Packard Corporation may make or buy the electronic circuitry, cases, and printer heads for its printers. Boeing recently sold some of its commercial aircraft factories in an effort to cut production costs and focus instead on engineering and final assembly rather than manufacturing. The decision to make or buy components should be made on the basis of incremental analysis.

To illustrate the analysis, assume that Baron Company incurs the following annual costs in producing 25,000 ignition switches for motor scooters.

Illustration 9-5 Annual product cost data

Direct materials	$ 50,000
Direct labor	75,000
Variable manufacturing overhead	40,000
Fixed manufacturing overhead	60,000
Total manufacturing costs	$225,000
Total cost per unit ($225,000 ÷ 25,000)	**$9.00**

Or, instead of making its own switches, Baron Company might purchase the ignition switches from Ignition, Inc. at a price of $8 per unit. The question again is, "What should management do?"

At first glance, it appears that management should purchase the ignition switches for $8, rather than make them at a cost of $9. However, a review of operations indicates that if the ignition switches are purchased from Ignition, Inc., *all* of Baron's variable costs but only $10,000 of its fixed manufacturing costs will be eliminated (avoided). Thus, $50,000 of the fixed manufacturing costs will remain if the ignition switches are purchased. The relevant costs for incremental analysis, therefore, are as follows.

Illustration 9-6 Incremental analysis—make or buy

Incremental Analysis - Make or buy.xls

File Edit View Insert Format Tools Data Window Help

	A	B	C	D
1		**Make**	**Buy**	**Net Income Increase (Decrease)**
2	Direct materials	$ 50,000	$ 0	**$ 50,000**
3	Direct labor	75,000	0	**75,000**
4	Variable manufacturing costs	40,000	0	**40,000**
5	Fixed manufacturing costs	60,000	50,000	**10,000**
6	Purchase price (25,000 × $8)	0	200,000	**(200,000)**
7	Total annual cost	$225,000	$250,000	**$ (25,000)**
8				

ETHICS NOTE

In the make-or-buy decision it is important for management to take into account the social impact of its choice. For instance, buying may be the most economically feasible solution, but such action could result in the closure of a manufacturing plant that employs many good workers.

This analysis indicates that Baron Company will incur $25,000 of additional cost by buying the ignition switches. Therefore, Baron should continue to make the ignition switches, even though the total manufacturing cost is $1 higher than the purchase price. The reason is that if the company purchases the ignition switches, it will still have fixed costs of $50,000 to absorb.

OPPORTUNITY COST

The foregoing make-or-buy analysis is complete only if it is assumed that the productive capacity used to make the ignition switches cannot be converted to another purpose. If there is an opportunity to use this productive capacity in some other manner, then this opportunity cost must be considered. As indicated earlier, **opportunity cost** is the potential benefit that may be obtained by following an alternative course of action.

To illustrate, assume that through buying the switches, Baron Company can use the released productive capacity to generate additional income of $28,000 from producing a different product. This lost income is an additional cost of continuing to make the switches in the make-or-buy decision. This opportunity cost therefore is added to the "Make" column, for comparison. As shown, it is now advantageous to buy the ignition switches.

Illustration 9-7
Incremental analysis—make or buy, with opportunity cost

Incremental Analysis - Make or buy with opportunity cost.xls

	A	B	C	D
1		Make	Buy	Net Income Increase (Decrease)
2	Total annual cost	$225,000	$250,000	$(25,000)
3	**Opportunity cost**	**28,000**	0	**28,000**
4	Total cost	$253,000	$250,000	$ 3,000
5				

The qualitative factors in this decision include the possible loss of jobs for employees who produce the ignition switches. In addition, management must assess how well the supplier will be able to satisfy the company's quality control standards at the quoted price per unit.

INTERNATIONAL INSIGHT

These Wheels Have Miles before Installation

Consider the make-or-buy decision faced by Superior Industries International, Inc., a big aluminum-wheel maker in Van Nuys, California. For years, president Steve Borick had ignored the possibility of Chinese manufacturing. Then Mr. Borick started getting a blunt message from General Motors and Ford, with whom Superior does 85% of its business: Match the prices that they were seeing at Chinese wheel suppliers. If Superior did not want to agree to new terms at those lower prices, both auto makers said separately that they could go directly to Chinese manufacturers or could turn to another North American wheel-maker that would.

Stories like this, repeated in various industries, illustrate why manufacturers engage in overseas outsourcing. (Some refer to this as *off-shoring.*) For example, compare the relative labor costs in major auto-producing nations, in dollars per hour, to see why incremental analysis often leads to outsourcing production to countries like China.

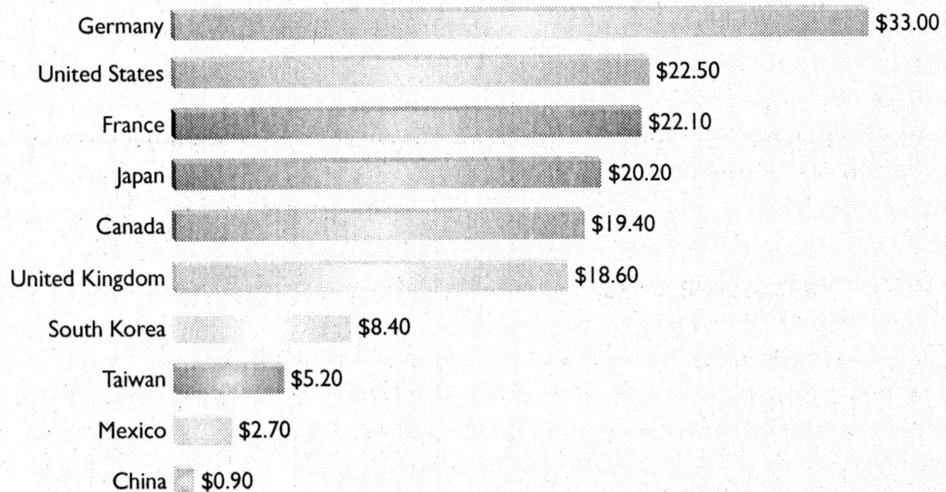

Source: Norihiko Shirouzu, "Big Three's Outsourcing Plan: Make Parts Suppliers Do It," *Wall Street Journal* (June 10, 2004), p. A1.

What are the disadvantages of outsourcing to a foreign country?

Sell or Process Further

STUDY OBJECTIVE 5

Identify the relevant costs in determining whether to sell or process materials further.

Many manufacturers have the option of selling products at a given point in the production cycle or continuing to process with the expectation of selling them at a later point at a higher price. For example, a bicycle manufacturer such as Schwinn could sell its 10-speed bicycles to retailers either unassembled or assembled. A furniture manufacturer such as Ethan Allen could sell its dining room sets to furniture stores either unfinished or finished. The sell-or-process-further decision should be made on the basis of incremental analysis. The basic decision rule is: **Process further as long as the incremental revenue from such processing exceeds the incremental processing costs.**

SINGLE-PRODUCT CASE

Assume, for example, that Woodmasters Inc. makes tables. The cost to manufacture an unfinished table is $35, computed as follows.

Illustration 9-8 Per unit cost of unfinished table

Direct materials	$15
Direct labor	10
Variable manufacturing overhead	6
Fixed manufacturing overhead	4
Manufacturing cost per unit	**$35**

The selling price per unfinished unit is $50. Woodmasters currently has unused productive capacity that is expected to continue indefinitely. What are the relevant costs? Management concludes that some of this capacity may be used to finish the tables and sell them at $60 per unit. For a finished table, direct materials will increase $2 and direct labor costs will increase $4. Variable manufacturing overhead costs will increase by $2.40 (60% of direct labor). No increase is anticipated in fixed manufacturing overhead.

The incremental analysis on a per unit basis is as follows.

Illustration 9-9 Incremental analysis—sell or process further

Incremental Analysis - Sell or process further.xls

File Edit View Insert Format Tools Data Window Help

	A	B	C	D
1		**Sell**	**Process Further**	**Net Income Increase (Decrease)**
2	Sales per unit	$50.00	$60.00	**$10.00**
3	Cost per unit			
4	Direct materials	15.00	17.00	**(2.00)**
5	Direct labor	10.00	14.00	**(4.00)**
6	Variable manufacturing overhead	6.00	8.40	**(2.40)**
7	Fixed manufacturing overhead	4.00	4.00	**0.00**
8	Total	35.00	43.40	**(8.40)**
9	Net income per unit	$15.00	$16.60	**$ 1.60**
10				

HELPFUL HINT

Current net income is known. Net income from processing further is an estimate. In making its decision, management could add a "risk" factor for the estimate.

It would be advantageous for Woodmasters to process the tables further. The incremental revenue of $10.00 from the additional processing is $1.60 higher than the incremental processing costs of $8.40.

MULTIPLE-PRODUCT CASE

Sell-or-process-further decisions are particularly applicable to production processes that produce multiple products simultaneously. In many industries, a number of end-products are produced from a single raw material and a common production process. These multiple end-products are commonly referred to as **joint products**. For example, in the meat-packing industry, a single sheep produces meat, internal organs, hides, bones, and fat. In the petroleum industry, crude oil is refined to produce gasoline, lubricating oil, kerosene, paraffin, and ethylene.

Illustration 9-10 presents a joint product situation for Marais Creamery involving a decision **to sell or process further** cream and skim milk. Cream and skim milk are products that result from the processing of raw milk.

Illustration 9-10 Joint production process—Creamery

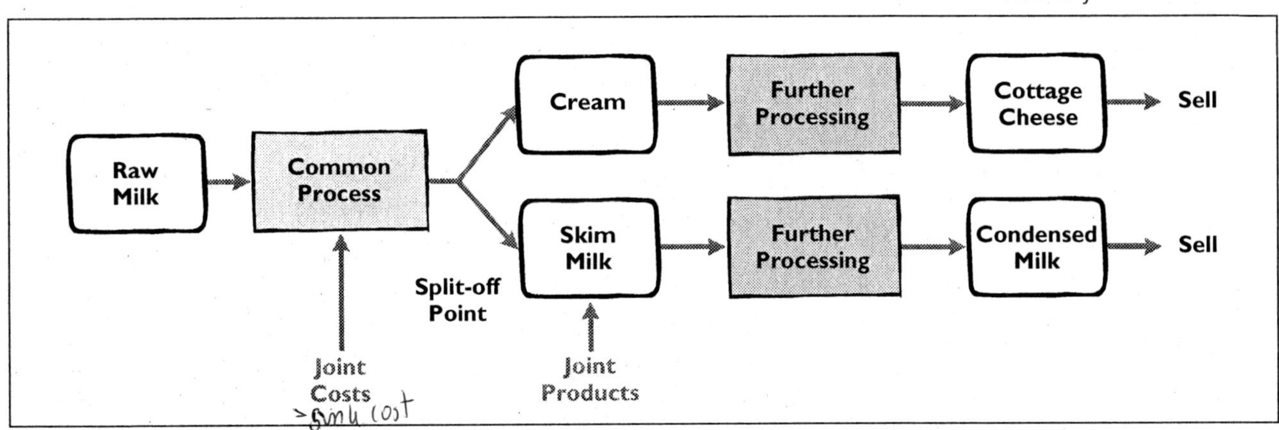

Marais incurs many costs prior to the manufacture of the cream and skim milk. All costs incurred prior to the point at which the two products are separately identifiable (the *split-off point*) are called **joint costs**. For purposes of determining the cost of each product, joint product costs must be allocated to the individual products. This is frequently done based on the relative sales value of the joint products. While this allocation is important for determination of product cost, it is irrelevant for any sell-or-process-further decisions. The reason is that these joint product costs **are sunk costs**. That is, they have already been incurred, and they cannot be changed or avoided by any subsequent decision.

Illustration 9-11 shows the daily cost and revenue data for Marais Creamery.

Illustration 9-11 Cost and revenue data per day

Costs (per day)	
Joint cost allocated to cream	$ 9,000
Joint cost allocated to skim milk	5,000
Processing cream into cottage cheese	10,000
Processing skim milk into condensed milk	8,000
Expected Revenues from Products (per day)	
Cream	$19,000
Skim milk	11,000
Cottage cheese	27,000
Condensed milk	26,000

From this information we can determine whether the company should simply sell the cream and skim milk, or process them further into cottage cheese and condensed milk. Illustration 9-12 (page 416) provides the analysis necessary to determine whether to sell the cream or process it further into cottage cheese.

Illustration 9-12 Analysis of whether to sell cream or process into cottage cheese

Incremental Analysis - Sell or process further - Cottage cheese.xls

	A	B	C	D
1		Sell	Process Further	Net Income Increase (Decrease)
2	Sales per day	$19,000	$27,000	$ 8,000
3	Cost per day			
4	Processing cream into cottage cheese	0	10,000	(10,000)
5		$19,000	$17,000	$ (2,000)
6				

From this analysis we can see that Marais should not process the cream further because it will sustain an incremental loss of $2,000. Illustration 9-13, however, shows that Marais Company should process the skim milk into condensed milk, as it will increase net income by $7,000.

Illustration 9-13 Analysis of whether to sell skim milk or process into condensed milk

Incremental Analysis - Sell or process further - Skim milk or process condensed milk.xls

	A	B	C	D
1		Sell	Process Further	Net Income Increase (Decrease)
2	Sales per day	$11,000	$26,000	$15,000
3	Cost per day			
4	Processing skim milk into condensed milk	0	8,000	(8,000)
5		$11,000	$18,000	$ 7,000
6				

Note that the amount of joint costs allocated to each product ($9,000 to the cream and $5,000 to the skim milk) is irrelevant in deciding whether to sell or process further. Why? The joint costs remain the same whether or not further processing is performed.

Retain or Replace Equipment

STUDY OBJECTIVE 6

Identify the relevant costs to be considered in retaining or replacing equipment.

Management often has to decide whether to continue using an asset or replace it. To illustrate, assume that Jeffcoat Company has a factory machine with a book value of $40,000 and a remaining useful life of four years. It is considering replacing this machine with a new machine. A new machine is available that costs $120,000. It is expected to have zero salvage value at the end of its four-year useful life. If the new machine is acquired, variable manufacturing costs are expected to decrease from $160,000 to $125,000 annually, and the old unit will be scrapped. The incremental analysis for the **four-year period** is as follows.

Illustration 9-14 Incremental analysis—retain or replace equipment

Incremental Analysis - Retain or replace equipment.xls

	A	B	C	D	E	F
1		Retain Equipment		Replace Equipment		Net Income Increase (Decrease)
2	Variable manufacturing costs	$640,000	a	$500,000	b	$140,000
3	New machine cost			120,000		(120,000)
4	Total	$640,000		$620,000		$ 20,000
5						
6	[a](4 years × $160,000)					
7	[b](4 years × $125,000)					
8						

In this case, it would be to the company's advantage to replace the equipment. The lower variable manufacturing costs due to replacement more than offset the cost of the new equipment.

One other point should be mentioned regarding Jeffcoat's decision: **The book value of the old machine does not affect the decision.** Book value is a **sunk cost**, which is a cost that cannot be changed by any present or future decision. **Sunk costs are not relevant in incremental analysis.** In this example, if the asset is retained, book value will be depreciated over its remaining useful life. Or, if the new unit is acquired, book value will be recognized as a loss of the current period. Thus, the effect of book value on current and future earnings is the same regardless of the replacement decision. **Any trade-in allowance or cash disposal value of the existing asset, however, is relevant** to the decision, because this value will not be realized if the asset remains in use.

Eliminate an Unprofitable Segment

STUDY OBJECTIVE 7

Identify the relevant costs in deciding whether to eliminate an unprofitable segment.

Management sometimes must decide whether to eliminate an unprofitable business segment. For example, in recent years many airlines have quit servicing certain cities or have cut back on the number of flights; and Goodyear recently quit producing several brands in the low-end tire market. Again, the key is to **focus on the relevant costs—the data that change under the alternative courses of action**. To illustrate, assume that Martina Company manufactures tennis racquets in three models: Pro, Master, and Champ. Pro and Master are profitable lines. Champ (highlighted in color in the table below) operates at a loss. Condensed income statement data are as follows.

Illustration 9-15 Segment income data

	Pro	Master	Champ	Total
Sales	$800,000	$300,000	$100,000	$1,200,000
Variable costs	520,000	210,000	90,000	820,000
Contribution margin	280,000	90,000	10,000	380,000
Fixed costs	80,000	50,000	30,000	160,000
Net income	$200,000	$ 40,000	$ (20,000)	$ 220,000

HELPFUL HINT

A decision to discontinue a segment based solely on the bottom line—net loss—is inappropriate.

It might be expected that total net income will increase by $20,000, to $240,000, if the unprofitable Champ line of racquets is eliminated. However, **net income may actually decrease if the Champ line is discontinued**. The reason is that the fixed costs allocated to the Champ racquets will have to be absorbed by the other products. To illustrate, assume that the $30,000 of fixed costs applicable to the unprofitable segment are allocated ⅔ to the Pro model and ⅓ to the Master model if the Champ model is eliminated. Fixed costs will increase to $100,000 ($80,000 + $20,000) in the Pro line and to $60,000 ($50,000 + $10,000) in the Master line. The revised income statement is:

Illustration 9-16 Income data after eliminating unprofitable product line

	Pro	Master	Total
Sales	$800,000	$300,000	$1,100,000
Variable costs	520,000	210,000	730,000
Contribution margin	280,000	90,000	370,000
Fixed costs	100,000	60,000	160,000
Net income	$180,000	$ 30,000	$ 210,000

Total net income has decreased $10,000 ($220,000 − $210,000). This result is also obtained in the following incremental analysis of the Champ racquets.

Illustration 9-17
Incremental analysis—eliminating an unprofitable segment

Incremental Analysis - Eliminating an unprofitable segment.xls

	A	B	C	D
1		Continue	Eliminate	Net Income Increase (Decrease)
2	Sales	$100,000	$ 0	$(100,000)
3	Variable costs	90,000	0	90,000
4	Contribution margin	10,000	0	(10,000)
5	Fixed costs	30,000	30,000	0
6	Net income	$ (20,000)	$(30,000)	$ (10,000)
7				

The loss in net income is attributable to the Champ line's contribution margin ($10,000) that will not be realized if the segment is discontinued.

In deciding on the future status of an unprofitable segment, management should consider the effect of elimination on related product lines. It may be possible for continuing product lines to obtain some or all of the sales lost by the discontinued product line. In some businesses, services or products may be linked—for example, free checking accounts at a bank, or coffee at a donut shop. In addition, management should consider the effect of eliminating the product line on employees who may have to be discharged or retrained.

MANAGEMENT INSIGHT

Time to Move to a New Neighborhood?

If you have ever moved, then you know how complicated and costly it can be. Now consider what it would be like for a manufacturing company with 260 employees and a 170,000-square foot facility to move from southern California to Idaho. That is what Buck Knives did in order to save its company from financial ruin. Electricity rates in Idaho were half those in California, workers' compensation was one-third the cost, and factory wages were 20% lower. Combined, this would reduce manufacturing costs by $600,000 per year. Moving the factory would cost about $8.5 million, plus $4 million to move key employees. Offsetting these costs was the estimated $11 million selling price of the California property. Based on these estimates, the move would pay for itself in three years.

Ultimately, the company received only $7.5 million for its California property, only 58 of 75 key employees were willing to move, construction was delayed by a year which caused the new plant to increase in price by $1.5 million, and wages surged in Idaho due to low unemployment. Despite all of these complications, though, the company considers the move a great success.

Source: Chris Lydgate, "The Buck Stopped," *Inc. Magazine*, May 2006, pp. 87–95.

What were some of the factors that complicated the company's decision to move? How should the company have incorporated such factors into its incremental analysis?

DECISION TOOLKIT

Decision Checkpoints	Info Needed for Decision	Tool to Use for Decision	How to Evaluate Results
Which alternative should the company choose?	All relevant costs and opportunity costs	Compare relevant cost of each alternative.	Choose the alternative that maximizes net income.

Before You Go On...

REVIEW IT

1. Give three examples of how incremental analysis might be used.
2. What is the decision rule in deciding to sell or process products further?
3. How may the elimination of an unprofitable segment decrease the overall net income of a company?

DO IT

Cobb Company incurs a cost of $28 per unit, of which $18 is variable, to make a product that normally sells for $42. A foreign wholesaler offers to buy 5,000 units at $25 each. Cobb will incur shipping costs of $1 per unit. Compute the increase or decrease in net income Cobb will realize by accepting the special order, assuming Cobb has excess operating capacity.

Action Plan

- Identify all revenues that will change as a result of accepting the order.
- Identify all costs that will change as a result of accepting the order, and net this amount against the change in revenues.

Solution

	Reject	Accept	Net Income Increase (Decrease)
Revenues	$-0-	$125,000	$125,000
Costs	-0-	95,000*	(95,000)
Net income	$-0-	$ 30,000	$ 30,000

*(5,000 × $18) + (5,000 × $1)

Given the result of the analysis, Cobb Company should accept the special order.

Related exercise material: *BE9-3, E9-2, E9-3, and E9-4.*

The Navigator

OTHER CONSIDERATIONS IN DECISION MAKING

Qualitative Factors

In this chapter we have focused primarily on the quantitative factors that affect a decision—those attributes that can be easily expressed in terms of numbers or dollars. However, many of the decisions involving incremental analysis have important qualitative features; though not easily measured, they should not be ignored.

Consider, for example, the potential effects of the make-or-buy decision or of the decision to eliminate a line of business on existing employees and the community in which the plant is located. The cost savings that may be obtained from outsourcing or from eliminating a plant should be weighed against these qualitative attributes. One example would be the cost of lost morale that might result. Al "Chainsaw" Dunlap was a so-called "turnaround" artist who went into many companies, identified inefficiencies (using incremental analysis techniques), and tried to correct these problems to improve corporate profitability. Along the way he laid off thousands of employees at numerous companies. As head of Sunbeam, it was Al Dunlap who lost his job because his Draconian approach failed to improve Sunbeam's profitability. It was widely reported that Sunbeam's employees openly rejoiced for days after his departure. Clearly, qualitative factors can matter.

Relationship of Incremental Analysis and Activity-Based Costing

Many companies have shifted to activity-based costing to allocate overhead costs to products. The primary reason for using activity-based costing is that it results in a more accurate allocation of overhead. The concepts presented in this chapter are completely consistent with the use of activity-based costing. In fact, activity-based costing will result in better identification of relevant costs and, therefore, better incremental analysis.

MANAGEMENT INSIGHT

What Is the Real Cost of Packaging Options?

The existence of excess plant capacity is frequently the incentive for management to add new products. Adding one new product may not add much incremental cost. But continuing to add products will at some point create new constraints, perhaps requiring additional investments in people, equipment, and facilities.

The effects of product and product line proliferation are generally understood. But the effect on incremental overhead costs of *changes in servicing customers* is less understood. For example, if a company newly offers its customers the option of product delivery by case or by pallet, the new service may appear to be simple and low in cost. But, if the manufacturing process must be realigned to package in two different forms; if two sets of inventory records must be maintained; and if warehousing, handling, and shipping require two different arrangements or sets of equipment, the additional costs of this new option could be as high as a whole new product. If the customer service option were adopted for all products, the product line could effectively be doubled—but so might many overhead costs.

Source: Elizabeth Haas Edersheim and Joan Wilson, "Complexity at Consumer Goods Companies: Naming and Taming the Beast," *Journal of Cost Management.*

If your marketing director suggests that, in addition to selling your cereal in a standard-size box, you should sell a jumbo size and an individual size, what issues must you consider?

Before You Go On...

REVIEW IT

1. What are some qualitative factors that should be considered in an incremental analysis decision?
2. What is the relationship between incremental analysis and activity-based costing?

Be sure to read **ALL ABOUT YOU: *What Is a Degree Worth?*** on the next page for information on how topics in this chapter apply to you.

all about YOU

What Is a Degree Worth?

It may not have occurred to you at the time, but you already made a huge decision in your life that was ideally suited to managerial accounting. No, it's not your choice of whether to have pizza or Chinese food at lunch today. We are referring to your decision to pursue a post–high-school degree. If you weren't going to college, you could be working full-time. School costs money, which is an expenditure that you could have avoided. Also, if you did not go to college, many of you would avoid mountains of school-related debt. While you cannot go back and redo your initial decision, we can look at some facts to evaluate the wisdom of your decision.

Some Facts

- Over a lifetime of work, high-school graduates earn an average of $1.2 million, associate's degree holders earn an average of $1.6 million, and people with bachelor's degrees earn about $2.1 million.
- A year of tuition at a public four-year college costs about $8,655, and a year of tuition at a public two-year college costs about $1,359.
- There has also been considerable research on other, less-tangible benefits of post–high-school education. For example, some have suggested that there is a relationship between higher education and good health. Research also suggests that college-educated people are more optimistic.
- About 600,000 students drop out of four-year colleges each year.

About the Numbers

Tuition is very expensive. As a result, many students have high "unmet needs"—the portion of college expenses not provided by family or student aid. The graph below suggests that in the coming decade an increasing number of students with high "unmet" financial needs will decide not to pursue any form of post–high-school education. This has obvious implications for their long-term personal financial well-being. It also has significant implications for the well-being of the United States as a society. Research shows that people with post–high-school degrees pay more in taxes. Also, without adequate educational training of its citizenry, the United States will be less able to compete in a high-tech world.

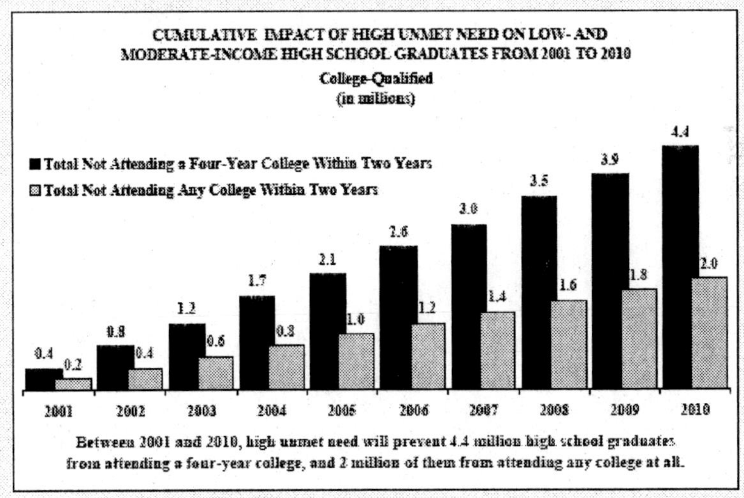

Between 2001 and 2010, high unmet need will prevent 4.4 million high school graduates from attending a four-year college, and 2 million of them from attending any college at all.

Source: "Empty Promises: The Myth of College Access in America," A Report of the Advisory Committee on Student Financial Assistance, June 2002, *www.ed.gov/about/bdscomm/list/acsfa/emptypromises.pdf*, p. 28 (accessed August 2006).

What Do You Think?

Each year many students decide to drop out of school. Many of them never return. Suppose that you are working two jobs and going to college and that you are not making ends meet. Your grades are suffering due to your lack of available study time. You feel depressed. Should you drop out of school?

YES: You can always go back to school. If your grades are bad, and you are depressed, what good is school doing you anyway?

NO: Once you drop out, it is very hard to get enough momentum to go back. Dropping out will dramatically reduce your long-term opportunities. It is better to stay in school, even if you take only one class per semester.

Sources: Kathleen Porter, "The Value of a College Degree," ERIC Clearinghouse on Higher Education, Washington DC, *www.ericdigests.org/2003-3/value.htm* (accessed August 2006).

The authors' comments on this situation appear on page 440.

Using the Decision Toolkit

Suppose Hewlett-Packard Company must decide whether to make or buy some of its components from Solectron Corp. The cost of producing 50,000 electrical connectors for its printers is $110,000, broken down as follows.

Direct materials	$60,000	Variable manufacturing overhead	$12,000
Direct labor	30,000	Fixed manufacturing overhead	8,000

Instead of making the electrical connectors at an average cost per unit of $2.20 ($110,000 ÷ 50,000), the company has an opportunity to buy the connectors at $2.15 per unit. If the connectors are purchased, all variable costs and one-half of the fixed costs will be eliminated.

Instructions

(a) Prepare an incremental analysis showing whether the company should make or buy the electrical connectors.

(b) Will your answer be different if the released productive capacity resulting from the purchase of the connectors will generate additional income of $25,000?

Solution

(a)

	Make	Buy	Net Income Increase (Decrease)
Direct materials	$ 60,000	$ -0-	$ 60,000
Direct labor	30,000	-0-	30,000
Variable manufacturing costs	12,000	-0-	12,000
Fixed manufacturing costs	8,000	4,000	4,000
Purchase price	-0-	107,500	(107,500)
Total cost	$110,000	$111,500	$ (1,500)

This analysis indicates that Hewlett-Packard will incur $1,500 of additional costs if it buys the electrical connectors. H-P therefore would choose to make the connectors.

(b)

	Make	Buy	Net Income Increase (Decrease)
Total cost	$110,000	$111,500	$(1,500)
Opportunity cost	25,000	-0-	25,000
Total cost	$135,000	$111,500	$23,500

Yes, the answer is different. The analysis shows that if additional capacity is released, net income will be increased by $23,500 if the electrical connectors are purchased. In this case, H-P would choose to purchase the connectors.

SUMMARY OF STUDY OBJECTIVES

1 **Identify the steps in management's decision-making process.** Management's decision-making process consists of (a) identifying the problem and assigning responsibility for the decision, (b) determining and evaluating possible courses of action, (c) making the decision, and (d) reviewing the results of the decision.

2 **Describe the concept of incremental analysis.** Incremental analysis identifies financial data that change under alternative courses of action. These data are relevant to the decision because they will vary in the future among the possible alternatives.

3 **Identify the relevant costs in accepting an order at a special price.** The relevant costs are those that change if the order is accepted. These are typically variable manufacturing costs. The relevant information in accepting an order at a special price is the difference between the variable manufacturing costs to produce the special order and expected revenues.

4 **Identify the relevant costs in a make-or-buy decision.** In a make-or-buy decision, the relevant costs are (a) the variable manufacturing costs that will be saved, (b) the purchase price, and (c) opportunity costs.

5 **Identify the relevant costs in determining whether to sell or process materials further.** The decision rule for whether to sell or process materials further is: Process further as long as the incremental revenue from processing exceeds the incremental processing costs.

6 **Identify the relevant costs to be considered in retaining or replacing equipment.** The relevant costs to be considered in determining whether equipment should be retained or replaced are the effects on variable costs and the cost of the new equipment. Also, any disposal value of the existing asset must be considered.

7 **Identify the relevant costs in deciding whether to eliminate an unprofitable segment.** In deciding whether to eliminate an unprofitable segment, the relevant costs are the variable costs that drive the contribution margin, if any, produced by the segment. Disposition of the segment's fixed expenses must also be considered.

DECISION TOOLKIT—A SUMMARY

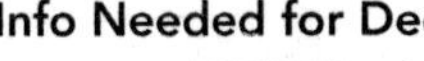

Decision Checkpoints	Info Needed for Decision	Tool to Use for Decision	How to Evaluate Results
	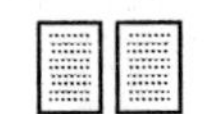		
Which alternative should the company choose?	All relevant costs and opportunity costs	Compare the relevant cost of each alternative.	Choose the alternative that maximizes net income.

GLOSSARY

Incremental analysis The process of identifying the financial data that change under alternative courses of action. (p. 409).

Joint costs For joint products, all costs incurred prior to the point at which the two products are separately identifiable (known as the *split-off point*). (p. 415).

Joint products Multiple end-products produced from a single raw material and a common production process. (p. 415).

Opportunity cost The potential benefit that is lost when one course of action is chosen rather than an alternative course of action. (p. 410).

Relevant costs Those costs and revenues that differ across alternatives. (p. 410).

Sunk cost A cost that cannot be changed by any present or future decision. (p. 410).

Demonstration Problem

Walston Company produces kitchen cabinets for homebuilders across the western United States. The cost of producing 5,000 cabinets is as follows.

Materials	$ 500,000
Labor	250,000
Variable overhead	100,000
Fixed overhead	400,000
Total	$1,250,000

Walston also incurs selling expenses of $20 per cabinet. Wellington Corp. has offered Walston $165 per cabinet for a special order of 1,000 cabinets. The cabinets would be sold to homebuilders in the eastern United States and thus would not conflict with Walston's current sales. Selling expenses per cabinet would be only $5 per cabinet. Walston has available capacity to do the work.

Instructions

(a) Prepare an incremental analysis for the special order.

(b) Should Walston accept the special order? Why or why not?

action plan

✓ Determine the relevant cost per unit of the special order.

✓ Identify the relevant costs and revenues for the units to be produced.

✓ Compare the results related to accepting the special order versus rejecting the special order.

Solution

(a) Relevant costs per unit would be:

Materials	\$500,000/5,000 =	\$100
Labor	250,000/5,000 =	50
Variable overhead	100,000/5,000 =	20
Selling expenses		5
Total relevant cost per unit		\$175

	Reject Order	Accept Order	Net Income Increase (Decrease)
Revenues	\$0	\$ 165,000	\$165,000
Costs	\$0	\$ 175,000	(\$175,000)
Net Income	\$0	\$ (10,000)	(\$ 10,000)

(b) Walston should reject the offer. The incremental benefit of \$165 per cabinet is less than the incremental cost of \$175. By accepting the order, Walston's net income would actually decline by \$10,000.

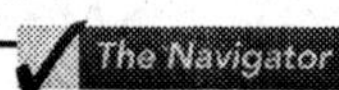

SELF-STUDY QUESTIONS

Answers are at the end of the chapter.

(SO 1) **1.** Three of the steps in management's decision making process are (1) review results of decision, (2) determine and evaluate possible courses of action, and (3) make the decision. The steps are prepared in the following order:
a. (1), (2), (3).
b. (3), (2), (1).
c. (2), (1), (3).
d. (2), (3), (1).

(SO 2) **2.** Incremental analysis is the process of identifying the financial data that:
a. do not change under alternative courses of action.
b. change under alternative courses of action.
c. are mixed under alternative courses of action.
d. No correct answer is given.

(SO 3) **3.** It costs a company \$14 of variable costs and \$6 of fixed costs to produce product Z200 that sells for \$30. A foreign buyer offers to purchase 3,000 units at \$18 each. If the special offer is accepted and produced with unused capacity, net income will:
a. decrease \$6,000.
b. increase \$6,000.
c. increase \$12,000.
d. increase \$9,000.

(SO 3) **4.** It costs a company \$14 of variable costs and \$6 of fixed costs to produce product Z200. Product Z200 sells for \$30. A buyer offers to purchase 3,000 units at \$18 each. The seller will incur special shipping costs of \$5 per unit. If the special offer is accepted and produced with unused capacity, net income will:
a. increase \$3,000.
b. increase \$12,000.
c. decrease \$12,000.
d. decrease \$3,000.

(SO 4) **5.** In a make-or-buy decision, relevant costs are:
a. manufacturing costs that will be saved.
b. the purchase price of the units.
c. opportunity costs.
d. all of the above.

6. The decision rule in a sell-or-process-further decision is: process further as long as the incremental revenue from processing exceeds: (SO 5)
a. incremental processing costs.
b. variable processing costs.
c. fixed processing costs.
d. No correct answer is given.

7. In a decision to retain or replace equipment, the book value of the old equipment is a (an): (SO 6)
a. opportunity cost.
b. sunk cost.
c. incremental cost.
d. marginal cost.

8. If an unprofitable segment is eliminated: (SO 7)
a. net income will always increase.
b. variable expenses of the eliminated segment will have to be absorbed by other segments.
c. fixed expenses allocated to the eliminated segment will have to be absorbed by other segments.
d. net income will always decrease.

9. A segment of Hazard Inc. has the following data. (SO 7)

Sales	\$200,000
Variable expenses	140,000
Fixed expenses	100,000

If this segment is eliminated, what will be the effect on the remaining company? Assume that 50% of the fixed expenses will be eliminated and the rest will be allocated to the segments of the remaining company.
a. \$120,000 increase.
b. \$10,000 decrease.
c. \$50,000 increase.
d. \$10,000 increase.

Go to the book's website, **www.wiley.com/college/weygandt**, for Additional Self-Study questions.

QUESTIONS

1. What steps are frequently involved in management's decision-making process?
2. Your roommate, Mike Myer, contends that accounting contributes to most of the steps in management's decision-making process. Is your roommate correct? Explain.
3. "Incremental analysis involves the accumulation of information concerning a single course of action." Do you agree? Why?
4. Sara Gura asks for your help concerning the relevance of variable and fixed costs in incremental analysis. Help Sara with her problem.
5. What data are relevant in deciding whether to accept an order at a special price?
6. Son Ly Company has an opportunity to buy parts at $7 each that currently cost $10 to make. What manufacturing costs are relevant to this make-or-buy decision?
7. Define the term "opportunity cost." How may this cost be relevant in a make-or-buy decision?
8. What is the decision rule in deciding whether to sell a product or process it further?
9. What are joint products? What accounting issue results from the production process that creates joint products?
10. How are allocated joint costs treated when making a sell-or-process-further decision?
11. Your roommate, Vanessa Hunt, is confused about sunk costs. Explain to your roommate the meaning of sunk costs and their relevance to a decision to retain or replace equipment.
12. Erm Paris Inc. has one product line that is unprofitable. What circumstances may cause overall company net income to be lower if the unprofitable product line is eliminated?

BRIEF EXERCISES

WILEY PLUS

Identify the steps in management's decision-making process.
(SO 1)

BE9-1 The steps in management's decision-making process are listed in random order below. Indicate the order in which the steps should be executed.

____ Make a decision
____ Identify the problem and assign responsibility
____ Review results of the decision
____ Determine and evaluate possible courses of action

Determine incremental changes.
(SO 2)

BE9-2 Anna Company is considering two alternatives. Alternative A will have revenues of $150,000 and costs of $100,000. Alternative B will have revenues of $185,000 and costs of $125,000. Compare Alternative A to Alternative B showing incremental revenues, costs, and net income.

Determine whether to accept a special order.
(SO 3)

BE9-3 In Sydney Company it costs $30 per unit ($20 variable and $10 fixed) to make a product at full capacity that normally sells for $45. A foreign wholesaler offers to buy 3,000 units at $24 each. Sydney will incur special shipping costs of $2 per unit. Assuming that Sydney has excess operating capacity, indicate the net income (loss) Sydney would realize by accepting the special order.

Determine whether to make or buy a part.
(SO 4)

BE9-4 Emil Manufacturing incurs unit costs of $7.50 ($4.50 variable and $3 fixed) in making a sub-assembly part for its finished product. A supplier offers to make 10,000 of the assembly part at $5 per unit. If the offer is accepted, Emil will save all variable costs but no fixed costs. Prepare an analysis showing the total cost saving, if any, Emil will realize by buying the part.

Determine whether to sell or process further.
(SO 5)

BE9-5 Green Inc. makes unfinished bookcases that it sells for $60. Production costs are $35 variable and $10 fixed. Because it has unused capacity, Green is considering finishing the bookcases and selling them for $70. Variable finishing costs are expected to be $8 per unit with no increase in fixed costs. Prepare an analysis on a per unit basis showing whether Green should sell unfinished or finished bookcases.

Determine whether to sell or process further, joint products.
(SO 5)

BE9-6 Each day, Dunham Corporation processes 1 ton of a secret raw material into two resulting products, AB1 and XY1. When it processes 1 ton of the raw material the company incurs joint processing costs of $60,000. It allocates $25,000 of these costs to AB1 and $35,000 of these costs to XY1. The resulting AB1 can be sold for $90,000. Alternatively, it can be processed further to make AB2 at an additional processing cost of $50,000, and sold for $150,000. Each day's batch of XY1 can be sold for $90,000. Alternatively, it can be processed further to create XY2, at an additional processing cost of $50,000, and sold for $130,000. Discuss what products Dunham Corporation should make.

Determine whether to retain or replace equipment.
(SO 6)

BE9-7 Chudzick Company has a factory machine with a book value of $90,000 and a remaining useful life of 4 years. A new machine is available at a cost of $250,000. This machine will have a 4-year useful life with no salvage value. The new machine will lower annual variable manufacturing costs from $600,000 to $500,000. Prepare an analysis showing whether the old machine should be retained or replaced.

Determine whether to eliminate an unprofitable segment.
(SO 7)

BE9-8 Bitterman, Inc., manufactures golf clubs in three models. For the year, the Big Bart line has a net loss of $5,000 from sales $200,000, variable costs $175,000, and fixed costs $30,000. If the Big Bart line is eliminated, $20,000 of fixed costs will remain. Prepare an analysis showing whether the Big Bart line should be eliminated.

EXERCISES

Analyze statements about decision making and incremental analysis.
(SO 1, 2)

E9-1 Pender has prepared the following list of statements about decision making and incremental analysis.

1. The first step in management's decision-making process is, "Determine and evaluate possible courses of action."
2. The final step in management's decision-making process is to actually make the decision.
3. Accounting's contribution to management's decision-making process occurs primarily in evaluating possible courses of action and in reviewing the results.
4. In making business decisions, management ordinarily considers only financial information because it is objectively determined.
5. Decisions involve a choice among alternative courses of action.
6. The process used to identify the financial data that change under alternative courses of action is called incremental analysis.
7. Costs that are the same under all alternative courses of action sometimes affect the decision.
8. When using incremental analysis, some costs will always change under alternative courses of action, but revenues will not.
9. Variable costs will change under alternative courses of action, but fixed costs will not.

Instructions

Identify each statement as true or false. If false, indicate how to correct the statement.

Make incremental analysis for special-order decision.
(SO 3)

E9-2 Innova Company produces golf discs which it normally sells to retailers for $7 each. The cost of manufacturing 20,000 golf discs is:

Materials	$ 10,000
Labor	30,000
Variable overhead	20,000
Fixed overhead	40,000
Total	$100,000

Innova also incurs 5% sales commission ($0.35) on each disc sold.

Mudd Corporation offers Innova $4.75 per disc for 5,000 discs. Mudd would sell the discs under its own brand name in foreign markets not yet served by Innova. If Innova accepts the offer, its fixed overhead will increase from $40,000 to $45,000 due to the purchase of a new imprinting machine. No sales commission will result from the special order.

Instructions

(a) Prepare an incremental analysis for the special order.
(b) Should Innova accept the special order? Why or why not?
(c) What assumptions underlie the decision made in part (b)?

Use incremental analysis for special order.
(SO 3)

E9-3 Quick Company manufactures toasters. For the first 8 months of 2008, the company reported the following operating results while operating at 75% of plant capacity:

Sales (350,000 units)	$4,375,000
Cost of goods sold	2,500,000
Gross profit	1,875,000
Operating expenses	875,000
Net income	$1,000,000

Cost of goods sold was 70% variable and 30% fixed; operating expenses were also 70% variable and 30% fixed.

In September, Quick Company receives a special order for 15,000 toasters at $7.50 each from Ortiz Company of Mexico City. Acceptance of the order would result in an additional $3,000 of shipping costs but no increase in fixed operating expenses.

Instructions

(a) Prepare an incremental analysis for the special order.
(b) Should Quick Company accept the special order? Why or why not?

Use incremental analysis for special order.
(SO 3)

E9-4 Hardy Fiber Company is the creator of Y-Go, a technology that weaves silver into its fabrics to kill bacteria and odor on clothing while managing heat. Y-Go has become very popular as an undergarment for sports activities. Operating at capacity, the company can produce 1,000,000 undergarments of Y-Go a year. The per unit and the total costs for an individual garment when the company operates at full capacity are as follows.

	Per Undergarment	Total
Direct materials	$2.00	$2,000,000
Direct labor	0.50	500,000
Variable manufacturing overhead	1.00	1,000,000
Fixed manufacturing overhead	1.50	1,500,000
Variable selling expenses	0.25	250,000
Totals	$5.25	$5,250,000

The U.S. Army has approached Hardy Fiber and expressed an interest in purchasing 200,000 Y-Go undergarments for soldiers in extremely warm climates. The Army would pay the unit cost for direct materials, direct labor, and variable manufacturing overhead costs. In addition, the Army has agreed to pay an additional $1 per undergarment to cover all other costs and provide a profit. Presently, Hardy Fiber is operating at 70 percent capacity and does not have any other potential buyers for Y-Go. If Hardy Fiber accepts the Army's offer, it will not incur any variable selling expenses related to this order.

Instructions

Using incremental analysis, determine whether Hardy Fiber should accept the Army's offer.

Use incremental analysis for make-or-buy decision.
(SO 4)

E9-5 Stahl Inc. has been manufacturing its own shades for its table lamps. The company is currently operating at 100% of capacity, and variable manufacturing overhead is charged to production at the rate of 70% of direct labor cost. The direct materials and direct labor cost per unit to make the lamp shades are $5 and $6, respectively. Normal production is 30,000 table lamps per year.

A supplier offers to make the lamp shades at a price of $15.50 per unit. If Stahl Inc. accepts the supplier's offer, all variable manufacturing costs will be eliminated, but the $45,000 of fixed manufacturing overhead currently being charged to the lamp shades will have to be absorbed by other products.

Instructions

(a) Prepare the incremental analysis for the decision to make or buy the lamp shades.
(b) Should Stahl Inc. buy the lamp shades?
(c) Would your answer be different in (b) if the productive capacity released by not making the lamp shades could be used to produce income of $35,000?

Use incremental analysis for make-or-buy decision.
(SO 4)

E9-6 SY Telc has recently started the manufacture of RecRobo, a three-wheeled robot that can scan a home for fires and gas leaks and then transmit this information to a mobile phone. The cost structure to manufacture 20,000 RecRobo's is as follows.

	Cost
Direct materials ($40 per robot)	$ 800,000
Direct labor ($30 per robot)	600,000
Variable overhead ($6 per robot)	120,000
Allocated fixed overhead ($25 per robot)	500,000
Total	$2,020,000

SY Telc is approached by Chen Inc. which offers to make RecRobo for $90 per unit or $1,800,000.

Instructions

(a) Using incremental analysis, determine whether SY Telc should accept this offer under each of the following independent assumptions.

(1) Assume that $300,000 of the fixed overhead cost can be reduced (avoided).

(2) Assume that none of the fixed overhead can be reduced (avoided). However, if the robots are purchased from Chen Inc., SY Telc can use the released productive resources to generate additional income of $300,000.

(b) Describe the qualitative factors that might affect the decision to purchase the robots from an outside supplier.

Use incremental analysis for further processing of materials decision.

(SO 5)

E9-7 Wanda Sublette recently opened her own basketweaving studio. She sells finished baskets in addition to the raw materials needed by customers to weave baskets of their own. Wanda has put together a variety of raw material kits, each including materials at various stages of completion. Unfortunately, owing to space limitations, Wanda is unable to carry all varieties of kits originally assembled and must choose between two basic packages.

The basic introductory kit includes undyed, uncut reeds (with dye included) for weaving one basket. This basic package costs Wanda $14 and sells for $28. The second kit, called Stage 2, includes cut reeds that have already been dyed. With this kit the customer need only soak the reeds and weave the basket. Wanda is able to produce the second kit by using the basic materials included in the first kit and adding one hour of her own time, which she values at $20 per hour. Because she is more efficient at cutting and dying reeds than her average customer, Wanda is able to make two kits of the dyed reeds, in one hour, from one kit of undyed reeds. The Stage 2 kit sells for $35.

Instructions

Determine whether Wanda's basketweaving shop should carry the basic introductory kit with undyed and uncut reeds or the Stage 2 kit with reeds already dyed and cut. Prepare an incremental analysis to support your answer.

Determine whether to sell or process further, joint products.

(SO 5)

E9-8 Benson, Inc. produces three separate products from a common process costing $100,000. Each of the products can be sold at the split-off point or can be processed further and then sold for a higher price. Shown below are cost and selling price data for a recent period.

	Sales Value at Split-off Point	Cost to Process Further	Sales Value After Further Processing
Product 12	$50,000	$100,000	$190,000
Product 14	10,000	30,000	35,000
Product 16	60,000	150,000	220,000

Instructions

(a) Determine total net income if all products are sold at the split-off point.

(b) Determine total net income if all products are sold after further processing.

(c) Using incremental analysis, determine which products should be sold at the split-off point and which should be processed further.

(d) Determine total net income using the results from **(c)** and explain why the net income is different from that determined in **(b)**.

Determine whether to sell or process further, joint products.

(SO 5)

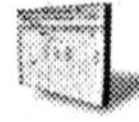

E9-9 Shynee Minerals processes materials extracted from mines. The most common raw material that it processes results in three joint products: Sarco, Barco, and Larco. Each of these products can be sold as is, or it can be processed further and sold for a higher price. The company incurs joint costs of $180,000 to process one batch of the raw material that produces the three joint products. The following cost and sales information is available for one batch of each product.

	Sales Value at Split-off Point	Allocated Joint Costs	Cost to Process Further	Sales Value of Processed Product
Sarco	$200,000	$40,000	$120,000	$300,000
Barco	300,000	60,000	89,000	400,000
Larco	400,000	80,000	250,000	800,000

Instructions
Determine whether each of the three joint products should be sold as is, or processed further.

Use incremental analysis for retaining or replacing equipment decision.

(SO 6)

E9-10 On January 2, 2008, Lucas Hospital purchased a $100,000 special radiology scanner from Faital Inc. The scanner has a useful life of 5 years and will have no disposal value at the end of its useful life. The straight-line method of depreciation is used on this scanner. Annual operating costs with this scanner are $105,000.

Approximately one year later, the hospital is approached by Alliant Technology salesperson, Becky Bishop, who indicated that purchasing the scanner in 2008 from Faital Inc. was a mistake. She points out that Alliant has a scanner that will save Lucas Hospital $27,000 a year in operating expenses over its 4-year useful life. She notes that the new scanner will cost $120,000 and has the same capabilities as the scanner purchased last year. The hospital agrees that both scanners are of equal quality. The new scanner will have no disposal value. Bishop agrees to buy the old scanner from Lucas Hospital for $30,000.

Instructions
(a) If Lucas Hospital sells its old scanner on January 2, 2009, compute the gain or loss on the sale.
(b) Using incremental analysis, determine if Lucas Hospital should purchase the new scanner on January 2, 2009.
(c) Explain why Lucas Hospital might be reluctant to purchase the new scanner, regardless of the results indicated by the incremental analysis in (b).

Use incremental analysis for retaining or replacing equipment decision.

(SO 6)

E9-11 Twyla Enterprises uses a computer to handle its sales invoices. Lately, business has been so good that it takes an extra 3 hours per night, plus every third Saturday, to keep up with the volume of sales invoices. Management is considering updating its computer with a faster model that would eliminate all of the overtime processing.

	Current Machine	New Machine
Original purchase cost	$15,000	$25,000
Accumulated depreciation	$ 6,000	—
Estimated annual operating costs	$24,000	$18,000
Useful life	5 years	5 years

If sold now, the current machine would have a salvage value of $5,000. If operated for the remainder of its useful life, the current machine would have zero salvage value. The new machine is expected to have zero salvage value after five years.

Instructions
Should the current machine be replaced?

Make incremental analysis concerning elimination of division.

(SO 7)

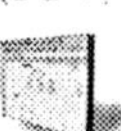

E9-12 Maggie Sharrer, a recent graduate of Rolling's accounting program, evaluated the operating performance of Poway Company's six divisions. Maggie made the following presentation to Poway's Board of Directors and suggested the Erie Division be eliminated. "If the Erie Division is eliminated," she said, "our total profits would increase by $24,500."

	The Other Five Divisions	Erie Division	Total
Sales	$1,664,200	$100,000	$1,764,200
Cost of goods sold	978,520	76,500	1,055,020
Gross profit	685,680	23,500	709,180
Operating expenses	527,940	48,000	575,940
Net income	$ 157,740	$ (24,500)	$ 133,240

In the Erie Division, cost of goods sold is $60,000 variable and $16,500 fixed, and operating expenses are $25,000 variable and $23,000 fixed. None of the Erie Division's fixed costs will be eliminated if the division is discontinued.

Instructions
Is Maggie right about eliminating the Erie Division? Prepare a schedule to support your answer.

Make incremental analysis for elimination of a product line.
(SO 7)

E9-13 Shatner Company makes three models of phasers. Information on the three products is given below.

	Stunner	Double-Set	Mega-Power
Sales	$300,000	$500,000	$200,000
Variable expenses	150,000	200,000	140,000
Contribution margin	150,000	300,000	60,000
Fixed expenses	120,000	225,000	90,000
Net income	$ 30,000	$ 75,000	$(30,000)

Fixed expenses consist of $300,000 of common costs allocated to the three products based on relative sales, and additional fixed expenses of $30,000 (Stunner), $75,000 (Double-Set), and $30,000 (Mega-Power). The common costs will be incurred regardless of how many models are produced. The other fixed expenses would be eliminated if a model is phased out.

Jim Kirk, an executive with the company, feels the Mega-Power line should be discontinued to increase the company's net income.

Instructions

(a) Compute current net income for Shatner Company.
(b) Compute net income by product line and in total for Shatner Company if the company discontinues the Mega-Power product line. (*Hint:* Allocate the $300,000 common costs to the two remaining product lines based on their relative sales.)
(c) Should Shatner eliminate the Mega-Power product line? Why or why not?

Identify relevant costs for different decisions.
(SO 3, 4, 5, 6, 7)

E9-14 The costs listed below relate to a variety of different decision situations.

Cost	Decision
1. Unavoidable fixed overhead	Eliminate an unprofitable segment
2. Direct labor	Make or buy
3. Original cost of old equipment	Equipment replacement
4. Joint production costs	Sell or process further
5. Opportunity cost	Accepting a special order
6. Segment manager's salary	Eliminate an unprofitable segment. Manager will be terminated.
7. Cost of new equipment	Equipment replacement
8. Incremental production costs	Sell or process further
9. Direct materials	Equipment replacement. The amount of materials required does not change.
10. Rent expense	Purchase or lease a building

Instructions

For each cost listed above, indicate if it is relevant or not to the related decision. For those costs determined to be irrelevant, briefly explain why.

EXERCISES: SET B

Visit the book's website at **www.wiley.com/college/weygandt**, and choose the Student Companion site, to access Exercise Set B.

PROBLEMS: SET A

WILEY PLUS

Make incremental analysis for special order and identify non-financial factors in the decision.
(SO 3)

P9-1A Pro Sports Inc. manufactures basketballs for the National Basketball Association (NBA). For the first 6 months of 2008, the company reported the following operating results while operating at 90% of plant capacity and producing 112,500 units.

	Amount
Sales	$4,500,000
Cost of goods sold	3,600,000
Selling and administrative expenses	450,000
Net income	$ 450,000

Fixed costs for the period were: cost of goods sold $1,080,000, and selling and administrative expenses $225,000.

In July, normally a slack manufacturing month, Pro Sports receives a special order for 10,000 basketballs at $28 each from the Italian Basketball Association (IBA). Acceptance of the order would increase variable selling and administrative expenses $0.50 per unit because of shipping costs but would not increase fixed costs and expenses.

Instructions

(a) Prepare an incremental analysis for the special order. (a) NI increase $31,000

(b) Should Pro Sports Inc. accept the special order? Explain your answer.

(c) What is the minimum selling price on the special order to produce net income of $4.10 per ball?

(d) What nonfinancial factors should management consider in making its decision?

Make incremental analysis related to make or buy, consider opportunity cost, and identify nonfinancial factors.

(SO 4)

P9-2A The management of Borealis Manufacturing Company is trying to decide whether to continue manufacturing a part or to buy it from an outside supplier. The part, called WISCO, is a component of the company's finished product.

The following information was collected from the accounting records and production data for the year ending December 31, 2008.

1. 7,000 units of WISCO were produced in the Machining Department.
2. Variable manufacturing costs applicable to the production of each WISCO unit were: direct materials $4.80, direct labor $4.30, indirect labor $0.43, utilities $0.40.
3. Fixed manufacturing costs applicable to the production of WISCO were:

Cost Item	Direct	Allocated
Depreciation	$2,100	$ 900
Property taxes	500	200
Insurance	900	600
	$3,500	$1,700

All variable manufacturing and direct fixed costs will be eliminated if WISCO is purchased. Allocated costs will have to be absorbed by other production departments.

4. The lowest quotation for 7,000 WISCO units from a supplier is $70,000.
5. If WISCO units are purchased, freight and inspection costs would be $0.40 per unit, and receiving costs totaling $1,250 per year would be incurred by the Machining Department.

Instructions

(a) Prepare an incremental analysis for WISCO. Your analysis should have columns for (1) Make WISCO, (2) Buy WISCO, and (3) Net Income Increase/(Decrease). (a) NI (decrease) $(1,040)

(b) Based on your analysis, what decision should management make?

(c) Would the decision be different if Borealis Company has the opportunity to produce $5,000 of net income with the facilities currently being used to manufacture WISCO? Show computations. (c) NI increase $3,960

(d) What nonfinancial factors should management consider in making its decision?

Determine if product should be sold or processed further.

(SO 5)

P9-3A Mesa Industrial Products Co. (MIPC) is a diversified industrial-cleaner processing company. The company's Verde plant produces two products: a table cleaner and a floor cleaner from a common set of chemical inputs (CDG). Each week 900,000 ounces of chemical input are processed at a cost of $210,000 into 600,000 ounces of floor cleaner and 300,000 ounces of table cleaner. The floor cleaner has no market value until it is converted into a polish with the trade name FloorShine. The additional processing costs for this conversion amount to $250,000.

FloorShine sells at $20 per 30-ounce bottle. The table cleaner can be sold for $25 per 30-ounce bottle. However, the table cleaner can be converted into two other products by adding 300,000 ounces of another compound (TCP) to the 300,000 ounces of table cleaner. This joint process will yield 300,000 ounces each of table stain remover (TSR) and table polish (TP). The additional processing costs for this process amount to $100,000. Both table products can be sold for $18 per 30-ounce bottle.

The company decided not to process the table cleaner into TSR and TP based on the following analysis.

	Table Cleaner	Process Further: Table Stain Remover (TSR)	Table Polish (TP)	Total
Production in ounces	(300,000)	300,000	300,000	
Revenue	$250,000	$180,000	$180,000	$360,000
Costs:				
CDG costs	70,000*	52,500	52,500	105,000**
TCP costs	0	50,000	50,000	100,000
Total costs	70,000	102,500	102,500	205,000
Weekly gross profit	$180,000	$ 77,500	$ 77,500	$155,000

*If table cleaner is not processed further it is allocated 1/3 of the $210,000 of CDG cost, which is equal to 1/3 of the total physical output.
**If table cleaner is processed further, total physical output is 1,200,000 ounces. TSR and TP combined account for 50% of the total physical output and are each allocated 25% of the CDG cost.

Instructions

(a) Determine if management made the correct decision to not process the table cleaner further by doing the following.
   (1) Calculate the company's total weekly gross profit assuming the table cleaner is not processed further.
   (2) Calculate the company's total weekly gross profit assuming the table cleaner is processed further.
   (3) Compare the resulting net incomes and comment on management's decision.
(b) Using incremental analysis, determine if the table cleaner should be processed further.

(2) Gross profit $200,000

(CMA adapted)

Compute gain or loss, and determine if equipment should be replaced.

(SO 6)

P9-4A Last year (2008) Calway Condos installed a mechanized elevator for its tenants. The owner of the company, Cab Calway, recently returned from an industry equipment exhibition where he watched a computerized elevator demonstrated. He was impressed with the elevator's speed, comfort of ride, and cost efficiency. Upon returning from the exhibition, he asked his purchasing agent to collect price and operating cost data on the new elevator. In addition, he asked the company's accountant to provide him with cost data on the company's elevator. This information is presented below.

	Old Elevator	New Elevator
Purchase price	$120,000	$180,000
Estimated salvage value	0	0
Estimated useful life	6 years	5 years
Depreciation method	Straight-line	Straight-line
Annual operating costs other than depreciation:		
Variable	$ 35,000	$ 12,000
Fixed	23,000	8,400

Annual revenues are $240,000, and selling and administrative expenses are $29,000, regardless of which elevator is used. If the old elevator is replaced now, at the beginning of 2009, Calway Condos will be able to sell it for $25,000.

Instructions

(a) Determine any gain or loss if the old elevator is replaced.
(b) Prepare a 5-year summarized income statement for each of the following assumptions:
   (1) The old elevator is retained.
   (2) The old elevator is replaced.
(c) Using incremental analysis, determine if the old elevator should be replaced.
(d) Write a memo to Cab Calway explaining why any gain or loss should be ignored in the decision to replace the old elevator.

(b)(2) NI $698,000

(c) NI increase $33,000

P9-5A Lewis Manufacturing Company has four operating divisions. During the first quarter of 2008, the company reported aggregate income from operations of $176,000 and the following divisional results.

Compute contribution margin and prepare incremental analysis concerning elimination of divisions.

(SO 7)

	Division			
	I	II	III	IV
Sales	$250,000	$200,000	$500,000	$400,000
Cost of goods sold	200,000	189,000	300,000	250,000
Selling and administrative expenses	65,000	60,000	60,000	50,000
Income (loss) from operations	$ (15,000)	$ (49,000)	$140,000	$100,000

Analysis reveals the following percentages of variable costs in each division.

	I	II	III	IV
Cost of goods sold	70%	90%	80%	75%
Selling and administrative expenses	40	70	50	60

Discontinuance of any division would save 50% of the fixed costs and expenses for that division.

Top management is very concerned about the unprofitable divisions (I and II). Consensus is that one or both of the divisions should be discontinued.

Instructions

(a) Compute the contribution margin for Divisions I and II. (a) I $84,000

(b) Prepare an incremental analysis concerning the possible discontinuance of (1) Division I and (2) Division II. What course of action do you recommend for each division?

(c) Prepare a columnar condensed income statement for Lewis Manufacturing, assuming Division II is eliminated. Use the CVP format. Division II's unavoidable fixed costs are allocated equally to the continuing divisions. (c) Income III $133,850

(d) Reconcile the total income from operations ($176,000) with the total income from operations without Division II.

PROBLEMS: SET B

P9-1B Oakbrook Company is currently producing 18,000 units per month, which is 80% of its production capacity. Variable manufacturing costs are currently $13.20 per unit, and fixed manufacturing costs are $72,000 per month. Oakbrook pays a 9% sales commission to its sales people, has $30,000 in fixed administrative expenses per month, and is averaging $432,000 in sales per month.

Make incremental analysis for special order and identify nonfinancial factors in the decision.

(SO 3)

A special order received from a foreign company would enable Oakbrook Company to operate at 100% capacity. The foreign company offered to pay 80% of Oakbrook's current selling price per unit. If the order is accepted, Oakbrook will have to spend an extra $2.00 per unit to package the product for overseas shipping. Also, Oakbrook Company would need to lease a new stamping machine to imprint the foreign company's logo on the product, at a monthly cost of $5,000. The special order would require a sales commission of $4,000.

Instructions

(a) Compute the number of units involved in the special order and the foreign company's offered price per unit.

(b) What is the manufacturing cost of producing one unit of Oakbrook's product for regular customers?

(c) Prepare an incremental analysis of the special order. Should management accept the order? (c) NI increase $9,000

(d) What is the lowest price that Oakbrook could accept for the special order to earn net income of $1.20 per unit?

(e) What nonfinancial factors should management consider in making its decision?

P9-2B The management of Dunham Manufacturing Company has asked for your assistance in deciding whether to continue manufacturing a part or to buy it from an outside supplier. The part, called Tropica, is a component of Dunham's finished product.

Make incremental analysis related to make or buy, consider opportunity cost, and identify nonfinancial factors.

(SO 4)

An analysis of the accounting records and the production data revealed the following information for the year ending December 31, 2008.

1. The Machinery Department produced 35,000 units of Tropica.
2. Each Tropica unit requires 10 minutes to produce. Three people in the Machinery Department work full time (2,000 hours per year) producing Tropica. Each person is paid $12 per hour.
3. The cost of materials per Tropica unit is $2.20.
4. Manufacturing costs directly applicable to the production of Tropica are: indirect labor, $6,000; utilities, $1,500; depreciation, $1,800; property taxes and insurance, $1,000. All of the costs will be eliminated if Tropica is purchased.
5. The lowest price for a Tropica from an outside supplier is $4 per unit. Freight charges will be $0.50 per unit, and a part-time receiving clerk at $8,500 per year will be required.
6. If Tropica is purchased, the excess space will be used to store Dunham's finished product. Currently, Dunham rents storage space at approximately $0.80 per unit stored per year. Approximately 5,000 units per year are stored in the rented space.

Instructions

(a) NI decrease $2,700

(a) Prepare an incremental analysis for the make or buy decision. Should Dunham make or buy the part? Why?

(b) NI increase $9,300

(b) Prepare an incremental analysis, assuming the released facilities can be used to produce $12,000 of net income in addition to the savings on the rental of storage space. What decision should now be made?

(c) What nonfinancial factors should be considered in the decision?

Determine if product should be sold or processed further.

(SO 5)

P9-3B Bonita Household Products Co. is a diversified household cleaner processing company. The company's Poway plant produces two products: a glass cleaner and a metal cleaner from a common set of chemical inputs, (TLC). Each week 1,000,000 ounces of chemical input are processed at a cost of $200,000 into 750,000 ounces of metal cleaner and 250,000 ounces of glass cleaner. The metal cleaner has no market value until it is converted into a polish with the trade name MetalShine. The additional processing costs for this conversion amount to $270,000. MetalShine sells at $15 per 25-ounce bottle.

The glass cleaner can be sold for $24 per 25-ounce bottle. However, the glass cleaner can be converted into two other products by adding 250,000 ounces of another compound (MST) to the 250,000 ounces of glass cleaner. This joint process will yield 250,000 ounces each of plastic cleaner (PC) and plastic polish (PP). The additional processing costs for this process amount to $140,000. Both plastic products can be sold for $20 per 25-ounce bottle.

The company decided not to process the glass cleaner into PC and PP based on the following analysis.

		Process Further		
	Glass Cleaner	Plastic Cleaner (PC)	Plastic Polish (PP)	Total
Production in ounces	(250,000)	(250,000)	(250,000)	
Revenue	$240,000	$200,000	$200,000	$400,000
Costs:				
TLC costs	50,000*	40,000	40,000	80,000**
MST costs	0	70,000	70,000	140,000
Total costs	50,000	110,000	110,000	220,000
Weekly gross profit	$190,000	$ 90,000	$ 90,000	$180,000

*If glass cleaner is not processed further it is allocated ¼ of the $200,000 of TLC cost, which is equal to ¼ of the total physical output.

**If glass cleaner is processed further, total physical output is 1,250,000 ounces. PC and PP combined account for 40% of the total physical output and are each allocated 20% of the TLC cost.

Instructions

(a) Determine if management made the correct decision to not process the glass cleaner further by doing the following.

(1) Calculate the company's total weekly gross profit assuming the glass cleaner is not processed further.

(2) Calculate the company's total weekly gross profit assuming the glass cleaner is processed further. (2) Gross profit $240,000

(3) Compare the resulting net incomes and comment on management's decision.

(b) Using incremental analysis, determine if the glass cleaner should be processed further.

(CMA adapted)

P9-4B Quik Press Inc. offers one-day dry cleaning. At the beginning of 2008, the company purchased a mechanized pressing machine. The owner of the company, Jill Jabowski, recently returned from an industry equipment exhibition where she watched a computerized press demonstrated. She was impressed with the machine's speed, efficiency, and quality of output. Upon returning from the exhibition, she asked her purchasing agent to collect price and operating cost data on the new press. In addition, she asked the company's accountant to provide her with cost data on the company's press. This information is presented below.

Compute gain or loss, and determine if equipment should be replaced.

(SO 6)

	Old Press	New Press
Purchase price	$120,000	$150,000
Estimated salvage value	0	0
Estimated useful life	6 years	5 years
Depreciation method	Straight-line	Straight-line
Annual operating expenses other than depreciation:		
Variable	$30,000	$10,000
Fixed	20,000	7,000

Annual revenues are $200,000, and selling and administrative expenses are $24,000, regardless of which press is used. If the old press is replaced now, at the beginning of 2009, Quik Press will be able to sell it for $10,000.

Instructions

(a) Determine any gain or loss if the old press is replaced.

(b) Prepare a 5-year summarized income statement for each of the following assumptions:

(1) The old press is retained.

(2) The old press is replaced. (b)(2) NI $555,000

(c) Using incremental analysis, determine if the old press should be replaced. (c) NI increase $25,000

(d) Write a memo to Jill Jabowski explaining why any gain or loss should be ignored in the decision to replace the old press.

P9-5B Hindu Manufacturing Company has four operating divisions. During the first quarter of 2008, the company reported total income from operations of $36,000 and the following results for the divisions.

Compute contribution margin and prepare incremental analysis concerning elimination of divisions.

(SO 7)

	Division			
	Taos	Boseman	Salem	Olympia
Sales	$405,000	$730,000	$920,000	$500,000
Cost of goods sold	400,000	480,000	576,000	390,000
Selling and administrative expenses	100,000	207,000	246,000	120,000
Income (loss) from operations	$(95,000)	$ 43,000	$ 98,000	$(10,000)

Analysis reveals the following percentages of variable costs in each division.

	Taos	Boseman	Salem	Olympia
Cost of goods sold	90%	80%	90%	95%
Selling and administrative expenses	60	60	70	80

Discontinuance of any division would save 70% of the fixed costs and expenses for that division.

Top management is deeply concerned about the unprofitable divisions (Taos and Olympia). The consensus is that one or both of the divisions should be eliminated.

Instructions

(a) Compute the contribution margin for the two unprofitable divisions. (a) Olympia $33,500

(b) Prepare an incremental analysis concerning the possible elimination of (1) the Taos Division and (2) the Olympia Division. What course of action do you recommend for each division?

(c) Income Salem $86,000

(c) Prepare a columnar condensed income statement using the CVP format for Hindu Manufacturing Company, assuming (1) the Taos Division is eliminated, and (2) the unavoidable fixed costs and expenses of the Taos Division are allocated 30% to Boseman, 50% to Salem, and 20% to Olympia.

(d) Compare the total income from operations with the Taos Division ($36,000) to total income from operations without this division.

PROBLEMS: SET C

Visit the book's website at **www.wiley.com/college/weygandt**, and choose the Student Companion site, to access Problem Set C.

WATERWAYS CONTINUING PROBLEM

(This is a continuation of the Waterways Problem from previous chapters.)

WCP9 Waterways Corporation is considering various business opportunities. It wants to make best use of its production facilities to maximize income. This problem asks you to help Waterways do incremental analysis on these various opportunities.

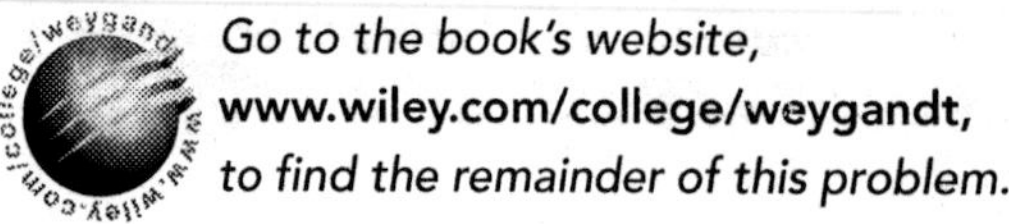

Go to the book's website,
www.wiley.com/college/weygandt,
to find the remainder of this problem.

BROADENING YOUR PERSPECTIVE

DECISION MAKING ACROSS THE ORGANIZATION

BYP9-1 Castle Company is considering the purchase of a new machine. The invoice price of the machine is $125,000, freight charges are estimated to be $4,000, and installation costs are expected to be $6,000. Salvage value of the new equipment is expected to be zero after a useful life of 4 years. Existing equipment could be retained and used for an additional 4 years if the new machine is not purchased. At that time, the salvage value of the equipment would be zero. If the new machine is purchased now, the existing machine would have to be scrapped. Castle's accountant, Shaida Fang, has accumulated the following data regarding annual sales and expenses with and without the new machine.

1. Without the new machine, Castle can sell 12,000 units of product annually at a per unit selling price of $100. If the new machine is purchased, the number of units produced and sold would increase by 20%, and the selling price would remain the same.
2. The new machine is faster than the old machine, and it is more efficient in its usage of materials. With the old machine the gross profit rate will be 25% of sales, whereas the rate will be 30% of sales with the new machine.
3. Annual selling expenses are $180,000 with the current equipment. Because the new equipment would produce a greater number of units to be sold, annual selling expenses are expected to increase by 10% if it is purchased.
4. Annual administrative expenses are expected to be $100,000 with the old machine, and $113,000 with the new machine.
5. The current book value of the existing machine is $36,000. Castle uses straight-line depreciation.

Instructions

With the class divided into groups, prepare an incremental analysis for the 4 years showing whether Castle should keep the existing machine or buy the new machine. (Ignore income tax effects.)

MANAGERIAL ANALYSIS

BYP9-2 Technology Plus manufactures private-label small electronic products, such as alarm clocks, calculators, kitchen timers, stopwatches, and automatic pencil sharpeners. Some of the products are sold as sets, and others are sold individually. Products are studied as to their sales potential, and then cost estimates are made. The Engineering Department develops production plans, and then production begins. The company has generally had very successful product introductions. Only two products introduced by the company have been discontinued.

One of the products currently sold is a multi-alarm alarm clock. The clock has four alarms that can be programmed to sound at various times and for varying lengths of time. The company has experienced a great deal of difficulty in making the circuit boards for the clocks. The production process has never operated smoothly. The product is unprofitable at the present time, primarily because of warranty repairs and product recalls. Two models of the clocks were recalled, for example, because they sometimes caused an electric shock when the alarms were being shut off. The Engineering Department is attempting to revise the manufacturing process, but the revision will take another 6 months at least.

The clocks were very popular when they were introduced, and since they are private-label, the company has not suffered much from the recalls. Presently, the company has a very large order for several items from Kmart Stores. The order includes 5,000 of the multi-alarm clocks. When the company suggested that Kmart purchase the clocks from another manufacturer, Kmart threatened to rescind the entire order unless the clocks were included.

The company has therefore investigated the possibility of having another company make the clocks for them. The clocks were bid for the Kmart order based on an estimated $6.65 cost to manufacture:

Circuit board, 1 each @ $2.00	$2.00
Plastic case, 1 each @ $0.75	0.75
Alarms, 4 @ $0.10 each	0.40
Labor, 15 minutes @ $12/hour	3.00
Overhead, $2.00 per labor hour	0.50

Technology Plus could purchase clocks to fill the Kmart order for $11 from Silver Star, a Korean manufacturer with a very good quality record. Silver Star has offered to reduce the price to $7.50 after Technology Plus has been a customer for 6 months, placing an order of at least 1,000 units per month. If Technology Plus becomes a "preferred customer" by purchasing 15,000 units per year, the price would be reduced still further to $4.50.

Alpha Products, a local manufacturer, has also offered to make clocks for Technology Plus. They have offered to sell 5,000 clocks for $4 each. However, Alpha Products has been in business for only 6 months. They have experienced significant turnover in their labor force, and the local press has reported that the owners may face tax evasion charges soon. The owner of Alpha Products is an electronic engineer, however, and the quality of the clocks is likely to be good.

If Technology Plus decides to purchase the clocks from either Silver Star or Alpha, all the costs to manufacture could be avoided, except a total of $5,000 in overhead costs for machine depreciation. The machinery is fairly new, and has no alternate use.

Instructions

(a) What is the difference in profit under each of the alternatives if the clocks are to be sold for $14.50 each to Kmart?

(b) What are the most important nonfinancial factors that Technology Plus should consider when making this decision?

(c) What do you think Technology Plus should do in regard to the Kmart order? What should it do in regard to continuing to manufacture the multi-alarm alarm clocks? Be prepared to defend your answer.

REAL-WORLD FOCUS

BYP9-3 Founded in 1983, Beverly Hills Fan Company is located in Woodland Hills, California. With 23 employees and sales of less than $10 million, the company is relatively small. Management feels that there is potential for growth in the upscale market for ceiling fans and lighting. They are particularly optimistic about growth in Mexican and Canadian markets.

Presented below is information from the president's letter in the company's annual report.

> **BEVERLY HILLS FAN COMPANY**
> President's Letter
>
> An aggressive product development program was initiated during the past year resulting in new ceiling fan models planned for introduction this year. Award winning industrial designer Ron Rezek created several new fan models for the Beverly Hills Fan and L.A. Fan lines, including a new Showroom Collection, designed specifically for the architectural and designer markets. Each of these models has received critical acclaim, and order commitments for this year have been outstanding. Additionally, our Custom Color and special order fans continued to enjoy increasing popularity and sales gains as more and more customers desire fans that match their specific interior decors. Currently, Beverly Hills Fan Company offers a product line of over 100 models of contemporary, traditional, and transitional ceiling fans.

Instructions

(a) What points did the company management need to consider before deciding to offer the special-order fans to customers?

(b) How would incremental analysis be employed to assist in this decision?

EXPLORING THE WEB

BYP9-4 Outsourcing by both manufacturers and service companies is becoming increasingly common. There are now many firms that specialize in outsourcing consulting.

Address: www.trowbridgegroup.net, or go to **www.wiley.com/college/weygandt**

Instructions

Go to the Web page of The Trowbridge Group at the address shown above, and answer the following questions.

(a) What are some of the ways that outsourcing can "strengthen the overall performance of the company"?

(b) What are some of the potential problems that arise when companies outsource?

COMMUNICATION ACTIVITY

BYP9-5 Jeff Howell is a production manager at a metal fabricating plant. Last night he read an article about a new piece of equipment that would dramatically reduce his division's costs. Jeff was very excited about the prospect, and the first thing he did this morning was to bring the article to his supervisor, Nathan Peas, the plant manager. The following conversation occurred:

Jeff: Nathan, I thought you would like to see this article on the new PDD1130; they've made some fantastic changes that could save us millions of dollars.

Nathan: I appreciate your interest Jeff, but I actually have been aware of the new machine for two months. The problem is that we just bought a new machine last year. We spent $2 million on that machine, and it was supposed to last us 12 years. If we replace it now we would have to write its book value off of the books for a huge loss. If I go to top management now and say that I want a new machine, they will fire me. I think we should use our existing machine for a couple of years, and then when it becomes obvious that we have to have a new machine, I will make the proposal.

Instructions

Jeff just completed a course in managerial accounting, and he believes that Nathan is making a big mistake. Write a memo from Jeff to Nathan explaining Nathan's decision-making error.

ETHICS CASE

BYP9-6 Robert Buey became Chief Executive Officer of Phelps Manufacturing two years ago. At the time, the company was reporting lagging profits, and Robert was brought in to "stir things up." The company has three divisions, electronics, fiber optics, and plumbing supplies. Robert has no interest in plumbing supplies, and one of the first things he did was to put pressure on his accountants to reallocate some of the company's fixed costs away from the other two divisions to the plumbing division. This had the effect of causing the plumbing division to report losses during the last two years; in the past it had always reported low, but acceptable, net income. Robert felt that this reallocation would shine a favorable light on him in front of the board of directors because it meant that the electronics and fiber optics divisions would look like they were improving. Given that these are "businesses of the future," he believed that the stock market would react favorably to these increases, while not penalizing the poor results of the plumbing division. Without this shift in the allocation of fixed costs, the profits of the electronics and fiber optics divisions would not have improved. But now the board of directors has suggested that the plumbing division be closed because it is reporting losses. This would mean that nearly 500 employees, many of whom have worked for Phelps their whole lives, would lose their jobs.

Instructions

(a) If a division is reporting losses, does that necessarily mean that it should be closed?
(b) Was the reallocation of fixed costs across divisions unethical?
(c) What should Robert do?

"ALL ABOUT YOU" ACTIVITY

BYP9-7 Managerial accounting techniques can be used in a wide variety of settings. As we have frequently pointed out, you can use them in many personal situations. They also can be useful in trying to find solutions for societal issues that appear to be hard to solve.

Instructions

Read the *Fortune* article, "The Toughest Customers: How Hardheaded Business Metrics Can Help the Hard-core Homeless," by Cait Murphy, available at *http://money.cnn.com/magazines/fortune/fortune_archive/2006/04/03/8373067/index.htm.* Answer the following questions.

(a) How does the article define "chronic" homelessness?
(b) In what ways does homelessness cost a city money? What are the estimated costs of a chronic homeless person to various cities?
(c) What are the steps suggested to address the problem?
(d) What is the estimated cost of implementing this program in New York? What results have been seen?
(e) In terms of incremental analysis, frame the relevant costs in this situation.

Answers to Insight and Accounting Across the Organization Questions

These Wheels Have Miles Before Installation, p. 413

Q: What are the disadvantages of outsourcing to a foreign country?

A: *Possible disadvantages of outsourcing are that the supplier loses control over the quality of the product, as well as the timing of production. Also, the company exposes itself to price changes caused by changes in the value of the foreign currency. In addition, shipping large, heavy products such as tires is costly, and disruptions in shipping (due to strikes, weather, etc.) can cause delays in final assembly of vehicles. As a result of the outsourcing, the company will have to reassign, or even lay off, many skilled workers. Not only is this very disruptive to the lives of those employees, it also hurts morale of the remaining employees. As more U.S. employers begin to use robotic automation in their facilities, they are able to reduce the amount of labor required, and thus are beginning to be able to compete more favorably with foreign suppliers.*

Time to Move to a New Neighborhood? p. 418

Q: What were some of the factors that complicated the company's decision to move? How should the company have incorporated such factors into its incremental analysis?

A: *The company received only $7.5 million for its California property, only 58 of 75 key employees were willing to move, construction was delayed by a year which caused the new plant to increase in price by $1.5 million, and wages surged in Idaho due to low unemployment. In performing incremental analysis of the decision to move, a company should perform sensitivity analysis. This would include evaluating the impact on the decision if all costs were, for example, 10% higher than expected or if cost savings were 10% lower than expected.*

What Is the Real Cost of Packaging Options? p. 420

Q: If your marketing director suggests that, in addition to selling your cereal in a standard-size box, you should sell a jumbo size and an individual size, what issues must you consider?

A: *In evaluating this decision, you should identify the incremental revenues as well as incremental costs. The marketing manager is most likely focusing on the fact that by offering alternative packaging options, the company can market the product to a broader range of customers. However, alternative packaging options will also result in additional costs. It will increase the number of setups, require different types of storage and handling, and increase the need for additional storage space for the packages and the packaged products.*

Authors' Comments on *All About You*: What Is a Degree Worth? (p. 421)

This is a very difficult decision. All of the evidence suggests that your short-term and long-term prospects will be far greater with some form of post–high-school degree. Because of this, we feel strongly that you should make every effort to continue your education. Many of the discussions provided in this text present ideas on how to get control of your individual financial situation. We would encourage you to use these tools to identify ways to reduce your financial burden in order to continue your education. We also want to repeat that even taking only one course a semester is better than dropping out. Your instructors and advisors frequently provide advice to students who are faced with the decision about whether to continue with their education. If you are in this situation, we would encourage you to seek their advice since the implications of this decision can be long-lasting.

Answers to Self-Study Questions

1. d **2.** b **3.** c **4.** d **5.** d **6.** a **7.** b **8.** c **9.** b

Remember to go back to the Navigator box on the chapter-opening page and check off your completed work.

Chapter 10

Planning for Capital Investments

STUDY OBJECTIVES

After studying this chapter, you should be able to:

1. Discuss capital budgeting evaluation, and explain inputs used in capital budgeting.
2. Describe the cash payback technique.
3. Explain the net present value method.
4. Identify the challenges presented by intangible benefits in capital budgeting.
5. Describe the profitability index.
6. Indicate the benefits of performing a post-audit.
7. Explain the internal rate of return method.
8. Describe the annual rate of return method.

The Navigator

Scan **Study Objectives**	☐
Read **Feature Story**	☐
Read **Preview**	☐
Read text and answer **Before You Go On** p. 452 ☐ p. 462 ☐	
Work **Using the Decision Toolkit**	☐
Review **Summary of Study Objectives**	☐
Work **Demonstration Problem**	☐
Answer **Self-Study Questions**	☐
Complete **Assignments**	☐

Feature Story

SOUP IS GOOD FOOD

When you hear the word *Campbell*, what is the first thing that comes to mind? Soup. Campbell *is* soup. It sells 38% of all the soup—including homemade—consumed in the United States.

But can a company survive on soup alone? In an effort to expand its operations and to lessen its reliance on soup, Campbell Soup Company (*www.campbellsoup.com*) in 1990 began searching for an additional line of business. Campbell's management believed it saw an opportunity in convenient meals that were low in fat, nutritionally rich, and had therapeutic value for heart patients and diabetics. This venture would require a huge investment—but the rewards were potentially tremendous.

The initial investment required building food labs, hiring nutritional scientists, researching prototype products, constructing new production facilities, and marketing the new products. Management predicted that with an initial investment of roughly $55 million, the company might generate sales of $200 million per year.

By 1994 the company had created 24 meals, and an extensive field-study revealed considerable health benefits from the products. Unfortunately, initial sales of the new product line, called Intelligent Quisine, were less than stellar. In 1997 Campbell hired a consulting firm to evaluate whether to continue the project. Product development of the new line was costing $20 million per year—a sum that some managers felt could be better spent developing new products in other divisions or expanding overseas operations. In 1998 Campbell discontinued the project.

Campbell was not giving up on growth, but simply had decided to refocus its efforts on soup. The company's annual report stated management's philosophy: "Soup will be our growth engine." Campbell has sold off many of its nonsoup businesses, and in a recent year introduced 20 new soup products.

Source: Vanessa O'Connell, "Food for Thought: How Campbell Saw a Break-through Menu Turn into Leftovers," *Wall Street Journal,* October 6, 1998.

The Navigator

Inside Chapter 10

- **Investing for the Future** (p. 445)
- **It Need Not Cost an Arm and a Leg** (p. 455)
- **Are You Ready for the 50-Inch Screen?** (p. 458)
- **Seeing the Big Picture** (p. 459)
- ***All About You:* The Risks of Adjustable Rates** (p. 463)

Preview of Chapter 10

Companies like Campbell Soup must constantly determine how to invest their resources. Other examples: Hollywood studios recently built 25 new sound stage projects to allow for additional filming in future years. Starwood Hotels and Resorts Worldwide, Inc. committed a total of $1 billion to renovate its existing hotel properties, while at roughly the same time, the hotel industry canceled about $2 billion worth of *new* construction. Union Pacific Resources Group Inc. announced that it would cut its planned capital expenditures by 19% in order to use the funds to reduce its outstanding debt.

The process of making such capital expenditure decisions is referred to as capital budgeting. Capital budgeting involves choosing among various capital projects to find the one(s) that will maximize a company's return on its financial investment. The purpose of this chapter is to discuss the various techniques used to make effective capital budgeting decisions.

The content and organization of this chapter are as follows.

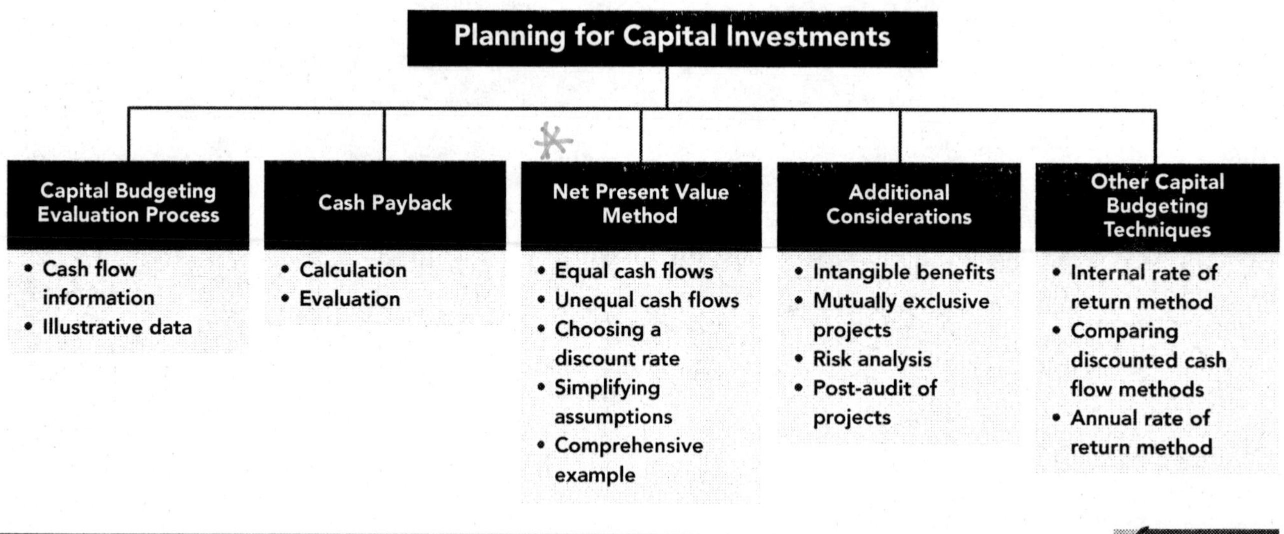

THE CAPITAL BUDGETING EVALUATION PROCESS

STUDY OBJECTIVE 1

Discuss capital budgeting evaluation, and explain inputs used in capital budgeting.

Many companies follow a carefully prescribed process in capital budgeting. At least once a year, top management requests proposals for projects from each department. A capital budgeting committee screens the proposals and submits its findings to the officers of the company. The officers, in turn, select the projects they believe to be most worthy of funding. They submit this list of projects to the board of directors. Ultimately, the directors approve the capital expenditure budget for the year. Illustration 10-1 (next page) shows this process.

The involvement of top management and the board of directors in the process demonstrates the importance of capital budgeting decisions. These decisions often have a significant impact on a company's future profitability. In fact, poor capital budgeting decisions can cost a lot of money, as the Campbell Soup Feature Story demonstrated. Such decisions have even led to the bankruptcy of some companies.

1. Project proposals are requested from departments, plants, and authorized personnel.

2. Proposals are screened by a capital budget committee.

3. Officers determine which projects are worthy of funding.

4. Board of directors approves capital budget.

Illustration 10-1
Corporate capital budget authorization process

MANAGEMENT INSIGHT

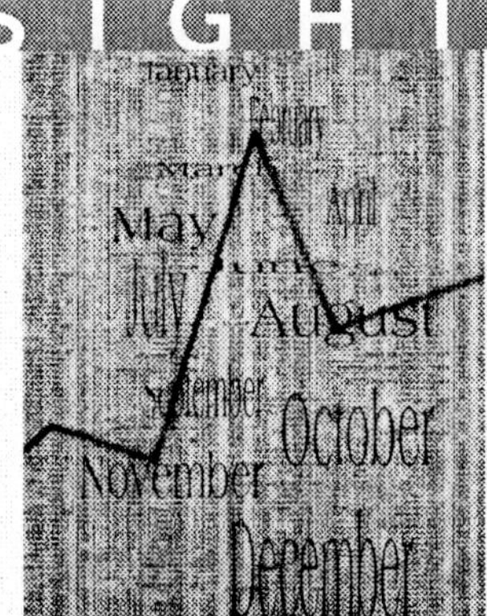

Investing for the Future

Monitoring capital expenditure amounts is one way to learn about a company's growth potential. Few companies can grow if they don't make significant capital investments. Here is a list of well-known companies and the amounts and types of their capital expenditures in a recent year.

Company Name	Amount	Type of Expenditures
Campbell Soup Company	$283 million	Acquisitions and plant expansions.
Barrick Gold Corporation	$228 million	Land acquisition and mine expansion.
Dell Computer Corporation	$329 million	Manufacturing and office facilities.
Sears, Roebuck and Co.	$925 million	New stores.
NIKE, Inc.	$186 million	Warehouse locations, management information systems.

Why is it important for top management to constantly monitor the nature, amount, and success of a company's capital expenditures?

Cash Flow Information

In this chapter we will look at several methods that help companies make effective capital budgeting decisions. Most of these methods employ **cash flow numbers**, rather than accrual accounting revenues and expenses. Remember from your financial accounting course that accrual accounting records *revenues* and *expenses*, rather than cash inflows and cash outflows. In fact, revenues and expenses measured during a period often differ significantly from their cash flow counterparts. Accrual accounting has advantages over cash accounting in many contexts. **For purposes of capital budgeting, though, estimated cash inflows and outflows are the preferred inputs**. Why? Because ultimately, the value of all financial investments is determined by the value of cash flows received and paid.

Sometimes cash flow information is not available. In this case, companies can make adjustments to accrual accounting numbers to estimate cash flow. Often, they estimate net annual cash flow by adding back depreciation expense to net income.

Depreciation expense is added back because it is an expense that does not require an outflow of cash. By adding back to net income the depreciation expense that was deducted in determining net income, companies determine net annual cash flow. Suppose, for example, that Reno Company's net income of $13,000 includes a charge for depreciation expense of $26,000. Its estimated net annual cash flow would be $39,000 ($13,000 + $26,000).

Illustration 10-2 lists some typical cash outflows and inflows related to equipment purchase and replacement.

Illustration 10-2
Typical cash flows relating to capital budgeting decisions

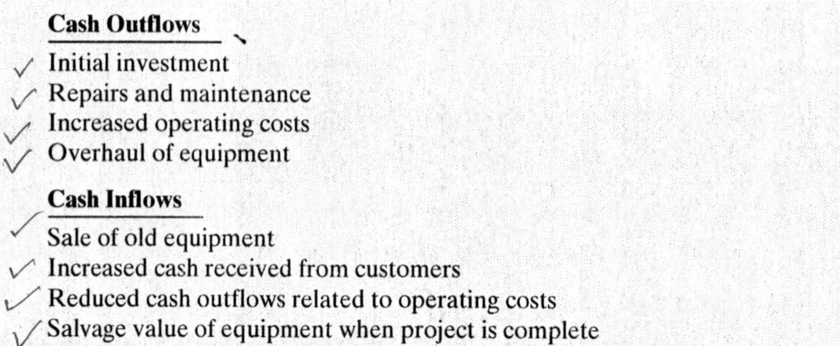

Cash Outflows

Initial investment
Repairs and maintenance
Increased operating costs
Overhaul of equipment

Cash Inflows

Sale of old equipment
Increased cash received from customers
Reduced cash outflows related to operating costs
Salvage value of equipment when project is complete

These cash flows are the inputs that are considered relevant in capital budgeting decisions.

The capital budgeting decision, under any technique, depends in part on a variety of considerations:

- **The availability of funds:** Does the company have unlimited funds, or will it have to ration capital investments?
- **Relationships among proposed projects:** Are proposed projects independent of each other, or does the acceptance or rejection of one depend on the acceptance or rejection of another?
- **The company's basic decision-making approach:** Does the company want to produce an accept-reject decision or a ranking of desirability among possible projects?
- **The risk associated with a particular project:** How certain are the projected returns? The certainty of estimates varies with such issues as market considerations or the length of time before returns are expected.

Illustrative Data

For our initial discussion of quantitative capital budgeting techniques, we will use a continuing example, which will enable us to compare the results of the various techniques. Assume that Stewart Soup Company is considering an investment of $130,000 in new equipment. The new equipment is expected to last 10 years. It will have a zero salvage value at the end of its useful life. The annual cash inflows are $200,000, and the annual cash outflows are $176,000. Illustration 10-3 summarizes these data.

Illustration 10-3
Investment information for Stewart Soup example

Initial investment	$130,000
Estimated useful life	10 years
Estimated salvage value	–0–
Estimated annual cash flows	
Cash inflows from customers	$200,000
Cash outflows for operating costs	176,000
Net annual cash flow	$ 24,000

In the following two sections we will examine two popular techniques for evaluating capital investments: cash payback and the net present value method.

CASH PAYBACK

STUDY OBJECTIVE 2

Describe the cash payback technique.

The **cash payback technique** identifies the time period required to recover the cost of the capital investment from the net annual cash flow produced by the investment. Illustration 10-4 presents the formula for computing the cash payback period.

Cost of Capital Investment	÷	Net Annual Cash Flow	=	Cash Payback Period

Illustration 10-4
Cash payback formula

The cash payback period in the Stewart Soup example is 5.42 years, computed as follows.

$$\$130,000 \div \$24,000 = 5.42 \text{ years}$$

HELPFUL HINT

Net annual cash flow can also be approximated by "Net cash provided by operating activities" from the statement of cash flows.

The evaluation of the payback period is often related to the expected useful life of the asset. For example, assume that at Stewart Soup a project is unacceptable if the payback period is longer than 60% of the asset's expected useful life. The 5.42-year payback period in this case is a bit over 50% of the project's expected useful life. Thus, the project is acceptable.

It follows that when the payback technique is used to decide among acceptable alternative projects, **the shorter the payback period, the more attractive the investment.** This is true for two reasons: First, the earlier the investment is recovered, the sooner the company can use the cash funds for other purposes. Second, the risk of loss from obsolescence and changed economic conditions is less in a shorter payback period.

The preceding computation of the cash payback period assumes **equal** net annual cash flows in each year of the investment's life. In many cases, this assumption is not valid. In the case of **uneven** net annual cash flows, the company determines the cash payback period when the cumulative net cash flows from the investment equal the cost of the investment.

To illustrate, assume that Chen Company proposes an investment in a new website that is estimated to cost $300,000. Illustration 10-5 shows the proposed investment cost, net annual cash flows, cumulative net cash flows, and the cash payback period.

Year	Investment	Net Annual Cash Flow	Cumulative Net Cash Flow
0	$300,000		
1		$ 60,000	$ 60,000
2		90,000	150,000
3		90,000	240,000
4		120,000	360,000
5		100,000	460,000

Cash payback period = 3.5 years

Illustration 10-5
Cash inflow schedule

As Illustration 10-5 shows, at the end of year 3, cumulative cash inflow of $240,000 is less than the investment cost of $300,000, but at the end of year 4 the cumulative cash inflow of $360,000 exceeds the investment cost. The cash inflow needed in year 4 to equal the investment cost is $60,000 ($300,000 − $240,000). Assuming the cash inflow occurred evenly during year 4, we then divide this amount by the net annual cash flow in year 4 ($120,000) to determine the point during the year when the cash payback occurs. Thus, we get 0.50 ($60,000/$120,000), or half of the year, and the cash payback period is 3.5 years.

The cash payback technique may be useful as an initial screening tool. It may be the most critical factor in the capital budgeting decision for a company that desires a fast turnaround of its investment because of a weak cash position. It also is relatively easy to compute and understand.

However, cash payback should not ordinarily be the only basis for the capital budgeting decision because it ignores the expected profitability of the project. To illustrate, assume that Projects A and B have the same payback period, but Project A's useful life is double the useful life of Project B. Project A's earning power, therefore, is twice as long as Project B's. A further—and major—disadvantage of this technique is that it ignores the time value of money.

NET PRESENT VALUE METHOD

STUDY OBJECTIVE 3

Explain the net present value method.

Recognition of the time value of money can make a significant difference in the long-term impact of the capital budgeting decision. For example, cash flows that occur early in the life of an investment will be worth more than those that occur later—because of the time value of money. Therefore it is useful to recognize the timing of cash flows when evaluating projects.

Capital budgeting techniques that take into account both the time value of money and the estimated net cash flow from an investment are called **discounted cash flow techniques**. They are generally recognized as the most informative and best conceptual approaches to making capital budgeting decisions. The expected net cash flow used in discounting cash flows consists of the annual net cash flows plus the estimated liquidation proceeds (salvage value) when the asset is sold for salvage at the end of its useful life.

The primary discounted cash flow technique is the **net present value method**. A second method, discussed later in the chapter, is the **internal rate of return**. At this point, before you read on, **we recommend that you examine Appendix C** at the end of the book to review time value of money concepts, upon which these methods are based.

The **net present value (NPV) method** involves discounting net cash flows to their present value and then comparing that present value with the capital outlay required by the investment. The difference between these two amounts is referred to as **net present value (NPV)**. Company management determines what interest rate to use in discounting the future net cash flows. This rate, often referred to as the **discount rate** or **required rate of return** is discussed in a later section.

The NVP decision rule is this: **A proposal is acceptable when net present value is zero or positive.** At either of those values, the rate of return on the investment equals or exceeds the required rate of return. When net present value is negative, the project is unacceptable. Illustration 10-6 (next page) shows the net present value decision criteria.

When making a selection among acceptable proposals, **the higher the positive net present value, the more attractive the investment**. The application of this method to two cases is described in the next two sections. In each case, we will assume that the investment has no salvage value at the end of its useful life.

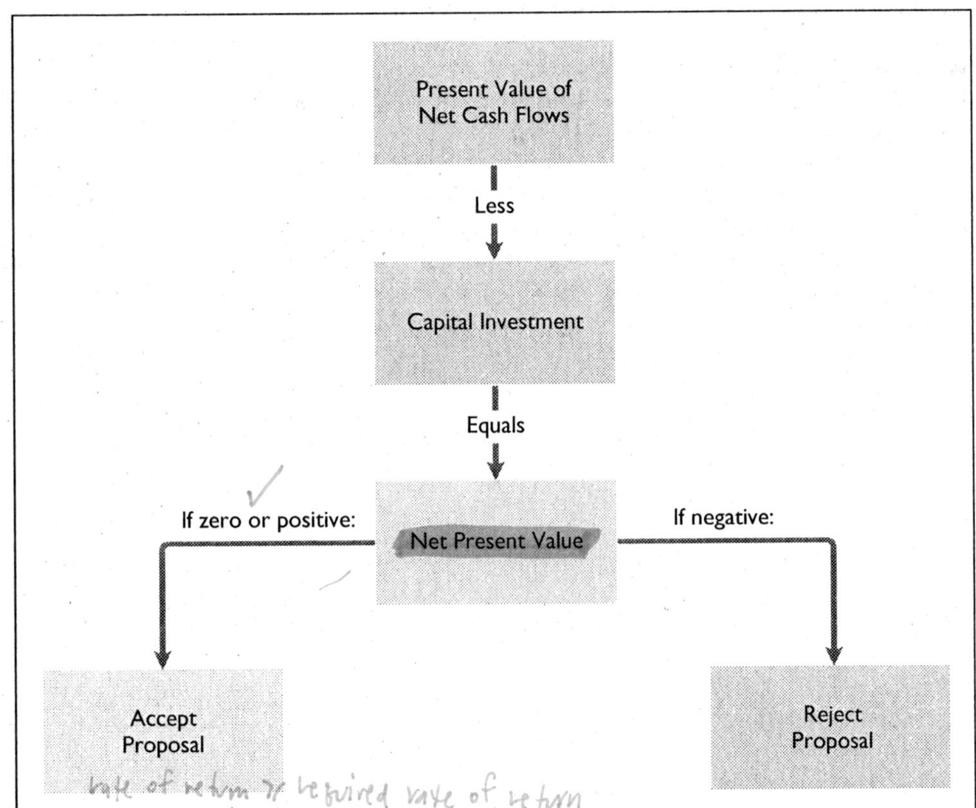

Illustration 10-6
Net present value decision criteria

Equal Annual Cash Flows

In our Stewart Soup Company example, the company's net annual cash flows are $24,000. If we assume this amount **is uniform over the asset's useful life**, we can compute the present value of the net annual cash flows by using the present value of an annuity of 1 for 10 periods (from Table 4, Appendix C). Assuming a discount rate of 12%, the present value of net cash flows are as shown in Illustration 10-7 (rounded to the nearest dollar).

HELPFUL HINT

The ABC Co. expects equal cash flows over an asset's 5-year useful life. What discount factor should it use in determining present values if management wants (1) a 12% return or (2) a 15% return? Answer: Using Table 4, the factors are (1) 3.60478 and (2) 3.35216.

Illustration 10-7
Computation of present value of equal net annual cash flows

	Present Value at 12%
Discount factor for 10 periods	5.65022
Present value of net cash flows:	
$24,000 × 5.65022	$135,605

The analysis of the proposal by the net present value method is as follows.

Illustration 10-8
Computation of net present value—equal net annual cash flows

	12%
Present value of net cash flows	$135,605
Capital investment	130,000
Net present value	$ 5,605

The proposed capital expenditure is acceptable at a required rate of return of 12% because the net present value is positive.

Unequal Annual Cash Flows

When net annual cash flows are unequal, we cannot use annuity tables to calculate their present value. Instead, we use tables showing the **present value of a single future amount for each annual cash flow**.

To illustrate, assume that Stewart Soup Company expects the same total net cash flows of $240,000 over the life of the investment. But because of a declining market demand for the new product over the life of the equipment, the net annual cash flows are higher in the early years and lower in the later years. The present value of the net annual cash flows is calculated as follows, using Table 3 in Appendix C.

HELPFUL HINT
Appendix C demonstrates the use of a financial calculator to solve time value of money problems.

Illustration 10-9
Computation of present value of unequal annual cash flows

Year	Assumed Net Annual Cash Flows	Discount Factor 12%	Present Value 12%
	(1)	(2)	(1) × (2)
1	$ 34,000	.89286	$ 30,357
2	30,000	.79719	23,916
3	27,000	.71178	19,218
4	25,000	.63552	15,888
5	24,000	.56743	13,618
6	22,000	.50663	11,146
7	21,000	.45235	9,499
8	20,000	.40388	8,078
9	19,000	.36061	6,852
10	18,000	.32197	5,795
	$240,000		$ 144,367

Therefore, the analysis of the proposal by the net present value method is as follows.

Illustration 10-10
Computation of net present value—unequal annual cash flows

	12%
Present value of net cash flows	$144,367
Capital investment	130,000
Net present value	**$ 14,367**

In this example, the present value of the net cash flows is greater than the $130,000 capital investment. Thus, the project is acceptable at a 12% required rate of return. The difference between the present values using the 12% rate under equal cash flows ($135,605) and unequal cash flows ($144,367) is due to the pattern of the flows. Since more money is received sooner under this particular uneven cash flow scenario, its present value is greater.

Choosing a Discount Rate

Now that you understand how companies apply the net present value method, it is logical to ask a related question: How is a discount rate (required rate of return) determined in real capital budgeting decisions? In most instances a company uses a required rate of return equal to its **cost of capital**—that is, the rate that it must pay to obtain funds from creditors and stockholders.

The cost of capital is a weighted average of the rates paid on borrowed funds as well as on funds provided by investors in the company's common stock and preferred stock. If management believes a project is riskier than the company's usual line of business, the discount rate should be increased. That is, the discount rate has two elements, a cost of capital element and a risk element. Often companies assume the risk element is equal to zero.

HELPFUL HINT
Cost of capital is the rate that management expects to pay on all borrowed and equity funds. It does not relate to the cost of funding a *specific* project.

Using an incorrect discount rate can lead to incorrect capital budgeting decisions. Consider again the Stewart Soup example in Illustration 10-8, where we used a discount rate of 12%. Suppose that this rate does not take into account the fact that this project is riskier than most of the company's investments. A more appropriate discount rate, given the risk, might be 15%. Illustration 10-11 compares the net present values at the two rates. At the higher, more appropriate discount rate of 15%, the net present value is negative, and the company should reject the project.

Illustration 10-11
Comparison of net present values at different discount rates

	Present Values at Different Discount Rates	
	12%	15%
Discount factor for 10 periods	5.65022	5.01877
Present value of net cash flows:		
$24,000 × 5.65022	$135,605	
$24,000 × 5.01877		$120,450
Capital investment	130,000	130,000
Positive (negative) net present value	$ 5,605	$ (9,550)

The discount rate is often referred to by alternative names, including the **required rate of return**, the **hurdle rate**, and the **cutoff rate**. Determination of the cost of capital varies somewhat depending on whether the entity is a for-profit or not-for-profit enterprise. Calculation of the cost of capital is discussed more fully in advanced accounting and finance courses.

Simplifying Assumptions

In our examples of the net present value method, we have made a number of simplifying assumptions:

- **All cash flows come at the end of each year.** In reality, cash flows will come at uneven intervals throughout the year. However, it is far simpler to assume that all cash flows come at the end (or in some cases the beginning) of the year. In fact, this assumption is frequently made in practice.
- **All cash flows are immediately reinvested in another project that has a similar return.** In most capital budgeting situations, companies receive cash flows during each year of a project's life. In order to determine the return on the investment, some assumption must be made about how the cash flows are reinvested in the year that they are received. It is customary to assume that cash flows received are reinvested in some other project of similar return until the end of the project's life.
- **All cash flows can be predicted with certainty.** The outcomes of business investments are full of uncertainty, as the Campbell Soup Feature Story shows. There is no way of knowing how popular a new product will be, how long a new machine will last, or what competitors' reactions might be to changes in a product. But, in order to make investment decisions, analysts must estimate future

outcomes. In this chapter we have assumed that future amounts are known with certainty.[1] In reality, little is known with certainty. More advanced capital budgeting techniques deal with uncertainty by considering the probability that various outcomes will occur.

Before You Go On...

REVIEW IT

1. What is the cash payback technique? What are its strengths and weaknesses?
2. What is the net present value decision rule to determine whether a project is acceptable?
3. What are common assumptions made in capital budgeting decisions?

DO IT

Watertown Paper Corporation is considering adding another machine for the manufacture of corrugated cardboard. The machine would cost $800,000. It would have an estimated life of 7 years and a salvage value of $40,000. The company estimates that annual cash inflows would increase by $400,000 and that annual cash outflows would increase by $190,000. Management believes a discount rate of 9% is appropriate. Using the net present value technique, should Watertown Paper accept the project?

Action Plan

- Use the NPV technique to calculate the difference between the present value of net cash flows and the initial investment.
- Accept the project if the net present value is positive.

Solution

Estimated annual cash inflows	$400,000
Estimated annual cash outflows	190,000
Net annual cash flow	$210,000

	Cash Flows	×	9% Discount Factor	=	Present Value
Present value of net annual cash flows	$210,000	×	5.03295[a]	=	$1,056,920
Present value of salvage value	$ 40,000	×	.54703[b]	=	21,881
Present value of net cash flows					1,078,801
Capital investment					800,000
Net present value					$ 278,801

[a]Table 4, Appendix C.
[b]Table 3, Appendix C.

Since the net present value is positive, the project is acceptable.

Related exercise material: *BE10-2, BE10-3, BE10-4, BE10-5, E10-1, E10-2, and E10-3.*

Comprehensive Example

Best Taste Foods is considering investing in new equipment to produce fat-free snack foods. Management believes that although demand for fat-free foods has leveled off, fat-free foods are here to stay. The following estimated costs, cost

[1]One exception is a brief discussion of sensitivity analysis later in the chapter.

of capital, and cash flows were determined in consultation with the marketing, production, and finance departments.

Illustration 10-12 Investment information for Best Taste Foods example

Initial investment	$1,000,000
Cost of equipment overhaul in 5 years	$200,000
Salvage value of equipment in 10 years	$20,000
Cost of capital (discount rate)	15%
Estimated annual cash flows	
Cash inflows received from sales	$500,000
Cash outflows for cost of goods sold	$200,000
Maintenance costs	$30,000
Other direct operating costs	$40,000

Remember that we are using cash flows in our analysis, not accrual revenues and expenses. Thus, for example, the direct operating costs would not include depreciation expense, since depreciation expense does not use cash. Illustration 10-13 presents the computation of the net annual cash flows of this project.

Illustration 10-13 Computation of net annual cash flow

Cash inflows received from sales	$ 500,000
Cash outflows for cost of goods sold	(200,000)
Maintenance costs	(30,000)
Other direct operating costs	(40,000)
Net annual cash flow	**$ 230,000**

Illustration 10-14 shows computation of the net present value for this proposed investment.

Illustration 10-14 Computation of net present value for Best Taste Foods investment

Event	Time Period	Cash Flow	×	15% Discount Factor	=	Present Value
Equipment purchase	0	$1,000,000		1.00000		$(1,000,000)
Equipment overhaul	5	200,000		.49718		(99,436)
Net annual cash flow	1–10	230,000		5.01877		1,154,317
Salvage value	10	20,000		.24719		4,944
Net present value						**$ 59,825**

Because the net present value of the project is positive, Best Taste should accept the project.

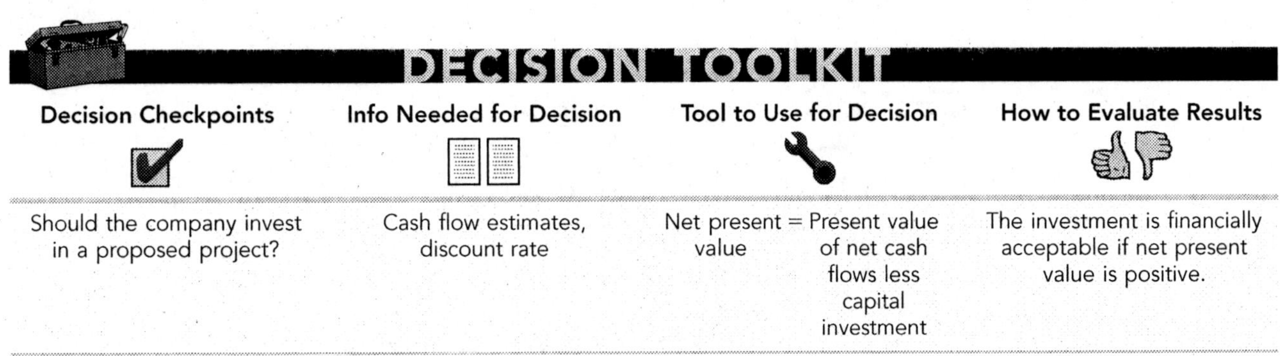

DECISION TOOLKIT
Decision Checkpoints
Info Needed for Decision
Tool to Use for Decision
How to Evaluate Results
Should the company invest in a proposed project?
Cash flow estimates, discount rate
Net present value = Present value of net cash flows less capital investment
The investment is financially acceptable if net present value is positive.

ADDITIONAL CONSIDERATIONS

Now that you understand how the net present value method works, we can add some "additional wrinkles." Specifically, these are: the impact of intangible benefits, a way to compare mutually exclusive projects, refinements that take risk into account, and the need to conduct post-audits of investment projects.

Intangible Benefits

STUDY OBJECTIVE 4

Identify the challenges presented by intangible benefits in capital budgeting.

The NPV evaluation techniques employed thus far rely on tangible costs and benefits that can be relatively easily quantified. Some investment projects, especially high-tech projects, fail to make it through initial capital budget screens because only the project's tangible benefits are considered. *Intangible benefits* might include increased quality, improved safety, or enhanced employee loyalty. By ignoring intangible benefits, capital budgeting techniques might incorrectly eliminate projects that could be financially beneficial to the company.

To avoid rejecting projects that actually should be accepted, analysts suggest two possible approaches:

1. Calculate net present value ignoring intangible benefits. Then, if the NPV is negative, ask whether the project offers any intangible benefits that are worth at least the amount of the negative NPV.
2. Project rough, conservative estimates of the value of the intangible benefits, and incorporate these values into the NPV calculation.

EXAMPLE

Assume that Berg Company is considering the purchase of a new mechanical robot to be used for soldering electrical connections. Illustration 10-15 shows the estimates related to this proposed purchase.

Illustration 10-15
Investment information for Berg Company example

Initial investment	$200,000				
Annual cash inflows	$ 50,000				
Annual cash outflows	20,000				
Net annual cash flow	**$ 30,000**				
Estimated life of equipment	10 years				
Discount rate	12%				

	Cash Flows	×	12% Discount Factor	=	Present Value
Present value of net cash flows	$30,000	×	5.65022	=	$169,507
Initial investment					200,000
Net present value					**$ (30,493)**

Based on the negative net present value of $30,493, the proposed project is not acceptable. This calculation, however, ignores important information. First, the company's engineers believe that purchasing this machine will dramatically improve the electrical connections in the company's products. As a result, future warranty costs will be reduced. Also, the company believes that higher quality will translate into higher future sales. Finally, the new machine will be much safer than the previous one.

Berg can incorporate this new information into the capital budgeting decision in the two ways listed earlier. First, management might simply ask whether the reduced warranty costs, increased sales, and improved safety benefits have an estimated total present value to the company of at least $30,493. If yes, then the project is acceptable.

Alternatively, analysts can estimate the annual cash flows of these benefits. In our initial calculation, we assumed each of these benefits to have a value of zero. It seems likely that their actual values are much higher than zero. Given the difficulty of estimating these benefits, however, conservative values should be assigned to them. If, after using conservative estimates, the net present value is positive, Berg should accept the project.

To illustrate, assume that Berg estimates that improved sales will increase cash inflows by $10,000 annually as a result of an increase in perceived quality. Berg also estimates that annual cost outflows would be reduced by $5,000 as a result of lower warranty claims, reduced injury claims, and missed work. Consideration of the intangible benefits results in the following revised NPV calculation.

Illustration 10-16
Revised investment information for Berg Company example, including intangible benefits

Initial investment	$200,000
Annual cash inflows (revised)	$ 60,000
Annual cash outflows (revised)	15,000
Net annual cash flow	**$ 45,000**
Estimated life of equipment	10 years
Discount rate	12%

	Cash Flows	×	12% Discount Factor	=	Present Value
Present value of net annual cash flows	$45,000	×	5.65022	=	$254,260
Initial investment					200,000
Net present value					**$ 54,260**

Using these conservative estimates of the value of the additional benefits, Berg should accept the project.

ETHICS INSIGHT

It Need Not Cost an Arm and a Leg

Most manufacturers say that employee safety matters above everything else. But how many back up this statement with investments that improve employee safety? Recently a woodworking hobbyist who also happens to be a patent attorney with a Ph.D. in physics invented a mechanism that automatically shuts down a power saw when the saw blade comes in contact with human flesh. The blade stops so quickly that only minor injuries result.

Power saws injure 40,000 Americans each year, and 4,000 of those injuries are bad enough to require amputation. Therefore, one might think that power-saw companies would be lined up to incorporate this mechanism into their saws. But, in the words of one power-tool company, "Safety doesn't sell." Since existing saw manufacturers were unwilling to incorporate the device into their saws, eventually the inventor started his own company to build the devices and sell them directly to businesses that use power saws.

Source: Melba Newsome, "An Edgy New Idea," *Time: Inside Business*, May 2006, p. A16.

In addition to the obvious humanitarian benefit of reducing serious injuries, how else might the manufacturer of this product convince potential customers of its worth?

Mutually Exclusive Projects

In theory, companies should accept all projects with positive NPVs. However, companies rarely are able to adopt all positive-NPV proposals. First, proposals often are **mutually exclusive**. This means that if the company adopts one proposal, it would be impossible also to adopt the other proposal. For example, a company may be considering the purchase of a new packaging machine and is looking at various brands and models. It needs only one packaging machine. Once the company has determined which brand and model to purchase, the others will not be purchased—even though they also may have positive net present values.

Even in instances where projects are not mutually exclusive, managers often must choose between various positive-NPV projects because of **limited resources**. For example, the company might have ideas for two new lines of business, each of which has a projected positive NPV. However, both of these proposals require skilled personnel, and the company determines that it will not be able to find enough skilled personnel to staff both projects. Management will have to choose the project it thinks is a better option.

When choosing between alternative proposals, it is tempting simply to choose the project with the higher NPV. Consider the following example of two mutually exclusive projects. Each is assumed to have a 10-year life and a 12% discount rate.

Illustration 10-17
Investment information for mutually exclusive projects

	Project A	Project B
Initial investment	$40,000	$ 90,000
Net annual cash inflow	10,000	19,000
Salvage value	5,000	10,000
Present value of net cash flows		
($10,000 × 5.65022) + ($5,000 × .32197)	58,112	
($19,000 × 5.65022) + ($10,000 × .32197)		110,574

From the information in Illustration 10-17, we can compute the net present values of Project A and Project B as shown in Illustration 10-18.

Illustration 10-18
Net present value computation

	Project A	Project B
Present value of net cash flows	$58,112	$110,574
Initial investment	40,000	90,000
Net present value	$18,112	$ 20,574

Project B has the higher NPV, and so it would seem that the company should adopt B. Note, however, that Project B also requires more than twice the original investment of Project A. In choosing between the two projects, the company should also include in its calculations the amount of the original investment.

STUDY OBJECTIVE 5
Describe the profitability index.

One relatively simple method of comparing alternative projects is the **profitability index**. This method takes into account both the size of the original investment and the discounted cash flows. The profitability index is calculated by dividing the present value of net cash flows that occur after the initial investment by the amount of the initial investment.

Present Value of Net Cash Flows	÷	Initial Investment	=	Profitability Index

Illustration 10-19
Formula for profitability index

The profitability index allows comparison of the relative desirability of projects that require differing initial investments. Note that any project with a positive NPV will have a profitability index above 1. The profitability index for each of the mutually exclusive projects is calculated below.

$$\text{Profitability Index} = \frac{\text{Present Value of Net Cash Flows}}{\text{Initial Investment}}$$

Project A	Project B
$\frac{\$58{,}112}{\$40{,}000} = 1.45$	$\frac{\$110{,}574}{\$90{,}000} = 1.23$

Illustration 10-20
Calculation of profitability index

In this case the profitability index of Project A exceeds that of Project B. Thus, Project A is more desirable. Again, if these were not mutually exclusive projects, and if resources were not limited, then the company should invest in both projects, since both have positive NPVs. Additional considerations related to preference decisions are discussed in more advanced courses.

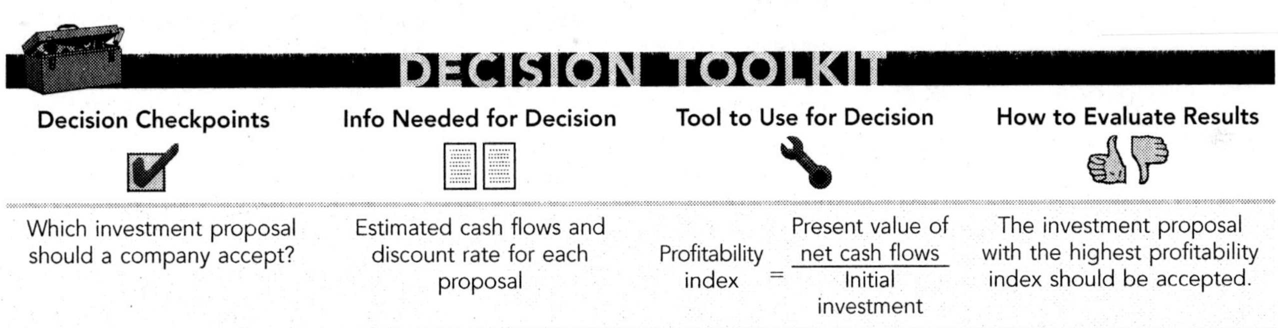

DECISION TOOLKIT

Decision Checkpoints	Info Needed for Decision	Tool to Use for Decision	How to Evaluate Results
Which investment proposal should a company accept?	Estimated cash flows and discount rate for each proposal	Profitability index = Present value of net cash flows / Initial investment	The investment proposal with the highest profitability index should be accepted.

Risk Analysis

A simplifying assumption made by many financial analysts is that projected results are known with certainty. In reality, projected results are only estimates based upon the forecaster's belief as to the most probable outcome. One approach for dealing with such uncertainty is **sensitivity analysis.** Sensitivity analysis uses a number of outcome estimates to get a sense of the variability among potential returns. An example of sensitivity analysis was presented in Illustration 10-11, where we illustrated the impact on NPV of different discount rate assumptions. A higher-risk project would be evaluated using a higher discount rate.

Similarly, to take into account that more distant cash flows are often more uncertain, a higher discount rate can be used to discount more distant cash flows. Other techniques to address uncertainty are discussed in advanced courses.

MANAGEMENT INSIGHT

Are You Ready for the 50-Inch Screen?

Building a new factory to produce 50-inch-plus TV screens can cost $4 billion at a time when prices for flat screens are tumbling. Now the makers of those giant liquid-crystal displays are wondering whether such investments are worth the gamble.

If LCD makers decide to hold off on building new factories, price declines for wide-screen TVs could slow in two or three years as production falls behind added consumer demand. Experts also say a slowdown in factory building could also bring welcome relief for the industry by reducing its volatile profit swings.

Since 2000, LCD makers have been on a nonstop construction binge, building new factories to produce the latest generation of screens arriving every 18 months or so. . . . Now, with the eighth generation of screens, the cost to build new factories is higher than ever—running between $3 billion to $4 billion each. And this generation of factories is optimized for screens measuring 50 inches or more diagonally, which so far is a much smaller potential market than that targeted by previous screen generations.

Source: Evan Ramstad, "The 50-Inch Screen Poses a Gamble," *Wall Street Journal*, June 8, 2006, p. B3.

? In building factories to manufacture 50-inch TV screens, how might companies build risk factors into their financial analyses?

Post-Audit of Investment Projects

STUDY OBJECTIVE 6

Indicate the benefits of performing a post-audit.

Any well-run organization should perform an evaluation, called a **post-audit**, of its investment projects after their completion. A post-audit is a thorough evaluation of how well a project's actual performance matches the original projections. An example of a post-audit is seen in the Feature Story about Campbell Soup. The company made the original decision to invest in the Intelligent Quisine line based on management's best estimates of future cash flows. During the development phase of the project, Campbell hired an outside consulting firm to evaluate the project's potential for success. Because actual results during the initial years were far below the estimated results, and because the future also did not look promising, the project was terminated.

Performing a post-audit is important for a variety of reasons. First, if managers know that the company will compare their estimates to actual results, they will be more likely to submit reasonable and accurate data when they make investment proposals. This clearly is better for the company than for managers to submit overly optimistic estimates in an effort to get pet projects approved. Second, as seen with Campbell Soup, a post-audit provides a formal mechanism by which the company can determine whether existing projects should be supported or terminated. Third, post-audits improve future investment proposals because, by evaluating past successes and failures, managers improve their estimation techniques.

A post-audit involves the same evaluation techniques used in making the original capital budgeting decision—for example, use of the NPV method. The difference is that, in the post-audit, analysts insert actual figures, where known, and they revise estimates of future amounts based on new information. The managers responsible for the estimates used in the original proposal must explain the reasons for any significant differences between their estimates and actual results.

Post-audits are not foolproof. In the case of Campbell Soup, some observers suggested that the company was too quick to abandon the project. Industry analysts suggested that with more time and more advertising expenditures, the company might have enjoyed a success.

MANAGEMENT INSIGHT

Seeing the Big Picture

Inaccurate trend forecasting and market positioning are more detrimental to capital investment decisions than using the wrong discount rate. Ampex patented the VCR, but failed to see its market potential. Westinghouse made the same mistake with the flat-screen video display. More often, companies adopt projects or businesses only to discontinue them in response to market changes. Texas Instruments announced it would stop manufacturing computer chips, after it had made substantial capital investments that enabled it to become one of the world's leading suppliers. The company has dropped out of some 12 business lines in recent years.

Source: World Research Advisory Inc. (London, August 1998), p. 4.

? How important is the choice of discount rate in making capital budgeting decisions?

OTHER CAPITAL BUDGETING TECHNIQUES

Some companies use capital budgeting techniques other than, or in addition to, the cash payback and net present value methods. In this section we will briefly discuss these other approaches.

Internal Rate of Return Method

STUDY OBJECTIVE 7

Explain the internal rate of return method.

The **internal rate of return method** differs from the net present value method in that it finds the **interest yield of the potential investment**. The **internal rate of return (IRR)** is the interest rate that will cause the present value of the proposed capital expenditure to equal the present value of the expected net annual cash flows (that is, NPV equal to zero). Because it recognizes the time value of money, the internal rate of return method is (like the NPV method) a discounted cash flow technique.

How does one determine the internal rate of return? One way is to use a financial calculator (see Appendix C) or computerized spreadsheet to solve for this rate. Or, one can use a trial-and-error procedure.

To illustrate, assume that Stewart Soup Company is considering the purchase of a new front-end loader at a cost of $244,371. Net annual cash flows from this loader are estimated to be $100,000 a year for three years. To determine the internal rate of return on this front-end loader, the company finds the discount rate that results in a net present value of zero. As Illustration 10-21 below shows, at a rate of return of 10%, Stewart Soup has a positive net present value of $4,315. At a rate of return of

Illustration 10-21
Estimation of internal rate of return

Year	Net Annual Cash Flows	Discount Factor 10%	Present Value 10%	Discount Factor 11%	Present Value 11%	Discount Factor 12%	Present Value 12%
1	$100,000	.90909	$ 90,909	.90090	$ 90,090	.89286	$ 89,286
2	$100,000	.82645	82,645	.81162	81,162	.79719	79,719
3	$100,000	.75132	75,132	.73119	73,119	.71178	71,178
			248,686		244,371		240,183
Less: Initial investment			244,371		244,371		244,371
Net present value			$ 4,315		$ -0-		$ (4,188)

12%, it has a negative net present value of $4,188. At an 11% rate, the net present value is zero. Therefore 11% is the internal rate of return for this investment.

An easier approach to solving for the internal rate of return can be used if the net annual cash flows are **equal**, as in the Stewart Soup example. In this special case, we can find the internal rate of return using the following formula.

Illustration 10-22
Formula for internal rate of return—even cash flows

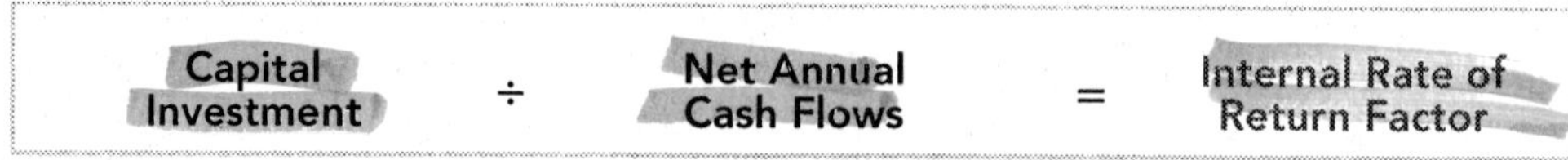

Applying this formula to the Stewart Soup example, we find:

$244,371 ÷ $100,000 = 2.44371

We then look up the factor 2.44371 in Table 4 of Appendix C in the three-period row and find it under 11%. Row 3 is reproduced below for your convenience.

TABLE 4 PRESENT VALUE OF AN ANNUITY OF 1

(*n*) Periods	4%	5%	6%	8%	9%	10%	11%	12%	15%
3	2.77509	2.72325	2.67301	2.57710	2.53130	2.48685	**2.44371**	2.40183	2.28323

Recognize that if the cash flows are **uneven**, then a trial-and-error approach or a financial calculator or computerized spreadsheet must be used.

Once managers know the internal rate of return, they compare it to the company's required rate of return (the discount rate). The IRR decision rule is as follows: **Accept the project when the internal rate of return is equal to or greater than the required rate of return. Reject the project when the internal rate of return is less than the required rate of return**. Illustration 10-23 shows these relationships. The internal rate of return method is widely used in practice, largely because most managers find the internal rate of return easy to interpret.

Illustration 10-23
Internal rate of return decision criteria

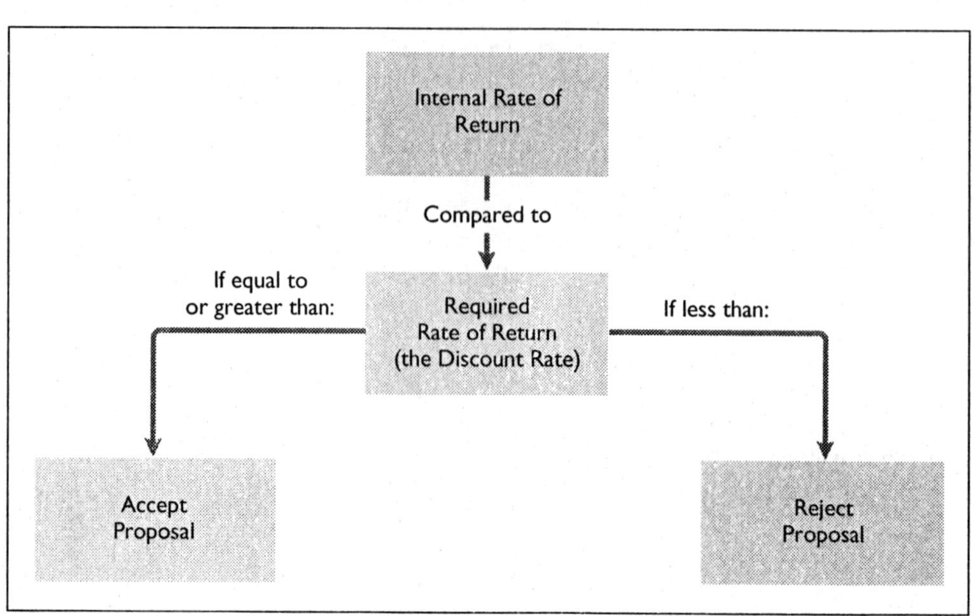

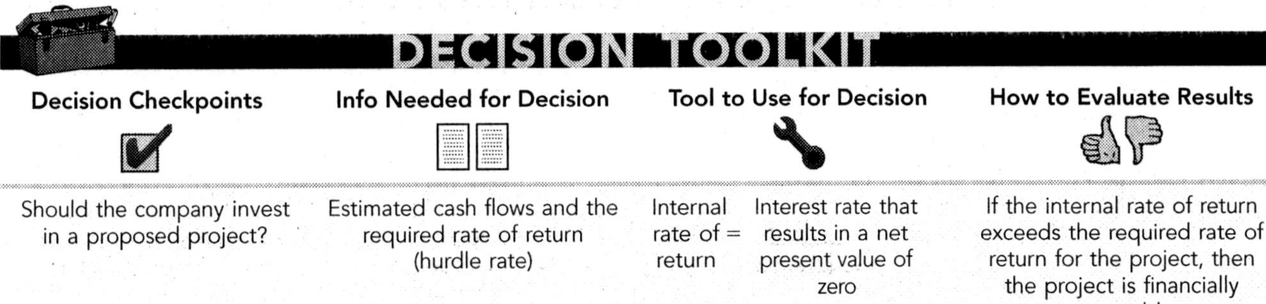

DECISION TOOLKIT

Decision Checkpoints	Info Needed for Decision	Tool to Use for Decision	How to Evaluate Results
Should the company invest in a proposed project?	Estimated cash flows and the required rate of return (hurdle rate)	Internal rate of return = Interest rate that results in a net present value of zero	If the internal rate of return exceeds the required rate of return for the project, then the project is financially acceptable.

Comparing Discounted Cash Flow Methods

Illustration 10-24 compares the two discounted cash flow methods—net present value and internal rate of return. When properly used, either method will provide management with relevant quantitative data for making capital budgeting decisions.

Illustration 10-24
Comparison of discounted cash flow methods

	Net Present Value	Internal Rate of Return
1. Objective	Compute net present value (a dollar amount).	Compute internal rate of return (a percentage).
2. Decision rule	If net present value is zero or positive, accept the proposal. If net present value is negative, reject the proposal.	If internal rate of return is equal to or greater than the required rate of return, accept the proposal. If internal rate of return is less than the required rate of return, reject the proposal.

Annual Rate of Return Method

STUDY OBJECTIVE 8
Describe the annual rate of return method.

The final capital budgeting technique we will look at is the **annual rate of return method**. It is based directly on accrual accounting data rather than on cash flows. It indicates **the profitability of a capital expenditure** by dividing expected annual net income by the average investment. Illustration 10-25 shows the formula for computing annual rate of return.

Illustration 10-25
Annual rate of return formula

Expected Annual Net Income	÷	Average Investment	=	Annual Rate of Return

Assume that Reno Company is considering an investment of $130,000 in new equipment. The new equipment is expected to last five years and have zero salvage value at the end of its useful life. Reno uses the straight-line method of depreciation for accounting purposes. The expected annual revenues and costs of the new product that will be produced from the investment are:

Illustration 10-26
Estimated annual net income from Reno Company's capital expenditure

Sales		$200,000
Less: Costs and expenses		
Manufacturing costs (exclusive of depreciation)	$132,000	
Depreciation expense ($130,000 ÷ 5)	26,000	
Selling and administrative expenses	22,000	180,000
Income before income taxes		20,000
Income tax expense		7,000
Net income		$ 13,000

Reno's expected annual net income is $13,000. Average investment is derived from the following formula.

Illustration 10-27
Formula for computing average investment

$$\text{Average Investment} = \frac{\text{Original Investment} + \text{Value at End of Useful Life}}{2}$$

The value at the end of useful life is equal to the asset's salvage value, if any. For Reno, average investment is $65,000 [($130,000 + $0) ÷ 2]. The expected annual rate of return for Reno's investment in new equipment is therefore 20%, computed as follows.

$$\$13,000 \div \$65,000 = 20\%$$

Management then compares the annual rate of return with its **required rate of return** for investments of similar risk. The required rate of return is generally based on the company's cost of capital. The decision rule is: **A project is acceptable if its rate of return is greater than management's required rate of return. It is unacceptable when the reverse is true.** When companies use the rate of return technique in deciding among several acceptable projects, **the higher the rate of return for a given risk, the more attractive the investment.**

The principal advantages of this method are the simplicity of its calculation and management's familiarity with the accounting terms used in the computation. A major limitation of the annual rate of return method is that it does not consider the time value of money. For example, no consideration is given as to whether cash inflows will occur early or late in the life of the investment. As explained in Appendix C, recognition of the time value of money can make a significant difference between the future value and the discounted present value of an investment. A second disadvantage is that this method relies on accrual accounting numbers rather than expected cash flows.

HELPFUL HINT
A capital budgeting decision based on only one technique may be misleading. It is often wise to analyze an investment from a number of different perspectives.

Before You Go On...

REVIEW IT

1. When is a proposal acceptable under (a) the net present value method and (b) the internal rate of return method?
2. How does the internal rate of return method differ from the net present value method?
3. What is the formula for and the decision rule in using the annual rate of return method? What are the drawbacks to the annual rate of return method?

Be sure to read **ALL ABOUT YOU: *The Risks of Adjustable Rates*** on the next page for information on how topics in this chapter apply to you.

all about YOU

The Risks of Adjustable Rates

It is likely that the biggest single capital expenditure decision you ever make will be the purchase of a home. As home prices rose rapidly between 2000 and 2005, many people found that they could not afford to buy a home using traditional fixed interest rate loans. Lenders encouraged some people to use less-conventional loans such as ARMs—adjustable-rate mortgages.

The lender periodically adjusts the interest rate on an ARM to reflect changes in market interest rates. The advantage of ARMs to home buyers is that the initial rate on an ARM is below the rate charged on a fixed-rate loan. This can enable the buyer to purchase a home that he or she otherwise could not afford. If market interest rates rise, however, the rate on the ARM can rise well above the initial rate. This will result in much higher mortgage payments. Rising rates can be a problem for homeowners who have not planned for them.

Some Facts

* 35% of people with ARMs do not know how much the rate could increase at one time, and 41% are not sure of the maximum rate they could face.
* 28% of people with ARMs do not know which index of interest rates is used to determine their adjustments.
* ARMs represented about one-third of all loans granted during 2004 and 2005, which was substantially higher than most previous years.
* Borrowers with less income or education were more likely not to know their mortgage terms. Borrowers with less income faced the largest change in their ARM payment, as a percentage of income, when interest rates changed.
* Subprime borrowers—people with weak credit histories—spend nearly 37% of their after-tax income on mortgage payments, insurance, and property taxes, whereas prime borrowers spend about 17% of after-tax income.
* Hundreds of thousands of families who purchased homes using adjustable-rate mortgages with low initial rates have lost their homes to foreclosure as interest rates increased and the mortgage rates readjusted. At the end of 2006 more than 450,000 loans were either in foreclosure or more than three months behind on payments.

About the Numbers

Although a high percentage of loans granted during 2004 and 2005 were adjustable-rate loans, these loans still represent a relatively small percentage of all loans outstanding. Many people who are initially granted an adjustable-rate loan subsequently refinance their loan to get a fixed-rate loan that will offer no unpleasant surprises in later years.

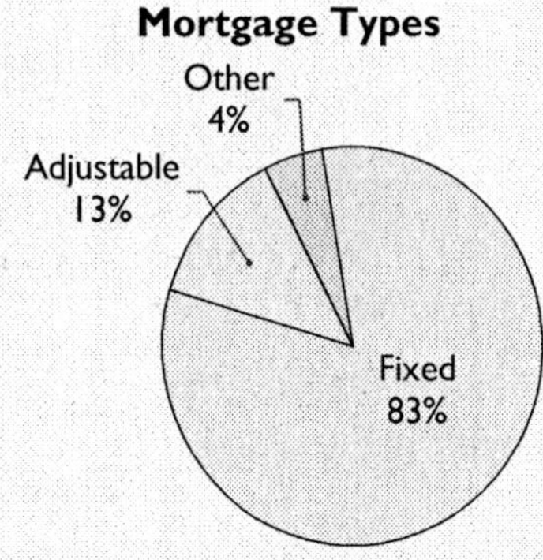

Source: Brian Bucks and Karen Pence, "Do Homeowners Know Their House Values and Mortgage Terms?," Federal Reserve Board of Governors, January 2006, *www.federalreserve.gov/pubs/feds/2006/200603/200603pap.pdf.*

What Do You Think?

Suppose that you are planning to buy your first home for $200,000. The payment on a 30-year, 7% fixed-rate loan of $180,000 (after a down payment of $20,000) would be $1,198 per month, which is more than you qualify for with the lender. The lender has suggested that you could instead use an ARM. The interest rate would be 5.5%, resulting in payments of $1,022 per month for the first three years. After that, the interest rate would be adjusted annually and could increase by as much as 2% each year, with an upper-end rate of 10.5%. Should you buy the home using adjustable-rate financing?

YES: House prices are just going to keep going up, up, up. If you don't get into the market now, you may never be able to.

NO: This nontraditional loan has too much uncertainty tied to it. If interest rates go up, your payment could get so high that you wouldn't be able to make the payment, in which case you would lose the house.

Sources: James R. Hagerty, "The Home-Mortgage Muddle; Some Borrowers Are Confused by Terms of Adjustable-Rate Loans," *Wall Street Journal*, March 11, 2006, p. B4; and Eduardo Porter and Vikas Bajaj, "Mortgage Trouble Clouds Homeownership Dream," *New York Times* (*nytimes.com*) March 17, 2007.

The authors' comments on this situation appear on page 479.

Using the Decision Toolkit

Campbell Soup is considering expanding its international presence. It sells 38% of the soup consumed in the United States, but only 2% of soup worldwide. Thus the company believes that it has great potential for international sales. Recently, 20% of Campbell's sales were in foreign markets (and nearly all of that was in Europe). Its goal is to have 30% of its sales be in foreign markets. In order to accomplish this goal, the company will have to invest heavily.

In recent years Campbell has spent between $300 and $400 million on capital expenditures. Suppose that Campbell is interested in expanding its South American presence by building a new production facility. After considering tax, marketing, labor, transportation, and political issues, Campbell has determined that the most desirable location is either in Buenos Aires or Rio de Janeiro. The following estimates have been provided. (All amounts are stated in U.S. dollars.)

	Buenos Aires	Rio de Janeiro
Initial investment	$2,500,000	$1,400,000
Estimated useful life	20 years	20 years
Annual revenues (accrual)	$500,000	$380,000
Annual expenses (accrual)	$200,000	$180,000
Annual cash inflows	$550,000	$430,000
Annual cash outflows	$222,250	$206,350
Estimated salvage value	$500,000	$0
Discount rate	9%	9%

Instructions

Evaluate each of these mutually exclusive proposals employing (a) cash payback, (b) net present value, (c) the profitability index, (d) the internal rate of return, and (e) annual rate of return. Discuss the implications of your findings.

Solution

	Buenos Aires		Rio de Janeiro
(a) Cash payback	$\frac{\$2,500,000}{\$327,750} = 7.63$ years		$\frac{\$1,400,000}{\$223,650} = 6.26$ years
(b) Net present value			
Present value of net cash flows			
$327,750 × 9.12855 =	$2,991,882		$223,650 × 9.12855 = $2,041,600
$500,000 × 0.17843 =	89,215		
	3,081,097		
Less: Initial investment	2,500,000		1,400,000
Net present value	$ 581,097		$ 641,600
(c) Profitability index	$\frac{\$3,081,097}{\$2,500,000} = 1.23$		$\frac{\$2,041,600}{\$1,400,000} = 1.46$

(d) Internal rate of return: The internal rate of return can be approximated by experimenting with different discount rates to see which one comes the closest to resulting in a net present value of zero. Doing this, we find that Buenos Aires has an internal rate of return of approximately 12%, while the internal rate of return of the Rio de Janeiro location is approximately 15% as shown below. Rio, therefore, is preferable.

	Buenos Aires			Rio de Janeiro	
Internal rate of return					
Cash Flows ×	12% Discount Factor =	Present Value	Cash Flows ×	15% Discount Factor =	Present Value
$327,750 ×	7.46944 =	$2,448,109	$223,650 ×	6.25933 =	$1,399,899
$500,000 ×	0.10367 =	51,835			
		$2,499,944			
Less: Capital investment		2,500,000			1,400,000
Net present value		$ (56)			$ (101)

(e) Annual rate of return

Average investment

$$\frac{(\$2{,}500{,}000 + \$500{,}000)}{2} = \$1{,}500{,}000 \qquad \frac{(\$1{,}400{,}000 + \$0)}{2} = \$700{,}000$$

$$\text{Annual rate of return} \quad \frac{\$300{,}000}{\$1{,}500{,}000} = .20 = 20\% \qquad \frac{\$200{,}000}{\$700{,}000} = .286 = 28.6\%$$

Implications: Although the annual rate of return is higher for Rio de Janeiro, this method has the disadvantage of ignoring time value of money, as well as using accrual numbers rather than cash flows. The cash payback of Rio de Janeiro is also shorter, but this method also ignores the time value of money. Thus, while these two methods can be used for a quick assessment, neither should be relied upon as the sole evaluation tool.

From the net present value calculation it would appear that the two projects are nearly identical in their acceptability. However, the profitability index indicates that the Rio de Janeiro investment is far more desirable because it generates its cash flows with a much smaller initial investment. A similar result is found by using the internal rate of return. Overall, assuming that the company will invest in only one project, it would appear that the Rio de Janeiro project should be chosen.

SUMMARY OF STUDY OBJECTIVES

1 **Discuss capital budgeting evaluation, and explain inputs used in capital budgeting.** Management gathers project proposals from each department; a capital budget committee screens the proposals and recommends worthy projects. Company officers decide which projects to fund, and the board of directors approves the capital budget. In capital budgeting, estimated cash inflows and outflows, rather than accrual-accounting numbers, are the preferred inputs.

2 **Describe the cash payback technique.** The cash payback technique identifies the time period required to recover the cost of the investment. The formula when net annual cash flows are equal is: Cost of capital investment ÷ Estimated net annual cash flow = Cash payback period. The shorter the payback period, the more attractive the investment.

3 **Explain the net present value method.** The net present value method compares the present value of future cash inflows with the capital investment to determine net present value. The NPV decision rule is: Accept the project if net present value is zero or positive. Reject the project if net present value is negative.

4 **Identify the challenges presented by intangible benefits in capital budgeting.** Intangible benefits are difficult to quantify, and thus are often ignored in capital budgeting decisions. This can result in incorrectly rejecting some projects. One method for considering intangible benefits is to calculate the NPV, ignoring intangible benefits; if the resulting NPV is below zero, evaluate whether the benefits are worth at least the amount of the negative net present value. Alternatively, intangible benefits can be incorporated into the NPV calculation, using conservative estimates of their value.

5 **Describe the profitability index.** The profitability index is a tool for comparing the relative merits of alternative capital investment opportunities. It is computed as: Present value of net cash flows ÷ Initial investment. The higher the index, the more desirable the project.

6 **Indicate the benefits of performing a post-audit.** A post-audit is an evaluation of a capital investment's actual performance. Post-audits create an incentive for managers to make accurate estimates. Post-audits also are useful for determining whether a company should continue, expand, or terminate a project. Finally, post-audits provide feedback that is useful for improving estimation techniques.

7 Explain the internal rate of return method. The objective of the internal rate of return method is to find the interest yield of the potential investment, which is expressed as a percentage rate. The IRR decision rule is: Accept the project when the internal rate of return is equal to or greater than the required rate of return. Reject the project when the internal rate of return is less than the required rate of return.

8 Describe the annual rate of return method. The annual rate of return uses accrual accounting data to indicate the profitability of a capital investment. It is calculated as: Expected annual net income ÷ Amount of the average investment. The higher the rate of return, the more attractive the investment.

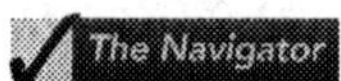

DECISION TOOLKIT—A SUMMARY

Decision Checkpoints	Info Needed for Decision	Tool to Use for Decision	How to Evaluate Results
Should the company invest in a proposed project?	Cash flow estimates, discount rate	Net present value = Present value of net cash flows less capital investment	The investment is financially acceptable if net present value is positive.
Which investment proposal should a company accept?	Estimated cash flows and discount rate for each proposal	Profitability index = Present value of net cash flows / Initial investment	The investment proposal with the highest profitability index should be accepted.
Should the company invest in a proposed project?	Estimated cash flows and the required rate of return (hurdle rate)	Internal rate of return = Interest rate that results in a net present value of zero	If the internal rate of return exceeds the required rate of return for the project, then the project is financially acceptable.

GLOSSARY

Annual rate of return method The determination of the profitability of a capital expenditure, computed by dividing expected annual net income by the average investment. (p. 461)

Capital budgeting The process of making capital expenditure decisions in business. (p. 444)

Cash payback technique A capital budgeting technique that identifies the time period required to recover the cost of a capital investment from the net annual cash flow produced by the investment. (p. 447)

Cost of capital The average rate of return that the firm must pay to obtain funds from creditors and stockholders. (p. 450)

Discounted cash flow technique A capital budgeting technique that considers both the estimated net cash flows from the investment and the time value of money. (p. 448)

Discount rate The interest rate used in discounting the future net cash flows to determine present value. (p. 448)

Internal rate of return (IRR) The interest rate that will cause the present value of the proposed capital expenditure to equal the present value of the expected net annual cash flows. (p. 459)

Internal rate of return (IRR) method A method used in capital budgeting that results in finding the interest yield of the potential investment. (p. 459)

Net present value (NPV) The difference that results when the original capital outlay is subtracted from the discounted net cash flows. (p. 448)

Net present value (NPV) method A method used in capital budgeting in which net cash flows are discounted to their present value and then compared to the capital outlay required by the investment. (p. 448)

Post-audit A thorough evaluation of how well a project's actual performance matches the original projections. (p. 458)

Profitability index A method of comparing alternative projects that takes into account both the size of the investment and its discounted future net cash flows. It is computed by dividing the present value of net future cash flows by the initial investment. (p. 456)

Required rate of return The rate of return management expects on investments; also called the *discount rate* or *cost of capital*. (p. 462)

Demonstration Problem

Sierra Company is considering a long-term capital investment project called ZIP. ZIP will require an investment of $120,000, and it will have a useful life of 4 years. Annual net income is expected to be $9,000 a year. Depreciation is computed by the straight-line method with no salvage value. The company's cost of capital is 12%. (*Hint:* Assume cash flows can be computed by adding back depreciation expense.)

Instructions

(Round all computations to two decimal places.)

(a) Compute the cash payback period for the project. (Round to two decimals.)
(b) Compute the net present value for the project. (Round to nearest dollar.)
(c) Compute the annual rate of return for the project.
(d) Should the project be accepted? Why?

Solution

(a) $120,000 ÷ $39,000, ($9,000 + $30,000), = 3.08 years

(b)

	Present Value at 12%
Discount factor for 4 periods	3.03735
Present value of net cash flows:	
$39,000 × 3.03735	$118,457
Capital investment	120,000
Negative net present value	$ (1,543)

(c) $9,000 ÷ $60,000 ($120,000 ÷ 2) = 15%

(d) The annual rate of return of 15% is good. However, the cash payback period is 77% of the project's useful life, and net present value is negative. The recommendation is to reject the project.

action plan

- ✓ Calculate the time it will take to pay back the investment: cost of the investment divided by net annual cash flows.
- ✓ When calculating NPV, remember that net annual cash flow equals annual net income plus annual depreciation expense.
- ✓ Be careful to use the correct discount factor in using the net present value method.
- ✓ Calculate the annual rate of return: expected annual net income divided by average investment.

✓ The Navigator

SELF-STUDY QUESTIONS

Answers are at the end of the chapter.

(SO 1) **1.** Which of the following is *not* an example of a capital budgeting decision?
   a. Decision to build a new plant.
   b. Decision to renovate an existing facility.
   c. Decision to buy a piece of machinery.
   d. All of these are capital budgeting decisions.

(SO 1) **2.** What is the order of involvement of the following parties in the capital budgeting authorization process?
   a. Plant managers, officers, capital budget committee, board of directors.
   b. Board of directors, plant managers, officers, capital budget committee.
   c. Plant managers, capital budget committee, officers, board of directors.
   d. Officers, plant managers, capital budget committee, board of directors.

3. What is a weakness of the cash payback approach? (SO 2)
   a. It uses accrual-based accounting numbers.
   b. It ignores the time value of money.
   c. It ignores the useful life of alternative projects.
   d. Both (b) and (c) are true.

4. Which is a true statement regarding using a higher discount rate to calculate the net present value of a project? (SO 3)
   a. It will make it less likely that the project will be accepted.
   b. It will make it more likely that the project will be accepted.
   c. It is appropriate to use a higher rate if the project is perceived as being less risky than other projects being considered.
   d. It is appropriate to use a higher rate if the project will have a short useful life relative to other projects being considered.

(SO 3) 5. A positive net present value means that the:
a. project's rate of return is less than the cutoff rate.
b. project's rate of return exceeds the required rate of return.
c. project's rate of return equals the required rate of return.
d. project is unacceptable.

(SO 3) 6. Which of the following is *not* an alternative name for the discount rate?
a. Hurdle rate.
b. Required rate of return.
c. Cutoff rate.
d. All of these are alternative names for the discount rate.

(SO 4) 7. If a project has intangible benefits whose value is hard to estimate, the best thing to do is:
a. ignore these benefits, since any estimate of their value will most likely be wrong.
b. include a conservative estimate of their value.
c. ignore their value in your initial net present value calculation, but then estimate whether their potential value is worth at least the amount of the net present value deficiency.
d. either (b) or (c) is correct.

8. A post-audit of an investment project should be performed: (SO 6)
a. on all significant capital expenditure projects.
b. on all projects that management feels might be financial failures.
c. on randomly selected projects.
d. only on projects that enjoy tremendous success.

9. A project should be accepted if its internal rate of return exceeds: (SO 7)
a. zero.
b. the rate of return on a government bond.
c. the company's required rate of return.
d. the rate the company pays on borrowed funds.

10. Which of the following is *incorrect* about the annual rate of return technique? (SO 8)
a. The calculation is simple.
b. The accounting terms used are familiar to management.
c. The timing of the cash inflows is not considered.
d. The time value of money is considered.

Go to the book's website, **www.wiley.com/college/weygandt**, for Additional Self-Study questions.

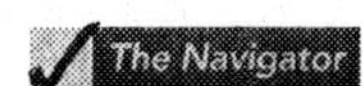

QUESTIONS

1. Describe the process a company may use in screening and approving the capital expenditure budget.
2. What are the advantages and disadvantages of the cash payback technique?
3. Walter Shea claims the formula for the cash payback technique is the same as the formula for the annual rate of return technique. Is Walter correct? What is the formula for the cash payback technique?
4. Two types of present value tables may be used with the discounted cash flow techniques. Identify the tables and the circumstance(s) when each table should be used.
5. What is the decision rule under the net present value method?
6. Discuss the factors that determine the appropriate discount rate to use when calculating the net present value.
7. What simplifying assumptions were made in the chapter regarding calculation of net present value?
8. What are some examples of potential intangible benefits of investment proposals? Why do these intangible benefits complicate the capital budgeting evaluation process? What might happen if intangible benefits are ignored in a capital budgeting decision?
9. What steps can be taken to incorporate intangible benefits into the capital budget evaluation process?
10. What advantages does the profitability index provide over direct comparison of net present value when comparing two projects?
11. What is a post-audit? What are the potential benefits of a post-audit?
12. Identify the steps required in using the internal rate of return method when the net annual cash flows are equal.
13. Waterville Company uses the internal rate of return method. What is the decision rule for this method?
14. What are the strengths of the annual rate of return approach? What are its weaknesses?
15. Your classmate, Kurt Snyder, is confused about the factors that are included in the annual rate of return technique. What is the formula for this technique?
16. Stella Waite is trying to understand the term "cost of capital." Define the term and indicate its relevance to the decision rule under the internal rate of return technique.

BRIEF EXERCISES

WILEY PLUS

Compute the cash payback period for a capital investment.
(SO 2)

BE10-1 Marcus Company is considering purchasing new equipment for $450,000. It is expected that the equipment will produce net annual cash flows of $55,000 over its 10-year useful life. Annual depreciation will be $45,000. Compute the cash payback period.

BE10-2 Nien Company accumulates the following data concerning a proposed capital investment: cash cost $220,000, net annual cash flows $40,000, present value factor of cash inflows for 10 years 5.65 (rounded). Determine the net present value, and indicate whether the investment should be made.

Compute net present value of an investment.

(SO 3)

BE10-3 Timo Corporation, an amusement park, is considering a capital investment in a new exhibit. The exhibit would cost $136,000 and have an estimated useful life of 5 years. It will be sold for $70,000 at that time. (Amusement parks need to rotate exhibits to keep people interested.) It is expected to increase net annual cash flows by $25,000. The company's borrowing rate is 8%. Its cost of capital is 10%. Calculate the net present value of this project to the company.

Compute net present value of an investment.

(SO 3)

BE10-4 Michener Bottling Corporation is considering the purchase of a new bottling machine. The machine would cost $200,000 and has an estimated useful life of 8 years with zero salvage value. Management estimates that the new bottling machine will provide net annual cash flows of $35,000. Management also believes that the new bottling machine will save the company money because it is expected to be more reliable than other machines, and thus will reduce downtime. How much would the reduction in downtime have to be worth in order for the project to be acceptable? Assume a discount rate of 9%. (*Hint:* Calculate the net present value.)

Compute net present value of an investment and consider intangible benefits.

(SO 3, 4)

BE10-5 Harry Company is considering two different, mutually exclusive capital expenditure proposals. Project A will cost $395,000, has an expected useful life of 10 years, a salvage value of zero, and is expected to increase net annual cash flows by $70,000. Project B will cost $270,000, has an expected useful life of 10 years, a salvage value of zero, and is expected to increase net annual cash flows by $50,000. A discount rate of 9% is appropriate for both projects. Compute the net present value and profitability index of each project. Which project should be accepted?

Compute net present value and profitability index.

(SO 3, 5)

BE10-6 Martelle Company is performing a post-audit of a project completed one year ago. The initial estimates were that the project would cost $250,000, would have a useful life of 9 years, zero salvage value, and would result in net annual cash flows of $45,000 per year. Now that the investment has been in operation for 1 year, revised figures indicate that it actually cost $260,000, will have a useful life of 11 years, and will produce net annual cash flows of $38,000 per year. Evaluate the success of the project. Assume a discount rate of 10%.

Perform a post-audit.

(SO 6)

BE10-7 Frost Company is evaluating the purchase of a rebuilt spot-welding machine to be used in the manufacture of a new product. The machine will cost $170,000, has an estimated useful life of 7 years, a salvage value of zero, and will increase net annual cash flows by $33,740. What is its approximate internal rate of return?

Calculate internal rate of return.

(SO 7)

BE10-8 Vintech Corporation is considering investing in a new facility. The estimated cost of the facility is $2,045,000. It will be used for 12 years, then sold for $600,000. The facility will generate annual cash inflows of $400,000 and will need new annual cash outflows of $160,000. The company has a required rate of return of 7%. Calculate the internal rate of return on this project, and discuss whether the project should be accepted.

Calculate internal rate of return.

(SO 7)

BE10-9 Engles Oil Company is considering investing in a new oil well. It is expected that the oil well will increase annual revenues by $130,000 and will increase annual expenses by $80,000 including depreciation. The oil well will cost $490,000 and will have a $10,000 salvage value at the end of its 10-year useful life. Calculate the annual rate of return.

Compute annual rate of return.

(SO 8)

EXERCISES

WILEY PLUS

E10-1 Dobbs Corporation is considering purchasing a new delivery truck. The truck has many advantages over the company's current truck (not the least of which is that it runs). The new truck would cost $56,000. Because of the increased capacity, reduced maintenance costs, and increased fuel economy, the new truck is expected to generate cost savings of $8,000. At the end of 8 years the company will sell the truck for an estimated $28,000. Traditionally the company has used a rule of thumb that a proposal should not be accepted unless it has a payback period that is less than 50% of the asset's estimated useful life. Hal Michaels, a new manager, has suggested that the company should not rely solely on the payback approach, but should also employ the net present value method when evaluating new projects. The company's cost of capital is 8%.

Compute cash payback and net present value.

(SO 2, 3)

Instructions

(a) Compute the cash payback period and net present value of the proposed investment.

(b) Does the project meet the company's cash payback criteria? Does it meet the net present value criteria for acceptance? Discuss your results.

Compute cash payback period and net present value.

(SO 2, 3)

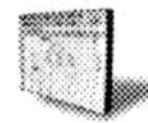

E10-2 Jack's Custom Manufacturing Company is considering three new projects, each requiring an equipment investment of $21,000. Each project will last for 3 years and produce the following net annual cash flows.

Year	AA	BB	CC
1	$ 7,000	$ 9,500	$13,000
2	9,000	9,500	10,000
3	15,000	9,500	11,000
Total	$31,000	$28,500	$34,000

The equipment's salvage value is zero, and Jack uses straight-line depreciation. Jack will not accept any project with a cash payback period over 2 years. Jack's required rate of return is 12%.

Instructions

(a) Compute each project's payback period, indicating the most desirable project and the least desirable project using this method. (Round to two decimals and assume in your computations that cash flows occur evenly throughout the year.)

(b) Compute the net present value of each project. Does your evaluation change? (Round to nearest dollar.)

Compute net present value and profitability index.

(SO 3, 5)

E10-3 TLC Corp. is considering purchasing one of two new diagnostic machines. Either machine would make it possible for the company to bid on jobs that it currently isn't equipped to do. Estimates regarding each machine are provided below.

	Machine A	Machine B
Original cost	$78,000	$190,000
Estimated life	8 years	8 years
Salvage value	–0–	–0–
Estimated annual cash inflows	$20,000	$40,000
Estimated annual cash outflows	$5,000	$9,000

Instructions

Calculate the net present value and profitability index of each machine. Assume a 9% discount rate. Which machine should be purchased?

Determine internal rate of return.

(SO 7)

E10-4 Kendra Corporation is involved in the business of injection molding of plastics. It is considering the purchase of a new computer-aided design and manufacturing machine for $425,000. The company believes that with this new machine it will improve productivity and increase quality, resulting in an increase in net annual cash flows of $95,000 for the next 6 years. Management requires a 10% rate of return on all new investments.

Instructions

Calculate the internal rate of return on this new machine. Should the investment be accepted?

Determine internal rate of return.

(SO 7)

E10-5 Summer Company is considering three capital expenditure projects. Relevant data for the projects are as follows.

Project	Investment	Annual Income	Life of Project
22A	$240,000	$15,000	6 years
23A	270,000	24,400	9 years
24A	280,000	21,000	7 years

Annual income is constant over the life of the project. Each project is expected to have zero salvage value at the end of the project. Summer Company uses the straight-line method of depreciation.

Instructions

(a) Determine the internal rate of return for each project. Round the internal rate of return factor to three decimals.

(b) If Summer Company's required rate of return is 11%, which projects are acceptable?

E10-6 Mane Event is considering opening a new hair salon in Pompador, California. The cost of building a new salon is $300,000. A new salon will normally generate annual revenues of $70,000, with annual expenses (including depreciation) of $40,000. At the end of 15 years the salon will have a salvage value of $75,000.

Calculate annual rate of return.

(SO 8)

Instructions

Calculate the annual rate of return on the project.

E10-7 Alameda Service Center just purchased an automobile hoist for $41,000. The hoist has an 8-year life and an estimated salvage value of $3,000. Installation costs and freight charges were $3,300 and $700, respectively. Alameda uses straight-line depreciation.

The new hoist will be used to replace mufflers and tires on automobiles. Alameda estimates that the new hoist will enable his mechanics to replace five extra mufflers per week. Each muffler sells for $72 installed. The cost of a muffler is $34, and the labor cost to install a muffler is $12.

Compute cash payback period and annual rate of return.

(SO 2, 8)

Instructions

(a) Compute the cash payback period for the new hoist.

(b) Compute the annual rate of return for the new hoist. (Round to one decimal.)

E10-8 Morgan Company is considering a capital investment of $180,000 in additional productive facilities. The new machinery is expected to have a useful life of 6 years with no salvage value. Depreciation is by the straight-line method. During the life of the investment, annual net income and net annual cash flows are expected to be $20,000 and $50,000 respectively. Morgan has a 15% cost of capital rate which is the required rate of return on the investment.

Compute annual rate of return, cash payback period, and net present value.

(SO 2, 3, 8)

Instructions

(Round to two decimals.)

(a) Compute (1) the cash payback period and (2) the annual rate of return on the proposed capital expenditure.

(b) Using the discounted cash flow technique, compute the net present value.

EXERCISES: SET B

Visit the book's website at **www.wiley.com/college/weygandt**, and choose the Student Companion site, to access Exercise Set B.

PROBLEMS: SET A

WILEY PLUS

P10-1A The Three Stooges partnership is considering three long-term capital investment proposals. Each investment has a useful life of 5 years. Relevant data on each project are as follows.

Compute annual rate of return, cash payback, and net present value.

(SO 2, 3, 8)

	Project Moe	Project Larry	Project Curly
Capital investment	$150,000	$160,000	$200,000
Annual net income:			
Year 1	13,000	18,000	27,000
2	13,000	17,000	22,000
3	13,000	16,000	21,000
4	13,000	12,000	13,000
5	13,000	9,000	12,000
Total	$ 65,000	$ 72,000	$ 95,000

Depreciation is computed by the straight-line method with no salvage value. The company's cost of capital is 15%. (Assume that cash flows occur evenly throughout the year.)

Instructions

(b) L $(2,368); C $1,407

(a) Compute the cash payback period for each project. (Round to two decimals.)
(b) Compute the net present value for each project. (Round to nearest dollar.)
(c) Compute the annual rate of return for each project. (Round to two decimals.) (*Hint*: Use average annual net income in your computation.)
(d) Rank the projects on each of the foregoing bases. Which project do you recommend?

Compute annual rate of return, cash payback, and net present value.

(SO 2, 3, 8)

P10-2A Tony Siebers is an accounting major at a midwestern state university located approximately 60 miles from a major city. Many of the students attending the university are from the metropolitan area and visit their homes regularly on the weekends. Tony, an entrepreneur at heart, realizes that few good commuting alternatives are available for students doing weekend travel. He believes that a weekend commuting service could be organized and run profitably from several suburban and downtown shopping mall locations. Tony has gathered the following investment information.

1. Five used vans would cost a total of $75,000 to purchase and would have a 3-year useful life with negligible salvage value. Tony plans to use straight-line depreciation.
2. Ten drivers would have to be employed at a total payroll expense of $48,000.
3. Other annual out-of-pocket expenses associated with running the commuter service would include Gasoline $16,000, Maintenance $4,300, Repairs $5,000, Insurance $5,200, Advertising $2,500.
4. Tony has visited several financial institutions to discuss funding. The best interest rate he has been able to negotiate is 8%. Use this rate for cost of capital.
5. Tony expects each van to make ten round trips weekly and carry an average of six students each trip. The service is expected to operate 30 weeks each year, and each student will be charged $12.00 for a round-trip ticket.

Instructions

(a) (1) $2,000
(b) (1) 2.78 years

(a) Determine the annual (1) net income and (2) net annual cash flows for the commuter service.
(b) Compute (1) the cash payback period and (2) the annual rate of return. (Round to two decimals.)
(c) Compute the net present value of the commuter service. (Round to the nearest dollar.)
(d) What should Tony conclude from these computations?

Compute net present value, profitability index, and internal rate of return.

(SO 3, 5, 7)

P10-3A Carolina Clinic is considering investing in new heart monitoring equipment. It has two options: Option A would have an initial lower cost but would require a significant expenditure for rebuilding after 4 years. Option B would require no rebuilding expenditure, but its maintenance costs would be higher. Since the option B machine is of initial higher quality, it is expected to have a salvage value at the end of its useful life. The following estimates were made of the cash flows. The company's cost of capital is 11%.

	Option A	Option B
Initial cost	$160,000	$227,000
Annual cash inflows	$75,000	$80,000
Annual cash outflows	$35,000	$30,000
Cost to rebuild (end of year 4)	$60,000	$0
Salvage value	$0	$12,000
Estimated useful life	8 years	8 years

Instructions

(a) (1) NPV A $6,321
(3) IRR B 15%

(a) Compute the (1) net present value, (2) profitability index, and (3) internal rate of return for each option. (*Hint:* To solve for internal rate of return, experiment with alternative discount rates to arrive at a net present value of zero.)
(b) Which option should be accepted?

Compute net present value considering intangible benefits.

(SO 3, 4)

P10-4A Prestige Auto Care is considering the purchase of a new tow truck. The garage doesn't currently have a tow truck, and the $60,000 price tag for a new truck would represent a major expenditure. Jenna Lind, owner of the garage, has compiled the following estimates in trying to determine whether the tow truck should be purchased.

Initial cost	$60,000
Estimated useful life	8 years
Net annual cash flows from towing	$8,000
Overhaul costs (end of year 4)	$5,000
Salvage value	$15,000

Jenna's good friend, Reid Shaw, stopped by. He is trying to convince Jenna that the tow truck will have other benefits that Jenna hasn't even considered. First, he says, cars that need towing need to be fixed. Thus, when Jenna tows them to her facility her repair revenues will increase. Second, he notes that the tow truck could have a plow mounted on it, thus saving Jenna the cost of plowing her parking lot. (Reid will give her a used plow blade for free if Jenna will plow Reid's driveway.) Third, he notes that the truck will generate goodwill; people who are rescued by Jenna's tow truck will feel grateful and might be more inclined to use her service station in the future, or buy gas there. Fourth, the tow truck will have "Prestige Auto Care" on its doors, hood, and back tailgate — a form of free advertising wherever the tow truck goes. Reid estimates that, at a minimum, these benefits would be worth the following.

Additional annual net cash flows from repair work	$3,000
Annual savings from plowing	500
Additional annual net cash flows from customer "goodwill"	1,000
Additional annual net cash flows resulting from free advertising	500

The company's cost of capital is 9%.

Instructions

(a) Calculate the net present value, ignoring the additional benefits described by Reid. Should the tow truck be purchased? (a) NPV $(11,735)

(b) Calculate the net present value, incorporating the additional benefits suggested by Reid. Should the tow truck be purchased? (b) NPV $15,939

(c) Suppose Reid has been overly optimistic in his assessment of the value of the additional benefits. At a minimum, how much would the additional benefits have to be worth in order for the project to be accepted?

Compute net present value and internal rate of return with sensitivity analysis.

(SO 3, 7)

P10-5A Bonita Corp. is thinking about opening a soccer camp in southern California. To start the camp, Bonita would need to purchase land and build four soccer fields and a sleeping and dining facility to house 150 soccer players. Each year the camp would be run for 8 sessions of 1 week each. The company would hire college soccer players as coaches. The camp attendees would be male and female soccer players ages 12–18. Property values in southern California have enjoyed a steady increase in value. It is expected that after using the facility for 20 years, Bonita can sell the property for more than it was originally purchased for. The following amounts have been estimated.

Cost of land	$300,000
Cost to build soccer fields, dorm and dining facility	$600,000
Annual cash inflows assuming 150 players and 8 weeks	$950,000
Annual cash outflows	$840,000
Estimated useful life	20 years
Salvage value	$1,500,000
Discount rate	8%

Instructions

(a) Calculate the net present value of the project. (a) NPV $501,822

(b) To gauge the sensitivity of the project to these estimates, assume that if only 125 players attend each week, annual cash inflows will be $800,000 and annual cash outflows will be $770,000. What is the net present value using these alternative estimates? Discuss your findings.

(c) Assuming the original facts, what is the net present value if the project is actually riskier than first assumed, and a 11% discount rate is more appropriate?

(d) Assume that during the first 5 years the annual net cash flows each year were only $45,000. At the end of the fifth year the company is running low on cash, so management decides to sell the property for $1,300,000. What was the actual internal rate of return on the project? Explain how this return was possible given that the camp did not appear to be successful. (d) IRR 12%

PROBLEMS: SET B

P10-1B The partnership of Lou and Bud is considering three long-term capital investment proposals. Relevant data on each project are as follows.

Compute annual rate of return, cash payback, and net present value.

(SO 2, 3, 8)

	Project		
	Brown	**Red**	**Yellow**
Capital investment	$200,000	$225,000	$250,000
Annual net income:			
Year 1	25,000	20,000	26,000
2	16,000	20,000	24,000
3	13,000	20,000	23,000
4	10,000	20,000	22,000
5	8,000	20,000	20,000
Total	$ 72,000	$100,000	$115,000

Salvage value is expected to be zero at the end of each project. Depreciation is computed by the straight-line method. The company's required rate of return is the company's cost of capital which is 12%. (Assume that cash flows occur evenly throughout the year.)

Instructions

(a) Compute the cash payback period for each project. (Round to two decimals.)

(b) NPV B $(584); Y $14,286

(b) Compute the net present value for each project. (Round to nearest dollar.)

(c) Compute the annual rate of return for each project. (Round to two decimals.) (*Hint*: Use average annual net income in your computation.)

(d) Rank the projects on each of the foregoing bases. What project do you recommend?

Compute annual rate of return, cash payback, and net present value.

(SO 2, 3, 8)

P10-2B Jo Quick is managing director of the Tot Lot Day Care Center. Tot Lot is currently set up as a full-time child care facility for children between the ages of 12 months and 6 years. Jo Quick is trying to determine whether the center should expand its facilities to incorporate a newborn care room for infants between the ages of 6 weeks and 12 months. The necessary space already exists. An investment of $20,000 would be needed, however, to purchase cribs, high chairs, etc. The equipment purchased for the room would have a 5-year useful life with zero salvage value.

The newborn nursery would be staffed to handle 11 infants on a full-time basis. The parents of each infant would be charged $125 weekly, and the facility would operate 52 weeks of the year. Staffing the nursery would require two full-time specialists and five part-time assistants at an annual cost of $60,000. Food, diapers, and other miscellaneous supplies are expected to total $6,000 annually.

Instructions

(a) (1) 1,500

(a) Determine (1) annual net income and (2) net annual cash flows for the new nursery.

(b) (1) 3.64 years

(b) Compute (1) the cash payback period for the new nursery and (2) the annual rate of return. (Round to two decimals.)

(c) Compute the net present value of incorporating a newborn care room. (Round to the nearest dollar.) Tot Lot's cost of capital is 10%.

(d) What should Jo Quick conclude from these computations?

Compute net present value, profitability index, and internal rate of return.

(SO 3, 5, 7)

P10-3B Aqua Tech Testing is considering investing in a new testing device. It has two options: Option A would have an initial lower cost but would require a significant expenditure for rebuilding after 5 years. Option B would require no rebuilding expenditure, but its maintenance costs would be higher. Since the option B machine is of initial higher quality, it is expected to have a salvage value at the end of its useful life. The following estimates were provided. The company's cost of capital is 9%.

	Option A	**Option B**
Initial cost	$90,000	$170,000
Annual cash inflows	$180,000	$140,000
Annual cash outflows	$160,000	$108,000
Cost to rebuild (end of year 5)	$26,500	$0
Salvage value	$0	$27,500
Estimated useful life	8 years	8 years

Instructions

(a) (1) NPV A $3,473
(3) IRR B 12%

(a) Compute the (1) net present value, (2) profitability index, and (3) internal rate of return for each option. (*Hint:* To solve for internal rate of return, experiment with alternative discount rates to arrive at a net present value of zero.)

(b) Which option should be accepted?

P10-4B The Watertown Sanitation Company is considering the purchase of a garbage truck. The $77,000 price tag for a new truck would represent a major expenditure for the company. Kalia Vang, owner of the company, has compiled the following estimates in trying to determine whether the garbage truck should be purchased.

Compute net present value considering intangible benefits.

(SO 3, 4)

Initial cost	$77,000
Estimated useful life	10 years
Net annual cash flows	$12,000
Overhaul costs (end of year 5)	$7,000
Salvage value	$15,000

One of the employees is trying to convince Kalia that the truck has other merits that were not considered in the initial estimates. First, the new truck will be more efficient, with lower maintenance and operating costs. Second, it will be safer. Third, it has the ability to handle recycled materials at the same time as trash, thus offering a new revenue source. Estimates of the minimum value of these benefits are as follows.

Annual savings from reduced operating costs	$400
Annual savings from reduced maintenance costs	800
Additional annual net cash savings from reduced employee absence	500
Additional annual net cash inflows from recycling	300

The company's cost of capital is 10%.

Instructions

(a) Calculate the net present value, ignoring the additional benefits. Should the truck be purchased?

(a) NPV $(1,828)

(b) Calculate the net present value, incorporating the additional benefits. Should the truck be purchased?

(b) NPV $10,461

(c) Suppose management has been overly optimistic in the assessment of the value of the additional benefits. At a minimum, how much would the additional benefits have to be worth in order for the project to be accepted?

P10-5B Benjamin Corp. is thinking about opening an ice hockey camp in Idaho. In order to start the camp the company would need to purchase land and build two ice rinks and a dormitory-type sleeping and dining facility to house 200 players. Each year the camp would be run for 8 sessions of 1 week each. The company would hire college hockey players as coaches. The camp attendees would be male and female hockey players ages 12–18. Property values in Idaho have enjoyed a steady increase in recent years. Benjamin Corp. expects that after using the facility for 15 years, the rinks will have to be dismantled, but the land and buildings will be worth more than they were originally purchased for. The following amounts have been estimated.

Compute net present value and internal rate of return with sensitivity analysis.

(SO 3, 7)

Cost of land	$300,000
Cost to build ice rinks, dorm and dining hall	$600,000
Annual cash inflows assuming 200 players and 8 weeks	$920,000
Annual cash outflows	$760,000
Estimated useful life	15 years
Salvage value	$1,200,000
Discount rate	11%

Instructions

(a) Calculate the net present value of the project.

(a) NPV $501,339

(b) To gauge the sensitivity of the project to these estimates, assume that if only 150 players attend each week, annual cash inflows will be $700,000 and annual cash outflows will be $650,000. What is the net present value using these alternative estimates? Discuss your findings.

(c) Assuming the original facts, what is the net present value if the project is actually riskier than first assumed, and a 15% discount rate is more appropriate?

(d) Assume that during the first 6 years the annual net cash flows each year were only $84,000. At the end of the sixth year the company is running low on cash, so management decides to sell the property for $1,100,000. What was the actual internal rate of return on the project? Explain how this return was possible given that the camp did not appear to be successful.

(d) IRR 12%

PROBLEMS: SET C

Visit the book's website at **www.wiley.com/college/weygandt**, and choose the Student Companion site, to access Problem Set C.

WATERWAYS CONTINUING PROBLEM

(This is a continuation of the Waterways Problem from previous chapters.)

WCP10 Waterways Corporation puts much emphasis on cash flow when it plans for capital investments. The company chose its discount rate of 8% based on the rate of return it must pay its owners and creditors. Using that rate, Waterways then uses different methods to determine the best decisions for making capital outlays. Waterways is considering buying five new backhoes to replace the backhoes it now has. This problem asks you to evaluate that decision, using various capital budgeting techniques.

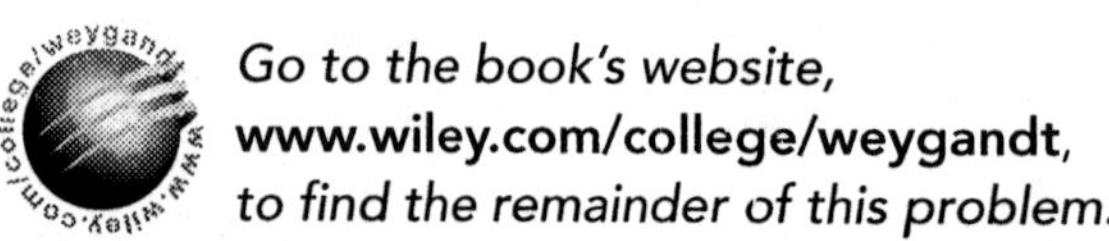

Go to the book's website,
www.wiley.com/college/weygandt,
to find the remainder of this problem.

BROADENING YOUR PERSPECTIVE

DECISION MAKING ACROSS THE ORGANIZATION

BYP10-1 Migami Company is considering the purchase of a new machine. Its invoice price is $117,000, freight charges are estimated to be $3,000, and installation costs are expected to be $5,000. Salvage value of the new machine is expected to be zero after a useful life of 4 years. Existing equipment could be retained and used for an additional 4 years if the new machine is not purchased. At that time, the salvage value of the equipment would be zero. If the new machine is purchased now, the existing machine would be scrapped. Migami accountant, Caitlyn Lahr, has accumulated the following data regarding annual sales and expenses with and without the new machine.

1. Without the new machine, Migami can sell 10,000 units of product annually at a per unit selling price of $100. If the new unit is purchased, the number of units produced and sold would increase by 20%, and the selling price would remain the same.
2. The new machine is faster than the old machine, and it is more efficient in its usage of materials. With the old machine the gross profit rate will be 28.5% of sales, whereas the rate will be 30% of sales with the new machine.
3. Annual selling expenses are $160,000 with the current equipment. Because the new equipment would produce a greater number of units to be sold, annual selling expenses are expected to increase by 10% if it is purchased.
4. Annual administrative expenses are expected to be $100,000 with the old machine, and $112,000 with the new machine.
5. The current book value of the existing machine is $30,000. Migami uses straight-line depreciation.
6. Migami management has a required rate of return of 15% on its investment and a cash payback period of no more than 3 years.

Instructions

With the class divided into groups, answer the following. (Ignore income tax effects.)

(a) Calculate the annual rate of return for the new machine. (Round to two decimals.)
(b) Compute the cash payback period for the new machine. (Round to two decimals.)

(c) Compute the net present value of the new machine. (Round to the nearest dollar.)
(d) On the basis of the foregoing data, would you recommend that Migami buy the machine? Why?

MANAGERIAL ANALYSIS

BYP10-2 Tony Skateboards is considering building a new plant. James Bott, the company's marketing manager, is an enthusiastic supporter of the new plant. Alyssa Minh, the company's chief financial officer, is not so sure that the plant is a good idea. Currently the company purchases its skateboards from foreign manufacturers. The following figures were estimated regarding the construction of a new plant.

Cost of plant	$4,000,000	Estimated useful life	15 years
Annual cash inflows	4,000,000	Salvage value	$2,000,000
Annual cash outflows	3,550,000	Discount rate	11%

James Bott believes that these figures understate the true potential value of the plant. He suggests that by manufacturing its own skateboards the company will benefit from a "buy American" patriotism that he believes is common among skateboarders. He also notes that the firm has had numerous quality problems with the skateboards manufactured by its suppliers. He suggests that the inconsistent quality has resulted in lost sales, increased warranty claims, and some costly lawsuits. Overall, he believes sales will be $200,000 higher than projected above, and that the savings from lower warranty costs and legal costs will be $80,000 per year. He also believes that the project is not as risky as assumed above, and that a 9% discount rate is more reasonable.

Instructions

Answer each of the following.

(a) Compute the net present value of the project based on the original projections.
(b) Compute the net present value incorporating James' estimates of the value of the intangible benefits, but still using the 11% discount rate.
(c) Compute the net present value using the original estimates, but employing the 9% discount rate that James suggests is more appropriate.
(d) Comment on your findings.

REAL-WORLD FOCUS

BYP10-3 Tecumseh Products Company has its headquarters in Tecumseh, Michigan. It describes itself as "a global multinational corporation producing mechanical and electrical components essential to industries creating end-products for health, comfort, and convenience." The following was excerpted from the management discussion and analysis section of a recent annual report.

TECUMSEH PRODUCTS COMPANY
Management Discussion and Analysis

The company has invested approximately $50 million in a scroll compressor manufacturing facility in Tecumseh, Michigan. After experiencing setbacks in developing a commercially acceptable scroll compressor, the Company is currently testing a new generation of scroll product. The Company is unable to predict when, or if, it will offer a scroll compressor for commercial sale, but it does anticipate that reaching volume production will require a significant additional investment. Given such additional investment and current market conditions, management is currently reviewing its options with respect to scroll product improvement, cost reductions, joint ventures and alternative new products.

Instructions

Discuss issues the company should consider and techniques the company should employ to determine whether to continue pursuing this project.

EXPLORING THE WEB

BYP10-4 Campbell Soup Company is an international provider of soup products. Management is very interested in continuing to grow the company in its core business, while "spinning off" those businesses that are not part of its core operation.

Address: www.campbellsoups.com, or go to **www.wiley.com/college/weygandt**

Steps

1. Go to the home page of Campbell Soup Company at the address shown above.
2. Choose the current annual report.

Instructions

Review the financial statements and management's discussion and analysis, and answer the following questions.

(a) What was the total amount of capital expenditures in the current year, and how does this amount compare with the previous year?
(b) What interest rate did the company pay on new borrowings in the current year?
(c) Assume that this year's capital expenditures are expected to increase cash flows by $42 million. What is the expected internal rate of return (IRR) for these capital expenditures? (Assume a 10-year period for the cash flows.)

COMMUNICATION ACTIVITY

BYP10-5 Refer back to E10-7 to address the following.

Instructions

Prepare a memo to Mary Ann Griffin, your supervisor. Show your calculations from E10-7, (a) and (b). In one or two paragraphs, discuss important nonfinancial considerations. Make any assumptions you believe to be necessary. Make a recommendation based on your analysis.

ETHICS CASE

BYP10-6 Impro Company operates in a state where corporate taxes and workers' compensation insurance rates have recently doubled. Impro's president has just assigned you the task of preparing an economic analysis and making a recommendation relative to moving the entire operation to Missouri. The president is slightly in favor of such a move because Missouri is his boyhood home and he also owns a fishing lodge there.

You have just completed building your dream house, moved in, and sodded the lawn. Your children are all doing well in school and sports and, along with your spouse, want no part of a move to Missouri. If the company does move, so will you because the town is a one-industry community and you and your spouse will have to move to have employment. Moving when everyone else does will cause you to take a big loss on the sale of your house. The same hardships will be suffered by your coworkers, and the town will be devastated.

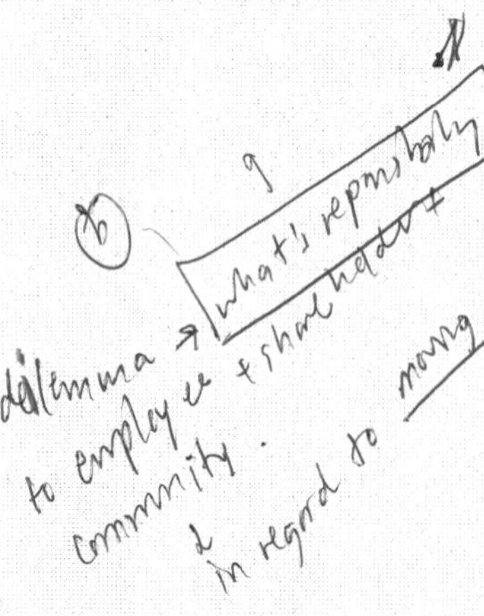

In compiling the costs of moving versus not moving, you have latitude in the assumptions you make, the estimates you compute, and the discount rates and time periods you project. You are in a position to influence the decision singlehandedly.

Instructions

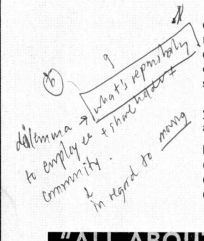

(a) Who are the stakeholders in this situation?
(b) What are the ethical issues in this situation?
(c) What would you do in this situation?

"ALL ABOUT YOU" ACTIVITY

BYP10-7 Numerous articles have been written that identify early warning signs that you might be getting into trouble with your personal debt load. You can find many good articles on this topic on the Web.

Instructions

Find an article that identifies early warning signs of personal debt trouble. Write up a summary of the article and bring your summary and the article to class to share.

Answers to Insight and Accounting Across the Organization Questions

Investing for the Future, p. 445

Q: Why is it important for top management to constantly monitor the nature, amount, and success of a company's capital expenditures?

A: *In order to remain competitive, and to grow, companies must continually invest in new opportunities. However, not all projects will be successful, so management must continually monitor projects to ensure that continuation of the investment is in the company's best interest.*

It Need Not Cost an Arm and a Leg, p. 455

Q: In addition to the obvious humanitarian benefit of reducing serious injuries, how else might the manufacturer of this product convince potential customers of its worth?

A: *Serious injuries cost employers huge sums, which can sometimes force small companies out of business. In addition to the obvious humanitarian benefit, the manufacturer can demonstrate that this device is a sound financial investment in terms of reduced health-care and workers' compensation costs and fewer hours missed due to injury. Also, as the device gains wider acceptance, employers that do not have the device may ultimately be found negligent with regard to worker safety.*

Are You Ready for the 50-Inch Screen?, p. 458

Q: In building factories to manufacture 50-inch TV screens, how might companies build risk factors into their financial analyses?

A: *One approach is to use sensitivity analysis. Sensitivity analysis uses a number of outcome estimates to get a sense of the variability among potential returns. In addition, more distant cash flows can be discounted using a higher rate because of their high uncertainty.*

Seeing the Big Picture, p. 459

Q: How important is the choice of discount rate in making capital budgeting decisions?

A: *The point of this discussion is that errors in implementation, as well as the accuracy of the estimated future benefits and costs as measured by cash inflows and outflows, is what matters the most when making capital expenditure decisions. While the choice of discount rates will result in incremental differences in present value calculations, "missing the big picture" has the potential to cause much bigger decision errors. Underestimating potential future cash inflows can result in missed opportunities. Underestimating future costs can result in failed investments.*

Authors' Comments on *All About You*: The Risks of Adjustable Rates, p. 463

A big part of the American dream is home ownership. In the past, homes have enjoyed a relatively steady and safe increase in value; thus many people are eager to quit renting and become homeowners.

But home ownership is not without risks. In recent years home prices increased so much that economists expect that in some parts of the country home prices could fall by as much as 30%. In the example above, if the house lost 30% of its value it would be worth only $140,000—much less than the amount owed. Another risk is that, as interest rates increase, people with adjustable-rate mortgages can experience huge increases in their mortgage payments. In the example given here, if the loan rate hit the cap of 10.5%, the monthly payment would jump to $1,647. That represents a 61% increase. We don't want to discourage you from home ownership, but we do want to encourage you to get educated about mortgage terms.

Answers to Self-Study Questions

1. d **2.** c **3.** d **4.** a **5.** b **6.** d **7.** d **8.** a **9.** c **10.** d

Remember to go back to the Navigator box on the chapter-opening page and check off your completed work.

Chapter 11

Pricing

STUDY OBJECTIVES

After studying this chapter, you should be able to:

1. Compute a target cost when the market determines a product price.
2. Compute a target selling price using cost-plus pricing.
3. Use time-and-material pricing to determine the cost of services provided.
4. Determine a transfer price using the negotiated, cost-based, and market-based approaches.
5. Explain issues involved in transferring goods between divisions in different countries.

The Navigator

The Navigator

- Scan **Study Objectives**
- Read **Feature Story**
- Read **Preview**
- Read text and answer **Before You Go On** p. 488 p. 491 p. 499
- Work **Using the Decision Toolkit**
- Review **Summary of Study Objectives**
- Work **Demonstration Problem**
- Answer **Self-Study Questions**
- Complete **Assignments**

Feature Story

"I'LL CALL YOUR BLUFF, AND RAISE YOU 46%"

If you own a PC, then there is a roughly 85% chance that the microprocessor chip that runs your machine was made by Intel. For as long as most people can remember, Intel has had at least an 85% share of the market for PC computer chips. It isn't that nobody else makes computer chips; it's just that the competition can't seem to get a foothold.

Intel's primary competition comes from a scrappy company called Advanced Micro Devices (AMD). At one time, Intel made a couple of missteps that caused it to lose a few points of market share to AMD. First, Intel had two product recalls on its chips. Then it had problems meeting demand. In the meantime, AMD was boasting that it had a chip that was more powerful than Intel's, and that it had plenty of supply to meet demand. The result was that Intel's market share fell—to 82%.

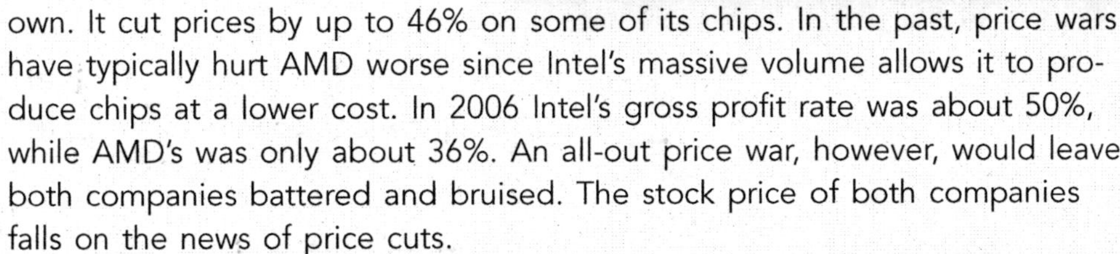

To those familiar with Intel, its response was easily predicted. It cut prices by up to 26%. One analyst noted, "When Intel screws up, they can't send flowers, so they cut prices." Said another analyst, "Intel has drawn a line in the sand at 85% market share, and they will use price to regain that share."

AMD had little choice but to respond with price cuts of its own. It cut prices by up to 46% on some of its chips. In the past, price wars have typically hurt AMD worse since Intel's massive volume allows it to produce chips at a lower cost. In 2006 Intel's gross profit rate was about 50%, while AMD's was only about 36%. An all-out price war, however, would leave both companies battered and bruised. The stock price of both companies falls on the news of price cuts.

Source: Molly Williams, "Intel Cuts Prices, Prompts AMD to Answer the Call." *Wall Street Journal*, October 17, 2000.

The Navigator

Inside Chapter 11

- **What's the Price on the Internet?** (p. 483)
- **Wal-Mart Says the Price Is Too High** (p. 484)
- **Losing Money with Every Sale** (p. 488)
- **Transferring Profits and Reducing Taxes** (p. 499)
- ***All About You:* Is the Price Right?** (p. 500)

Preview of Chapter 11

As the Feature Story about Intel and AMD indicates, few management decisions are more important than setting prices. Intel, for example, must sell computer chips at a price that is high enough to cover its costs and ensure a reasonable profit. But if the price is too high, the chips will not sell. In this chapter, we examine two types of pricing situations. The first part of the chapter addresses pricing for goods sold or services provided to external parties. The second part of the chapter addresses pricing decisions managers face when they sell goods to other divisions within the company.

The content and organization of this chapter are as follows.

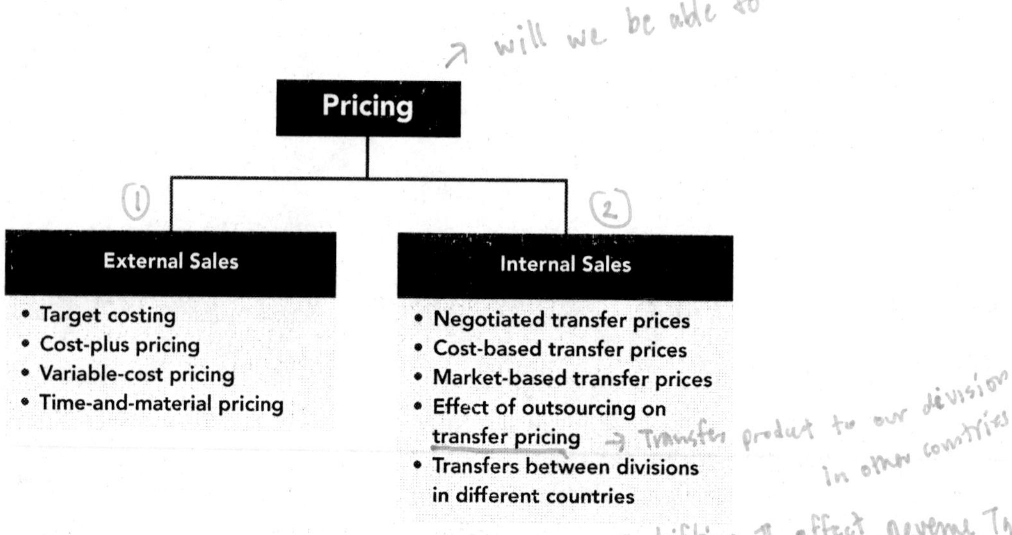

The Navigator

SECTION 1 External Sales

Establishing the price for any good or service is affected by many factors. Take the pharmaceutical industry as an example. Its approach to profitability has been to spend heavily on research and development in an effort to find and patent a few new drugs, price them high, and market them aggressively. Due to the AIDS crisis in Africa, the drug industry has been under considerable pressure recently to lower prices on drugs used to treat AIDS. For example, Merck Co. lowered the price of its AIDS drug Crixivan to $600 per patient in these countries. This compares with the $6,016 it typically charges in the United States.[1] As a consequence, individuals in the United States are questioning whether prices in the U.S. market are too high. The drug companies counter that to cover their substantial financial risks to develop these products, they need to set the prices high. Illustration 11-1 (next page) indicates the many factors that can affect pricing decisions.

In the long run a company must price its product to cover its costs and earn a reasonable profit. But to price its product appropriately, it must have a good understanding of market forces at work. In most cases, a company does not set the prices. Instead the price is set by the competitive market (the laws of supply and demand). For example, a company such as ChevronTexaco or ExxonMobil

[1] "AIDS Gaffes in Africa Come Back to Haunt Drug Industry at Home," *Wall Street Journal* (April 23, 2001), p. 1.

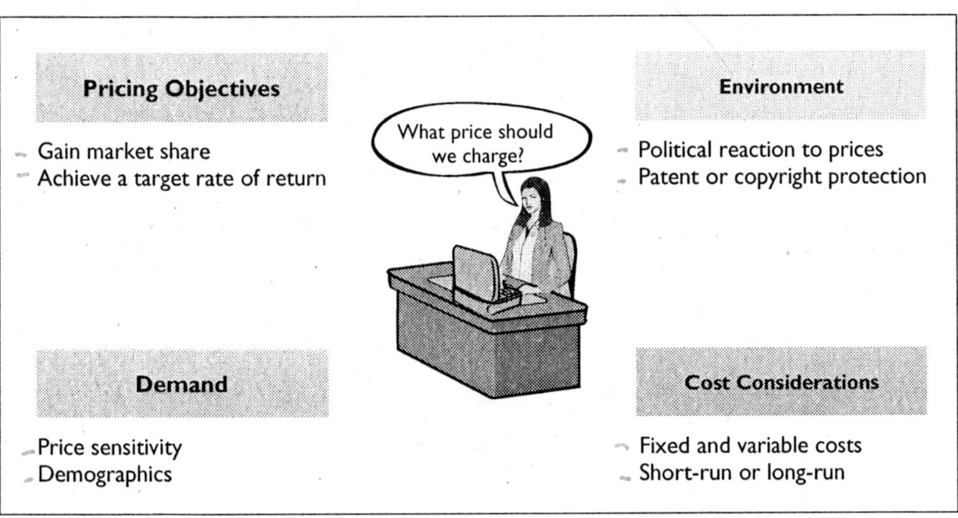

Illustration 11-1
Pricing factors

cannot set the price of gasoline by itself. These companies are called **price takers** because the price of gasoline is set by market forces (the supply of oil and the demand by customers). This is the case for any product that is not easily differentiated from competing products, such as farm products (corn or wheat) or minerals (coal or sand).

In other situations the company sets the prices. This would be the case where the product is specially made for a customer, as in a one-of-a-kind product such as a designer dress by Zoran or Armani. This also occurs when there are few or no other producers capable of manufacturing a similar item. An example would be a company that has a patent or copyright on a unique process, such as the case of computer chips by Intel. However, it is also the case when a company can effectively differentiate its product or service from others. Even in a competitive market like coffee, Starbucks has been able to differentiate its product and charge a premium for a cup of java.

MANAGEMENT INSIGHT

What's the Price on the Internet?

How has the Internet affected pricing? The answer isn't simple, because of two conflicting forces. On the one hand, the Internet allows customers to easily compare prices, thus driving prices down. In fact, many companies feared that the Internet would squeeze all profits out of their businesses. However, e-business has also allowed many businesses to more effectively target their customers and differentiate their products, thus allowing them to avoid severe price competition by striving to create customer-focused "markets of one." E-business technology conveniently provides up-to-date information about "buying behaviors and the level of real-time local demand. Also, e-businesses are able to customize offerings by rebundling related services and products—often from a number of different companies—into attractive 'baskets'."

Source: M. V. Deise et al., *Executive's Guide to E-Business: From Tactics to Strategy* (New York: John Wiley & Sons, Inc., 2000), p. 195.

How does the Internet affect product prices?

TARGET COSTING

STUDY OBJECTIVE 1

Compute a target cost when the market determines a product price.

Automobile manufacturers like Ford or Toyota face a competitive market. The price of an automobile is affected greatly by the laws of supply and demand, so no company in this industry can affect the price to a significant degree. Therefore, to earn a profit, companies in the auto industry must focus on controlling costs. This requires setting a **target cost** that provides a desired profit. Illustration 11-2 shows the relationship and importance of a target cost to the price and desired profit.

Illustration 11-2
Target cost as related to price and profit

Market Price	−	Desired Profit	=	Target Cost

If General Motors, for example, can produce its automobiles for the target cost (or less), it will meet its profit goal. If it cannot achieve its target cost, it will fail to produce the desired profit (and will most likely "get hammered" by stockholders and the market). In a competitive market, a company chooses the segment of the market it wants to compete in—that is, its market niche. For example, it may choose between selling luxury goods or economy goods in order to focus its efforts on one segment or the other.

Once the company has identified its segment of the market, it conducts market research to determine the target price. This target price is the price that the company believes would place it in the optimal position for its target audience. Once the company has determined this target price, it can determine its target cost by setting a desired profit. The difference between the target price and the desired profit is the target cost of the product. (This computation is shown in Illustration 11-2.) After the company determines the target cost, it assembles a team of employees with expertise in a variety of areas (production and operations, marketing, and finance). The team's task is to design and develop a product that can meet quality specifications while not exceeding the target cost. The target cost includes all product and period costs necessary to make and market the product or service.

MANAGEMENT INSIGHT

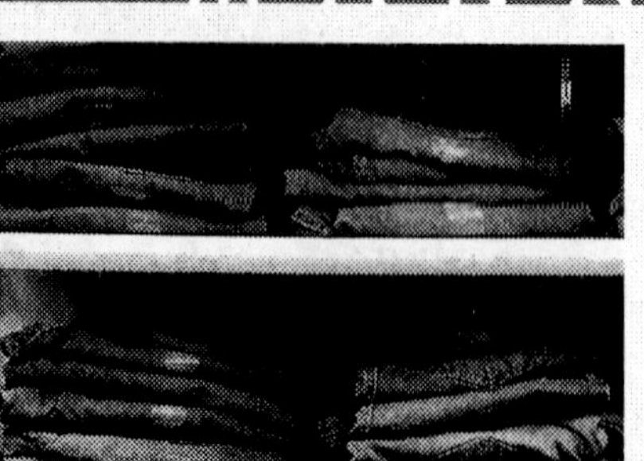

Wal-Mart Says the Price Is Too High

"And the price should be $19 per pair of jeans instead of $23," said the retailer Wal-Mart to jean maker Levi Strauss. What happened to Levi Strauss is what happens to many manufacturers who deal with Wal-Mart. Wal-Mart often sets the price, and the manufacturer has to find out how to make a profit, given that price. In Levi Strauss's case, it revamped its distribution and production to serve Wal-Mart and improve its overall record of timely deliveries. Producing a season of new jeans styles, from conception to store shelves, used to take Levi 12 to 15 months. Today it takes just 10 months for Levi Strauss signature jeans; for regular Levi's, the time is down to 7 1/2 months. As the chief executive of Levi Strauss noted, "We had to change people and practice. It's been somewhat of a D-Day invasion approach."

Source: "In Bow to Retailers' New Clout, Levi Strauss Makes Alterations," *Wall Street Journal*, June 17, 2004, p A1.

What are some issues that Levi should consider in deciding whether it should agree to meet Wal-Mart's target price?

DECISION TOOLKIT

Decision Checkpoints	Info Needed for Decision	Tool to Use for Decision	How to Evaluate Results
	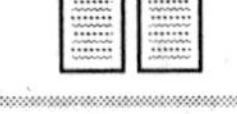		
How does management use target costs to make decisions about manufacturing products or providing services?	Target selling price, desired profit, target cost	Target selling price less desired profit equals target cost	If actual cost exceeds target cost, the company will not earn desired profit. If desired profit is not achieved, company must evaluate whether to manufacture the product or provide the service.

COST-PLUS PRICING

STUDY OBJECTIVE 2

Compute a target selling price using cost-plus pricing.

As discussed, in a competitive, common-product environment the market price is already set, and the company instead must set a target cost. But, in a less competitive or noncompetitive environment, the company may be faced with the task of setting its own price. When the company sets the price, price is commonly a function of the cost of the product or service. That is, the typical approach is to use **cost-plus pricing**. This approach involves establishing a cost base and adding to this cost base a **markup** to determine a **target selling price**. The size of the markup (the "plus") depends on the desired return on investment (ROI = net income ÷ invested assets) for the product line, product, or service. In determining the proper markup, the company must also consider competitive and market conditions, political and legal issues, and other relevant risk factors. The cost-plus pricing formula is expressed as follows.

$$\text{Cost} + \begin{array}{c}\text{Markup Percentage}\\ \times\\ \text{Cost}\end{array} = \text{Target Selling Price}$$

Illustration 11-3
Cost-plus pricing formula

To illustrate, assume that Cleanmore Products, Inc. is in the process of setting a selling price on its new top-of-the-line, 3-horsepower, 16-gallon, variable-speed wet/dry shop vacuum. The per unit variable cost estimates for the new shop vacuum are as follows.

Illustration 11-4
Variable costs per unit

	Per Unit
Direct materials	$23
Direct labor	17
Variable manufacturing overhead	12
Variable selling and administrative expenses	8
Variable cost per unit	$60

In addition, Cleanmore has the following (page 486) fixed costs per unit at a budgeted sales volume of 10,000 units.

Illustration 11-5
Fixed cost per unit, 10,000 units

	Total Costs	÷	Budgeted Volume	=	Cost Per Unit
Fixed manufacturing overhead	$280,000	÷	10,000	=	$28
Fixed selling and administrative expenses	240,000	÷	10,000	=	24
Fixed cost per unit					$52

Cleanmore has decided to price its new shop vacuum to earn a 20% return on its investment (ROI) of $1,000,000. Therefore, Cleanmore expects to receive income of $200,000 (20% × $1,000,000) on its investment. On a per unit basis, the desired ROI is $20 ($200,000 ÷ 10,000). Given the per unit costs shown above, Cleanmore then computes the sales price to be $132, as follows.

Illustration 11-6
Computation of selling price, 10,000 units

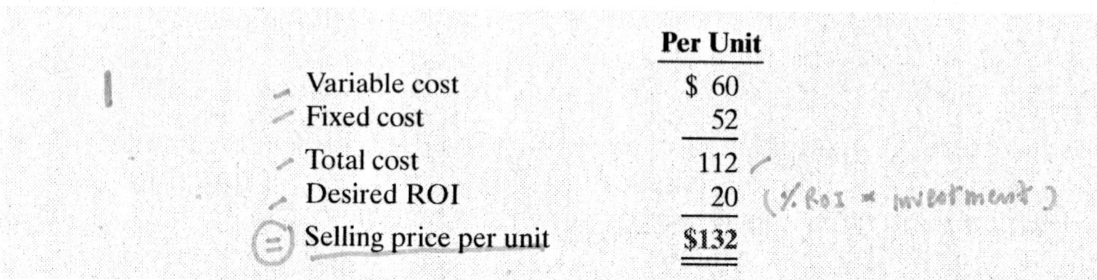

	Per Unit
Variable cost	$ 60
Fixed cost	52
Total cost	112
Desired ROI	20
Selling price per unit	$132

In most cases, companies like Cleanmore will use a percentage markup on cost to determine the selling price. The formula to compute the markup percentage to achieve a desired ROI of $20 per unit is as follows.

Illustration 11-7
Computation of markup percentage

Desired ROI Per Unit	÷	Total Unit Cost	=	Markup Percentage
$20	÷	$112	=	17.86%

Using a 17.86% markup on cost, Cleanmore Products would compute the target selling price as follows.

Illustration 11-8
Computation of selling price—markup approach

Total Unit Cost	+	(Total Unit Cost	×	Markup Percentage)	=	Target Selling Price Per Unit
$112	+	($112	×	17.86%)	=	$132

Cleanmore should set the price for its wet/dry vacuum at $132 per unit.

Limitations of Cost-Plus Pricing

The cost-plus pricing approach has a major advantage: It is simple to compute. However, the cost model does not give consideration to the demand side. That is, will customers pay the price Cleanmore computed for its vacuums? In addition, sales volume plays a large role in determining per unit costs. The lower the sales volume, for example, the higher the price Cleanmore must charge to meet its desired ROI. To illustrate, if the budgeted sales volume was 8,000 instead of 10,000, Cleanmore's variable cost per unit would remain the same. However, the fixed cost per unit would change as follows.

Illustration 11-9
Fixed cost per unit, 8,000 units

	Total Costs	÷	Budgeted Volume	=	Cost Per Unit
Fixed manufacturing overhead	$280,000	÷	8,000	=	$35
Fixed selling and administrative expenses	240,000	÷	8,000	=	30
Fixed cost per unit					$65

As indicated in Illustration 11-5, fixed costs per unit for 10,000 units were $52. However, at a lower sales volume of 8,000 units, fixed costs per unit increase to $65. Cleanmore's desired 20% ROI now results in a $25 ROI per unit [(20% × $1,000,000) ÷ 8,000]. Cleanmore computes the selling price at 8,000 units as follows.

Illustration 11-10
Computation of selling price, 8,000 units

	Per Unit
Variable cost	$ 60
Fixed cost	65
Total cost	125
Desired ROI	25
Selling price per unit	$150

As shown, the lower the budgeted volume, the higher the per unit price. The reason: Fixed costs and ROI are spread over fewer units, and therefore the fixed cost and ROI per unit increase. In this case, at 8,000 units, Cleanmore would have to mark up its total unit costs 20% to earn a desired ROI of $25 per unit, as shown below.

$$20\% = \frac{\$25 \text{ (desired ROI)}}{\$125 \text{ (total unit cost)}}$$

The target selling price would then be $150, as indicated earlier:

$$\$125 + (\$125 \times 20\%) = \$150$$

The opposite effect will occur if budgeted volume is higher (say, at 12,000 units) because fixed costs and ROI can be spread over more units. As a result, the cost-plus model of pricing will achieve its desired ROI only when Cleanmore sells the quantity it budgeted. If actual volume is much less than budgeted volume, Cleanmore may sustain losses unless it can raise its prices.

VARIABLE-COST PRICING

In determining the target price for Cleanmore's shop vacuum, we calculated the cost base by including all costs incurred. This approach is referred to as **full-cost pricing**. Instead of using full costs to set prices, some companies simply add a markup to their variable costs. Using **variable-cost pricing** as the basis for setting prices avoids the problem of using uncertain cost information (as shown in Illustration 11-9) related to fixed-cost-per-unit computations. Variable-cost pricing also is helpful in pricing special orders or when excess capacity exists.

The major disadvantage of variable-cost pricing is that managers may set the price too low and consequently fail to cover their fixed costs. In the long run, failure to cover fixed costs will lead to losses. As a result, companies that use variable-cost pricing must adjust their markups to make sure that the price set will provide a fair return. An example of how variable costs are used as the basis for setting prices is discussed in the appendix to this chapter.

MANAGEMENT INSIGHT

Losing Money with Every Sale

During 2006 the sale of high-definition television sets exploded. It would seem that this was good news for the makers of the flat-screens that are used in these televisions. But the reality was that those companies were losing money almost as fast as they were making TV screens. The problem is that there are a number of flat-screen manufacturers, and they all increased capacity because they expected sales volume to increase even more than it did. In order to avoid getting stuck with inventory, they then cut prices severely, so the companies actually had huge losses even as they were selling a record number of screens. The prices of high-definition TVs have continued to fall, which will make it unlikely that the flat-screen manufacturers will be able to increase their prices. Instead, they must look for ways to cut their costs by as much as 30%.

? If prices continue to tumble, and sales do not increase at a more rapid rate, what will probably happen to the manufacturers of flat-screen TVs?

DECISION TOOLKIT

Decision Checkpoints 	Info Needed for Decision 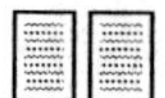	Tool to Use for Decision 	How to Evaluate Results 
What factors should be considered in determining selling price in a less competitive environment?	Total cost per unit and desired profit (cost-plus pricing)	Total cost per unit plus desired profit equals target selling price	Does company make its desired profit? If not, does the profit shortfall result from less volume?

Before You Go On...

REVIEW IT

1. What is a target cost, and how does management use it?
2. What is the general formula for determining the target selling price with cost-plus pricing?
3. How is the per unit return on investment determined?

DO IT

Air Corporation produces air purifiers. The following per unit cost information is available: direct materials \$16; direct labor \$18; variable manufacturing overhead \$11; fixed manufacturing overhead \$10; variable selling and administrative expenses \$6; and fixed selling and administrative expenses \$10. Using a 45% markup percentage on total per unit cost, compute the target selling price.

Action Plan

- Calculate the total cost per unit.
- Multiply the total cost per unit by the markup percentage, then add this amount to the total cost per unit to determine the target selling price.

Solution

Direct materials	$16
Direct labor	18
Variable manufacturing overhead	11
Fixed manufacturing overhead	10
Variable selling and administrative expenses	6
Fixed selling and administrative expenses	10
Total unit cost	$71

Total unit cost	+	(Total unit cost	×	Markup percentage)	=	Target selling price
$71	+	($71	×	45%)	=	$102.95

Related exercise material: *BE11-2, BE11-3, BE11-4, BE11-5, E11-3, E11-4, E11-5, E11-6, and E11-7.*

TIME-AND-MATERIAL PRICING

STUDY OBJECTIVE 3

Use time-and-material pricing to determine the cost of services provided.

Another variation on cost-plus pricing is called **time-and-material pricing**. Under this approach, the company sets two pricing rates—one for the **labor** used on a job and another for the **material**. The labor rate includes direct labor time and other employee costs. The material charge is based on the cost of direct parts and materials used and a **material loading charge** for related overhead costs. Time-and-material pricing is widely used in service industries, especially professional firms such as public accounting, law, engineering, and consulting firms, as well as construction companies, repair shops, and printers.

To illustrate a time-and-material pricing situation, assume the following data for Lake Holiday Marina, a boat and motor repair shop.

Illustration 11-11
Total annual budgeted time and material costs

LAKE HOLIDAY MARINA
Budgeted Costs for the Year 2008

	Time Charges	Material Loading Charges*
Mechanics' wages and benefits	$103,500	–
Parts manager's salary and benefits	–	$11,500
Office employee's salary and benefits	20,700	2,300
Other overhead (supplies, depreciation, property taxes, advertising, utilities)	26,800	14,400
Total budgeted costs	$151,000	$28,200

*The material loading charges exclude the invoice cost of the materials.

Using time-and-material pricing involves three steps: (1) calculate the per hour labor charge, (2) calculate the charge for obtaining and holding materials, and (3) calculate the charges for a particular job.

Step 1: Calculate the Labor Charge. The first step for time-and-material pricing is to determine a charge for labor time. The charge for labor time is expressed as a rate per hour of labor. This rate includes: (1) the direct labor cost of the employee, including hourly rate or salary and fringe benefits; (2) selling, administrative, and similar overhead costs; and (3) an allowance for a desired profit or ROI per hour of employee time. In some industries, such as auto, boat, and farm equipment repair shops, a company charges the same hourly labor rate regardless of which employee performs the work. In other industries, a company charges the rate according to classification or level of the employee. A public accounting firm, for example, would charge the services of an assistant, senior, manager, or partner at different rates; a law firm would charge different rates for the work of a paralegal, associate, or partner.

Illustration 11-12 shows computation of the hourly charges for Lake Holiday Marina during 2008. The marina budgets 5,000 hours of repair time in 2008, and it desires a profit margin of $8 per hour of labor.

Illustration 11-12
Computation of hourly time-charge rate

Lake Holiday Marina.xls

File Edit View Insert Format Tools Data Window Help

	A	B	C	D	E	F
1	Per Hour	Total Cost	÷	Total Hours	=	Per Hour Charge
2	Hourly labor rate for repairs					
3	Mechanics' wages and benefits	$103,500	÷	5,000	=	$20.70
4	Overhead costs					
5	Office employee's salary and benefits	20,700	÷	5,000	=	4.14
6	Other overhead	26,800	÷	5,000	=	5.36
7	Total hourly cost	$151,000	÷	5,000	=	30.20
8	Profit margin					8.00
9	Rate charged per hour of labor					$38.20
10						

The marina multiplies this rate of $38.20 by the number of hours of labor used on any particular job to determine the labor charge for that job.

Step 2: Calculate the Material Loading Charge. The charge for materials typically includes the invoice price of any materials used on the job plus a material loading charge. The **material loading charge** covers the costs of purchasing, receiving, handling, and storing materials, plus any desired profit margin on the materials themselves. The material loading charge is expressed as a **percentage** of the total estimated costs of parts and materials for the year. To determine this percentage, the company does the following: (1) It estimates its total annual costs for purchasing, receiving, handling, and storing materials. (2) It divides this amount by the total estimated cost of parts and materials. (3) It adds a desired profit margin on the materials themselves.

Illustration 11-13 shows computation of the material loading charge used by Lake Holiday Marina during 2008. The marina estimates that the total invoice cost

Illustration 11-13
Computation of material loading charge

Lake Holiday Marina.xls

File Edit View Insert Format Tools Data Window Help

	A	B	C	D	E	F
1		Material Loading Charges	÷	Total Invoice Cost, Parts and Materials	=	Material Loading Percentage
2	Overhead costs					
3	Parts manager's salary and benefits	$11,500				
4	Office employee's salary	2,300				
5		13,800	÷	$120,000	=	11.50%
6						
7	Other overhead	14,400	÷	120,000	=	12.00%
8		$28,200	÷	120,000	=	23.50%
9	Profit margin					20.00%
10	Material loading percentage					43.50%
11						

of parts and materials used in 2008 will be $120,000. The marina desires a 20% profit margin on the invoice cost of parts and materials.

The marina's material loading charge on any particular job is 43.50% multiplied by the cost of materials used on the job. For example, if the marina used $100 of parts, the additional material loading charge would be $43.50.

Step 3: Calculate Charges for a Particular Job. The charges for any particular job are the sum of (1) the labor charge, (2) the charge for the materials, and (3) the material loading charge. For example, suppose that Lake Holiday Marina prepares a price quotation to estimate the cost to refurbish a used 28-foot pontoon boat. Lake Holiday Marina estimates the job will require 50 hours of labor and $3,600 in parts and materials. Illustration 11-14 shows the marina's price quotation.

Illustration 11-14
Price quotation for time and material

LAKE HOLIDAY MARINA
Time-and-Material Price Quotation

Job: Marianne Perino, repair of 28-foot pontoon boat		
Labor charges: 50 hours @ $38.20		$1,910
Material charges		
Cost of parts and materials	$3,600	
Material loading charge (43.5% × $3,600)	1,566	5,166
Total price of labor and material		$7,076

Included in the $7,076 price quotation for the boat repair and refurbishment are charges for labor costs, overhead costs, materials costs, materials handling and storage costs, and a profit margin on both labor and parts. Lake Holiday Marina used labor hours as a basis for computing the time rate. Other companies, such as machine shops, plastic molding shops, and printers, might use machine hours.

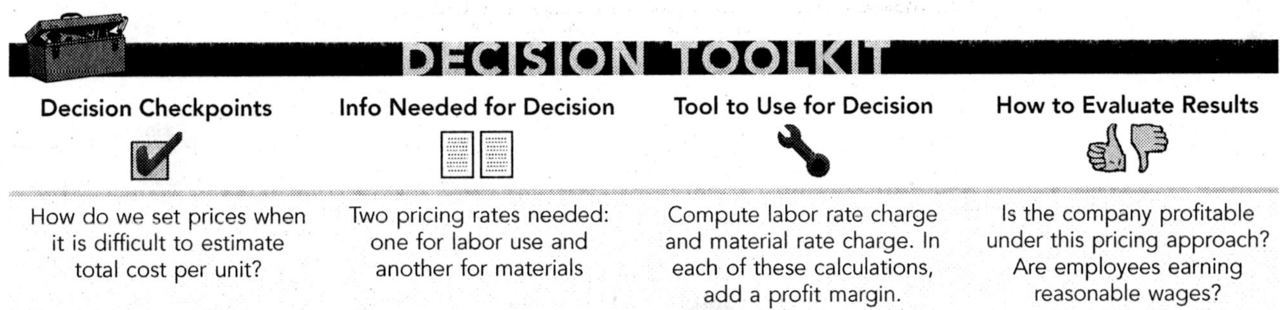

DECISION TOOLKIT

Decision Checkpoints	Info Needed for Decision	Tool to Use for Decision	How to Evaluate Results
How do we set prices when it is difficult to estimate total cost per unit?	Two pricing rates needed: one for labor use and another for materials	Compute labor rate charge and material rate charge. In each of these calculations, add a profit margin.	Is the company profitable under this pricing approach? Are employees earning reasonable wages?

Before You Go On...

REVIEW IT

1. What is time-and-material pricing? Where is it often used?
2. What is a material loading charge?

DO IT

Presented below are data for Harmon Electrical Repair Shop for next year.

Repair-technicians' wages	$130,000
Fringe benefits	30,000
Overhead	20,000

The desired profit margin per labor hour is $10. The material loading charge is 40% of invoice cost. Harman estimates that 8,000 labor hours will be worked next year. If Harmon repairs a TV that takes 4 hours to repair and uses parts of $50, compute the bill for this job.

Action Plan

- Calculate the labor charge.
- Calculate the material loading charge.
- Compute the bill for specific repair.

Solution

	Total Cost	÷	Total Hours	=	Per Hour Charge
Repair-technician's wages	$130,000	÷	8,000	=	$16.25
Fringe benefits	30,000	÷	8,000	=	3.75
Overhead	20,000	÷	8,000	=	2.50
	$180,000	÷	8,000	=	22.50
Profit margin					10.00
Rate charged per hour of labor					$32.50

Materials cost	$50
Materials loading charge ($50 × 40%)	20
Total materials cost	$70
Cost of TV repair	
Labor costs ($32.50 × 4)	$130
Materials cost	70
Total repair cost	$200

Related exercise material: *BE11-6, E11-8, E11-9, and E11-10.*

SECTION 2 Internal Sales

In today's global economy, growth is vital to survival. Frequently growth is "vertical," meaning the company expands in the direction of either its suppliers or its customers. For example, a manufacturer of bicycles, like Trek, may acquire a chain of bicycle shops. A movie production company like Walt Disney or Time Warner may acquire a movie theater chain or a cable television company.

Divisions within vertically integrated companies normally transfer goods or services to other divisions within the same company, as well as make sales to customers outside the company. When companies transfer goods internally, the price used to record the transfer between the two divisions is the **transfer price**. Illustration 11-15 (next page) highlights these transactions for Aerobic Bicycle Company. Aerobic Bicycle has a Bicycle Assembly Division and a Bicycle Component Division.

The pricing issues presented by transfer pricing are similar to those related to outside pricing issues. The objective is to maximize the return to the whole company. In addition, in the transfer-pricing situation, it is important that divisional performance not decline because of internal transfers. As a result, setting a transfer price is complicated because of competing interests among divisions within the company. For example, setting the transfer price high will benefit the Bicycle Component Division (the selling division), but will hurt the Bicycle Assembly Division (the purchasing division).

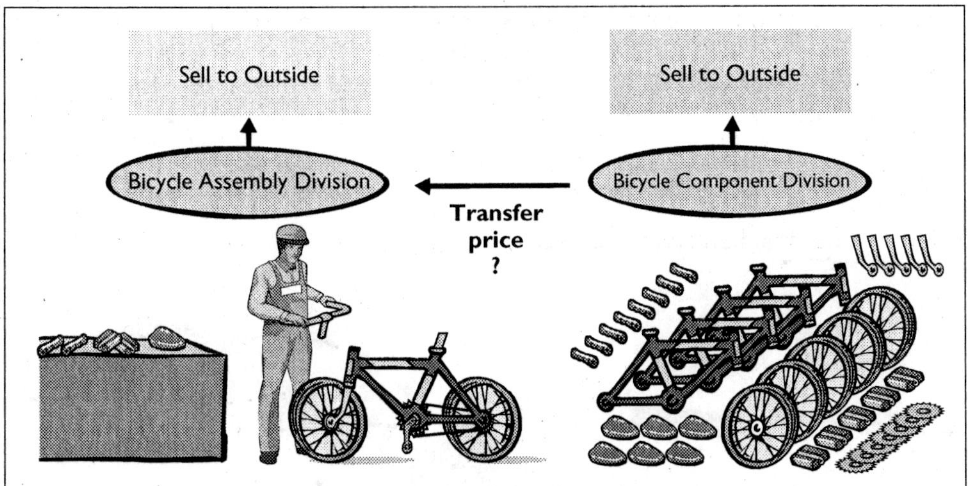

Illustration 11-15
Transfer-pricing example

There are three possible approaches for determining a transfer price:

1. Negotiated transfer prices.
2. Cost-based transfer prices.
3. Market-based transfer prices.

Conceptually, a negotiated transfer price should work best, but due to practical considerations, companies often use the other two methods.

NEGOTIATED TRANSFER PRICES

STUDY OBJECTIVE 4
Determine a transfer price using the negotiated, cost-based, and market-based approaches.

The **negotiated transfer price** is determined through agreement of division managers. To illustrate negotiated transfer pricing, we will examine Alberta Company. Until recently Alberta focused exclusively on making rubber soles for work boots and hiking boots. It sold these rubber soles to boot manufacturers. However, last year the company decided to take advantage of its strong reputation by expanding into the business of making hiking boots. As a consequence of this expansion, the company is now structured as two independent divisions, the Boot Division and the Sole Division. The company compensates the manager of each division based on achievement of profitability targets for his or her division.

The Sole Division continues to make rubber soles for both hiking boots and work boots and sells these soles to other boot manufacturers. The Boot Division manufactures leather uppers for hiking boots and attaches these uppers to rubber soles. During its first year the Boot Division purchased its rubber soles from *outside suppliers* so as not to disrupt the operations of the Sole Division. However, top management now wants the Sole Division to provide at least some of the soles used by the Boot Division. Illustration 11-16 shows the computation of the contribution margin per unit for each division when the Boot Division purchases soles from an outside supplier.

Boot Division		Sole Division	
Selling price of hiking boots	$90	Selling price of sole	$18
Variable cost of manufacturing boot (not including sole)	35	Variable cost per sole	11
Cost of sole purchased from outside suppliers	17		
Contribution margin per unit	**$38**	**Contribution margin per unit**	**$ 7**
Total contribution margin per unit		$45 ($38 + $7)	

Illustration 11-16
Computation of contribution margin for two divisions, when Boot Division purchases soles from an outside supplier

This information indicates that the contribution margin per unit for the Boot Division is $38 and for the Sole Division is $7. The total contribution margin per unit is $45 ($38 + $7).

Now let's ask the question, "What would be a fair transfer price if the Sole Division sold 10,000 soles to the Boot Division?" The answer depends on how busy the Sole Division is—that is, whether it has excess capacity.

No Excess Capacity

As indicated in Illustration 11-16, the Sole Division charges $18 and derives a contribution margin of $7 per sole. The Sole Division has **no excess capacity** and produces and sells 80,000 units (soles) to outside customers. Therefore, the Sole Division must receive from the Boot Division a payment that will at least cover its variable cost per sole **plus** its lost contribution margin per sole. (This lost contribution margin is often referred to as **opportunity cost.**) If the Sole Division cannot cover that amount—called the **minimum transfer price**—it should not sell its soles to the Boot Division. The minimum transfer price that would be acceptable to the Sole Division is $18, as shown below.

Illustration 11-17
Minimum transfer price—no excess capacity

Variable Cost	+	Opportunity Cost	=	Minimum Transfer Price
$11	+	$7	=	$18

From the perspective of the Boot Division (the buyer), the most it will pay is what the sole would cost from an outside supplier. In this case, therefore, the Boot Division would pay no more than $17. As shown in Illustration 11-18, an acceptable transfer price is not available in this situation.

Illustration 11-18
Transfer price negotiations—no deal

Excess Capacity

What happens if the Sole Division **has excess capacity?** For example, assume the Sole Division can produce 80,000 soles but can sell only 70,000 soles in the open market. As a result, it has available capacity of 10,000 units. In this situation, the Sole Division does not lose its contribution margin of $7 per unit and, therefore, the minimum price it would now accept is $11, as shown below.

Illustration 11-19
Minimum transfer price formula—excess capacity

Variable Cost	+	Opportunity Cost	=	Minimum Transfer Price
$11	+	$0	=	$11

In this case, the Boot Division and the Sole Division should negotiate a transfer price within the range of $11 to $17, as shown in Illustration 11-20.

Illustration 11-20
Transfer pricing negotiations—deal

Given excess capacity, Alberta Company will increase its overall net income if the Boot Division purchases the 10,000 soles internally. This is true as long as the Sole Division's variable cost is less than the outside price of $17. The Sole Division will receive a positive contribution margin from any transfer price above its variable cost of $11. The Boot Division will benefit from any price below $17. At any transfer price above $17 the Boot Division will go to an outside supplier, a solution that would be undesirable to both divisions, as well as to the company as a whole.

Variable Costs

In the minimum transfer price formula, **variable cost is defined as the variable cost of units sold *internally*.** In some instances the variable cost of units sold internally will differ from the variable cost of units sold externally. For example, companies often reduce variable selling expenses when units are sold internally. In this case, the variable cost of units sold internally will be lower than that of units sold externally.

Alternatively, the variable cost of units sold internally could be higher if the internal division requests a special order that requires more expensive materials or additional labor. For example, assume that the Boot Division would like to make 5,000 new high-margin, heavy-duty boots. The sole required for this boot will be made of a denser rubber with an intricate lug design. Alberta Company is not aware of any supplier that currently makes such a sole, nor does it feel that any other supplier can meet the quality expectations. As a consequence, there is no available market price to use as the transfer price.

We can, however, still employ the formula for the minimum transfer price to assist in arriving at a reasonable solution. After evaluating the special sole, the Sole Division determines that its variable cost would be $19 per sole. The Sole Division is at full capacity. The Sole Division's opportunity cost at full capacity is the $7 ($18 − $11) per sole that it earns producing the standard sole and selling it to an outside customer. Therefore, the minimum transfer price that the Sole Division would be willing to accept for the special-order sole would be:

Variable Cost	+	Opportunity Cost	=	Minimum Transfer Price
$19	+	$7	=	$26

Illustration 11-21
Minimum transfer price formula—special order

The transfer price of $26 provides the Sole Division with enough revenue to cover its increased variable cost and its opportunity cost (contribution margin on its standard sole).

Summary of Negotiated Transfer Pricing

Under negotiated transfer pricing, the selling division establishes a minimum transfer price, and the purchasing division establishes a maximum transfer price. This system provides a sound basis for establishing a transfer price because both divisions are better off if the proper decision rules are used. However, companies often do not use negotiated transfer pricing because:

- Market price information is sometimes not easily obtainable.
- A lack of trust between the two negotiating divisions may lead to a breakdown in the negotiations.
- Negotiations often lead to different pricing strategies from division to division which is cumbersome and sometimes costly to implement.

Many companies, therefore, often use simple systems based on cost or market information to develop transfer prices.

COST-BASED TRANSFER PRICES

One method of determining transfer prices is to base the transfer price on the costs incurred by the division producing the goods or services. If the company uses a **cost-based transfer price**, the transfer price may be based on variable costs alone, or on variable costs plus fixed costs. The selling division may add a markup.

Under a cost-based approach, divisions sometimes use improper transfer prices. This leads to a loss of profitability for the company and unfair evaluations of division performance. To illustrate, assume that Alberta Company requires the division to use a transfer price based on the variable cost of the sole. With no excess capacity, the contribution margins per unit for the two divisions are:

Illustration 11-22
Cost-based transfer price—10,000 units

Boot Division		Sole Division	
Selling price of hiking boots	$90	Selling price of sole	$11
Variable cost of manufacturing boot (not including sole)	35	Variable cost per sole	11
Cost of sole purchased from sole division	11	**Contribution margin per unit**	**$ 0**
Contribution margin per unit	**$44**		
Total contribution margin per unit		$44 ($44 + $0)	

This cost-based transfer system is a bad deal for the Sole Division, as it reports no profit on the transfer of 10,000 soles to the Boot Division. If the Sole Division could sell these soles to an outside customer, it would make $70,000 [10,000 × ($18 − $11)]. The Boot Division, on the other hand, is delighted: its contribution margin per unit increases from $38 to $44, or $6 per boot. The Sole Division lost a contribution margin per unit of $7 (Illustration 11-16, page 493), and the Boot Division experienced only a $6 increase in its contribution margin per unit. Overall, Alberta Company loses $10,000 [10,000 boots × ($7 − $6)]. Illustration 11-23 (page 497) illustrates this deficiency.

The overall results change if the Sole Division **has excess capacity**. In this case, the Sole Division continues to report a zero profit on these 10,000 units but does not lose the $7 per unit of contribution margin (because it had excess capacity). The Boot Division gains $6. So overall, the company is better off by $60,000 (10,000 × $6). However, with a cost-based system, the Sole Division continues to report a zero profit on these 10,000 units.

We can see that a cost-based system does not reflect the division's true profitability. What's more, it does not even provide adequate incentive for the Sole Division to control costs. The division's costs are simply passed on to the next division.

Illustration 11-23
Cost-based transfer price results—no excess capacity

Notwithstanding these disadvantages, the cost system is simple to understand and easy to use because the information is already available in the accounting system. In addition, market information is sometimes not available, so the only alternative is some type of cost-based system. As a result, it is the most common method used by companies to establish transfer prices.

MARKET-BASED TRANSFER PRICES

The **market-based transfer price** is based on existing market prices of competing goods or services. A market-based system is often considered the best approach because it is objective and generally provides the proper economic incentives. For example, if the Sole Division can charge the market price, it is indifferent as to whether soles are sold to outside customers or internally to the Boot Division—it does not lose any contribution margin. Similarly, the Boot Division pays a price for the soles that is at or reasonably close to market.

When the Sole Division has no excess capacity, the market-based system works reasonably well. The Sole Division receives market price, and the Boot Division pays market price.

If the Sole Division has excess capacity, however, the market-based system can lead to actions that are not in the best interest of the company. For example, the minimum transfer price that the Sole Division should receive is its variable cost plus opportunity cost. Given that the Sole Division has excess capacity, its opportunity cost is zero. However, under the market-based system, the Sole Division transfers the goods at the market price of $18, for a contribution margin per unit of $7. The Boot Division manager then has to accept the $18 sole price. The Boot Division must recognize, however, that this price is not the cost of the sole, given that the Sole Division had excess capacity. As a result, the Boot Division may overprice its boots in the market if it uses the market price of the sole plus a markup in setting the price of the boot. This action can lead to losses for Alberta overall.

As indicated earlier, in many cases, there simply is not a well-defined market for the good or service being transferred. As a result, a reasonable market value cannot be developed, and therefore companies resort to a cost-based system.

EFFECT OF OUTSOURCING ON TRANSFER PRICING

An increasing number of companies rely on **outsourcing**. Outsourcing involves contracting with an external party to provide a good or service, rather than performing the work internally. Some companies have taken outsourcing to the extreme by outsourcing all of their production. These so-called **virtual companies** have well-established brand names, though they do not manufacture any of their own products. Companies use incremental analysis (Chapter 9) to determine whether outsourcing is profitable. As companies increasingly rely on outsourcing, fewer components are transferred internally between divisions reducing the need for transfer prices.

TRANSFERS BETWEEN DIVISIONS IN DIFFERENT COUNTRIES

STUDY OBJECTIVE 5

Explain issues involved in transferring goods between divisions in different countries.

As more companies "globalize" their operations, an increasing number of transfers are between divisions that are located in different countries. For example, one estimate suggests that 60% of trade between countries is simply transfers between divisions. Differences in tax rates across countries can complicate the determination of the appropriate transfer price.

Companies must pay income tax in the country where they generate the income. In order to maximize income and minimize income tax, many companies prefer to report more income in countries with low tax rates, and less income in countries with high tax rates. They accomplish this by adjusting the transfer prices they use on internal transfers between divisions located in different countries. They allocate more contribution margin to the division in the low-tax-rate country, and allocate less to the division in the high-tax-rate country.

To illustrate, suppose that Alberta's Boot Division is located in a country with a corporate tax rate of 10%, and the Sole Division is located in a country with a tax rate of 30%. Illustration 11-24 demonstrates the after-tax contribution margin to the company as a whole assuming first, that the company transfers the soles at a transfer price of $18, and second, that it transfers them at a transfer price of $11.

Illustration 11-24
After-tax contribution margin per unit under alternative transfer prices

At $18 Transfer Price

Boot Division		**Sole Division**	
Selling price of hiking boots	$90.00	Selling price of sole	$18.00
Variable cost of manufacturing boot (not including sole)	35.00	Variable cost per sole	11.00
Cost of sole purchased internally	18.00		
Before-tax contribution margin	37.00	Before-tax contribution margin	7.00
Tax at 10%	3.70	Tax at 30%	2.10
After-tax contribution margin	$33.30	After-tax contribution margin	$ 4.90

Before-tax total contribution margin per unit to company = $37 + $7 = $44
After-tax total contribution margin per unit to company = $33.30 + $4.90 = $38.20

At $11 Transfer Price

Boot Division		**Sole Division**	
Selling price of hiking boots	$90.00	Selling price of sole	$11.00
Variable cost of manufacturing boot (not including sole)	35.00	Variable cost per sole	11.00
Cost of sole purchased internally	11.00		
Before-tax contribution margin	44.00	Before-tax contribution margin	0.00
Tax at 10%	4.40	Tax at 30%	0.00
After-tax contribution margin	$39.60	After-tax contribution margin	$ 0.00

Before-tax total contribution margin per unit to company = $44 + $0 = $44
After-tax total contribution margin per unit to company = $39.60 + $0 = $39.60

Note that the *before-tax* total contribution margin to Alberta Company is $44 regardless of whether the transfer price is $18 or $11. However, the *after-tax* total contribution margin to Alberta Company is $38.20 using the $18 transfer price, and

$39.60 using the $11 transfer price. The reason: When Alberta uses the $11 transfer price, more of the contribution margin is attributed to the division that is in the country with the lower tax rate.

As this analysis shows, Alberta Company would be better off using the $11 transfer price. However, this presents some concerns. First, the Sole Division manager won't be happy with an $11 transfer price. This price may lead to unfair evaluations of the Sole Division's manager. Second, the company must ask whether it is legal and ethical to use an $11 transfer price when the market price clearly is higher than that.

Additional consideration of international transfer pricing is presented in advanced accounting texts.

ETHICS INSIGHT

Transferring Profits and Reducing Taxes

International transfer pricing issues create a huge headache for the Internal Revenue Service. Some estimates suggest that the United States loses over $25 billion in underpaid taxes due to transfer price abuses. Occasionally violators are caught. Toyota, for example, reportedly paid a $1 billion dollar settlement. But enforcement is complicated and time-consuming, and many foreign firms are reluctant to give access to their records.

U.S. companies have also been accused of transfer pricing abuse. It has been noted that at one time U.S. giant Westinghouse booked over 25% of its profit in the tiny island of Puerto Rico. At the time, the corporate tax rate there was zero. The rules require that the transfer price be based on the current market price that a nonrelated party would pay for the goods. But often this current market price is difficult to determine.

What are the implications for other taxpayers if companies reduce their taxes by using improper transfer prices to shift profits to lower-tax countries?

DECISION TOOLKIT

Decision Checkpoints 	Info Needed for Decision 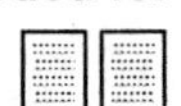	Tool to Use for Decision 	How to Evaluate Results 
What price should be charged for transfer of goods between divisions of a company?	Variable costs, opportunity costs, market prices	Variable cost plus opportunity cost provides minimum transfer price for seller.	If income of division provides fair evaluation of managers, then transfer price is useful. Also, income of the company overall should not be reduced due to the transfer pricing approach.

Before You Go On...

REVIEW IT

1. What are the objectives of transfer pricing?
2. What are the three approaches to transfer pricing? What are the advantages and disadvantages of each?
3. How do some companies reduce their tax payments through their choice of transfer price?

Be sure to read **ALL ABOUT YOU: *Is the Price Right?*** on page 500 for information on how topics in this chapter apply to you.

all about YOU

Is the Price Right?

The right price can make a big difference to companies. For example, at Coca-Cola a 4% increase in the price received for its products would increase net income significantly.

As indicated in the chapter, a company has to choose a price for its products that will cover its variable costs and make some contribution to fixed overhead in the short run. In the long run, the company must price its products to cover all costs. But pricing products to achieve these objectives is complex, given the nature of consumer behavior.

Some Facts

* Prices come in all forms such as tuition for school, fees for medical care, premiums for insurance, user fees for tolls. In some cases we can influence the price by our behavior (e.g., buying airplane tickets online rather than through a travel agent); in other cases, it is more difficult to influence price (e.g., the price of cable TV).
* In one survey, marketing managers rated pricing as their biggest problem. Other issues such as new competition, product differentiation, and selling expenses were not as stressful. Reasons for the stress are the importance of getting the price right to ensure overall profitability and the difficulty of getting it right.
* Do you buy products based on expected savings from rebates? If so, do you actually file for the rebate? Some 40% of rebates do not get redeemed. Many people do not bother to fill out the form and process the receipts. And some companies do not make it easy: They make up complex rules, demand original copies of bills, set short expiration periods, and delay sending checks. In some cases, the companies send the check with another company's name on the envelope in hope you will not recognize it and tear it up.
* Retailers use price-optimization software to assess difficult situations. For example: In a store with a variety of paintbrushes, the best seller was the cheapest one, at $1. But after inputting many variables, the store stopped selling the $1 brushes, which enabled it to sell more high-priced (and more profitable) paintbrushes. Why? The key factor in whether a customer bought a paintbrush was whether he or she was buying paint, not the price of the brush.

Some useful sites for pricing information are *www.consumerreports.org, www.pricescan.com, www.consumerworld.org, www.consumer.gov,* and *www.ftc.gov.*

About the Numbers

At your local grocery store, you may see items that are identified as fair-traded. Fair-traded means that the retailer paid a minimum price to the producer to ensure a fair profit for the producer. Most individuals believe that by paying the fair-trade price, you are helping some struggling farmer, often in a less-developed country.

To better understand how pricing works in a fair-trade situation, here is an example of how the price is set for one pound of fair-trade coffee computed by wholesaler roaster **Dean's Beans.**

$1.41 Price paid to grower, includes 5-cent fair-trade premium
0.39 Administrative costs and shipping
0.36 Shrinkage during roasting
2.50 Operating and maintenance costs
0.14 Packaging and misc. cost
$4.80 Wholesale roaster cost

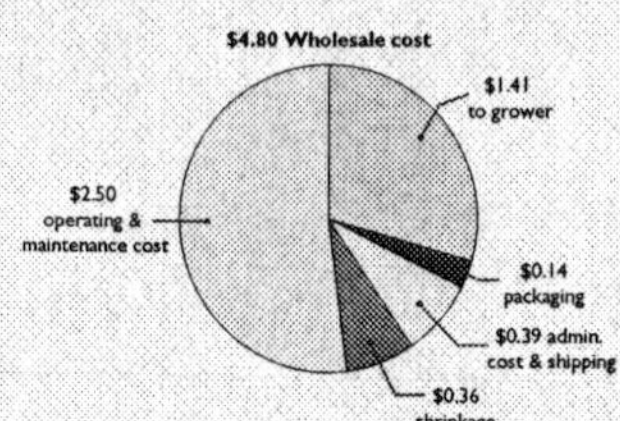

The price at which Dean's sells to the grocery store is $5.00, for a profit of $0.20 to the wholesaler. The retailer sells the pound of coffee to you for $8.49, for a profit of $3.49 profit before expenses. So next time you are considering a fair-traded product, you might ask, How much does that poor struggling farmer receive in relation to the markup that the retailer receives when the product is fair-traded?

Source: Steve Stecklow and Erin White, "What Price Virtue? At Some Retailers, 'Fair Trade' Carries a Very High Cost: Stores Charge Big Markups on Goods Intended to Help Farmers in Poor Countries; Bananas at $2.74 a Bunch," *Wall Street Journal,* June 8, 2004, p. Al.

What Do You Think?

One issue that always raises many questions is the pricing of medical drugs. For example, we often hear about the fact that certain drugs sold by U.S. companies cost much less overseas than in the United States. And there are certain drugs in the United States that seem extremely expensive. For example, Avantis is a cancer-reducing drug that costs patients $55,000 a year. Congress continues to study the issue of drug pricing. Do you think that high pricing of pharmaceuticals is fair?

YES: Drug companies have to spend substantial amounts of money to create new therapies. In addition to the heavy research and development costs involved, the lead time from discovery to actual use of new drugs on patients can exceed 10 years. In short, the drug companies must recover these costs by charging high prices.

NO: The drug companies are profitable. How can they expect individuals to pay very high prices for some of these live-saving drugs? Furthermore, how can a drug sold in the United States often sell for much less in another part of the world?

Sources: Brian Bergstein, "It's Buyer Beware in Stores," Wisconsin State Journal, April 28, 2007, p. A9; Marilyn Chase, "How Genentech Wins At Blockbuster Drugs," Wall Street Journal, June 6, 2007, p. B1; Brian Grow, "The Great Rebate Runaround,' Business Week, December 5, 2005.

The authors' comments on this situation appear on page 527.

Using the Decision Toolkit

Cedarburg Lumber specializes in building "high-end" playhouses for kids. It builds the components in its factory, and then ships the parts to the customer's home. It has contracted with carpenters across the country to do the final assembly. Each year the company introduces a new model. This year's model looks like a miniature castle, complete with spires and drawbridge. The accounting department provided the following cost estimates for this new product for a budgeted volume of 1,000 units.

	Per Unit	Total
Direct materials	$ 840	
Direct labor	$1,600	
Variable manufacturing overhead	$ 400	
Fixed manufacturing overhead		$540,000
Variable selling and administrative expenses	$ 510	
Fixed selling and administrative expenses		$320,000

Cedarburg Lumber uses cost-plus pricing to set its selling price. Management also directs that the target price be set to provide a 25% return on investment (ROI) on invested assets of $4,200,000.

Instructions

(a) Compute the markup percentage and target selling price on this new playhouse.

(b) Assuming that the volume is 1,500 units instead of 1,000 units, compute the markup percentage and target selling price that will allow Cedarburg Lumber to earn its desired ROI of 25%.

Solution

(a)

Variable cost per unit

	Per Unit
Direct materials	$ 840
Direct labor	1,600
Variable manufacturing overhead	400
Variable selling and administrative expenses	510
Variable cost per unit	$3,350

Fixed cost per unit

	Total Costs	÷	Budgeted Volume	=	Cost Per Unit
Fixed manufacturing overhead	$540,000	÷	1,000	=	$540
Fixed selling and administrative expenses	320,000	÷	1,000	=	320
Fixed cost per unit	$860,000				$860

Computation of selling price (1,000 units)

Variable cost per unit	$3,350
Fixed cost per unit	860
Total unit cost	4,210
Desired ROI per unit*	1,050
Selling price	$5,260

*($4,200,000 × .25) ÷ 1,000

The markup percentage is:

$$\frac{\text{Desired ROI per unit}}{\text{Total unit cost}} = \frac{\$1,050}{\$4,210} = 24.9\%$$

(b) If the company produces 1,500 units, its selling price and markup percentage would be:

Computation of selling price (1,500 units)	
Variable cost per unit	$3,350
Fixed cost per unit ($860,000 ÷ 1,500)	573
Total unit cost	3,923
Desired ROI per unit*	700
Selling price	$4,623

*($4,200,000 × .25) ÷ 1,500

The markup percentage would be:

$$\frac{\text{Desired ROI per unit}}{\text{Total unit cost}} = \frac{\$700}{\$3,923} = 17.8\%$$

SUMMARY OF STUDY OBJECTIVES

WILEY PLUS

1 **Compute a target cost when the market determines a product price.** To compute a target cost, the company determines its target selling price. Once the target selling price is set, it determines its target cost by setting a desired profit. The difference between the target price and desired profit is the target cost of the product.

2 **Compute a target selling price using cost-plus pricing.** Cost-plus pricing involves establishing a cost base and adding to this cost base a markup to determine a target selling price. The cost-plus pricing formula is expressed as follows: Target selling price = Cost + (Markup percentage × Cost).

3 **Use time-and-material pricing to determine the cost of services provided.** Under time-and-material pricing, two pricing rates are set—one for the labor used on a job and another for the material. The labor rate includes direct labor time and other employee costs. The material charge is based on the cost of direct parts and materials used and a material loading charge for related overhead costs.

4 **Determine a transfer price using the negotiated, cost-based, and market-based approaches.** The negotiated price is determined through agreement of division managers. Under a cost-based approach, the transfer price may be based on variable cost alone or on variable cost plus fixed costs. Companies may add a markup to these numbers. The cost-based approach often leads to poor performance evaluations and purchasing decisions. The advantage of the cost-based system is its simplicity. A market-based transfer price is based on existing competing market prices and services. A market-based system is often considered the best approach because it is objective and generally provides the proper economic incentives.

5 **Explain issues involved in transferring goods between divisions in different countries.** Companies must pay income tax in the country where they generate the income. In order to maximize income and minimize income tax, many companies prefer to report more income in countries with low tax rates, and less income in countries with high tax rates. This is accomplished by adjusting the transfer prices they use on internal transfers between divisions located in different countries.

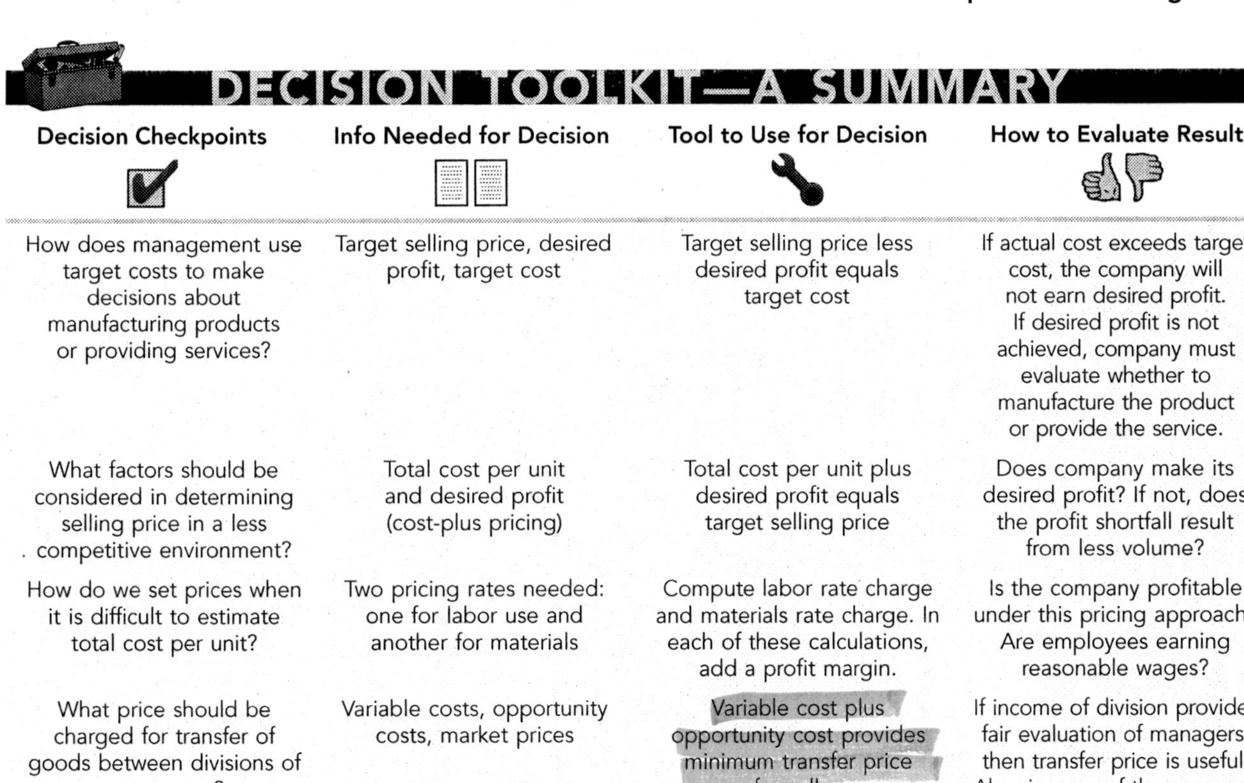

DECISION TOOLKIT—A SUMMARY

Decision Checkpoints	Info Needed for Decision	Tool to Use for Decision	How to Evaluate Results
How does management use target costs to make decisions about manufacturing products or providing services?	Target selling price, desired profit, target cost	Target selling price less desired profit equals target cost	If actual cost exceeds target cost, the company will not earn desired profit. If desired profit is not achieved, company must evaluate whether to manufacture the product or provide the service.
What factors should be considered in determining selling price in a less competitive environment?	Total cost per unit and desired profit (cost-plus pricing)	Total cost per unit plus desired profit equals target selling price	Does company make its desired profit? If not, does the profit shortfall result from less volume?
How do we set prices when it is difficult to estimate total cost per unit?	Two pricing rates needed: one for labor use and another for materials	Compute labor rate charge and materials rate charge. In each of these calculations, add a profit margin.	Is the company profitable under this pricing approach? Are employees earning reasonable wages?
What price should be charged for transfer of goods between divisions of a company?	Variable costs, opportunity costs, market prices	Variable cost plus opportunity cost provides minimum transfer price for seller.	If income of division provides fair evaluation of managers, then transfer price is useful. Also, income of the company overall should not be reduced due to the transfer pricing approach.

APPENDIX Other Cost Approaches to Pricing

STUDY OBJECTIVE 6

Determine prices using absorption-cost pricing and variable-cost pricing.

In determining the target price for Cleanmore's shop vacuum in the chapter, we calculated the cost base **by including all costs incurred**. This approach is referred to as **full-cost pricing**. Using total cost as the basis of the markup makes sense conceptually because in the long run the price must cover all costs and provide a reasonable profit. However, total cost is difficult to determine in practice. This is because period costs (selling and administrative expenses) are difficult to trace to a specific product. Activity-based costing can be used to overcome this difficulty to some extent.

In practice, companies use two other cost approaches: (1) absorption-cost pricing, and (2) variable-cost pricing. Absorption-cost pricing is more popular than variable-cost pricing.[1] We will illustrate both of them, though, because both have merit.

ABSORPTION-COST PRICING

Absorption-cost pricing is consistent with generally accepted accounting principles (GAAP). The reason: It includes both variable and fixed manufacturing costs as product costs. **It excludes from this cost base both variable and fixed selling and administrative costs**. Thus, companies must somehow provide for selling and administrative costs plus the target ROI, and they do this through the markup.

[1] For a discussion of cost-plus pricing, see Eunsup Skim and Ephraim F. Sudit, "How Manufacturers Price Products," *Management Accounting* (February 1995), pp. 37–39; and V. Govindarajan and R. N. Anthony, "How Firms Use Cost Data in Pricing Decisions," *Management Accounting,* 65, no. 1, pp. 30–36.

The **first step** in absorption-cost pricing is to compute the unit **manufacturing cost**. For Cleanmore Products, Inc., this amounts to $80 per unit at a volume of 10,000 units, as shown in Illustration 11A-1.

Illustration 11A-1
Computation of unit manufacturing cost

	Per Unit
Direct materials	$23
Direct labor	17
Variable manufacturing overhead	12
Fixed manufacturing overhead ($280,000 ÷ 10,000)	28
Total unit manufacturing cost (absorption cost)	$80

In addition, Cleanmore provided the following information regarding selling and administrative expenses per unit and desired ROI per unit.

Illustration 11A-2
Other information

Variable selling and administrative expenses	$8
Fixed selling and administrative expenses ($240,000 ÷ 10,000)	$24
Desired ROI per unit	$20

The **second step** in absorption-cost pricing is to compute the markup percentage using the formula in Illustration 11A-3. Note that when companies use manufacturing cost per unit as the cost base to compute the markup percentage, the **percentage must cover the desired ROI and also the selling and administrative expenses**.

Illustration 11A-3
Markup percentage—absorption-cost pricing

Desired ROI Per Unit	+	Selling and Administrative Expenses Per Unit	=	Markup Percentage	×	Manufacturing Cost Per Unit
$20	+	$32	=	**MP**	×	$80

Solving we find:

$$MP = (\$20 + \$32) \div \$80 = 65\%$$

The **third** and final **step** is to set the target selling price. Using a markup percentage of 65% and absorption cost pricing, Cleanmore computes the target selling price as shown in Illustration 11A-4.

Illustration 11A-4
Computation of target price—absorption-cost pricing

Manufacturing Cost per Unit	+	(Markup Percentage	×	Manufacturing Cost Per Unit)	=	Target Selling Price
$80	+	(65%	×	$80)	=	$132

Using a target price of $132 will produce the desired 20% return on investment for Cleanmore Products on its 3-horsepower, wet/dry shop vacuum at a volume level of 10,000 units, as shown in Illustration 11A-5.

Illustration 11A-5
Proof of 20% ROI—absorption-cost pricing

CLEANMORE PRODUCTS, INC.
Budgeted Absorption-Cost Income Statement

Revenue (10,000 units × $132)	$1,320,000
Cost of goods sold (10,000 units × $80)	800,000
Gross profit	520,000
Selling and administrative expenses [10,000 units × ($8 + $24)]	320,000
Net income	$ 200,000

Budgeted ROI

$$\frac{\text{Net income}}{\text{Invested assets}} = \frac{\$200{,}000}{\$1{,}000{,}000} = 20\%$$

Markup Percentage

$$\frac{\text{Net income} + \text{Selling and administrative expenses}}{\text{Cost of goods sold}} = \frac{\$200{,}000 + \$320{,}000}{\$800{,}000} = 65\%$$

Because of the fixed-cost element, if Cleanmore sells more than 10,000 units, the ROI will be greater than 20%. If it sells fewer than 10,000 units, the ROI will be less than 20%. The markup percentage is also verified by adding $200,000 (the net income) and $320,000 (selling and administrative expenses) and then dividing by $800,000 (the cost of goods sold or the cost base).

Most companies that use cost-plus pricing use either absorption cost or full cost as the basis. The reasons for this tendency are as follows.

1. Absorption-cost information is most readily provided by a company's cost accounting system. Because absorption-cost data already exist in general ledger accounts, it is cost-effective to use the data for pricing.
2. Basing the cost-plus formula on only variable costs could encourage managers to set too low a price to boost sales. There is the fear that if managers use only variable costs, they will substitute variable costs for full costs, which can lead to suicidal price cutting.
3. Absorption-cost or full-cost pricing provides the most defensible base for justifying prices to all interested parties—managers, customers, and government.

VARIABLE-COST PRICING

Under variable-cost pricing, the cost base consists of all of the **variable costs** associated with a product, including variable selling and administrative costs. **Because fixed costs are not included in the base, the markup must provide for fixed costs (manufacturing, and selling and administrative) and the target ROI.** Variable-cost pricing is more useful for making short-run decisions because it considers variable cost and fixed cost behavior patterns separately.

The **first step** in variable-cost pricing is to compute the unit variable cost. For Cleanmore Products, Inc., this amounts to $60 per unit as shown in Illustration 11A-6.

Illustration 11A-6
Computation of unit variable cost

	Per Unit
Direct materials	$23
Direct labor	17
Variable manufacturing overhead	12
Variable selling and administrative expense	8
Total unit variable cost	$60

The **second step** in variable-cost pricing is to compute the markup percentage. Illustration 11A-7 shows the formula for the markup percentage. For Cleanmore, fixed costs include fixed manufacturing overhead of $28 per unit ($280,000 ÷ 10,000) and fixed selling and administrative expenses of $24 per unit ($240,000 ÷ 10,000).

Illustration 11A-7
Computation of markup percentage—variable-cost pricing

Desired ROI Per Unit	+	Fixed Costs Per Unit	=	Markup Percentage	×	Variable Cost Per Unit
$20	+	($28 + $24)	=	**MP**	×	$60

Solving, we find:

$$MP = \frac{\$20 + (\$28 + \$24)}{\$60} = 120\%$$

The **third step** is to set the target selling price. Using a markup percentage of 120% and the contribution approach, Cleanmore computes the selling price as shown in Illustration 11A-8.

Illustration 11A-8
Computation of target price—variable-cost pricing

Variable Cost Per Unit	+	(Markup Percentage	×	Variable Cost Per Unit)	=	Target Selling Price
$60	+	(120%	×	$60)	=	$132

Using a target price of $132 will produce the desired 20% return on investment for Cleanmore Products on its 3-horse power, wet/dry shop vacuum at a volume level of 10,000 units, as shown in Illustration 11A-9.

Illustration 11A-9
Proof of 20% ROI—contribution approach

CLEANMORE PRODUCTS, INC.
Budgeted Variable-Cost Income Statement

Revenue (10,000 vacuums × $132)		$1,320,000
Variable costs (10,000 vacuums × $60)		600,000
Contribution margin		720,000
Fixed manufacturing overhead (10,000 vacuums × $28)	$280,000	
Fixed selling and administrative expenses (10,000 vacuums × $24)	240,000	520,000
Net income		**$ 200,000**

Budgeted ROI

$$\frac{\text{Net income}}{\text{Invested assets}} = \frac{\$200{,}000}{\$1{,}000{,}000} = \mathbf{20\%}$$

Markup Percentage

$$\frac{\text{Net income + Fixed costs}}{\text{Variable costs}} = \frac{\$200{,}000 + \$520{,}000}{\$600{,}000} = \mathbf{120\%}$$

Under any of the three pricing approaches we have looked at (full-cost, absorption-cost, and variable-cost), the desired ROI will be attained only if the budgeted sales volume for the period is attained. None of these approaches guarantees a profit or a desired ROI. Achieving a desired ROI is the result of many factors, some of which are beyond the company's control, such as market conditions, political and legal issues, customers' tastes, and competitive actions.

Because absorption-cost pricing includes allocated fixed costs, it does not make clear how the company's costs will change as volume changes. To avoid blurring the effects of cost behavior on net income, some managers therefore prefer variable-cost pricing. The specific reasons for using variable-cost pricing, even though the basic accounting data are less accessible, are as follows.

1. Variable-cost pricing, being based on variable cost, is more consistent with cost-volume-profit analysis used by managers to measure the profit implications of changes in price and volume.
2. Variable-cost pricing provides the type of data managers need for pricing special orders. It shows the incremental cost of accepting one more order.
3. Variable-cost pricing avoids arbitrary allocation of common fixed costs (such as executive salaries) to individual product lines.

SUMMARY OF STUDY OBJECTIVE FOR APPENDIX

6 **Determine prices using absorption-cost pricing and variable-cost pricing.** Absorption-cost pricing uses total manufacturing cost as the cost base and provides for selling and administrative costs plus the target ROI through the markup. The target selling price is computed as: Manufacturing cost per unit + (Markup percentage × Manufacturing cost per unit).

Variable-cost pricing uses all of the variable costs, including selling and administrative costs, as the cost base and provides for fixed costs and target ROI through the markup. The target selling price is computed as: Variable cost per unit + (Markup percentage × Variable cost per unit).

GLOSSARY

Absorption-cost pricing An approach to pricing that defines the cost base as the manufacturing cost; it excludes both variable and fixed selling and administrative costs. (p. 503)

Cost-based transfer price A transfer price that uses as its foundation the costs incurred by the division producing the goods. (p. 496)

Cost-plus pricing A process whereby a product's selling price is determined by adding a markup to a cost base. (p. 485)

Full-cost pricing An approach to pricing that defines the cost base as all costs incurred. (p. 487)

Market-based transfer price A transfer price that is based on existing market prices of competing products. (p. 497)

Markup The percentage applied to a product's cost to determine the product's selling price. (p. 485)

Material loading charge A charge added to cover the cost of purchasing, receiving, handling, and storing materials, plus any desired profit margin on the materials themselves. (p. 490)

Negotiated transfer price A transfer price that is determined by the agreement of the division managers. (p. 493)

Outsourcing Contracting with an external party to provide a good or service, rather than performing the work internally. (p. 497)

Target cost The cost that will provide the desired profit on a product when the seller does not have control over the product's price. (p. 484)

Target selling price The selling price that will provide the desired profit on a product when the seller has the ability to determine the product's price. (p. 485)

Time-and-material pricing An approach to cost-plus pricing in which the company uses two pricing rates, one for the labor used on a job and another for the material. (p. 489)

Transfer price The price used to record the transfer of goods between two divisions of a company. (p. 492)

Variable-cost pricing An approach to pricing that defines the cost base as all variable costs; it excludes both fixed manufacturing and fixed selling and administrative costs. (pp. 487, 505)

Demonstration Problem

Revco Electronics is a division of International Motors, an automobile manufacturer. Revco produces car radio/CD players. Revco sells its products to International Motors, as well as to other car manufacturers and electronics distributors. The following information is available regarding Revco's car radio/CD player.

Selling price of car radio/CD player to external customers	$49
Variable cost per unit	$28
Capacity	200,000 units

Instructions

Determine whether the goods should be transferred internally or purchased externally and what the appropriate transfer price should be under each of the following **independent** situations.

(a) Revco Electronics is operating at full capacity. There is a saving of $4 per unit for variable cost if the car radio is made for internal sale. International Motors can purchase a comparable car radio from an outside supplier for $47.

(b) Revco Electronics has sufficient existing capacity to meet the needs of International Motors. International Motors can purchase a comparable car radio from an outside supplier for $47.

(c) International Motors wants to purchase a special-order car radio/CD player that also includes a tape deck. It needs 15,000 units. Revco Electronics has determined that the additional variable cost would be $12 per unit. Revco Electronics has no spare capacity. It will have to forgo sales of 15,000 units to external parties in order to provide this special order.

action plan

- ✓ Determine whether company is at full capacity or not.
- ✓ Find the minimum transfer price, using formulas.
- ✓ Compare maximum price the buyer would pay to the minimum price for the seller.
- ✓ Determine if a deal can be made.

Solution

(a) Revco Electronics' opportunity cost (its lost contribution margin) would be $21 ($49 − $28). Using the formula for minimum transfer price, we determine:

Minimum transfer price	=	Variable cost	+	Opportunity cost
$45	=	($28 − $4)	+	$21

Since this minimum transfer price is less than the $47 it would cost if International Motors purchases from an external party, internal transfer should take place. Revco Electronics and International Motors should negotiate a transfer price between $45 and $47.

(b) Since Revco Electronics has available capacity, its opportunity cost (its lost contribution margin) would be $0. Using the formula for minimum transfer price, we determine the following.

Minimum transfer price	=	Variable cost	+	Opportunity cost
$28	=	$28	+	$0

Since International Motors can purchase the unit for $47 from an external party, the most it would be willing to pay would be $47. It is in the best interest of the company as a whole, as well as the two divisions, for a transfer to take place. The two divisions must reach a negotiated transfer price between $28 and $47 that recognizes the costs and benefits to each party and is acceptable to both.

(c) Revco Electronics' opportunity cost (its lost contribution margin per unit) would be $21 ($49 − $28). Its variable cost would be $40 ($28 + $12). Using the formula for minimum transfer price, we determine the following.

Minimum transfer price	=	Variable cost	+	Opportunity cost
$61	=	$40	+	$21

Note that in this case Revco Electronics has no available capacity. Its management may decide that it does not want to provide this special order because to do so will require that it cut off the supply of the standard unit to some of its existing customers. This may anger those customers and result in the loss of customers.

✓ The Navigator

*Note: All **asterisked** Questions, Exercises, and Problems relate to material in the appendix to the chapter.

SELF-STUDY QUESTIONS

Answers are at the end of the chapter.

(SO 2) **1.** Cost-plus pricing means that:
a. Selling price = Variable cost + (Markup percentage + Variable cost).
b. Selling price = Cost + (Markup percentage × Cost).
c. Selling price = Manufacturing cost + (Markup percentage + Manufacturing cost).
d. Selling price = Fixed cost + (Markup percentage × Fixed cost).

(SO 1) **2.** Target cost related to price and profit means that:
a. cost and desired profit must be determined before selling price.
b. cost and selling price must be determined before desired profit.
c. price and desired profit must be determined before costs.
d. costs can be achieved only if the company is at full capacity.

(SO 1) **3.** Classic Toys has examined the market for toy train locomotives. It believes there is a market niche in which it can sell locomotives at $80 each. It estimates that it could sell 10,000 of these locomotives annually. Variable costs to make a locomotive are expected to be $25. Classic anticipates a profit of $15 per locomotive. The target cost for the locomotive is:
a. $80. **c.** $40.
b. $65. **d.** $25.

(SO 2) **4.** Adler Company is considering developing a new product. The company has gathered the following information on this product.

Expected total unit cost	$25
Estimated investment for new product	$500,000
Desired ROI	10%
Expected number of units to be produced and sold	1,000

Given this information, the desired markup percentage and selling price are:
a. markup percentage 10%; selling price $55.
b. markup percentage 200%; selling price $75.
c. markup percentage 10%; selling price $50.
d. markup percentage 100%; selling price $55.

(SO 2) **5.** Mystique Co. provides the following information for the new product it recently introduced.

Total unit cost	$30
Desired ROI per unit	$10
Target selling price	$40

What would be Mystique Co.'s percentage markup on cost?
a. 125%. **c.** 33 ⅓%.
b. 75%. **d.** 25%.

(SO 3) **6.** Crescent Electrical Repair has decided to price its work on a time-and-material basis. It estimates the following costs for the year related to labor.

Technician wages and benefits	$100,000
Office employee's salary and benefits	$ 40,000
Other overhead	$ 80,000

Crescent desires a profit margin of $10 per labor hour and budgets 5,000 hours of repair time for the year. The office employee's salary, benefits, and other overhead costs should be divided evenly between time charges and material loading charges. Crescent labor charge per hour would be:
a. $42. **c.** $32.
b. $34. **d.** $30.

7. The Plastics Division of Weston Company manufactures plastic molds and then sells them to customers for $70 per unit. Its variable cost is $30 per unit, and its fixed cost per unit is $10. Management would like the Plastics Division to transfer 10,000 of these molds to another division within the company at a price of $40. The Plastics Division is operating at full capacity. What is the minimum transfer price that the Plastics Division should accept? (SO 4)
a. $10. **c.** $40.
b. $30. **d.** $70.

8. Assume the same information as question 7, except that the Plastics Division has available capacity of 10,000 units for plastic moldings. What is the minimum transfer price that the Plastics Division should accept? (SO 4)
a. $10. **c.** $40.
b. $30. **d.** $70.

***9.** AST Electrical provides the following cost information related to its production of electronic circuit boards. (SO 6)

	Per Unit
Variable manufacturing cost	$40
Fixed manufacturing cost	$30
Variable selling and administrative expenses	$8
Fixed selling and administrative expenses	$12
Desired ROI per unit	$15

What is its markup percentage assuming that AST Electrical uses absorption-cost pricing?
a. 16.67%. **c.** 54.28%.
b. 50%. **d.** 118.75%.

***10.** Assume the same information as question 9 and determine AST Electrical's markup percentage using variable-cost pricing. (SO 6)
a. 16.67%. **c.** 54.28%.
b. 50%. **d.** 118.75%.

Go to the book's website, **www.wiley.com/college/weygandt**, for Additional Self-Study questions.

QUESTIONS

1. What are the two types of pricing environments for sales to external parties?
2. In what situation does a company place the greatest focus on its target cost? How is the target cost determined?
3. What is the basic formula to determine the target selling price in cost-plus pricing?
4. Stine Corporation produces a filter that has a per unit cost of $17. The company would like a 30% markup. Using cost-plus pricing, determine the per unit selling price.
5. What is the basic formula for the markup percentage?
6. What are some of the factors that affect a company's desired ROI?
7. Livingston Corporation manufactures an electronic switch for dishwashers. The cost base per unit, excluding selling and administrative expenses, is $60. The per unit cost of selling and administrative expenses is $20. The company's desired ROI per unit is $6. Calculate its markup percentage on total unit cost.
8. Estevan manufactures a standard cabinet for a DVD player. The variable cost per unit is $15. The fixed cost per unit is $9. The desired ROI per unit is $6. Compute the markup percentage on total unit cost and the target selling price for the cabinet.
9. In what circumstances is time-and-material pricing most often used?
10. What is the material loading charge? How is it expressed?
11. What is a transfer price? Why is determining a fair transfer price important to division managers?
12. When setting a transfer price, what objective(s) should the company have in mind?
13. What are the three approaches for determining transfer prices?
14. Describe the cost-based approach to transfer pricing. What is the strength of this approach? What are the weaknesses of this approach?
15. What is the general formula for determining the minimum transfer price that the selling division should be willing to accept?
16. When determining the minimum transfer price, what is meant by the "opportunity cost"?
17. In what circumstances will a negotiated transfer price be used instead of a market-based price?
18. Explain how companies use transfer pricing between divisions located in different countries to reduce tax payments, and discuss the propriety of this approach.

*19. What costs are excluded from the cost base when absorption-cost pricing is used to determine the markup percentage?

*20. Kay Corporation manufactures a fiber optic connector. The variable cost per unit is $15. The fixed cost per unit is $9. The company's desired ROI per unit is $3. Compute the markup percentage using variable-cost pricing.

BRIEF EXERCISES

WILEY PLUS

Compute target cost. (SO 1)

BE11-1 Russell Company manufactures computer hard drives. The market for hard drives is very competitive. The current market price for a computer hard drive is $45. Russell would like a profit of $14 per drive. How can Russell Company accomplish this objective?

Use cost-plus pricing to determine selling price. (SO 2)

BE11-2 Gruner Corporation produces snowboards. The following per unit cost information is available: direct materials $12; direct labor $8; variable manufacturing overhead $6; fixed manufacturing overhead $14; variable selling and administrative expenses $4; and fixed selling and administrative expenses $12. Using a 32% markup percentage on total per unit cost, compute the target selling price.

Compute ROI per unit. (SO 2)

BE11-3 Travis Corporation produces high-performance rotors. It expects to produce 50,000 rotors in the coming year. It has invested $10,000,000 to produce rotors. The company has a required return on investment of 18%. What is its ROI per unit?

Compute markup percentage. (SO 2)

BE11-4 Shandling Corporation produces microwave units. The following per unit cost information is available: direct materials $36; direct labor $24; variable manufacturing overhead $18; fixed manufacturing overhead $42; variable selling and administrative expenses $14; and fixed selling and administrative expenses $28. Its desired ROI per unit is $30. Compute its markup percentage using a total-cost approach.

Compute ROI and markup percentage. (SO 2)

BE11-5 During the current year Bierko Corporation expects to produce 10,000 units and has budgeted the following: net income $300,000; variable costs $1,100,000; and fixed costs $100,000. It has invested assets of $1,500,000. The company's budgeted ROI was 20%. What was its budgeted markup percentage using a full-cost approach?

BE11-6 Swayze Small Engine Repair charges $45 per hour of labor. It has a material loading percentage of 40%. On a recent job replacing the engine of a riding lawnmower, Swayze worked 10.5 hours and used parts with a cost of $700. Calculate Swayze's total bill.

Use time-and-material pricing to determine bill.

(SO 3)

BE11-7 The Heating Division of ITA International produces a heating element that it sells to its customers for $42 per unit. Its variable cost per unit is $19, and its fixed cost per unit is $10. Top management of ITA International would like the Heating Division to transfer 15,000 heating units to another division within the company at a price of $29. The Heating Division is operating at full capacity. What is the minimum transfer price that the Heating Division should accept?

Determine minimum transfer price.

(SO 4)

BE11-8 Use the data from BE11-7, but assume that the Heating Division has sufficient excess capacity to provide the 15,000 heating units to the other division. What is the minimum transfer price that the Heating Division should accept?

Determine minimum transfer price with excess capacity.

(SO 4)

BE11-9 Use the data from BE11-7, but assume that the units being requested are special high-performance units, and that the division's variable cost would be $24 per unit (rather than $19). What is the minimum transfer price that the Heating Division should accept?

Determine minimum transfer price for special order.

(SO 4)

***BE11-10** Using the data in BE11-4, compute the markup percentage using absorption-cost pricing.

Compute markup percentage using absorption-cost pricing.

(SO 6)

***BE11-11** Using the data in BE11-4, compute the markup percentage using variable-cost pricing.

Compute markup percentage using variable-cost pricing.

(SO 6)

EXERCISES

WILEY PLUS

E11-1 Culver Cheese Company has developed a new cheese slicer called Slim Slicer. The company plans to sell this slicer through its catalog, which it issues monthly. Given market research, Culver believes that it can charge $15 for the Slim Slicer. Prototypes of the Slim Slicer, however, are costing $22. By using cheaper materials and gaining efficiencies in mass production Culver believes it can reduce Slim Slicer's cost substantially. Culver wishes to earn a return of 30% of the selling price.

Compute target cost.

(SO 1)

Instructions

(a) Compute the target cost for the Slim Slicer.
(b) When is target costing particularly helpful in deciding whether to produce a given product?

E11-2 LaserLook is involved in producing and selling high-end golf equipment. The company has recently been involved in developing various types of laser guns to measure yardages on the golf course. One small laser gun, called LittleLaser, appears to have a very large potential market. Because of competition, LaserLook does not believe that it can charge more than $90 for LittleLaser. At this price, LaserLook believes it can sell 100,000 of these laser guns. LittleLaser will require an investment of $8,500,000 to manufacture, and the company wants an ROI of 20%.

Compute target cost.

(SO 1)

Instructions

Determine the target cost for one LittleLaser.

E11-3 Mucky Duck makes swimsuits and sells these suits directly to retailers. Although Mucky Duck has a variety of suits, it does not make the All-Body suit used by highly skilled swimmers. The market research department believes that a strong market exists for this type of suit. The department indicates that the All-Body suit would sell for approximately $110. Given its experience, Mucky Duck believes the All-Body suit would have the following manufacturing costs.

Compute target cost and cost-plus pricing.

(SO 1, 2)

Direct materials	$ 25
Direct labor	30
Manufacturing overhead	45
Total costs	$100

Instructions

(a) Assume that Mucky Duck uses cost-plus pricing, setting the selling price 25% above its costs. (1) What would be the price charged for the All-Body swimsuit? (2) Under what circumstances might Mucky Duck consider manufacturing the All-Body swimsuit given this approach?

(b) Assume that Mucky Duck uses target costing. What is the price that Mucky Duck would charge the retailer for the All-Body swimsuit?

(c) What is the highest acceptable manufacturing cost Mucky Duck would be willing to incur to produce the All-Body swimsuit, if it desired a profit of $25 per unit? (Assume target costing.)

Use cost-plus pricing to determine selling price.

(SO 2)

E11-4 Selleck Corporation makes a commercial-grade cooking griddle. The following information is available for Selleck Corporation's anticipated annual volume of 30,000 units.

	Per Unit	Total
Direct materials	$17	
Direct labor	$8	
Variable manufacturing overhead	$11	
Fixed manufacturing overhead		$360,000
Variable selling and administrative expenses	$4	
Fixed selling and administrative expenses		$150,000

The company uses a 40% markup percentage on total cost.

Instructions

(a) Compute the total cost per unit.

(b) Compute the target selling price.

Use cost-plus pricing to determine various amounts.

(SO 2)

E11-5 Marlowe Corporation makes a mechanical stuffed alligator that sings the Martian national anthem. The following information is available for Marlowe Corporation's anticipated annual volume of 500,000 units.

	Per Unit	Total
Direct materials	$7	
Direct labor	$9	
Variable manufacturing overhead	$15	
Fixed manufacturing overhead		$3,300,000
Variable selling and administrative expenses	$14	
Fixed selling and administrative expenses		$1,500,000

The company has a desired ROI of 25%. It has invested assets of $24,000,000.

Instructions

(a) Compute the total cost per unit.

(b) Compute the desired ROI per unit.

(c) Compute the markup percentage using total cost per unit.

(d) Compute the target selling price.

Use cost-plus pricing to determine various amounts.

(SO 2)

E11-6 Roxy's Recording Studio rents studio time to musicians in 2-hour blocks. Each session includes the use of the studio facilities, a digital recording of the performance, and a professional music producer/mixer. Anticipated annual volume is 1,000 sessions. The company has invested $2,058,000 in the studio and expects a return on investment (ROI) of 20%. Budgeted costs for the coming year are as follows.

	Per Session	Total
Direct materials (tapes, CDs, etc)	$20	
Direct labor	$400	
Variable overhead	$50	
Fixed overhead		$950,000
Variable selling and administrative expenses	$40	
Fixed selling and administrative expenses		$500,000

Instructions

(a) Determine the total cost per session.

(b) Determine the desired ROI per session.

(c) Calculate the mark-up percentage on the total cost per session.

(d) Calculate the target price per session.

E11-7 Caan Corporation produces industrial robots for high-precision manufacturing. The following information is given for Caan Corporation.

Use cost-plus pricing to determine various amounts.

(SO 2)

	Per Unit	Total
Direct materials	$380	
Direct labor	$290	
Variable manufacturing overhead	$72	
Fixed manufacturing overhead		$1,800,000
Variable selling and administrative expenses	$55	
Fixed selling and administrative expenses		$327,000

The company has a desired ROI of 20%. It has invested assets of $49,600,000. It anticipates production of 3,000 units per year.

Instructions

(a) Compute the cost per unit of the fixed manufacturing overhead and the fixed selling and administrative expenses.
(b) Compute the desired ROI per unit. (Round to the nearest dollar.)
(c) Compute the target selling price.

E11-8 Padong Remanufacturing rebuilds spot welders for manufacturers. The following budgeted cost data for 2008 is available for Padong.

Use time-and-material pricing to determine bill.

(SO 3)

	Time Charges	Material Loading Charges
Technicians' wages and benefits	$228,000	–
Parts manager's salary and benefits	–	$42,500
Office employee's salary and benefits	38,000	9,000
Other overhead	15,200	24,000
Total budgeted costs	$281,200	$75,500

The company desires a $35 profit margin per hour of labor and a 25% profit margin on parts. It has budgeted for 7,600 hours of repair time in the coming year, and estimates that the total invoice cost of parts and materials in 2008 will be $400,000.

Instructions

(a) Compute the rate charged per hour of labor.
(b) Compute the material loading percentage. (Round to three decimal places.)
(c) Lindy Corporation has requested an estimate to rebuild its spot welder. Padong estimates that it would require 40 hours of labor and $2,500 of parts. Compute the total estimated bill.

E11-9 Justin's Custom Electronics (JCE) sells and installs complete security, computer, audio, and video systems for homes. On newly constructed homes it provides bids using time-and-material pricing. The following budgeted cost data are available.

Use time-and-material pricing to determine bill.

(SO 3)

	Time Charges	Material Loading Charges
Technicians' wages and benefits	$150,000	–
Parts manager's salary and benefits	–	$34,000
Office employee's salary and benefits	28,000	12,000
Other overhead	15,000	42,000
Total budgeted costs	$193,000	$88,000

The company has budgeted for 6,000 hours of technician time during the coming year. It desires a $38 profit margin per hour of labor and a 100% profit on parts. It estimates the total invoice cost of parts and materials in 2008 will be $700,000.

Instructions

(a) Compute the rate charged per hour of labor. (Round to two decimal places.)
(b) Compute the material loading percentage. (Round to two decimal places.)

(c) JCE has just received a request for a bid from R.J. Builders on a $1,200,000 new home. The company estimates that it would require 80 hours of labor and $40,000 of parts. Compute the total estimated bill.

Use time-and-material pricing to determine bill.

(SO 3)

E11-10 Karl's Klassic Kars restores classic automobiles to showroom status. Budgeted data for the current year are:

	Time Charges	Material Loading Charges
Restorers' wages and fringe benefits	$270,000	
Purchasing agent's salary and fringe benefits		$ 67,500
Administrative salaries and fringe benefits	54,000	21,960
Other overhead costs	21,600	75,600
Total budgeted costs	$345,600	$165,060

The company anticipated that the restorers would work a total of 12,000 hours this year. Expected parts and materials were $1,260,000.

In late January, the company experienced a fire in its facilities that destroyed most of the accounting records. The accountant remembers that the hourly labor rate was $68.80 and that the material loading charge was 93.10%.

Instructions

(a) Determine the profit margin per hour on labor.

(b) Determine the profit margin on materials.

(c) Determine the total price of labor and materials on a job that was completed after the fire that required 150 hours of labor and $60,000 in parts and materials.

Determine minimum transfer price.

(SO 4)

E11-11 Allied Company's Small Motor Division manufactures a number of small motors used in household and office appliances. The Household Division of Allied then assembles and packages such items as blenders and juicers. Both divisions are free to buy and sell any of their components internally or externally. The following costs relate to small motor LN233 on a per unit basis.

Fixed cost per unit	$5
Variable cost per unit	$8
Selling price per unit	$30

Instructions

(a) Assuming that the Small Motor Division has excess capacity, compute the minimum acceptable price for the transfer of small motor LN233 to the Household Division.

(b) Assuming that the Small Motor Division does not have excess capacity, compute the minimum acceptable price for the transfer of the small motor to the Household Division.

(c) Explain why the level of capacity in the Small Motor Division has an effect on the transfer price.

Determine effect on income from transfer price.

(SO 4)

E11-12 The Cycle Division of TravelVelocity Company has the following per unit data related to its most recent cycle called Roadbuster.

Selling price		$2,200
Variable cost of goods sold		
Body frame	$300	
Other variable costs	900	1,200
Contribution margin		$1,000

Presently, the Cycle Division buys its body frames from an outside supplier. However TravelVelocity has another division, FrameBody, that makes body frames for other cycle companies. The Cycle Division believes that FrameBody's product is suitable for its new Roadbuster cycle. Presently, FrameBody sells its frames for $350 per frame. The variable cost for FrameBody is $250. The Cycle Division is willing to pay $275 to purchase the frames from FrameBody.

Instructions

(a) Assume that FrameBody has excess capacity and is able to meet all of the Cycle Division's needs. If the Cycle Division buys 1,000 frames from FrameBody, determine the following:

(1) effect on the income of the Cycle Division; (2) effect on the income of FrameBody; and (3) effect on the income of TravelVelocity.

(b) Assume that FrameBody does not have excess capacity and therefore would lose sales if the frames were sold to the Cycle Division. If the Cycle Division buys 1,000 frames from FrameBody, determine the following: (1) effect on the income of the Cycle Division; (2) effect on the income of FrameBody; and (3) effect on the income of TravelVelocity.

Determine minimum transfer price. (SO 4)

E11-13 NuVox Corporation manufactures car stereos. It is a division of RustBucket Motors, which manufactures vehicles. NuVox sells car stereos to RustBucket, as well as to other vehicle manufacturers and retail stores. The following information is available for NuVox's standard unit: variable cost per unit $34; fixed cost per unit $23; and selling price to outside customer $85. RustBucket currently purchases a standard unit from an outside supplier for $80. Because of quality concerns and to ensure a reliable supply, the top management of RustBucket has ordered NuVox to provide 200,000 units per year at a transfer price of $34 per unit. NuVox is already operating at full capacity. NuVox can avoid $4 per unit of variable selling costs by selling the unit internally.

Instructions

Answer each of the following questions.

(a) What is the minimum transfer price that NuVox should accept?
(b) What is the potential loss to the corporation as a whole resulting from this forced transfer?
(c) How should the company resolve this situation?

Compute minimum transfer price. (SO 4)

E11-14 The Bathtub Division of Korey Plumbing Corporation has recently approached the Faucet Division with a proposal. The Bathtub Division would like to make a special "ivory" tub with gold-plated fixtures for the company's 50-year anniversary. It would make only 5,000 of these units. It would like the Faucet Division to make the fixtures and provide them to the Bathtub Division at a transfer price of $160. If sold externally, the estimated variable cost per unit would be $135. However, by selling internally the Faucet Division would save $6 per unit on variable selling expenses. The Faucet Division is currently operating at full capacity. Its standard unit sells for $50 per unit and has variable costs of $29.

Instructions

Compute the minimum transfer price that the Faucet Division should be willing to accept, and discuss whether it should accept this offer.

Determine minimum transfer price. (SO 4)

E11-15 The Appraisal Department of Mega-Mortgage Bank performs appraisals of business properties for loans being considered by the bank and appraisals for home buyers that are financing their purchase through some other financial institution. The department charges $160 per home appraisal, and its variable costs are $126 per appraisal.

Recently, Mega-Mortgage Bank has opened its own Home-Loan Department and wants the Appraisal Department to perform 1,200 appraisals on all Mega-Mortgage Bank–financed home loans. Bank management feels that the cost of these appraisals to the Home-Loan Department should be $150. The variable cost per appraisal to the Home-Loan Department would be $6 less than those performed for outside customers due to savings in administrative costs.

Instructions

(a) Determine the minimum transfer price, assuming the Appraisal Department has excess capacity.
(b) Determine the minimum transfer price, assuming the Appraisal Department has no excess capacity.
(c) Assuming the Appraisal Department has no excess capacity, should management force the department to charge the Home-Loan Department only $150? Discuss.

Compute total cost per unit, ROI, and markup percentages using absorption-cost pricing and variable-cost pricing. (SO 6)

***E11-16** Information for Marlowe Corporation is given in E11-5.

Instructions

Using the information given in E11-5, answer the following.

(a) Compute the total cost per unit.
(b) Compute the desired ROI per unit.
(c) Using absorption-cost pricing, compute the markup percentage.
(d) Using variable-cost pricing, compute the markup percentage.

Compute markup percentage using absorption-cost pricing and variable-cost pricing.
(SO 6)

***E11-17** Firefly Corporation produces outdoor portable fireplace units. The following per unit cost information is available: direct materials $21; direct labor $26; variable manufacturing overhead $16; fixed manufacturing overhead $22; variable selling and administrative expenses $9; and fixed selling and administrative expenses $15. The company's ROI per unit is $20.

Instructions
Compute Firefly Corporation's markup percentage using (a) absorption-cost pricing and (b) variable-cost pricing.

Compute various amounts using absorption-cost pricing and variable-cost pricing.
(SO 6)

***E11-18** Information for Caan Corporation is given in E11-7.

Instructions
Using the information given in E11-7, answer the following.

(a) Compute the cost per unit of the fixed manufacturing overhead and the fixed selling and administrative expenses.
(b) Compute the desired ROI per unit. (Round to the nearest dollar.)
(c) Compute the markup percentage and target selling price using absorption-cost pricing. (Round the markup percentage to three decimal places.)
(d) Compute the markup percentage and target selling price using variable-cost pricing. (Round the markup percentage to three decimal places.)

EXERCISES: SET B

Visit the book's website at **www.wiley.com/college/weygandt**, and choose Student Companion site, to access Exercise Set B.

PROBLEMS: SET A

Use cost-plus pricing to determine various amounts.
(SO 2)

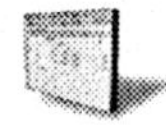

P11-1A Lafluer Corporation needs to set a target price for its newly designed product M14–M16. The following data relate to this new product.

	Per Unit	Total
Direct materials	$20	
Direct labor	$42	
Variable manufacturing overhead	$10	
Fixed manufacturing overhead		$1,440,000
Variable selling and administrative expenses	$5	
Fixed selling and administrative expenses		$1,040,000

These costs are based on a budgeted volume of 80,000 units produced and sold each year. Lafluer uses cost-plus pricing methods to set its target selling price. The markup percentage on total unit cost is 30%.

Instructions

(a) Variable cost per unit $77

(a) Compute the total variable cost per unit, total fixed cost per unit, and total cost per unit for M14 – M16.
(b) Compute the desired ROI per unit for M14–M16.
(c) Compute the target selling price for M14–M16.
(d) Compute variable cost per unit, fixed cost per unit, and total cost per unit assuming that 60,000 M14 – M16s are sold during the year. (Round to two decimal places.)

Use cost-plus pricing to determine various amounts.
(SO 2)

P11-2A Bolus Computer Parts Inc. is in the process of setting a selling price on a new component it has just designed and developed. The following cost estimates for this new component have been provided by the accounting department for a budgeted volume of 50,000 units.

	Per Unit	Total
Direct materials	$50	
Direct labor	$25	
Variable manufacturing overhead	$20	
Fixed manufacturing overhead		$600,000
Variable selling and administrative expenses	$18	
Fixed selling and administrative expenses		$400,000

Bolus Computer Parts management requests that the total cost per unit be used in cost-plus pricing its products. On this particular product, management also directs that the target price be set to provide a 25% return on investment (ROI) on invested assets of $1,200,000.

Instructions

(Round all calculations to two decimal places.)

(a) Compute the markup percentage and target selling price that will allow Bolus Computer Parts to earn its desired ROI of 25% on this new component.

(b) Assuming that the volume is 40,000 units, compute the markup percentage and target selling price that will allow Bolus Computer Parts to earn its desired ROI of 25% on this new component.

(b) Target selling price $145.50

P11-3A Hawks Electronic Repair Shop has budgeted the following time and material for 2008.

Use time-and-material pricing to determine bill.

(SO 3)

HAWKS ELECTRONIC REPAIR SHOP
Budgeted Costs for the Year 2008

	Time Charges	Material Loading Charges
Shop employees' wages and benefits	$108,000	—
Parts manager's salary and benefits	—	$25,400
Office employee's salary and benefits	20,000	13,600
Overhead (supplies, depreciation, advertising, utilities)	26,000	18,000
Total budgeted costs	$154,000	$57,000

Hawks budgets 5,000 hours of repair time in 2008 and will bill a profit of $5 per labor hour along with a 30% profit markup on the invoice cost of parts. The estimated invoice cost for parts to be used is $100,000.

On January 5, 2008 Hawks is asked to submit a price estimate to fix a 72-inch big-screen TV. Hawks estimates that this job will consume 20 hours of labor and $500 in parts.

Instructions

(a) Compute the labor rate for Hawks Electronic Repair Shop for the year 2008.

(b) Compute the material loading charge percentage for Hawks Electronic Repair Shop for the year 2008.

(c) Prepare a time-and-material price quotation for fixing the big-screen TV.

(c) $1,651

P11-4A Wordsmith is a publishing company with a number of different book lines. Each line has contracts with a number of different authors. The company also owns a printing operation called Pronto Press. The book lines and the printing operation each operate as a separate profit center. The printing operation earns revenue by printing books by authors under contract with the book lines owned by Wordsmith, as well as authors under contract with other companies. The printing operation bills out at $0.01 per page, and a typical book requires 500 pages of print. A manager from Business Books, one of the Wordsmith's book lines, has approached the manager of the printing operation offering to pay $0.007 per page for 1,200 copies of a 500-page book. The book line pays outside printers $0.009 per page. The printing operation's variable cost per page is $0.006.

Determine minimum transfer price with no excess capacity and with excess capacity.

(SO 4)

Instructions

Determine whether the printing should be done internally or externally, and the appropriate transfer price, under each of the following situations.

(a) Assume that the printing operation is booked solid for the next 2 years, and it would have to cancel an obligation with an outside customer in order to meet the needs of the internal division.

(b) Assume that the printing operation has available capacity.

(c) The top management of Wordsmith believes that the printing operation should always do the printing for the company's authors. On a number of occasions it has forced the printing operation to cancel jobs with outside customers in order to meet the needs of its own lines. Discuss the pros and cons of this approach.

(d) Loss to company $600

(d) Calculate the change in contribution margin to each division, and to the company as a whole, if top management forces the printing operation to accept the $0.007 per page transfer price when it has no available capacity.

Determine minimum transfer price with no excess capacity.

(SO 4)

P11-5A Zapp Manufacturing Company makes various electronic products. The company is divided into a number of autonomous divisions that can either sell to internal units or sell externally. All divisions are located in buildings on the same piece of property. The Board Division has offered the Chip Division $20 per unit to supply it with chips for 40,000 boards. It has been purchasing these chips for $21 per unit from outside suppliers. The Chip Division receives $22.50 per unit for sales made to outside customers on this type of chip. The variable cost of chips sold externally by the Chip Division is $14. It estimates that it will save $4 per chip of selling expenses on units sold internally to the Board Division. The Chip Division has no excess capacity.

Instructions

(a) Calculate the minimum transfer price that the Chip Division should accept. Discuss whether it is in the Chip Division's best interest to accept the offer.

(b) Total loss to company $100,000

(b) Suppose that the Chip Division decides to reject the offer. What are the financial implications for each division, and for the company as a whole, of this decision?

Determine minimum transfer price under different situations.

(SO 4)

P11-6A Commcenter Manufacturing (CM) is a division of Worldwide Communications, Inc. CM produces pagers and other personal communication devices. These devices are sold to other Worldwide divisions, as well as to other communication companies. CM was recently approached by the manager of the Personal Communications Division regarding a request to make a special pager designed to receive signals from anywhere in the world. The Personal Communications Division has requested that CM produce 10,000 units of this special pager. The following facts are available regarding the Commcenter Manufacturing Division.

Selling price of standard pager	$95
Variable cost of standard pager	$50
Additional variable cost of special pager	$35

Instructions

For each of the following independent situations, calculate the minimum transfer price, and discuss whether the internal transfer should take place or whether the Personal Communications Division should purchase the pager externally.

(a) The Personal Communications Division has offered to pay the CM Division $105 per pager. The CM Division has no available capacity. The CM Division would have to forgo sales of 10,000 pagers to existing customers in order to meet the request of the Personal Communications Division.

(b) Minimum price $148

(b) The Personal Communications Division has offered to pay the CM Division $160 per pager. The CM Division has no available capacity. The CM Division would have to forgo sales of 14,000 pagers to existing customers in order to meet the request of the Personal Communications Division.

(c) The Personal Communications Division has offered to pay the CM Division $105 per pager. The CM Division has available capacity.

Compute the target price using absorption-cost pricing and variable-cost pricing.

(SO 6)

***P11-7A** Fast Buck Corporation needs to set a target price for its newly designed product EverReady. The following data relate to this new product.

	Per Unit	Total
Direct materials	$20	
Direct labor	$40	
Variable manufacturing overhead	$10	
Fixed manufacturing overhead		$1,400,000
Variable selling and administrative expenses	$5	
Fixed selling and administrative expenses		$1,120,000

The costs shown on page 518 are based on a budgeted volume of 80,000 units produced and sold each year. Fast Buck uses cost-plus pricing methods to set its target selling price. Because some managers prefer absorption-cost pricing and others prefer variable-cost pricing, the accounting department provides information under both approaches using a markup of 50% on absorption cost and a markup of 75% on variable cost.

Instructions

(a) Compute the target price for one unit of EverReady using absorption-cost pricing. (a) Markup $43.75

(b) Compute the target price for one unit of EverReady using variable-cost pricing. (b) Markup $56.25

***P11-8A** Weather Guard Windows Inc. is in the process of setting a target price on its newly designed tinted window. Cost data relating to the window at a budgeted volume of 4,000 units are as follows.

Compute various amounts using absorption-cost pricing and variable-cost pricing.

(SO 6)

	Per Unit	Total
Direct materials	$100	
Direct labor	$70	
Variable manufacturing overhead	$20	
Fixed manufacturing overhead		$120,000
Variable selling and administrative expenses	$10	
Fixed selling and administrative expenses		$102,000

Weather Guard Windows uses cost-plus pricing methods that are designed to provide the company with a 30% ROI on its tinted window line. A total of $700,000 in assets is committed to production of the new tinted window.

Instructions

(a) Compute the markup percentage under absorption-cost pricing that will allow Weather Guard Windows to realize its desired ROI. (a) 40%

(b) Compute the target price of the window under absorption-cost pricing, and show proof that the desired ROI is realized.

(c) Compute the markup percentage under variable-cost pricing that will allow Weather Guard Windows to realize its desired ROI. (Round to three decimal places.)

(d) Compute the target price of the window under variable-cost pricing, and show proof that the desired ROI is realized.

(e) Since both absorption-cost pricing and variable-cost pricing produce the same target price and provide the same desired ROI, why do both methods exist? Isn't one method clearly superior to the other?

PROBLEMS: SET B

P11-1B Wamser Corporation needs to set a target price for its newly designed product E2-D2. The following data relate to this new product.

Use cost-plus pricing to determine various amounts.

(SO 2)

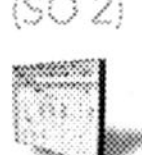

	Per Unit	Total
Direct materials	$18	
Direct labor	$30	
Variable manufacturing overhead	$8	
Fixed manufacturing overhead		$1,440,000
Variable selling and administrative expenses	$4	
Fixed selling and administrative expenses		$1,080,000

These costs are based on a budgeted volume of 90,000 units produced and sold each year. Wamser uses cost-plus pricing methods to set its target selling price. The markup percentage on total unit cost is 25%.

Instructions

(a) Compute total variable cost per unit, total fixed cost per unit, and total cost per unit for E2-D2. (a) Variable cost per unit $60

(b) Compute the desired ROI per unit for E2-D2.

(c) Compute the target selling price for E2-D2.

(d) Compute variable cost per unit, fixed cost per unit, and total cost per unit assuming that 80,000 E2-D2s are sold during the year.

Use cost-plus pricing to determine various amounts.

(SO 2)

P11-2B Bosworth Electronics Inc. is in the process of setting a selling price on a new CDL component it has just developed. The following cost estimates for this component have been provided by the accounting department for a budgeted volume of 50,000 units.

	Per Unit	Total
Direct materials	$38	
Direct labor	$24	
Variable manufacturing overhead	$18	
Fixed manufacturing overhead		$450,000
Variable selling and administrative expenses	$12	
Fixed selling and administrative expenses		$360,000

Bosworth's management uses cost-plus pricing to set its selling price. Management also directs that the target price be set to provide a 20% return on investment (ROI) on invested assets of $1,500,000.

Instructions

(Round all calculations to two decimal places.)

(a) Compute the markup percentage and target selling price on this new CDL component.

(b) Target selling price $119.75

(b) Assuming that the volume is 40,000 units, compute the markup percentage and target selling price that will allow Bosworth Electronics to earn its desired ROI of 20%.

Use time-and-material pricing to determine bill.

(SO 3)

P11-3B Zip's Auto Body Shop has budgeted the following time and material for 2008.

ZIP'S AUTO BODY SHOP
Budgeted Costs for the Year 2008

	Time Charges	Material Loading Charges
Shop employees' wages and benefits	$111,000	—
Parts manager's salary and benefits	—	$26,600
Office employee's salary and benefits	21,000	12,000
Overhead (supplies, depreciation, advertising, utilities)	24,600	15,000
Total budgeted costs	$156,600	$53,600

Zip's budgets 6,000 hours of repair time in 2008. It will bill a profit of $7 per labor hour along with a 40% profit markup on the invoice cost of parts. Zip's anticipates using $200,000 of parts in 2008.

On January 10, 2008, Zip's is asked to submit a price estimate for the repair of a 2005 Chevrolet Blazer that was damaged in a head-on collision. Zip's estimates that this repair will consume 61 hours of labor and $4,200 in parts and materials.

Instructions

(a) Compute the labor rate for Zip's Auto Body Shop for the year 2008.

(b) Compute the material loading charge percentage for Zip's Auto Body Shop for the year 2008. (Round to three decimal places.)

(c) $9,024.70

(c) Prepare a time-and-material price quotation for the repair of the 2005 Blazer.

Determine minimum transfer price with no excess capacity and with excess capacity.

(SO 4)

P11-4B Cosmic Sounds is a record company with a number of record labels. Each record label has contracts with a number of recording artists. It also owns a recording studio called Blast Off. The record labels and the recording studio operate as separate profit centers. The studio earns revenue by recording artists under contract with the labels owned by Cosmic Sounds, as well as artists under contract with other companies. The studio bills out at $1,100 per hour, and a typical CD requires 80 hours of studio time. A manager from Big Bang, one of the Cosmic Sounds' record labels, has approached the manager of the recording studio offering to pay $800 per hour for an 80-hour session. The record label pays outside studios $1,000 per hour. The recording studio's variable cost per hour is $600.

Instructions

Determine whether the recording should be done internally or hired externally, and the appropriate transfer price, under each of the following situations.

(a) Assume that the recording studio is booked solid for the next 3 years, and it would have to cancel an obligation with an outside customer in order to meet the needs of the internal division.

(b) Assume that the recording studio has available capacity.

(c)  The top management of Cosmic Sounds believes that the recording studio should always do the recording for the company's artists. On a number of occasions it has forced the recording studio to cancel jobs with outside customers in order to meet the needs of its own labels. Discuss the pros and cons of this approach.

(d) Calculate the change in contribution margin to each division, and to the company as a whole, if top management forces the recording studio to accept the $800 transfer price when it has no available capacity.

(d) Loss to company $8,000

P11-5B Chula Vista Pump Company makes irrigation pump systems. The company is divided into a number of autonomous divisions that can either sell to internal units or sell externally. All divisions are located in buildings on the same piece of property. The Pump Division has offered the Washer Division $4 per unit to supply it with the washers for 50,000 units. It has been purchasing these washers for $4.30 per unit from outside suppliers. The Washer Division receives $4.60 per unit for sales made to outside customers on this type of washer. The variable cost of units sold externally by the Washer Division is $3.20. It estimates that it will save 70 cents per unit of selling expenses on units sold internally to the Pump Division. The Washer Division has no excess capacity.

Determine minimum transfer price with no excess capacity.

(SO 4)

Instructions

(a) Calculate the minimum transfer price that the Washer Division should accept. Discuss whether it is in the Washer Division's best interest to accept the offer.

(b) Suppose that the Washer Division decides to reject the offer. What are the financial implications for each division, and the company as a whole, of the decision to reject the offer?

(b) Total loss to company $20,000

P11-6B Heartland Engines is a division of EverGreen Lawn Equipment Company. Heartland makes engines for lawn mowers, snow blowers, and other types of lawn and garden equipment. It sells its engines to the Lawn Mower Division and the Snow Blower Division of the company, as well as to other lawn equipment companies. It was recently approached by the manager of the Lawn Mower Division with a request to make a special, high-performance engine for a lawn mower designed to mow heavy brush. The Lawn Mower Division has requested that Heartland produce 8,500 units of this special engine. The following facts are available regarding the Heartland Engine Division.

Determine minimum transfer price under different situations.

(SO 4)

Selling price of standard lawn mower engine	$88
Variable cost of standard lawn mower engine	$55
Additional variable cost of special engine	$41

Instructions

For each of the following independent situations, calculate the minimum transfer price, and discuss whether the internal transfer should take place or whether the Lawn Mower Division should purchase its goods externally.

(a) The Lawn Mower Division has offered to pay the Heartland Engine Division $110 per engine. Heartland Engine has no available capacity. Heartland Engine would have to forgo sales of 8,500 units to existing customers in order to meet the request of the Lawn Mower Division.

(a) $129

(b) The Lawn Mower Division has offered to pay the Heartland Engine Division $170 per engine. Heartland has no available capacity. Heartland Engine would have to forgo sales of 12,000 units to existing customers in order to meet the request of the Lawn Mower Division. (Round to two decimal places.)

(b) $142.59

(c) The Lawn Mower division has offered to pay the Heartland Engine Division $110 per engine. Heartland Engine Division has available capacity.

(c) $96

***P11-7B** Wamser Corporation needs to set a target price for its newly designed product E2-D2. The following data relate to this new product.

Compute the target price using absorption-cost pricing and variable-cost pricing.

(SO 6)

	Per Unit	Total
Direct materials	$18	
Direct labor	$30	
Variable manufacturing overhead	$8	
Fixed manufacturing overhead		$1,440,000
Variable selling and administrative expenses	$4	
Fixed selling and administrative expenses		$1,080,000

The costs shown on page 521 are based on a budgeted volume of 90,000 units produced and sold each year. Wamser uses cost-plus pricing methods to set its target selling price. Because some managers prefer to work with absorption-cost pricing and other managers prefer variable-cost pricing, the accounting department provides information under both approaches using a markup of 50% on absorption cost and a markup of 80% on variable cost.

Instructions

(a) Markup $36
(b) Markup $48

(a) Compute the target price for one unit of E2-D2 using absorption-cost pricing.
(b) Compute the target price for one unit of E2-D2 using variable-cost pricing.

Compute various amounts using absorption-cost pricing and variable-cost pricing.
(SO 6)

***P11-8B** Santana Furniture Inc. is in the process of setting a target price on its newly designed leather recliner sofa. Cost data relating to the sofa at a budgeted volume of 3,000 units are as follows.

	Per Unit	Total
Direct materials	$140	
Direct labor	$80	
Variable manufacturing overhead	$40	
Fixed manufacturing overhead		$180,000
Variable selling and administrative expenses	$20	
Fixed selling and administrative expenses		$ 90,000

Santana Furniture uses cost-plus pricing methods that are designed to provide the company with a 30% ROI on its stuffed furniture line. A total of $700,000 in assets are committed to production of the new leather recliner sofa.

Instructions

(a) 37.5%

(a) Compute the markup percentage under absorption-cost pricing that will allow Santana Furniture to realize its desired ROI.
(b) Compute the target price of the sofa under absorption-cost pricing, and show proof that the desired ROI is realized.
(c) Compute the markup percentage under variable-cost pricing that will allow Santana Furniture to realize its desired ROI. (Round to three decimal places.)
(d) Compute the target price of the sofa under variable-cost pricing, and show proof that the desired ROI is realized.
(e) Since both absorption-cost pricing and variable-cost pricing produce the same target price and provide the same desired ROI, why do both methods exist? Isn't one method clearly superior to the other?

PROBLEMS: SET C

Visit the book's website at **www.wiley.com/college/weygandt**, and choose the Student Companion site, to access Problem Set C.

WATERWAYS CONTINUING PROBLEM

(This is a continuation of the Waterways Problem from previous chapters.)

WCP11 Waterways Corporation competes in a market economy in which its products must be sold at market prices. Its emphasis is therefore on manufacturing its products at a cost that allows the company to earn its desired profit. This problem asks you to consider various pricing situations for Waterways' projects.

Go to the book's website, **www.wiley.com/college/weygandt,** *to find the remainder of this problem.*

BROADENING YOUR PERSPECTIVE

DECISION MAKING ACROSS THE ORGANIZATION

BYP11-1 Aurora Manufacturing has multiple divisions that make a wide variety of products. Recently the Bearing Division and the Wheel Division got into an argument over a transfer price. The Wheel Division needed bearings for garden tractor wheels. It normally buys its bearings from an outside supplier for $24 per set. The company's top management recently initiated a campaign to persuade the different divisions to buy their materials from within the company whenever possible. As a result, Steve Hamblin, the purchasing manager for the Wheel Division, received a letter from the vice president of Purchasing, ordering him to contact the Bearing Division to discuss buying bearings from this division.

To comply with this request, Steve from the Wheel Division called Terry Tompkin of the Bearing Division, and asked the price for 15,000 bearings. Terry responded that the bearings normally sell for $35 per set. However, Terry noted that the Bearing Division would save $3 on marketing costs by selling internally, and would pass this cost savings on to the Wheel Division. He further commented that they were at full capacity, and therefore would not be able to provide any bearings presently. In the future, if they had available capacity, they would be happy to provide bearings.

Steve responded indignantly, "Thanks but no thanks." He said, "We can get all the bearings we need from Falk Manufacturing for $24 per set." Terry snorted back, "Falk makes junk. It costs us $22 per set just to make our bearings. Our bearings can withstand heat of 2,000 degrees centigrade, and are good to within .00001 centimeters. If you guys are happy buying junk, then go ahead and buy from Falk."

Two weeks later, Steve's boss from the central office stopped in to find out whether he had placed an order with the Bearing Division. Steve responded that he would sooner buy his bearings from his worst enemy than from the Bearing Division.

Instructions

With the class divided into groups, prepare answers to the following questions.

(a) Why might the company's top management want the divisions to start doing more business with one another?

(b) Under what conditions should a buying division be forced to buy from an internal supplier? Under what conditions should a selling division be forced to sell to an internal division, rather than to an outside customer?

(c) The vice president of Purchasing thinks that this problem should be resolved by forcing the Bearing Division to sell to the Wheel Division at its cost of $22. Is this a good solution for the Wheel Division? Is this a good solution for the Bearing Division? Is this a good solution for the company?

(d) Provide at least two other possible solutions to this problem. Discuss the merits and drawbacks of each.

MANAGERIAL ANALYSIS

BYP11-2 Construction on the Atlantis Full-Service Car Wash is nearing completion. The owner is Jay Leer, a retired accounting professor. The car wash is strategically located on a busy street that separates an affluent suburban community from a middle-class community. It has two state-of-the-art stalls. Each stall can provide anything from a basic two-stage wash and rinse to a five-stage luxurious bath. It is all "touchless," that is, there are no brushes to potentially damage the car. Outside each stall there is also a 400 horse-power vacuum. Jay likes to joke that these vacuums are so strong that they will pull the carpet right out of your car if you aren't careful.

Jay has some important decisions to make before he can open the car wash. First, he knows that there is one drive-through car wash only a 10-minute drive away. It is attached to a gas station; it charges $5 for a basic wash, and $4 if you also buy at least 8 gallons of gas. It is a "brush"-type wash with rotating brush heads. There is also a self- serve "stand outside your car and spray until you are soaked" car wash a 15-minute drive away from Jay's location. He went over and tried this out. He went through $3 in quarters to get the equivalent of a basic wash. He knows that both of these locations always have long lines, which is one reason why he decided to build a new car wash.

Jay is planning to offer three levels of wash service—Basic, Deluxe, and Premium. The Basic is all automated; it requires no direct intervention by employees. The Deluxe is all automated except that at the end an employee will wipe down the car and will put a window treatment on the windshield that reduces glare and allows rainwater to run off more quickly. The Premium level is a "pampered" service. This will include all the services of the Deluxe, plus a special wax after the machine wax, and an employee will vacuum the car, wipe down the entire interior, and wash the inside of the windows. To provide the Premium service, Jay will have to hire a couple of "car wash specialists" to do the additional pampering.

Jay has pulled together the following estimates, based on data he received from the local Chamber of Commerce and information from a trade association.

	Per Unit	Total
Direct materials per Basic wash	$0.25	
Direct materials per Deluxe wash	$0.75	
Direct materials per Premium wash	$1.05	
Direct labor per Basic wash	na	
Direct labor per Deluxe wash	$0.40	
Direct labor per Premium wash	$2.40	
Variable overhead per Basic wash	$0.10	
Variable overhead per Deluxe and Premium washes	$0.20	
Fixed overhead		$112,500
Variable selling and administrative expenses all washes	$0.10	
Fixed selling and administrative expenses		$121,500

The total estimated number of washes of any type is 45,000. Jay has invested assets of $324,000. He would like a return on investment (ROI) of 25%.

Instructions

Answer each of the following questions.

(a) Identify the issues that Jay must consider in deciding on the price of each level of service of his car wash. Also discuss what issues he should consider in deciding on what levels of service to provide.

(b) Jay estimates that of the total 45,000 washes, 20,000 will be Basic, 20,000 will be Deluxe, and 5,000 will be Premium. Calculate the selling price, using cost-plus pricing, that Jay should use for each type of wash to achieve his desired ROI of 25%.

(c) During the first year, instead of selling 45,000 washes, Jay sold 43,000 washes. He was quite accurate in his estimate of first-year sales, but he was way off on the types of washes that he sold. He sold 3,000 Basic, 31,000 Deluxe, and 9,000 Premium. His actual total fixed expenses were as he expected, and his variable cost per unit was as estimated. Calculate Jay's actual net income and his actual ROI. (Round to two decimal places.)

(d) Jay is using a traditional approach to allocate overhead. As a consequence, he is allocating overhead equally to all three types of washes, even though the Basic wash is considerably less complicated and uses very little of the technical capabilities of the machinery. What should Jay do to determine more accurate costs per unit? How will this affect his pricing and, consequently, his sales?

REAL-WORLD FOCUS

BYP11-3 Merck & Co., Inc. is a global, research-driven pharmaceutical company that discovers, develops, manufactures, and markets a broad range of human and animal health products. The following are excerpts from the financial review section of the company's annual report.

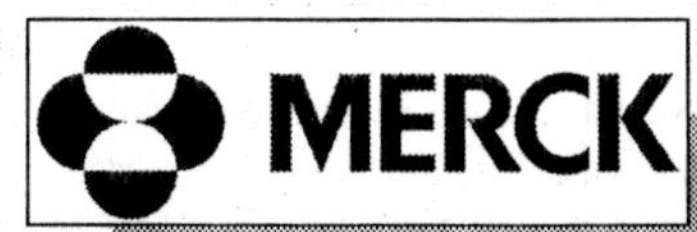

MERCK & CO., INC.
Financial Review Section (partial)

In the United States, the Company has been working with private and governmental employers to slow the increase of health care costs.

Outside of the United States, in difficult environments encumbered by government cost containment actions, the Company has worked with payers to help them allocate scarce resources to optimize health care outcomes, limiting potentially detrimental effects of government actions on sales growth.

Several products face expiration of product patents in the near term.

The Company, along with other pharmaceutical manufacturers, received a notice from the Federal Trade Commission (FTC) that it was conducting an investigation into pricing practices.

Instructions

Answer each of the following questions.

(a) In light of the above excerpts from Merck's annual report, discuss some unique pricing issues faced by companies that operate in the pharmaceutical industry.

(b) What are some reasons why the same company often sells identical drugs for dramatically different prices in different countries? How can the same drug used for both humans and animals cost significantly different prices?

(c) Suppose that Merck has just developed a revolutionary new drug for the treatment of arthritis. Discuss the steps it would go through in setting a price. Include a discussion of the information it would need to gather, and the issues it would need to consider.

EXPLORING THE WEB

BYP11-4 Shopping "robots" have become very popular on the Web. These are sites that will find the price of a specified product that is listed by retailers on the Web ("e-tailers"). This allows the customer to search for the lowest possible price.

Address: www.dealtime.com or go to **www.wiley.com/college/weygandt**

Steps

1. Go to the Web page of DealTime.
2. Under the heading "**Electronics**," click on **DVD players**.
3. Choose one of the models.

Instructions

(a) Write down the name of the retailer and the price of the two lowest-priced units and the two highest-priced units.

(b) As a consumer, what concerns might you have in clicking on the "buy" button?

(c) Why might a consumer want to purchase a unit from a retailer that isn't offering the lowest price?

(d) What implications does the existence of these sites have for retailers?

COMMUNICATION ACTIVITY

BYP11-5 Judy Prest recently graduated from college with a degree in landscape architecture. Her father runs a tree, shrub, and perennial-flower nursery, and her brother has a business delivering topsoil, mulch, and compost. Judy has decided that she would like to start a landscape business. She believes that she can generate a nice profit for herself, while providing an opportunity for both her brother's and father's businesses to grow.

One potential problem that Judy is concerned about is that her father and brother tend to charge the highest prices of any local suppliers for their products. She is hoping that she can demonstrate that it would be in her interest, as well as theirs, for them to sell to her at a discounted price.

Instructions

Write a memo to Judy explaining what information she must gather, and what issues she must consider in working out an arrangement with her father and brother. In your memo, discuss how this situation differs from a "standard" transfer pricing problem, but also, how it has many of the characteristics of a transfer pricing problem.

ETHICS CASE

BYP11-6 Giant Airlines operates out of three main "hub" airports in the United States. Recently Mosquito Airlines began operating a flight from Reno, Nevada, into Giant's Metropolis hub for $190. Giant Airlines offers a price of $425 for the same route. The management of Giant is not happy about Mosquito invading its turf. In fact, Giant has driven off nearly every other competing airline from its hub, so that today 90% of flights into and out of Metropolis are Giant Airline flights. Mosquito is able to offer a lower fare because its pilots are paid less, it uses older planes, and it has lower overhead costs. Mosquito has been in business for only 6 months, and it services only two other cities. It expects the Metropolis route to be its most profitable.

Giant estimates that it would have to charge $210 just to break even on this flight. It estimates that Mosquito can break even at a price of $160. Within one day of Mosquito's entry into the market, Giant dropped its price to $140, whereupon Mosquito matched its price. They both maintained this fare for a period of 9 months, until Mosquito went out of business. As soon as Mosquito went out of business, Giant raised its fare back to $425.

Instructions

Answer each of the following questions.

(a) Who are the stakeholders in this case?
(b) What are some of the reasons why Mosquito's breakeven-point is lower than that of Giant?
(c) What are the likely reasons why Giant was able to offer this price for this period of time, while Mosquito couldn't?
(d) What are some of the possible courses of action available to Mosquito in this situation?
(e) Do you think that this kind of pricing activity is ethical? What are the implications for the stakeholders in this situation?

"ALL ABOUT YOU" ACTIVITY

BYP11-7 In the "All About You" feature in this chapter, you learned that pricing is a difficult and complex task both from the seller's and the consumer's sides. One issue that you will face is making sure that you receive a fair price for the goods that you are interested in buying. In some cases, price is not necessarily the deciding factor. Your wealth level, the quality of the product, the convenience of the product, the warranty, and the reputation of the manufacturer all may play an important role in your decision. As a result, it often is important to do solid research before you make your decision. Fortunately there are now a number of services that provide comparisons on price and quality for many products.

Instructions

Suppose you are interested in golf and want to buy a new driver and three dozen golf balls. (Hopefully that number of golf balls will last the season.) Go to *www.golfdigest.com/hotlist/* and see whether you can find any information that will help you make a decision on the driver and golf balls you might purchase.

Answers to Business Insight and Accounting Across the Organization Questions

What's the Price on the Internet? p. 483

Q: How does the Internet affect product prices?

A: *The Internet can result in lower product prices because it is easier for customers to compare prices across different retailers. However, the Internet also makes it possible for companies to offer a wider variety of products and to differentiate their products in a variety of ways. Providing customized alternatives allows retailers to offset some of the downward pressure on prices.*

Wal-Mart Says the Price Is Too High, p. 484

Q: What are some issues that Levi should consider in deciding whether it should agree to meet Wal-Mart's target price?

A: *Levi may be tempted to reduce the quality of its product, or it may be forced to move more of its operations to low-wage suppliers. A big concern is that other retailers may complain that Levi is selling its jeans to Wal-Mart at a price that is lower than they receive. Also, customers may no longer be willing to pay for Levi's other models of higher-priced jeans that it sells in other stores because they can get the low-price jeans (those with the lower gross margin) at Wal-Mart. All of these are issues that a manufacturer must consider in deciding whether to be a supplier to Wal-Mart.*

Losing Money with Every Sale, p. 488

Q: If prices continue to tumble, and sales do not increase at a more rapid rate, what will probably happen to the manufacturers of flat-screen TVs?

A: *Right now the industry has more capacity than is warranted by customer demand. As a consequence, suppliers are not able to build a sufficient return into their product price. If prices continue to fall, and sales volume does not increase at a more rapid pace, then the least-cost-efficient suppliers will eventually be forced out of business. As this occurs, there will be less downward price pressure on the remaining suppliers. Their increased efficiency, combined with less price pressure, should enable them to charge a price that provides a reasonable return.*

Transferring Profits and Reducing Taxes, p. 499

Q: What are the implications for other taxpayers if companies reduce their taxes by using improper transfer prices to shift profits to lower-tax countries?

A: *If companies reduce their taxes by using improper transfer prices, then more of the tax burden will fall on law-abiding companies or on individual taxpayers. As countries such as Ireland, for example, have drawn increased foreign investment by non-Irish companies, many other European countries have complained that Ireland is using unfair tax incentives. Many countries are beginning to scrutinize the transfer-pricing practices of multinational companies more closely in order to reduce cheating and increase tax revenues.*

Authors' Comments on *All About You*: Is the Price Right?, p. 500

The questions that Congress faces about pricing are difficult. Consumers (voters) are asking for relief from high drug prices. Many note that one reason for the high cost of the Medicare program is the cost of drugs, especially new ones. Others argue that Congress should permit the use of more generic drugs in the marketplace.

On the other hand, a company like Genentech argues that since 1976 the biotech industry has lost over $90 billion. Although Genentech has done well, most drug companies have not. The reason is that it takes a long time from creation of a new drug to use. For example, it took Genentech from 1982 untill 1999 to bring its breast cancer drug to market. Another way to look at the issue is to ask how much society is willing to invest in fighting disease. Consumers presently spend $15 billion a year on cancer drugs in the United States, which is 1/800th of the gross national product of the United States, spent on the leading cause of death for those under the age of 85.

There is no easy answer to the question posed here. Certainly, some people do not receive drugs because they cannot afford them. On the other hand, many are able to benefit from their use. As indicated in the story, the problem is even more complicated because some of these drugs are sold for lower prices overseas. Some argue that consumers are subsidizing individuals overseas. On the other hand, the prices have to be lower because some countries simply would not be able to afford these drugs, and the incremental revenue received does reduce the overall cost.

Answers to Self-Study Questions

1. b **2.** c **3.** b **4.** b **5.** c **6.** a **7.** d **8.** b **9.** b **10.** d

Remember to go back to the Navigator box on the chapter-opening page and check off your completed work.

Specimen Financial Statements: Tootsie Roll Industries, Inc.

The Annual Report

Once each year a corporation communicates to its stockholders and other interested parties by issuing a complete set of audited financial statements. The **annual report**, as this communication is called, summarizes the financial results of the company's operations for the year and its plans for the future. Many annual reports are attractive, multicolored, glossy public relations pieces, containing pictures of corporate officers and directors as well as photos and descriptions of new products and new buildings. Yet the basic function of every annual report is to report financial information, almost all of which is a product of the corporation's accounting system.

WILEY PLUS
Tootsie Roll Annual Report Walkthrough

The content and organization of corporate annual reports have become fairly standardized. Excluding the public relations part of the report (pictures, products, and propaganda), the following items are the traditional financial portions of the annual report:

Financial Highlights
Letter to the Stockholders
Management's Discussion and Analysis
Financial Statements
Notes to the Financial Statements
Management's Report on Internal Control
Management Certification of Financial Statements
Auditor's Report
Supplementary Financial Information

In this appendix we illustrate current financial reporting with a comprehensive set of corporate financial statements that are prepared in accordance with generally accepted accounting principles and audited by an international independent certified public accounting firm. We are grateful for permission to use the actual financial statements and other accompanying financial information from the annual report of a large, publicly held company, Tootsie Roll Industries, Inc.

Financial Highlights

Companies usually present the financial highlights section inside the front cover of the annual report or on its first two pages. This section generally reports the total or per share amounts for five to ten financial items for the current year and one or more previous years.

The financial information herein is reprinted with permission from the Tootsie Roll Industries, Inc. 2007 Annual Report. The complete financial statements for Tootsie Roll Industries are also available on the book's companion website.

Corporate Profile

Tootsie Roll Industries, Inc. has been engaged in the manufacture and sale of confectionery products for 111 years. Our products are primarily sold under the familiar brand names: Tootsie Roll, Tootsie Roll Pops, Caramel Apple Pops, Child's Play, Charms, Blow Pop, Blue Razz, Cella's chocolate covered cherries, Mason Dots, Mason Crows, Junior Mints, Junior Caramels, Charleston Chew, Sugar Daddy, Sugar Babies, Andes, Fluffy Stuff cotton candy, Dubble Bubble, Razzles, Cry Baby, Nik-L-Nip and El Bubble.

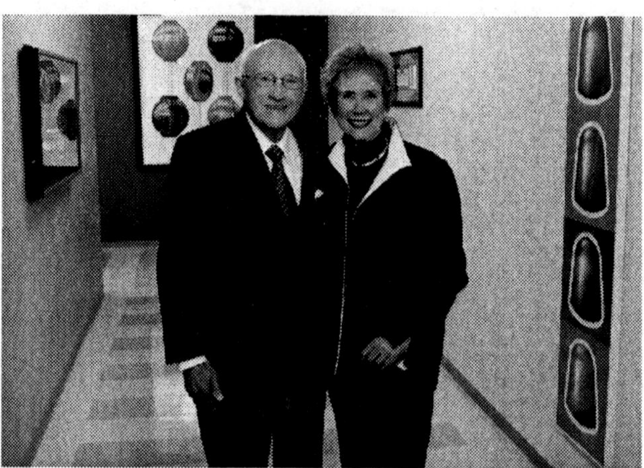

Melvin J. Gordon, Chairman and Chief Executive Officer and Ellen R. Gordon, President and Chief Operating Officer.

Corporate Principles

We believe that the differences among companies are attributable to the caliber of their people, and therefore we strive to attract and retain superior people for each job.

We believe that an open family atmosphere at work combined with professional management fosters cooperation and enables each individual to maximize his or her contribution to the Company and realize the corresponding rewards.

We do not jeopardize long-term growth for immediate, short-term results.

We maintain a conservative financial posture in the deployment and management of our assets.

We run a trim operation and continually strive to eliminate waste, minimize cost and implement performance improvements.

We invest in the latest and most productive equipment to deliver the best quality product to our customers at the lowest cost.

We seek to outsource functions where appropriate and to vertically integrate operations where it is financially advantageous to do so.

We view our well known brands as prized assets to be aggressively advertised and promoted to each new generation of consumers.

We conduct business with the highest ethical standards and integrity which are codified in the Company's "Code of Business Conduct and Ethics."

Financial items from the income statement and the balance sheet that typically are presented are sales, income from continuing operations, net income, net income per share, dividends per common share, and the amount of capital expenditures. The financial highlights section from **Tootsie Roll Industries' Annual Report** is shown on page A-3. Above, we have also included Tootsie Roll's discussion of its corporate principles and corporate profile.

Letter to the Stockholders

Nearly every annual report contains a letter to the stockholders from the chairman of the board or the president, or both. This letter typically discusses the company's accomplishments during the past year and highlights significant events such as mergers and acquisitions, new products, operating achievements, business philosophy, changes in officers or directors, financing commitments, expansion plans, and future prospects. The letter to the stockholders signed by Melvin J. Gordon, Chairman of the Board and Chief Executive Officer, and Ellen R. Gordon, President and Chief Operating Officer, of Tootsie Roll Industries is shown on the next pages.

To Our Shareholders

To Our Shareholders:

Product sales in 2007 were $493 million compared with 2006 sales of $496 million. Sales increased in many of our core products and we had a strong Halloween selling season. These gains were offset by the conclusion of a contract to manufacture product under a private label for a third party and a non-recurring sale of certain inventory to a foreign distributor in 2006.

Net earnings in 2007 were $52 million compared to 2006 net earnings of $66 million. On a per share basis, earnings were $.94 in 2007 and $1.18 in 2006. Average shares outstanding declined as a result of share repurchases in 2007. As discussed in more detail later in this letter, the food industry has experienced extreme cost increases in many key ingredients. This was our experience as well. Substantially all of our principal ingredients as well as packaging and energy costs were significantly higher in 2007. In addition, the weakened U.S. dollar translated into higher costs in our Canadian manufacturing plants. All of these factors adversely impacted our margins and profitability.

At Tootsie Roll we have always maintained a bottom line focus and continually review all facets of our operations in order to increase efficiencies and eliminate waste. As a result of significantly higher input costs, we have also adjusted selling prices or package weights on some items and will continue to take other steps to increase profitability. We do, however, take a long-term view of the business and are mindful not to let our reactions to current market conditions jeopardize the Company's future prospects.

We are a value-oriented branded confectioner and deem it essential to be the low cost producer in each of our major product lines. To that end we continue to implement production technologies that are state-of-the-art, or even better. Accordingly, in 2007 $15 million of capital was invested in operations.

We ended the year with cash and investments of $157 million in excess of interest bearing debt. This strong financial position enables us to continue to distribute dividends, repurchase stock, support our brands in the marketplace, develop new products, invest in operating assets, and consider business acquisition opportunities.

During 2007, we paid cash dividends of 32 cents per share and again distributed a 3% stock dividend. This was the sixty-fifth consecutive year in which cash dividends have been paid and the forty-third consecutive year in which a 3% stock dividend has been distributed. Our record of paying dividends once again earned us the distinction of being named a Mergent "Dividend Achiever," an honor shared with only 3% of U.S. listed dividend paying companies.

During the year we also repurchased $27 million of our common stock in the open market.

Sales and Marketing

During 2007, we once again used targeted consumer and trade promotions to emphasize the high quality and attractive values that our well known brands provide. Carefully executed promotions of this kind move our product into distribution and, with high sell-through, subsequently move them off the retailer's shelf to the consumer.

Our portfolio of highly recognized brands remains popular across all classes of trade. We offer something for virtually all major consumer demographics and continually add new items or introduce new packs in response to changing consumer preferences in the highly competitive confectionery market.

Halloween continues to be our largest selling period. Through product offerings such as large bags of mixed product assortments and merchandising presentations such as pallet packs and display-ready cases we continue to enjoy high sales volume in our Halloween packaged goods line. We see

Financial Highlights

	December 31, 2007	2006
	(in thousands except per share data)	
Net Product Sales	**$492,742**	$495,990
Net Earnings	**51,625**	65,919
Working Capital	**141,754**	128,706
Net Property, Plant and Equipment	**201,401**	202,898
Shareholders' Equity	**638,230**	630,681
Average Shares Outstanding*	**54,980**	55,800
Per Share Items*		
Net Earnings	**$0.94**	$1.18
Cash Dividends Paid	**.32**	.32

*Adjusted for stock dividends.

good results in major trade classes including grocery, mass merchandisers, warehouse clubs, dollar stores and drug chains.

We also see continued consumer acceptance of our theater and home video box line in the super market, dollar store, mass merchandiser and drug store trade classes. Based on sales data tracked by Information Resources, Inc. in 2007 we had ten of the fifty top selling theater and home video box products, including Junior Mints and Dots, the #1 and #2 best selling items in this area.

Our theater and home video box line was expanded in 2007 to include DUBBLE BUBBLE. This iconic brand is offered in both the traditional pink "chunk" format and in colorful gumballs.

New Theater Boxes of DUBBLE BUBBLE

Seasonal offerings were also added in the theater box format. These included Peppermint Crunch Junior Mints, a dual-mint combination of real Junior Mints sprinkled with the refreshing crunch of peppermint candies.

Peppermint Crunch Junior Mints

Another new seasonal theater box item was Holiday Tootsie Mini Chews. These are mini Tootsie Rolls enrobed in a delicious white chocolaty coating and packed in boxes that feature red and green Christmas graphics. Both of these items are perfect for snacking on the go or for holiday gift bowls to share with friends.

Holiday Tootsie Mini Chews

Trick or treaters enjoyed frightfully fun Ghost Dots which were introduced for Halloween 2007. The five assorted flavor remain a mystery—masked behind a ghostly green translucent color!

Ghost Dots

Caramel Apple Sugar Babies were another seasonal addition to the theater box line. These are luscious caramel Sugar Babies with a tart green apple candy shell that are perfect for snacking!

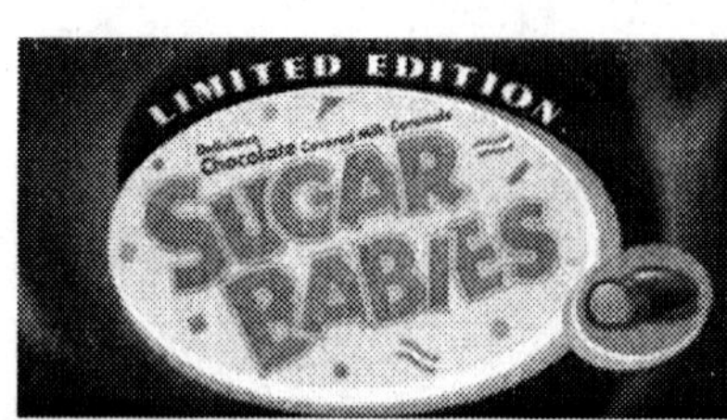

Caramel Apple Sugar Babies

Two additions to our gift box line were introduced in 2007—Cella's Dark and Junior Mint Deluxe. Both items capitalize on the market trend with dark chocolate shells. Cella's Dark are filled with a maraschino cherry bathed in our unique 100% liquid center. Junior Mint Deluxe are filled with a creamy smooth mint fondant. These top shelf items make perfect gifts for any occasion.

Cella's Dark and Junior Mint Deluxe

We also introduced new items in the Andes line during 2007. Sugar free Andes is a traditional three layer mint thin made without sugar to appeal to consumers who must restrict their sugar intake.

Andes Sugar Free and Andes Trio

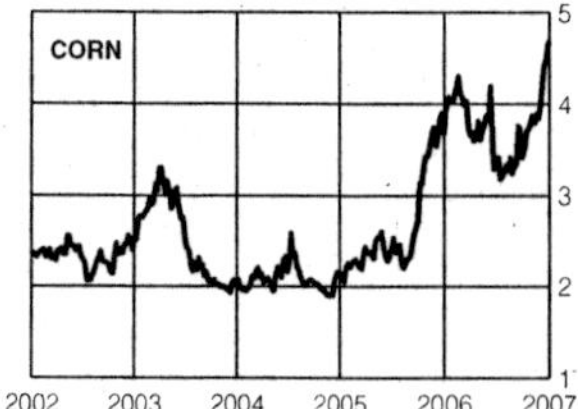

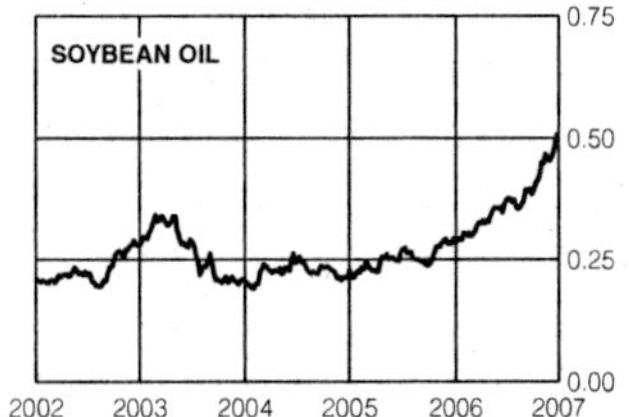

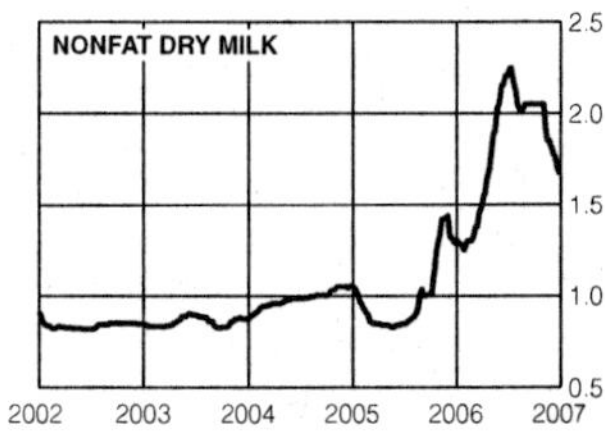

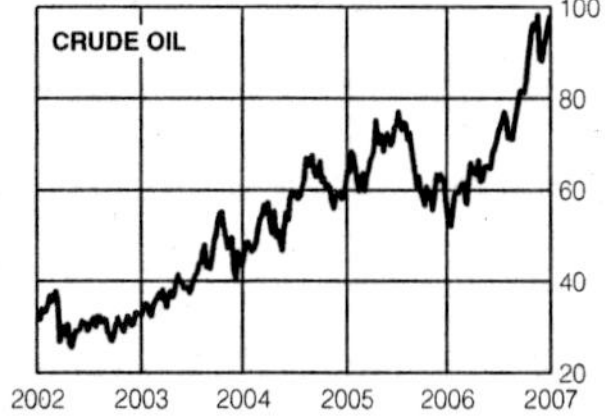

Andes Trio is a gusseted bag filled with three popular Andes flavors—traditional Crème de Menthe, refreshing Peppermint Crunch and coffee flavor Mocha Mint—that is targeted to the warehouse club class of trade.

Advertising and Public Relations

We again promoted our longstanding "How Many Licks" Tootsie Pop theme through campaigns on several children's channels on cable television. Also on cable, several of our products received extensive exposure through showings of popular special interest features including segments on the Food Network's *Unwrapped* program, a segment exploring "snack food technology" on The History Channel's *Modern Marvels,* and John Ratzenberger's *Made in America* show on the Travel Channel.

The Company's listing by KLD on the Domini 400 Social Index was affirmed in recognition of our leadership in the areas of corporate and social responsibility.

Purchasing

While 2007 was another year of generally modest consumer price inflation as measured by the Consumer Price Index, food producers experienced extreme increases in many of the commodities that we buy.

The accompanying charts depict the prices of three key commodities, oil and the Canadian dollar over the past five years. Corn is, of course, the key ingredient in corn syrup which is one of our highest volume commodities. Milk and soybean oil are also important ingredients used in Tootsie Rolls and other products that we manufacture.

Oil is used for fuel in transportation of both inbound and outbound shipments. Our Canadian operations are sensitive to the exchange rate between the U.S. and Canadian dollar for all labor, fringe benefits, and certain other factors of production.

The accompanying charts do not precisely mirror our actual costs of these commodities due to hedging and other programs that insulate the Company from short term fluctuations in market prices. Still, these techniques are limited in their ability to overcome significant cost trends over the long-term and our operating results reflect the impact of these higher costs.

We continue to use competitive bidding, volume purchases and other means to mitigate commodity and other cost increases to the fullest extent possible just as we strive to make operating improvements, increase our selling prices and take other actions to restore and improve profitability.

Supply Chain

We continue to invest capital and resources in projects and processes that keep our production and distribution facilities as efficient as possible, support growing product lines and changing distribution patterns and improve the quality of our products. Further, as technology continues to evolve, we have continued to realize benefits through automation.

During 2007, we embarked on a company wide upgrade of our ERP software. This multi-year project is consistent with our Corporate Principle to invest in our operations. We continue to examine every opportunity to search for operational improvements.

International

All of our international businesses grew profitably during 2007. Mexico had another strong sales year and higher profits. Our Canadian division experienced sales growth, improved distribution and increased profitability. Additionally, our export division, which reaches more than 50 countries in Europe, Asia, and

South and Central America, had higher sales and profits.

In Appreciation

We wish to thank our many loyal employees, customers, suppliers, sales brokers and domestic as well as foreign distributors for their contributions during 2007. We also thank our fellow shareholders for their support over the years. Excellence and dedication is required at every level of the organization in order to meet the challenges of today's business environment and we are committed to both.

Melvin J. Gordon

Melvin J. Gordon
Chairman of the Board and
Chief Executive Officer

Ellen R. Gordon

Ellen R. Gordon
President and
Chief Operating Officer

Management Discussion and Analysis

The management discussion and analysis (MD&A) section covers three financial aspects of a company: its results of operations, its ability to pay near-term obligations, and its ability to fund operations and expansion. Management must highlight favorable or unfavorable trends and identify significant events and uncertainties that affect these three factors. This discussion obviously involves a number of subjective estimates and opinions. The MD&A section of Tootsie Roll's annual report is presented below.

Management's Discussion and Analysis of Financial Condition and Results of Operations

(in thousands except per share, percentage and ratio figures)

FINANCIAL REVIEW

This financial review discusses the Company's financial condition, results of operations, liquidity and capital resources, significant accounting policies and estimates, new accounting pronouncements, market risks and other matters. It should be read in conjunction with the Consolidated Financial Statements and related footnotes that follow this discussion.

FINANCIAL CONDITION

The Company's overall financial position was further strengthened by its 2007 net earnings and related cash flows provided by operating activities.

During 2007, the Company's cash flows from operating activities aggregated $90,064. The Company used these cash flows to pay cash dividends of $17,542, repurchase and retire $27,300 of its outstanding shares, and make capital expenditures of $14,767.

The Company's net working capital increased from $128,706 at December 31, 2006 to $141,754 at December 31, 2007, an increase of $13,048.

As of December 31, 2007, the Company's aggregate cash, cash equivalents and investments, including all long-term investments in marketable securities, was $164,906, compared to $130,841 at December 31, 2006, an increase of $34,065. These amounts include approximately $32,800 and $30,800 of trading securities as of December 31, 2007 and 2006, respectively, in which the Company has invested to hedge its deferred compensation liabilities, as further discussed in Note 7 to the financial statements.

Shareholders' equity increased from $630,681 at December 31, 2006 to $638,230 as of December 31, 2007, principally reflecting 2007 net earnings of $51,625 less cash dividends and share repurchases of $17,542 and $27,300, respectively.

The Company has a relatively straight-forward financial structure and has historically maintained a conservative financial position. Except for an immaterial amount of operating leases, the Company has no special financing arrangements or "off-balance sheet" special purpose entities. Cash flows from operations plus maturities of short term investments are expected to be adequate to meet the Company's overall financing needs, including capital expenditures, in 2008. The Company considers possible appropriate acquisitions on an ongoing basis, and if the Company were to pursue and complete such an acquisition, that could result in bank borrowings.

Results of Operations

2007 vs. 2006

Net product sales were $492,742 in 2007 compared to $495,990 in 2006, a decrease of $3,248 or 1%. This decline principally reflects the conclusion of a contract to manufacture product under a private label for a third party, which accounted for approximately $2,200 in net product sales in 2006, and a non-recurring sale of certain inventory in the amount of approximately $1,000 to a new foreign distributor in the first quarter of 2006.

Product cost of goods sold as a percentage of net sales increased from 62.8% in 2006 to 66.5% in 2007. This increase principally reflects significant cost increases in major ingredients, as well as increases in packaging materials, and labor and fringe benefits, including health insurance. In 2007, increases in ingredient and packaging costs approximated $10,500 and $1,500, respectively. The Company generally experienced significant cost increases in substantially all of its major ingredients, including corn syrup, vegetable oils, sugar, dextrose, milk products, and gum base inputs. In addition, the adverse effects of foreign currency exchange on products manufactured in Canada is estimated to have been $1,800 in 2007.

Due to the seasonal nature of the Company's business and corresponding variations in product mix, gross margins have historically been lower in the second half of the year, and second half 2007 and 2006 were consistent with this trend.

Selling, marketing and administrative expenses were $97,821 in 2007 compared to $101,032 in 2006, a decrease of $3,211 or 3%. This decrease principally reflects the Company's cost reduction efforts as well as lower expenses that directly relate to the 1% sales decline. In addition, prior year 2006 operating expenses reflect approximately $1,500 of additional marketing expenses associated with the transition to new pack sizes and government mandated labeling changes. Additionally, higher freight, delivery and warehousing expenses, principally relating to higher energy and fuel costs, adversely impacted 2007 operating expenses compared to 2006.

Selling, marketing and administrative expenses as a percent of net product sales favorably decreased from 20.4% of net product sales in 2006 to 19.9% of product sales in 2007. These expenses include $41,775 and $40,353 of freight, warehousing and distribution expenses in 2007 and 2006, respectively. Freight, warehousing and distribution expenses increased from 8.1% of net product sales in 2006 to 8.5% of net product sales in 2007, primarily reflecting higher energy input costs and increased warehousing expenses in 2007.

Reported earnings from operations were $70,852 in 2007 compared to $87,529 in 2006, a decrease of $16,677 or 19.1%. This decrease principally reflects the decrease in gross profit resulting from higher input costs, principally ingredients, as discussed above.

The Company performs its annual impairment testing of its intangible assets, trademarks and goodwill, during the fourth quarter of each year. The Company believes that the carrying values of its trademarks and goodwill have indefinite lives as they are expected to generate cash flows indefinitely. There were no impairments in 2006 or 2007.

Other income, net, was $6,315 in 2007 compared to $7,186 in 2006, a decrease of $871. This is due to a decline in income from the Company's 50% interest in a joint venture, accounted for under the equity method, from $921 in 2006 to $182 in 2007.

The consolidated effective tax rate was 33.1% and 30.7% in 2007 and 2006, respectively. This increase in the effective tax rate principally reflects higher foreign income tax expense in 2007. During 2007 and 2006, the Company recorded $3,145 and $3,481 of valuation allowances, respectively, relating to foreign subsidiary tax loss carry-forwards to reduce the future income tax benefits to amounts expected to be realized. In addition, the 2007 effective tax rate was adversely impacted by $1,040 relating to the adoption of FASB Interpretation No. 48, "Accounting for Uncertainty in Income Taxes—an Interpretation of FASB Statement No. 109" (FIN 48) (see also section entitled New Accounting Pronouncements).

Net earnings were $51,625 in 2007 compared to $65,919 in 2006, and earnings per share were $.94 and $1.18 in 2007 and 2006, respectively. Twelve months 2007 results were adversely affected by lower sales and higher input costs, primarily relating to ingredients, as discussed above. Earnings per share did benefit from a reduction in average shares outstanding resulting from common stock purchases in the open market by the Company. Average shares outstanding decreased from 55,800 in 2006 to 54,980 in 2007.

The Company has taken actions and implemented programs, including selected price increases as well as cost reduction programs, with the objective of recovering some of these higher input costs. However these actions have not allowed the Company to recover all of these increases in ingredient and other input costs in 2007.

2006 vs. 2005

Net product sales were $495,990 in 2006, a new record, compared to $487,739 in 2005, reflecting an increase of $8,251 or 2%. Although this sales increase includes some selective price increases, the Company achieved record "back to school" and pre-Halloween product sales in third quarter 2006.

Product cost of goods sold as a percentage of net sales increased from 61.4% in 2005 to 62.8% in 2006. This increase reflects significant cost increases in major ingredients, as well as increases in packaging materials, labor and fringe benefits, and overall plant overhead. In 2006, increases in ingredient and packaging costs approximated $4,882 and $730, respectively. In addition, the adverse effect of foreign exchange on products manufactured in Canada is estimated to have been $2,200 in 2006.

Selling, marketing and administrative expenses were $101,032 in 2006 compared to $97,595 in 2005, an increase of $3,437 or 3.5%. This increase principally reflects significantly higher freight and delivery expenses due to higher energy costs. In addition, marketing expenses associated with the transition to new pack sizes and government mandated labeling changes also added approximately $1,500 to these expenses. Selling, marketing and administrative expenses as a percent of net product sales increased slightly from 20.0% of sales in 2005 to 20.4% of sales in 2006. These expenses include $40,353 and $37,836 of freight, warehousing and distribution expenses in 2006 and 2005, respectively. The amount for 2006 reflects higher fuel surcharges due to higher energy input costs.

Reported earnings from operations were $87,529 in 2006, compared to $110,232 in 2005. Prior year 2005 operating earnings benefited from a $21,840 pre-tax gain on the sale of surplus real estate partially offset by a $4,743 pre-tax charge relating to the impairment of a minor trademark and related goodwill. There were no impairments in 2006. Excluding the nonrecurring net benefit in 2005 described above, earnings from operations were $87,529 in 2006 compared to $93,135 in 2005, a decrease of $5,606 or 6%. This decrease principally reflects the decrease in gross profit margin and higher freight and delivery expenses as discussed above.

Other income, net was $7,186 in 2006 compared to $3,420 in 2005, an increase of $3,766. This net increase principally reflects $1,524 of increased investment income and $1,811 of decreased interest expense due to the pay down of bank debt.

The consolidated effective tax rate was 30.7% and 32.3% in 2006 and 2005, respectively. The decrease in the effective tax rate principally reflects the effects of additional taxes in 2005 relating to the repatriation of foreign dividends as allowed by the American Jobs Creation Act of 2004, as well as a minor reduction in rates relating to increased investment income from tax-exempt municipal bonds and lower state taxes. During 2006, the Company also recorded a $3,481 valuation allowance relating to foreign subsidiary tax loss carry-forwards to reduce the future income tax benefits to amounts expected to be realized.

Net earnings were $65,919 in 2006 compared to $77,227 in 2005, and earnings per share were $1.18 and $1.36 in 2006 and 2005, respectively, a decrease of $.18 per share or 13%. Both fourth quarter and twelve months 2005 periods benefited from a nonrecurring net after-tax gain $10,053 or $.18 per share relating to the sale of surplus real estate, net of the $4,743 write-off of a minor trademark and related goodwill and additional income taxes relating to repatriated foreign dividends. Earnings per share also benefits from a reduction in average shares outstanding resulting from common stock purchases in the open market by the Company. Average shares outstanding decreased from 56,732 in 2005 to 55,800 in 2006.

LIQUIDITY AND CAPITAL RESOURCES

Cash flows from operating activities were $90,064, $55,656, and $82,524 in 2007, 2006 and 2005, respectively. The $34,408 increase in 2007 from 2006 reflects changes in certain operating assets and liabilities. 2007 cash provided by operating activities principally benefited from a $13,481 increase in taxes payable and deferred, $6,506 decrease in inventories, and $2,591 decrease in accounts receivable. However, a $3,234 decrease in accounts payable and accrued liabilities negatively impacted 2007 cash flows from operating activities compared to 2006.

Cash flows from investing activities reflect capital expenditures of $14,767, $39,207 and $14,690 in 2007, 2006 and 2005 respectively, including $25,241 relating to investment of the proceeds of a sale of surplus real estate in like-kind real estate in 2006. 2005 cash flows also included $22,559 relating to the proceeds of such sale of surplus real estate. Cash flows from investing activities also reflect the 2005 recovery of $6,755 for a minimum working capital deficiency adjustment relating to the purchase of Concord Confections Inc. and certain of its affiliates in 2004.

Cash flows from financing activities reflect the repayment of various bank loans of $32,001 and $98,400 in 2006 and 2005, respectively, and bank borrowing of $38,401 in 2005. The Company had no bank borrowing or repayments in 2007, and has no outstanding bank borrowings as of December 31, 2007.

Financing activities also include common stock repurchases and retirements of $27,300, $30,694, and $17,248 in 2007, 2006 and 2005, respectively. Cash dividends of $17,542, $17,264, and $15,132 were paid in 2007, 2006 and 2005, respectively.

SIGNIFICANT ACCOUNTING POLICIES AND ESTIMATES

Preparation of the Company's financial statements involves judgments and estimates due to uncertainties affecting the application of accounting policies, and the likelihood that different amounts would be reported under different conditions or using different assumptions. The Company bases its estimates on historical experience and other assumptions, as discussed herein, that it believes are reasonable. If actual amounts are ultimately different from previous estimates, the revisions are included in the Company's results of operations for the period in which the actual amounts become known. The Company's significant accounting policies are discussed in Note 1 to the financial statements.

Following is a summary and discussion of the more significant accounting policies which management believes to have a significant impact on the Company's operating results, financial position, cash flows and footnote disclosure.

Revenue recognition

Revenue, net of applicable provisions for discounts, returns, allowances, and certain advertising and promotional costs, is recognized when products are delivered to customers based on a customer purchase order, and collectibility is reasonably assured. The accounting for such promotional programs is discussed below.

Provisions for bad debts are recorded as selling, marketing and administrative expenses. Such provisions have generally not exceeded 0.2% of net sales for 2007, 2006 and 2005 and, accordingly, have not been significant to the Company's financial position or results of operations.

Intangible assets

The Company's intangible assets consist primarily of acquired trademarks and related goodwill. In accordance with SFAS No. 142, goodwill and other indefinite lived assets are not amortized, but are instead subjected to annual testing for impairment. The Company performs its annual impairment testing in the fourth quarter of each year.

This determination is made by comparing the carrying value of the asset with its estimated fair value, which is calculated using estimates including discounted projected future cash flows. These projected future cash flows are dependent on a number of factors including the execution of business plans, achievement of projected sales, including but not limited to future price increases, projected operating margins, and projected capital expenditures. Such operating results are also dependent upon future ingredient and packaging material costs, exchange rates for products manufactured in foreign countries, operational efficiencies, cost savings initiatives, and competitive factors. Although the majority of the Company's trademarks relate to well established brands with a long history of consumer acceptance, projected cash flows are inherently uncertain. A change in the assumptions underlying the impairment analysis, including but not limited to a reduction in projected cash flows, the use of a different discount rate to discount future cash flows or a different royalty rate applied to the Company's trademarks, could cause impairment in the future. No impairments were recorded in 2007 or 2006, however, the Company recorded a pre-tax impairment charge of $4,743 during 2005 with respect to a minor trademark and related goodwill.

Customer incentive programs, advertising and marketing

Advertising and marketing costs are recorded in the period to which such costs relate. The Company does not defer the recognition of any amounts on its consolidated balance sheet with respect to such costs. Customer incentives and other promotional costs are recorded at the time of sale based upon incentive program terms and historical utilization statistics, which are generally consistent from year to year.

The liabilities associated with these programs are reviewed quarterly and adjusted if utilization rates differ from management's original estimates. Such adjustments have not historically been material to the Company's operating results.

Split dollar officer life insurance

The Company provides split dollar insurance benefits to certain executive officers and records an asset equal to the cumulative premiums paid on the related policies, as the Company will fully recover these premiums under the terms of the plan. The Company retains a collateral assignment of the cash surrender values and policy death benefits payable to insure recovery of these premiums.

Valuation of long-lived assets

Long-lived assets, primarily property, plant and equipment, are reviewed for impairment as events or changes in business circumstances occur indicating that the carrying value of the asset may not be recoverable. The estimated cash flows produced by the asset or asset groups are compared to the asset carrying value to determine whether impairment exists. Such estimates involve considerable management judgment and are based upon assumptions about expected future operating performance. As a result, actual cash flows could differ from management's estimates due to changes in business conditions, operating performance, and economic conditions. The Company has recorded no such impairments in the years presented.

Income taxes

Deferred income taxes are recognized for future tax effects of temporary differences between financial and income tax reporting using tax rates in effect for the years in which the differences are expected to reverse. The Company records valuation allowances in situations where the realization of deferred tax assets is not likely. The Company, along with third-party tax advisors, periodically reviews assumptions and estimates of the Company's probable tax obligations using informed judgment and historical experience.

Other matters

In the opinion of management, other than contracts for raw materials, including commodity hedges and outstanding purchase orders for packaging, ingredients supplies, and operational services, all entered into in the ordinary course of business, the Company does not have any significant contractual obligations or future commitments. The Company's outstanding contractual commitments as of December 31, 2007, all of which are normal and recurring in nature, are summarized in the chart on page 10 (textbook page A-12).

RECENT ACCOUNTING PRONOUNCEMENTS

FASB Interpretation No. 48 "Accounting for Uncertainty in Income Taxes—an interpretation of FASB Statement 109." (FIN 48)

In July 2006, the FASB issued FIN 48 which prescribes a comprehensive model for recognizing, measuring, presenting and disclosing in the financial statements tax positions taken by the Company on its tax returns. Although the adoption of FIN 48 on January 1, 2007 had no impact on the Company's retained earnings, it did result in the recognition of $14,987 of unrecognized tax benefits which was consistent with those recorded in current income taxes payable at December 31, 2006. This includes $7,802 of unrecognized tax benefits the Company recorded with a corresponding increase in the amount of deferred income tax assets. As of January 1, 2007, the Company's liability for uncertain tax positions included $3,382 of accrued interest relating to its uncertain tax positions.

During 2007, the Company recorded approximately $1,040 of additional income tax expense, including $577 of additional accrued interest and penalties, relating to uncertain tax positions. The Company is not currently subject to a U.S. federal or foreign income tax examination, however, the Company is currently subject to various state tax examinations. Although the Company is unable to determine the ultimate outcome of these examinations, the Company believes that its liability for uncertain tax positions relating to these tax jurisdictions for such years is adequate.

SFAS No. 157, "Fair Value Measurements" (SFAS No. 157)

In September 2006, the FASB issued SFAS No. 157 which establishes a common definition for fair value to be applied to U.S. GAAP guidance requiring use of fair value, establishes a framework for measuring fair value, and expands disclosure about such fair value measurements. SFAS No. 157 is effective for fiscal years beginning after November 15, 2007. The Company is currently assessing the impact of SFAS No. 157 and has not yet made any determination as to the effects, if any, that it may have on the Company's financial position and results of operations.

SFAS No. 159, "The Fair Value Option for Financial Assets and Financial Liabilities-including an amendment to FSAB Statement No. 115," (SFAS No. 159)

In February 2007, the FASB issued SFAS No. 159 which permits entities to choose to measure many financial instruments and certain other items at fair value that are not currently required to be measured at fair value. SFAS No. 159 is effective for fiscal years beginning after November 15, 2007. The Company is currently assessing the impact of SFAS No. 159 and has not yet made any determination as to the effects, if any, that it may have on the Company's financial position and results of operations.

MARKET RISKS

The Company is exposed to market risks related to commodity prices, interest rates, investments in marketable securities, equity prices and foreign exchange.

Commodities

Commodity price risks relate to ingredients, primarily sugar, cocoa, chocolate, corn syrup, dextrose, vegetable oils, milk, whey and gum base ingredients. The Company believes its competitors face similar risks, and the industry has historically adjusted prices to compensate for adverse fluctuations in commodity costs. The Company, as well as competitors in the confectionery industry, have taken actions, including price increases and selective product weight declines (indirect price increases) to mitigate rising input costs for ingredients, transportation, fuel and energy. Although management seeks to substantially recover cost increases over the long term, there is risk that price increases and weight declines cannot be fully passed on to customers and, to the extent they are passed on, they could adversely affect customer and consumer acceptance and resulting sales volume.

The Company utilizes commodity futures contracts as well as annual supply agreements to hedge anticipated purchases of certain ingredients, including sugar, in order to mitigate commodity cost fluctuations. Such commodity future contracts are cash flow hedges and are effective as hedges as defined by Statement of Financial Accounting Standards (SFAS) 133, "Accounting for Derivative Instruments and Hedging Activities." The unrealized gains and losses on such contracts are deferred as a component of accumulated other comprehensive earnings (loss) and are recognized as a component of product cost of goods sold when the related inventory is sold.

The potential change in fair value of commodity derivative instruments (primarily sugar futures contracts) held by the Company, assuming a 10% change in the underlying commodity price, was $535. This analysis only includes commodity derivative instruments and, therefore, does not consider the offsetting effect of changes in the price of the underlying commodity. This amount is not significant compared with the net earnings and shareholders' equity of the Company.

Interest rates

Interest rate risks primarily relate to the Company's investments in tax exempt marketable securities, including auction rate securities (ARS), with maturities or auction dates of generally up to three years. Auction dates, generally every 35 days, are similar to maturity dates in that the interest rate of the ARS is then reset based on current market conditions or, conversely, the holder of the security also can redeem the ARS at face value.

The majority of the Company's investments have historically been held to maturity or to auction date, which limits the Company's exposure to interest rate fluctuations. The accompanying chart summarizes the maturities or auction dates of the Company's investments in debt securities at December 31, 2007.

Less than 1 year	$41,245
1–2 years	19,939
2–3 years	12,685
Over 3 years	525
Total	$74,394

The Company had no outstanding debt at December 31, 2007 other than $7,500 in an IRB note in which interest rates reset each week based on the current market rate. Therefore, the Company does not believe that it has significant interest rate risk with respect to its interest bearing debt.

Investment in marketable securities

As stated above, the Company invests primarily in tax exempt marketable securities, including ARS, with maturities or auction dates generally up to three years. The Company utilizes professional money managers and maintains investment policy guidelines which emphasize quality and liquidity in order to minimize the potential loss exposures that could result in the event of a default or other adverse event, including failed auctions.

The Company believes that it has taken adequate measures to prevent a loss or impairment in the market value of such securities. However, given recent events in the municipal bond and ARS markets, including failed auctions, the Company continues to monitor these investments and markets, as well as investment policies.

As of December 31, 2007, the Company had $27,250 of ARS included in short-tem Investments. Subsequently, $13,700 of these ARS were redeemed at auction at face value. However, $13,550 of such ARS at December 31, 2007 have experienced a successful auction followed by a failed auction subsequent to December 31, 2007.

The Company presently believes that its ARS will not become impaired, given their high investment quality. Nonetheless, due to illiquidity in the ARS market the Company may be forced to hold its ARS for a longer period than originally anticipated. Furthermore, the financial markets seem to be experiencing unprecedented events, and a favorable ultimate outcome cannot be assured.

Equity price

Equity price risk relates to the Company's investments in mutual funds which are principally used to fund and hedge the Company's deferred compensation liabilities. At December 31, 2007, the Company has investments in mutual funds, classified as trading securities, of $32,800. Any change in the fair value of these trading securities would be completely offset by a corresponding change in the respective hedged deferred compensation liability.

Foreign currency exchange

Foreign currency exchange risk principally relates to the Company's foreign operations in Canada and Mexico, as well as periodic purchase commitments of machinery and equipment from foreign sources.

Certain of the Company's Canadian manufacturing costs, including local payroll and a portion of its packaging, ingredients and supplies are sourced in Canadian dollars. The Company uses its Canadian dollar collections on Canadian sales as a partial hedge of its overall Canadian manufacturing obligations sourced in Canadian dollars. The Company also periodically purchases Canadian dollars to facilitate the risk management of these currency changes.

From time to time the Company may use forward foreign exchange contracts and derivative instruments to mitigate its exposure to foreign exchange risk, as well as those related to firm commitments to purchase equipment from foreign vendors. As of December 31, 2007 the Company did not have any material outstanding foreign exchange contracts.

RISK FACTORS

The Company's operations and financial results are subject to a number of risks and uncertainties that could adversely affect the Company's operating results and financial condition. Significant risk factors, without limitation, that could impact the Company are the following: (i) significant competitive activity, including advertising, promotional and price competition, and changes in consumer demand for the Company's products; (ii) fluctuations in the cost and availability of various ingredients and packaging materials; (iii) inherent risks in the marketplace, including uncertainties about trade and consumer acceptance and seasonal events such as Halloween; (iv) the effect of acquisitions on the Company's results of operations and financial condition; (v) the effect of changes in foreign currencies on the Company's foreign subsidiaries operating results, and the effect of the Canadian dollar on products manufactured in Canada and marketed and sold in the United States in U.S. dollars; (vi) the Company's reliance on third-party vendors for various goods and services; (vii) the Company's ability to successfully implement new production processes and lines; (viii) the effect of changes in assumptions, including discount rates, sales growth and profit

Open Contractual Commitments as of December 31, 2007

Payable in	Total	Less than 1 year	1 to 3 Years	3 to 5 Years	More than 5 Years
Commodity hedges	$ 5,351	$ 5,351	$ —	$ —	$ —
Purchase obligations ...	35,309	35,309	—	—	—
Interest bearing debt	7,500	—	—	—	7,500
Operating leases	5,154	1,177	1,897	998	1,082
Total	$53,314	$41,837	$1,897	$998	$8,582

Note: the above amounts exclude deferred income tax liabilities of $35,940, liabilities for uncertain tax positions of $20,056, postretirement health care and life insurance benefits of $13,214 and deferred compensation and other liabilities of $39,813 because the timing of payments relating to these items cannot be reasonably determined.

margins, and the capability to pass along higher ingredient and other input costs through price increases, relating to the Company's impairment testing and analysis of its goodwill and trademarks; (ix) changes in the confectionery marketplace including actions taken by major retailers and customers; (x) customer and consumer response to marketing programs and price and product weight adjustments, and new products; (xi) dependence on significant customers, including the volume and timing of their purchases, and availability of shelf space; (xii) increases in energy costs, including freight and delivery, that cannot be passed along to customers through increased prices due to competitive reasons; (xiii) any significant labor stoppages, strikes or production interruptions; and (xiv) changes in governmental laws and regulations including taxes and tariffs.

The Company's results may be affected by general factors, such as economic conditions, financial and securities' market factors, political developments, currency exchange rates, interest and inflation rates, accounting standards, taxes, and laws and regulations affecting the Company in markets where it competes, and those factors described in Part 1, Item 1A "Risk Factors" and elsewhere in the Company's Annual Report on Form 10-K and in other Company filings, including quarterly reports on Form 10-Q, with the Securities and Exchange Commission.

Forward-looking statements

This discussion and certain other sections contain forward-looking statements that are based largely on the Company's current expectations and are made pursuant to the safe harbor provisions of the Private Securities Litigation Reform Act of 1995. Forward-looking statements can be identified by the use of words such as "anticipated," "believe," "expect," "intend," "estimate," "project," and other words of similar meaning in connection with a discussion of future operating or financial performance and are subject to certain factors, risks, trends and uncertainties that could cause actual results and achievements to differ materially from those expressed in the forward-looking statements. Such factors, risks, trends and uncertainties, which in some instances are beyond the Company's control, including the overall competitive environment in the Company's industry, changes in assumptions and judgments discussed above under the heading "Significant Accounting Policies and Estimates", and factors identified and referred to above under the heading "Risk Factors."

The risk factors identified and referred to above are believed to be significant factors, but not necessarily all of the significant factors that could cause actual results to differ from those expressed in any forward-looking statement. Readers are cautioned not to place undue reliance on such forward-looking statements, which are made only as of the date of this report. The Company undertakes no obligation to update such forward-looking statements.

Management's Report on Internal Control and Management Certifications of Financial Statements

The Sarbanes-Oxley Act of 2002, requires managers of publicly traded companies to establish and maintain systems of internal control on the company's financial reporting processes. In addition, the Act requires the company's top management to provide certifications regarding the accuracy of the financial statements. The reports of Tootsie Roll are shown below.

Management's Report on Internal Control Over Financial Reporting

The management of Tootsie Roll Industries, Inc. is responsible for establishing and maintaining adequate internal control over financial reporting, as such term is defined in the Securities Exchange Act of 1934 (SEC) Rule 13a-15(f). Our management conducted an evaluation of the effectiveness of the Company's internal control over financial reporting as of December 31, 2007 as required by SEC Rule 13a-15(c). In making this assessment, we used the criteria established in *Internal Control—Integrated Framework* issued by the Committee of Sponsoring Organizations of the Treadway Commission (the COSO criteria). Based on our evaluation under the COSO criteria, our management concluded that our internal control over financial reporting was effective as of December 31, 2007.

The effectiveness of the Company's internal control over financial reporting as of December 31, 2007 has been audited by PricewaterhouseCoopers LLP, an independent registered public accounting firm, as stated in their report which appears on page 22 (textbook pages A-27 to A-28).

Tootsie Roll Industries, Inc.

Chicago, Illinois
February 28, 2008

Required Certifications

In 2007, the Company's Chief Executive Officer submitted to the New York Stock Exchange the required Annual CEO Certification certifying that he was not aware of any violation by the Company of the exchange's corporate governance listing standards.

The Company filed with the Securities and Exchange Commission the certifications required of the Company's Chief Executive Officer and Chief Financial Officer under Section 302 of the Sarbanes-Oxley Act of 2002 as exhibits to the Form 10-K for the year ended December 31, 2007.

Financial Statements and Accompanying Notes

The standard set of financial statements consists of: (1) a comparative income statement for three years, (2) a comparative balance sheet for two years, (3) a comparative statement of cash flows for three years, (4) a statement of retained earnings (or stockholders' equity) for three years, and (5) a set of accompanying notes that are considered an integral part of the financial statements. The auditor's report, unless stated otherwise, covers the financial statements and the accompanying notes. The financial statements and accompanying notes plus some supplementary data and analyses for Tootsie Roll Industries follow.

CONSOLIDATED STATEMENT OF

Earnings, Comprehensive Earnings and Retained Earnings

TOOTSIE ROLL INDUSTRIES, INC. AND SUBSIDIARIES

(in thousands except per share data)

	For the year ended December 31,		
	2007	2006	2005
Net product sales	$492,742	$495,990	$487,739
Rental and royalty revenue	4,975	5,150	3,345
Total revenue	497,717	501,140	491,084
Product cost of goods sold	327,695	311,267	299,683
Rental and royalty cost	1,349	1,312	671
Total costs	329,044	312,579	300,354
Product gross margin	165,047	184,723	188,056
Rental and royalty gross margin	3,626	3,838	2,674
Total gross margin	168,673	188,561	190,730
Selling, marketing and administrative expenses	97,821	101,032	97,595
Impairment charges	—	—	4,743
Gain on sale of real estate	—	—	(21,840)
Earnings from operations	70,852	87,529	110,232
Other income, net	6,315	7,186	3,420
Earnings before income taxes	77,167	94,715	113,652
Provision for income taxes	25,542	28,796	36,425
Net earnings	$ 51,625	$ 65,919	$ 77,227
Net earnings	$ 51,625	$ 65,919	$ 77,227
Other comprehensive earnings (loss)	810	(3,697)	2,984
Comprehensive earnings	$ 52,435	$ 62,222	$ 80,211
Retained earnings at beginning of year	$169,233	$164,236	$149,055
Net earnings	51,625	65,919	77,227
Cash dividends ($.32, $.32 and $.29 per share, respectively)	(17,421)	(17,170)	(15,406)
Stock dividends	(46,685)	(43,694)	(46,640)
Cumulative effect of SAB 108	—	(58)	—
Retained earnings at end of year	$156,752	$169,233	$164,236
Earnings per share	$0.94	$ 1.18	$ 1.36
Average common and class B common shares outstanding	54,980	55,800	56,732

(The accompanying notes are an integral part of these statements.)

CONSOLIDATED STATEMENT OF

Financial Position

TOOTSIE ROLL INDUSTRIES, INC. AND SUBSIDIARIES

(in thousands)

Assets

	December 31, 2007	December 31, 2006
CURRENT ASSETS:		
Cash and cash equivalents	$ 57,606	$ 55,729
Investments	41,307	23,531
Accounts receivable trade, less allowances of $2,287 and $2,322	32,371	35,075
Other receivables	2,913	3,932
Inventories:		
Finished goods and work-in-process	37,031	42,146
Raw materials and supplies	20,371	21,811
Prepaid expenses	6,551	6,489
Deferred income taxes	1,576	2,204
Total current assets	199,726	190,917
PROPERTY, PLANT AND EQUIPMENT, at cost:		
Land	19,398	19,402
Buildings	88,225	87,273
Machinery and equipment	270,070	259,049
	377,693	365,724
Less—Accumulated depreciation	176,292	162,826
Net property, plant and equipment	201,401	202,898
OTHER ASSETS:		
Goodwill	73,237	74,194
Trademarks	189,024	189,024
Investments	65,993	51,581
Split dollar officer life insurance	74,944	73,357
Investment in joint venture	8,400	9,668
Total other assets	411,598	397,824
Total assets	$812,725	$791,639

(The accompanying notes are an integral part of these statements.)

(in thousands except per share data)

Liabilities and Shareholders' Equity

	December 31, 2007	2006
CURRENT LIABILITIES:		
Accounts payable	$ 11,572	$ 13,102
Dividends payable	4,344	4,300
Accrued liabilities	42,056	43,802
Income taxes payable	—	1,007
Total current liabilities	57,972	62,211
NONCURRENT LIABILITIES:		
Deferred income taxes	35,940	40,864
Postretirement health care and life insurance benefits	13,214	12,582
Industrial development bonds	7,500	7,500
Liability for uncertain tax positions	20,056	—
Deferred compensation and other liabilities	39,813	37,801
Total noncurrent liabilities	116,523	98,747
SHAREHOLDERS' EQUITY:		
Common stock, $.69-4/9 par value— 120,000 shares authorized— 35,404 and 35,364, respectively, issued	24,586	24,558
Class B common stock, $.69-4/9 par value— 40,000 shares authorized— 18,892 and 18,390, respectively, issued	13,120	12,771
Capital in excess of par value	457,491	438,648
Retained earnings, per accompanying statement	156,752	169,233
Accumulated other comprehensive loss	(11,727)	(12,537)
Treasury stock (at cost)— 63 shares and 62 shares, respectively	(1,992)	(1,992)
Total shareholders' equity	638,230	630,681
Total liabilities and shareholders' equity	$812,725	$791,639

CONSOLIDATED STATEMENT OF

Cash Flows

TOOTSIE ROLL INDUSTRIES, INC. AND SUBSIDIARIES (in thousands)

	For the year ended December 31,		
	2007	2006	2005
CASH FLOWS FROM OPERATING ACTIVITIES:			
Net earnings	$ 51,625	$ 65,919	$ 77,227
Adjustments to reconcile net earnings to net cash provided by operating activities:			
Depreciation	15,859	15,816	14,687
Gain on sale of real estate	—	—	(21,840)
Impairment charges	—	—	4,743
Excess of earnings from joint venture over dividends received	—	(921)	(267)
Return on investment in joint venture	1,419	—	—
Amortization of marketable securities	521	909	1,680
Purchase of trading securities	(84)	(749)	(1,141)
Changes in operating assets and liabilities:			
Accounts receivable	2,591	(4,368)	(1,846)
Other receivables	7	(4,125)	1,519
Inventories	6,506	(8,451)	3,947
Prepaid expenses and other assets	283	(1,912)	(4,357)
Accounts payable and accrued liabilities	(3,234)	(3,688)	(1,868)
Income taxes payable and deferred	13,481	(3,984)	8,423
Postretirement health care and life insurance benefits	1,272	971	708
Deferred compensation and other liabilities	(12)	382	1,251
Other	(170)	(143)	(342)
Net cash provided by operating activities	90,064	55,656	82,524
CASH FLOWS FROM INVESTING ACTIVITIES:			
Working capital adjustment from acquisition	—	—	6,755
Proceeds from sale of real estate and other assets	434	1,343	22,559
(Increase) decrease in restricted cash	—	22,330	(22,330)
Return of investment in joint venture	1,206	—	—
Capital expenditures	(14,767)	(39,207)	(14,690)
Purchase of available for sale securities	(59,132)	(35,663)	(16,772)
Sale and maturity of available for sale securities	28,914	62,223	46,350
Net cash provided by (used in) investing activities	(43,345)	11,026	21,872
CASH FLOWS FROM FINANCING ACTIVITIES:			
Proceeds from bank loan	—	—	38,401
Repayment of bank loan	—	(32,001)	(98,400)
Shares repurchased and retired	(27,300)	(30,694)	(17,248)
Dividends paid in cash	(17,542)	(17,264)	(15,132)
Net cash used in financing activities	(44,842)	(79,959)	(92,379)
Increase (decrease) in cash and cash equivalents	1,877	(13,277)	12,017
Cash and cash equivalents at beginning of year	55,729	69,006	56,989
Cash and cash equivalents at end of year	$ 57,606	$ 55,729	$ 69,006
Supplemental cash flow information:			
Income taxes paid	$ 11,343	$ 29,780	$ 26,947
Interest paid	$ 537	$ 733	$ 2,537
Stock dividend issued	$ 46,520	$ 43,563	$ 46,310

(The accompanying notes are an integral part of these statements.)

Notes to Consolidated Financial Statements

TOOTSIE ROLL INDUSTRIES, INC. AND SUBSIDIARIES

($ in thousands except per share data)

NOTE 1—SIGNIFICANT ACCOUNTING POLICIES:

Basis of consolidation:

The consolidated financial statements include the accounts of Tootsie Roll Industries, Inc. and its wholly-owned subsidiaries (the Company), which are primarily engaged in the manufacture and sale of candy products. All significant intercompany transactions have been eliminated.

The preparation of financial statements in conformity with generally accepted accounting principles in the United States of America requires management to make estimates and assumptions that affect the reported amounts of assets and liabilities and disclosure of contingent assets and liabilities at the date of the financial statements and the reported amounts of revenues and expenses during the reporting period. Actual results could differ from those estimates.

Certain reclassifications have been made to the prior year financial statements to conform to the current year presentation.

Revenue recognition:

Products are sold to customers based on accepted purchase orders which include quantity, sales price and other relevant terms of sale. Revenue, net of applicable provisions for discounts, returns, allowances, and certain advertising and promotional costs, is recognized when products are delivered to customers and collectibility is reasonably assured. Shipping and handling costs of $41,775, $40,353 and $37,836 in 2007, 2006 and 2005, respectively, are included in selling, marketing and administrative expenses. Accounts receivable are unsecured. Revenues from a major customer aggregated approximately 22.4%, 23.7% and 24.0% of net product sales during the years ended December 31, 2007, 2006 and 2005, respectively.

Cash and cash equivalents:

The Company considers temporary cash investments with an original maturity of three months or less to be cash equivalents.

Restricted cash represents the net proceeds received from the sale of surplus real estate in 2005 which was held by a third party intermediary and earmarked for reinvestment in like-kind real estate as provided under U.S. Internal Revenue Code Section 1031. During 2006, the Company reinvested such restricted cash in like-kind real estate.

Investments:

Investments consist of various marketable securities with maturities of generally up to four years. The Company classifies debt and equity securities as either available for sale or trading. Available for sale are not actively traded and are carried at fair value. Unrealized gains and losses on these securities are excluded from earnings and are reported as a separate component of shareholders' equity, net of applicable taxes, until realized. Trading securities relate to deferred compensation arrangements and are carried at fair value. The Company invests in trading securities to hedge changes in its deferred compensation liabilities.

Hedging activities:

From time to time, the Company enters into commodities futures contracts that are intended and effective as hedges of market price risks associated with the anticipated purchase of certain raw materials (primarily sugar). To qualify as a hedge, the Company evaluates a variety of characteristics of these transactions, including the probability that the anticipated transaction will occur. If the anticipated transaction were not to occur, the gain or loss would then be recognized in current earnings. The Company does not engage in trading or other speculative use of derivative instruments. The Company does assume the risk that counter parties may not be able to meet the terms of their contracts. The Company does not expect any losses as a result of counter party defaults.

The Company's commodities futures contracts are being accounted for as cash flow hedges and are recorded on the balance sheet at fair value. Changes therein are recorded in other comprehensive earnings and are reclassified to earnings in the periods in which earnings are affected by the hedged item. Substantially all amounts reported in accumulated other comprehensive earnings (loss) are expected to be reclassified to cost of goods sold.

Inventories:

Inventories are stated at cost, not to exceed market. The cost of substantially all of the Company's inventories ($54,367 and $61,092 at December 31, 2007 and 2006, respectively) has been determined by the last-in, first-out (LIFO) method. The excess of current cost over LIFO cost of inventories approximates $11,284 and $7,350 at December 31, 2007 and 2006, respectively. The cost of certain foreign inventories ($3,036 and $2,865 at December 31, 2007 and 2006, respectively) has been determined by the first-in, first-out (FIFO) method. Rebates, discounts and other cash consideration received from a vendor related to inventory purchases is reflected as a reduction in the cost of the related inventory item, and is therefore reflected in cost of sales when the related inventory item is sold.

Property, plant and equipment:

Depreciation is computed for financial reporting purposes by use of the straight-line method based on useful lives of 20 to 35 years for buildings and 5 to 20 years for machinery and equipment. Depreciation expense was $15,859, $15,816, and $14,687 in 2007, 2006 and 2005, respectively.

Carrying value of long-lived assets:

The Company reviews long-lived assets to determine if there are events or circumstances indicating that the amount of the asset reflected in the Company's balance sheet may not be recoverable. When such indicators are present, the Company compares the carrying value of the long-lived asset, or asset group, to the future undiscounted cash flows of the underlying assets to determine if an impairment exists. If applicable, an impairment charge would be recorded to write down the carrying value to its fair value. The determination of fair value involves the use of estimates of future cash flows that involve considerable management judgment and are based upon assumptions about expected future operating performance. The actual cash flows could differ from management's estimates due to changes in business conditions, operating performance, and economic conditions. No impairment charges were recorded by the Company during 2007, 2006 or 2005.

Postretirement health care and life insurance benefits:

The Company provides certain postretirement health care and life insurance benefits. The cost of these postretirement benefits is accrued during employees' working careers. The Company also provides split dollar life insurance benefits to certain executive officers. The Company records an asset equal to the cumulative insurance premiums that will be recovered upon the death of a covered employee(s) or earlier under the terms of the plan. Split dollar premiums paid were $1,586, $3,002, and $3,678 in 2007, 2006 and 2005, respectively.

Goodwill and intangible assets:

The Company accounts for intangible assets in accordance with SFAS No. 142, "Goodwill and Other Intangible Assets." In accordance with this statement, goodwill and intangible assets with indefinite lives are not amortized, but rather tested for impairment at least annually. All trademarks have been assessed by management to have indefinite lives because they are expected to generate cash flows indefinitely. The Company has completed its annual impairment testing of its goodwill and trademarks during the fourth quarter of each of the years presented, and recorded an impairment of $4,743 in the fourth quarter of 2005 relating to a minor trademark and related goodwill. No impairments were recorded in either 2007 or 2006.

Income taxes:

Deferred income taxes are recorded and recognized for future tax effects of temporary differences between financial and income tax reporting. The Company records valuation allowances in situations where the realization of deferred tax assets is not likely. Federal income taxes are provided on the portion of income of foreign subsidiaries that is expected to be remitted to the U.S. and become taxable, but not on the portion that is considered to be permanently invested in the foreign subsidiary.

Foreign currency translation:

The Company has determined the functional currency for each foreign subsidiary. The U.S. dollar is used as the functional currency where a substantial portion of the subsidiary's business is indexed to the U.S. dollar or where its manufactured products are principally sold in the U.S. All other foreign subsidiaries use the local currency as their functional currency. Where the U.S. dollar is used as the functional currency, foreign currency translation adjustments are recorded as a charge or credit to other income in the statement of earnings. Where the foreign currency is used as the functional currency, translation adjustments are recorded as a separate component of comprehensive earnings (loss).

Joint venture:

The Company's 50% interest in two companies is accounted for using the equity method. The Company records an increase in its investment in the joint venture to the extent of its share of the joint venture's earnings, and reduces its investment to the extent of dividends received. Dividends of $861, $1,946 and $651 were paid in 2007, 2006 and 2005, respectively, by the joint venture. The $1,946 dividend declared in 2006 was not received by the Company until after December 31, 2006; this amount is included in other receivables at December 31, 2006.

Comprehensive earnings:

Comprehensive earnings includes net earnings, foreign currency translation adjustments and unrealized gains/losses on commodity hedging contracts, available for sale securities and certain postretirement benefit obligations.

Earnings per share:

A dual presentation of basic and diluted earnings per share is not required due to the lack of potentially dilutive securities under the Company's simple capital structure. Therefore, all earnings per share amounts represent basic earnings per share.

The Class B Common Stock has essentially the same rights as Common Stock, except that each share of Class B Common Stock has ten votes per share (compared to one vote per share of Common Stock), is not traded on any exchange, is restricted as to transfer and is convertible on a share-for-share basis, at any time and at no cost to the holders, into shares of Common Stock which are traded on the New York Stock Exchange.

Recent accounting pronouncements:

In September 2006, the FASB issued SFAS No. 157, "Fair Value Measurements" (SFAS 157), SFAS 157 establishes a common definition for fair value to be applied to U.S. GAAP guidance requiring use of fair value, establishes a framework for measuring fair value, and expands disclosure about such fair value measurements. SFAS 157 is effective for fiscal years beginning after November 15, 2007. The Company is currently assessing the impact of SFAS 157 and has not yet made any determination as to the effects, if any, that they may have on the Company's financial position and results of operations.

In February 2007, the FASB issued SFAS No. 159. "The Fair Value Option for Financial Assets and Financial Liabilities—including an amendment to FASB Statement No. 115" (SFAS No. 159), which permits entities to choose to measure many financial instruments and certain other items at fair value that are not currently required to be measured at fair value SFAS No. 159 is effective for fiscal years beginning after November 15, 2007. The Company is currently assessing the impact of SFAS No. 159 and has not yet made any determination as to the effects, if any, that it may have on the Company's financial position and results of operations.

NOTE 2—ACCRUED LIABILITIES:

Accrued liabilities are comprised of the following:

	December 31, 2007	December 31, 2006
Compensation	$12,072	$12,923
Other employee benefits	2,843	5,631
Taxes, other than income	1,802	1,781
Advertising and promotions	17,808	17,854
Other	7,531	5,613
	$42,056	$43,802

NOTE 3—BANK LOAN AND INDUSTRIAL DEVELOPMENT BONDS:

Industrial development bonds are due in 2027. The average floating interest rate was 3.8% and 3.6% in 2007 and 2006, respectively.

NOTE 4—INCOME TAXES:

The domestic and foreign components of pretax income are as follows:

	2007	2006	2005
Domestic	$69,250	$81,514	$103,725
Foreign	7,917	13,201	9,927
	$77,167	$94,715	$113,652

The provision for income taxes is comprised of the following:

	2007	2006	2005
Current:			
Federal	$21,785	$14,358	$33,036
Foreign	(702)	944	1,151
State	737	1,050	1,990
	21,820	16,352	36,177
Deferred:			
Federal	2,671	10,962	1,038
Foreign	918	1,196	(849)
State	133	286	59
	3,722	12,444	248
	$25,542	$28,796	$36,425

Significant components of the Company's net deferred tax liability at year end were as follows:

	December 31, 2007	December 31, 2006
Deferred tax assets:		
Accrued customer promotions	$ 4,765	$ —
Deferred compensation	9,993	10,644
Post retirement benefits	4,658	3,938
Reserve for uncollectible accounts	560	567
Other accrued expenses	7,275	3,008
Foreign subsidiary tax loss carry forward	5,922	5,172
Foreign tax credit carry forward	3,651	4,900
Marked to market on investments	—	573
Inventory reserves	2,154	—
Other	1,485	687
	40,463	29,489
Valuation reserve	(7,556)	(4,329)
Total deferred tax assets	$32,907	$25,160

	December 31, 2007	December 31, 2006
Deferred tax liabilities:		
Depreciation	$23,143	$22,330
Deductible goodwill and trademarks	25,050	22,447
Accrued export company commissions	4,100	3,974
Employee benefit plans	777	897
Inventory reserves	4,262	2,591
Prepaid insurance	430	627
Accounts receivable	914	—
Deferred gain on sale of real estate	7,972	7,972
Other	624	2,982
Total deferred tax liabilities	$67,272	$63,820
Net deferred tax liability	$34,365	$38,660

At December 31, 2007, the tax benefits of foreign subsidiary tax loss carry forwards expiring by year are as follows: $1,287 in 2011, $3,150 in 2015 and $498 in 2026 and $987 in 2027. A valuation allowance has been established for these tax loss carry forwards to reduce the future income tax benefits to amounts expected to be realized.

Also at December 31, 2007, the amounts of the foreign subsidiary tax credit carry forwards expiring by year are as follows: $147 in 2008, $173 in 2009, $331 in 2010, $351 in 2011, $334 in 2012, $274 in 2013, $340 in 2014, $1,220 in 2015 and $481 in 2016. A valuation allowance has been established for these carry forward credits to reduce the future income tax benefits to amounts expected to be realized.

The effective income tax rate differs from the statutory rate as follows:

	2007	2006	2005
U.S. statutory rate	**35.0%**	35.0%	35.0%
State income taxes net	**0.9**	0.9	1.2
Exempt municipal bond interest	**(1.4)**	(0.8)	(0.6)
Foreign tax rates	**(1.6)**	(2.8)	(2.8)
Qualified domestic production activities deduction	**(1.9)**	(0.8)	(0.9)
Repatriation of accumulated foreign earnings	**—**	—	0.7
Reserve for uncertain tax benefits	**1.3**	—	—
Other, net	**0.8**	(0.8)	(0.3)
Effective income tax rate	**33.1%**	30.7%	32.3%

The Company has not provided for U.S. federal or foreign withholding taxes on $4,743 and $6,561 of foreign subsidiaries' undistributed earnings as of December 31, 2007 and December 31, 2006, respectively, because such earnings are considered to be permanently reinvested. It is not practicable to determine the amount of income taxes that would be payable upon remittance of the undistributed earnings.

American Jobs Creation Act of 2004 created a temporary incentive for U.S. corporations to repatriate accumulated income earned abroad by providing an 85% dividends received deduction for certain dividends from controlled foreign corporations. In 2005, the Company repatriated accumulated income earned abroad by its controlled foreign corporations in the amount of $21,200 and incurred a U.S. tax expense of $800 net of foreign tax credits.

The Company adopted the provisions of FASB Interpretation No. 48, "Accounting for Uncertainty in Income Taxes" (FIN 48) effective January 1, 2007. The adoption of FIN 48 is reflected in the accompanying financial statements. At January 1, 2007, the Company had unrecognized tax benefits of $14,987. Included in this balance is $7,160 of unrecognized tax benefits that, if recognized, would favorably affect the annual effective income tax rate. The Company recognizes interest and penalties related to unrecognized tax benefits in the provision for income taxes on the Consolidated Statement of Earnings. As of January 1, 2007, $3,382 of interest and penalties were included in the Liability for Uncertain Tax Positions.

At December 31, 2007, the Company had unrecognized tax benefits of $15,867. Included in this balance is $7,622 of unrecognized tax benefits that, if recognized, would favorably affect the annual effective income tax rate. As of December 31, 2007, $4,189 of interest and penalties were included in the Liability for Uncertain Tax Positions.

A reconciliation of the beginning and ending balances of the total amounts of unrecognized tax benefits is as follows:

Unrecognized tax benefits at January 1, 2007	$14,987
Increases in tax positions for the current year	1,895
Reductions in tax positions for lapse of statute of limitations	(1,015)
Unrecognized tax benefits at December 31, 2007	$15,867

The Company is subject to taxation in the U.S. and various state and foreign jurisdictions. The Company remains subject to examination by U.S. federal and state and foreign tax authorities for the years 2004 through 2006. With few exceptions, the Company is no longer subject to examinations by tax authorities for the year 2003 and prior.

The Company is not currently subject to a U.S. federal or foreign income tax examination, however, the Company is currently subject to various state tax examinations. Although the Company is unable to determine the ultimate outcome of these examinations, the Company believes that its liability for uncertain tax positions relating to these jurisdictions for such years is adequate.

Beginning in 2008, statutory income tax rates in Canada will be reduced five percentage points with the final rate adjustment coming in 2012. Accordingly, the Company's Canadian subsidiary has revalued its deferred tax assets and liabilities based on the rate in effect for the year the differences are expected to reverse.

NOTE 5—SHARE CAPITAL AND CAPITAL IN EXCESS OF PAR VALUE:

	Common Stock		Class B Common Stock		Treasury Stock		Capital in excess of par value
	Shares	Amount	Shares	Amount	Shares	Amount	
	(000's)		(000's)		(000's)		
Balance at January 1, 2005	34,760	$24,139	17,515	$12,163	(58)	$(1,992)	$397,745
Issuance of 3% stock dividend	1,033	717	524	364	(2)	—	45,229
Conversion of Class B common shares to common shares	39	27	(39)	(27)	—	—	—
Purchase and retirement of common shares	(577)	(400)	—	—	—	—	(16,849)
Balance at December 31, 2005	35,255	24,483	18,000	12,500	(60)	(1,992)	426,125
Issuance of 3% stock dividend	1,048	727	539	375	(2)	—	42,461
Conversion of Class B common shares to common shares	149	104	(149)	(104)	—	—	—
Purchase and retirement of common shares	(1,088)	(756)	—	—	—	—	(29,938)
Balance at December 31, 2006	35,364	24,558	18,390	12,771	(62)	(1,992)	438,648
Issuance of 3% stock dividend	1,056	733	550	383	(1)	—	45,404
Conversion of Class B common shares to common shares	48	34	(48)	(34)	—	—	—
Purchase and retirement of common shares	(1,064)	(739)	—	—	—	—	(26,561)
Balance at December 31, 2007	35,404	$24,586	18,892	$13,120	(63)	$(1,992)	$457,491

Average shares outstanding and all per share amounts included in the financial statements and notes thereto have been adjusted retroactively to reflect annual three percent stock dividends.

While the Company does not have a formal or publicly announced stock repurchase program, the Company's board of directors periodically authorizes a dollar amount for share repurchases.

Based upon this policy, shares were purchased and retired as follows:

Year	Total Number Of Shares Purchased	Average Price Paid Per Share
2007	1,064	$25.61
2006	1,088	$28.17
2005	577	$29.87

NOTE 6—OTHER INCOME, NET:

Other income (expense) is comprised of the following:

	2007	2006	2005
Interest and dividend income	**$5,495**	$5,155	$3,631
Interest expense	**(535)**	(726)	(2,537)
Joint venture income	**182**	921	918
Foreign exchange gains	**656**	453	852
Capital gains (losses)	**228**	678	166
Insurance recovery	**128**	300	326
Miscellaneous, net	**161**	405	64
	$6,315	$7,186	$3,420

NOTE 7—EMPLOYEE BENEFIT PLANS:

Pension plans:

The Company sponsors defined contribution pension plans covering certain nonunion employees with over one year of credited service. The Company's policy is to fund pension costs accrued based on compensation levels. Total pension expense for 2007, 2006 and 2005 was $3,589, $3,364 and $3,362, respectively. The Company also maintains certain profit sharing and retirement savings-investment plans. Company contributions in 2007, 2006 and 2005 to these plans were $873, $916 and $905, respectively.

The Company also contributes to a multi-employer defined benefit pension plan for its union employees in the U.S. Such contributions aggregated $1,257, $1,084 and $1,011 in 2007, 2006 and 2005, respectively. Although the Company has been advised that the plan is currently in an underfunded status, the relative position of each employer associated with the multi-employer plan with respect to the actuarial present value of benefits and net plan assets is not determinable by the Company.

Deferred compensation:

The Company sponsors three deferred compensation plans for selected executives and other employees: (i) the Excess Benefit Plan, which restores retirement benefits lost due to IRS limitations on contributions to tax-qualified plans, (ii) the Supplemental Savings Plan, which allows eligible employees to defer the receipt of eligible compensation until designated future dates and (iii) the Career Achievement Plan, which provides a deferred annual incentive award to selected executives. Participants in these plans earn a return on amounts due them based on several investment options, which mirror returns on underlying investments (primarily mutual funds). The Company hedges its obligations under the plans by investing in the actual underlying investments. These investments are classified as trading securities and are carried at fair value. At December 31, 2007 and 2006, these investments totaled $32,800 and $30,800, respectively. All gains and losses in these investments are equally offset by corresponding gains and losses in the Company's deferred compensation liabilities.

Postretirement health care and life insurance benefit plans:

The Company provides certain postretirement health care and life insurance benefits for corporate office and management employees. Employees become eligible for these benefits based upon their age and service and if they agree to contribute a portion of the cost. The Company has the right to modify or terminate these benefits. The Company does not fund postretirement health care and life insurance benefits in advance of payments for benefit claims.

Amounts recognized in accumulated other comprehensive loss (pre-tax) at December 31, 2007 are as follows:

Prior service credit	$(1,127)
Net actuarial loss	1,812
Net amount recognized in accumulated other comprehensive loss	$ 685

The estimated actuarial loss, prior service credit and transition obligation to be amortized from accumulated other comprehensive income into net periodic benefit cost during 2008 are $158, $(125) and $0, respectively.

The changes in the accumulated postretirement benefit obligation at December 31, 2007 and 2006 consist of the following:

	December 31,	
	2007	2006
Benefit obligation, beginning of year	$12,582	$ 9,924
Service cost	667	524
Interest cost	694	539
Actuarial (gain)/loss	(550)	2,101
Benefits paid	(179)	(506)
Benefit obligation, end of year	$13,214	$12,582

Net periodic postretirement benefit cost included the following components:

	2007	2006	2005
Service cost—benefits attributed to service during the period	$ 667	$524	$474
Interest cost on the accumulated postretirement benefit obligation	694	539	519
Net amortization	90	(84)	(74)
Net periodic postretirement benefit cost	$1,451	$979	$919

For measurement purposes, the 2007 annual rate of increase in the per capita cost of covered health care benefits was assumed to be 8.0% for pre-age 65 retirees, 9.5% for post-age 65 retirees and 11.0% for prescription drugs; these rates were assumed to decrease gradually to 5.0% for 2014 and remain at that level thereafter. The health care cost trend rate assumption has a significant effect on the amounts reported. The weighted-average discount rate used in determining the accumulated postretirement benefit obligation was 5.70% and 5.60% at December 31, 2007 and 2006, respectively.

Increasing or decreasing the health care trend rates by one percentage point in each year would have the following effect on:

	1% Increase	1% Decrease
Postretirement benefit obligation	$1,814	$(1,497)
Total of service and interest cost components	$ 236	$ (190)

The Company estimates future benefit payments will be $453, $483, $569, $598 and $677 in 2008 through 2012, respectively, and a total of $4,723 in 2013 through 2017. The future benefit payments are net of the annual Medicare Part D subsidy of approximately $1,095 beginning in 2008.

NOTE 8—COMMITMENTS:

Rental expense aggregated $1,090, $1,132 and $1,090 in 2007, 2006 and 2005, respectively.

Future operating lease commitments are not significant.

NOTE 9—SEGMENT AND GEOGRAPHIC INFORMATION:

The Company operates as a single reportable segment encompassing the manufacture and sale of confectionery products. Its principal manufacturing operations are located in the United States and Canada, and its principal market is the United States. The Company also manufactures and sells confectionery products in Mexico, and exports products to Canada as well as to over 50 countries worldwide.

The following geographic data include net sales summarized on the basis of the customer location and long-lived assets based on their physical location.

	2007	2006	2005
Net Product Sales:			
United States	$445,820	$450,591	$445,405
Foreign	46,922	45,399	42,334
	$492,742	$495,990	$487,739
Long-lived assets:			
United States	$296,277	$282,490	$246,721
Foreign	54,461	55,014	57,160
	$350,738	$337,504	$303,881

NOTE 10—DISCLOSURES ABOUT THE FAIR VALUE AND CARRYING AMOUNT OF FINANCIAL INSTRUMENTS:

The carrying amount approximates fair value of cash and cash equivalents because of the short maturity of those instruments. The fair values of investments are estimated based on quoted market prices. The fair value of the Company's industrial development bonds approximates their carrying value because they have a floating interest rate.

The carrying amount and estimated fair values of the Company's financial instruments are as follows:

	2007		2006	
	Carrying Amount	Fair Value	Carrying Amount	Fair Value
Cash and cash equivalents	$57,606	$57,606	$55,729	$55,729
Investments available for sale	74,456	74,456	44,351	44,351
Investments in trading securities	32,844	32,844	30,761	30,761
Bank loan and industrial development bonds	7,500	7,500	7,500	7,500

A summary of the aggregate fair value, gross unrealized gains, gross unrealized losses and amortized cost basis of the Company's investment portfolio by major security type is as follows:

	December 31, 2007			
	Amortized	Fair	Unrealized	
Available for sale:	Cost	Value	Gains	Losses
Municipal bonds	$74,228	$74,394	$166	$ —
Mutual funds	57	62	5	—
	$74,285	$74,456	$171	$ —

	December 31, 2006			
	Amortized	Fair	Unrealised	
Available for sale:	Cost	Value	Gains	Losses
Municipal bonds	$44,532	$44,293	$ —	$(239)
tual funMuds	57	58	1	—
	$44,589	$44,351	$ 1	$(239)

Investments available for sale included $27,250 and $0 of auction based municipal bonds as of year end 2007 and 2006, respectively. Subsequent to December 31, 2007, $13,700 of such bonds were redeemed at auction at face value. The remaining $13,550 experienced a successful auction followed by a failed auction, and the Company may be forced to hold them for a longer period than originally anticipated. There were no securities with maturities greater than four years. The sale of available for sale securities resulted in realized gains of $118 and $684 in 2007 and 2006, respectively.

NOTE 11—COMPREHENSIVE INCOME:

The following table sets forth information with respect to accumulated other comprehensive income (loss):

		Unrealized Gain (Loss) on			
	Foreign Currency Translation Adjustment	Investments	Derivatives	Postretirement and Pension Benefits	Accumulated Other Comprehensive Earnings (Loss)
Balance at January 1, 2005	$(11,964)	$ 209	$ 824	$ —	$(10,931)
Unrealized gains (losses)	1,036	(184)	4,186	—	5,038
(Gains) losses reclassified to net earnings	—	36	(946)	—	(910)
Tax effect	—	55	(1,199)	—	(1,144)
Net of tax amount	1,036	(93)	2,041	—	2,984
Balance at December 31, 2005	(10,928)	116	2,865	—	(7,947)
Unrealized gains (losses)	(296)	263	880	—	847
(Gains) losses reclassified to net earnings	—	(684)	(5,856)	—	(6,540)
Tax effect	—	156	1,840	—	1,996
Net of tax amount	(296)	(265)	(3,136)	—	(3,697)
Adoption of SFAS 158 (Note 7)	—	—	—	(893)	(893)
Balance at December 31,2006	(11,224)	(149)	(271)	(893)	(12,537)
Unrealized gains (losses)	(272)	469	(462)	588	323
(Gains) losses reclassified to net earnings	—	(61)	1,202	—	1,141
Tax effect	—	(151)	(273)	(230)	(654)
Net of tax amount	(272)	257	467	358	810
Balance at December 31, 2007	$(11,496)	$ 108	$ 196	$(535)	$(11,727)

NOTE 12—GAIN ON SALE OF REAL ESTATE:

During 2005, the Company sold surplus real estate and realized a pre-tax gain of $21,840. During 2006, the Company invested the net proceeds of $22,330 in new real estate investments in compliance with U.S. Internal Revenue Code (IRC) Section 1031 resulting in the deferral of income tax payable on such gain.

NOTE 13—SEC STAFF ACCOUNTING BULLETIN NO. 108:

In September 2006, the SEC issued Staff Accounting Bulletin No. 108, "Considering the Effects of Prior Year Misstatements when Quantifying Misstatements in Current Year Financial Statements" (SAB 108). Traditionally, there have been two widely-recognized methods for quantifying the effects of financial statement misstatements: the "roll-over" method and the "iron curtain" method. Prior to its application of the guidance in SAB 108, the Company used the "roll-over" method for quantifying financial statement misstatements, which focused primarily on the impact of a misstatement on the income statement (and net earnings), including the reversing effects, if any, of prior year misstatements. SAB 108 permits companies to initially apply its provisions by recording the cumulative effect of any misstatements as adjustments to the carrying values of assets and liabilities as of January 1, 2006 with an offsetting adjustment recorded to the opening balance of retained earnings. The Company previously evaluated these items under the "roll-over" method and concluded they were quantitatively and qualitatively immaterial, individually and in the aggregate. The following table, and accompanying footnotes, summarizes the effects of applying the guidance in SAB 108:

	Period in which the Misstatement Originated			
	Cumulative Prior to January 1, 2004	Year Ended December 31, 2004	2005	Adjustment Recorded as of January 1, 2006
Current assets (1)	$ 3,252	$ —	$ —	$ 3,252
Noncurrent assets (2)	2,184	(464)	1,446	3,166
Current liabilities (3)	(1,625)	(242)	—	(1,867)
Noncurrent liabilities (4)	(2,280)	—	(2,329)	(4,609)
Impact on net income (5)	$ 1,531	$(706)	$ (883)	
Net decrease to retained earnings (6)				$ (58)

(1) Primarily includes adjustments to (a) inventory relating to the calculation of a valuation reserve of $333 and (b) accounts receivable for the classification of estimated collectible accounts on the balance sheet which were previously classified as an offset to an accrued liability of $2,635.

(2) Primarily includes adjustments to (a) property, plant and equipment for a computational correction relating to depreciation expense over several prior years of $1,500, the timing of the recognition of a loss associated with the abandonment and disposal of certain machinery and equipment of ($464), and the timing of the recognition of a minor asset retirement obligation of $1,446 which is partially offset by the related liability discussed in Note 4 (c) below, and (b) other assets relating to the carrying value of cumulative split-dollar life insurance premiums paid by the Company of $587.

(3) Primarily includes adjustments to (a) accounts payable relating to certain estimated liabilities recorded during various acquisition purchase accounting transactions which were not subsequently adjusted for the lower actual amounts paid of $940. (b) accrued liabilities resulting from higher estimates which were not subsequently adjusted to lower actual amounts of $809, and the classification on the balance sheet of estimated collectible accounts of ($2,635) as described in Note 1(b) above, and (c) income taxes payable and deferred to reflect the income tax impact of recording the items described herein of ($981).

(4) Primarily includes adjustments to (a) employee benefit obligations relating to the unintentional misapplication of certain technical GAAP requirements surrounding the establishment of employee disability obligations of $1,575, and of the timing of the recognition of liabilities relating to employee severance obligations of ($1,982), each of which are substantially offsetting, (b) deferred income tax liabilities for computational differences relating to the calculation and reconciliation of deferred tax liabilities of ($2,059), and (c) other long term liabilities relating to the timing of the recognition of a minor asset retirement obligation of ($2,143).

(5) Represents the net after-tax effect for the indicated periods resulting from the above-described items.

(6) Represents the net after tax impact on retained earnings as of January 1, 2006 to record the initial application of SAB 108.

Auditor's Report

All publicly held corporations, as well as many other enterprises and organizations (both profit and not-for-profit, large and small) engage the services of independent certified public accountants for the purpose of obtaining an objective, expert report on their financial statements. Based on a comprehensive examination of the company's accounting system, accounting records, and the financial statements, the outside CPA issues the auditor's report.

The standard auditor's report consists of three sections: (1) an introduction, (2) a scope section, and (3) the opinion. In the **introduction,** the auditor identifies who and what was audited and indicates the responsibilities of management and the auditor relative to the financial statements. In the **scope section** the auditor states that the audit was conducted in accordance with generally accepted auditing standards and discusses the nature and limitations of the audit. In the **opinion,** the auditor expresses an informed opinion as to (1) the fairness of the financial statements and (2) their conformity with generally accepted accounting principles. The Report of PricewaterhouseCoopers LLP appearing in Tootsie Roll's Annual Report is shown here.

Report of Independent Registered Public Accounting Firm

To the Board of Directors and Shareholders of Tootsie Roll Industries, Inc.:

In our opinion, the accompanying consolidated balance sheets and the related consolidated statements of earnings, comprehensive earnings, retained earnings, and cash flows present fairly, in all material respects, the financial position of Tootsie Roll Industries, Inc. and its subsidiaries at December 31, 2007 and December 31, 2006, and the results of their operations and their cash flows for each of the three years in the period ended December 31, 2007 in conformity with accounting principles generally accepted in the United States of America. Also in our opinion, the Company maintained, in all material respects, effective internal control over financial reporting as of December 31, 2007, based on criteria established in *Internal Control—Integrated Framework* issued by the Committee of Sponsoring Organizations of the Treadway Commission (COSO). The Company's management is responsible for these financial statements, for maintaining effective internal control over financial reporting and for its assessment of the effectiveness of internal control over financial reporting, included in Management's Report on Internal Control Over Financial Reporting in the accompanying Annual Report. Our responsibility is to express opinions on these financial statements and on the Company's internal control over financial reporting based on our integrated audits. We conducted our audits in accordance with the standards of the Public Company Accounting Oversight Board (United States). Those standards require that we plan and perform the audits to obtain reasonable assurance about whether the financial statements are free of material misstatement and whether effective internal control over financial reporting was maintained in all material respects. Our audits of the financial statements included examining, on a test basis, evidence supporting the amounts and disclosures in the financial statements, assessing the accounting principles used and significant estimates made by management, and evaluating the overall financial statement presentation. Our audit of internal control over financial reporting included obtaining an understanding of internal control over financial reporting, assessing the risk that a material weakness exists, and testing and evaluating the design and operating effectiveness of internal control based on the assessed risk. Our audits also included performing such other procedures as we considered necessary in the circumstances. We believe that our audits provide a reasonable basis for our opinions.

As discussed in Note 4 to the consolidated financial statements, the Company changed its method of accounting for uncertainty in income taxes as of January 1, 2007.

A company's internal control over financial reporting is a process designed to provide reasonable assurance regarding the reliability of financial reporting and the preparation of financial statements for external purposes in accordance with generally accepted accounting principles. A company's internal control over financial reporting includes those policies and procedures that (i) pertain to the maintenance of records that, in reasonable detail, accurately and fairly reflect the transactions and dispositions of the assets of the company; (ii) provide reasonable assurance that transactions are recorded as necessary to permit preparation of financial statements in accordance with generally accepted accounting principles, and that receipts and expenditures of the company are being made only in accordance with authorizations of management and directors of the company; and (iii) provide reasonable assurance regarding prevention or timely detection of unauthorized acquisition, use, or disposition of the company's assets that could have a material effect on the financial statements.

Because of its inherent limitations, internal control over financial reporting may not prevent or detect misstatements. Also, projections of any evaluation of effectiveness to future periods are subject to the risk that controls may become inadequate because of changes in conditions, or that the degree of compliance with the policies or procedures may deteriorate.

PricewaterhouseCoopers LLP

Chicago, Illinois
February 28, 2008

Supplementary Financial Information

In addition to the financial statements and the accompanying notes, companies often present supplementary financial information. Tootsie Roll has provided stock performance information, quarterly financial data, and a five-year summary of earnings and financial highlights.

Performance Graph

The following performance graphs compare the Company's cumulative total shareholder return on the Company's Common Stock for a five-year period (December 31, 2002 to December 31, 2007) and a ten-year period (December 31, 1997 to December 31, 2007 with the cumulative total return of Standard & Poor's 500 Stock Index ("S&P 500") and the Dow Jones Industry Food Index ("Peer Group," which includes the Company), assuming (i) $100 invested on December 31 of the first year of the chart in each of the Company's Common Stock, S&P 500 and the Dow Jones Industry Food Index and (ii) the reinvestment of dividends.

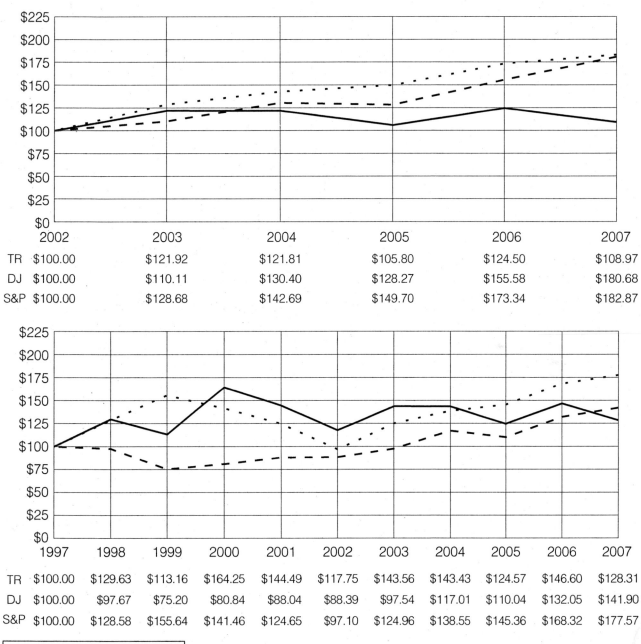

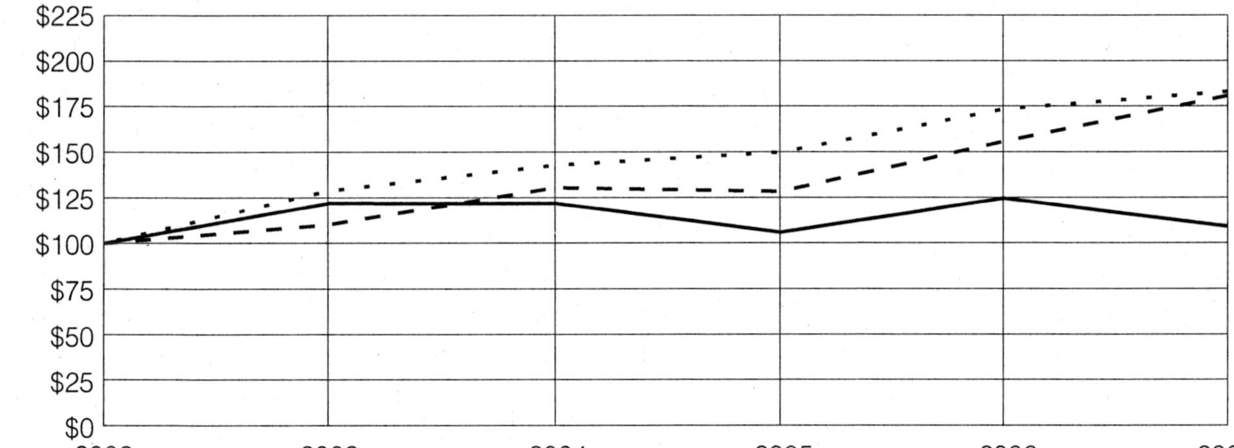

	2002	2003	2004	2005	2006	2007
TR	$100.00	$121.92	$121.81	$105.80	$124.50	$108.97
DJ	$100.00	$110.11	$130.40	$128.27	$155.58	$180.68
S&P	$100.00	$128.68	$142.69	$149.70	$173.34	$182.87

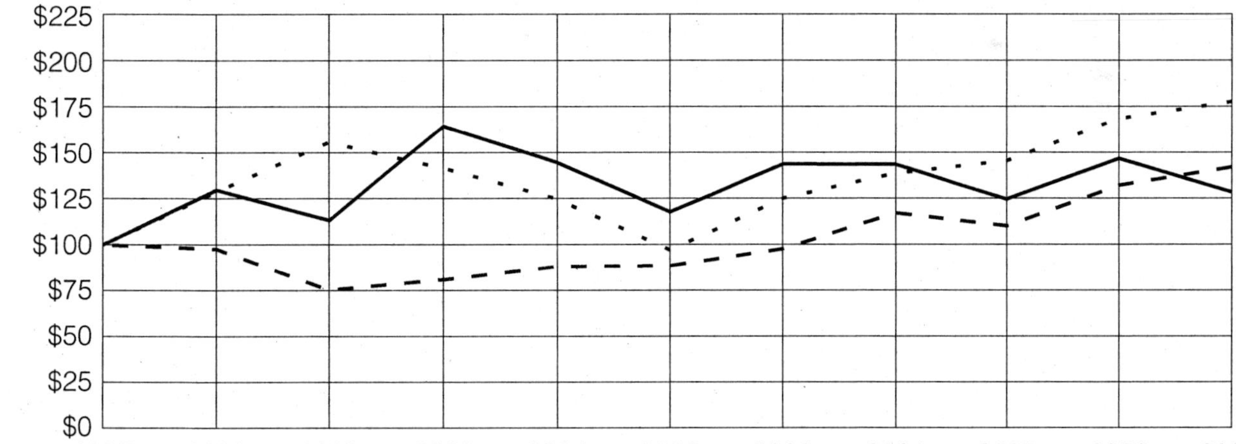

	1997	1998	1999	2000	2001	2002	2003	2004	2005	2006	2007
TR	$100.00	$129.63	$113.16	$164.25	$144.49	$117.75	$143.56	$143.43	$124.57	$146.60	$128.31
DJ	$100.00	$97.67	$75.20	$80.84	$88.04	$88.39	$97.54	$117.01	$110.04	$132.05	$141.90
S&P	$100.00	$128.58	$155.64	$141.46	$124.65	$97.10	$124.96	$138.55	$145.36	$168.32	$177.57

Legend

——— Tootsie Roll

- - - - - DJ Food Producers

.... S&P 500 Composite

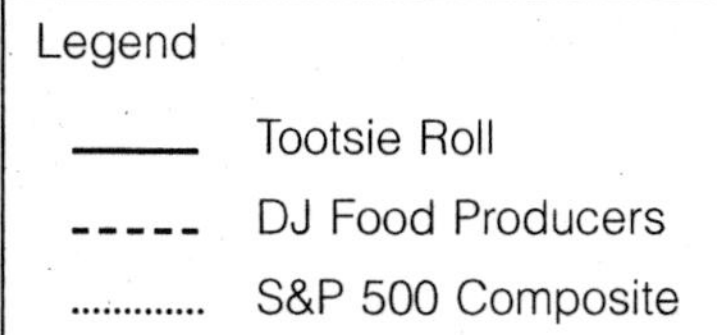

Quarterly Financial Data (Unaudited)

TOOTSIE ROLL INDUSTRIES, INC. AND SUBSIDIARIES

(Thousands of dollars except per share data)

2007	First	Second	Third	Fourth	Total
Net product sales	$92,914	$101,901	182,917	115,010	492,742
Gross product margin	33,178	34,425	60,659	36,785	165,047
Net earnings	9,811	10,226	23,432	8,156	51,625
Net earnings per share	.18	.19	.43	.15	.94
2006					
Net product sales	$103,822	$94,944	$186,403	$110,821	$495,990
Gross product margin	39,074	38,166	70,042	37,441	184,723
Net earnings	12,362	12,858	28,969	11,730	65,919
Net earnings per share	.22	.23	.52	.21	1.18
2005					
Net product sales	$97,925	$103,627	$173,692	$112,495	$487,739
Gross product margin	39,589	41,414	67,333	39,720	188,056
Net earnings	12,506	13,731	27,665	23,325	77,227
Net earnings per share	.22	.24	.49	.41	1.36

Net earnings per share is based upon average outstanding shares as adjusted for 3% stock dividends issued during the second quarter of each year. The sum of the per share amounts may not equal annual amounts due to rounding.

2007-2006 QUARTERLY SUMMARY OF TOOTSIE ROLL INDUSTRIES, INC. STOCK PRICE AND DIVIDENDS PER SHARE

STOCK PRICES*

	2007		2006	
....	High	Low	High	Low
1st Qtr	**$32.69**	**$28.19**	$29.71	$26.98
2nd Qtr	**$30.50**	**$27.65**	$31.42	$28.23
3rd Qtr	**$30.85**	**$25.03**	$29.75	$26.35
4th Qtr	**$27.44**	**$23.55**	$33.26	$29.08

*NYSE—Closing Price

Estimated Number of shareholders at February 2008:

Common Stock	18,000
Class B Common Stock	5,000

DIVIDENDS

	2007	2006
1st Qtr	**$.08**	$.08
2nd Qtr	**$.08**	$.08
3rd Qtr	**$.08**	$.08
4th Qtr	**$.08**	$.08

NOTE: In addition to the above cash dividends, a 3% stock dividend was issued on April 12, 2007 and April 13, 2006. Cash dividends are not restated to reflect 3% stock dividends.

Five Year Summary of Earnings and Financial Highlights

TOOTSIE ROLL INDUSTRIES, INC. AND SUBSIDIARIES

(Thousands of dollars except per share, percentage and ratio figures)

(See Management's Comments starting on page 5 [textbook page A-6])

	2007	2006	2005	2004	2003
Sales and Earnings Data (2)					
Net product sales	$ 492,742	$495,990	$487,739	$420,110	$392,656
Gross product margin	165,047	184,723	188,056	174,539	168,833
Interest expense	535	726	2,537	912	172
Provision for income taxes	25,542	28,796	36,425	30,514	32,933
Net earnings	51,625	65,919	77,227	64,174	65,014
% of net product sales	10.5%	13.3%	15.8%	15.3%	16.6%
% of shareholders' equity	8.1%	10.5%	12.5%	11.3%	12.1%
Per Common Share Data (1)					
Net earnings	$ .94	$ 1.18	$ 1.36	$ 1.12	$ 1.12
Cash dividends declared	.32	.32	.29	.27	.25
Stock dividends	3%	3%	3%	3%	3%
Additional Financial Data					
Working capital	$ 141,754	$128,706	$132,940	$110,376	$180,818
Net cash provided by operating activities	90,064	55,656	82,524	76,228	83,466
Net cash provided by (used in) investing activities	(43,345)	11,026	21,872	(164,039)	(50,383)
Net cash provided by (used in) financing activities	(44,842)	(79,959)	(92,379)	60,716	(54,506)
Property, plant & equipment additions	14,767	39,207	14,690	17,948	12,150
Net property, plant & equipment	201,401	202,898	178,760	178,750	129,163
Total assets	812,725	791,639	813,696	811,753	665,297
Long term debt	7,500	7,500	7,500	93,167	7,500
Shareholders' equity	638,230	630,681	617,405	570,179	536,581
Average shares outstanding (1)	54,980	55,800	56,732	57,111	58,202

(1) Adjusted for annual 3% stock dividends.
(2) Certain reclassifications have been made to prior year numbers to conform to current year presentation.

appendix 

Specimen Financial Statements: Hershey Foods Corporation

THE HERSHEY COMPANY

CONSOLIDATED STATEMENTS OF INCOME

For the years ended December 31, In thousands of dollars except per share amounts	2007	2006	2005
Net Sales	**$4,946,716**	$4,944,230	$4,819,827
Costs and Expenses:			
Cost of sales	**3,315,147**	3,076,718	2,956,682
Selling, marketing and administrative	**895,874**	860,378	912,986
Business realignment and impairment charges, net	**276,868**	14,576	96,537
Total costs and expenses	**4,487,889**	3,951,672	3,966,205
Income before Interest and Income Taxes	**458,827**	992,558	853,622
Interest expense, net	**118,585**	116,056	87,985
Income before Income Taxes	**340,242**	876,502	765,637
Provision for income taxes	**126,088**	317,441	277,090
Net Income	**$ 214,154**	$ 559,061	$ 488,547
Net Income Per Share—Basic—Class B Common Stock	**$ .87**	$ 2.19	$ 1.85
Net Income Per Share—Diluted—Class B Common Stock	**$ .87**	$ 2.17	$ 1.84
Net Income Per Share—Basic—Common Stock	**$ .96**	$ 2.44	$ 2.05
Net Income Per Share—Diluted—Common Stock	**$ .93**	$ 2.34	$ 1.97
Cash Dividends Paid Per Share:			
Common Stock	**$ 1.1350**	$ 1.030	$ .9300
Class B Common Stock	**1.0206**	.925	.8400

The notes to consolidated financial statements are an integral part of these statements.

The financial information herein is reprinted with permission from the Hershey Foods Corporation 2007 Consolidated Financial Statements and Management's Discussion and Analysis. The complete financial statements for Hershey Foods, including notes, are available on the book's companion website.

THE HERSHEY COMPANY

CONSOLIDATED BALANCE SHEETS

December 31, In thousands of dollars	2007	2006
ASSETS		
Current Assets:		
Cash and cash equivalents	**$ 129,198**	$ 97,141
Accounts receivable—trade	**487,285**	522,673
Inventories	**600,185**	648,820
Deferred income taxes	**83,668**	61,360
Prepaid expenses and other	**126,238**	87,818
Total current assets	**1,426,574**	1,417,812
Property, Plant and Equipment, Net	**1,539,715**	1,651,300
Goodwill	**584,713**	501,955
Other Intangibles	**155,862**	140,314
Other Assets	**540,249**	446,184
Total assets	**$ 4,247,113**	$ 4,157,565
LIABILITIES, MINORITY INTEREST AND STOCKHOLDERS' EQUITY		
Current Liabilities:		
Accounts payable	**$ 223,019**	$ 155,517
Accrued liabilities	**538,986**	454,023
Accrued income taxes	**373**	—
Short-term debt	**850,288**	655,233
Current portion of long-term debt	**6,104**	188,765
Total current liabilities	**1,618,770**	1,453,538
Long-term Debt	**1,279,965**	1,248,128
Other Long-term Liabilities	**544,016**	486,473
Deferred Income Taxes	**180,842**	286,003
Total liabilities	**3,623,593**	3,474,142
Commitments and Contingencies	**—**	—
Minority Interest	**30,598**	—
Stockholders' Equity:		
Preferred Stock, shares issued: none in 2007 and 2006	**—**	—
Common Stock, shares issued: 299,095,417 in 2007 and 299,085,666 in 2006	**299,095**	299,085
Class B Common Stock, shares issued: 60,806,327 in 2007 and 60,816,078 in 2006	**60,806**	60,816
Additional paid-in capital	**335,256**	298,243
Retained earnings	**3,927,306**	3,965,415
Treasury—Common Stock shares, at cost: 132,851,893 in 2007 and 129,638,183 in 2006	**(4,001,562)**	(3,801,947)
Accumulated other comprehensive loss	**(27,979)**	(138,189)
Total stockholders' equity	**592,922**	683,423
Total liabilities, minority interest and stockholders' equity	**$ 4,247,113**	$ 4,157,565

The notes to consolidated financial statements are an integral part of these balance sheets.

THE HERSHEY COMPANY

CONSOLIDATED STATEMENTS OF CASH FLOWS

For the years ended December 31, In thousands of dollars	2007	2006	2005
Cash Flows Provided from (Used by) Operating Activities			
Net income	**$ 214,154**	$ 559,061	$ 488,547
Adjustments to reconcile net income to net cash provided from operations:			
Depreciation and amortization	**310,925**	199,911	218,032
Stock-based compensation expense, net of tax of $10,634, $14,524 and $19,716, respectively	**18,987**	25,598	34,449
Excess tax benefits from exercise of stock options	**(9,461)**	(9,275)	(20,186)
Deferred income taxes	**(124,276)**	4,173	71,038
Business realignment and impairment charges, net of tax of $144,928, $4,070, and $44,975, respectively	**267,653**	7,573	74,021
Contributions to pension plans	**(15,836)**	(23,570)	(277,492)
Changes in assets and liabilities, net of effects from business acquisitions and divestitures:			
Accounts receivable—trade	**40,467**	(14,919)	(130,663)
Inventories	**45,348**	(12,461)	(60,062)
Accounts payable	**62,204**	(13,173)	16,715
Other assets and liabilities	**(31,329)**	275	47,363
Net Cash Provided from Operating Activities	**778,836**	723,193	461,762
Cash Flows Provided from (Used by) Investing Activities			
Capital additions	**(189,698)**	(183,496)	(181,069)
Capitalized software additions	**(14,194)**	(15,016)	(13,236)
Business acquisitions	**(100,461)**	(17,000)	(47,074)
Proceeds from divestitures	**—**	—	2,713
Net Cash (Used by) Investing Activities	**(304,353)**	(215,512)	(238,666)
Cash Flows Provided from (Used by) Financing Activities			
Net change in short-term borrowings	**195,055**	(163,826)	475,582
Long-term borrowings	**—**	496,728	248,318
Repayment of long-term debt	**(188,891)**	(234)	(278,236)
Cash dividends paid	**(252,263)**	(235,129)	(221,235)
Exercise of stock options	**50,497**	37,111	81,632
Excess tax benefits from exercise of stock options	**9,461**	9,275	20,186
Repurchase of Common Stock	**(256,285)**	(621,648)	(536,997)
Net Cash (Used by) Financing Activities	**(442,426)**	(477,723)	(210,750)
Increase in Cash and Cash Equivalents	**32,057**	29,958	12,346
Cash and Cash Equivalents as of January 1	**97,141**	67,183	54,837
Cash and Cash Equivalents as of December 31	**$ 129,198**	$ 97,141	$ 67,183
Interest Paid	**$ 126,450**	$ 105,250	$ 88,077
Income Taxes Paid	**253,977**	325,451	206,704

The notes to consolidated financial statements are an integral part of these statements.

THE HERSHEY COMPANY
CONSOLIDATED STATEMENTS OF STOCKHOLDERS' EQUITY

In thousands of dollars	Preferred Stock	Common Stock	Class B Common Stock	Additional Paid-in Capital	Unearned ESOP Compensation	Retained Earnings	Treasury Common Stock	Accumulated Other Comprehensive Income (Loss)	Total Stockholders' Equity
Balance as of January 1, 2005	$—	$299,060	$60,841	$171,413	$(6,387)	$3,374,171	$(2,762,304)	$ 309	$1,137,103
Net income						488,547			488,547
Other comprehensive (loss)								(9,631)	(9,631)
Comprehensive income									478,916
Dividends:									
Common Stock, $.93 per share						(170,147)			(170,147)
Class B Common Stock, $.84 per share						(51,088)			(51,088)
Conversion of Class B Common Stock into Common Stock		23	(23)						—
Incentive plan transactions				236			1,161		1,397
Stock-based compensation				35,764					35,764
Exercise of stock options				44,759			73,258		118,017
Employee stock ownership trust/benefits transactions				202	3,194		19		3,415
Repurchase of Common Stock							(536,997)		(536,997)
Balance as of December 31, 2005	—	299,083	60,818	252,374	(3,193)	3,641,483	(3,224,863)	(9,322)	1,016,380
Net income						559,061			559,061
Other comprehensive income								9,105	9,105
Comprehensive income									568,166
Adjustment to initially apply SFAS No. 158, net of tax								(137,972)	(137,972)
Dividends:									
Common Stock, $1.03 per share						(178,873)			(178,873)
Class B Common Stock, $.925 per share						(56,256)			(56,256)
Conversion of Class B Common Stock into Common Stock		2	(2)						—
Incentive plan transactions				840			3,250		4,090
Stock-based compensation				34,374					34,374
Exercise of stock options				9,732			39,992		49,724
Employee stock ownership trust/benefits transactions				923	3,193		1,322		5,438
Repurchase of Common Stock							(621,648)		(621,648)
Balance as of December 31, 2006	—	299,085	60,816	298,243	—	3,965,415	(3,801,947)	(138,189)	683,423
Net income						214,154			214,154
Other comprehensive income								110,210	110,210
Comprehensive income									324,364
Dividends:									
Common Stock, $1.135 per share						(190,199)			(190,199)
Class B Common Stock, $1.0206 per share						(62,064)			(62,064)
Conversion of Class B Common Stock into Common Stock		10	(10)						—
Incentive plan transactions				1,426			2,082		3,508
Stock-based compensation				29,790					29,790
Exercise of stock options				5,797			54,588		60,385
Repurchase of Common Stock							(256,285)		(256,285)
Balance as of December 31, 2007	$—	$299,095	$60,806	$335,256	$ —	$3,927,306	$(4,001,562)	$ (27,979)	$ 592,922

The notes to consolidated financial statements are an integral part of these statements.

Time Value of Money

STUDY OBJECTIVES

After studying this appendix, you should be able to:

1 Distinguish between simple and compound interest.
2 Solve for future value of a single amount.
3 Solve for future value of an annuity.
4 Identify the variables fundamental to solving present value problems.
5 Solve for present value of a single amount.
6 Solve for present value of an annuity.
7 Compute the present values in capital budgeting situations.
8 Use a financial calculator to solve time value of money problems.

Would you rather receive $1,000 today or a year from now? You should prefer to receive the $1,000 today because you can invest the $1,000 and earn interest on it. As a result, you will have more than $1,000 a year from now. What this example illustrates is the concept of the **time value of money**. Everyone prefers to receive money today rather than in the future because of the interest factor.

NATURE OF INTEREST

STUDY OBJECTIVE 1
Distinguish between simple and compound interest.

Interest is payment for the use of another person's money. It is the difference between the amount borrowed or invested (called the **principal**) and the amount repaid or collected. The amount of interest to be paid or collected is usually stated as a rate over a specific period of time. The rate of interest is generally stated as an annual rate.

The amount of interest involved in any financing transaction is based on three elements:

1. **Principal (*p*)**: The original amount borrowed or invested.
2. **Interest Rate (*i*)**: An annual percentage of the principal.
3. **Time (*n*)**: The number of years that the principal is borrowed or invested.

Simple Interest

Simple interest is computed on the principal amount only. It is the return on the principal for one period. Simple interest is usually expressed as shown in Illustration C-1 (page C2).

Illustration C-1
Interest computation

Interest	=	Principal p	×	Rate i	×	Time n

For example, if you borrowed $5,000 for 2 years at a simple interest rate of 12% annually, you would pay $1,200 in total interest computed as follows:

$$\begin{aligned}\text{Interest} &= p \times i \times n \\ &= \$5{,}000 \times .12 \times 2 \\ &= \$1{,}200\end{aligned}$$

Compound Interest

Compound interest is computed on principal **and** on any interest earned that has not been paid or withdrawn. It is the return on (or growth of) the principal for two or more time periods. Compounding computes interest not only on the principal but also on the interest earned to date on that principal, assuming the interest is left on deposit.

To illustrate the difference between simple and compound interest, assume that you deposit $1,000 in BankOne, where it will earn simple interest of 9% per year, and you deposit another $1,000 in CityCorp, where it will earn compound interest of 9% per year compounded annually. Also assume that in both cases you will not withdraw any interest until three years from the date of deposit. The computation of interest to be received and the accumulated year-end balances are indicated in Illustration C-2.

Illustration C-2
Simple vs. compound interest

BankOne

Simple Interest Calculation	Simple Interest	Accumulated Year-end Balance
Year 1 $1,000.00 × 9%	$ 90.00	$1,090.00
Year 2 $1,000.00 × 9%	90.00	$1,180.00
Year 3 $1,000.00 × 9%	90.00	$1,270.00
	$ 270.00	

CityCorp.

Compound Interest Calculation	Compound Interest	Accumulated Year-end Balance
Year 1 $1,000.00 × 9%	$ 90.00	$1,090.00
Year 2 $1,090.00 × 9%	98.10	$1,188.10
Year 3 $1,188.10 × 9%	106.93	$1,295.03
	$ 295.03	

$25.03 Difference

Note in the illustration above that simple interest uses the initial principal of $1,000 to compute the interest in all three years. Compound interest uses the accumulated balance (principal plus interest to date) at each year-end to compute interest in the succeeding year—which explains why your compound interest account is larger.

Obviously if you had a choice between investing your money at simple interest or at compound interest, you would choose compound interest, all other things—especially risk—being equal. In the example, compounding provides $25.03 of additional interest income. For practical purposes, compounding assumes that unpaid interest earned becomes a part of the principal, and the accumulated balance at the end of each year becomes the new principal on which interest is earned during the next year.

As can be seen in Illustration C-2, you should invest your money at CityCorp, which compounds interest annually. Compound interest is used in most business situations. Simple interest is generally applicable only to short-term situations of one year or less.

SECTION 1 Future Value Concepts

FUTURE VALUE OF A SINGLE AMOUNT

STUDY OBJECTIVE 2

Solve for future value of a single amount.

The **future value of a single amount** is the value at a future date of a given amount invested assuming compound interest. For example, in Illustration C-2, $1,295.03 is the future value of the $1,000 at the end of three years at 9% interest. The $1,295.03 could be determined more easily by using the following formula.

Illustration C-3
Future value computation

$$FV = p \times (1 + i)^n$$

where

FV = future value of a single amount
p = principal
i = interest rate for one period
n = number of periods

The future value of the CityCorp deposit in Illustration C-2 is computed as follows.

$$\begin{aligned} FV &= p \times (1 + i)^n \\ &= \$1{,}000 \times (1 + .09)^3 \\ &= \$1{,}000 \times 1.29503 \\ &= \$1{,}295.03 \end{aligned}$$

The 1.29503 is computed by multiplying (1.09 × 1.09 × 1.09). The amounts in this example can be depicted in the following time diagram.

Illustration C-4
Time diagram

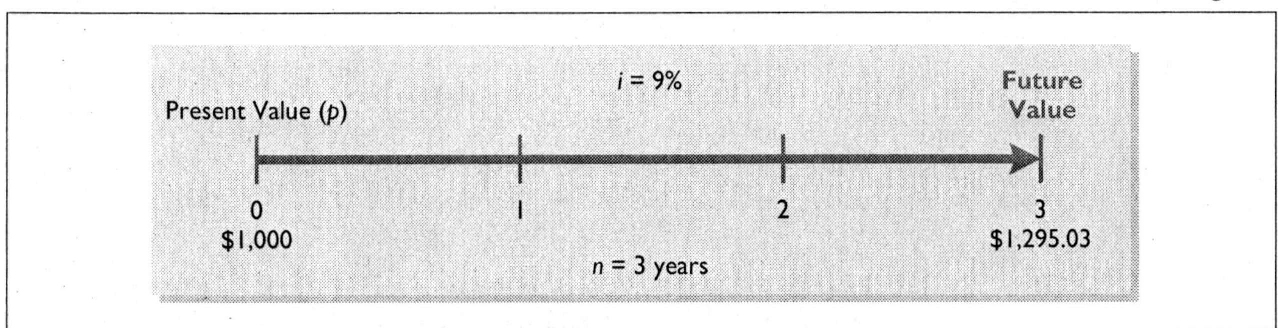

Another method that may be used to compute the future value of a single amount involves the use of a compound interest table. This table shows the future value of 1 for n periods. Table 1, shown at the top of the next page, is such a table.

TABLE 1
Future Value of 1

(n) Periods	4%	5%	6%	8%	9%	10%	11%	12%	15%
1	1.04000	1.05000	1.06000	1.08000	1.09000	1.10000	1.11000	1.12000	1.15000
2	1.08160	1.10250	1.12360	1.16640	1.18810	1.21000	1.23210	1.25440	1.32250
3	1.12486	1.15763	1.19102	1.25971	1.29503	1.33100	1.36763	1.40493	1.52088
4	1.16986	1.21551	1.26248	1.36049	1.41158	1.46410	1.51807	1.57352	1.74901
5	1.21665	1.27628	1.33823	1.46933	1.53862	1.61051	1.68506	1.76234	2.01136
6	1.26532	1.34010	1.41852	1.58687	1.67710	1.77156	1.87041	1.97382	2.31306
7	1.31593	1.40710	1.50363	1.71382	1.82804	1.94872	2.07616	2.21068	2.66002
8	1.36857	1.47746	1.59385	1.85093	1.99256	2.14359	2.30454	2.47596	3.05902
9	1.42331	1.55133	1.68948	1.99900	2.17189	2.35795	2.55803	2.77308	3.51788
10	1.48024	1.62889	1.79085	2.15892	2.36736	2.59374	2.83942	3.10585	4.04556
11	1.53945	1.71034	1.89830	2.33164	2.58043	2.85312	3.15176	3.47855	4.65239
12	1.60103	1.79586	2.01220	2.51817	2.81267	3.13843	3.49845	3.89598	5.35025
13	1.66507	1.88565	2.13293	2.71962	3.06581	3.45227	3.88328	4.36349	6.15279
14	1.73168	1.97993	2.26090	2.93719	3.34173	3.79750	4.31044	4.88711	7.07571
15	1.80094	2.07893	2.39656	3.17217	3.64248	4.17725	4.78459	5.47357	8.13706
16	1.87298	2.18287	2.54035	3.42594	3.97031	4.59497	5.31089	6.13039	9.35762
17	1.94790	2.29202	2.69277	3.70002	4.32763	5.05447	5.89509	6.86604	10.76126
18	2.02582	2.40662	2.85434	3.99602	4.71712	5.55992	6.54355	7.68997	12.37545
19	2.10685	2.52695	3.02560	4.31570	5.14166	6.11591	7.26334	8.61276	14.23177
20	2.19112	2.65330	3.20714	4.66096	5.60441	6.72750	8.06231	9.64629	16.36654

In Table 1, n is the number of compounding periods, the percentages are the periodic interest rates, and the decimal numbers in the respective columns are the future value of 1 factors. To use Table 1, multiply the principal amount by the future value factor for the specified number of periods and interest rate. For example, the future value factor for two periods at 9% is 1.18810. Multiplying this factor by \$1,000 equals \$1,188.10, which is the accumulated balance at the end of year 2 in the CityCorp example in Illustration C-2. The \$1,295.03 accumulated balance at the end of the third year can be calculated from Table 1 by multiplying the future value factor for three periods (1.29503) by the \$1,000.

The following demonstration problem illustrates how to use Table 1.

Illustration C-5
Demonstration Problem—
Using Table 1 for FV of 1

John and Mary Rich invested $20,000 in a savings account paying 6% interest at the time their son, Mike, was born. The money is to be used by Mike for his college education. On his 18th birthday, Mike withdraws the money from his savings account. How much did Mike withdraw from his account?

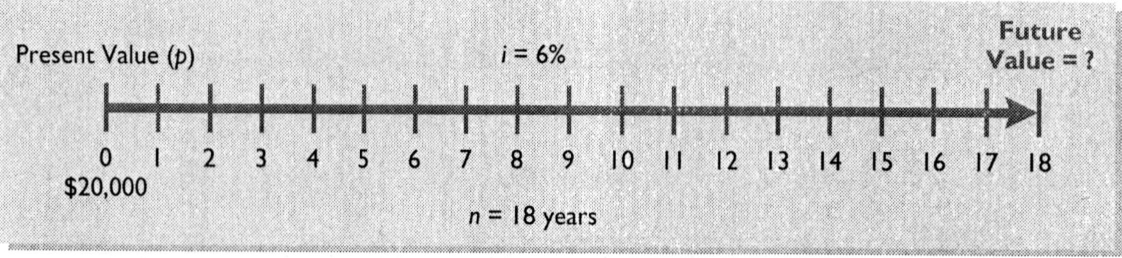

Answer: The future value factor from Table 1 is 2.85434 (18 periods at 6%). The future value of $20,000 earning 6% per year for 18 years is **$57,086.80** ($20,000 × 2.85434).

FUTURE VALUE OF AN ANNUITY

STUDY OBJECTIVE 3

Solve for future value of an annuity.

The preceding discussion involved the accumulation of only a single principal sum. Individuals and businesses frequently encounter situations in which a series of equal dollar amounts are to be paid or received periodically, such as loans or lease (rental) contracts. Such payments or receipts of equal dollar amounts are referred to as **annuities**. The **future value of an annuity** is the sum of all the payments (receipts) plus the accumulated compound interest on them. In computing the future value of an annuity, it is necessary to know (1) the interest rate, (2) the number of compounding periods, and (3) the amount of the periodic payments or receipts.

To illustrate the computation of the future value of an annuity, assume that you invest $2,000 at the end of each year for three years at 5% interest compounded annually. This situation is depicted in the time diagram in Illustration C-6.

Illustration C-6
Time diagram for a three-year annuity

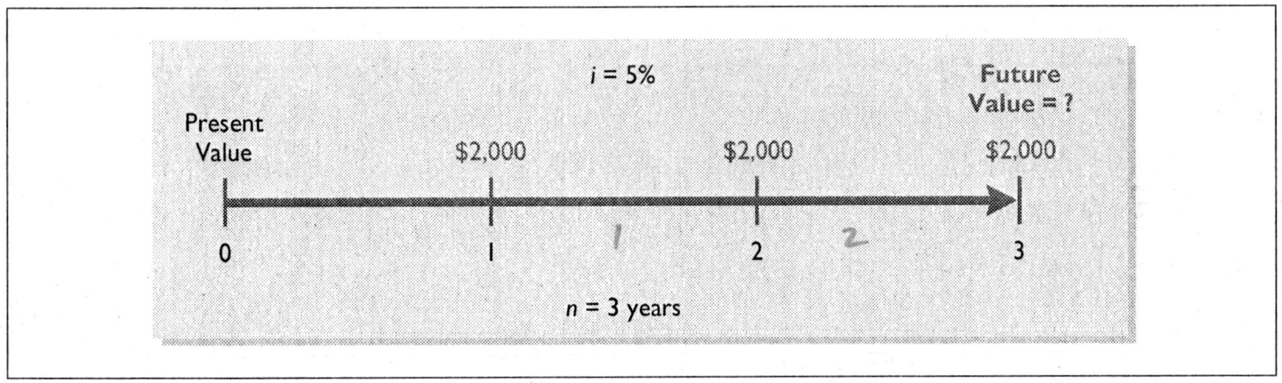

As can be seen in Illustration C-6, the $2,000 invested at the end of year 1 will earn interest for two years (years 2 and 3), and the $2,000 invested at the end of year 2 will earn interest for one year (year 3). However, the last $2,000 investment (made at the end of year 3) will not earn any interest. The future value of these periodic payments could be computed using the future value factors from Table 1 as shown in Illustration C-7.

Illustration C-7
Future value of periodic payments

Year Invested	Amount Invested	×	Future Value of 1 Factor at 5%	=	Future Value
1	$2,000	×	1.10250	=	$ 2,205
2	$2,000	×	1.05000	=	2,100
3	$2,000	×	1.00000	=	2,000
			3.15250		**$6,305**

The first $2,000 investment is multiplied by the future value factor for two periods (1.1025) because two years' interest will accumulate on it (in years 2 and 3). The second $2,000 investment will earn only one year's interest (in year 3) and therefore is multiplied by the future value factor for one year (1.0500). The final $2,000 investment is made at the end of the third year and will not earn any interest. Consequently, the future value of the last $2,000 invested is only $2,000 since it does not accumulate any interest.

This method of calculation is required when the periodic payments or receipts are not equal in each period. However, when the periodic payments (receipts) are the same in each period, the future value can be computed by using a future value of an annuity of 1 table. Table 2, shown on page C6, is such a table.

TABLE 2
Future Value of an Annuity of 1

(n) Periods	4%	5%	6%	8%	9%	10%	11%	12%	15%
1	1.00000	1.00000	1.00000	1.00000	1.00000	1.00000	1.00000	1.00000	1.00000
2	2.04000	2.05000	2.06000	2.08000	2.09000	2.10000	2.11000	2.12000	2.15000
3	3.12160	3.15250	3.18360	3.24640	3.27810	3.31000	3.34210	3.37440	3.47250
4	4.24646	4.31013	4.37462	4.50611	4.57313	4.64100	4.70973	4.77933	4.99338
5	5.41632	5.52563	5.63709	5.86660	5.98471	6.10510	6.22780	6.35285	6.74238
6	6.63298	6.80191	6.97532	7.33592	7.52334	7.71561	7.91286	8.11519	8.75374
7	7.89829	8.14201	8.39384	8.92280	9.20044	9.48717	9.78327	10.08901	11.06680
8	9.21423	9.54911	9.89747	10.63663	11.02847	11.43589	11.85943	12.29969	13.72682
9	10.58280	11.02656	11.49132	12.48756	13.02104	13.57948	14.16397	14.77566	16.78584
10	12.00611	12.57789	13.18079	14.48656	15.19293	15.93743	16.72201	17.54874	20.30372
11	13.48635	14.20679	14.97164	16.64549	17.56029	18.53117	19.56143	20.65458	24.34928
12	15.02581	15.91713	16.86994	18.97713	20.14072	21.38428	22.71319	24.13313	29.00167
13	16.62684	17.71298	18.88214	21.49530	22.95339	24.52271	26.21164	28.02911	34.35192
14	18.29191	19.59863	21.01507	24.21492	26.01919	27.97498	30.09492	32.39260	40.50471
15	20.02359	21.57856	23.27597	27.15211	29.36092	31.77248	34.40536	37.27972	47.58041
16	21.82453	23.65749	25.67253	30.32428	33.00340	35.94973	39.18995	42.75328	55.71747
17	23.69751	25.84037	28.21288	33.75023	36.97351	40.54470	44.50084	48.88367	65.07509
18	25.64541	28.13238	30.90565	37.45024	41.30134	45.59917	50.39593	55.74972	75.83636
19	27.67123	30.53900	33.75999	41.44626	46.01846	51.15909	56.93949	63.43968	88.21181
20	29.77808	33.06595	36.78559	45.76196	51.16012	57.27500	64.20283	72.05244	102.44358

Table 2 shows the future value of 1 to be received periodically for a given number of end-of-period payments. You can see from Table 2 that the future value of an annuity of 1 factor for three periods at 5% is 3.15250. The future value factor is the total of the three individual future value factors as shown in Illustration C-7. Multiplying this amount by the annual investment of $2,000 produces a future value of $6,305.

The demonstration problem in Illustration C-8 illustrates how to use Table 2.

Illustration C-8
Demonstration Problem—
Using Table 2 for FV of an annuity of 1

Henning Printing Company knows that in four years it must replace one of its existing printing presses with a new one. To ensure that some funds are available to replace the machine in four years, the company is depositing $25,000 in a savings account at the end of each of the next four years (4 deposits in total). The savings account will earn 6% interest compounded annually. How much will be in the savings account at the end of four years when the new printing press is to be purchased?

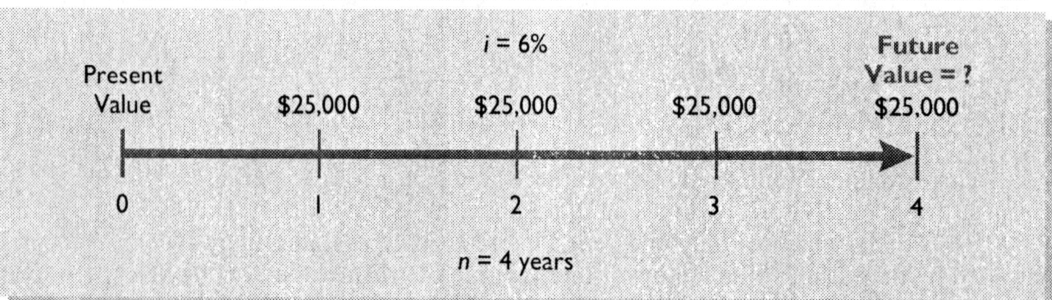

Answer: The future value factor from Table 2 is 4.37462 (4 periods at 6%). The future value of $25,000 invested at the end of each year for four years at 6% interest is **$109,365.50** ($25,000 × 4.37462).

SECTION 2 Present Value Concepts

PRESENT VALUE VARIABLES

STUDY OBJECTIVE 4

Identify the variables fundamental to solving present value problems.

The present value is the value now of a given amount to be received in the future, assuming compound interest. Like the future value, it is based on three variables: (1) the dollar amount to be received (future amount), (2) the length of time until the amount is received (number of periods), and (3) the interest rate (the discount rate). The process of determining the present value is referred to as discounting the future amount.

In this textbook, present value computations are used in measuring several items. For example, capital budgeting and other investment proposals are evaluated using present value computations. All rate of return and internal rate of return computations involve present value techniques.

PRESENT VALUE OF A SINGLE AMOUNT

STUDY OBJECTIVE 5

Solve for present value of a single amount.

To illustrate present value concepts, assume that you want to invest a sum of money today that will provide $1,000 at the end of one year. What amount would you need to invest today to have $1,000 one year from now? If you want a 10% rate of return, the investment or present value is $909.09 ($1,000 ÷ 1.10). The computation of this amount is shown in Illustration C-9.

Illustration C-9
Present value computation—$1,000 discounted at 10% for one year

Present Value = **Future Value ÷ (1 + i)^1**

$$PV = FV \div (1 + .10)^1$$
$$PV = \$1{,}000 \div 1.10$$
$$PV = \$909.09$$

The future amount ($1,000), the discount rate (10%), and the number of periods (1) are known. The variables in this situation can be depicted in the following time diagram.

Illustration C-10
Finding present value if discounted for one period

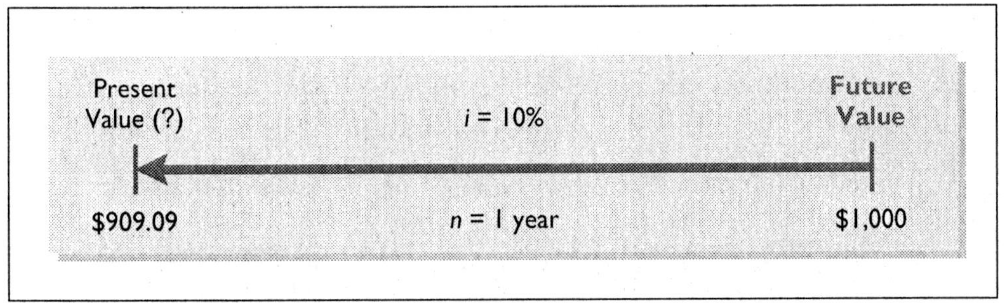

If the single amount of $1,000 is to be received **in two years** and discounted at 10% [PV = $1,000 ÷ (1 + .10)^2], its present value is $826.45 [($1,000 ÷ 1.10) ÷ 1.10], as shown in Illustration C-11 (page C8).

Illustration C-11
Finding present value if discounted for two periods

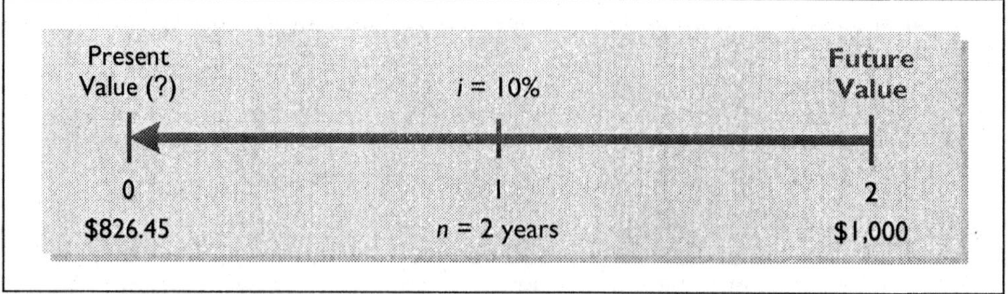

The present value of 1 may also be determined through tables that show the present value of 1 for *n* periods. In Table 3, *n* is the number of discounting periods involved. The percentages are the periodic interest rates or discount rates, and the five-digit decimal numbers in the respective columns are the present value of 1 factors.

TABLE 3
Present Value of 1

(*n*) Periods	4%	5%	6%	8%	9%	10%	11%	12%	15%
1	.96154	.95238	.94340	.92593	.91743	.90909	.90090	.89286	.86957
2	.92456	.90703	.89000	.85734	.84168	.82645	.81162	.79719	.75614
3	.88900	.86384	.83962	.79383	.77218	.75132	.73119	.71178	.65752
4	.85480	.82270	.79209	.73503	.70843	.68301	.65873	.63552	.57175
5	.82193	.78353	.74726	.68058	.64993	.62092	.59345	.56743	.49718
6	.79031	.74622	.70496	.63017	.59627	.56447	.53464	.50663	.43233
7	.75992	.71068	.66506	.58349	.54703	.51316	.48166	.45235	.37594
8	.73069	.67684	.62741	.54027	.50187	.46651	.43393	.40388	.32690
9	.70259	.64461	.59190	.50025	.46043	.42410	.39092	.36061	.28426
10	.67556	.61391	.55839	.46319	.42241	.38554	.35218	.32197	.24719
11	.64958	.58468	.52679	.42888	.38753	.35049	.31728	.28748	.21494
12	.62460	.55684	.49697	.39711	.35554	.31863	.28584	.25668	.18691
13	.60057	.53032	.46884	.36770	.32618	.28966	.25751	.22917	.16253
14	.57748	.50507	.44230	.34046	.29925	.26333	.23199	.20462	.14133
15	.55526	.48102	.41727	.31524	.27454	.23939	.20900	.18270	.12289
16	.53391	.45811	.39365	.29189	.25187	.21763	.18829	.16312	.10687
17	.51337	.43630	.37136	.27027	.23107	.19785	.16963	.14564	.09293
18	.49363	.41552	.35034	.25025	.21199	.17986	.15282	.13004	.08081
19	.47464	.39573	.33051	.23171	.19449	.16351	.13768	.11611	.07027
20	.45639	.37689	.31180	.21455	.17843	.14864	.12403	.10367	.06110

When Table 3 is used, the future value is multiplied by the present value factor specified at the intersection of the number of periods and the discount rate. For example, the present value factor for one period at a discount rate of 10% is .90909, which equals the $909.09 ($1,000 × .90909) computed in Illustration C-9. For two periods at a discount rate of 10%, the present value factor is .82645, which equals the $826.45 ($1,000 × .82645) computed previously.

Note that a higher discount rate produces a smaller present value. For example, using a 15% discount rate, the present value of $1,000 due one year from now is $869.57 versus $909.09 at 10%. It should also be recognized that the further removed from the present the future value is, the smaller the present value. For example, using the same discount rate of 10%, the present value of $1,000 due in **five** years is $620.92 versus $1,000 due in **one** year is $909.09.

The following two demonstration problems (Illustrations C-12, C-13) illustrate how to use Table 3.

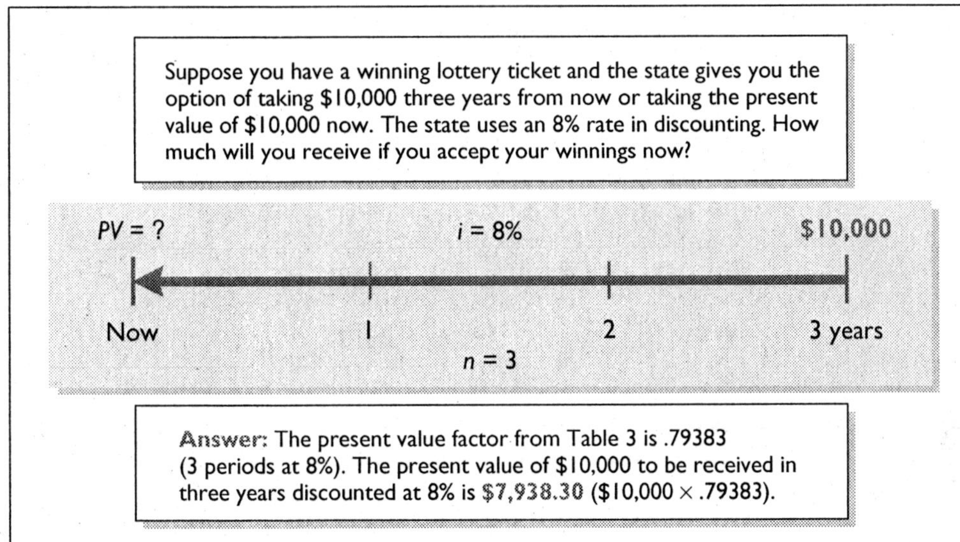

Suppose you have a winning lottery ticket and the state gives you the option of taking $10,000 three years from now or taking the present value of $10,000 now. The state uses an 8% rate in discounting. How much will you receive if you accept your winnings now?
PV = ?
i = 8%
$10,000
Now
1
2
3 years
n = 3
Answer: The present value factor from Table 3 is .79383 (3 periods at 8%). The present value of $10,000 to be received in three years discounted at 8% is $7,938.30 ($10,000 × .79383).

Illustration C-12
Demonstration Problem—
Using Table 3 for PV of 1

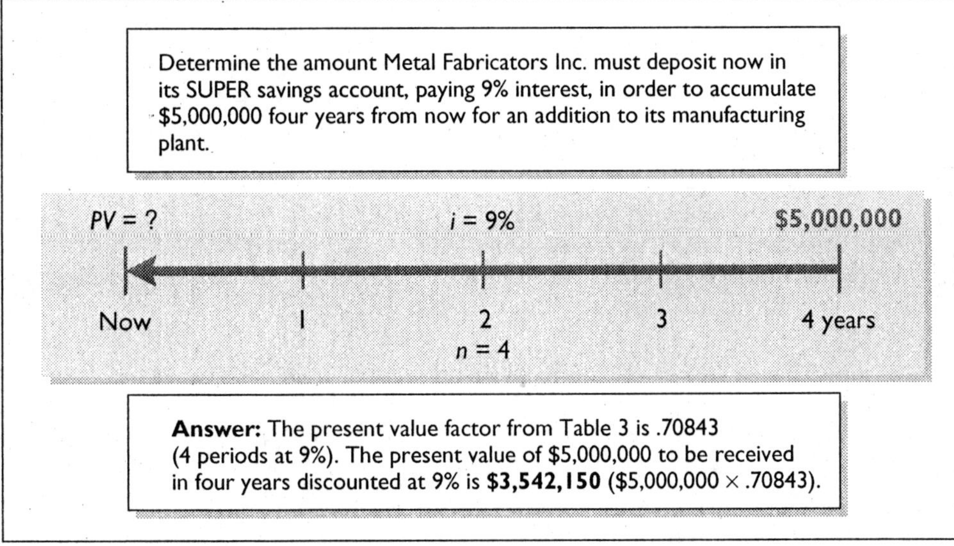

Determine the amount Metal Fabricators Inc. must deposit now in its SUPER savings account, paying 9% interest, in order to accumulate $5,000,000 four years from now for an addition to its manufacturing plant.
PV = ?
i = 9%
$5,000,000
Now
1
2
3
4 years
n = 4
Answer: The present value factor from Table 3 is .70843 (4 periods at 9%). The present value of $5,000,000 to be received in four years discounted at 9% is $3,542,150 ($5,000,000 × .70843).

Illustration C-13
Demonstration Problem—
Using Table 3 for PV of 1

PRESENT VALUE OF AN ANNUITY

STUDY OBJECTIVE 6

Solve for present value of an annuity.

The preceding discussion involved the discounting of only a single future amount. Businesses and individuals frequently engage in transactions in which a series of equal dollar amounts are to be received or paid periodically. Examples of a series of periodic receipts or payments are loan agreements, installment sales, mortgage notes, lease (rental) contracts, and pension obligations. These series of periodic receipts or payments are called **annuities**. The **present value of an annuity** is the value now of a series of future receipts or payments, assuming compound interest. In computing the present value of an annuity, it is necessary to know (1) the discount rate, (2) the number of discount periods, and (3) the amount of the periodic receipts or payments.

To illustrate the computation of the present value of an annuity, assume that you will receive $1,000 cash annually for three years at a time when the discount rate is 10%. This situation is depicted in the time diagram in Illustration C-14 (page C10).

Illustration C-14
Time diagram for a three-year annuity

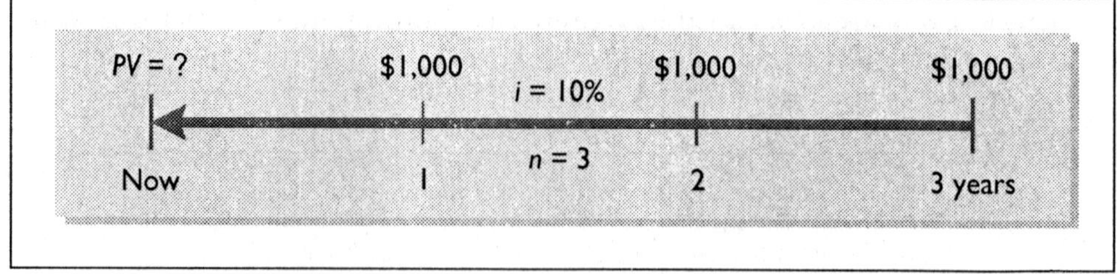

The present value in this situation may be computed as follows.

Illustration C-15
Present value of a series of future amounts computation

Future Amount	×	Present Value of 1 Factor at 10%	=	Present Value
$1,000 (One year away)	×	.90909	=	$ 909.09
1,000 (Two years away)	×	.82645	=	826.45
1,000 (Three years away)	×	.75132	=	751.32
		2.48686		$2,486.86

This method of calculation is required when the periodic cash flows are not uniform in each period. However, when the future receipts are the same in each period, there are two other ways to compute present value. First, the annual cash flow can be multiplied by the sum of the three present value factors. In the previous example, $1,000 × 2.48686 equals $2,486.86. Second, annuity tables may be used. As illustrated in Table 4 below, these tables show the present value of 1 to be received periodically for a given number of periods.

TABLE 4
Present Value of an Annuity of 1

(n) Periods	4%	5%	6%	8%	9%	10%	11%	12%	15%
1	.96154	.95238	.94340	.92593	.91743	.90909	.90090	.89286	.86957
2	1.88609	1.85941	1.83339	1.78326	1.75911	1.73554	1.71252	1.69005	1.62571
3	2.77509	2.72325	2.67301	2.57710	2.53130	2.48685	2.44371	2.40183	2.28323
4	3.62990	3.54595	3.46511	3.31213	3.23972	3.16986	3.10245	3.03735	2.85498
5	4.45182	4.32948	4.21236	3.99271	3.88965	3.79079	3.69590	3.60478	3.35216
6	5.24214	5.07569	4.91732	4.62288	4.48592	4.35526	4.23054	4.11141	3.78448
7	6.00205	5.78637	5.58238	5.20637	5.03295	4.86842	4.71220	4.56376	4.16042
8	6.73274	6.46321	6.20979	5.74664	5.53482	5.33493	5.14612	4.96764	4.48732
9	7.43533	7.10782	6.80169	6.24689	5.99525	5.75902	5.53705	5.32825	4.77158
10	8.11090	7.72173	7.36009	6.71008	6.41766	6.14457	5.88923	5.65022	5.01877
11	8.76048	8.30641	7.88687	7.13896	6.80519	6.49506	6.20652	5.93770	5.23371
12	9.38507	8.86325	8.38384	7.53608	7.16073	6.81369	6.49236	6.19437	5.42062
13	9.98565	9.39357	8.85268	7.90378	7.48690	7.10336	6.74987	6.42355	5.58315
14	10.56312	9.89864	9.29498	8.24424	7.78615	7.36669	6.98187	6.62817	5.72448
15	11.11839	10.37966	9.71225	8.55948	8.06069	7.60608	7.19087	6.81086	5.84737
16	11.65230	10.83777	10.10590	8.85137	8.31256	7.82371	7.37916	6.97399	5.95424
17	12.16567	11.27407	10.47726	9.12164	8.54363	8.02155	7.54879	7.11963	6.04716
18	12.65930	11.68959	10.82760	9.37189	8.75563	8.20141	7.70162	7.24967	6.12797
19	13.13394	12.08532	11.15812	9.60360	8.95012	8.36492	7.83929	7.36578	6.19823
20	13.59033	12.46221	11.46992	9.81815	9.12855	8.51356	7.96333	7.46944	6.25933

You can see from Table 4 that the present value of an annuity of 1 factor for three periods at 10% is 2.48685.[1] This present value factor is the total of the three individual present value factors as shown in Illustration C-15. Applying this amount to the annual cash flow of $1,000 produces a present value of $2,486.85.

The following demonstration problem (Illustration C-16) illustrates how to use Table 4.

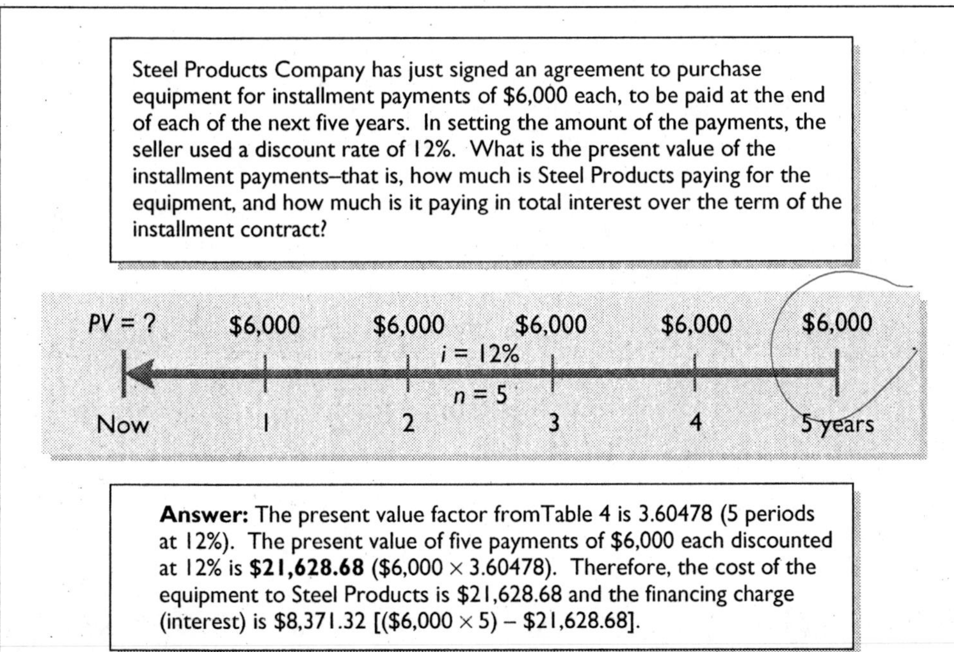

Steel Products Company has just signed an agreement to purchase equipment for installment payments of $6,000 each, to be paid at the end of each of the next five years. In setting the amount of the payments, the seller used a discount rate of 12%. What is the present value of the installment payments–that is, how much is Steel Products paying for the equipment, and how much is it paying in total interest over the term of the installment contract?

Answer: The present value factor fromTable 4 is 3.60478 (5 periods at 12%). The present value of five payments of $6,000 each discounted at 12% is **$21,628.68** ($6,000 × 3.60478). Therefore, the cost of the equipment to Steel Products is $21,628.68 and the financing charge (interest) is $8,371.32 [($6,000 × 5) – $21,628.68].

Illustration C-16
Demonstration Problem—
Using Table 4 for PV of an annuity of 1

TIME PERIODS AND DISCOUNTING

In the preceding calculations, the discounting has been done on an annual basis using an annual interest rate. Discounting may also be done over shorter periods of time such as monthly, quarterly, or semiannually. When the time frame is less than one year, it is necessary to convert the annual interest rate to the applicable time frame.

Assume, for example, that the investor in Illustration C-15 received $500 **semiannually** for three years instead of $1,000 annually. In this case, the number of periods becomes six (3 × 2), the discount rate is 5% (10% ÷ 2), the present value factor from Table 4 is 5.07569 (6 periods at 5%), and the present value of the future cash flows is $2,537.85 (5.07569 × $500). This amount is slightly higher than the $2,486.86 computed in Illustration C-15 because interest is computed twice during the same year. That is, interest is earned on the first half year's interest.

[1] The difference of .00001 between 2.48686 and 2.48685 is due to rounding.

COMPUTING THE PRESENT VALUES IN A CAPITAL BUDGETING DECISION

STUDY OBJECTIVE 7

Compute the present values in capital budgeting situations.

The decision to make long-term capital investments is best evaluated using discounting techniques that recognize the time value of money. To do this, many companies calculate the present value of the cash flows involved in a capital investment.

To illustrate, Nagel-Siebert Trucking Company, a cross-country freight carrier in Montgomery, Illinois, is considering adding another truck to its fleet because of a purchasing opportunity. Navistar Inc., Nagel-Siebert's primary supplier of overland rigs, is overstocked and offers to sell its biggest rig for $154,000 cash payable upon delivery. Nagel-Siebert knows that the rig will produce a net cash flow per year of $40,000 for five years (received at the end of each year), at which time it will be sold for an estimated salvage value of $35,000. Nagel-Siebert's discount rate in evaluating capital expenditures is 10%. Should Nagel-Siebert commit to the purchase of this rig?

The cash flows that must be discounted to present value by Nagel-Siebert are as follows.

Cash payable on delivery (now): $154,000.

Net cash flow from operating the rig: $40,000 for 5 years (at the end of each year).

Cash received from sale of rig at the end of 5 years: $35,000.

The time diagrams for the latter two cash flows are shown in Illustration C-17.

Illustration C-17
Time diagrams for Nagel-Siebert Trucking Company

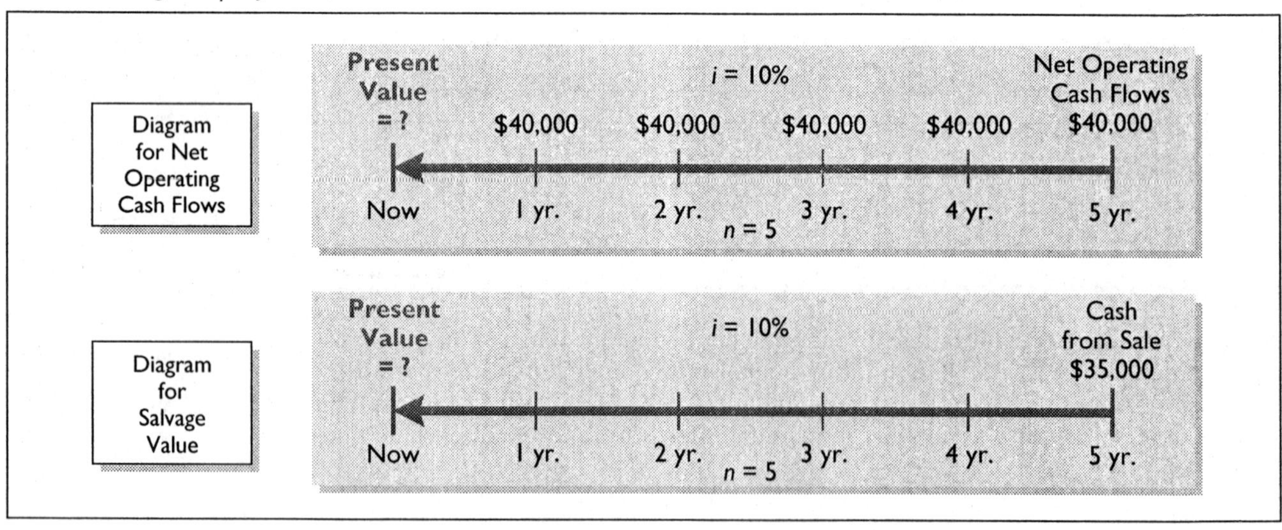

Notice from the diagrams that computing the present value of the net operating cash flows ($40,000 at the end of each year) is **discounting an annuity** (Table 4), while computing the present value of the $35,000 salvage value is **discounting a single sum** (Table 3). The computation of these present values is shown in Illustration C-18 (next page).

Because the present value of the cash receipts (inflows) of $173,363.80 ($151,631.60 + $21,732.20) exceeds the present value of the cash payments

Illustration C-18
Present value computations at 10%

Present Values Using a 10 Percent Discount Rate	
Present value of net operating cash flows received annually over 5 years:	
$40,000 × PV of 1 received annually for 5 years at 10%	
$40,000 × 3.79079 =	$151,631.60
Present value of salvage value (cash) to be received in 5 years	
$35,000 × PV of 1 received in 5 years at 10%	
$35,000 × .62092 =	21,732.20
Present value of cash **inflows**	173,363.80
Present value cash **outflows** (purchase price due now at 10%):	
$154,000 × PV of 1 due now	
$154,000 × 1.00000 =	154,000.00
Net present value	**$19,363.80**

(outflows) of $154,000.00, the net present value of $19,363.80 is positive, and **the decision to invest should be accepted.**

Now assume that Nagel-Siebert uses a discount rate of 15%, not 10%, because it wants a greater return on its investments in capital assets. The cash receipts and cash payments by Nagel-Siebert are the same. The present values of these receipts and cash payments discounted at 15% are shown in Illustration C-19.

Illustration C-19
Present value computations at 15 percent

Present Values Using a 15 Percent Discount Rate	
Present value of net operating cash flows received annually over 5 years at 15%:	
$40,000 × 3.35216	$134,086.40
Present value of salvage value (cash) to be received in 5 years at 15%	
$35,000 × .49718	17,401.30
Present value of cash **inflows**	$151,487.70
Present value of cash **outflows** (purchase price due now at 15%):	
$154,000 × 1.00000	154,000.00
Net present value	**$ (2,512.30)**

Because the present value of the cash payments (outflows) of $154,000 exceeds the present value of the cash receipts (inflows) of $151,487.70 ($134,086.40 + $17,401.30), the net present value of $2,512.30 is negative, and **the investment should be rejected.**

The above discussion relied on present value tables in solving present value problems. As we show in the next section, calculators may also be used to compute present values without the use of these tables. Some calculators, especially the "business" or financial calculators, have present value (PV) functions that allow you to calculate present values by merely identifying the proper amount, discount rate, periods, and pressing the PV key.

SECTION 3 Using Financial Calculators

STUDY OBJECTIVE 8

Use a financial calculator to solve time value of money problems.

Business professionals, once they have mastered the underlying concepts in sections 1 and 2, often use a financial (business) calculator to solve time value of money problems. In many cases, they must use calculators if interest rates or time periods do not correspond with the information provided in the compound interest tables.

To use financial calculators, you enter the time value of money variables into the calculator. Illustration C-20 shows the five most common keys used to solve time value of money problems.[2]

Illustration C-20
Financial calculator keys

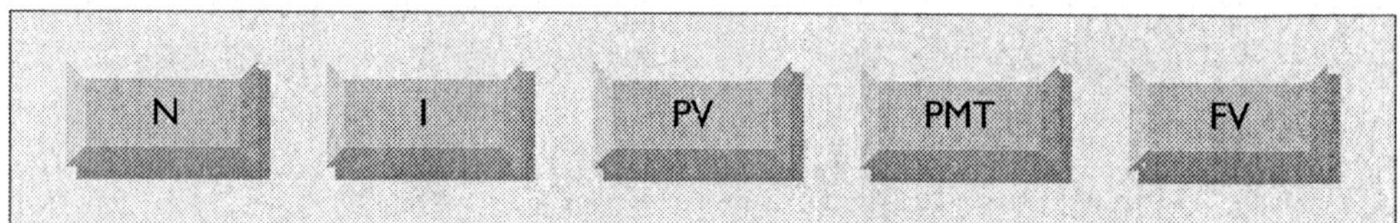

where

N = number of periods

I = interest rate per period (some calculators use I/YR or i)

PV = present value (occurs at the beginning of the first period)

PMT = payment (all payments are equal, and none are skipped)

FV = future value (occurs at the end of the last period)

In solving time value of money problems in this appendix, you will generally be given three of four variables and will have to solve for the remaining variable. The fifth key (the key not used) is given a value of zero to ensure that this variable is not used in the computation.

PRESENT VALUE OF A SINGLE SUM

To illustrate how to solve a present value problem using a financial calculator, assume that you want to know the present value of $84,253 to be received in five years, discounted at 11% compounded annually. Illustration C-21 pictures this problem.

Illustration C-21
Calculator solution for present value of a single sum

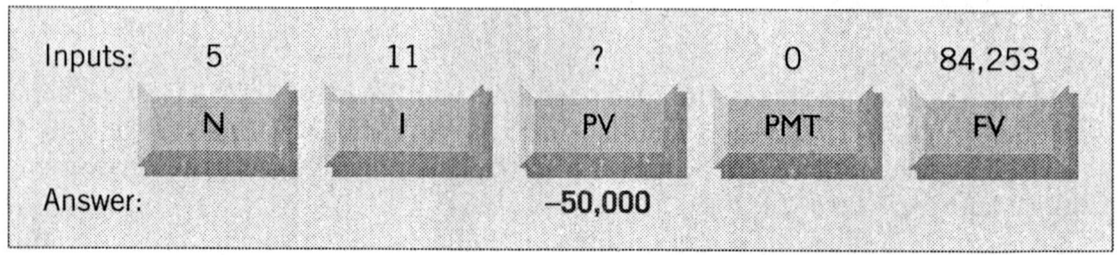

[2]On many calculators, these keys are actual buttons on the face of the calculator; on others they appear on the display after the user accesses a present value menu.

The diagram shows you the information (inputs) to enter into the calculator: N = 5, I = 11, PMT = 0, and FV = 84,253. You then press PV for the answer: −$50,000. As indicated, the PMT key was given a value of zero because a series of payments did not occur in this problem.

Plus and Minus

The use of plus and minus signs in time value of money problems with a financial calculator can be confusing. Most financial calculators are programmed so that the positive and negative cash flows in any problem offset each other. In the present value problem above, we identified the $84,253 future value initial investment as a positive (inflow); the answer −$50,000 was shown as a negative amount, reflecting a cash outflow. If the 84,253 were entered as a negative, then the final answer would have been reported as a positive 50,000.

Hopefully, the sign convention will not cause confusion. If you understand what is required in a problem, you should be able to interpret a positive or negative amount in determining the solution to a problem.

Compounding Periods

In the problem above, we assumed that compounding occurs once a year. Some financial calculators have a default setting, which assumes that compounding occurs 12 times a year. You must determine what default period has been programmed into your calculator and change it as necessary to arrive at the proper compounding period.

Rounding

Most financial calculators store and calculate using 12 decimal places. As a result, because compound interest tables generally have factors only up to five decimal places, a slight difference in the final answer can result. In most time value of money problems, the final answer will not include more than two decimal places.

PRESENT VALUE OF AN ANNUITY

To illustrate how to solve a present value of an annuity problem using a financial calculator, assume that you are asked to determine the present value of rental receipts of $6,000 each to be received at the end of each of the next five years, when discounted at 12%, as pictured in Illustration C-22.

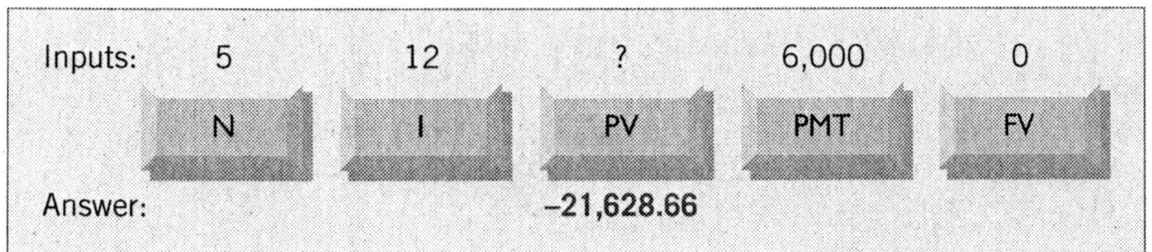

Illustration C-22
Calculator solution for present value of an annuity

In this case, you enter N = 5, I = 12, PMT = 6,000, FV = 0, and then press PV to arrive at the answer of $21,628.66.

USEFUL APPLICATIONS OF THE FINANCIAL CALCULATOR

With a financial calculator you can solve for any interest rate or for any number of periods in a time value of money problem. Here are some examples of these applications.

Auto Loan

Assume you are financing a car with a three-year loan. The loan has a 9.5% nominal annual interest rate, compounded monthly. The price of the car is $6,000, and you want to determine the monthly payments, assuming that the payments start one month after the purchase. This problem is pictured in Illustration C-23.

Illustration C-23
Calculator solution for auto loan payments

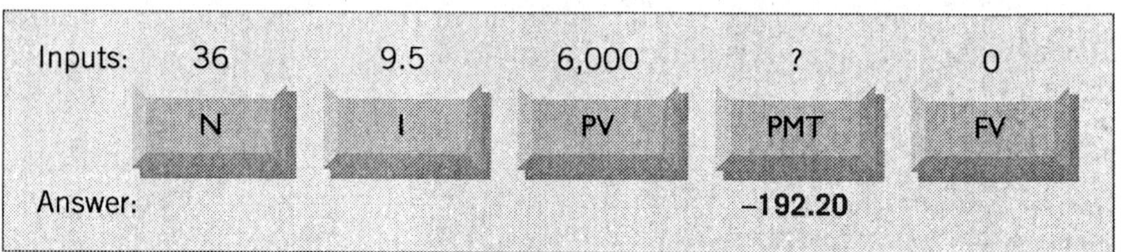

To solve this problem, you enter N = 36 (12 × 3), I = 9.5, PV = 6,000, FV = 0, and then press PMT. You will find that the monthly payments will be $192.20. Note that the payment key is usually programmed for 12 payments per year. Thus, you must change the default (compounding period) if the payments are other than monthly.

Mortgage Loan Amount

Let's say you are evaluating financing options for a loan on a house. You decide that the maximum mortgage payment you can afford is $700 per month. The annual interest rate is 8.4%. If you get a mortgage that requires you to make monthly payments over a 15-year period, what is the maximum purchase price you can afford? Illustration C-24 depicts this problem.

Illustration C-24
Calculator solution for mortgage amount

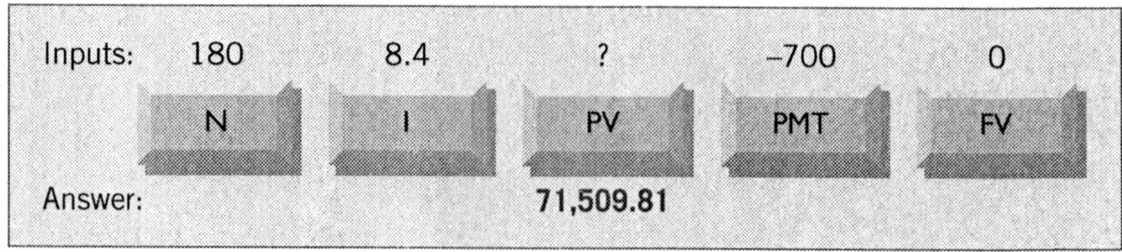

You enter N = 180 (12 × 15 years), I = 8.4, PMT = −700, FV = 0, and press PV. With the payments-per-year key set at 12, you find a present value of $71,509.81—

SUMMARY OF STUDY OBJECTIVES

1 **Distinguish between simple and compound interest.** Simple interest is computed on the principal only while compound interest is computed on the principal and any interest earned that has not been withdrawn.

2 **Solve for future value of a single amount.** Prepare a time diagram of the problem. Identify the principal amount, the number of compounding periods, and the interest rate. Using the future value of 1 table, multiply the principal amount by the future value factor specified at the intersection of the number of periods and the interest rate.

3 **Solve for future value of an annuity.** Prepare a time diagram of the problem. Identify the amount of the periodic payments (annuities), the number of compounding periods, and the interest rate. Using the future value of an annuity of 1 table, multiply the amount of the annuity by the future value factor specified at the intersection of the number of periods and the interest rate.

4 **Identify the variables fundamental to solving present value problems.** The following three variables are fundamental to solving present value problems: (1) the future amount, (2) the number of periods, and (3) the interest rate (the discount rate).

5 **Solve for present value of a single amount.** Prepare a time diagram of the problem. Identify the future amount, the number of discounting periods, and the discount (interest) rate. Using the present value of 1 table, multiply the future amount by the present value factor specified at the intersection of the number of periods and the discount rate.

6 **Solve for present value of an annuity.** Prepare a time diagram of the problem. Identify the future amounts (annuities), the number of discounting periods, and the discount (interest) rate. Using the present value of an annuity of 1 table, multiply the amount of the annuity by the present value factor specified at the intersection of the number of periods and the interest rate.

7 **Compute the present values in capital budgeting situations.** Compute the present values of all cash inflows and all cash outflows related to the capital budgeting proposal (an investment-type decision). If the **net** present value is positive, accept the proposal (make the investment). If the **net** present value is negative, reject the proposal (do not make the investment).

8 **Use a financial calculator to solve time value of money problems.** Financial calculators can be used to solve the same and additional problems as those solved with time value of money tables. One enters into the financial calculator the amounts for all of the known elements of a time value of money problem (periods, interest rate, payments, future or present value) and solves for the unknown element. Particularly useful situations involve interest rates and compounding periods not presented in the tables.

GLOSSARY

Annuity A series of equal dollar amounts to be paid or received periodically. (p. C5)

Compound interest The interest computed on the principal and any interest earned that has not been paid or withdrawn. (p. C2)

Discounting the future amount(s) The process of determining present value. (p. C7)

Future value of a single amount The value at a future date of a given amount invested assuming compound interest. (p. C3)

Future value of an annuity The sum of all the payments or receipts plus the accumulated compound interest on them. (p. C5)

Interest Payment for the use of another's money. (p. C1)

Present value The value now of a given amount to be received in the future, assuming compound interest. (p. C7)

Present value of an annuity The value now of a series of future receipts or payments, assuming compound interest. (p. C9)

Principal The amount borrowed or invested. (p. C1)

Simple interest The interest computed on the principal only. (p. C1)

BRIEF EXERCISES

Use tables to solve Brief Exercises 1 through 23.
Use a financial calculator to solve Brief Exercises 24 through 28.

BEC-1 Don Smith invested $5,000 at 6% annual interest, and left the money invested without withdrawing any of the interest for 10 years. At the end of the 10 years, Don withdrew the accumulated amount of money.

Compute the future value of a single amount.
(SO 2)

(a) What amount did Don withdraw assuming the investment earns simple interest?
(b) What amount did Don withdraw assuming the investment earns interest compounded annually?

Use future value tables.
(SO 2, 3)

BEC-2 For each of the following cases, indicate (a) to what interest rate columns and (b) to what number of periods you would refer in looking up the future value factor.

1. In Table 1 (future value of 1):

	Annual Rate	Number of Years Invested	Compounded
(a)	6%	5	Annually
(b)	8%	4	Semiannually

2. In Table 2 (future value of an annuity of 1):

	Annual Rate	Number of Years Invested	Compounded
(a)	5%	10	Annually
(b)	4%	6	Semiannually

Compute the future value of a single amount.
(SO 2)

BEC-3 Porter Company signed a lease for an office building for a period of 10 years. Under the lease agreement, a security deposit of $10,000 is made. The deposit will be returned at the expiration of the lease with interest compounded at 4% per year. What amount will Porter receive at the time the lease expires?

Compute the future value of an annuity.
(SO 3)

BEC-4 Gordon Company issued $1,000,000, 10-year bonds and agreed to make annual sinking fund deposits of $75,000. The deposits are made at the end of each year into an account paying 6% annual interest. What amount will be in the sinking fund at the end of 10 years?

Compute the future value of a single amount and of an annuity.
(SO 2, 3)

BEC-5 David and Kathy Hatcher invested $5,000 in a savings account paying 6% annual interest when their daughter, Sue, was born. They also deposited $500 on each of her birthdays until she was 18 (including her 18th birthday). How much will be in the savings account on her 18th birthday (after the last deposit)?

Compute the future value of a single amount.
(SO 2)

BEC-6 Ron Watson borrowed $20,000 on July 1, 2000. This amount plus accrued interest at 8% compounded annually is to be repaid on July 1, 2008. How much will Ron have to repay on July 1, 2008?

Use present value tables.
(SO 5, 6)

BEC-7 For each of the following cases, indicate (a) to what interest rate columns and (b) to what number of periods you would refer in looking up the discount rate.

1. In Table 3 (present value of 1):

	Annual Rate	Number of Years Involved	Discounts Per Year
(a)	12%	5	Semiannually
(b)	10%	15	Annually
(c)	8%	8	Semiannually

2. In Table 4 (present value of an annuity of 1):

	Annual Rate	Number of Years Involved	Number of Payments Involved	Frequency of Payments
(a)	12%	20	20	Annually
(b)	10%	5	5	Annually
(c)	8%	4	8	Semiannually

Determine present values.
(SO 5, 6)

BEC-8 (a) What is the present value of $10,000 due 4 periods from now, discounted at 8%? (b) What is the present value of $10,000 to be received at the end of each of 6 periods, discounted at 9%?

BEC-9 Smolinski Company is considering an investment which will return a lump sum of $500,000, 5 years from now. What amount should Smolinski Company pay for this investment to earn a 12% return?

Compute the present value of a single amount investment.

(SO 5)

BEC-10 Pizzeria Company earns 9% on an investment that will return $600,000, 8 years from now. What is the amount Pizzeria should invest now to earn this rate of return?

Compute the present value of a single amount investment.

(SO 5)

BEC-11 Kilarny Company is considering investing in an annuity contract that will return $20,000 annually at the end of each year for 18 years. What amount should Kilarny Company pay for this investment if it earns a 6% return?

Compute the present value of an annuity investment.

(SO 6)

BEC-12 Zarita Enterprises earns 8% on an investment that pays back $110,000 at the end of each of the next 4 years. What is the amount Zarita Enterprises invested to earn the 8% rate of return?

Compute the present value of an annuity investment.

(SO 6)

BEC-13 Hernandez Railroad Co. is about to issue $100,000 of 10-year bonds paying a 10% interest rate, with interest payable semiannually. The discount rate for such securities is 8%. How much can Hernandez expect to receive from the sale of these bonds?

Compute the present value of bonds.

(SO 5, 6)

BEC-14 Assume the same information as BEC-13 except that the discount rate was 10% instead of 8%. In this case, how much can Hernandez expect to receive from the sale of these bonds?

Compute the present value of bonds.

(SO 5, 6)

BEC-15 Caledonian Taco Company receives a $50,000, 6-year note bearing interest of 8% (paid annually) from a customer at a time when the discount rate is 9%. What is the present value of the note received by Caledonian?

Compute the present value of a note.

(SO 5, 6)

BEC-16 Galway Bay Enterprises issued 10%, 7-year, $2,000,000 par value bonds that pay interest semiannually on October 1 and April 1. The bonds are dated April 1, 2008, and are issued on that date. The discount rate of interest for such bonds on April 1, 2008, is 12%. What cash proceeds did Galway Bay receive from issuance of the bonds?

Compute the present value of bonds.

(SO 5, 6)

BEC-17 Barney Googal owns a garage and is contemplating purchasing a tire retreading machine for $14,280. After estimating costs and revenues, Barney projects a net cash flow from the retreading machine of $2,900 annually for 8 years. Barney hopes to earn a return of 11% on such investments. What is the present value of the retreading operation? Should Barney Googal purchase the retreading machine?

Compute the present value of a machine for purposes of making a purchase decision.

(SO 7)

BEC-18 Hung-Chao Yu Company issues an 8%, 6-year mortgage note on January 1, 2008 to obtain financing for new equipment. Land is used as collateral for the note. The terms provide for semiannual installment payments of $85,242. What were the cash proceeds received from the issuance of the note?

Compute the present value of a note.

(SO 6)

BEC-19 Ramos Company is considering purchasing equipment. The equipment will produce the following cash flows: Year 1, $30,000; Year 2, $40,000; Year 3, $50,000. Ramos requires a minimum rate of return of 12%. What is the maximum price Ramos should pay for this equipment?

Compute the maximum price to pay for a machine.

(SO 7)

BEC-20 Kerry Rodriguez invests $3,555.40 now and will receive $10,000 at the end of 12 years. What annual rate of interest will Kerry earn on her investment? (*Hint:* Use Table 3.)

Compute the interest rate on a single amount.

(SO 5)

BEC-21 Maloney Cork has been offered the opportunity of investing $20,462 now. The investment will earn 12% per year and will at the end of that time return Maloney $100,000. How many years must Maloney wait to receive $100,000? (*Hint:* Use Table 3.)

Compute the number of periods of a single amount.

(SO 5)

BEC-22 Annie Dublin purchased an investment of $9,818.15. From this investment, she will receive $1,000 annually for the next 20 years starting one year from now. What rate of interest will Annie's investment be earning for her? (*Hint:* Use Table 4.)

Compute the interest rate on an annuity.

(SO 6)

BEC-23 Andy Sanchez invests $8,863.25 now for a series of $1,000 annual returns beginning one year from now. Andy will earn a return of 5% on the initial investment. How many annual payments of $1,000 will Andy receive? (*Hint:* Use Table 4.)

Compute the number of periods of an annuity.

(SO 6)

BEC-24 Reba McEntire wishes to invest $19,000 on July 1, 2008, and have it accumulate to $49,000 by July 1, 2018.

Determine interest rate.

(SO 8)

Instructions

Use a financial calculator to determine at what exact annual rate of interest Reba must invest the $19,000.

Determine interest rate.

(SO 8)

BEC-25 On July 17, 2008, Tim McGraw borrowed $42,000 from his grandfather to open a clothing store. Starting July 17, 2009, Tim has to make 10 equal annual payments of $6,500 each to repay the loan.

Instructions

Use a financial calculator to determine what interest rate Tim is paying.

Determine interest rate.

(SO 8)

BEC-26 As the purchaser of a new house, Patty Loveless has signed a mortgage note to pay the Memphis National Bank and Trust Co. $14,000 every 6 months for 20 years, at the end of which time she will own the house. At the date the mortgage is signed the purchase price was $198,000, and Loveless made a down payment of $20,000. The first payment will be made 6 months after the date the mortgage is signed.

Instructions

Using a financial calculator, compute the exact rate of interest earned on the mortgage by the bank.

Various time value of money situations.

(SO 8)

BEC-27 Using a financial calculator, solve for the unknowns in each of the following situations.

(a) On June 1, 2008, Shelley Long purchases lakefront property from her neighbor, Joey Brenner, and agrees to pay the purchase price in seven payments of $16,000 each, the first payment to be payable June 1, 2009. (Assume that interest compounded at an annual rate of 7.35% is implicit in the payments.) What is the purchase price of the property?

(b) On January 1, 2008, Cooke Corporation purchased 200 of the $1,000 face value, 8% coupon, 10-year bonds of Howe Inc. The bonds mature on January 1, 2018, and pay interest annually beginning January 1, 2009. Cooke purchased the bonds to yield 10.65%. How much did Cooke pay for the bonds?

Various time value of money situations.

(SO 8)

BEC-28 Using a financial calculator, provide a solution to each of the following situations.

(a) Bill Schroeder owes a debt of $35,000 from the purchase of his new sport utility vehicle. The debt bears annual interest of 9.1% compounded monthly. Bill wishes to pay the debt and interest in equal monthly payments over 8 years, beginning one month hence. What equal monthly payments will pay off the debt and interest?

(b) On January 1, 2008, Sammy Sosa offers to buy Mark Grace's used snowmobile for $8,000, payable in five equal annual installments, which are to include 8.25% interest on the unpaid balance and a portion of the principal. If the first payment is to be made on December 31, 2008, how much will each payment be?

Appendix D

Standards of Ethical Conduct for Management Accountants

Management accountants have an obligation to the organizations they serve, their profession, the public, and themselves to maintain the highest standards of ethical conduct. In recognition of this obligation, the **Institute of Management Accountants** has published and promoted the following standards of ethical conduct for management accountants.

IMA STATEMENT OF ETHICAL PROFESSIONAL PRACTICE

Members of IMA shall behave ethically. A commitment to ethical professional practice includes: overarching principles that express our values, and standards that guide our conduct.

Principles

IMA's overarching ethical principles include: Honesty, Fairness, Objectivity, and Responsibility. Members shall act in accordance with these principles and shall encourage others within their organizations to adhere to them.

Standards

A member's failure to comply with the following standards may result in disciplinary action.

I. COMPETENCE

Each member has a responsibility to:

1. Maintain an appropriate level of professional expertise by continually developing knowledge and skills.
2. Perform professional duties in accordance with relevant laws, regulations, and technical standards.
3. Provide decision support information and recommendations that are accurate, clear, concise, and timely.
4. Recognize and communicate professional limitations or other constraints that would preclude responsible judgment or successful performance of an activity.

II. CONFIDENTIALITY

Each member has a responsibility to:

1. Keep information confidential except when disclosure is authorized or legally required.
2. Inform all relevant parties regarding appropriate use of confidential information. Monitor subordinates' activities to ensure compliance.
3. Refrain from using confidential information for unethical or illegal advantage.

III. INTEGRITY

Each member has a responsibility to:

1. Mitigate actual conflicts of interest. Regularly communicate with business associates to avoid apparent conflicts of interest. Advise all parties of any potential conflicts.
2. Refrain from engaging in any conduct that would prejudice carrying out duties ethically.
3. Abstain from engaging in or supporting any activity that might discredit the profession.

IV. CREDIBILITY

Each member has a responsibility to:

1. Communicate information fairly and objectively.
2. Disclose all relevant information that could reasonably be expected to influence an intended user's understanding of the reports, analyses, or recommendations.
3. Disclose delays or deficiencies in information, timeliness, processing, or internal controls in conformance with organization policy and/or applicable law.

Resolution of Ethical Conflict

In applying the Standards of Ethical Professional Practice, you may encounter problems identifying unethical behavior or resolving an ethical conflict. When faced with ethical issues, you should follow your organization's established policies on the resolution of such conflict. If these policies do not resolve the ethical conflict, you should consider the following courses of action:

1. Discuss the issue with your immediate supervisor except when it appears that the supervisor is involved. In that case, present the issue to the next level. If you cannot achieve a satisfactory resolution, submit the issue to the next management level. If your immediate superior is the chief executive officer or equivalent, the acceptable reviewing authority may be a group such as the audit committee, executive committee, board of directors, board of trustees, or owners. Contact with levels above the immediate superior should be initiated only with your superior's knowledge, assuming he or she is not involved. Communication of such problems to authorities or individuals not employed or engaged by the organization is not considered appropriate, unless you believe there is a clear violation of the law.
2. Clarify relevant ethical issues by initiating a confidential discussion with an IMA Ethics Counselor or other impartial advisor to obtain a better understanding of possible courses of action.
3. Consult your own attorney as to legal obligations and rights concerning the ethical conflict.

Source: Institute of Management Accountants, *www.imanct.org/pdf/981.pdf*. Reprinted by permission.

company index

A
ABC, 239
Abitibi Consolidated Inc., 32
Adelphia, 67
Advanced Micro Devices (AMD), 480–481
Ag-Chem, 186
AIG, 8
Allied Signal, 239
Alternative Distributor Corp., 217
Amazon.com, 14
AMD, *see* Advanced Micro Devices
American Airlines, 278
American Eagle Outfitters, 85
American Pharmaceutical Partners, 61
American Van Lines, 357
Ampex, 459
AOL Time Warner, Inc., 51
Aptara Corp., 229

B
Bally Total Fitness, 39
Bank of America, 39, 218, 289
Bank One Corporation, 108
Best Buy Company, 47, 54–67, 71, 72, 99
Blockbuster Inc., 93–94
Bob Evans Farms, Inc., 79
Boeing Capital Corporation, 39
Boeing Company, 82, 97, 98, 227
Briggs and Stratton, 383
Buck Knives, 418

C
Cal State-Northridge Student Union, 32
Callaway Golf Company, 61, 83
Campbell Soup Company, 37, 442–443, 451, 458, 464
Canadian National Railway Company, 155
Cedarburg Lumber, 501
Chase Manhattan, 37
Chase, 108
ChevronTexaco, 482, 483
Chicago Bears, 114, 158
Chicago Cubs, 114, 158
Chieftain International, Inc., 155
Chiquita Brands International, 239
Circuit City Stores, Inc., 55, 59–61, 63, 75–76
Cisco Systems, 13, 366
Citigroup, 5, 58
Coca-Cola, 229, 239, 500, 383
Compaq Computer, 220–221, 232
Cooper Tire & Rubber Company, 51
Corel, 155
Cott, 155
CSU Corporation, 18

D
DaimlerChrysler, 228, 229
Dayton Hudson, 186
Dean's Beans, 500
Dell Computer, 221, 224, 225, 228, 232, 238
Deloitte and Touche, 42, 69
Delta Air Lines, Inc., 66, 185–186
Dick's Sporting Goods, 231
Digital Equipment, 221, 232, 236
Doman Industries Ltd., 155, 156
Dow Chemical, 13
Duke Energy Corporation, 8, 353, 357, 369
Dunkin' Donuts, Inc., 66
Dynegy, Inc., 8

E
Eastman Kodak Company, 61, 184
Eli Lilly, 163, 383
Enron Corporation, 8, 69, 226
Eskimo Pie Corporation, 31
Ethan Allen, 414
ExxonMobil, 5, 226, 482, 483

F
Fannie Mae, 108
Fidelity Investments, 101, 111, 129, 239
FlightServe, 284
Ford Motor Company, 8, 120, 228, 241, 278, 289, 484, 369
Fox Manufacturing Company, 360–363, 370

G
Gap, Inc., 96
GE, *see* General Electric
General Electric (GE), 158, 226
General Motors (GM), 5, 7, 61, 98, 102, 103, 228, 229, 239, 406, 408, 411, 413, 484
Gibson Greetings, Inc., 407
Global Crossing, 69, 226
GM, *see* General Motors
Goodyear, 417
Google, 13, 289
Grant Thronton LLP, 32

H
H.J. Heinz Company, 82
Hayes Company, 315–326, 356
HealthSouth, 8
Hershey Foods Corporation, 24, 41, 95, 154
Hewlett-Packard (HP) Corporation, 58, 221, 224, 228, 241, 406, 411, 422
Hilton Hotels Corporation, 238, 240
Hollywood, 376
Honda Civic, 289
HP, *see* Hewlett-Packard Corporation

I
IBM, 44, 227, 241
Inco, 155
Intel Corporation, 480–481, 483
Intelligent Quisine, 443, 458
International Business Machines, *see* IBM
International Outsourcing Services, LLC, 116
IT&T, 3

J
JCPenney Company, Inc., 186

K
Kansas Farmers' Vertically Integrated Cooperative, Inc. (K-VIC), 130–132
Kellogg Company, 35, 90–91, 278
Kiley Enterprises, 86–87
Kohl's Department Stores, 198
KPMG, 226
Kraft Foods, 116
Krispy Kreme Doughnuts, Inc., 144
K-VIC, *see* Kansas Farmers' Vertically Integrated Cooperative, Inc.

L
Levi Strauss, 484
Louis Vuitton, 224

M
Marriott Hotels, 357
Massachusetts General Hospital, 272
Mattel Corporation, 191–192
McDonnell Douglas, 97, 227
McKesson Corporation, 171
McKinsey Global Institute, 241
Merck and Co., 33, 482
Merrill Lynch, 8
Microsoft Corporation, 5, 61, 98, 103, 118, 158, 223
Motley Fool, 47
Motorola, 227
Movie Gallery Inc., 93–94

N
Nagel-Siebert Trucking Company, C12–C13
NationsBank, 218
Navistar, Inc., C12
Net Nanny Software International Inc., 94
Nike, Inc., 36, 227, 406
Nissan, 229
Nordstrom, Inc., 84
Northwest Airlines Corporation, 39

O
Oracle Corporation, 32
Oral-B Laboratories, 408

P
PairGain Technologies, 47
PepsiCo, Inc., 116
Philip Morris, 407
Positively-You.com, 308–309, 312
Pratt & Whitney, 237
PricewaterhouseCoopers, 44
Procter & Gamble Co., 8, 53, 231, 366
Prudential Real Estate, 8
Pujols Manufacturing, 383

Q
Quaker Oats, 408

R
REL Consultancy Group, 60
Resorts Worldwide, Inc., 444
Rhino Foods, 7
Rolling Stones, 288

S
San Diego Zoo, 363
SAP AG, 238
Sara Lee, 229, 406
Schering-Plough, 227
Schwinn, 414
Sears Holdings Corporation, 61
Sharp, 500
Sheraton Hotels, 444
Siebel Systems, 377
Siemens AG, 383
Solectron Corporation, 407, 422
Southwest Airlines Co., 32, 50, 272
Sportsco Investments, 32
Springfield ReManufacturing Corporation, 3
Starwood Hotels and Resorts Worldwide, Inc., 444
Stephanie's Gourmet Coffee and More, 161–162, 167, 169
Sunbeam, 420
SunTrust Banks, Inc., 184
Superior Industries International, Inc., 413

T
Target Corporation, 89
Texas Instruments Inc., 83, 459
The Coca-Cola Company, 5
The North Face, Inc., 37
Thomas Moser, 274
Thomson Corporation, 155
Timberland, 289
Time Warner, 314
Tootsie Roll Industries, Inc., 3, 5, 10, 11, 19–24, 30, 41, 43, 78, 95, 102, 137, 154
Toyota, 229, 237, 289, 484, 499
Toys "R" Us, 184
Tweeter Home Entertainment, 71–72

U
U-Haul, 276
Union Pacific Resources Group Inc., 444
United Airlines, 272
United States Steel Corp., 278

W
Wal-Mart, 89, 240, 484
Walt Disney Productions, 66
Waste Management Company, 108
Wells Fargo & Company, 162
Westinghouse, 499, 459
Willard & Shullman Group Ltd., 312
WorldCom, Inc., 8, 69, 170, 226

X
Xerox Corporation, 42, 161, 162, 189
XM Satellite Radio Holdings, 321

Y
Yahoo!, Inc., 50, 86

subject index

A

ABC, *see* Activity-based costing
ABM, *see* Activity-based management
Absorption-cost pricing, 503–505, 507
Account(s), 110–111. *See also* Accounts payable; Accounts receivable
  in accounting information system, 111–114
    debits and credits, 111–114
    expansion of basic equation, 115
    stockholders' equity relationships, 114
  chart of, 120, 133
  debit and credit, columns in, 111
  defined, 133
  T accounts, 110–111, 133
Accounting, 25
  accrual, 448
  and budgeting, 310–311
  and non-accounting careers, 8
  as recruiting tool, 7
  cash, 445
  defined, 6
  double-entry system, 111–114
  importance of knowing basic, 3
  responsibility, 365–377
Accounting information, *see* Financial information
Accounting information system, 102
  accounting transactions in, 102–109
    analyzing, 103–104
    dividend payments, 108
    employee salaries cash payments, 108–109
    and hiring of new employees, 108
    insurance policy cash purchases, 107
    investment of cash by stockholders, 104–105
    note issues in exchange for cash, 105
    office equipment cash purchases, 105
    receipt of cash in advance from customer, 105–106
    rent payments, 107
    services rendered for cash, 106–107
    supplies purchases (credit), 107
  accounts in:
    debits and credits, 111–114
    expansion of basic equation, 115
    stockholders' equity relationships, 114
  defined, 133
  recording process:
    chart of accounts, 120
    illustration of, 120–128
    journal, 116–118
    journalizing, 116–118
    ledger entries, 119
    posting, 120
  trial balance, 129
Accounting transactions, 102–109, 133. *See also* Transaction analysis
Accounts payable:
  defined, 11
Accounts receivable, 11, 106
Accrual accounting: cash accounting vs., 445
Accumulated depreciation, 51
Activities:
  assignment of related, 165–166
  business, *see* Business activities
Activity index, 272
  for flexible budgets, 359–360
  relevant range of, 275
Activity-based costing (ABC), 239
  and incremental analysis, 420
Adjustable-rate mortgages (ARMs), 378, 463
Adjusted cash balance, 182, 183
Adjusted cash balance per books, 182
Adjusting entries
  for bank reconciliation, 180–184
Administrative expense budget selling and, 319–320
Administrative expenses, 11
Airline industry, 284
Analysis. *See also* Financial statement analysis
  cost behavior, 272–278
  break-even, 282–285
  cost-volume-profit, 279–291
  incremental, 406–423
  sensitivity, 457
Annual rate of return method, 461–462
Annual reports, 21–23
  auditor's report section of, 22–23
  defined, 25
  MD&A section of, 22
  notes to financial statements section of, 22
  for Tootsie Roll Industries, Inc., A1–A22
Annuities, C9
  present value of, C9–C11
  future value of, C5–C6
  discounting, C12
ARMs, *see* Adjustable-rate mortgages
ASEAN, 236
Assets, 25
  debit/credit procedures for, 111–114
  intangible, *see* Intangible assets
  long-lived, *see* Long-lived assets
  operating, 374–376
  record keeping and custody of, 166
Associate's degree, 421
Assumptions:
  economic entity, 67, 73
  going concern, 68, 73
  monetary unit, 68, 73
  time period, 67–68, 73
Audit committees, 227
Auditor(s):
  defined, 23
  internal, 170
Auditor's report, 22–23, 25–26, A23
Auto loans, C16
Automation, 237, 238
Automobile industry, 289

B

B2B (business-to-business) e-commerce, 238
Bachelor's degree, 421
Balance sheet(s), 14, 17, 26, 233–234
  budgeted, 325–326
  classified, 48–53, 58–61
    current assets on, 49–50
    current liabilities on, 52
    defined, 74
    intangible assets on, 51
    long-term investments on, 50
    long-term liabilities on, 53
    property, plant, and equipment on, 51
    stockholders' equity on, 53
  defined, 12
  for Hershey Foods Corporation, B2
  or liquidity on, 59
  solvency on, 60–61
  for Tootsie Roll Industries, Inc., 20–21
  using, 58–61
Balanced scorecard, 240
Banks, 179
  errors by, 180, 182
  use of, 179–184
Bank memoranda, 182
Bank reconciliation, 180–184, 195
Bank statements, 179–180, 195
Bankruptcies
  due to medical bills, 378
Basic accounting equation:
  defined, 26
  expansion of, 115

Beginning work in process inventory, 232
Behavior: and budgeting, 312–313
  and performance evaluations, 377
Boards of directors, 226
Bonding, 170, 195
Bonds payable, 10
Book value, 417
Borick, Steve, 413
Bottlenecks, 239
Bounced checks, *see* NSF checks
Bowline, Lyle, 308–309
Brand pricing, 500
Break-even analysis, 282–285
  contribution margin technique for, 283–284
  and CVP analysis, 282–285
  and CVP graph, 284–285
  defined, 282
Break-even point, 282
  defined, 282
  in sales units, 282
  identifying, 283
  in sales dollars, 283
Brock, Paula, 363
Budget committees, 312
Budget period, 311–312
Budget reports, 354
  flexible, 362–363
  for responsibility accounting, 367–369
Budget(s), 310. *See also* Budgeting
  master, 314–315
  production, 316–317
  direct materials, 317–318
  selling and administrative expense, 319–320
  operating, 314–321
  cash, 322–325
  financial, 322–327
  personal, 330, 378
  defined, 310
  sales, 316
  direct labor, 318
  manufacturing overhead, 319
Budgetary control, 354–364
  with static budget reports, 355–357
  with flexible budgets, 357–364
  defined, 354
Budgetary slack, 313
Budgeted balance sheet, 325–326
Budgeted income statement, 321
Budgeting, 310–315. *See also* Capital budgeting
  and accounting, 310–311
  human behavior affected by, 312–313
  merchandisers, 327–328
  for nonmanufacturing companies, 327–329
  not-for-profit organizations, 328–329
  benefits of, 311
  effective, 311
  process of, 312
  long-range planning vs., 314
  service enterprises, 328
  for housing costs, 378
Bulletin boards, online, 47
Burden, *see* Manufacturing overhead
Business activities, 10–11
  financing, 10, 15
    on statement of cash flows, 61–62
  investing, 10, 16
    on statement of cash flows, 61
  operating, 11
    on statement of cash flows, 61, 73
Business calculators, *see* Financial calculators
Business ethics, 226–227
Businesses
  manufacturing, 244–247, 406–407,
  nonmanufacturing, 327–329
  virtual, 497
  small, 312
Business organizations, 4–5
  See also Forms of business organization
Business-to-business (B2B) e-commerce, 238

C

Calculators, *see* Financial calculators
California energy crisis, 353
Canceled checks, 179
Capital:
  working, 59, 75
Capital budgeting, 442–466
  information, 445–446
  evaluation process for, 444–447
  cash payback technique used in, 447–448
  net present value method used in, 448–453
  intangible benefits in, 454–455
  with mutually exclusive projects, 456–457
  internal rate of return method used in, 459–461
  annual rate of return method used in, 461–462
  computing time and present values in, C12–C14
  authorization process, 445
  and sensitivity analysis, 457
  and post-audits, 458
Capital: cost of, 450–451
Capital stock. *See also* Common stock
Carbon dioxide, 289
Cash, 10, 195. *See also* Statement of cash flows
  as asset, 61–63
  cash equivalents, 185–186, 195
  crediting/debiting, 111
  defined, 173
  electronic funds transfer (EFT), 184
  employee salaries paid by, 108–109
  insurance policy purchase by, 107
  internal control of, 173–186
    bank statements, 179–180
    disbursements, 176–180
    receipts, 173–176
    reconciling bank accounts, 180–184
    use of banks, 179–184
  managing/monitoring, 186–190
  notes issued in exchange for, 105
  office equipment purchased by, 105
  petty cash fund, 178, 193–195
  reporting, 185–186
  restricted, 186
  services rendered for, 106–107
  stockholders' investment by, 104–105
Cash accounting, 445
Cash advances, 105
Cash budgets, 195, 322–325
Cash disbursements section (of cash budget), 322
Cash equivalents, 185–186, 195
Cash flow information, 445–446
Cash flow numbers, 445, 460
Cash flow techniques, 448
Cash flow(s). *See also* Statement of cash flows
  inflows, 445, 446
  outflows, 445, 446
  and capital budgeting, 445–446
  net annual, 447
  discounted, 448
Cash inflows, 445, 446
Cash management, principles of, 187–188
Cash outflows, 445, 446
Cash payback technique, 447–448
Cash receipts section (of cash budget), 322
CEO (chief executive officer), 226
Certified Public Accountants (CPAs), 23, 26, 241
CFO (chief financial officer), 226
Charges, job, 491
Chart of accounts, 120, 133

Check register, 177
Checks:
  canceled, 179
  NSF (not sufficient funds), 183
  outstanding, 182
Chief executive officer (CEO), 226
Chief financial officer (CFO), 226
China, 51, 236
CIM (computer-integrated manufacturing), 238
Classified balance sheet(s), 48–53, 58–61
  current assets on, 49–50
  current liabilities on, 52
  defined, 74
  intangible assets on, 51
  long-term investments on, 50
  long-term liabilities on, 53
  property, plant, and equipment on, 51
  stockholders' equity on, 53
Closing entries, 246
Collaboration, 366
College degree, value of, 421
Collusion, 172
Common-size analysis, *see* Vertical analysis
Common stock, 26, 53
  debit/credit procedures for, 112–113
  defined, 10
Companies, *see* Businesses
Company officers
  treasurer, 187, 196
  as users of financial information, 6
Comparability of information, 66, 67, 74
Comparative statements, 19
  defined, 26
Comparisons:
  industry-average, 54
  intercompany, 54
  intracompany, 54
Compensation programs, 366
Competence, D1
Compound interest, C2–C4
Compounding periods, C4, C15
Computer-integrated manufacturing (CIM), 238
Computerization, 237, 238
Confidentiality, D2
Conflict resolution, D2
Conservatism, 74
Conservatism constraint, 70
Consistency of information, 66–67, 74
Constraints, theory of, 239
Contribution margin
  ratios, 281–282
  per unit, 281
Control device, budgets as, 310
Controllable costs, 364, 366–367
Controllable items, 364
Controllable margin, 371, 375
Controllable revenues, 366–367
Controller, 226
Controlling, as management function, 225
Corporate fraud, 226
Corporations, 4–5, 26
  defined, 26
Correct cash balance, 181
Cost(s). *See also* Expenses
Cost behavior analysis, 272–278
  fixed costs in, 273–274
  relevant range in, 274–276
  mixed costs in, 276–278
  in, 273
  and identification of variable and fixed costs, 278
Cost centers, 369, 370
Cost determination, 223
Cost of capital, 450–451
Cost of goods manufactured, 231, 232
Cost of goods manufactured schedule, 232, 233
Cost of goods purchased, 231
Cost of goods sold, 11
Cost principle, 68–69, 74
Cost systems: absorption costing
  and cost-plus pricing, 485–487
  target costing, 484
  activity-based, *see* Activity-based costing (ABC)
  job order costing, *see* Job order cost systems
  process costing, *see* Process cost systems
  variable, *see* Variable costing
Cost(s), 228–230. *See also* Standard costs
  variable, 273, 277–278, 495,
  controllable vs. noncontrollable, 364, 366–367
  opportunity, 410, 412–413, 494,
  sunk, 410, 415, 417
  manufacturing, 228–229, 231–236,
  direct materials, 228–229
  in financial statements, 231–236
  relevant, 410, 411
  direct labor, 229
  overhead, 229
  product vs. period, 230
  reducing, 241
  joint, 415
  of morale, 420
  of degrees, 421
  target, 484
Cost-based transfer price, 496–497
Costing and costing systems, *see* Cost systems
Cost-plus pricing, 485–487
Cost-volume-profit (CVP) analysis, 279–291
  and break-even analysis, 282–285
  income, 286–287
  margin of safety in, 287–288
  components of, 279
  assumptions of, 280
Cost-volume-profit (CVP) graph, 284, 287
Cost-volume-profit (CVP) income statement, 280–282
  contribution margin ratio, 281–282
  contribution margin per unit, 281
CPAs (certified public accountants), 241
Credibility, D2
Cr., *see* Credits
Credit:
  supplies purchases by, 107
Credits (Cr.), 111
  defined, 133
  procedures:
    for assets, 112
    for dividends, 113
    for expenses, 113
    for retained earnings, 113
    for revenues, 113
    for stockholders' equity, 112–114
  tax, 289
  on worksheets, 245
Credit balances:
  defined, 102
  in liability accounts, 112
  in revenue accounts, 114
Creditors, 7, 10
Current assets:
  on classified balance sheet, 49–50
  defined, 74
  types of, 50
Current liability(-ies)
  on classified balance sheet, 52
  defined, 74
Current ratios, 59
  defined, 74
Custody of assets, recordkeeping and, 166
Customers:
  as users of financial information, 7–8
Cutoff rate, *see* Discount rate
CVP analysis, *see* Cost-volume-profit analysis
CVP graph, *see* Cost-volume-profit graph
CVP income statement, *see* Cost-volume-profit income statement

D

Debits (Dr.), 111, 245
  defined, 133
  procedures:
    for assets, 112
    for dividends, 113
    for retained earnings, 113
    for revenues, 113
    for stockholders' equity, 112–114
Debit balances
  on asset accounts, 111
  defined, 132
  in expense accounts, 114
Debiting, 112
Debt, *see* Liability(-ies)
Debt financing, 60
Debt to total assets ratio, 60–61, 74
Decentralization, 366
Departmental overhead costs (report), 355
Deposits in transit, 181–182, 195
Depreciation
  defined, 51
Direct fixed costs, 371
Direct labor, 229
  as manufacturing cost, 229
  and overhead
Direct labor budget, 318
Direct materials, 228–229
Direct materials budget, 317–318
Directing, as management function, 224, 225
Disbursements, cash, 176–180
Discount rate (required rate of return, hurdle rate, cutoff rate), 448, 450–451
Discounted cash flow techniques, 448
Discounting, C11
Discounting the future amount, C7
Dividend(s), 26
  debit/credit procedures for, 113
  defined, 13
  payment of, 112
Documents:
  controls for, 167–168
  prenumbering of, 167
  source, 116, 167
Double-entry system, 111, 133
Dr., *see* Debits
Dunlap, Al "Chainsaw," 420
Duties, segregation of, 165–167

E

Earnings per share (EPS), 55–56, 74
Earnings retained, *see* Retained earnings
E-businesses, 483
E-commerce, business-to-business (B2B), 238
Economic entity assumption, 67, 74
Economic planners, 8
EDP (electronic data processing), 102
EFT (electronic funds transfer), *see* Electronic funds transfer
Electric utility industry, 353
Electronic data processing (EDP) systems, 102
Electronic funds transfer (EFT), 184, 196
Employees:
  cash salary payments to, 108–109
  hiring of, 108
  fraud by, 226
  safety of, 455
Ending work in process inventory, 232
Enterprise resource planning (ERP) software systems, 237–238
EPS, *see* Earnings per share
Equipment. *See also* Property, plant, and equipment
  incremental analysis for, 416–417
  office, 105
  replacement of, 416–417
  retention of, 416–417
ERP (enterprise resource planning) software systems, 237–238
Errors:
  in bank accounts, 182
Ethics issues, 8–9
  and budgeting, 313
  and business, 226–227
  and standards, D1–D2
  and IMA, D1–D2
  and incentives, 227
  and taxes, 499
  of transferring profits, 499
  and competence, D1
  principles of, D1
  and confidentiality, D2
  and conflict resolution, D2
  and credibility, D2
  and integrity, D2
  in financial reporting, 8–9
  time lags, 180
European Union, 236
Evaluation process (capital budgeting), 444–447
Excess capacity, 494–495
Exotic Newcastle Disease, 363
Expenditures:
  timing of, 188
Expense(s), 26. *See also* Cost(s)
  debit/credit procedures for, 113
  defined, 11
  and stockholders' equity, 114
Expense accounts, debit balances in, 114
External sales, 482–491
  cost-plus pricing for, 485–487
  time-and-material pricing for, 489–491
  and target costing, 484
  variable-cost pricing for, 487
External users of financial information, 7–8

F

Factory overhead, *see* Manufacturing overhead
FASB, *see* Financial Accounting Standards Board
FIFO (Last-in, First-out), *see* First-In, First-Out
Finance directors, as users of financial information, 6
Financial accounting, 223
Financial Accounting Standards Board (FASB), 65, 74
Financial budgets, 314, 322–327
  cash budget, 322–325
  budgeted balance sheet, 325–326
Financial calculators, C13–C16
  keys on, C13, C14
  present value function on, C13
  and compounding period, C15
  minus signs on, C15
  plus signs on, C15
  rounding on, C15
  applications of, C16
Financial executives, 223
Financial information, 6, 409. *See also* Accounting information system; Financial reporting
  external users of, 7–8
  internal users of, 6–7
  usefulness of information, 67
Financial pressure (in fraud triangle), 163
Financial reporting, *See also* Financial statements
  assumptions in, 67–69
  comparability of, 66, 67
  consistency of, 67–68
  constraints in, 69–70
  defined, 65
  ethics in, 8–9. *See also* Ethics issues
  fraud, 226
  objectives of, 66, 67
  principles in, 67–69
  relevance in, 65–66
  reliability in, 66
Financial statements, 10–25. *See also specific statements*
  analysis of. *See also specific headings*
    classified balance sheet, 48–53
    income statements, 55–56
    ratio analysis, 54

and ratio analysis, 54
statement of cash flows, 61–65
statement of stockholders' equity, 56–57
annual report information on, 21–22
balance sheet, 14–15, 17, 233–234
classified balance sheet, 48–53
comparative analysis:
consolidated
for Tootsie Roll Industries, Inc., A13–A15
for Hershey Foods Corporation, B1–B4
income statement, 13, 17, 231–233
income statements, 55–56
interrelationships of, 16
ratio analysis, 54
and ratio analysis, 54
reflected in, 231–236
responsibility for, 227
retained earnings statement, 13, 17
statement of cash flows, 12, 61–65
statement of stockholders' equity, 56–57
for Tootsie Roll Industries, Inc., 19, A13–A15
types of, 12
Financing. *See also* Financing activities
debt, 60
Financing activities, 10, 15
Financing section (of cash budget), 322
Fixed assets, 11. *See also* Property, plant, and equipment
Fixed costs (traceable costs):
in cost behavior analysis, 273–274
computing with high-low method, 277–278
behavior analysis, 278
accounting, 371
Fixed-rate loans, 463
Flexible budget reports, 362–363
Flexible budget(s), 357–364
development of, 359–360
case study, 360–362
budgetary control with, 357–364
with management by exception, 363–364
Food budgets, 330
Forecasts, sales, *see* Sales forecasts
Foreclosure, 463
Forms of business organization:
corporations, 4–5. *See also* Corporations
partnerships, 4–5
sole proprietorships, 4, 5
Fraud, 162–163, 196, 226. *See also* Internal control
defined, 162
Fraud triangle, 162–163, 196
Free cash flow, 62–63, 74
Free on board destination, *see* FOB destination
Free on board shipping point, *see* FOB shipping point
Full-cost pricing, 487, 503
Full disclosure principle, 69, 74
Future value: of annuities, C5–C6
of single amounts, C3–C4

G

GAAP, *see* Generally accepted accounting principles
Gardner, Tom and David, 47
General journal, 116–118, 133
defined, 133
General ledger, 119
defined, 133
Generally accepted accounting principles (GAAP), 64, 503
defined, 74
General managers, 8
Globalization, 498–499
Going concern assumption, 68, 74
Goods manufactured, cost of, 231, 232
Goodwill, 51
Government budgets, 329
Green, Harold, 3
Growth, 492

H

HDTV industry, 488
High-low method, 277–278
High-school graduates, 421
Hiring, recording of, 108
Housing costs, 330, 378
Human behavior, 312–313
Human element, for internal control, 172
Hurdle rate, *see* Discount rate
Hybrid vehicles, 289

I

IASB, *see* International Accounting Standards Board
iGAAP, 65
IMA (Institute of Management Accountants), 227, D2
IMA Ethics Counselor, D2
IMA Statement of Ethical Professional Practice, 227, D1–D2
Immaterial items, 69
Incentives, 227
Income:
net, 11
defined, 26
target net, 286–287
residual, 382–383
Income (margin) measure, 374
Income statement(s), 13, 17, 231–233, 355
CVP, 280–282
budgeted, 321
defined, 26
for Hershey Foods Corporation, B1
of Tootsie Roll Industries, Inc., 19
using, 55–56
Income taxes payable, 11
Incremental analysis, 406–423
qualitative factors in, 419–420
for outsourcing, 497–498
in virtual companies, 497–498
approach used in, 409–410
for make-or-buy decision, 411–413
for sell-or-process-further decision, 413–416
for equipment retention/replacement, 416–417
unprofitable segments, 417–418
defined, 409
types of, 410
with special orders, 411
and activity-based costing, 420
Independent internal verification, 169–170
India, 236
Indirect fixed costs, 371
Indirect labor, 229
Indirect manufacturing costs, *see* Manufacturing overhead
Indirect materials, 228–229
Industry average comparisons, 54
Information, *see* Financial information
Insourcing, 241
Institute of Management Accountants (IMA), 227, D2
Insurance:
purchase of, 107
Intangible assets
on classified balance sheet, 51
defined, 74
Integrity, D2
Intercompany comparisons, 54
Interest, C1–C4
simple, C1–C2
compound, C2–C4
Interest coverage, *see* Times interest earned ratio
Interest expenses, 11
Interest payable, 11
Interest rates, 378, C1
Interest revenues, 11

Internal audit staff, 226
Internal auditors, 170, 196
Internal control, 163–173, 196
bonding of employees handling cash, 170
of cash, 173–186
bank statements, 179–180
disbursements, 176–180
receipts, 173–176
reconciling bank accounts, 180–184
use of banks, 179–184
documentation procedures, 167–168
and establishment of responsibility, 164–165
human element, 172
independent internal verification, 169–170
limitations of, 171–172
for petty cash replacement, 194–195
physical, 168–169
requiring vacations, 170
rotating duties, 170
and segregation of duties, 165–167
with voucher system, 177–178
Internal rate of return (IRR), 459
Internal rate of return method, 459–461
net present value method vs., 459, 461
decision rule for, 460, 462
advantages of, 462
Internal sales, 492. *See also* Transfer pricing
Internal users of financial information, 6–7
International Accounting Standards Board (IASB), 65, 74
International not-for-profits, 9
Internet, 238
bulletin boards, 47
e-commerce, 238
airline industry and B2B, 284
and pricing, 483
Intracompany comparisons, 54
Inventory(-ies), 11
Inventory methods: just-in-time, 238
periodic, 231–233
Inventory(-ies), 221
product costs as, 230
beginning work in process, 232
Investing activities, 10, 16
on statement of cash flows, 61
Investment centers, 369, 372–376
Investment(s): in common stocks, interest, C2
Investments, 10
of cash, 188
long-term
on classified balance sheets, 50
defined, 74
Investors, 7

J

JIT (just-in-time) inventory method, 238
JIT processing, *see* Just-in-time processing
Job assignment, *see* Assigning manufacturing costs
Jobs (employment), 241
Joint costs, 415
Journal, 116–118, 133
Journalizing, 116–118
account titles in, 118
defined, 133
illustration of, 127–128
Just-in-time (JIT) inventory method, 238

L

Labor costs: calculating, with time-and-material pricing, 489–490
Labor reports, 355
Labor: direct, 229, 318
indirect, 229
Labor unions, 7
LCDs (liquid crystal displays), 458
Ledger, 116, 119, 133
Lee, Bryan, 118
Legal liability, form of business and, 5
Liability(-ies)
current
on classified balance sheets, 52
defined, 74
debit/credit procedures for, 112
defined, 10, 26, 74
delayed payment of, 187
long-term
on classified balance sheets, 53
Line positions, 226
Liquid crystal displays (LCDs), 458
Liquid investments, 188
Liquidity, 74
on balance sheet, 59
defined, 74
Liquidity ratios, 58
current ratio, 59, 74
defined, 74
working capital, 59
Loans: auto, C16
mortgage, 378, 463, C16
fixed-rate, 463
calculating amounts of, C16
Long-range planning, 314
Long-term investments
on classified balance sheet, 50
defined, 74
Long-term liability(-ies)
bonds:
on classified balance sheet, 53
defined, 74
Losses:
net, 11, 26

M

Madison Square Garden, 316
Mail receipts, 176
Make-or-buy decision: incremental analysis for, 411–413
and outsourcing, 406, 413
opportunity cost in, 412–413
Management (managers), functions of, 224, 225
decision-making process of, 408–410
and financial statements, 227
Management accounting, *see* Managerial accounting
Management by exception, 363–364
Management discussion and analysis (MD&A), 22
defined, 26
for Tootsie Roll Industries, Inc., 22, A6–A10
Management issues:
theft, 172
Managerial accountants, 223
Managerial accounting (management accounting), 222–223
current trends in, 236–240
activities of, 222
defined, 222
financial accounting vs., 223
Manufacturing, 228
merchandising vs., 228
and outsourcing, 241
Manufacturing companies: accounting cycle for, 244–247
outsourcing by, 406–407
Manufacturing costs, 228–229, 231–236. *See also* Manufacturing overhead
materials, 228–229
in financial statements, 231–236
direct labor, 229
calculating, for absorption-cost pricing, 504
Manufacturing operations:
operating cycle for, 186–187
Manufacturing overhead, 229
Manufacturing overhead budget, 319
Manufacturing Summary account, 246
Margin (income) measure, 374
Margin of safety, 287–288

Margin of safety ratio, 288
Market positioning, 459
Market-based transfer price, 497
Marketable securities, *see* Short-term investments
Marketing, and pricing, 500
Marketing department, 8
Marketing expenses, 11
Marketing managers, 6
Markup, 485
  calculating, for absorption-cost pricing, 504
  calculating, for variable-cost pricing, 506
Master budgets, 314–315
  reports for, 355–357
  sales point in, 316
Material loading charge, 489, 490
  calculating, 490–491
  for overhead costs, 489
Material(s): direct, 228
  indirect, 228–229
  pricing, 489–491
  raw, 228
Material items, 69–70
Materiality, 69–70, 74, 364
MBA calculators, *see* Financial calculators
McCollick, Sharon, 186–187
MD&A, *see* Management discussion and analysis
Merchandise purchases budget, 327–328
Merchandisers, 327–328
Merchandising, 228
Minimum transfer price, 494
Minus signs (in time value of money problems), C15
Misinformation, 47
Mixed costs, 276–278
Monetary unit assumption, 67, 74
Money, time value of, *see* Time value of money
Morale, cost of, 420
Mortgage loans: adjustable-rate mortgages, 378, 463
  calculating, C16
Moser, Thomas, 274
Multiple products, 413–416
Mutually exclusive projects, 456–457

N

NAFTA, 236
Negotiated transfer prices, 493–496
  with excess capacity, 494–495
  with no excess capacity, 494
  variable costs in, 495
Net annual cash flow, 447
  target, 286–287
Net income. *See also* Income statement(s); Statement of cash flows
  defined, 26
Net losses, 26
Net present value (NPV), 448
Net present value method, 448–453
  assumptions of, 452–452
  intangible benefits in, 454–455
  with mutually exclusive projects, 456–457
  internal rate of return method vs., 459, 461
  for equal annual cash flows, 449
  for unequal annual cash flows, 450
  and sensitivity analysis, 457
  and post-auditing, 458
Net realizable value, *see* Cash realizable value
No excess capacity, 494
Nominal accounts, *see* Temporary accounts
Noncontrollable costs, 364
Nonfinancial information, 409
Nonmanufacturing companies, 327–329
  merchandisers, 327–328
  not-for-profit organizations, 328–329
  service enterprises, 328
Normal range, *see* Relevant range
Not-for-profit organizations, 328–329
Notes payable, 10
Notes receivable
  collection of, 182–183
Notes to the financial statements, 22
  defined, 26
  for Tootsie Roll Industries, Inc., A17–A22
Not-for-profits, international, 9
NPV (net present value), 448. *See also* Net present value method
NSF (not sufficient funds) checks, 183, 196

O

Office equipment, 105
Officers, company, *see* Company officers
Olympic Games, 324
Online investor bulletin boards, 47
Open-book management, 3
Operating activities, 10, 11, 16
  on statement of cash flow, 61
Operating assets: reducing average of, 375–376
  valuation of, 374
Operating budgets, 315–321
  production budget, 316–317
  direct materials budget, 317–318
  selling and administrative expense budget, 319–320
  planning for, 315–321
  preparation of, 315–321
  defined, 314
  sales budget, 316
  direct labor budget, 318
  manufacturing overhead budget, 319
  income statement, 321
Operating cycle, 50
  defined, 74
  in manufacturing vs. merchandising companies, 186–187
Opinions, unqualified, 23
Opportunity (in fraud triangle), 162–163
Opportunity costs, 410
  in make-or-buy decision, 412–413
  capacity, 494
Orders: accepting, at special prices, 411
  incremental analysis for, 411
Organization charts, 225
Organizational structure, 225–226
Other assets, *see* Intangible assets
Outsourcing, 241, 497
  by manufacturers, 406–407
  and transfer pricing, 497–498
  in make-or-buy decision, 413
Outstanding checks, 182, 196
Over-the-counter receipts, 173–175
Overhead, departmental overhead costs, 355
Overspending, in government budgets, 329

P

Participative budgeting, 312–313
Partnerships, 4–5, 26
Payables, *see* Accounts payable; Notes payable
Payback period, 447
PCAOB, *see* Public Company Accounting Oversight Board
Performance evaluation, 376–377
Performance measures, 371
Period costs, 230
Period(s): average collection budget, 311–312
  compounding, C4, C15
  payback, 447
Periodic inventory system, 231–233
Personal budgets, 330, 378
Petty cash fund, 178, 193–195
  defined, 196
  establishment of, 194
  payments from, 194–195
  replenishing, 194–195

Pfeiffer, Eckhard, 220–221
Pharmaceutical industry, 482
Physical controls, 168–169
Planning, as management function, 224
Plasma screens, 458
Plus signs (in time value of money problems), C15
Post-audits, 458
Posting, 120
  defined, 133
  illustration of, 127–128
Practical range, *see* Relevant range
Practice, D2
Prenumbered documents, 167
Present value, C7. *See also* under Net present value
  of annuities, C9–C11
  in capital budgeting decisions, C12–C14
  of single sums, C14–C15
  of single amounts, C7–C9
  functions for, in calculators, C12
  variables affecting, C7
Price takers, 483
Price-optimization software, 500
Pricing, 480–507
  cost-plus costing, 485–487
  for external sales, 482–491
  time-and-material pricing, 489–491
  target costing, 484
  variable-cost pricing, 487
Principal, C1
Product costs: as inventory, 230
  magnitudes affecting, 229
  period costs vs., 230
Product quality, 238
Production budget, 316–317
Production supervisors, 6
Profit centers, 369, 371–372
Profitability index, 456–457
Profitability ratios, 55
  defined, 74
Program controls, computer, 168
Property, plant, and equipment, 10. *See also* Equipment; Plant assets
  on classified balance sheet, 51
  defined, 74
Property taxes payable, 11
Public Company Accounting Oversight Board (PCAOB), 65, 74
PV (present value) key, C13

Q

Quick ratios, *see* Acid-test ratios

R

"Rate caps," 353
Rate of return on sales, *see* Profit margin
Ratio, 54, 74
Ratio analysis, 54
  defined, 74
Rationalization (in fraud triangle), 163
Raw materials, 228
Real accounts, *see* Permanent accounts
Real estate brokers, 8
Receipts, cash, 173–176
Recording industry, 16
Recording process (accounting information system):
  chart of accounts, 120
  illustration of, 120–128
  journal, 116–118
  journalizing, 116–118
  ledger entries, 119
  posting, 120
Recordkeeping, custody of assets and, 166
Regulatory agencies, 7–8
Related activities, assignment of, 165–166
Relevance of information, 74
Relevant costs, 410, 411
Relevant range: of activity index, 275
  in cost behavior analysis, 274–276
Reliability of information, 66, 74
Rent, payment of, 107
Reporting: determining costs vs., 223
  performance evaluation, 377
Required rate of return, *see* Discount rate
Residual income, 382–383
  defined, 382
Responsibility accounting, 365–377. *See also* Responsibility centers
  with controllable vs. noncontrollable revenues and costs, 366–367
  reporting system for, 367–369
  performance evaluation in, 376–377
Responsibility centers, 369–376
  profit centers, 371–372
  investment centers, 372–376
  cost centers, 370
  behavior affecting, 377
Responsibility, establishment of, 164–165
Responsibility reporting system, 367–369
  centers, 371–372
  for investment centers, 373–374
Restatements, 13
Restricted cash, 186, 196
Retailers, 500
Retained earnings, 12, 53
  debit/credit procedures for, 113
  defined, 26
  stockholders' equity in, 113
Retained earnings statement, 12, 13, 17
  defined, 26
  of Tootsie Roll Industries, Inc., 19–20
Return on investment (ROI), 373
  improvement of, 375–376
  residual income vs., 382–383
  judgmental factors in, 374
  disadvantage of, 382
Revenue(s):
  controllable vs. noncontrollable, 366–367
  debit/credit procedures for, 114
  defined, 11, 26
  interest, 11
  recording of, 106–107
  sales, 11
  service, 11
  and stockholders' equity, 114
Revenue accounts, credit balances in, 114
Revenue recognition principle, 22
Risk analysis, 457
Robotic equipment, 238
ROI, *see* Return on investment
ROI vs., 382–383
  weakness of, 383
Rounding, C15

S

Safety: employee, 455
  margin of, 287–288
Salaries:
  payment of cash for, 108–109
Sales budgets, 316
Sales dollars: break-even point in, 283
  for target net income, 286, 287
Sales forecasts, 312, 316
Sales reports, 355
Sales revenues, 11
Sales tax payable, 11
Sales units: break-even point in, 283
  for target net income, 286
Sales: external, 482–491
  internal, 492.
Sarbanes-Oxley Act (SOX), 9, 13, 26, 163, 196, 227
Scrap reports, 355
SEC, *see* Securities and Exchange Commission
Securities and Exchange Commission (SEC), 64, 65, 74
Segments, 366

Segregation of duties, 165–167
Selling and administrative expense budget, 319–320
Selling expenses, 11
Selling expenses (report), 355
Sell-or-process-further decision, 413–416
 for multiple products, 413–416
 for single products, 413
Sensitivity analysis, 457
Service charges, bank, 183–184
Service enterprises, 328
Service industry: activity-based costing in, current trends in, 236–237
Service revenues, 11
Services, revenue from, 11
Shareholders, *see* Stockholders
Simple interest, C1–C2
Single amount: future value of, C3–C4
 present value of, C7–C9
Single sum: discounting, C12
 present value of, C14–C15
Size of business, and theft, 172
Small businesses, 312
Sole proprietorships, 4
Solvency:
 on balance sheet, 60–61
 defined, 74
Solvency ratios, 60–61, 74
 debt to total assets ratio, 60–61
 defined, 74
Source documents, 116
South Korea, 65
SOX, *see* Sarbanes-Oxley Act, 227
Staff positions, 226
Stack, Jack, 3
Stated rate, *see* Contractual interest rate
Statements, *see* Bank statements; Financial statements
Statement of cash flows, 12, 16, 17, 26
 analysis of, 61–63
 business activities on, 61
 defined, 26
 financing activities on, 61–62
 for Hershey Foods Corporation, B3
 for Tootsie Roll Industries, Inc., 21, A16
Statement of stockholders' equity:
 analysis of, 56–57
 defined, 74–75
 for Hershey Foods Corporation, B4
Static budget reports, 355–357
Static budget(s), 355–357. *See also* Master budgets
 defined, 355
 evaluation, 358
Stock(s). *See also* Common stock
 amounts received from issuing, 13
 common, 53
  debit/credit procedures for, 112–113
  defined, 10, 26
Stockholders, 4–5, 226
 cash investment by, 104–105
 creditors owed and claims of, 10
Stockholders' equity, 14, 53
 on classified balance sheet, 53
 common stock, 112–113
 debit/credit procedures for, 112–114
 defined, 26, 74–75
 dividends, 113
 recording change to, 109
 relationships of accounts affecting, 114
 retained earnings, 113
 revenues and expenses, 114
Subprime borrowers, 463
Sunk costs, 410, 415, 417
Supplies:
 credit purchases of, 107

T

T accounts, 110–111, 133
Target costs, 484
Target net income, 286–287
 in sales dollars, 286, 287
 formula for, 286
 sales units for, 286
 and cost-volume-profit graph, 287
 contribution margin technique for, 287
Target price, 484
Target selling price, 485
 calculating, for absorption-cost pricing, 504–505
 calculating, for variable-cost pricing, 506
Tax credits, for hybrid vehicles, 289
Tax rates, global differences in, 498
Taxes:
 income, 11
 property, 11
 sales, 11
Taxes payable, 11
Taxing authorities, 7
Technology, 237–238
Television screen manufacturers, 488
Theft, 172. *See also* Internal control
Theory of constraints, 239
Time, C1
Time value of money, C1–C17
 present value of an annuity, C9–C11
 present values in capital budgeting decisions, C12–C14
 present value of a single sum, C14–C15
 and interest, C1–C3
 future value of a single amount, C3–C4
 future value of an annuity, C5–C6
 present value of a single amount, C7–C9
 and discounting, C11
 and use of financial calculators, C16
 present value variables, C7
Time-and-material pricing, 489–491
Time lags (in bank accounts), 180
Time period assumption, 67–68, 75
Total cost of work in process, 232
Total manufacturing costs, 232
Total quality management (TQM) systems, 238–239
Toyota Prius, 289
TQM systems, *see* Total quality management systems
Traceable costs, *see* Fixed costs
Transactions, accounting, 133
Transaction analysis, 102–109
 defined, 103
 hiring of new employees as, 108
 investment of cash by stockholders as, 104–105
 note issued in exchange for cash as, 105
 payments:
  of cash for employee salaries as, 108–109
  of dividend as, 108
  of rent as, 107
 purchases:
  of insurance policy in cash as, 107
  of office equipment for cash as, 105
  of supplies on account as, 107
 receipt of cash in advance from customer as, 105–106
 services provided for cash as, 106–107
Transfer prices, 492
Transfer pricing, 492–502
 variable-cost, 487, 505–506
 time-and-material, 489–491
 negotiated, 493–496
 cost-based, 496–497
 and outsourcing, 497–498
 in global environment, 498–499
 transfer, 492–502
 market-based, 497
 tax rates affecting, 498
 abuse of, 499
Treasurer, 196, 226

Trend analysis, *see* Horizontal analysis
Trend forecasting, 459
Trial balance, 129
- defined, 133
- limitations of, 129
- purpose of, 129

Tuition, 421

U

Unit costs: with activity-based costing, calculating, for variable-cost pricing, 505–506
Unqualified opinions (auditor's), 23
Unprofitable segments: elimination of, 417–418
- incremental analysis for, 417–418

Users/uses of financial information:
- communicating with, 12–16
- ethical issues related to, 7–9
- external, 7–8
- internal, 6–7

V

Value chain, 237
- and technology, 238
- and theory of constraints, 239

Value(s), 224
- present, C7–C15
- time value of money, C1–C17
- future, C3–C6
- adding, 224
- measurement of, 224
- book, 417
- net present, 448

Variable cost(s): computing, with high-low method, 277–278
- in cost behavior analysis, 273
- identifying, with cost behavior analysis, 278
- in negotiated transfer pricing, 495

Variable-cost pricing, 487, 505–506
Verification, independent internal, 169–170
Vertical growth, 492
Vice president of operations, 226
Virtual companies, 497
Vouchers, 177, 196
Voucher register, 177
Voucher system, 177–178, 196

W

Wages payable, 11
Working capital, 59, 75
Worksheets: closing entries on, 246
- preparation of, 245